国家出版基金项目
NATIONAL PUBLICATION FOUNDATION

产品寿命预测力学与设计
Mechanics and Design for Product Life Prediction Ⅰ

江永瑞 著

重庆大学出版社

图书在版编目（CIP）数据

产品寿命预测力学与设计 = Mechanics and Design
for Product Life Prediction：英文／江永瑞著. --
重庆：重庆大学出版社，2022.1
（自主品牌汽车实践创新丛书）
ISBN 978-7-5689-1917-3

Ⅰ.①产…　Ⅱ.①江…　Ⅲ.①汽车—零部件—产品寿
命—力学—研究—英文　Ⅳ.U463

中国版本图书馆 CIP 数据核字（2020）第 001261 号

产品寿命预测力学与设计

CHANPIN SHOUMING YUCE LIXUE YU SHEJI

（Ⅰ）

江永瑞　著

策划编辑:杨粮菊　鲁　黎

责任编辑:陈　力　张慧梓　　版式设计:杨粮菊
责任校对:邹　忌　　　　　责任印制:张　策

*

重庆大学出版社出版发行
出版人:饶帮华
社址:重庆市沙坪坝区大学城西路 21 号
邮编:401331
电话:（023）88617190　88617185（中小学）
传真:（023）88617186　88617166
网址:http://www.cqup.com.cn
邮箱:fxk@ cqup.com.cn（营销中心）
全国新华书店经销
重庆升光电力印务有限公司印刷

*

开本:889mm×1194mm　1/16　总印张:60.5　总字数:1975 千
2022 年 1 月第 1 版　2022 年 1 月第 1 次印刷
ISBN 978-7-5689-1917-3　总定价:368.00 元（全 3 卷）

自主品牌汽车创新实践丛书

编委会

汽车产业是各国科技、经济的"主战场"。汽车产业是国家和区域经济发展中的支柱产业,具有科技含量高、经济产值大、产业链长、影响面广等诸多特征。特别是当今,随着信息技术、人工智能、新材料等高科技的广泛运用,电动化、智能化、网联化、共享化等"新四化"已成为全球汽车产业发展大趋势。当今的汽车产品也已经超出了交通工具的范畴,成为智能移动空间,是智能交通和智慧城市的重要组成部分,在国民经济与社会发展中扮演着更加重要的角色。汽车产业不仅是未来人们消费的热点,也是供给侧改革的重点。党的十九大报告指出,"深化供给侧结构性改革……把提高供给体系质量作为主攻方向"。作为 GDP 总量世界第二的中国,汽车产业不可缺席,中国自主品牌汽车企业必须参与到全球竞争中去,在竞争中不断崛起和创新发展。

自主品牌汽车的发展是加快建设创新型国家、实施"创新驱动"国家战略的一个重要方面。党的十九大报告提出"加快建设创新型国家""建立以企业为主体、市场为导向、产学研深度融合的技术创新体系"。2016 年 5 月,中共中央、国务院发布的《国家创新驱动发展战略纲要》指出,推动产业技术体系创新、创造发展新优势,强化原始创新、增强源头供给,优化区域创新布局、打造区域经济增长极,从而明确企业、科研院所、高校、社会组织等各类创新主体功能定位,构建开放、高效的创新网络。发展新能源汽车是我国从汽车大国迈向汽车强国的必由之路,是应对气候变化、推动绿色发展的战略举措。2012 年国务院发布《节能与新能源汽车产业发展规划(2012—2020 年)》。为深入贯彻落实党中央、国务院重要部署,顺应新一轮科技革命和产业变革趋势,抓住产业智能化发展战略机遇,加快推进智能汽车创新发展,国家发改委 2020 年 2 月发布的《智能汽车创新发展战略》请各省、自治区、直辖市、计划单列市结合实际制定促进智能汽车创新发展的政策措施,着力推动各项战略任务有效落实。可见,我国汽车产业的发展,尤其是自主品牌汽车企业的发展是加快建设创新型国家、实现中国制造向中国创造转型的重要一环。

重庆自主品牌汽车协同创新中心由重庆大学牵头,联合重庆长安汽车股份有限公司、中国汽车工程研究院股份有限公司、青山工业、超力高科、西南铝业、重庆理工大学、重庆邮电大学等核心企业、零部件供应商及院校共同组建。2014 年 10 月,教育部、财政部联合发文,认定"重庆自主品牌汽车协同创新中心"为国家级"2011 协同创新中心",成为三个国家级"2011 汽车协同创新中心"之一。"2011 计划"是继"211 工程""985 工程"之后,国家在高等教育系统又一项体现国家意志的重大创新战略举措,其建设以协同创新中心为基本载体,服务国家、行业、区域重大创新战略需求。汽车领域有 3 个国家级的"2011 协同创新中心",其中重庆自主品牌汽车协同创新中心面向区域汽车产业发展的前沿技术研发与创新人才培养共性需求,围绕汽车节能环保、安全舒适、智能网联三大方向开展协同创新和前沿技术研发,取得系列重要协同创新成果。其支撑长安汽车成为中国自主品牌汽车领头羊和自主研发技术标杆,支撑中国汽研成为国内一流汽车科技研发与行业服务机构,支撑重庆大学等高校成为汽车领域高层次创新人才培养基地。

重庆自主品牌汽车协同创新中心联合重庆大学出版社共同策划组织了大型、持续性出版项目"自主品牌汽车实践创新丛书",丛书选题涵盖节能环保、安全舒适、智能网联、可靠耐久4个大方向和15个子方向。3个主要协同单位的首席专家担任总主编,分别是刘庆(重庆自主品牌汽车协同创新中心第一任主任)、刘波(重庆长安汽车股份有限公司原副总裁)、任晓常(中国汽车工程研究院股份有限公司原董事长)。系列丛书集中体现了重庆自主品牌汽车协同创新中心的核心专家、学者在多个领域的前沿技术水平,属汽车领域系列学术著作,这些著作主题从实际问题中来,成果也已应用到设计和生产实际中,能够帮助和指导中国汽车企业建设和提升自主研发技术体系,具有现实指导意义。

本系列著作的第一辑,包括8本著作(6本中文著作,2本英文著作),选题涉及智能网联汽车人机交互理论与技术、汽车产品寿命预测、汽车可靠性及可持续性设计、高塑性镁合金材料及其在汽车中的应用、动力总成悬置系统工程设计、汽车风洞测试、碰撞与安全等。中文著作分别是中国工程院院士、重庆大学潘复生教授团队撰写的《高塑性镁合金材料》、长安汽车赵会博士团队撰写的《汽车安全性能设计》、重庆大学郭钢教授团队撰写的《智能网联汽车人机交互理论与技术》、中国汽车工程研究院朱习加博士团队撰写的《汽车风洞测试技术》、重庆大学刘永刚教授团队撰写的《新能源汽车能量管理与优化控制》、重庆理工大学付江华副教授团队撰写的《动力总成悬置系统工程设计及实例详解》。

本系列著作具有以下特点:

1.知识产权的自主性。本系列著作是自主品牌汽车协同创新中心专家团队研究开发的技术成果,且由专家团队亲自撰写,具有鲜明的知识产权自主性。其中,一些著作以英文写作,出版社已与国际知名出版企业合作出版,拟通过版权输出的形式向全世界推介相关成果,这将有利于我国汽车行业自主技术的国际交流,提升我国汽车行业的国际影响力。

2.技术的前沿性。本系列著作立足于我国自主品牌汽车企业的创新实践,在各自领域反映了我国汽车自主技术的前沿水平,是专家团队多年科研的结晶。

3.立足于产学研的融合创新。本系列著作脱胎于"2011协同创新平台",这就决定了其具有"产学研融合"的特点。著作主题从工程问题中来,其成果已应用到整车及零部件设计和生产的实际中去,相关成果在进行理论梳理和技术提炼的同时,更突出体现在实践上的应用创新。

4.服务目标明确。本系列著作不过分追求技术上的"高精尖",而更注重服务于我国自主品牌汽车研发创新知识与技术体系的形成,对于相关行业的工程研究人员以及相关专业高层次人才的培养具有非常高的参考价值。

本系列著作若有不妥或具争议之处,愿与读者商榷。

《自主品牌汽车实践创新丛书》编委会

2021年9月

Purpose The challenge going forward in the automotive industry is not only who provides the ultimate technology but also who best realizes the updated multi-disciplinary technology timely in a way that fits people with the most exciting and delightful products. Since the advent of the 21st century design and reliability engineers have been in search of the following goals:

(a) Design: Calculated products with minimal physical tests.

(b) Reliability: Equal life expectancy for product components.

As a textbook for university graduate students and a reference manual for practitioners in the automotive industry, the book is intended to help them achieve these two goals by providing a full range of knowledge in "understanding of physics" for whoever are interested in reliability engineering.

Calculated Products Finite element methods and other numerical methods in combination with realistic material data provide the most prominent nonlinear analysis under various electro-magneto-thermo-mechanical loadings have rendered calculated products to the reality. It is the attempt herein to put together the updated material for design in the lecture contents that lay the technical foundation for practical product life prediction using finite element methods and material failure theories. Hopefully, this will help readers speed up realizing their product life prediction for design and validation in the real world of virtual reality.

Equal Life Expectancy The growth of the automotive industry has spurred dramatic changes in the automotive parts, which comprise the products/systems that the public buys. Increases in speed and loadings, reductions in feature size and weight, more innovative electromagnetic devices, highly complex software and control, and changes in assembly and packaging technologies are becoming events that occur annually. Consequently, some of the automotive parts, which have a life cycle that is significantly shorter than the expected life cycle of the vehicle, ruin the vehicle and bring the other thousands of "good" parts to the junkyard, causing a tremendous loss to the society. Understanding each component's behaviors in its lifetime and being able to predict its service life during the design stage have come into the ages and they will eventually lead to a product made up to the life expectancy.

Data Accuracy Material property data used herein are obtained from various sources.

Nominal values of true stress-strain curves, in contrast to the engineering stresses and strains in paradox, are tabulated as standing in need of the automotive electro-magneto-thermo-mechanical works. Because material properties vary according to its chemical composition, production conditions, and the working environment, data given in the book are for reference only. Exactly accurate data of specific material properties used for design should be measured or obtained directly from the material manufacturer.

Living Reference Correction does much, but encouragement everything. Each chapter herein is as concise as possible such that a person can find the theories he/she wants in minutes. This book can be improved through readers' constructive criticisms and suggestions and it will be perfected in the future versions accordingly. Henry Ford said, "Failure is simply the opportunity to begin again, this time more intelligently."

Acknowledgements Authors of the technical papers that contain original theories and data cited in the references are deeply appreciated for helping bring calculated products and equal-life design into reality.

Young Chiang, PhD
College of Mechanical and Vehicle Engineering
Chongqing University

Nomenclature

A (MPa)   Yield strength at 1 s^{-1} (strain rate) and 23 ℃

A_f Final cross-sectional area of the specimen center at fracture in tensile tests

Ar Archimedes number

B (Tesla = Wb/m^2)   Magnetic flux density

B Strain hardening coefficient at 1 s^{-1} (strain rate) and 23 ℃

b, b_o Normal and shear fatigue strength exponents, respectively

C Strain-rate hardening coefficient at 23 ℃

c, c_o Normal and shear fatigue ductility exponents, respectively

C_d Aerodynamic drag coefficient

C_e Equivalent damping coefficient

C_p (J/kg/℃)   Specific heat capacity at constant pressure

C_v Damping coefficient (viscous)

C_v (J/m^3/℃)   Specific heat capacity at constant volume

$C_{10}, C_{01}, C_{20}, C_{30}$ Hyperelastic constants of Mooney-Rivlin's and Yeoh's material models

C_m Moisture concentration

$C_{m,24}$ Moisture concentration after 24-hour immersion in the fluid

$C_{m,sat}$ Saturated moisture concentration

D, d (mm)   Diameter

D_{min} (mm)   Cross-sectional diameter in the thinnest part of the neck in tensile tests

d_f (mm, μm)   Fiber diameter

d_{ij} (pm/V, C/N)   Piezoelectric charge constants

E (V/m, Nm/C)   Electric field intensity

E (GPa)   Modulus of elasticity or Young's modulus (Mechanics)

E_{11}, E_{22}, E_{33} (GPa)   Moduli of elasticity, namely Young's moduli, for orthotropic materials

E_T (GPa)   Tensile modulus of elasticity

E_C (GPa)   Compressive modulus of elasticity

E_D (GPa)   Dynamic modulus; $E_D = E_S(1 + \tan \delta)^{\frac{1}{2}}$

E_S (GPa)   Storage modulus; $E_S = E_D/(1 + \tan \delta)^{\frac{1}{2}}$

E^* (GPa)   Complex modulus

E' (GPa)   Storage modulus

E'' (GPa)   Loss modulus

E_k Electric field strength, $k = 1, 2, 3$ in the (1, 2, 3) coordinate system

e_{ij} (MPa · m/V)   Piezoelectric stiffness

F (N)   Force (Newton)

$f(\text{Hz}; \text{s}^{-1})$	Frequency; 1 Hz = 1 cycle/s
$G(\text{GPa})$	Shear modulus of elasticity
Gr	Grashof number
$G_x, g_x(\text{mm/s}^2; \text{m/s}^2)$	Gravity per unit volume in X-direction
$G_y, g_y(\text{mm/s}^2; \text{m/s}^2)$	Gravity per unit volume in Y-direction
$G_z, g_z(\text{mm/s}^2; \text{m/s}^2)$	Gravity per unit volume in Z-direction
$G'(\text{GPa})$	Storage shear modulus
$G''(\text{GPa})$	Loss shear modulus
$G^*(\text{GPa})$	Complex shear modulus
$G_{23}, G_{31}, G_{12}(\text{GPa})$	Shear moduli of elasticity for orthotropic materials
$g_{ij}(\text{Vm/N}, \text{m}^2/\text{C})$	Piezoelectric voltage constants
H, h, hr	Hour
H	Magnetic field intensity, having the unit of ampere/m
H_A, H_D	Shore A or Shore D hardness: diamond-tipped hammer rebound
$H_B(\text{kgf/mm}^2)$	Brinell hardness: spherical indenter
$H_K(\text{kgf/mm}^2)$	Knoop hardness: pyramidal indenter
$H_M(\text{MPa})$	Martens hardness
$H_R(\text{kgf/mm}^2)$	Rockwell hardness
$H_{RA}(\text{kgf/mm}^2)$	Rockwell hardness (A scale)
$H_{Rc}(\text{kgf/mm}^2)$	Rockwell hardness (C scale): spheroconical indenter
$H_{RR}(\text{kgf/mm}^2)$	Rockwell hardness (R scale)
$H_V(\text{kgf/mm}^2)$	Vickers hardness: rectangular pyramidal indenter
H_r	Relative humidity
$h(\text{N/s/mm/°C}, \text{W/m}^2/\text{°C})$	Heat convection coefficient
$I_{\text{zod}}(\text{kJ/m}^2)$	Izod notched impact strength at 23 °C (ISO 180/1A)
$K(\text{MPa})$	Bulk modulus
K_S	Surface factor
K_R	Residual stress factor
K_T	Treatment factor such as heat treatment and shot-peening
$K_{\mathrm{I}}, K_{\mathrm{IC}}(\text{MPa-m}^{\frac{1}{2}})$	Mode Ⅰ fracture toughness and critical fracture toughness
$K_{\mathrm{II}}, K_{\mathrm{IIC}}(\text{MPa-m}^{\frac{1}{2}})$	Mode Ⅱ fracture toughness and critical fracture toughness
$K_{\mathrm{III}}, K_{\mathrm{IIIC}}(\text{MPa-m}^{\frac{1}{2}})$	Mode Ⅲ fracture toughness and critical fracture toughness
$K'(\text{MPa})$	Cyclic Strain hardening coefficient
$k(\text{W/m/°C})$	Thermal conductivity
$k_x, k_y, k_z(\text{W/m/°C})$	Thermal conductivities in x-, y-, and z-directions, respectively
$k_1, k_2, k_3(\text{W/m/°C})$	Thermal conductivities in 1-, 2-, and 3-directions, respectively
MAPP	Methyl Acetylene Propadiene Stabilized
M_S	Sprung mass
M_U	Unsprung mass
m	Strain softening exponent with respect to temperature variation

$m_{ij}(\text{Ns/V/C})$	Magneto-electric coefficient
n	Strain hardening exponent at 23 ℃
n'	Cyclic strain hardening exponent
N_b	Number of repeated blocks leading to failure
N_c	Number of cycles
N_{cutoff}	Number of reversals at cutoff as no apparent knee point is available
N_f	Number of reversals at endurance limit, or cutoff if no apparent knee point
N_{fi}	Number of fatigue reversals to fatigue failure
$2N_f(\text{Cycles})$	Number of loading cycles at fatigue (endurance limit)
Nu	Nusselt number
$p_{e,i}(\text{C/m}^2/℃)$	Pyroelectric coefficients
$P_{er}(\text{L/m}^2/\text{d/atm}))$	Permeability in He (Helium) at 4 ounces/yard^2
$p_{m,i}(\text{T/℃})$	Pyromagnetic coefficient
pphr	Parts Per Hundred Rubber parts by weight
Pr	Prandtl number
$P_r(\text{C/m}^2 \text{ or } \mu\text{C/m}^2)$	Polarization
$Q(\text{J})$	Heat energy
$Q(\text{J/mol})$	Activation energy
$R(8.314 \text{ J/mol/℃})$	Universal gas constant
$R(\text{mm;m})$	Radius
R	Load ratio, stress ratio (S-N fatigue), or strain ratio (ε-N fatigue); $R=-1$ for fully reversed tension-compression fatigue test
Ra	Rayleigh number
$R_a(\mu\text{m})$	Surface roughness- Average
$R_{\text{rms}}(\mu\text{m})$	Surface roughness- Root Mean Squared (rms)
$R_z(\mu\text{m})$	Surface roughness- Maximum
Re	Reynolds number
S	Multiaxial path-independent damage parameter
$S_e(\text{MPa})$	Ideal fatigue strength (endurance limit)
ST	Solution-treated
STA	Solution-treated and aged
$T(℃),\text{Temp}(℃)$	Temperature in ℃
$T_k(\text{K})$	Temperature in K
$T(\text{t})$	Mass for mm-sec-ton system
$t(\text{s})$	Time
$T_c(℃)$	Curie temperature, at which ferromagnetic becomes paramagnetic
$T_g(℃)$	Glass transition point (Temperature)
$T_m(℃)$	Melting point (Temperature)
$T_{\text{room}}(℃)$	Room temperature (23 ℃)
$T_x,T_y,T_z(\text{N}\cdot\text{m}; \text{N}\cdot\text{mm})$	Torques in the x-, y-, and z-direction, respectively
$\tan\delta$	Loss tangent, also called loss factor

$u, v, w \, (\mathrm{m}; \, \mathrm{mm})$	Displacements in x, y, and z directions, respectively
V	Volts
V_f, V_F	Volume fraction of fibers- percentage by volume
V_p	Volume fraction of particulates/particles- percentage by volume
V_v	Volume fraction of voids
$V_x, V_y, V_z \, (\mathrm{m/s})$	Velocities or speeds in x-, y-, and z-directions, respectively
W_A	Water absorption (24-hour test), following ASTM D570
W_f, W_F	Weight fraction of fibers- percentage by weight
WIV	Wave-induced vibrations
$(X, Y, Z), (x, y, z)$	Cartesian coordinate system
$\alpha \, (\mu\mathrm{m/m/^\circ C})$	Coefficient of linear thermal expansion; $\perp$ and $/\!/$ to mold or casting flow
$\alpha \, (\mu\mathrm{m/m/^\circ C})$	$\perp$ and $/\!/$ crystal (a, b, c) axes, as applied to crystal structures
$\alpha_x, \alpha_y, \alpha_z \, (\mu\mathrm{m/m/^\circ C})$	Coefficients of linear thermal expansion in x-, y-, and z-directions
$\alpha_1, \alpha_2, \alpha_3 \, (\mu\mathrm{m/m/^\circ C})$	Coefficients of linear thermal expansion in 1-, 2-, and 3-directions
$\alpha_\mu \, (\mathrm{MPa}^{-1})$	Pressure-dynamic viscosity coefficient
$\beta \, (\mu\mathrm{m/m/\%})$	Swelling coefficient of linear moisture expansion
$\beta_1, \beta_2, \beta_3 \, (\mu\mathrm{m/m/\%})$	Swelling coefficients of linear moisture expansion of a composite lamina
$\mathrm{d}\sigma_n, \Delta\sigma_n \, (\mathrm{MPa}, \mathrm{Pa})$	Stress recursion on and $\perp$ the critical plane
Δ_{22}	Compression set, after 22 hours constantly under 25% deflection
$\epsilon \, (\epsilon_o \text{ or } \mathrm{C/N/m}^2)$	Electric permittivity
ϵ'	Electric permittivity- real part
ϵ''	Electric permittivity- imaginary part
$\epsilon_r (\epsilon_o)$	Relative permittivity
$\epsilon_o \, (\mathrm{C/N/m}^2)$	Permittivity of the vacuum, $\epsilon_o = 8.854 \times 10^{-12} \, \mathrm{C/N/m}^2$
μ	10^{-6}
μ	Coefficient of Coulomb friction (Mechanics)
$\mu \, (\mathrm{H/m} \text{ or } \mu_o)$	Magnetic permeability (Electronics)
μ'	Magnetic permeability- real part
μ''	Magnetic permeability- imaginary part
$\mu_r (\mu_o)$	Relative permittivity
$\mu_o \, (\mathrm{H/m})$	Permeability of the vacuum, $\mu_o = 4\pi \times 10^{-7} \, \mathrm{H/m}$
μ_D	Dynamic coefficient of friction
μ_d	Dynamic viscosity (fluid only)
μ_{d0}	Dynamic viscosity at ambient pressure
μ_{dg}	Dynamic viscosity at glass transition temperature
μ_f	Frictional factor
μ_k	Kinematic viscosity
μ_S	Static coefficient of friction
ε	Strain
ε_{creep}	Creep rupture strain
$\varepsilon^e \ \& \ \varepsilon_e$	Elastic strain

ε^{p} & ε_{p}	Plastic strain
$\varepsilon_{\mathrm{eq}}$	Equivalent strain
$\varepsilon_{\mathrm{eq}}^{\mathrm{p}}$	Equivalent plastic strain
$\mathrm{d}\varepsilon_{\mathrm{eq}}^{\mathrm{p}}/\mathrm{d}t$	Equivalent plastic strain rate obtained in reference to a strain rate of 1 sec^{-1}
$\varepsilon_{\mathrm{f}}'$	Fatigue ductility coefficient
$\varepsilon_{xx},\varepsilon_{yy},\varepsilon_{zz}$	Normal strains
$\varepsilon_{yz},\varepsilon_{zx},\varepsilon_{xy}$	Shear strains
$\varepsilon_{\mathrm{ucs}}$	Ultimate compressive strain
$\varepsilon_{\mathrm{uts}}$	Ultimate tensile strain
$\varepsilon_1,\varepsilon_2,\varepsilon_3$	Principal strains
$\varepsilon_{11},\varepsilon_{22},\varepsilon_{33}$	Normal strains defined in the (1, 2, 3) coordinate system
$\varepsilon_{23},\varepsilon_{31},\varepsilon_{12}$	Shear strains (tensor) defined in the (1, 2, 3) coordinate system
$\varepsilon_{11\mathrm{c}},\varepsilon_{22\mathrm{c}},\varepsilon_{33\mathrm{c}}$	Ultimate compressive strains along the primary orthotropic material axes
$\varepsilon_{11\mathrm{t}},\varepsilon_{22\mathrm{t}},\varepsilon_{33\mathrm{t}}$	Ultimate tensile strains along the primary orthotropic material axes
$\varepsilon_{23\mathrm{u}},\varepsilon_{31\mathrm{u}},\varepsilon_{12\mathrm{u}}$	Ultimate shear strains in primary orthotropic material coordinates (1,2,3)
$\Delta\varepsilon$	Fluctuating strain, as $\Delta\varepsilon = \Delta\varepsilon^{\mathrm{e}} + \Delta\varepsilon^{\mathrm{p}}$
$\Delta\varepsilon^{\mathrm{e}}$ or $\Delta\varepsilon_{\mathrm{e}}$	Fluctuating (equivalent) elastic strain
$\Delta\varepsilon^{\mathrm{p}}$ or $\Delta\varepsilon_{\mathrm{p}}$	Fluctuating (equivalent) plastic strain
ϵ (C/N/m^2 or ϵ_{o})	Permittivity
ϵ_{o} (C/N/m^2)	Permittivity of vacuum, $\epsilon_{\mathrm{o}} = 8.85 \times 10^{-12}$ C/(N $\cdot$ m^2)
$\epsilon_{\mathrm{r}}(\epsilon_{\mathrm{o}})$	Relative permittivity of material
ϕ (m, mm)	Mechanical displacement
ϕ_{ϵ} (V, N $\cdot$ m/C)	Electric potential
ϕ_{μ} (V $\cdot$ s/m)	Magnetic vector potential or magnetic potential
γ (Nmm/T/℃ , J/kg/℃)	Specific heat capacity
γ_{f} (Nmm/T/℃ , J/kg/℃)	Specific heat of fibers in a composite
γ_{m} (Nmm/T/℃ , J/kg/℃)	Specific heat of matrix in a composite
λ_i ($i = 1, 2, 3$)	Stretch ratio along i-axis, i.e. deviatorial principal stretches
$\rho,\rho_{\mathrm{f}},\rho_{\mathrm{m}}$ (g/cm^3)	Density (overall), density of fiber, and density of matrix, respectively
$\rho_{\mathrm{E}},\rho_{\mathrm{e}}$ (Ωm, Ωmm)	Electric resistivity
ξ	Damping factor
σ (MPa)	Stress
$\sigma_{\mathrm{a}},\sigma_{\mathrm{A}}$ (MPa)	Stress amplitude
$\sigma_{\mathrm{ccs},10000}$ (MPa)	Creep compressive strength (rupture in compression) at 10000 hours
$\sigma_{\mathrm{creep},1\%,1000}$ (MPa)	Creep strength or limiting creep strength; creep = 1% at 1000 hours
$\sigma_{\mathrm{creep},1\%,10000}$ (MPa)	Creep strength or limiting creep strength; creep = 1% at 10000 hours
$\sigma_{\mathrm{creep},5\%,1000}$ (MPa)	Creep strength or limiting creep strength; creep = 5% at 1000 hours
$\sigma_{\mathrm{creep},5\%,10000}$ (MPa)	Creep strength or limiting creep strength; creep = 5% at 10000 hours
σ_{crs} (MPa)	Creep rupture strength
$\sigma_{\mathrm{crs},1000}$ (MPa)	Creep rupture strength at 1000 hours ($\approx$ 41.7 days)
$\sigma_{\mathrm{crs},10000}$ (MPa)	Creep rupture strength at 10000 hours ($\approx$ 417 days)

$\sigma_{cts,10000}(\text{MPa})$	Creep tensile strength in tension at 10000 hours
$\sigma_E(\Omega\text{m}^{-1},\Omega\text{mm}^{-1})$	Electric conductivity, also called specific conductance, as $\sigma_E = 1/\rho_E$
$\sigma_{eq}(\text{MPa})$	Equivalent stress, e.g. von Mises stress
$\sigma_f(\text{MPa})$	Fatigue limit, also called endurance limit
$\sigma_f'(\text{MPa})$	Fatigue strength coefficient
$\sigma_M(\text{MPa})$	Mean stress
$\sigma_R(\text{MPa})$	Rupture strength, resulting from 3-point bending tests for brittle materials
$\sigma_{100\%},\sigma_{300\%}(\text{MPa})$	Stresses at 100% and 300% strains, defined mainly for rubbers
$\sigma_{us}(\text{MPa})$	Ultimate strength
$\sigma_{uts}(\text{MPa})$	Ultimate tensile strength
$\sigma_{ucs}(\text{MPa})$	Ultimate compressive strength
$(\sigma_{ucs},\varepsilon_{ucs})..(\sigma_{uts},\varepsilon_{uts})$	Stress-strain curve data ranging from ultimate compression to tension
$\sigma_{xx},\sigma_{yy},\sigma_{zz}(\text{MPa})$	Normal stresses
$\sigma_{xy},\sigma_{yz},\sigma_{zx}(\text{MPa})$	Shear stresses
$\sigma_y,\sigma_{0.2\%}(\text{MPa})$	Yield strength, i.e. stress at 0.2% (tensile) or$-$0.2% (compressive) strain
$\sigma_{YC}(\text{MPa})$	Yield strengths in compression
$\sigma_{YT}(\text{MPa})$	Yield strengths in tension
$\sigma_1,\sigma_2,\sigma_3(\text{MPa})$	Principal stresses
$\sigma_{11c},\sigma_{22c},\sigma_{33c}(\text{MPa})$	Ultimate compressive stresses along the primary orthotropic material axes
$\sigma_{11t},\sigma_{22t},\sigma_{33t}(\text{MPa})$	Ultimate tensile stresses along the primary orthotropic material axes
$\sigma_{23u},\sigma_{31u},\sigma_{12u}(\text{MPa})$	Ultimate shear stresses in primary orthotropic material coordinates (1,2,3)
$\tau,\tau_{yz},\tau_{zx},\tau_{xy}(\text{MPa})$	Shear stresses
$\theta\ (\text{J}/^{\circ}\text{C})$	Entropy
ν	Poisson's ratio
$\nu_{23},\nu_{31},\nu_{12}$	Poisson's ratios of composite materials
$\nu_{yz},\nu_{zx},\nu_{xy}$	Poisson's ratios of composite materials
$\omega,\Omega(\text{Hz or s}^{-1})$	Frequency
$\omega_D,\omega_d(\text{Hz or s}^{-1})$	Damped natural frequency
$\omega_N,\omega_n(\text{Hz or s}^{-1})$	Undamped natural frequency
χ_e	Electric susceptibility
χ_m	Magnetic susceptibility
(1,2,3)	Primary material coordinate system, defined mainly for composites

Acronyms

AC	Alternating current
AFM	Atomic force microscope
AHSS	Advanced high strength steels
AS	As sintered
ASTM	American Society of Materials
BGA	Ball grid array
BH	Bake hardenable
BHN	Brinell hardness
BLDC	Brushless direct-current motor
BPA	Bisphenol-A
BPC	Bisphenol-C
BNNT	Boron nitride nanotube
C	Carbon
CB	Carbon black such as N110, ···, N990 (ISO classification)
CD	Cold-drawn
CLD	Constant Life Diagram
CMOS	Complementary metal-oxide-semiconductor
CNT	Carbon nanotube
COB	Chip-on-board
COG	Chip-on-glass
COUR	Cost of unreliability
CP	Complex phase
CR	Cold-rolled
CSM	Chopped strand mat; fibers laid randomly and held together by a binder
CVD	Chemical vapor deposit
CW	Cold-worked
DAM	Dry as molded
DBTT	Ductile-brittle transition temperature
DC	Die cast (mechanical engineering) or direct current (electric engineering)
DF or DOF	Degree of freedom
DFMEA	Design failure modes and effect analysis
DGEBA	Diglycidyl ether of bisphenol A (commercial epoxy)
DIN	Deutsche Industrial Normale (German)
DMA	Dynamical mechanical analysis
DOD	Depth of discharge

DoD	Department of Defense
DP	Dual phase
DSC	Differential scanning calorimetry
EBPVD	Electron beam vapor deposition
emf or EMF	Electromotive force
EMI	Electromagnetic interference
ETP	Electrolytic touch pitch copper
Exp or exp	Exponential
F	Force
F	As fabricated
FB	Ferritic-bainitic
FB, Flexural B.	Flexural bending fatigue test via cantilever impact
FCBGA	Flip-chip ball grid array
FDS	Fatigue damage spectrum
FOM	Figure of merit
FRF	Frequency response function
FZ	Fusion zone
G	Gravity
Gf or GF	Glass fiber
Gl	Glass
Gr	Graphite
GPa	10^9 pascals
GTAW	Gas tungsten arc welding
G2V and V2G	Grid to vehicle and vehicle to grid
g	Gram
H	Hardening Symbol, such as H12, H14, H16, H18, H22, H24, H26, H28, H32, H34, H36, H38 for 1×××, 3×××, and 5××× series aluminum alloys:

1st digit:

    0-No cold worked

    1-Cold worked only

    2-Cold worked and annealed

    3-Cold worked and stabilized

2nd digit:

    1-Annealed

    $2-\dfrac{1}{4}$ Hard

    $4-\dfrac{1}{2}$ Hard

    $6-\dfrac{3}{4}$ Hard

    8-Hard

	9-Extra Hard
HAZ	Heat affected zone
HD	Hot-drawn
HF	Hot-formed
HIP	Hot Isostatic pressing
HM	High modulus
HR	Hot-rolled
HR	Humidity, relative
HS	High strength
HSLA	High strength low alloy (SAE J1392 JUN 84)
HT	Heat treatment
HVAC	Heat ventilation and air conditioner
Hz	Herz (cycles per second)
IF	Interstitial free
IGBT	Insulated gate bipolar transistor
IRI	International roughness index
ISO	International Standards Organization
J	Joule
kg	Kilogram
kPa	Kilo Pascals
M or m	Meter
Max (Subscript)	Maximum
MCM	Multi-chip module
MAG	Metal active gas welding
MIG	Metal inert gas welding
min	Minute
MM or mm	Millimeter
min (Subscript)	Minimum
mmf or MMF	Magneto motive force
MOE	Modulus of elasticity
MOR	Modulus of rupture
MOSFET	Metal-oxide-semiconductor field-effect transistor
MPa	Mega-Pascals
MPB	Morphotropic phase boundary
MS	Martensitic
MWCNT or MWNT	Multi-walled carbon nanotubes
N	Newton
O	Annealed, soft (a heat treatment condition)
PCB	Printed circuit boards
PF	Powder forged
PH	Precipitation hardening

PM	Powder metallurgy
PM	Permanent mold cast
PoF	Physics of failure
pphr	Parts per hundred rubber parts by weight
PSD	Power spectral density
PTMG	Polyoxytetramethylene glycol
PWHT	Post-weld heat treatment
Q&T or QT	Quench and tempering
Q&T&C or QTC	Quench, tempering, and carburizing
Rad	Radian
RH	Relative humidity
RHA	Rolled homogeneous armor- steel for military applications, e.g. armors
RoHS	Restriction of Hazardous Substances Directive 2002/95/EC
Rotating B.	Rotating beam bending fatigue test
RTM	Resin transfer molding
R-3p, 3p Bending	3-point bending fatigue test
R-4p, 4p Bending	4-point bending fatigue test
S, s, Sec, sec	Second
SAC	Sine amplitude converter
SC	Sand cast
SEAT	Seat effective amplitude transmission
SIP	System in package
SOC	State of charge
SOH	State of health
SOL	State of life
ST	Solution-treated
SWNT	Single-walled nano-carbon tube
T	Temperature
T	Ton
T	Heat Treatment, such as T1, T2, T3, T4, T5, T6, T7, T8, T9, T10 for $2\times\times\times$, $4\times\times\times$, $6\times\times\times$, $7\times\times\times$, and $8\times\times\times$ aluminum alloys
T1	Cooled from elevated temperatures and naturally aged
T2	Cooled from elevated temperature and artificially aged
T3	Solution-heat-treated, cold worked, and naturally aged
T4	Solution-heat-treated and naturally aged
T5	Cooled from elevated temperatures and artificially aged
T6	Solution-heat-treated and artificially aged
T7	Solution-heat-treated and over-aged/stabilized
T8	Solution-heat-treated, cold worked, and artificially aged
T9	Solution-heat-treated, artificially aged, and cold worked
T10	Cooled from an elevated temperature, cold worked, and artificially aged

TGA	Thermogravimetric Analysis
TGMDA	Diglycidyl ether of bisphenol A; an epoxy for aerospace applications
TGO	Thermally grown oxide
TIG	Tungsten inert gas welding
TM	Trade mark
TPC	Thermoplastic copolyester
TPE	Thermoplastic elastomer
TPE-s	Styrenic block copolymers
TPG	Thermal pyrolytic graphite
TPI	Thermoplastic polyamides
TPO	Thermoplastic olefin (Polyolefin blends)
TPU	Thermoplastic polyurethanes
TPV, TPE-v	Thermoplastic vulcanizates, i.e. thermoplastic alloys
TRIP	Transformation-induced plasticity
TTSF	Time-temperature shift factors
TTSP	Time-temperature superposition principle
TWIP	Twinning-induced plasticity
t	Time
VDV	Vibration dose values
VIV	Vortex-induced vibrations
W	Watt
W	Solution heat-treated only
X-fem	Extended finite element method
xxA	Shore A durometer hardness, e.g. 70A is Shore A hardness 70
ZVS	Zero voltage switching

Chapter 5 Fracture Mechanics

Chapter 6 Creep and Oxidation

Chapter 7　Random Vibration Fatigue and Impact Engineering

Chapter 15   *Failure of Composites*

Chapter 16   *Indentation Engineering and Fretting Fatigue*

Index

Chapter 3　Finite Element Methods in Composites

Chapter 4　Mechanical Fatigue

Chapter 5　Fracture Mechanics

Chapter 6　Creep and Oxidation

Chapter 1

Material Reliability and Sustainability

1.1　Predictive Engineering Analytics

Predictive engineering is the application of multidisciplinary engineering simulations and tests to developing virtual reality that can predict the real-world behavior of products throughout the product lifecycle. It includes both the product life management strategy, simulation tools, and test validations that one can leverage to expand experimental design verification and validation into calculated products in support of systems-driven product development.

Predictive engineering for automotive manufacturers deals with the complex nature of today's vehicles and product development environments, which combine various functional requirements based on Materials Science, mechanics, electronics, magnetism, thermal analytics, control, and related software. For example, applications of the finite element method have been extended from elastic homogeneous solids to composite materials, computational fluid dynamics (CFD), multibody dynamics, vibration and acoustic effect, analytics of electromagnetic field, creep, corrosion and other degradation mechanisms, and material data analytics. Nowadays, predictive engineering has been moving into a managed context to support the engineering and development of vehicles.

Since the advent of the 21st century, calculated products with minimal physical tests have prevailed in most industries including the automotive industry. Electric vehicles are emerging from low mileage per charge and getting into the main stream market, but product reliability and sustainability of EV/HEV are to be further explored extensively. Design for reliability and sustainability based on material-based fatigue lifetime estimation is in urgent need while virtual prototyping can lead to shorter design cycles, reduced design costs, and superior performance. Fault tree analysis is a powerful live tool for system optimization according to the vehicle-driving conditions.

Computer-aided engineering (CAE) methods have been focused on product data, form and fit. The multiplying consumer uses of CAE tools have business people thinking long and hard about how and where the technology could fit in the enterprise. Within such a virtual-reality process, yet there is a need to exploit an effective approach to justifying the design features that have significant influences on the functional performance of a specific product and its potential failure modes consequently. Many researchers reveal that understanding the physics of material is the key to success.

1.1.1　Deterministic Product Life Prediction Based on Mechanics of Materials

Automotive engineering materials are classified as follows: elastomers, thermoplastics, thermoset plastics, metals, C (including diamond, graphite and carbon), ceramics, electromagnetic materials, natural materials, and fluids. The cost of materials may account for about 70% of manufacturing cost. Reliability of smart (electro-magneto-thermo-mechanical) materials and adaptation of natural materials in the automotive industry are the two emerging challenges ahead. Effectively, it is deemed that predictive engineering analytics requires disciplined comprehension of fundamental material behaviors including their performance and failure mechanisms, of which hand-on experience, in-depth engineering skills, and excelling knowledge from many different fields of mechanics of materials. The following entails these basic theories of how to apply the deterministic approach to product life prediction:

(1) Material Reliability and Sustainability.

(2) Elastoplastics.

(3) Finite Element Methods in Orthotropic Composites.

(4) Mechanical Fatigue.

(5) Fracture Mechanics.

(6) Creep and Oxidation.

(7) Random Vibration Fatigue and Impact Engineering.

(8) Tribology.

(9) Structural Instability.

(10) Micromechanics.

(11) Thermal Loadings.

(12) Moisture Diffusion.

(13) Elastomeric Composites.

(14) Dielectric Materials.

(15) Failure of Composites.

(16) Indentation Engineering and Fretting Fatigue.

Of course, the above is also a list of multidisciplinary fundamental curriculums in mechanics and design for reliability required for implementing CAE (computer-aided engineering) and CAD (computer-aided design), which are taking a tremendous role for practicing engineers in both design and analysis context. CAE has been widely applied to various engineering and science curriculums and virtual prototyping offers analysis on components as designed, as manufactured, and as a comparison between the two. They provide an opportunity to explore conceptual design without the initial expense of prototypes and/or pilot facilities. Examples include durability and crashworthiness, vehicle ride and handling, noise and vibration and harshness, structural integrity and weight control.

1.1.2   Stochastic Product Life Management Based on Reliability Engineering

Product life prediction requires an elaborated systematic approach based on reliability engineering to the stochastic nature of products. It consists of a series of proactive steps towards resolving the stochastic variation in material and manufacturing. In accordance with product development operations, reliability engineering for automobiles may involve the following:

1. Functional requirements analysis of products (including both hardware and software) at both system and component levels.
2. Nominal product life prediction based on natural sciences and test validations.
3. Variational analysis of product and derived requirements and specifications.
4. Product fault tree analysis and related cost analysis.
5. Product availability and mission readiness analysis, including manufacturing requirement allocation.
6. Autonomous System diagnostics.
7. Fault tolerant systems (e.g. designing with redundancy).
8. Predictive and preventive maintenance such as reliability-centered maintenance, including their effect on the discernible potential zero-kilometer (zero hour) quality.
9. Product life studies and derived requirements to prevent the product from potential maintenance-induced failures, potential transport-induced failures, potential storage-induced failures, and potential software (systematic) failures.
10. Reliability tests and derived requirements at plants.
11. Field failure monitoring and corrective actions.
12. Distribution control, including production part availability and spare parts stocking.
13. Technical documentation, including caution and warning messages.
14. Human factors, including human-machine interactions and errors.
15. An organizing system with a disciplined data and information acquisition process for malfunction reporting, failure analyses, taking corrective actions, and implementing proper preventive mechanisms such as FRACAS.

These product development activities of necessity must be implemented in order to achieve the desired reliability and sustainability goals when developing a vehicle.

1.1.3　Lifetime Prognostics

Lifetime estimation based on physics of material is to be addressed in the book. A case study on the power module harnessed on an electric vehicle is employed hereupon to illustrate the work procedure. The methodology is versatile for analyzing most mechanical and electromagnetic systems/components. Key life tests (KLT) of material sustainability at various loading conditions are essential for validating product life prediction.

The power electronics system translates its commands into electric signals to operate the electromagnetic devices (e. g. electric motors) that subsequently drive various mechanical components, while the overall functional operation is governed by a control system. Fluidic cooling is sometimes required for most working conditions as another form of energy exchange. Energy-converting behaviors are governed by energy exchanges, containment or minimization principles. They are therefore referred to as "conservative". The control equations, referred to as "non-conservative", often stay in state variable form that is basically not energy-related.

1.1.4　Field Lifetime Estimation

The optimal method for crack initiation life prediction for complex multiaxial variable amplitude loading has been found to utilize the critical plane approach based on maximum normal strain plane and damage quantification by cracking energy density on that plane, obtained either from experimental tests or finite element methods (Chapter 3). Fundamental mechanics based on true stress-strain is a key prerequisite (Chapter 2). The rainflow cycle counting algorithm and Miner's linear damage rule may be used for predicting fatigue life under variable amplitude loadings in the field (Chapter 4). The fracture mechanics approach (Chapter 5) is used for total fatigue life prediction of the component based on specimen crack growth data and finite element simulation results. Creep and oxidation ought to be considered in the lifetime estimation (Chapters 6) as they complicate the fatigue mechanism and cut back at the product life. Structures may fail when subjected to random vibrations, of which the load spectrum (in frequency domain) is available instead of time series, and the fatigue life prediction has to be accessed in the frequency domain such as spectral methods for fatigue (Chapter 7). Impact loading may cause another catastrophic failure mode (Chapter 7). Tribological phenomena (Chapter 8) are another complex product life-threatening syndrome to deal with, while structural instability (buckling, snapping, and dynamic instability) may cause a structure to collapse as a catastrophic failure (Chapter 9). Micromechanics of composites is addressed in Chapter 10 since more and more composite materials are used in vehicles. Plastic composites, elastomeric materials, and "smart" dielectrics (Chapters 10, 13, and 14, respectively) are addressed to unveil their perspective requirements for individual applications. Thermal loadings (Chapter 11) and material degradation due to moisture absorption (Chapter 12) have been a threat to composites, specially for automotive power electronics, and they render another kind of failure mode. Theories for failure modes of composite materials are in demand for the product life prediction of composites (Chapter 15). Modern indentation methods for measuring mechanical properties and monitoring structural health provide a convenient venue for the acquisition of material properties (Chapter 16).

As an example, the field lifetime estimation of the power modules of electric vehicles is given here to illustrate the work procedure. One may ask, "How are active power cycling and non-destructive thermal measurements used by engineers to predict the expected lifetime of power modules in application for operational use?" The flow chart for field lifetime estimation is depicted in Fig. 1.1.1 to answer this question.

The component can be an IGBT (insulated-gate bipolar transistor) in an automotive power module or a MOSFET (metal-oxide-semiconductor field-effect transistor) in a renewable energy photovoltaic inverter module under different operating modes over a lifetime of drive cycles. Both of them are weak links up to the reliability concern in an EV. The lifetime of EV power electronics can be defined as the number of operating hours, by which the module (e.g. battery, electric motor, inverter, harness, etc.) can survive various specified loading conditions. The automotive drive cycle against the life span test is generally employed to determine the load cycle on IGBTs and MOSFETs based on chip junction temperature variations (ΔT_j) via the resulting temperature cycle profile. Note that the load can be stress, strain, temperature, and/or acceleration. Potential thermal shock failure diagnosis using thermal transient measurement techniques is also required.

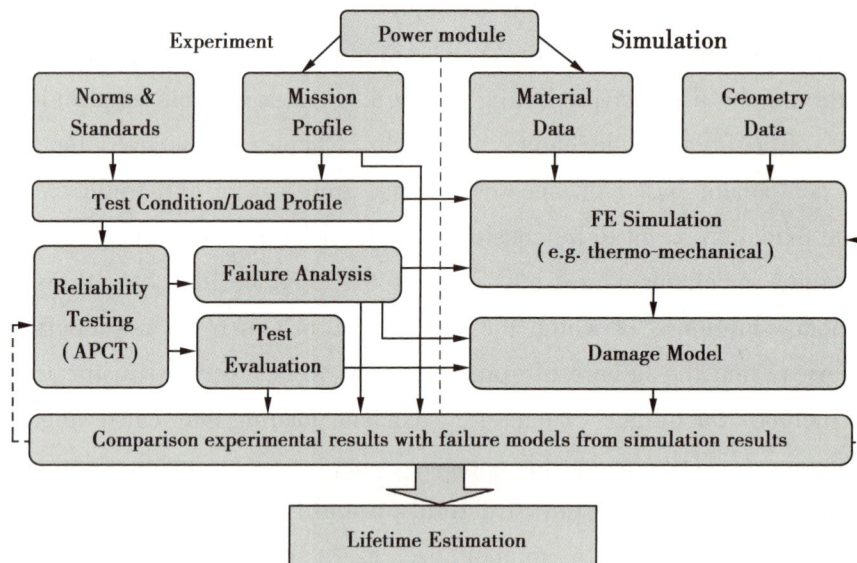

Fig. 1.1.1 Flow Chart for Field Lifetime Estimation of a Power Module

While power cycle test profiles are defined with a given target operational duty cycle, also called mission profile, reliability engineering fills the role of lifetime management for applications under coupled electro-magneto-thermo-mechanical-coupled loadings. Aiming reliability analysis at the system failure prevention is a tremendous enhancement to the maximum lifetime testing, if not a replacement. Stresses at junctions invited by the mismatches of thermal expansions between the parts of an IGBT (Fig. 1.1.2) are a critical threat, especially the bonding of the aluminum wire to silicon wafer and all solder joints.

Active power cycling results in thermal cycling that imposes junction temperature cycles, which in turn change the mechanical, thermal, electric, and even magnetic performance profiles of EV electronic modules that control the active power cycling. As illustrated in Fig. 1.1.3, in order to make a lifetime estimation of such electronic components, one may follow the procedure given below:

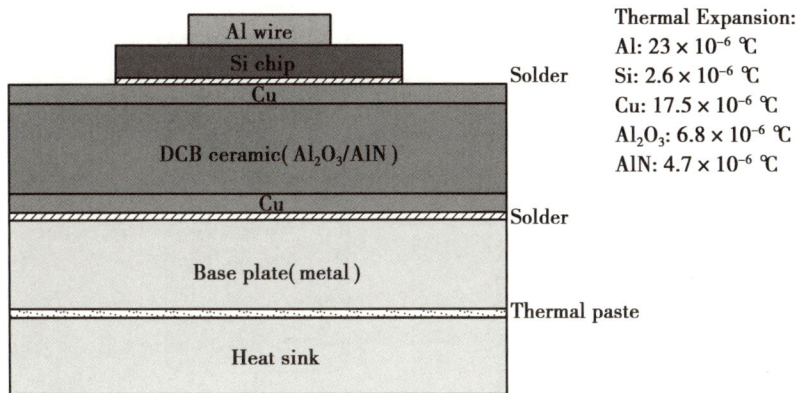

Fig. 1.1.2   **Schematic Drawing of an IGBT with Coefficients of Thermal Expansion** [Busca]

(a) Mission profile is the loading function of time, which originates from the drive cycle such as electric generator from the wind turbine or ECU of an EV motor.

(b) Power electronics process the signals.

(c) Loss modeling handles all possible energy losses and their heating mechanism.

(d) Thermal analysis predicts the temperature profile at junctions of concern.

(e) Generating the temperature profile form measurement or numerical analysis at the locations of interest subject to drive cycles in service.

(f) Applying counting algorithms such as the rainflow method to count the numbers of temperature fluctuations to obtain the means and fluctuating amplitudes.

(g) Seeking for component lifetime curves (e.g. fatigue, creep, oxidation, moisture) and introduce the corresponding models into to lifetime estimation, including the exploration of the electro-magneto-thermo-mechanical coupling and resolving limiting issues.

(h) Quantifying accumulated damage using rules such as the Miner's equation.

(i) Calculating the remaining life or its potential life span.

The procedure given above applies to most power electronics and mechanical components such as electric vehicles and wind turbine systems [Blaabjerg et al.]. Finite element analysis may be implemented in step (c) to translate the thermal loads (temperature fluctuations) into a fatigue criterion that is correlated to the life cycles, instead of simply ε-N or S-N curves. Step (d) will receive the number of temperature cycles corresponding to individual temperature levels from step (b). The methodology is explained in details in the next chapter. The strain or stress fluctuations will often be calculated numerically or recorded in testing in addition to temperature variations for prognosis of mechanical components.

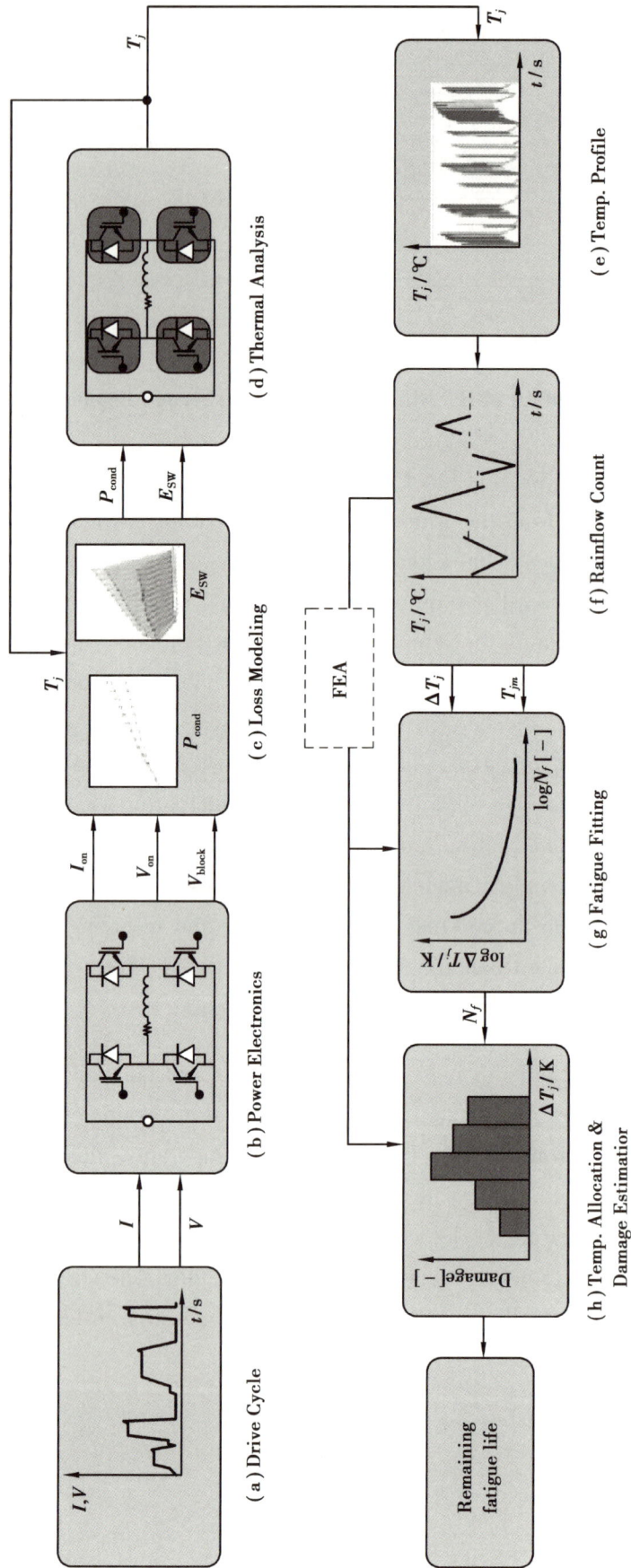

Fig. 1.1.3 Fatigue Life Estimation on Thermomechanical Failure [Nicola] [Hayes et al.]

1.1.5   Cost of Unreliability

The cost of unreliability, as shown in Fig. 1.1.4, tells a big-picture view of cost in correction and re-correction after the product is launched. Failures must be addressed from a financial view point and not a gear-head approach of simply counting the number of failures. One must speak the language of cost of unreliability, which describes events in monetary measures over a period of time, such as for a design facility as if the key elements are simplified to a series of block diagrams for reducing the cost of failures as a portion of the tactical plan. An automotive design engineer always pontificates about the importance of designing a vehicle for reliability, maintainability, and operability that will result in minimal life cycle cost.

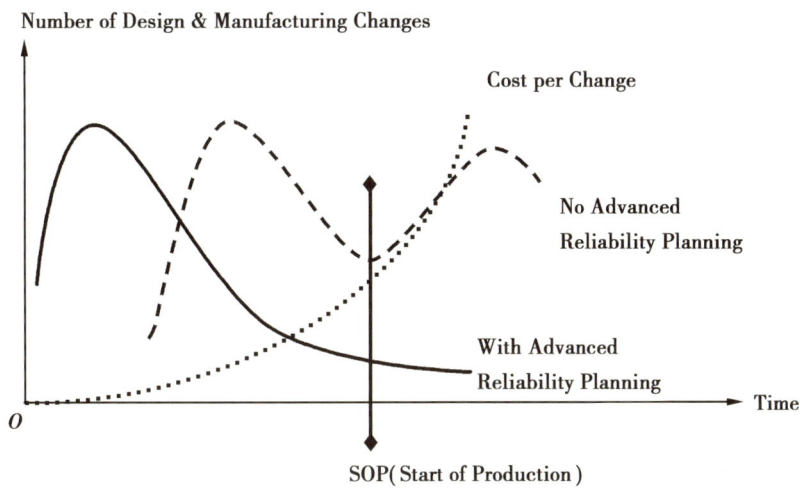

Fig. 1.1.4   Designing with Reliability for Product Research and Development

The cost of unreliability is a direct concern connected to program management's two favorite metrics: time and money. Without advanced reliability planning, the engineering change number (ECN) increases tremendously as shown in Fig. 1.1.4. Once a product gets to the customer after SOP (start of production), the cost of each corrective activity can be thousand-fold as much as when it is still in the research and development center. Improvements in reliability made by a supplier early in the product life cycle may result in higher research and development costs being passed on to the customer in the product acquisition costs. However, this can be more than offset as the customer benefits by having lower operational costs with increased reliability and up time that results in greater productivity.

1.2 Coupled Mechanics of Materials

Physical products are made of materials after all. Design for reliability and sustainability begins with a fundamental understanding of the physics of how such as why a technology can fail. Material sustainability is fundamental to a product life assessment. All in all, the first intuitive fundamental questions would be asked with regard to a product failure: Is the material proper?

Material specifications for a part are intended to satisfy functional performance, reliability, sustainability, aesthetic, and eventually economic requirements by controlling variations in the final product [Bittence]. Functionalities of engineering materials can be classified into five general categories: electric, magnetic, mechanical, thermal and optical effects. Interactions among the first four effects are depicted in Fig. 1.2.1. They are frequently described by differential equations that interact with one another through power conversion and exchange between any two

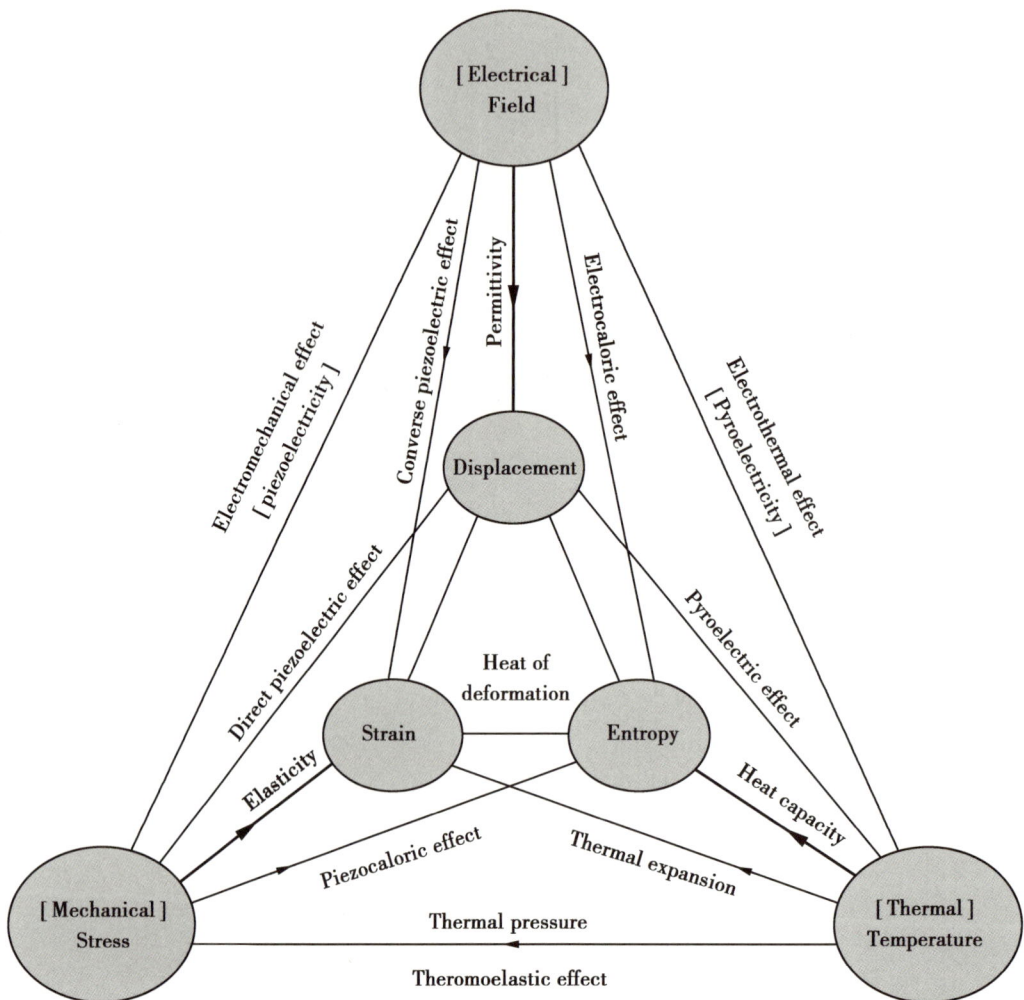

Fig. 1.2.1　Material Infrastructure for Electro-magneto-thermo-mechanical Coupling Effects [Nye]

of the electric, magnetic, fluid, and mechanical fields, which are both time- and temperature-dependent.

1.2.1   Material Infrastructure

More AI (artificial intelligence) functions are motivated to run in a vehicle means more electro-magneto-thermo-mechanical coupling effects are to be utilized. Miniaturization of automotive sensors, actuators, and electric components also relies on these coupling effects. Mechanics is thus herein defined as the branch of science concerned with the behaviors of physical bodies when subjected to forces (displacements), electric fields (electric displacements), magnetic fields (magnetic flux densities), and their coupled. As the study of mechanics of materials evolves, some interesting changes in the last several decades are given as follows:

(a) Thermodynamic connections among electric field, magnetic field, and mechanical stress complicate the promised functional requirements in product design.

(b) Anisotropy found in most electro-magneto-mechanical properties, though mostly orthotropic or transversely isotropic, is another hurdle.

(c) Multi-domain structures are engineered to have properties that may not be found in nature, such as designing with meta-materials that offer great potential to realize novel electromagnetic functionality in products ranging from thermal detectors, large bandwidth energy-harvesters, acoustic tuning, to reconfigurable cloaks.

(d) Composite materials have gained the momentum of attack to structural components in the real world, but fabrication and failure theories are yet to be explored further.

(e) One interesting finding is that orthotropic materials for negative or zero Poisson's ratios (compressibility) are feasible. This is called auxetic materials, that exhibit improved mechanical properties such as impact resistance, fracture toughness, hardness and shear modulus over conventional materials of the same stiffness with a positive Poisson's ratio.

(f) Spontaneous stiction and adhesion by van der Waals attraction, capillary attraction, or plastic strain are more and more practical.

(g) Calculated design based on statistical tolerance analysis, finite element methods, and other virtual reality tools becomes reality for not-so-sophisticated products but remains challenging.

(h) Printing of 3-dimensional parts including micro- and nano-structures directly from 3-dimensional solid models is encouraging, but how to haul in with reality needs more diversified multidisciplinary skills.

(i) Temperature-, strain-, and frequency-dependent failure modes, such as fatigue, creep, oxidation, stiction, moisture diffusion, resonance, and phase transformation, rise to the challenge for product reliability and fabrication, especially for heterogeneous materials.

1.2.2 Timing on Energy Conversion between Fields

All fields involved in the general energy-converting electro-magneto-thermo-mechanical processes have their own specific time scale, as depicted in Fig. 1.2.2. For example, in the electric-thermal interaction, the temperature seemingly has not changed at all in a short time duration like 1 second while the electric current in PWM switches in an extremely dynamic manner. The typical ratio of a large time constant to a small time constant may be as large as 10^{10}. Obviously, it has a major consequence for computational algorithms in the coupled fields.

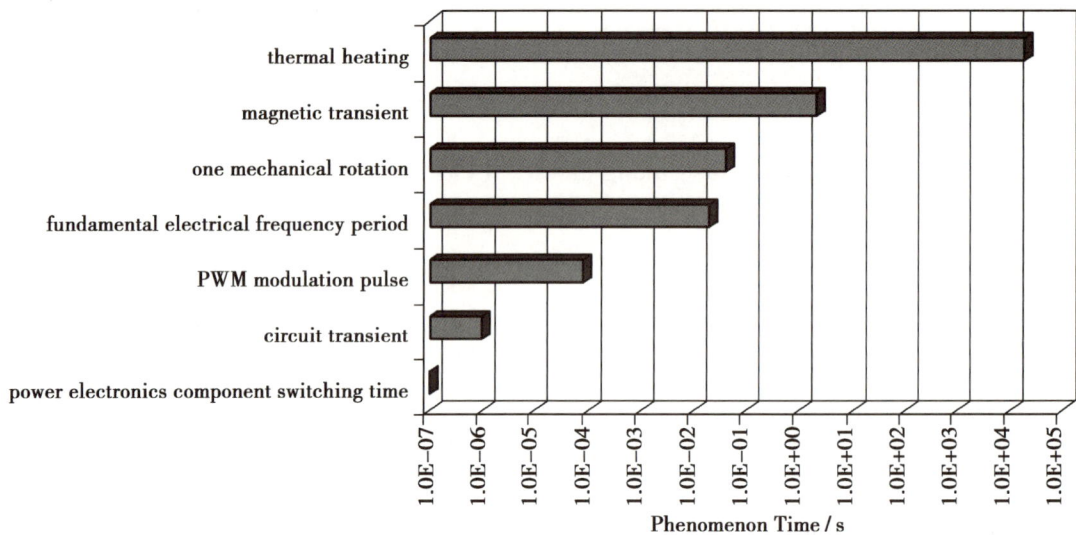

Fig. 1.2.2 Processing Time Required for Different Energy-Converting Operations [Moha]

1.3 Finite Element Methods

FEM (Finite element method) is part of Computer-Aided Engineering (CAE). In fact, more than 80% of comprehensive CAE technologies in practice fall into the category of FEM. This powerful analysis tool has tremendously improved both the standard of engineering design and the methodology of the design process in many industrial applications, especially automotive engineering. Finite element analysis (FEA) essentially consists of the following four major steps:

(a) A piecewise approximation of a physical function (variable), e.g. displacements for structural analysis, temperature for heat transfer, pressure for acoustic analysis, stream function for fluid flow, velocities for impact, electric displacement for electricity, and magnetic flux density for magnetism, by means of polynomials and/or exponentials defined over a small region of the continuum (namely element) and interpolated from certain fixed points (namely nodes) of the element.

(b) Interactions between adjacent elements are connected by the nodes in terms of a physical quantity and/or its derivatives following physical and/or chemical laws. In other words, an assembly of all the nodes in the physical system must be made.

(c) Solution schemes for solving the simultaneous equations associated with nodes are then implemented.

(d) The solved numerical data for the physical quantity for all the nodes are eventually used to obtain other correlated defining physical quantities such as fatigue damage, degree of cure for curing rubber, and buckling modes.

A common use of FEA is originally for the computation of stresses induced by mechanical and thermal deformations in mechanical devices and structural systems, while it gradually becomes an effective tool for solving more complex problems involving the coupling of structural behavior, heat transfer, fluid flow and electromagnetic effects. Application of FEA/CAE to fluid mechanics is also called CFD (Computational Fluid Dynamics) and FEA/CAE used for mechanism-oriented dynamic systems is often called MBD (Multi-body Dynamics). The implementation of finite element methods is usually divided into three phases:

Pre-processing: Doing finite element meshing of the geometry, with prescribed materials and boundary conditions, including mechanical loadings (i.e., displacements, forces, pressures, and shear tractions), initial temperature, initial speeds/accelerations, and other environmental work conditions. It also does the checking of mesh quality.

Processing: Employing finite element methods to solve finite element models, comprises the four steps, (a)~(d), mentioned above.

Post-processing: Using visualization tools to make inferences from the calculated result. Failure analysis such as fatigue, noise (acoustic pressure), buckling, or any other potential failure mode should be the follow-up step included in post-processing. The final goal of finite element analysis is in pursuit of a design value such as product life prediction, more than just "stress analysis".

Even if one knows in advance that a dynamic or nonlinear analysis is required, a linear static analysis is normally conducted first. A linear static in the steady state analysis is easy to run and can be used for debugging the preprocessor-built finite element model and refinement of mesh in the critical area before progressing to a more complex, time consuming, and expensive dynamic or nonlinear analysis.

1.4　Experimental Mechanics

Experimental mechanics is the category of disciplines and sub-disciplines in the field of mechanics that are concerned with the observation of mechanical phenomena based on physical experiments. As an application example, experimental mechanics procedures have led to a much more direct identification of fatigue testing of aircraft structures and then to develop it into a flying aircraft health and usage monitoring system. Methods vary from discipline to discipline, from simple experiments and observations such as the material hardness experiment, to more complicated ones such as

- (a) Strain-gages: Strain-gaging, strain indicators, wiring techniques, sensors, and transducers.
- (b) Moiré's methods: Moiré's interferometry and sharpening/multiplication techniques.
- (c) Photoelasticity: Three-dimensional photoelasticity, dynamic photoelasticity, scattered-light technique, birefringent coatings, and birefringent materials.
- (d) Holography: Holographic interferometry, speckle interferometry, and dynamic holophotoelastic method.
- (e) Nanoindentation: Identifying mechanical properties of materials such as stress-strain curves, creep, and fracture toughness by indentation. See Chapter 16 for details.

If virtual-reality knowledge of how to engineer systems and components to minimize or prevent failure is to aim at modern demanding product performance and the zero tolerance of failure, experimental mechanics is a real-world tool to explore and validate the potential for material performance and damage of such engineering products.

To see is to believe. "The solution of the increasingly complex engineering problems must rely more and more on experimental mechanics studies to indicate limitations in current theories, to formulate more realistic and general, yet simple, assumptions required for developing new theories, and later to check the compatibility of these new theories with still newer engineering situations or simulations thereof," as part of the editorial in the first issue of *Experimental Mechanics*, published by the Society of Experimental Mechanics. The then called new theories include new algorithms in numerical analysis such as finite element methods and finite difference methods.

1.5　Consistent Units

Units for engineering calculations such as finite element methods for structural stiffness, mechanical vibration, vehicle dynamics, thermal conduction, moisture diffusion, fluid flow, electric current flow, and magnetic field have been complicated by the unit of length in the automotive industry. Universally mm (millimeter) has been used for parts and their assemblies on automotive engineering drawings. Conversions of units between mm-based (millimeter) systems and m-based (meter) systems are complicated by the fact of even-ordered differential equations for dynamics and odd-ordered differential equations for heat transfer by nature. Usage of consistent units for engineering analysis is more complex than it appears. Units given in Table 1.5.1, are based on the dilemma that the units of time, temperature, and force are always second (s), centigrade (℃), and Newton (N), respectively, no matter whether mm (millimeter) or m (meter) is used for length. The derivative units are illustrated using generic steel data as unit-conversion examples, shown in the last column of the table.

Table 1.5.1   Recommended Units for Automotive Engineering Practice.

Variable	Unit/mm	Unit/m	Generic Steel (Example)
Time, t	s or sec	s or sec	s or sec
Temperature, T	℃ or K	℃ or K	℃
Force, F	N	N	N
Frequency, f	Hz(s^{-1})	Hz	Hz
Angular velocity, ω or Ω	rad/s	rad/s	rad/s
Length, L	mm	m	$1 \text{ mm} = 10^{-3} \text{ m}$
Mass, M	t(Ton)	kg	$1 \text{ t} = 10^{3} \text{ kg}$
Torque, T_x, T_y, T_z	N · mm	N · m	$1 \text{ N} \cdot \text{mm} = 10^{-3} \text{ N} \cdot \text{m}$
Velocity, V	mm/s	m/s	$1 \text{ mm/s} = 10^{-3} \text{ m/s}$
Acceleration, a	mm/s^2	m/s^2	$\text{mm/s}^2 = 10^{-3} \text{ m/s}^2$
Gravity, g	g	g	$1 \text{ g} = 9\ 807 \text{ mm/s}^2 = 9.807 \text{ m/s}^2$
Work, W	N · mm	J(N · m)	$1 \text{ N} \cdot \text{mm} = 10^{-3} \text{ J}$
Power, P	N · mm/s	W(J/s)	$1 \text{ N} \cdot \text{mm/s} = 10^{-3} \text{ W}$
Spring constant, K	N/mm	N/m	$1 \text{ N/mm} = 10^{3} \text{ N/m}$
Stress, σ	MPa(N/mm^2)	Pa(N/m^2)	$1 \text{ MPa} = 10^{6} \text{ Pa}$
Body force	N/mm^3	N/m^3	$1 \text{ N/mm}^3 = 10^{9} \text{ N/m}^3$
Strain, ε	—	—	—
Density, ρ	t/mm^3	kg/m^3	$7.83 \times 10^{-9} \text{ t/mm}^3 = 7\ 830 \text{ kg/m}^3$
Tensile modulus of elasticity, E_T	MPa(N/mm^2)	Pa(N/m^2)	$206 \text{ GPa} = 206 \times 10^{3} \text{ MPa} = 206 \times 10^{9} \text{ Pa}$

continued

Variable	Unit/mm	Unit/m	Generic Steel（Example）
Ultimate tensile strength, σ_{uts}	MPa	Pa	370 MPa＝370×10^6 Pa
Ultimate tensile strain, ε_{uts}	—	—	0.235 or 23.5%
Poisson's ratio, ν	—	—	0.29
Fatigue limit, σ_f	MPa	Pa	190 MPa＝190×10^6 Pa
Damping coefficient（viscous）, C_v	N・s/mm	N・s/m	N・s/mm＝10^3 N・s/m
C. of linear thermal expansion, α	μmm/mm/℃	μm/m/℃	12 μmm/mm/℃＝12 μm/m/℃
C. of linear moisture expansion, β	mm/mm/%	m/m/%	（3.3×10^{-3} mm/mm/℃ for PA6）
Specific heat capacity, γ	N・mm/T/℃	J/kg/℃	473×10^6N・mm/T/℃＝473 J/kg/℃
Thermal conductivity, k	N/S/℃	W/m/℃	42 N/S/℃＝42 W/m/℃
Heat convection coefficient, h	N/S/mm/℃	W/m^2/℃	9×10^{-3} N/S/mm/℃＝9 W/m^2/℃
Capacitance, C	—	F（Farad）	—
Electric charge, Q	—	C（Coulomb）	—
Electric conductance, G	—	S（Siemens）	—
Electric conductivity, σ_e	—	S/m	—
Electric current, I	—	A（Ampere.C/s）	—
Electric displacement, D	—	C/m^2	—
Electric field intensity, E	—	V/m or N・m/C	—
Electric potential, V	—	V（Volt）	—
Electric resistance/impedance, R/Z	—	Ω（Ohm）	—
Electric resistivity, ρ_e	—	Ω・m	—
Electric susceptibility, χ_e	—	Dimensionless	—
Electric permittivity, ϵ	—	C/N/m^2	—
Electromotive force, ΔE, V or U	—	V（Volt）	—
Inductance, L or M	—	H（Henry）	—
Magnetic field intensity, E	—	A/m or W/m/H	—
Magnetic flux, Φ_m	—	Wb（Weber）	—

continued

Variable	Unit/mm	Unit/m	Generic Steel(Example)
Magnetic flux density, $B(=V.s)$	—	$T(Tesla=Wb/m^2)$	—
Magnetic permeability, μ	—	Dimensionless	—
Magnetic susceptibility, χ_m	—	Dimensionless	—
Magnetization of material, M	—	A/m	—
Magnetization intensity J	—	$Tesla=Wb/m^2$	—

References

SWIFT T K, 2016. Plastics and Polymer Composites in Light Vehicles[J]. Dept. of Economics & Statistics, American Chemistry Council, July 2016:1-20.

ARDITO R, CORIGLIANO A, FRANGI A, et al, 2014. Computation of Adhesive Forces Due to Van Der Waals and Capillary Effects on Realistic Rough Surfaces. European Journal of Mechanics, A/Solids, 47: 298-308.

BATHE K J, 1976. Numerical Methods in Finite Element Analysis[J]. Mathematics of Computation, 31(139): S140.

BAYERER R, et al, 2008. Model for Power Cycling Lifetime of IGBT Modules: Various Factors Influencing Lifetime, CIPS 2008, Nuremberg, 2008:1-6.

BIANCHI N, 2005. Electrical Machine Analysis Using Finite Elements[M]. Power Electronics and Applications Series, Taylor and Francis.

BITTENCE J C, 1978. Specifying Materials Statistically[J]. Machine Design, 50(2):79-83.

BLAABJERG F, 2012. Power Electronics Converters for Wind Turbine Systems[J]. IEEE Transactions on Industrial Applications, 48(2):708-719.

BRUNDELL-FREIJ K, ERICSSON E. May 2005. Influence of Street Characteristics, Driver Category and Car Performance on Urban Driving Patterns[J]. Transportation Research Part D: Transport and Environment, 10 (3):213-229.

BUSCA C, 2011. Modeling Lifetime of High Power IGBTs in Wind Power Applications: An Overview, 2011 IEEE International Symposium of Industrial Electronics, Gdansk.

CALKINS D E, 1996. Learning All about Knowledge-Based Engineering[J]. Product Design and Development, Chilton Company, September:30-32.

CAO X, LU G, NGO K, 2012. Planar Power Module with Low Thermal Impedance and Low Thermomechanical Stress[J]. IEEE Trans. Components, Packaging and Manufacturing Technology, 2(8):1247-1259.

CHASKALOVIC J, 2008. Finite Elements Methods for Engineering Sciences: Theoretical Approach and Problem Solving Techniques[M]. Springer Verlag, 2008.

CHIANG Y J, BARBER G C, 1997. Self-Threading Bolts Tapped into Temperature-Dependent Plastic Bosses [J]. Int'l Journal of Materials and Product Technology, 12(2-3):110-123.

CHIANG Y J, TANG C, 1995. Accuracy Assessment to Applying 20-node Solid Elements to Pressurized Composite Shells[J]. Finite Elements in Analysis and Design, 20(4):219-232.

CHIANG Y J, LEE, Y L, 1994. Evaluation of Modeling Accuracy of 20-Node Solid Elements by Statistical Factorial Design[J]. Computers and Structures, 52(6):1309-1314.

COOK R D, 1995. Finite Element Modeling For Stress Analysis[M]. John Wiley & Sons.

COOK R D, MALKUS D S, PLESHA M E, 1993. Concepts and Applications in Finite Element Analysis[M]. 4th edition, McGraw-Hill, New York, NY, USA.

COOK W A, 1974. Body Oriented (Natural) Coordinates for Generating Three-dimensional Meshes[J]. Int'l Journal for Numerical Methods in Engineering, Vol. 8:27-43.

COOK W A, OAKES W R, 1982. Mapping Methods for Generating 3-Dimensional meshes[J]. Computers in Mechanical Engineering, August:67-72.

COULD J, 1998. CAD and CAM Integration[M]. Desktop Engineering, September:24-33.

DARVISH K K, TAKHOUNTS E G, MATHEWS B T, et al, 1999. A Nonlinear Viscoelastic Model for Polyurethane Foams[C]. SAE 1999-01-0299.

DUBARRY M, DEVIE A, MCKENZIE K, 2017. Durability and Reliability of Electric Vehicle Batteries under Electric Utility Grid Operations: Bidirectional Charging Impact Analysis[J]. Journal of Power Sources, 358: 39-49.

DUBENSKY R G, 1998. Simultaneous Engineering- Accurate Material Properties Leads to Effect Simulation [J]. SAE 980378.

DUPONT, 1992. Design Handbook for Dupont Engineering Polymers: Module 1- General Design Principles [M].15-23.

ERKKINEN T, 1999. Developing High-Integrity Software in C and Ada[R]. SAE 1999-01-0265.

FOO G, ZHANG X, 2017. Robust Direct Torque Control of Synchronous Reluctance Motor Drives in the Field Weakening Region, IEEE Transactions on Power Electronics, 32(2):1289-1298.

GOSS J, et al, 2010. The Design of AC Permanent Magnet Motors for Electric Vehicles: A Computationally Efficient Model of the Operational Envelope[C]. Bristol University.

HAYES J G, 2011. Simplified Electric Vehicle Powertrain Models and Range Estimation, IEEE Vehicle Power and Propulsion Conference (VPPC), Chicago, IL.

INFINEON, 2008. Thermal Equivalent Circuit Models[M]. Application NoteAN2008-03.

KARYA Y, OTSUKA M, 1998. Mechanical Fatigue Characteristics of $SnAg_X$ Solder Alloys[J]. Journal of Electronic Materials, 27(11):1229-1235.

KEENAN T, 1998. Modular Mania, Automotive Industries, November:34-37. SAE 2012-01-1027.

KIM N, et al, 2012. Comparison of Powertrain Configuration Options for Plug-in HEVs from a Fuel Economy Perspective[J]. SAE-2012-01-1027.

KISS T, LUSTBADER J, LEIGHTON D, 2015. Modeling of an Electric Vehicle Thermal Management System in MATLAB/Simulink[J], (11):35-36.

KOVACH J, 1996. Enterprise Integration, Actionline, Automotive Industry Action Group[J]. 16(5):32-35.

MCLEAN H, 2009. HALT, HASS, and HASA Explained[M]. ASQ Quality Press.

MELLOR P, WROBEL R, HOLLIDAY D, 2009. A Computationally Efficient Iron Loss Model for Brushless AC Machines that Caters for Rated Flux and Field Weakened Operation[C]. Proceedings of IEEE Int'l Electric Machines and Drives Conference, IEMDC '09:490-494.

MOHAN N, UNDELAND T, ROBBINS W, 1995. Power Electronics, Converters, Applications and Design [M]. 2nd edition, Wiley, NY.

MÜNZER M, THOBEN M, VETTER A, et al, 2006. Suitability of Power Semiconductor Modules for HEV Applications, Automotive Power Electronics.

NICOLA L, 2013. Lifetime Estimation of IGBT Power Modules, Master Thesis, Aalborg University, Aalborg.

NYE J F, 1957. Physical Properties of Crystals[M]. Clarendon Press, Oxford, UK.

ORLANDO M J, 1999. Modular Vehicle Approach[J]. SAE 1999-01-1255.

PATERA A T, 1984. A Spectral Element Method for Fluid Dynamics- Laminar Flow in a Channel Expansion [J]. Journal of Computational Physics, 54(3):468-488.

PERVIN S, et al, 2012. Newton-Raphson Based Computation of i_d in the Field Weakening Region of IPM Motor Incorporating the Stator Resistance to Improve the Performance[C]//Industry Applications Society Meeting IEEE.

RASK E, LOHSE-BUSCH H, DUOBA M, et al, 2014. Ford Focus BEV In-depth (Level 2) Testing and Analysis[C]. DOE Annual Merit Review Presentation.

SHOOK S O, 1990. Fabricating a Magnesium Part:An Overview, SAE 900790.

SMITH K, et al, 2013. Models for Battery Reliability and Lifetime:Applications in Design and Health

Management, NREL/PR-5400-58550, Battery Congress, April 15-16, Ann Arbor, MI.

SRAJBER D, LUKASCH W, 1992. The Calculation of the Power Dissipation for the IGBT and the Inverse Diode[C]//Electronica Conference.

THOBEN M, et al, 2008. From Vehicle Drive Cycle to Reliability Testing of Power Modules for Hybrid Vehicle Inverter[C]//PCIM Europe 2008.

TOLBERT L M, et al, 1998. Multilevel Inverters for Electric Vehicle Applications[C]//Power Electronics in Transportation IEEE, Dearborn, MI:79-85.

SMET E, et al, 2011. Ageing and Failure Modes of IGBT Modules in High-temperature Power Cycling, IEEE Transactions on Industrial Electronics, 58:4931-4941.

WANG P Z, et al, 1999. Quantitative Characterization of Scratch Damage in Polypropylene (TPO) for Automotive Interior Applications, SAE 1999-01-0243.

WARNER J D, MILLER A G, 1990. Advanced Composite Use Experience-The Basis for Future Applications, SAE 901938.

ZIENKIEWICZ O C, TAYLOR R L, ZU J Z, 2005. The Finite Element Method: Its Basis and Fundamentals [J]. Butterworth-Heinemann.

Chapter 2

Elastoplastics

2.1　Thermomechanical Properties

Engineering of vehicular systems and parts needs sophisticated defining analytics and testing to assure that the materials can meet various loading requirements in the working environment. Abrupt fractures, fatigue, creep, resonance, buckling, fretting, corrosion, oxidation and other degradation are potential failure modes of great concern when making a mechanical or electromagnetic design decision on product reliability and sustainability. Vibration and noises are anti-ergonomic and must be also taken into consideration. Nevertheless, a product is fundamentally made of materials at all events. Thermomechanical properties of both mechanical and electromagnetic components are essential for analyzing and synthesizing these potential failure modes, which are dominated by stochastic nonlinear behaviors of materials as a function of strain, strain rate, strain energy, temperature, moisture, time, and space. Among all, elastoplastic properties of these materials are the foundation. The stress-strain curves of PA6,6/33GF (Nylon 6, 6 reinforced with 33% by volume), which is a popular material used for vehicular parts such as door handles, interior trims, and sensors are given in Fig. 2.1.1 to demonstrate the influence of temperature.

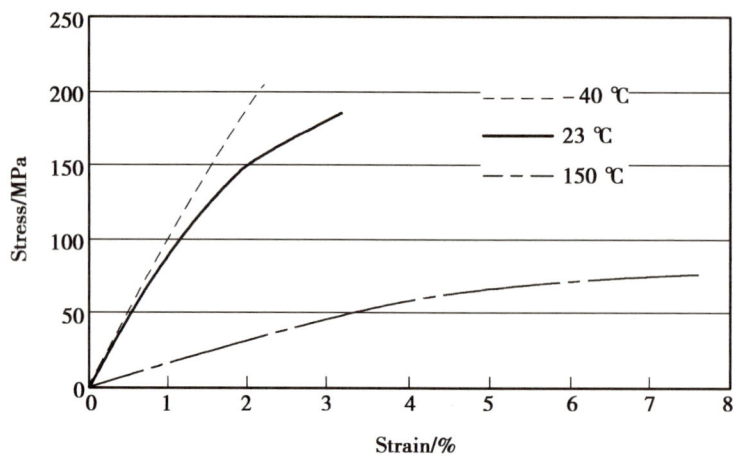

Fig. 2.1.1　Stress-Strain Curves of Dry-as-Molded PA6, 6/33GF ［DuPont］ at Different Working Temperatures

2.2　Density, ρ

Density is the most important engineering parameter. The weight of a vehicle is a combination of each "density × volume" of its individual constituents. Specific weight is defined as the ratio of the material density to the cool water at 4 ℃. The unit of material density given in g/cm^3 is in compliance with its specific weight, for convenience. Ground-vehicle parts are usually dimensioned in mm (millimeter) and the part weight is measured by kg (Kilogram) in practice. The resulting value of density used for engineering calculations has to be in t/mm^3. For example, the density of aluminum (specific weight = 2.7) to be used for engineering calculations ought to be

2.7×10^{-9} t/mm^3, in contrast to 2700 kg/m^3 if the traditional metric system (e.g. meter and kg) is used. The strength of engineering materials as a function of density is depicted in Fig. 2.2.1.

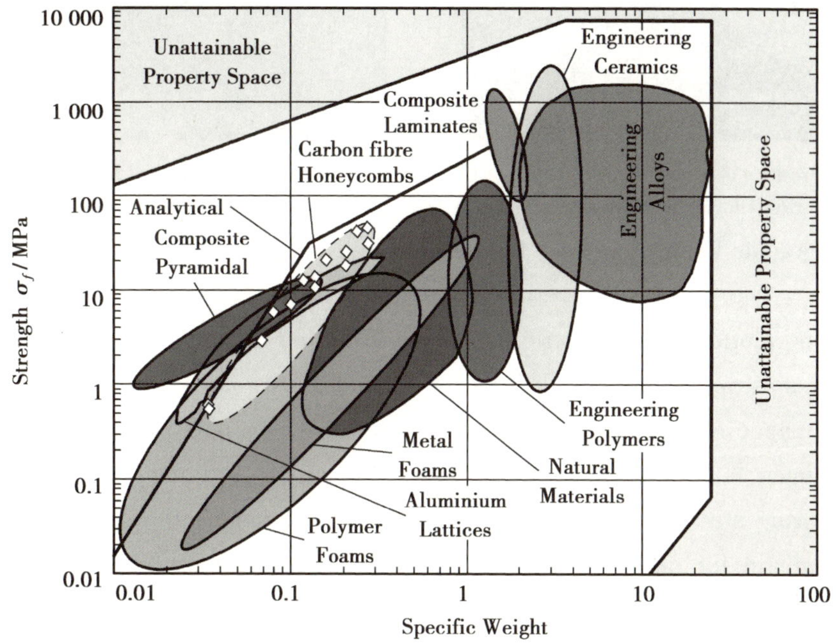

Fig. 2.2.1   Strength of Materials as a Function of Density [Ashby & Bréchet 2003]

2.3   Stress-Strain Curves

The commonly accepted method in evaluation of the mechanical properties of a solid would be the uniaxial test in tension or compression. The amount of strain is then derived from the measure length change and its corresponding stress are then computed accordingly. The engineering measures of stress and strain, denoted here as σ_e and ε_e respectively, are determined from the measured load and defection using the original specimen cross-sectional area A_o and length L_o as

$$\sigma_e \equiv \frac{F}{A_o} \tag{2.3.1}$$

and $$\varepsilon_e \equiv \frac{L - L_o}{L_o} = \frac{L}{L_o} - 1 \tag{2.3.2}$$

where

F: Applied constant load;

A_o: Original specimen cross-section;

L_o: Original specimen length considered;

L: Updated instantaneous length after being elongated.

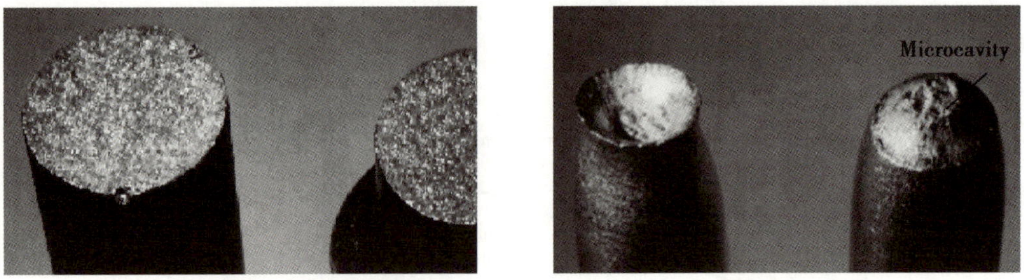

(a) Breaking of Atomic Bonds along
Crystallographic Planes

(b) Necking-induced Microcavities
due to Plastic Deformation

Fig. 2.3.1　Fractographic Features of (a) Brittle Steel and (b) Ductile Steel

When stress σ_e is plotted against strain ε_e, it is called an engineering stress-strain curve (Fig. 2.3.1). Stress-strain curves at different temperatures are required for analyzing the mechanical performance of automotive parts and systems. The stress is usually lower at the same strain if the specimen temperature is raised. Since the cross-sectional area varies with the load level, the engineering stress and strain are hypothetical. It means that engineering stress-strain curves are not realistic for doing product analysis, though engineering stresses and strains are typical formats given in some available literature for characterizing material properties.

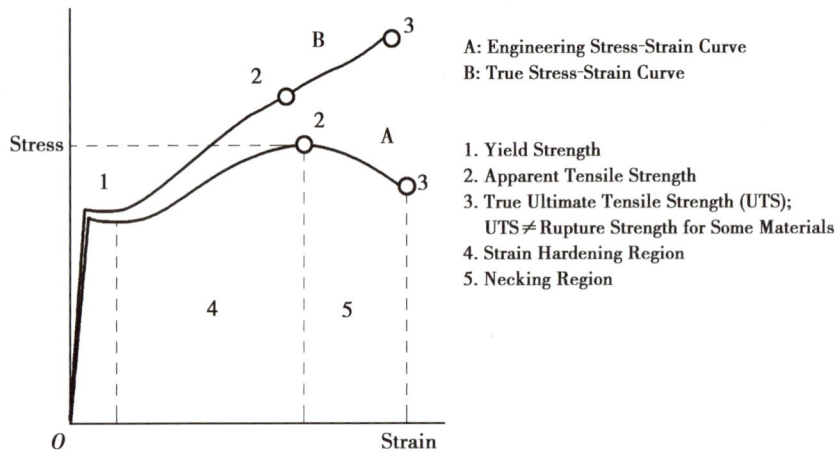

A: Engineering Stress-Strain Curve
B: True Stress-Strain Curve

1. Yield Strength
2. Apparent Tensile Strength
3. True Ultimate Tensile Strength (UTS);
   UTS ≠ Rupture Strength for Some Materials
4. Strain Hardening Region
5. Necking Region

Fig. 2.3.2　Typical Stress-Strain Curves of Ductile Carbon Steel in Tension

True stresses and strains are realistic physically and they are in the proper sense of product life prediction by means of failure analysis. Consider uniaxial loading in tension of a uniform rod section of length z as measured. An incremental change in the gage length with respect to its length is defined as the strain increment,

$$\mathrm{d}\varepsilon = \frac{\mathrm{d}z}{z} \tag{2.3.3}$$

An integration of the strain increment from the original length (L_o) to the current length (L) yields the total strain as

$$\varepsilon = \int d\varepsilon = \int_{L_o}^{L} \left(\frac{dz}{z} \right) = \ln \frac{L}{L_o} \tag{2.3.4a}$$

i.e. $\quad \dfrac{L}{L_o} = e^{\varepsilon}$ $\tag{2.3.4b}$

The strain defined above is called true strain, natural strain, logarithmic strain, or Hencky strain. It is also an indicator of material ductility. Substituting Eq. (2.3.2) into Eq. (2.3.4) gives the relationship between the true strain and engineering strain,

$$\varepsilon_{true} = \ln(1 + \varepsilon_e) \tag{2.3.5}$$

It means that a true strain can be calculated by taking a natural logarithm of its corresponding engineering strain. The true stress is defined as the instantaneous force change with respect to the corresponding area change as

$$\sigma_{true} = \lim_{\Delta A \to 0} \frac{\Delta F}{\Delta A} \approx \frac{F}{A} \tag{2.3.6}$$

of which A is the updated cross-sectional area. The true stress of a material is an indicator of its mechanical, based on the assumption of volume conservation that

$$A\,L = A_o\,L_o \tag{2.3.7a}$$

or $\quad A = \dfrac{A_o\,L_o}{L}$ $\tag{2.3.7b}$

Substituting Eq. (2.3.7) back into Eq. (2.3.4b) leads to the updated instantaneous cross-sectional area [Holoman]

$$A = A_o\,e^{-\varepsilon} \approx A_o(1 - \varepsilon) \tag{2.3.8}$$

The above approximating equation can be obtained using the Taylor's series expansion that $e^{-\varepsilon} = 1 - \varepsilon + \varepsilon^2/2 - \cdots \approx (1-\varepsilon)$ on the condition that ε is significantly small. Substituting Eq. (2.3.7) into Eq. (2.3.6), one has

$$\sigma_{true} \approx \frac{F}{A} = \frac{F}{A_o} \frac{A_o}{A} = \sigma_e \frac{L}{L_o} = \sigma_e \frac{L_o + \Delta L}{L_o} = \sigma_e(1 + \varepsilon_e) \tag{2.3.9}$$

Thus, the true stress is brought into correspondence with an engineering stress as being scaled up in token of the true strain. The initial slope of a stress-strain curve is its modulus of elasticity, also called Young's modulus. The unit for stress and modulus of elasticity is MPa or Pa, but there is no unit for strain. The schematic drawing of a typical engineering stress-strain curve of steel is the lower A curve depicted in Fig. 2.3.2. Some mechanical strength points of great significance are identified as follows:

(a) Proportional limit: Point that the stress is still related to the strain linearly.

(b) Elastic limit: Point that the strain can be recovered completely once unloaded.

(c) Yield point: Equivalent to elastic limit or at the stress point taken at 0.2% strain.

(d) Ultimate strength: Peak stress point of the stress-strain curve.

(e) Rupture strength: Facture initiation point.

(f) Actual rupture strength: Rupture strength on the true stress-strain curve.

The actual rupture strength (either tensile or compressive) is the ultimate design point, as shown in the true stress-strain curve, i.e., the upper B curve in Fig. 2.3.2. The true stress-strain relationship ought to be used for failure analysis. This is mandated by some FEA (finite element analysis) codes such as Abaqus to use true stresses and strains. Engineering stress-strain curves are applicable only for small deformations. In such cases true stress-strain and engineering stress-strain curves coincide within reasonable tolerances.

Ultimate strengths, denoted as σ_{uts} or σ_{ucs} and ultimate strains denoted as ε_{uts} or ε_{ucs} are the stress and strain levels, at which the material fractures under pure tension and compression, respectively. Most materials reach a yield point, at which the strain begins to increase rapidly with a less corresponding increase in stress. Nevertheless, the yield strength (σ_y) is evaluated at a strain of 0.2% for steel and some other metals in practice. Most true stress-strain curves grow asymptotically based on a quasi-static monotonic stress-strain tests and therefore a data set of three points selected properly is generally considered adequate to approximate a stress-strain curve before the peak stress level is reached. They are denoted as $(0, 0)$, $(\sigma_y, 0.2\%)$, and $(\sigma_{us}, \varepsilon_{us})$ for metals and engineering plastics, while special material constants are used for rubber-like materials (elastomers) in order to account for its incompressibility. If ε_{us} is far larger than 0.2%, arbitrary intermediate loading points $(\sigma_i, \varepsilon_i)$ may be taken instead, such that data points $(0, 0)$, $(\sigma_y, 0.2\%)$, $\cdots$, $(\sigma_i, \varepsilon_i)$, $\cdots$, $(\sigma_{us}, \varepsilon_{us})$ can represent the entire stress-strain curve properly.

2.4　Onset of Necking

Plastic strain starts at the very onset of necking, which begins at the maximum load where the increase in stress due to the decrease in the cross-sectional area of the specimen becomes greater than the increase in the load-carrying ability of the specimen due to strain hardening. A general true plastic stress-strain curve increases monotonically and it can be approximated by the following power expression of stress flow according to [Hollomon]:

$$\sigma = \sigma_e + K \varepsilon_p^n \tag{2.4.1}$$

or $\quad \sigma - \sigma_e = K \varepsilon_p^n$ (2.4.2)

where

σ: True stress;

σ_e: Elastic stress;

ε_p: Plastic strain (a true strain);

K: Static strength coefficient;

n: Work hardening exponent.

Exponent n is also called strain hardening parameter. When $n = 0$, it is a perfect plastic deformation. When $n = 1$, the plastic stress increases linearly with respect to the plastic strain. Generally speaking, $n = 0.5$ for a FCC (Face Center Cubic), $n = 0.15$ for BCC (Body Centered Cubic), and $n = 0.05$ for HCP (Hexagonal Close Packed) structures, respectively, for the majority of common metals. In the range of $0 < n < 1$, it presents a uniform elongation, necking and post-necking behavior sequentially. It can be ascertained that a uniform elongation is prolonged as strain hardening parameter n increases for most common metals. By taking a natural log on both sides of Eq.(2.4.2) and a differentiation of ln (σ) with respect to ln (ε), one has an explicit equation for the work hardening exponent as

$$n = \frac{d(\ln \sigma)}{d(\ln \varepsilon_p)} \tag{2.4.3}$$

The true stress is the ratio of the applied force to its corresponding true cross-sectional area after deformation. Thus, in light of Eq. (2.4.1) the applied static force can be attributed to two distinct components: the elastic deformation and fully plastic deformation, shown as below:

$$F = A \sigma = A \sigma_e + A K \varepsilon_p^n = F_e + F_p \tag{2.4.4}$$

On the other hand, substituting Eq. (2.3.9) into Eq. (2.4.2) yields

$$F_p = A (\sigma - \sigma_e) = K A_o e^{-\varepsilon_p} \varepsilon_p^n \tag{2.4.5}$$

Thus　$\ln (F_p) = \ln(K) + \ln(A_o) - \varepsilon_p + n \ln(\varepsilon_p)$ \hfill (2.4.6)

Taking a differentiation of the terms on both sides of the above equation with respect to the true strain, one has

$$\frac{d(\ln F_p)}{d\varepsilon_p} = 0 + 0 - 1 + \frac{n}{\varepsilon_p} = \frac{n}{\varepsilon_p} - 1 \tag{2.4.7}$$

The onset of necking takes place when the internal plastic force reaches the maximum value. At the moment when $d(\ln(F_p))/d\varepsilon_p = 0$, Eq. (2.4.7) reduces to

$$n = (\varepsilon_p)_{fractured} = \varepsilon_{us} \tag{2.4.8}$$

of which ε_{us} is the ultimate strain (true strain). The above equation is called Considere's criterion that diffused necking starts at the point of maximum stress on the engineering stress-strain curve, resulting in that the magnitude of the corresponding true strain (mainly plastic strain) is equal to the work hardening exponent n. In other words, the physical meaning of hardening exponent n is ultimate true strain ε_{us} as given by Eq. (2.4.8) at the onset of necking. One may jumps to the conclusion that the greater the strain-hardening exponent, the greater is the effort for the plastic strain to reach the diffused necking [Choung & Cho].

2.5　Correction Factor for Triaxial State of Uniaxially Loaded Specimens

As a specimen is conducted on a uniaxial stress-strain curve tester, it is necessary to correct the true stress calculation for necking effect, which exhibits a multiaxial stress state. Schematic drawings of two different specimens for test of material properties, i.e., HCF (High Cycle Fatigue) and LCF (Low Cycle Fatigue) specimens are depicted in Fig. 2.5.1(a) and Fig. 2.5.1(b), respectively.

2.5.1　Bridgman Equation

In reference to Fig. 2.5.1(a) the axial stress in the loading direction (σ_z), radial stress (σ_r), and tangential stress (σ_t) on the cross-sectional plane of the minimal cross-sectional area in the cylindrical coordinate system are, respectively given as follows [Bridgman]:

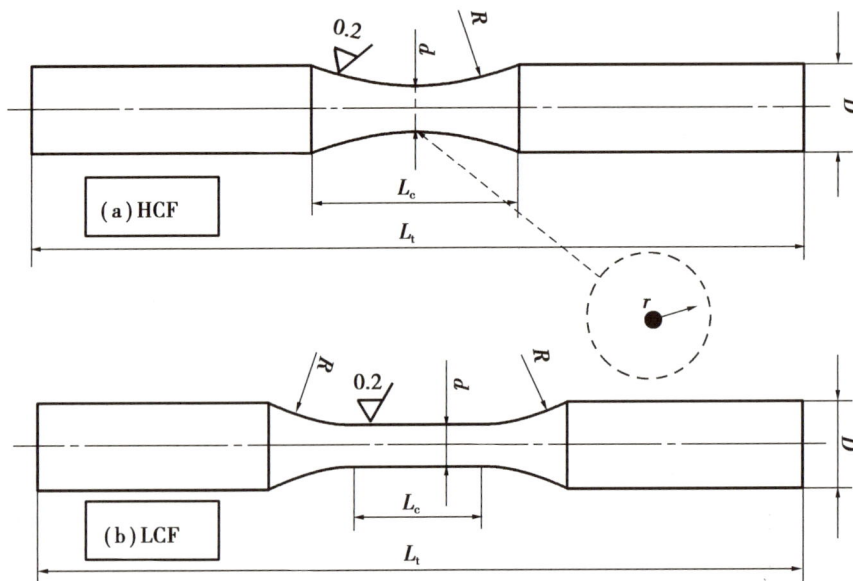

Fig. 2.5.1　Test Specimens Used for Material Properties for (a) High Cycle Fatigue (HCF) and (b) Low Cycle Fatigue (LCF)

$$\sigma_z(r) = \frac{\left(\dfrac{F_f}{A_f}\right)\left[1 + \ln\left(\dfrac{d_{min}^2 + 4\,R\,d_{min} - 4\,r}{4\,R\,d_{min}}\right)\right]}{\left(1 + \dfrac{4\,R}{d_{min}}\right)\ln\left(1 + \dfrac{d_{min}}{4R}\right)} \qquad (2.5.1)$$

$$\sigma_r(r) = \sigma_t(r) = \frac{\dfrac{F_f}{A_f}\ln\left(\dfrac{d_{min}^2 + 4\,R\,d_{min} - 4\,r}{4\,R\,d_{min}}\right)}{\left(1 + \dfrac{4\,R}{d_{min}}\right)\ln\left(1 + \dfrac{d_{min}}{4R}\right)} \qquad (2.5.2)$$

where

F_f: Final load at fracture;

A_f: Final cross-sectional area of the specimen center at fracture;

R: Radius of neck curvature;

d_{min}: Diameter of the minimal cross-section as necking develops, i.e., d in Fig. 2.5.1(a);

r: Radius variable in the minimal cross-sectional area, as shown in Fig. 2.5.1(a).

The Bridgman correction factor may be used to calculate exactly an equivalent true stress (such as von Mises stress), compensating for the triaxial state of stress as applied to cylindrical specimens as

$$\sigma_{true} = \frac{\dfrac{F_f}{A_f}}{\left(1 + \dfrac{4\,R}{d_{min}}\right)\ln\left(1 + \dfrac{d_{min}}{4R}\right)} \qquad (2.5.3)$$

Bridgman correction method can also predict the true stress-strain relationship beyond necking fairly well providing that the radius of curvature is accurately measured [Zhang and Li]. A stress-strain curve can be in tension or compression. Bridgman's correction is not easy to use in practice, as it requires the updated radius of curvature R and the diameter of the minimal cross-section radius (d_{min}). Both parameters are difficult to measure with sufficient degree of accuracy, with increasing variation of tensile loading even for a round specimen. In order to overcome this difficulty, LeRoy et al. proposed an empirical equation that

$$\frac{d_{min}}{2\,R} = 1.1\,(\varepsilon - \varepsilon_u) \qquad (2.5.4)$$

The ratio of $1/2d_{min}$ to R in the necked region is proportional to the difference between the current true strain (ε) and the true ultimate strain (ε_u), at which the onset of necking takes place as the internal force reaches its maximum value. When $\varepsilon = \varepsilon_u$, the specimen is fractured and could be tumbled to pieces ($d_{min} = 0$).

2.5.2　Cyclic Loading

The cyclic stress-strain curve has to be used for fatigue analysis instead of quasi-static monotonic loading. Results from finite element analysis of HSLA350 steel based on LCF specimens using the cyclic stress-strain curve under cyclic loading are demonstrated in Figs. (2.5.2) and (2.5.3). It shows that the stress level due to cyclic loading is generally higher than the quasi-static one due to cyclic hardening.

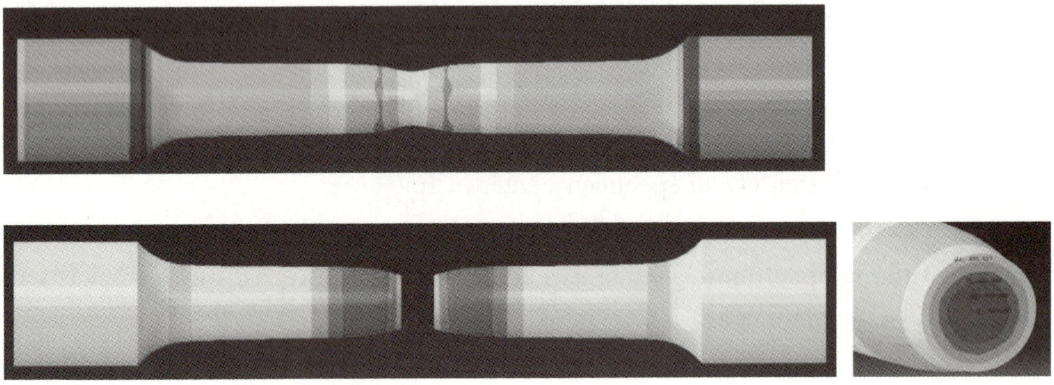

Fig. 2.5.2　Finite Element Analysis of HSLA350 Steel Based on LCF Specimens under Cyclic Stress-Strain Curve

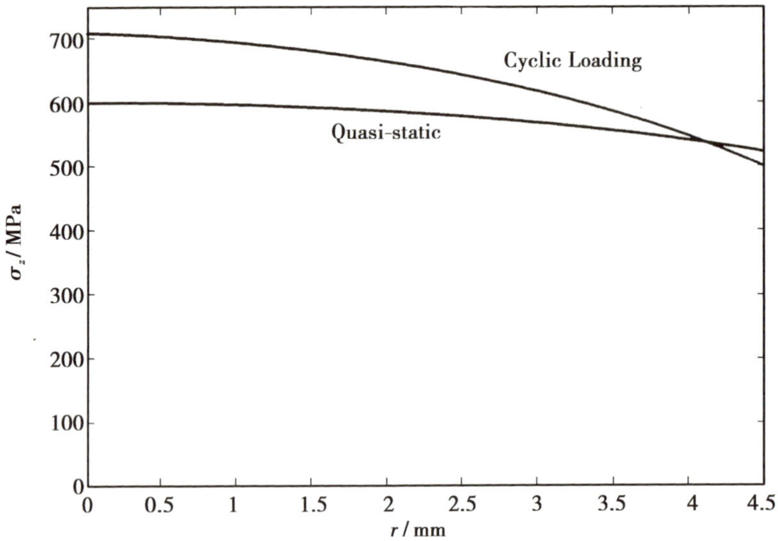

Fig. 2.5.3　Comparison of Axial Forces between Cyclic Stress-Strain Curve（Finite Element Analysis）and the Bridgman Equation for Quasi-Static Case Using the LCF Specimens

2.6   Constitutive Equations of Elasticity in Isotropic Homogeneous Material

The constitutive equations of elasticity are defined to describe the relationship between physical quantities which pertains to the elastic deformation range of the material. These physical quantities, for example, can be stresses, strains, Young's modulus, Poisson's ratio, and shear modulus.

2.6.1   Poisson's Ratio

When a solid is stretched in one direction, it tends to contract in the plane perpendicular to the stretching direction. In terms of strains induced in a solid under a simple unidirectional load along x-axis, it is defined as the ratio of the normal stress in y-direction to the normal stress in x-direction, such that

$$\nu = \frac{-\varepsilon_{yy}}{\varepsilon_{xx}} \tag{2.6.1}$$

2.6.2   Stress-Strain Relationship

Poisson's ratio falls between 0 and 0.5 for a homogeneous continuum. For homogeneous material, the 3-dimensional stress-strain relationships in the (x, y, z) coordinate system can be described by six equations in the 3-dimensional space. In case of known stresses, the strains can be calculated as

$$\varepsilon_{xx} = \frac{\sigma_{xx} - \nu\,\sigma_{yy} - \nu\,\sigma_{zz}}{E} \tag{2.6.2}$$

$$\varepsilon_{yy} = \frac{\sigma_{yy} - \nu\,\sigma_{zz} - \nu\,\sigma_{xx}}{E} \tag{2.6.3}$$

$$\varepsilon_{zz} = \frac{\sigma_{zz} - \nu\,\sigma_{xx} - \nu\,\sigma_{yy}}{E} \tag{2.6.4}$$

$$\gamma_{xy} = 2\,\varepsilon_{xy} = \frac{\tau_{xy}}{G} \tag{2.6.5}$$

$$\gamma_{yz} = 2\,\varepsilon_{yz} = \frac{\tau_{yz}}{G} \tag{2.6.6}$$

and $\quad \gamma_{zx} = 2\,\varepsilon_{zx} = \dfrac{\tau_{zx}}{G} \tag{2.6.7}$

In case of known strains, the stresses can be calculated as

$$\sigma_{xx} = \frac{E}{(1 - 2\nu)(1 + \nu)}[(1 - \nu)\,\varepsilon_{xx} + \nu\,\varepsilon_{yy} + \nu\,\varepsilon_{zz}] \tag{2.6.8}$$

$$\sigma_{yy} = \frac{E}{(1 - 2\nu)(1 + \nu)}[\nu\,\varepsilon_{xx} + (1 - \nu)\,\varepsilon_{yy} + \nu\,\varepsilon_{zz}] \tag{2.6.9}$$

$$\sigma_{zz} = \frac{E}{(1 - 2\nu)(1 + \nu)}[\nu\,\varepsilon_{xx} + \nu\,\varepsilon_{yy} + (1 - \nu)\,\varepsilon_{zz}] \tag{2.6.10}$$

$$\tau_{xy} = G\,\gamma_{xy} = 2G\,\varepsilon_{xy} \tag{2.6.11}$$

$$\tau_{yz} = G\,\gamma_{yz} = 2G\,\varepsilon_{yz} \tag{2.6.12}$$

and $\quad \tau_{zx} = G\,\gamma_{zx} = 2G\,\varepsilon_{zx} \tag{2.6.13}$

Tensile (compressive) modulus of elasticity E is the initial slope of the stress-strain curve in tension (compression). Its corresponding shear modulus of elasticity G is

$$G = \frac{E}{2(1 + \nu)} \tag{2.6.14}$$

A stress-strain curve for the material is mostly obtained from the frictionless, low-speed uniaxial tensile or compression test at the room temperature, though triaxial or biaxial tests are desired.

2.6.3　Principal Stresses

The principal stresses in the space are the three stress components corresponding to a stress state in a special coordinate system, in which the shear stresses disappear. Given that the six stress components in the 3-dimensional space are σ_{xx}, σ_{yy}, σ_{zz}, σ_{xy}, σ_{yz}, and σ_{zx}, the principal stresses in 3-dimensional space will be calculated from the following three equations

$$\sigma_1 = \frac{I_1}{3} + \frac{2}{3}(I_1^2 - 3I_2)^{\frac{1}{2}}\cos\theta \tag{2.6.15}$$

$$\sigma_2 = \frac{I_1}{3} + \frac{2}{3}(I_1^2 - 3I_2)^{\frac{1}{2}}\cos\left(\theta - \frac{2}{3}\pi\right) \tag{2.6.16}$$

and $\quad \sigma_3 = \dfrac{I_1}{3} + \dfrac{2}{3}(I_1^2 - 3I_2)^{\frac{1}{2}}\cos\left(\theta - \dfrac{4}{3}\pi\right) \tag{2.6.17}$

where

$$I_1 = \sigma_{xx} + \sigma_{yy} + \sigma_{zz} = \sigma_1 + \sigma_2 + \sigma_3 \tag{2.6.18}$$

$$I_2 = \sigma_{xx}\,\sigma_{yy} + \sigma_{yy}\,\sigma_{zz} + \sigma_{zz}\,\sigma_{xx} - \sigma_{xy}^2 - \sigma_{yz}^2 - \sigma_{zx}^2 = \sigma_1\,\sigma_2 + \sigma_2\,\sigma_3 + \sigma_3\,\sigma_1 \tag{2.6.19}$$

$$I_3 = \sigma_{xx}\,\sigma_{yy}\,\sigma_{zz} - \sigma_{xx}\,\sigma_{yz}^2 - \sigma_{yy}\,\sigma_{zx}^2 - \sigma_{zz}\,\sigma_{xy}^2 + 2\,\sigma_{xy}\,\sigma_{yz}\,\sigma_{zx} = \sigma_1\,\sigma_2\,\sigma_3 \tag{2.6.20}$$

$$\text{and} \quad \theta = \frac{1}{3}\cos^{-1}\left[\frac{2\,I_1^3 - 9\,I_1\,I_2 + 27\,I_3}{2(I_1^2 - 3\,I_2)^{\frac{3}{2}}}\right] \tag{2.6.21}$$

Note that parameters I_1, I_2, and I_3 are called stress variants. Angle θ is the angle required for the directional cosines of the new coordinate system (x', y', z') relative to the original (x, y, z) coordinate system. This operation is called a stress transformation. There are three direction cosines involved in a general 3-dimensional strain transformation.

Next consider the 2-dimensional stress transformation in the state of plane stress. as shown in Fig. 2.6.1. Assume that the three stress components at a point in the two-dimensional domain with an arbitrary Cartesian coordinate system (x, y, z) are σ_{xx}, σ_{yy}, and σ_{xy}. Due to the Mohr's circle method, these normal and shear after being rotated from the (x, y, z) coordinate system to a new coordinate denoted as (x', y', z') about the z-axis (i.e., $z'=z$), the new stress components are

$$\sigma_{x'x'} = \frac{1}{2}(\sigma_{xx} + \sigma_{yy}) + \frac{1}{2}(\sigma_{xx} - \sigma_{yy})\cos 2\theta + \tau_{xy}\sin 2\theta \tag{2.6.22}$$

$$\sigma_{y'y'} = \frac{1}{2}(\sigma_{xx} + \sigma_{yy}) - \frac{1}{2}(\sigma_{xx} - \sigma_{yy})\cos 2\theta - \tau_{xy}\sin 2\theta \tag{2.6.23}$$

$$\text{and} \quad \tau_{x'y'} = -\frac{1}{2}(\sigma_{xx} - \sigma_{yy})\sin 2\theta + \tau_{xy}\cos 2\theta \tag{2.6.24}$$

where

$\sigma_{x'x'}$: Normal stress along x'-axis;

$\tau_{x'y'}$: Engineering shear stress.

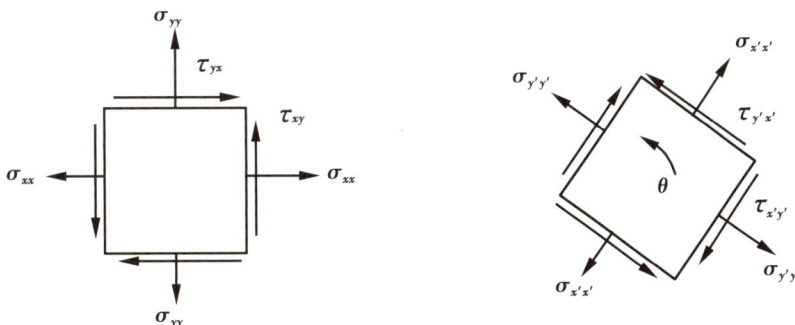

Fig. 2.6.1   Mohr's Circle Method for 2-D Stress Transformation in Plane Stress State

Then the principal stresses can be calculated when $\tau_{x'y'} = 0$, which yields

$$\theta = \frac{1}{2}\tan^{-1}\left[\frac{\tau_{xy}}{\frac{1}{2}(\sigma_{xx} - \sigma_{yy})}\right] \tag{2.6.25}$$

Plugging the above equation into Eq. (2.6.22) yields

$$\sigma = \frac{1}{2}(\sigma_{xx} + \sigma_{yy}) \pm \left\{\left[\frac{1}{2}(\sigma_{xx} - \sigma_{yy})\right]^2 + \tau_{xy}^2\right\}^{\frac{1}{2}} \tag{2.6.26}$$

Two principal stresses will be obtained from the above equation, while their calculated values have to be compared with the other component "$\sigma = 0$" for ranking the order as

$$\sigma_1 \geqslant \sigma_2 \geqslant \sigma_3 \tag{2.6.27}$$

The maximum shear stress is then,

$$\tau_{max} = \left\{\left[\frac{1}{2}(\sigma_{xx} - \sigma_{yy})\right]^2 + \tau_{xy}^2\right\}^{\frac{1}{2}} = \frac{1}{2}(\sigma_1 - \sigma_3) \tag{2.6.28}$$

2.6.4 Principal Strains

The principal stresses in the space are the three strain components corresponding to a strain state in a special coordinate system, in which the shear strains disappear. Given that the six strain components in the 3-dimensional space are ε_{xx}, ε_{yy}, ε_{zz}, ε_{xy}, ε_{yz}, and ε_{zx}, the principal strains will be calculated from the following three equations

$$\varepsilon_1 = \frac{J_1}{3} + \frac{2}{3}(J_1^2 - 3J_2)^{\frac{1}{2}}\cos\theta_\varepsilon \tag{2.6.29}$$

$$\varepsilon_2 = \frac{J_1}{3} + \frac{2}{3}(J_1^2 - 3J_2)^{\frac{1}{2}}\cos\left(\theta_\varepsilon - \frac{2\pi}{3}\right) \tag{2.6.30}$$

and $$\varepsilon_3 = \frac{J_1}{3} + \frac{2}{3}(J_1^2 - 3J_2)^{\frac{1}{2}}\cos\left(\theta_\varepsilon - \frac{4\pi}{3}\right) \tag{2.6.31}$$

where

$$J_1 = \varepsilon_{xx} + \varepsilon_{yy} + \varepsilon_{zz} \tag{2.6.32}$$

$$J_2 = \varepsilon_{xx}\varepsilon_{yy} + \varepsilon_{yy}\varepsilon_{zz} + \varepsilon_{zz}\varepsilon_{xx} - \varepsilon_{xy}^2 - \varepsilon_{yz}^2 - \varepsilon_{zx}^2 \tag{2.6.33}$$

$$J_3 = \varepsilon_{xx}\varepsilon_{yy}\varepsilon_{zz} - \varepsilon_{xx}\varepsilon_{yz}^2 - \varepsilon_{yy}\varepsilon_{zx}^2 - \varepsilon_{zz}\varepsilon_{xy}^2 + 2\varepsilon_{xy}\varepsilon_{yz}\varepsilon_{zx} \tag{2.6.34}$$

and $\quad \theta_\varepsilon = \dfrac{1}{3}\cos^{-1}\left[\dfrac{2\,J_1^3 - 9\,J_1\,J_2 + 27\,J_3}{2(J_1^2 - 3\,J_2)^{\frac{3}{2}}}\right]$ $\hspace{2cm}$ (2.6.35)

Note that parameters J_1, J_2, and J_3 are called strain variants. Angle θ is the angle required for the directional cosines of the new coordinate system (x', y', z') relative to the original (x, y, z) coordinate system. This operation is called a strain transformation. There are three direction cosines involved in a general 3-dimensional strain transformation.

Next consider the 2-dimensional strain transformation in the state of plane stress. Assume that the three strain components at a point in the two-dimensional domain with an arbitrary Cartesian coordinate system (x, y, z) are ε_{xx}, ε_{yy}, and ε_{xy}. Due to the Mohr's circle method, these normal and shear after being rotated from the (x, y, z) coordinate system to a new coordinate denoted as (x', y', z') about the z-axis (i.e., $z' = z$), the new stress components are

$$\varepsilon_{x'x'} = \frac{1}{2}\,(\varepsilon_{xx} + \varepsilon_{yy}) + \frac{1}{2}\,(\varepsilon_{xx} - \varepsilon_{yy})\,\cos 2\theta + \varepsilon_{xy}\sin 2\theta \qquad (2.6.36)$$

$$\varepsilon_{y'y'} = \frac{1}{2}\,(\varepsilon_{xx} + \varepsilon_{yy}) - \frac{1}{2}\,(\varepsilon_{xx} - \varepsilon_{yy})\,\cos 2\theta - \varepsilon_{xy}\sin 2\theta \qquad (2.6.37)$$

and $\quad \varepsilon_{x'y'} = \dfrac{1}{2}\,\gamma_{x'y'} = -\dfrac{1}{2}\,(\varepsilon_{xx} - \varepsilon_{yy})\sin 2\theta + \varepsilon_{xy}\cos 2\theta$ $\hspace{1.5cm}$ (2.6.38)

where

$\varepsilon_{x'x'}$: Normal strain along x'-axis;

$\varepsilon_{x'y'}$: Tensor shear strain;

$\gamma_{x'y'}$: Engineering shear strain.

Note that $\gamma_{xy} = 2\varepsilon_{xy}$. The principal strains can be calculated at the moment when $\gamma_{x'y'} = 0$. That yields

$$\theta = \frac{1}{2}\tan^{-1}\left[\frac{\varepsilon_{xy}}{\dfrac{1}{2}\,(\varepsilon_{xx} - \varepsilon_{yy})}\right] \qquad (2.6.39)$$

The above equation is derived from Eq. (2.6.38). Plugging the above equation into Eq. (2.6.36) yields

$$\varepsilon = \frac{1}{2}\,(\varepsilon_{xx} + \varepsilon_{yy}) \pm \left\{\left[\frac{1}{2}\,(\varepsilon_{xx} - \varepsilon_{yy})\right]^2 + \varepsilon_{xy}^2\right\}^{\frac{1}{2}} \qquad (2.6.40)$$

Two principal stresses will be obtained from the above equation, while their calculated values have to be compared with the other component "$\varepsilon = 0$" for ranking the order as

$$\varepsilon_1 \geqslant \varepsilon_2 \geqslant \varepsilon_3 \tag{2.6.41}$$

The maximum engineering shear strain (γ_{13}) and tensor shear strain (ε_{13}) are then,

$$\frac{1}{2}\gamma_{13,\max} = \varepsilon_{13,\max} = \left\{\left[\frac{1}{2}(\varepsilon_{xx} - \varepsilon_{yy})\right]^2 + \varepsilon_{xy}^2\right\}^{\frac{1}{2}} = \frac{1}{2}(\varepsilon_1 - \varepsilon_3) \tag{2.6.42}$$

2.6.5　Principal Strains Using Measured Data Obtained from Rectangular Rosette Gage

A rectangular rosette gage is oriented with gages labeled A, B, and C at an angle of $45°$ apart （Fig. 2.6.2（a）） such that gage A and gage C are perpendicular to each other. The principal strains and the angle going from the 1st principal strain to the gage A can be calculated using the measured data, respectively as

$$\varepsilon = \frac{1}{2}(\varepsilon_A + \varepsilon_C) \pm \left\{\left[\frac{1}{2}(\varepsilon_A - \varepsilon_B)\right]^2 + \left[\frac{1}{2}(\varepsilon_B - \varepsilon_C)\right]^2\right\}^{\frac{1}{2}} \tag{2.6.43}$$

and $\quad \psi = \frac{1}{2}\tan^{-1}\left[\dfrac{\varepsilon_A - 2\varepsilon_B + \varepsilon_C}{\varepsilon_A - \varepsilon_C}\right] \tag{2.6.44}$

where

ε_A: Strain measured at gage A;

ε_B: Strain measured at gage B;

ε_C: Strain measured at gage C;

ψ: Angle measured from the first principal stress ε_1 to gage A.

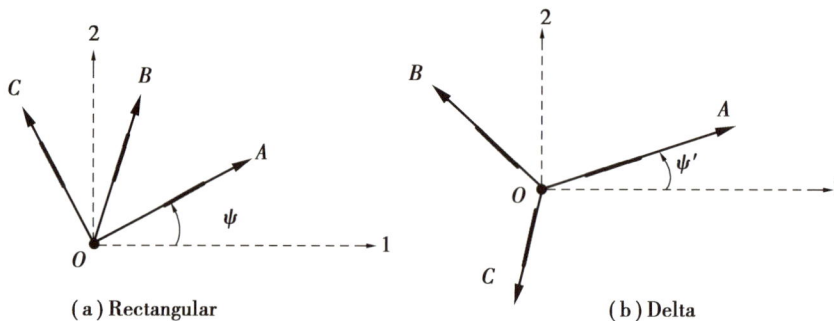

(a) Rectangular　　　　　　　(b) Delta

Fig. 2.6.2　**Orientations of Rosette Gages**

2.6.6　Principal Strains Using Measured Data Obtained from Delta Rosette Gage

A rectangular rosette gage is oriented with gages labeled A, B, and C at an angle of $120°$ apart ［Fig. 2.6.2（b）］. The principal strains and the angle going from the 1st principal strain to the gage A can be calculated using the measured data, respectively as

$$\varepsilon = \frac{\varepsilon_A + \varepsilon_B + \varepsilon_C}{3} \pm \frac{\left\{2\left[(\varepsilon_A - \varepsilon_B)^2 + (\varepsilon_B - \varepsilon_C)^2 + (\varepsilon_C - \varepsilon_A)^2\right]\right\}^{\frac{1}{2}}}{3} \quad (2.6.45)$$

and $\quad \psi' = \frac{1}{2}\tan^{-1}\left[\dfrac{3^{\frac{1}{2}}(\varepsilon_C - \varepsilon_B)}{2\varepsilon_A - \varepsilon_B - \varepsilon_C}\right] \qquad (2.6.46)$

where

ε_A: Strain measured at gage A;

ε_B: Strain measured at gage B;

ε_C: Strain measured at gage C;

ψ': Angle measured from the first principal stress ε_1 to gage A.

2.7   Crack Nucleation under Static Loadings

Two fundamental fracture criteria on predicting the onset of material yielding and crack initiation are described here. They are von Mises stress criterion for ductile homogeneous materials and modified-Mohr theory for homogeneous materials.

2.7.1   von Mises Stress for Ductile Homogeneous Materials

Strain energy density consists of two components: volumetric (dilatational) and distortional. Volumetric component is accountable for volume change without any change in shape, while distortional component causes shape shape change. The distortion-energy theory based on von Mises stress has been accepted for evaluating ductile homogeneous materials such as aluminum alloys and ferrous alloys that are subjected to multiaxial stress states. The von Mises yield criterion suggests that the yielding of material begins when the distortional component, or called second deviatoric stress invariant, exceeds a limit. Prior to yield, material response is assumed to be elastic. Considering the principal directions as the coordinate axes, a plane whose normal vector makes equal angles with each of the principal axes is called an octahedral plane. There are a total of eight ($2 \times 2 \times 2$) octahedral planes corresponding to $\pm\sigma_1$, $\pm\sigma_2$, $\pm\sigma_3$, of which plane ($+\sigma_1$, $+\sigma_2$, $+\sigma_3$) as shown in Fig. 2.7.1. The normal and shear components of the stress tensor on these planes are called octahedral normal stress (σ_{oct}) and octahedral shear stress (τ_{oct}). Thus, one of the eight octahedral planes will be the critical plane for failure analysis based on the von Mises stress. The critical plane is defined as the particular plane in a material, of which the loaded material is likely to experience the most damage.

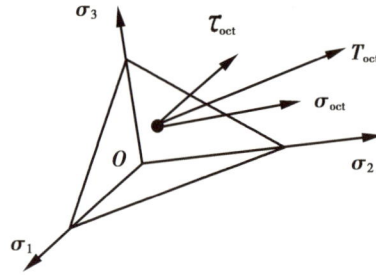

Fig. 2.7.1   The Octohedral Stress Plane in the First Octant

Von Mises stress, as the most used equivalent stress flow when the material is subjected to multiaxial loadings, is defined by the maximum octahedral shear stress criterion that yielding occurs whenever the distortion energy in a unit volume equals the distortion energy in the same volume when uniaxially stressed to the yield strength. In terms of the three principal stresses, $(\sigma_1, \sigma_2, \sigma_3)$, the von Mises stress can be written as

$$\sigma_{eq} = \left\{ \frac{1}{2} \left[(\sigma_1 - \sigma_2)^2 + (\sigma_2 - \sigma_3)^2 + (\sigma_3 - \sigma_1)^2 \right] \right\}^{\frac{1}{2}} \tag{2.7.1}$$

The von Mises equivalent stress given above is a combined shear effect attributable to the three principal stress in the 3-dimensional space. It is an extension from the maxiumum shear stress attributable to the two principal stresses on a 2-dimensional plane as described by Eq. (2.6.28). The corresponding von Mises strain is obtained from principal strains $(\varepsilon_1, \varepsilon_2, \varepsilon_3)$ as

$$\varepsilon_{eq} = \frac{\left\{ \frac{1}{2} \left[(\varepsilon_1 - \varepsilon_2)^2 + (\varepsilon_2 - \varepsilon_3)^2 + (\varepsilon_3 - \varepsilon_1)^2 \right] \right\}^{\frac{1}{2}}}{1 + \nu} \tag{2.7.2}$$

In a Cartesian coordinate system, von Mises stress can be also calculated from the three normal-stress components $(\sigma_{xx}, \sigma_{yy}, \sigma_{zz})$ and the three shear-stress components $(\sigma_{xy}, \sigma_{yz}, \sigma_{zx})$ as follows:

$$\sigma_{eq} = \frac{\left\{ \left[(\sigma_{xx} - \sigma_{yy})^2 + (\sigma_{yy} - \sigma_{zz})^2 + (\sigma_{zz} - \sigma_{xx})^2 \right] + 6 \left(\sigma_{xy}^2 + \sigma_{yz}^2 + \sigma_{zx}^2 \right) \right\}^{\frac{1}{2}}}{3} \tag{2.7.3}$$

Similarly, the maximum octahedral shearing strain can be a material-yielding criterion. The yielding occurs whenever the distortion energy in a unit volume equals the distortion energy in the same volume when uniaxially loaded to the yield strain. von Mises strain can be calculated using the following equation:

$$\varepsilon_{eq} = \frac{\left\{ \left[(\varepsilon_{xx} - \varepsilon_{yy})^2 + (\varepsilon_{yy} - \varepsilon_{zz})^2 + (\varepsilon_{zz} - \varepsilon_{xx})^2 \right] + 6 \left(\varepsilon_{xy}^2 + \varepsilon_{yz}^2 + \varepsilon_{zx}^2 \right) \right\}^{\frac{1}{2}}}{3(1 + \nu)} \tag{2.7.4}$$

In case of known stresses induced in the plastic range, the strains given by Eqs. (2.6.2) and (2.6.7) can be expanded into

$$\varepsilon_{xx} = \frac{\sigma_{xx} - \nu\,\sigma_{yy} - \nu\,\sigma_{zz}}{E} + \frac{\varepsilon^{\mathrm{p}}_{\mathrm{eq}}\left(\sigma_{xx} - \dfrac{1}{2}\,\sigma_{yy} - \dfrac{1}{2}\,\sigma_{zz}\right)}{\sigma_{\mathrm{eq}}} \qquad (2.7.5)$$

$$\varepsilon_{yy} = \frac{\sigma_{yy} - \nu\,\sigma_{zz} - \nu\,\sigma_{xx}}{E} + \frac{\varepsilon^{\mathrm{p}}_{\mathrm{eq}}\left(\sigma_{yy} - \dfrac{1}{2}\,\sigma_{zz} - \dfrac{1}{2}\,\sigma_{xx}\right)}{\sigma_{\mathrm{eq}}} \qquad (2.7.6)$$

$$\varepsilon_{zz} = \frac{\sigma_{zz} - \nu\,\sigma_{xx} - \nu\,\sigma_{yy}}{E} + \frac{\varepsilon^{\mathrm{p}}_{\mathrm{eq}}\left(\sigma_{zz} - \dfrac{1}{2}\,\sigma_{xx} - \dfrac{1}{2}\,y\,\sigma_{zz}\right)}{\sigma_{\mathrm{eq}}} \qquad (2.7.7)$$

$$\gamma_{xy} = 2\varepsilon_{xy} = \frac{\tau_{xy}}{G} + \frac{3\,\varepsilon^{\mathrm{p}}_{\mathrm{eq}}\,\sigma_{xy}}{2\,\sigma_{\mathrm{eq}}} \qquad (2.7.8)$$

$$\gamma_{yz} = 2\varepsilon_{yz} = \frac{\tau_{yz}}{G} + \frac{3\,\varepsilon^{\mathrm{p}}_{\mathrm{eq}}\,\sigma_{yz}}{2\,\sigma_{\mathrm{eq}}} \qquad (2.7.9)$$

and $\quad \gamma_{zx} = 2\varepsilon_{zx} = \dfrac{\tau_{zx}}{G} + \dfrac{3\,\varepsilon^{\mathrm{p}}_{\mathrm{eq}}\,\sigma_{zx}}{2\,\sigma_{\mathrm{eq}}} \qquad (2.7.10)$

where

σ_{eq}: Equivalent stress such as the von Mises stress, i.e., Eq. (2.7.3);

$\varepsilon^{\mathrm{p}}_{\mathrm{eq}}$: Equivalent plastic strain, can be obtained from Eq. (2.7.4) with plastic strains only as

$$\varepsilon^{\mathrm{p}}_{\mathrm{eq}} = \frac{\left\{\left[(\varepsilon^{\mathrm{p}}_{xx} - \varepsilon^{\mathrm{p}}_{yy})^2 + (\varepsilon^{\mathrm{p}}_{yy} - \varepsilon^{\mathrm{p}}_{zz})^2 + (\varepsilon^{\mathrm{p}}_{zz} - \varepsilon^{\mathrm{p}}_{xx})^2\right] + 6\left[(\varepsilon^{\mathrm{p}}_{xy})^2 + (\varepsilon^{\mathrm{p}}_{yz})^2 + (\varepsilon^{\mathrm{p}}_{zx})^2\right]\right\}^{\frac{1}{2}}}{3(1+\nu)}$$

$$(2.7.11)$$

When the material is stressed in the plastic range, the total strain increment include both the elastic strain and plastic strain increments

$$d\varepsilon = d\varepsilon_{\mathrm{e}} + d\varepsilon_{\mathrm{P}} \qquad (2.7.12)$$

where

$$d\varepsilon_{\mathrm{e}} = E^{-1}d\sigma \qquad (2.7.13)$$

and $\quad d\varepsilon_{\mathrm{p}} = E_{\mathrm{p}}^{-1}\,d\sigma = H^{-1}\,d\sigma \qquad (2.7.14)$

Note that plastic modulus E_{p} is often written as H, which is defined as the gradient of "the point of interest on the stress-strain curve" due to plastic deformation only in the plastic range, as shown in Fig. 2.7.2. As illustrated in Fig. 2.7.2, the differential forms of both the normal and shear strains corresponding to Eqs. (2.7.5)-(2.7.10) are expressed explicitly as, respectively

$$d\varepsilon = (E^{-1} + E_p^{-1}) \, d\sigma = (E^{-1} + H^{-1}) d\sigma = E_T^{-1} \, d\sigma \qquad (2.7.15)$$

and $d\gamma = (G^{-1} + G_p^{-1}) \, d\tau = (G^{-1} + 3E_p^{-1}) \, d\tau = (G^{-1} + 3H^{-1}) d\tau = G_T^{-1} \, d\sigma \qquad (2.7.16)$

where

$$H \equiv E_p = \frac{d\sigma_{eq}}{d\varepsilon_{eq}^P} = \frac{d\sigma_{eq}}{\left(\dfrac{d\sigma_{eq}}{E_T}\right)^{\frac{1}{n}}} \qquad (2.7.17)$$

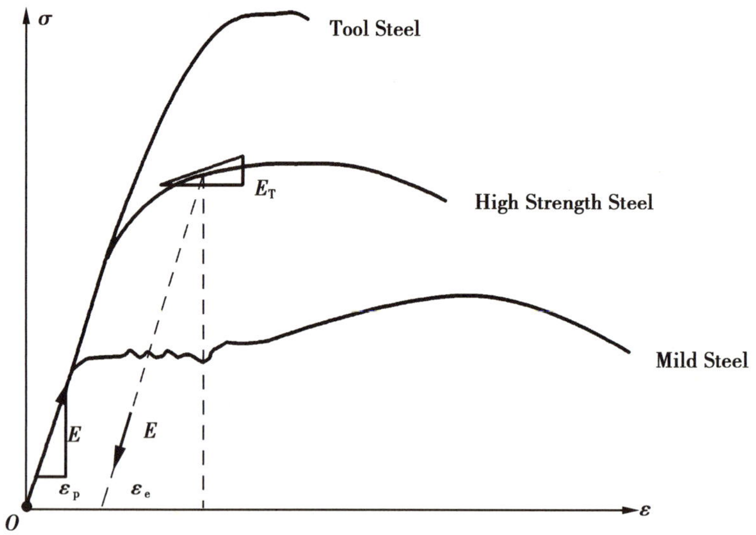

Fig. 2.7.2   Nominal Stress-Strain Curves in the Plastic Range of Steels

Since the Poissin's ratio reaches 0.5 ($\nu_p = 0.5$) in the fully plastic range, shear modulus G_p is related to normal modulus E_p by

$$G_p = \frac{E_p}{2(1 + \nu_p)} = \frac{E_p}{3} \qquad (2.7.18)$$

In light of Eqs. (2.7.15) and (2.7.16), the equations that relate the tangential moduli to elastic moduli and plastic moduli for both normal and shear modes are, respectively

$$E_T^{-1} = E^{-1} + H^{-1} \quad (\text{Normal Mode}) \qquad (2.7.19)$$

and $G_T^{-1} = E^{-1} + 3H^{-1} \quad (\text{Shear Mode}) \qquad (2.7.20)$

Eqs. (2.7.1)-(2.7.20) are derived under the quasi-static conditions and they can be applied to multiaxial fatigue life prediction for material subjected to proportional loadings. The additional cyclic hardening due to nonproportional loadings is not accommodated by the von Mises stress and strain. The following incremental approach to the kinematic cyclic hardening based on subsequently incremental-iterative methods due to [Mroz] [Garud] is recommended for accommodating the behavior of cyclic hardening

$$\Delta \varepsilon = E^{-1} \Delta \sigma + \left(\frac{\Delta \sigma_{eq}}{H \, \sigma_{eq}} \right) \sigma \qquad (2.7.21)$$

and $\quad \Delta \gamma = G^{-1} \Delta \tau + \left(\frac{3 \, \Delta \sigma_{eq}}{H \, \sigma_{eq}} \right) \tau \qquad (2.7.22)$

Modulus H given above has to be updated at each load increment. The Ramberg-Osgood relation for cyclic loadings is discussed in Chapter 4.

2.7.2 Modified-Mohr Theory for Brittle Homogeneous Materials

The modified Mohr theory is the preferred failure theory for brittle homogeneous materials, e.g. cast irons, subjected to static multiaxial stress states. Assume that σ_1, σ_2, and σ_3 are the three principal stresses and $\sigma_1 \geqslant \sigma_2 \geqslant \sigma_3$. Taking the maximum principal stress (σ_1) and minimal principal stress (σ_3) in consideration, one can jump to the conclusion that the material is safe as long as the following conditions are satisfied:

(1) Both principal stresses are positive (1st quadrant, Fig. 2.7.3):

$$\sigma_1 < \sigma_{uts} \qquad (2.7.23)$$

(2) $\sigma_1 \leqslant 0$ and $\sigma_3 \geqslant 0$ (2nd quadrant, Fig. 2.7.3): This doesn't exist, since $\sigma_1 \geqslant \sigma_2 \geqslant \sigma_3$.

(3) $\sigma_1 \leqslant 0$ and $\sigma_3 \leqslant 0$ (3rd quadrant, Fig. 2.7.3):

$$\sigma_1 \geqslant \sigma_3 > \sigma_{ucs} \qquad (2.7.24)$$

(4) $\sigma_1 \geqslant 0$ and $\sigma_3 \leqslant 0$ (4th quadrant, Fig. 2.7.3): $\sigma_1 < \sigma_{uts}$

and $\quad \sigma_1 < \dfrac{-(\sigma_3 + \sigma_{ucs})}{1 - \dfrac{\sigma_{ucs}}{\sigma_{uts}}} \qquad (2.7.25)$

When the stress state in the 4th quadrant is of concern, the factor of safety (S_f) is derived from the smaller one of the following two values:

$$S_f = \frac{\sigma_{uts}}{\sigma_1} \qquad (2.7.26)$$

or $\quad S_f = \dfrac{|\sigma_{ucs}| \sigma_{uts}}{|\sigma_{ucs}| \sigma_1 - \dfrac{\sigma_{uts} \sigma_1}{\sigma_3}}$　　　　　　　　　　　　　(2.7.27)

where

σ_{uts} : Ultimate tensile strength, always positive;

σ_{ucs} : Ultimate compressive strength, always negative;

σ_1 : Maximum principal stress;

σ_3 : Minimum principal stress.

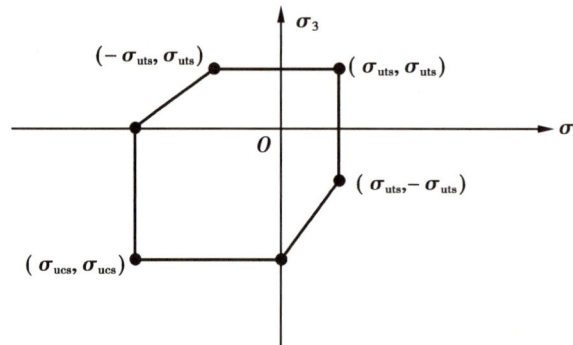

Fig. 2.7.3　Modified-Mohr Criteria for Brittle Homogeneous Materials

---

Example 2.7.1　The stress components at a critical location of a diesel engine block made of cast iron (Class 20) are $\sigma_{xx} = 50$ MPa, $\sigma_{yy} = 0$ MPa and are $\tau_{xy} = 30$ MPa. How much is the safety factor?

Solution:

The tensile and compressive strengths of cast iron (Class 20) are $\sigma_{uts} = 152$ MPa and $\sigma_{ucs} = -572$ MPa, respectively. Based on the Mohr's circle, one has the following equation for principal stresses,

$$\sigma = \frac{1}{2}(\sigma_{xx} + \sigma_{yy}) \pm \left\{\left[\frac{1}{2}(\sigma_{xx} - \sigma_{yy})\right]^2 + \tau_{xy}^2\right\}^{\frac{1}{2}}$$

$$= \frac{1}{2}(50 + 0) \pm \left\{\left[\frac{1}{2}(50 - 0)\right]^2 + 30^2\right\}^{\frac{1}{2}}$$

Thus, $\sigma_1 = 64.05$ MPa and $\sigma_3 = -14.05$ MPa.

It means that the stress state falls in the 4th quadrant (Fig. 2.7.1). Based on Eq. (2.7.6), the factor of safety is smaller of the following two calculated values

$$S_f = \frac{\sigma_{uts}}{\sigma_1} = \frac{152}{64.05} = 2.36$$

and $\quad S_f = \dfrac{\mid \sigma_{ucs} \mid \sigma_{uts}}{\mid \sigma_{ucs} \mid \sigma_1 - \dfrac{\sigma_{uts}\,\sigma_1}{\mid \sigma_3 \mid}} = \dfrac{572 \times 152}{572 \times 64.05 - 152 \times \dfrac{64.05}{14.05}} = 2.42$

Thus, the safety factor is 2.36.

2.8   Residual Stresses

A residual stress is a stress that remains in a solid material after the original loading function has been removed. Undesirable residual stresses may be induced by the following processes: castings, welding, cold-drawing, fabrication of thin films, coating, heat treatments (e. g. quenching), and curing of composites. The strength behavior of components is influenced by their existing residual stresses without showing any visible signs. Residual stresses may have combined critically with the applied stresses, or because together with the presence of undetected defects they have dangerously lowered the applied stress, at which failure may occur [Withers].

Residual stresses may come from a variety of mechanisms such as plastic deformations, temperature gradients, and phase transformation. For example, castings may have large residual stresses due to temperature gradients (uneven cooling) if heat treatment is not well-done. There are several ways to find out residual stresses:

(a) Nondestructive methods: X-ray, ultrasonic, magnetic, and neutrons.
(b) Indentation method: To detect residual stresses using successive indentations.
(c) Hole-drilling method: Strain-gaged; drilling a small hole (e.g. 1-2 mm in diameter) into the center of a 3-element strain rosette. The hole changes the initial strain allowing redistribution of the residual stresses originally existing in the material.
(d) Ring-coring method: Strain-gaged; drilling a core (e. g. 4-5 mm in diameter) surrounding a 3-element strain rosette. The core changes the initial strain allowing redistribution of the residual stresses originally existing in the material.

Besides the above methods, another way is to use destructive methods. It is based on a strain release principle: cutting the measurement specimen to relax the residual stresses and then measuring the deformed shape.

Residual stresses are sometimes desirable. Desired residual-stress-embedded products include toughened glass, toughened steels (by shot pinning, laser pinning, or ultrasonic mechanical attrition), pre-stressed concretes, compound cylinders (e.g. gun barrels), swords (having a martensite cutting edge and soft back).

2.8.1　Excision Method for Measuring Residual Stresses

For excision from a relatively thin (plane stress) plate provided that the stress is completely relaxed, the original principal stresses can be inferred from strains measured using a standard three gauge rectangular rosette ($0°$, $45°$ and $90°$) as [Schajer 2001] :

$$\sigma_{max} = -\frac{1}{2} E \left\{ \frac{\varepsilon_1 + \varepsilon_3}{1 - \nu} + \frac{[(\varepsilon_1 - \varepsilon_3)^2 + (\varepsilon_1 + \varepsilon_3 - 2\varepsilon_2)^2]^{\frac{1}{2}}}{1 + \nu} \right\} \tag{2.8.1}$$

and $\quad \sigma_{min} = -\frac{1}{2} E \left\{ \frac{\varepsilon_1 + \varepsilon_3}{1 - \nu} - \frac{[(\varepsilon_1 - \varepsilon_3)^2 + (\varepsilon_1 + \varepsilon_3 - 2\varepsilon_2)^2]^{\frac{1}{2}}}{1 + \nu} \right\} \tag{2.8.2}$

where

σ_{max} : Maximum principal stress;

σ_{min} : Minimum principal stress;

ε_1, ε_2 & ε_3 : Principal strains calculated from the readings of rosette gauges.

The method can be differentiated between excision and sectioning [Schajer]. Upon excision the removed block is small thus becoming stress free, but only partial strain relaxations occur by sectioning for that more sophisticated analyses are necessary.

2.8.2　Hole-Drilling Method

The hole-drilling method [Mathar] involves drilling a shallow hole, around which local surface deformations are measured by a specially designed strain-gauge rosette. Provided that the stress is essentially constant over the drill depth the residual stress that originally existed at the hole can then be calculated from the measured strain relaxations ε_1, ε_2 and ε_3 around it using

$$\sigma_{max} = -\frac{1}{2} E \left\{ \frac{\varepsilon_1 + \varepsilon_3}{a(1 - \nu)} + \frac{[(\varepsilon_1 - \varepsilon_3)^2 + (\varepsilon_1 + \varepsilon_3 - 2\varepsilon_2)^2]^{\frac{1}{2}}}{b} \right\} \tag{2.8.3}$$

and $\quad \sigma_{min} = -\frac{1}{2} E \left\{ \frac{\varepsilon_1 + \varepsilon_3}{a(1 - \nu)} - \frac{[(\varepsilon_1 - \varepsilon_3)^2 + (\varepsilon_1 + \varepsilon_3 - 2\varepsilon_2)^2]^{\frac{1}{2}}}{b} \right\} \tag{2.8.4}$

Parameters a and b given in the above equations are dimensionless calibration constants that depend on the diameter and depth of the hole [Schajer]. It is the most widely employed destructive method for measuring residual stresses.

2.9   Oscillatory Stress-Strain Behavior

An oscillatory stress-strain curve may be obtained during dynamic recrystallization when the strain required to initiate recrystallization is greater than the strain required to completely recrystallize the material [Lutton & Sellars].

2.10   Flexural Modulus of Rupture

Some materials such as ceramics and rocks are hard to measure the axial tensile and/or compressive properties, if not impossible. The flexural modulus of rupture is recommended as an alternative for reference as it cannot be used for the design purpose. There are three commonly used methods for measuring the flexural modulus and they are described as follows:

(a) 3-point bending test.
(b) 4-point bending test.
(c) Ball-on-ring biaxial flexure test.

2.10.1   3-Point Bend Test

A three-point loading test may be conducted to determine its flexural strength and modulus based on the piston-on-three-balls method as shown in Fig. 2.10.1. The flexural strength under a load in a three-point bending setup, also called modulus of rupture, is calculated as

$$\sigma_R = \frac{3 F L}{2 b h^2} \tag{2.10.1}$$

F is the applied force in the middle of the supporting span. Dimensions b (depth) and h (height) of the rectangular cross-section is shown in Fig. 2.10.1.

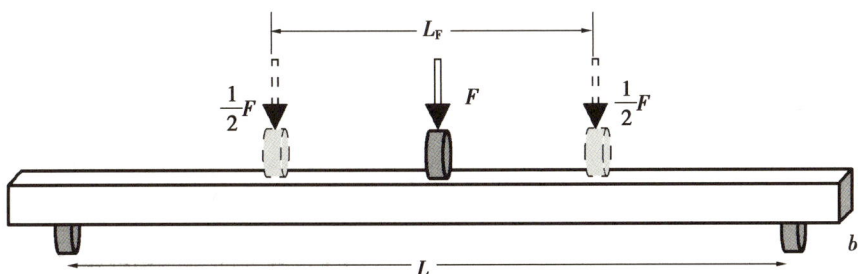

Fig. 2.10. 1   3-point (Solid-Line Load F) and 4-point $\left(\text{Dashed-Line Load } \frac{1}{2}F \right)$ Bending Tests for Moduli of Rupture of Brittle Materials

2.10.2 4-point Bend Test

Another flexural strength is a 4-point bend setup, Fig. 2.10.1. If the loading span (distance between the two loading points) is L_F, the modulus of rupture is

$$\sigma_R = \frac{3\,F(L - L_F)}{2\,b\,h^2} \tag{2.10.2}$$

Traditional compression tests are used for ceramics on compressive stress-strain relationship. Subjected to embedded porosities in nature, the compressive strength of a ceramic is much higher than its tensile strength. Since the three-point or four-point bending is subjected both tension and compression, the flexural strength (modulus of rupture) derived by either Eq. (2.10.1) or Eq. (2.10.2) is expected to be higher than the actual tensile strength.

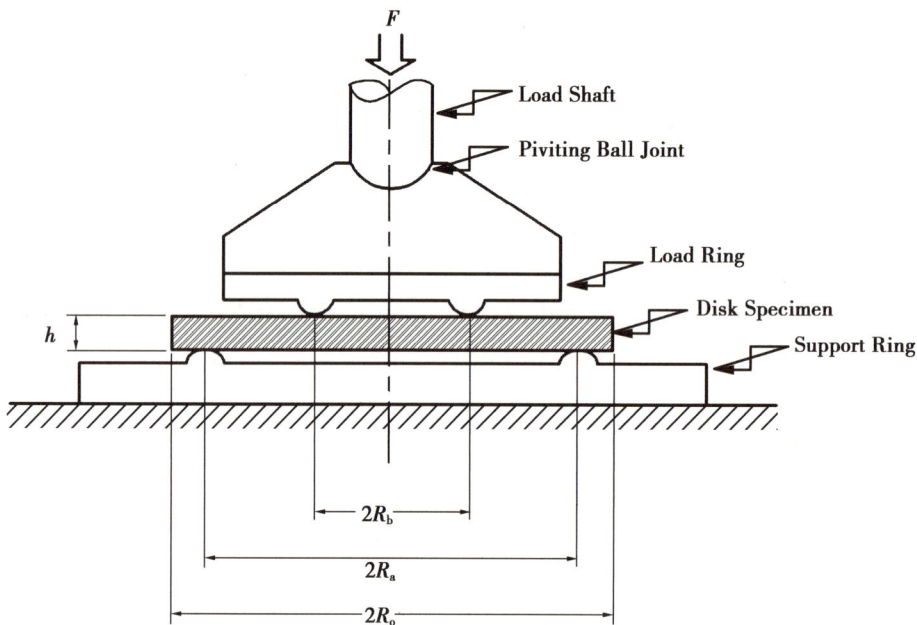

Fig. 2.10.2   Flexure Strength by Biaxial Ball-on-Ring Test

2.10.3 Ball-Disk-on-Ring Test

A more accurate equation for the flexural strength was suggested by [Shetty et al.]. Consider a thin, circular disk specimen with an outer radius of R_o, which is pushed onto a ring of radius R_r ($<R_o$) under a central load (ball). The maximum radial stress and maximum tangential stress at the center (Fig. 2.10.2) are equal and they can be calculated as [Kristein & Woolley] [Alder & Mihora]

$$\sigma_{\max} = \sigma_{rr} = \sigma_{\theta\theta} = \frac{3F}{4\pi\, h^2}\left[2(1+\nu)\,\ln\frac{R_a}{R_b} + (1-\nu)\left(\frac{R_a^2 - R_b^2}{R_o^2}\right)\right] \tag{2.10.3}$$

where

$F(\mathrm{N})$: Load at fracture;

$h(\mathrm{mm})$: Thickness of the thin disk (specimen);

$R_a(\mathrm{mm})$: Radius of the support ring circle in contact with the disk bottom;

$R_b(\mathrm{mm})$: Radius of the load ring circle (piston ball) in contact with the disk top;

ν: Poisson's ratio;

$R_o(\mathrm{mm})$: Outer radius of the disk specimen.

2.11   Material Hardening Rules and Bauschinger Effect

In case of multi-axial loading, subsequent loading after first yield produces further plastic deformation that can result in a modification of the shape and/or position of the yield surface. The yield function depends on the stresses but also the plastic strains and a hardening parameter K. The way in which the plastic strains modify the yield function is defined by hardening rules:

(1) Isotropic hardening rule: The yield surface increases in size but maintains its original shape under loading conditions.

(2) Kinematic hardening rule: The original yield surface is translated to a new position in stress space with no change of its shape and size. This plays an important role in modelling cyclic behavior for fatigue analysis.

The hardening behaviors of these two different hardening rules are illustrated in domain of principal stresses, as shown in Fig. 2.11.1. The combination of the two principal hardening rules leads to a mixed hardening rule, where the initial yield surface both reshapes and translates as a consequence of plastic flow.

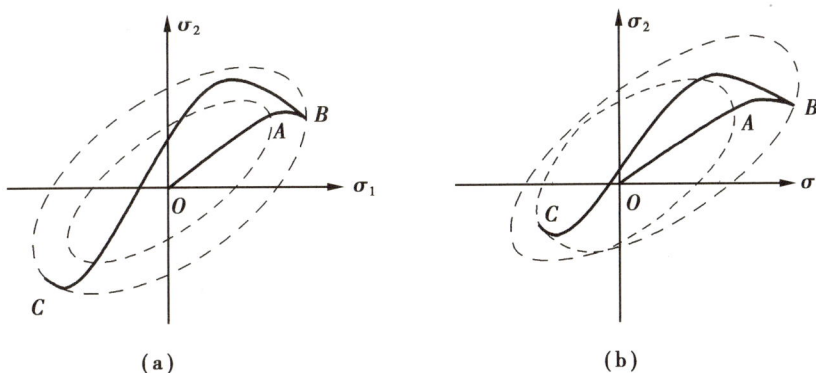

(a)   (b)

Fig. 2.11.1   Material Hardening Rules: (a) Isotropic and (b) Kinematic

However, the plastic deformation of most polycrystalline and some semi-polycrystalline metals in one direction will affect subsequent plastic response in another direction. This phenomenon is called Bauschinger effect [Mughrabi]. As depicted in Fig. 2.11.2, the current yielding point may be lower than the previous one when subjected to a cyclic tension-compression test. That is more phenomenal in the early test period. As the strain is applied in one direction, the dislocation is aided by the "springback" — strain that nucleates at the dislocation barrier during the previous cold work. The greater the compressive cold work, the greater the compressive yield strength; but the Bauschinger effect applies to small strains only, not valid in the range of plastic deformation. Influences of such internal strains on stress-strain relationships observed in monotonic and reversed stressing can be described as a combination of isotropic and kinematic components.

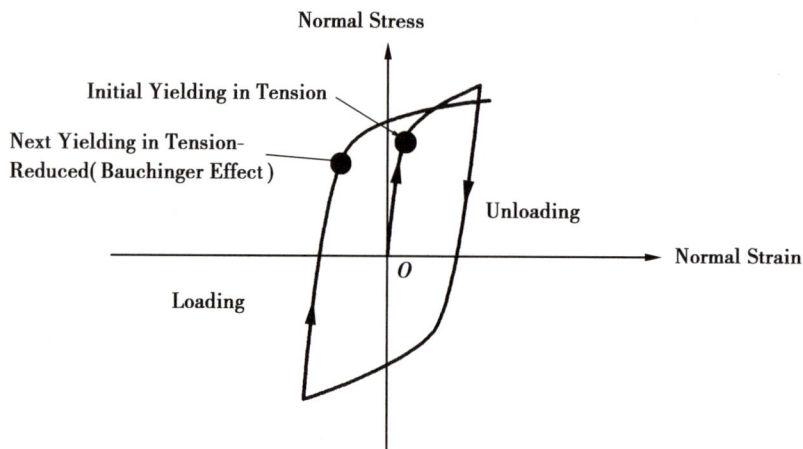

Fig. 2.11.2　Bauschinger Effect of Material under Tension-Compression Test

2.12　Heat Treatments

Heat treatment is used to harden or soften material by altering its physical, and sometimes chemical, properties by a controlled heating/cooling process in a controlled environment. Heat treatment techniques include anneal, precipitation strengthening, tempering, normalizing, quenching, and case hardening.

2.12.1　Anneal

Anneal involves heating the material to above its recrystallization temperature, maintaining at a suitable specified temperature, and then cooling it down. Anneal can induce ductility, soften material, relieve internal stresses, refine the structure by making it homogeneous, and improve cold working properties. In the cases of copper, steel, silver, and brass, this process is performed by heating the material, generally until glowing, for a while and then slowly letting it cool to room temperature in still air. According to temperature requirements, for example, anneal of steel can be classified into the following three processes:

(a) In-process Anneal (Intermediate Anneal): Steel is heated to a temperature below the austenitic temperature (260-760 ℃) such that some of the ductility is restored to a product during the process of cold working.

(b) Normalization: Normalization involves heating the steel to 20-50 ℃ above its upper critical point. The steel is soaked for a short period at that temperature and then allowed to cool in air. It is applicable to steels of less than 0.4% carbon to transform austenite into ferrite, pearlite, and sorbite. Smaller grains form to produce a tougher and more ductile material. It improves machinability of a component and provides dimensional stability if subjected to further heat treatment processes.

(c) Full Anneal: Steel is heated to 50 ℃ above the austenitic temperature and held for sufficient time to allow the material to fully form austenite or austenite-cementite grain structure.

2.12.2   Quenching

The alloy is rapidly cooled to retain as much of the alloying elements in solution as possible. Quenching produces a supersaturated solid solution that is not an equilibrium structure, as the atoms do not have time to diffuse to potential nucleation sites.

2.12.3   Tempering

Tempering means to impart some toughness to brittle material (e.g. steel) by heating it to a temperature below its critical temperature, ranging from 200 ℃ to 700 ℃ for steel for example, depending on the desired result. The yield strength is lowered after tempering. Quenched parts need to be tempered in general practice.

2.12.4   Solution Treatment

Solution treatment involves heating the alloy to a temperature just below the lowest melting point of the alloy, holding it at this temperature until the base metal dissolves a significant amount of the alloying elements.

Full solution treatment of stainless steels, by heating to about 1080 ℃ followed by rapid cooling, may eliminate most residual stresses. However, full solution treatment is not practically feasible for most large or complex fabrications.

2.12.5　Ageing

Ageing is a metallurgical process, which renders the state of supersaturation in a solid solution that arises after the cooling of an alloy from high temperatures inasmuch as the solubility of admixtures. Ageing is an essential step that ensures that the materials in the alloy do not revert to their original configuration after a prolonged period of time. High-carbon steels used for spring and rope wire are frequently given strain-ageing treatments to increase their strength. Strain ageing occurs when strained steel is heated in the range of 200-400 ℃.

On the other hand, ageing has been also extensively studied and many manufacturers work towards perfecting the ability to accelerate and increase the ageing (weathering) process to bring the metal surface to a desired texture and color.

2.12.6　Precipitation Hardening（PH）

PH (Precipitation Hardening) is a three-staged heat treatment process, applied only to those groups of alloys, which are heat treatable such as aluminum 2×××, 6××× and 7××× wrought series.

(1) Firstly, a supersaturated condition is produced by solution treatment.
(2) Secondly, quenching is carried out.
(3) Finally "ageing" process that occurs after quenching may be accelerated by heating the supersaturated alloy below the solvos' temperature until a second-and-coherent phase is precipitated. This coherent phase strengthens the alloys by obstructing the movements of dislocations and yields a finely dispersed precipitate in the alloy.

With regard to precipitation hardening, there are three operating criteria: (a) thoroughly experiencing appreciable maximum solubility, (b) following a solubility curve that reduces quickly with temperature, and (c) composing an alloy that is less than the maximum solubility.

2.12.7　Case Hardening

Case hardening is a thermo-chemical diffusion process, via which an alloying element (e.g. carbon or nitrogen) diffuses into the surface of a monolithic metal. The resulting interstitial solid solution is harder than the base material. The strength and wear resistance may be improved without sacrificing global toughness by case hardening.

References

ALDER W F, MIHORA D J, 1992, Biaxial Flexural Testing: Analysis and Experimental Results[M]. Fracture

Mechanics of Ceramics, Vol. 10 (Edited by R.C. Bradt el al.), 227, Plenum Press, New York.

ARONOFSKY J, 1951. Evaluation of Stress Distribution in the Symmetric Neck of Flat Tensile Bar[J]. Journal of Applied Mechanics:75-84.

ASHBY M F, 2005. Materials Selection in Mechanical Design[M]. 3rd Edition, Elsevier, New York, NY.

ASHBY M F, ASHBY, BRÉCHET Y J M, 2003. Designing Hybrid Materials[J]. Acta Materialia, 51(19): 5801-5821.

ASTM D638-10 2010. Standard Test Method for Tensile Properties of Plastics[M]. ASTM International, West Conshohocken, PA, USA.

BACKMAN D G, WILLIAMS J C, 1992. Advanced Materials for Aircraft Engine Applications[J]. Science, 255:1082-1087.

BAUMEISTER T, AVALLONE E, BAUMEISTER T. Marks' Standard Handbook for Mechanical Engineers [M]. 3rd Edition. McGraw-Hill, New York, NY, USA.

BEER F, et al, 2009. Mechanics of Materials[M]. 7th Edition, McGraw-Hill, New York, NY, USA.

BESSON J, STEGLICH D, BROCKS W, 2003, Modeling of Plain Strain Ductile Rupture[J]. International Journal of Plasticity, (1910):1517-1541.

BLAZINSKI T Z, 1983. Applied Elastoplasticity of Solids[M]. Macmillan, Hong Kong.

BOYER H E, 1987. Atlas of Stress-strain Curves[M]. ASM International, Metals Park, OH, USA.

BRIDGMAN P W, 1952. Studies in Large Plastic Flow and Fracture[M]. McGraw Hill, NY.

CALLISTER W D, 1991. Materials Science and Engineering[M]. 2nd edition, John Wiley and Sons, New York, NY, USA.

CHARLES J A, CRANE F A A, FURNESS J A G, 1997. Selection and Use of Engineering Materials[M]. 3rd Edition, Butterworth Heinemann, New York, NY, USA.

CHEN C P, LAKES R C, 1993. Viscoelastic Behavior of Composite materials with Conventional or Negative Poisson's Ratio Foam as One phase[J]. Journal of Materials Science, 28: 4288-4298.

CHIANG Y J, 1996. Robust Design of the Iosipescu Shear Test Specimen for Composites[J]. Journal of Testing and Evaluation, 24(1):1-11.

CAMPO A, 2008, Selection of Polymeric Materials[M]. PDL Handbook Series.

CHEN P C T, 1986. The Bauschinger and Hardening Effect on Residual Stresses in an Autofrettaged Thick-Walled Cylinder[M]. Journal of Pressure Vessel Technology, 108:108-112.

COURTNEY T H, 1990. Mechanical Behavior of Materials[M]. McGraw-Hill, New York, NY, USA.

CHOUNG J M, CHO S R, 2008. Study on True Stress Correction from Tensile Tests[J]. Journal of Mechanical Science and Technology, 22: 1039-1051.

DANIEL J, MAYKUTH, 1984. Structural Alloys Handbook, Mechanical Properties Data Center[M]. Battelle Columbus Laboratory, Columbus, OH, USA.

DASKO J, 1977. Materials in Design and Manufacturing[M]. Malloy, Ann Arbor, MI, USA.

DIETER G E, 1989. Mechanical Metallurgy[M]. McGraw Hill, New York.

DIETER G E, 1991. Engineering Design, a Materials and Processing Approach[M]. 2nd edition, McGraw-Hill, New York, NY, USA.

DUBENSKY R G, 1998. Simultaneous Engineering-Accurate Material Properties Leads to Effect Simulation[J]. SAE 980378.

FARAG M M, 1997. Materials Selections for Engineering Design[M]. London: Prentice Hall.

FENTON J, 1996. Handbook of Vehicle Design Analysis[J]. SAE, Warrendale, PA, USA.

GERLACH J, PAUL U, BLUMEL K, 2001. How the Modeling of Virtual Materials Can Secure Part Feasibility, SAE 2001-01-3051.

GILLEO K, 2001. Area Array Packaging Processes for BGA[M]. Flip Chip, and CSG, McGraw-Hill Professor.

GRASSIA L, D'AMORE A, SIMON S, 2010. On the Viscoelastic Poisson's Ratio in Amorphous Polymers[J]. Journal of Rheology, 54(5):1009-1022.

HARPER C A, 2001. Handbook of Materials for Product Design[M]. 3rd Edition, McGraw-Hill, New York, NY, USA.

HILL R, 1950. The Mathematical Theory of Plasticity[M]. Clarendon, Oxford, UK.

HOLLOMON J H, 1945. Tensile Deformation[J]. Transactions of AIME, 162, 268-290.

JOHNSON W, MELLOR P B, 1973. Engineering Plasticity[C]. VDM, 2010.

KORKMAZ S, 2010. Uniform Material Law: Extension to High-Strength Steels[C]. VDM, 2010.

KRISTEIN A, WOOLLEY R, 1967. Symmetric Bending of Thin Circular Plates on Equally Spaced Point Supports[J]. Journal of Research, 71C:1-10, National Bureau of Standards, USA.

LEE H H, et al, 2005. A Study of Failure Characteristic of Spherical Pressure Vessels[J]. Journal of Material Processing Technology, 164/165:882-888.

LEE Y L, CHIANG Y J, WONG H H, 1995. A Constitutive Model for Estimating Multiaxial Notch Strains[J]. Journal of Engineering Materials and Technology. 117(1):33-40.

LEIPHOLZ H, 1974. Theory of Elasticity[M]. Dictionary Geotechnical Engineering/wörterbuch Geotechnik, 42(4): 1385.

LEROY G, EMBURY J, EDWARDS G, et al, 1981. A Model of Ductile Fracture Based on the Nucleation and Growth of Voids[J]. Acta Metallurgical, 29(8):1509-1522.

LEWIS R, MARSHALL M B, DWYER-JOYCE R S, 2005. Measurement of Interface Pressure in Interference Fits[J]. ARCHIVE Proceedings of the Institution of Mechanical Engineers Part C Journal of Mechanical Engineering Sciences, 1989—1996(Vols 203-210), 219(2):127-139.

LINBERG R A, 1990. Processes and Materials of Manufacture[M]. Allyn and Bacon, Needham Heights, MA, USA.

LING Y, 1996. Uniaxial True Stress-Strain after Necking[J]. AMP Journal of Technology, Vol. 5. 37-48.

LUBLINER J, 1990. Plasticity Theory[M]. MacMillan, New York, NY, USA.

LUTTON M J, SELLARS C M, 1969. Acta Metall[J]. 17:1033-1043.

MAJZOOBI G H, et al, 2003. A Finite Element Simulation and an Experimental Study of Autofrettage for Strain Hardened Thick-walled Cylinders[J]. Materials Science and Engineering, A, 359(1-2):326-331.

MAYVILL R A, FINNIE I, 1982. Uniaxial Stress-Strain Curves from a Bending Test[J]. Experimental Mechanics, 22(6):197-201.

MATHAR J, 1934. Determination of Initial Stresses by Measuring the Deformation around Drilled Holes[J]. Transactions of ASME, 56:249-254.

MUGHRABI H, 1987. Johann Bauschinger, Pioneer of Modern Materials Testing[J]. Materials Forum, 10 (1):5-10.

PARSONS B, WILSON E A, 1970. A Method for Determining the Surface Contact Stresses Resulting from Interference Fits[J]. Journal of Engineering for Industry:208-218.

RAGAB A R, BAYOMI, S E, 1998. Engineering Solid Mechanics, Fundamentals and Applications[M]. CRC Press, Boca Raton.

ROMEU J L, GRETHLEIN A, 2000. A Practical Guide to Statistical Analysis of Materials Property Data[M]. AMTIAC (AMPT-14).

SCHAJER G S, 2001. Residual Stresses: Destructive Measurements[J]. Encyclopedia of Materials Science and Technology, Edited by Buschow, K. H. J, et al, Elsevier, Oxford, UK,2001:3703-3707.

SCHEIDER I, BROCKS W, CORNEC A, 2004. Procedure for the Determination of True Stress-Strain Curves from Tensile Tests with Rectangular Cross-Section Specimens[J]. Journal of Engineering Materials and Technology, 126:70-76.

SHACKELFORD J F, ALEXANDER W, PARK J S, 1994. CRC Materials Science and Engineering Handbook [M]. CRC Press, Boca Raton, FL, USA.

SCHAJER G S, 1988. Measurement of Non-uniform Residual Stresses Using the Hole-drilling Method Part Ⅰ [J]. Journal of Engineering Materials and Technology, 103:338-343.

SCHAJER G S, 1988. Measurement of Non-uniform Residual Stresses Using the Hole-drilling Method Part Ⅱ [J]. Journal of Engineering Materials and Technology, 103:344-349.

SEIFERT T, MAIER G, 2008. Linearization and Finite Element Implementation of an Incrementally Objective Canonical Form Return Mapping Algorithm for Large Deformation Inelasticity.

SEN S, AKSAKAL B, 2004. Stress Analysis of Interference Fitted Shaft-Hub System under Transient Heat Transfer Conditions[J]. Materials and Design, 25(5):407-417.

SHIGLEY J E, MISCHKE C R, 2001. Mechanical Engineering Design[M]. McGraw-Hill, New York, NY, USA.

SMITH W F, HASHEMI J, 2005. Foundations of Materials Science and Engineering [M]. 4th Edition, McGraw-Hill, New York, NY, USA.

STAMENKOVIC D, et al, 2001. Investigation of the Pressfit Joint by the Tribology Aspect [J]. Facta Universitatis, Series: Mechanical Engineering, 1(8):1057-1064.

STRAND H, 2005. Design, Testing, and Analysis of Journal Bearings for Construction Equipment[M]. PhD Dissertation, Royal Institute of Technology, Stockholm, Sweden.

TAMARIN Y, 2002. Atlas of Stress-Strain Curves[M]. 2nd Edition, ASM International, Metals Park, OH, USA.

TIMOSHENKO S P, GERE J M, 1972. Mechanics of Materials[M]. Van Nostrand Reinbold Litton Education Publishing.

TSENG A A, 1990. Material Characterization and Finite Element Simulation for Forming Miniature Metal Parts [J]. Finite Element in Analysis and Design, 6(3):251-265.

TVERGAARD V, 1993. Necking in Tensile Bars with Rectangular Cross-Section [J]. Computer Methods in Applied Mechanics and Engineering, 103(1-2):273-290.

VON MISES R, 1913. Mechanik der festen Körper im plastisch deformablen[J]. Zustand Göttin. Nachr. Math. Phys., Vol. 1:582-592.

WITHERS P J, 2007. Residual Stress and Its Role in Failure[J]. Reports on Progress in Physics, 70(12): 2211-2264.

YANG G, et al, 2001. Influence of Roughness on Characteristics of Tight Interference Fit of a Shaft and a Hub [J]. International Journal of Solids and Structures, 38(42-43):7691-7701.

ZHANG K S, HAUGE M, ODEGARD J, et al, 1999. Determining Material True Stress-Strain Curve from Tensile Specimens with Rectangular Cross Section [J]. International Journal of Solids and Structures, 36 (23):3497-3516.

ZHANG K S, LI Z H, 1994. Numerical Analysis of the Stress-Strain Curve and Fracture Initiation for Ductile Material [J]. Engineering Fracture Mechanics, 49(2):235-241.

Chapter 3

Finite Element Methods in Composites

3.1　Orthotropic Elasticity of Composites

Through experiments that were carried out under a uniaxial cyclic load, Williams and Svensson has demonstrated that the yield locus (yield surface) is not elliptical anymore if the specimen is loaded by torsion prior to tension. This anisotropy via memorizing past plastic deformations cannot be neglected in cyclic plasticity modeling for fatigue life prediction. Nevertheless, the material behavior is usually orthotropic rather than randomly anisotropic. In the meanwhile, most composites used for automobiles, such as tires, car body, under-body beams, bumpers, leaf springs, brake pads/shoes, suspension components, sensors, stamped parts, and even the cast iron are no more complicated than an orthotropic material in the manner of anisotropy; so are the composites for aviation. In light of these reasons, it is imperative to understand the mechanical behaviors of orthotropic material and the related FEA (finite element analysis) techniques. The derivation of thermomechanical strains and stresses using finite element methods is a versatile approach [Geng et al.] to assessing the product life in terms of fatigue nucleation, crack growth, creep, oxidation, corrosion, etc. The finite element formulation for 3-dimensional orthotropic composites is theorized here for generalizing the strain (stress) state associated with potential crack nucleation and the corresponding crack propagation for a product life prediction.

3.1.1　Orthotropic Compliances

Orthotropic materials are a subset of anisotropic materials; their properties depend on the direction in which they are measured. Orthotropic materials possess three orthogonal planes of symmetry. If the material properties along the 1-axis, 2-axis, and 3-axis are mutually different in the orthogonal material coordinate system, it is an orthotropic material.

There are nine independent material properties associated with an orthotropic material. By convention, the elastic constants in orthotropic constitutive equations are comprised of Young's moduli E_{11}, E_{22}, E_{33}, Poisson's ratios ν_{12}, ν_{23}, ν_{31}, ν_{21}, ν_{32}, ν_{13}, and shear moduli G_{12}, G_{23}, G_{31}, G_{21}, G_{32}, G_{13}, based on the primary material coordinate system denoted as (1, 2, 3). A layer of unidirectional fiber-reinforced lamina, shown in Fig. 11.1.2 can be described using the following orthotropic stress-strain relationships in the primary material coordinate system:

$$\varepsilon_{11} = \frac{1}{E_{11}}\sigma_{11} + \frac{-\nu_{21}}{E_{22}}\sigma_{22} + \frac{-\nu_{31}}{E_{33}}\sigma_{33} + \alpha_1 \Delta T + \beta_1 \Delta C_{\mathrm{m}} \tag{3.1.1}$$

$$\varepsilon_{22} = \frac{-\nu_{12}}{E_{11}}\sigma_{11} + \frac{1}{E_{22}}\sigma_{22} + \frac{-\nu_{32}}{E_{33}}\sigma_{33} + \alpha_2 \Delta T + \beta_2 \Delta C_{\mathrm{m}} \tag{3.1.2}$$

$$\varepsilon_{33} = \frac{-\nu_{13}}{E_{11}} \sigma_{11} + \frac{-\nu_{23}}{E_{22}} \sigma_{22} + \frac{1}{E_{33}} \sigma_{33} + \alpha_3 \Delta T + \beta_3 \Delta C_m \qquad (3.1.3)$$

$$\gamma_{23} = \frac{\tau_{23}}{G_{23}} \qquad (3.1.4)$$

$$\gamma_{31} = \frac{\tau_{31}}{G_{31}} \qquad (3.1.5)$$

$$\text{and} \quad \gamma_{12} = \frac{\tau_{12}}{G_{12}} \qquad (3.1.6)$$

where

1-axis: Along the longitudinal direction of fibers in the unidirectional lamina;

2-axis: Transverse to the longitudinal direction of fibers in the lamina plane;

3-axis: Perpendicular to the lamina plane;

E_{11}, E_{22}, E_{33}(GPa): Young's moduli in axial, transverse, and out-of-plane directions;

G_{12}, G_{23}, G_{31}, G_{21}, G_{12}, G_{23}(GPa): Shear moduli of a unidirectional lamina;

ν_{12}, ν_{23}, ν_{31}, ν_{21}, ν_{13}, ν_{32}: Poisson's ratios of a unidirectional lamina;

ΔT: Temperature variation;

ΔC_m: Variation in concentration of moisture.

Note that the tensor shear strains ε_{ij} and the engineering shear strains γ_{ij} are related by the following three equations:

$$\gamma_{12} = 2\varepsilon_{12} \qquad (3.1.7)$$

$$\gamma_{23} = 2\varepsilon_{23} \qquad (3.1.8)$$

$$\text{and} \quad \gamma_{31} = 2\varepsilon_{31} \qquad (3.1.9)$$

The elastic constants in Eqs. (3.1.1)-(3.1.6) can be regrouped into a compliance matrix, $[s_{ij}]$, based on tensor shear strain without taking the hydrothermal (both temperature and moisture) effects into consideration, as follows:

$$\varepsilon = s_{ij}\sigma \qquad (3.1.10)$$

$$\text{i.e.} \quad \begin{Bmatrix} \varepsilon_{11} \\ \varepsilon_{22} \\ \varepsilon_{33} \\ \varepsilon_{23} \\ \varepsilon_{31} \\ \varepsilon_{12} \end{Bmatrix} = \begin{bmatrix} s_{11} & s_{12} & s_{13} & 0 & 0 & 0 \\ s_{12} & s_{22} & s_{23} & 0 & 0 & 0 \\ s_{13} & s_{23} & s_{33} & 0 & 0 & 0 \\ 0 & 0 & 0 & s_{44} & 0 & 0 \\ 0 & 0 & 0 & 0 & s_{55} & 0 \\ 0 & 0 & 0 & 0 & 0 & s_{66} \end{bmatrix} \begin{Bmatrix} \sigma_{11} \\ \sigma_{22} \\ \sigma_{33} \\ \sigma_{23} \\ \sigma_{31} \\ \sigma_{12} \end{Bmatrix} \qquad (3.1.11)$$

where

$$s_{11} = \frac{1}{E_{11}}$$

(3.1.12)

$$s_{22} = \frac{1}{E_{22}}$$

(3.1.13)

$$s_{33} = \frac{1}{E_{33}}$$

(3.1.14)

$$s_{12} = -\frac{\nu_{21}}{E_{22}} = s_{21} = -\frac{\nu_{12}}{E_{11}}$$

(3.1.15)

$$s_{23} = -\frac{\nu_{32}}{E_{33}} = s_{32} = -\frac{\nu_{23}}{E_{22}}$$

(3.1.16)

$$s_{31} = -\frac{\nu_{13}}{E_{11}} = s_{13} = -\frac{\nu_{31}}{E_{33}}$$

(3.1.17)

$$s_{44} = \frac{1}{2G_{23}}$$

(3.1.18)

$$s_{55} = \frac{1}{2G_{31}}$$

(3.1.19)

and $s_{66} = \frac{1}{2G_{12}}$

(3.1.20)

The compliance matrix is symmetric and must be positive definite for the strain energy density to be positive. The factor $1/2$ multiplying the shear moduli in the compliance matrix results from the difference between tensor shear strain and engineering shear strain, as described by Eqs. (3.1.7)-(3.1.9).

3.1.2 Orthotropic Elastic Constants

As given in Eqs. (3.1.1)-(3.1.6), there are 15 elastic constants for an orthotropic material. However, there are six special relationships for the elastic constants of an orthotropic material. They are given here without detailed derivations. The reciprocal theory relating Young's moduli to Poisson's ratios holds for an orthotropic material,

$$\nu_{ij} E_{jj} = \nu_{ji} E_{ii} \quad (i = 1, 2, 3 \, \& \, j = 1, 2, 3; \, i \neq j)$$

(3.1.21)

i.e. $\nu_{21} = \frac{\nu_{12} E_{22}}{E_{11}}$

(3.1.21a)

$$\nu_{32} = \frac{\nu_{23}\,E_{33}}{E_{22}} \tag{3.1.21b}$$

$$\text{and} \quad \nu_{13} = \frac{\nu_{31}\,E_{11}}{E_{33}} \tag{3.1.21c}$$

So does the reciprocal relation hold for shear moduli

$$G_{ij} = G_{ji}(i = 1,\, 2,\, 3 \ \& \ j = 1,\, 2,\, 3;\ i \ne j) \tag{3.1.22}$$

$$\text{i.e.} \quad G_{21} = G_{12} \tag{3.1.22a}$$

$$G_{31} = G_{13} \tag{3.1.22b}$$

$$\text{and} \quad G_{32} = G_{23} \tag{3.1.22c}$$

Enlightened by the reciprocal equations given above, there are only 9 independent elastic constants. By convention, the 9 independent elastic constants in orthotropic constitutive equations are the three Young's moduli, three Poisson's ratios, and the three shear moduli given as follows:

  (a) Young's moduli: E_{11}, E_{22}, and E_{33}.
  (b) Poisson's ratios: ν_{12}, ν_{23}, and ν_{31}.
  (c) Shear moduli: G_{12}, G_{23}, and G_{31}.

Elastic constants, thermal properties (namely thermal conductivities and specific heat capacities), hydrothermal properties (i.e., heat and moisture expansions), and mechanical strengths of commonly used reinforcing fibers for automobiles are listed in Tables 3.1.1, 3.1.2, and 3.1.3, respectively. Note that a reinforcing fiber (or particulate) itself may be orthotropic, transversely isotropic, or isotropic.

3.1.3   Orthotropic Stiffness

The stiffness of an orthotropic material, denoted by c_{ij}, can be derived by inverting Eqs. (3.1.1)-(3.1.6) without considering the hydroscopic (i.e., both thermal and moisture) effects,

$$\sigma_{11} = c_{11}\,\varepsilon_{11} + c_{12}\,\varepsilon_{22} + c_{13}\,\varepsilon_{33} \tag{3.1.23}$$

$$\sigma_{22} = c_{12}\,\varepsilon_{11} + c_{22}\,\varepsilon_{22} + c_{23}\,\varepsilon_{33} \tag{3.1.24}$$

$$\sigma_{33} = c_{13}\,\varepsilon_{11} + c_{23}\,\varepsilon_{22} + c_{33}\,\varepsilon_{33} \tag{3.1.25}$$

$$\tau_{23} = c_{44}\,\varepsilon_{23} \tag{3.1.26}$$

$$\tau_{31} = c_{55}\,\varepsilon_{31} \tag{3.1.27}$$

and $\quad \tau_{12} = c_{66} \, \varepsilon_{12}$ (3.1.28)

Individual stiffness elements are related to the elastic constants as

$$c_{11} = \frac{1 - \nu_{23} \, \nu_{32}}{E_{22} \, E_{33} \, \Delta}$$ (3.1.29)

$$c_{22} = \frac{1 - \nu_{31} \, \nu_{13}}{E_{33} \, E_{11} \, \Delta}$$ (3.1.30)

$$c_{33} = \frac{1 - \nu_{12} \, \nu_{21}}{E_{11} \, E_{22} \, \Delta}$$ (3.1.31)

$$c_{12} = \frac{\nu_{21} - \nu_{23} \, \nu_{32}}{E_{22} \, E_{33} \, \Delta} = c_{21} = \frac{\nu_{12} - \nu_{13} \, \nu_{32}}{E_{33} \, E_{11} \, \Delta}$$ (3.1.32)

$$c_{13} = \frac{\nu_{31} - \nu_{21} \, \nu_{32}}{E_{22} \, E_{33} \, \Delta} = c_{31} = \frac{\nu_{13} - \nu_{12} \, \nu_{23}}{E_{11} \, E_{22} \, \Delta}$$ (3.1.33)

$$c_{23} = \frac{\nu_{32} - \nu_{31} \, \nu_{12}}{E_{33} \, E_{11} \, \Delta} = c_{32} = \frac{\nu_{23} - \nu_{13} \, \nu_{12}}{E_{11} \, E_{22} \, \Delta}$$ (3.1.34)

$$c_{44} = 2G_{23}$$ (3.1.35)

$$c_{55} = 2G_{31}$$ (3.1.36)

and $\quad c_{66} = 2G_{12}$ (3.1.37)

where

$$\Delta = \frac{1 - \nu_{12} \, \nu_{21} - \nu_{23} \, \nu_{32} - \nu_{31} \, \nu_{13} - 2 \, \nu_{12} \, \nu_{23} \, \nu_{31}}{E_{11} \, E_{22} \, E_{33}}$$ (3.1.38)

The stiffness coefficients given in Eqs. (3.1.29)-(3.1.37) can be regrouped into a stiffness matrix, namely $[c]$, which represents the orthotropic elasticity tensor, as

$$\boldsymbol{\sigma} = \mathbf{c}\boldsymbol{\varepsilon}$$ (3.1.39)

i.e.
$$\begin{Bmatrix} \sigma_{11} \\ \sigma_{22} \\ \sigma_{33} \\ \tau_{23} \\ \tau_{31} \\ \tau_{12} \end{Bmatrix} = \begin{bmatrix} c_{11} & c_{12} & c_{13} & 0 & 0 & 0 \\ c_{12} & c_{22} & c_{23} & 0 & 0 & 0 \\ c_{13} & c_{23} & c_{33} & 0 & 0 & 0 \\ 0 & 0 & 0 & c_{44} & 0 & 0 \\ 0 & 0 & 0 & 0 & c_{55} & 0 \\ 0 & 0 & 0 & 0 & 0 & c_{66} \end{bmatrix} = \begin{Bmatrix} \varepsilon_{11} \\ \varepsilon_{22} \\ \varepsilon_{33} \\ \varepsilon_{23} \\ \varepsilon_{31} \\ \varepsilon_{12} \end{Bmatrix}$$ (3.1.40)

3.1.4   Transversely Isotropic Materials

If the material properties are the same in any direction in the $(1, 2)$ plane, but different along the 3-axis in the orthogonal material coordinate system, the composite is called transversely isotropic. As a special case of orthotropic materials, there are only five independent elastic constants, namely E_{11}, E_{33}, ν_{12}, ν_{13}, and G_{13}, because

$$E_{22} = E_{11} \tag{3.1.41}$$

$$\nu_{21} = \nu_{12} \tag{3.1.42}$$

$$\nu_{23} = \nu_{13} \tag{3.1.43}$$

$$G_{23} = G_{13} \tag{3.1.44}$$

and $$G_{12} = \frac{E_{11}}{2(1 + \nu_{12})} \tag{3.1.45}$$

Barium titanate ($BaTiO_3$, a piezoelectric material) and unidirectional fiber-reinforced composite are typical examples of transversely isotropic materials.

3.1.5   Isotropic Materials

If each material property along all directions in the orthogonal material coordinate system is identical, the composite is called isotropic. It means that the material is homogeneous. There are only two independent elastic constants as shown below:

$$E = E_{11} = E_{22} = E_{33} \tag{3.1.46}$$

$$\nu = \nu_{12} = \nu_{23} = \nu_{31} = \nu_{21} = \nu_{32} = \nu_{13} \tag{3.1.47}$$

and $$G = G_{23} = G_{31} = G_{12} = \frac{E}{2(1 + \nu)} \tag{3.1.48}$$

3.1.6   Finite Element Formulation for Composites

The finite element method is an ideal tool for determining structural strains and stresses, due to its versatility to model different and complex structures. It also represents an excellent alternative to the experimental approach since it is not required to have the physical model or the real component to be analyzed. For the application of FEA in the automotive industry, quadratic 20-node and linear 8-node elements are the two most used elements. When orthotropic thermal expansion coefficients are present in shell type structures, the modeling with shell or plate elements leads to results that are inconsistent with six stress (strain) components mandated by the nature, or sometimes even incorrect results. Only solid elements robustly present the realistic physical behavior. A detailed finite element formulation for composites with 20-node elements is addressed here and the procedure can be extended to the 8-node element and other solid elements. There are two schools of thought in the finite element world:

1. Use lots of lower order elements in areas with high stress gradients to obtain an accurate solution, called h-method.
2. Use fewer, but higher-order (smarter) elements in areas of high stress gradients to obtain an accurate solution, called p-method.

Smarter elements (higher order) have shape functions that can better approximate the deformation of the element. If, for example, someone has another node in the center of an element edge, there is a quadratic shape function, which would handle a constant acceleration load much more accurately [Cook et al.]. However, that additional accuracy comes at a price as higher order elements are more computationally expensive.

3.2 Strain-Displacement Relationship

For the 3-dimensional linear case, the six strain components in the (x, y, z) coordinate system can be obtained from the three linear displacements as follows:

$$\varepsilon_{xx} = \frac{\partial u}{\partial x} \tag{3.2.1}$$

$$\varepsilon_{yy} = \frac{\partial v}{\partial y} \tag{3.2.2}$$

$$\varepsilon_{zz} = \frac{\partial w}{\partial z} \tag{3.2.3}$$

$$\gamma_{xy} = \gamma_{yx} = 2\varepsilon_{xy} = 2\varepsilon_{yx} = \frac{\partial u}{\partial y} + \frac{\partial v}{\partial x} \tag{3.2.4}$$

$$\gamma_{yz} = \gamma_{zy} = 2\varepsilon_{yz} = 2\varepsilon_{zy} = \frac{\partial v}{\partial z} + \frac{\partial w}{\partial y} \tag{3.2.5}$$

and $$\gamma_{zx} = \gamma_{xz} = 2\varepsilon_{zx} = 2\varepsilon_{xz} = \frac{\partial w}{\partial z} + \frac{\partial u}{\partial z} \tag{3.2.6}$$

where

x, y, z: Cartesian coordinates;

u, v, w: Displacements along the x-, y-, and z-axis, respectively;

ε_{xx}, ε_{yy}, ε_{zz}: Normal strains;

ε_{xy}, ε_{yz}, ε_{zx}: Tensor shear strains;

γ_{xy}, γ_{yz}, γ_{zz}: Engineering shear strains.

The above six equations constitute the compatibility conditions in linear elasticity with small displacements or deformations. It is observed that there are six strain-displacement relations, also called linear compatibility equations, which are functions of only three unknown displacements in the 3-dimenisional space.

3.2.1   Shape Functions

Shape functions are interpolation functions, which relate the nodal displacements to the displacements of any point of the element after the nodes and elements are formed by discretizing the continuum. Let ξ, η and ζ be three curvilinear natural (body) coordinates attached to the isoparametric quadratic solid element, Fig. 3.2.1. Assume that these three coordinates vary between -1 and 1 which are located on respective faces of the element. The displacement field u, v, and w defined in the x, y, and z directions of the global Cartesian coordinates can be interpolated by

$$u = \sum_{i=1}^{20} N_i u_i \qquad\qquad (3.2.7a)$$

$$v = \sum_{i=1}^{20} N_i v_i \qquad\qquad (3.2.7b)$$

$$\text{and} \quad w = \sum_{i=1}^{20} N_i w_i \qquad\qquad (3.2.7c)$$

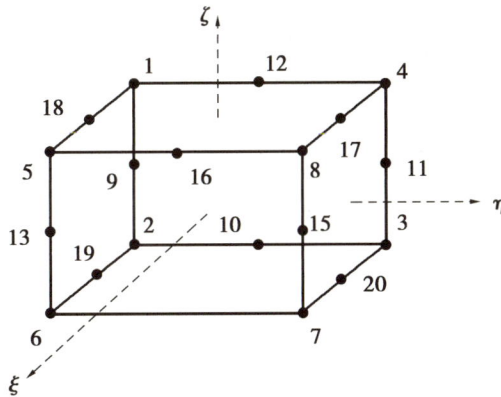

Fig. 3.2.1   Local Numbering Sequence of Nodes of a 20-node Solid Element

Note that u_i, v_i, and w_i are the three discrete variables at individual nodes. For nodes on $\xi_i = 0$, $\eta_i = 0$, and $\zeta_i = 0$, respectively,

$$N_i = \frac{1}{4}(1 - \xi^2)(1 + \eta\,\eta_i)(1 + \zeta\,\zeta_i), \quad i = 9, 11, 13, 15 \tag{3.2.8}$$

$$N_i = \frac{1}{4}(1 + \xi\xi_i)(1 - \eta^2)(1 + \zeta\,\zeta_i), \quad i = 17, 18, 19, 20 \tag{3.2.9}$$

and $\quad N_i = \dfrac{1}{4}(1 + \xi\xi_i)(1 + \eta\,\eta_i)(1 - \zeta^2), \quad i = 10, 12, 14, 16$ (3.2.10)

For corner nodes,

$$N_i = \frac{(1 + \xi\xi_i)(1 + \eta\,\eta_i)(1 + \zeta\,\zeta_i)(\xi\xi_i + \eta\,\eta_i + \zeta\,\zeta_i - 2)}{8} \tag{3.2.11}$$

where
i: Subscript, ranging from 1 to 20;
N_i: Shape functions;
u_i, v_i, w_i: Global displacements of node i in the Cartesian coordinates;
ξ, η, ζ: Natural coordinate system attached to the element of concern;
ξ_i, η_i, ζ_i: Natural coordinate system of node i.

By differentiating Eq. (3.2.7) with respect to the three body coordinates (ξ, η, ζ), and stacking the them into a vector column, one has

$$
\begin{Bmatrix}
\dfrac{\partial u}{\partial \xi} \\[4pt]
\dfrac{\partial u}{\partial \eta} \\[4pt]
\dfrac{\partial u}{\partial \zeta} \\[4pt]
\dfrac{\partial v}{\partial \xi} \\[4pt]
\dfrac{\partial v}{\partial \eta} \\[4pt]
\dfrac{\partial v}{\partial \zeta} \\[4pt]
\dfrac{\partial w}{\partial \xi} \\[4pt]
\dfrac{\partial w}{\partial \eta} \\[4pt]
\dfrac{\partial w}{\partial \zeta}
\end{Bmatrix}
=
\begin{bmatrix}
\dfrac{\partial N_i}{\partial \xi} & 0 & 0 \\[4pt]
\dfrac{\partial N_i}{\partial \eta} & 0 & 0 \\[4pt]
\dfrac{\partial N_i}{\partial \zeta} & 0 & 0 \\[4pt]
0 & \dfrac{\partial N_i}{\partial \xi} & 0 \\[4pt]
0 & \dfrac{\partial N_i}{\partial \eta} & 0 \\[4pt]
0 & \dfrac{\partial N_i}{\partial \zeta} & 0 \\[4pt]
0 & 0 & \dfrac{\partial N_i}{\partial \xi} \\[4pt]
0 & 0 & \dfrac{\partial N_i}{\partial \eta} \\[4pt]
0 & 0 & \dfrac{\partial N_i}{\partial \zeta}
\end{bmatrix}
\begin{Bmatrix}
u_i \\ v_i \\ w_i
\end{Bmatrix}
\tag{3.2.12}
$$

The same interpolation functions are employed to model the geometric shape,

$$x = \sum_{i=1}^{20} N_i \, x_i \tag{3.2.13a}$$

$$y = \sum_{i=1}^{20} N_i \, y_i \tag{3.2.13b}$$

and $\quad z = \sum_{i=1}^{20} N_i \, z_i \tag{3.2.13c}$

where (x_i, y_i, z_i) denotes the coordinates of node i of an element. When displacements and coordinates of all nodes of an element are packed together in a column, they can be rearranged in form of,

$$\begin{Bmatrix} u \\ v \\ w \end{Bmatrix} = [N] \{\phi\} \tag{3.2.14a}$$

and $\quad \begin{Bmatrix} x \\ y \\ z \end{Bmatrix} = [N] \{e\} \tag{3.2.14b}$

where

$$\{\phi\}^{\mathrm{T}} = (u_1 \quad v_1 \quad w_1 \quad u_2 \quad v_2 \quad w_2 \quad \cdots \quad u_{20} \quad v_{20} \quad w_{20}) \tag{3.2.15}$$

$$\{e\}^{\mathrm{T}} = (x_1 \quad y_1 \quad z_1 \quad x_2 \quad y_2 \quad z_2 \quad \cdots \quad x_{20} \quad y_{20} \quad z_{20}) \tag{3.2.16}$$

and $\quad [N] = \begin{pmatrix} N_1 & 0 & 0 & N_2 & 0 & 0 & N_3 & 0 & 0 & \cdots & N_{20} & 0 & 0 \\ 0 & N_1 & 0 & 0 & N_2 & 0 & 0 & N_3 & 0 & \cdots & 0 & N_{20} & 0 \\ 0 & 0 & N_1 & 0 & 0 & N_2 & 0 & 0 & N_3 & \cdots & 0 & 0 & N_{20} \end{pmatrix}_{3 \times 60} \tag{3.2.17}$

The next step is to find the relationship between strains and displacements of an element. This requires that the coordinate transformation of derivatives of displacements measured by the global Cartesian coordinates, (x, y, z), be established and expressed in terms of natural coordinates (ξ, η, ζ),

$$\begin{Bmatrix} \dfrac{\partial u}{\partial \xi} \\[2mm] \dfrac{\partial u}{\partial \eta} \\[2mm] \dfrac{\partial u}{\partial \zeta} \end{Bmatrix} = [J] \begin{Bmatrix} \dfrac{\partial u}{\partial x} \\[2mm] \dfrac{\partial u}{\partial y} \\[2mm] \dfrac{\partial u}{\partial z} \end{Bmatrix} \tag{3.2.18a}$$

$$\begin{Bmatrix} \dfrac{\partial v}{\partial \xi} \\[2mm] \dfrac{\partial v}{\partial \eta} \\[2mm] \dfrac{\partial v}{\partial \zeta} \end{Bmatrix} = [J] \begin{Bmatrix} \dfrac{\partial v}{\partial x} \\[2mm] \dfrac{\partial v}{\partial y} \\[2mm] \dfrac{\partial v}{\partial z} \end{Bmatrix} \tag{3.2.18b}$$

and
$$\left\{\begin{array}{c} \dfrac{\partial w}{\partial \xi} \\[6pt] \dfrac{\partial w}{\partial \eta} \\[6pt] \dfrac{\partial w}{\partial \zeta} \end{array}\right\} = [J] \left\{\begin{array}{c} \dfrac{\partial w}{\partial x} \\[6pt] \dfrac{\partial w}{\partial y} \\[6pt] \dfrac{\partial w}{\partial z} \end{array}\right\}$$
(3.2.18c)

of which $[J]$ is the Jacobian matrix, defined as

$$[J] = \begin{bmatrix} J_{11} & J_{12} & J_{13} \\ J_{21} & J_{22} & J_{13} \\ J_{31} & J_{32} & J_{33} \end{bmatrix} = \begin{bmatrix} \dfrac{\partial x}{\partial \xi} & \dfrac{\partial y}{\partial \xi} & \dfrac{\partial z}{\partial \xi} \\[8pt] \dfrac{\partial x}{\partial \eta} & \dfrac{\partial y}{\partial \eta} & \dfrac{\partial z}{\partial \eta} \\[8pt] \dfrac{\partial x}{\partial \zeta} & \dfrac{\partial y}{\partial \zeta} & \dfrac{\partial z}{\partial \zeta} \end{bmatrix}$$
(3.2.19)

For example, $J_{12} = \partial y/\partial \xi = (\partial N_1/\partial \xi) \, y_1 + (\partial N_2/\partial \xi) \, y_2 + \cdots + (\partial N_{20}/\partial \xi) \, y_{20}$. Let $[L] = [J]^{-1}$ be the inverse of the Jacobian matrix, then

$$\left\{\begin{array}{c} \dfrac{\partial u}{\partial x} \\[6pt] \dfrac{\partial u}{\partial y} \\[6pt] \dfrac{\partial u}{\partial z} \end{array}\right\} = [L] \left\{\begin{array}{c} \dfrac{\partial u}{\partial \xi} \\[6pt] \dfrac{\partial u}{\partial \eta} \\[6pt] \dfrac{\partial u}{\partial \zeta} \end{array}\right\}$$
(3.2.20a)

$$\left\{\begin{array}{c} \dfrac{\partial v}{\partial x} \\[6pt] \dfrac{\partial v}{\partial y} \\[6pt] \dfrac{\partial v}{\partial z} \end{array}\right\} = [L] \left\{\begin{array}{c} \dfrac{\partial v}{\partial \xi} \\[6pt] \dfrac{\partial v}{\partial \eta} \\[6pt] \dfrac{\partial v}{\partial \zeta} \end{array}\right\}$$
(3.2.20b)

and
$$\left\{\begin{array}{c} \dfrac{\partial w}{\partial x} \\[6pt] \dfrac{\partial w}{\partial y} \\[6pt] \dfrac{\partial w}{\partial z} \end{array}\right\} = [L] \left\{\begin{array}{c} \dfrac{\partial w}{\partial \xi} \\[6pt] \dfrac{\partial w}{\partial \eta} \\[6pt] \dfrac{\partial w}{\partial \zeta} \end{array}\right\}$$
(3.2.20c)

Or put them together as,

$$
\begin{Bmatrix}
\dfrac{\partial u}{\partial x} \\[4pt]
\dfrac{\partial u}{\partial y} \\[4pt]
\dfrac{\partial u}{\partial z} \\[4pt]
\dfrac{\partial v}{\partial x} \\[4pt]
\dfrac{\partial v}{\partial y} \\[4pt]
\dfrac{\partial v}{\partial z} \\[4pt]
\dfrac{\partial w}{\partial x} \\[4pt]
\dfrac{\partial w}{\partial y} \\[4pt]
\dfrac{\partial w}{\partial z}
\end{Bmatrix}
=
\begin{bmatrix}
L_{11} & L_{12} & L_{13} & 0 & 0 & 0 & 0 & 0 & 0 \\
L_{21} & L_{22} & L_{23} & 0 & 0 & 0 & 0 & 0 & 0 \\
L_{31} & L_{32} & L_{33} & 0 & 0 & 0 & 0 & 0 & 0 \\
0 & 0 & 0 & L_{11} & L_{12} & L_{13} & 0 & 0 & 0 \\
0 & 0 & 0 & L_{21} & L_{22} & L_{23} & 0 & 0 & 0 \\
0 & 0 & 0 & L_{31} & L_{32} & L_{33} & 0 & 0 & 0 \\
0 & 0 & 0 & 0 & 0 & 0 & L_{11} & L_{12} & L_{13} \\
0 & 0 & 0 & 0 & 0 & 0 & L_{21} & L_{22} & L_{23} \\
0 & 0 & 0 & 0 & 0 & 0 & L_{31} & L_{32} & L_{33}
\end{bmatrix}
\begin{Bmatrix}
\dfrac{\partial u}{\partial \xi} \\[4pt]
\dfrac{\partial u}{\partial \eta} \\[4pt]
\dfrac{\partial u}{\partial \zeta} \\[4pt]
\dfrac{\partial v}{\partial \xi} \\[4pt]
\dfrac{\partial v}{\partial \eta} \\[4pt]
\dfrac{\partial v}{\partial \zeta} \\[4pt]
\dfrac{\partial w}{\partial \xi} \\[4pt]
\dfrac{\partial w}{\partial \eta} \\[4pt]
\dfrac{\partial w}{\partial \zeta}
\end{Bmatrix}
= [L]'
\begin{Bmatrix}
\dfrac{\partial u}{\partial \xi} \\[4pt]
\dfrac{\partial u}{\partial \eta} \\[4pt]
\dfrac{\partial u}{\partial \zeta} \\[4pt]
\dfrac{\partial v}{\partial \xi} \\[4pt]
\dfrac{\partial v}{\partial \eta} \\[4pt]
\dfrac{\partial v}{\partial \zeta} \\[4pt]
\dfrac{\partial w}{\partial \xi} \\[4pt]
\dfrac{\partial w}{\partial \eta} \\[4pt]
\dfrac{\partial w}{\partial \zeta}
\end{Bmatrix}
\tag{3.2.21}
$$

3.2.2 Relating Element Strains to Nodal Displacements

Based on linear elasticity for small deformation, the engineering strains can be expressed in terms of displacements as

$$
\{\varepsilon\} =
\begin{Bmatrix}
\varepsilon_{xx} \\
\varepsilon_{yy} \\
\varepsilon_{zz} \\
\gamma_{xy} \\
\gamma_{yz} \\
\gamma_{zx}
\end{Bmatrix}
=
\begin{bmatrix}
1 & 0 & 0 & 0 & 0 & 0 & 0 & 0 & 0 \\
0 & 0 & 0 & 0 & 1 & 0 & 0 & 0 & 0 \\
0 & 0 & 0 & 0 & 0 & 0 & 0 & 0 & 1 \\
0 & 1 & 0 & 1 & 0 & 0 & 0 & 0 & 0 \\
0 & 0 & 0 & 0 & 0 & 1 & 0 & 1 & 0 \\
0 & 0 & 1 & 0 & 0 & 0 & 1 & 0 & 0
\end{bmatrix}
\begin{Bmatrix}
\dfrac{\partial u}{\partial x} \\[4pt]
\dfrac{\partial u}{\partial y} \\[4pt]
\dfrac{\partial u}{\partial z} \\[4pt]
\dfrac{\partial v}{\partial x} \\[4pt]
\dfrac{\partial v}{\partial y} \\[4pt]
\dfrac{\partial v}{\partial z} \\[4pt]
\dfrac{\partial w}{\partial x} \\[4pt]
\dfrac{\partial w}{\partial y} \\[4pt]
\dfrac{\partial w}{\partial z}
\end{Bmatrix}
= [H]
\begin{Bmatrix}
\dfrac{\partial u}{\partial x} \\[4pt]
\dfrac{\partial u}{\partial y} \\[4pt]
\dfrac{\partial u}{\partial z} \\[4pt]
\dfrac{\partial v}{\partial x} \\[4pt]
\dfrac{\partial v}{\partial y} \\[4pt]
\dfrac{\partial v}{\partial z} \\[4pt]
\dfrac{\partial w}{\partial y} \\[4pt]
\dfrac{\partial w}{\partial y} \\[4pt]
\dfrac{\partial w}{\partial z}
\end{Bmatrix}
\tag{3.2.22}
$$

Substituting Eq. (3.2.12) into Eq. (3.2.21), and then into Eq. (3.2.22), one can find the relationship between strains and displacements,

$$\{\varepsilon\} = \sum_{i=1}^{20} [H][L'] \begin{bmatrix} \dfrac{\partial N_i}{\partial \xi} & 0 & 0 \\[2mm] \dfrac{\partial N_i}{\partial \eta} & 0 & 0 \\[2mm] \dfrac{\partial N_i}{\partial \zeta} & 0 & 0 \\[2mm] 0 & \dfrac{\partial N_i}{\partial \xi} & 0 \\[2mm] 0 & \dfrac{\partial N_i}{\partial \eta} & 0 \\[2mm] 0 & \dfrac{\partial N_i}{\partial \zeta} & 0 \\[2mm] 0 & 0 & \dfrac{\partial N_i}{\partial \xi} \\[2mm] 0 & 0 & \dfrac{\partial N_i}{\partial \eta} \\[2mm] 0 & 0 & \dfrac{\partial N_i}{\partial \zeta} \end{bmatrix} \begin{Bmatrix} u_i \\ v_i \\ w_i \end{Bmatrix} = \sum_{i=1}^{20} [B_i] \begin{Bmatrix} u_i \\ v_i \\ w_i \end{Bmatrix} \qquad (3.2.23)$$

or expressed in another format with every node packed into an array,

$$\{\varepsilon\} = [[B_1] \quad [B_2] \quad [B_3] \quad \cdots \quad [B_{20}]] \begin{Bmatrix} u_1 \\ v_1 \\ w_1 \\ \vdots \\ u_{20} \\ v_{20} \\ w_{20} \end{Bmatrix} \qquad (3.2.24)$$

When the displacements at each node i is compacted into a single column for an entire element, the strain-displacement relationship in the above equation becomes

$$\{\varepsilon\}_{6\times 1} = [B]_{6\times 60} \{\phi\}_{60\times 1} \qquad (3.2.25)$$

and displacement vector $\{g\}^{\mathrm{T}} \equiv \{u, v, w\}$ at any point of this element is related to nodal displacement vector $\{\phi\}$ by the corresponding shape matrix $[N]$,

$$\{g\}_{3\times1} = [N]_{6\times60}\{\phi\}_{60\times1} \qquad (3.2.26)$$

3.3　Energy Formulation for Small Deformations

Taking initial stresses $\{\sigma_0\}$ and initial strains $\{\varepsilon_0\}$ into consideration, one can obtain the relationship between current stresses $\{\sigma\}$ and strains $\{\varepsilon\}$ as

$$\{\sigma\} = [c] (\{\varepsilon\} - \{\varepsilon_0\}) + \{\sigma_0\} \qquad (3.3.1)$$

The initial strain $\{\varepsilon_0\}$ in the above equation may include the thermal, moisture, plastic and creeping strains in a nonlinear large deformation. The corresponding strain energy per unit volume is

$$U_0 = \iiint_V dU_0 = \iiint_V \{\sigma\}^T\{d\varepsilon\} = \frac{1}{2}\{\varepsilon\}^T[c]\{\varepsilon\} - \{\varepsilon\}^T[c]\{\varepsilon_0\} + \{\varepsilon\}^T\{\sigma_0\} \qquad (3.3.2)$$

Based on the formula for strains $\{\varepsilon\}$ expressed in terms of nodal displacements $\{\phi\}$ as described by Eq. (3.2.25), the strain energy per unit volume can be further extended into

$$U_0 = \frac{1}{2}\{\phi\}^T[B]^T[c][B]\{\phi\} - \{\phi\}^T[B]^T[c]\{\varepsilon_0\} + \{\phi\}^T[B]^T\{\sigma_0\} \qquad (3.3.3)$$

Furthermore, the total potential of a continuum with volume domain V and surface domain S consists of four parts, i. e. strain energy, and works done by body forces $\{b\}$, surface tractions $\{S\}$ and concentrated forces $\{Q\}$,

$$\prod = \iiint_V U_0 \, dV - \iiint_V \{g\}^T\{b\} \, dV - \iint_S \{g\}^T\{S\} \, dS - \{\Phi\}^T\{Q\} \qquad (3.3.4)$$

Since the concentrated forces in $\{Q\}$ are usually expressed in the global Cartesian coordinate system and independent of integration, the total displacement vector for the entire structure $\{\Phi\}$ is used as its corresponding displacement. Substitution of Eq. (3.3.1) and Eq. (3.3.3) into the above equation yields

$$\prod = \iiint_V \left(\frac{1}{2}\{\phi\}^T[B]^T[c][B]\{\phi\} - \{\phi\}^T[B]^T[c]\{\varepsilon_0\} + \{\phi\}^T[B]^T\{\sigma_0\} \right) dV$$

$$- \iiint_V \{\phi\}^T[N]^T\{b\} \, dV - \iint_S \{\phi\}^T[N]^T\{S\} \, dS - \{\Phi\}^T\{Q\} \qquad (3.3.5)$$

in which the summation means the contribution from all elements assembled. Then the total potential of the entire structure is

$$\prod = \frac{1}{2}\sum\{\phi\}^T[k]\{\phi\} - \sum\{\phi\}^T\{f\} - \sum\{\Phi\}^T\{Q\} \qquad (3.3.6)$$

where

$$[k] = \iiint_V [B]^T[c][B] \, dV \tag{3.3.7}$$

and

$$\{f\} = \iiint_V [B]^T[c]\{\varepsilon_o\} \, dV$$
$$- \iiint_V [B]\{\sigma_o\} \, dV + \iiint_V [N]^T\{b\} \, dV + \iint_S [N]^T\{S\} \tag{3.3.8}$$

By stacking the elemental displacements $\{\phi\}$ into a vector column to form the total displacement vector $\{\Phi\}$ according to the sequence of element numbers, the above equation can be rewritten as

$$\prod = \frac{1}{2}\{\Phi\}^T[K]\{\Phi\} - \{\Phi\}^T\{F\} \tag{3.3.9}$$

and taking the first derivative with respect to the total displacement vector $\{\Phi\}$ to obtain the equation of equilibrium,

$$[K]\{\Phi\} = \{F\} \tag{3.3.10}$$

It means that static equilibrium prevails with variation principle, when $\{\Phi\}$ satisfies the above set of simultaneous equations. The total stiffness $[K]$ and total load $[F]$ are assembled from individual elements,

$$[K] = \text{Assembled } [k] \tag{3.3.11}$$

and $\{F\} = \text{directed } \{Q\} + \text{assembled } \{f\}$ $\tag{3.3.12}$

Based on the linear elasticity the stiffness matrix $[k]$ of an element is formulated as Eq. (3.3.7), while each element might contain several layers of orthotropic laminae with different fiber orientations. $\{Q\}$ is a vector of forces directly applied. A composite element or super element could be an economic approach to the calculation and prediction of structural performance, especially for the modal analysis and dynamic transient response. Both composite and super elements (as super-positioned) are to be addressed.

3.4   Composite Elements

A composite element is defined as a finite element with layered laminae of which the material properties are assembled together according to the lamination theory as shown in. For the kth ply, the corresponding stresses $\{\sigma_{ij}\}_k$ can be written in terms of strains $\{\varepsilon_{ij}\}_k$ as

$$\{\sigma_{ij}\}_k = [C]_k\{\varepsilon_{ij}\}_k \tag{3.4.1}$$

$[C]_k$ is the stiffness referring to the axes of orthotropic material of kth ply. From the formulae for engineering strains, the above equation has the following expression in the primary material coordinates $(1, 2, 3)$,

$$
\begin{Bmatrix} \sigma_{11} \\ \sigma_{22} \\ \sigma_{33} \\ \tau_{23} \\ \tau_{31} \\ \tau_{12} \end{Bmatrix}_k =
\begin{bmatrix}
C_{11}^k & C_{12}^k & C_{13}^k & 0 & 0 & 0 \\
C_{21}^k & C_{22}^k & C_{23}^k & 0 & 0 & 0 \\
C_{31}^k & C_{32}^k & C_{33}^k & 0 & 0 & 0 \\
0 & 0 & 0 & C_{44}^k & 0 & 0 \\
0 & 0 & 0 & 0 & C_{55}^k & 0 \\
0 & 0 & 0 & 0 & 0 & C_{66}^k
\end{bmatrix}
\begin{Bmatrix} \varepsilon_{11} \\ \varepsilon_{22} \\ \varepsilon_{33} \\ \gamma_{23} \\ \gamma_{31} \\ \gamma_{12} \end{Bmatrix}
\tag{3.4.2}
$$

and
$$
C_{11}^k = \frac{E_{11}^k(1 - \nu_{23}^k \nu_{32}^k)}{\nu_t^k}
\tag{3.4.3}
$$

$$
C_{12}^k = \frac{E_{22}^k(\nu_{12}^k - \nu_{13}^k \nu_{32}^k)}{\nu_t^k}
\tag{3.4.4}
$$

$$
C_{22}^k = \frac{E_{22}^k(1 - \nu_{13}^k \nu_{31}^k)}{\nu_t^k}
\tag{3.4.5}
$$

$$
C_{23}^k = \frac{E_{33}^k(\nu_{23}^k - \nu_{21}^k \nu_{13}^k)}{\nu_t^k}
\tag{3.4.6}
$$

$$
C_{33}^k = \frac{E_{33}^k(1 - \nu_{12}^k \nu_{23}^k)}{\nu_t^k}
\tag{3.4.7}
$$

$$
C_{13}^k = \frac{E_{33}^k(\nu_{13}^k - \nu_{12}^k \nu_{23}^k)}{\nu_t^k}
\tag{3.4.8}
$$

$$
C_{44}^k = G_{23}^k
\tag{3.4.9}
$$

$$
C_{55}^k = G_{31}^k
\tag{3.4.10}
$$

$$
C_{66}^k = G_{12}^k
\tag{3.4.11}
$$

where
$$
\nu_t^k = 1 - \nu_{12}^k \nu_{21}^k - \nu_{13}^k \nu_{31}^k - \nu_{23}^k \nu_{32}^k - \nu_{13}^k \nu_{31}^k - \nu_{12}^k \nu_{23}^k \nu_{31}^k - \nu_{21}^k \nu_{13}^k \nu_{32}^k
\tag{3.4.12}
$$

Let θ denote the angle of fiber direction, i.e., the 1-axis of the kth ply with respect to the natural coordinate ξ-axis, while the plane formed by the material coordinates 2-axis and 3-axis is coincident with that formed by natural coordinates η-axis and ζ-axis. A simple coordinate transformation matrix for strains is [Cook et al.] [Chiang & Tang]

$$[T_\varepsilon]_k = \begin{bmatrix} c^2 & s^2 & 0 & cs & 0 & 0 \\ s^2 & c^2 & 0 & -cs & 0 & 0 \\ 0 & 0 & 0 & 0 & 0 & 0 \\ -2cs & 2cs & 0 & c^2-s^2 & 0 & 0 \\ 0 & 0 & 0 & 0 & c & -s \\ 0 & 0 & 0 & 0 & s & c \end{bmatrix}_k \tag{3.4.13}$$

would relate the stiffness matrix $[\hat{C}]_k$ in the natural coordinate system to the stiffness matrix $[C]_k$ in the material coordinate system,

$$[\hat{C}]_k = [T_\varepsilon]_k^T [C]_k [T_\varepsilon]_k \tag{3.4.14}$$

This can be regarded as a ply of monoclinic material in a set of natural coordinates,

$$\begin{Bmatrix} \sigma_{11} \\ \sigma_{22} \\ \sigma_{33} \\ \tau_{23} \\ \tau_{31} \\ \tau_{12} \end{Bmatrix}_k = \begin{bmatrix} C_{11}^k & C_{12}^k & C_{13}^k & 0 & 0 & 0 \\ C_{21}^k & C_{22}^k & C_{23}^k & 0 & 0 & 0 \\ C_{31}^k & C_{32}^k & C_{33}^k & 0 & 0 & 0 \\ 0 & 0 & 0 & C_{44}^k & 0 & 0 \\ 0 & 0 & 0 & 0 & C_{55}^k & 0 \\ 0 & 0 & 0 & 0 & 0 & C_{66}^k \end{bmatrix} \begin{Bmatrix} \varepsilon_{11} \\ \varepsilon_{22} \\ \varepsilon_{33} \\ \gamma_{23} \\ \gamma_{31} \\ \gamma_{12} \end{Bmatrix}_k \tag{3.4.15}$$

where
$$C_{ij}^k = C_{ji}^k, \quad i \neq j$$

By considering a representative small element of a laminated medium and imposing the conditions of continuity of stresses and displacements at interfacial surfaces of each layer, the 3-dimensional lamination theories presented in [Jones] can be used to compute the equivalent material properties for an element containing a stack of layers. Thus, the equivalent constitutive equation for a composite element is

$$\{\sigma_{ij}\} = [E]\{\varepsilon_{ij}\} = [\hat{C}]\{\varepsilon_{ij}\} \tag{3.4.16}$$

It means that $[\hat{C}]$ is the $[E]$ matrix in the above equation, used to compute the element stiffness matrix.

3.5 Super Element

A super element for composites is defined as a finite element with layered laminae, of which the material properties are used to calculate the stiffness matrix in Eq. (3.4.2) for each individual layer, and then stacked up additively. A change of variables from the Cartesian coordinates to the natural coordinates in Eq. (3.3.7) yields

$$[k] = \int_{-1}^{1}\int_{-1}^{1}\int_{-1}^{1} [B]^{\mathrm{T}}[E][B] \mid J \mid \mathrm{d}\xi\ \mathrm{d}\eta\ \mathrm{d}\zeta \tag{3.5.1}$$

where $\mid J \mid$ is the determinant of Jacobian matrix between natural and Cartesian coordinates, i.e., Eq. (3.2.13).

It is assumed that each layer of the element is stacked with its norm in the ζ-direction. However, the elasticity matrix is not uniform and geometrical discontinuity happens from layer to layer along the stacking ζ-direction. It is assumed that each layer is integrated individually and added up to account for the entire through-thickness stiffness matrix without considering the interactions of material properties in a triaxial-stressed state along the interfacial surfaces. Another change of variable for the ζ-coordinate is required for this algorithm,

$$\zeta = -1 + \frac{1}{h}\left[-h_{k}(1-\zeta_{k}) + 2\sum_{j=1}^{k} h_{j}\right] \tag{3.5.2}$$

and $\quad \mathrm{d}\zeta = \dfrac{h_{k}}{h}\mathrm{d}\zeta_{k}$ $\hspace{5cm}$ (3.5.3)

where h_{k} is the thickness of layer k and h is the total thickness throughout the stacked laminate. With the above substitutions, Eq. (3.5.1) becomes

$$[k] = \sum_{k=1}^{N}\int_{-1}^{1}\int_{-1}^{1}\int_{-1}^{1} [B]^{\mathrm{T}}[\hat{C}]_{k}[B] \mid J \mid (h_{k}/h)\ \mathrm{d}\xi\ \mathrm{d}\eta\ \mathrm{d}\zeta_{k} \tag{3.5.4}$$

3.6   Nodal Loads

Nodal loads, as shown in Eq. (3.3.12) that are derived from energy formulation and variational principle, are called consistent loads. Those loads might include body forces, surface traction, line forces, concentrated forces, and forces responsible for initial stresses and strains. Body forces and surface traction are discussed in this section. Note that line forces and concentrated forces do not exist in the real world and they are assumed to be possible artificially by fictitious imagination. Forces associated with initial stresses and strains are usually related to material nonlinearity.

3.6.1   Body forces

Body forces are generally measured in terms of amplitude per unit volume of mass, i. e., gravitational force, magnetic force. They can be integrated out directly using the Gauss-quadrature rule in the natural coordinate system. If the components of body forces are known in the global Cartesian coordinates, a coordinate transformation is required before the integration for body forces in Eq. (3.3.12) is performed,

$$\begin{Bmatrix} b_\xi \\ b_\eta \\ b_\zeta \end{Bmatrix} = [\,T_c\,]_{3\times3} \begin{Bmatrix} b_x \\ b_y \\ b_z \end{Bmatrix} \tag{3.6.1}$$

where

$$T_c = \begin{pmatrix} l_1 & m_1 & n_1 \\ l_2 & m_2 & n_2 \\ l_3 & m_3 & n_3 \end{pmatrix} \tag{3.6.2}$$

3.6.2　Surface Tractions

Surface tractions are measured in terms of amplitude per unit surface area for finite element analysis, i.e., pressure and pure shear forces.

3.6.2.1　Pressure

The pressure is always normal to surfaces which it is acting on. Assume the surface $\zeta = -1$ (or $\zeta = 1$) is under pressure p, then the two face-tangent vectors V_1 and V_2 in the direction (i, j, k) of the global Cartesian coordinates are

$$V_1 = (x,_\xi i + y,_\xi j + z,_\xi k)d = (J_{11} i + J_{12} j + J_{13} k)d \tag{3.6.3}$$

and　$V_2 = (x,_\eta i + y,_\eta j + z,_\eta k)d = (J_{21} i + J_{22} j + J_{23} k)d \tag{3.6.4}$

where $J_{\alpha\beta}$, $\alpha = 1, 2$ and $\beta = 1, 2, 3$ are defined in Eq. (3.2.13). Let $\{l, m, n\}$ be the vector of direction cosines of a unit vector normal to the surface $\zeta = -1$ (or $\zeta = 1$),

$$l\, i + m\, j + n\, k = \frac{V_1 \times V_2}{|\,V_1 \times V_2\,|} = \frac{V_1 \times V_2}{dS} \tag{3.6.5}$$

Thus the term contributed by pressure p, as part of the surface traction shown in Eq. (3.3.8), becomes

$$\iint_S [N] \{S\} \, dS = \iint_S N_i \begin{pmatrix} l \\ m \\ n \end{pmatrix} p \, dS \tag{3.6.6}$$

so that the x, y and z components of consistent loads due to pressure p_i at node i are evaluated by

$$
\begin{Bmatrix} f_{xi} \\ f_{yi} \\ f_{zi} \end{Bmatrix} = \int_{-1}^{1}\int_{-1}^{1} N_i\, p_i \begin{Bmatrix} J_{12}\ J_{23}\ -J_{13}\ J_{22} \\ J_{13}\ J_{21}\ -J_{11}\ J_{23} \\ J_{11}\ J_{22}\ -J_{12}\ J_{21} \end{Bmatrix} \mathrm{d}\xi\ \mathrm{d}\eta
\tag{3.6.7}
$$

in which N_i and all the $J_{\alpha\beta}$ are evaluated at $\zeta=-1$ (or $\zeta=1$), and i ranges over all nodes on surface $\zeta=-1$ (or $\zeta=1$). Similarly, the x, y and z components of consistent loads for pressure p_i at node i on surface $\xi=-1$ (or $\xi=1$) are

$$
\begin{Bmatrix} f_{xi} \\ f_{yi} \\ f_{zi} \end{Bmatrix} = \int_{-1}^{1}\int_{-1}^{1} N_i\, p_i \begin{Bmatrix} J_{32}\ J_{13}\ -J_{33}\ J_{12} \\ J_{33}\ J_{11}\ -J_{31}\ J_{13} \\ J_{31}\ J_{12}\ -J_{32}\ J_{11} \end{Bmatrix} \mathrm{d}\xi\ \mathrm{d}\eta
\tag{3.6.8}
$$

and on surface $\eta=-1$ (or $\eta=1$) are

$$
\begin{Bmatrix} f_{xi} \\ f_{yi} \\ f_{zi} \end{Bmatrix} = \int_{-1}^{1}\int_{-1}^{1} N_i\, p_i \begin{Bmatrix} J_{22}\ J_{33}\ -J_{23}\ J_{32} \\ J_{23}\ J_{31}\ -J_{21}\ J_{33} \\ J_{21}\ J_{32}\ -J_{22}\ J_{31} \end{Bmatrix} \mathrm{d}\xi\ \mathrm{d}\eta
\tag{3.6.9}
$$

3.6.2.2   Traction

The shear traction in shear is always tangent to surfaces which it is acting on. It can always be decomposed into 2 components directed along the 2 facetangent vectors. The x, y and z components of consistent loads for the traction in V_1 direction at node i on surface $\zeta=-1$ (or $\zeta=1$) are

$$
\begin{Bmatrix} f_{xi} \\ f_{yi} \\ f_{zi} \end{Bmatrix} = \int_{-1}^{1}\int_{-1}^{1} N_i\, p_i \begin{Bmatrix} J_{11} \\ J_{12} \\ J_{13} \end{Bmatrix} \mathrm{d}\xi\ \mathrm{d}\eta
\tag{3.6.10}
$$

and in V_2 direction at node i on surface $\zeta=-1$ (or $\zeta=1$) are

$$
\begin{Bmatrix} f_{xi} \\ f_{yi} \\ f_{zi} \end{Bmatrix} = \int_{-1}^{1}\int_{-1}^{1} N_i\, p_i \begin{Bmatrix} J_{21} \\ J_{22} \\ J_{23} \end{Bmatrix} \mathrm{d}\xi\ \mathrm{d}\eta
\tag{3.6.11}
$$

Similarly, the x, y and z components of consistent loads for a traction in V_1 direction at node i on surface $\xi=-1$ (or $\xi=1$) are

$$
\begin{Bmatrix} f_{xi} \\ f_{yi} \\ f_{zi} \end{Bmatrix} = \int_{-1}^{1}\int_{-1}^{1} N_i\, p_i \begin{Bmatrix} J_{11} \\ J_{12} \\ J_{13} \end{Bmatrix} \mathrm{d}\eta\ \mathrm{d}\zeta
\tag{3.6.12}
$$

and in V_2 direction at node i on surface $\xi=-1$ (or $\xi=1$) are

$$\begin{Bmatrix} f_{xi} \\ f_{yi} \\ f_{zi} \end{Bmatrix} = \int_{-1}^{1} \int_{-1}^{1} N_i \, p_i \begin{Bmatrix} J_{21} \\ J_{22} \\ J_{23} \end{Bmatrix} d\eta \, d\zeta \qquad (3.6.13)$$

Finally the x, y and z components of consistent loads for a traction in V_1 direction at node i on surface $\eta=-1$ (or $\eta=1$) are

$$\begin{Bmatrix} f_{xi} \\ f_{yi} \\ f_{zi} \end{Bmatrix} = \int_{-1}^{1} \int_{-1}^{1} N_i \, p_i \begin{Bmatrix} J_{11} \\ J_{12} \\ J_{13} \end{Bmatrix} d\zeta \, d\xi \qquad (3.6.14)$$

and in V_2 direction at node i on surface $\eta=-1$ (or $\xi=1$) are

$$\begin{Bmatrix} f_{xi} \\ f_{yi} \\ f_{zi} \end{Bmatrix} = \int_{-1}^{1} \int_{-1}^{1} N_i \, p_i \begin{Bmatrix} J_{21} \\ J_{22} \\ J_{23} \end{Bmatrix} d\zeta \, d\xi \qquad (3.6.15)$$

3.7 Coordinate Transformations

Coordinate transformations between the global and natural coordinates are required for the calculations of material stiffness and loading. A method for finding a natural coordinate system for an 8-node linear isoparametric solid element is given in [Cook et al.]. The following procedure is employed to formulate the transformation matrix and implement transformation for the 20-node quadratic isoparametric solid element [Chiang & Tang].

1. For each of the six faces, locate the central point by taking the average of all the nodes on the surface.

2. Form three vector components a_1, a_2 and a_3 by connecting the two central points of opposite faces. Compute lengths of all three connected line segments, L_1, L_2, and L_3 and the vector sum $L=L_1+L_2+L_3$. Normalize each vector,

$$v_1 = \frac{a_1}{L}; \qquad (3.7.1)$$

$$v_2 = \frac{a_2}{L}; \qquad (3.7.2)$$

$$v_3 = \frac{a_3}{L} \tag{3.7.3}$$

3. Use the following weighted averaging scheme to compute three new vectors that are closer to being orthogonal than the vectors v_i, $i = 1, 2, 3$,

$$u_1 = \frac{(L_2 + L_3)(v_2 \times v_3) + L_1 v_1}{L} \tag{3.7.4}$$

$$u_2 = \frac{(L_3 + L_1)(v_3 \times v_1) + L_2 v_2}{L} \tag{3.7.5}$$

$$u_3 = \frac{(L_1 + L_2)(v_1 \times v_2) + L_3 v_3}{L} \tag{3.7.6}$$

4. Test for convergence. Is $u_1 \approx v_1$, $u_2 \approx v_2$ and $u_3 \approx v_3$? The criterion used here are that each component of vectors u_1, u_2 and u_3 must not differ from its corresponding components in v_1, v_2 and v_3 by more than a tolerance, 0.001 is a good example. If convergence is met, go to step 7; otherwise go to step 5.

5. Normalize the u vectors.

6. Replace the v vectors by the normalized u vectors, using the following under-relaxation equation to speed up convergence, for the nth iteration,

$$(a_1)_{n+1} = \frac{1}{2n}(a_i)_n + \frac{2n-1}{2n}(b_i)_n, i = 1, 2, 3 \tag{3.7.7}$$

Return to step 3.

7. Make sure that the unit vectors are orthogonal. Define a 3×3 transformation matrix $[T]$ whose rows are the three vectors of v_1, v_2 and v_3.

$$[T] = \begin{bmatrix} v_{11} & v_{12} & v_{13} \\ v_{21} & v_{22} & v_{23} \\ v_{31} & v_{32} & v_{33} \end{bmatrix} \tag{3.7.8}$$

8. Calculate the center of an element, (x_o, y_o, z_o) by taking the average of overall nodes of this element. Compute the new coordinates for each node with origin at (x_o, y_o, z_o), then put them in

$$[X]_g = \begin{bmatrix} x_1 & x_2 & x_3 & \cdots & x_{20} \\ y_1 & y_2 & y_3 & \cdots & y_{20} \\ z_1 & z_2 & z_3 & \cdots & z_{20} \end{bmatrix} \tag{3.7.9}$$

9. Transform the global coordinate system of each node of this element to the local, natural coordinate system by

$$[X]_1 = [T] [X]_g \tag{3.7.10}$$

10. Transform the force vector, $\{F\}_g$ in the global coordinate system, to that in the local natural coordinate system, $\{F\}_1$,

$$\{F\}_1 = [T] \{F\}_g \tag{3.7.11}$$

11. Form the element stiffness matrix $[k]_1$ and force vector $\{f\}_1$ in the natural coordinate system. Prior to assemblage, transform them back to the global coordinate system, $[k]_g$ and $\{f\}_g$,

$$[k]_g = [T^*]^{\mathrm{T}} [k]_1 [T^*] \tag{3.7.12}$$

$$[f]_g = [T^*]^{\mathrm{T}} \{f\}_1 \tag{3.7.13}$$

and

$$[T^*]_{60 \times 60} = \begin{bmatrix} [T] & & & & & \\ & [T] & & & & \\ & & 0 & & & \\ & & & 0 & & \\ & & & & [T] & \\ & & & & & [T] \end{bmatrix} \tag{3.7.14}$$

12. Solve the whole assembled simultaneous equations for the whole global nodal displacements $\{\Phi\}_g$ from which the global nodal displacements $\{\phi\}_g$ of an individual element can be extracted.

13. Strains and stresses are computed from the deformations in local, natural coordinate system

$$\{\phi\}_1 = [T] \{\phi\}_g \tag{3.7.15}$$

then strains and stresses are transformed back to the global coordinate system,

$$\{\varepsilon\}_g = [T_\varepsilon]^{\mathrm{T}} \{\varepsilon\}_1 [T_\varepsilon] \tag{3.7.16}$$

$$\{\sigma\}_g = [T_\sigma]^{\mathrm{T}} \{\sigma\}_1 [T_\sigma] \tag{3.7.17}$$

3.8   Integration for Elemental Matrices

Integrations have to be carried out numerically for elemental matrices and loads given by Eqs. (3.3.7) and (3.3.8). The numerical integrations shown above for various mechanical properties can be implemented based on the Gauss-quadrature formulae in terms of natural coordinates, as

$$\iiint_V f(x, y, z)\,\mathrm{d}V = \int_{-1}^{1}\int_{-1}^{1}\int_{-1}^{1} f(\xi, \eta, \zeta) J(\xi, \eta, \zeta)\,\mathrm{d}\xi\,\mathrm{d}\eta\,\mathrm{d}\zeta$$

$$= \sum_i \sum_j \sum_k w_i\,w_j\,w_k\,f(\xi_i, \eta_j, \zeta_k)\,J(\xi_i, \eta_j, \zeta_k) \qquad (3.8.1)$$

where

$f(\xi_i, \eta_j, \zeta_k)$ & $J(\xi_i, \eta_j, \zeta_k)$: Values to be computed at sampling point (ξ_i, η_j, ζ_k);

w_i, w_j, w_k: Weighting function for Gauss-quadrature integral;

i, j, k: Subscripts to number the integration order.

An integration point is the point within an element, at which integrals are evaluated numerically. These points are chosen in such a way that the results for a particular numerical integration scheme are the most accurate. Subscripts for 20-noded solid element may range from 1 to 3 for all three directions for full integration, i.e., 3×3×3 integration and from 1 to 2 for all 3 directions for reduced integration, i.e., 2×2×2 integration. Depending on the integration scheme used the location of these points will vary. The 20-noded solid also has a special type of integration point scheme, called to 14-point integration in addition to 3×3×3 and 2×2×2 integrations. This scheme places points close to each of the 8 corner nodes and close to the centers of the 6 faces for a total of 14 points.

3.8.1   Numerical Integration to Form Elemental Matrices and Vectors

Finite element displacements are most accurate at the nodes. However, the derivatives (i.e., stresses and strains) tend to be quite accurate at the integration points and less accurate at the nodes sometimes. Of course, the accuracy of nodal strains is dependent on the mesh size dearly, so with an adequate mesh it shouldn't matter.

3.8.2   Hourglass Effect

Hourglass effect, also called shear-locking, is essentially a spurious deformation mode of a finite element mesh, resulting from the excitation of zero-energy degrees of freedom. It typically manifests as a patchwork of zig-zag or hourglass like element shapes (Fig. 3.8.1), where individual elements are severely deformed, while the overall mesh section is undeformed. This happens to hexahedral 3D solid elements with reduced 2×2×2 integration, as well as to the respective tetrahedral 3D shell elements and 2D solid elements.

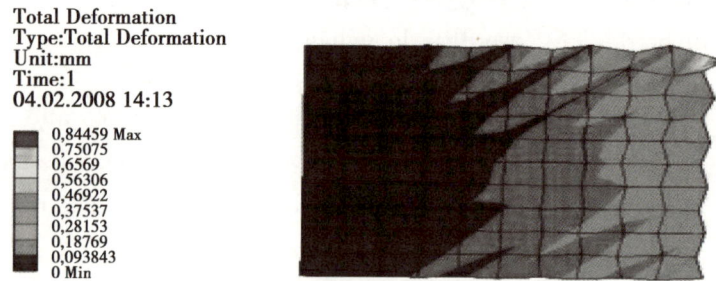

Total Deformation
Type:Total Deformation
Unit:mm
Time:1
04.02.2008 14:13

0,84459 Max
0,75075
0,6569
0,56306
0,46922
0,37537
0,28153
0,18769
0,093843
0 Min

Fig. 3.8.1   Hourglass Effect：Elements Severely Deformed，but Overall Mesh Undeformed ［Esocaetwikplus］

One way to fix this is to split the stiffness matrix into two parts and use different integration rules for each part. If the stiffness matrix in Eq. （3.5.1） is split into two diagonal 3×3 sub-matrices

$$[k] = \iiint_V [B]^T [E] [B] \, dV = \iiint_V [B]^T ([E]_N + [E]_S) [B] \qquad (3.8.2)$$

The two diagonal sub-matrices represent the relationship between the direct "normal" stresses and strains （upper left） and the shear stresses and strains （lower right）. The two off-diagonal blocks consist mostly of zeroes for isotropic materials, while it is not so for composites but may be neglected sometimes. Using the 2-point integration for the "normal stress-strain"-related matrix and 1-point integration for the "shear stress-strain"- related matrix. If it is a dynamic problem, the mass matrix doesn't suffer from this problem and a 2×2×2 integration rule works fine ［Cook et al.］.

3.8.3   Incompressible Materials

Nearly incompressible materials such as rubber where the lack of zero energy modes severely impedes convergence, numerical integration has the beneficial effect of reducing the rank of some stiffness matrices assuring thereby the presence of discrete zero modes.

3.9   Element/Node Assembly and Solution Schemes

Element matrices and nodal loads are assembled using Eqs. （3.3.11） and （3.3.12） according to the solution scheme to be taken. There are various numerical solution algorithms that can be classified into two broad categories：direct and iterative solvers. These algorithms are designed to exploit the sparsity of matrices that depend on the choices of variational formulation and discretization strategy.

3.9.1   Skyline Direct Solver

The skyline direct solver is intended to handle only the non-zero entries in the $[K]$ matrix. It is straight forward like taking the inverse of the $[K]$ matrix while omitting "zero" calculations. Due to its inefficiency in solving a large number of simultaneous equations as formulated for practical problems, it is not recommended.

3.9.2   Frontal Solver

Computations are to be carried out in the sequence of elements. Assembly-elimination process of variables (nodes)-analogous to the paging of a virtual memory operating system to keep memory requirement minimum. Variables that are needed for computation are loaded into memory, and variables that are no longer needed are eliminated, moved to the virtual space, or written to files so that the memory requirement is kept to a minimum. This minimum memory is called the wavefront limit. The ideal model size when using Frontal Solver is less than fifty thousand degrees of freedom. It is not suitable for an extremely large model.

3.9.3   Iterative Solver

Nowadays, nonlinear equilibrium equations of structures are usually solved by using the traditional and modified Newton-Raphson methods for monotonic load-displacement behaviors complimented with incremental-iterative solution techniques. The arc-length methods, spherical or elliptical, are applied when solving problems with structural instability. Iterative solvers are based on the conjugate gradient method. The residual force vector, which is defined as the imbalance of the assembled simultaneous equations, i.e., Eq. (3.3.10), at the ith iteration can be reset as

$$\{R_i\} = \{F\} - [K]\{\Phi_i\} \tag{3.9.1}$$

It is generally assumed that the starting vector is the zero vector, i.e., $\{D_o\} = 0$, if no preconditioning is performed. Convergence is satisfied if

$$\frac{\{R_i\}^T\{R_i\}}{\{F\}^T\{F\}} < \text{error} \tag{3.9.2}$$

where error is the tolerance, i.e., tolerable numerical error to be assigned by the user. Conjugate gradient method is a preconditioning technique used for refining the equations in order to solve the equations faster.

3.10 Stress Computation

Based on the displacements, $\{\phi\}$, obtained from the solver one can determine the strains. To determine stresses, one passes it through the stress-strain elastic relationship, including the initial strains $\{\varepsilon\}_o$. Stresses $\{\sigma\}$ in an element can be calculated by

$$\{\sigma\} = [E] ([B]^T\{\phi\} - \{\varepsilon\}_o) + \{\sigma\}_o \tag{3.10.1}$$

Of which $\{\sigma\}_o$ is the initial stress vector. Where stresses should be calculated? Often they are least accurate at element corners, more accurate at the midside or midface, and most accurate at certain interior points. These interior points can be used to define a stress field that can be extrapolated to yield stresses at nodes on element boundaries. It was shown that the stresses at Gauss points are almost as accurate as nodal displacement [Cook et al.]. If reduced integration is adopted in the evaluation of element stiffness matrix, local smoothing has some theoretical justification and can be considered as a natural method for sampling stresses.

For the isoparametric quadratic solid element, the smoothed stresses $\{\Psi\}$ are assumed to have a trilinear variation over the element as given by the expression

$$\Psi(\xi, \eta, \zeta) = [1 \quad \xi \quad \eta \quad \zeta \quad \xi\eta \quad \eta\zeta \quad \zeta\xi \quad \xi\eta\zeta]\begin{Bmatrix} a_1 \\ a_2 \\ a_3 \\ a_4 \\ a_5 \\ a_6 \\ a_7 \\ a_8 \end{Bmatrix} \tag{3.10.2a}$$

or $\quad \Psi = [G] \{a\}$ $\tag{3.10.2b}$

Following the numbering of Gauss points corresponding to the isoparametric quadratic solid element (Fig. 3.2.1), the relation matrix $[G]$ may be estimated from the 8 equations with $\{\Psi_{I-VIII}\} = \{\sigma_I, \sigma_{II}, \sigma_{III}, \sigma_{IV}, \sigma_V, \sigma_{VI}, \sigma_{VII}, \sigma_{VIII}\}$ at 8 Gauss points corresponding to locations at $\pm 3^{-\frac{1}{2}}$ for each coordinate,

$$\begin{Bmatrix} \sigma_{\mathrm{I}} \\ \sigma_{\mathrm{II}} \\ \sigma_{\mathrm{III}} \\ \sigma_{\mathrm{IV}} \\ \sigma_{\mathrm{V}} \\ \sigma_{\mathrm{VI}} \\ \sigma_{\mathrm{VII}} \\ \sigma_{\mathrm{VIII}} \end{Bmatrix} = \begin{bmatrix} 1 & -p & -p & p & p^2 & -p^2 & -p^2 & p^3 \\ 1 & -p & -p & -p & p^2 & p^2 & p^2 & -p^3 \\ 1 & -p & p & -p & -p^2 & p^2 & -p^2 & p^3 \\ 1 & -p & p & p & -p^2 & -p^2 & p^2 & -p^3 \\ 1 & p & -p & p & -p^2 & p^2 & -p^2 & -p^3 \\ 1 & p & -p & -p & -p^2 & -p^2 & p^2 & p^3 \\ 1 & p & p & -p & p^2 & -p^2 & -p^2 & -p^3 \\ 1 & p & p & p & p^2 & p^2 & p^2 & p^3 \end{bmatrix} \begin{Bmatrix} a_1 \\ a_2 \\ a_3 \\ a_4 \\ a_5 \\ a_6 \\ a_7 \\ a_8 \end{Bmatrix} \qquad (3.10.3)$$

of which $p = 3^{-\frac{1}{2}}$. Looking for the inverse of $[G]$ matrix in the above equation and substitute $\boldsymbol{a}$ back into Eq. (3.10.2), one has

$$\{\Psi_i\} = \begin{bmatrix} 1 & \xi_i & \eta_i & \zeta_i & \xi_i\eta_i & \eta_i\zeta_i & \zeta_i\xi_i & \xi_i\eta_i\zeta_i \end{bmatrix} [G]^{-1} \{\sigma_{\mathrm{I-VIII}}\} \qquad (3.10.4)$$

in which i ranges from 1 to 20 for every node of the element. For example, stresses at 8 corner nodes are interpolated as

$$\begin{Bmatrix} \Psi_1 \\ \Psi_2 \\ \Psi_3 \\ \Psi_4 \\ \Psi_5 \\ \Psi_6 \\ \Psi_7 \\ \Psi_8 \end{Bmatrix} = \begin{bmatrix} a & b & c & b & b & c & d & c \\ b & a & b & c & c & b & c & d \\ c & b & a & b & d & c & b & c \\ b & c & b & a & c & d & c & b \\ b & c & d & c & a & b & c & b \\ c & b & c & d & b & a & b & c \\ d & c & b & c & c & b & a & b \\ c & d & c & b & b & c & b & a \end{bmatrix} \begin{Bmatrix} \sigma_{\mathrm{VI}} \\ \sigma_{\mathrm{VII}} \\ \sigma_{\mathrm{III}} \\ \sigma_{\mathrm{II}} \\ \sigma_{\mathrm{V}} \\ \sigma_{\mathrm{VIII}} \\ \sigma_{\mathrm{IV}} \\ \sigma_{\mathrm{I}} \end{Bmatrix} \qquad (3.10.5)$$

where

$$a = \frac{5 + 3^{\frac{3}{2}}}{4} \qquad (3.10.6a)$$

$$b = \frac{-1 - 3^{\frac{1}{2}}}{4} \qquad (3.10.6b)$$

$$c = \frac{-1 + 3^{\frac{1}{2}}}{4} \qquad (3.10.6c)$$

and $\quad d = \dfrac{5 - 3^{\frac{3}{2}}}{4} \qquad (3.10.6d)$

In elements with material discontinuities or incompatible modes, extrapolated stresses at interfacial nodes may be inaccurate. Elements, which share a node on an interfacial surface can be expected to predict different stresses at that node. Usually the averaged value from various elements sharing the same node can be more reliable than any individual one of the contributing stresses. However, averaging between dissimilar materials or across sudden changes of thickness must be avoided.

The element shape function is used to extrapolate the integration point stresses out to the element nodes-these are in a useful location like a fillet radius free surface or a hole edge. The six components of stresses at any point P in an element are found by the interpolation of shape function from these 20 nodes

$$\sigma_P = \sum_{i=1}^{20} N_i \, \Psi_i \tag{3.10.7}$$

Adjacent elements combined with their shape functions will predict different stress values at their common nodes. The question then arises which stress do you believe? Most FEA packages average the stresses for each element connected at the node.

3.11 Geometric Nonlinearity

As is often the case for buckling that experience large displacements, the six strain components in the (x, y, z) coordinate system can be obtained from the three displacements as follows:

$$\varepsilon_{xx} = \frac{\partial u}{\partial x} + \frac{1}{2}\left[\left(\frac{\partial u}{\partial x}\right)^2 + \left(\frac{\partial v}{\partial x}\right)^2 + \left(\frac{\partial w}{\partial x}\right)^2\right] \tag{3.11.1}$$

$$\varepsilon_{yy} = \frac{\partial v}{\partial y} + \frac{1}{2}\left[\left(\frac{\partial u}{\partial y}\right)^2 + \left(\frac{\partial v}{\partial y}\right)^2 + \left(\frac{\partial w}{\partial y}\right)^2\right] \tag{3.11.2}$$

$$\varepsilon_{zz} = \frac{\partial w}{\partial z} + \frac{1}{2}\left[\left(\frac{\partial u}{\partial z}\right)^2 + \left(\frac{\partial v}{\partial z}\right)^2 + \left(\frac{\partial w}{\partial z}\right)^2\right] \tag{3.11.3}$$

$$\gamma_{xy} = \gamma_{yx} = 2\varepsilon_{xy} = 2\varepsilon_{yx} = \frac{\partial u}{\partial y} + \frac{\partial v}{\partial x} + \frac{\partial u}{\partial x} \cdot \frac{\partial u}{\partial y} + \frac{\partial v}{\partial x} \cdot \frac{\partial v}{\partial y} + \frac{\partial w}{\partial x} \cdot \frac{\partial w}{\partial y} \tag{3.11.4}$$

$$\gamma_{yz} = \gamma_{zy} = 2\varepsilon_{yz} = 2\varepsilon_{zy} = \frac{\partial v}{\partial z} + \frac{\partial w}{\partial y} + \frac{\partial u}{\partial y} \cdot \frac{\partial u}{\partial z} + \frac{\partial v}{\partial y} \cdot \frac{\partial v}{\partial z} + \frac{\partial w}{\partial y} \cdot \frac{\partial w}{\partial z} \tag{3.11.5}$$

and $$\gamma_{zx} = \gamma_{xz} = 2\varepsilon_{zx} = 2\varepsilon_{xz} = \frac{\partial w}{\partial z} + \frac{\partial u}{\partial z} + \frac{\partial u}{\partial z} \cdot \frac{\partial u}{\partial x} + \frac{\partial v}{\partial x} \cdot \frac{\partial v}{\partial x} + \frac{\partial w}{\partial x} \cdot \frac{\partial w}{\partial x} \tag{3.11.6}$$

The six strain components given above are also called Green's strains or Green-Lagrange strains that are capable of handling large displacements.

Repeating the derivation procedure for finite element formulation (Section 3.2) with these nonlinear compatibility equations, i.e., Eqs. (3.11.1)-(3.11.6), one can derive the following equation for the six Green's strain components as functions of the 60 nodal displacements

$$\{\varepsilon\}_{6\times1} = \left([B]_{6\times60} + \frac{1}{2}[B_N]\right)\{\phi\}_{60\times1} \tag{3.11.7}$$

where

$[B_N]$: Nonlinear elemental strain-nodal displacement relationship.

Eq. (3.11.7) is an extension from Eq. (3.2.25) and it can be substituted into Eq. (3.3.2) to obtain the stiffness matrices induced by the geometric nonlinearity in addition to the linear stiffness matrix. The strain energy per unit volume, given by Eq. (3.3.2), is subsequently expanded as

$$U_o = \frac{1}{2}\{\varepsilon\}^T[c]\{\varepsilon\} - \{\varepsilon\}^T[c]\{\varepsilon_o\} + \{\varepsilon\}^T\{\sigma_o\}$$

$$= \frac{1}{2}\{\phi\}^T\left([B] + \frac{1}{2}[B_N]\right)^T[c]\left([B] + \frac{1}{2}[B_N]\right)\{\phi\} -$$

$$\{\phi\}^T\left([B] + \frac{1}{2}[B_N]\right)^T[c]\{\varepsilon_o\} + \{\phi\}^T\left([B] + \frac{1}{2}[B_N]\right)^T\{\sigma_o\} \tag{3.11.8}$$

or

$$U_o \approx \frac{1}{2}\{\phi\}^T([B]^T[c][B] + [B]^T[c][B_N])\{\phi\} -$$

$$\{\phi\}^T\left([B] + \frac{1}{2}[B_N]\right)^T[c]\{\varepsilon_o\} + \{\phi\}^T\left([B] + \frac{1}{2}[B_N]\right)^T\{\sigma_o\} \tag{3.11.9}$$

The above equation is obtained by assuming that the quadratic nonlinear terms $[B_N]^T[c][B_N]$ in Eq. (3.11.8) is approximately zero. Formulations for nonlinear finite element matrices and vectors can be advanced upon the procedure presented in Section 3.3, by substituting Eq. (3.11.9) into Eq. (3.3.4) and continuing the process.

3.12   Elastoplastic Nonlinearity of Orthotropic Materials

The other nonlinearity next to geometric nonlinearity is material nonlinearity, which is involved with finite strain or large strain. It means that the evolving strains are not infinitesimal and thus the shape change of elements need be taken into account. Finite (or large) strain analyses deal with the cases that the associated displacements are not small anymore and the stiffness variations resulting from changes in elemental shape and orientation play a significant role in solution accuracy. These are frequently associated with material nonlinearities such as loaded tires and metal forming, in which the strains can easily go large e.g. 5%.

In elastoplasticity, it is reasonable to assume that the total differential strain is a combination of differential elastic strain and differential plastic strain additively. The strain increment is then decoupled into two components as

$$d\varepsilon = d\varepsilon_e + d\varepsilon_p \qquad (3.12.1)$$

where

$d\varepsilon$: Total strain increment;

$d\varepsilon_e$: Elastic strain increment;

$d\varepsilon_p$: Plastic strain increment.

However, the general problem of non-linear structural analysis can be effectively linearized if the load is applied in sufficiently small increments. After due consideration of Eq. (3.3.9) enlightened by the incremental-iterative approach, the total potential of the entire structure associated with displacement Φ_p without concentrated load q can be written as

$$\prod = \frac{1}{2}\{\Phi\}^T[K]\{\Phi\} - \{\Phi\}^T\{F\}$$
$$\approx \frac{1}{2}\{\Phi_p\}^T[K_p]\{\Phi_p\} + \{\Phi_p\}^T\sum_{h=1}^{p-1}[K_h]\{\Phi_h\} - \{\Phi_p\}^T\sum_{h=1}^{p}\{F_h\} \qquad (3.12.2)$$

where

$\{\Phi_p\}$: Displacement vector due to incrementally applied load $\sum\{F_h\}$, where $h = 1, 2, \cdots, p$;

$\{F_h\}$: Vector of incremental loads at the hth incremental step, where $h = 1, 2, \cdots, p$;

$\{\Phi_h\}$: Displacement vector corresponding to $\{F_h\}$;

$[K_h]$: Tangential stiffness matrix, which is a function of displacements and loads.

The force equilibrium equation can be obtained from minimizing potential energy $\prod$ with respect to displacements $\{\Phi_p\}$ at the $(i+1)$th iteration [Mottershead],

$$[K_p]_i\{\Delta\Phi_p\}_{i+1} = \sum_{h=1}^{p}\{F_h\} - \sum_{h=1}^{p-1}[K_h]\{\Phi_h\} - [K_p]_i\sum_{j=1}^{i}\{\Delta\Phi_p\}_j \qquad (3.12.3)$$

and

$$\{\Phi_p\} = \sum_{j=1}^{N}\{\Delta\Phi_p\}_j \qquad (3.12.4)$$

where

N: Number of iterations required for completing increment h;

j: Iteration number, $j = 1, 2, \cdots, N$.

Tangential stiffness matrix $[K_h]$ is to be updated either each increment or iteration, depending on the algorithm taken by the analyst. The iteration process may cease after N iterations if $\{\Delta\Phi_p\}_N$ is negligibly small. The Cauchy stress increments $d\sigma_{ij}(d\sigma_{11}, d\sigma_{22}, d\sigma_{33}, d\tau_{23}, d\tau_{31}, d\tau_{12})$ are to be used for updating the composite stiffness matrix and they are given by the generalized Hooke's law as follows:

$$d\sigma_{11} = \frac{1 - \nu_{23}\nu_{32}}{E_{22}E_{33}\Delta}d\varepsilon_{11} + \frac{\nu_{21} - \nu_{23}\nu_{32}}{E_{22}E_{33}\Delta}d\varepsilon_{22} + \frac{\nu_{31} - \nu_{21}\nu_{32}}{E_{22}E_{33}\Delta}d\varepsilon_{33} \qquad (3.12.5)$$

$$d\sigma_{22} = \frac{\nu_{12} - \nu_{13}\nu_{32}}{E_{33}E_{11}\Delta}d\varepsilon_{11} + \frac{1 - \nu_{31}\nu_{13}}{E_{33}E_{11}\Delta}d\varepsilon_{22} + \frac{\nu_{32} - \nu_{31}\nu_{12}}{E_{33}E_{11}\Delta}d\varepsilon_{33} \qquad (3.12.6)$$

$$d\sigma_{33} = \frac{\nu_{13} - \nu_{12}\nu_{23}}{E_{11}E_{22}\Delta}d\varepsilon_{11} + \frac{\nu_{23} - \nu_{13}\nu_{12}}{E_{11}E_{22}\Delta}d\varepsilon_{22} + \frac{1 - \nu_{12}\nu_{21}}{E_{11}E_{22}\Delta}d\varepsilon_{33} \qquad (3.12.7)$$

$$d\tau_{23} = G_{23}d\gamma_{23} = 2G_{23}d\varepsilon_{23} \qquad (3.12.8)$$

$$d\tau_{31} = G_{31}d\gamma_{31} = 2G_{31}d\varepsilon_{31} \qquad (3.12.9)$$

and $\quad d\tau_{12} = G_{12}d\gamma_{12} = 2G_{21}d\varepsilon_{21} \qquad (3.12.10)$

The total normal strain increments of that consist of mechanical, thermal expansion, and moisture swelling components, are given as follows:

$$d\varepsilon_{11} = d\varepsilon_{11,\text{mech}} + \alpha_1\,dT + \beta_1\,dC_m \qquad (3.12.11)$$

$$d\varepsilon_{22} = d\varepsilon_{22,\text{mech}} + \alpha_2\,dT + \beta_2\,dC_m \qquad (3.12.12)$$

and $\quad d\varepsilon_{33} = d\varepsilon_{33,\text{mech}} + \alpha_3\,dT + \beta_3\,dC_m \qquad (3.12.13)$

Since the internal forces has to be equal to the external so as to achieve an equilibrium. Therefore, in the case where the solution process for $([K]+[K_\sigma])\ \{\phi\} = \{F\}$ enters the nonlinear state for the first time, by assuming that the stiffness is elastic but in reality it is not, the resulting unbalanced force $\{F_{\text{unbalanced}}\} = \{F_{\text{ext}}\} - \{F_{\text{int}}\}$ which must be balanced. This is where the implicit solution starts by re-solving for the unbalanced forces after you update the "tangential" stiffness matrix due to material nonlinearity when the Newton-Raphson method is applied. This is done internally until the unbalanced forces are relatively small as defined using a convergence criterion. When the convergence is reached one can move to the next load step and perform the same procedure.

3.13   Contact Nonlinearity

The finite element model involved with contact elements requires a nonlinear solver, as the force equilibrium and displacement compatibility vary with respect to the change of contact conditions including contact loads, areas, and state variables (strains, stress, friction, etc.). This is called contact nonlinearity. Contact nonlinearity occurs when, due to the deformation of one or more parts in contact (pushing or pulling on each other) produces a deformation leading to a change in the geometry of the part that translates into a change of stiffness $[K]$ or on the forces (action and reaction) between the parts in contact demanding another iteration on approaching the solution. The range of automotive application includes crash analysis of cars, tire-road interactions, bolted joints, braking mechanisms, shaft bearings, metal forming, drilling problems, and cooling of electronic devices.

The numerical treatment of contact problems involves the formulation of the geometry, the statement of interface laws, the variational formulation, and the development of algorithms. As generalized for most applications, a geometrical formulation for contact has to be valid for large deformations and the interface laws will be able to deal with both normal and tangential stress components in frictional-contact areas [Chiang et al.]. Several of these different techniques are reviewed in [Wriggers]. Fundamental contact kinematics and contact algorithms for 3-dimensional contact problems are detailed in [Mottershead et al.].

An artificial small gap aligned with the "contact normals", e.g. 0.01mm or 0.001mm, can be instated between two potentially-to-be-in-contact bodies to initiate the smooth transition when solving a contact or impact problem using finite element methods, though they are actually in contact in the real product and its drawings.

3.13.1　Generalized 3-Dimensional Contact Topology

Consider the case of two contacting meshed patches, namely the contacter and the target, although the theory is basically ready for multi-body contact problems. Target nodes will be allowed to overlap into the contactor mesh but contactor nodes are not allowed to penetrate into the target mesh. Therefore, the contact algorithm provides the following functions:

(a) to detect the penetration of new contactor nodes into the target mesh;
(b) to remove such overlaps with proper justification of the contact state-sticking contact, sliding contact, or separation.

As the natural coordinate (ξ, η, ζ) is attached to the element as described for the shape functions of the isoparametric 20-noded (or 8-noded) solid element, a surface boundary is depicted by one of the local coordinates (ξ, η, ζ) that takes the values of ± 1. Consider contactor node k. Its global Cartesian coordinates are identified as (x_k, y_k, z_k) where is the position of node k after the ith iteration, and it is to be checked with the updated target element $(x_{T1} \quad y_{T1} \quad z_{T1} \quad x_{T2} \quad y_{T2} \quad z_{T2} \cdots \quad x_{T20} \quad y_{T20} \quad z_{T20})$ using Eq. (3.2.14) equipped with the shape functions defined by Eqs. (3.2.8)-(3.2.11) for a target element,

$$\begin{Bmatrix} x_k \\ y_k \\ z_k \end{Bmatrix} = [N_T(\xi_k, \eta_k, \zeta_k)] \{ e_T \} \tag{3.13.1}$$

and $\quad \{ e_T \}^T = \{ x_{T1} \quad y_{T1} \quad z_{T1} \quad x_{T2} \quad y_{T2} \quad z_{T2} \quad \cdots \quad x_{T20} \quad y_{T20} \quad z_{T20} \}$ (3.13.2)

where

x_k, y_k, z_k: Cartesian coordinates of contacter node k;

$\{ e_T \}^T$: Nodal position vector of the target element in Cartesian coordinate system;

$N_T(\xi_k, \eta_k, \zeta_k)$: Shape functions evaluated at point k' on the surface of the target element.

Note that subscript T of e_T stands for the "target" element, while superscript T of $\{ e_T \}^T$ is "transpose" operation for the vector or matrix. The above equation can be solved explicitly for ξ_k, η_k, ζ_k directly for 8-noded linear solid elements, but a solver based on an iterative process similar to New-Raphson method has to be taken for 20-noded quadratic elements [Mottershead et al.]. Based on the isoparametric nature of the element, if the inequality that

$$-1 < \xi_k, \eta_k, \zeta_k < 1 \tag{3.13.3}$$

is true, contactor node k has penetrated into the target element. Since any penetration is not allowed, an overlap-corresponding corrective displacement vector, denoted here by $\{ \delta u_k \quad \delta v_k \quad \delta w_k \}$, has to be applied to in the $(i+1)$ th iteration when an incremental-iterative approach is applied. The corrective displacement vector, defined as $\{ \Delta u_x \quad \Delta v_y \quad \Delta w_z \}$, is equal and opposite to the overlap vector. The corrective action to be taken in the $(i+1)$ th iteration is to relocate contacter node k to point k' on the boundary surface of the target element,

$$\begin{Bmatrix} \delta u_k \\ \delta v_k \\ \delta w_k \end{Bmatrix} = \begin{Bmatrix} u_k \\ v_k \\ w_k \end{Bmatrix} - [N_T(\xi_{k'}, \eta_{k'}, \zeta_{k'})] \{ \phi_T \} \tag{3.13.4}$$

and $\quad \{ \phi_T \}^T = \{ u_{T1} \quad v_{T1} \quad w_{T1} \quad u_{T2} \quad v_{T2} \quad w_{T2} \quad \cdots \quad u_{T20} \quad v_{T20} \quad w_{T20} \}$ (3.13.5)

where

δu_k, δv_k, δw_k: Corrective displacements for contacter node k after the ith iteration;

u_k, v_k, w_k: Displacements of contacter node k after the ith iteration;

$\{ \phi_T \}^T$: Nodal displacement vector of the target element in Cartesian coordinate system;

$N_T(\xi_{k'}, \eta_{k'}, \zeta_{k'})$: Shape functions evaluated at point k' on the surface of the target element.

Note that the $(i+1)$ th iteration is a corrective action. The local natural co-ordinates $(\xi_{k'}, \eta_{k'}, \zeta_{k'})$ can be found from the intercept of the updated target surface (i.e., resulting from the ith iteration) and the line joining the current coordinates (after the ith iteration) and the previous coordinates（after the $(i-1)$th iteration）of contactor node k, based on the shape functions of the target element.

$$
\begin{Bmatrix} \xi_{k'} \\ \eta_{k'} \\ \zeta_{k'} \end{Bmatrix} = \begin{Bmatrix} \xi_{k,i-1} \\ \eta_{k,i-1} \\ \zeta_{k,i-1} \end{Bmatrix} + \psi \begin{Bmatrix} \xi_{k,i} - \xi_{k,i-1} \\ \eta_{k,i} - \eta_{k,i-1} \\ \zeta_{k,i} - \zeta_{k,i-1} \end{Bmatrix}
\tag{3.13.6}
$$

of which ψ is the positioning parameter. The corrective displacement vector is then applied in the $(i+1)$th iteration as a constraint to the displacement vector of contacter node k in compliance with surface node k' of the target element. Note that the normal component of the corrective displacement vector must be constrained to ensure that the overlap is removed, while the normal direction is defined by the position vector of k' with respect to k after the ith iteration is completed. The tangent plane is supposedly perpendicular to the normal direction.

When such a constraint is applied, the related contact force vector can be calculated at the nodes of concern. The contact forces vector is to be used to decide the state of contact-sticking or sliding where the friction can be applied. Since the path of sliding contact lies along a tangent plane to the curved target surface, a separation or overlap may occur again and they ought to be removed in the subsequent iterations. It means that there is no need to impose constraints in the tangent plane.

3.13.2　Reposition Overlapped Contacter Nodes

Obviously, point k' on a boundary surface of the particular target element of concern represents the initial contact position between contactor node k and the target element and it is to be located by positioning parameter ψ in light of Eq. （3.13.5）, which can be realigned as

$$
\psi = \begin{Bmatrix} \dfrac{\xi_{k'} - \xi_{k,i-1}}{\xi_{k,i} - \xi_{k,i-1}} \\[2ex] \dfrac{\eta_{k'} - \eta_{k,i-1}}{\eta_{k,i} - \eta_{k,i-1}} \\[2ex] \dfrac{\zeta_{k'} - \zeta_{k,i-1}}{\zeta_{k,i} - \zeta_{k,i-1}} \end{Bmatrix}
\tag{3.13.7}
$$

Since each boundary surface is formed to be isoparametric using only two local parameters, k' can be established using any one of the following general criteria:

    a. $(\xi=\pm1,\eta=\pm1)$
    b. $(\eta=\pm1,\zeta=\pm1)$
    c. $(\zeta=\pm1,\xi=\pm1)$

Substituting the three "boundary conditions" given above into Eq. (3.13.7) lead to the solution of positioning parameter ψ,

$$\psi = \frac{\pm 1 - \xi_{i-1}}{\xi_i - \xi_{i-1}} \quad \text{and} \quad \psi = \frac{\pm 1 - \eta_{i-1}}{\eta_i - \eta_{i-1}} \tag{3.13.8}$$

$$\psi = \frac{\pm 1 - \eta_{i-1}}{\eta_i - \eta_{i-1}} \quad \text{and} \quad \psi = \frac{\pm 1 - \zeta_{i-1}}{\zeta_i - \zeta_{i-1}} \tag{3.13.9}$$

or $\quad \psi = \dfrac{\pm 1 - \zeta_{i-1}}{\zeta_i - \zeta_{i-1}} \quad \text{and} \quad \psi = \dfrac{\pm 1 - \xi_{i-1}}{\xi_i - \xi_{i-1}} \tag{3.13.10}$

3.13.3   Displacement Constraints

Assume that contacter node k is now relocated to the point k' position after positioning parameter Ψ is sought out. In light of Eq. (3.13.4), the updated constraint equation can be applied to the next iteration, i.e., $(i+1)$th iteration, as follows:

(1) For adhesive contact (also called sticking contact): Applying Eq. (3.13.4) directly as

$$\begin{Bmatrix} \delta u_{k,i} \\ \delta v_{k,i} \\ \delta w_{k,i} \end{Bmatrix}_{3\times1} - \begin{Bmatrix} u_{k,i+1} \\ v_{k,i+1} \\ w_{k,i+1} \end{Bmatrix}_{3\times1} + [N_T(\xi_{k',i}, \eta_{k',i}, \zeta_{k',i})]_{3\times60} \{\phi_T\}_{i+1,60\times1} = \{0\}_{3\times1} \tag{3.13.11}$$

The above equation can be rewritten in a short form as

$$\{\delta\Phi_i\} - [L_i] \{\Delta\Phi_p\}_{i+1} = \{0\} \tag{3.13.12}$$

(2) For sliding contact: The displacement constraint is applied only to the direction that is normal to the surface at point k'. Let $\{l, m, n\}$ be the vector of direction cosines of a unit vector normal to the surface at point k'

$$\{l,m,n\}_{1\times3} \begin{Bmatrix} u_{k,i+1} \\ v_{k,i+1} \\ w_{k,i+1} \end{Bmatrix}_{3\times1} - \{lmn\}_{1\times3} [N_T(\xi_{k',i}, \eta_{k',i}, \zeta_{k',i})]_{3\times60} \{\phi_T\}_{i+1,60\times1} = \{0\}_{1\times1}$$

$$\tag{3.13.13}$$

where $\{l, m, n\}$ is the vector of direction cosines of a unit vector normal to the surface. For example, if the contact surface is $\zeta=-1$ (or $\zeta=1$), Eq. (3.6.5) can be used for calculating the direction cosines. Note that Eq. (3.3.13) is a special case of (3.13.11) and thus both can be represented by Eq. (3.13.12).

3.13.4　Constitutive Equations for Contact Interface

Contact stresses ought to obey the constraint equations （i.e., meeting the need of compatibility） given above, but both contact bodies as observed in the contact area lead to their associated interfacial constitutive equations. Nevertheless, one has to deal with the inequality such as Eq. （3.13.13）, when solving the contact nonlinearity. Both the penalty function method and Lagrange multiplier method have been in use for this purpose in commercial FEM codes such as Abaqus, Ansys, and Nastran, converting constrained problems into unconstrained problems.

3.13.4.1　Penalty Function Method

Many constraints in the real world of finite element analysis are so "soft" in the sense that they need not be satisfied exactly, especially when the load is applied incrementally. The penalty function approach is well-suited to this type of approximation. The total potential energy including the associated penalty function can be obtained from summing up the terms in Eq. （3.12.2） and the penalty function-related constraint as described by Eq. （3.13.12） as

$$
\begin{aligned}
\Pi_p \approx \frac{1}{2} & \left(\sum_{j=1}^{i+1} \{\Delta\Phi_p\}_j^{\mathrm{T}}[K_p] \right) \left(\sum_{j=1}^{i+1} \{\Delta\Phi_p\}_j \right) + \left(\sum_{j=1}^{i+1} \{\Delta\Phi_p\}_j^{\mathrm{T}} \right) \left(\sum_{h=1}^{p-1} [K_h] \{\Phi_h\} \right) - \\
& \left(\sum_{j=1}^{i+1} \{\Delta\Phi_p\}_j^{\mathrm{T}} \right) \left(\sum_{h=1}^{p} \{F_h\} + \sum_{h=1}^{p-1} \{C_h\} + \sum_{j=1}^{i} \{C_p\}_j \right) + \frac{1}{2}\alpha(\{\delta\Phi_i\} - \\
& [L_i]\{\Delta\Phi_p\}_{i+1})^{\mathrm{T}}(\{\delta\Phi_i\} - [L_i]\{\Delta\Phi_p\}_{i+1})
\end{aligned}
\tag{3.13.14}
$$

where

$1/2\alpha$: Penalty number, selected arbitrarily;

$\{\delta\Phi_i\}$: $\{\delta\Phi_i\} = \{\delta u_{k,i}, \delta v_{k,i}, \delta w_{k,i}\}^{\mathrm{T}}$, penetrating displacements or penetration vector;

$\{C_h\}$: Contact force after h increments;

$\{C_p\}_j$: Contact force after p increments at interaction j.

The force equilibrium equation corresponding to the potential energy given above can be obtained by minimizing the potential with respect to the displacement vector; $\mathrm{d}\Pi_p/\mathrm{d}\{\Delta\Phi_p\}_{i+1}=0$ results in

$$
([K_p]_i + \alpha [L_i]^{\mathrm{T}}[L_i]) \{\Delta\Phi_p\}_{i+1} = - \sum_{h=1}^{p} [K_h]_i\{\Phi_p\} - [K_p]_i \sum_{j=1}^{i} \{\Delta\phi_p\}_j +
$$

$$
\alpha [L_i]^{\mathrm{T}}\{\delta\Phi_i\} + \sum_{h=1}^{p} \{F_h\} +
$$

$$
\sum_{h=1}^{p-1} \{C_h\} + \sum_{j=1}^{i} \{C_p\}_j
\tag{3.13.15}
$$

In general, applying penalty enforcement may ease the convergence difficulty encountered in the process of finite element analysis when dealing with contact problems with friction, as evidenced by the practice using Abaqus.

3.13.4.2   Lagrange Multiplier Method

The total potential energy including the associated potential energy due to Lagrange multiplier can be obtained from Eq. (3.12.2) as

$$
\begin{aligned}
\Pi_p \approx \frac{1}{2} \left(\sum_{j=1}^{i+1} \{\Delta\Phi_p\}_j^{\mathrm{T}} \right) [K_p] \left(\sum_{j=1}^{i+1} \{\Delta\Phi_p\}_j^{\mathrm{T}} \right) + \left(\sum_{j=1}^{i+1} \{\Delta\Phi_p\}_j^{\mathrm{T}} \right) \left(\sum_{h=1}^{p-1} [K_h] \{\Phi_h\} \right) - \\
\left(\sum_{j=1}^{i+1} \{\Delta\Phi_p\}^{\mathrm{T}} \right) \left(\sum_{h=1}^{p} \{F_h\} \right) - \left(\sum_{j=1}^{i+1} \{\Delta\Phi_p\}^{\mathrm{T}} \right) \left(\sum_{h=1}^{p-1} \{C_h\} + \sum_{j=1}^{i} \{C_p\}_j \right) + \\
\lambda_{i+1} (\{\delta\Phi_i\} - [L_i] \{\Delta\Phi_p\}_{i+1})
\end{aligned}
\tag{3.13.16}
$$

where

λ_{i+1} : Lagrange multiplier at the $(i+1)$th iteration.

A Lagrange multiplier is treated as an additional variable in the problem-solving process and it represents a force function. The force equilibrium equations can be obtained by setting that $\mathrm{d}\Pi_p / \mathrm{d}\{\Delta\Phi_p\}_{i+1} = 0$ and $\mathrm{d}\Pi_p / \mathrm{d}\lambda_{i+1} = 0$, as

$$
\sum_{h=1}^{p-1} [K_h] \{\Phi_h\} + [K_p]_i \left(\sum_{j=1}^{i+1} \{\Delta\phi_p\}_j \right) = \sum_{h=1}^{p} \{F_h\} + \sum_{h=1}^{p-1} \{C_h\} + \sum_{j=1}^{i} \{C_p\}_j + [L_i]^{\mathrm{T}} \lambda_{i+1}
\tag{3.13.17}
$$

and $\{\delta\Phi_i\} - [L_i] \{\Delta\Phi_p\}_{i+1} = \{0\}.$ (3.13.18)

3.13.5   Contact Force

It is necessary to calculate contact forces of the previous iterations and load steps by the penalty function method and Lagrange multiplier method. The contact force vector resulting from increment p iteration $i+1$ can be obtained from subtracting the externally applied force vector from the vector of element stress resultants as follows [Mottershead]:

$$
\{C_p\}_{i+1} = - \sum_{h=1}^{p-1} \{C_p\}_{i+1} - \sum_{j=1}^{i} \{C_{p,j}\} - \sum_{h=1}^{p} \{F_h\} + \sum_{h=1}^{p-1} [K_h] \{\phi_h\} + [K_p]_i \sum_{j=1}^{i+1} \{\Delta\phi_p\}_j
\tag{3.13.19}
$$

3.13.6   Contact Modeling as Implemented in Abaqus

One is allowed to use "general contact" in Abaqus in search for a performance hit, but designated contact pairs are more feasible. If you know the potential "contact pairs" and deem the extra user work is worth the computational time savings then go for it. Contact modeling based on 3-dimensional finite elements deals with interfacial behaviors between two meshed surfaces in contact or to be in contact. A to-be-contact zone between any two surface groups is identified first and then modeled by two types of contact meshes, as parts of the 3-dimensional elemental meshes: A master-surface (i.e., contactor surface) that containing "contactor elements" and a slave-surface (i.e., target surface) containing "target elements". Two different algorithms are implemented in Abaqus:

(a) *Small sliding*: Each slave node interacts with its own tangent plane on the master surface and consequently slave nodes are not monitored for possible contact along the entire master surface. Thus, the small sliding is less expensive computationally than the finite sliding contact.

(b) *Finite sliding*: The finite sliding contact requires that master surfaces be smooth and have a unique surface normal at all points.

The contact properties must be defined in an input table like material properties, e.g. friction and penetration allowance. Friction coefficients can be specified based on the underlying surface properties and a combinatorial rule. Geometry and loading data are not applicable to these elements, but initial contact stresses in Abaqus/Standard can be computed based on user-specified stress in elements underlying the contact surface. If the contact zone can be split in several contact areas, which do not have any mutual interaction, the slave contact elements in separated areas can be identified and put in different contact sets. Penalty methods are used in general to solve the contact problems. Each slave node can transfer load to any nodes on the master surface in the finite sliding, but it can only transfer load to a limited number of nodes on the master surface for the small sliding. The scalar integration of contact pressure over the surface is available.

If a "minor" penetration of a slave node into the master surface is detected, an additional constraint is added to realign the node to lie on the master surface exactly. A "major" penetration causes the FEA software to scale back the applied load increment and tries the contact algorithm again.

3.14　3-Dimensional Finite Element Meshing

Solid elements are the most frequently used elements for 3-dimensional modeling as solid elements with 3-dimensional geometry and material properties could satisfy the natural need of prediction for performance of complex structures in the real world. The family of frequently used solid elements in practice consists of

(a) linear hexahedral solid element (8 nodes per element).
(b) quadratic hexahedral solid element (20 nodes per element), as shown in Fig. 3.14.1(a).

(c) linear tetrahedral solid element (4-nodes per element).

(d) quadratic tetrahedral solid element (10-nodes per element), as shown in Fig. 3.14.1(b).

Discretization of the geometry and approximation to the physical value generated by the finite element formulation based on displacement method automatically enforce some equilibrium and compatibility conditions. Isoparametric hexahedral solid elements (20 nodes or 8 nodes per element) with linear and quadratic shape functions are demonstrated to be adequate for general modeling, even for very thin orthotropic shells [Chiang]. Hexahedral elements perform better than tetrahedral elements. It is suggested that 4-noded tetrahedral solid elements should not be used in zones of load transfer, an abrupt change of cross sections, and junctions (e.g. spar-rib and skin-rib connections). In general, quadratic elements outperform linear elements in modeling accuracy because they are not subjected to the hourglass effect.

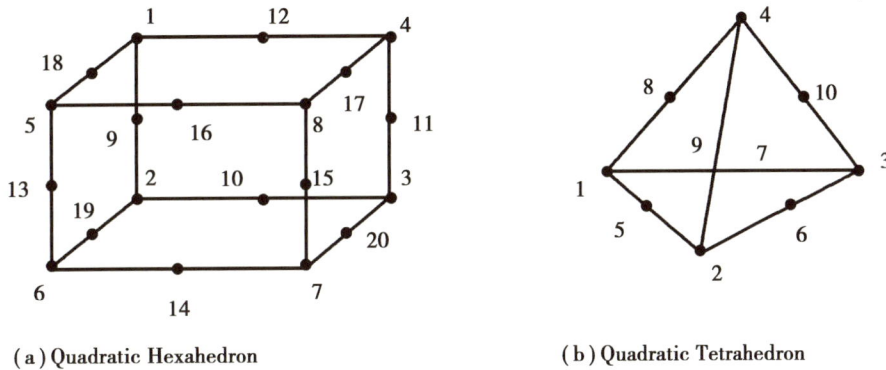

(a) Quadratic Hexahedron　　　　　　　　(b) Quadratic Tetrahedron

Fig. 3.14.1　Local Numbering Sequence of Nodes of 20-Node and 10-Node Solid Elements

3.14.1　20-Noded 3-Dimensional Solid Element

The isoparametric quadratic element with 20 nodes, having 60 degrees of freedom, is very valuable. With a possible alternative choice of full (either 3×3×3 Gauss-quadrature or 14 points) and reduced (2×2×2 Gauss-quadrature) integration rules for this element, design engineers can use just one kind of element to model various structures, such as straight and curved beams, plates, shells and solids. The merits could be attributed to the following characteristics:

(1) Satisfying validity conditions: compatibility, rigid body motion, and linear strain state.

(2) Retaining an ability to account for all the six components of coupled strains and stresses.

(3) Accommodating curved surfaces and edges of a structure.

In addition to the advantages listed above, the isoparametric quadratic solid element can also interface with the geometric data generated from the solid modeling schemes in a CAD/CAM package. Although this element can be used to model various structures, the following situations must be considered cautiously:

(a) A full integration rule is a better choice for the modeling of straight beams to avoid the generation of singular stiffness.

(b) A reduced integration rule is a better choice for the modeling of curved and twisted beams.

(c) A reduced integration rule is a better choice for the modeling of plates and shells. Finer mesh must be used to achieve the desired accuracy, when applied to thin plates and shells.

(d) While both full and reduced integration rules work for solid structures, the reduced one is an economic choice.

(e) The 14-point integration rule is an economic substitute for the $3\times3\times3$ Gauss-quadrature integration rule, if the full integration rule is the right choice.

(f) As the Poisson's ratio approaches 0.5 when modeling rubber-like materials, a reduced integration rule must be employed to avoid the generation of singular stiffness matrix.

The formulation of finite element analysis for orthotropic composites based on the displacement method is illustrated above. Linear or cubic hexahedral solid elements could be formulated without too much further effort by following the same procedure. The finite element formulation for modeling tetrahedral solid elements, shell/plate elements, beam elements, or pipe elements can be achieved following the same process.

3.14.2　8-Noded 3-Dimensional Solid Element

The 8-node solid element has been the most frequently used finite element in the automotive industry. It includes the first 8 nodes of the 20-node solid element shown in Fig. 3.14.1(a) and has the same merit as the 20-node solid element. Nevertheless, dense mesh is expected for modeling zones with a high strain (stress) gradient. Furthermore, it is required to have at least three elements across the thickness or any other dimension for a "shell-shaped" structure in order to avoid the hourglass effect, which means the structure is artificially stiffened due to coarse mesh.

First, consider a body modeled with a single 8-node solid element subjected to a concentrated force as shown in Fig. 3.14.2. The applied force tends to pull the loaded element in the arrow direction and enforces both free edges to deform into the two curves with sharp corner at the loading point if the material is compressible. However, the linear shape functions can only allow a displacement of the loaded node to move along the circular arc, which is perpendicular to the force direction. Such a complication results in "incompressibility" locking that induces an almost zero deformation. This phenomenon is called hourglass effect. Thus, at least three layers of linear solid elements should be enforced for rendering a robust model.

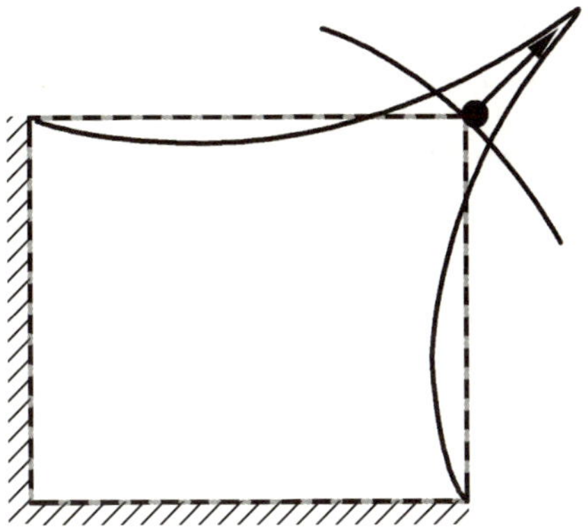

Fig. 3.14.2   Hourglass Effect Rendering Incompressibility Locking

Models with only one 20-noded element with midside nodes using a $2 \times 2 \times 2$ mesh of integration points have been seen to generate spurious zero energy (hourglassing) modes [Cook et al.].

3.14.3   4-Noded 3-Dimensional Solid Element

Although 4-noded solid elements are suggested not to be used in zones of load transfer, a certain change of cross sections, and junctions (e.g. spar-rib and skin-rib connections), they are often used for the sake of being much easier for meshing. It takes the first four nodes given in Fig. 3.14.1 (b). Sometimes, it is very difficult, if not impossible, to model a body with extremely irregular geometry and the automatic mesh generation for tetrahedral elements is the merit to meet this need.

3.14.4   10-Noded 3-Dimensional Solid Element

The 10-noded solid element is shown in Fig. 3.14.1 (b). Engineers are encouraged to use 10-nodes tetrahedrons instead of 4-node tetrahedrons in zones having a high strain gradient, if it is impossible to mesh it with hexahedral elements.

3.14.5   Implicit Codes

An implicit nonlinear finite element analysis uses Newton-Raphson iterations to enforce equilibrium of the internal structure forces with the externally applied loads. The equilibrium check is performed by iteration since the displacements at the new time result from the displacements and accelerations at the previous step. The equilibrium is usually enforced to a certain user-specified tolerance. The calculation also requires formation and inversion of global model mass (if the problem is dynamic) and stiffness matrices before equilibrium calculations can commence. However, since it can be unconditionally stable one may be able to choose a relatively larger increment step. This is a great advantage. Also, this type of analysis can handle problems better such as cyclic loading, snap through, and snap back so long as sophisticated control methods such as arc length control or generalized displacement control are used. One drawback of the method is that during the Newton-Raphson iterations the stiffness matrix for the next iteration will be updated and reconstructed. Since it can be unconditionally stable the engineer may be able to choose a large time step.

There are many finite element software packages available, some are free and some proprietary. Major general-purpose implicit FEA codes used in the automotive industry are:

    （1）Abaqus.
    （2）Ansys.
    （3）Nastran.
    （4）Hyperview.
    （5）COMSOL.
    （6）Algor.

A wide variety of analyses are available as appropriate for an engineer's work scope. These range from mechanical stress analysis, heat transfer, thermal stress analysis, stability/buckling, dynamic analysis, fluid flow, electric conduction, and electromagnetic analysis. Abaqus 2018 has three unified FEA products: Abaqus/CAE (pre-processor and solid modeling), Abaqus/Standard (implicit codes) for static and low-speed dynamic events, Abaqus/Explicit for solving high-speed, highly nonlinear and transient response events.

When dealing with slow-speed dynamic problems, one may find out that the solution time spans a period of time considerably longer than the time it takes the mechanical vibration wave to propagate through an element. The solution in this case is dominated by the lower frequencies of the structure. This class of problems covers most problems with structural dynamics, low-speed metal forming problems, low-speed crush analysis, earthquake response and biomedical problems. Should the explicit method be used for such problems the resulting number of time steps will be excessive, unless mass-scaling is applied, or the loads are artificially applied over a shorter time frame. No such modifications are needed in the implicit method. Hence, the implicit method is the optimal choice.

A large number of dynamics problems cannot be fully classified as either slow-speed or high-speed dynamic. This includes many crash problems, drop tests and high-speed metal forming problems. For these problems both solution methods are comparable, though the explicit codes are preferred. However, when the time step is relatively large and there are no convergence difficulties, the use of the implicit solution method is the proper way of doing analysis.

3.14.5.1　Meshing Guidelines for Implicit Codes

FEM utilizes the divide-and-conquer technique. Simple linear equations like $\{F\} = [K]\{R\}$ don't fit a complex part but they can be fit for a small zone of the part. When the divided small zones are piece wisely connected in both geometry and applied physical quantities, they "conquer" the part. Meshing is the process of discretizing the part with the selected elements. For the sake of the survival of the fittest, the following meshing guidelines for dividing the part are suggested:

(a) Start from the most complicated feature and not the simple one or a corner of the part.

(b) No component thickness penetration or part intersection is allowed. Keep the element mesh as orthogonal to the centerline of the part as possible.

(c) 3D elements should be used, because of 3-dimensional solids can capture all the minute details accurately. Should the 2-dimensional FEA be applied, the element mesh would be on the mid-plane of the cross-section of the component thickness cross section of the component thickness. The mid-plane is established by offsetting the geometry by 1/2 of the gage thickness in the direction that the material is shown in the cross section of the drawing.

(d) Element size should be uniform whenever possible, element length and overall mesh pattern should be consistent. Maintain a smooth transition from coarse mesh to fine mesh.

(e) Bend radii of concern are to be modeled at least 1 element spanning over a 15° angle for 8-node solid elements, while minimum 2 elements on a fillet for 20-noded hexahedral or 10-noded tetrahedral solid elements. Bend radii of no concern can be modeled as a sharp corner angle.

(f) When modeling a sectional structure component, use a minimum of 3 rows of elements to get a good in-plane bending, avoiding hourglass effect, if linear elements are used. When modeling a sectional structure component for buckling analysis, use at least 5 rows of elements.

(g) Mid nodes should lie exactly on the geometry, if quadratic elements are applied. This is extremely when meshing the parts in contact with each other.

(h) Use as less tetrahedral elements as possible because tetrahedral elements are stiffer than hexahedral elements, particularly when modeling in coarse meshes. Irregular tetrahedral solids may jeopardize the contact surface profiles.

(i) Point load produces infinite stress locally, but it is meaningless. Instead, use tractions (e. g. pressure, pulling normal stress, and shear stresses) or even equivalent displacements. Displacements are user-friendly loading, since the implicit finite element formulation is built on nodal displacements.

3.14.5.2 Mesh Quality Check

The accuracy of finite element calculations depends on the mesh quality. Degenerated elements with small volumes in conjunction with large displacements of the associated nodes may lead to large local errors of the solution. How do I know if my mesh is good enough? Most commercial finite element codes, e.g. Abaqus CAE module, allow the user to conduct quality checks during the pre-processing phase. It is recommended that one should verify the quality of the finite element mesh model, both prior to the analysis and after results have been generated.

(1) Aspect ratio is defined as the ratio of the longest edge of an element to its shortest edge of each hexahedral element. It is expected to be less than 5 : 1, though 3 : 1 or below is preferred.

(2) Skew angle should be less than 60°. Abaqus, for example, checks the distortion of each solid element through the angle between isoparametric lines of each element face. If dihedral angles approach π or $0°$, convergence to the exact solution may fail.

(3) Warpage is defined as the amount by which an element or a solid element face deviates from being planar. It should be less than 15°.

(4) Jacobian is a measure of the deviation of an element from the ideally shaped. The Jacobian is calculated by taking the partial derivatives of the hexahedron shape functions with respect to the Cartesian coordinate system. The resulting index ranges from 0 to 100%, where 100% represents a perfectly shaped element. This value is expected to be greater than 60%.

(5) Frobenius-norm-based measures of coherence and asymmetry by the averaged condition number of the transformation matrix from an isosceles configuration for each of the eight corner-tetrahedra of a hexahedral solid element.

(6) Boundary check to assure that no interior splits or cracks appear in the mesh of solid elements for traditional FEM, but this is allowed for applying X-FEM.

(7) Align element "norms" for each component in 1-direction.

(8) Eliminate duplicate elements and free 1-D elements.

(9) Eliminate rigid dependency, rigid loops, or circular dependency.

3.14.6　Adaptivity of Mesh and Nodes

The use of nodal and mesh refinement has been especially effective in super nonlinear analyses such as metal cutting, welding process, fluid transport and aerodynamic simulations for accurately capturing material flow and discontinuities. Adaptivity involves the following possible variations to a traditional finite element formulation and/or solution process:

(a) h-adaptation (mesh refined): The element size varies while the orders of the shape functions are the same. Each individual element is subdivided without altering the original position.

(b) p-adaptation (polynomial orders of shape functions elevated): The element size is the same while the polynomial orders of shape functions increased such as going from 8-noded to 20-noded solid elements.

(c) h-p adaptation (mesh refined and orders of shape function elevated): It is expected to render exponential convergence rates.

(d) r-adaptation (remeshing): It is expected to improve the element quality for a nonlinear solution process to converge when getting involved with extremely large deformations that may distort the original mesh numerically.

(e) Spectral element: A formulation of the finite element method (FEM) that uses high-ordered piecewise polynomials as basic functions such as orthogonal Chebyshev polynomials or very high-ordered Legendre polynomials. In SEM (Spectral Element Method) as part of FEM, computational error decreases exponentially as the order of approximating polynomial, therefore a fast convergence of solution to the exact solution is realized with fewer degrees of freedom of the structure in comparison with FEM [Patera]. The SEM with fewer degrees of freedom per node, can be useful for detecting small flaws for the purpose of structural health monitoring.

(f) X-FEM (Extended Finite Element Method): Crack propagation is modeled using modified nodal displacements yet based the implicit finite element formulation. This engenders additional degrees of freedom that are tied to the nodes of the involved finite elements to be intersected by the crack to model the presence of a crack (Chapter 4).

3.15   Finite Element Accuracy of 20-Node Solid Elements in Composites

It is well accepted by researchers to predict the behaviors of composite "solids" by 20-node isoparametric elements, but the application to composite shells is dubious. Lack of adequate understanding can lead to puzzling and misleading results. On the finite element accuracy, a factorial analysis is conducted to explore the impact of the following five factors [Chiang & Tang]:

(a) Aspect ratio: Ratio of length (average of four side) to width (average of four side) of an element.

(b) Radius-to-thickness ratio: Ratio of radius (on the centroidal surface, averaged) to thickness (averaged) of an element; its inverse can be used as a measure of curvature.

(c) Material anisotropy: Ratio of Young's modulus in the fiber direction to that in the transverse direction.

(d) Fiber angle: Fiber alignment measured from the longitudinal axis of shell.

(e) Integration order: Reduced integration ($2\times2\times2$) and full integration ($3\times3\times3$) in Gauss quadrature formulae.

The case study is done on the application of 20-node isoparametric solid elements to a clamped composite cylindrical shell (baseline data: axial length of 508 mm, radius of 508 mm, and thickness of 25.4 mm) subjected to internal pressure ($p=0.02758$ MPa). The full factorial design, 2^5, with no confounding patterns, is deployed and their corresponding design levels are listed in Table 3.15.1. The objective is to check the finite element accuracy as measured by the radial displacement at the central cross-section, when the cylinder is subjected to factorial variations.

Table 3.15.1　Factors and Levels Used for the Study on FEA on Composite Shells ［Chiang & Tang］.

Factor	Level （-）	Level （+）	Variate
A: Aspect ratio	1.25	5.00	$a = \dfrac{A-3.125}{1.875}$
B: Radius-to-thickness ratio	20	200	$b = \dfrac{B-110}{90}$
C: Material anisotropy	Glass/epoxy[*]	Graphite/epoxy[*]	$c_{-1} = \dfrac{G_l}{E_p}$; $c_1 = \dfrac{G_r}{E_p}$
D: Fiber angle （degrees）	90°	0°	$d = \dfrac{D-45}{45}$
E: Integration order	2×2×2	3×3×3	$e_{-1} = 2×2×2$; $e_1 = 3×3×3$

Notes: * Glass/epoxy: $E_{11} = 51.7$ GPa, $E_{22} = E_{33} = 13.8$ GPa;

$$G_{12} = G_{13} = G_{23} = 8.62 \text{ GPa}; \ \nu_{12} = \nu_{13} = \nu_{23} = 0.25$$

* Graphite/epoxy: $E_{11} = 51.7$ GPa, $E_{22} = E_{33} = 13.8$ GPa;

$$G_{12} = G_{13} = G_{23} = 6.42 \text{ GPa}; \ \nu_{12} = \nu_{13} = \nu_{23} = 0.25$$

All the finite element calculations, including pre- and post-processors were performed on an in-house finite element computer program, namely CADOCS (Computer-Aided Design of Composite Structures). Solutions to obtain simultaneous equations were derived according to the columnwise skyline algorithm ［Cook & Bretl］. The validity of the finite element program has been confirmed repeatedly since it was originally developed for tire modeling and body panels by the first author of ［Chiang & Tang］. Note that the skew angle was kept zero throughout the experimental design. On this example, with the integration order 3×3×3, the calculated radial displacement at the central cross-section under internal pressure $p = 0.02758$ MPa is 0.00928 mm, which correlates extremely well with the exact solution 0.00932 mm, derived from the closed form-solution ［Kraus］.

Calculations on statistic inferences are performed according to contrast coefficients based on design of experiments ［Box et al.］. Since there is no replication, the statistical sample standard error is formed by pooling the small 4- and 5-factorial interactions together. The final assessment equation for the finite element error based on the balanced design of experiments for this case study can be summarized as ［Chaing & Tang］

$$Y_p = 0.163 + 0.11a + 0.153b - 0.025d - 0.140e + 0.093ab - 0.084ae - 0.123be + 0.024de - 0.064abc \tag{3.15.1}$$

This case study proves that 20-node isoparametric solid elements can be used to model thin shells such as all the tire components and composite vehicle bodies. Although shell finite elements can also be applied, but they are not able to predict the interlaminar normal stress naturally. On average, the maximum radial displacement predicted by 20-node isoparametric solid elements is 16.3% on this case study, but it can be improved tremendously by using the right calculating parameters. Some interesting findings are listed as follows:

(1) Increasing either the aspect ratio or the radius-to-thickness ratio tends to damage the finite element accuracy. When both are increased, their interaction does more damage to the finite element accuracy. However, the effectiveness of the three-factor interaction (aspect ratio × radius-to-thickness ratio × integration order) shows that the $3 \times 3 \times 3$ integration will relieve some of the damage done by increasing both aspect ratio and radius-to-thickness ratio.

(2) It seems that the anisotropy of material has little influence on the finite element accuracy, at lease within the range of $E_{11}/E_{22} = 3.75$ and $E_{11}/E_{22} = 14.6$. This is contradictory to what claimed by [Noor & Camin], in which one factor-at-a-time methodology is applied. However, aligning fibers along the curved edges makes the finite element accuracy worse. This can be explained by the fact that successive coordinate transformations made from the material axes the natural (body) coordinates, then to the global coordinate, have damaged the finite element accuracy over a subtended angle of a curve.

(3) Integration order is also a significant main effect, as proven mathematically. The change of integration order from $2 \times 2 \times 2$ to $3 \times 3 \times 3$ improves the finite element accuracy very much. Consider the two-factor interactions. The $3 \times 3 \times 3$ integration order can recover some damage done by high aspect ratio and high radius-to-thickness ratio.

3.16   Solution Methods for Nonlinear Finite Element Analysis

As nonlinear finite element formulations are applied to continuum mechanics, the continuation-based solution scheme is not just a possible game but also the only game [Felippa]. The behavior of nonlinear systems is not subject to the principle of superposition, as linear systems are. Solution procedures for nonlinear implicit finite element analysis are founded on the algorithm of advancing the approximating scheme by continuation of the load-displacement curve (or curves), of which the load factor and angle between predictor and corrector surfaces may be utilized for stabilizing numerical stability [Rezaiee-Pajand & Afsharimoghadam] or speeding up the convergence.

3.16.1 Solution Procedure

The fundamental is to make sense of the equilibrium response of the to-be-resolved system in terms of geometric nonlinearity and material nonlinearity, as well as to circumvent potential divergence in solution. Approaches are enlightened by the desired control parameters and/or state variables that advance while following three different solution steps (Fig. 3.16.1) as follows:

(1) Stages: The solution are divided into several stages, also called load steps. A load step is a set of loading and boundary conditions to define an analysis problem. Multiple load steps can be used to define a sequence of loading conditions. For example, tire modeling for virtual proving ground application can be divided into the following stages: (A) Tire inflation with composite fiber reinforcement and netting adjustment, (B) Assembly of tires to vehicle axles and getting vehicle tires deflected against the flat ground, (C) Letting the vehicle run on the designated path (such as Belgium road).

(2) Increments: Within an increment, an iterative process (e.g., NR method) is used to find nonlinear solution. Success in a corrective process done by a Newton-Raphson method, for example, may hinge on having a good initial guess supplied by the predictor and the presence of point- or path-dependent effects restricts increment sizes because of history-tracing constraints. The incremental size close to yielding and bifurcation points are typically point-dependence, while friction-based contact problems are path dependent. Thus, the number of increments of the assigned load-control variables of each load for the Newton-Raphson method or the arc length/scale factor for the arc-length control method play an important role in solution convergence. Load increments have to be handled with caution, when the finite element procedure is conducted for the following cases: (a) the linear analysis concerning the maximum load, (b) the nonlinear analysis depends on load path (history) and (c) the applied load gradually increased. In general, it needs about 10 increments for mild nonlinearity and 10-100 increments for rough nonlinearity. Most finite element codes utilize an automatic load increment scheme, where the size of load increment is usually not uniform. For example, if a solution converges in less than 4 iterations, the increment is to be increased by 25% and If a solution converges in more than 8 iterations, the increment is to be reduced by 25%. When it diverges, the load increment is halved and tried again.

(3) Iterations: Corrections may be applied in each increment, which is also called a predictor step when using the Newton-Raphson method, and thus one or more iterations within each increment in required. Both predictors and the related correctors are applied iteratively in order to eliminate or reduce the residual drifting error. The number of iterations required for each increment depends on the solution scheme, convergence algorithm and desired accuracy. An upper limit of the number of iterations (e.g. 100 or

200) may be prescribed by the user to quit the run, in case it stands no chance against convergence.

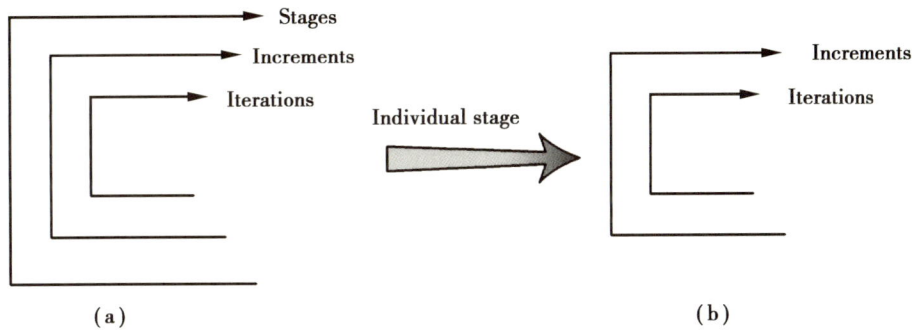

(a)   (b)

Fig. 3.16.1   Solution Steps for Nonlinear Finite Element Analysis [Fellipa]

3.16.2   Error Smoothing

Assume that there are N degrees of freedom in the discretized system during a nonlinear finite element analysis. Consider the Newton-Raphson method. The solution basically "marches" along a load-displacement curve in each stage, as shown in Fig. 3.16.2(a). After n incremental steps have been completed and the last accepted displacement solution is $\{\phi\}_n$, which corresponds to the load value $\{R\}_n$(or load factor λ_n) of the stage control parameter. Performing the $(n+1)$th step entails the calculation of the increments

$$\{\Delta\phi\}_n = \{\phi\}_{n+1} - \{\phi\}_n \tag{3.16.1}$$

and $$\{\Delta R\}_n = \{R\}_{n+1} - \{R\}_n \tag{3.16.2}$$

where
$\{\phi\}_n$: Displacement vector after n incremental steps;
$\{R\}_n$: Load vector after n incremental steps.

The load control strategy is usually a closure in light of error message that can be expressed in general form as the following error-constraint condition

$$e(\{\Delta\phi\}_n, \{\Delta R\}_n) \to 0 \tag{3.16.3}$$

of which "$\to$" means that the error approaches zero within a numerical tolerance assigned by the programmer or user. Eq. (3.9.2) is a fulfillment of the above equation and it is representative of the convergence criterion for Newton-Raphson method.

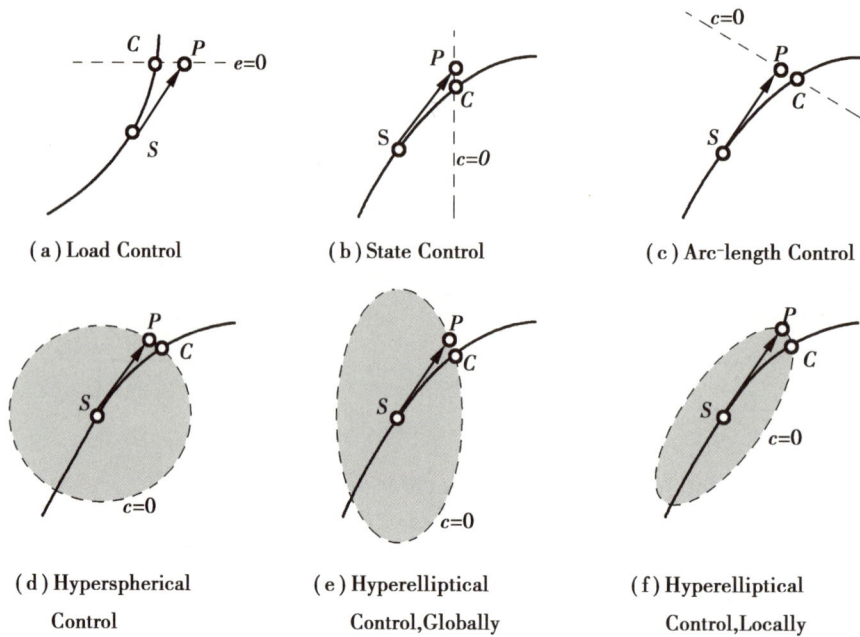

(a) Load Control   (b) State Control   (c) Arc-length Control

(d) Hyperspherical
Control

(e) Hyperelliptical
Control, Globally

(f) Hyperelliptical
Control, Locally

Fig. 3.16.2 Six Feasible Constraints for Nonlinear Finite Element Solutions, as Modified from [Fellipa]

There are six feasible control methods as schematically demonstrated in Fig. 3.16.2. The Newton-Raphson method follows the load control algorithm and has been successfully used for approaching mildly nonlinear finite element problems with monotonically-increasing or -decreasing load-displacement curves. The load control or displacement (state) control method, Fig. 3.16.2(a) and (b), frequently diverges when getting close to the limit points of a structure. The arc-length control method and others are then used for modeling nonlinear bifurcation (buckling) and snapping behaviors, and other structurally unstable phenomenon. The arc-length control method and others, as shown in Fig. 3.16.2(c), (d), (e), and (f), utilize both the load and displacement as the guide along a "2-dimensional curve" on the load-displacement chart to search for the converging point. They are to be addressed in Chapter 9.

The force-control procedure [Fig. 3.16.2(b)] is a versatile approach to solving linear problems using finite element methods, while the displacement-control procedure is more stable for nonlinear analysis. Applied forces can be also calculated from the reaction forces, when needed. The traditional convergence criterion relies on the residual load to check the equilibrium between internal forces and external forces when implicit codes are used. It is preferred for the case shown in Fig. 3.16.2(a), where the load-displacement curve is concave upwards. Displacement, strain, stress, and energy can be also used as a convergence criterion; it is called state-control method. Among them, the displacement convergence criterion is preferred for and the case as shown in Fig. 3.16.2(b), where the load-displacement curve is concave downwards, as well as for load-insensitive systems.

3.16.3   Meshing for Nonlinear Large Deformations

It is best to make discretize the continuum in such a way that the mesh quality can be maintained after deformation, as experience counts. Initial good mesh may be distorted during a large deformation. When distorted too much, the finite element codes have to stop the analysis. Most commercial finite element codes provide remeshing capability, but it is hard to control the accuracy well or becomes extremely inconvenient.

3.16.4   Newton-Raphson Method

The Newton-Raphson method is an algorithm of successive approximations simultaneously to the "zeros" (e.g. roots of nonlinear simultaneous polynomials) of real-valued functions. The algorithm is here illustrated using a one-degree-of-freedom problem-solving process. Let $y = f(x)$, which is a nonlinear continuous function. The solution to the equation is to find out the root of $f(x) = 0$ as illustrated in Fig. 13.5.1. After the initial point of the curve is selected, namely (x_1, y_1), the slope of the curve at this point is then

$$\frac{df(x_1)}{dx} = \frac{y - f(x_1)}{x - x_1} \qquad (3.16.4)$$

Given that $x \neq x_1$, then there is a slope of finite value. Assume that the tangent (slope) of the curve at x_1 intersects the x-axis at point $(x_2, y_2 = 0)$. At point $(x_2, 0)$, Eq. (3.16.4) reduces to

$$x_2 = x_1 - \frac{f(x_1)}{\dfrac{df(x_1)}{dx}} \qquad (3.16.5)$$

After repeating the above process r times, one has

$$x_{r+1} = x_r - \frac{f(x_r)}{\dfrac{df(x_r)}{dx}} \qquad (3.16.6)$$

As long as curve $f(x)$ is monotonically increasing or decreasing, the intersecting point gets closer to the root (i.e., $y = 0$) after each iteration, as shown in Fig. 3.16.3. The x_{r+1} is to be the root numerically when the following convergence criterion is satisfied

$$| x_{r+1} - x_r | \leq \text{Tolerance} \qquad (3.16.7)$$

of which "Tolerance" is a small value (e.g. 0.1%), representative of the allowable error, that depends on the desired computational accuracy.

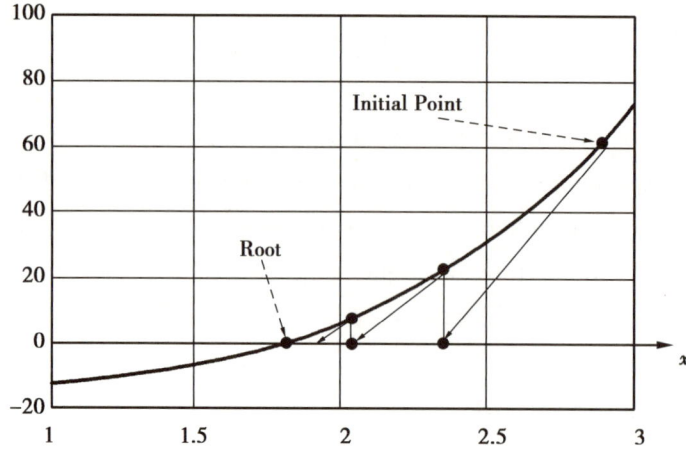

Fig. 3.16.3　Newton-Raphson Schematics for $f(x) = x^4 + 3x - 16$.

The Newton-Raphson method and its modified versions based on the incremental-iterative technique are popular approaches to solving nonlinear finite element problems [Chama et al.]. Assume that displacement vector $\{\phi\}_i$ at the ith iteration in a given load increment is known. The next iteration is to seek out $\{\phi\}_{i+1}$ from the first-order Taylor's series expansion,

$$\{P(\{\phi\}_{i+1})\} \approx \{P(\{\phi\}_i)\} + [K(\{\phi\}_i)]_T \{\Delta\phi\}_i = \{F\} \tag{3.16.8}$$

and $\quad [K(\{\phi\}_i)]_T = \dfrac{\partial\{P(\{\phi\}_i)\}}{\partial\{\phi\}_i}$ $\tag{3.16.9}$

where

$\{F\}$: Applied force vector, i.e., $\{F\}_{N \times 1}$, where subscript N is the total number of equations;

$\{\phi\}_i$: Displacement at iteration i;

$\{\Delta\phi\}_i$: Displacement advance in increment at iteration i;

$[K(\{\phi\}_i)]_T$: Tangential stiffness matrix at iteration I, also called Jacobian matrix.

The tangential stiffness matrix will be updated for each iteration. The next step is to solve the incremental equation, i.e., Eq. (3.16.8), which can be rearranged with the unbalanced force (called residual force) on the right side of the " = " sign as

$$[K(\{\phi\}_i)]_T \{\Delta\phi\}_i = \{R\}_i \tag{3.16.10}$$

where

$$\{R\}_i = \{F\} - \{P(\{\phi\}_i)\} \tag{3.16.11}$$

for the next displacement advance $\{\Delta\phi\}_{i+1}$. The next step is to update the displacement as follows:

$$\{\phi\}_{i+1} \approx \{\phi\}_i + \{\Delta\phi\}_{i+1} \tag{3.16.12}$$

After displacement $\{\phi\}_{i+1}$ is obtained, it can be substituted into the following equation for displacement $\{\phi\}_{i+2}$ and Eq. (3.16.8) is updated to be

$$\{P(\{\phi\}_{i+2})\} \approx \{P(\{\phi\}_{i+1})\} + [K(\{\phi\}_{i+1})]_T \{\Delta\phi\}_{i+1} = \{F\} \qquad (3.16.13)$$

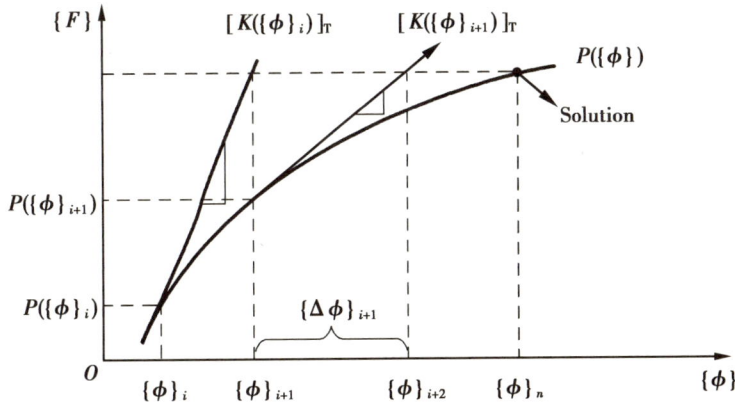

Fig. 3.16.4   Newton-Raphson Schematics for Solving Nonlinear Finite Element Equations

As shown in Fig. 3.16.4, this process is repeated until one or both of the following two convergence tolerances are met.

$$\text{Convergence}_1 = \frac{\sum_{n=1}^{N} [(R_n)_{r+1}]^2}{1 + \sum_{n=1}^{N} (F_n)^2} \leqslant \text{Tolerance} \qquad (3.16.14)$$

$$\text{and} \quad \text{Convergence}_2 = \frac{\sum_{n=1}^{N} [(\Delta\phi_n)_{r+1}]^2}{1 + \sum_{n=1}^{N} [(\Delta\phi_n)_0]^2} \leqslant \text{Tolerance} \qquad (3.16.15)$$

where

N: Total number of equations (degrees of freedom) associated with Eq. (3.16.8);

n: Subscript n is the equation number, ranging from 1 to N;

r: Subscript r is the number of repetitions;

0: Subscript 0 is the original;

$(\Delta\phi_n)_0$: Original displacement vector calculated before the repetition.

The Newton-Raphson method assumes a constant curvature locally.

When a sign of curvature changes around the solution, the residual often changes signs between two successive iterations. The solution procedure may diverge after several oscillating iterations. The arc-length control procedure [Fig. 3.16.2(c)] can then be applied instead.

3.16.5   Boundary Conditions

Spring elements and "soft" solid elements are super useful for constraining an unconstrained "body" in the 3-dimensional space, e. g. ship on the sea, in order to fix its six degrees of freedom.

3.17   Dynamic Problems: Implicit, Explicit, and Coupled Codes

The dynamic response as a time series at each structural location of concern need be considered in order to accurately predict damage when a system is subjected to significant time-varying loadings. The dynamic analysis (either transient or modal analysis) follows a governing equation which looks like

$$[M] \frac{d^2 y}{dt^2} + [C] \frac{dy}{dt} + [K] \{y\} = \{F\} \tag{3.17.1}$$

Where

$\{y\}$: Vector of dependent variables;

$[M]$: Mass matrix;

$[C]$: Damping matrix;

$[K]$: Stiffness matrix;

$\{F\}$: Forcing vector.

3.17.1   Implicit Codes for Dynamics

The dynamic solution using implicit FEA codes is based on the iterative scheme, in which the calculation of current quantities in one time step relies on the quantities calculated in the previous time step. This approach requires the calculation of the inverse of stiffness matrix and calculation of an inverse is a computationally intensive step. This is especially so when non linearities are present, as the stiffness matrix itself will become a function of x. An implicit algorithm looks like

$$f(y_{n+1}, y_n, y_{n-1}, \cdots) = 0 \tag{3.17.2}$$

which is a nonlinear equation involving the next unknown state y_{i+1} and is to be solved iteratively. Although one calculation step of an implicit algorithm takes more time than one step of an explicit one, the user can use larger time steps, less number of steps, and at the end the implicit algorithms are faster compared to explicit algorithms. The implicit method is not sensitive to such small elements. Hence for all such situations, Implicit algorithms are quite efficient for dynamic analysis in the low frequency range, e.g. a vehicle body subjected to a forced vibration at a frequency lower than 1/3 of the fundamental natural frequency [Cook et al.].

3.17.2   Explicit Codes for Dynamics

In an explicit analysis, instead of solving for $\{y\}$, we go for solving d^2y/dt^2. The inversion of the complex stiffness matrix $[K]$ is bypassed, while the mass matrix $[M]$ is inverted instead. Explicit algorithms are more suitable for high-speed dynamic problems. In case lower order elements are used, which is preferred when using explicit codes, the mass matrix is also a lumped matrix, or a diagonal matrix, whose inversion is a single step process of just making the diagonal elements reciprocal. This class of problems covers most wave propagation problems, explosives problems, and high-speed impact problems (e.g. car crash tests). The explicit algorithm does not need a small-time increment in time integration but it is defined by the highest eigenfrequency. An explicit algorithm looks like

$$y_{n+1} = f(y_n, y_{n-1}, \cdots) \tag{3.17.3}$$

It means that the next new unknown y_{i+1} is to be found from previous known states at y_n, y_{n-1}, and so on. If the implicit method uses a similar time step it will be much slower; and if it uses a much larger time step it will introduce other solution errors since it may not be able to capture the pertinent detailed features of the solution. Hence, the explicit method is the optimal choice for high-speed dynamic problems. The quality of the results obtained from both the explicit algorithm with correct step size and the implicit algorithm with the same step size should be the same though it takes longer time to complete. Since the size of explicit time step depends on the length of the smallest element, one excessively small element will reduce the size of stable time step for the whole model. Nevertheless, mass-scaling can be applied to these small elements to improve the solution stability.

Explicit methods cannot be applied to some problems, though they are not able to handle behaviors of bifurcation and snapping (both snap-through and snap-back) and hardly do cyclic loads. Perhaps more importantly, explicit methods do not enforce the equilibrium of internal structural forces and externally applied loads as implicit methods do. Conclusively, a good number of steps are required for explicit methods, as the solution time is comparable to the time required for the wave to propagate through the structure. It can handle rapid changes in contact state as well as material failure much more effectively than the implicit dynamics scheme [Duni et al.].

Most applications of explicit FEA codes to vehicle dynamics are to serve the following purposes: durability, noise, and crashworthiness. VPG (virtual proving ground) testing for the durability of a vehicle body using Abaqus Explicit Codes is illustrated in Fig. 3.17.1 (a), via which the acceleration profile as shown in Fig. 3.17.1(b) acquired form the explicit codes can be input into the quasi-static Abaqus Standard for fatigue analysis [Surendranath].

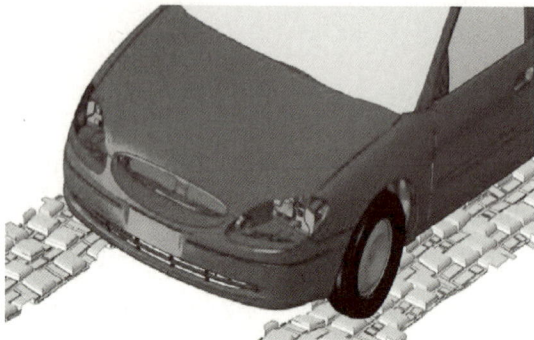

| (a) Road Profile of Belgium Blocks | (b) Vertical Acceleration at Wheel Center |

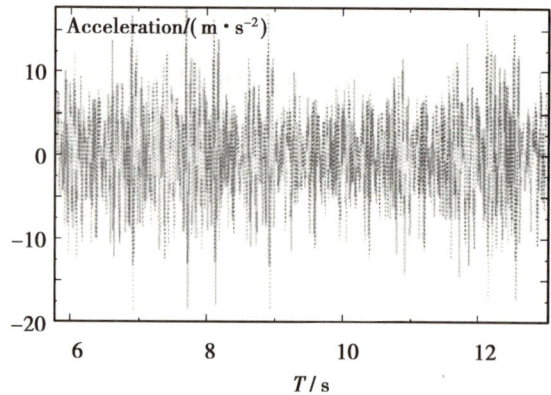

Fig. 3.17.1   VPG (Virtual Proving Ground) Testing on the Belgium Blocks [Surendranath]

The stability limit for the central-difference method (the largest time increment that can be taken without the method generating large, rapidly growing errors) is closely related to the time required for a stress wave to cross the smallest element dimension in the model. Therefore, the time increment in an explicit dynamic analysis can be very short if the mesh contains small elements or if the stress wave speed in the material is high. The explicit method can handle rapid changes in contact state as well as material failure much more effectively than the implicit dynamics scheme.

3.17.3   Coupled Implicit-Explicit Methodology for Dynamics

A growing trend in FEA is the simulation of large-scale motion using finite element models. Simulating large-scale motion is crucial for accurately replicating the real-world behavior of many mechanisms and for determining how components will perform under conditions of impact, contact or other loads of concern. A co-simulation method allows users to combine implicit and explicit solvers into a single simulation, substantially reducing computation time. For example, automotive engineers can now combine a substructure representation of a vehicle body with a model of the tires and suspension systems to evaluate the durability of a vehicle running over Belgium blocks as shown in Fig. 3.17.1 using Abaqus Standards and Abaqus Explicit.

3.17.4   Nonlinear FEA Coupled with Elastic Multibody Systems

Although most OEMs use detailed models in FEA for VPG tests yet simulating the entire vehicle model and road profile with FEA is very time-consuming. The computation time required for a full FEA of a typical vehicle running over a pothole, as shown in Fig. 3.17.2, using Abaqus explicit codes takes around 50 hours on 38 CPUs [Christl et al.]. The major idea is to replace bigger parts of the FEA model by computational-reduced MBS (Multibody Systems) with rigid body members (or elastic superelements) and the coupled model is simulated in a single application. All critical components with nonlinear deformations can still be calculated using Abaqus Standard with the same accuracy as in the full FEA model. It takes 8 hours on 9 CPUs based on the FEA-MBS coupled model.

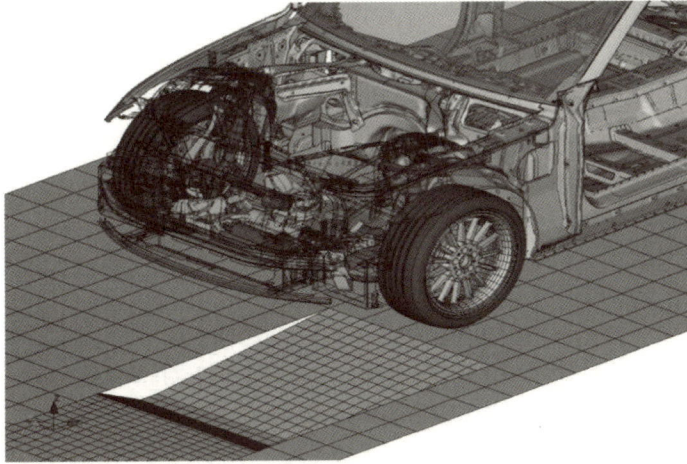

Fig. 3.17.2   VPG (Virtual Proving Ground) Testing on a Pothole [Christl et al.]

In a finite-element model, certain relatively stiff parts can be represented by rigid bodies if their stress distributions and wave propagation are not of concern. A rigid body can be connected to other rigid bodies via joint elements. It can also be connected to flexible bodies to model mixed rigid-flexible body dynamics. An advantage of using rigid bodies rather than deformable finite elements is computational efficiency since elements that belong to the rigid bodies have no associated internal forces or stiffness. The motion of a rigid body is determined by a maximum of six degrees of freedom at the pilot node with no mass or moments of inertia [Ansys]. For dynamic problems, an effective way to present the effect of rigid-body mass is to add the point mass element on the gravity center of a rigid body, where the center of mass and rotary inertia properties of the actual rigid body can be estimated.

Connector elements, also called connectors, can be applied in Abaqus models at either the part level or the assembly level in a FEA model. Connector elements operate on components of motion local to the connection, and nodal coordinate transformations can be defined for either node connected to the connector element or the other way around. These transformations affect only the nodal degrees of freedom, but their use does not affect the behavior of connector elements. The connector element force, moment, and kinematic output is defined in connector element library [Abaqus]. These output quantities include total, elastic, viscous, and friction forces and moments. Simultaneously, reaction forces and moments caused by connector stops and locks are available as well as connector contact forces used for friction calculation. Multiple connector elements may be used in parallel to obtain output in different coordinate systems or for other purposes.

References

ANSYS, INC, 2018. Ansys/DesignSpace, Ansys/LS-DYNA, Ansys/CFD[M]. Canonsburg, PA, USA.

BATHE K J, 2014. Finite Element Procedures[M]. 2nd Edition, Klaus-Jürgen Bathe, 2014.

BELYTSCHKO T, CRACIE R, VENTURA G, 2009. A Review of Extended/Generalized Finite Element Methods for Material Modeling[M]. Modeling and Simulation of Materials Science and Engineering, 17(4):1-24.

CAO J, et al, 2008. Characterization of Mechanical Behavior of Woven Fabrics: Experimental Methods and Benchmark Results[J]. Composites, Part A Applied Science & Manufacturing, 39(6):1037-1053.

CHAMA A, et al, 2018. Newton-Raphson Solver for Finite Element Methods Featuring Nonlinear Hysteresis Models[J]. IEEE Transactions on Magnetics, 54(1): 1-8.

CHANDRUPATLA T R, BELEGUNDU A D, 2011. Introduction to Finite Elements in Engineering[M]. 4th Edition, Prentice Hall (Pearson).

CHEN X, XU S, HUANG D, 1999. Critical Plane-Strain Energy Density Criterion of Multiaxial Low-Cycle Fatigue Life[J]. Fatigue & Fracture Engineering for Materials & Structures, 22:679-686.

CHIANG Y J, TANG C, 1995. Accuracy Assessment to Applying 20-Node Solid Elements to Pressurized Composite Shells[J]. Finite Elements in Analysis and Design, 20(4):219-231.

CHRISTL J, et al, 2015. FEA-MBS-Coupling-Approach for Vehicle Dynamics, NAFEMS European Conference, Turin, Italy.

COOK R D, MALKUS D S, PLESHA M E, et al, 2001. Concepts and Applications of Finite Element Analysis [M]. 4th Edition, John Wiley and Sons, NY, USA.

COOK R D, BRETL J L, 1979. A New Eight Node Solid Element, International Journal of Numerical Methods in Engineering[J]. 14(4):593-615.

DANTULURI V, et al, 2007. Cohesive Modeling of Delamination in *Z*-pin Reinforced Composite Laminates[J]. Composites Science & Technology, 67:616-631.

DASSAULT SYSTÈMES SIMULIA CORP, 2018. Abaqus/CAE, Abaqus/Standard, Abaqus/Explicit, Abaqus/CFD, and Abaqus/Electromagnetic, Johnston, Rhode Island, USA.

DUNI E, TONIATO G, SMERIGLIO P, et al, 2010. Vehicle Dynamic Solution Based on Finite Element Tire/Road Interaction Implemented through Implicit/Explicit Sequential and Co-Simulation Approach, SAE Paper

2010-01-1138.

FELIPPA C A, 1999. Chapter 20: Overview of Solution Methods, Nonlinear Finite Element Methods, Lecture Notes, Department of Aerospace Engineering Sciences, University of Colorado-Boulder.

GENG L, SHEN Y, WAGONER R, 2002. Anisotropic Hardening equations Derived from Reverse-Bend Testing [J]. International Journal of Plasticity, 18(5-6):743-767.

HUANG H, WAAS A M, 2009. Compressive Response of Z-pinned Woven Glass Fiber Textile Composite Laminates, Modeling and Computations[J]. Composites Science & Technology, 69(14):2338-2344.

KRAUS H, 1967. Thin Elastic Shells[J]. Journal of Appllied Mechanics, 35(3):624.

MOTTERSHEAD J E, PASCOE S K, ENGLISH R G, 1992. A General Finite Element Approach for Contact Stress Analysis[J]. International Journal of Numerical Methods in Engineering, 33:765-779.

NIKISHKOV G, et al, 2013. Finite Element Mesh Generation for Composites with Ply Waviness Based on X-ray Computed Tomography[J]. Advances in Engineering Software, 58(apr):35-44.

NISHIKAWA M, OKABE T, TAKEDA N, 2007. Numerical Simulation of Interlaminar Damage Propagation in CFRP Cross-ply Laminates under Transverse Loading[J]. International Journal of Solids and Structures, 44: 3101-3113.

NOOR A K, CAMIN R A, 1976. Symmetry Considerations for Anisotropic Shells[J]. Computer Methods in Applied Mechanics and Engineering, 9(3):317-335.

REDDY J N, 2004. An Introduction to Nonlinear Finite Element Analysis[M]. Oxford University. Press.

REZAIEE-PAJAND M, AFSHARIMOGHADAM H, 2017. Optimization Formulation for Nonlinear Structural Analysis[J]. International of Optimization in Civil Engineering, International Journal of Optimization in Civil Engineering, 7(1):109-127.

RIKS E, 1979. An Incremental Approach to the Solution of Snapping and Buckling Problems[J]. International Journal of Solids and Structures, 15(7):524-551.

ROGERS D F, ADAMS J A, 1990. Mathematical Elements for Computer Graphics[M]. Chapter 3, 2nd Edition, McGraw Hill, New York, NY, USA.

SONG M C, et al, 2013. Finite Element Analysis of Delamination in Woven Composites under Quasi-Static Indentation[J]. CMC, 35(1):67-85.

SRINIVASAN R, PERUCCHIO R, 1994. Finite Element Analysis of Anisotropic Non-Linear Incompressible Elastic Solid by a Mixed Model[J]. International Journal of Numerical Methods in Engineering, 37(18): 3075-3092.

SURENDRANATH H, 2013. Vehicle Dynamics and Durability Simulations Using Ansa and Abaqus, 5th ANSA & μETA International Conference, Thessaloniki, Greece.

VASILIEV V, 2007. Advanced Mechanics of Composite Materials[M]. 2nd Edition, Elsevier Ltd.

WILLIAMS J, SVENSSON N, 1971. An Experimental Analysis of the Neck of the Femur[J]. Medical and Biological Engineering, 9(5):479-493.

WILSON E L, et al, 1974. Direct Solution of Large Systems of Linear Equations[J]. Computers and Structures, 4(2):363.

WINKLER D C, ACCORSI M L, 1997. Application of the Patch Test to Incompatible Laminated Finite Elements[J]. International Journal for Numerical Methods in Engineering, 40(22):4239-4257.

WIRGGERS P, 1995. Finite Element Algorithms for Contact Problems[J]. Archives of Computational Methods in Engineering, 2(4):1-49.

Chapter 4

Mechanical Fatigue

4.1   Stress and Strain State Due at Fatigue

One important aspect for evaluating an engineering material is fatigue, which involves considerations in addition to yielding flow and creep flow. A fatigue failure is due to repeated or cyclic loading and unloading or fluctuating reversal in loading after a large number of cycles. It is a material-based phenomenon that causes failure in a mechanical part at a stress-strain level much lower than the corresponding yield strength of the material. Fatigue failures are estimated to occur in 80%-90% of all machine component failures and account for a 4% loss in the gross domestic product of the United States and Europe [Draper 2002]. Fatigue cracks initiate through the release of strain energy, especially in the shear mode. It is shown in Fig. 4.1.1 how the shear stresses result in local plastic deformation along slip planes. As the cyclic loading fluctuates, the slip planes move back and forth like a pack of cards, resulting in small extrusions and intrusions on the crystal surface. These surface disturbances range from 1 μm to 10 μm in height approximately and constitute embryonic cracks.

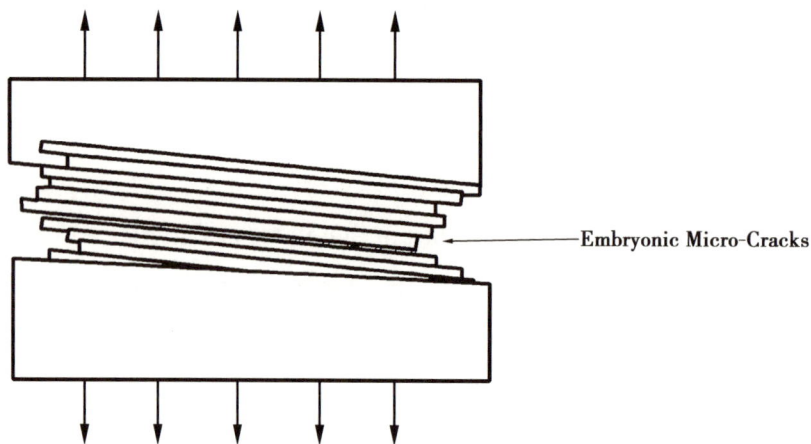

—Embryonic Micro-Cracks

Fig. 4.1.1   Slip Bands Form along Planes of Maximum Shear Giving Rise to Localized Plastic Deformation under Fluctuating Loading

Fatigue is the progressive and localized structural damage that occurs when a material is subjected to cyclic loading. At high frequencies with short hold times, the fatigue mode dominates and failures start near the surface and propagate transgranularly. As the hold time increases or relatively the frequency decreases, the creep component begins to play a role in increasing creep-fatigue interaction, resulting in fractures of a mixed mode involving both fatigue cracking and creep cavitation.

A typical initial stress-strain curve for a uniaxial fatigue test under constant-amplitude loading is illustrated in Fig. 4.1.2. It is specified in ISO 12106—2017 how to conduct fully reversed uniaxial tension-compression cycle test under stress control at constant amplitude and uniform temperature, as shown in Fig. 4.1.2. Note that both strain range $\Delta\varepsilon$ and strain amplitude ε_a can be taken into consideration for the strain-life approach, while $\Delta\varepsilon = 2\varepsilon_a$.

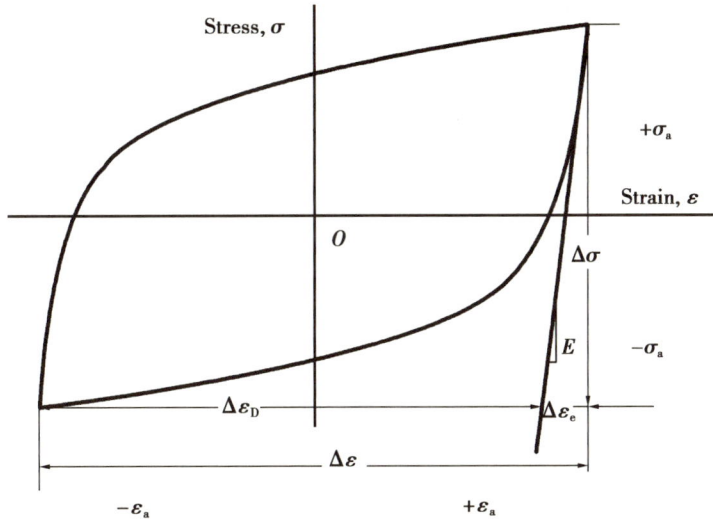

Fig. 4.1.2　Typical Uniaxial Stress-Strain Curve for Fatigue under Constant-Amplitude Loading

Two algorithms currently available for predicting fatigue life of materials are the crack nucleation approach and the crack growth approach.

 (a) Crack nucleation method: This is to predict the service time duration up to the moment when the crack is initiated. The early development of slip bands and deepening of initial cracks. This is more appropriate for evaluating fatigue life under complex loading and analyzing the spatial distribution of fatigue life in metals, rubber, and structural plastics.

 (b) Crack growth method: This algorithm is suitable to the case where the crack location, growth path, and crack shape are assumed to have been well identified [Saintier et al. 2006a]. This approach is quite applicable to ceramics, concretes, and rubbers subjected to ageing as cracks are not indiscernible in these materials. This is detailed in the study area of fracture mechanics.

For proper fatigue characterization of a material for a given application, it is necessary to obtain data in a test whose loading mimics the expected cyclic load that will be experienced by the material in the specific application. There are two key fatigue tests, i.e., fully reversed uniaxial (tension-compression) and fully reversed torsional (also called pure torsion) tests. They can be either controlled by the strain at a constant strain or by the stress at a constant stress for identifying the fatigue life. Their responsive principal stress and strain states are addressed herein.

4.1.1 Fully Reversed Uniaxial （Tension-Compression） Fatigue Test

The fully reversed uniaxial condition means that the specimen is under a constant fluctuating load in terms of strain or stress amplitude with a zero mean value, i.e., $\varepsilon_{min} = -\varepsilon_{max}$ or $\sigma_{min} = -\sigma_{max}$. Both stress- and strain-controlled uniaxial fatigue tests have been in use for refereeing the fatigue life of a part under multiaxial loadings in the real world. A schematic drawing of crack nucleation and propagation of a circular cross-section starting from the edge is given in Fig. 4.1.3. The final fracture surface is rough as it is pulled off and the final fractured cross-section is tapered 45° with respect to the pulling direction.

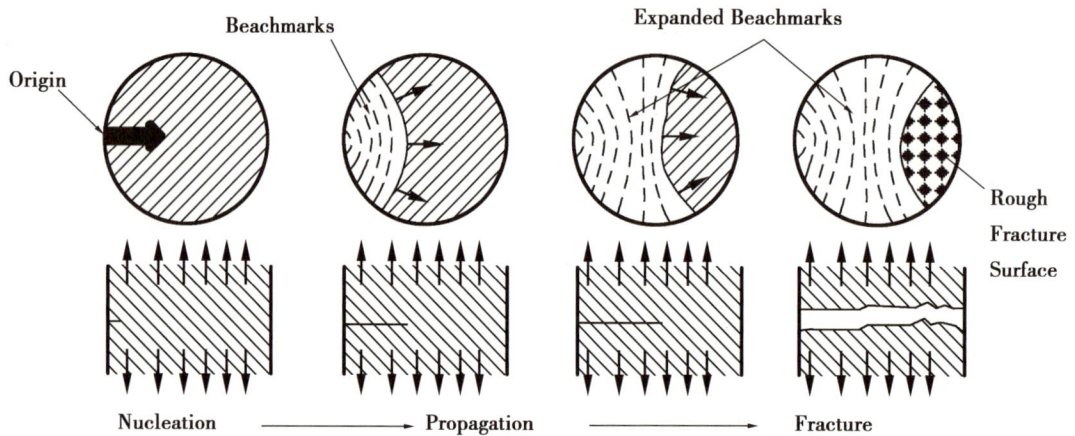

Fig. 4.1.3 Schematic Drawing of Crack Nucleation and Propagation Subjected to Uniaxial Fatigue

Strain-controlled fatigue test results can be used in the formulation of empirical relationships between the cyclic variables of stress, total strain, plastic strain, and fatigue life. They are useful in various areas such as materials research and development, electromechanical design and product performance, process and quality control, and failure analysis. For a fully reversed axial fatigue test controlled by the strain, of which the strain amplitude is ε_{a1}. The principal strains and locating angle θ_ε can be calculated from Eqs. （2.6.24）-（2.6.26）, respectively as

$$\varepsilon_1 = \frac{J_1}{3} + \frac{2}{3}(J_1^2 - 3J_2)^{\frac{1}{2}}\cos\theta_\varepsilon = \varepsilon_{a1} \tag{4.1.1}$$

$$\varepsilon_2 = \frac{J_1}{3} + \frac{2}{3}(J_1^2 - 3J_2)^{\frac{1}{2}}\cos\left(\theta_\varepsilon - \frac{2\pi}{3}\right) = 0 \tag{4.1.2}$$

and $\quad\varepsilon_3 = \frac{J_1}{3} + \frac{2}{3}(J_1^2 - 3J_2)^{\frac{1}{2}}\cos\left(\theta_\varepsilon - \frac{4\pi}{3}\right) = 0 \tag{4.1.3}$

where

$$J_1 = \varepsilon_{xx} + \varepsilon_{yy} + \varepsilon_{zz} = \varepsilon_{a1} \tag{4.1.4}$$

$$J_2 = 0 \tag{4.1.5}$$
$$J_3 = 0 \tag{4.1.6}$$

and $\quad \theta_\varepsilon = \dfrac{1}{3} \cos^{-1} \dfrac{2J_1^3 - 9J_1 J_2 + 27J_3}{2(J_1^2 - 3J_2)^{\frac{3}{2}}} = \dfrac{\cos^{-1}(1)}{3} = 0 \tag{4.1.7}$

Thus, $\quad \varepsilon_1 = \varepsilon_{al}$, $\varepsilon_2 = 0$, $\varepsilon_3 = 0$, and $\theta_\varepsilon = 0$. The mean of the principal strains is

$$\varepsilon_v = \varepsilon_{ave} = \frac{\varepsilon_1 + \varepsilon_2 + \varepsilon_3}{3} = \frac{\varepsilon_{al}}{3} \tag{4.1.8}$$

The mean strain given above is also called the volumetric strain (ε_v) or dilatation. The principal stresses can be calculated from the principal strains using Eqs. (2.6.15)-(2.6.17),

$$\sigma_1 = \frac{E}{(1-2\nu)(1+\nu)} \left[(1-\nu)\varepsilon_1 + \nu\varepsilon_2 + \nu\varepsilon_3 \right] = \frac{E(1-\nu)}{(1-2\nu)(1+\nu)} \varepsilon_{al} \tag{4.1.9}$$

$$\sigma_2 = \frac{E}{(1-2\nu)(1+\nu)} \left[\nu\varepsilon_1 + (1-\nu)\varepsilon_2 + \nu\varepsilon_3 \right] = \frac{E\nu}{(1-2\nu)(1+\nu)} \varepsilon_{al} \tag{4.1.10}$$

and $\quad \sigma_3 = \dfrac{E}{(1-2\nu)(1+\nu)} \left[\nu\varepsilon_1 + \nu\varepsilon_2 + (1-\nu)\varepsilon_3 \right] = \dfrac{E\nu}{(1-2\nu)(1+\nu)} \varepsilon_{al} \tag{4.1.11}$

The mean of the principal stresses is called hydrostatic stress (or hydrostatic pressure if negative) and it is calculated as

$$\sigma_{ave} = \frac{\sigma_1 + \sigma_2 + \sigma_3}{3} = \frac{E}{3(1-2\nu)} \varepsilon_{al} = K\varepsilon_{al} \tag{4.1.12}$$

where K is called bulk modulus, defined as

$$K = \frac{E}{3(1-2\nu)} \tag{4.1.13}$$

The maximum stress fluctuation is then calculated as

$$\Delta\sigma_{max} = \sigma_1 - \sigma_2 = \frac{E}{1+\nu} \varepsilon_{al} \tag{4.1.14}$$

The angle of rotation from the original Cartesian coordinate system to the principal stress plane (i.e., maximum stress range) is

$$\text{and} \quad \theta = \frac{1}{3}\cos^{-1}\left[\frac{2 I_1^3 - 9 I_1 I_2 + 27 I_3}{2 (I_1^2 - 3 I_2)^{\frac{3}{2}}}\right] \neq 0 \tag{4.1.15}$$

where

$$I_1 = \sigma_1 + \sigma_2 + \sigma_3 \tag{4.1.16}$$
$$I_2 = \sigma_1 \sigma_2 + \sigma_2 \sigma_3 + \sigma_3 \sigma_1 \tag{4.1.17}$$
$$I_3 = \sigma_1 \sigma_2 \sigma_3 \tag{4.1.18}$$

Next, consider a fully reversed axial fatigue test controlled by the stress, of which the strain amplitude is ε_{al}. The principal stresses are listed as follows:

$$\sigma_1 = \sigma_{al}, \ \sigma_2 = 0, \ \text{and} \ \sigma_3 = 0 \tag{4.1.19}$$

The mean of the principal stresses is

$$\sigma_{ave} = \frac{\sigma_1 + \sigma_2 + \sigma_3}{3} = \frac{\sigma_{al}}{3} \tag{4.1.20}$$

The maximum stress fluctuation is calculated as

$$\Delta\sigma_{max} = \sigma_1 - \sigma_2 = \sigma_{al} \tag{4.1.21}$$

The principal stress angle is

$$\theta = 0 \tag{4.1.22}$$

The principal strains can be calculated using the principal stresses based on Eqs. (2.6.2) and (2.6.4) as

$$\varepsilon_1 = \frac{\sigma_1 - \nu \sigma_2 - \nu \sigma_3}{E} = \frac{\sigma_{al}}{E} \tag{4.1.23}$$

$$\varepsilon_2 = \frac{\sigma_2 - \nu \sigma_3 - \nu \sigma_1}{E} = \frac{\nu \sigma_{al}}{E} \tag{4.1.24}$$

$$\text{and} \quad \varepsilon_3 = \frac{\sigma_3 - \nu \sigma_1 - \nu \sigma_2}{E} = \frac{\nu \sigma_{al}}{E} \tag{4.1.25}$$

where

$$J_1 = \varepsilon_1 + \varepsilon_2 + \varepsilon_3 = \frac{1+2\nu}{E} \varepsilon_{al} \tag{4.1.26}$$

$$J_2 = \varepsilon_1 \varepsilon_1 + \varepsilon_2 \varepsilon_3 + \varepsilon_3 \varepsilon_1 = \frac{1+2\nu^2}{E^2} \varepsilon_{al}^2 \tag{4.1.27}$$

$$J_3 = \varepsilon_1 \, \varepsilon_2 \, \varepsilon_3 = \frac{\nu^2}{E^3} \, \varepsilon_{al}^3 \tag{4.1.28}$$

and $\quad \theta_\varepsilon = \frac{1}{3} \, \cos^{-1} \left[\dfrac{2 \, J_1^3 - 9 \, J_1 \, J_2 + 27 \, J_3}{2 \, (J_1^2 - 3 \, J_2)^{\frac{3}{2}}} \right] \neq 0 \tag{4.1.29}$

The mean of the principal strains is thus

$$\varepsilon_v = \varepsilon_{ave} = \frac{\varepsilon_1 + \varepsilon_2 + \varepsilon_3}{3} = \frac{3(1 - 2\nu)}{E} \varepsilon_{al} = \frac{\varepsilon_{al}}{\dfrac{E}{3\,(1 - 2\nu)}} = \frac{\varepsilon_{al}}{K} \tag{4.1.30}$$

of which K is the bulk modulus.

4.1.2   Fully Reversed Torsional Fatigue Test

A torsion fatigue test rig, that consists of a base, hydraulic rotary actuator, and torque cell, can be constructed to experimentally characterize the fatigue behavior of materials that fail due to oscillating shear stresses. Tests are usually carried out in torque-controlled mode and the prescribed torque amplitudes are controlled through commercial software. For a fully reversed pure torsion fatigue test controlled by the shear strain γ_{xy}, of which the strain amplitude is γ_{al}. The principal strains and locating angle θ_ε can be calculated from Eqs. (2.6.24)-(2.6.26). Strain invariants and principal direction of strain are, respectively

$$J_1 = \varepsilon_{xx} + \varepsilon_{yy} + \varepsilon_{zz} = 0 \tag{4.1.31}$$

$$J_2 = \varepsilon_{xx} \, \varepsilon_{yy} + \varepsilon_{yy} \, \varepsilon_{zz} + \varepsilon_{zz} \, \varepsilon_{xx} - \varepsilon_{xy}^2 - \varepsilon_{yz}^2 - \varepsilon_{zx}^2 = \varepsilon_{xy}^2 = \frac{1}{4} \, \gamma_{al}^2 \tag{4.1.32}$$

$$J_3 = \varepsilon_{xx} \, \varepsilon_{yy} \, \varepsilon_{zz} - \varepsilon_{xx} \, \varepsilon_{yz}^2 - \varepsilon_{yy} \, \varepsilon_{zx}^2 - \varepsilon_{zz} \, \varepsilon_{xy}^2 + 2\varepsilon_{xy} \, \varepsilon_{yz} \, \varepsilon_{zx} = 0 \tag{4.1.33}$$

and $\quad \theta_\varepsilon = \frac{1}{3} \cos^{-1} \dfrac{2 \, J_1^3 - 9 \, J_1 \, J_2 + 27 \, J_3}{2(J_1^2 - 3 \, J_2)^{\frac{3}{2}}} = 0 \tag{4.1.34}$

Hence $\quad \varepsilon_1 = 0, \; \varepsilon_2 = 0, \; \varepsilon_3 = 0, \; \text{and} \; \theta_\varepsilon = 0. \tag{4.1.35}$

The mean of the principal strains is thus

$$\varepsilon_v = \varepsilon_{ave} = \frac{\varepsilon_1 + \varepsilon_2 + \varepsilon_3}{3} = 0 \tag{4.1.36}$$

The principal stresses can be calculated using Eqs. (2.6.15)-(2.6.17),

$$\sigma_1 = \frac{E}{(1-2\nu)(1+\nu)}\left[(1-\nu)\,\varepsilon_1 + \nu\,\varepsilon_2 + \nu\,\varepsilon_3\right] = 0 \tag{4.1.37}$$

$$\sigma_2 = \frac{E}{(1-2\nu)(1+\nu)}\left[\nu\,\varepsilon_1 + (1-\nu)\,\varepsilon_2 + \nu\,\varepsilon_3\right] = 0 \tag{4.1.38}$$

and $\quad \sigma_3 = \dfrac{E}{(1-2\nu)(1+\nu)}\left[\nu\,\varepsilon_1 + \nu\,\varepsilon_2 + (1-\nu)\,\varepsilon_3\right] = 0 \tag{4.1.39}$

The mean stress of the principal stresses is

$$\sigma_{ave} = \frac{\sigma_1 + \sigma_2 + \sigma_3}{3} = 0 \tag{4.1.40}$$

The above equation means that no hydrostatic effect is generated from shearing. The maximum stress fluctuation is then calculated as

$$\Delta\sigma_{max} = \sigma_1 - \sigma_2 = 0 \tag{4.1.41}$$

The angle of rotation from the original Cartesian coordinate system to the principal stress plane (i.e., maximum stress range) is then

and $\quad \theta = \dfrac{1}{3}\cos^{-1}\left[\dfrac{2\,I_1^3 - 9\,I_1\,I_2 + 27\,I_3}{2(I_1^2 - 3\,I_2)^{\frac{3}{2}}}\right] = 0 \tag{4.1.42}$

Since

$$I_1 = \sigma_1 + \sigma_2 + \sigma_3 = 0 \tag{4.1.43}$$
$$I_2 = \sigma_1\,\sigma_2 + \sigma_2\,\sigma_3 + \sigma_3\,\sigma_1 = 0 \tag{4.1.44}$$

and $\quad I_3 = \sigma_1\,\sigma_2\,\sigma_3 = 0 \tag{4.1.45}$

4.1.3 Influence of Hydrostatic Stress on Fatigue Life

As described by the von Mises failure criterion, the hydrostatic stress, i.e., $(\sigma_1 + \sigma_2 + \sigma_3)/3$, has no impact on the yield strength. It means that the hydrostatic stress has no influence on the stress flow at all in the elastoplastic range. This is evidenced by the fact that no discernible increase or reduction in fatigue life is observed by the superposition of the hydrostatic stress under a fully reversed loading [Ohji et al.]. In other words, the von Mises stress is a valid equivalent stress for presenting a general case under multiaxial fatigue loadings in a quasi-static condition. However, there is a significant increase of fatigue life of a part under zero-to-tension loading as shown in Fig. 4.1.4 [Sakane & Itoh]. The influence is also evidenced by the work done by [Cu & Chen

2018]. Based on physical tests, there are three prominent findings [Ohji et al.] [Cristalli et al. 2017], given below:

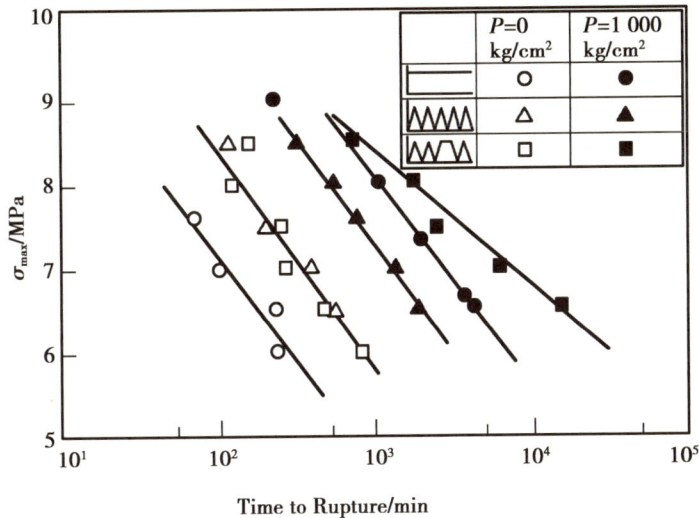

Fig. 4.1.4   Creep-Fatigue Life of Pure Copper Plate with a 0.5 mm Center Hole under Hydrostatic Pressure (*P*=Hydrostatic Pressure) **at 270 ℃** [Onamia & Sarane] [Sarane & Itoh]

(a) On fatigue under zero-to-tension loading: The presence of hydrostatic stress will reduce influence of the triaxial stress state and suppress void nucleation and thus result in an increase in the tensile or torsional ductility [Ohji et al.]. This is important when applying the fatigue theory to mechanical springs, which may work totally under a hydrostatic stress in their service lifetime.

(b) On creep-fatigue under zero-to-tension loading: The presence of hydrostatic stress changes the slope of the stress-life curve when creep-fatigue loading is exerted to pure copper at an elevated temperature under zero-to-tension loading. This phenomenon is validated by [Cristalli et al.] when creep-fatigue loading is applied to P91 steel at a high temperature under zero-to-tension loading.

(c) On creep-fatigue under zero-to-compression loading: The presence of hydrostatic pressure also has a great influence on the creep-fatigue life of P91 steel at a high temperature under zero-to-compression loading [Cristalli et al.]. It elongates the creep-fatigue life.

4.1.4   Procedure for Fatigue Analysis

The general procedure for fatigue life prediction, as shown in Fig. 4.1.5, based on strain-life or stress-life analysis in regard of crack nucleation consists of the following steps:

```
┌─────────────────────────────────────┐   ┌─────────────────────────────────────┐
│ Material properties：                │   │ Loading：                           │
│ 1. Cyclic stress-strain             │   │ 1. Uniaxial, pure shear, or         │
│ 2. Creep/relaxation, oxidation,     │   │    multaxial?                       │
│    corrosion, etc.                  │   │ 2. Mechnaical loads?                │
│ 3. Environmental conditions         │   │ 3. Temperature?                     │
│ 4. Parameters of fatigue predictors │   │ 4. Load risers, e.g. roughness &    │
│    (e.g. Morrow's)                  │   │    notches?                         │
└─────────────────────────────────────┘   └─────────────────────────────────────┘
```

Applied loads (force, strain, stress, temperature, displacement, etc.)

Compute stresses and strains：
A. Transient thermomechanical stress-strain data,
   if to be analyzed in time domain.
   Tools: FEA, closed-form solution, strain
   gaging, etc.
B. Spectral analysis, if to be analyzed in
   frequency domain.
   Tools: FEA, spectral density function

Locating the critical plane (in-phase)
or critical planes (out-of-phase)

Compute fatigue damage

Ranflow counting of fatigue cycles/
reversals (or other similar methods)
based on strain (stress) amplitude,
mean strain (stress), strain energy,
maximun shear strain, etc.

Progressive damage parameters, e.g. stiffness, strength,
creep, oxidation, and corrosion degradations

Fatigue life prediction or remaining life prediction

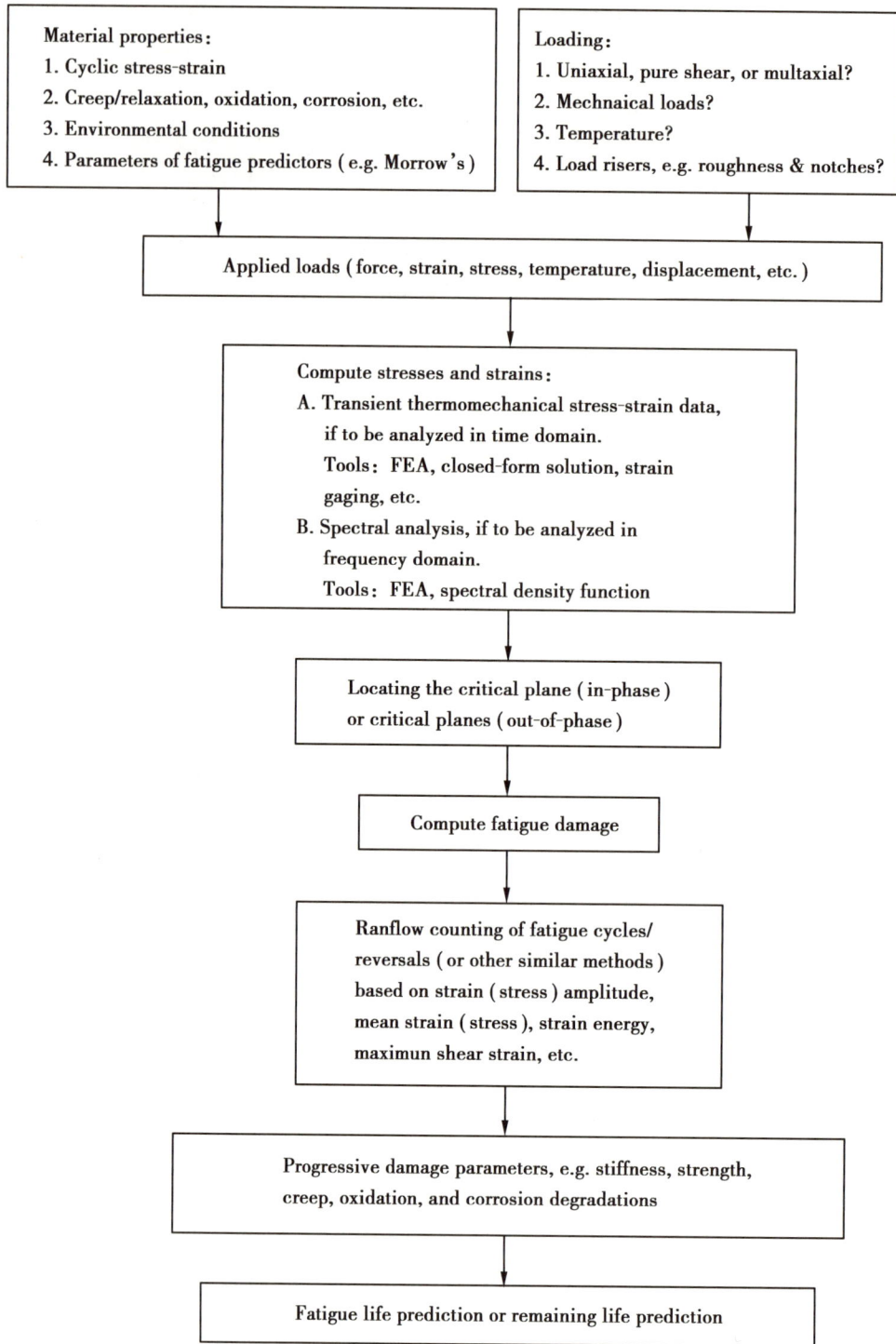

Fig. 4.1.5　Flowchart for Fatigue Life Prediction

(a) Defining applied loadings (i.e., stresses, strains, temperatures, corrosives, etc.) in time history or power spectral density.

(b) Identifying life predictors.

(c) Selecting material properties.

(d) Computing the stresses and strains of concern (e.g. FEA and experimental mechanics).

(e) Calculating fatigue damage.

(f) Searching for possible failure planes.

(g) Developing progressive damage parameter if the loading sequence is important.

(h) Doing the product life prediction or predicting the remaining life.

4.2   *S-N* (Stress-Life) Approach Based on Fatigue Strength

Fatigue-cracking results from cyclic stresses that are below the ultimate tensile stress, or even below the yield stress, of the material. The ratio of the fatigue limit to the tensile strength is called the fatigue ratio. Two distinct rupture zones are evident in a fatigue-failed cross-section. One is the fatigue zone and the other is the fracture zone. The fatigue zone is the smooth and wavy area of the crack propagation. As being over-stressed, the area of final failure is due to instantaneous fracture, which yields the material ductility, loading type, and loading direction. The relative size of the fracture zone compared with the fatigue zone is related to the degree of overstress applied to the structure.

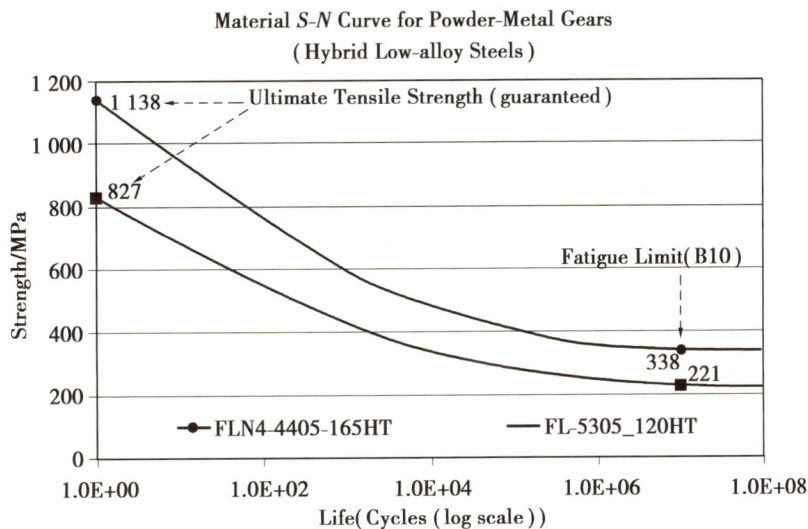

Fig. 4.2.1   *S-N* Curves of Powder Steel Gears with No Mean Stress

Fatigue life, N, is the number of stress cycles of a specified character that a specimen sustains before failure of a specified nature occurs. Fatigue strength is the "knee point" of an *S-N* (stress versus number of cycles) curve in steel, as illustrated in Fig. 4.2.1. Most metals exhibit distinct fatigue strength. Some materials don't have clear fatigue strength as their *S-N* curves have no "knee point". However, the "conceptual fatigue strength" for designing automotive components made of such materials may be taken at 10^8 cycles (2×10^8 reversals) or more depending on applications. A simple theory for fatigue analysis is to define the fatigue damage function, $G(\sigma_a)$, in terms of stress amplitude σ_a,

$$G(\sigma_a) = \frac{\sigma_a}{\sigma_f} < 100\% \tag{4.2.1}$$

where

σ_f: Fatigue strength, also called endurance limit;

σ_a: Stress amplitude.

Stress amplitude σ_a gets to be smaller than fatigue limit σ_f in order to guarantee a forever fatigue life according to Eq. (4.2.1). When subject to variable-amplitude loading, only those cycles exceeding a certain stress-peak threshold will contribute to fatigue damage. The threshold is usually taken at a stress level lower than the fatigue strength, e.g. 40% of the ultimate tensile strength for metals is suggested by researchers.

General speaking, the stress amplitude at 10^6 cycles without mean stress is reckoned to be the fatigue strength for alloy steels, which can be obtained [Roessle & Fatemi] from the following regression models as a function of Brinell hardness (H_B):

$\sigma_f(\text{MPa}) @ 10^6$ Cycles (Normalized Alloy Steels)
$$= 0.18H_B + 0.5348C + 2.183\text{Mn} - 20.53\text{S} - 0.464\text{Si} + 13.37\text{Ni} -$$
$$0.5656\text{Cr} - 0.3804\text{Mo} + 36.1 \qquad (\pm 4.6) \tag{4.2.2}$$

and $\quad \sigma_f(\text{MPa}) @ 10^6$ Cycles (Quench and Tempered Alloy Steels)
$$= 2.52H_B + 6.744C + 3.886\text{Mn} - 40.62\text{S} - 12.25\text{Si} + 3.55\text{Ni} + 2.101\text{Cr} -$$
$$22.6\text{Mo} + 5.702\text{Al} - 15.9\text{V} - 476.48 \qquad (\pm 27.94) \tag{4.2.3}$$

4.3　Influence of Mean Stress on Fatigue Life

A part such as an electro-mechanical relay or mechanical spring may be preloaded to a certain stress level that is never removed during the application lifetime of the part. The part works between the maximum stress level and the preload set as installed. Besides the stress amplitude, the mean stress is another decisive factor on the fatigue life. The mean stress (σ_m) is the average level of a constant amplitude cyclic loading, and the stress amplitude (σ_a) is the variation about this mean. The amplitude is nominally taken at half of the overall stress range $\Delta\sigma$. The maximum stress, minimum stress, and load ratio of a fatigue test are then defined as shown in Fig. 4.3.1, respectively

$$\sigma_{max} = \sigma_m + \sigma_a \quad (\text{Maximum stress}) \tag{4.3.1}$$

$$\sigma_{min} = \sigma_m - \sigma_a \quad (\text{Minimum stress}) \tag{4.3.2}$$

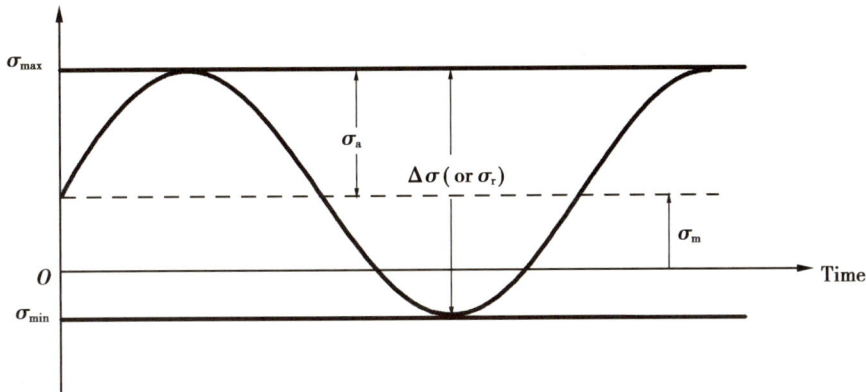

Fig. 4.3.1   Cyclic Loadings

When the vibration amplitude is fixed, a single stress ratio (also called load ratio) and a single fluctuation can be used to represent the entire process. Stress ratio is defined as the ratio of the applied minimum stress to maximum stress as

$$\text{and} \quad R = \frac{\sigma_{min}}{\sigma_{max}} \quad (\text{Stress ratio or load ratio}) \qquad (4.3.3)$$

Note that $R = -1$ is the fully reversed tension-compression fatigue test for a normal load of constant amplitude and zero mean normal stress. The fatigue limit of material is generally defined at $R = -1$, if not noted down otherwise. The following relationships can be derived easily from Eqs. (4.3.1)-(4.3.3),

$$\sigma_a = \frac{1}{2}(\sigma_{max} - \sigma_{min}) = \frac{1}{2}\sigma_{max}(1 - R) \qquad (4.3.4)$$

$$\sigma_m = \frac{1}{2}(\sigma_{max} + \sigma_{min}) = \frac{1}{2}\sigma_{max}(1 + R) \qquad (4.3.5)$$

Stress fluctuation is defined as the ratio of the stress amplitude to the mean stress as

$$A = \frac{\sigma_a}{\sigma_m} \qquad (4.3.6)$$

4.3.1   Metals

The next criterion of fatigue analysis is to include the mean stress effect, other than Eq. (4.2.1). The fatigue damage function is then defined in terms of both mean stress σ_m and stress amplitude σ_a such that $G(\sigma_a, \sigma_m)$ has to be smaller than 100% to guarantee a forever fatigue life,

$$G(\sigma_a, \sigma_m) = \frac{\sigma_a}{\sigma_f} + \left(\frac{\sigma_m}{\sigma_{uts}}\right)^\alpha < 100\% \qquad (4.3.7)$$

where

σ_f: Fatigue strength, also called endurance limit;

σ_{uts}: Ultimate tensile strength;

α: Exponent.

Eq. (4.3.6) is defined for uniaxial loadings. However, values of σ_m and σ_a based on von Mises stress can be applied directly to the above equation as the first approximation to multiaxial loadings, although they are supposed to be derived from multiaxial failure tensors. The suitable value of exponent α depends on the material type and ductility,

(a) If $\alpha = 1$, Eq. (4.3.6) is called Goodman equation. Although simple, the Goodman equation appears to be a promising equation for fatigue life prediction of some metals. Nevertheless, the Goodman relationship gives poor results, usually being excessively conservative for tensile mean stresses, but not conservative for the limited data available at compressive mean stresses.

(b) If $\alpha = 2$, Eq. (4.3.6) is called Gerber parabolic equation, which has been traditionally used for strength-controlled materials under high cycle fatigue tests.

4.3.2 Plastics

Instead of the Goodman and Geber relations, a parabolic equation is proposed by [Oka et al.] on the fatigue life prediction of engineering plastics reinforced with short fibers randomly and other ductile material such as ductile iron castings. Under cyclic loading with a high mean stress, creep prevails as it contributes to ratcheting deformation of plastics reinforced with short fibers randomly as

$$O(\sigma_a, \sigma_m) = \frac{\sigma_a}{\sigma_f} + \left(\frac{\sigma_m}{\sigma_{creep}}\right)^\alpha < 100\% \qquad (4.3.8)$$

where

σ_{creep}: Creep rupture strength;

α: Exponent, while $\alpha = 2$ for PBT reinforced with short fibers randomly [Oka et al.].

The above equation is proven to be valid for engineering plastics randomly reinforced with short glass fibers [Oka et al.]. The creep rupture strength (σ_{creep}) is estimated at the rupture of material under a continuously applied constant stress at a point, which eventually leads to fracture due to creep. It stays below the tensile strength. Fatigue strengths for most plastics fall between 20% and 30% of their corresponding ultimate tensile strengths respectively. Fatigue strength decreases at an elevated temperature, at a higher loading frequency, and with a higher content of moisture [Brockway and Martin], yet to be explored quantitatively with regard to individual plastics.

Creep of plastics may be worse if less crystallinity is developed or more voids are embedded in during the injection molding process. Mold temperature, compression pressure, and timing are all significant contributors. Exponent α in Eq. (4.3.8) varies accordingly.

4.4   Factors Affecting Fatigue Strength

Variability in fatigue life has ranged from almost a factor of one to over several orders of magnitude for a given test or service condition. For a given molecular (metallurgical) structure, surface roughness, stress concentration, temperature, vibration frequency, residual stress, oxidation, and corrosion can affect the propensity to fatigue, in addition to mean stress and stress amplitude. Phase transformation at the crack tip may occur. All in all, the fatigue strength obtained from test specimens under perfect physical conditions, denoted by Se herein, has to be modified accordingly, and lowered mostly. The modified fatigue strength (σ'_f) has to be used for estimating the fatigue life of a structural component. The impact function of mechanical fatigue strength-reduction factors is given here as a general guideline as follows:

$$\sigma'_f = f(K_S, K_Z, K_R, K_f, K_h) \sigma_f \tag{4.4.1}$$

where

σ_f: Ideal fatigue strength or ideal endurance limit;

K_S: Surface factor;

K_Z: Size factor;

K_R: Residual stress factor;

K_f: Fatigue notch factor;

K_h: Treatment factor such as heat treatment.

Individual effects and interactions among these strength-reduction factors in $f(K_S, K_Z, K_R, K_f, K_h)$ are yet to be discovered. For the purpose of reference, though the following equation is generally employed to explain their engineering influences

$$f(K_S, K_Z, K_R, K_f, K_h) = K_S \times K_Z \times K_R \times K_f \times K_h \tag{4.4.1a}$$

4.4.1 K_S(Surface Factor, Including Surface Roughness)

The maximum stress usually occurs at the outer surface in response to common types of loading such as bending and torsion. Surface roughness is important to fatigue strength by default. Fretting and wear on the part's surface will shorten an applicable fatigue life. Experimental tests were conducted on SAE 3130 steel subject to a fully reversed stress amplitude of 655 MPa ($R = -1$) to understand the effects of finish operations by [Fluck]. The results are given as follows:

Finish Operation	Surface Roughness	Fatigue Life (Median)
Lathe-formed	2.67 μm	2.4×10^4 Cycles
Partially Hand-Polished	0.15 μm	9.1×10^4 Cycles
Hand Polished	0.13 μm	1.37×10^5 Cycles
Ground	0.18 μm	2.17×10^5 Cycles
Ground and Polished	0.05 μm	2.34×10^5 Cycles
Super-finished	0.18 μm	2.12×10^5 Cycles

In light of the table given above, the surface roughness due to the machining process has a significant influence on the part's fatigue life. The following equation can be used for estimating the surface factor to modify the fatigue limit of steel subject to different operations:

$$K_S = \alpha \,|\, \sigma_{us} \,|^{\beta} \qquad (4.4.2)$$

where
Forged: $\alpha = 272$ and $\beta = -0.995$;
Ground: $\alpha = 1.58$ and $\beta = -0.085$;
Hot-rolled: $\alpha = 57.7$ and $\beta = -0.718$;
Machined: $\alpha = 4.51$ and $\beta = -0.265$;
σ_{us}: Ultimate strength, which can be σ_{uts} or σ_{ucs} according to the type of loading.

4.4.2 K_Z (Size Factor)

The larger a part is, the more is its material imperfection. In other words, a large volume of material under stress is of greater likelihood to encounter potential microstructural defects. Based on experiments done on alloy steels under axial tension-compression loading, it was found that the diameter of a steel rod (d) affects the fatigue life as follows:

$$
\begin{cases}
K_Z = 1 & \text{if} \quad d < 10 \text{ mm} \\
K_Z = 0.9 & \text{if} \quad 10 \text{ mm} < d < 50 \text{ mm} \\
K_Z = 1 - \dfrac{d}{380} & \text{if} \quad 50 \text{ mm} < d < 230 \text{ mm}
\end{cases}
$$

$$(4.4.3a)$$
$$(4.4.3b)$$
$$(4.4.3c)$$

Note that the size of most fastening bolts for a sedan falls between 6 mm and 12 mm.

4.4.3 K_R (Residual Stress Factor)

Operations such as shot peening and cold rolling that produce compressive residual stresses at the surface have a positive impact on the fatigue life; vice versa such as residual stresses in tension induced by forging, stamping, and grinding.

Shot peening is a cold working process used to produce a compressive residual stress layer and modify mechanical properties of metals. It entails impacting a surface with shot (round metallic, glass, ceramic particles, or cavitation bubble collapse) with force sufficient to create plastic deformation. Material with high yield strength is found to respond better to shot peening for improvement in fatigue life, especially for high cycle fatigue situation. This is because a high residual stress level can be maintained in these materials. Besides, the higher value of strain hardening exponent appears to have a favorable effect. Shot peening is effective for low-stressed high-cycle fatigue components (stress amplitude < 60% of yield stress) and low temperature applications (temperature < 20% of melting temperatures in ℃ for steel and aluminum). The lower the stress level the smaller the shot-peening effect is, if corrosion is taken into consideration. In the very high cycle regime shot-peening effect cannot be expected when corrosion and corrosion pit initiate easily even compressive residual stress remains on surface layer of the specimen. The fatigue limit usually increases by 10%-20% for high strength alloys steels due to shot peening, especially spring steels.

Peening by cavitation bubble collapse, called cavitation shotless peening (CSP), can be used to improve the fatigue strength just in the same way as shot peening. The peened surface by CSP is not as rough as the shot-peened ones. The fatigue limit of ASTM 356.0 aluminum alloy has been improved by 56% using CSP, but by 20% by ball-shot peening [Soyama et al.].

Deep rolling is a process that utilizes cold working and non-uniform plastic strain to control surface hardness and residual stress to result in parts with improved fatigue resistance. Deep rolling also can be used to improve surface finish and radial profiles in fillets. Crankshafts, axle shafts, and fasteners have been the primary products of interest for the application of deep rolling. Assume that σ_e is the cold-rolled forged part. The quantitative effect of surface treatments on the endurance limit for steels is given as follows:

Finish	Shot-peened	Cold-rolled	Nitrided
Cast	$1.4\ \sigma_e$	$1.0\ \sigma_e$	$2.0\ \sigma_e$
Forged	$2.0\ \sigma_e$	$1.0\ \sigma_e$	$2.0\ \sigma_e$
Ground	$1.2\ \sigma_e$	$1.0\ \sigma_e$	$2.0\ \sigma_e$
Hot-rolled	$1.4\ \sigma_e$	Not Applicable	$2.0\ \sigma_e$
Machined	$1.3\ \sigma_e$	$1.7\ \sigma_e$	$2.0\ \sigma_e$
Polished	$1.15\ \sigma_e$	$1.5\ \sigma_e$	$2.0\ \sigma_e$
Ground	$1.2\ \sigma_e$	$1.0\ \sigma_e$	$2.0\ \sigma_e$

Laser peening provides significant fatigue life extension through shock wave mechanics which plastically deform the surface of the metal component changing the material properties. Shot peening imparts residual compressive stresses approximately 0.13 mm deep, while laser peening imparts residual compressive stresses from 1.0-2.5 mm deep [Cao etc.].

4.4.4 K_f(Fatigue Notch Factor)

The fatigue notch factor is dependent not only upon the component geometry, but also on the material properties and the mode of loading. For example, Ti-alloys are not so sensitive to notch as steels. Local stress-strain behavior may be determined by the following methods:

(a) Strain gage measurements.
(b) Finite element analysis.
(c) Simplified analysis using stress concentration factor K_t or fatigue notch factor K_f.

Effect of stress concentration on fatigue is affected by the severity of stress concentration. The notch strain amplitude resulting from the dynamic cyclic equation is then used in the strain-life equation to calculate the fatigue life. The degree of difference between K_f and K_t is of practical interest to engineers, and is frequently expressed using the notch sensitivity, q, given as [Stephens at al.]

$$K_f = 1 + \frac{K_t - 1}{1 + \dfrac{a}{r}} \qquad (4.4.4)$$

where
K_f: Fatigue notch factor;
K_t: Stress concentration factor;
r (mm): Notch root radius;
a: Material constant.

The material constant, a, is obtained from the following empirical relation originally developed for wrought steel [SAE Fatigue Design Handbook]:

$$a = 0.0254 \left(\frac{2070}{\sigma_{uts}} \right)^{1.8} \qquad (4.4.5)$$

where σ_{uts} is the ultimate strength in MPa. If $r \gg a$, then $K_f = K_t$, i.e., the material is fully notch sensitive. Notch sensitivity reduces with increasing ultimate tensile strength as shown in Eq. (4.4.5), as slip occurrence is less in stronger materials.

$K_t = 2.045$ may be taken as the first approximation corresponding to a single spherical hole in an infinite body, such as an isolated cast porosity [Hardin & Beckermann].

4.4.5　K_h (Treatment such as Heat Treatment)

Carburizing and nitriding produce higher mechanical strength and hardness on the surface and thus improves fatigue life, following the increase of ultimate strength.

4.4.6　Temperature

The influence of temperature on fatigue strength is expected and should be identified and dealt with independently since it cannot be presented as a simple strength modifier. In general, the part stiffness is softened at a high temperature and the fatigue life is reduced.

The fatigue life of a part may be worsened by cracks propagating in the brittle state at a low temperature, as more rapidly than propagating in the ductile state at room temperature.

4.4.7　Loading

Crack surfaces, that grow through the grain structure, are generally irregular shaped at the microscopic level. This results in interlocking between crack surfaces and the related frictional resistance during cyclic shear loading. On the other hand, a tensile stress perpendicular to the crack surfaces tends to separate the crack surfaces and reduces the interlocking effect and frictional resistance. Thus, another key factor that has a great influence on the fatigue life is the type of loading, namely strain amplitude, stress amplitude, load ratio, stress type (normal or shear), load phase (proportional or non-proportional), strain rate including frequency of vibration, loading wave form, and loading sequence.

4.4.8　Harsh Environment

Harsh environments such as corrosion and oxidization may speed up the fatigue, but they usually change the material itself rather than only the fatigue strength of the neat material originally.

4.5　$\varepsilon\text{-}N$ (Strain-Life) Approach

Equations given in Section 4.3 may be used for checking if the material under a certain loading has infinitive life or not. Yet the life expectancy of a material is not infinitive, it may be estimated using its strain-life cycles, known as $\varepsilon\text{-}N$ curves where strain ε may be elastic and/or elastoplastic. Recently strain-life approach has been widely used in product development for calculation of number of reversals to crack initiation, denoted by $2N_f$ as a general practice, especially in the automotive industry. The strain-life approach measures life in terms of reversals,

$2N_f$, whereas the stress-life method tends to use cycles (N_f). A reversal is one-half of a full cycle and two reversals of the same magnitude to make a cycle.

At long fatigue lives the fatigue strength σ'_f/E controls the fatigue performance and the strain-life and stress-life approaches may give essentially similar results. For short fatigue lives, plastic strain is dominant and fatigue ductility (ε'_f) controls the fatigue performance. The optimum material is therefore the one that has both high ductility and high strength. Unfortunately, there is usually a trade-off between these two properties and a compromise must be made for the expected load or strain conditions being considered.

4.5.1 Persistent Slip Bands

The fatigue behavior of material is described using the dislocation theory as part of ε-N approach. Dislocations that accumulate near stressed surface form certain structures called persistent slip bands (PSB) after a certain number of loading cycles. PSB are areas that rise above (extrusion) or fall below (intrusion) the surface of the component due to movement of material along slip planes. This phenomenon entails tiny curvatures and discontinuities upon the surface and serves as stress risers where tiny cracks initiate. These tiny cracks that may be detected by Magnaflux or X-ray inspection nucleate along planes of high shear stress, which is often aligned 45° to the loading direction. With continued cyclic loading, the growth of dominant cracks will continue until the remaining uncracked section of the component can no longer support the load. At this point, the fracture toughness is once exceeded and the remaining cross-section of the material will experience a rapid fracture.

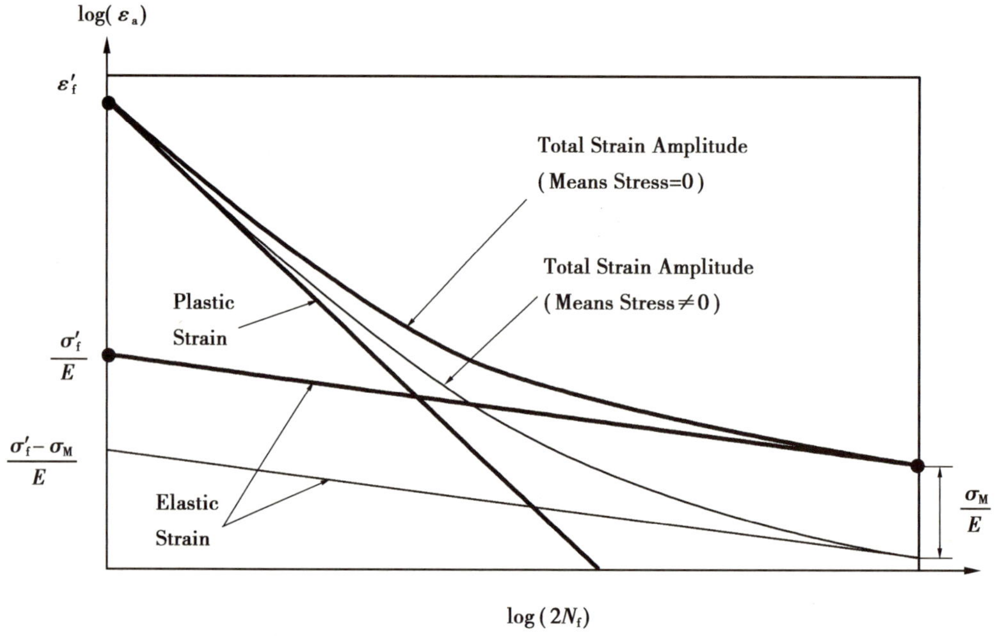

Fig. 4.5.1 Influence of Strain Amplitude and Mean Stress on the Fatigue Life

4.5.2   Manson-Coffin Equation for Fully Reversed Uniaxial (Tension-Compression) Test

Empirical Manson-Coffin equation has been in practice for fatigue life prediction for metals under moderate and high life cycles at room temperature with both elastic and plastic strains for years. As an empirical equation by curve fitting, it is given here without any derivation that

$$\varepsilon_a = \frac{\sigma'_f}{E}(2N_f)^b + \varepsilon'_f(2N_f)^c \tag{4.5.1}$$

and

$$\varepsilon_a = \varepsilon_a^e + \varepsilon_a^p \tag{4.5.2}$$

where

$2N_f$: Number of reversals, while 1 life cycle = 2 reversals of the same amplitude;

b: Fatigue strength exponent, negative slope of the log-log curve in the elastic range;

c: Fatigue strain exponent; negative slope of the log-log curve with plastic strain mainly;

σ'_f: Fatigue strength coefficient, stress at which the material fails in one cycle;

E: Modulus of elasticity (Young's modulus);

ε'_f: Fatigue strain coefficient, i.e., strain, at which the material fails in one cycle;

ε_a: Amplitude of the fluctuating strain, not the total fluctuation;

ε_a^e: Amplitude of the fluctuating elastic strain;

ε_a^p: Amplitude of the fluctuating plastic strain.

Note that σ'_f, ε'_f, b, and c are to be determined from dynamic cycling tests under zero mean stress ($R = -1$), i.e., fully reversed tests. Strain-life curves of some sigh-end carbon steels are presented in Fig. 4.5.2. If the Brinell hardness (H_B) is a known material parameter, Eq. (4.5.1) can be approximated by a linear regression model [Roessle & Fetimi] for steel as

$$\varepsilon_a = \frac{4.25H_B + 225}{E}(2N_f)^{-0.09} + \frac{0.32H_B^2 - 487\,H_B + 191000}{E}(2N_f)^{-0.56} \tag{4.5.3}$$

The von Mises strain (stress), an equivalent flow strain (stress) based on the maximum octahedral shearing stress, may be used for calculating the equivalent plastic strain $\varepsilon_{a,eq}^p$ instead of ε_a^p in Eq. (4.5.2), if a multiaxial fatigue is in focus. Signed von Mises strain and stress are used when the material is in tension or compression, respectively,

$$\text{Signed } \sigma_{eq} = \frac{\sigma_1}{|\sigma_1|}\sigma_{eq} \tag{4.5.4}$$

and

$$\text{Signed } \varepsilon_{eq} = \frac{\varepsilon_1}{|\varepsilon_1|}\varepsilon_{eq} \tag{4.5.5}$$

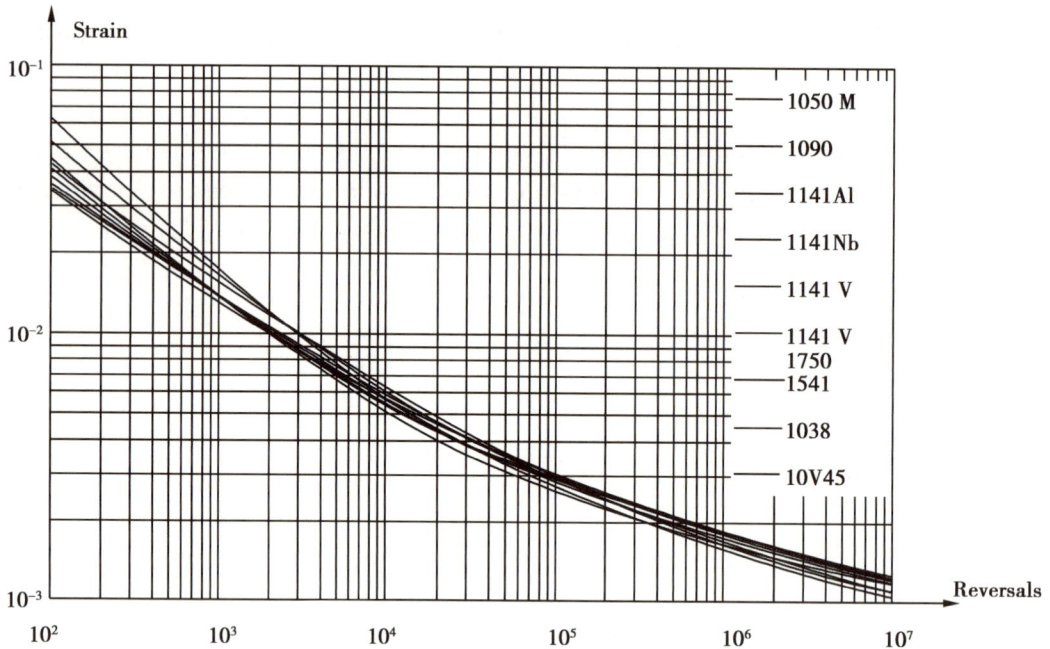

Fig. 4.5.2   Strain-Life Curves of High-End Carbon Steels

4.5.3   Manson-Coffin Equation for Pure-Torsion Test

Eq. (4.5.1) is applicable to a fully reversed uniaxial (tension-compression) fatigue analysis, its counterpart for pure-torsion fatigue is given as follows:

$$\gamma_a = \frac{\tau_f'}{G}(2N_f)^{b_\gamma} + \gamma_f'(2N_f)^{c_\gamma} \qquad (4.5.6)$$

and $\gamma_a = \gamma_a^e + \gamma_a^p$ 　　　　　　　　　　　　　　　　　　　(4.5.7)

where

$2N_f$: Number of reversals, while 1 life cycle = 2 reversals of the same amplitude;

b_γ: Fatigue shear strength exponent in the elastic range;

c_γ: Fatigue shear strain exponent associated with plastic strain;

τ_f': Fatigue strength coefficient, shear stress at which the material fails in one cycle;

G: Modulus of elasticity (Shear modulus) and $G = 1/[2(1+\nu)]$;

γ_f': Fatigue shear strain coefficient, i.e., shear strain, at which the material fails in 1 cycle;

γ_a: Amplitude of the fluctuating shear strain, not the total fluctuation;

γ_a^e: Amplitude of the fluctuating elastic shear strain;

γ_a^p: Amplitude of the fluctuating plastic shear strain.

The γ-N curve is mainly recommended to model fatigue damage in materials that are sensitive to shear strains with a zero mean shear strain. Since most fatigue data are presented on the basis on

ε-N curves and data for b_γ & c_γ are not available for immediate need, the following equation can be a convenient substitute for Eq. (4.5.6)

$$\gamma_a = \frac{2(1 + \nu)\, \sigma'_f}{\sqrt{3}\, E}(2N_f)^b + \sqrt{3}\, \gamma'_f(2N_f)^c \qquad (4.5.8)$$

where

$$\tau'_f \approx \frac{\sigma'_f}{\sqrt{3}}$$

$$\gamma'_f \approx \sqrt{3}\, \varepsilon'_f$$

$$b \approx b_\gamma$$

and $\quad c \approx c_\gamma$

4.5.4 Low Cycle Fatigue (LCF)

Low cycle fatigue is referred to situations where the fatigue failure occurs at a life less than 10^4 loading cycles. After the elastic term is dropped from Eq. (4.5.1), the number of loading cycles may be rewritten in another form as

$$2N_f = \left(\frac{\varepsilon^p_a}{\varepsilon'_f}\right)^{\frac{1}{c}} \qquad (4.5.9)$$

of which ε^p_a is the amplitude of fluctuating plastic flow strain or equivalent plastic flow strain. Note that the above strain-life equation was independently found by Manson and Coffin in the 1950s.

In the range of low cycle fatigue life prediction, [Xue] presented a modified Manson-Coffin equation dropping the contribution from elastic deformation while adding an exponential complication as

$$\log \varepsilon^p_a = -m^{-1}\left(\log 2N_f + \log \frac{2\lambda}{e^\lambda - 1}\right)\log \varepsilon'_f \qquad (4.5.10)$$

The additional parameter λ represents the nonlinear exponential form in the range of low fatigue life. Since plastic strain prevails in the low-cycle range, elastic strain is excluded in the above equation. Parameter m in Eq. (4.5.10) provides the exponential effect, so does parameter c in Eq. (4.5.1).

4.5.5 Influence of Loading Frequency on Fatigue Life

If the loading frequency and thermal effect due to a temperature variation are considered, Eq. (4.5.8) may be modified [Wei and Chow] as

$$2N_f = \frac{\omega}{\omega_o}\left(\frac{\varepsilon_a^p}{\varepsilon_f'}\right)^{\frac{1}{c}} \qquad\qquad (4.5.11)$$

where

ω: Frequency of the loading function;

ω_o: Reference frequency.

The above equation has been effectively applied to thermal analysis of electronic solders for packaging [Wei and Chow]. Note that the growth in bulk volume due to thermal expansions does not cause damage if there is no constraint.

4.5.6 Effect of Mean Stress

It was first proposed by [Morrow] to modify the baseline strain-life curve derived by [Manson and Coffin] to account for the effect of mean stress. The approach is to alter the value of the fatigue strength coefficient in the elastic component of the stress-strain relationship proposed as

$$\varepsilon_a = \frac{\sigma_f' - \sigma_m}{E}(2N_f)^b + \varepsilon_f'(2N_f)^c \qquad\qquad (4.5.12)$$

of which σ_m is the mean stress or signed equivalent mean stress if von Mises stress is applied. The above equation is called Morrow's equation or Manson-Coffin-Basquin-Morrow equation and its representative curve is demonstrated in Fig. 4.5.1. Generic fatigue properties based on Eq. (4.5.12) for materials are given in Table 4.5.1. If the load sequence is of concern, or saying that it is a load order-oriented fatigue process, Eq. (4.5.12) can be modified as

$$\varepsilon_a = \frac{\sigma_f' - \sigma_m}{E(1 - D)}(2N_f)^b + \varepsilon_f'(2N_f)^c \qquad\qquad (4.5.13)$$

Damage parameter is called the diffusion damage, and $D<1$ before the structure loses the entire stiffness. Initially $D_0 = 0$ at time $= 0$. Then,

$$D = \sum \Delta D \qquad\qquad (4.5.14)$$

where

$$\Delta D = f(2N_f, \Delta t, \sigma_a, R) \qquad\qquad (4.5.15)$$

The above equation tells that diffusion damage interval ΔD is a function of cycle $2N_f$, hold-time duration Δt (e.g. creep phenomenon), stress amplitude σ_a, and stress ratio R. As proposed by [Zhang, W. et al.], the damage growth rate equation is prescribed following the form of the Kachanov-Rabotnov equation,

$$\frac{\mathrm{d}D}{\mathrm{d}N} = \frac{A\left(\dfrac{\sigma_a^*}{1 - \sigma_m^*}\right)^n}{(1 - D)^B} \tag{4.5.16}$$

$$\sigma_a^* = \frac{\sigma_a}{\sigma_{eq}} \tag{4.5.17}$$

$$\text{and} \quad \sigma_m^* = \frac{\sigma_m}{\sigma_{eq}} \tag{4.5.18}$$

where

A: Coefficient, to be obtained from regression of test data;

B: Exponent, to be obtained from regression of test data;

n: Exponent, to be obtained from regression of test data;

σ_a^* : Dimensionless stress amplitude;

σ_m^* : Dimensionless mean stress;

σ_{eq} : Equivalent stress, e.g. Von Mises Stress.

Note that A, B, and n are material-dependent. After Eq. (4.5.18) is derived, $\mathrm{d}D/\mathrm{d}N$ can be approximated using $\Delta D/\Delta N$, which is to be applied to Eq. (4.5.14).

Morrow's mean stress correction are consistent with the experimental observations that the mean stress effect is significant in the elastic range having low plasticity, while it has little influence in the range of low cycle fatigue as shown in Fig. 4.5.1. However, it violates one observation that the loop of stress-strain hysteresis is independent of the mean stress.

Fatigue parameters E, σ_f', ε_f', b, and c are determined from isothermal fatigue experiments at room temperature. Thereby, it is assumed that all experiments at an elevated temperature show a similar or shorter fatigue life than at room temperature. In some cases the fatigue life reduction may be further complicated due to the oxidation and creep damage at high temperatures. Eq. (4.5.13) can be further extended to different applications as follows [Dowling]:

$$\varepsilon_a = \frac{\sigma_f'}{E}\left(1 - \frac{\sigma_m}{\sigma_f'}\right)(2N_f)^b + \varepsilon_f'(2N_f)^c \quad \text{for ferrous} \tag{4.5.19}$$

$$\text{or} \quad \varepsilon_a = \frac{\sigma_f'}{E}\left(1 - \frac{\sigma_m}{\sigma_b}\right)(2N_f)^b + \varepsilon_f'(2N_f)^c \quad \text{for nonferrous} \tag{4.5.20}$$

Denominator σ_b in the above equation is the true stress at fracture as subscript "b" stands for "break" that may not exactly be the ultimate tensile strength (σ_{uts}), which occurs at the peak instead. Note that Eq. (4.5.19) is exactly Eq. (4.5.12). In general, the extended Morrow fatigue life predictors, i.e., Eq. (4.5.19) and (4.5.20), give considerably better results than the Goodman's in most applications [Dowling]. Eq. (4.5.19) has a proven track in modeling ferrous materials, while Eq. (4.5.20) has to be used for the nonferrous. The correction is due to the fact that σ_f' is significantly larger than σ_b for the nonferrous. Some data available for reference from [Dowling] are given below:

Material	σ_f'/MPa	b	σ_b/MPa	σ_{uts}/MPa
SAE1015	801	−0.113	726	415
SAE 1045	3050	−0.098	2717	2248
AISI 4340	1758	−0.098	1634	1103
Ti-6Al-4V	2749	−0.144	1362	978
2014-T6	1120	−0.122	580	494
2024-T3	1602	−0.154	610	497
2024-T4	1294	−0.142	631	476
7075-T6	—	—	730	567

4.5.7　Advantages of Fatigue Life Prediction Based on ε-N Curves

The cyclic stress-strain relation (to be presented in the next section) is considered in the ε-N approach and it can be extrapolated to complex geometry under both low-cycle (high strain level) and high-cycle (low strain level) loads with variable strain amplitudes as measured. Its team-up with damage accumulation algorithms (e.g. Miner's rule, to be presented later) leads to more accurate results versus the S-N approach. Residual strains (stresses), phenomena such as creep and oxidation at high temperatures, and transient material models can be incorporated into the analysis. As an example for the purpose of reference, the fatigue data for thermoplastic PEEK are listed as follows [Wang et al.]:

Elasticity modulus	E/GPa	3.8
Shear elasticity modulus	G/GPa	1.3
Poisson ratio	ν	0.4
Axial fatigue strength coefficient,	σ_f'/MPa	60.34
Axial fatigue ductility coefficient,	ε_f'	0.00713
Axial fatigue strength exponent,	b	−0.03314
Axial fatigue ductility exponent,	c	−0.1528
Shear fatigue strength coefficient,	τ_f'/MPa	34.2
Shear fatigue ductility coefficient,	γ_f'	0.0445
Shear fatigue strength exponent,	b_γ	−0.0462
Shear fatigue ductility exponent,	c_γ	−0.1537

4.6   Cyclic Stress-Strain Relationship

The cyclic stress-strain curve defines the relationship between stress and strain under cyclic loading conditions. Material exhibits a different behavior under cyclic loading in comparison with that under monotonic loading. Note that the hysteresis loop is defined using values ($\Delta\sigma$, $\Delta\varepsilon$) that are relative to some point (σ, ε) in the stress-strain space. Massing's Hypothesis states that the stabilized hysteresis loop may be obtained by doubling the stress and strain values from the cyclic stress-strain curve.

4.6.1   Primary Cyclic Stress-Strain Relationship

When subjected to strain-controlled cyclic loading, the stress-strain response of a material can change with the number of applied cycles. There are four different kinds of phenomenal responses:

(a) Stabilized after several cycles: For a stable cyclic stress-strain relationship, points 1, 3 and 5 in Fig. 4.6.1 are coincident at one location in the hysteresis loop chart.

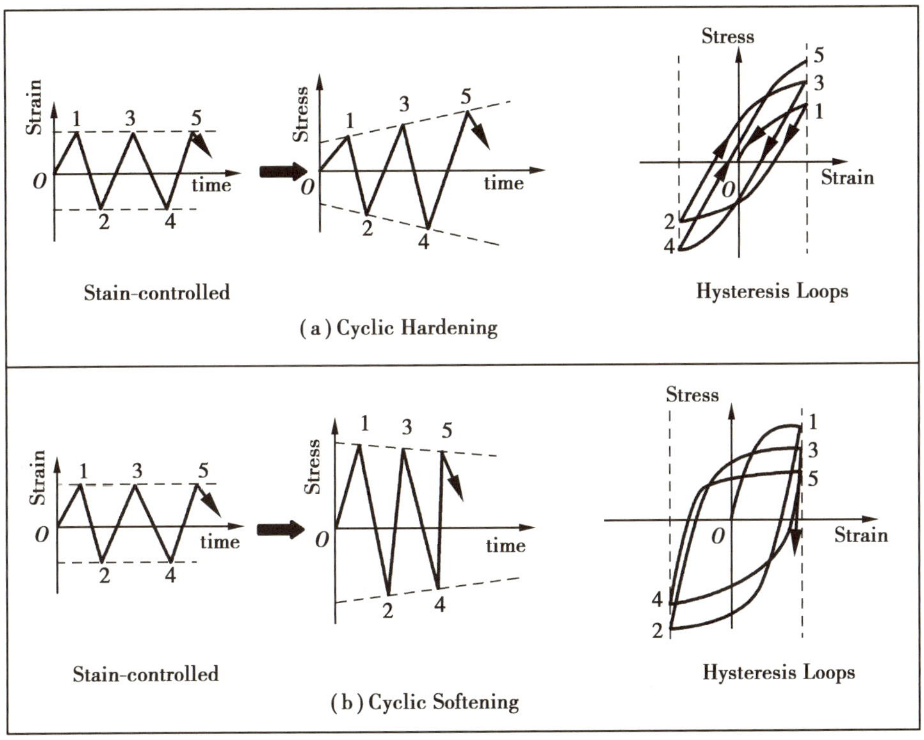

Fig. 4.6.1   Strain-controlled Cyclic Stress-Strain Relationship Represented by Hysteresis Loops

(b) Cyclic hardening: It takes higher stress to create the same strain in the next loop. It means that the stress range (amplitude) increases relative to the previous cycle at a fixed strain as shown in Fig. 4.6.1(a). If $\sigma_{uts}/\sigma_y > 1.4$, the material tends to cyclically harden.

（c）Cyclic softening: It takes less stress to create the same strain in the next loop. It means that the stress range（amplitude）decreases relative to the previous cycle at a fixed strain as shown in Fig. 4.6.1(b). If $\sigma_{uts}/\sigma_y < 1.2$, the material tends to cyclically soften.

（d）Kinetic rule: The yield surface subject to strain hardening or softening may shift. It means that the centroid of the hysteresis loop is not centered anymore.

4.6.2　Ramberg-Osgood Equation

Although mean stress adjustments are needed in making strain-based fatigue life estimates, the materials properties needed to apply a strain-based approach are obtained from tests under completely reversedly controlled strain, with mean stresses in the tests being at or near zero. The specimen is subjected to blocks of gradually increasing and decreasing strain amplitudes. The locus connecting the hysteresis loop tips as shown in Fig. 4.6.2(a) traces out a cyclic stress-strain curve [Nachtigall]. A representative cyclic stress-strain curve of aluminum alloys is given in Fig. 4.6.2(b) for demonstration. Such test results provide a cyclic stress-strain curve and a strain-life curve, which are usually represented by Ramberg-Osgood equation. Again, there is a corresponding number of loading reversals（1 cycle=2 reversals）in response to each given strain amplitude when a material is under cyclic loading. While the four material parameters in Eqs. (4.5.9)-(4.5.11) are used to account for the fatigue damage, the following cyclic relationship between the stress and strain with two more fatigue material parameters（K' and n'）have to be used for describing hysteresis cycles under proportional loadings [Ramberg & Osgood] [Jiang & Sehitoglu]

$$\varepsilon_a = \frac{\sigma_a}{E} + \left(\frac{\sigma_a}{K'}\right)^{\frac{1}{n'}} + \varepsilon_{creep} \tag{4.6.1}$$

where

ε_a: Stain amplitude;

σ_a: Stress amplitude;

K': Cyclic hardening coefficient;

n': Cyclic hardening exponent;

ε_{creep}: Creep strain.

The above equation（Ramberg-Osgood relation）is adequate to model most metals, including bi-modulus materials such as grey cast iron, with different compressive and tensile cyclic loadings.

As argued by [Dowling] that theoretical relationships among the six fitting constants in these two "dissimilar" equations are not invoked, it is recommended that Eq. (4.6.1) and Eq. (4.5.9) should be fitted separately to stress-strain-life test data, for the purpose of accurately representing each curve.

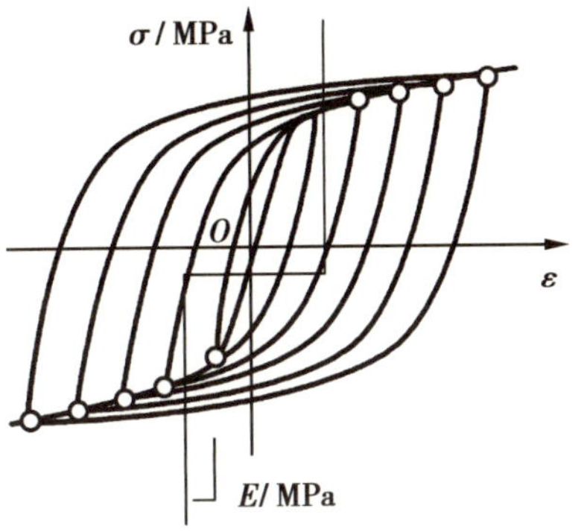

(a) Stabilized Cyclic σ-ε Curves 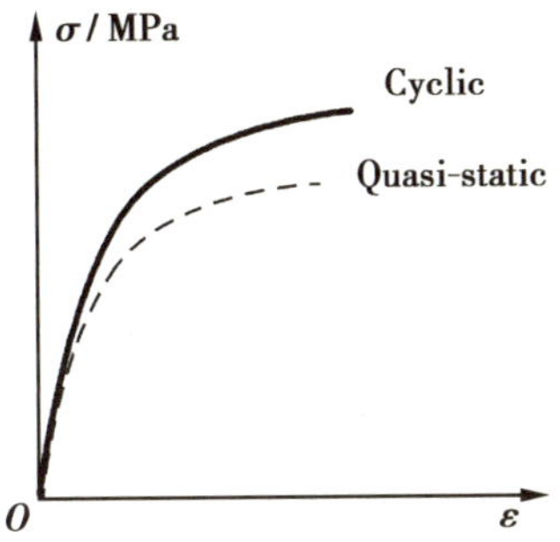   (b) Typical σ-ε Curves for Al-alloys

Fig. 4.6.2   Cyclic σ-ε Curves versus Quasi-Static σ-ε Curves

Although K' and n' of a material are supposedly obtained from a curve fit of its cyclic stress-strain data, the following relationships may be used as the first approximation if no experimental data is available:

$$n' = \frac{b}{c} \tag{4.6.2}$$

and
$$K' = \frac{\sigma'_f}{(\varepsilon'_f)^{n'}} \tag{4.6.3}$$

Note that the strain amplitude (ε_a) may fall in the plastic range and thus nonlinear finite element analysis is quested out. If a linear finite element analysis is conducted (though not recommended), the following Neuber's equation can be used for estimating the total strain (plastic strain + elastic strain)

$$\sigma_\varepsilon = K_t^2 \, \varepsilon_{el} \, \sigma_{el} = K_t^2 \, E \, \varepsilon_{el}^2 \tag{4.6.4}$$

where

K_t: Elastic stress concentration factor, and $K_t = 1$ assumed for an ideal theoretical analysis;

ε_{el}: Nominal elastic strain (or equivalent strain), obtained from linear analysis;

σ_{el}: Nominal elastic stress (or equivalent stress), obtained from linear analysis.

4.6.3   Chaboche Model for Inelastic Strain Rate

Once a material works at a high strain rate, its time-dependent behavior cannot be neglected. Ramberg-Osgood relation is not applicable anymore. Chaboche nonlinear kinematic hardening model has been developed to account for the effect of strain rate as

$$\sigma_a = k + K \left| \frac{d\varepsilon_{a,inelastic}}{dt} \right|^{\frac{1}{n}} \tag{4.6.5}$$

and
$$\frac{d\varepsilon_{a,\,inelastic}}{dt} = \frac{d\varepsilon_a}{dt}\left(1 - \frac{\dfrac{\partial\sigma_a}{\partial\varepsilon_a}}{E}\right) \tag{4.6.6}$$

where

k (MPa): Material Constant;

K (MPa.$S^{\frac{1}{n}}$): Material Constant;

N: Exponent;

E (MPa): Young's modulus.

Material constants of Chaboche model for some materials that have been used at high strain rate and high temperature are given below:

Material	T/℃	E/MPa	k/MPa	K/MPa $\cdot$ $S^{\frac{1}{n}}$	n
Ti-6242	20	200000	1028	325	8.5
316 (SS)	650	145000	129	103	8.03
$2\frac{1}{4}$Cr-1Mo	600	155000	75	230	8.54
IN 738LC	850	164000	0	1510	4.75
IN 738LC	900	164000	0	1156	5.635

4.6.4 Dynamic Strain Ageing （DSA）

There are two different strain ageing processes: SSA (Static Strain Ageing) and DSA (Dynamic Strain Ageing). SSA (Static strain ageing) is a hardening phenomenon occurs in a cold plastic-deformed material during ageing such as a part of heat treatment. SSA may result in higher yield strength.

DSA (Dynamic Strain Ageing) happens to alloys with small amounts of interstitial elements. It is the interaction between dislocation movement and interstitial atoms in the alloy at an elevated temperature and the ageing level varies with the strain rate. It is typical of DSA alloy to exhibit serrated stress-strain curves, which is called jerky flow stress [Protevin & LeChatelier].

As known, the diffusion of carbon and nitrogen atoms in metals in the temperature range between 150 ℃ and 450 ℃ may lead to strain ageing in metals. For example, under the influence of dynamic strain ageing (DSA), at 300 ℃ 316L stainless steel exhibits: primary cyclic hardening due to a significant increase in dislocation density and the incidence of profuse point defects, then cyclic softening due to dislocation re-arrangement, and finally an almost stabilized response stage or secondary cyclic hardening [Phama & Holdswortha]. As an example, the formation of irreversibly dislocated structures and stacking faults can contribute to the second hardening in the stress response curve in the material such as duplex stainless steel S32705. It consequently increases the fatigue life in the low-cycle fatigue region [Chai & Anderson] as given below:

$T/{}^\circ\mathrm{C}$	$\varepsilon = 0.4\%$	$\varepsilon = 0.42\%$	$\varepsilon = 0.7\%$	$\varepsilon = 0.84\%$
Room	7867 cycles	—	2333 cycles	—
200	—	10032 cycles	—	1697 cycles
250	11638 cycles	—	2665 cycles	—
350	—	9394 cycles	—	2456 cycles

4.7 Damage Accumulation Models

Material damage due to mechanical cycles is quantified by considering strain-life (or stress-life) from constant amplitude tests and by employing an approach that covers the influence of mean stresses. Cycle counting is a procedure for determining damaging events under variable amplitude loading. Closed hysteresis loops are registered in cyclic stress-strain paths. These loops are treated as one cycle of the corresponding constant amplitude loading. Damage accumulation models result from variable strain (stress) amplitude can be divided into three categories: strain (stress)-independent linear model, strain (stress)-dependent linear model, and strain (stress)-dependent nonlinear model.

4.7.1 Strain (Stress)-Independent Linear Damage Model: Miner's Rule

Damage summation is done according to Miner's rule, sometimes called the Palmgren-Miner linear damage hypothesis. Assume that there are k different strain (or stress) amplitudes in a loading spectrum, ε_k (or σ_k) where $1 \leqslant k \leqslant K$, each contributing $n_k(\varepsilon_k)$ [or $n_k(\sigma_k)$] reversals in the damage counts. Note that 1 reversal = 1/2 cycle. If $N_{\mathrm{f}k}(\varepsilon_k)$ or $N_{\mathrm{f}k}(\sigma_k)$, is the number of reversals to failure in response to constant-strain-amplitude (or constant-stress amplitude) loading at kth strain (stress) amplitude, failure occurs when the following equation is met [Miner]:

$$\left[\sum_{k=1}^{K} \left(\frac{n_k}{N_{\mathrm{f}k}} \right) \right] M = \left[\frac{n_1}{N_{\mathrm{f}1}} + \frac{n_2}{N_{\mathrm{f}2}} + \cdots + \frac{n_k}{N_{\mathrm{f}k}} \right] M = C \qquad (4.7.1)$$

where

M: Total number of the repeated time-series sections leading to failure;

K: Number of load blocks in each time series section;

$N_{\mathrm{f}k}$: Number of cycles to failure at the $(\sigma_k, \varepsilon_k)$ load level;

C: 100%, generally.

Parameter C on the right side of the above equation is assumed to be 100% for the design purpose, though parameter C is experimentally found to be between 70% and 220%. The denominator $(N_{\mathrm{f}k})$ is calculated from ε-N or S-N curves, such as Eq. (4.5.7), i.e., Manson-

Coffin-Basquin-Morrow equation, for each strain amplitude ε_k, should an ε-N approach to the fatigue calculation under proportional loadings is to be carried out. The numerator, n_k, is obtained from the load spectrum for each load case. Two methods have been applied to computing the load spectrum for counting effective n_k and they are time-domain approach and frequency-domain approach. The strain (stress) independent model predicts quite well the fatigue life of both steel and unidirectional composites for high cycle fatigue [Fragoudakis & Saigal].

4.7.2 Strain (Stress)-Independent Linear Damage Model: Extended Miner's Rule

In the case both cyclic and creep effects have to be taken into account. The following weighted linear damage summations extend from Miner's rule applies [ASME Code Case 13331-5]:

$$\left[\sum_{i=1}^{I} \frac{n_i}{N_{fi}} + w_{creep} \sum_{j=1}^{J} \frac{t_j}{T_{fj}} \right] M = 100\% \tag{4.7.2}$$

where
T_{fj}: Creep time to failure;
t_j: Creep time in the jth stage of creep, corresponding to T_{fj};
w_{creep}: Weight put on creep;
M: Repeated time-series sections, of which each contains I load blocks and J creep blocks.

For most practical situations, the creep-fatigue interaction has a nonlinear character. Detailed fatigue analysis involving creep phenomena is given in Chapter 6.

4.7.3 Stress-Dependent Linear Damage Model: Broutman-Sahu Model

A stress-dependent model to explain the order of stress levels was proposed by [Broutman & Sahu] as

$$\left(\sum_{k=1}^{K} \frac{n_k}{N_{fk}} \cdot d_k \right) M = 100\% \tag{4.7.3}$$

of which d_k is the stress-dependent or strain-dependent factor of each load case and it is defined as

$$d_k = \frac{\sigma_{uts} - \sigma_k}{\sigma_{uts} - \sigma_{k+1}} \quad \text{(Stress-dependent)} \tag{4.7.4}$$

or $\quad d_k = \dfrac{\varepsilon_{uts} - \varepsilon_k}{\varepsilon_{uts} - \varepsilon_{k+1}} \quad \text{(Strain-dependent)} \tag{4.7.5}$

The stress-dependent linear model given above predicts damage accumulation for low cycle fatigue in the high-stressed range more accurately than the stress-independent linear model does according to [Fragoudakis & Saigal] on the testing of SAE 6150 (i.e., AISI 6150) alloy steel. SAE 6150 is chromium-vanadium steel commonly used in leaf-springs for heavy duty vehicles. Nevertheless, both models, Eq. (4.7.2) and Eq. (4.7.3), are also good for predicting damage accumulation for high cycle fatigue in the low-stressed range.

4.7.4   Strain (Stress)-Dependent Nonlinear Damage Model: Hashin-Rotem Model

Composites behave very differently from metals in fatigue. The strength of composites decreases slowly in the early fatigue life and as failure approaches the strength decreases at a rapid rate. The ensemble of attempts to calculate the damage caused by cycling for composites and its accumulation when cycling includes more than one stress amplitudes is summarized using the following stress-dependent nonlinear model [Hashin & Rotem]:

$$\sum_{k=1}^{K} \left[\frac{n_k}{N_{f,k}} + \left(\frac{n_{m-1}}{N_{f,m-1}} \right)^{\frac{1}{d_{m-1}}} \right] M = 100\% \qquad (4.7.6)$$

and $d_{m-1} = \dfrac{\sigma_{uts} - \sigma_{m-1}}{\sigma_{uts} - \sigma_m}$ (Stress-dependent) $\qquad (4.7.7)$

or $d_{m-1} = \dfrac{\varepsilon_{uts} - \varepsilon_{m-1}}{\varepsilon_{uts} - \varepsilon_m}$ (Strain-dependent) $\qquad (4.7.8)$

where
d_{m-1}: Accountable damage due to the previous load block;
m: Each individual number of the repeated load blocks leading to failure, $m = 1, 2, \cdots, M$.

It was reported by [Epaarachchi] and [Fragoudakis & Saigal] that the stress-dependent nonlinear model predicts damage accumulation for fiber-reinforced plastic composites more accurately than the stress-dependent linear model.

4.8   Counting Damaging Cycles

Counting algorithms have initially been developed for the study of fatigue damage generated in aeronautical structures. It is well known that fatigue damage depends more on the effective strain (stress) amplitude and mean strain (stress) than on the applied load. Every effective strain (stress) cycle accountable for material fatigue in the load history must be included in the damage accumulation model. An actual measured strain history is depicted in Fig. 4.8.1: (1) The truck is loaded in the park gear, (2) The truck runs at the full load, (3) The truck comes back at no load.

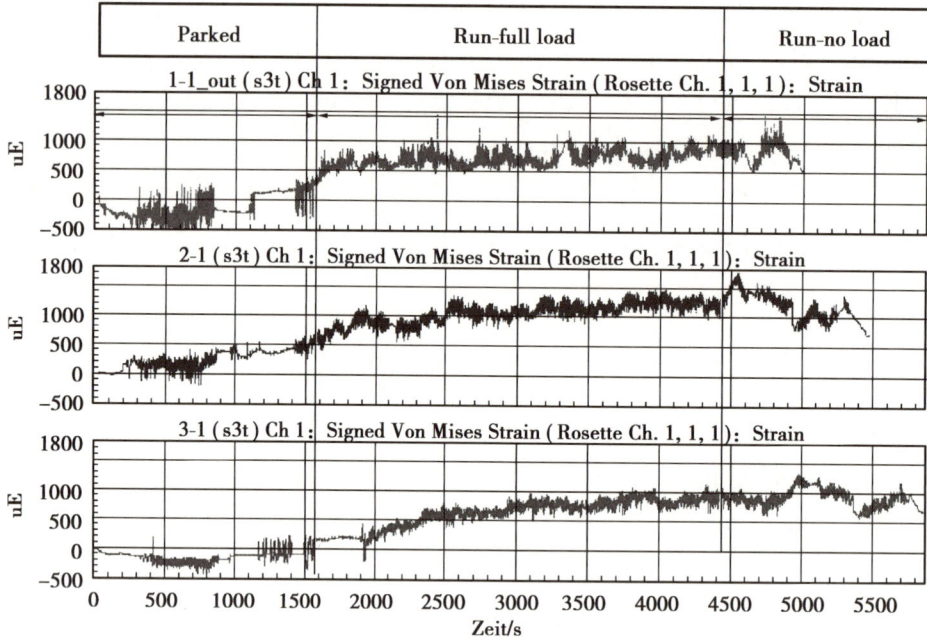

Fig. 4.8.1　Measured Real-Time Strain History（Rosette）of the Truck Frame Welding Point on a Highly Irregular Mining Route（Vertical Axis- Strain, μm/m; Horizontal Axis- Time, sec）

4.8.1　Load Bock

When a specimen is loaded periodically until failure, the rainflow counting algorithm is a time-domain approach to converting an irregular fluctuating load（acceleration, strain, stress, or temperature）history into a load histogram ［ASTM E-1049］. When "similar" loads are grouped together, they form a load block. In many loading cases such as the one shown in Fig. 4.8.1, a vehicle（or product）undergoes a number of load blocks of fluctuating loads repeatedly. The example time series of strains shown in Fig. 4.8.2 are allocated into five blocks according to the strain range.

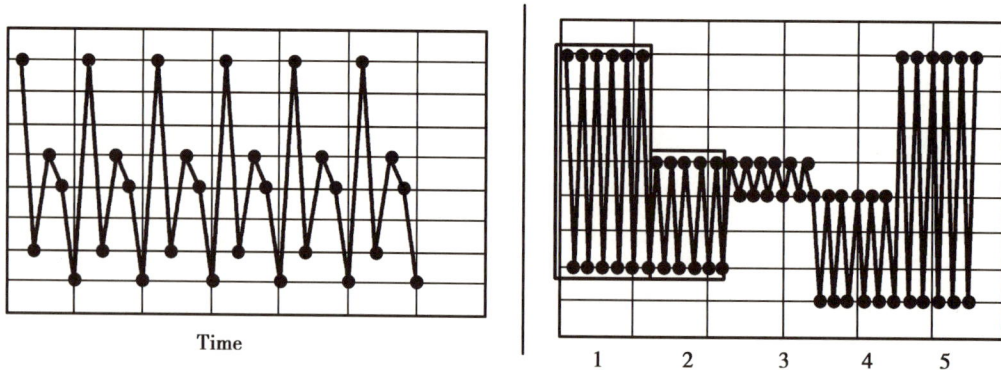

Fig. 4.8.2　Five Load Blocks Allocated According to the Range ［WIKI］

In practice, the total data in each section of sequential time series is divided into $C_1 \times C_2$ classes of constant-width interval or steps in a 2-dimensional arrays, and all the extreme values（peaks and valleys) located in a given load block are replaced by the representative values in terms of mean value and fluctuating amplitude. Standard practice in industry is to take $C_1 \times C_2 = 8 \times 8 = 64$ [Schlitz et al.]. An example classification of load blocks based on mean strain and strain amplitude is depicted in Fig. 4.8.3, which is obtained from the repeating strain history of a load section that is expressed in terms of μm/m as a function of time shown in the excerption. Each load block that exceeds a predefined threshold will be taken into consideration for fatigue analysis in terms of its mean value, amplitude, and loading sequence.

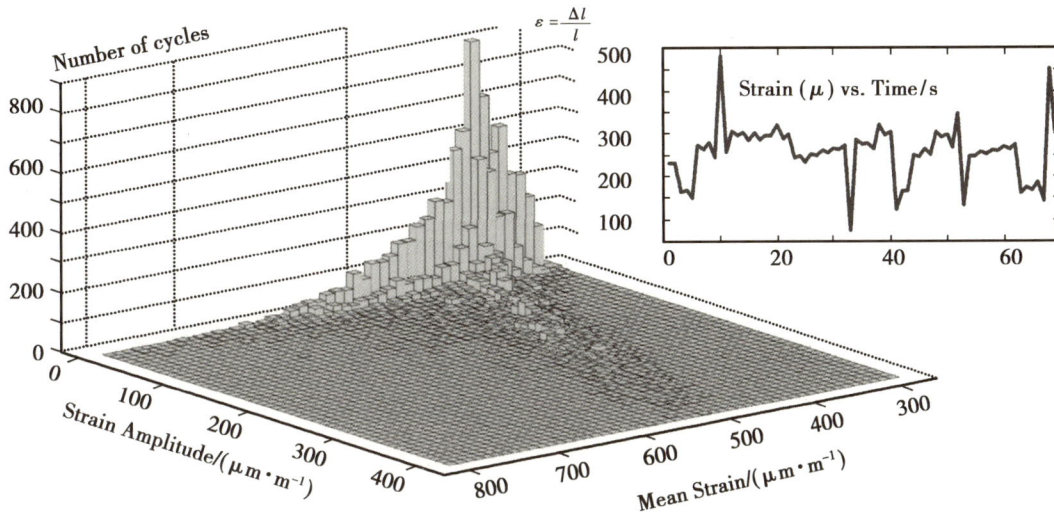

Fig. 4.8.3   Allocating Load-Block Spectrum as a Function of Strain Amplitude and Mean Strain in μm/m

4.8.2   Rainflow Counting Algorithm of Proportional Stress/Strain Fluctuations in Time Domain

Before conducting the rainflow counting method, one has to orderly convert the loading cycles of a spectrum of the varying design variable (e.g. strain, stress, strain energy, and/or temperature) into a set of simple design variable reversals [Matsuishi & Endo] [ASTM]. It means that the design variable history such as strain $\varepsilon(t)$, stress $\sigma(t)$, strain energy $E(t)$, or temperature $T(t)$, is transformed to a time series having various extrema-peaks and valleys. The rainflow method, as an algorithm for counting fatigue cycles from a response time history that comprises of strain, stress, equivalent strain, equivalent stress, energy and/or temperature reversals, is then carried out to count the number of reversals (or cycles) that has a 'similar' damaging capacity. The rainflow begins successively at the inside of each peak or valley, and every part of the history is counted once and only once [Glinka and Kam]. One may imagine how the rain runs along a 2-dimensional pagoda roof while applying the rainflow counting algorithm. Assume that the design variable is strain. The number of total cyclic reversals (half-cycles) can be counted as follows:

1. Reduce the time history to a sequence of peaks and valleys.
2. Turn the strain-time history (from left to right) clockwise 90°, and now it looks like a pagoda roof (the strain at the earliest time being on top), as shown in Fig. 4.8.4.

3. Each peak is perceived as a source of water that "drips" down the pagoda. Count the number of reversals by looking for terminations in the flow occurring when either:
   (a) It reaches the end of the time history;
   (b) It merges with a flow that started at an earlier tensile peak; or
   (c) It flows when an opposite tensile peak has greater magnitude.
4. Repeat the above step for valleys.
5. The strain difference between its start and termination is identified as a reversal.
6. Pair up reversals of identical magnitude (but opposite sense) to count the number of complete cycles. There are residual reversals usually.

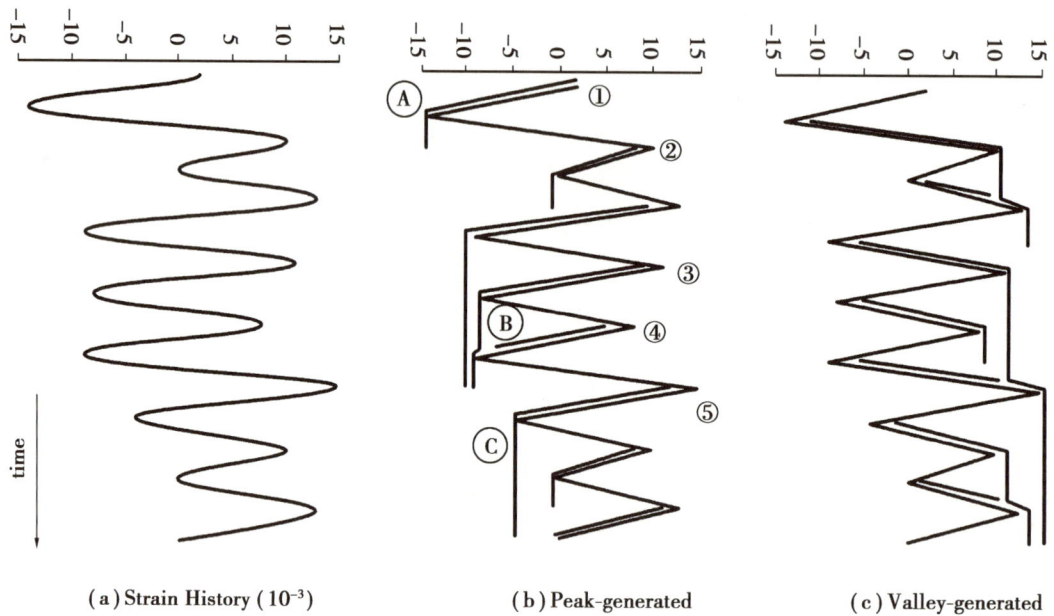

(a) Strain History (10⁻³)   (b) Peak-generated   (c) Valley-generated

Fig. 4.8.4   Conceptual Pagoda Roof to Identify Fluctuating Reversals for Fatigue Analysis

The peaks are in either tension or compression, and so are the valleys. There are two fundamental assumptions made in order to rearrange the loads into blocks using the rainflow counting method. Loads are independent of each other and the load order is not rigorously taken into consideration. This method has been given a mathematical definition by [Rychlik] and thus the analytic closed-form calculation based on the statistical properties of the designated design variable, also called signal, can be carried out.

The rainflow method allows the application of Miner's rule or other accumulation methods to assess the fatigue life of a mechanical structure subject to complex loadings in either stationary or nonstationary vibrational state. It may also be used to calculate a Miner's rule-like relative damage index for acceleration response cycles. There are two different approaches to implementing the rainflow counting algorithm: (a) 4-point method and (b) 3-point method. They are supposed to produce the same result [McInners & Meehan].

4.8.3   4-Point Method

The 4-point method is the commonly used rainflow counting algorithm. Both amplitude and mean values of strain (or stress) variations are to be counted while using the rainflow counting algorithm for either ε-N or S-N fatigue analysis. Let ε represent a strain component and the recorded strain data are the consecutive values $\varepsilon_i (1 \leqslant i \leqslant N)$ of the peaks and valleys of the sequence. Assume that the cycles made of the first four points appear as a close-looped stress-strain curve as shown Fig. 4.8.5, which shows that two possible types of cycle that can occur. The principle of the extraction of a cycle based on four successive points, namely ε_1, ε_2, ε_3, and ε_4, is illustrated as follows [Amzallag et al.]:

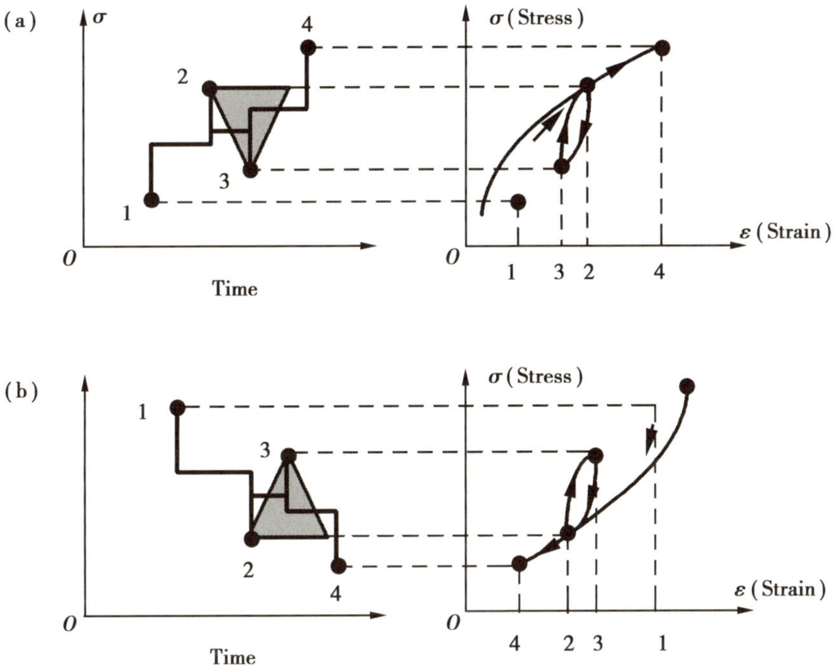

Fig. 4.8.5   Cycle Extraction Based on Four Point Method: (a) Bottom-up and (b) Top-down

(a) Three consecutive ranges are determined using four points: $\Delta\varepsilon_a = |\varepsilon_2 - \varepsilon_1|$, $\Delta\varepsilon_b = |\varepsilon_3 - \varepsilon_2|$, and $\Delta\varepsilon_c = |\varepsilon_4 - \varepsilon_3|$. If $\Delta\varepsilon_b \leqslant \Delta\varepsilon_a$ and $\Delta\varepsilon_b \leqslant \Delta\varepsilon_c$, the cycle represented by stress range $(\varepsilon_2, \varepsilon_3)$ is extracted. Then, both point ε_2 and point ε_3 are discarded from the picture. Point ε_1 is then connected directly to point ε_4.

(b) If "$\Delta\varepsilon_b \leqslant \Delta\varepsilon_a$ and $\Delta\varepsilon_b \leqslant \Delta\varepsilon_c$" is not true, read the next point (ε_5). Reversal $\varepsilon_1 - \varepsilon_2$ is a residue (reversal). Then, use $\Delta\varepsilon_a = |\varepsilon_3 - \varepsilon_2|$, $\Delta\varepsilon_b = |\varepsilon_4 - \varepsilon_3|$, and $\Delta\varepsilon_c = |\varepsilon_5 - \varepsilon_4|$ to detect the next feasible cycle.

(c) The procedure, i.e., steps (a) and (b), is repeated until the last point of the sequence is reached. Once all the comparisons are completed, the remaining points constitute the so-called residue. Note that the maximum number of points cannot exceed $2L-1$, where L is the number of possible levels.

(d) The resulting counted-cycles are then input into a matrix that stores the following three pieces of information: mean value, amplitude (range), and number of cycles.

The comparison of design ranges (4-point method), instead of the relative design levels (3-point method), simplifies the algorithm when using the 4-point method rather than the 3-point method, though both are proven to generate the same result.

Example 4.8.1　A series of 24 strain extrema measured at the critical location of a steel part are listed as: 0.0004, 0.0007, 0.0002, 0.0010, 0.0005, 0.0009, 0.0003, 0.0004, 0.0002, 0.0012, 0.0005, 0.0011, 0.0001, 0.0004, 0.0003, 0.0010, 0.0006, 0.0012, 0.0004, 0.0008, 0.0001, 0.0009, 0.0004, 0.0006

Note that the yield strength of steel is 0.002 or 0.2%. They are plotted as follows:

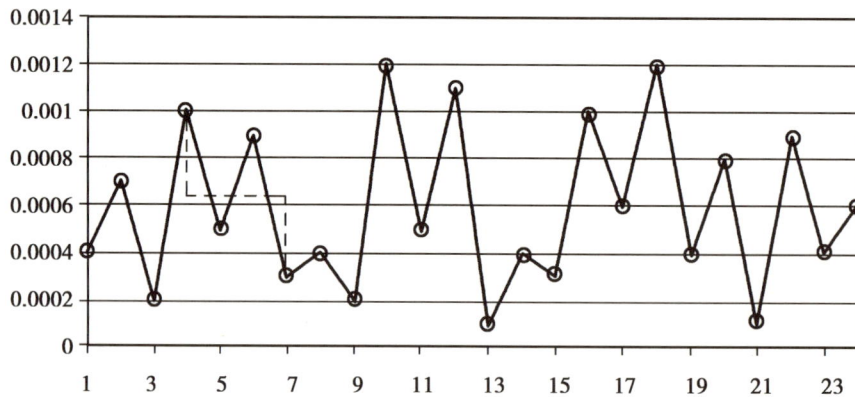

Extract the cycles and residues.

Solution:

(a) Consider the first 4 points. Since $\Delta\varepsilon_a = |\varepsilon_2 - \varepsilon_1| = 0.03\%$, $\Delta\varepsilon_b = |\varepsilon_3 - \varepsilon_2| = 0.05\%$ and $\Delta\varepsilon_c = |\varepsilon_4 - \varepsilon_3| = 0.08\%$, "$\Delta\varepsilon_b \leqslant \Delta\varepsilon_a$ and $\Delta\varepsilon_b \leqslant \Delta\varepsilon_c$" is not true. Thus, $\varepsilon_1 - \varepsilon_2$, going from 0.0002 to 0.0010, is a residue (reversal) and no cycle is extracted.

(b) Read the next piece of data, i.e., ε_5, then the new 4 points are ε_2, ε_3, ε_4 and ε_5. Since $\Delta\varepsilon_a = |\varepsilon_3 - \varepsilon_2| = 0.05\%$, $\Delta\varepsilon_b = |\varepsilon_4 - \varepsilon_3| = 0.08\%$ and $\Delta\varepsilon_c = |\varepsilon_5 - \varepsilon_4| = 0.05\%$, "$\Delta\varepsilon_b \leqslant \Delta\varepsilon_a$ and $\Delta\varepsilon_b \leqslant \Delta\varepsilon_c$" is not true. Thus, $\varepsilon_2 - \varepsilon_3$ is a residue (reversal), going from 0.0007 to 0.0002, no cycle is extracted.

(c) Read the next piece of data, i.e., ε_6, then the new 4 points are ε_3, ε_4, ε_5 and ε_6. Since $\Delta\varepsilon_a = |\varepsilon_4 - \varepsilon_3| = 0.08\%$, $\Delta\varepsilon_b = |\varepsilon_5 - \varepsilon_4| = 0.05\%$ and $\Delta\varepsilon_c = |\varepsilon_6 - \varepsilon_5| = 0.04\%$, "$\Delta\varepsilon_b \leqslant \Delta\varepsilon_a$ and $\Delta\varepsilon_b \leqslant \Delta\varepsilon_c$" is not true. Thus, $\varepsilon_3 - \varepsilon_4$ is a residue (reversal), going from 0.0002 to 0.0010, no cycle is extracted.

(d) Read the next piece of data, i.e., ε_7, then the new 4 points are ε_4, ε_5, ε_6 and ε_7. Since

$\Delta\varepsilon_a = |\varepsilon_5 - \varepsilon_4| = 0.05\%$, $\Delta\varepsilon_b = |\varepsilon_6 - \varepsilon_5| = 0.04\%$, and $\Delta\varepsilon_c = |\varepsilon_7 - \varepsilon_6| = 0.06\%$, "$\Delta\varepsilon_b \leqslant \Delta\varepsilon_a$ and $\Delta\varepsilon_b \leqslant \Delta\varepsilon_c$" is true. the cycle represented by strain range $(\varepsilon_5, \varepsilon_6) = (0.0005, 0.0009)$ that has mean = 0.0007 and amplitude = 0.0002 is extracted. Then, both point ε_5 and point ε_6 are discarded from the picture. Point ε_4 is then connected directly to point ε_7.

(e) Read the next 2 pieces of data and the new 4 points are ε_4, ε_7, ε_8 and ε_9. Since $\Delta\varepsilon_a = |\varepsilon_7 - \varepsilon_4| = 0.07\%$, $\Delta\varepsilon_b = |\varepsilon_8 - \varepsilon_7| = 0.01\%$, and $\Delta\varepsilon_c = |\varepsilon_9 - \varepsilon_8| = 0.02\%$, "$\Delta\varepsilon_b \leqslant \Delta\varepsilon_a$ and $\Delta\varepsilon_b \leqslant \Delta\varepsilon_c$" is true. The cycle represented by strain range $(\varepsilon_7, \varepsilon_8) = (0.0003, 0.0004)$ that has mean = 0.00035 and amplitude = 0.00005 is extracted. Then, both point ε_7 and point ε_8 are discarded from the picture. Point ε_4 is then connected directly to point ε_9.

(f) Read the next 2 pieces of data and the new 4 points are ε_4, ε_9, ε_{10} and ε_{11}. Since $\Delta\varepsilon_a = |\varepsilon_9 - \varepsilon_4| = 0.08\%$, $\Delta\varepsilon_b = |\varepsilon_{10} - \varepsilon_9| = 0.10\%$ and $\Delta\varepsilon_c = |\varepsilon_{11} - \varepsilon_{10}| = 0.07\%$, "$\Delta\varepsilon_b \leqslant \Delta\varepsilon_a$ and $\Delta\varepsilon_b \leqslant \Delta\varepsilon_c$" is not true. Thus, $\varepsilon_9 - \varepsilon_{10}$ is a residue (reversal), going from 0.0002 to 0.0012, no cycle is extracted.

(g) Read the next piece of data, i.e., ε_{12} and the new 4 points are ε_4, ε_{10}, ε_{11} and ε_{12}. Since $\Delta\varepsilon_a = |\varepsilon_{10} - \varepsilon_4| = 0.10\%$, $\Delta\varepsilon_b = |\varepsilon_{11} - \varepsilon_{10}| = 0.07\%$, and $\Delta\varepsilon_c = |\varepsilon_{12} - \varepsilon_{11}| = 0.06\%$, "$\Delta\varepsilon_b \leqslant \Delta\varepsilon_a$ and $\Delta\varepsilon_b \leqslant \Delta\varepsilon_c$" is not true. Thus, $\varepsilon_9 - \varepsilon_{10}$ is a residue (reversal), going from 0.0002 to 0.0012, no cycle is extracted.

(h) Read the next piece of data, i.e., ε_{13}, then the new 4 points are ε_{10}, ε_{11}, ε_{12} and ε_{13}. Since $\Delta\varepsilon_a = |\varepsilon_{11} - \varepsilon_{10}| = 0.07\%$, $\Delta\varepsilon_b = |\varepsilon_{12} - \varepsilon_{11}| = 0.06\%$, and $\Delta\varepsilon_c = |\varepsilon_{13} - \varepsilon_{12}| = 0.10\%$, "$\Delta\varepsilon_b \leqslant \Delta\varepsilon_a$ and $\Delta\varepsilon_b \leqslant \Delta\varepsilon_c$" is true. The cycle represented by strain range $(\varepsilon_{11}, \varepsilon_{12}) = (0.0005, 0.0011)$ that has mean = 0.0008 and amplitude = 0.0003 is extracted. Then, both point ε_{11} and point ε_{12} are discarded from the picture. Point ε_{10} is then connected directly to point ε_{13}.

(i) Read the next 2 pieces of data, i.e., ε_{14} and ε_{15}, then the new 4 points are ε_{10}, ε_{13}, ε_{14} and ε_{15}. Since $\Delta\varepsilon_a = |\varepsilon_{13} - \varepsilon_{10}| = 0.11\%$, $\Delta\varepsilon_b = |\varepsilon_{14} - \varepsilon_{13}| = 0.03\%$, and $\Delta\varepsilon_c = |\varepsilon_{15} - \varepsilon_{14}| = 0.01\%$, "$\Delta\varepsilon_b \leqslant \Delta\varepsilon_a$ and $\Delta\varepsilon_b \leqslant \Delta\varepsilon_c$" is not true. Thus, $\varepsilon_{10} - \varepsilon_{13}$ is a residue (reversal), going from 0.0012 to 0.0001, no cycle is extracted.

(j) Read the next piece of data, i.e., ε_{16}, then the new 4 points are ε_{13}, ε_{14}, ε_{15} and ε_{16}. Since $\Delta\varepsilon_a = |\varepsilon_{14} - \varepsilon_{13}| = 0.03\%$, $\Delta\varepsilon_b = |\varepsilon_{15} - \varepsilon_{14}| = 0.01\%$, and $\Delta\varepsilon_c = |\varepsilon_{16} - \varepsilon_{15}| = 0.07\%$, "$\Delta\varepsilon_b \leqslant \Delta\varepsilon_a$ and $\Delta\varepsilon_b \leqslant \Delta\varepsilon_c$" is true. The cycle represented by strain range $(\varepsilon_{14}, \varepsilon_{15}) = (0.0004, 0.0003)$ that has mean = 0.00035 and amplitude = 0.00005 is extracted. Then, both point ε_{14} and point ε_{15} are discarded from the picture. Point ε_{13} is then connected directly to point ε_{16}.

(k) Read the next 2 pieces of data, i.e., ε_{17} and ε_{18}, then the new 4 points are ε_{13}, ε_{16}, ε_{17} and ε_{18}. Since $\Delta\varepsilon_a = |\varepsilon_{16} - \varepsilon_{13}| = 0.09\%$, $\Delta\varepsilon_b = |\varepsilon_{17} - \varepsilon_{16}| = 0.04\%$, and $\Delta\varepsilon_c = |\varepsilon_{18} - \varepsilon_{17}| = 0.06\%$, "$\Delta\varepsilon_b \leqslant \Delta\varepsilon_a$ and $\Delta\varepsilon_b \leqslant \Delta\varepsilon_c$" is true. The cycle represented by strain range $(\varepsilon_{16}, \varepsilon_{17}) = (0.0010, 0.0006)$ that has mean = 0.0008 and amplitude = 0.0002 is extracted. Then, both point ε_{16} and point ε_{17} are discarded from the picture. Point ε_{13} is then connected directly to point ε_{18}.

(l) Read the next 2 pieces of data, i.e., ε_{19} and ε_{20}, then the new 4 points are ε_{13}, ε_{18}, ε_{19} and ε_{20}. Since $\Delta\varepsilon_a = |\varepsilon_{18}-\varepsilon_{13}| = 0.11\%$, $\Delta\varepsilon_b = |\varepsilon_{19}-\varepsilon_{18}| = 0.08\%$, and $\Delta\varepsilon_c = |\varepsilon_{20}-\varepsilon_{19}|$ $=0.04\%$, "$\Delta\varepsilon_b \leqslant \Delta\varepsilon_a$ and $\Delta\varepsilon_b \leqslant \Delta\varepsilon_c$" is not true. Thus, $\varepsilon_{13} - \varepsilon_{18}$ is a residue (reversal), going from 0.0001 to 0.0012, no cycle is extracted.

(m) Read the next piece of data, i.e., ε_{21}, then the new 4 points are ε_{18}, ε_{19}, ε_{20} and ε_{21}. Since $\Delta\varepsilon_a = |\varepsilon_{19}-\varepsilon_{18}| = 0.08\%$, $\Delta\varepsilon_b = |\varepsilon_{20}-\varepsilon_{19}| = 0.04\%$, and $\Delta\varepsilon_c = |\varepsilon_{21}-\varepsilon_{20}| = 0.07\%$, "$\Delta\varepsilon_b \leqslant \Delta\varepsilon_a$ and $\Delta\varepsilon_b \leqslant \Delta\varepsilon_c$" is true. The cycle represented by strain range $(\varepsilon_{19}, \varepsilon_{20}) = (0.0004, 0.0008)$ that has mean = 0.0006 and amplitude = 0.0002 is extracted. Then, both point ε_{19} and point ε_{20} are discarded from the picture. Point ε_{18} is then connected directly to point ε_{21}.

(n) Read the next 2 pieces of data, i.e., ε_{22} and ε_{23}, then the new 4 points are ε_{18}, ε_{21}, ε_{22} and ε_{23}. Since $\Delta\varepsilon_a = |\varepsilon_{21}-\varepsilon_{18}| = 0.11\%$, $\Delta\varepsilon_b = |\varepsilon_{22}-\varepsilon_{21}| = 0.08\%$, and $\Delta\varepsilon_c = |\varepsilon_{23}-\varepsilon_{22}|$ $=0.05\%$, "$\Delta\varepsilon_b \leqslant \Delta\varepsilon_a$ and $\Delta\varepsilon_b \leqslant \Delta\varepsilon_c$" is not true. Thus, $\varepsilon_{18} - \varepsilon_{21}$ is a residue (reversal), going from 0.0012 to 0.0001, no cycle is extracted.

(o) Read the next piece of data, i.e., ε_{24}, then the new 4 points are ε_{21}, ε_{22}, ε_{23} and ε_{24}. Since $\Delta\varepsilon_a = |\varepsilon_{22}-\varepsilon_{21}| = 0.08\%$, $\Delta\varepsilon_b = |\varepsilon_{23}-\varepsilon_{22}| = 0.05\%$, and $\Delta\varepsilon_c = |\varepsilon_{24}-\varepsilon_{23}| = 0.02\%$, "$\Delta\varepsilon_b \leqslant \Delta\varepsilon_a$ and $\Delta\varepsilon_b \leqslant \Delta\varepsilon_c$" is not true. Thus, $\varepsilon_{21}-\varepsilon_{22}$ is a residue (reversal), going from 0.0001 to 0.0009, no cycle is extracted.

(p) Read the next piece of data, i.e., ε_1, then the new 4 points are ε_{22}, ε_{23}, ε_{24} and ε_1. Since $\Delta\varepsilon_a = |\varepsilon_{23}-\varepsilon_{22}| = 0.05\%$, $\Delta\varepsilon_b = |\varepsilon_{24}-\varepsilon_{23}| = 0.02\%$, and $\Delta\varepsilon_c = |\varepsilon_1-\varepsilon_{24}| = 0.02\%$, "$\Delta\varepsilon_b \leqslant \Delta\varepsilon_a$ and $\Delta\varepsilon_b \leqslant \Delta\varepsilon_c$" is true. The cycle represented by strain range $(\varepsilon_{23}, \varepsilon_{24}) = (0.0004, 0.0006)$ that has mean = 0.0005 and amplitude = 0.0001 is extracted. Then, both point ε_{19} and point ε_{20} are discarded from the picture. Point ε_{18} is then connected directly to point ε_{21}.

In summary:	Cycles/Reversal	Range	Mean	Amplitude
	2	$(\varepsilon_5, \varepsilon_6) = (0.0005, 0.0009)$	0.0007	0.0002
	2	$(\varepsilon_7, \varepsilon_8) = (0.0003, 0.0004)$	0.00035	0.00005
	2	$(\varepsilon_{11}, \varepsilon_{12}) = (0.0005, 0.0011)$	0.0008	0.0003
	2	$(\varepsilon_{14}, \varepsilon_{15}) = (0.0004, 0.0003)$	0.00035	0.00005
	2	$(\varepsilon_{16}, \varepsilon_{17}) = (0.0010, 0.0006)$	0.0008	0.0002
	2	$(\varepsilon_{19}, \varepsilon_{20}) = (0.0004, 0.0008)$	0.0006	0.0002
	1	$\varepsilon_1{\rightarrow}\varepsilon_2(0.0002, 0.0010)$	0.0006	0.0004
	1	$\varepsilon_2{\rightarrow}\varepsilon_3(0.0007, 0.0002)$	0.00045	0.00025
	1	$\varepsilon_3{\rightarrow}\varepsilon_4(0.0002, 0.0010)$	0.0006	0.0004
	1	$\varepsilon_9{\rightarrow}\varepsilon_{10}(0.0002, 0.0012)$	0.0007	0.0005
	1	$\varepsilon_{10}{\rightarrow}\varepsilon_{13}(0.0012, 0.0001)$	0.00065	0.00055

1	$\varepsilon_{13} \rightarrow \varepsilon_{18}(0.0001,\ 0.0012)$	0.00065	0.00055
1	$\varepsilon_{18} \rightarrow \varepsilon_{21}(0.0012,\ 0.0001)$	0.00065	0.00055
1	$\varepsilon_{21} \rightarrow \varepsilon_{22}(0.0001,\ 0.0009)$	0.0005	0.0004
1	$\varepsilon_{22} \rightarrow \varepsilon_{23}(0.0009,\ 0.0004)$	0.00065	0.00025
1	$\varepsilon_{23} \rightarrow \varepsilon_{24}(0.0004,\ 0.0006)$	0.0005	0.0001

Assume that the mean strain and strain amplitude are the two fatigue parameters of concern without considering the loading sequence. The data shown above exhibit two additional cycles, i.e., ($\varepsilon_{13} \rightarrow \varepsilon_{18}$, $\varepsilon_{18} \rightarrow \varepsilon_{21}$) and ($\varepsilon_1 \rightarrow \varepsilon_2$, $\varepsilon_3 \rightarrow \varepsilon_4$) can be regrouped into the following patterns

Cycles/Reversal	Range	Mean	Amplitude
2	$(\varepsilon_1 \rightarrow \varepsilon_2,\ \varepsilon_3 \rightarrow \varepsilon_4)$	0.0006	0.0004
2	$(\varepsilon_5,\ \varepsilon_6) = (0.0005,\ 0.0009)$	0.0007	0.0002
2	$(\varepsilon_7,\ \varepsilon_8) = (0.0003,\ 0.0004)$	0.00035	0.00005
2	$(\varepsilon_{11},\ \varepsilon_{12}) = (0.0005,\ 0.0011)$	0.0008	0.0003
2	$(\varepsilon_{13} \rightarrow \varepsilon_{18},\ \varepsilon_{18} \rightarrow \varepsilon_{21})$	0.00065	0.00055
2	$(\varepsilon_{14},\ \varepsilon_{15}) = (0.0004,\ 0.0003)$	0.00035	0.00005
2	$(\varepsilon_{16},\ \varepsilon_{17}) = (0.0010,\ 0.0006)$	0.0008	0.0002
2	$(\varepsilon_{19},\ \varepsilon_{20}) = (0.0004,\ 0.0008)$	0.0006	0.0002
1	$\varepsilon_2 \rightarrow \varepsilon_3(0.0007,\ 0.0002)$	0.00045	0.00025
1	$\varepsilon_9 \rightarrow \varepsilon_{10}(0.0002,\ 0.0012)$	0.0007	0.0005
1	$\varepsilon_{10} \rightarrow \varepsilon_{13}(0.0012,\ 0.0001)$	0.00065	0.00055
1	$\varepsilon_{21} \rightarrow \varepsilon_{22}(0.0001,\ 0.0009)$	0.0005	0.0004
1	$\varepsilon_{22} \rightarrow \varepsilon_{23}(0.0009,\ 0.0004)$	0.00065	0.00025
1	$\varepsilon_{23} \rightarrow \varepsilon_{24}(0.0004,\ 0.0006)$	0.0005	0.0001

4.8.4　3-Point Method

The 3-point method constitutes another rainflow counting method. It follows the guideline given below:

If　$|\varepsilon_{i+1} - \varepsilon_i| > |\varepsilon_i - \varepsilon_{i-1}|$, one cycle is identified.

of which i is one of the strain extrema. It is here demonstrated using the case study on IGBT connections for an electronic power module done by [Nicola]. The temperature of the weak link (an IGBT connection) in an electronic power module is frequently identified as the design variable, whose amplitude and mean value are to be counted using the rainflow counting algorithm. Though not required for every case of study, the amplitude and mean value of time intervals can be also counted.

(a) A history of temperature fluctuating between 20 ℃ and 60 ℃ has been recorded as shown in Fig. 4.8.6(a), including seventeen peaks and valleys.

(b) The seventeen extremities, connected as shown in Fig. 4.8.6(b), are given as follows:

$P_1 = 34.8$ ℃ $\quad$ $P_2 = 45.8$ ℃ $\quad$ $P_3 = 22.3$ ℃ $\quad$ $P_4 = 45.3$ ℃ $\quad$ $P_5 = 23.7$ ℃

$P_6 = 48.2$ ℃ $\quad$ $P_7 = 26.2$ ℃ $\quad$ $P_8 = 49$ ℃ $\quad$ $P_9 = 26.7$ ℃ $\quad$ $P_{10} = 51.2$ ℃

$P_{11} = 28.7$ ℃ $\quad$ $P_{12} = 51.8$ ℃ $\quad$ $P_{13} = 29$ ℃ $\quad$ $P_{14} = 53.4$ ℃ $\quad$ $P_{15} = 30.5$ ℃

$P_{16} = 53.8$ ℃ $\quad$ $P_{17} = 27.4$ ℃

(c) Check in the first 3 points, i.e., P_1, P_2, and P_3. Since $|P_3 - P_2| > |P_2 - P_1|$, P_1 is discarded and a reversal (half cycle) is designated to $P_1 - P_2$, as shown in Fig. 4.8.6(c), of which

$$\frac{1}{2}\Delta T = \frac{P_2 - P_1}{2} = \frac{45.8 - 34.8}{2} = 5.5 \text{ ℃} \quad (\text{Amplitude})$$

$$T_{\text{mean}} = \frac{P_2 + P_1}{2} = \frac{45.8 + 34.8}{2} = 40.3 \text{ ℃} \quad (\text{Mean})$$

Discard P_1 and check in the next point (P_4). P_2 is the new starting point. Since $|P_4 - P_3| < |P_3 - P_2|$, no cycle or reversal is identified. Check in the next point (P_5). Since $|P_5 - P_4| < |P_4 - P_3|$, no cycle or reversal is identified. Check in the next point (P_6). Since $|P_6 - P_5| > |P_5 - P_4|$, a cycle at "$P_4 - P_5$" level is formed as

$$\frac{1}{2}\Delta T = \frac{|P_5 - P_4|}{2} = \frac{|23.7 - 45.3|}{2} = 10.8 \text{ ℃} \quad (\text{Amplitude})$$

$$T_{\text{mean}} = \frac{P_5 + P_4}{2} = \frac{23.7 + 45.3}{2} = 34.5 \text{ ℃} \quad (\text{Mean})$$

(d) P_4 and P_5 are discarded and P_3 is connected to P_6. Now the new 3 points of concern is $P_2 - P_3 - P_6$, as shown in Fig. 4.8.6(d). Since $|P_6 - P_3| > |P_3 - P_2|$, a reversal is identified at $P_2 - P_3$ level,

$$\frac{1}{2}\Delta T = \frac{|P_3 - P_2|}{2} = \frac{|22.3 - 45.8|}{2} = 11.75 \text{ ℃} \quad (\text{Amplitude})$$

$$T_{\text{mean}} = \frac{P_3 + P_2}{2} = \frac{22.3 - 45.8}{2} = 34.05 \text{ ℃} \quad (\text{Mean})$$

(e) Check in the next point (P_7), discard P_2, and P_3 is the new starting point. The new 3 points of concern is $P_3-P_6-P_7$, as shown in Fig. 4.8.6(e). Since $|P_7-P_6| < |P_6-P_3|$, no cycle or reversal is identified. Discard P_3 and check in the next point (P_8). Since $|P_7 -P_6| < |P_8-P_7|$, a cycle at "P_6-P_7" level is formed as

$$\frac{1}{2}\Delta T = \frac{|P_7 - P_6|}{2} = \frac{|26.2 - 48.2|}{2} = 11 \ ℃ \quad (\text{Amplitude})$$

$$T_{\text{mean}} = \frac{P_7 + P_6}{2} = \frac{26.2 + 48.2}{2} = 37.2 \ ℃ \quad (\text{Mean})$$

(f) P_6 and P_7 are discarded and P_3 is connected to P_8. Now the 3 points of concern is $P_3-P_8-P_9$, as shown in Fig. 4.8.6(f). Since $|P_9-P_8| < |P_8-P_3|$, no cycle or reversal is identified. Discard P_3 and check in the next point (P_{10}). Since $|P_{10}-P_9|>|P_9-P_8|$, a cycle at 'P_8-P_9' level is formed as

$$\frac{1}{2}\Delta T = \frac{|P_9 - P_8|}{2} = \frac{|26.7 - 49|}{2} = 11.15 \ ℃ \quad (\text{Amplitude})$$

$$T_{\text{mean}} = \frac{P_9 + P_8}{2} = \frac{26.7 + 49}{2} = 37.85 \ ℃ \quad (\text{Mean})$$

(g) P_8 and P_9 are discarded. P_{10} and P_{11} are checked in, P_3 is connected to P_{10}. Now the 3 points of concern is formed, i.e., $P_3-P_{10}-P_{11}$, as shown in Fig. 4.8.6(g). Since $|P_{11}-P_{10}|<|P_{10}-P_3|$, no cycle or reversal is identified. P_3 is discarded, P_{12} is checked in, and the new 3 points of concern is $P_{10}-P_{11}-P_{12}$. Since $|P_{12}-P_{11}|>|P_{11}-P_{10}|$, a cycle at "$P_{10}-P_{11}$" level is formed as

$$\frac{1}{2}\Delta T = \frac{|P_{11} - P_{10}|}{2} = \frac{|28.7 - 51.2|}{2} = 11.25 \ ℃ \quad (\text{Amplitude})$$

$$T_{\text{mean}} = \frac{P_{11} + P_{10}}{2} = \frac{28.7 + 51.2}{2} = 39.95 \ ℃ \quad (\text{Mean})$$

(h) P_{10} and P_{11} are discarded. P_3 is connected to P_{12}. Now the 3 points of concern is formed, i.e., $P_3-P_{12}-P_{13}$, as shown in Fig. 4.8.6(h). Since $|P_{13}-P_{12}| < |P_{12}-P_3|$, no cycle or reversal is identified. P_3 is neglected, P_{14} is checked in, and the new 3 points of concern is $P_{12}-P_{13}-P_{14}$. Since $|P_{14}-P_{13}|>|P_{13}-P_{12}|$, a cycle at "$P_{12}-P_{13}$" level is formed as

$$\frac{1}{2}\Delta T = \frac{|P_{13} - P_{12}|}{2} = \frac{|29 - 51.8|}{2} = 11.4 \ ℃ \quad (\text{Amplitude})$$

$$T_{\text{mean}} = \frac{P_{13} + P_{12}}{2} = \frac{29 + 51.8}{2} = 40.4 \ ℃ \quad (\text{Mean})$$

(ⅰ) P_{12} and P_{13} are discarded. P_3 is connected to P_{14}. Now the 3 points of concern is formed, i.e., P_3–P_{14}–P_{15}, as shown in Fig. 4.8.6(ⅰ). Since $|P_{15}–P_{14}| < |P_{14}–P_3|$, no cycle or reversal is identified. P_3 is neglected, P_{16} is checked in, and the new 3 points of concern is P_{14}–P_{15}–P_{16}. Since $|P_{16}–P_{15}| > |P_{15}–P_{14}|$, a cycle at "$P_{12}$–$P_{13}$" level is formed as

$$\frac{1}{2}\Delta T = \frac{|P_{15} - P_{14}|}{2} = \frac{|30.5 - 53.4|}{2} = 11.45 \ ℃ \quad (\text{Amplitude})$$

$$T_{mean} = \frac{P_{15} + P_{14}}{2} = \frac{30.5 + 53.4}{2} = 41.95 \ ℃ \quad (\text{Mean})$$

(ⅰ) P_{14} and P_{15} are discarded. P_3 is connected to P_{14}. Now the 3 points of concern is P_3–P_{16}–P_{17}, as shown in Fig. 4.8.6(ⅰ). Since $|P_{17}–P_{16}| < |P_{16}–P_3|$, no cycle or reversal is identified. P_3 is neglected, but no more point to be checked in. Here one may assume there are two reversals: one at P_3–P_{16} level and the other at P_{16}–P_{17} level, respectively, having

$$\frac{1}{2}\Delta T = \frac{|P_{15} - P_{14}|}{2} = \frac{|30.5 - 53.4|}{2} = 11.45 \ ℃ \quad (\text{Amplitude})$$

$$T_{mean} = \frac{P_{15} + P_{14}}{2} = \frac{30.5 + 53.4}{2} = 41.95 \ ℃ \quad (\text{Mean})$$

and $$\frac{1}{2}\Delta T = \frac{|P_{15} - P_{14}|}{2} = \frac{|30.5 - 53.4|}{2} = 11.45 \ ℃ \quad (\text{Amplitude})$$

$$T_{mean} = \frac{P_{15} + P_{14}}{2} = \frac{30.5 + 53.4}{2} = 41.95 \ ℃ \quad (\text{Mean})$$

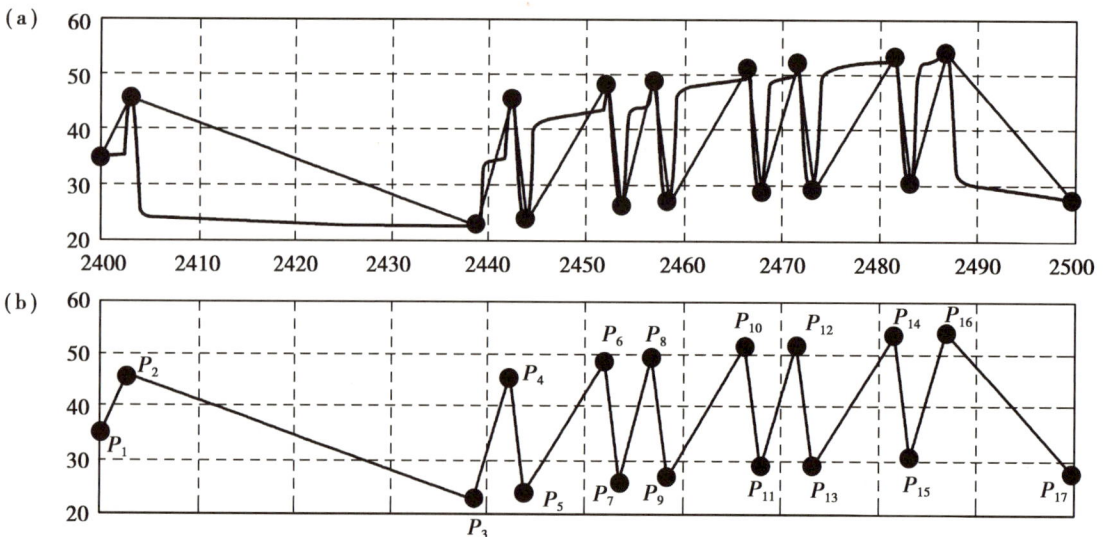

(c)
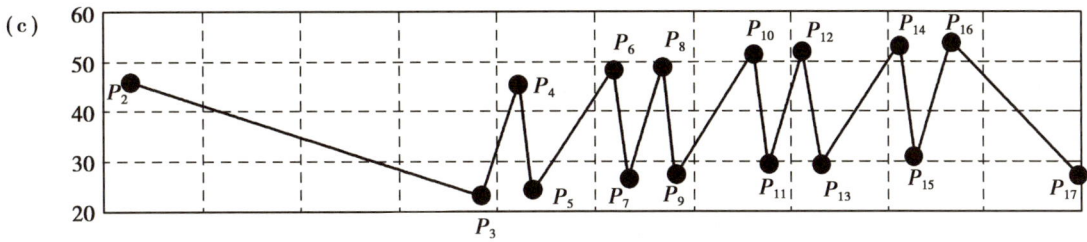

(d)

(e)
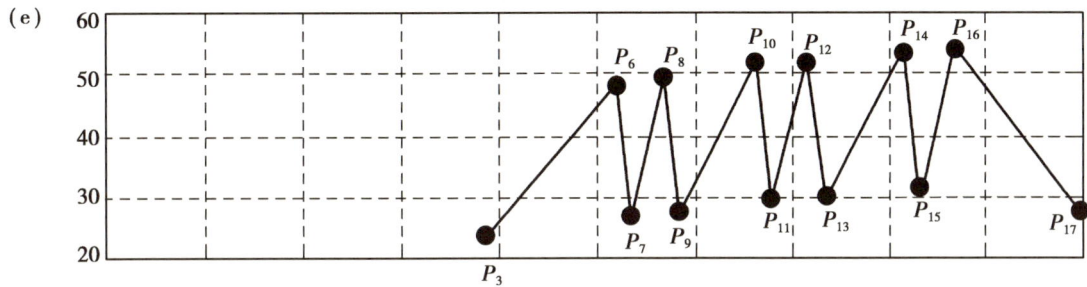

(f)
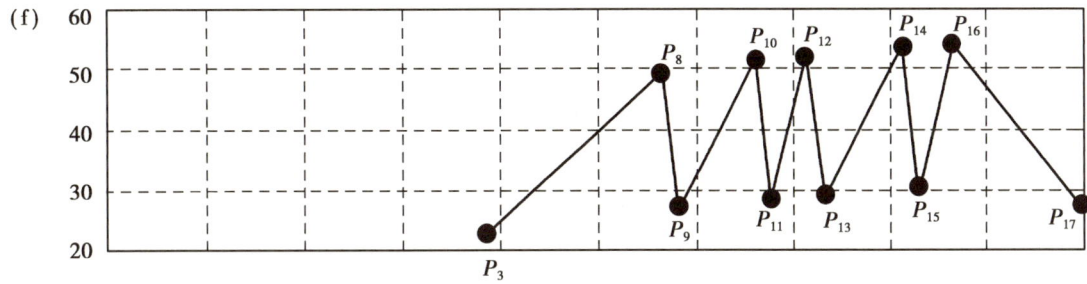

(g)
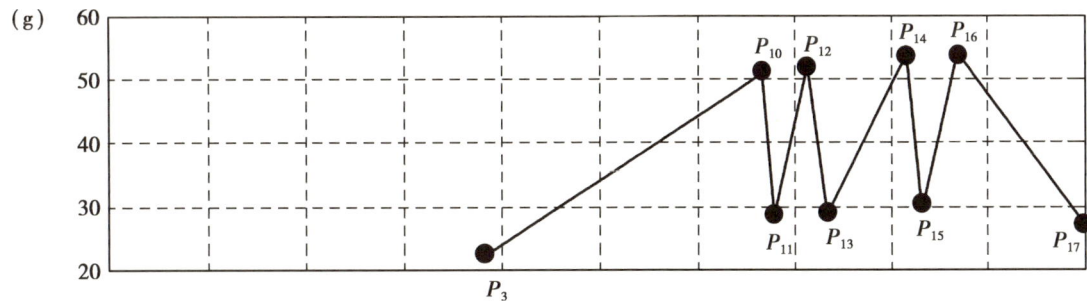

(h)
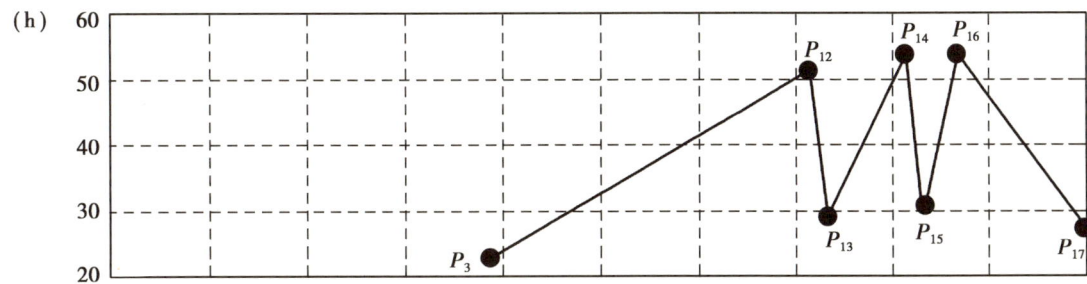

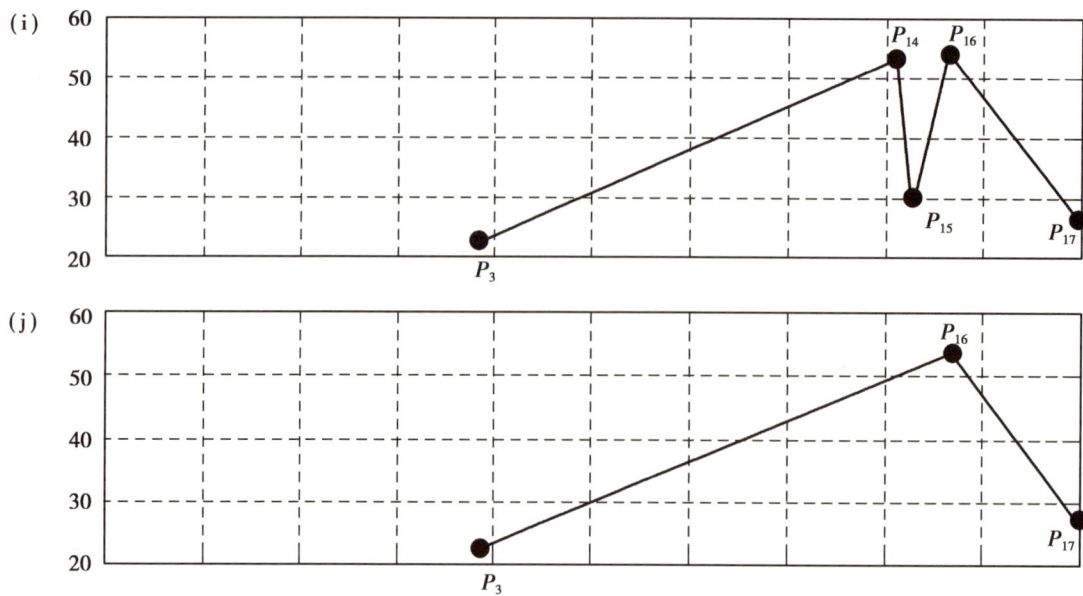

Fig. 4.8.6 Rainflow Counting of Temperature Fluctuations at an IGBT Junction ［Nicola］

4.8.5 Reconstruction of Loading Sequence

Damage by fatigue is usually interpreted as micro-crack growth in opening and/or sliding modes, while the effective strain (stress) value results from the crack closure phenomenon due to which the applied stress range is reduced; such a mechanism strongly depends on the load history. The rainflow counting method emerges as an examination procedure that can be used to store service measurements in a form suitable for fatigue life prediction of materials and structures, as well as for reconstructing a sequence from the data in order to provide prominent loading data for fatigue life testing. Cycles with small amounts of mean value and fluctuating amplitude are to be truncated. The decision on the threshold of "being small" depends on the material fatigue properties.

4.9 Nonproportional Loading and Strain Ratcheting

Some parts such as rotating shafts and mounted gears (e.g. engine crankshafts and connecting rods/bearings), vehicle axles with vehicle stability control mechanisms (including ABS and traction control), pressure vessels, and machine tools, experience multiaxial loads in operation, of which bending moment and torsional torque are applied at a frequency different from the rotational frequency. This is called nonproportional loading. The amount of out-of-phase in terms of phase angle, that lowers the allowable strain amplitude as shown in Fig. 4.9.1, is a key destructive factor to the fatigue life of materials.

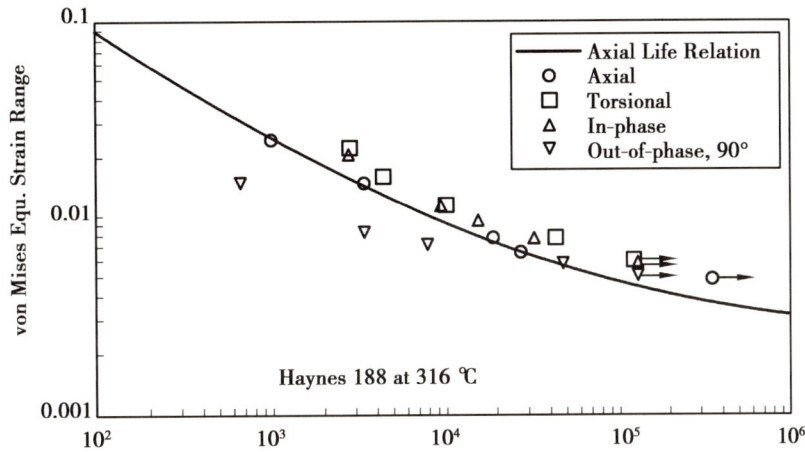

Fig. 4.9.1   Lowered Allowable Fluctuating Strain Amplitude for Out-of-Phase Loading Relative to Others [Kalluri & Bonacuse]

The loads are not proportional when the six strain components are not in phase with each other and their resulting principal strain (stress) angle is not constant. For example, normal strain $\varepsilon = \varepsilon_{\circ}$ $\sin(\omega t)$ in combination with shear strain $\gamma = \gamma_{\circ} \sin(\omega t + \psi)$, of which $\psi \neq 0$. The influence of nonproportionality on fatigue is to cause more damage than proportional loading for most cases. Its impact on the mechanism of dislocation evolution is the main cause of the decrease of fatigue strength and the reduction in the fatigue limit [Skibicki]. Nevertheless, there is also the influence of nonproportionality on the course of structural changes (e.g. phase transformations in steel) induced by plastic strain [Skibicki & Dymski].

4.9.1   Nonproportional Loading

A promising fully reversedly combined torsion and bending test for out-of-phase fatigue life prediction of high-strength structural steel SM45C at intermediate to high cycles was developed by [Lee] and it is presented in [ASTM STP853]. Examples 4.9.1-4.9.4 are given to clarify the concept of nonproportionality.

Assume that a rotating shaft experiences significant torsional and bending strains that can be represented by the following three components: ε_{xx}, ε_{yy} and γ_{xy}. The rotating phase angle will be illustrated using the Mohr's circles for principal strains, i.e., Eqs. (2.6.38)-(2.6.39). Sine and cosine loading waves are proposed by [Chattopadhyay & Nathan] to explain the concepts of proportionality and nonproportionality based on such rotating shafts that experience time-varying loads such as transmission shafts, connecting rods, and crankshafts under multiaxial loads.

Example 4.9.1   Given that ε_{xx}, $= 7000 \sin \omega t \ \mu m/m$, $\varepsilon_{yy} = 0 \ \mu m/m$ and $\varepsilon_{xy} = 4000 \sin \omega t \ \mu m/m$ (i.e., $\gamma_{xy} = 8000 \sin \omega t \ \mu m/m$). How does the phase angle vary in the space?

Solution:

According to Eqs. (2.6.38) and (2.6.39), the principal strain angle and principal strain are, respectively

$$\theta = \frac{1}{2}\tan^{-1}\left[\frac{\varepsilon_{xy}}{\frac{1}{2}(\varepsilon_{xx} - \varepsilon_{yy})}\right] = \frac{1}{2}\tan^{-1}\left(\frac{4000\sin\omega t}{3500\sin\omega t}\right) = 24.4°$$

and

$$\varepsilon = \frac{1}{2}(\varepsilon_{xx} + \varepsilon_{yy}) \pm \left\{\left[\frac{1}{2}(\varepsilon_{xx} - \varepsilon_{yy})\right]^2 + \varepsilon_{xy}^2\right\}^{\frac{1}{2}}$$

$$= 3500\sin\omega t \pm (3500^2\sin^2\omega t + 4000^2\sin^2\omega t)^{\frac{1}{2}}$$

Thus, $\varepsilon_1 = 8815\sin\omega t$ μm/m and $\varepsilon_2 = -1815\sin\omega t$ μm/m.

The phase angle is constant while the principal strains vary with respect to time. This is a proportional load case.

Example 4.9.2   Given that $\varepsilon_{xx} = 4000$ μm/m, $\varepsilon_{yy} = 0$ μm/m and $\varepsilon_{xy} = 2000\sin\omega t$ μm/m (i.e., $\gamma_{xy} = 4000\sin\omega t$ μm/m). How does the phase angle vary in the space?

Solution:

According to Eqs. (2.6.38) and (2.6.39), the principal strain angle and principal strain are, respectively

$$\theta = \frac{1}{2}\tan^{-1}\left[\frac{\varepsilon_{xy}}{\frac{1}{2}(\varepsilon_{xx} - \varepsilon_{yy})}\right] = \frac{1}{2}\tan^{-1}\left(\frac{2000\sin\omega t}{2000}\right) = \frac{1}{2}\tan^{-1}(\sin\omega t)$$

and

$$\varepsilon = \frac{1}{2}(\varepsilon_{xx} + \varepsilon_{yy}) \pm \left\{\left[\frac{1}{2}(\varepsilon_{xx} - \varepsilon_{yy})\right]^2 + \varepsilon_{xy}^2\right\}^{\frac{1}{2}}$$

$$= 2000 \pm (2000^2 + 2000^2\sin^2\omega t)^{\frac{1}{2}}$$

$$= 2000 \pm 2000(1 + \sin^2\omega t)^{\frac{1}{2}}$$

Thus, $\varepsilon_1 = 2000\left[1 + (1 + \sin^2\omega t)^{\frac{1}{2}}\right]$ μm/m   (1st   Principal Strain)

$\varepsilon_3 = 2000\left[1 - (1 + \sin^2\omega t)^{\frac{1}{2}}\right]$ μm/m   (3rd   Principal Strain)

$\Delta\varepsilon = (\varepsilon_1 - \varepsilon_3) = 4000(1 + \sin^2\omega t)^{\frac{1}{2}}$ μm/m   (Strain Range)

$$\varepsilon_a = \frac{1}{2}(\varepsilon_1 - \varepsilon_3) = 2000\,(1 + \sin^2 \omega t)^{\frac{1}{2}}\ \mu m/m \qquad\qquad (\text{Strain Amplitude})$$

$$\varepsilon_m = \frac{1}{2}(\varepsilon_1 + \varepsilon_3) = 2000\ \mu m/m \qquad\qquad (\text{Mean Strain})$$

$$\text{and}\quad \varepsilon_{13max} = \frac{1}{2}(\varepsilon_1 - \varepsilon_3) = 2000\,(1 + \sin^2 \omega t)^{\frac{1}{2}}\ \mu m/m \qquad\qquad (\text{Max. Shear Strain})$$

The phase angle is not constant. This is a nonproportional load case. Note that the 2nd principal strain is zero ($\varepsilon_2 = 0$) and the maximum shear strain (ε_{13max}) is of the same magnitude as the fluctuating amplitude of normal strain (ε_a). Assume that $\omega = 2\pi$ and 2π (i.e., 1 Hz and 2 Hz). The variations of the phase angle and strain amplitude with respect to time for both angular speeds can be plotted in Figs. 4.9.2 and 4.9.3, respectively.

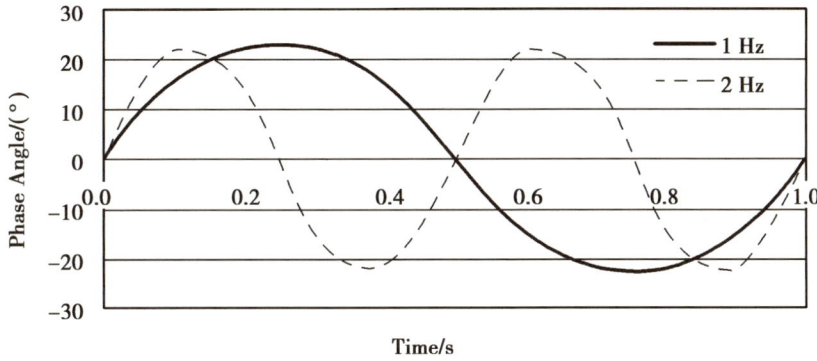

Fig. 4.9.2　Plots of Phase Angle versus Time at Two Angular Speeds (1 Hz and 2 Hz)

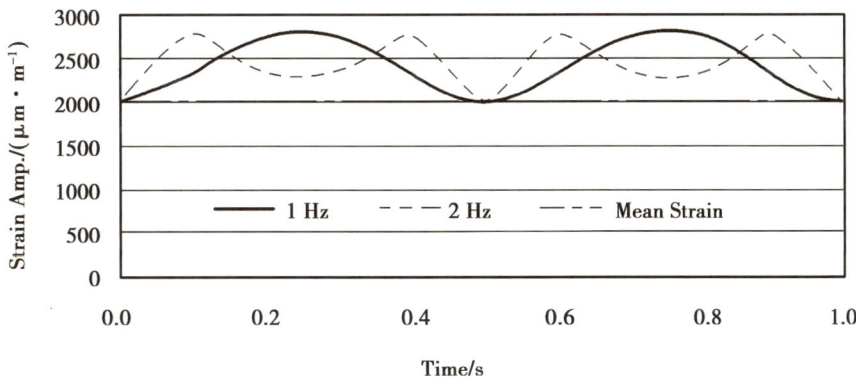

Fig. 4.9.3　Plots of Normal Strain Amplitude versus Mean Strain as Functions of Time at Two Angular Speeds (1 Hz and 2 Hz)

Example 4.9.3　Given that $\varepsilon_{xx} = 4000\ \mu m/m$, $\varepsilon_{yy} = 2000 \sin \omega t\ \mu m/m$ and $\varepsilon_{xy} = 0\ \mu m/m$. How does the phase angle vary in the space?

Solution:

According to Eqs. (2.6.38) and (2.6.39), the principal strain angle and principal strain are, respectively

$$\theta = \frac{1}{2}\tan^{-1}\frac{\varepsilon_{xy}}{\frac{1}{2}(\varepsilon_{xx} - \varepsilon_{yy})} = \frac{1}{2}\tan^{-1}\frac{0}{2000(1 - \sin\omega t)} = \frac{1}{2}\tan^{-1}0 = 0$$

The phase angle is constant. This is a proportional load case.

Example 4.9.4   Given that $\varepsilon_{xx} = 4000\ \mu m/m$, $\varepsilon_{yy} = 2000\sin\omega t\ \mu m/m$ and $\varepsilon_{xy} = 2000\ \mu m/m$. How does the phase angle vary in the space?

Solution:

According to Eqs. (2.6.38) and (2.6.39), the principal strain angle is

$$\theta = \frac{1}{2}\tan^{-1}\frac{\varepsilon_{xy}}{\frac{1}{2}(\varepsilon_{xx} - \varepsilon_{yy})} = \frac{1}{2}\tan^{-1}\frac{2000}{2000(1 - \sin\omega t)} = \frac{1}{2}\tan^{-1}\frac{1}{1 - \sin\omega t}$$

The phase angle is not constant, as plotted in Fig. 4.9.4. This is a nonproportional load case.

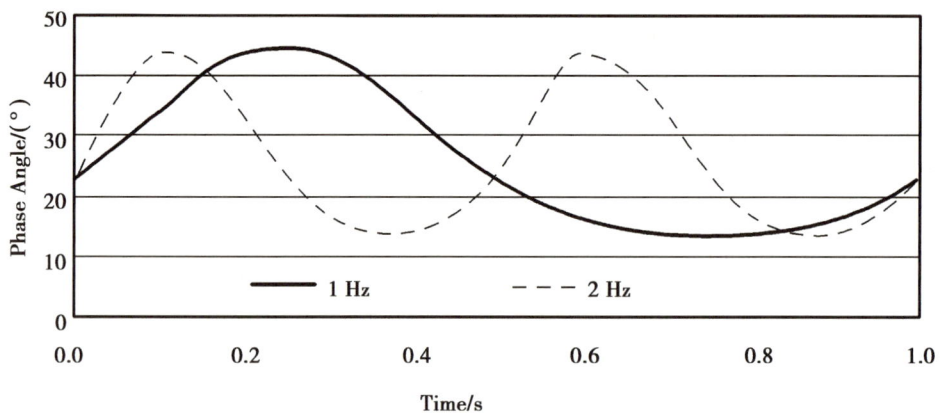

Fig. 4.9.4   Plots of Phase Angle versus Time at Two Angular Speeds (1 Hz and 2 Hz)

4.9.2   Strain Ratcheting Due to Asymmetric Loads and Non-Zero Mean Strain

When mechanical components are subjected to asymmetric cyclic loads even at zero mean strain (or stress), the loaded material starts accumulating plastic strain and leads to strain ratcheting, which may happen at room temperature or at an elevated temperature. Creep ratcheting is a phenomenon that applies at the moment when both creep and strain ratcheting occur.

Uniaxial ratcheting under zero mean stress is characterized by an open hysteresis loop and it is a result of different nonlinear behaviors of the material in tension and compression. On the other hand, in a uniaxial fatigue test under a controlled load with non-zero mean strain (or mean stress) the accumulation of axial plastic strain may also occur cycle by cycle. An asymmetric cyclic loading of specimens was carried out at a frequency of 0.1 Hz in a stress-controlled mode up to 1200 cycles by [Borodii et al.]. The results are shown in Fig. 4.9.5. When gap δ [Fig. 4.9.5 (b)] is getting smaller and smaller, it is a strain hardening process. The "$3^{\frac{1}{2}}$" is employed to balance the scales of horizontal and vertical axes according to the definition of von Mises equivalent stress (strain) for the combination of a single normal stress (strain) and a single shear stress (strain) as follows:

(a) Uniaxial Tension-Comperssion Load(σ_m=106.1 MPa & σ_a=265.3 MPa)

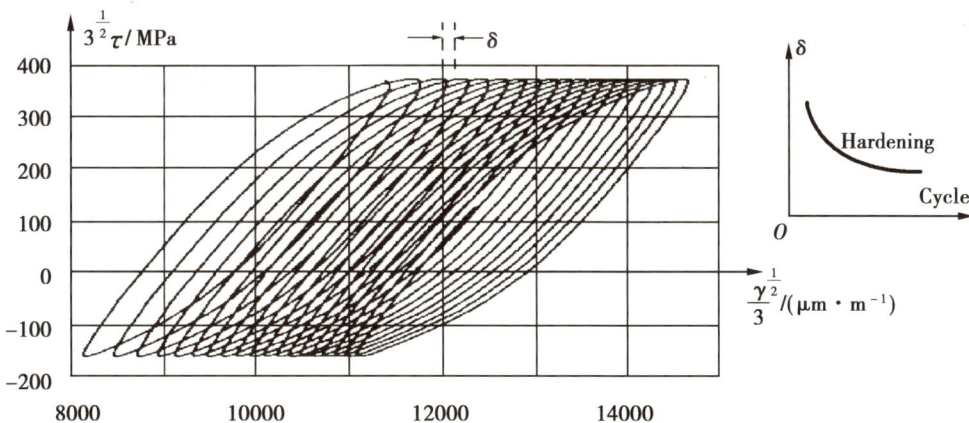

(b) Torsional Load($3^{\frac{1}{2}}\tau_m$=106.1 MPa & $3^{\frac{1}{2}}\tau_a$=265.3 MPa)

Fig. 4.9.5   Strain Ratcheting of SAE 1020 Steel under Stress-Controlled Tests with Asymmetric Loading [Borodii et al.]

$$\sigma_{eq} = (\sigma_{11}^2 + 3\tau_{12}^2)^{\frac{1}{2}} = [\sigma_{11}^2 + (3^{\frac{1}{2}}\tau_{12})^2]^{\frac{1}{2}} \qquad (4.9.1)$$

$$\text{and} \quad \varepsilon_{eq} = \left(\varepsilon_{11}^2 + \frac{\gamma_{12}^2}{3}\right)^{\frac{1}{2}} = \left[\varepsilon_{11}^2 + \left(\frac{\gamma_{12}}{3^{\frac{1}{2}}}\right)^2\right]^{\frac{1}{2}}$$

$$= \left(\varepsilon_{11}^2 + \frac{4\varepsilon_{12}^2}{3}\right)^{\frac{1}{2}} = \left[\varepsilon_{11}^2 + \left(\frac{2\varepsilon_{12}}{3^{\frac{1}{2}}}\right)^2\right]^{\frac{1}{2}} \qquad (4.9.2)$$

of which σ_{11} and ε_{11} are axial stress and strain respectively, and τ_{12} and γ_{12} are shear stress and strain, respectively. Note that ε_{12} is the tensor shear strain and $\varepsilon_{12} = \gamma_{12}/2$. The von Mises equivalent stress (strain) is the main driving force that accounts for strain ratcheting. The hydrostatic stress has no noticeable impact on strain ratcheting, as it has no influence on the dislocation sliding [Sakane & Itoh].

4.9.3 Strain Hardening/Softening and Ratcheting due to Nonproportional Loads

When the material is subjected to nonproportional loading, the principal strains (or stresses) rotate as dictated by the phase angle and more slip planes are energized interactively. A test with nonproportional tension-compression/torsional loads, as illustrated by Figs. 4.9.21-4.9.4, concludes that bi-axial strain hardening is associated with strain ratcheting in addition to the proportional-strain hardening [Doquet & Clavel].

Strain ratcheting due to nonproportional loads generates a resultant strain with non-zero mean value that accumulates cycle after cycle. Uniaxial ratcheting under zero mean stress is also characterized by hysteresis loops, as shown in Fig. 4.9.5.

Conception of non-proportional hardening represents material ratcheting resulting from nonproportional loads, as demonstrated by the tension-compression/torsion loading. The additional hardening due to nonproportional loading is defined as the ratio of the increased strain to the strain hardening subjected to proportional loading,

$$\alpha_{np} = \frac{\varepsilon_{a,nonpro} - \varepsilon_{a,pro}}{\varepsilon_{a,pro}} \qquad (4.9.3)$$

or $\quad \varepsilon_{a,nonpro} = (1 + \alpha_{np})\varepsilon_{a,pro} \qquad (4.9.4)$

where

α_{np}: Nonproportionality due to material;

$\varepsilon_{a,nonpro}$: Max. equivalent strain amplitude (i.e., von Mises) under proportional loading;

$\varepsilon_{a,pro}$: Max. Equivalent strain amplitude (i.e., von Mises) under proportional loading.

Nonproportionality due to material hardening happens to well-spaced planar slip bands with low fault stacking energy, such as austenitic stainless steels. In this kind of materials, crossed slip bands are further energized by the rotation of the maximum shear planes in various directions. On the other hand for materials having crossed bands with high existing fault stacking energy, such as aluminum alloys, the α_{np} is small. Carbon steels falls between these two extrema. The following data are given for reference:

Wrought Al 7075	SAE 1045 steel	SAE 316 Stainless Steel
$\alpha_{np} \approx 0$	$\alpha_{np} \approx 0.3$	$\alpha_{np} \approx 1.0$

However, the degree of non-proportional hardening also depends on the loading path as described by the following equation

$$\varepsilon_{a,\text{nonpro}} = (1 + \alpha\, F_{np})\, \varepsilon_{a,\text{pro}} = (1 + \alpha F_{np})\, \varepsilon_{a,\text{pro}} \tag{4.9.5}$$

where

$\varepsilon_{a,\text{nonpro}}$: Max. equivalent strain amplitude (i.e., von Mises) under nonproportional loading;

$\varepsilon_{a,\text{pro}}$: Max. equivalent strain amplitude (i.e., von Mises) under proportional loading;

F_{np}: Nonproportionality subject to load path.

The equivalent strain amplitude is the radius of the minimum circle that circumscribes the loading path in the deviatoric strain space, as shown in Fig. 4.9.6. The non-proportional factor is defined as the ratio of the minor axis length (R_b) to the major axis length (R_a) of the ellipse tracing the loading path [Li & deFreitas],

$$F_{np} = \frac{R_b}{R_a} \tag{4.9.6}$$

of which F_{np} falls between 0 and 1, i.e., $0 \leqslant F_{np} \leqslant 1$. The variation of the equivalent strain (stress) amplitude and mean strain (stress) due to nonproportionality in loading is to be illustrated using Example 4.9.5, without considering the potential material phase transformation.

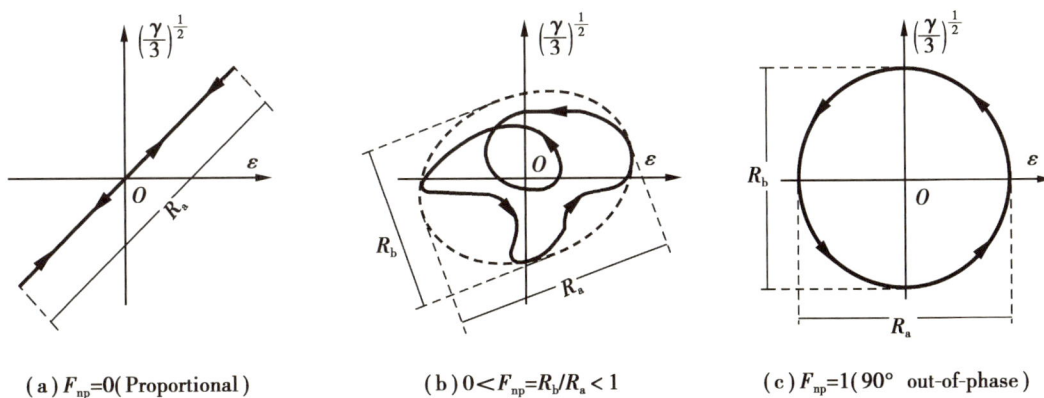

(a) $F_{np}=0$ (Proportional)   (b) $0 < F_{np}=R_b/R_a < 1$ (c) $F_{np}=1$ (90° out-of-phase)

Fig. 4.9.6   Deviatoric Strain Space for Identifying the Equivalent Strain Amplitude [Meggiolar et al.]

Example 4.9.5　Given that $\varepsilon_{xx} = 4000 \sin 2\pi t$ μm/m, $\varepsilon_{yy} = 0$ μm/m and $\varepsilon_{xy} = 2000 \sin(2\pi t + \theta)$ μm/m. How much is the equivalent strain amplitude and equivalent mean strain by Eqs. (4.9.1) and (4.9.2) if (a) $\theta = 0°$, (b) $\theta = 45°$, and (c) $\theta = 90°$?

Solution:

$$\varepsilon_{eq} = \left(\frac{\varepsilon_{11}^2 + 4\varepsilon_{12}^2}{3} \right)^{\frac{1}{2}} = \left[4000^2 \sin^2 2\pi t + \frac{4}{3} \cdot 2000^2 \sin^2(2\pi t + \theta) \right]^{\frac{1}{2}}$$

$$= \left[4000^2 \sin^2 2\pi t + \frac{4}{3} \cdot 2000^2 \sin^2(2\pi t + \theta) \right]^{\frac{1}{2}}$$

The equivalent mean strains (ε_{eq}), i.e., averaged magnitudes), corresponding to phase angles of $0°$, $30°$, $45°$, $60°$, and $90°$ are calculated from the above equation and listed as follows:

$\theta/(°)$	0	30	45	60	90	120	135	150	180
$\varepsilon_{eq,ave}/(\mu m \cdot m^{-1})$	2585	2870	2977	3059	3129	3059	2977	2870	2585

A plot of the variation of the equivalent strain amplitude versus phase angle shows that the maximum increase of loading due to the phase angle is at $90°$, as shown in Fig. 4.9.7. The resultant equivalent strains versus the given normal and shear strains are plotted in Fig. 4.9.8.

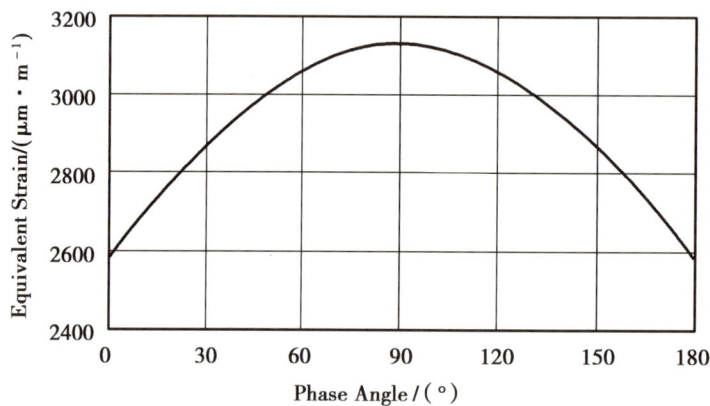

Fig. 4.9.7　Variation of Equivalent Strain Amplitude versus Phase Angle by Example 4.9.5

(a) Proportional

(b) Phase angle=45°

(c) Phase angle=90°

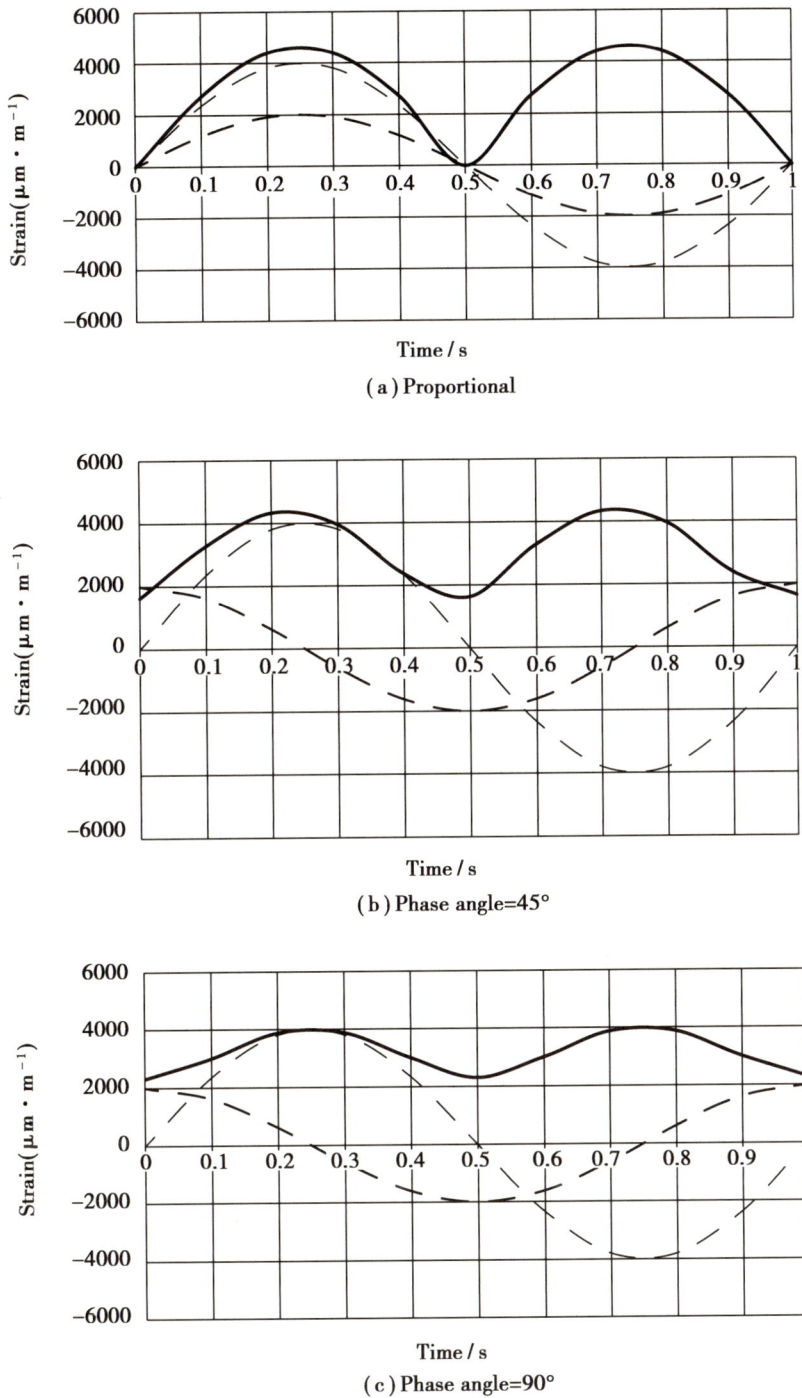

Fig. 4.9.8   Resultant Equivalent Strain Amplitudes (Solid) versus Normal and Shear Strains：

(a) Proportional，(b) Phase Angle＝45°，and (c) Phase Angle＝90°(Example 4.9.5)

4.9.4　Modified Ramberg-Osgood Equation for Nonproportionality

The nonproportional hardening can be modeled using the same Ramberg-Osgood plastic exponent n' from the uniaxial cyclic σ-ε curve, but using a new denominator to represent the nonproportional hardening

$$\varepsilon_a = \frac{\sigma_a}{E} + \left(\frac{\sigma_a}{K'_{np}}\right)^{\frac{1}{n'}} + \varepsilon_{creep} \tag{4.9.7}$$

where
$$K'_{np} = K' \cdot (1 + \alpha_{np} F_{np}) \tag{4.9.8}$$

Note that K' is the uniaxial Ramberg-Osgood plastic coefficient. Note that the nonproportional hardening factor, i.e., $1 + \alpha_{np} F_{np}$, may go as high as 200%. A plot of relative stress-strain curves for quasi-static, cyclic and proportional, and cyclic and nonproportional loadings is given in Fig. 4.9.9.

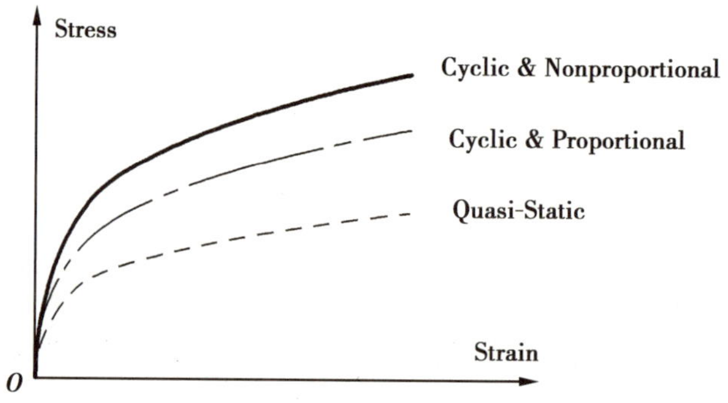

Fig. 4.9.9　Relative Stress-Strain Curves for a Generic Carbon Steel

4.9.5　Counting Methods of Nonproportional Stress/Strain Fluctuations in Time Domain

Identification of looped hysteresis cycles is complex in multiaxial loading cases, while out-of-phase cycling further complicates the problem. Most approaches use equivalent strain/stress quantities to reduce the multiaxial problem to a pseudo-uniaxial one. Its applicability is limited to isotropic materials and it is not feasible to take out-of-phase loadings into consideration.

The second approach is to take a major strain (or stress) component to define the time interval for a cycle and segment other strain (or stress) components accordingly. According to the experimental observation by [Wang Y. et al.], fatigue cycles can be counted based on a main destructive means such as the maximum principal strain. The rainflow counting algorithm is therefore only applied to the maximum principal strain ranges ($\Delta\varepsilon_{1,max}$) and it is assumed that the starting and ending points of the other components of each cycle are identical to those of the maximum principal strain. The extrema of each sub-component are evaluated using the data in this time interval, as shown in Fig. 4.9.10. A normal-strain cycle in a multiaxial domain may cover only a fraction of shear-strain cycle or many cycles.

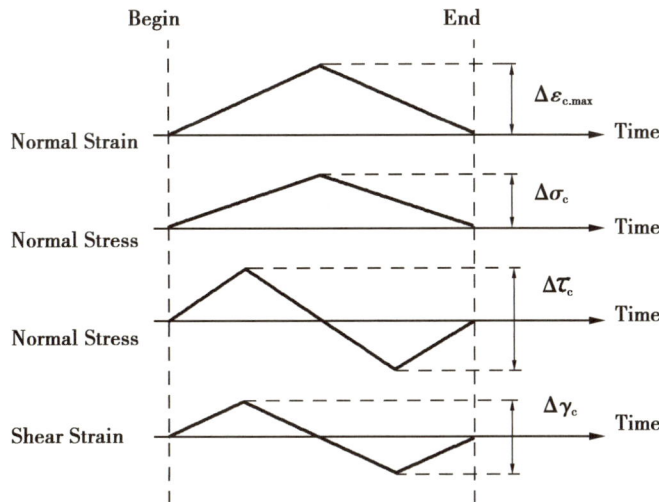

Fig. 4.9.10   Counting Multi-Strains and Multi-Stresses on the Critical Plane

4.10   Stress and Strain Transformations from Freed Surface to the Critical Plane

When the applied multiaxial loading is nonproportional, the critical plane method is an effective approach [Miller & Brown] to identifying the potential failure plane, called critical plane that incurs the most damage. The critical plane method is utilized to identify the failure plane, and resolve and project the strain (stress) components at the potential failure location onto the plane for predicting the potential failure modes including opening, shearing and tearing behaviors. There are two potential crack-initiating modes based on the considered critical plane:

(A) Crack propagating along the surface of the specimen.
(B) Crack growing away from the surface into the specimen.

Once the critical plane is identified, stress and strain components on the plane can be computed via 2-dimensional principal stress algorithm (i.e., Mohr's circle method) for a plane stress case. For a general 3-dimensional case the tensor coordinate transformations are required (see Chapter 3 for details for 3-dimensional coordinate transformations). Two major advantages of the critical plane method over others are two folds: (a) handling multiaxial out-of-phase loadings and (b) dealing with crack closure.

4.10.1　Where is the Critical Plane?

Fatigue occurs mostly on the surface where one of the principal stresses does not exist (zero). Most multiaxial fatigue problems are consequently biaxial in nature. Where is the critical plane, when the material is subjected to multiaxial loads? The criteria have been divided into three categories [Karolczuk & Macha]:

- (a) Stresses: Maximum normal stress, maximum shear stress, and maximum octahedral shear stress are assumed to be effective to locate the critically plane individually.
- (b) Strains: Maximum normal strain, maximum shear strain, and maximum octahedral shear strain are assumed to be effective to locate the critically plane individually. The maximum shear strain energy is the most used criterion for locating the critical plane.
- (c) Strain energy density: Normal strain energy, shear strain energy, and hydrostatic strain energy (mean normal strain energy) can be combined into one equation because each energy term is a scalar. How to relate the energy terms to the two fundamental fatigue cycle tests (fully revered uniaxial tension-compression and pure torsion fatigue tests) for identifying the number to failure will be the next bridge to be built. The approach based on [Liu & Mahadevan] and [Wei] will be rephrased in the next section.

4.10.2　Stress and Strain Transformations in the State of Plane Stress

The methodology based on the plane stress assumption is discussed here. As usual in most homogeneous plastics and metallic alloys, a fatigue failure is associated with a single dominant crack originating from the free surface, of which the following free surface conditions on stresses and strains hold:

$$\text{Stresses:}\ \tau_{xz} = 0,\ \tau_{yz} = 0,\ \tau_{xy} \neq 0,\ \sigma_{xx} \neq 0,\ \sigma_{yy} \neq 0,\ \sigma_{zz} = -p \tag{4.10.1}$$

$$\text{and}\quad \text{Strains:}\ \gamma_{xz} = 0,\ \gamma_{yz} = 0,\ \gamma_{xy} \neq 0,\ \varepsilon_{xx} \neq 0,\ \varepsilon_{yy} \neq 0,\ \varepsilon_{zz} \neq 0 \tag{4.10.2}$$

where
x, y, and z: Coordinates at the free surface and z is perpendicular to the free surface;
p: Pressure applied onto the free surface.

Let (x, y) be the free surface plane. First rotate the stresses and strains on the plane tangent to the surface around the z-axis ($\perp$ the surface plane) at angle θ and obtain the stresses and strains in the new (x', y', z') coordinate system, in which the maximum normal stress amplitude (or range) can be obtained. Then rotating them around the y'-axis (new y-axis after first rotation) at angle ϕ from the surface onto another plane, as illustrated in Fig. 4.10.1, one has a new plane (x'', y''), which is here defined as the "candidate" critical plane. Note that angle ϕ is here to be obtained using Eq. (4.10.13). After the stresses and strains on the free surface are projected onto this "candidate" critical plane [Meggiolaroa et al.], they are related to the original stresses and strains as [Cook]

$$\tau_A(\theta, \phi) = \left[\tau_{xy}\cos 2\theta - \frac{1}{2}(\sigma_{xx} - \sigma_{yy})\sin 2\theta\right]\sin \phi \qquad (4.10.3)$$

$$\tau_B(\theta, \phi) = \frac{1}{2}[\sigma_{xx}\cos^2\theta + \sigma_{yy}\sin^2\theta + p + \tau_{xy}\sin 2\theta]\sin 2\phi \qquad (4.10.4)$$

$$\sigma_\perp(\theta, \phi) = [\sigma_{xx}\cos^2\theta + \sigma_{yy}\sin^2\theta + \tau_{xy}\sin 2\theta]\sin^2\phi - p\cos^2\phi \qquad (4.10.5)$$

$$\gamma_A(\theta, \phi) = [\gamma_{xy}\cos 2\theta - (\varepsilon_{xx} - \varepsilon_{yy})\sin 2\theta]\sin \phi \qquad (4.10.6)$$

$$\gamma_B(\theta, \phi) = \left[\varepsilon_{xx}\cos^2\theta + \varepsilon_{yy}\sin^2\theta - \varepsilon_{zz} + \frac{1}{2}\gamma_{xy}\sin 2\theta\right]\sin 2\phi \qquad (4.10.7)$$

and $$\varepsilon_\perp(\theta, \phi) = \left(\varepsilon_{xx}\cos^2\theta + \varepsilon_{yy}\sin^2\theta + \frac{1}{2}\gamma_{xy}\sin 2\theta\right)\sin^2\phi + \varepsilon_{zz}\cos^2\phi \qquad (4.10.8)$$

where

$\sigma_\perp$ and $\varepsilon_\perp$: Normal stress and strain perpendicular to the critical plane such that the potential crack that lies on the critical plane is in opening mode (mode-I), if there is no other stress or strain;

τ_A and γ_A: Shear stress and strain on the critical plane and parallel to the free surface, responsible for initiating a crack on the critical plane in shear mode-II;

τ_B and γ_B: Shear stress and strain on the critical plane and perpendicular to τ_A and γ_A, Respectively and they are responsible for initiating a crack on the critical plane in shear mode-III.

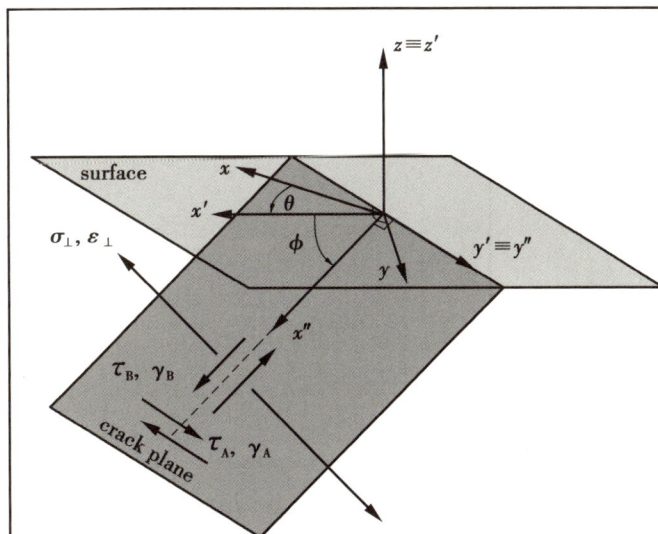

Fig. 4.10.1 Stress Transformations between Free Surface and Critical Plane [Meggiolaroa et al.]

The critical plane is defined traditionally as the maximum shear plane that has the maximum shear strain [Smith, Watson, & Topper]. The maximum normal strain, maximum normal stress, maximum normal strain range, or maximum normal stress range on that plane are then regraded as key damaging parameters.

4.10.3 Nonproportional In-Plane Loading with No Pressure on the Free Surface

Regardless of the load history that is either proportional or nonproportional, τ_A, $\sigma_\perp$, γ_A, or $\varepsilon_\perp$ reach their potential maximum value at $\phi = 90°$ as long as there is no pressure applied onto the "free surface". It means that the critical plane is perpendicular to the free surface when $\phi = 90°$, as shown in Fig. 4.10.2. A shallow straight fracture pattern is therefore expected for either mode-Ⅰ or mode-Ⅱ crack.

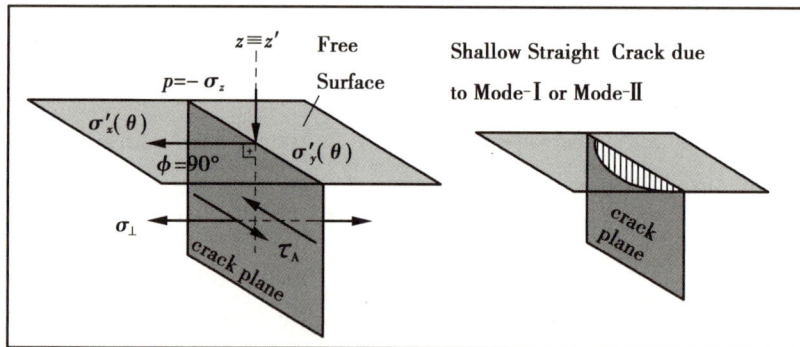

Fig. 4.10.2 Fracture on the Free Surface in Mode-Ⅰ and/or Mode-Ⅱ [Meggiolaroa et al.]

The next step is to demonstrate the impact of phase angle, when the load case is nonproportional. Consider the critical plane based on the assumption of plane stress [Findley], on which the principal normal strain (ε_{xx}) on the critical plane and its associated shear strain (γ_{xy}), in the (x, y, z) coordinate system, can be written, respectively as

$$\varepsilon_{xx} = \varepsilon_A \sin \omega t \tag{4.10.9}$$

and $$\gamma_{xy} = \gamma_A \sin(\omega t - \psi) = \lambda \, \varepsilon_A \sin(\omega t - \psi) \tag{4.10.10}$$

where

ω: Angular speed;

t: Time;

ψ: Phase angle between the shear strain and normal strain;

λ: Ratio of the shear strain amplitude to normal strain amplitude, i.e., $\lambda = \gamma_A / \varepsilon_A$.

The normal strains along y- and z-directions can be calculated using the effective Poisson's ratio

(ν_{eff}) in terms of ε_{xx} as

$$\varepsilon_{yy} = -\nu_{\text{eff}}\,\varepsilon_{xx} \qquad\qquad (4.10.11)$$

and $\quad \varepsilon_{zz} = -\nu_{\text{eff}}\,\varepsilon_{xx} \qquad\qquad (4.10.12)$

Next consider the rotation of stress components in a 2-dimensional plane stress field where $\sigma_{zz} = \tau_{yz} = \tau_{zx} = 0$, around the z-axis from coordinate $(x,\,y,\,z)$ to coordinate $(x',\,y',\,z')$,

$$\sigma_{x'x'} = \frac{1}{2}\,(\sigma_{xx} + \sigma_{yy}) + \frac{1}{2}\,(\sigma_{xx} - \sigma_{yy})\cos 2\theta + \tau_{xy}\sin 2\theta \qquad\qquad (4.10.13)$$

Note that $z \equiv z'$ as z is the rotating axis. Since $\sigma_{yy} = 0$ on the critical plane, the above equation reduces to

$$\sigma_{x'x'} = \frac{1}{2}\,\sigma_{xx}(1 + \cos 2\theta) + \tau_{xy}\sin 2\theta \qquad\qquad (4.10.14)$$

The strains in the $(x,\,y,\,z)$ coordinate system on the surface at angle θ relative to x-axis are thus derived through general coordinate transformations as

$$\varepsilon_{x'x'} = \frac{1}{2}\,(\varepsilon_{xx} + \varepsilon_{yy}) + \frac{1}{2}\,(\varepsilon_{xx} - \varepsilon_{yy})\cos 2\theta + \frac{1}{2}\,\gamma_{xy}\sin 2\theta \qquad\qquad (4.10.15)$$

and $\quad \gamma_{x'y'} = -(\varepsilon_{xx} - \varepsilon_{yy})\sin 2\theta + \gamma_{xy}\cos 2\theta \qquad\qquad (4.10.16)$

Because $\varepsilon_{yy} = -\nu_{\text{eff}}\varepsilon_{xx}$, the above two equations reduce to

$$\varepsilon_{x'x'} = \frac{1}{2}(1 - \nu_{\text{eff}})\,\varepsilon_{xx} + \frac{1}{2}\,(1 + \nu_{\text{eff}})\varepsilon_{xx}\cos 2\theta + \frac{1}{2}\gamma_{xy}\sin 2\theta \qquad\qquad (4.10.17)$$

and $\quad \gamma_{x'y'} = -(1 + \nu_{\text{eff}})\varepsilon_{xx}\sin 2\theta + \gamma_{xy}\cos 2\theta \qquad\qquad (4.10.18)$

Substituting Eqs. (4.10.9) and (4.10.10) into the above two equations leads to [Shang et al.] [Li et al.]

$$\frac{\varepsilon_{x'x'}}{\varepsilon_A} = \frac{1}{2}\{[2\,(1 + \nu_{\text{eff}})\cos^2\theta - 2\nu_{\text{eff}} + \lambda\,\sin 2\theta\,\cos\psi]^2 + (\lambda\,\sin 2\theta\,\sin\psi)^2\}^{\frac{1}{2}}$$
$$[1 + \cos(\xi + \eta)] \qquad\qquad (4.10.19)$$

$$\frac{\gamma_{x'y'}}{\varepsilon_A} = \{[\lambda\,\cos 2\theta\,\cos\psi - (1 + \nu_{\text{eff}})\sin 2\theta]^2 + (\lambda\,\cos 2\theta\,\sin\psi)^2\}^{\frac{1}{2}} \qquad\qquad (4.10.20)$$

where

$$\xi = \tan^{-1} \frac{\lambda \sin 2\theta \sin \psi}{(1 + \nu_{eff}) \cos 2\theta + (1 - \nu_{eff}) + \lambda \sin 2\theta \cos \psi} \qquad (4.10.21)$$

$$\text{and} \quad \eta = \tan^{-1} \frac{-\lambda \cos 2\theta \sin \psi}{-(1 + \nu_{eff}) \sin 2\theta + \lambda \cos 2\theta \cos \psi} \qquad (4.10.22)$$

Differentiation of the dimensionless shear stress, $\gamma_{x'y'}/\varepsilon_A$ in Eq. (4.10.19), with respect to θ leads to attaining the maximum shear strain at angle θ_{max},

$$\theta_{max} = \frac{1}{4}\tan^{-1} \frac{2\lambda(1 + \nu_{eff})\cos \psi}{(1 + \nu_{eff})^2 - \lambda^2} \qquad (4.10.23)$$

This is traditionally defined as the critical plane, i. e., $\theta_{critical} = \theta_{max}$. As demonstrated in Fig. 4.10.3, which is a schematic depiction of Eq. (4.10.20) to show how the shear strain varies with respect to the changing phase angle (ψ) and so does the location of the critical plane. When the phase angle is zero ($\psi = 0$), the critical plane is fixed at a location where Eq. (4.10.20) reduces to

$$\frac{\gamma_{x'y'}}{\varepsilon_A} = \lambda \cos 2\theta - (1 + \nu_{eff}) \sin 2\theta \qquad (4.10.24)$$

Note that $\gamma_{x'y'}/\varepsilon_A$ is not a function of phase angle ψ anymore.

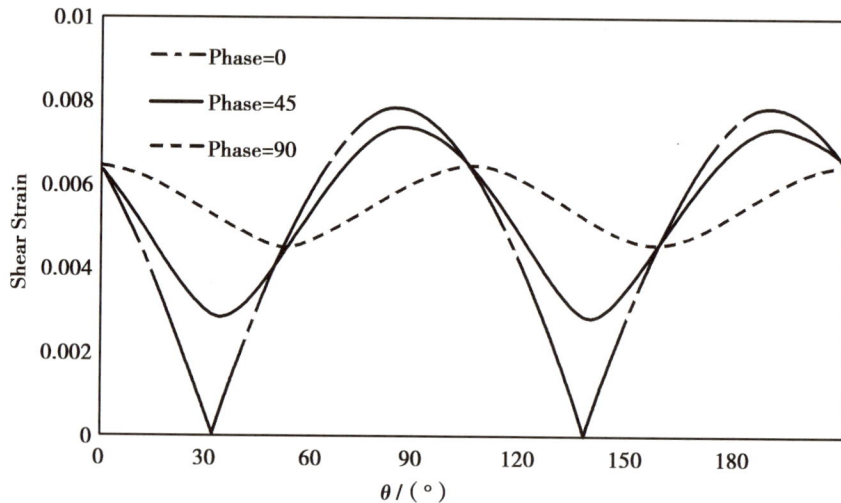

Fig. 4.10.3　Shear Strain Plots for Locating the Critical Plane at Three Given Phase Angles

4.10.4　Mode-Ⅲ: Out-of-Plane Shearing

The presence of significant $\tau_B(\theta, \phi = 45°)$ parallel to the critical plane along its crack depth makes the surface fracture dominated by mode-Ⅲ (Fig. 4.10.4) much deeper than the fracture dominated by mode-I and mode-II. The stress and strain components at $\phi = 45°$ are, respectively

$$\tau_A(\theta, 45°) = \frac{\tau_{xy}\cos 2\theta - \dfrac{1}{2}(\sigma_{xx} - \sigma_{yy})\sin 2\theta}{2^{\frac{1}{2}}} \tag{4.10.25}$$

$$\tau_B(\theta, 45°) = \frac{1}{2}(\sigma_{xx}\cos^2\theta + \sigma_{yy}\sin^2\theta + p + \tau_{xy}\sin 2\theta) \tag{4.10.26}$$

$$\sigma_\perp(\theta, 45°) = \frac{1}{2}(\sigma_{xx}\cos^2\theta + \sigma_{yy}\sin^2\theta - p + \tau_{xy}\sin 2\theta) \tag{4.10.27}$$

$$\gamma_A(\theta, 45°) = \frac{\gamma_{xy}\cos 2\theta - (\varepsilon_{xx} - \varepsilon_{yy})\sin 2\theta}{2^{\frac{1}{2}}} \tag{4.10.28}$$

$$\gamma_B(\theta, 45°) = \left(\varepsilon_{xx}\cos^2\theta + \varepsilon_{yy}\sin^2\theta - \varepsilon_{zz} + \frac{1}{2}\gamma_{xy}\sin 2\theta\right) \tag{4.10.29}$$

and $$\varepsilon_\perp(\theta, 45°) = \varepsilon_{xx}\cos^2\theta + \varepsilon_{yy}\sin^2\theta + \varepsilon_{zz} + \frac{1}{2}\gamma_{xy}\sin 2\theta \tag{4.10.30}$$

However, a combination of all shear stresses (strains) τ_A and τ_B (or γ_A and γ_B, if the strain criterion is preferred) can be the main cause of mode-III crack initiation in light of the above equations. It can be shown that $\tau_B(\theta, 45°) - \sigma_\perp(\theta, 45°) = 2p$. It may be accompanied by the influence of the maximum and mean normal stress $\sigma_\perp$ (or $\varepsilon_\perp$) due to the opening and closure of micro cracks [Meggiolaroa et al.].

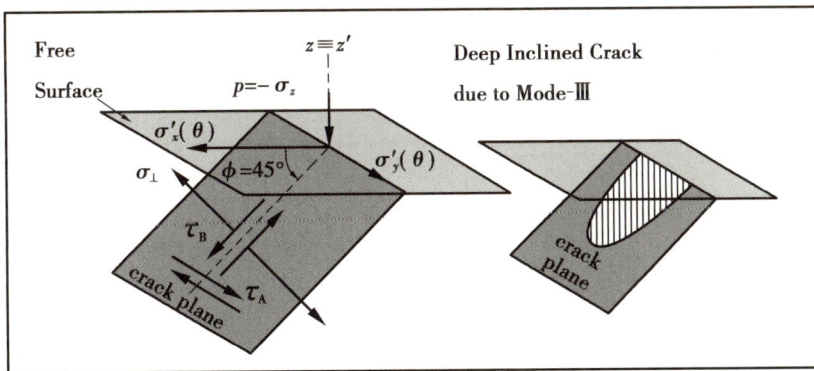

Fig. 4.10.4 Fracture on the Free Surface due to Out-of-Plane Shearing [Meggiolaroa et al.]

4.10.5 Rainflow Counting on the Critical Plane after Transformations

A multiaxial fatigue life prediction related to fatigue damage to strains and stresses on a critical plane is called a critical plane model. This model can predict the fatigue life and the orientation of the crack in all three crack propagation modes. Rainflow counting on the critical plane can be an effective tool for multiaxial non-proportional loading cases with variable amplitude [Bannantine & Socie] [Langlais et al.]. Different damage parameters using strains, stresses, or energy quantities have been used to evaluate damage on the critical plane. As identified by [Meggiolaro et al.], the following strain and stress components are to be counted on the critical plane in order to meet the need of specific predictive models for fatigue life:

Model	Strains and Reversals	Stresses, Reversals, and Others
Brown-Wang	$\varepsilon_\perp, \Delta\varepsilon_\perp, \gamma_A, \Delta\gamma_A, \gamma_B, \Delta\gamma_B$	—
Fatemi-Socie	$\gamma_A, \Delta\gamma_A, \gamma_B, \Delta\gamma_B$	$\sigma_\perp, \sigma_{\perp\,max}$
Goodman, Modified	—	$\sigma_\perp, \Delta\sigma_\perp, \sigma_{\perp\,mean}(=\sigma_\perp-\Delta\sigma_\perp)$
Liu	$\varepsilon_\perp, \Delta\varepsilon_\perp, \gamma_A, \Delta\gamma_A, \gamma_B, \Delta\gamma_B$	$\sigma_\perp, \Delta\sigma_\perp, \sigma_{\perp\,mean}, R, \tau_A, \Delta\tau_A, \tau_B, \Delta\tau_B$
McDiarmid-Findley	—	$\sigma_\perp, \sigma_{\perp\,max}, \tau_A, \Delta\tau_A, \tau_B, \Delta\tau_B$
Smith-Watson-Topper	$\varepsilon_\perp, \Delta\varepsilon_\perp$	$\sigma_\perp, \sigma_{\perp,max}$

4.11　Critical Plane Method Based on Strain Energy

In order to fully capture certain characteristics of the loading that can occur under complex, non-proportional load paths, which can be observed through careful examination of experimental data, including torsional mean stresses, let us consider the phase characteristics between the shear and normal stresses, and the influence of cyclic normal stresses on the critical plane. These effects, not inclusively discovered by [Findley], are taken into consideration and accounted for by recent researchers in the development of new critical plane parameters.

4.11.1　Energy Algorithm to Locate the Critical Plane

When the material is subjected to multiaxial loads, it involves 3-dimensional stress and strain components in the space. Via the critical plane method the 3-dimensional complexity is reduced and solved like a 2-dimensional problem. The material damage has been quested out in terms of plane stress, plane strain, or energy. An energy based fatigue limit criterion is presented by [Liu & Mahadevan], in which the critical plane can be located as long as the influence of the hydrostatic pressure disappears from the following equation:

$$\frac{\sigma_a \varepsilon_a}{\sigma_{al} \varepsilon_{al}} + \frac{\tau_a \gamma_a}{\tau_{al} \gamma_{al}} + A\frac{\sigma_{ap} \varepsilon_{ap}}{\sigma_{al} \varepsilon_{al}} = B \tag{4.11.1}$$

where

σ_a, ε_a: Normal stress and strain amplitudes in 3-D space under multiaxial loadings;

τ_a, γ_a: Shear stress and shear strain amplitudes in 3-D space under multiaxial loadings;

$\sigma_{ap}, \varepsilon_{ap}$: Hydrostatic stress (pressure) and strain amplitudes in 3-D space;

$\sigma_{a1}, \varepsilon_{a1}$: Uniaxial stress and strain amplitudes;

τ_{a1}, γ_{a1}: Uniaxial shear stress and shear strain amplitudes;

A: Coefficient, to be determined from uniaxial and pure torsional fatigue tests;

B: Constant, to be determined from uniaxial and pure torsional fatigue tests.

Hydrostatic effect is produced by uniaxial tension-compression loading only, as proven in Examples 2.7.1-2.7.3. The above equation means that the damage done to the material is an accumulation of damages done by the three different energy components. The critical plane is then defined to be the plane, on which the contribution from the hydrostatic stress and strain components is minimized or reaches zero. If $A = 0$, Eq. (4.11.1) reduces to

$$\frac{\sigma_a \varepsilon_a}{\sigma_{a1} \varepsilon_{a1}} + \frac{\tau_a \gamma_a}{\tau_{a1} \gamma_{a1}} = B \tag{4.11.2}$$

4.11.2 Locating the Critical Plane

Assume that the material is isotropically homogeneous and let ϕ denote the angle between the critical plane and the maximum normal stress plane. According to a fully reversed uniaxial tension-compression fatigue test ($R = -1$) controlled by the stress, the stress and strain components are due out on the fatigue limit as follows [Liu & Mahadevan]:

$$\sigma_a = \frac{1}{2}\sigma_{a1} + \frac{1}{2}\sigma_{a1}\cos 2\phi \tag{4.11.3}$$

$$\tau_a = -\sigma_{a1}\sin 2\phi \tag{4.11.4}$$

$$\varepsilon_a = \frac{1}{2}(1 + \nu_{eff})\varepsilon_{a1} + \frac{1}{2}(1 + \nu_{eff})\varepsilon_{a1}\cos 2\phi \tag{4.11.5}$$

and $$\gamma_a = -(1 + \nu_{eff})\varepsilon_{a1}\sin 2\phi \tag{4.11.6}$$

where

σ_{a1}: Principal stress in the principal coordinate system;

σ_a: Normal stress on the critical plane, i.e., perpendicular to the critical plane;

τ_a: Shear stress on the critical plane;

ε_{a1}: Principal strain in the principal coordinate system;

ε_a: Normal strain on the critical plane, i.e., perpendicular to the critical plane;

γ_a: Shear strain on the critical plane;

ϕ: Rotating angle from the maximum stress (principal stress) plane to the critical plane.

Parameter ν_{eff} is the effective Poisson's ratio that is a combination of the Poisson's ratios due to elastic strain ε_{e} and plastic strain ε_{p}, i.e., ν_{e} and ν_{p}, respectively.

$$\nu_{\text{eff}} = \frac{\nu_{\text{e}} \varepsilon_{\text{e}} + \nu_{\text{p}} \varepsilon_{\text{p}}}{\varepsilon_{\text{e}} + \varepsilon_{\text{p}}} \tag{4.11.7}$$

Because it is hard to identify ν_{p} that varies with respect to the material plasticity, the effective Poisson's ratio is sometimes approximated using the following equation [Wang & Brown] for convenience as

$$\nu_{\text{eff}} = 0.5 - \frac{(0.5 - \nu_{\text{e}}) \sigma_{\text{eq}}}{E \varepsilon_{\text{eq}}} \tag{4.11.8}$$

Note that $\nu_{\text{p}} = 0.5$ when working in the fully plastic range. Similarly, according to a fully reversed pure torsion fatigue test controlled by the shear strain ($R = -1$), the stress and strain components are given as follows:

$$\sigma_{\text{a}} = \tau_{\text{al}} \cos 2\phi \tag{4.11.9}$$

$$\tau_{\text{a}} = -\tau_{\text{al}} \sin 2\phi \tag{4.11.10}$$

$$\varepsilon_{\text{a}} = \frac{1}{2} \gamma_{\text{al}} \cos 2\phi \tag{4.11.11}$$

and $\quad \gamma_{\text{a}} = -\gamma_{\text{al}} \sin 2\phi \tag{4.11.12}$

The next step is to look for the angle of rotation (ϕ) from the maximum stress range plane to the critical plane. One can substitute Eqs. (4.11.3)-(4.11.6) into Eq. (4.11.2) and Eqs. (4.11.9)-(4.11.12) into Eq. (4.11.2), respectively, to obtain two simultaneous equations with two unknowns, i.e., B and ϕ. Angle ϕ results from these two equations is shown below:

$$\phi = \frac{1}{2} \cos^{-1} \frac{-1 + \left\{ 1 - \left[(5 + \nu_{\text{eff}}) - 2s - \frac{2(1 + \nu_{\text{eff}})}{s} \right] \left[(-3 - \nu_{\text{eff}}) + \frac{2(1 + \nu_{\text{eff}})}{s} \right] \right\}^{\frac{1}{2}}}{(1 + \nu_{\text{eff}}) - 2s - \frac{2(1 + \nu_{\text{eff}})}{s} + 4} \tag{4.11.13}$$

where

$$s = \frac{\tau_{\text{al}} \gamma_{\text{al}}}{\sigma_{\text{al}} \varepsilon_{\text{al}}} \tag{4.11.14}$$

As defined by the above equation, parameter s is the strain energy ratio of the pure shearing energy to the uniaxial tension-compression energy, of which the load ratio is $R=-1$. It is supposedly to be a positive number and can only be derived from these two fatigue tests. Thus, angle ϕ is a function of material properties and applied stress components. Assume that ν_{eff} falls between 0.3333 and 0.5. In order to have a real solution, the combined terms in the $\cos(*)$ must fall between 0 and 1, since angle ϕ sits between $0°$ and $90°$. Plugging these two ν_{eff} values into Eq. (4.11.13) leads to

$$0.4144 < s < 0.5129 \quad \text{when} \quad \nu_{\text{eff}} = 0.3333 \tag{4.11.14a}$$

$$\text{and} \quad 0.47 < s < 0.5732 \quad \text{when} \quad \dot{\nu}_{\text{eff}} = 0.5 \tag{4.11.14b}$$

Thus, the influence of the hydrostatic stress can only be neglected when the s value meets the requirement given by the above constraint equations for the case with $\nu_{\text{eff}} = 0.3333$ and 0.5, which provide a reasonable range of s value for steel.

4.11.3   Locating the Critical Plane in Ductile Materials

As the plasticity develops, it is known that a ductile (plastic) material will eventually fail along the plane of maximum shear strength, which is therefore the easily identifiable critical plane. Assume that the material is isotropic and homogeneous, the plane of maximum shear strength is at an angle of $\phi = 45°$ relative to the plane of maximum tensile strength at the last moment when it fails. Again, first consider the uniaxial tension-compression fatigue test ($R=-1$) controlled by the normal strain, the stress and strain components at the moment when the fatigue limit is reached,

$$\sigma_a = \frac{1}{2} \sigma_{a1} \tag{4.11.15}$$

$$\tau_a = \frac{1}{2} \sigma_{a1} \tag{4.11.16}$$

$$\sigma_{ap} = \frac{\sigma_{a1}}{3} \tag{4.11.17}$$

$$\varepsilon_a = \frac{1}{2} (1 + \nu_{\text{eff}}) \varepsilon_{a1} \tag{4.11.18}$$

$$\gamma_a = \frac{1}{2} (1 + \nu_{\text{eff}}) \varepsilon_{a1} \tag{4.11.19}$$

$$\text{and} \quad \varepsilon_{ah} = \frac{(1 - 2\nu_{\text{eff}}) \varepsilon_{a1}}{3} \tag{4.11.20}$$

Next, examination of the pure torsional fatigue test （$R = -1$） results in the following stress and strain components at the moment when the fatigue limit is reached, are respectively

$$\sigma_a = 0 \tag{4.11.21}$$

$$\tau_a = \tau_{al} \tag{4.11.22}$$

$$\sigma_{ap} = 0 \tag{4.11.23}$$

$$\varepsilon_a = 0 \tag{4.11.24}$$

$$\gamma_a = \gamma_{al} \tag{4.11.25}$$

and $\quad \varepsilon_{ah} = 0 \tag{4.11.26}$

One can substitute Eqs. （4.11.15）-（4.11.20） into Eq. （4.11.1） and Eqs. （4.11.21）-（4.11.26） into Eq. （4.11.1）, respectively, to obtain two simultaneous equations and solve the equations for A and B as follows:

$$A = \frac{9\left[1 - \dfrac{1}{4}(1 + \nu_{eff})\left(1 + \dfrac{1}{s}\right)\right]}{1 - 2\nu_{eff}} \tag{4.11.27}$$

and $\quad B = 1 \tag{4.11.28}$

In order to warrant that $A \geqslant 0$, which means that the fatigue damage grows monotonically in the nature of things, Eq. （4.11.27） reduces to

$$s \geqslant \frac{1 + \nu_{eff}}{3 - \nu_{eff}} \tag{4.11.29}$$

The above equation is here examined using the steel, of which the effective Poisson's ratio falls between 0.3333 and 0.5, respectively. Thus, numerically

$$s \geqslant 0.5, \quad \text{if} \quad \nu_{eff} = 0.3333 \tag{4.11.29a}$$

and $\quad s \geqslant 0.6, \quad \text{if} \quad \nu_{eff} = 0.5 \tag{4.11.29b}$

4.11.4　Locating the Critical Plane in Brittle Materials

As already known that a fully brittle material will fail along the plane of maximum tensile strength, which is therefore the identifiable critical plane. Assume that the material is isotropical and homogeneous. The critical plane is thus perpendicular to the maximum tensile stress, i.e., $\phi = 90°$ relative to the plane of maximum tensile strength. First consider the uniaxial tension-compression fatigue test ($R = -1$) controlled by the normal stress, the stress and strain components at the moment when the fatigue limit is reached, are respectively

$$\sigma_a = \sigma_{al} \qquad (4.11.30)$$

$$\tau_a = 0 \qquad (4.11.31)$$

$$\sigma_{ap} = \frac{\sigma_{al}}{3} \qquad (4.11.32)$$

$$\varepsilon_a = \varepsilon_{al} \qquad (4.11.33)$$

$$\gamma_a = 0 \qquad (4.11.34)$$

and $\quad \varepsilon_{ah} = \dfrac{(1 - 2\nu_{eff})\,\varepsilon_{al}}{3} \qquad (4.11.35)$

Next, examination of the pure torsional fatigue test ($R = -1$) results in the following stress and strain components at the moment when the fatigue limit is reached,

$$\sigma_a = \tau_{al} \qquad (4.11.36)$$

$$\tau_a = 0 \qquad (4.11.37)$$

$$\sigma_{ap} = 0 \qquad (4.11.38)$$

$$\varepsilon_a = \frac{1}{2}\,\gamma_{al} \qquad (4.11.39)$$

$$\gamma_a = 0 \qquad (4.11.40)$$

and $\quad \varepsilon_{ah} = 0 \qquad (4.11.41)$

One can substitute Eqs. (4.11.30)-(4.11.25) into Eq. (4.11.1) and Eqs. (4.11.36)-(4.11.41) into Eq. (4.11.1), respectively, to obtain two simultaneous equations and solve the equations for A and B as follows:

$$A = \frac{9\left(\dfrac{1}{2}s - 1\right)}{1 - 2\nu_{eff}} \qquad (4.11.42)$$

and $\quad B = \dfrac{1}{2}s \qquad (4.11.43)$

Constant A must be greater than zero ($A > 0$), in order to warrant that the fatigue damage grows monotonically in the nature of things. In light of Eq. (4.11.42), $s>2$ for brittle material. At $s=2$, $A=0$ and $B=1$, and therefore there is no contribution from hydrostatic stress/strain components.

4.12　Fatigue Life Predictors under Multiaxial Loadings

When the vibration amplitude is not fixed, the strain (stress) ratio and fluctuation vary over time. The fatigue loading that causes the maximum damage cannot be easily figured out and thus cumulative damage calculations including cycle counting (such as the rainflow technique) and damage accumulation (such as Miner's rule) have to be carried out to determine the total amount of fatigue damage and which cycle combinations cause the damage. A rainflow chart is a 3-D histogram—recording the number of counts for a given strain (stress) amplitude and mean strain (stress), as shown in Fig. 4.8.3. The Z-axis corresponds to the percentage of damage of each load block, which consists of a certain alternating strain amplitude (or stress amplitude) and mean strain (or mean stress) denoted along the X-axis and Y-axis, respectively. The chart is a measure of the composition of a load history without considering the loading sequence and each rainflow chart may be required at every (or at least the most damaging) work temperature. Note that the loading sequence is important for some applications.

When normal strain (stress) components and the accompanying shear strain (stress) components are in phase of each other, it is called proportional loading condition. For example, if $\psi = 0$, the combined load of the normal stress in Eq. (4.10.9) and the shear stress in Eq. (4.10.10) forms a proportional loading condition. The Manson-Coffin-Basquin-Morrow model has been an effective model in use for fatigue life prediction for material under proportional loading conditions. Nevertheless, more fatigue life predictors in addition to Manson-Coffin-Basquin-Morrow model are presented in the following subsections. No cycle counting has to be done if there is only one constant strain (stress) amplitude of vibration. Four different load ratios are suggested for checking up the validity of stress-life curve (i.e., Haigh diagram) by [Steinweger et al.]: $R=-1$, $R=-0.4$, $R=-0.2$, $R=0$ as illustrated in Fig. 4.12.1, while $R=0.2$ is the special checkup for rubber or other materials with a severe contrast in tensile and compressive stress-strain curves.

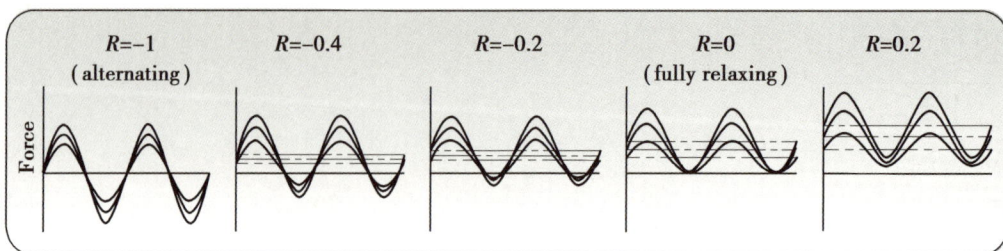

Fig. 4.12.1　Load Ratios for Diagnostic Checking of a Stress-Life Curve

The ratio of a shear strain (stress) component to a normal strain (stress) component and their relative phase angle have a strong influence on fatigue damage and consequently in fatigue life. Additional strain hardening observed in a nonproportional load block does not appear when the material is under proportional loading conditions. Even when the loading is of constant amplitude but nonproportional, the principal strain (stress) axes vary from one load case to another. A change in the direction or magnitude of the applied load in a nonproportional multiaxial cyclic loading case. causes a change in the stress contour (or distribution). The critical fatigue location may occur at a spatial location that is not easily spotted while just looking into the strain (stress) state generated by an individual load. More sophisticated theories for fatigue life may be employed with more material parameters when relative time-varying phase angles in a dynamic multiaxial loading system are considered [Lee & Chiang]. For example, strain hardening of stainless steel 304 under non-proportional axial-torsional loadings in contrast to the corresponding proportional loading is given in Fig. 4.12.2 [Jiang et al.]. A stabilized strain (stress) amplitude under nonproportional loading will do a greater damage than that of the same size under proportional loadings, while the 90° out-of-phase loading is the worst. The fatigue life of material subjected to nonproportional loadings is significantly shortened relative to other loading conditions as shown in Fig. 4.12.2. Some available material data are listed in Table 4.12.1 [Wang et al.] [Zhang and Yao] [Zhang, et al.].

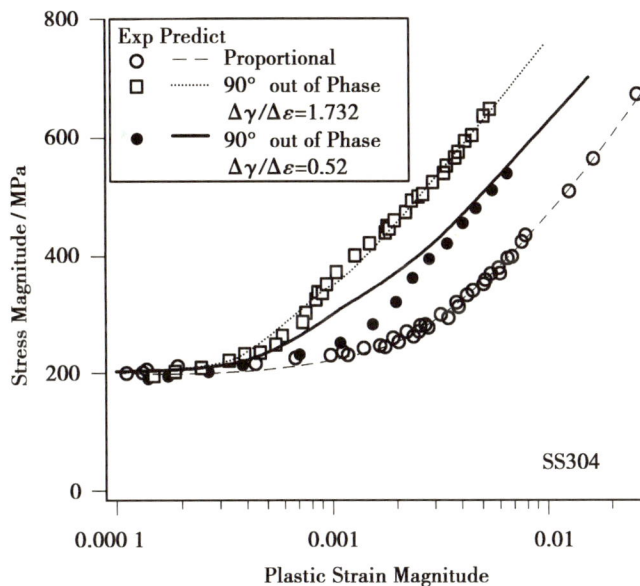

Fig. 4.12.2   Strain Hardening of Material Subjected to Non-Proportional Loading [**Jiang et al.**]

A study on fatigue life prediction under non-proportional loading with non-constant amplitude has to be dealt with case by case. Not only is the spatial location of critical fatigue life to be sought, but also what combination of loads would cause the most damage. Two major difficulties are encountered in dealing with multiaxial fatigue life evaluation in the case of variation with variable amplitudes: （1）lack of a reliable and consistent definition of an effective damage parameter, and （2）lack of consistent cycle identification or cycle counting procedure.

Advanced cycle counting algorithms such as path-independent methods or multiaxial critical plane methods are being sought by researchers.

When a structure is subjected to multiaxial loads, the strain and stress responses at a point in terms of time may compose of multidirectional loadings that do not have the same time-varying load factor. Under the condition of multiaxial loading, nonlinear transient responses following the complete load history is required to obtain stress and strain histories in a general case. One way to deal with such a problem is to find the equivalent strain （or stress）that would summarize the potential damage due to individual strain （or stress）components such that the rainflow counting algorithm can be easily implemented like a uniaxial load case. The other is to utilize the dominant strain （or stress）component to do the rainflow counting, the other strain/stress components are to be chopped accordingly in the time domain. Recent fatigue life predictors that acquire rainflow counting on the critical plane（s）under multiaxial loadings are to be presented herein.

4.12.1　Equivalent Strain Approach: Simple Power Equation

As a path-independent peak-counting algorithm, the equivalent strain method is recommended ［Wang & Borg］［Li & de Freitas］for fatigue life prediction. The equivalent strain amplitude is defined in terms of the von Mises strain. A multiaxial low cycle fatigue life prediction method available for both proportional and non-proportional loading conditions was proposed by ［Surajit］, by which the equivalent strain amplitude teamed up with a simple power law equation,

$$\varepsilon_{\text{eq,ave}} = B(2N_{\text{f}})^{\text{h}} \tag{4.12.1}$$

where

B: Coefficient;

h: Exponent.

$$\text{and} \quad \varepsilon_{\text{eq,ave}} = \frac{\int_0^{\Delta T} \varepsilon_{\text{eq}} \text{d}t}{\Delta T} \tag{4.12.2}$$

The model requires only two material constants, i.e., B and h, which are directly and explicitly related to the basic fatigue experiments under fully reversed tension-compression and torsional tests. Nevertheless, the regression model based on a biaxial test will be a more proper way to generate these two constants. The proposed model is able to facilitate its application to fatigue life prediction with a constant strain amplitude under general multiaxial fatigue loading without a highly tedious operating procedure. The influence of waveform and creep duration can also be accommodated while using Eq. (4.12.2). The following is a list of (B, h) data of some engineering materials [Surajit] for Eq. (4.12.1):

Parameter	Ti(Pure)	SAE 1045 Steel	30CrNiMo8	GH4169 Nickel Alloy
B	0.548	0.33	0.14	0.03
h	−0.646	−0.65	−0.459	−0.31

4.12.2   Equivalent Strain Approach: Modified Manson-Coffin-Basquin-Morrow Equation

Another equivalent strain (stress) amplitude model has been proposed by [Li & de Freitas] is also simple to use and it is a conservative approach to the life prediction in the domain of high cycle fatigue. Making a minor modification to Manson-Coffin-Basquin-Morrow equation, they gave the following equation:

$$\varepsilon_{a,np} = \frac{\sigma'_f - \sigma_m}{E}(2N_f)^b + \varepsilon'_f(2N_f)^c \tag{4.12.3}$$

where $\varepsilon_{a,np}$ is the equivalent non-proportional loading amplitude derived from the equivalent strain amplitude (e.g. von Mises stress) as

$$\varepsilon_{a,np} = (1 + \alpha F_{np}) \, \varepsilon_{a,eq} \tag{4.12.4}$$

where

α: Material constant accounting for hardening (or softening) as the material is stressed;

F_{np}: Non-proportional factor to be obtained from the loading path;

$\varepsilon_{a,eq}$: Equivalent strain amplitude.

It was reported that the Morrow's mean stress correction in Eq. (4.12.3) for the stress-life prediction is suitable for steel alloys, but it is too aggressive to be a good predictor for aluminum alloys [Dowling]. When only the elastic strain amplitude is to be corrected in order to accommodate the influence of mean stress, the following is proposed for the equivalent strain amplitude for more accurate results [Ince & Glinka],

$$\varepsilon_{a,eq} = \frac{\sigma_{max}}{\sigma'_f} \cdot \frac{1}{2}\Delta\varepsilon_e + \frac{1}{2}\Delta\varepsilon_p \tag{4.12.5}$$

where

$\Delta\varepsilon_e$: Elastic strain range;

$\Delta\varepsilon_p$: Plastic strain range.

4.12.3   Shear Strain Approach: Sofie's Criterion

It was postulated that the nucleation and growth of small fatigue cracks are driven primarily by cyclic shear stresses [Findley]. That has been verified by experimental observations of slip band formation under shear loading within individual grains. Three different criteria, i.e., principal shear strain, principal normal strain, and total strain energy on the critical plane can be employed to evaluate the damage. On such a critical plane, the following fatigue damage model including the effect of mean stress has been proposed as [Socie]

$$\Delta\gamma_p^* + k\Delta\varepsilon_{p,n}^* + \frac{\sigma_{m,n}^*}{E} = f(2N_f) \qquad\qquad (4.12.6)$$

where

γ_p^* : Plastic shear strain;

$\varepsilon_{p,n}^*$: Plastic normal strain for the crack to propagate from the surface into the specimen;

$\sigma_{m,n}^*$: Mean normal stress, perpendicular to the critical plane;

k : Constant;

E : Tensile modulus of elasticity;

$f(2N_f)$: Function of fatigue cycles.

The plastic normal strain ($\varepsilon_{p,n}^*$) is a vector perpendicular to the critical plane and the plastic shear strain (γ_p^*) lies on the critical plane, although damage done to a part subject to most loadings is usually located on the outer surface of the part body. By letting $k = 0$, it can be shown that the method based on shear strain in combination with mean normal stress turns out to be a suitable approach algorithm for the material under multiaxial loadings as demonstrated in Fig. 4.12.3.

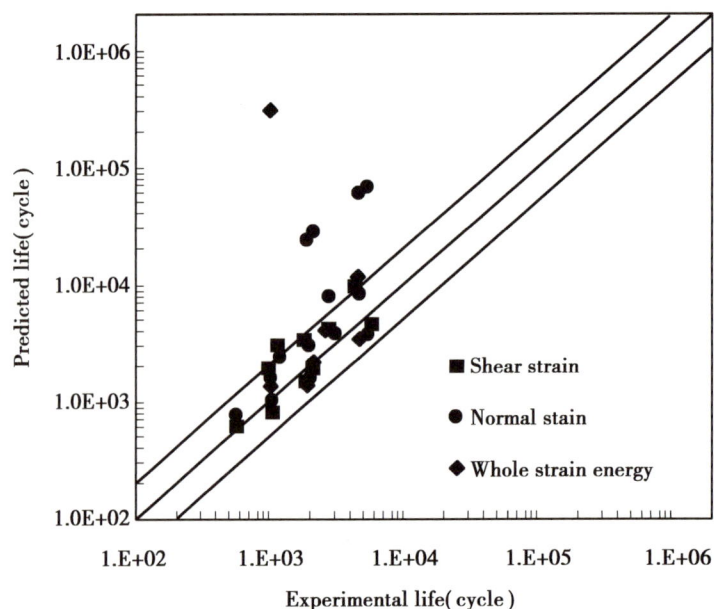

Fig. 4.12.3   Comparison of Three Different Methods for Defining a Critical Plane

4.12.4   Equivalent Strain Approach: Brown-Miller Equation

As being inspired by the Socie's criterion and Manson-Coffin equation, a strain-life equation can be written in a general form in terms of the shear strain amplitude and normal strain amplitude as follows:

$$\frac{1}{2}\Delta\gamma_{max} + \frac{1}{2}\Delta\varepsilon_n = c_1 \frac{\sigma'_f}{E}(2N_f)^b + c_2\varepsilon'_f(2N_f)^c \tag{4.12.7}$$

where

$\Delta\gamma_{max}$: Maximum shear strain range;

$\Delta\varepsilon_n$: Normal strain perpendicular to the critical plane;

c_1 & c_2: Constants.

Consider a uniaxial plane stress case that the principal strains are related to each other by $\varepsilon_2 = \varepsilon_3 = -\nu\,\varepsilon_1$, when loaded along the 1-axis. Then

$$\gamma_{max} = \frac{1}{2}(\varepsilon_1 - \varepsilon_3) = (1 + \nu)\,\varepsilon_1 \tag{4.12.8}$$

and $\quad \varepsilon_n = \frac{1}{2}(\varepsilon_1 + \varepsilon_2) = (1 - \nu)\,\varepsilon_1 \tag{4.12.9}$

For steel, $\nu = 0.3$ in the elastic range, in which c_1 is the only coefficient of concern (c_2 neglected). Plugging the Poisson's ratio into Eqs. (4.12.7) and (4.12.8),

$$\gamma_{max} = \frac{1}{2}(\varepsilon_1 - \varepsilon_3) = (1 + \nu)\varepsilon_1 = 1.3\varepsilon_1$$

and $\quad \varepsilon_n = \frac{1}{2}(\varepsilon_1 + \varepsilon_2) = \frac{1}{2}(1 - \nu)\,\varepsilon_1 = 0.35\varepsilon_1$

Thus, $c_1 = 1.65$ can be obtained from the data given above. Similarly, letting $\nu = 0.5$ in the fully plastic range, one can obtain that $\gamma_{max} = 1/2(\varepsilon_1 - \varepsilon_3) = (1+\nu)\varepsilon_1 = 1.5\varepsilon_1$, $\varepsilon_n = 1/2(\varepsilon_1 + \varepsilon_2) = 1/2(1-\nu)\,\varepsilon_1 = 0.25\varepsilon_1$, and $c_2 = 1.75$. Hence, Eq. (4.12.7) for steels reduces to

$$\frac{1}{2}\Delta\gamma_{max} + \frac{1}{2}\Delta\varepsilon_n = 1.65\frac{\sigma'_f}{E}(2N_f)^b + 1.75\varepsilon'_f(2N_f)^c \tag{4.12.10}$$

The above equation is a complete Brown-Miller equation for steel. With Morrow's mean stress correction, the Brown-Miller strain-life equation for steel can be rewritten as follows:

$$\frac{1}{2}\Delta\gamma_{\max} + \frac{1}{2}\Delta\varepsilon_n = 1.65\frac{\sigma_f' - \sigma_{n,m}}{E}(2N_f)^b + 1.75\varepsilon_f'(2N_f)^c \qquad (4.12.11)$$

of which $\sigma_{n,m}$ is the mean normal stress exerted on the critical plane and perpendicular to the critical plane. A "stress-hardening factor" was introduced to account for nonproportional cyclic hardening effect into the Brown-Miller equation [Li, J. et al.]. The modified Brown-Miller equation is

$$\frac{1}{2}\Delta\gamma_{\max} + \frac{1}{2}\Delta\varepsilon_n\left(1 + \frac{\sigma_{n,\max}}{\sigma_y}\right) = \left[\frac{\sigma_f'}{E}(2N_f)^b + \varepsilon_f'(2N_f)^c\right]\left[1 + \frac{\sigma_f'}{\sigma_y}(2N_f)^b\right] \qquad (4.12.12)$$

where

$\sigma_{n,\max}$: Maximum normal stress perpendicular to the critical plane;

σ_y : Yield strength.

4.12.5　Strain Energy Approach: Generalized Criterion for Fatigue Life Prediction

When each term in Eq. (4.11.1) is multiplied by the strain energy density due to the uniaxial fatigue test, i.e., $\frac{1}{2}\sigma_{al}\varepsilon_{al}$, it becomes [Wei] [Liu & Mahadevan]

$$\left(\frac{1}{2}\sigma_a\varepsilon_a + \frac{1}{2}s^{-1}\tau_a\gamma_a + \frac{1}{2}A\sigma_{ap}\varepsilon_{ap}\right)B^{-1} = \frac{1}{2}\sigma_{al}\varepsilon_{al} \qquad (4.12.13)$$

or $\quad\left[\frac{1}{2}\sigma_a\varepsilon_a + \frac{1}{2}\left(\frac{\tau_{al}\gamma_{al}}{\sigma_{al}\varepsilon_{al}}\right)^{-1}\tau_a\gamma_a + \frac{1}{2}A\sigma_{ap}\varepsilon_{ap}\right]B^{-1} = \frac{1}{2}\sigma_{al}\varepsilon_{al} \qquad (4.12.14)$

When A and B are obtained using Eqs. (4.11.27) and (4.11.28) for brittle materials and Eqs. (4.11.42)-(4.11.43) for ductile materials, one can set the energy-fatigue curves using the following four approximating uniaxial (tension-compression) and pure torsion test results as

$$\sigma_{al} \approx \sigma_{Nf} \qquad (4.12.15)$$

$$\varepsilon_{al} \approx \varepsilon_{Nf} \qquad (4.12.16)$$

$$\tau_{al} \approx \tau_{Nf} \qquad (4.12.17)$$

and $\quad \gamma_{al} \approx \gamma_{Nf} \qquad (4.12.18)$

Thus, substituting the above four equations into Eq. (4.11.45) yields

$$\left[\frac{1}{2}\sigma_a\varepsilon_a + \frac{1}{2}\left(\frac{\tau_{Nf}\gamma_{Nf}}{\sigma_{Nf}\varepsilon_{Nf}}\right)^{-1}\tau_a\gamma_a + \frac{1}{2}A\sigma_{ap}\varepsilon_{ap}\right]B^{-1} = \frac{1}{2}\sigma_{Nf}\varepsilon_{Nf} \qquad (4.12.19)$$

Once the fundamental multiaxial fatigue test data, including fully reversed uniaxial test controlled by stress, fully reversed uniaxial test controlled by strain, fully reversed pure torsion test controlled by stress, and fully reversed torsion test controlled by strain, are available, one can obtain σ_{Nf}, ε_{Nf}, τ_{Nf}, and γ_{Nf}. The equation is then used for fatigue life prediction.

4.12.6 Strain Energy Approach: SWT [Smith, Watson, & Topper] Equation and the Modified One

It is postulated that fatigue life is a function of strain energy [Smith, Watson, & Topper], i.e., half of the product of the strain amplitude and maximum stress specifically in a loading cycle. The SWT model resembles the Manson-Coffin-Basquin-Morrow equation and its fatigue strength exponent and ductility exponent, i.e., b and c respectively. As a simplified theory derived from Eq. (4.12.13), the SWT criterion leads to a strain energy-life relationship

$$\varepsilon_{1a,eq}\,\sigma_{max} = \frac{(\sigma_f')^2}{E}(2N_f)^{2b} + \varepsilon_f'\sigma_f'(2N_f)^{b+c} \tag{4.12.20}$$

where

ε_{1a}: First principal strain amplitude;

σ_{max}: Maximum stress on the maximum principal strain plane;

ε_f': Axial fatigue ductility coefficient;

σ_f': Axial fatigue strength coefficient.

The SWT equation given above provides good results for the case studies on a variety of metals [Dowling]. When it is desired to choose one simple strain (or stress) amplitude-mean equation for metals, SWT would be the preferred choice. In light of Eq. (4.12.5), the following equation has been proposed by [Ince & Glinka] as a modified SWT equation

$$\frac{\sigma_{max}}{\sigma_f'} \cdot \frac{1}{2}\Delta\varepsilon_e + \frac{1}{2}\Delta\varepsilon_p = \frac{\sigma_f'}{E}(2N_f)^{2b} + \varepsilon_f'(2N_f)^c \tag{4.12.21}$$

If the fatigue life data are collected from stress-life tests, the following alternative SWT equation may be used for fatigue analysis [Dowling et al. 2009]

$$\varepsilon_{a,eq} = \frac{\sigma_f'}{E}\left\{\frac{1}{2}(1-R)^{\frac{1}{2}}(2N_f)^b + \varepsilon_f'\left[\frac{1}{2}(1-R)^{\frac{1}{2}}\right]^{\frac{c}{b}}(2N_f)^c\right\} \tag{4.12.22}$$

A fatigue damage model based on tensile components for SWT equation has been in practice for a while, but it may overestimate fatigue lives of materials under non-proportional loadings. Nevertheless, the combined normal and shear stress model usually underestimate fatigue lives of materials and it is hard to differentiate the contributions from normal and shear stresses [Chen et al.]. Experimental validations using eight kinds of materials show that the effective strain energy density (ESED) model can give satisfactory fatigue life predictions under the non-proportional loading [Li et al.]. Another option is to calculate $\varepsilon_{a,eq}$ using Eq. (4.12.5), and then Eq. (4.12.4) if nonproportional loading is involved.

4.12.7　Strain Energy Approach: CXH [Chen, Xu, & Huang] Equation

As being simplified from Eq. (4.12.13), the following strain energy-life relationship has been postulated by [Chen, Xu, & Huang]

$$\sigma_{ac}\,\varepsilon_{ac,max} + \tau_{ac}\gamma_{ac} = B(2N_f)^d \tag{4.12.23}$$

$$\text{or}\quad \Delta\sigma_c\Delta\varepsilon_{c,max} + \Delta\tau_c\Delta\gamma_c = K(2N_f)^d \tag{4.12.24}$$

for fatigue life prediction. Eq. (4.12.24) is the original form given by [Chen, Xu, & Huang], while $K = 4B$. CXH employs normal and shear components of both stresses and strains on the critical plane. $\Delta\varepsilon_{c,max}$ is the range of maximum principal strain, and $\Delta\varepsilon_{c,max}$, $\Delta\sigma_c$, $\Delta\gamma_c$, and $\Delta\tau_c$ are the ranges of normal strain, normal stress, shear strain, and shear stress on a critical plane, respectively. An application of CXH model to an engine mount rubber leads to [Chung & Kim]

$$\Delta\sigma_c\Delta\varepsilon_{c,max} + \Delta\tau_c\Delta\gamma_c = 134.73(2N_f)^{-0.339} \quad \text{(from Biaxial Test)} \tag{4.12.25}$$

4.12.8　Strain Energy Approach: SCLW (Sun-Chiang-Li-Wang) Equation

For multiaxial Loading, either a proportional or non-proportional case, the following empirical equation in terms of strain and stress amplitudes can be applied [Sun et al.]

$$\varepsilon_a\sigma_a + P'\gamma_a\,\tau_a\frac{\gamma'_f}{\varepsilon'_f}\left(1 + \frac{\Delta\sigma_n}{2\sigma'_f}\right) = \frac{(\sigma'_f - \sigma_{n,m})^2}{E}(2N_f)^{2b} + (\sigma'_f - \sigma_{n,m})\,\varepsilon'_f(2N_f)^{b+c} +$$

$$\frac{(\tau'_f)^2}{G}(2N_f)^{2b\gamma} + \gamma'_f\tau'_f(2N_f)^{b\gamma+c\gamma} \tag{4.12.26}$$

where
σ_n: Normal stress exerted on and perpendicular to the critical plane;
$\Delta\sigma_n$: Maximum normal stress range;
$\sigma_{n,m}$: Mean normal stress;
b: Torsional fatigue strength exponent;
c: Torsional fatigue strain exponent, mainly associated with plastic strain;
σ'_f: Normal fatigue strength coefficient;
ε'_f: Normal ductility coefficient;
$b\gamma$: Torsional fatigue strength exponent;
$c\gamma$: Torsional fatigue strain exponent, mainly associated with plastic strain;
τ'_f: Shear fatigue strength coefficient;
γ'_f: Shear fatigue ductility coefficient;

E: Young's modulus;

G: Shear modulus of elasticity;

σ_a: Normal stress amplitude;

ε_a: Normal strain amplitude;

τ_a: Shear stress amplitude;

γ_a: Shear strain amplitude;

P': Correction factor.

If the loading is proportional, i.e., multiaxial loads synchronized with the same phase angle, the critical fatigue location can be ascertained by looking into a single set of FEA (Finite Element Analysis) or physical test results.

Coefficient P' is a correction factor addressing the fixture effect in torsional fatigue tests. The outer edge of a part tends to elongate when it is twisted, but it is restrained to move axially. It represents the plastic shear strain correction for the varying hardening exponent that starts at the very onset of material necking. It may range from 1.1 to 1.4 for most materials [LeRoy et al.], while $P' = 1.1$ is generally taken by default for compensation. However, there are not ample test data available for torsional fatigue analysis to validate it.

4.12.8.1   Sun-Chiang-Li-Wang Equation for Uniaxial (Tension-Compression) Loading

For uniaxial (tension-compression) loads, the following equation is recommended [Sun et al.]

$$\varepsilon_a \sigma_a = \frac{(\sigma'_f - \sigma_m)^2}{E}(2N_f)^{2b} + (\sigma'_f - \sigma_m)\varepsilon'_f(2N_f)^{b+c} \qquad (4.12.27)$$

It is shown in Fig. 4.12.4 that the above equation prevails as compared with the traditional Manson-Coffin-Basquin-Morrow approach. All the input data for material properties are the same as those for Manson-Coffin-Basquin-Morrow Model.

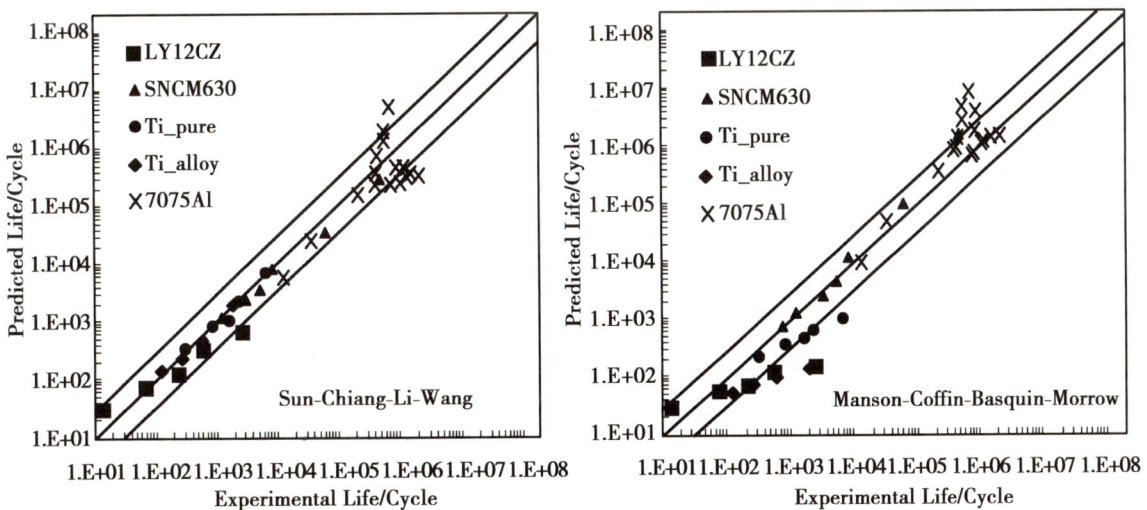

Fig. 4.12.4   Validity of Eq. (4.12.21) for Different Materials Subject to Uniaxial Loading, as Compared with Manson-Coffin-Basquin-Morrow Model [Sun, Chiang, & Li]

4.12.8.2 Sun-Chiang-Li-Wang Equation for Torsional Loading

For torsional loading, the following equation is recommended [Sun et al.]：

$$P'\gamma_a \tau_a \frac{\gamma'_f}{\varepsilon'_f} = \frac{(\tau'_f)^2}{G}(2N_f)^{2b\gamma} + \gamma'_f \tau'_f (2N_f)^{b\gamma+c\gamma} \tag{4.12.28}$$

It is shown in Fig. 4.12.5 that the above equation is valid for predicting fatigue life.

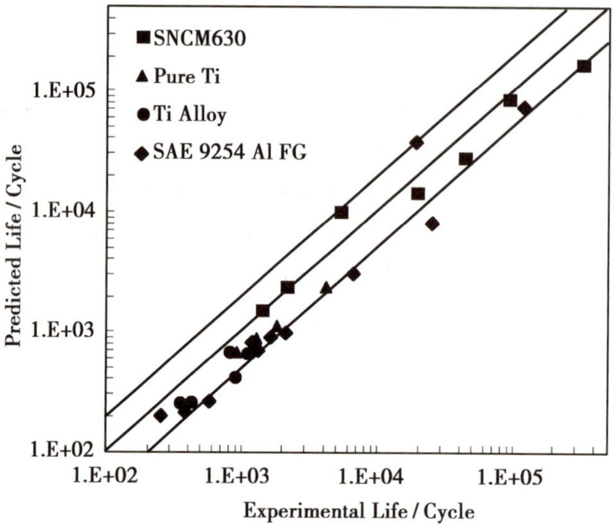

Fig. 4.12.5　Validity of Eq. （4.12.22） for Different Materials Subject to Torsional Loading ［Sun, Chiang & Li］

4.13　Estimation of Strain-Controlled Fatigue Parameters by Hardness

Based on experimentally obtained fatigue parameters, the relationship between the monotonic Brinell hardness, denoted by H_B, and the fatigue parameters have been identified and established by ［Basan et al.］. From these models of regression, values of fatigue parameters σ'_f, ε'_f, b and c can be determined as a function of Brinell hardness, respectively, as follows：

$$\frac{\sigma'_f}{E} = \frac{\sigma'_f}{E(H_B)} \tag{4.13.1}$$

$$\varepsilon'_f = \varepsilon'_f(H_B) \tag{4.13.2}$$

$$b = b(H_B) \tag{4.13.3}$$

and　$c = c(H_B)$ \tag{4.13.4}

One major advantage of the approach is that the fatigue parameters are not individually estimated, i.e., they are independent of one another. If there are no experimental data available ever since, for an alloy steel with a Brinell hardness (H_B) between 150 and 700, the following regressive polynomials on hardness may be used to estimate σ'_f and ε'_f[Roessle & Fetimi], respectively

$$\sigma'_f = 4.25(H_B)^2 + 225 \text{ MPa} \tag{4.13.5}$$

and $\quad \varepsilon'_f = \dfrac{0.32\,(H_B)^2 - 487\,(H_B) + 191000}{E} \tag{4.13.6}$

In general, b varies between -0.057 to -0.14 for most metals; and c, which is not as well defined in terms of other parameters, varies between -0.39 and -1.04 for most metals. Fairly ductile metals ($\varepsilon'_f \sim 1.0$) have c values close to -0.7 and brittle metals ($\varepsilon'_f \sim 0.5$) have c values close to -0.5.

4.14   Commercial Codes for Fatigue Life Prediction

Fatigue modules have recently been integrated into commercial FEA codes that include Abaqus, Algor, Ansys, COMSOL, COSMOSWorks, Nastran, and Pro/E. Three commercial codes seem to be used most in the North American industry. They are nCode, Fesafe, and MSC Nastran.

4.14.1   nCode DesignLife

nCode DesignLife is a CAE-based software solution for fatigue and durability analysis. DesignLife works with all leading finite element (FE) codes and produces realistic predictions of fatigue hotspots and fatigue life. DesignLife shares an environment with nCode GlyphWorks, a graphical test data processing software, to provide an unparalleled integration of test and CAE data. Its core functionality includes the following:

1. Virtual Strain Gauge: This enables correlation between test and finite element results. Single or rosette gauges may be graphically positioned and oriented on finite models as a post-processing step. Time histories due to applied loads can then be extracted for direct correlation with your measured strain data.
2. Schedule Create: This lets the user build and process multiple cases that model a duty cycle. Through an intuitive interface, Schedule Create makes it easy to create a complete durability schedule.
3. Signal Processing: This includes nCode fundamentals functionality for basic data manipulation, analysis and visualization.
4. Materials Manager: This enables materials data to be added, edited and plotted. A default

database with fatigue properties for many commonly used materials is also provided.

5. Crack Growth: provides a complete fracture mechanics capability using industry standard methodologies for specified locations on an FE model. Built-in growth laws include NASGRO (Fracture Codes), Forman, Paris, Walker, and more. Select from a provided library of geometries or supply custom stress intensity factors.

6. Customization:

(6a) Python Scripting. This enables Python scripting to be used to extend existing analysis capabilities rather than needing to code fatigue analysis from scratch. Perfect for proprietary methods or research projects. Available for all the major analysis types including SN, EN, and short fiber composites and also for all the main loading types including vibration.

(6b) FE Input Glyph. This passes FE file results directly into the GlyphWorks environment to allow custom analysis development within the standard scripting glyph with either Python or Matlab.

4.14.2　Fe-Safe

It is a basic durability analysis software for finite element models [Simulia]. It can be used for calculating fatigue lives at every point on a finite element model, producing contour plots to reveal fatigue lives and crack sites. It also provides a proprietary technique of superimposing multiaxial power spectral densities (PSDs) upon critical plane analysis. The following modules can be added to the basic FE-Safe:

(1) Fatigue of Welded Joints.
(2) Creep Fatigue.
(3) Fatigue of Rubber.

4.14.3　FEMFAT

It has been a tool for multiaxial fatigue assessment of axles, suspension systems, frames, engine components, BIWs, etc., widely used in Magna. It has multi-interfaces for history data from multibody simulation and measurement data software. Applications include both isotropic materials and fibrous composites. Specialty capabilities in weld fatigue analysis (spot and arc welding) are available.

References

AMZALLAG C, GEREY J P, ROBERT J L, et al, 1994. Standardization of the Rainflow Counting Method for Fatigue Analysis[J]. International Journal of Fatigue, 16(4):287-293.

ANDREW W, 1995. Fatigue and Tribological Properties of Plastics and Elastomers[M]. William Andrew, UK.

ANTHES R J, 1997. Modified rainflow counting keeping the load sequence[J]. International Journal of Fatigue, 19(7):529-535.

ASM International 2002. Fatigue Failures, Failure Analysis and Prevention[J]. Vol. 11, ASM Handbook.

ASTM D7791-10 2010. Standard Test Method for Uniaxial Fatigue Properties of Plastics[M]. ASTM International, West Conshohocken, PA, USA.

ASTM E1049-85 (Reapproved 2005). Standard Practices for Cycle Counting in Fatigue Analysis[M]. ASTM International, West Conshohocken, PA, USA.

ASTM Standard E606, 2004ε1, 2010. Standard Practice for Strain-Controlled Fatigue Testing[M]. ASTM International, West Conshohocken, PA, USA.

BANNANTINE J A, SOCIE D F, 1992. A Multiaxial Fatigue Life Estimation Technique[J]. ASTM STP (1122):75.

BARBASH K P, MARS W V, 2016. Critical Plane Analysis of Rubber Bushing under Road Loads[R]. Sae world congress & Exhibition.

BASAN R, RUBEŠA D, FRANULOVIĆ M, et al, 2010. A Novel Approach to the Estimation of Strain Life Fatigue Parameters[J]. Procedia Engineering, 2(1):417-426.

BASQUIN O H, 1910. The Exponential Law of Endurance Tests[J]. Proc ASTM(10):625-630.

BATHIAS C, 1999. There is No Infinite Fatigue Life in Metallic Materials[J]. Fatigue and Fracture of Engineering Materials and Structures.

BENDAT J S, 1964. Probability Functions for Random Responses[J]. NASA report on contract NAS-5-4590.

BERGMANN J, KLEE S, SEEGER T, 1977. Effect of Mean Strain and Mean Stress on the Cyclic Stress-Strain and Fracture Behavior of Steel StE70[J]. Journal of Engineering Materials and Technology, 9:10-17.

BISHOP N, HU Z, 1991. The Fatigue Analysis of Wind Turbine Blades Using Frequency Domain Techniques [J]. European Wind Energy Conference, EWEC '91, Amsterdam:246-250.

BISHOP N W M, SHERRATT F, 1990. A Theoretical Solution for the Estimation of Rainflow Ranges from Power Spectral Density Data[J]. Fatigue and Fracture of Engineering Materials and Structures, 13(4):311-326.

BOILER H E, 1986. Atlas of Fatigue Curves[M]. ASM International, Metals Park, OH, USA.

BONACUSE P J, KALLURI S, 1995. Elevated Temperature Axial and Torsional Fatigue Behavior of Haynes 188[J]. Journal of Engineering Materials and Technology, 117(2):191-199.

BORODII M V, et al, 2014. An Axial Experimental Study of Ratcheting Effect under Multiaxial Proportional

Loading[J]. Strength of Materials, 46(1):97-104.

BROUTMAN L J, SAHU S A, 1972. A New Theory to Predict Cumulative Fatigue Damage in Fiberglass Reinforced Plastics[J]. Composite Materials: Testing and Design (2nd Conference), ASTM STP 497: ASTM, Anaheim, April 20-22, 1972:170-188.

BROWN M W, MILLER K J, 1973. A Theory for Fatigue Failure under Multiaxial Stress-Strain Conditions[J]. ARCHIVE: Proceedings of the Institute of Mechanical Engineers, 1847-1982(Vols1-196).

BROWN M W, SUKER D K, WANG C H, 1996. An Analysis of Mean Stress in Multiaxial Random Fatigue [J]. Fatigue and Fracture of Engineering Materials and Structures, 19(2-3):323-333.

BYRNE T P, MORANDIN G D, 1998. A Multiaxial Fatigue Cycle Counting Technique Based on the Rainflow Method[J]. PVP-Vol.370, Finite Element Applications: Linear, Non-Linear, Optimization and Fatigue and Fracture, 19-25.

CAHI G, ANDERSSON M, 2013. Secondary Hardening Behavior in Super Duplex Stainless Steels during LCF in Dynamic Strain Ageing Regime[J]. Procedia Engineering, 55:123-127.

CALDWELL J, et al, 2009. Fatigue Countermeasures in Aviation[J]. Aviation Space and Environmental Medicine, 80(1):29-59.

CAO Y, XIE X, ANTONAGLIA J, et al, 2015. Laser Shock Peening on Zr-based Bulk Metallic Glass and Its Effect on Plasticity: Experiment and Modeling[J]. Scientific Reports 5.

CHABOCHE J L, 1989. Constitutive Equations for Cyclic Plasticity and Cyclic Viscoplasticity[J]. International Journal of Plasticity, 5(3):247.

CHABOCHE J L, 1991. On Some Modifications of Kinematic Hardening to Improve the Description of Ratcheting Effects[J]. International Journal of Plasticity, 7(7):661-678.

CHATTOPADHYAY A, et al, 2011. Stress Analysis and Fatigue of Welded Structures[J]. Welding in the World, 55(7-8):2-21.

CHATTOPADHYAY S, NATHAN R, 2013. Illustrating Rotating Principal Stresses in a Materials Science Course[C]. 120th ASEE Annual Conference and Exhibition, 23-678.

CHEN X, XU S, HUANG D, 1999. A Critical Plane-Strain Energy Density Criterion for Multiaxial Low-Cycle Fatigue Life under Non-Proportional Loading[J]. Fatigue of Engineering Materials and Structures, 22:679-686.

CHEN X, GAO Q, SUN X F, 1994. Damage Analysis of Low-Cycle Fatigue under Non-Proportional Loading [J]. International Journal of Fatigue, 16(3):221-225.

CHEN X, et al, 1996. Evaluation of Low Cycle fatigue under Non-Proportional Loading[J]. Fatigue and Fracture of Engineering Materials and Structures, 19(10):1161-1168.

CHO J, et al, 2015. Fatigue Life Assessment of Fabric Braided Composite Rubber Hose in Complicated Large Deformation Cyclic Motion[J]. Finite Elements in Analysis and Design, 100(aug):65-76.

CHOW C L, WEI Y, 1999. Constitutive Modeling of Material Damage for Fatigue Failure Prediction[J]. International Journal of Damage Mechanics, 8(4):355-375.

COFFIN J R. L F, 1954. A Study of the Effects of Cyclic Thermal Stresses on a Ductile Metal[J]. Transaction of American Society for Testing and Materials, Vol. 76:931-950.

COJOCARU D, KARLSSON A M, 2009. Assessing Plastically Dissipated Energy as a Condition for Fatigue Crack Growth[J]. International Journal of Fatigue, 31(7):1154-1162.

CONSTANTINESCU A, VAN K D, MAITOURNAM M H, 2003. A Unified Approach for High and Low Cycle Fatigue Based on Shakedown Concepts[J]. Fatigue and Fracture of Engineering Materials and Structures, 26 (6):1-8.

CU J, CHEN P, 2018. A Failure Criterion for Homogeneous and Isotropic Materials Distinguishing the Different Effects of Hydrostatic Tension and Compression[J]. European Journal of Mechanics, A/Solids, 70:15-22.

DELA'O J D, GUNDLACH R B, TARTAGLIA J M, Strain-Life Fatigue Properties Database for Cast Iron, (DVD), RR08DVD.

DINEGDAE Y H, et al, 2015. Mechanics-Based Top-Down Fatigue Cracking Initiation Prediction Framework for Asphalt Pavements[J]. Road Materials and Pavement Design, 16(4).

DING J, et al, 2008. Finite Element Simulation of Fretting Wear Fatigue Interaction in Spline Couplings[J]. Tribology, 2(1):10-24.

DIRLIK T, 1985. Application of Computers in Fatigue Analysis[M]. PhD Dissertation, University of Warwick.

DOQUET V, CLAVEL M, 1996. Stacking-Fault Energy and Cyclic Hardening of FCC Solid Solutions under Multiaxial Non-Proportional Loadings[J]. Multiaxial Fatigue and Design (Edited by Pineau, Cailletaud, & Lindley), Mechanical Engineering Publication, London:43-60.

D'ORING R, et al, 2006. Short Fatigue Crack Growth under Nonproportional Multiaxial Elastic-Plastic Strains [J]. International Journal of Fatigue, 28(9):972-982.

DOWLING N E, 2007. Mechanical Behavior of Materials: Engineering Methods for Deformation, Fracture and Fatigue, Prentice Hall.

DOWLING N E, 2004. Mean Stress Effects in Stress-Life and Strain-Life Fatigue[J]. SAE Technical Paper, 2004, 32(12):1004−1019.

DOWNING S D, SOCIE D F, 1982. Simple Rainflow Counting Algorithms[J]. International Journal of Fatigue, 1(1):31-40.

DRAPER J, 2008. Modern Metal Fatigue Analysis[M]. EMAS.

DRAPER J, 2002. New Ideas in Fatigue Analysis, Machine Design, December 12, ASME.

EL KADI H, ELLYIN F, 1994. Effect of Stress Ratio on the Fatigue of Unidirectional Glass Fiber/Epoxy Composite Laminae[J]. Composites, 25(10):917-924.

EPAARACHCHI J A, 2006. A Study on Estimation of Damage Accumulation of Glass Fiber Reinforced Plastic (GFRP) Composites under a Block Loading Situation[J]. Composite Structures, 75(1/4):88-92.

FATEMI A, PLASEIED A, KHOSROVANEH A K, 2005. Application of Bi-linear Log-log S-N Model to Strain-Controlled Fatigue Data of Aluminum Alloys and Its Effect on the Life Predictions[J]. International Journal of Fatigue, 27(9):1040-1050.

FATEMI A, SOCIE D F, 1988. A Critical Plane Approach to Multiaxial Fatigue Damage Including Out-of-Phase Loading[J]. Fatigue and Fracture of Engineering Materials and Structures, 11(3):149-165.

FAYARD J, et al, 1996. Fatigue Design Criterion for Welded Structures [J]. Fatigue and Fracture of Engineering Materials and Structures, 19(6):723-729.

FINDLEYW N, 1959. A Theory for the Effect of Mean Stress on Fatigue of Metals under Combined Torsion and Axial Load or Bending[J]. Journal of Engineering for Industry, 81(4):301-306.

FRAGOUDAKIS R, SAIGAL A, 2011. Predicting the Fatigue Life in Steel and Glass Fiber Reinforced Plastics Using Damage Models[J]. Materials Sciences & Applications, 2(6):596-604.

GAIERA C, DANNBAUERA H, 2003. Fatigue Analysis of Multiaxially Loaded Components with the FE-Postprocessor FEMFAT-MAX[J]. European Structural Integrity Society, 31(3):223-240.

GARUD Y S, 1981. A New Approach to the Evaluation of Fatigue under Multiaxial Loadings[J]. Journal of Engineering Materials and Technology, 103(2):118-125.

GERY D, LONG H, MAROPOULOS P, 2005. Effects of Welding Speed, Energy Input and Heat Source Distribution on Temperature Variations in Butt Joint Welding [J]. Journal of Materials Processing Technology, 167(2-3):393-401.

GLINKA G, et al, 1995. A Multiaxial Fatigue Strain Energy Density Parameter Related to the Critical Fracture Plane[J]. Fatigue and Fracture of Engineering Materials and Structures, 18(1):37-46.

GLINKA G, WANG G, PLUMTREE A, 1995. Mean Stress Effects in Multiaxial Fatigue[J]. Fatigue and Fracture of Engineering Materials and Structures.

GLINKA G, KAM J, 1987. Rainflow Counting Algorithm for Very Long Stress Histories[J]. International Journal of Fatigue, 9(4):223-228.

GOCMEZ T, et al, 2010. A New Low Cycle Fatigue Criterion for the Isothermal and Out-of-Phase Thermomechanical Loading[J]. International Journal of Fatigue, 32(4):769-779.

GOLDEN P J, CALCATERRA J R, 2006. A Fracture Mechanics Life Prediction Methodology Applied to

Dovetail Fretting[J]. Tribology International, 39(10):1172-1180.

GOODMAN J, 1930. Mechanics Applied to Engineering[J]. Vol. 1, 9th Edition, Longmans Green and Co., London.

GUAGLIANO M, VERYANI L, 2004. An Approach for Prediction of Fatigue Strength of Shot Peened Components[J]. Engineering Fracture Mechanics, 71(4):501-512.

HALFPENNY KIM, 2010. Rainflow Cycle Counting and Acoustic Fatigue Analysis Techniques for Random Loading[J]. RASD 2010 Conference, Southampton, UK.

HAN C, CHEN X, KIM K, 2002. Evaluation of Multiaxial Fatigue Criteria under Irregular Loading[J]. International Journal of Fatigue, 24(9):913-922.

HASHIN Z, ROTEM A, 1978. A Cumulative Damage Theory of Fatigue Failure[J]. Materials Science and Engineering, 34(2):147-160.

HASHIN Z, ROTEM A, 1973. A Fatigue Failure Criterion for Fiber Reinforced Materials[J]. Journal of Composite Materials, 7(4):448-464.

HECKEL T K, et al, 2010. Thermomechanical Fatigue of the TiAl Intermetallic Alloy TNB-V2 [J]. Experimental Mechanics, 50(6):717-724.

HONG N, 1991. A Modified Rainflow Counting Method[J]. International Journal of Fatigue, 13(6):465-469.

HU W, et al, 2016. A Model of BGA Thermal Fatigue Life Prediction Considering Load Sequence Effects[J]. Materials, 9(10): 860.

HUANG X, TORGEIR M, CUI W, 2008. An Engineering Model of Fatigue Crack Growth under Variable Amplitude Loading[J]. International Journal of Fatigue, 30(1):2-10.

INCE A, GLINKA G, 2011. A Modification of Morrow and Smith-Watson-Topper Mean Stress Correction Models [J]. Fatigue and Fracture of Engineering Materials, 34(11):854-867.

IRVINE T, 2009.An Introduction to the Vibration Response Spectrum[M]. Revision D, Vibrationdata.

JAGLINSKI T, et al, 2007.Study of Bolt Load Loss in Bolted Aluminum Joints[J]. Journal of Engineering Materials and Technology, 129(1):48-54.

JIANG Y, et al, 2009.Fatigue Life Predictions by Integrating EVICD Fatigue Damage Model and an Advanced Cyclic Plasticity Theory[J]. International Journal of Plasticity, 25:780-801.

JIANG Y, ZHANG J, 2008. Benchmark Experiments and Characteristic Cyclic Plastic Deformation Behavior [J]. International Journal of Plasticity, 24(9):1481-1515.

JIANG Y, HERTEL O, VORMWALD M, 2007.An Experimental Evaluation of Three Critical Plane Multiaxial Fatigue Criteria[J]. International Journal of Fatigue:1490-1502.

JIANG Y, SEHITOGLU H, 1996. Modeling of Cyclic Ratcheting Plasticity, Part Ⅰ: Development of Constitutive Equations[J]. Journal of Applied Mechanics, 63:720-725.

JIANG Y, KURATH P, 1997. Nonproportional Cyclic Deformation: Critical Experiments and Analytic Modeling [J]. International Journal of Plasticity, 13(8-9):743-763.

JOHANNESON P, SVENSSON T, DE MARE J, 2005. Fatigue Life Prediction Based on Variable Amplitude Test-Methodology[J]. International Journal of Fatigue, 27.

KALLURI S, BONACUSE P, 1994. Estimation of Fatigue Life Under Axial-Torsional 1. Loading[J]. ASME PVP, Vol. 290, Material Durability/Life Prediction Modeling: Materials for the 21st Century, Edited by Zamrik, S. & Halford, 17-33.

KAROLCZUK A, MACHA E, 2005. A Review of Critical Plane Orientation in Multiaxial Fatigue Failure Criteria of Metallic Materials[J]. International Journal of Fatigue, 134(3-4):267-304.

KIM H S, 2016. Mechanics of Solids and Fracture[M]. 2nd Edition, Ventus Publishing.

KIM K S, et al, 2002. Estimation Methods for Fatigue Properties of Steels under Axial and Torsional Loading [J]. International Journal of Fatigue, 24(7):783-793.

KIM W D, LEE H J, KIM J Y, et al, 2004. Fatigue Life Estimation of an Engine Rubber Mount[J]. International Journal of Fatigue, 26:553-560.

KOCABICAK U, FIRAT M, 2004. A Simple Approach for Multiaxial Fatigue Damage Prediction Based on FEM Post-Processing[J]. Materials and Design, 25(1):73-82.

KONG NIE, 1991. A Modified Rainflow Counting Method[J]. International Journal of Fatigue, 13(6):465-469.

KORKMAZ S, 2011. A Methodology to Predict Fatigue Life of Cast Iron: Uniform Material Law for Cast Iron [J]. International Journal of Iron and Steel Research, 18(8):42-45.

KUBOTA M, NOYAMA N, SAKAE C, et al, 2006. Fretting Fatigue in Hydrogen Gas [J]. Tribology International, 39(10):1241-1247.

KUGUEL R, 1961. A Relation between Theoretical Stress Concentration Factor and Fatigue Notch Deduced from the Concept of Highly Stresses Volume[J]. Proceeding of ASTM, 461:732-748.

KUMAR P S, et al, 2013. Structural Fatigue Strength Evaluation of Commercial Vehicle Structures by Calculating Damage Due to Road Load Inputs[J]. Bodies & Structures.

LAGODA T, MACHA E, BEDKOWSKI W, 1999. A Critical Plane Approach Based on Energy Concepts: Application to Biaxial Random Tension-Compression High-Cycle Fatigue Regime[J]. International Journal of Fatigue, 21(5):431-443.

LAGODA T, MACHA E, 2012. Fatigue Life under Biaxial Stress State with Different Cross-Correlation

Coefficients of Normal Stresses[J]. Proceedings of 9th International Conference of Fracture, 1997:1371-1377.

LALANNE C, 2009. Fatigue Damage[M]. ISTE, Wiley and Sons.

LANGLAIS T, VOGEL J, CHASE T, 2003. Multiaxial Cycle Counting for Critical Plane Methods [J]. International Journal of Fatigue, 25(7):641-647.

LEE B L, KIM K S, NAM K M, 2003. Fatigue Analysis under Variable Amplitude Loading Using an Energy Parameter[J]. International Journal of Fatigue, 25(7):621-631.

LEE D, et al, 2005. Fatigue Life Evaluation of Press-Fitted Specimens by Using Multiaxial Fatigue Theory at Contact Edge[J]. Key Engineering Materials, 297-300:108-114.

LEE S B, 1985. A Criterion for Fully Reversed Out-of-Phase Torsion and Bending[M]. ASTM STP853.

LEE Y L, BARKEY M E, KANG H T, 2011. Metal Fatigue Analysis Handbook[M]. Elsevier Burlington, MA, USA.

LEE Y L, PAN J, HATHAWAY R, et al, 2005. Fatigue Testing and Analysis: Theory and Practice[M]. Elsevier, Burlington, MA, USA.

LEE Y L, CHIANG Y J, WONG H H, 1995. A Constitutive Model for Estimating Multiaxial Notch Strains[J]. Journal of Engineering Materials and Technology, 117(1):33-40.

LEE YUNG-LI, WOLFENDEN A, CHIANG Y J, 1991. Fatigue Predictions for Components under Biaxial Reversed Loading[J]. Journal of Testing and Evaluation, 19(5):359-367.

LEHTOVAARA A, RABB R, 2008. A Numerical Model for the Evaluation of Fretting Fatigue Crack Initiation in Rough Point Contact[J]. Wear, 264(9):750-756.

LEROY G, EMBURY J, EDWARDS G, et al, 1981. A Model of Ductile Fracture Based on the Nucleation and Growth of Voids[J]. Acta Metallurgica, 29(18):1509-1522.

LI B, REIS L, DE FREITAS M, 2006. Simulation of Cyclic Stress/Strain Evolution for Multiaxial Fatigue Life Prediction[J]. International Journal of Fatigue, 28(5/6):451-458.

LI B, DE FREITAS M, 2002. A Procedure for Fast Evaluation of High-Cycle Fatigue under Multiaxial Random Loading[J]. Journal of Mechanical Design, 124(3):558-563.

LI J, et al, 2011. A Modification of Smith-Watson-Topper Damage Parameter for Fatigue Life Prediction under Non-Proportional Loading[J]. Fatigue and Fracture of Engineering Materials and Structures, Online since 1 SEP 2011 (Early On-line Version).

LI J, et al, 2011. Multiaxial Fatigue Life Predictions for Various Metallic Materials Based on the Critical Plane Approach[J]. International Journal of Fatigue, 33(2):90-101.

LI J, ZHANG Z P, SUN Q, et al, 2009. A New Multiaxial Fatigue Damage Model for Various Metallic Materials under the Combined Tension and Torsion Loadings[J]. International Journal of Fatigue, 31(4):776-781.

LI Q, et al, 2009. Fatigue Life Prediction of a Rubber Mount Based on Test of Material Properties and Finite Element Analysis[J]. Engineering Failure Analysis, 16(7):2304-2310.

LI Q M, 2001. Strain Energy Density Failure Criterion[J]. International Journal of Solids and Structures, 38 (38):6997-7013.

LIAN W, YAO W, 2010. Fatigue Life Prediction of Composite Laminates by FEA Simulation Method[J]. International Journal of Fatigue, 32(1):123-133.

LINDGREN G, RYDEN J, 2002. Transfer Function Approximations of the Rainflow Filter[J]. Mechanical Systems and Signal Processing, 16(6):979-989.

LING Y, et al, 2011. Stochastic Prediction of Fatigue Loading Using Real-Time Monitoring Data[J]. International Journal of Fatigue, 33(7):868-879.

LIU K C, WANG J A, 2001. An Energy Method for Predicting Fatigue Life, Crack Orientation, and Crack Growth under Multiaxial Loading Condition[J]. International Journal of Fatigue, 23(supp-s1):129-134.

LIU K C, 1993. A Method Based on Virtual Strain-Energy Parameters for Multiaxial Fatigue Life Prediction, Advances in Multiaxial Fatigue, ASTM, STP1191:67-84.

LIU Y, MAHADEVAN S, 2005. Strain-Based Multiaxial Fatigue Damage Modeling[J]. Fatigue and Fracture of Engineering Materials and Structures, 28(12):1177-1189.

LIU Y, MAHADEVAN S, 2005. Multiaxial High-Cycle Fatigue Criterion and Life Prediction for Metals[J]. International Journal of Fatigue, 27(7):790-800.

MANSON S S, et al, 1965. Further Investigation of a Relation for Cumulative Fatigue Damage in Bending[J]. Journal of Engineering for Industry, Series B, 87(1):25-35.

MARS W V, FATEMI A, 2004. Factors That Affect the Fatigue Life of Rubber: A Literature Survey, Rubber Chemistry and Technology, 77(3):391-412.

MARS W V, FATEMI A, 2002. A Literature Survey on Fatigue Analysis Approaches for Rubber[J]. International Journal of Fatigue, 24(9):949-961.

MATSUISHI M, ENDO T, 1968. Fatigue of Metals Subjected to Varying Stress[J]. Japanese Society of Mechanical Engineering.

MCDIARMID D L, 1994. A Shear Stress Based Critical-Plane Criterion of Multiaxial Fatigue Failure for Design and Life Prediction[J]. Fatigue and Fracture of Engineering Materials and Structures, 17(12):1475-1484.

MCINNERS C, MEEHAN P, 2008. Equivalence of Four-Point and Three-Point Rainflow Cycle Counting Algorithm[J]. International Journal of Fatigue, 30(3):547-559.

MEGGIOLAROA M, CASTRO J, WU H, 2015. Invariant-Based and Critical-Plane Rainflow Approaches for Fatigue Life Prediction under Multiaxial Variable Amplitude Loading[J]. Procedia Engineering, 101:69-76.

MINER M A, 1945. Cumulative Damage in Fatigue[J]. Journal of Applied Mechanics, 12:159-164.

MORROW J, 1965. Cyclic Plastic Strain Energy and Fatigue of Metals[J]. in International Friction, Damping, and Cyclic Plasticity, ASTM STP 378, ASTM.

MROZ Z, 1967. On the Description of Anisotropic Workhardening[J]. Journal of Mech. Phys. Solids, 15(3): 163-175.

MRŠNIK M, SLAVIČ J, BOLTEŽAR M, 2016. Multiaxial Vibration Fatigue: A Theoretical and Experimental Comparison[J]. Mechanical Systems and Signal Processing.

MRŠNIK M, SLAVIČ J, BOLTEŽAR M, 2012. Frequency-Domain Methods for a Vibration-Fatigue-Life Estimation: Application to Real Data[J]. International Journal of Fatigue, 47:8-17.

MURALIDHARAN U, MANSON S S, 1988. A Modified Universal Slopes Equation for Estimation of Fatigue Characteristics[J]. Journal of Engineering Materials and Technology, 110(1):55-58.

NACHTIGALL A J, 1977. Cyclic Stress-Strain Determination for D6AC Steel by Three Methods, NASA TM-73825, Lewis Research Center, Cleveland, 44135.

NAGODE M, HACK M, 2011. The Damage Operator Approach: Fatigue, Creep and Viscoplasticity Modeling in Thermomechanical Fatigue[J]. SAE International Journal of Materials and Manufacturing, 4(1):632-637.

NEUBER H, 1961. Theory of Stress Concentration for Shear-Strained Prismatic Bodies with Arbitrary Nonlinear Stress-Strain Laws[J]. Journal of Applied Mechanics, 28(4):544-550.

NIESLONY A, 2003. Rainflow Counting Algorithm[J]. MATLAB File Exchange Central, 17.

NOWELL D, DINI D, HILLS D, 2006. Recent Developments in the Understanding of Fretting Fatigue[J]. Engineering Fracture Mechanics, 73(2):207-222.

OHJI K, et al, 1972. Development of a Push-Pull Fatigue Testing under High Pressure and the Results of Preliminary Fatigue Tests[J]. Journal of Materials Science, Japan, 21(227):772-777.

OKA H, et al, 2007. Effect of Mean Stress on Fatigue Strength of Short Glass Fiber Reinforced Polybuthyleneterephthalate[J]. Key Engineering Materials, 340/341(Pt1):537-542.

ONAMI M, SAKANE M, 2008. A Study on Creep-Fatigue Interaction of Polycrystalline Metals at Elevated Temperatures[J]. Journal of Materials Science, Japan, 20(139):1-8.

PALMGREN A, 1924.Die Lebensdauer von Kugellagern[J]. ZVDI, 68:339-341.

PAN W F, HUNG C Y, CHEN L L, 1999. Fatigue Life Estimation under Multiaxial Loading[J]. International

Journal of Fatigue, 21:3-10.

PAPADOPOULOS I V, DAVOLI P, GORLA C, 1997. A Comparative Study of Multiaxial High-Cycle Fatigue Criteria for Metals[J]. International Journal of Fatigue, 19(3):219-235.

PARK J, NELSON D, 2000. Evaluation of an Energy-Based Approach and a Critical Plane Approach for Predicting Constant Amplitude Multiaxial Fatigue Life[J]. International Journal of Fatigue, 22(1):23-39.

PETERMAN J, PLUMTREE A, 2001. A Unified Fatigue Failure Criterion for Unidirectional Laminates[J]. Composites, Part A, 32(1):107-118.

PHAMA M S, HOLDSWORTHA S R, 2012. Dynamic Strain Ageing of AISI 316L during Cyclic Loading at 300 ℃: Mechanism, Evolution, and Its Effects[J]. Materials Science and Engineering, A, 556(OCT, 30):122-133.

PITOISET X, PREUMONT A, 2000. Spectral Methods for Multiaxial Random Fatigue Analysis of Metallic Structures[J]. International Journal of Fatigue, 22(7):541-550.

POOK L, 2007. Metal Fatigue, What It Is, Why It Matters, Springer[M]. PO Box 17, 3300 Dordrecht, The Netherlands.

PORTEVIN A, LE-CHATELIER F, 1923. Sur un phénomèneobservélors de l'essai de traction d'alliages en cours de transformation[J]. Compt. Rend. Acad. Sci., Paris, 176:507-510.

QUIGLEY J, LEE Y, 2012. Assessing Dirlik's Fatigue Damage Estimation Method for Automotive Applications [J]. SAE International Journal of Passenger Cars- Mechanical Systems, 5(2):911-920.

RAMBERG W, OSGOOD W E, 1943. Description of Stress Strain Curves by Three Parameters[J]. NACA Technical Notes 902.

REEMSNYDER H S, 1982. Constant Amplitude Fatigue Life Assessment Models[J]. SAE Transactions, 2337-2350.

ROESSLE M, FETIMI A, 2000. Strain-Controlled Fatigue Properties of Steels and Some Simple Approximations [J]. International Journal of Fatigue, 22:495-511.

ROLOVIC R, TIPTON S M, 1999. An Energy Based Critical Plane Approach to Multiaxial Fatigue Analysis [J]. Fatigue and Fracture Mechanics, ASTM, STP 1332:599-613.

RYCHLIK I, 1987. A New Definition of the Rainflow Cycle Counting Method[J]. International Journal of Fatigue, 9(2):119-121.

SAKANE M, ITOH T, 2005. Effect of Hydrostatic Stress on Low Cycle Fatigue Life[J]. Proceedings of PVP2005, Paper No. PVP2005-71756:279-285.

SALEMI S, et al, 2008. Physics-of-Failure Based Handbook of Microelectronic Systems, Defense Technical Info Center/Air Force Research Lab Report, U of MD and RIAC, Utica, NY.

SAMD M, ALI A, 2010. Simulation Work of Fatigue Life Prediction of Rubber Automotive Components[J]. IOP Conf. Series: Materials Science and Engineering, 11, 012009.

SCHIJVE J, 2009. Fatigue of Structures and Materials[M]. 2nd Edition with CD-Rom, Springer.

SCHLITZ D, KLITSCHKE H, STEINHILBER H, et al, 1990. Standardized Load Sequences for Car Wheel Suspension Components-Car Loading Standard CARLOS, final report. Suspension Systems.

SCHLUTER L, 1991. Programmer's Guide for LIFE2's Rainflow Counting Algorithm, Sandia Report SAND90-2260.

SHAMSAEI N, FATEMI A, 2011. Fatigue Life Predictions under General Multiaxial Loading Based on Simple Material Properties[J]. Sae International Journal of Materials & Manufacturing, 4(1):651-658.

SHANG D G, 2009. Measurement of Fatigue Damage Based on the Natural Frequency for Spotwelded Joints[J]. Materials and Design, 30(4):1008-1013.

SHANG D G, et al, 2007. Creep-Fatigue Life Prediction under Fully-Reversed Multiaxial Loading at High Temperatures[J]. International Journal of Fatigue, 29(4):705-712.

SHANG D G, SUN G Q, WANG D J, 2007. Multiaxial Fatigue Damage Parameter and Life Prediction for Medium-Carbon Steel Based on the Critical Plane Approach[J]. International Journal of Fatigue, 29(12):2200-2207.

SHANG D G, WANG D J, YAO W X, 1999. Study on Nonlinear Continuum Multiaxial Fatigue Cumulative Damage Model[J]. Chinese Journal of Solid Mechanics, 20:241-245.

SKIBICKI D, 2014. Phenomena and Computational Models for Nonporportional Fatigue of Materials[M]. Springer.

SKIBICKI D, DYMSKI S, 2010. The Influence of Fatigue Loading on the Microstructure of an Austenitic Stainless Steel[J]. Materials Testing, 52(11):787-794.

SMITH J O, 1942. Effect of Range of Stress on Fatigue Strength of Metals[J]. University of Illinois, Engineering Experiment Station, Bull No. 334:39(26).

SMITH K N, WATSON P, TOPPER T H, 1970. A Stress Strain Function for the Fatigue of Metal[J]. Journal of Materials, 5:767-778.

SOCIE D F, MARQUIS G B, 2000. Multiaxial Fatigue[J]. SAE R-234.

SOCIE D F, 1993. In Advances in Multiaxial Fatigue[M]. ASTM STP 1191:7-36, MCDOWELL D L. and ELLIS R. (Eds.), American Society for Testing and Materials, Philadelphia, PA.

SOCIE D F, 1987. Multiaxial Fatigue Damage Models[J]. Journal of Engineering Materials and Technology, 109(4):292-298.

SOYAMA H, SAITO K, SAKA M, 2002. Improvement of Fatigue Strength of Aluminum Alloy by Cavitation Shotless Peening[J]. Journal of Engineering Materials and Technology, 124(2):135-139.

SONSINO C M, et al, 2012. Notch Stress Concepts for the Fatigue Assessment of Welded Joints-Background and Applications[J]. International Journal of Fatigue, 34(1):2-16.

SONSINO C M, 2007.Fatigue Test under Variable Loading[J]. International Journal of Fatigue, 29(6):1080-1089.

STEPHENS R I, FUCHS H O, 2001. Metal Fatigue in Engineering[M]. 2nd Edition, John Wiley & Sons, Inc., NYC.

STEINWEGER T. et al. 2005. Four Tests to Characterize a Haigh-Diagram for Damage Calculations[C]. in Austrell, P.-E. (Editor): Constitutive Models for Rubber Ⅳ, Proceedings of the 4th European Conf. on Constitutive Models for Rubber, ECCMR 2005, Stockholm, Sweden.

SUMEL L, 2010. A Simple and Efficient Numerical Algorithm to Determine the Orientation of the Critical Plane in Multiaxial Fatigue Problems[J]. International Journal of Fatigue, 32(11):1875-1883.

SUN G Q, SHANG D G, 2010. Prediction of Fatigue Lifetime under Multiaxial Cyclic Loading Using Finite Element Analysis[J]. Materials and Design, 31(1):126-133.

SUN N N, CHIANG Y J, LI G X, et al, 2014. A Comparative Study of Fatigue Criteria for Engineering Application[J]. Applied Mechanics and Materials, 538:356-359.

SUSMEL L, TOVO R, 2011. Estimating Fatigue Damage under Variable Amplitude Multiaxial Fatigue Loading [J]. Fatigue and Fracture of Engineering Materials and Structures, 34(12):1053-1077.

SUSMEL L, 2010. A Simple and Efficient Numerical Algorithm to Determine the Orientation of the Critical Plane in Multiaxial Fatigue Problems[J]. International Journal of Fatigue, 32(11):1875-1883.

TOPPER T H, WETZEL R M, MORROW J, 1969. Neuber's Rule Applied to Fatigue Notched Specimens[J]. Journal of Materials, 4(1):200-209.

TOPPER T H, WETZEL R M, 1972. Fatigue-Damage Evaluation for Mild Steel Incorporating Mean Stress and Overload Effects[J]. Experimental Mechanics, 12(1):11-17.

UPADHYAYA Y S, SRIDHAR B K, 2012. Strain Controlled Fatigue Life Prediction of Materials [J]. International Journal of Research in Engineering and Technology, 1(3):153-157.

VARVANI-FARAHANI A, 2000. A New Energy-Critical Plane Parameter for Fatigue Life Assessment of Various Metallic Materials Subjected to In-Phase and Out-of-Phase Multiaxial Fatigue Loading Conditions [J]. International Journal of Fatigue, 22(4):295-305.

VARVANI-FARAHANI A, TOPPER T H, 2000. A New Multiaxial Fatigue Life and Crack Growth Rate Model for Various In-Phase and Out-of-Phase Strain Paths [J]. Multiaxial Fatigue Deformation: Testing and Prediction, ASTM, STP 1387:305-322.

WALKER K, 1970. The Effect of Stress Ratio During Crack Propagation and Fatigue for 2024-T3 and 7075-T6 Aluminum, Effects of Environment and Complex Load History on Fatigue Life, ASTM STP 462, ASTM, West Conshohocken, PA:1-14.

WANG C H, BROWN M W, 1996. Life Prediction Techniques for Variable Amplitude Multiaxial Fatigue—Part 1: Theories[J]. Journal of Engineering Materials and Technology, 118(3):367-370.

WANG C H, BROWN M W, 1996. Life Prediction Techniques for Variable Amplitude Multiaxial Fatigue—Part 2: Comparison with Experimental Results[J]. Journal of Engineering Materials and Technology, 118:371-374.

WANG C H, BROWN M W, 1993. A Path-Independent Parameter for Fatigue under Proportional and Nonproportional Loadings[J]. Fatigue and Fracture of Engineering Materials and Structures, 16:1285-1298.

WANG C, SHANG D, WANG X, 2015. A New Multiaxial Fatigue Criterion Based on the Critical Plane for Ductile and Brittle Materials[J]. Journal of Materials Engineering and Performance, 24(2):816-824.

WANG J, LEVKOVITCH V, REUSCH F, et al, 2008. On the Modeling of Hardening in Metals during Non-Proportional Loading[J]. International Journal of Plasticity, 24(6):1039-1070.

WANG L, et al, 2014. Evaluation of Multiaxial Fatigue Life Prediction Criteria for PEEK, Theoretical and Applied Fracture Mechanics, 73:128-135.

WANG Y, YU W, CHEN X, et al, 2008. Fatigue Life Prediction of Vulcanized Natural Rubber under Proportional and Non-Proportional Loading, Fatigue and Fracture of Engineering Materials and Structures, 31:38.

WEI H, 2017. A Critical Plane-Energy Model for Multiaxial Fatigue Life Prediction of Homogeneous and Heterogeneous Materials, Fatigue & Fracture of Engineering Materials & Structures, 40(12):1973-1983.

WEI Y, CHOW C L, 2006. Isothermal Fatigue Damage Model for Lead-Free Solder[J]. International Journal of Damage Mechanics, 15(2):109-119.

WILLIAMS J, SVENSSON N, 1971. An Experimental Analysis of the Neck of the Femur[J]. Medical and Biological Engineering, 9(5):479-493.

WU Z R, HU X T, SONG Y D, 2013. Multiaxial Fatigue Life Prediction Model Based on Maximum Shear Strain Amplitude and Modified SWT Parameter[J]. Journal of Mechanical Engineering, 49:59-66.

XIA Z, KUJAWSKI D, ELLYIN F, 1996. Effect of Mean Stress and Ratcheting Strain on Fatigue Life of Steel, International Journal of Fatigue, 18(5):335-341.

XUE L, 2008.A Unified Expression for Low Cycle Fatigue and Extremely Low Cycle Fatigue and Its Implication for Monotonic Loading[J]. International Journal of Fatigue, 30(10-11):1691-1698.

YOUNG D G, 1991. Fatigue and Fracture of Elastomeric Materials, Rubber World; (United States), 204: 1.

ZHANG C C, YAO W X, 2008. Additional Hardening and Life Prediction under Multiaxial Non-Proportional Loading, Proceedings of the 14th National Conference on Fatigue and Fracture, 2008:327-330.

ZHANG W, ZHOU Z, SCARPA F, et al, 2016. A Fatigue Damage Mesomodel for Fiber-Reinforced Composites with Stress Ratio Effect[J]. Materials and Design, 107(Oct.5):212-220.

ZHANG Y H, MADDOX S J, 2009. Investigation of Fatigue Damage to Welded Joints under Variable Amplitude Loading Spectra[J]. International Journal of Fatigue, 31(1):138-152.

ZHAO W, BAKER M, 1992. On the Probability Density Function of Rainflow Stress Range for Stationary Gaussian Processes[J]. International Journal of Fatigue, 14(2):121-135.

ZHAO T, JIANG Y, 2008. Fatigue of 7075-T651 Aluminum Alloy[J]. International Journal of Fatigue, 30 (5):834-849.

ZHU H B, 2010. Calculation Methods for Equivalent Fatigue Stress Amplitude Based on Corten-Dolan Accumulative Damage Rule[J]. Advanced Materials Research, 156-157:1271.

Problems

4.8.1　Follow the rainflow counting algorithm. Please identify that there are five peak-generated reversals and 3 valley-generated reversals in the following figure (Fig.P.4.8.1).

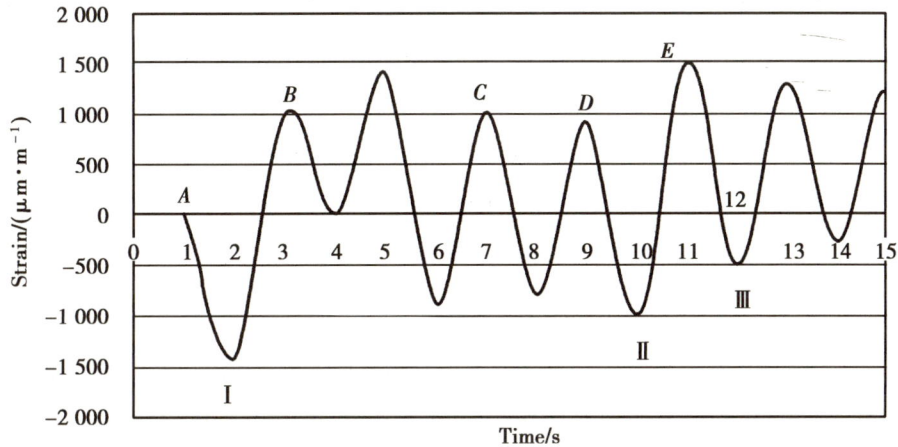

Fig. P.4.8.1　A Time Series of Stress History Used for Illustrating the Rainflow Counting Algorithm: Peak-Generated Reversals (A-E) and Valley-Generated Reversals (I -Ⅲ)

Solution: Following the guiding steps from (A) to (H), one can obtain the following:

Stress Level/MPa	No. of Cycles	No. of Reversals
27	0	1
24	0	1
22	0	1
20	0	1
19	1	0
17	0	2
16	0	2
13	0	1
10	2	0
Total	3	9

Table 4.5.1　Generic ε-N Material Parameters Materials Based on Manson-Coffin-Basquin-Morrow Equation.

Material	$T/℃$	$d\varepsilon/dt$	σ'_f	ε'_f	b	c	K'	n'	$\sigma_f@2N_f$	R
Ferrous	23	—	$1.5\sigma_{uts}$	0.59^*	-0.087	-0.58	$1.65\sigma_{uts}$	0.15	$\sigma_f@10^8$	-1
Al Alloys	23	—	$1.67\sigma_{uts}$	0.35	-0.095	-0.69	$1.61\sigma_{uts}$	0.11	$\sigma_f@10^8$	-1
Ti Alloys	23	—	$1.61\sigma_{uts}$	0.35	-0.095	-0.69	$1.61\sigma_{uts}$	0.11	$\sigma_f@10^8$	-1
General Metals	23	—	Eq.(4.13.1)	Eq.(4.13.2)	-0.12	-0.6	$\dfrac{\sigma'_f}{(\varepsilon'_f)^{n'}}$	$\dfrac{b}{c}$	$\sigma_f@10^8$	-1

Notes：* Ferrous：$\varepsilon'_f=0.59$, if $\sigma_{uts}\leqslant 0.3\%E$

$$=0.59\left(1.375-\frac{125\sigma_{uts}}{E}\right),\ 0.3\%E<\text{if }\sigma_{uts}<1.02\%E;$$

$$=0.059,\ \text{if }\sigma_{uts}\geqslant 1.02\%\ E,\ \text{where }E\text{ is the Young's modulus};$$

$2N_f$(Cycles)：Number of cycles at endurance limit or cutoff point；

K' (MPa)：Strain hardening coefficient；

n'：Strain hardening exponent.

Table 4.12.1　Experimental Data for Material Fatigue under Nonproportional Loadings ［Zhang & Yaw］［Wang et al.］［Zhang et al.］.

Material	Run$R$	σ_a/MPa	σ_m/MPa	τ_a	τ_m	$\psi/(°)$	Life (cycles)
Al 7075−T651	1	138.9	156.6	69.5	78.3	0	819255
	1	137.9	155.5	79.6	89.8	30	974032

Chapter 5

Fracture Mechanics

5.1 Fracture Failure

Material subjected to a single static load is likely to break as the static stress exceeds a certain limit, beyond which the failure mode is called fracture failure. The vast majority of the released strain energy of a crack induced by fracture failure is absorbed not only by creating new surfaces, but also by energy dissipation due to plastic flow in the material near the crack tip. Fracture failure of general steel can be divided into three stages:

(1) Crack nucleation;
(2) Crack-growth;
(3) Ultimate ductile failure.

The fracture threshold in a static system subjected to uniaxial loading is generally called tensile strength, compressive strength, or shear strength, depending on the loading mode. The surface of either brittle or ductile fracture tends to be perpendicular to the first principal stress (i.e. σ_1, mostly in tension) although other stress components can be assisting factors.

5.1.1 Fracture Surface-Ductile Fracture

Transgranular fracture generally occurs in a ductile material, as exhibited by most metals that cracks passing through grains. Faceted texture appears in the fractured surface due to different orientation of cleavage planes in grains, as observed in Fig. 5.1.1(a). A ductile material usually experiences extensive plastic strain-hardening deformation before fracture nucleates, as such a crack resists extension unless the applied stress is increased. In ductile crystalline metals and plastics, the crack top extends by means of microscopically resolved shear stress that creates an angled crack surface that is not perpendicular to the maximum principal stress. The fracture surface is dull and fibrous. There is a permanent deformation at the tip of the advancing crack that leaves distinct patterns in SEM (Scanning Electron Microscopy) images.

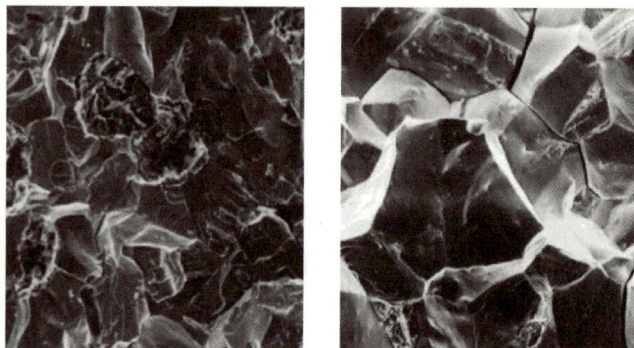

(a) Transgranular Fracture   (b) Intergranular Fracture

Fig. 5.1.1   Fractographic Features of Fracture Surface: Transgranular and Intergranular

5.1.2   Fracture Surface-Brittle Fracture

When material is brittle, crack propagation goes along grain boundaries that may be weakened as embrittled by impurity segregation etc. as shown in Fig. 5.1.1(b) and exhibited by most ceramics and cold metals and cold plastics. Little plastic deformation is observed. Crack propagates rapidly even with little increase in the applied stress and it propagates nearly perpendicular to the direction of the applied stress by cleavage-breaking of atomic bonds along specific crystallographic planes. Characteristic-crack-advance-markings on the brittle-fractured surface frequently point to wherever the fracture originated from. The path which the crack follows depends on the material's structure. Cleavage shows up clearly in the SEM (Scanning Electron Microscopy). There is no gross permanent deformation of brittle material.

5.1.3   Dynamic Fracture

Material subjected to a cyclic dynamic load is likely to fail at a lower stress than when the same load amplitude is applied statically, especially after the load is repeated for a large number of cycles. The failure mode is called fatigue failure. Fatigue analysis may be based on one of the following criteria:

(A) Stress-Life Approach: This approach is often referred to as the *S-N* approach and is appropriate for long life situations (more elastic deformation) when the material strength and the nominal stress control the fatigue life. Note that *S* stands for stress and *N* is the number of fatigue cycles.

(B) Strain-Life Approach: This approach is often referred to as the *ε-N* approach and is used for finite fatigue lives in ductile materials where plastic deformation prevails. Strain-life methods are often considered crack initiation life estimates. Note that *ε* stands for strain.

(C) Energy-Life Approach: The strain energy is considered in addition to stress and/or strain components. This is the more promising criterion for predicting crack initiation.

(D) Crack Growth Approach: Fracture mechanics is used to determine how much time it takes for a crack to grow to the critical size. The theory starts with linear elastic fracture mechanics (LEFM).

(E) Impact Fracture: Under a dynamic impact load, the impact energy is transferred from a moving object to a stationary object and breaks it. The fracture threshold in such a dynamic system is generally measured by fracture toughness.

Whether stress-yielding flow, strain-yielding flow, creep flow, oxidation, ageing, and fracture toughness (e. g. stress-crack) need be considered in the fatigue life prediction of a product depends on the material itself, applied stress and strain amplitudes, static/dynamic loading states, and working temperature. Multifactorial analyses can be considered, especially for plastics and rubber. If the operating temperature is significantly high, e.g. above 50% of the absolute melting temperature of the material (K), creep of metals becomes the primary contributor to the failure.

5.2 Fracture Toughness and Impact Tests

Instantaneous crack propagation to failure originating from one or more of the original cracks is called a brittle fracture. If there is fatigue loading, the initial cracks grow slowly until one crack reaches a critical size that results in a total fracture immediately after then. Fracture toughness based on fracture mechanics is thus defined to measure the material toughness ranging from brittle fracture and ductile fracture. In other words, fracture toughness is a material property that presents the ability to resist fracture when there is a crack.

The measurement of fracture toughness relies on impact tests. Under dynamic loading, the transfer of energy from a device such as a drop weight or a swinging specimen to the deforming or breaking specimen is equated to the impact energy, traditionally called fracture toughness. It is also a test for material brittleness. An Izod impact testing machine or Charpy impact testing machine (Figs. 5.2.1 and 5.2.2) may be used for evaluating this impact energy and its related fracture toughness. However, the fracture toughness is also defined as the energy required for creating a crack based on fracture mechanics described in the next section.

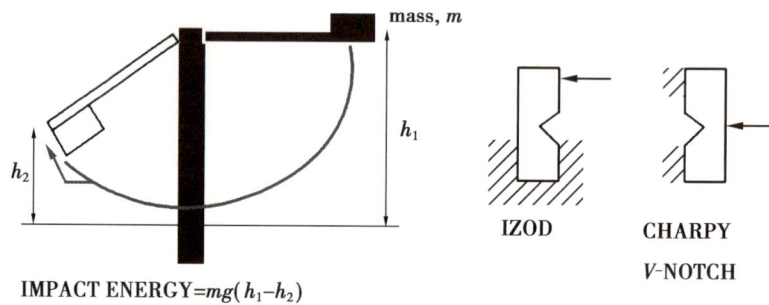

IMPACT ENERGY$=mg(h_1-h_2)$

Fig. 5.2.1   Schematic of Izod Impact Testing and Charpy Impact Testing [ASTM]

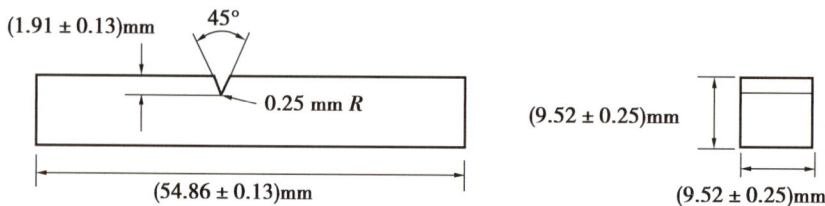

Fig. 5.2.2   Dimensions of Charpy V-Notch Specimens

The Charpy impact testing machine consists of a rigid specimen holder and a swinging pendulum hammer for striking the impact blow to a V-notched specimen (Fig. 5.2.2) as shown in Fig. 5.2.1. Beside dynamic effects, another aspect is that the material properties may be merged to downgrade the fracture toughness as brittleness develops. Failure modes due to low fracture toughness are addressed as follows:

(a) Intergranular fracture embrittlement: Cracks follow grain boundaries. Typical examples include phosphor or antimony in hard steels, seasoned cracking of brass by ammonia, liquid metal embrittlement during soldering, and sensitization of stainless steels.

(b) Quench-aged embrittlement: During cooling of carbon or low-alloyed steels from subcritical temperatures, precipitation of carbides within the microstructure may raise the strength but reduce the toughness.

(c) Blue brittleness: Within the temperature range of 230-470 ℃ blue-purple oxides can form on steels. As formed, these precipitates enhance the tensile strength and hardness while reducing the ductility and toughness.

(d) Temper embrittlement: Quenched steels containing appreciable amounts of manganese, silicon, nickel or chromium are susceptible to temper embrittlement if they contain even trace amounts of antimony, tin or arsenic. Embrittlement of susceptible steels can occur after being heated up to a temperature between 370 ℃ and 575 ℃. The embrittlement proceeds rapidly in the temperature range between 450 ℃ and 475 ℃.

(e) Sigma-phase embrittlement: The prolonged service at a temperature ranging from 560 ℃ to 980 ℃ can cause formation of the hard, brittle, sigma phase in ferritic and austenitic stainless steels and similar alloys.

(f) Graphitization: Graphitization happens when the pearlite in steels begins to decompose into ferrite and graphite following very long, high temperature service.

(g) Internal oxidation: This is one of the common failure modes at a high temperature, as exposed to oxidizing conditions. A typical failure example is engine exhaust manifolds made of G3500 gray iron, i.e. GJB-400 (also called QT-400in China).

(h) Intermetallic-compound embrittlement: Intermetallic compounds can form inside a metal or ceramic when certain other metals penetrate by diffusion. An example would be galvanized steel where the zinc has diffused into the steel, of which the temperature stays in the vicinity of 420 ℃.

(i) Hydrogen embrittlement: The material (e.g. steel) become brittle and has low fracture toughness due to the introduction and subsequent diffusion of hydrogen into it. It is a whole subject unto itself, having several origins and several different effects.

(j) Order-disorder reactions: These embrittling reactions at the crystal level are common in nonferrous alloys, but not common in bulky steels.

5.3   Stress Intensity Factors

All materials contain cracks of some size on a microscopic scale due to the manufacturing process and material nature. Not all interior and surface flaws found in a product are unstable under service conditions. Fracture mechanics is to analyze these flaws to find out what are safe and what are liable to crack propagation. The stress intensity factor, traditionally noted down as K, is used in fracture mechanics to predict the stress intensity near the tip of a crack due to remote loading functions. It is applied to materials that exhibit a linear elastic deformation and small-scale elastoplastic yielding at a crack tip. Cracks may grow in three distinct dislocation modes as shown in Fig. 5.3.1: opening, in-plane sliding, and out-of-plane tearing. The 2-dimensional view of an arbitrary-depicted contour path around the Mode-I crack tip is shown in Fig. 5.3.2. The three corresponding stress intensity factors are defined as follows:

$$K_{\mathrm{I}} = \lim_{r \to 0}(2\pi r)^{\frac{1}{2}} \sigma_{yy}(r,0)$$

$$K_{\mathrm{II}} = \lim_{r \to 0}(2\pi r)^{\frac{1}{2}} \tau_{yx}(r,0)$$

and $\quad K_{\mathrm{III}} = \lim_{r \to 0}(2\pi r)^{\frac{1}{2}} \tau_{yz}(r,0)$

where

K_{I}: Mode-I stress intensity factor, opening mode;

K_{II}: Mode-II stress intensity factor, in-plane sliding mode;

K_{III}: Mode-III stress intensity factor, out-of-plane tearing;

r: Crack length along the x-axis;

σ_{yy}, τ_{yx}, and τ_{yz}: Normal, in-plane shear, and out-of-plane shear stresses, respectively.

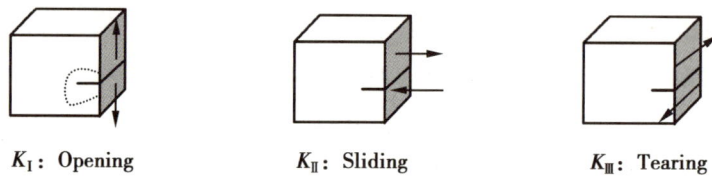

K_{I}: Opening K_{II}: Sliding K_{III}: Tearing

Fig. 5.3.1   Three Fracture Modes-Relative Dislocation Directions Represented by Arrows

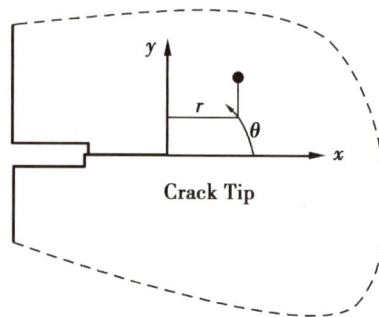

Fig. 5.3.2   Stress Field around a Crack Tip of a 2-Dimensional Fracture

5.3.1   Stress Components around a Crack Tip

First of all, let's consider the opening mode, also called Mode-I fracture. It occurs more often than the other two. The origin of the coordinates is purposely located at the crack tip as shown in Fig. 5.3.2. In the relevant Cartesian coordinate system (x, y, z) and polar coordinate system (r, θ, z), the three stress components at the "dot point" in the vicinity of the crack tip for Mode-I fracture corresponding to plane strain case are

$$\sigma_{xx} = \frac{K_{\text{I}}}{(2\pi r)^{\frac{1}{2}}}\cos\frac{\theta}{2}\left[1 - \sin\frac{\theta}{2}\sin\frac{3\theta}{2}\right] + O(r^{\frac{1}{2}}) \tag{5.3.1}$$

$$\sigma_{yy} = \frac{K_{\text{I}}}{(2\pi r)^{\frac{1}{2}}}\cos\frac{\theta}{2}\left[1 + \sin\frac{\theta}{2}\sin\frac{3\theta}{2}\right] + O(r^{\frac{1}{2}}) \tag{5.3.2}$$

and $\quad \tau_{xy} = \dfrac{K_{\text{I}}}{(2\pi r)^{\frac{1}{2}}}\cos\dfrac{\theta}{2}\sin\dfrac{\theta}{2}\cos\dfrac{3\theta}{2} + O(r^{\frac{1}{2}}) \tag{5.3.3}$

For Mode II corresponding to plane strain case are

$$\sigma_{xx} = \frac{K_{\text{II}}}{(2\pi r)^{\frac{1}{2}}}\sin\frac{\theta}{2}\left[2 + \cos\frac{\theta}{2}\cos\frac{3\theta}{2}\right] + O(r^{\frac{1}{2}}) \tag{5.3.4}$$

$$\sigma_{yy} = \frac{K_{\text{II}}}{(2\pi r)^{\frac{1}{2}}}\sin\frac{\theta}{2}\cos\frac{\theta}{2}\cos\frac{3\theta}{2} + O(r^{\frac{1}{2}}) \tag{5.3.5}$$

and $\quad \tau_{xy} = \dfrac{K_{\text{II}}}{(2\pi r)^{\frac{1}{2}}}\cos\dfrac{\theta}{2}\left[1 - \sin\dfrac{\theta}{2}\sin\dfrac{3\theta}{2}\right] + O(r^{\frac{1}{2}}) \tag{5.3.6}$

of which term $O(r^{1/2})$ comprises of the higher-order terms. In the crack plane (i.e. $y = 0$ plane) where $r = x$ and $\theta = 0$ ahead of the crack tip, Eqs. (5.3.1)-(5.3.3) corresponding to Mode-I reduce to

$$\sigma_{xx} = \sigma_{yy} = \frac{K_{\text{I}}}{(2\pi x)^{\frac{1}{2}}} \tag{5.3.7}$$

and $\quad \tau_{xy} = 0 \tag{5.3.8}$

Eqs. (5.3.1)-(5.3.8) that are derived on the basis of LEFM (Linear Engineering Fracture Mechanics) are only valid if the plastic zone with finite strains is much smaller than the singularity zones.

Each dislocation mode does not present itself as a catastrophic failure until its corresponding crack size under a certain stress has reached the critical value. The critical values of these three dislocation modes, i.e. K_{IC}, $K_{ⅡC}$, and $K_{ⅢC}$, are Mode-Ⅰ, Mode-Ⅱ, and Mode-Ⅲ of fracture toughness, respectively shown in Fig. 5.3.1. They are mathematically defined as

$$K_{IC} = \sigma_{xx}(\pi a)^{\frac{1}{2}} \tag{5.3.9}$$

$$K_{ⅡC} = \tau_{yx}(\pi a)^{\frac{1}{2}} \tag{5.3.10}$$

and $\quad K_{ⅢC} = \tau_{yz}(\pi a)^{\frac{1}{2}} \tag{5.3.11}$

where

K_{IC}: Critical stress intensity factor in opening mode (Mode-Ⅰ);
$K_{ⅡC}$: Critical stress intensity factor in in-plane sliding mode (Mode-Ⅱ);
$K_{ⅢC}$: Critical stress intensity factor in out-of-plane tearing mode (Mode-Ⅲ);
a: Crack length;

σ_{xx}, τ_{yx}, and τ_{yz}: Normal, in-plane shear, and out-of-plane shear stresses, respectively.

K_{IC} (MPa-m$^{1/2}$) usually occurs more often than the other two dislocation failure modes and is used to represent the fracture toughness. It denotes crack opening mode under a normal tensile stress perpendicular to the crack extension based on the linear-elastic fracture toughness, at which the material begins to grow significantly. K_{IC} monotonically decreases with increasing thickness for thin samples but it converges to a stabilized value called plain strain fracture toughness, as shown in Fig. 5.3.3. Data of fracture toughness given in this publication are plane strain fracture toughness unless denoted otherwise.

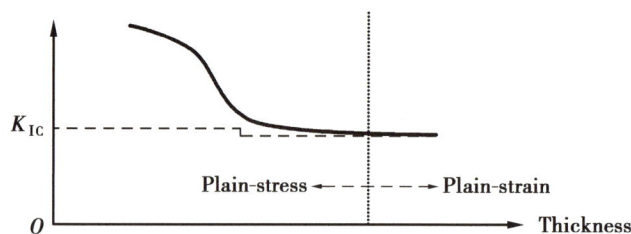

Fig. 5.3.3 Schematic Drawing of Fracture Toughness versus Specimen Thickness

5.3.2 Experimental Determination of Fracture Toughness: Three-Point Bend Test

The fracture toughness of a specimen can be determined using a three-point flexural test as shown in Fig. 5.3.4. The length of the crack is measured as the specimen is loaded monotonically. A plot of the load versus the crack opening displacement is used to determine the loading force (F) at which the crack starts growing. The stress intensity factor at the crack tip of a single edge notch

bending specimen [Bower] is given as

$$K_{IC} = \left[1.6 \left(\frac{a}{h} \right)^{\frac{1}{2}} - 2.6 \left(\frac{a}{h} \right)^{\frac{3}{2}} + 12.3 \left(\frac{a}{h} \right)^{\frac{5}{2}} - 21.2 \left(\frac{a}{h} \right)^{\frac{7}{2}} + 21.8 \left(\frac{a}{h} \right)^{\frac{9}{2}} \right] \left(\frac{\pi}{h} \right)^{\frac{1}{2}} \left(\frac{4F}{b} \right)$$

$$(5.3.12)$$

where

F: Applied force;

b: Thickness of the specimen;

a: Crack length;

h: Height of the specimen.

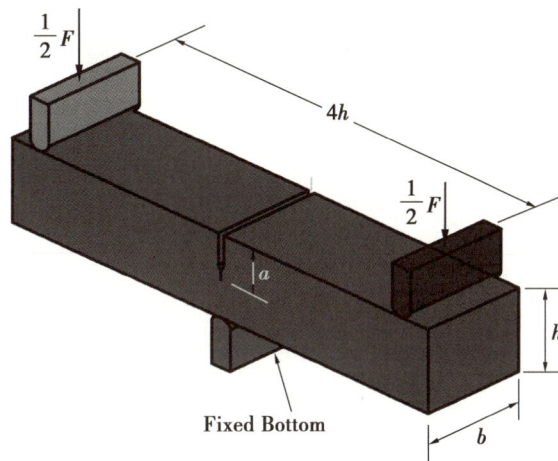

Fig. 5.3.4   Three-Point Bend Test for Fracture Toughness K_{IC} [Wikipedia]

This load is then substituted into the above formula to find out the fracture toughness in the opening mode. By such a three-point bend test, a fatigue crack is first created at the tip of the notch by cyclic loading if a fluctuating load is applied.

5.3.3   Experimental Determination of Fracture Toughness: Compact Tension Test

Another commonly applied test for acquiring the Mode-I stress intensity factor at the crack tip of a single edge notch is the compact tension test [Bower], as shown in Fig. 5.3.5. The stress intensity factor in the opening mode is given as

$$K_{IC} = \left[16.7 \left(\frac{a}{w} \right)^{\frac{1}{2}} - 104.7 \left(\frac{a}{w} \right)^{\frac{3}{2}} + 369.9 \left(\frac{a}{w} \right)^{\frac{5}{2}} - 573.8 \left(\frac{a}{w} \right)^{\frac{7}{2}} + 360.5 \left(\frac{a}{w} \right)^{\frac{9}{2}} \right] \left(\frac{\pi}{w} \right)^{\frac{1}{2}} \frac{F}{b}$$

$$(5.3.13)$$

where

F: Applied force;

b: Thickness of the specimen;

a: Crack length;

w: Width of the specimen.

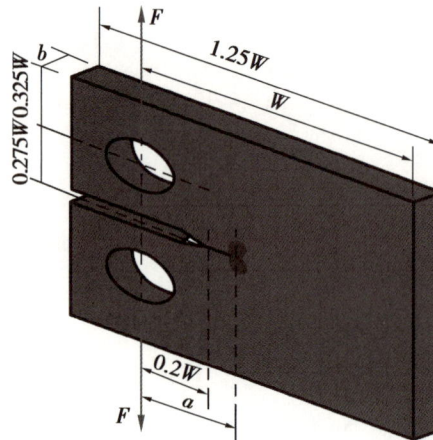

Fig. 5.3.5   Three-Point Bend Test for Fracture Toughness K_{IC} [Wikipedia 2/5/2018]

5.3.4 Stress-Corrosion Cracking

Cracks may develop and propagate far below K_{IC} in the presence of a corrodent. The damage is magnified and controlled by K_{ISCC} (Intensity of Stress-Corrosion Cracking) instead of K_{IC}. K_{ISCC} is much smaller than K_{IC} because of chemical energy release during the crack propagation. A list of stress-corrosion cracking mechanisms to be considered in the real-world design is given as follows [Jewett] :

Alloy	Stress-Corrosion Cracking Environment
Austenitic Stainless-Steel	NaCl
Aluminum Alloys	Aqueous Halides
Copper Alloys	NH_4OH (pH7)
High-Strength Structural Steel	NaCl
Ti-6Al-4V	KCl

5.4   Strain Energy Release Rate and *R*-Curve

An energy approach to fracture mechanics was first sought by [Griffith 1921] in a paper for analyzing the brittle fracture of glass. It is found that the energy required for creating an additional differential crack length (i.e. da) of thickness h in 2-dimensional domain is equivalent to the differential potential energy variation over that extended differential crack area. This is quantified by the definition of strain energy release rate in the linear elastic stage, which is defined as shown below

$$G = \frac{-\mathrm{d}(U - W)}{h\,\mathrm{d}a}$$

(5.4.1)

where

G: Strain energy release rate;

$U(\mathrm{J},\ \mathrm{Nm},\ \text{or}\ \mathrm{Nmm})$: Potential energy;

$W(\mathrm{J},\ \mathrm{Nm},\ \text{or}\ \mathrm{Nmm})$: Work done by external forces;

$h(\mathrm{m}\ \text{or}\ \mathrm{mm})$: Thickness;

$a(\mathrm{m}\ \text{or}\ \mathrm{mm})$: Crack length.

Note that $\mathrm{d}(ha)=h\mathrm{d}a$, of which h is constant is the differential crack surface created. His work was extended to metals by [Irwin 1957], who showed that the strain energy release rate (G_{I}) for a Mode-I crack can be related to stress intensity (K_{I}) in the linear elastic range using the Young's modulus and Poisson's ratio as

$$G_{\mathrm{I}} = \frac{K_{\mathrm{I}}^2}{E} \quad (\text{Plane stress}) \tag{5.4.2}$$

$$G_{\mathrm{I}} = \frac{K_{\mathrm{I}}^2}{[E(1-\nu^2)]} \quad (\text{Plane strain}) \tag{5.4.3}$$

where

E: Young's modulus;

ν: Poisson's ratio.

The energy release rate failure criterion states that a crack will grow when the available energy release rate is greater than or equal to the critical value, namely G_{IC}, G_{IIC}, and G_{IIIC}, depending on the failure mode. The critical fracture energy term, G_{IC}, G_{IIC}, and G_{IIIC} are considered to be a material property, which is independent of the applied loads and the geometry of the body. The failure criteria for each individual failure mode based on the energy release rate are expressed as

$G_{\mathrm{I}} \geqslant G_{\mathrm{IC}}$, which is similar to $K_{\mathrm{I}} \geqslant K_{\mathrm{IC}}$

$G_{\mathrm{II}} \geqslant G_{\mathrm{IIC}}$, which is similar to $K_{\mathrm{II}} \geqslant K_{\mathrm{IIC}}$

or $G_{\mathrm{III}} \geqslant G_{\mathrm{IIIC}}$, which is similar to $K_{\mathrm{III}} \geqslant K_{\mathrm{IIIC}}$

R value is another terminology defined as the material's resistance to crack extension. The energy release rate G of most materials rises asymptotically with respect to crack size while the material working in the LEFM (Linear Elastic Fracture Mechanics) range. A plot of fracture energy ($\mathrm{J/m^2}$ or $\mathrm{N/m}$) versus crack extension is called R-curve, i.e. a crack resistance curve of the material. At the moment when an R-curve goes flat, the crack reaches the critical strain energy release rate. However, a falling R-curve may occur when metal fails by cleavage, by which strain wave propagation is unstable due to a decreasing supporting mass and excites a very high strain rate near the crack tip that suppresses plastic deformation.

The damage evolution for mixed-mode failure is defined based on the power law criterion, which is established in terms of an interaction between the energy release rates [Camacho & Davila]

$$\left(\frac{G_{\mathrm{I}}}{G_{\mathrm{IC}}}\right)^{n} + \left(\frac{G_{\mathrm{II}}}{G_{\mathrm{IIC}}}\right)^{n} = 1 \qquad (5.4.4)$$

of which, exponent n is a material property. The above equation is originally derived from composite materials. In finite element analysis, energy release rates G_{I} and G_{II} refer to the work done by the traction along the crack surface and the conjugate relative displacement between the two crack surfaces in the normal and shear direction, respectively. When linear solid elements are applied, G_{I} and G_{II} can be calculated, respectively as

$$G_{\mathrm{I}} = \lim_{\Delta \to 0}\left[\frac{F_{i}(v_{k} - v'_{k})}{2\Delta}\right] \qquad (5.4.5)$$

and $\quad G_{\mathrm{II}} = \lim_{\Delta \to 0}\left[\frac{F_{i}(u_{k} - u'_{k})}{2\Delta}\right] \qquad (5.4.6)$

When quadratic solid elements are applied, G_{I} and G_{II} can be calculated, respectively as

$$G_{\mathrm{I}} = \lim_{\Delta \to 0}\frac{[F_{iy}(v_{k} - v'_{k}) + F_{iy}(v_{k} - v'_{k})]}{2\Delta} \qquad (5.4.7)$$

and $\quad G_{\mathrm{II}} = \lim_{\Delta \to 0}\frac{[F_{ix}(u_{k} - u'_{k}) + F_{ix}(u_{k} - u'_{k})]}{2\Delta} \qquad (5.4.8)$

where

Δ: Size of the mesh around the tip, as being uniformly meshed as shown in Fig. 5.4.1;

v_{k}: Displacement in the opening mode (along the y-direction) on one side of the crack;

v'_{k}: Displacement in the opening mode (along the y-direction) on the other side;

u_{k}: Displacement in mode Ⅱ (along the x-direction) on one side of the crack;

u'_{k}: Displacement in mode Ⅱ (along the x-direction) on the other side;

F_{ix} and F_{iy}: Nodal forces at the crack tip along the x-and y-directions, respectively.

Subscripts k and k' denote node k and k' on the crack surfaces. This method is called decohesive zone model in finite element methods [Camacho & Davila]. The technique requires that the finite element meshes along the crack path immediately before and after the crack tip are of the same size Δ, as shown in Fig. 5.4.1.

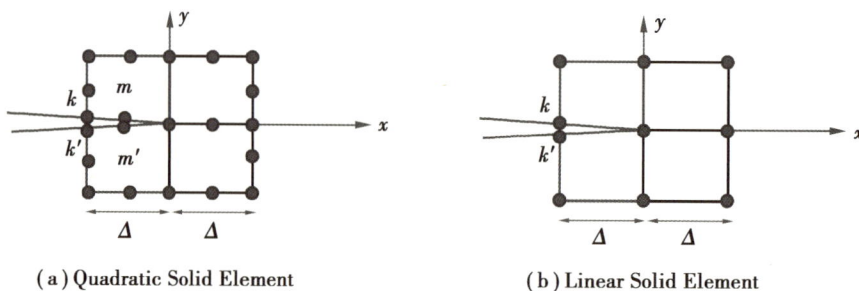

(a) Quadratic Solid Element   (b) Linear Solid Element

Fig. 5.4.1　Decohesive Zone Model in Finite Element Methods (4-Noded Solid Elements)

According to a sensitivity study on the mesh size by [Quaresimin & Ricotta], element size Δ can be set at 0.03 mm in order to balance the need for a sufficient number of elements through the lamina and adhesive thickness, and also generate a reasonable result (SERR) that is independent of the mesh size. Unrealistic oscillatory behavior of stress and displacement fields in the neighborhood of the crack tip [Sun & Jih] even based on implicit FEM, if element size Δ is too small.

5.5   Crack Propagation and Stress Intensity Factor Range

The fracture mechanics approach is based on the assumption that there are pre-existing cracks. Fracture development may be divided into three stages: crack initiation, crack propagation, and then fracture failure.

(a) Crack initiation: The initial crack occurs in this stage. The crack is generally intrinsically caused by slip bands or dislocations intersecting the surface as a result of previous cyclic loading or work hardening. It may be as well created by surface defects caused by tooling or handling. USA Navy defines arbitrarily that the presence of a crack of 0.25 mm in length is the onset of crack initiation.

(b) Crack propagation: The crack continues to grow during this stage as a result of continuously applied stresses.

(c) Fracture failure: Failure occurs when the material that has not been affected by the crack cannot withstand the applied stress. This stage happens rapidly.

During the stage of crack propagation the fatigue crack growth rate is of great concern, for it is used for predicting the fatigue life of material. The fatigue crack growth rate with respect to fluctuating loading cycles can be related to its driving stress intensity factor range, ΔK, as

$$\frac{\mathrm{d}a}{\mathrm{d}N_{\mathrm{p}}} = f(R) \left| \Delta K - \Delta K_{\mathrm{th}} \right|^{m} \tag{5.5.1}$$

where

a: Crack size;

N_{p}: Number of cycles in the crack propagation stage;

ΔK: Stress intensity factor range;

K_{max} and K_{min}: Maximum and minimum stress intensity factors under cyclic loading;

ΔK_{th}: Threshold stress intensity factor range, which is strongly influenced by corrosion;

m: Stress intensity factor exponent;

R: Load ratio, $R = K_{\mathrm{min}}/K_{\mathrm{max}}$;

$f(R)$: Parameter as a function of load ratio R.

The stress intensity factor range given above may be due to anyone of the following failure mode: opening, in-plane sliding, and out-of-plane tearing. The approach to life prediction based on fracture mechanics can account for pre-existing cracks. As shown in Fig. 5.5.1, the crack propagation can be divided into three stages: (1) initial crack (ΔK_{th}), (2) steady-state crack propagation, and (3) final eruption stage. Influential parameters for crack growth based on Eq. (5.5.1) for some common materials are in given in the tables of individual materials scattered in the book. In general, the material failure pattern of a fractured cross-section has a distinct feature that varies with the stress intensity range (ΔK) as follows:

(a) Low ΔK: Crystallographic.
(b) Medium ΔK: Striation.
(c) High ΔK: Striation and Dimples.

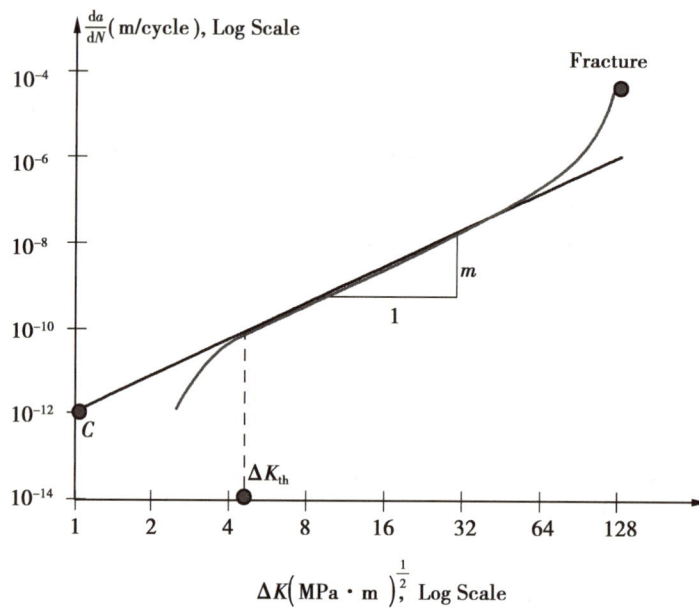

Fig. 5.5.1　Schematic Plot of Fatigue Crack Growth as a Function of Stress Intensity Factor Range

5.5.1　Paris Equation

A simplified model can be derived from Eq. (5.5.1), called the modified Paris equation that accounts for the stress ratio (R), due to [Kurihara],

$$\frac{da}{dN_p} = C \left| \frac{\Delta K}{1-R} \right|^m \quad \text{if} -5.0 \leqslant R \leqslant 0.5 \tag{5.5.2}$$

or $\quad \dfrac{da}{dN_p} = C |\Delta K|^m \quad$ if $R > 0.5$ $\hfill$ (5.5.3)

The integration of Eq. (5.5.1), for estimating N_p that is the number of fluctuations (cycles) of the applied dynamic load for a crack to propagate from the initial crack size to the critical crack size, leads to

$$N_p = \int_{a_i}^{a_c} C^{-1} |\Delta K - \Delta K_{th}|^{-m} \, da \tag{5.5.4}$$

where

a_c: Critical crack size;

a_i: Initial crack size.

The above equation is to be justified by the fracture toughness of the material. The critical crack size (a_c) is a material property and its size depends on the loading type, i.e. opening, in-plane shearing, or out-of-plane shearing mode. The total life cycle is a combined fatigue cycles to the crack nucleation (from $a = 0$ to a_i) and the fracture propagation cycles (from a_i to a_c),

$$N = N_i + N_p \tag{5.5.5}$$

where

N: Total useful product life cycles;

N_i: Fatigue life to initiating a crack;

N_p: Life cycles accounting for allowable crack propagation.

Note that opening failure mode occurs more often than the other two (in-plane sliding and out-of-plane shearing). Parameter ΔK bears the same format for the fracture toughness K, referring to Eqs. (5.3.9)-(5.3.11), as

$$\Delta K = Y' \Delta \sigma_{max} (\pi a')^{\frac{1}{2}} \tag{5.5.6}$$

where

Y': Correction factor subject to crack tip configuration;

$\Delta \sigma_{max}$: Maximum fluctuating stress component;

a': Crack length in response to elastoplastic deformation (See Section 5.6.1 for details).

Assume that $f(R)$ in Eq. (5.5.1) is a constant and $\Delta K_{th} = 0$. Consider the case with crack propagation that has only minor plastic effect (brittle materials), then $a' \rightarrow a$. Substituting Eq.(5.5.6) into Eq. (5.5.4) gives

$$
\begin{aligned}
N_p &= \int_{a_i}^{a_c} C^{-1} (\Delta K)^{-m} \, da = \int_{a_i}^{a_c} C^{-1} [Y' \Delta \sigma_{max} (\pi a)^{\frac{1}{2}}]^{-m} da \\
&= C^{-1} [Y' \Delta \sigma_{max} \pi^{\frac{1}{2}}]^{-m} \int_{a_i}^{a_c} a^{-\frac{m}{2}} \, da \\
&= \frac{2[a_c^{1-\frac{m}{2}} - a_i^{1-\frac{m}{2}}]}{(2-m) C [Y' \Delta \sigma_{max} \pi^{\frac{1}{2}}]^m}
\end{aligned} \tag{5.5.7}
$$

Yet the Y' is employed here as a geometry correction factor related to crack configuration around the crack tip. In other words, Y' is employed here to modify the "smooth sharp" crack front assumed for Eqs. (5.3.9)-(5.3.11). In the meanwhile parameter a' is used for correcting the elastoplastic deformation at the crack tip in contrast to the elastic brittle crack tip for Eqs. (5.5.3)-(5.5.5). Explicit formulae for stress intensity factor ranges corresponding to cracks of four fundamental geometries subjected to remote tension, as shown in Fig. 5.5.2, are given as follows:

(a) Edge crack of length a' in a semi-infinite plate.

$$\Delta K = 1.12 \Delta \sigma (\pi a')^{\frac{1}{2}} \tag{5.5.8}$$

(b) Central coin-shaped crack of radius a' in an infinite body.

$$\Delta K = 2 \Delta \sigma \left(\frac{a'}{\pi} \right)^{\frac{1}{2}} = \frac{2}{\pi} \Delta \sigma (\pi a')^{\frac{1}{2}} \approx 0.637 (\pi a')^{\frac{1}{2}} \tag{5.5.9}$$

(c) Center crack, length $2a'$ in plate of width w.

$$\Delta K = \Delta \sigma \left[w \tan \frac{\pi a'}{w} \right]^{\frac{1}{2}} \tag{5.5.10}$$

(d) 2 symmetrical edge cracks of length a' each, in a plate of total width w.

$$\Delta K = \Delta \sigma \left[w \tan \frac{\pi a'}{w} + 0.1 \, w \sin \frac{2\pi a'}{w} \right]^{\frac{1}{2}} \tag{5.5.11}$$

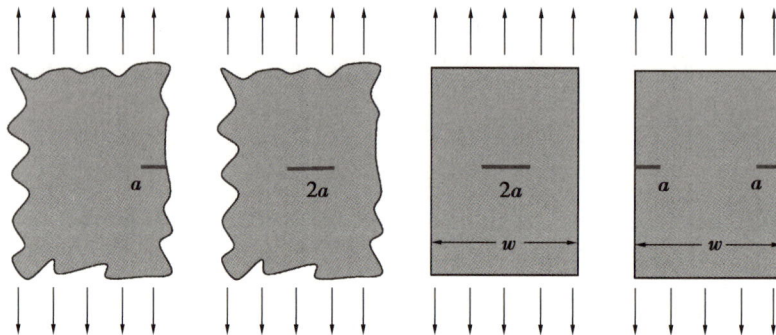

Fig. 5.5.2   Fundamentals of Cracks Subjected to Remote Tension

Numerous explicit formulae of modifiers for stress intensity factors under various loadings have been established [Murakami et al.] and the principle of superposition can be applied in the linear elastic range. Nevertheless, the finite element methods can be a better approach to assessing the stress intensity factors. As cracks induced in the manufacturing process are relatively much smaller than the substrate in size, a comparison between Eqs. (5.5.8) and (5.5.9) unveils that a microcrack on the surface does more damage than an embedded microcrack.

Example 5.5.1   A steel plate ($E = 207$ GPa and $\nu = 0.27$) is subjected to a fluctuating load, ranging from $\sigma_{min} = -40$ MPa to $\sigma_{max} = 140$ MPa at 15 Hz. If the plate contains an initial through-thickness edge crack of 0.5 mm in length, how many fatigue cycles are required to break the plate for the following material:

Mild steel, $\mathrm{d}a/\mathrm{d}N$ (m/cycle) $= 6.8 \times 10^{-12} (\Delta K_{\mathrm{I}})^{2.4}$ and $K_{\mathrm{IC}} = 90$ MPa $\cdot$ m$^{\frac{1}{2}}$

and $Y' = 1.12$ (a semi-infinite plate)?

Solution:

(1) First, the critical length of crack has to be determined using Eq. (5.3.9)

$$K_{\mathrm{IC}} = \sigma_{xx}(\pi a_{\mathrm{c}})^{\frac{1}{2}}$$

$$90 \text{ MPa} \cdot \text{m}^{\frac{1}{2}} = [140 - (-40)] \text{ MPa}[\pi(a_{\mathrm{c}})]^{\frac{1}{2}}$$

Thus, $\quad a_{\mathrm{c}} = \dfrac{1}{4\pi} = 0.07958$ m

(2) Given that $m = 2.4$, $a_i = 0.000\ 5$ m (0.5 mm), $\Delta\sigma_{\max} = 140$ MPa $- (-40$ MPa$) = 180$ MPa, $Y' = 1.12$, and $C = 6.8 \times 10^{-12}$. Following Eq. (5.5.7), one has

$$N_{\mathrm{p}} = \frac{2\left[a_{\mathrm{c}}^{1-\frac{m}{2}} - a_i^{1-\frac{m}{2}}\right]}{(2-m)\ C\left[Y'\Delta\sigma_{\max}\pi^{\frac{1}{2}}\right]^{m}} = \frac{2\left[0.07958^{1-\frac{2.4}{2}} - 0.0005^{1-\frac{2.4}{2}}\right]}{(2-2.4) \times 6.8 \times 10^{-12} \times [1.12(180)\pi^{\frac{1}{2}}]^{2.4}}$$

$$= 1.598 \times 10^{5} \text{Cycles}$$

$$= 29.594 \text{ h}$$

5.5.2 $\Delta K_{\mathrm{th}} : \neq 0$

Consider the case that the threshold stress intensity factor range is significant and the crack propagation involves with only minor plastic effect (brittle materials), then $a' \to a$. Substituting Eq. (5.5.6) into Eq. (5.5.4) gives

$$N_{\mathrm{p}} = \int_{a_i}^{a_{\mathrm{c}}} C^{-1}(\Delta K - \Delta K_{\mathrm{th}})^{-m}\ \mathrm{d}a = \int_{a_i}^{a_{\mathrm{c}}} C^{-1}[Y'\Delta\sigma_{\max}(\pi a)^{\frac{1}{2}} - \Delta K_{\mathrm{th}}]^{-m}\mathrm{d}a \qquad (5.5.12)$$

Let $\quad t = Y'\Delta\sigma_{\max}(\pi a)^{\frac{1}{2}} - \Delta K_{\mathrm{th}} \qquad (5.5.13)$

then $\quad a = \left(\dfrac{t + \Delta K_{\mathrm{th}}}{\pi^{\frac{1}{2}} Y'\Delta\sigma_{\max}}\right)^{2} \qquad (5.5.14)$

Thus，
$$\text{d}a = -\frac{2(t + \Delta K_{th})}{\pi(Y'\Delta\sigma_{max})^2}\text{d}t \tag{5.5.15}$$

Substituting the two above equations back into Eq. (5.5.12), i.e. changing the variable from crack length a to time t such that the integration limit goes from t_i (starting time) to t_c (time when the crack length becomes critic), yields

$$
\begin{aligned}
N_p &= \int_{t_i}^{t_c} C^{-1}\left[\frac{2(t + \Delta K_{th})}{\pi(Y'\Delta\sigma_{max})^2}\right]t^{-m}\text{d}t \\
&= \frac{2C^{-1}}{\pi(Y'\Delta\sigma_{max})^2}\left[\int_{t_i}^{t_c}t^{1-m}\text{d}t + \int_{t_i}^{t_c}(\Delta K_{th})t^{-m}\text{d}t\right] \\
&= \frac{2C^{-1}}{\pi(Y'\Delta\sigma_{max})^2}\left[\frac{t_c^{2-m} - t_i^{2-m}}{2-m} + \frac{t_c^{1-m} - t_i^{1-m}}{1-m}\Delta K_{th}\right]
\end{aligned} \tag{5.5.16}
$$

Example 5.5.2 A stainless steel plate ($E = 200$ GPa and $\nu = 0.27$) is subjected to a fluctuating load, ranging from $\sigma_{min} = -40$ MPa to $\sigma_{max} = 140$ MPa at 15 Hz. If the plate contained an initial through-thickness edge crack of 0.5 mm in length, how many fatigue cycles are required to break the plate for the following case:

Stainless steel, $\text{d}a/\text{d}N$ (m/cycle) $= 3.1 \times 10^{-13}(\Delta K_I - 11.4)^{3.3}$ and $K_{IC} = 60$ MPa $\cdot$ m$^{\frac{1}{2}}$

and $Y' = 1.12$ (a semi-infinite plate)?

Solution:

(1) The critical crack length to be determined using Eq. (5.3.9)

$$K_{IC} = \sigma_{xx}(\pi a_c)^{\frac{1}{2}}$$

$$60 \text{ MPa} \cdot \text{m}^{\frac{1}{2}} = [140 - (-40)] \text{ MPa}[\pi(a_c)]^{\frac{1}{2}}$$

Thus， $a_c = 0.03537$ m

(2) Substituting $a_i = 0.0005$ m (0.5 mm as given) and $a_c = 0.03537$ m (obtained above) into Eq. (5.5.14) leads to

$t_i = 244.47$ and $t_c = 2120$

(3) Given that $m = 3.3$, $t_i = 244.47$, $t_c = 2120$, $\Delta K_{th} = 11.4$, $\Delta\sigma_{max} = 140$ MPa $- (-40$ MPa$) = 180$ MPa, and $Y' = 1.12$, $C = 6.8 \times 10^{-12}$. Following Eq. (5.5.16), one has

$$N_p = \frac{2C^{-1}}{\pi(Y'\Delta\sigma_{max})^2}\left[\frac{t_c^{2-m}-t_i^{2-m}}{2-m}+\frac{t_c^{1-m}-t_i^{1-m}}{1-m}\Delta K_{th}\right]$$

$$= \frac{2\times(3.1\times10^{-13})^{-1}}{\pi[(1.12)180]^2}\left[\frac{t_c^{2-m}-t_i^{2-m}}{2-3.3}+\frac{t_c^{1-m}-t_i^{1-m}}{1-3.3}(11.4)\right]$$

$$= 4.326\times10^{10}\text{cycles}$$

$$= 8.01\times10^5\text{hours(at 15 Hz)}$$

5.5.3 Modified Crack Size to Accommodate Elastoplastic Deformation (a')

There is always a plastic zone formed at the crack tip when the dislocation theory is applied. If the plastic deformation of the material around the crack tip is significant, it can be accounted for by considering the plastic zone surrounding the crack tip

$$a_p = a \sec\left[\frac{1}{4}\pi(1-R)\frac{\Delta\sigma_{max}}{\sigma'_{uts}}-1\right] \tag{5.5.17}$$

The above equation is due to [Wilkinson] to include the plastic zone at the crack tip, such that a' in Eq. (5.5.6) can be written as

$$a' = a + a_p = a\left\{1 + \sec\left[\frac{1}{4}\pi(1-R)\frac{\Delta\sigma_{max}}{\sigma_o}-1\right]\right\} \tag{5.5.18}$$

Parameter σ_o is the stress measurable to account for the material damage due to dynamic cyclic hardening or softening, and it is given as follows:

(a) $\sigma_o = \sigma_y$, if plastic strain after yielding point is of concern under quasi-static loading;
(b) $\sigma_o = \sigma_f$, if fatigue strength is of concern;
(c) $\sigma_o = \sigma_{uts}$, if the material fails in one cycle.

5.5.4 Geometry Correction Factor, Y'

The geometry correction factor depends on the geometry around the crack tip and loadings (i.e. opening, in-plane shear, and out-of-plane shear mode). Assume that there is a semi-elliptical flaw in an extreme long finite plate subjected to uniform uniaxial tension (Mode-I). The geometry correction factor is [Anderson]

$$Y' = \left\{\frac{\left[\sin^2\phi+\left(\frac{a}{c}\right)^2\cos^2\phi\right]^{\frac{1}{4}}}{E(k,\phi)}\right\}P(w,h,\phi) \tag{5.5.19}$$

where

c: Crack depth;

a: Crack length;

ϕ: Angle of the polar expression for an elliptical equation, $\phi = 0$ for the crack tip;

$E(k, \phi)$: Complete elliptical integral of the 2nd kind;

$P(w, h, \phi)$: Geometry modifier resulting from the width w and thickness h.

The complete elliptical integral of the 2nd kind given in the denominator on the right side of Eq. (5.5.13) is given as follows [Hildebrand]:

$$E(k, \phi) = \int_0^\phi (1 - k^2 \sin^2\theta)^{\frac{1}{2}} \, d\theta \quad (0 < k < 1) \tag{5.5.20}$$

The corresponding geometry modifier in Eq. (5.5.14), subjected to the finite plate configuration having width w, thickness h and crack depth c, is [Anderson]

$$P(w, h, \phi) = \left\{ \begin{array}{l} \left[1.13 - 0.09\dfrac{c}{a} \right] + \left[-0.54 - \dfrac{0.89}{0.2 + \dfrac{c}{a}} \right] \left(\dfrac{c}{h} \right)^2 + \\[2em] \left[0.5 - \dfrac{1}{0.6 + \dfrac{c}{a}} + \dfrac{14}{\left(1 - \dfrac{c}{a} \right)^{24}} \right] \left(\dfrac{c}{h} \right)^4 \end{array} \right\}$$
$$\left\{ 1 + \left[0.1 + 0.35\left(\dfrac{c}{h} \right)^2 (1 - \sin\phi)^2 \right] \right\} \sec\left[\dfrac{1}{2} \dfrac{\pi a}{w} \left(\dfrac{c}{h} \right)^{\frac{1}{2}} \right] \tag{5.5.21}$$

5.5.5 Stress Intensity Factor Range with Notch Effect

An asymptotic solution to the stress intensity factor range as a function of crack size due to the notch effect was derived by [Liu & Mahadevan].

$$\Delta K = S \, \Delta\sigma \, \pi^{\frac{1}{2}} \{ a + d[1 - e^{-\frac{a(K_t^2 - 1)}{d}}] \}^{\frac{1}{2}} \tag{5.5.22}$$

where

a: Crack length;

d: Crack depth;

K_t: Stress concentration factor that accounts for notch effect;

S: Surface correction factor, and generally $S = 1.122$ [Liu & Mahadevan].

Eq. (5.5.17) is augmented by Fig. 5.5.3. The nonlinear variation of the two extreme cases: (1) Short Cracks: $d \gg a$ and (2) Long Cracks: $a \gg d$.

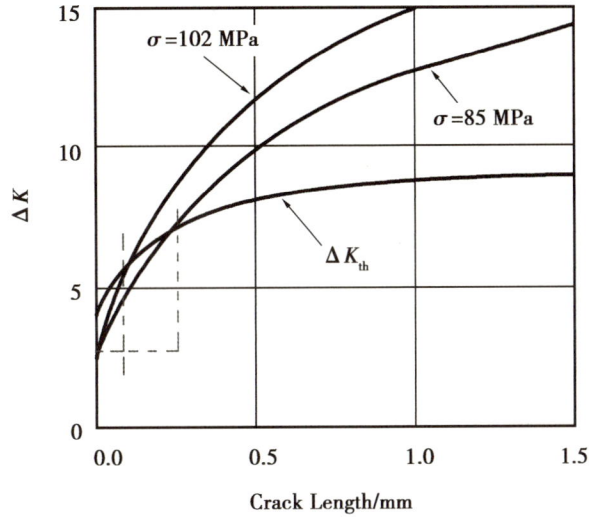

Fig. 5.5.3　Nonlinear Variation of Stress Intensity Factor versus Crack Length Based on Inconel 600 Material [Helmi & Attia]

(1) Short Cracks: $d \gg a$: If the crack is extremely short, the following approximating equation can be derived using the Taylor's series expansion,

$$1 - e^{\frac{-a(K_t^2 - 1)}{d}} \approx \frac{a(K_t^2 - 1)}{d} \tag{5.5.23}$$

Substituting the above equation into Eq. (5.5.21) yields

$$\Delta K = S\, K_t \Delta\sigma (\pi a)^{\frac{1}{2}} \tag{5.5.24}$$

(2) Long Cracks: $a \gg d$: If the crack is extremely long, the following approximating equation can be derived using the Taylor's series expansion,

$$1 - e^{\frac{-a(K_t^2 - 1)}{d}} = 1 \tag{5.5.25}$$

Substituting the above equation into Eq. (5.5.24) yields

$$\Delta K = S\, \Delta\sigma [\pi(a + d)]^{\frac{1}{2}} \tag{5.5.26}$$

A smooth specimen, without a notch, achieves its fatigue limit ($\Delta\sigma_{\text{f,smooth}}$) when the applied stress intensity reaches the threshold stress intensity factor. Similar to Eq. (5.5.24), the threshold stress intensity factor with an elliptical "micro" crack opening ($d \to d_m$) around a crack tip with a perfect smooth surface may be expressed as

$$\Delta K_{\text{th}} = Y\, \alpha\Delta\sigma_f\, \pi^{\frac{1}{2}} \left\{ a + d_m \left[1 - e^{-\frac{a}{d_m}\frac{K_t^2}{\alpha^2 - 1}} \right] \right\}^{\frac{1}{2}} \tag{5.5.27}$$

Note that d_m replaces d as the depth of the micro crack.

5.5.6 Fatigue Notch Factor (K_f)

Fatigue notch effect exhibits in a notched specimen subject to a cyclic fatigue test. It induces more damage than an unnotched specimen. The fatigue strength reduction factor falls between 1 and elastic stress concentration factor (K_t) and it is defined as

$$K_f = \frac{\text{Fatigue strength without notch}}{\text{Fatigue strength with notch}} = \frac{\Delta\sigma_{f,\text{smooth}}}{\Delta\sigma_{f,\text{notch}}} \tag{5.5.28}$$

Assume that Eq. (5.5.27) holds for the threshold stress intensity factor associated with a notch crack; with such a minor modification to Eq. (5.5.27),

$$\Delta K_{th} = Y\,\alpha\,\Delta\sigma_{f,\text{notch}}\,\pi^{\frac{1}{2}}\left\{a + d\left[1 - e^{-\frac{a}{d}\frac{K_t^2}{\alpha^2-1}}\right]\right\}^{\frac{1}{2}} \tag{5.5.29}$$

Equating Eq. (5.5.22) to Eq. (5.5.20) yields

$$
\begin{aligned}
K_f &= \frac{\Delta\sigma_{f,\text{smooth}}}{\Delta\sigma_{f,\text{notch}}} = \frac{\left\{1 + \dfrac{d}{a}\left[1 - e^{-\frac{a}{d}\frac{K_t^2}{\alpha^2-1}}\right]\right\}^{\frac{1}{2}}}{\left\{1 + \dfrac{d_m}{a}\left[1 - e^{-\frac{a}{d_m}\frac{K_t^2}{\alpha^2-1}}\right]\right\}^{\frac{1}{2}}} \\[2mm]
&= \frac{K_t}{\left\{1 + \dfrac{d_m}{a}\left[1 - e^{-\frac{a}{d_m}\frac{K_t^2}{\alpha^2-1}}\right]\right\}^{\frac{1}{2}}}
\end{aligned} \tag{5.5.30}
$$

Since part depth d is much larger than crack size a, plugging Eq. (5.5.23) into the numerator of the right-hand side of the above equation leads to

$$\left\{1 + \frac{d}{a}\left[1 - e^{-\frac{a}{d}\frac{K_t^2}{\alpha^2-1}}\right]\right\}^{\frac{1}{2}} \approx K_t \tag{5.5.31}$$

and $\quad K_f = \dfrac{K_t}{\left\{1 + \dfrac{d_m}{a}\left[1 - e^{-\frac{a}{d_m}\frac{K_t^2}{\alpha^2-1}}\right]\right\}^{\frac{1}{2}}}$ $\qquad\qquad$ (5.5.32)

or $\quad K_f = K_t\left\{1 + \dfrac{d_m}{a}\left[1 - e^{-\frac{a}{d_m}\frac{K_t^2}{\alpha^2-1}}\right]\right\}^{-\frac{1}{2}}$ $\qquad\qquad$ (5.5.33)

Thus, the ratio of fatigue concentration factor and stress concentration factor (K_f/K_t) falls between 1 and $1/K_t$. The following two special cases related to fatigue notch factor can be derived from the above equation:

(a) Case A: Deep crack with short crack size: If $d_m \gg a, K_f \approx 1$ (5.5.34)

(b) Case B: Shallow crack with long crack size: If $d_m \ll a, K_f = K_t$ (5.5.35)

Some material data of nominal d_m/a ratio are listed as follows [Xiang et al.]:

Material	d_m/a
2024-T3(Al alloy)	1.2
7075-T6(Al alloy)	2.5
4340(Alloy steel)	0.0
Ti-6Al-4V(Ti alloy)	0.8

Nevertheless, the extrinsic fracture toughness may be lowered due to porosities, oxidation, and foreign inclusions.

5.5.7 Orientation of Crack Extension

For predicting the crack orientation, one can follow the MTS (Maximum Tangential Stress) criterion based on stress intensity factors K_I and K_{II} for a 2-dimensional analysis [Erdogan & Sih], as

$$\theta_{crack} = \cos^{-1}\left\{\left[\frac{3K_{II}^2 + (K_I^4 + 8 \ K_I^2 \ K_{II}^2)^{\frac{1}{2}}}{K_I^2} + 9K_{II}^2\right]\right\} \tag{5.5.36}$$

of which θ_{crack} is the angle that is to follow the crack for each load increment. The sign convention is such that $\theta_c < 0$ when $K_{II} > 0$ and vice versa.

Another criterion is to assume that the potential crack extension will follow the direction that generates the maximum stress intensity range under mixed-mode loadings, ΔK, which can be derived as [Tanaka]

$$\Delta K_{eq} = \left[\frac{\Delta K_I^4 + 8 \ \Delta K_{II}^4 + 8 \ \Delta K_{III}^4}{1 - \nu}\right]^{\frac{1}{4}} \tag{5.5.37}$$

The third option for identifying the orientation of a potential crack extension is to apply the critical plane method that is addressed in Chapter 4. ΔK_{eq} can be used for a loading condition involving mixed modes in the Paris equation to obtain the crack growth rate and cycles to failure through integrations.

5.5.8 Rotating Shafts under Nonproportional Loading

In the case of rotating shafts, both normal and shear stress exist due to the bending moment subjected to the vertical work load and the torsional moment subjected to the torque transmission. The normal stress is usually higher than the shear stress because of the presence of notch effect. Thus, the threat mostly comes from the surface located distant from the neutral axis. Should there be a microcrack, the strain (stress) distribution near the crack tip can be allocated into three different categories, i.e. Modes I, II, and III in the Cartesian coordinate system, but more likely allocated into two categories, i.e. Mode I and Mode III in the polar coordinate system. Considering the equivalent stress intensity factor to account for crack propagation under nonproportional loading with phase angle ψ, [Tipton] proposed the following equation

$$\Delta K_{eq} = \Delta K_{\mathrm{I}} \left\{ 2 + 6 \left(\frac{\Delta K_{\mathrm{III}}}{\Delta K_{\mathrm{I}}} \right)^2 + \left[4 + 24 \left(\frac{\Delta K_{\mathrm{III}}}{\Delta K_{\mathrm{I}}} \right)^2 \cos(2\psi) + 9 \left(\frac{\Delta K_{\mathrm{III}}}{\Delta K_{\mathrm{I}}} \right)^4 \right]^{\frac{1}{2}} \right\}^{\frac{1}{2}} \qquad (5.5.38)$$

where ΔK_{I} and ΔK_{III} can be obtained from Eq. (5.5.6), of which the maximum normal stress range ($\Delta \sigma_{max}$) can be derived from finite element analysis.

5.6 Crack Propagation under Elastoplastic Yielding

Beyond the application limit of fatigue crack life prediction based on the stress intensity factor range, various substituting procedures have been explored. Different algorithms conceived for interpreting crack driving force parameters in elastoplastic fracture mechanics are to be discussed.

5.6.1 Strain-Based Stress Intensity Factor Range

An simple approach to fatigue crack propagation is to reformulate the stress intensity factor in terms of strain components in order to explain elastoplastic yielding around the crack tip. This is done by modifying Eq. (5.5.6),

$$\Delta K_{\varepsilon} = Y' (\Delta \varepsilon_{el} + \Delta \varepsilon_{pl})_{max} (\pi a')^{\frac{1}{2}} \qquad (5.6.1)$$

where
ΔK_{ε}: Stress intensity factor range in terms of strain ranges;
$\Delta \varepsilon_{el}$: Elastic strain range;
$\Delta \varepsilon_{pl}$: Plastic strain range.

Elastic and plastic strain ranges replace the stress range in stress intensity factor formulas of a given geometry.

5.6.2   *J*-Integral

The *J*-integral is a means to calculate the strain energy release rate, or work (energy) per unit fracture surface area, in a material [Rice]. *J*-integral represents the rate of change of net potential energy with respect to crack advance (per unit thickness of crack front) for a linear elastic or elastoplastic solid.

$$J \equiv -\frac{\mathrm{d}U}{\mathrm{d}a} = \int_S \left[U_\varepsilon \mathrm{d}y - T\frac{\mathrm{d}U_{\mathrm{tm}}}{\mathrm{d}x}\mathrm{d}s \right] \tag{5.6.2}$$

where

U: Total energy density, and $U = U_\varepsilon + u$;

U_ε: Strain energy per unit volume, as $\sigma_{ij} = \partial U_\varepsilon / \partial \varepsilon_{ij}$;

U_{tm}: Thermo-mechanical energy density applied;

a: Crack length;

T: Traction applied to the crack surface;

x & y: Cartesian coordinates;

s: Any closed-loop integration path, such as S_1 and S_2 identified in Fig. 5.3.2.

The *J*-integral has been developed to solve the difficulties involved in computing the stress close to a crack in a nonlinear elastic or elastoplastic material [Cherepanov]. It was shown by [Rice] that if monotonic loading was assumed (without any plastic unloading) then the *J*-integral could be used to compute the energy release rate of a plastic material, too. The *J*-integral can be also interpreted as a plastic analog to the stress intensity factor (K) that is used in linear elastic fracture mechanics, i.e., we can use a criterion such as $J > J_{\mathrm{IC}}$ as a crack growth criterion for Mode-I, when enduring elastoplastic formation at the crack tip. For a fully elastic homogeneous solid, the 2-dimensional *J*-integral J_I can be used for the calculation of stress intensity factor K_I as follows:

$$J_I = \left[\frac{1 - v^2}{E} \right] K_I^2 \tag{5.6.3}$$

Thus,
$$J_{IC} = \left[\frac{1 - v^2}{E} \right] K_{IC}^2 \tag{5.6.4}$$

where

$J_{IC}(\mathrm{J/m^2}, \mathrm{J/cm^2}, \text{ or } \mathrm{J/mm^2})$: Critical *J*-integral around a crack tip;

E: Young's modulus;

v: Poisson's ratio.

The above equation yields the potential maximum intrinsic fracture toughness K_{IC} by the *J*-integral without knowing the detailed geometry of any crack. The *J*-integral is thus capable of appropriating energy release rate for nonlinear elastoplastic materials in terms of the amount of energy required to initiate and propagate the crack. The critical J-integral value, denoted by J_{IC}, accounts for a threshold of holding the crack growth as K_{IC} does.

Since the J-Integral is independent of the path around the crack tip, it is more convenient to take the integration path along S_2 (or beyond) in the elastic zone to obtain the J_I value, refer to Fig. 5.6.1. Because the test specimen for acquiring the K_{IC} value [ASTM standard E399 (1974)] directly is large, a much smaller specimen based on J-integral algorithm is sometime measured for J_{IC} instead. Then, J_{IC} is used to calculate the K_{IC} value following Eq. (5.6.4). This approach has been validated by extensive testing. If the crack driving force is calculated numerically it is usually calculated using the J-Integral approach. The J-Integral algorithm is robust for being able to deal with the strains (stresses) in the elastic zone only and requiring no extremely detailed finite element mesh refinement.

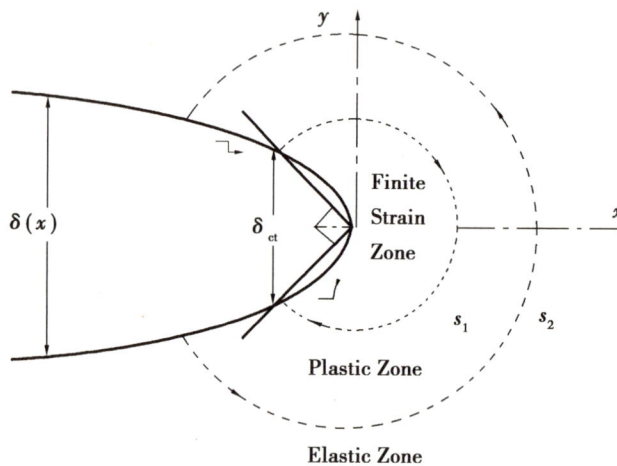

Fig. 5.6.1   Definition of Crack Tip Opening Displacement in Practice

Upon the given condition that the elastic strain is much smaller than the plastic strain developed around the crack tip, one can assume that the material is represented by the power law (resembling Romberg-Osgood model) as follows:

$$\frac{\varepsilon}{\varepsilon_o} = \lambda \left(\frac{\sigma}{\sigma_o} \right)^n \tag{5.6.5}$$

where

σ_o: Reference stress, for which yield stress may be used;

ε_o: Reference strain, for which yield strain may be used, as $\varepsilon_o = \sigma_o / E$;

λ: Coefficient;

n: Exponent.

[Hutchinson] and [Rice & Rosenberg] studied such a stress/strain field problem around a crack tip with the constitutive equation, Eq. (5.6.8). With appropriate boundary conditions, they jump to the conclusion that the stress and strain in the neighborhood of the crack tip can be written as

$$\sigma_{ij} = \sigma_0 \left(\frac{EJ}{\lambda \, \sigma_0^2 \, I_n \, r} \right)^{\frac{1}{n+1}} \sigma_{ij}(n, \theta) \tag{5.6.6}$$

$$\text{and} \quad \varepsilon_{ij} = \varepsilon_0 \left(\frac{EJ}{\lambda \, \sigma_0^2 \, I_n \, r} \right)^{\frac{1}{n+1}} \varepsilon_{ij}(n, \theta) \tag{5.6.7}$$

When plastic deformation is of concern, J_{IC} (J/m^2 or J/cm^2) is elastoplastic fracture toughness used to measure the energy required to grow a thin crack. Similar to K_{IC}, J_{IC} is due to mechanical energy that is also represented by fracture toughness that depend on the size and geometry of the test specimen [Vormwald et al.].

5.6.3 Inclusive Crack Tip Opening Displacement (CTOD) Algorithm

In order to explain the plastic deformation at the crack tip, [Schnitzler et al. 2012] formulated fatigue crack growth based on the cyclic crack tip opening displacement that is extracted from strip yield model calculations. It enables that the parametric criterion may asymptotically approach an objective functional relationship with the stress intensity factor, when going from large to small scale yielding conditions. The J-Integral fracture toughness and CTOD fracture toughness are related to each other through the following equation:

$$\delta_{ct} = \frac{J}{m \, \sigma_y} \tag{5.6.8}$$

where
m: Plastic constraint factor;
δ_{ct}: Crack tip opening displacement;
σ_y: Yield strength.

The plastic constraint factor, namely m, has been refined by ASTM based on the following regression model as

$$m = -0.111 + 0.817 \left(\frac{a}{w} \right) + 1.36 \left(\frac{\sigma_y}{\sigma_{uts}} \right) \tag{5.6.9}$$

where
a: Crack length;
w: Thickness of the test specimen;
σ_y: Yield strength;
σ_{uts}: Ultimate tensile strength.

The CTOD is thus a measure of fracture toughness and its variation due to each incremental load, ΔCTOD (i.e. $\Delta\delta_{ct}$), can be utilized for further exploring the driving force of crack propagation, even under multiaxial fracture characterization. The dentition of δ_{ct} is somewhat arbitrary since the opening displacement varies as the crack tip is approached. A commonly used operational dentition is in light of the 45°-inclined construction square depicted in Fig. 5.6.1 [Shih].

5.6.4 Crack Propagation by Δ *J*-Integral

In order to explain the plastic deformation at the crack tip, researchers formulated fatigue crack growth based on a complete closed-loop integration around the crack tip, i.e. the *J*-integral, as a simple path independent approach to fatigue crack propagation. *J*-integral gives a path independent value as a summarized measure of stresses and strains around the crack tip that are responsible for material crack propagation. By the same token as the stress intensity factor is replaced by stress intensity factor range for accommodating the "change" under a cyclic loading, the definition of the cyclic Δ*J*-integral is given by

$$\Delta J = \int_0^{\Delta\varepsilon_{ij}} \Delta\sigma_{ij} \, d\Delta\varepsilon_{ij} \quad \text{(Closed-loop integration)} \tag{5.6.10}$$

where
$\Delta\sigma_{ij}$: Stress variation;
$\Delta\varepsilon_{ij}$: Strain variation.

The integration task can be completed using far-field stresses and strains (not exactly at the crack tip), uncontaminated by numerical deficiencies. However, there are drawbacks in the Δ*J*-integral theorization. The path independence under a cyclic loading is violated if the material is not completely cyclically stabilized as pointed out by [Yoon & Saxena], especially in the presence of temperature gradients and temperature dependent material behavior. Furthermore, a valid Δ*J*-integral cannot be calculated for a reversal from the maximum load to the crack closure load, which is a phenomenon that prevails during a cyclic loading with large scale yielding, as shown in Fig. 5.6.2. The observed crack closure is governed by large cycles, while the crack is completely open during small cycles.

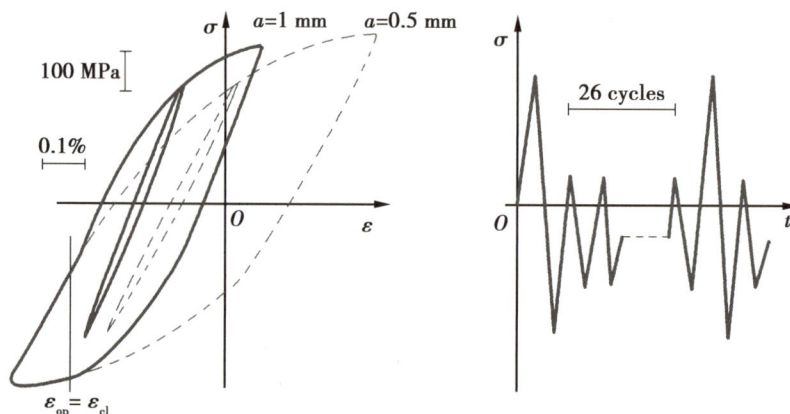

Fig. 5.6.2　Strain Fluctuations at Crack Tip Opening in a Variable Amplitude Test [Vormwald et al.]

5.7   Crack Propagation under Large Scale Yielding

Fracture toughness, stress intensity factor, and *J*-integral don't fit the fracture behavior well in the presence of excessive plasticity, especially when the fracture toughness depends on the size and geometry of the test specimen [Vormwald et al.]. New theoretical approaches, utilizing *T*-term effects and J-Q-M theory, are therefore proposed to model fracture mechanics with large scale yielding, where plasticity is not only located at the crack tip, but also extends to a larger area of the component.

5.7.1   Crack Closure under Large Scale Yielding

Both stress- and strain-based intensity factor ranges do not provide a measure of the strain singularity at the crack front, neither do the Δ*J*-integral algorithm and the CTOD approach, when the cyclic loading is involved with large scaled yielding [Vormwald 2014]. New parameters are yet sought for interpreting the crack driving force.

5.7.2   *T*-Term Effects

Near the tip of the crack, where the higher order terms of the series expansion are negligible, as the non-singular and bounded term for the stress near the crack tip, *T*-stress has to be included in the σ_{xx} for Mode I,

$$\sigma_{xx} = \frac{K_{\mathrm{I}}}{(2\pi r)^{\frac{1}{2}}}\cos\frac{\theta}{2}\left[1 - \sin\frac{\theta}{2}\sin\frac{3\theta}{2}\right] + T + O(r^{\frac{1}{2}}) \qquad (5.7.1)$$

Term *T* is a constant stress parallel to the crack, due to only a symmetric component of loading and it vanishes for pure Mode II [Larsson & Carlson]. A test specimen showing a positive *T*-stress has a higher constraint than those having a negative T-stress. It is found that both T-stress and Poisson's ratio ν of the material play important roles in the prediction of the crack propagation angle and the mixed mode fracture toughness of material [Mirsayar], including the size and shape of the plastic zone. [Du and Hancock] investigated the effect of the T-stress on the small-scale yielding field in elastic perfectly-plastic materials and [Betegon & Hancock] investigated the two-parameter (*J* -*T*) characterization of elastoplastic crack-tip fields and T-stress, which is derived from constraint, does not require the use of FEM but it can be determined from finite element analysis for both Mode I and Mode I / II loadings [Ayatollahi et al.]. [Chen et al.] discovered that the path independent integrals, in conjunction with hierarchical p-version finite element methods, provide a powerful and robust tool to obtain highly accurate numerical results for the T-stress.

In order to normalize the effect of term T relative to the stress intensity factor in Mode I, [Leevers & Radon] proposed a dimensionless parameter B, called biaxial ratio, which is defined as

$$B_{\mathrm{I}} = \frac{T(\pi a)^{\frac{1}{2}}}{K_{\mathrm{I}}} \tag{5.7.2}$$

$$\text{or} \quad B_{\mathrm{I}\text{-}\mathrm{II}} = \frac{T(\pi a)^{\frac{1}{2}}}{(K_{\mathrm{I}} + K_{\mathrm{II}})^{\frac{1}{2}}} \tag{5.7.3}$$

The T-stress is often significantly large in comparison with the singular terms in Eqs. (5.4.1) and (5.4.2) for some study cases. This occurs, for example, for an inclined internal crack where the angle β between the crack line and the loading direction tends towards zero. When the crack is parallel to the loading direction $(\beta=0)$, T-stress dominates the stress field in the body and all other terms in Eqs. (5.4.1) and (5.4.2) vanish [Haefele & Lee]. Consider Fig. 5.7.1, in which the far field stresses σ_{xx}^{∞} and σ_{yy}^{∞} are applied to an existing internal crack (on the z-x plane) of length $2a$. For the case of brittle crack,

$$T = \sigma_{yy}^{\infty} - \sigma_{xx}^{\infty}$$

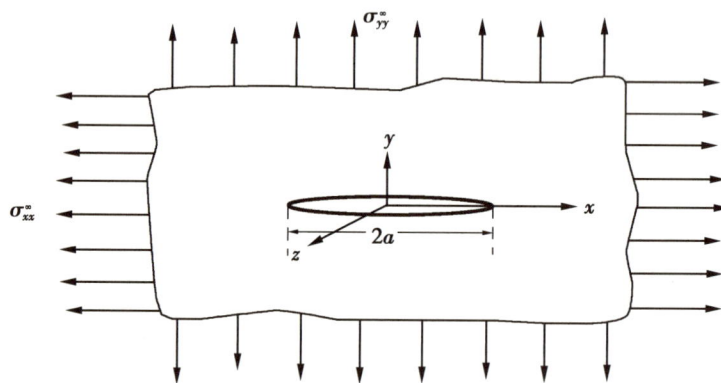

Fig. 5.7.1 Internal Crack (on the z-x Plane) Subjected to Far Field Stresses σ_{xx}^{∞} and σ_{yy}^{∞}

5.7.3 J-Q-M Theory

[O'Dowd & Shih] developed the J-Q theory (Q is a hydrostatic stress parameter) and found that the Q-family provides a framework for quantifying the evolution of constraint from small-scale yielding to full yielding conditions. They deduced a one-to-one correspondence between Q and T, which is valid in the case where the applied load and geometry affect Q only through T.

It has been shown by [Zhang et al.] [Leopold & Munier] that the crack growth rate of 316L stainless steel under large-scale yielding at varying temperature distributions is lower than the one calculated with an elastic calculation. The elastic calculation used to design and justify safety of real components is conservative. By using finite element analysis, one can establish a parameter, namely Q, to modify the stress field for a better solution when the plastic zone is growing. The new stress field is to be obtained as

$$\sigma_{ij} = \sigma_{ij} + Q \, \delta_{ij} + \sigma_{\text{yield}} \qquad\qquad (5.7.4)$$

where

σ_{ij}: Stress component, $\sigma_{ij} = 1$, when $i = j$; $\sigma_{ij} = 0$, when $i \neq j$;

σ_{yield}: Yield stress;

Q: a crack-growth parameter; Q usually takes values from -3 to 2.

Nevertheless, crack propagation needs to be estimated with adapted numerical models in the finite element analysis. A negative Q value greatly changes the geometry of the plastic zone. The J-Q-M theory includes another parameter, the mismatch parameter, which is used for welds to make up for the change in toughness of the weld metal (WM), base metal (BM) and heat affected zone (HAZ). This value is interpreted in the formula in a similar way as the Q-parameter, and the two are usually assumed to be independent of each other.

5.8   Finite Element Methods for Crack Propagation

To design a durable structure allowing for fatigue damage tolerance requires an understanding of fracture mechanics, where the fundamental crack tip parameters such as stress intensity factor, energy release rate, and J-integral in elastic, elastoplastic yielding, and large scale yielding have to be explored and their related potential crack propagation has to be predicted in the early design stage. Due to the complexity of geometry and boundary conditions involved with both the mechanical and electric components in an automotive vehicle, these fatigue crack driving force parameters can only be resolved using finite element methods and other numerical methods.

5.8.1   Quarter-Point Approach for Brittle Materials

The nodal point of a 20-node solid element, originally at the middle of an edge, can be moved to a certain location between the two ending nodes to create a desired singularity value. The finite element model does not extremely dense mesh to model the singularity. When it is relocated to a quarter of the edge length, so called quarter-point node, which can be used to induce the stress singularity at the crack-tip node (at one end of the edge) in a 3-dimensional crack analysis when it is practiced in the linear elastic range.

5.8.2　Crack-Tip Blunting Due to Material Ductility

This is a practice for applying standard implicit finite element formulation to seeking the fracture toughness. A crack must conform to the finite element mesh and remeshing is required to conduct crack propagation simulations. Crack-tip blunting under tensile loads （Mode-Ⅰ） and reshaping （owing to remeshing） of the crack-tip during unloading is one of the basic skills required for crack propagation in ductile materials ［Tvergaard］. A reference size of plastic zone developed around the crack tip can be estimated using the following fully plastic material model

$$R_{o} = (3\pi)^{-1} \left(\frac{K_{o}}{\sigma_{y}} \right)^{2} \tag{5.8.1}$$

5.8.3　X-FEM Method

The fundamental concept inherent in the formulation of the X-FEM method is to incorporate the discontinuity through additional terms in the conventional displacement approximation. By the X-FEM （Extended Finite Element Method）, crack propagation is modeled using modified nodal displacements yet based on the implicit finite element formulation. It engenders additional degrees of freedom that are tied to the nodes on the crack surfaces that intersect finite elements to denote the presence of a crack and its potential crack path. It is an effective algorithm to simulate the initiation and propagation of a crack along a solution-oriented path arbitrarily without remeshing. The X-FEM has been implemented in Abaqus and provides a powerful tool for simulating crack growth along arbitrary paths that do not correspond to element boundaries. In the automotive and aerospace industries, X-FEM can be used in combination with other Abaqus capabilities to predict the durability and damage tolerance of composite structures.

5.8.3.1　Finite Element Formulation

Being compatible with Eq. （12.13.8） for a 3-dimensional analysis, the nodal displacement interpolation for modeling the crack based on the X-FEM, as shown in Fig. 5.8.1, takes one or four more additional terms ［Moes et al. 1999］［Zi & Belytschkol］, respectively for the nodes surrounding the crack edge and tip as ［Belytschko & Black］

$$\begin{Bmatrix} u \\ v \\ w \end{Bmatrix} = [N]\{\phi\} + [N]H(x,y,z)\{q\} + [N]r^{\frac{1}{2}}\sin\left(\frac{1}{2}\theta\right)\{\phi_{a}\} + [N]r^{\frac{1}{2}}\cos\left(\frac{1}{2}\theta\right)\{\phi_{b}\} + $$

$$[N]r^{\frac{1}{2}}\sin\left(\frac{1}{2}\theta\right)\sin(\theta)\{\phi_{c}\} + [N]r^{\frac{1}{2}}\cos\left(\frac{1}{2}\theta\right)\sin(\theta)\{\phi_{d}\} \tag{5.8.2}$$

where

$H(x,y,z)$: Heaviside step function;

$[N]$: Shape function;

R and θ: Polar coordinates, as depicted in Fig. 5.3.2;

$\{\phi\}^T$: Classical nodal displacements;

$\{q\}^T$: Enriched nodal displacements surrounding the crack path, shown in Fig. 5.8.1;

$\{\phi_a\}^T, \{\phi_b\}^T, \{\phi_c\}^T, \& \{\phi_d\}^T$: Enriched nodal displacements surrounding the crack tip.

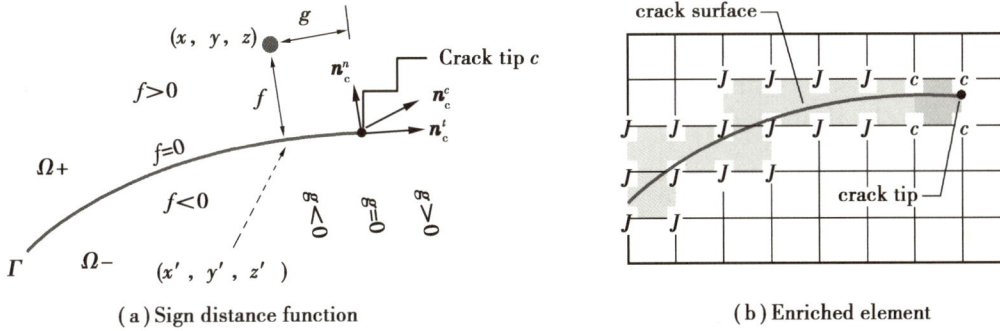

(a) Sign distance function   (b) Enriched element

Fig. 5.8.1 **Enrichment of Finite Element Nodes around a Crack Path and Tip** [Tsuda et al.]

The finite element formulation is the same as what described in Chapter 3 except that Eq. (3.2.7) is to be replaced by Eq. (5.8.2). In other words, the enriching stiffness of an enriched finite element will be added to its standard stiffness matrix. A numerical integration will be performed for the enriched elements that are cut by the crack. Then, the displacement, stress, and strain of all nodes will be calculated in a manner that is similar to the standard FEM method.

Since there are three degrees of freedom associated with each node of a solid element in the space, there will be 3 enriched nodal displacements for each enriched node surrounding the crack path and 12 enriched nodal displacements for each node surrounding the crack tip for a 3-dimensional model. For a p-noded isoparametric solid element, of which $p = 8$ or $p = 20$ for a standard FEM in practice, the nodal displacements can be expressed as

$$\{\phi\}^T = (u_1 \quad v_1 \quad w_1 \quad u_2 \quad v_2 \quad w_2 \cdots u_p \quad v_p \quad w_p) \tag{5.8.3}$$

$$\{q\}^T = (u_1^q \quad v_1^q \quad w_1^q \quad u_2^q \quad v_2^q \quad w_2^q \cdots u_p^q \quad v_p^q \quad w_p^q) \tag{5.8.4}$$

$$\{d^1\}^T = (u_1^1 \quad v_1^1 \quad w_1^1 \quad u_2^1 \quad v_2^1 \quad w_2^1 \cdots u_p^1 \quad v_p^1 \quad w_p^1) \tag{5.8.5}$$

$$\{d^2\}^T = (u_1^2 \quad v_1^2 \quad w_1^2 \quad u_2^2 \quad v_2^2 \quad w_2^2 \cdots u_p^2 \quad v_p^2 \quad w_p^2) \tag{5.8.6}$$

$$\{d^3\}^T = (u_1^3 \quad v_1^3 \quad w_1^3 \quad u_2^3 \quad v_2^3 \quad w_2^3 \cdots u_p^3 \quad v_p^3 \quad w_p^3) \tag{5.8.7}$$

$$\{d^4\}^T = (u_1^4 \quad v_1^4 \quad w_1^4 \quad u_2^4 \quad v_2^4 \quad w_2^4 \cdots u_p^4 \quad v_p^4 \quad w_p^4) \tag{5.8.8}$$

For modeling an existing crack in a homogeneous material, two different enrichment schemes are employed. Term $H(x,y,z)$, namely Heaviside function, is applied to the nodes surrounding the existing crack surfaces, while the other four terms with $r^{\frac{1}{2}}$ singularity is for nodes around the crack tips.

5.8.3.2 Jump（Heaviside）Function

Discontinuity based on the jump function, also called Heaviside function, is explicitly exerted to the nodes of all the elements cut by a crack. For an element completely cut by a crack, the Heaviside function $H(x)$ is employed such that

$$H(x,y,z) = 1, \text{ if above the crack} \tag{5.8.9}$$

and $\quad H(x,y,z) =- 1, \text{ if below the crack} \tag{5.8.10}$

As a discontinuous function is added to the nodal displacement vector across the crack as enrichment, the crack extension mechanism can be done numerically. The surface of discontinuity, Γ, is to be prescribed by a signed distance function. As being associated with the finite element meshes surrounding the crack tip c, the extension of the crack front is to be designated by the "+1" and "−1" signs, which is to be defined as

$$h(x,y,z) = \text{sign}\left\{ [(x,y,z) - (x',y',z')] \begin{Bmatrix} u^n_{xc} \\ u^n_{yc} \\ u^n_{zc} \end{Bmatrix} \right\} \min || \ (x,y,z) - (x',y',z') \ || \tag{5.8.11}$$

where
(x,y,z): Coordinates of an enriched node near the crack;
(x',y',z'): Coordinates of a point on the crack surface Γ that located closest to node (x,y,z);
$\{ u^n_{xc}, u^n_{yc}, u^n_{zc} \}$: Unit vector normal to the crack surface at crack tip c, as shown in Fig. 5.8.1;
$\min || (x,y,z)-(x',y',z') ||$: Shortest distance from the (x,y,z) to the crack surface.

The discontinuity corresponding to $h(x,y,z) = 0$ on Γ and the two opposite areas with different signs of $h(x,y,z)$ corresponding to two different domains across the crack surface are as shown in Fig. 5.8.1. The nodal displacement interpolation for modeling the elements cut through by the crack based on the X-FEM without considering the crack tip is then

$$\begin{Bmatrix} u \\ v \\ w \end{Bmatrix} = [N]\{\phi\} + [N] \ H(h(x,y,z))\{q\} \tag{5.8.12}$$

where $\quad H(h(x,y,z)) = 1 \quad$ when $h(x,y,z) > 0 \tag{5.8.13}$

and $\quad H(h(x,y,z)) =- 1 \quad$ when $h(x,y,z) \leqslant 0 \tag{5.8.14}$

5.8.3.3   Singular Functions

As suggested by the formulation using the singularity terms around the crack tip as $r^{\frac{1}{2}}$, the last four terms in Eq. (5.8.2) span the near-tip asymptotic fields. Nevertheless, the enrichment is valid only for linear elastic fracture mechanics that having a singularity of $-1/2$. In order to align the enrichment functions with the crack front, the crack plane where θ is zero must be tangent to the crack front. In other words, parameter g given in Fig. 5.8.1 must be a continuous function.

Hopefully, the X-FEM method may be extended to include crack propagation under elastoplastic yielding and even crack propagation under large scale yielding, where

(a) The crack tip opening mechanism is involved with varying singularities with changing phase angle (exhibiting the nonproportional stress-strain relationship) and load amplitude when subjected to cyclic loadings.
(b) The local material anisotropy and its gradients around the crack tip may develop for being highly strained in one direction, or two for some cases.

5.8.3.4   Crack Growth-Orientation

The orientation of a potential crack extension can be identified with the algorithms described in Chapter 4. However, it has to be superimposed to the original heading direction, i.e. $\boldsymbol{n}_c^t$, which is a unit vector tangential to the crack surface at the crack tip, as shown in Fig. 5.8.1. The g function for this need is defined as follows:

$$g(x,y,z) = \text{sign}\left\{ [(x,y,z) - (x_c,y_c,z_c)] \begin{Bmatrix} u_{xc}^t \\ u_{yc}^t \\ u_{zc}^t \end{Bmatrix} \right\} \min || (x,y,z) - (x_c,y_c,z_c) || \quad (5.8.15)$$

where
$\{u_{xc}^t, u_{yc}^t, u_{zc}^t\}$: Unit vector tangential to the crack surface at tip c, as shown in Fig. 5.8.1;
$\min || (x,y,z) - (x_c,y_c,z_c) ||$: Shortest distance from the (x,y,z) to the crack front.

When $g>0$, the crack tip looks forward; when $g<0$, the crack tip looks backward, as shown in Fig. 5.8.1. Unit cotangent vector $\boldsymbol{n}_c^c$, i.e. $(u_{xc}^{ct}, u_{yc}^{ct}, u_{zc}^{ct})$, is associated with the crack front that comprises divided front edges. Unit tangent vector $\boldsymbol{n}_c^t$, i.e. $(u_{xc}^t, u_{yc}^t, u_{zc}^t)$ for each crack tip c is the cross product of the unit normal vector and unit cotangent vector:

$$\boldsymbol{n}_c^t = \boldsymbol{n}_c^c \boldsymbol{x} \boldsymbol{n}_c^n \quad (5.8.16a)$$

or $\{u_{xc}^t, u_{yc}^t, u_{zc}^t\} = \{u_{xc}^{ct}, u_{yc}^{ct}, u_{zc}^{ct}\} \boldsymbol{x} \{u_{xc}^n, u_{yc}^n, u_{zc}^n\}$ $\quad (5.8.16b)$

The coordinate systems at the crack surface and crack front are illustrated in Fig. 5.8.2. The

2-dimensional snap shot shown in Fig. 5.8.1 is a cross-sectional view.

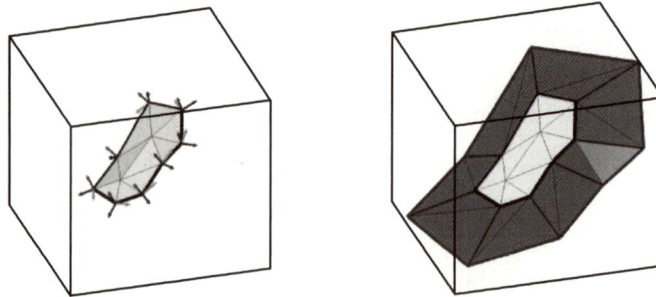

Fig. 5.8.2   Crack Surface Growth-Orientation and Extension ［Fries & Baydoun］

5.8.3.5   Crack Growth-Extension

The Paris crack growth model, as described by Eq. (5.5.1), can be used to determine the magnitude at which the crack will grow if it stays in the elastoplastic crack range. When the crack extension is justified, for example $\Delta K_{\mathrm{I}} > \Delta K_{\mathrm{Ic}}$ and/or $\sigma_{\mathrm{eq}} > \sigma_{\mathrm{eq, critical}}$ at each integration point surrounding the crack tip, and CTOD>CTOD$_{\mathrm{critical}}$, the crack tip will propagate across one mesh. When the crack tips jumps over the edge of an element, the element is to be failed.

5.9   Weak Stress Intensity Factor between Dissimilar Materials

Cracking along an interface between dissimilar materials is the primary cause of failure in microstructures like electronic packages, micro-electro-mechanical systems（MEMS）, and aviation composites ［Ioka］. A stress singularity may be at the interface corner, as shown in Fig.5.9.1 and its severity depends on the type of loadings in addition to the material properties.

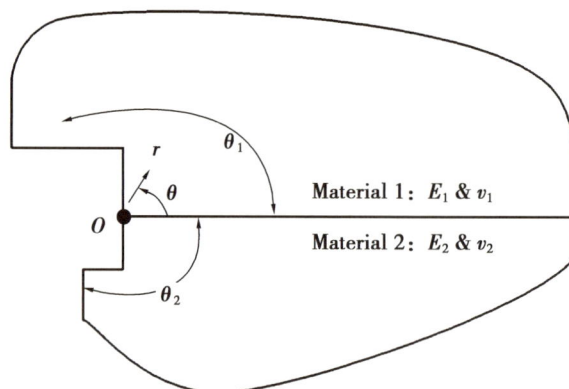

Fig. 5.9.1   Interfacial Singularity of Two Dissimilar Isotropic Materials

5.9.1   Stress Singularity between Dissimilar Isotropic Materials

The asymptotic stress components σ_{ij} at the interface between two dissimilar materials can be described [Mohammed & Liechti] by

$$\sigma_{ij} = \sum_{n=0}^{N} K_n \, r^{-\lambda_n} f_{ij,n}(\theta) \quad (i = 1, 2, 3 \text{ and } j = 1, 2, 3) \tag{5.9.1}$$

where

K_n: Stress intensity factors, $n = 0$, I, II, III, $\cdots$, N;

λ_n: Stress singularity, a complex number, and no singularity if the real part of $\lambda_n \leq 0$;

r: Radius from the singular tip to the point of interest;

$f_{ij,n}(\theta)$: Function of angle θ, referring to the x-axis (Figs. 5.9.1 and 5.4.2).

Note that λ_n is the order of stress singularity, which is determined by a combined effect of material and edge geometry. The H_n stress field dominates only the local region near the interface corner of the joint and it is called the free edge intensity factor. In combination with λ_n, the magnitude of H_n can be used to predict the initiation of failure at the interface corner in a manner similar to the use of conventional crack tip stress intensity factor for predicting the onset of crack growth. The stress intensity factors corresponding to the three failure modes of a crack in a homogeneous material are given by Eqs. (5.4.1)-(5.4.3). The polar coordinate (r, θ) is illustrated in Figs. 5.9.1 and 5.4.2. Note that $\lambda_n = 0.5$ around a crack tip of an elastic material is also used to denote the stress singularity.

In general the stress singularity at the interface between two dissimilar isotropic materials is weaker than 0.5, sometimes called weak stress singularity. Mathematically, it means that the real part of λ_n is smaller than 0.5. The stress intensity factor λ_n is obtained by solving the following equation according to [Bogy]:

$$\beta^2 A + 2 \alpha \beta B + \alpha^2 C - 2 \beta D - 2 \alpha E + F = 0 \tag{5.9.2}$$

where $A = 4 \{ \sin^2[\theta_1(1 - \lambda)] - (1 - \lambda)^2 \sin^2\theta_1 \} \{ \sin^2[\theta_2(1 - \lambda)] - (1 - \lambda)^2 \sin^2\theta_2 \}$

$$\tag{5.9.3}$$

$$B = 2 (1 - \lambda)^2 (\sin \theta_1 \{ \sin^2[\theta_2(1 - \lambda)] - (1 - \lambda)^2 \sin^2\theta_2 \} + \sin \theta_2 \{ \sin^2[\theta_1(1 - \lambda)] - (1 - \lambda)^2 \sin^2\theta_1 \})$$

$$\tag{5.9.4}$$

$$C = 4 \lambda (1 - \lambda)^2 (\lambda - 2) \sin^2\theta_1 \sin^2\theta_2 + \{ \sin^2[(1 - \lambda)(\theta_1 - \theta_2)] - (1 - \lambda)^2 \sin^2(\theta_1 - \theta_2) \}$$

$$\tag{5.9.5}$$

$$D = 2 (1 - \lambda)^2 (\sin^2\theta_1 \{ \sin^2[(1 - \lambda)\theta_2] - (1 - \lambda)^2 \sin^2\theta_2 \}^2 -$$

$$\sin^2\theta_2 \{ \sin^2 [(1 - \lambda)\theta_1] - (1 - \lambda)^2 \sin^2\theta_1 \}^2) \tag{5.9.6}$$

$$E = \{ \sin^2 [\theta_2 (1 - \lambda)] - (1 - \lambda)^2 \sin^2\theta_2 \} - \{ \sin^2 [\theta_1 (1 - \lambda)] - (1 - \lambda)^2 \sin^2\theta_1 \} - D \tag{5.9.7}$$

$$F = \sin^2 [(\theta_1 + \theta_2) (1 - \lambda)] - (1 - \lambda)^2 \sin^2 (\theta_1 + \theta_2) \tag{5.9.8}$$

Note that material parameters α and β consist of Young's moduli and Poisson's ratios. For plane strain, respectively

$$\alpha = \frac{E_1(1 + 4\nu_1) (1 + \nu_2) - E_2(1 + 4\nu_2) (1 + \nu_1)}{E_1(1 + 4\nu_1) (1 + \nu_2) + E_2(1 + 4\nu_2) (1 + \nu_1)} \tag{5.9.9}$$

and $\quad \beta = \dfrac{E_1(1 + 4\nu_1) \left(\dfrac{1}{2} - 2\nu_2 \right) (1 + \nu_2) - E_2(1 + \nu_1) \left(\dfrac{1}{2} - 2\nu_1 \right) (1 + 4\nu_2)}{E_1(1 + 4\nu_1) (1 + \nu_2) + E_2(1 + 4\nu_2) (1 + \nu_1)} \tag{5.9.10}$

On the other hand, material parameters α and β based on plane stress state are, respectively,

$$\alpha = \frac{E_1(1 - \nu_2^2) - E_2(1 - \nu_1^2)}{E_1(1 - \nu_2^2) + E_2(1 - \nu_1^2)} \tag{5.9.11}$$

and $\quad \beta = \dfrac{E_1 \left(\dfrac{1}{2} - \nu_2^2 \right) (1 + \nu_2) - E_2 \left(\dfrac{1}{2} - \nu_1^2 \right) (1 + \nu_1)}{E_1(1 - \nu_2^2) + E_2(1 - \nu_1^2)} \tag{5.9.12}$

Eq. (5.9.2) can be solved numerically for the smallest real eigenvalue λ in the range of $(0, 1)$. Its corresponding specific stress component around the potential crack tip will be

$$\sigma_{ij} = K r^{-\lambda} \tag{5.9.13}$$

For a single-lapped joint such as a socket joint shown in Fig. 5.9.2, the adhesive and the riser pipe forms a joint with $\theta_1 = \dfrac{1}{2}\pi$ and $\theta_2 = -\pi$. Eq. (5.9.2) hence reduces to

$$\beta^2 \left[\sin^2 \left(\frac{1}{2}\pi\lambda \right) - \lambda^2 \right]^2 + 2 \alpha \beta \lambda^2 \left[\sin^2 \left(\frac{1}{2}\pi\lambda \right) - \lambda^2 \right] + \alpha^2 \lambda^2 (\lambda^2 - 1) + \frac{1}{4} \sin^2 (\pi\lambda) = 0 \tag{5.9.14}$$

A plot of the above equation will reveal the singularity associated with the joint.

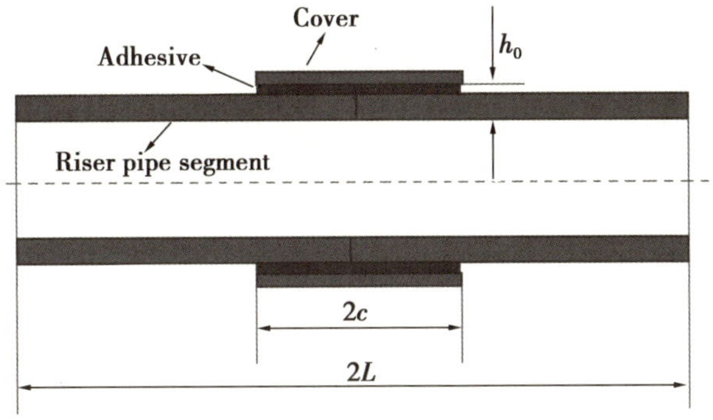

Fig. 5.9.2 Adhesive Bonded Socket Joint [Zhang et al.]

5.9.2 Convex Joint Design

A convex joint design, inspired by the shape and mechanics of trees and bamboo, allows for designing with least stress singularities at bi-material interfacial corners for engineering application. Consider two axis-symmetric cylinders of different but homogeneous materials that are joined together as shown in Fig. 5.9.3. Both ends are subjected to tension. It was found [Bogy] that the stress singularity relies only on the two corner angles of the two homogeneous materials at the joint, α_1 versus α_2, and the mismatch of structural rigidities, namely (E_1, ν_1,) versus (E_2, ν_2). Hence, a more generalized alternative to Eq. (5.9.2) can be written as

$$\lambda_n = f (\alpha_1, E_1, \nu_1, \alpha_2, E_2, \nu_2) \tag{5.9.15}$$

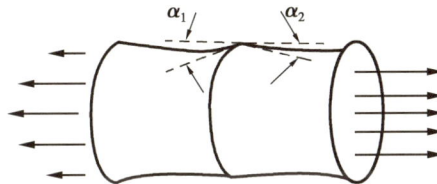

Fig. 5.9.3 Joint between Two Axis-Symmetrical Cylinders of Dissimilar Materials

Due to the complexity for solving the above equation and Eq. (5.9.2), the finite element analysis is recommended in order to reduce the stress singularity assuring a robust joint design [Xu et al.]. Given the structural properties of the two materials, one can figure out the two corner angles, i.e. α_1 and α_2 in search for minimum stress singularity. Nevertheless, it was shown by [Xu et al.] that minimizing stress singularity for most combinations of dissimilar engineering materials may be achieved as long as the interfacial joint angle is set between 45° and 65°.

5.9.3 Stress Singularities at Welded Joints

The type of welding in terms of stress intensity between two dissimilar materials (weld and base material) can also be argued using Figs. 5.9.1 and 5.9.2. Depending on the extensions of angles θ_1

and θ_2, the following welding patterns can be formed:

(a) Butt joint, if $\theta_1 = \dfrac{1}{2}\pi$ and $\theta_2 = -\dfrac{1}{2}\pi$ $\hspace{2cm}$ (5.9.16)

(b) Single-lapped joint, if $\theta_1 = \dfrac{1}{2}\pi$ and $\theta_2 = -\pi$ $\hspace{2cm}$ (5.9.17)

The uncertainty of welded joints mainly comes from the following three complicating factors:

(1) The welded joint made of dissimilar materials: Stress singularity results from weld reinforcement. A weld represents a stress concentration due to weak stress singularities at interfaces of dissimilar materials. Adjacent to the weld, the stress is several times higher than the normal stress in the base plate.

(2) The weld as a defect: Weld defects, such as undercut and slag micro-inclusions, occur during welding. The stress concentration at such a place may initiate fatigue cracks.

(3) Internal tensile stresses: Welding gives rise to internal tensile stresses due to irregular structural shapes, nonhomogeneous materials, and thermal differentials. As a result, the material adjacent to the weld is subjected to a higher stress than that corresponding to the applied load.

5.10 Fatigue of Spot Welds

Resistance spot welds are very commonly used in the fabrication of all manner of automotive components and structures. Approximately 90% of the welded joints used in an automobile are due to spot welds. A sedan uni-body may have more than 3000 spot welds that integrate panels and structural components together. Fatigue resistance of these joints impart a significant influence on the rigidity and durability of such a vehicle. The materials can be AHSS (Advanced High Strength Steel) and heavier gage components made of low carbon steels and HSLA (High Strength Low Alloy) materials. Conclusions obtained from the study by [Mohan Iyengaret et al.], based on both tensile-shear and coach-peel tests as shown in Fig. 5.10.1, are given as follows:

(a) Spot weld fatigue behavior is mainly controlled by geometric factors, such as nugget diameter, sheet thickness, and sheet width [Rudy et al.], while there is no effect of paint bake cycle. When the nugget diameter is reduced to 2 mm, the stress distribution is extremely concentrated. In the case of 6 mm in diameter, stress concentration is relieved dramatically [Ertas & Sonmez].

(b) Joints using both adhesive bonding and weld bonding have significantly improved fatigue strength over spot welding alone, although this improvement is in keeping with the actual increase in joint area gained by the addition of an adhesive layer.

(c) The base material strength has been studied by many researchers. Aa pointed out by [Lee et al.] that the base material having a higher strength benefits the fatigue performance in the LCF regime with diminishing effect in the HCF regime.

(d) The influence of heat-affected zones and the resulting residual stresses on the mechanical behavior of spot welds has to be taken into consideration.

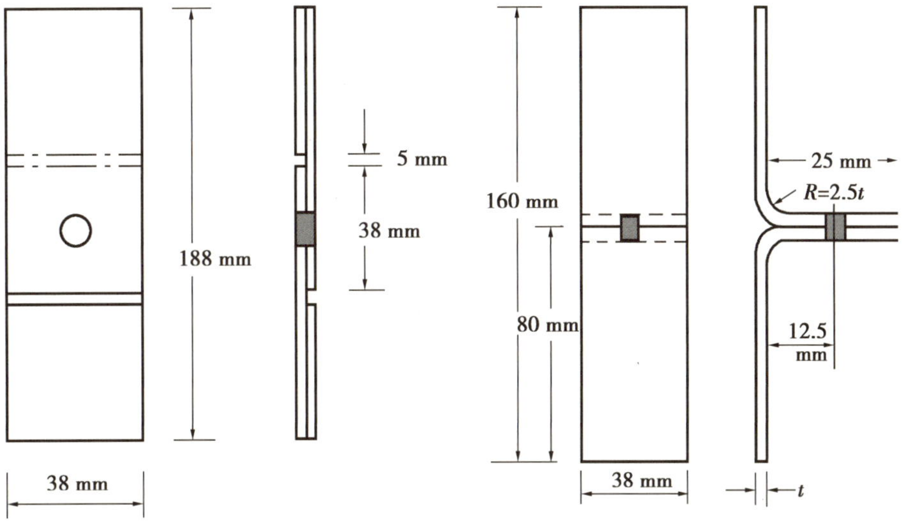

(a) Tensile–Shear Test   (b) Coach–Peel Test

Fig. 5.10.1   Fatigue Specimens for Durability of Spot Welds [Mohan Iyengaret et al.]

5.10.1   Semi-Empirical FEA

A well-educated semi-empirical approach to finite element analysis of spot welds based on shell/plate elements and rigid beams have been in practice in the automotive industry for a long time and the basic algorithm is summarized in [Dong] [Kang et al.]. A typical meshing pattern is presented in Fig. 5.10.2 [Kang et al.], which is incorporated into the finite element model of the entire welded joint for global analysis. The force and moment components exerted to the rigid beams derived from the global finite element analysis are then employed to do the fatigue or any other failure analysis locally. However, for models incorporating shell/plate elements, it is important to represent the welds in complex welded joints, not only in term of stiffness and thickness but also the geometric shape. This can be only accomplished using oblique shell elements. Note that every isoparametric solid element has three degrees of freedom at each node while shell elements have five degrees of freedom. When modeling the welds with shell elements that are adjacent to solid elements, a special technique is necessary to connect these two different types of elements. Finite element modeling has to be able to enforce that the bending moments induced in shell elements are transferred to solid elements. One way to accomplish it is to apply MPC (multi-point constraint) between them. The other way is to extend two or more shell elements into the adjacent solid elements like clamped cantilever shell elements and it is better done in the low-stressed areas. Nevertheless, the modeling accuracy using this approach is quite empirical and likely to depend on the pattern of rigid beams and mesh shapes that used for modeling the weld nugget [Song 2005].

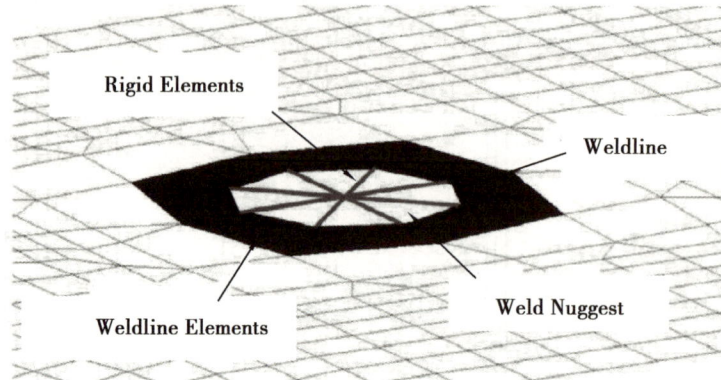

Fig. 5.10.2   Fatigue Analysis of Spot Weld Using Rigid Beams and Plate Elements [Kang et al.]

5.10.2   Full-Scaled Modeling Using 3-Dimensional Solid Elements

A better way is to model the entire welded joints using 3-dimensional isoparametric solid elements [Chiang & Tang] [Deng et al.] that may capture the material behaviors with strain singularities (or deep strain gradient) and orthotropic (or transversely isotropic) properties around the nugget boundaries.

5.11   Fatigue of Seam Welds

If a structural member is cut or joined using thermal methods such as laser, plasma, or gas cutting/welding, its fatigue strength is to be examined like a welded component. Although high strength steel has a higher fatigue limit, it is not better than mild steel if the following occurs:

   (a) The material is affected of weldments.
   (b) The material is cut using thermal methods.
   (c) The environment is corrosive.

The fatigue life is mainly controlled by the strain (stress) amplitude, mean strain (stress), and geometry of the welded joint, but the entire structure has to be also checked out for potential resonance at all possible working eigenfrequencies. For welds, the fatigue life is generally taken as being 10^7 cycles and above, while the time-history variation of the load plays an important role in it.

5.11.1   Weld Geometry and Defects

The geometry and embedded defects of a welded joint may dominate the fatigue strength, while both base material strength and filler material strength have little influence on fatigue life of a welded connection. Potential crack patterns of welded joints are illustrated in Fig. 5.11.1. Weld discontinuities such as porosity (e.g. embedded bubble and voids), slag inclusions (e.g. debris, dirt and oxides), oxidation, uneven cooling, undercuts, and rollovers are usually found in zones adjacent to the weld and on the weld crown. They may originate from one of the following problems:

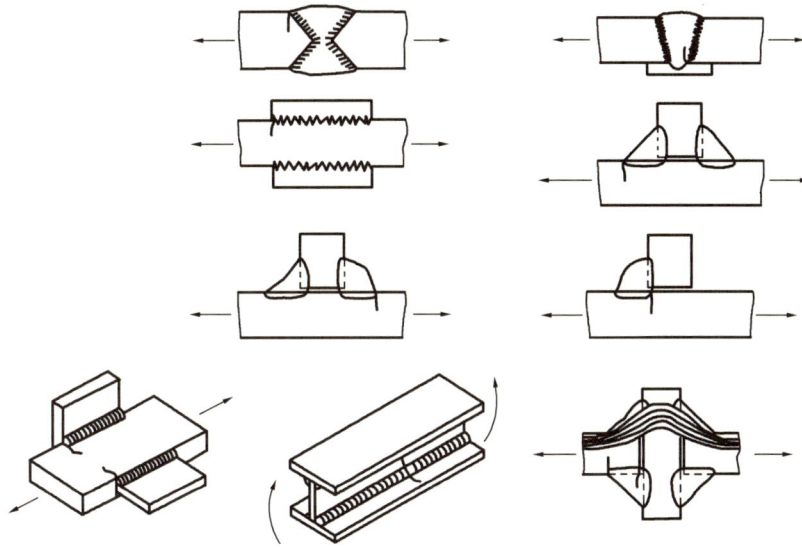

Fig. 5.11.1   Potential Failure Modes of Joints by Seam Welds

These discontinuities can create false crack indications, especially when trying to detect small cracks ($\leqslant 0.2$ mm). On welded connections, fatigue analysis shall be performed if the number of load cycles is expected to be higher than 10^3 cycles. The relative fatigue stress-life curves between the welded connections and cracks (Mode-I) induced bolted-joints are given in Fig. 5.11.2 [Lassen & Recho]. There is a significant decrease in the fatigue resistance of the welded joint when compared with its counter bolted joint.

Fig. 5.11.2   Relative Stress-Life Curves between Bolted and Welded Joints in Steel

The fatigue strength is generally proportional to the yield strength for untouched base material. The fatigue properties of a welded joint are different from those of the base material due to the following changes:

(a) Ill-conditioned geometry, such as microcracks and voids.

(b) Residual strains/stresses.

(c) Heterogeneous materials: slag inclusions, material transformations infusion zone and heat-affected zone.

5.11.2 Seam Welds-Hot Spot Stress by Finite Element Method

The finite element method is an ideal tool for determining structural strains in the hot spot area. It is possible to solve directly the linear strain distribution at the weld toe over the welded connection with both the membrane and bending strain components calculated using a 3D finite element modeling of a welded connection including the weld seam. This approach requires having a highly refined mesh to represent the weld profile in detail. For the studied welded joint, fine meshed solid element models yield more representative stress ranges at the hot spot points. Misalignment, skewness of base plates or other geometric imperfections can be taken care of using the finite element method. Stresses normal to the weld seam at toes or roots are taken into consideration. The distribution of the strain at the weld toe can then be linearized across the two dissimilar materials (hot spot and base), though there is a weak strain (or stress) singularity between them. This is the reason why it is a common practice to use extrapolation techniques to evaluate the hot spot strain components as a semi-empirical approach, even when using a 3D isoparametric solid element. The strain components are to be extrapolated on by one, but in practice von Mises stress or principal stresses can be extrapolated instead. It is yet to seek after how to capture the material behaviors with strain singularities (or deep strain gradient) and orthotropic (or transversely isotropic) properties [Shakoor & Zhenggan] around the seam boundaries.

Note that the so-called nominal stress method is not recommended for fatigue life estimate because it may provide calculations in agreement with test results only when the shear stress distribution over the welded section and the normal stress distribution over the structure are calculated correctly.

5.11.3 Seam Welds-Effective Notch Stress by Finite Element Analysis

This is to use of solid element models to accommodate the entire welded joint to evaluate the structural hot spot stresses in details with cut-out holes, as recommended by some researchers [Hobbacher] [Malikoutsakis & Savaidis] [Radaj et al.] [Schijve] [Sonsino] as shown in Fig. 5.11.3. Then, the complication by weak strain (or stress) singularity between dissimilar materials and other imperfect conditions can be excluded. The main purpose of this alternative methodology for applying finite element methods to welded connections is to utilize effective notch stresses as a tool for relative comparison. This effective notch stress method is relatively new, but it is gaining the momentum for comparative fatigue analysis of welded joints.

In a notched region, a hole with 1 mm in radius is introduced artificially without modeling its related embedded crack in the weld, as shown in Fig. 5.11.3. Detailed finite element models with fine meshes are encouraged, while sub-modeling techniques may be utilized cautiously. This approach is useful for comparing different design patterns of weldments, including geometry. Fatigue lifetime estimation of a welded joint using such "notched stress" finite element methods is still not well posted up.

How to conduct a "notched stress" finite element analysis of a welded joint has been a challenging issue. In order to reduce the influence of the geometric singularity at the hot spot location, the first interpolation point is positioned at 40% of the thickness and the element size is controlled to be less than 40% of thickness. As a rule of thumb, the influence of strain (stress) singularity is almost eliminated at about 2 or 3 elements away from the singularity. Second order (quadratic) solid elements are preferred. The size of each element around the hole opening is recommended to be less than 1/6 of the radius for 8-noded solid elements and 1/4 to 20-noded solid elements. Low aspect ratios on the element sides are expected, such as aspect ratio < 3. A smooth transition between small and large elements sizes is preferred.

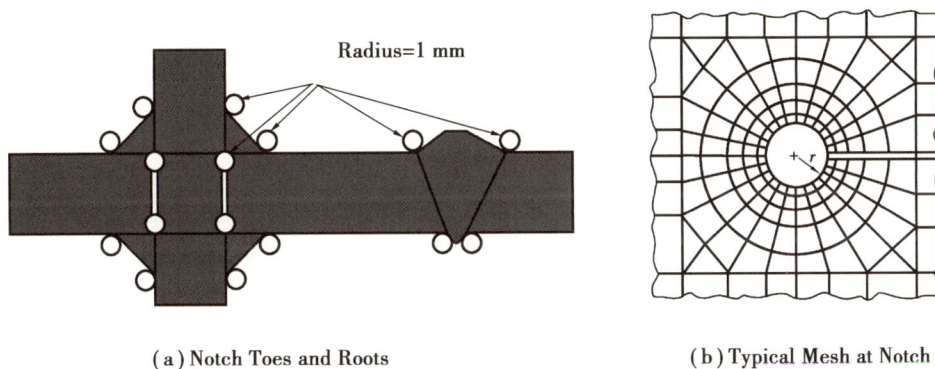

(a) Notch Toes and Roots   (b) Typical Mesh at Notch

Fig. 5.11.3   Notched Stress Method for Mining the Stress Distribution at Toes and Roots [Hobbacher]

5.11.4   Fracture Mechanics for Fatigue Analysis of Welded Joint

The fatigue property base material is generally represented by the number of cycles leading to crack initiation, while this is not true for a welded joint. Microcracks are introduced into the welded joint by nature after the welding process is completed, and thus the crack initiation phase has already passed. One way to estimate the fatigue life of a weld would be to assume a crack at the weld toe, of saying 0.1 mm, and use a fracture mechanics approach to estimating the number of lives to before it reaches the critical crack size. This method is sometime deemed to be more appropriate for the many cases, in which standard weld assessments don't appear to apply.

The crack path is modeled in reference to the cracks (size and direction) that can be detected under a nondestructive test. Around the crack tip, second-order solid elements with quarter nodes capable of modeling strain/stress singularities are to be constructed. Crack starts from the root or when there are other defects in the weld seam during welding. The stress intensity factor K_{I} and K_{II} are calculated for the given geometry and loading condition. Crack propagation is calculated using the modified Paris equation

$$\frac{\mathrm{d}a}{\mathrm{d}N_{\mathrm{p}}} = C \left| \frac{\Delta K}{1 - R} \right|^{m} \quad \text{if} - 5.0 \leqslant R \leqslant 0.5 \tag{5.11.1}$$

or $\quad \dfrac{\mathrm{d}a}{\mathrm{d}N_{\mathrm{p}}} = C \mid \Delta K \mid^{m} \quad \text{if } R > 0.5$ $\hfill$ (5.11.2)

Fracture occurs when the crack has grown to a size where $K_{\mathrm{I}} > K_{\mathrm{IC}}$. Crack growth rates subjected to complex loadings are too rapid to be counted on for added life at the design stage. A new design ought to pay primary attention to preventing crack initiation at localized geometric stress risers in highly stressed regions. One important information from the finite element analysis might be to get realistic estimates of critical crack lengths at various locations.

5.11.5 Stress Approach by Strain Measurement

The hot spot refers to the critical boundary in a welded connection where a fatigue crack is expected to occur due to a discontinuity and/or notch. It is due to the local temperature rise produced by cyclic plastic deformation prior to crack initiation. The hot spot stress approach is applied to the location where the fluctuation acts predominantly perpendicular to the weld toe (or the end of a discontinuous longitudinal weld). It is usually hard to measure the needed strain components at the notch; the measurement is undertaken at a certain distance away from the weld toe. The strain is to be extrapolated from the measured locations as shown in Fig. 5.11.4 to the weld toe following a polynomial model,

$$x^{n} + a_{n-1} x^{n-1} + \cdots + a_{0} = 0$$

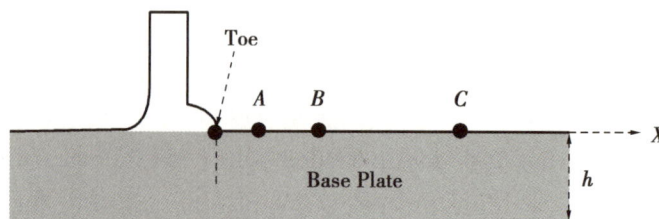

Fig. 5.11.4　Hot Spot Stress Interpolation Utilizing Measured Strains

Then, the strain at the weld toe is equal to constant c. For $d_A = 4$ mm, $d_B = 8$ mm, and $d_C = 12$ mm, according to [Niemi et al.] the strain at the weld toe is to be calculated as

$$\varepsilon_{Toe} = 3\varepsilon_A - 3\varepsilon_B + \varepsilon_C \tag{5.11.3}$$

After a series of six strain components at the weld toe are obtained and combed in the time history, the material damage can be conducted using the rainflow counting algorithm for fatigue life prediction.

5.11.6   Fatigue Strength Improvement

Welding, including spot and seam weld techniques, remains the most common joining method in the automobile industry, where it is used to weld sheet metal to form vehicle bodies and other parts. The virtual proving ground methodology with a full vehicle model based on finite elements methods can be used to form a diagnosis on the durability of welds, as shown in Fig. 5.11.5. There are several ways to improve the fatigue life for welded joints. Since most only apply to the toe, it assumed that the weld is designed in such a way that the toe is the critical area. The following common methods can be applied for improving the fatigue strength of a welded joint:

(a) Hammer-, needle-, shot-, brush-peening, and ultrasonic treatment.
(b) Laser-or plasma-dressing.
(c) Welding profiling-reshaping the weld geometry to reduce stress concentration.
(d) Grinding of weld to remove undercuts.
(e) Overstressing (proof stressing).
(f) Heat treatment to do post-weld stress relief.
(g) Painting or resin coating for environment protection.

Redundant design, load shedding, and multiple loading paths can significantly reduce the damage originating from a specific crack propagation and thereby improve the safety of a structure.

Fig. 5.11.5   VPG (Virtual Proving Ground) Vehicle on Belgian Road Profile [Son et al.]

References

ADNAN Özel Ş T, et al, 2005. Stress Analysis of Shrink-fitted Joints for Various Fit Forms via Finite Element Method[J]. Materials and Design, 26: 281-289.

AGGELIS D, et al, 2011. Monitoring of Metal Fatigue Damage Using Acoustic Emission and Thermography[J]. Journal of Acoustic Emission, 29: 113-122.

ANDERSON T L, 2005. Fracture Mechanics: Fundamentals and Applications[M]. CRC Press.

ASTM D5528-01 (Revised 2007), Mode Ⅰ Interlaminar Fracture Toughness of Unidirectional Fiber-Reinforced Polymer Matrix Composites[J]. ASTM International, W. Conshohocken, Pa.

ASTM Standards, Standard Test Methods for Notched Bar Impact Testing of Metallic Materials[J]. Vol. 3.01, E23-12C, ASTM Internation, West Conshohocken, PA.

AYATOLLAHI M R, et al, 1998. Determination of T-stress from Finite Element Analysis for Mode Ⅰ and Mixed Mode Ⅰ/Ⅱ Loading[J]. International Journal of Fracture, 91: 283-298.

BALADI A, Arezoodar F, 2011. The Effect of Materials Properties and Angle Junction on Stress Concentration at Interface of Dissimilar Materials[J]. world Academy of Science Engineering & Technology 29.79(2011): 47.

BARQUINS M. MAUGIS D, 1983. Adhesive Contact of Sectionally Smooth-ended Punches on Elastic Half-Spaces[J]. Theory and Experiment. Journal of Physics, Applied Physics, 1610.

BARQUIN O H, 1910. The Exponential Law of Endurance Tests[J]. ASTM, 10: 625-630.

BATHIAS C, DROUILLAC L, LEFRANÇOIS, P, 2001. How and Why the Fatigue S-N Curve Does not Approach a Horizontal Asymptote[J]. International Journal of Fatigue, 23(1S): 143.

BELYTSCHKO T. BLACK, T, 1999. Elastic Crack Growth in Finite Elements with Minimal Remeshing[J]. International Journal of Numerical Methods in Engineering, 45: 601-620.

BETEGÓN C J W. HANCOCK J, 1992. Two-Parameter Characterization of Elastic-Plastic Crack-Tip Fields[J]. Journal of Applied Mechanics, 58(1): 104-110.

BOGY D B, 1971. Two Edge-Bonded Elastic Wedges of Different Materials and Wedge Angles under Surface Traction[J]. Journal of Applied Mechanics, 38: 377-386.

BOWER A F. 2009. Applied Mechanics of Solids[M]. Boca Raton: CRC Press.

BRUCK H A, EVANS J J, PETERSON M L. 2002. The Role of Mechanics in Biological and Biologically Inspired Materials[J]. Experimental Mechanics, 42: 361-371.

CAMACHO P. DÁVILA C, 2002. Mixed-Mode Decohesion Finite Elements for the Simulation of Delamination in Composite Materials[J]. NASA/TM-2002-211737: 1-37.

CARDARIO A, AFREDSSON, B. 2007. Fatigue Growth of Short Cracks in Ti-17: Experiments and Simulation [J]. Engineering Fracture Mechanics, 74(15): 2293-2310.

CHAO Y J, 2003. Ultimate Strength and Failure Mechanism of Resistance Spot Wear Subjected to Tensile, Shear, or Combined Tensile/Shear Laods[J]. Journal of Engineering Materials and Technology, 125: 125-132.

CHEN S, et al, 2001, Numerical Assessment of T-stress Computation Using a p-version Finite Element Method [J]. International Journal of Fracture, 107(2): 177-199.

CHEREPANOV G P, 1967. The Propagation of Cracks in a Continuous Medium[J]. Journal of Applied Mathematics and Mechanics, 31(3): 503-512.

CHIANG Y J, TANG C, 1995. Accuracy Assessment to Applying 20-Node Solid Elements to Pressurized Composite Shells[M]. Elsevier Science Publishen B.V.: 1995.

CHIANG Y J, 1991. Crack-Speed Calculations for Unidirectional Laminae [J]. Journal of Composites Technology and Research, 13(3): 183-186.

CHOWDHURY S K R, et al, 1980. Journal of Physics, D: Applied Physics, 13: 1761.

CONNER B P et al, 2004. Application of a Fracture Mechanics Based Life Prediction Method for Contact Fatigue[J]. International Journal of Fatigue, 26(5): 511-520.

COOK L S, LAKES R S. 1995. Damping at High Homologous Temperature in Pure Cd, In, Pb, and Sn[J]. Scripta Metallurgical et Materialia, 32: 773-777.

CORUM J M, et al, 1998. Durability-Based Design Criteria for an Automotive Structural Composite: Part 1. Design Rules, ORNL-6930, Department of Energy, USA.

DENG X, et al, 2000. Three-dimensional Finite Element Analysis of the Mechanical Behavior of Spot Welds [J]. Finite Elements in Analysis and Design, 35(1): 17-39.

DONG P, 2001. A Structural Stress Definition and Numerical Implementation for Fatigue Analysis of Welded Joints[J]. International Journal of Fatigue, 23(1): 865-876.

DU Z, HANCOCK J, 1991. The effect of Non-singular Stresses on Crack-tip Constraint[J]. Journal of the Mechanics and Physics of Solids, 39(3): 555-567.

ERDOGAN F, SIH G C, 1997. On the Crack Extension in Plates under Plane Loading and Transverse Shear [J]. Journal of Basic Engineering, 85: 519-527.

EUFINGER J, et al, 2012. An Engineering Approach to Fatigue Analysis Based on Elastic-Plastic Fracture Mechanics[J]. Fatigue and Fracture of Engineering Materials and Structures, Article first published online: 27 APR 2012. 36(1): 65-74.

FLECK N A, SHIH C S, SMITH R A. 1985. Fatigue Crack Growth under Compressive Loading［J］. Engineering Fracture Mechanics, 21(1): 173-185.

FLUCK P G, 1951. American Society of Testing and Materials Proceedings, 51: 584-592.

FRIES T P, BAYDOUN M, 2011. Crack Propagation with the X-FEM and a Hybrid Explicit Implicit Crack Description［J］. International Journal for Numerical Methods in Engineering, 89(12): 1527-1558.

GIANNAKOPOULOS A E, VENKATESH T A, LINDLEY, et al, 1999. The Role of Adhesion in Contact Fatigue［J］. Acta Materia, 47(18): 4653-4664.

GLANCEY C, STEPHENS R, 2006. Fatigue Crack Growth and Life Prediction under Variable Amplitude Loading for a Cast and Wrought Aluminum Alloy［J］. International Journal of Fatigue, 28(1): 53-60.

GOODMAN M, COWIN S C, 1972. A Continuum Theory for Granular Materials［J］. Arch. Rat. Mech. Anal., 44(4): 249-266.

GORMAN M R, 2009. Acoustic Emission［J］. Encyclopedia of Structural Health Monitoring, Edited by Boller, Chang and Fujino, March 2009. 1(4): 79-100.

GRIFFITHS A A, 1920. The Theory of Rupture and Flow in Solids［J］. Philosophical Transactions of the Royal Society of London, A221(4): 198.

GROSS D, SEELIG T, 2011. Fracture Mechanics: With an Introduction to Micromechanics, Springer.

HOBBACHER A F, 2007. Recommendations for Fatigue Design of Welded Joints and Components［J］. International Institute of Welding-IIW/IIS., IIW document XIII-2151-07/ XV1254-07.

HABBACHER A, 1993. Stress Intensity Factors of Welded Joints［J］. Engineering Fracture Mechanics, 46(2): 173-182.

HAEFELE P M, LEE J D, 1995. The Constant Stress Term［J］. Engineering Fracture Mechanics, 50(5-6): 869-882.

HARDIN R A, BECKERMANN C, 2009. Prediction of the Fatigue Life of Cast Steel Containing Shrinkage Porosity［J］. Metallurgical and Materials Transactions, A, 40: 581-597.

HELMI A, ATTIA M, 2005. Prediction of Fretting Fatigue Behavior of Metals Using a Fracture Mechanics Approach with Special Consideration to the Contact Problem［J］. Journal of Tribology, 127(4): 685-693.

HILDEBRAND F B. 1976. Advanced Calculus for Applications, 2nd Edition, Prentice-Hall, Inc., Englewood Cliffs, NJ, USA.

HUANG X, et al, 2008. An Engineering Model for Fatigue Crack Growth under Variable Amplitude Loading［J］. International Journal of Fatigue, 30(1): 2-10.

HUTCHINSON J W, 1968. Singular Behavior at the End of a Tensile Crack in a Hardening Material, Journal of the Mechanics and Physics of Solids, 16(1): 13-31.

IOKA SEIJI et al, 2007. Free-Edge Stress Singularity of Bonded Dissimilar Materials with an Interlayer[J]. Key Engineering Materials: 353-358, 3104-3107.

JEWETT, R P, 1973. Hydrogen Environment Embrittlement of Metals[J]. NASA CR-2163.

KANG H, et al, 2007. Fatigue Analysis of Spot Welds Using a Mesh Insensitive Structural Stress Approach[J]. International Journal of Fatigue, 29,8(2007): 1546-1553.

KESHTGAR A. MOHAMMAD M, 2013. Detecting Crack Initiation Based on Acoustic Emission[J]. Chemical Engineering Transactions, 33: 547-552.

KURIHARA M, et al, 1986. Analysis on Fatigue Crack Growth Rates under a Wide Range of Stress Ratio[J]. Journal of Pressure Vessel Technology, 108(2): 209-213.

LARSSON S G, CARLSON A J, 1973. Influence of Non-singular Stress Terms and Specimen Geometry on Small Scale Yielding at Crack Tips in Elastic-Plastic Materials[J]. Journal of the Mechanics and Physics of Solids, 21(4): 263-277.

LASSEN T, RECHO N, 2006. Fatigue Life Analyses of Welded Structures, ISTE Ltd., Great Britain and USA.

LEE D S, et al, 2004. Fatigue Crack Detection in Cold Worked Aluminum Alloys using Acoustic Emission Technique[J]. Key Engineering Materials, 270/273: 537-542.

LEE Y, et al, 2012. Metal Fatigue Analysis Handbook[M]. Bufferworth-Heineman, Elsevier.

LEEVERS P S, RADON J C D, 1982. Inherent Stress Biaxiality in Various Fracture Specimen [J]. International Journal of Fracture, 19(4): 311-325.

LEHTOVAARA A, RABB R, 2008. A Numerical Model for the Evaluation of Fretting Fatigue Crack Initiation in Rough Point Contact[J]. Wear, 264(9-10): 750-756.

LEOPOLD C, MUNIER R, 2015. Crack Propagation in Large Scale Yielding (LSY) Conditions[J]. Procedia Engineering, 133: 681-687.

LIBBY H L, 1971. Introduction to Electromagnetic Nondestructive Test Methods, John Wiley & Sons, Inc., New York, NY.

LIU C, NAIRN J, 2000. Analytical and Experimental Methods for a Fracture Mechanics Interpretation of the Microbond Test Including the Effects of Friction and Thermal Stresses[J]. International Journal of Adhesion & Adhesives, 19(1): 59-70.

LIU M, et al, 2015. An Improved Semi-Analytical Solution for Stress at Round-tip Notches[J]. Engineering Fracture Mechanics, 149: 134-143.

LIU Y, MAHADEVAN S, 2009. Fatigue Limit Prediction of Notched Components Using Short Crack Growth Theory and Asymptotic Interpolation Method[J]. Engineering Fracture Mechanics, 76(15): 2317-2331.

MALIKOUTSAKIS M, SAVAIDIS G, 2011. Modeling and Fatigue Assessment of Weld Start-End Locations Based on the Effective Notch Stress Approach[J]. Material Science & Engineering Technology, 42(2011): 298-305.

MANSON S, 1953. Behavior of Materials under Conditions of Thermal Stress[J]. Heat Transfer Symposium, University of Michigan Engineering Research Institute.

MARTIN J, 2015. Mechanical Behavior of Engineering Materials, Prentice-Hall, Englewood Cliffs, N J[J]. USA: 224.

MARINES G L, et al, 2008. Fatigue Crack Growth from Small to Large Cracks on Very High Cycle Fatigue with Fish Eye Failure[J]. Engineering Fracture Mechanics, 75(6): 1657-1665.

MAYOR H, et al, 2005. Endurance Limit and Threshold Stress Intensity Factor of Magnesium and Aluminum Alloys at Elevated Temperatures[J]. International Journal of Fatigue, 27(9): 1076-1088.

MERATI A, ESTAUGH G, 2009. Determination of Fatigue Related to Discontinuity State of 7000 Series of Aerospace Aluminum Alloys[J]. Engineering Failure Analysis, 14(4): 673-685.

METKAR R, SUNNAPWAR V, HIWASE S, 2013. Fatigue Strength and Life Prediction of Forged Steel Crankshaft by Using Fracture Mechanics Approach[J]. SAE 2013-26-0141.

MIKHEEVSKIY, S, GLINKA G, 2009. Elastic-plastic Fatigue Crack Growth Analysis under Variable Amplitude Loading Spectra[J]. International Journal of Fatigue, 31(11-12): 1828-1836.

MIRSAYAR M M, 2015. Mixed Mode Fracture Analysis Using Extended Maximum Tangential Strain Criterion [J]. Materials & Design, 85CDE(5): 941-947.

MISCHKE C R, 1987. Prediction of Stochastic Endurance Strength[J]. Journal of Vibration, Acoustics, Stress, and Reliability in Design, 109(1): 113-122.

MOES N, et al, 1999. A Finite Element Method for Crack Growth without Remeshing[J]. International Journal for Numerical Methods in Engineering, 46(1): 131-150.

MOHAN I R, et al, 2008. Fatigue of Spot Fatigue of Spot-Welded Sheet Steel Joints: Welded Sheet Steel Joints: Physics, Mechanics, and Process Variability[J]. www.autosteel.org, retrieved 4/10/2018.

MOHAMMED I, LIECHTI K M, 2001. The Effect of Corner Angles in Bimaterial Structures[J]. International Journal of Solids and Structures, 38: 4375-4394.

MURAKAMI Y, et al, 1992, Stress Intensity Factors Handbook[M], 2nd Edition, Committee on Fracture Mechanics of the Society of Materials Science, Japan.

NEWMAN J C, et al, 1999. Fatigue Life Prediction Methodology Using Small-Crack Theory[J]. International Journal of Fatigue, 21(2): 109.

NIEMI E, FRICKEAND W, MADDOX S, 2006. Fatigue Analysis of Welded Components: Designer's Guide to the Structural Hot Spot Approach[M], Woodhead Publishing Ltd., USA.

NOROOZI A H, et al, 2007. A Study of the Stress Ratio Effects on the Fracture Crack Growth Using the Unified Two-Parameter Fatigue Crack Driving Force[J]. International Journal of Fatigue, 29(9-11): 1616.

O'DOWD N P, SHIH C F, 1991. Family of Crack-tip Fields Characterized by a Triaxiality Parameter-I. Structure of Fields[J]. Journal of the Mechanics and Physics of Solids. 39: 989-1015.

O'DOWD N P, SHIH C F, 1991. Family of Crack-tip Fields Characterized by a Triaxiality Parameter-II. Fracture Applications[J]. Journal of the Mechanics and Physics of Solids, 40: 939-963.

PARIS P C, ERDOGAN F, 1963. A Critical Analysis of Crack Propagation Laws[J]. Journal of Basic Engineering, D85: 528-534.

PUGNO N, et al, 2006. A Generalized Paris' Law for Fatigue Crack Growth[J]. Journal of the Mechanics and Physics of Solids, 54(7): 1333-1349.

QUARESIMIN M, RICOTTA M, 2006. Stress Intensity Factors and Strain Energy Release Rates in Single Lap Bonded Joints in Composite Materials[J]. Composites Science and Technology, 66(5): 647-656.

RABOTNOV Y N, 1969. Creep Problems of Structural Members, North-Holland.

RADAJ D, LAZZARIN P, BERTO F, 2013. Generalized Neuber Concept of Fictitious Notch Rounding[J]. International Journal of Fatigue, 51: 105-115.

REMMERS J, BORST R, de NEEDLEMAN A, 2003. A Cohesive Segments Method for the Simulation of Crack Growth[J]. Computational Mechanics, 31(1): 69-77.

RICE J R, 1968. A Path Independent Integral and the Approximate Analysis of Strain Concentration by Notches and Cracks[J]. Journal of Applied Mechanics, 35: 379-386.

RICE J R, ROSENGREN G F, 1968. Plane Strain Deformation near a Crack Tip in a Power-law Hardening Material[J]. Journal of the Mechanics and Physics of Solids, 16(1): 1-12.

RODOPOULOS C A, 2004. Optimization of Fatigue Resistance of 2024-T351 Aluminum Alloy by Controlled Shot Peening-Methodology, Results and Analysis[J]. International Journal of Fatigue, 26(8): 849-856.

RUDY J F, et al, 1965. The Behavior of Spot Welds under Stress[J]. Welding Journal, 35(2): 653-713.

RYCHLIK I, GUPTA S, 2007. Rain-flow Fatigue Damage for Transformed Gaussian Loads[J]. International Journal of Fatigue, 29(3): 406-420.

SAE Fatigue Design Handbook, 1968. Society of Automotive Engineers[J], Warrendale, PA, V. 4.

SAHARAN M R, MITRI H S, 2008. Numerical Procedure for Dynamic Simulation of Discrete Fractures Due to Blasting[J]. Rock Mechanics and Rock Engineering, 41(5): 641-670.

SCHIJVE J, 2012. Fatigue Predictions of Welded joints and the Effective Notch Stress Concept [J]. International Journal of Fatigue, 45: 31-38.

SHAKOOR A, ZHENGGAN Z, 2011. Investigation of 3D Anisotropic Electrical Conductivity in TIG Welded 5A06 Alloy using Eddy Currents[J]. Journal of Materials Processing Technology, 211(11):1736-1741.

SHI Z, et al, 2000. Characterization of Acoustic Emission Signals from Fatigue Fracture[J]. Proceedings of the Institution of Mechanical Engineers, Part C: Journal of Mechanical Engineering Science, 214(9): 1141-1149.

SHIH C F, 1982. Journal of the Mechanics and Physics of Solids, 29: 305-326.

SIH G C, MACDONALD B, 1974. Fracture Mechanics Applied to Engineering Problems-Strain Energy Density Fracture Criterion[J]. Engineering Fracture Mechanics, 6(2): 361-386.

SIH G C, PARIS P C, ERDOGAN F, 1962. Crack-tip Stress Intensity Factors for the Plane Extension and Plate Bending Problem[J]. Journal of Applied Mechanics, 29: 306-312.

SON K J, et al, 2003. Fatigue Strength Evaluation on Resistance Spot Welds of the Vehicle Body [J]. Mechanics Based Design of Structures and Machines, 31(1): 79-92.

SONG J H, 2005. Evaluation of Finite Element Modeling of a Spot-Welded Region for Crash Analysis[J]. International Journal of Automotive Technology, 7(3): 3293-3336.

SONG J, AREIAS P, BELYTSCHKO T, 2010. A Method for Dynamic Crack and Shear Band Propagation with Phantom Nodes[J]. International Journal for Numerical Methods in Engineering, 67(6): 868-893.

SONSINO C M, 2009. A Consideration of Allowable Equivalent Stresses for Fatigue Design of Welded Joints According to the Notch Stress Concept with the Reference Radii $r_r = 1.00$ and 0.05 mm[J]. Welding in the World, 53(3-4): R64-R75.

SUN C T, JIH C J, 1987. On Strain Energy Release Rates for Interfacial Cracks in Bimaterial Media[J]. Engineering Fracture Mechanics, 28: 13-20.

SURESH S, 1998. Fatigue of Materials[M]. 2nd Edition. Cambridge University Press, New York, NY.

TADA H, PARIS P, IRWIN G, 2000. The Stress Analysis of Cracks Handbook[M]. 3rd Edition, American Society of Mechanical Engineers.

TIPTON S M, 1985. Fatigue Behavior under Multiaxial Loading in the Presence of a Notch: Methodologies for the Prediction of Life to Crack Initiation and Life Spent in Crack Propagation[D]. Dissertation, Stanford University, Stanford, CA, USA.

TSUDA T, et al, 2015. Three Point Bending Crack Propagation Analysis of Beam Subjected to Eccentric Bending Impact Loading by X-FEM[J]. 10th LS-Dyna Conference, Wurzburg, Germany.

TVERGAARD V, 2007. Mesh Sensitivity Effects on Fatigue Crack Growth by Crack-tip Blunting and Resharpening[J]. International Journal of Solids and Structures, 44: 1891-1899.

VALLET C, CHAU T, STEPHAN J, 2012. Crack Propagation under High Thermal Amplitude Cycles in a Ductile Material[J]. Proceedings of ASME Pressure Vessels and Piping Conference.

VORMWALD M, 2014. Fatigue Crack Propagation under Large Cyclic Plastic Strain Conditions[J]. Procedia Materials Science, 3: 301-396.

VORMWALD M, HEULER P, SEEGER T, 1992. A Fracture Mechanics Based Model for Cumulative Damage Assessment as Part of Fatigue Life Prediction[J]. ASTM STP 1122: 28-43.

WILKINSON A J, 2001. Modeling the Effect of Texture in the Statistics of Stage Ⅰ Fatigue Crack Growth[J]. Philosophical Magazine, 81: 841-855.

XIANG Y, et al, 2009. Crack Growth-Based Fatigue Life Prediction Using an Equivalent Initial Flaw Model. Part Ⅰ: Uniaxial Loading[J]. International Journal of Fatigue.

XU J Q, MUTOH Y, 1996. Singular Residual Stress Field near the Interface Edge[J]. Japan Society of Mechanical Engineering, A-62(597): 1219-1225.

XU L R, et al, 2006. Computer Simulation and Experimental Investigation of a Novel Dissimilar Material Joint for Structural Applications[J]. Joint International Conference on Computing and Decision Making in Civil and Building Engineering, Montreal, Canada.

YAO W, XIA K, GU Y, 1995. On the Fatigue Notch Factor, K_f[J]. International Journal of Fatigue, 17(4): 245-251.

YOON K B, SAXENA A, 1991. An Interpretation of the ΔJ for Cyclically Unsaturated Materials [J]. International Journal of Fracture, 49: R3-R9.

ZHA T, JIANG Y, 2008. Fatigue of 7075-T651 Aluminum Alloy[J]. International Journal of Fatigue, 30(5): 834-849.

ZHANG W, et al, 2015. Mode-Ⅰ Crack Propagation under High Cyclic Loading in 316L Stainless Steel[J]. Procedia Materials Science, 3: 1197-1203.

ZHANG Y, QIN, T, NODA N, et al, 2013. Strength Analysis of Adhesive Joints of Riser Pipes in Deep Sea Environment Loadings[J]. Applied Adhesion Science,1(1): 9.

ZEHNDER A, 2012. Fracture Mechanics[M]. Springer.

ZHOU M, ZWERNEMAN F, 1997. Acoustic Emission Analysis on Fatigue Threshold Behavior[J]. SAE 971536.

ZHURKOV S, KUKSENKO V, 1975. The Micromechanics of Polymer Fracture[J]. International Journal of Fracture, 11(4): 629-639.

ZI G, BELYTSCHKO T, 2010. New Crack-tip Elements for X-FEM and Applications to Cohesive Cracks[J]. International Journal for Numerical Methods in Engineering, 57(15): 2221-2240.

Chapter 6

Creep and Oxidation

6.1　Introduction

Most automotive components such as batteries for EV, combustion engines, transmissions, tires, plastics of instrument panels must withstand severe cyclic mechanical and thermal loads throughout their life cycle. The combination of thermal transients with mechanical load cycles results in a complex evolution of damage, leading to thermomechanical fatigue (TMF) of the material and, after a certain number of loading cycles, to failure of the component. For example, loosened self-tapping screws observed in an instrument panel.

Creep and oxidation are the two major influential factors, which have a deciding impact on the product durability especially in a harsh environment involving high stress levels, high working temperatures, and eroding agents. Although numerous expensive and time-consuming bench tests are necessary to find the appropriate design and material that ensure the integrity of the component for a whole product life at elevated and high temperatures, there is a demand for reliable computational methods allowing the calculation of the lifetime of an automotive component and the optimization of the component design via computer simulations. When the transient temperature fields in the components are known from measurements or numerical calculations, computational methods for TMF life prediction comprise the following steps:

- (a) Transient stress and strain fields can be calculated from temperature fields as prescribed in finite element calculations.
- (b) Identify the material degradation (e.g. oxidation, creep, or others) due to both mechanical and thermal loads to update the status of coupled thermomechanical problem, including material properties.
- (c) Apply a lifetime-estimating model to predict the fatigue life of the component based on the true stresses and strains obtained from the converged finite element solution.

Thermal barrier coatings have been extensively used to protect parts that operate at high temperatures. They provide thermal insulation and a barrier for oxidation of underlying substrates, whose risky exposure to creep and oxidation can be reduced dramatically. The temperature difference between a thermal barrier coating and the protected alloyed-metallic substrate can be as high as 300 ℃ [Rigney]. Thermally grown oxide (TGO) between the coating and substrate can be an effective means to attenuate the complication of interfacial defects and surface roughness. Both the coating and the interfacial surface have been identified as the weak links concerning researchers [Miller] [Evans et al.].

6.1.1   Introduction to Creep

Creep is measured by permanent deformation of material at a constant load and it increases in time at constant stress except under hydrostatic stress. Unlike brittle fracture, creep deformation results from long-term stresses. Creep is also called cold flow because it may occur at room temperature though it gets worse at elevated temperatures even if there is no material phase transformation. Design for creep at elevated (high) temperatures has been of great concern [Penny & Marriott]. However, when metallic parts work at elevated temperatures where creep occurs, other microstructural changes may take place. Creep damage and microstructural degradation occur simultaneously. For carbon steels and carbon/Mo steels, iron carbide will decompose into graphite. For low-alloy steels such as T-11 and T-22, the carbide phase spheroidizes. Thus, creep failures will include the degraded microstructures of graphite or spheroidized carbides along with the grain-boundary voids and cracks characteristic of these high-temperature long-time failures.

The creep behavior of plastics and metals at elevated/high temperatures is one of the main deciding factors for a variety of applications that require a strict dimensional stability, including electrical and electronic parts and various automotive applications. However, obtaining or generating accurate creep data is very difficult for both material suppliers and product designers because the creep property is time-dependent. It may take several months or even years of time span. Hence a faster and more reliable method for predicting creep behavior of products working at elevated temperature is needed when designing with materials that will meet long-term loading requirements.

6.1.2   Introduction to Oxidation

Oxidation is a high-temperature corrosion. It denotes chemical deterioration of a material resulting from heating. This non-galvanic form of corrosion can occur when a metal is subjected to a hot atmosphere containing oxygen, sulfur, or other compounds capable of oxidizing the material. High temperature oxidation of metals occurs when the temperature is sufficient to allow inter-diffusion of metal and oxygen.

In some cases oxidation is to be avoided or only permitted until a protective oxide is produced. Areas of interest may be inside a jet engine, automotive engine components, and air leaks in a reducing or other gas furnace process such as hardening or annealing, and welding under a protective inert gas shield. Combining fatigue with corrosion becomes a catastrophic form of attack affecting metallics such as aluminum alloys.

On the other hand, high temperature oxidation of metals can be deliberately desired such as field oxide and gate oxide used to isolate the devices from one another in the manufacture of integrated circuits; furnace produced colored metal for controlled heat transfer characteristics (e. g. emissivity); growing a certain layer thicknesses of silicon oxide insulation or silicon oxy-nitride as a dielectric on semiconductor wafers; furnace oxidation method of cleaning contaminants off metals.

6.2   Creep and Relaxation

Materials may deform by plastic dislocation, diffusional flow, and power-law creep at an elevated temperature [Kassner], as shown in Fig. 6.2.1. Creep results in an increase in plastic strain even under constant stress. Stress relaxation means a decrease in stress under constant strain. Creep compliance and relaxation modulus are employed to characterize creep and stress relaxation, respectively.

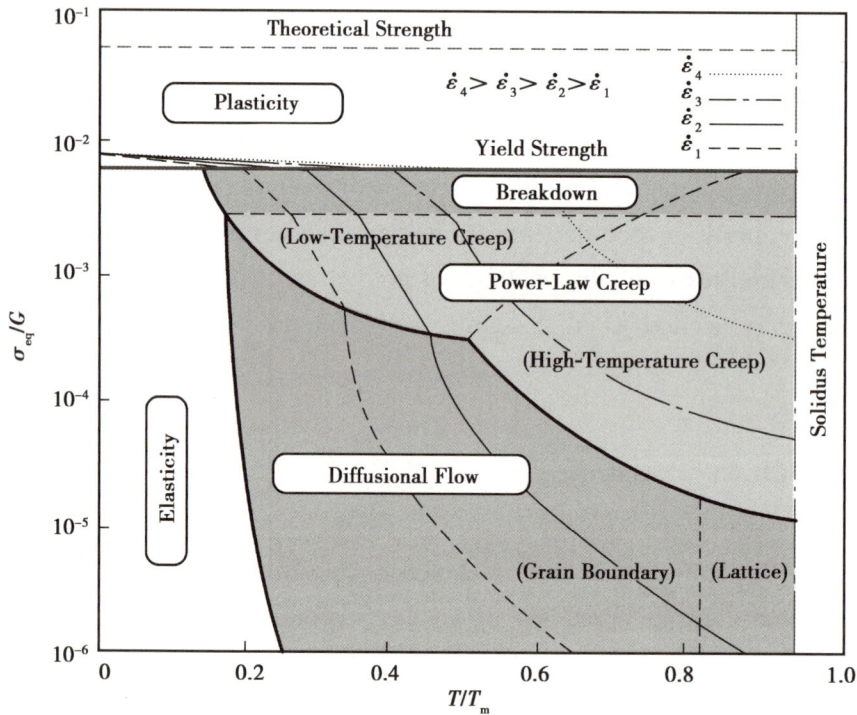

Fig. 6.2.1   Schematic Material Deformation Map［Frost & Ashby］［Graham & Walles］

A method for predicting the long-term creep behavior of materials using the short-term creep experimental data is in demand. For a quick and reliable prediction of long-term creep behavior of materials, time regional power-law model and time-stress modulus are introduced here. The ratio of strain to stress is called compliance. A time-varying strain, $\varepsilon(t)$, may arise from a constant stress, σ_0, and the ratio is called creep compliance as

$$C_{\text{creep}}(t) \equiv \frac{\varepsilon(t)}{\sigma_0} \tag{6.2.1}$$

Creep cavity nucleation, its growth and the rendered intergranular damage are the common characteristics of both the cyclic creep and static creep.

6.2.1 Creep

A typical strain-time curve due to creep at a constant uniaxial stress is depicted in Fig. 6.2.2. Creep strain is the total strain at any time produced by the applied stress during a creep test. There are three distinct stages: primary, secondary, and tertiary. Linear viscoelasticity in terms of strain creep can be described as follows:

$$\varepsilon(t) = \int_0^t C(t-s) \, \mathrm{d}\sigma = \int_0^t C(t-s)\left(\frac{\mathrm{d}\sigma}{\mathrm{d}s}\right) \mathrm{d}s \tag{6.2.2}$$

$$\text{or} \quad \varepsilon(t) = C_o \, \sigma(t) + \int_{0^+}^t C(t-s)\left(\frac{\mathrm{d}\sigma}{\mathrm{d}s}\right) \mathrm{d}s \tag{6.2.3}$$

where
C_o: Instantaneous compliance of relaxation;
C: Elastic compliance;
t: Time;
s: Dummy variable of time.

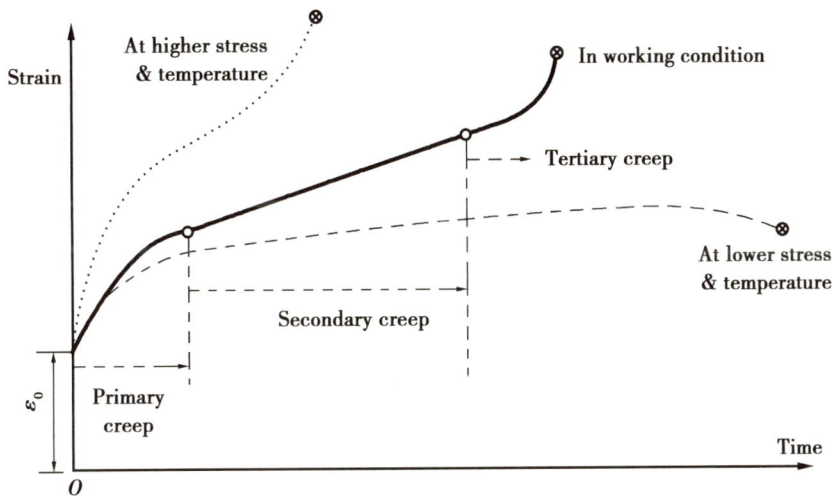

Fig. 6.2.2   Creep Strain-versus-Time Curve Subjected to a Constant Uniaxial Stress

An instantaneous deformation occurs once upon loading, i.e. ε_o in Fig. 6.2.2, and then the primary creep stage begins. The following equation is a model to describe the overall strain growth,

$$\varepsilon(t) = \varepsilon_o + \varepsilon_p \left(1 - e^{\frac{-t}{t_c}}\right) + \varepsilon_{\text{creep}} + \varepsilon_t \left(e^{\frac{t}{t_c}} - 1\right) \tag{6.2.4}$$

where

ε_0: Instantaneous strain upon loading;

ε_p: Stain magnitude related to primary creep (1st stage);

ε_{creep}: Creep strain in the steady-state stage, i.e. 2nd stage of creep;

ε_t: Strain magnitude related to tertiary creep;

t_p: Time parameter in the primary stage;

t_t: Time parameter in the tertiary stage.

6.2.2　Creep Worsened by High Working Temperature

Solid materials creep, especially at elevated temperatures. The ratio of the working temperature to melting temperature is called homologous temperature.

$$T_{hom} = \frac{T}{T_m} \tag{6.2.5}$$

where

T: Homologous temperature, which is dimensionless;

$T(K)$: Working temperature;

$T_m(K)$: Meting temperature.

A general design guide to the severity of creep is that once the dimensionless homologous temperature goes higher than 40%, the activation energy is closer to the activation energy of self-diffusion and it is likely to creep. An atom, jumping from material structure 1 into material structure 2, has to go through an energy activation (called activation energy) that causes its neighboring atoms to be moved elastically. For example, once steel is in use at a working temperature above 550 ℃, creep instead of yield strength will be the major design concern for a long-term application. As a general approximation for structural and boiler steels, the following is a list of initial creep temperatures:

(a) Plain carbon steels: $T > 350$ ℃.
(b) Carbon steel alloyed with Fe-0.5% Mo: $T > 450$ ℃.
(c) Alloyed steel with Fe-1.25%Cr-0.5%Mo: $T > 510$ ℃.
(d) Alloyed steel with Fe-2.25%Cr-1%Mo: $T > 540$ ℃.
(e) Stainless Steel: $T > 550$ ℃.

Aluminum alloys are subjected to creep at relatively low elevated temperatures, ranging from 200-300 ℃. Most plastics and rubber creep even at room temperature.

6.3   Stress Relaxation

Stress relaxation, defined as the observed decrease in stress in response to the same amount of strain applied, is a corollary to creep. In other words, stress relaxation is a decreased tendency for the material to return to its original shape when unloaded. The linear viscoelasticity can be represented in terms of relaxation modulus as follows:

$$\sigma(t) = \int_0^t E(t-s)\,\mathrm{d}\varepsilon = \int_0^t E(t-s)\,\frac{\mathrm{d}\varepsilon}{\mathrm{d}s}\mathrm{d}s \tag{6.3.1}$$

$$\text{or} \quad \sigma(t) = E_o\varepsilon(t) + \int_{0^*}^t E(t-s)\,\frac{\mathrm{d}\varepsilon}{\mathrm{d}s}\mathrm{d}s \tag{6.3.2}$$

where

E_o: Instantaneous elastic modulus of relaxation;

E: Elastic modulus;

T: Time;

s: Dummy variable of time.

The above equation means that the stress responses to an applied strain. Analogously with creep compliance, one may superimpose the relaxation curves by means of the "relaxation modulus" defined as

$$E_{\text{relaxation}}(t,\sigma,T) = \frac{\sigma(t)}{\varepsilon_0} \tag{6.3.3}$$

where

$E_{\text{relaxation}}$: Relaxation modulus as a function of time, stress, and temperature;

ε_0: Applied constant strain.

Given that the deformation is constant, the stress resisting that deformation will decrease with time even at a fixed temperature. It means that the relaxation modulus decreases as time goes on as depicted schematically in Fig. 6.3.1.

The physical mechanism that causes a plastic to undergo creep also applies to the phenomenon of stress relaxation. Design engineers have to obtain creep databases provided by suppliers and perform interpolation and extrapolation procedures to develop a complete nonlinear isochronous stress-strain curve as a function of time, stress, and temperature, resembling the curve shown in Fig. 6.3.1. Representing curves are then used replacing short-term stress-strain curves when designing for applications involving long-term static loading.

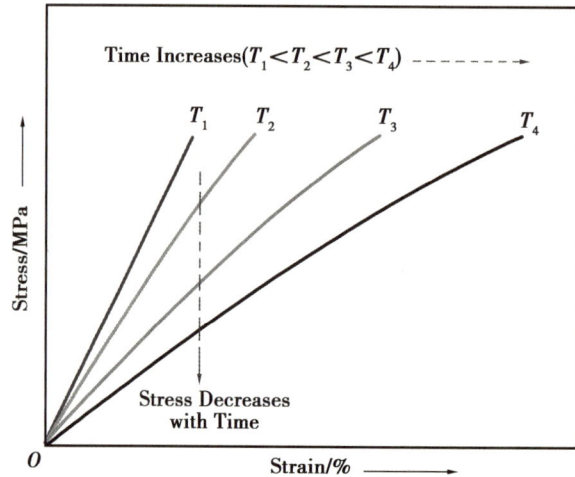

Fig. 6.3.1 Schematic Isochronous Curves Showing Stress Relaxation as a Function of Time

6.4 Standard Linear Solid Model for Viscoelastic Materials

When a stress is applied to a polymer, parts of the long polymer chain are relocated. This is one of the creep phenomena. For typical polymers whose conformational change is eventually limited by the network of entanglements or other types of junction points, more elaborate spring-dashpot models may be applied. An anelastic material is one that shows a temporal shift between an applied stress and the induced strain and the deformation is a function of time, strain, and strain rate. An anelastic material is a special case of a viscoelastic material that will fully recover to its original state when unloaded.

A viscous material is modeled as a spring and a dashpot in series with each other, both of which are in parallel with a lone spring, as shown in Fig. 6.4.1(a). This is called linear solid model if the behavior of the dashpot is Newtonian. Viscoelastic materials lose energy (or dissipate heat) when subjected to cyclic loads. Hysteresis is observed in the stress-strain curve as schematically depicted in Fig. 6.4.1(b) with the area of the loop representing the energy lost during the loading cycle due to the viscous effect. Material having low melting temperatures may fail due to the involved hysteretic heating.

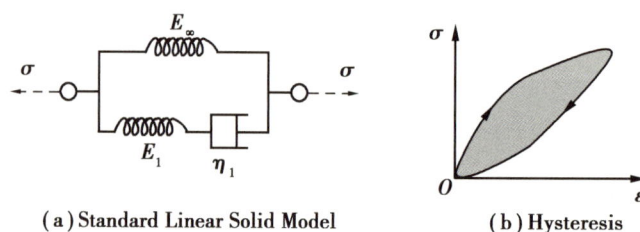

(a) Standard Linear Solid Model (b) Hysteresis

Fig. 6.4.1 Viscoelastic Models by Springs and Viscous Dashpots

6.4.1   Standard Linear Solid Model-Stress Relaxation

In the "spring-dashpot in series" unit, the stress in the spring is equal to the stress in the dashpot. Thus,

$$\sigma_1 = \eta_1 \frac{d\varepsilon_{dash}}{dt} = E_1(\varepsilon - \varepsilon_{dash}) \tag{6.4.1}$$

where

$\sigma_1(MPa)$: Stress induced in the spring-dashpot in series;

ε_{dash}: Strain due to the dashpot;

ε: Overall strain;

$E_1(MPa)$: Elastic modulus of spring 1, in series with dashpot 1;

$\eta_1(MPa\text{-}sec)$: Viscosity of the dashpot in series with spring 1.

For a case study on the relaxation subjected to a constant strain, $\varepsilon = \varepsilon_o$, Eq. (6.4.1) becomes

$$\eta_1 \frac{d\varepsilon_{dash}}{dt} = E_1(\varepsilon_o - \varepsilon_{dash})$$

i.e.
$$\frac{d\varepsilon_{dash}}{dt} + \frac{E_1}{\eta_1}\varepsilon_{dash} = \frac{E_1}{\eta_1}\varepsilon_o \tag{6.4.2}$$

of which ε_o is the initial strain applied at $t = 0$ and kept constant after then. With an initial condition that $\varepsilon_{dash} = 0$ at $t = 0$, Eq. (6.4.2) can be solved for ε_{dash},

$$\varepsilon_{dash} = \varepsilon_o \left[1 - \exp^{-\frac{t}{\tau_1}} \right] \tag{6.4.3}$$

of which τ_1 is the retardation time (or relaxation time) due to creep, and

$$\tau_1 = \frac{\eta_1}{E_1} \tag{6.4.4}$$

Thus the stress in the "spring-dashpot in series" unit can be obtained by substituting Eq. (6.4.3) back into Eq. (6.4.1) and

$$\sigma_1 = E_1(\varepsilon - \varepsilon_{dash}) = E_1\left\{ \varepsilon_o - \varepsilon_o\left[1 - \exp^{-\frac{t}{\tau_v}} \right] \right\} = E_1\varepsilon_o \exp\left(-\frac{t}{\tau_v} \right) \tag{6.4.5}$$

Since spring E_∞ is in parallel to the "spring E_1-dashpot η_1 in series", the overall stress is a sum of them as

$$\sigma = E_\infty \, \varepsilon_o + \sigma_1 = E_1(\varepsilon - \varepsilon_{dash}) = E_\infty \, \varepsilon_o + E_1 \, \varepsilon_o \exp\left(-\frac{t}{\tau_1}\right) \tag{6.4.6}$$

of which E_o and E_1 are the spring rate of the two springs given in Fig. 6.4.1(a).

6.4.2 Standard Linear Solid Model-Creep

Next, consider a special case of a sudden unit load (step function) that $\sigma = $ constant (initial constant stress), when $t \geqslant 0$ and $\sigma = 0$, when $t < 0$. The stress will be carried by both spring E_∞ and "spring-dashpot in series" as

$$\sigma = E_\infty \varepsilon + E_1(\varepsilon - \varepsilon_{dash}) \tag{6.4.7}$$

i.e. $\quad \varepsilon_{dash} = \dfrac{E_\infty}{E_1}\varepsilon - \dfrac{\sigma}{E_1} \tag{6.4.8}$

On the other hand the stress induced in the "spring-dashpot in series" is balanced as

$$E_1(\varepsilon - \varepsilon_{dash}) = \eta \frac{d\varepsilon_{dash}}{dt} \tag{6.4.9}$$

Substitution of Eq. (6.4.8) into the above equation leads to

$$\frac{d\varepsilon}{dt} + \frac{E_\infty E_1}{\eta(E_\infty + E_1)}\varepsilon + \frac{E_1}{\eta(E_\infty + E_1)}\sigma = 0 \tag{6.4.10}$$

The above equation can then be solved for the time-dependent strain and the material's creep compliance, exhibited by the material in response to an imposed constant normal stress, respectively as

$$\varepsilon(t) = \left[\frac{\sigma}{E_\infty + E_1}\right]\left(1 + \frac{E_1}{E_\infty}\right)\eta\left[1 - \exp\left(-\frac{t}{\tau_1}\right)\right] \tag{6.4.11}$$

where $\quad \tau_1 = \dfrac{\eta_1}{E_1} \tag{6.4.12}$

Define $\quad C_{creep}(t) = \dfrac{\varepsilon(t)}{\sigma_{in}} \tag{6.4.13}$

Then $\quad C_{creep}(t) = (E_\infty + E_1)^{-1}\left(1 + \frac{E_1}{E_\infty}\right)\eta\left[1 - \exp\left(-\frac{t}{\tau_1}\right)\right] \tag{6.4.14}$

The creep behavior subjected to a constant stress, following Eq. (6.4.11), is depicted in Fig. 6.4.2.

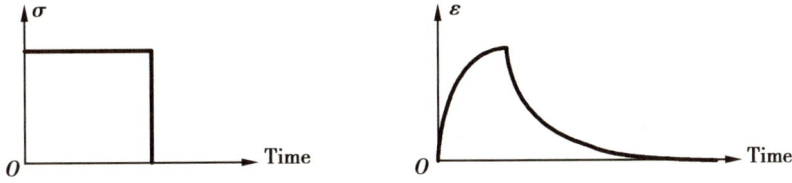

Fig. 6.4.2 Creep Behavior of Viscoelastic Material under a Constant Stress

6.4.3 Linear Solid Model-Characteristics

The behavior of a linear solid model can describe viscoelastic-material behaviors, including instantaneous stress in response to a sudden applied strain, instantaneous strain in response to a sudden applied stress, the time-dependent strain creep, and the time-dependent stress relaxation. If both $\sigma(t)$ and $\varepsilon(t)$ are time-dependent, then the governing equation becomes

$$\frac{d\varepsilon(t)}{dt} + \frac{E_\infty E_1}{\eta\,(E_\infty + E_1)}\varepsilon(t) + \frac{1}{E_\infty + E_1}\left[\frac{d\sigma(t)}{dt}\right] + \frac{E_1}{\eta\,(E_\infty + E_1)}\sigma(t) = 0 \qquad (6.4.15)$$

The shape of strain creep or stress relaxation can be described using a linear solid model, but the linear solid model is not versatile enough to cover various materials completely for general applications. An extension of the linear solid model called Prony series has been brought forth to overcome such inadequacy [Prony].

6.5 Prony Series

The time dependent constitutive equations of a solid viscoelastic material include the historic effect. The stress-strain history, the strain rate, and time of load application on the specimen are all needed to determine the constants in the constitutive equations. The most applied form for these constitutive equations is a Prony model, which comprises a series of relaxation moduli as shown in Fig. 6.5.1. A Prony series extracts valuable information from a uniformly sampled signal and builds a series of damped complex exponentials or sinusoids. It allows for the estimation of amplitude, frequency, phase and damping components of a signal.

If more "spring-dashpot in series" are inserted into the model in Fig. 6.4.1, it forms a Prony model for modulus of relaxation as shown in Fig. 6.5.1. When subjected to a constant strain, in light of Eq. (6.4.6), the following equation can be obtained,

$$\sigma = E_\infty\,\varepsilon_0 + \sum_{i=1}^{N} E_i\,\varepsilon_0\,\exp\left(-\frac{t}{\tau_i}\right) = \left[E_\infty + \sum_{i=1}^{N} E_i\,\exp\left(-\frac{t}{\tau_i}\right)\right]\varepsilon_0 \qquad (6.5.1)$$

and $\quad \tau_i = \left(1 + \dfrac{E_i}{E_\infty}\right)\dfrac{\eta_i}{E_i}$ $\qquad$ (6.5.2)

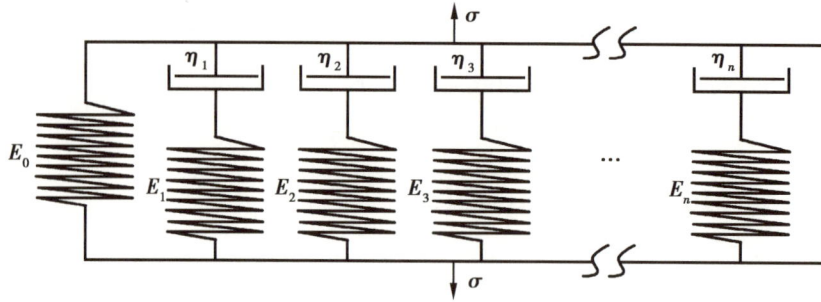

Fig. 6.5.1　Prony Model for Modulus of Relaxation

6.5.1　Prony Series for Modulus of Relaxation Under Infinitesimal Deformation

The Prony series is an array of "spring-dashpot in series" units, called Maxwell elements, in parallel with an extra spring (without a dashpot) also in parallel. Each term of the Prony series can be simply represented by one Maxwell element. Consider a one-dimensional relaxation test. The material is subjected to a sudden-stepped normal strain ($\varepsilon = 0, t \leqslant 0; \varepsilon = \varepsilon_0, t > 0$) that is kept constant over the test duration. The stress measured over time is assumed to be $\sigma(t) = E(t)\varepsilon$. The Prony series for the normal modulus of relaxation is originally given as

$$E(t) = E_\infty + \sum_{i=1}^{N} E_i \left[\exp\left(\dfrac{-t}{T_i}\right)\right]$$ $\qquad$ (6.5.3)

where

E_∞ : Long term normal modulus of elasticity in a totally relaxed state;

E_i : Coefficients of normal modulus of relaxation;

T_i : Characteristic time of normal modulus of relaxation.

The higher the T_i value is, the longer it takes for the stress to relax. Note that E_∞ is an unknown and hard-to-obtain parameter and ∞ in not defined in an engineering application. Define that $E_0 \equiv E(0)$. At $t = 0$, Eq. (6.5.3) reduces to

$$E_0 \equiv E(0) = E_\infty + \sum_{i=1}^{N} E_i$$ $\qquad$ (6.5.4)

It is easier to determine the Prony series from a stress relaxation test than to obtain load-displacement data at different strain rates, though both methods are feasible. Actual parameters can be calculated either using a built-in feature in an FEA software (e.g. Abaqus) or writing one's own computer program. Substituting Eq. (6.5.4) into Eq. (6.5.3) and eliminating E_∞, one has

$$E(t) = E_0 - \sum_{i=1}^{N} E_i \left[1 - \exp\left(-\frac{t}{T_i} \right) \right] = E_0 \left\{ 1 - \sum_{i=1}^{N} p_i \left[1 - \exp\left(-\frac{t}{T_i} \right) \right] \right\}$$

$$\equiv E_0 [1 - p(t)]$$ (6.5.5)

where $\quad p_i = \dfrac{E_i}{E_0}$ (6.5.6)

and $\quad p(t) = \displaystyle\sum_{i=1}^{N} p_i \left[1 - \exp\left(-\frac{t}{T_i} \right) \right]$ (6.5.7)

Thus, $\quad \dfrac{E(t)}{E_0} = 1 - p(t) = 1 - \displaystyle\sum_{i=1}^{N} p_i \left[1 - \exp\left(-\frac{t}{T_i} \right) \right]$ (6.5.8)

and Eq. (6.5.1) becomes

$$\sigma = \left[E_\infty + \sum_{i=1}^{N} E_i \exp\left(-\frac{t}{\tau_i} \right) \right] \varepsilon_0$$ (6.5.9)

A nonlinear least squares regression algorithm can be employed for fitting the load versus time test data with a sequence of different rate loading segments to a Prony series hereditary integral model. The measured data includes ramp loading, relaxation, and unloading stress-strain data.

Example 6.5.1   The following data are listed in the CAMPUS Datasheet by [DuPont] for Zytel 101L (PA6,6): $E_0 = 3.1$ GPa

　　　　　　　　Tensile creep modulus = 1.4 GPa at 1 hours

　　　　　　　　Tensile creep modulus = 0.82 GPa at 1000 h

What would be the 1st-order model (i.e. the linear solid model) based on Prony series for Zytel 101L?

Solution:

Given that $N=1$, the following equation is derived from Eq. (6.5.8):

$$\frac{E(t)}{E_0} = 1 - p(t) = 1 - p_1 \left[1 - \exp\left(-\frac{t}{T_1} \right) \right]$$

At $t = 1$ hour, $\quad \dfrac{1.4}{3.1} = 1 - p_1 \left[1 - \exp\left(-\frac{1}{T_1} \right) \right]$

At $t = 1000$ h, $\quad \dfrac{0.82}{3.1} = 1 - p_1 \left[1 - \exp\left(- \dfrac{1000}{T_1} \right) \right]$

The above two equations can be solved for the following two unknowns:

$p_1 = 0.7355$

and $\quad T_1 = 2.388$ h

Thus, $\dfrac{E(t)}{E_0} = 1 - 0.7355 \left[1 - \exp\left(- \dfrac{t}{2.388} \right) \right]$

6.5.2　Stress-Strain Relationship Based on Prony Series

As the strain is a function of time, the instantaneous stress $\sigma(t)$ of viscoelastic material is also a function of time and it is defined as

$$\sigma(t) = \int_0^t E(t - s)\, d\varepsilon = \int_0^t E(t - s)\, \frac{d\varepsilon}{ds}\, ds \tag{6.5.10}$$

where
$E(t-s)$: Relaxation modulus, in response to an applied strain function $\varepsilon(t)$;
t: Time;
s: Dummy variable of time.

Relaxation modulus $E(t-s)$ is time-dependent and it is used to characterize the material's time-delayed response, while parameter s is the amount of time delay that works like a dummy variable for time in the integration. The viscoelastic material property is "long-term elastic" in the sense that, after having been subjected to a constant strain for a very long time, even after the response settles down to a constant stress. Eventually E becomes E_∞ at $t = \infty$.

The constitutive behavior given by Eq. (6.5.7) can be illustrated by considering a relaxation test, in which a strain $\varepsilon(t)$ can be suddenly applied to a specimen and then held constant up to time t. In other words, $d\varepsilon/dt = 0$ for $t > 0$ while the strain is suddenly applied at $t = 0$. Plugging Eq.(6.5.3) into Eq.(6.5.7), one has

$$\sigma(t) = \int_0^t E_0 [1 - p(t - s)]\, \frac{d\varepsilon}{ds}\, ds \tag{6.5.11}$$

or $\quad \sigma(t) = E_0\, \varepsilon(t) - \displaystyle\int_{0+}^t E_0\, p(t - s)\, \frac{d\varepsilon}{ds}\, ds \tag{6.5.12}$

6.5.3   Prony Series Based on Shear Modulus

Some researchers prefer deviatoric (shear) modulus instead of Young's modulus (E). Normalized coefficients and characteristic times for deviatoric relaxation modulus $G(t)$ in the Prony series have a similar form to Eq. (6.5.1) as

$$G(t) = G_\infty + \sum_{i=1}^{N} G_i \left[\exp\left(-\frac{t}{T_i^g} \right) \right] \qquad (6.5.13)$$

or $\quad \dfrac{G(t)}{G_0} = 1 - \sum_{i=1}^{N} g_i \left[1 - \exp\left(-\frac{t}{T_i^g} \right) \right] \qquad (6.5.14)$

and $\quad g_i = \dfrac{G_i}{G_0} \qquad (6.5.15)$

where

G_∞ : Long term shear modulus of elasticity in totally relaxed state;

G_0 : Initial shear modulus of elasticity;

G_i : Coefficients of shear modulus of relaxation, respectively;

g_i : Normalized coefficients of shear modulus of relaxation, dimensionless;

T_i^g : Characteristic time of deviatoric (shear) modulus of relaxation.

Creep parameters p_i and T_i of Eq. (6.5.1), as well as g_i and T_i^g of Eq. (6.5.13), are to be determined using nonlinear regression. As an example, the deviatoric relaxation modulus of generic PVC are given below:

$$G(t) = 430 + 35.47 \exp\left(-\frac{t}{479.5} \right) + 56.45 \exp\left(-\frac{t}{4663} \right) + 138.2 \exp\left(-\frac{t}{41160} \right) +$$

$$151.1 \exp\left(-\frac{t}{138000} \right) + 44.64 \exp\left(-\frac{t}{1795000} \right) \qquad (6.5.16)$$

of which the units for time and shear modulus of elasticity are second and MPa, respectively.

6.5.4   Prony Series for Modulus of Relaxation under Finite-Strain Deformation

The resulting Prony series, which captures strain rate loading and unloading effects, can produce an excellent fit to a complex loading sequence. To determine the stress state in a viscoelastic material at a given time, the deformation history must be considered. For linear viscoelastic materials, a superposition of hereditary integrals describes the time dependent response. Consider a specimen that is load free prior to the time $t=0$, and then $\sigma(t)$ is applied at $t=0$.

Once the material goes through a finite-strain deformation, the 2nd term on the right hand side of the Eq. (6.5.11) cannot be neglected and it can be transformed using the integration by parts as

$$\sigma(t) = E_0 \, \varepsilon - \int_0^t \frac{dp}{dt} E_0 \, \varepsilon(t - s) \, ds = \sigma_0(t) - \int_0^t \frac{dp}{dt} \sigma_0(t - s) \, ds \qquad (6.5.17)$$

where $\sigma_0(t)$ is the instantaneous normal stress at time t. In the above equation the instantaneous stress, σ_0, applied at time $(t-s)$ results in the stress, σ, at time t. Therefore, in order to create a proper finite-strain formulation, it is necessary to map the stress that existed in the configuration at time $(t-s)$ into another configuration at time t. This form, Eq. (6.5.18), allows a straightforward generalization to a nonlinear elastic deformation composed of the linear elastic term, $\sigma_0 = E_0\varepsilon$, and the nonlinear elastic stress-strain relation $\sigma_0 = \sigma_0(\varepsilon)$. This generalization leads to linear viscoelasticity in the sense that the normal dimensionless stress relaxation function $p(t)$ is independent of the magnitude of the deformation. The stress relaxation modulus can then be obtained from creep data by solving the Laplace convolution integral, or through a numerical solution scheme.

The following is done by means of a mixed "push-forward" transformation with the relative deformation gradient $F_{t-s}(t)$ for the modulus of relaxation under finite-strain deformation in Abaqus as

$$F_{t-s}(t) = \frac{\partial x(t)}{\partial x(t - s)} \qquad (6.5.18)$$

The above deformation gradient is then substituted into Eq. (6.5.16). This will ensure that the stress remains symmetric with the following integral form [Dassault, Abaqus 6.10]:

$$\sigma(t) = \sigma_0(t) - \mathrm{Sym}\left[\int_0^t \frac{dp}{dt} F_t^{-1}(t - s) \; \sigma_0(t - s) F_t(t - s) \; ds\right] \qquad (6.5.19)$$

where

$\sigma(t)$: Deviatoric part of the Kirchhoff stress;

Sym: Symmetric.

6.6   Time-Temperature Superposition Principle

In the linear viscoelastic range, the strain response is proportional to the currently applied stress and independent of other strain levels subjected to existing or other simultaneous applied loads. The total strain estimated additively as described by the following equation in terms of relaxation modulus,

$$\varepsilon = \varepsilon_0 + \Delta\varepsilon_1 + \Delta\varepsilon_2 + \cdots + \Delta\varepsilon_n$$

$$= \frac{\sigma_0}{E_0} + \frac{\Delta\sigma_1}{E(t - t_1)} + \frac{\Delta\sigma_2}{E(t - t_2)} + \cdots + \frac{\Delta\sigma_n}{E(t - t_n)}$$

$$= \frac{\sigma_0}{E_0} + \frac{\sigma_1 - \sigma_0}{E(t - t_1)} + \frac{\sigma_2 - \sigma_1}{E(t - t_2)} + \cdots + \frac{\sigma_n - \sigma_{n-1}}{E(t - t_n)}$$

$$= \frac{\sigma_0}{E_0} + \sum_{i=1}^{N} \frac{\sigma_i - \sigma_{i-1}}{E(t - t_i)} \tag{6.6.1}$$

It can be also expressed in terms of creep compliance as

$$\varepsilon = C_0 \sigma_0 + C(t - t_1)(\sigma_1 - \sigma_0) + C(t - t_2)(\sigma_2 - \sigma_1) + \cdots + C(t - t_n)(\sigma_n - \sigma_{n-1})$$

$$= C_0 \sigma_0 + \sum_{i=1}^{N} C(t - t_i)(\sigma_i - \sigma_{i-1}) \tag{6.6.2}$$

where $E(t - t_i)$ is the relaxation modulus (or modulus of relaxation) and $C(t - t_i)$ is the compliance, which is characterized at a given temperature and initial stress (σ_0). Generally speaking, $C(t - t_i) \approx 1/[E(t - t_i)]$ for uniaxial loadings. As shown by Eq. (6.6.1), the total creep strain results from the superposition of initial strain and the follow-up stepwise strains that are attributed to different load steps denominated by the structural moduli of relaxation (or compliances) step by step. This is called Boltzmann superposition principle.

6.6.1   Time-Temperature Shift for Relaxation Modulus

Temperature has a dramatic influence on the rate of creep, and in practical work it is often necessary to adjust a creep analysis for varying temperature. Consider relaxation modulus E at two different temperatures T_1 and T_2. Given that $T_1 < T_2$, then $E_1(t, T_1) > E_2(t, T_2)$, where t is time. The time-temperature shift may be set up for materials working in the viscoelastic range such that

$$E_1(t, T_1) = E_2\left(\frac{t}{\alpha_T}, T_2\right) \tag{6.6.3}$$

Note that the temperature unit is K. Time denominator α_T is called horizontal time-temperature shift factor, which is a material property as a function of the two temperatures T_1 and T_2. Explicitly, a shift is presented in Fig. 6.6.1. Let T_1 be the selected reference temperature. Then,

$$\text{If } T_2 > T_1 \rightarrow \alpha_T < 1 \tag{6.6.4}$$

$$\text{and   If } T_2 < T_1 \rightarrow \alpha_T > 1 \tag{6.6.5}$$

The time-temperature superposition principle for relaxation modulus based on Williams-Landel-Ferry (WLF) method can be described mathematically as

$$\log(\alpha_T) = \log(t_{\text{reduced}}) - \log(t) \tag{6.6.6}$$

or $\quad \log(t_{\text{reduced}}) = \log(t) - \log(\alpha_T) \tag{6.6.7}$

where

α_T : time-temperature shift factor, depending on the current and reference temperatures;

$t_{\text{reduced}}(K)$: Reduced time at the desired temperature;

$t_{\text{ref}}(K)$: time at the reference temperature, e.g. room temperature.

In other words, relaxation modulus curves for these viscoelastic materials made at different temperatures may be superimposed upon one another by shifts along a logarithmic time scale to give a single master curve at the reference temperature covering a longer time span required for the purpose of design. The master curve is defined as a single curve that has the ample scope of creep behavior at a reference temperature. For the superposition principle to apply, the test sample must be linear viscoelastic under the deformations of interest, and more importantly the material is isotropic and homogeneous such as amorphous polymers.

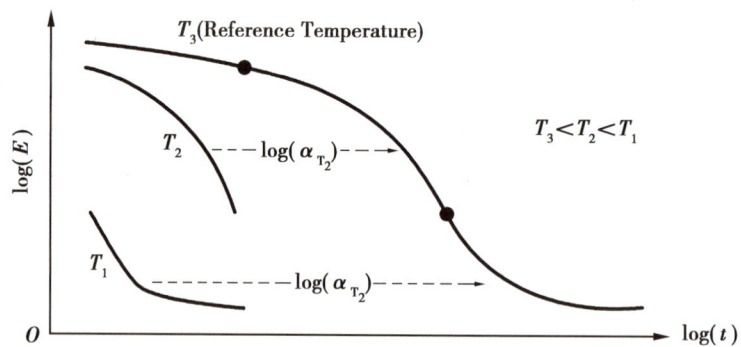

Fig. 6.6.1 Horizontal Time-Temperature Shift for Relaxation Modulus

6.6.2 Time-Temperature Shift for Creep Compliance

The "horizontal time-temperature shift factor" $\alpha_T(T)$ can be also defined as the horizontal shift that is to be applied to a creep compliance curve, i.e. creep (t), measured at an arbitrary temperature T in reference with moving it to the curve measured at a reference temperature (T_{ref}). The time-temperature shift may be set up for materials working in the viscoelastic range such that

$$C_1(t, T_1) = C_2\left(\frac{t}{\alpha_T}, T_2\right) \tag{6.6.8}$$

Again, time denominator α_T is called time-temperature shift factor, which is a function of temperature T. Let T_1 is the selected reference temperature. Then,

$\quad$ If $T_2 > T_1 \rightarrow \alpha_T < 1 \tag{6.6.9}$

and $\quad$ If $T_2 < T_1 \rightarrow \alpha_T > 1 \tag{6.6.10}$

Note that Eqs. (6.6.6) and (6.6.7) are also valid for creep compliance. The creep compliance time duration at the reference temperature is unshifted, while others will be shifted according to the time-temperature shift factor at the operating temperature relative to the reference temperature as shown in Fig. 6.6.2 [Goertzen & Kessler]. Curves representing data obtained at temperatures lower than the reference temperature appear at longer times are to be shifted to the right of the reference curve following Eq. (6.6.7), so they will have to shift to the left when the shift is positive. On the other hand, data obtained at temperatures higher than the reference temperature will have a negative shift, i.e. to shift right. Conversely a master curve for an amorphous polymer measured at a given temperature can be used as the reference to predict curves at different temperatures by applying a shift, i.e. a reverse of the flow arrow in Figs. 6.6.1 and 6.6.2.

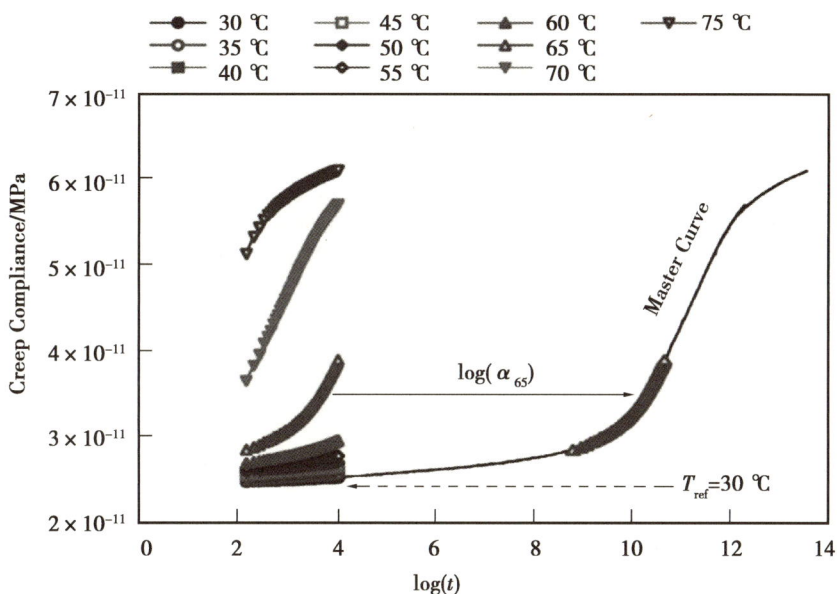

Fig. 6.6.2　Unshifted Creep Compliance Data and Corresponding Master Curve after Horizontal Shifts [Goertzen & Kessler]

6.6.3　Curve Fitting for the Master Curve

It is identified that reasonable continuities between adjacent creep curve segments are feasible only when shifting has been performed for the steady state regions of the involved creep curves. In other words, the creep data in the early period (e.g. up to 1 hour) can be omitted while TTSP is to be applied [Jeon et al.]. The procedure depicted in Fig. 6.6.3 was suggested by [Sihn & Tsai] and it is described as follows:

(a) A general linear least-square model of order m, e.g. $y(x) = a_0 + a_1 x + a_2 x^2 + \cdots + a_m x^m$, is used for fitting the data points at each temperature.

(b) After setting a reference curve at the reference temperature, the data points at an elevated temperature (T_i) are mapped and shifted onto the reference curve.

(c) The shifted data points along with the reference data points are fitted to form a new reference curve. If the new curve is not fitted well enough, the order of the polynomial (m) increases by one until it finds a best fit.

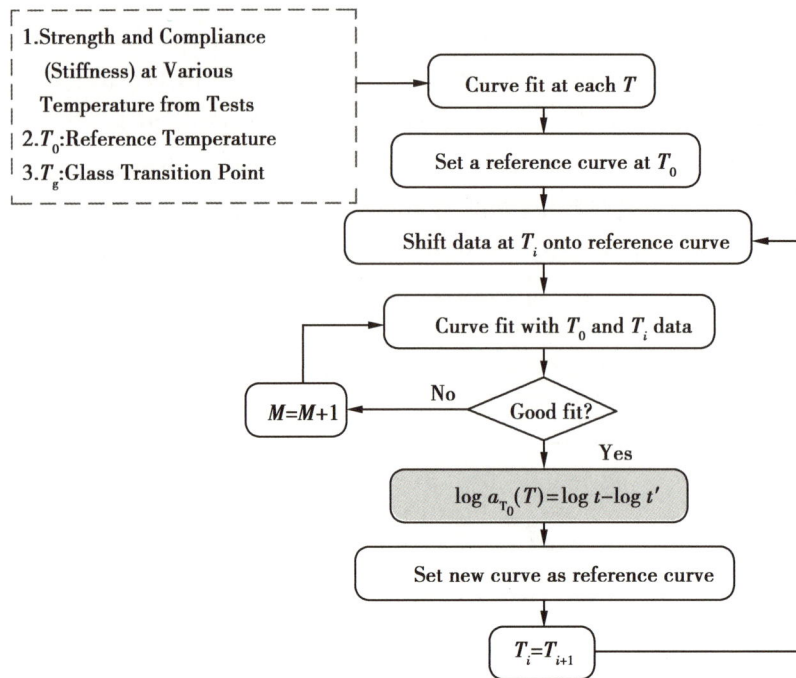

Fig. 6.6.3 Assembling Segmented Creep Test Data at Various Temperature (T_i) for the Master Curve by Curve Fitting [Sihn & Tsai]

6.6.4 Frequency-Temperature Shift for Relaxation Modulus

By the same token, the superposition principle for complex dynamic moduli (normal: $E^* = E + i\,E''$ or shear: $G^* = G + iG''$) at a fixed frequency ω can be obtained as

$$E_1'(\omega, T_1) = E_2'(\omega\,\alpha_T, T_2) \tag{6.6.11}$$

$$G_1'(\omega, T_1) = G_2'(\omega\,\alpha_T, T_2) \tag{6.6.12}$$

$$E_1''(\omega, T_1) = E_2''(\omega\,\alpha_T, T_2) \tag{6.6.13}$$

and $\quad G_1''(\omega, T_1) = G_2''(\omega\,\alpha_T, T_2) \tag{6.6.14}$

Due to edge effects, flow curve tests on polymer melts are not feasible for most molding processes (e.g. compression molding: 1-10 Hz, calendaring: 10-100 Hz, film extrusion: 100-1000 Hz, blow-molding: 100-10000 Hz, and Injection molding: 500-50000 Hz), whose shear rates are way higher than 10 s^{-1} (10 Hz). Dynamical mechanical analysis (DMA) is an experimental technique commonly used to study the frequency and temperature dependence of the mechanical properties of viscoelastic materials. Most applied master curves for frequency sweep functions with such high shear rates are determined at several test temperatures and then shifted with respect to the reference curve according to the TTSP, using the individual horizontal shift factor α_T and vertical shift β_T. Horizontal shifting along the axis of the angular frequency is dominant. The considerably smaller shift in vertical direction is caused mainly by the temperature-dependent density change of the polymer. The shape of the curves remains unchanged while shifted. Frequency sweeps of PS (Polystyrene) melt measured at different discrete temperatures, i.e. 170, 200, 230, and 260 ℃) are shown in Fig. 6.6.4(a), of which each of the measured curve segments covers four decades of the frequency range [Anton Paar]. The resulting "assembled" master curve that covers nine decades of the frequency range is depicted in Fig. 6.6.4(b).

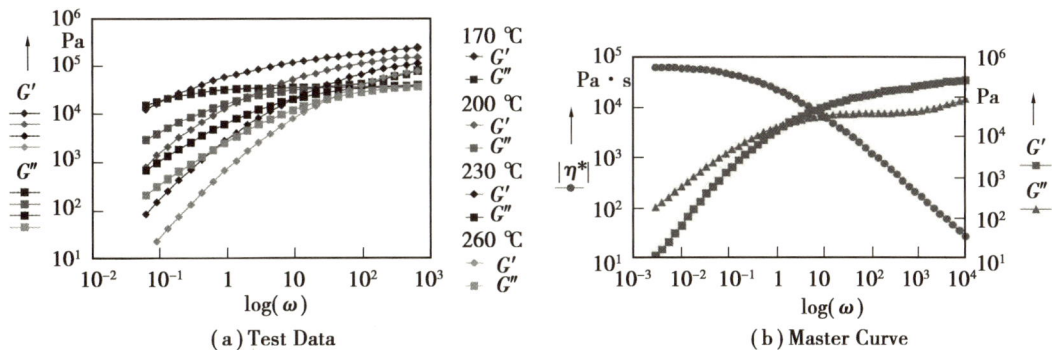

(a) Test Data   (b) Master Curve

Fig. 6.6.4   Frequency Sweeps of Polystyrene Melt at Discrete Temperatures and the Master Curve Based on Time-Temperature Shift Principle [Anton Paar]

6.6.5   Time-Temperature Shift Factor Based on Intrinsic Viscosity

Curves of the instantaneous modulus of viscoelastic materials as a function of time do not change shape as the temperature varies but appear only to shift left or right on the time scale. For simple amorphous materials, lowering the temperature is simply to shift the viscoelastic creep curve, plotted against $\log(t)$, to the right without change in shape. This is equivalent to increasing the relaxation time τ_s, without changing the glassy or rubbery moduli or compliances. Time-temperature superposition is then a procedure that has become important in the field of polymers to observe the dependence upon temperature on the change of viscosity of a polymeric fluid. Shift factor α_T can be determined from the molten polymer during continuous non-Newtonian flow, being regarded as a relative dimensionless viscosity [Hiemenz et al.] at two different temperatures

$$\alpha_T = \frac{\eta_T}{\eta_{T_0}} \tag{6.6.15}$$

where

η_T: Intrinsic viscosity at temperature T;

η_{T_0}: Intrinsic viscosity at reference temperature T_{ref}.

6.6.6 Time-Temperature Shift Factor Based on Thermo-Rheological Models

The impact of temperature on creep of such viscoelastic materials can simply be described by thermo-rheological models. This applies to simple-structured materials such as most amorphous thermoplastics and some rubbers (e.g. IIR), which have few complicating features (e.g. varying crystallinity with respect to temperature change) in their microstructure. The shift factor can be also determined from the following relationship [Hiemenz et al.],

$$\frac{\mathrm{d}\alpha_T}{\mathrm{d}T} = \frac{Q}{K_a} \tag{6.6.16}$$

where

Q(J/mole): Activation energy of the material;

K_a(J/K): Boltzmann constant, $K_a = 1.381 \times 10^{-23}$ J/K or 8.64×10^{-5} eV/K.

Thus, by plotting the shift factor α_T versus the reciprocal of temperature (in K), the slope of the curve can be interpreted as Q/K_b.

When $\log(\alpha_T)$ is plotted against $\log(T)$, it shows a bilinear curve with the separation point at T_g (glass transition point). Horizontal time-temperature shift factor α_T is then expressed using the Arrhenius model [Miyano et al. 2008] as

$$\alpha_T = \exp\left[\frac{E_a}{2.303R}\left(\frac{1}{T_k} - \frac{1}{T_{ref}}\right)\right] \quad \text{when} \quad T < T_g \tag{6.6.17a}$$

$$\text{or} \quad \alpha_T = \exp\left[\frac{E_a}{2.303R}\left(\frac{1}{T_g} - \frac{1}{T_{ref}}\right) + \frac{E'_a}{2.203R}\left(\frac{1}{T_k} - \frac{1}{T_g}\right)\right] \quad \text{when} \quad T > T_g \tag{6.6.17b}$$

where

E_a(J/mole): Activation energy at a temperature above glass transition point T_g;

E'_a(J/mole): Activation energy at a temperature below glass transition point T_g;

T_{ref}(K): Reference temperature;

$R(= 8.314$ J/mole/ ℃): Universal gas constant.

Vertical time-temperature shift factor β_T, which is mainly subjected to the density change with respect to the temperature variation, can be obtained as [Guedes 2014]

$$\text{and} \quad \beta_T = \frac{\rho\, T_k}{\rho_{ref}\, T_{ref}} = \frac{T_k}{T_{ref}}(1 + \alpha\, \Delta T)^3 \tag{6.6.18}$$

where

ρ (kg/m^3): Density at the desired temperature T_k;

$\rho_{ref}(kg/m^3)$: Density at the desired temperature T_{ref} ;

$\alpha(mm/mm)$: Coefficient of linear thermal expansion.

6.6.7   Time-Temperature Shift Factor by Williams-Landel-Ferry Equation

As an approximating alternative for relaxation modulus curves at temperatures near or above the glass temperature, another equation based on the same working principle is to directly use the WLF [Williams, Landel, & Ferry] relationship

$$\log(\alpha_T) = \frac{-c_1(T_k - T_{ref})}{c_2 + (T_k - T_{ref})} \tag{6.6.19}$$

where

α_T : time-temperature shift factor;

c_1 : Dimensionless coefficient, of which the value depends on the reference temperature;

$c_2(K)$: Constant, of which the value depends on the reference temperature.

All the temperatures given in the above equation are up to the K scale, as denoted by T_k. Both constants, c_1 and c_2, depend on the material and glass transition point (T_g). This relationship is approximately valid only in the temperature range between T_g and $T_g + 100$ ℃. Consider the relaxation modulus of a polymer as a special case. When the glass transition temperature (T_g) is chosen to be the reference temperature (T_{ref}), Eq. (6.6.19) fits well for a great variety of polymers with $c_1 = 17.44$ and $c_2 = 51.6$ K according to [Li] [Van Gurp & Palmenm], i.e.

$$\log(\alpha_{shit}) = \frac{-17.44(T_k - T_{ref})}{51.6 + (T_k - T_{ref})} \tag{6.6.20}$$

6.6.8   Concept of Effective Time Theory

Consider the two ends of a test curve from point a to point b. Then, the reduced time at each end can be derived from Eq. (6.6.7) as

$$\log(t_{reduced,a}) = \log(t_a) - \log(\alpha_T) \tag{6.6.21a}$$

i.e. $t_{reduced,b} = 10^{[\log(t_a)-\log(\alpha_T)]}$

and $\log(t_{reduced,b}) = \log(t_b) - \log(\alpha_T) \tag{6.6.21b}$

i.e. $t_{reduced,b} = 10^{[\log(t_b)-\log(\alpha_T)]}$

The effective time duration on the linear real time scale is obtained from Eqs. (6.6.21a) and (6.6.21b) as

$$\Delta t_{\text{reduced}} = t_{\text{reduced},b} - t_{\text{reduced},a} = 10^{[\log(t_b) - \log(\alpha_T)]} - 10^{[\log(t_a) - \log(\alpha_T)]} \qquad (6.6.22)$$

Example 6.6.1   As shown in Fig. 6.6.2, the time-temperature shift factor at 65 ℃ relative to reference temperature 30 ℃ is assumed to be 0.005. How many hours is the effective time equivalent to a one-temperature cycle test at 30 ℃?

Solution:

Following Eq. (6.6.21) and converting the test hours at 65 ℃ to its effective hours at reference temperature 30 ℃, one has the effective time duration

$$\Delta t_{\text{reduced}} = 10^{[\log(t_b) - \log(\alpha_T)]} - 10^{[\log(t_a) - \log(\alpha_T)]}$$

$$\Delta t_{\text{reduced}} = 10^{4.2 - \log(0.005)} - 10^{2 - \log(0.005)} = 3149786 \text{ s} = 0.1816 \text{ day}$$

The original test time duration is

$$\Delta t_{65} = 10^{\log(t_b)} - 10^{\log(t_a)} = 10^{4.2} - 10^2 = 15690 \text{ s} = 36.36 \text{ days}$$

Thus, the efficiency due to time-temperature shift by converting the test curve at 65 ℃ to the corresponding reduced curve at 30 ℃ for this case study by [Goertzen & Kessler] is $\Delta t_{\text{reduced}} / \Delta t_{65} \approx 20$.

6.7   Creep Strengths

Creep may result in two different failure modes, i.e. excessive deformation and fracture. Limiting creep strength and creep rupture strength are defined to counter against these two potential failure modes, respectively. Plastics may creep even at room temperature. As for steels, deformation under stress is plastic rather than elastic at elevated temperatures (e.g. $T > 482$ ℃ for most stainless steels). For service at an elevated temperature, the primary factor to be considered is the strength in the hot state and then the thermal stability that may set the limits of softening, oxidation and embrittlement.

6.7.1   Limiting Creep Strength

Limiting creep strength is defined as the stress level applied in a creep test at a specific temperature until the creep of specimen reaches a certain percentage at the specified time. For example, limiting creep strength of 100 MPa at 1% creep after 100000 hours may be specified for a certain type of bolted-joint for safety operation.

6.7.2 Creep Rupture Strength

At a certain temperature, application of a constant load to a component may produce continuous deformation or creep, which eventually leads to fracture if the load is maintained for a sufficient length of time. A failure resulting from such a condition is referred to as a creep failure or occasionally called a creep stress rupture. The yield point as determined by the short-term tensile test is usually higher than the creep rupture strength. Creep-stress-rupture tests are used to determine the time necessary to produce failure so stress rupture testing is always done until failure. Data of creep stress are plotted log-log as shown in Fig. 6.7.1. A best fit curve is usually obtained at each temperature of interest.

Creep rupture strength (σ_{crs}) is defined as the stress required to initiating a fracture in a creep test within a specified time at a specific temperature. The time duration to reach creep rupture strength is usually taken at 1000 hours (≈ 41.7 days), 10000 hours (≈ 417 days ≈ 13.9 months ≈ 1.14 years), or 100000 hours (≈ 11.4 years).

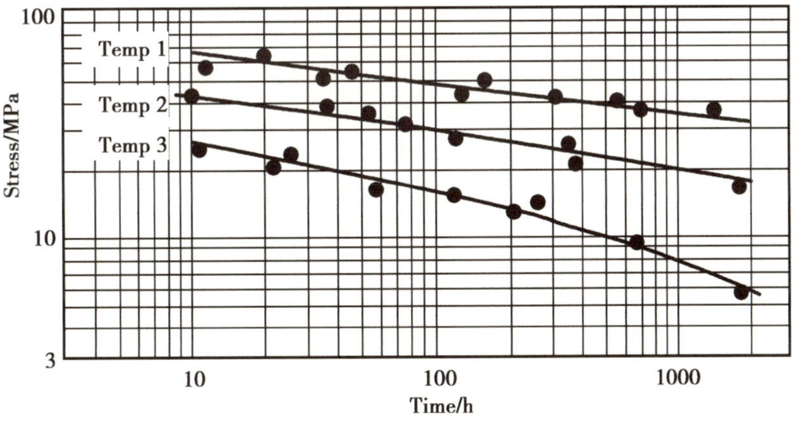

Fig. 6.7.1 Example Creep Rupture Strength as a Function of Time

6.7.3 Creep Life Prediction by Time-Temperature Superposition Principle

Recently an accelerated testing methodology has been established by [Miyano et al. 2006] [Miyano et al. 2008] to show how to apply the time-temperature superposition principle to do the creep life prediction at various temperature levels with the applicable stress ratio. The linear cumulative damage (LCD) law, which resembles the Miner's rule for fatigue, is applicable to the creep rupture strength by the monotonic loading sequence. The linear damage cumulative (LDC) law for creep can be introduced by the same token as Miner's equation for fatigue (Chapter 4). The creep life prediction can be done using the stress- and strain-based criteria, respectively:

$$\sum_{i=1}^{N} \frac{\Delta t_i(\sigma_m, \sigma_a, R, T)}{t_{crs}(\sigma_m, \sigma_a, R, T)} = 1 \tag{6.7.1}$$

or $\quad \displaystyle\sum_{i=1}^{N} \frac{\Delta t_i(\varepsilon_m, \varepsilon_a, R, T)}{t_{crs}(\varepsilon_m, \varepsilon_a, R, T)} = 1$ (6.7.2)

Linear viscoelasticity in terms of strain creep subjected to stress load $\sigma(t)$, described by Eq. (6.2.2), can be rewritten as:

or $\quad \varepsilon(t) = C_o\,\sigma(t) + C_1\displaystyle\int_{0^+}^{t}\left(\frac{t-s}{s_u}\right)^n \frac{\mathrm{d}\sigma(s)}{\mathrm{d}s}\mathrm{d}s$ (6.7.3)

where

$C_o(\mathrm{MPa}^{-1})$: Instantaneous compliance of relaxation;

$C_1(\mathrm{MPa}^{-1})$: Compliance of relaxation for $t>0$;

$\sigma(t)(\mathrm{MPa})$: Applied stress in time history;

n: Exponent;

t: Time;

s: Dummy variable of time for carrying out the integration;

s_u: time unit, e.g. second, minute, hour, day, etc.; thus, $(t-s)/s_u$ is dimensionless time.

The effectiveness of time-temperature superposition principle (TTSP) has been tested out using carbon fiber-reinforced epoxy [Miyano et al. 2006] and its validity is shown in Fig. 6.7.2. Among various theories with regard to the curve-fitting of the creep-rupture behavior, including the maximum strain method, maximum stress method, and distortional strain energy method and modified distortional strain energy method [Reiner & Weissenberg], the maximum strain criterion turns out to be the most fit to the time-temperature superposition principle. The total work done by the applied stress up to time t is to be obtained from integrating the stress with respect to the strain rate,

$$W(t) = \int_0^t \sigma(s)\,\frac{\partial\varepsilon(s)}{\partial s}\mathrm{d}s$$ (6.7.4)

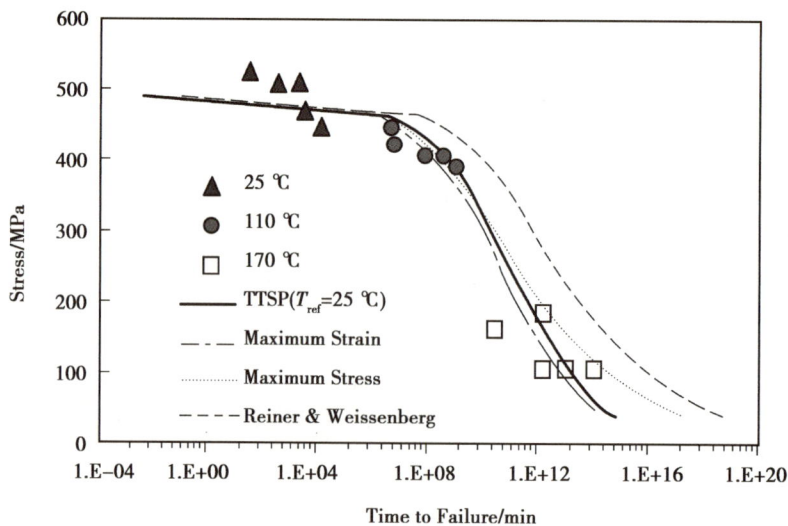

Fig. 6.7.2 **Validation of Creep Life Prediction of Twill-Woven *Ep/CF* (135/UT500) Composite Using Time-Temperature Superposition Principle via Various Criteria** [Miyano et al.]

The maximum strain criterion means that the strain has to be smaller than instantaneous rupture stress scaled by the instantaneous compliance, i.e.

$$\varepsilon(t) \leqslant C_{o}\, \sigma_{R} \tag{6.7.5}$$

The failure criteria for viscoelastic materials under creep due to constant stress and constant stress rate based on the maximum strain method [Guedes] are, respectively

$$\left(\frac{t_{f}}{s_{u}}\right)^{n} = \frac{C_{o}}{C_{1}}\left(\frac{\sigma_{R}}{Rt_{f}} - 1\right) \quad \text{(Constant stress)} \tag{6.7.6}$$

and $\quad \left(\frac{t_{f}}{s_{u}}\right)^{n} = (n + 1)\frac{C_{o}}{C_{1}}\left(\frac{\sigma_{R}}{Rt_{f}} - 1\right) \quad \text{(Constant stress rate)} \tag{6.7.7}$

of which σ_{R} is the instant rupture strength and R is the stress ratio under fatigue cycling. For reference, the material properties of two composites are listed as follows [Miyano et al. 2006] [Ren]:

Material	$T/℃$	s_{u}	C_{o}/MPa^{-1}	C_{1}/MPa^{-1}	n	σ_{R}/MPa
Epoxy/CF (135/UT500)	25	1 min	2.6×10^{-5}	2.55×10^{-8}	0.281	490
Urethane/GF	23	1 hour	1.06×10^{-4}	7.35×10^{-6}	0.196	120

6.7.4   Creep Fatigue Life Prediction by Time-Temperature Superposition Principle

It is feasible to calculate the creep strength master curve from the constant strain rate (CSR) strength master curve determined from relatively easy tests under CSR loading with a fixed strain rate at several elevated temperatures. The procedure is outlined as follows:

(1) Establish a master curve of the modulus at a reference temperature, as described in Section 6.6.

(2) Establish master curves of creep rupture strength at the desired constant strain rate.

(3) Establish the master curves of fatigue strength of the creep material (e.g. polymeric composites) at zero stress ratio. They are determined by conducting the fatigue tests at several stress levels, a single frequency, a single stress ratio (zero stress ratio), and several elevated temperatures.

(4) The creep rupture strength master curve at the desired constant strain rate is regarded as the fatigue strength master curve at one reversal, i.e. $N_{f} = 1/2$. The limiting creep strength applies, if the desired failure mode is the amount of creep such as a loosened bolted-joint.

(5) Finally, the creep and fatigue strengths at the desired frequency, stress ratio and temperature are obtained from the combined master curves of creep rupture strength and

fatigue strength at zero stress ratio.

The above procedure is applicable to most viscoelastic materials and their related composites, except some materials, such as PEEK/GF (high modulus pitched-based carbon fibers), in which the matrix crystallizes when loaded and the viscoelastic behaviors of the high modulus pitch-based carbon fibers [Miyano et al. 2008].

6.8　Creep Mechanisms and Creep Rates

The steady-state creep rate of the secondary stage (Fig. 6.2.2) is the major engineering design parameter of concern. Once the homologous temperature exceeds 50% the creep plays an important role in the life prediction of a product.

6.8.1　General Creep Rate Due to Dislocation

Creep of a material increases nonlinearly with an increasing stress and increasing temperature. Creep mechanisms involve dislocation and diffusional flow, but are primarily controlled by dislocation at a high-stressed level. Anelasticity is the material property of a solid that varies with respect to the strain (stress) and strain (stress) rate in addition to temperature. For an anelastic deformation, the following creep strain rate in the steady state at a certain temperature has been traditionally synthesized to include the time factor as

$$\frac{\mathrm{d}\varepsilon_{\mathrm{creep}}}{\mathrm{d}t} = A \, \sigma^n \, t^m \exp\left(\frac{-Q}{R \, T_k}\right) \tag{6.8.1}$$

where

$\varepsilon_{\mathrm{creep}}$: Uniaxial equivalent creep strain;

$A(\mathrm{MPa}^{-n} \, \mathrm{s}^{m-1})$: Constant;

$\sigma(\mathrm{MPa})$: Equivalent stress, applied;

n : Stress exponent, ranging roughly from 4 to 6;

m : Time exponent;

$Q(\mathrm{J/mole})$: Activation energy of the material creep mechanism;

$R(= 8.314 \, \mathrm{J/mole/\,℃})$: Universal gas constant;

$T_k(\mathrm{K})$: Temperature in Kelvin and $T_k = T + 273$;

$T(\mathrm{℃})$: Temperature in Celsius.

The above regression model is valid for creep due to dislocation of material subjected to stresses in a self-diffusion process. It means that it need possess enough energy (thermal energy) to break the bonds, squeeze through its neighbors, and settle down in a vacancy site. It signifies that for reactants to get dislocated by creep into another structure, they must first acquire a minimum amount of energy, called the activation energy Q. If the exponent of the stress exponent n is large (e.g. $n>10$), a threshold stress component may be introduced in order to generalize Eq. (6.8.1) ,

$$\frac{d\varepsilon_{creep}}{dt} = A\ (\sigma - \sigma_{th})^n\ t^m\ \exp\left(\frac{-Q}{RT_k}\right) \tag{6.8.2}$$

of which σ_{th} (MPa) is the threshold stress (an equivalent stress). No creep, if $\sigma < \sigma_{th}$. Eq. (6.8.2) is sometimes rewritten as

$$\frac{d\varepsilon_{creep}}{dt} = A\left(\frac{\sigma - \sigma_{th}}{E}\right)^n\ t^m - \exp\left(\frac{-Q}{RT_k}\right) \tag{6.8.3}$$

of which E is the modulus of elasticity (Young's modulus) that is also a temperature-dependent variable. Modulus E has to be converted to the same unit as σ and σ_{th}. Both Eqs. (6.8.2) and (6.8.3) have been in use for modeling the creep behavior.

6.8.2   Larson-Miller Parameters

Assume the material is under a uniaxial steady-state viscoelastic deformation. When the creep is not an explicit function of time, Eq. (6.8.1) reduces to

$$\frac{d\varepsilon_{creep}}{dt} = A\ \sigma^n\ \exp\left(\frac{-Q}{RT_k}\right) \tag{6.8.4}$$

Example 6.8.1   Steady-state creep data measured for a stainless steel experimentally at a stress level of 70 MPa are given as follows:

$$\frac{d\varepsilon_{creep}}{dt} = 10^{-5} \text{ at } T_k = 977 \text{ K} \tag{a}$$

and $\quad \dfrac{d\varepsilon_{creep}}{dt} = 2.5 \times 10^{-3} \text{ at } T_k = 1089 \text{ K} \tag{b}$

For a given value of the stress exponent, $n = 7.0$, what is the steady-state creep rate at 977 ℃ when it is loaded at a stress level of 50 MPa.

Solution:

Substituting Eqs. (a) and (b) into Eq. (6.8.4) leads to

$$10^{-5} = A \ (70)^7 \ \exp\left(-\frac{Q}{977 \ R}\right)$$

and $\quad 2.5 \times 10^{-3} = A \ (70)^7 \ \exp\left(\frac{-Q}{1089 \ R}\right)$

The above two equations can be solved for two unknowns A and (Q/R) as

$$A = 2.512 \times 10^5$$

and $\quad \dfrac{Q}{R} = 52452$

Thus, at $T_k = (977+273) \, \text{K} = 1250 \, \text{K}$ and $\sigma = 50$ MPa. Eq. (6.8.4) yields

$$\frac{\mathrm{d}\varepsilon_{\text{creep}}}{\mathrm{d}t} = A \ (50)^7 \ \exp\left(-\frac{Q}{1250R}\right) = 0.1173 \ \text{s}^{-1}$$

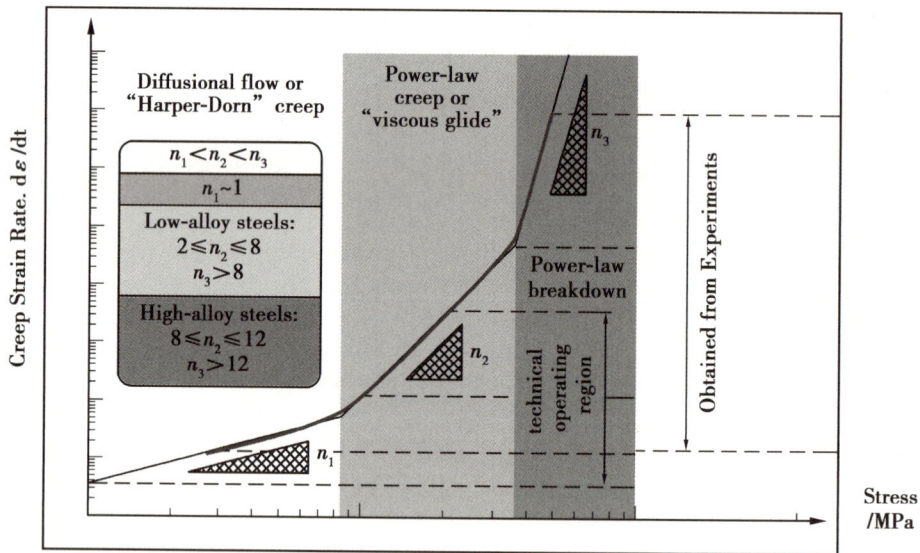

Fig. 6.8.1   Schematic Illustration of Creep Rate （$\mathrm{d}\varepsilon_{\text{creep}}/\mathrm{d}t$） versus Flow Stress σ for Alloy Steels

The physical meaning of "exponent n" is demonstrated in Fig. 6.8.1: (n_1-linear diffusional flow creep, n_2-power law creep, and n_3-power law breakdown). The thick line in Fig. 6.8.1 is obtained from experiments, while both extreme ends are "educated" extrapolations. Taking a natural log on both sides of Eq. (6.8.4) with a finite-deformation approximation to the uniaxial creep strain yields

$$\ln \frac{\Delta L}{\Delta t} = \ln(A) + n \ln(\sigma) - \frac{Q}{R \, T_k} \tag{6.8.5}$$

i.e. $\dfrac{Q}{R} = T_k \left[\ln\left(\dfrac{\Delta t}{\Delta L}\right) + \ln(A) + n \ln(\sigma) \right]$

$= T_k \left[\ln(\Delta t) + n \ln(\sigma) + \ln\left(\dfrac{A}{\Delta L}\right) \right]$

$= T_k \left[\ln\Delta(t) + n \ln(\sigma) + C \right]$ (6.8.6)

of which $C = \ln(A/\Delta L)$ and it is a constant. At a given constant stress level, the Larson-Miller parameter is then defined as

$P_{LM} = LMP = T_k \left[\ln(\Delta t) + C \right]$ (6.8.7)

i.e. $\Delta t = \exp\left(\dfrac{P_{LM}}{T_k - C}\right)$ (6.8.8)

where

C: Material constant, ranging from 20 to 22 for most metals;

P_{LM} or LMP: Larson-Miller parameter [Larson & Miller].

In other words, the natural log of creep rupture time plus a constant multiplied by the temperature (K) remains constant at a given creep rupture stress (σ_{crs}) level. The following polynomial can be entered as a polynomial function of stress as follows:

$P_{LM} = \displaystyle\sum_{n=0}^{N} P_n \sigma^n = P_0 + P_1 \sigma + P_2 \sigma^2 + P_3 \sigma^3 + \cdots + P_N \sigma^N$ (6.8.9)

The damage due to creep is then taken as the inverse of the creep life as follows:

$D_{creep} = P_{LM}^{-1}$ (6.8.10)

The total damage D is then the additive combination of creep damage D_{creep} and fatigue damage $D_{fatigue}$ (detailed in Chapter 4) as

$D = D_{fatigue} + D_{creep}$ (6.8.11)

6.8.3   Hyperbolic Power Law

It is also a matter of common practice for reliability study of solders, as well as implemented in Abaqus, that the creep strain rate of a material in a steady state of dislocation creep can be written as a hyperbolic power law

$\dfrac{d\varepsilon_{creep}}{dt} = A \left[\sin h(B\sigma)^n \right] \exp\left(-\dfrac{Q}{R T_k} \right)$ (6.8.12)

of which B is a constant and $\sin h$ is a hyperbolic sine. In the case of the small stress that $(B\sigma) \leqslant 0.39$, Eq. (6.8.8) reduces to Eq. (6.8.5) within $a \pm 1\%$ error.

6.8.4 Stress Relaxation via Creep

Under a fixed-strain condition such as a part clamped in a bolted joint, the total strain (ε_T) is a combination of elastic strain (ε_E) and creep strain (ε_{creep}),

$$\varepsilon_T = \varepsilon_E + \varepsilon_{creep} \tag{6.8.13}$$

Note that plastic and thermal strains are not considered here. In order to calculate the relaxed stress for a given time with a fixed strain, such as the need for knowing the bolt-joint relaxation, the stress has to be expressed as a function of time. At a fixed total displacement, the creep strain rate can be derived by taking a differentiation with respect to time as

$$0 = \frac{d\varepsilon_E}{dt} + \frac{d\varepsilon_{creep}}{dt} \tag{6.8.14}$$

The elastic stress-strain relationship is

$$\sigma = E_0 \, \varepsilon_E \tag{6.8.15}$$

Thus, $$\frac{d\varepsilon_E}{dt} = E_0^{-1} \left[\frac{d\sigma(t)}{dt} \right] \tag{6.8.16}$$

Substituting Eqs. (6.8.1) and (6.8.16) into Eq. (6.8.14), one has

$$E_0^{-1} \frac{d\sigma(t)}{dt} + A \, \sigma^n \, t^m \, \exp\left(\frac{-Q}{R \, T_k} \right) = 0 \tag{6.8.17}$$

Given that Q, R and T_k don't vary with respect to time, the nonlinear ordinary differential equation given above has a closed-form solution for $\sigma(t)$ as

$$\sigma(t) = \left\{ E_0 \, A \, \frac{n-1}{m+1} \exp\left[\frac{-Q}{RT_k} \right] t^{m+1} + C_0 \tan(t) \right\}^{-\frac{1}{n-1}} \tag{6.8.18}$$

of which C_0 is a constant that can be obtained using the initial condition that $\sigma(0) = \sigma_0$. Substituting the initial condition into Eq. (6.8.18) yields the instantaneous stress level,

$$\sigma(t) = \left\{ E_0 \, A \, \frac{n-1}{m+1} \exp\left[\frac{-Q}{RT_k} \right] t^{m+1} + \sigma_0 \exp[-n \ln(\sigma_0)] \right\} \tag{6.8.19}$$

The related creep strain can be calculated by substituting the above equation back into Eq. (6.8.10),

$$\varepsilon_{\text{creep}} = \frac{\sigma_0}{E_0} - \frac{\sigma(t)}{E_0} = \frac{\sigma_0 - \sigma(t)}{E_0} \tag{6.8.20}$$

Example 6.8.2   Steel bolts in a steam-pipe flange are so tightened that the initial tensile stress is $\sigma_0 = 200$ MPa at the working temperature of 525 ℃. The length of the bolts remains fixed in service. At 525 ℃, the steady-state creep strain rate of the steel follows the following equation: $d\varepsilon/dt = 3 \times 10^{-18} \sigma^4$ (in s^{-1} and MPa) and the initial elastic modulus $E_0 = 170$ GPa. What are the stresses in the bolts after 10000-hour and 100000-hour operations under the same working temperature? What is the creep strain after 100000-hour operation?

Solution:

By Eq. (6.8.15), after 10000-hour operation,

$$\sigma(10000) = \left\{ E_0 A \left[\frac{n-1}{m+1} \right] \exp\left[-\frac{Q}{RT_k} \right] t^{m+1} + \sigma_0 \exp[-n \ln(\sigma_0)] \right\}^{-\frac{1}{n-1}}$$

$$= \left\{ 170000 \times 3 \times 10^{-18} \times \frac{4-1}{1} \exp(0) \times 10000^1 + 200 \exp[-4 \ln(200)] \right\}^{-\frac{1}{3}}$$

$$= 192.45 \text{ MPa}$$

By the same token, after 100000-hour operation, $\sigma(100000) = 153.2$ MPa

Thus, $\varepsilon_{\text{creep}}(10000) = \dfrac{\sigma_0 - 10000\sigma}{E_0} = 0.00444\%$ (Note that 10000 hours = 1.14 year)

and $\varepsilon_{\text{creep}}(100000) = \dfrac{\sigma_0 - 100000\sigma}{E_0} = 0.0275\%$

6.8.5   Creep under Multiaxial Loading

Assume that σ_1, σ_2, and σ_3 are the three principal stresses loaded at the point of concern. Based on von Mises equivalent stress, i.e. the effective stress (flow stress)

$$\sigma_{\text{eff}} = \left\{ \frac{1}{2} \left[(\sigma_1 - \sigma_2)^2 + (\sigma_2 - \sigma_3)^2 + (\sigma_3 - \sigma_1)^2 \right] \right\}^{\frac{1}{2}} \tag{6.8.21}$$

Similarly, the equivalent von Mises equivalent strain is

$$\varepsilon_{\text{eff}} = \left\{ \frac{1}{2} \left[(\varepsilon_1 - \varepsilon_2)^2 + (\varepsilon_2 - \varepsilon_3)^2 + (\varepsilon_3 - \varepsilon_1)^2 \right] \right\}^{\frac{1}{2}} \tag{6.8.22}$$

The new apparent Young's modulus is then $\sigma_{\text{eff}}/\varepsilon_{\text{eff}}$. Taking a differential element of each principal strain, one has

$$d\varepsilon_1 = \frac{d\varepsilon_{\text{eff}}}{\sigma_{\text{eff}}} \left[\sigma_1 - \frac{1}{2}(\sigma_2 + \sigma_3) \right] \tag{6.8.23}$$

$$d\varepsilon_2 = \frac{d\varepsilon_{\text{eff}}}{\sigma_{\text{eff}}} \left[\sigma_2 - \frac{1}{2}(\sigma_3 + \sigma_1) \right] \tag{6.8.24}$$

$$\text{and} \quad d\varepsilon_3 = \frac{d\varepsilon_{\text{eff}}}{\sigma_{\text{eff}}} \left[\sigma_3 - \frac{1}{2}(\sigma_1 + \sigma_2) \right] \tag{6.8.25}$$

of which creep undergoes such a plastic deformation that Poisson ratio $\nu = 1/2$ appears. Dividing each of the three equations by dt, one gets the corresponding three creep-rates in the principal directions,

$$\frac{d\varepsilon_1}{dt} = \frac{d\varepsilon_{\text{eff}}/dt}{\sigma_{\text{eff}}} \left[\sigma_1 - \frac{1}{2}(\sigma_2 + \sigma_3) \right] \tag{6.8.26}$$

$$\frac{d\varepsilon_2}{dt} = \frac{d\varepsilon_{\text{eff}}/dt}{\sigma_{\text{eff}}} \left[\sigma_2 - \frac{1}{2}(\sigma_3 + \sigma_1) \right] \tag{6.8.27}$$

$$\text{and} \quad \frac{d\varepsilon_3}{dt} = \frac{d\varepsilon_{\text{eff}}/dt}{\sigma_{\text{eff}}} \left[\sigma_3 - \frac{1}{2}(\sigma_1 + \sigma_2) \right] \tag{6.8.28}$$

Thus, the multiaxial effective creep strain rate $(d\varepsilon_{\text{eff}}/dt)$, can be converted from an uniaxial test, which is redeemed as a deformation along the first principal axis as

$$\frac{d\varepsilon_{\text{eff}}}{dt} = \left[\frac{\sigma_{\text{eff}}}{\sigma_1 - \frac{1}{2}(\sigma_2 + \sigma_3)} \right] \frac{d\varepsilon_1}{dt} \tag{6.8.29}$$

Note that σ_2 and σ_3 exist even for a uniaxial test. Assume that the same format of Eq. (6.8.4) holds for multiaxial effective strain creep rate. Then

$$\frac{d\varepsilon_{\text{eff,creep}}}{dt} = A\, \sigma_{\text{eff}}^n \exp\left(-\frac{Q}{RT_k} \right) \tag{6.8.30}$$

The above equation shows how the onset of creep occurs regardless of individual principal stress levels. Substituting Eq. (6.8.30) back into Eqs. (6.8.26)-(6.8.28) yields the three equations of the creep rates of the three principal strains in response to the applied principal stresses,

$$\frac{d\varepsilon_{1,\text{creep}}}{dt} = A\,\sigma_{\text{eff}}^{n-1}\left[\sigma_1 - \frac{1}{2}\,(\sigma_2 + \sigma_3)\right]\exp\!\left(\frac{-Q}{RT_k}\right) \tag{6.8.31}$$

$$\frac{d\varepsilon_{2,\text{creep}}}{dt} = A\,\sigma_{\text{eff}}^{n-1}\left[\sigma_2 - \frac{1}{2}\,(\sigma_3 + \sigma_1)\right]\exp\!\left(\frac{-Q}{RT_k}\right) \tag{6.8.32}$$

and $$\frac{d\varepsilon_{3,\text{creep}}}{dt} = A\,\sigma_{\text{eff}}^{n-1}\left[\sigma_3 - \frac{1}{2}\,(\sigma_1 + \sigma_2)\right]\exp\!\left(\frac{-Q}{RT_k}\right) \tag{6.8.33}$$

6.8.6   Creep by Diffusion of Atoms

Diffusion creep refers to the deformation of crystalline solids by diffusing vacancies through the crystal lattice via plastic deformations. It occurs usually at high homologous temperatures and its creep rate is so sensitive to temperature that the creep activation energy correlates well with self-diffusion activation energy for a variety of materials, especially metals. The mechanism also depends very much on stress. For example, defective impurities in the vacancies may move through the crystal structure by stresses as being diffused in the crystal lattice effectively. Generally speaking, the existence of lobate grain boundaries is an evidence of diffusion creep. Another general equation of strain rate as a function of temperature, stress, and diffusion parameters is given as follows:

$$\frac{d\varepsilon_{\text{creep}}}{dt} = \frac{C\sigma^n}{d^b}\exp\!\left(\frac{-Q}{RT_k}\right) \tag{6.8.34}$$

where
C: Constant, depending on the type of creep mechanism;
d: Grain size of the material;
n: Exponent;
b: Exponent;
$K(\text{J}/\text{K})$: Boltzmann's constant, $K = 1.381\times10^{-23}\,\text{J}/\text{K}$.

6.8.6.1   Lattice Distorted

When atoms diffusion through the lattice distortion causing grains to elongate along the stress direction, the influence of the grain size is more than the stress. Eq. (6.8.34) reduces to

$$\frac{d\varepsilon_{\text{creep}}}{dt} = A\,\sigma\,d^{-2}\exp\!\left(\frac{-Q_L}{KT_k}\right) \tag{6.8.35}$$

6.8.6.2　Grain Boundary Distorted

When atoms diffusion through the grain boundary dislocation causing grains to elongate along the stress direction, the dependence of creep on the grain size is profound and Eq. (6.8.29) becomes

$$\frac{d\varepsilon_{creep}}{dt} = A\,\sigma\,d^{-3}\exp\!\left(\frac{-Q_G}{KT_k}\right) \tag{6.8.36}$$

of which Q_G(J/mole) is the activation energy of the creep due to atoms diffusion through the grain boundary and usually $Q_G < Q_L$.

6.8.6.3　Both Lattice and Grain Boundaries Distorted

A creep may consist of both lattice and grain boundary dislocations. The following equation has been used for the creep material model for evaluating cowl lip, which is made of copper, at elevated temperatures [Arya]:

$$\frac{d\varepsilon_{creep}}{dt} = A\!\left(\frac{\sigma}{E}\right)^{n} t^{m-1}\!\left[\exp\!\left(\frac{-Q_L}{KT_k}\right) + X\,\exp\!\left(\frac{-Q_G}{KT_k}\right)\right] \tag{6.8.37}$$

where

E(GPa): Young's modus, e.g. $E = 127.6 - 21.82\,T - 0.1517\,T^2$ GPa for copper;

α(μm/m): Coefficient of thermal expansion, e.g. $\alpha = 15.9 + 0.00278\,T$ μm/m for copper;

Q_L: Activation energy (lattice distortion), e.g. $Q_L = 2\times10^5$ J/mole for copper;

Q_G: Activation energy (grain boundary dislocation), e.g. $Q_G = 1.2\times10^5$ J/mole for copper;

A (sec^{-1}): Constant, e.g. $A = 3\times10^{24}$ s^{-1} for copper;

n: Exponent, e.g. $n = 5.0$ for copper;

m: Exponent, e.g. $m = 0.35$ for copper;

X: Constant, e.g. $X = 1.5\times10^{-5}$ for copper.

6.8.7　Creep of Concrete

Concrete creeps because of the calcium silicate hydrates (C-S-H) in the hardened Portland cement paste. It exhibits short-term (multi-month) hydration and long-term (multi-year) settling of C-S-H in the cement paste. The phenomenon is totally different from creep of metals and plastics.

6.9　Isochronous Stress-Strain Curves with Creep

Creep rupture strength tests are generally conducted over a series of loads ranging from those causing rupture in a few minutes to those requiring months or even years. By contrast, a tensile strength test is completed in mini-seconds with little time to develop the creep phenomenon. Typical creep rupture strength is presented in terms of a fraction of ultimate strength as a function of stress and time, Fig. 6.9.1. Once a potential mechanical failure is complicated by creep, the strain increment at time t is assumed to be a function of the loading time history and time. For a single-stepped creep test with stress amplitude σ, time-dependent creep strain ε_{creep} is then given by

$$\varepsilon_{creep} = \sum_{i=1}^{N} K_i(t)\sigma^{n_i} \tag{6.9.1}$$

The above equation can be used to generate an isochronous stress-strain curve with respect to both time and stress at certain temperature level. The exponent of Eq. (6.9.1), i.e. n_i, may be a real number instead of integers exactly. If n_i's are integers, Eq. (6.9.1) becomes Findley equation [Findley et al.], i.e.

$$\varepsilon_{creep} = \varepsilon_\sigma + f(\sigma, T)t^{m(\sigma,T)} \tag{6.9.2}$$

of which ε_σ is the instantaneous strain as a function of stress only. Note that $f(\sigma, T)$ and m are material constants as a function of stress and temperature. A simplified model derived from Eq. (6.9.2) is called Nutting equation, i.e.

$$\varepsilon_{creep} = K(T)\sigma\, t^{m(T)} \tag{6.9.3}$$

The above equation has been proven to be effective in modeling linear relaxation behavior of amorphous polymers at temperatures below T_g (glass transition temperature). The relationship among stress, strain and time described by Eq. (6.9.3) is demonstrated in Fig. 6.9.1. Isochronous, isometric, and creep curves are defined accordingly:

(a) Isochronous curves: Stress versus strain.
(b) Isometric curves: Stress versus time.
(c) Creep curves: Strain versus time.

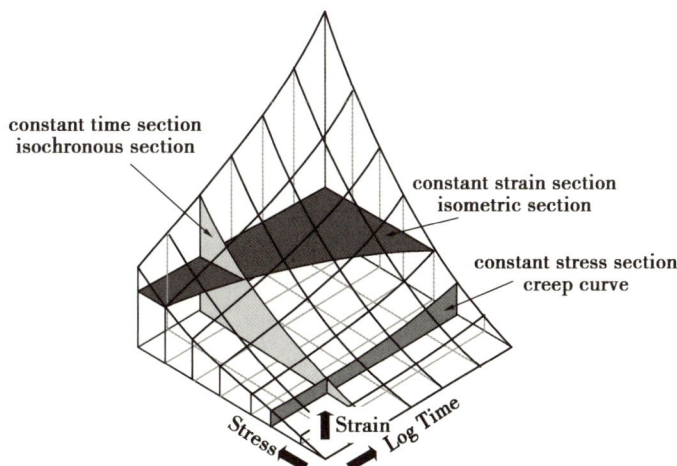

Fig. 6.9.1　Schematic Creep Rupture Strength as a Function of Strain, Stress, and Time. Ultimate Strength is Measured by Percentage of Ultimate Strength [ASTM D2990-01]

Creep of most plastics behaves linearly under a stress level at room temperature and quite nonlinearly once above that stress level, especially accelerated rapidly at elevated temperatures. As an example, a urethane mat reinforced with continuous glass fibers with a relative humidity of 50%, which has been extensively tested by US Department of Energy-Oak Ridge National Laboratory, exhibits a linear relaxation equation at room temperature subjected to one certain stress level only [Corum et al.] as follows:

$$\varepsilon_{creep} = 0.000735 \, \sigma \, t^{0.196} \quad (\sigma < 98 \text{ MPa for Urethane}) \tag{6.9.4}$$

of which the units for t and σ are hours and MPa, respectively. With multiple time durations and stress levels, nonlinear effects prevail as revealed by [Corum et al.],

$$\varepsilon_{creep} = (5.033 \times 10^{-9} + 7.353 \times 10^{-12} \, t^{0.196}) \sigma + 3.971 \times 10^{-26} \sigma^{3.589} \tag{6.9.5}$$

An individual isochronous stress-strain curve generated by the above equation at a given time and a given temperature can be used to approximate elastoplastic analysis for predicting creep deformations, especially convenient for finite element analyses.

6.10　Creep Fatigue

Creep is of great concern to engineers and metallurgists when evaluating components that operate at elevated and high temperatures under high strains (stresses) at a prolonged duration [Chrzanowski]. Application and environmental parameters, such as hardware temperatures and gas pressures, thermally induced stresses, uneven loading, flange distortion, and increased vibrations in motion, demand innovative creep- and/or fatigue-related solutions to ensure optimal performance of the thermal management systems. Creep fatigue problems drawing great attentions are given as follows:

(A) Plastics-based sensors and actuators: Most plastics creep even works at room temperatures. Creep fatigue of plastics due to thermomechanical loads including on-vehicle vibration and self-hysteretic heating have been observed.

(B) Semiconductors: Wafer level chip scale package has become a norm for electronic modules in the electric vehicles and hand-held devices. Solder joints subjected to thermal loads and vehicle vibration is the package reliability of concern. The working temperatures ranging from −40-125 ℃ are demanded by JESD22-A104D from JEDEC (Joint Electronic Devices Engineering Council).

(C) Compressor wheels: Aluminum alloy compressor wheels often fail by casing rubbing due to creep dilation at elevated temperatures, or by cracking due to the accumulation of cyclic creep-fatigue damage.

(D) Exhaust manifolds: Check if the material transformations (e.g. oxidation) occur. The creep-fatigue damage envelope in terms of the creep damage and fatigue damage coordinates that define the onset of cracking according to the material properties.

(E) Gas turbine blades: The endurance of components in high temperature environments where fatigue damage mechanisms, creep damage mechanisms, material transformations (e.g. oxidation) interact to reduce component life significantly.

Nevertheless, creep may or may not constitute a failure mode. For example, moderate creep in fibrous composites is mostly welcomed because it relieves tensile stresses that might otherwise lead to cracking between fibers and matrix.

6.10.1 Creep and Relaxation Fatigue Tests

An automotive engineer faces tremendous challenging problems due material creep, resulting from increasing demand in high-temperature applications and more stringent controls to advanced hardware configurations such as polymers-based composites for automobiles. Schematic loading profiles in response to two different fatigue tests, i.e. creep fatigue and relaxation fatigue, are presented in Fig. 6.10.1. They are addressed as follows:

(1) Creep fatigue (Fig. 6.10.2): If the stress level is held constant during hold periods of a cyclic fatigue test, it is called a creep fatigue test, the strain (or deformation) will vary and its tensile and compressive peaks will be a significant measure and they are the feedback signals during the hold durations, of which Δt_+ is the hold time in tension while Δt_- is the hold time in compression.

(2) Relaxation fatigue (Fig. 6.10.3): If the strain level is held constant during hold periods of a cyclic fatigue test, the load (stress) will vary and its tensile and compressive peaks will be a significant measure and they are the feedback signals during the hold durations.

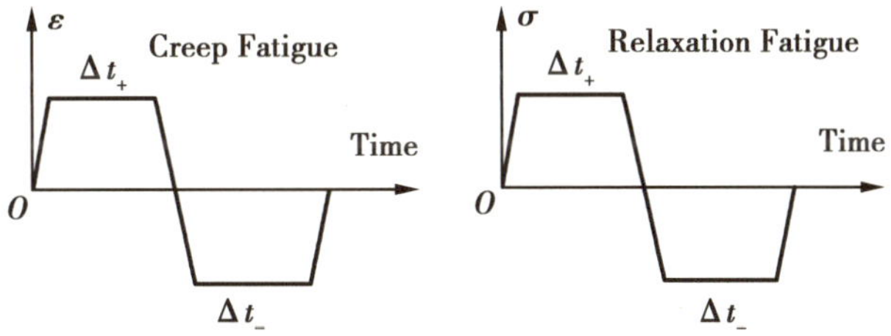

Fig. 6.10.1 Schematic Loading Profiles of Creep and Relaxation Fatigue Tests at $R = -1$

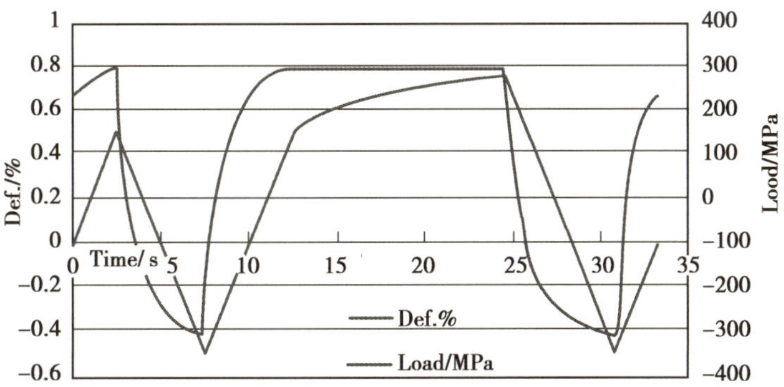

Fig. 6.10.2 Stress and Strain Variations during a Creep-Fatigue Test [Cristalli et al.]

In the case of creep fatigue, the hydrostatic stress significantly lowers the creep strain rate and elongates the creep rupture time and it also increases the creep-fatigue life under a fully reversed loading [Sakane & Itoh].

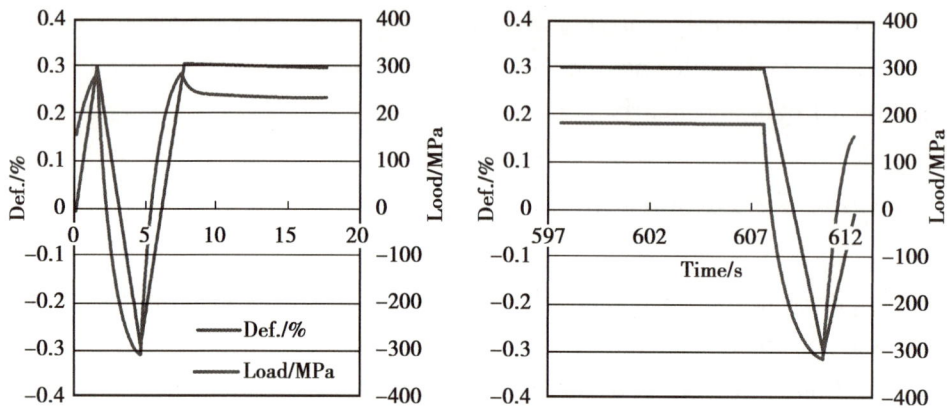

Fig. 6.10.3 Stress and Strain Variations during a Relaxation-Fatigue Test [Cristalli et al.]

6.10.2 Effect of Hold-Time Duration

What would be the potential dominating cause of failure: creep, fatigue, or creep-fatigue interaction? It has been reported by [Ogata] that the creep fatigue test, i.e. strain-controlled hold-time, has a great influence on the creep fatigue life. This has been validated by low-speed (0.1 Hz) LCF (low-cycle fatigue) tests based on P91 steel (Fe-9Cr-1Mo-V-Nb-..) at an elevated temperature of 550 ℃ conducted by [Cristalli et al.]. Two observations derived from the study by [Cristalli et al.] are given as follows:

(a) Creep fatigue: An increasing hold-time duration in tension under creep fatigue test yields a shorter fatigue life.

(b) Relaxation fatigue: An increasing hold-time duration in tension under relaxation fatigue test has no impact on the fatigue life, but the hold-time in compression under relaxation test does damage to the fatigue life significantly.

Creep-fatigue tests are strain-asymmetric while relaxation-fatigue is stress-asymmetric. When the applied mean strain (mean stress) is zero, the direction of strain accumulation due to ratcheting (Section 4.7) is dependent on the holding position, i.e. either peak tensile or peak compressive. On the other hand, if the mean strain (stress) is not zero, it will determine the direction of strain ratcheting, regardless of the holding position-compressive or tensile accumulation. Further research is in demand on the assessment of the influence of cyclic creep of strain (stress) state on the strain accumulation kinetics.

6.10.3   Effect of Temperature

With the increase in temperature, the stress rupture strength of material decreases rapidly to a value that may be considerably lower than its fatigue strength. The primary requirement of a material that will be subjected to elevated temperatures is that it has adequate stress-rupture strength.

6.10.4   Effect of Mean Strain Rate

Based on the ductility dissipation theory and effective stress concept of continuum mechanics, the mean strain rate at half-life is used as control parameter to propose a new model for strain-controlled creep-fatigue life prediction [Fan et al.] as

$$2N_f = k_1 \left(\frac{d\varepsilon_m}{dt} \right)^{k_2} \tag{6.10.1}$$

where

ε_m : Mean strain;

k_1 : Coefficient;

k_2 : Exponent.

The effect of mean strain (stress) on the interaction between cyclic dynamic and static creep phenomena is also taken into consideration in the above equation. The validity of Eq. (6.10.1) has been examined using the test data of three different low alloy steels at both room and elevated temperatures. They are

(a) 16MnR steel between 23 ℃ and 420 ℃ : $N_f = 10^{1.18716} \left(\dfrac{d\varepsilon_m}{dt} \right)^{-0.8529}$.

(b) ASTM A-516 Grade 70 steel at 23 ℃ : $N_f = 10^{7.704} \left(\dfrac{d\varepsilon_m}{dt} \right)^{-0.542}$.

(c) 1.25Cr 0.5Mo steel between 23 ℃ and 540 ℃ : $N_f = 10^{1.10304} \left(\dfrac{d\varepsilon_m}{dt} \right)^{-0.94178}$.

Most of the life prediction results fall within a factor of $\pm(\times 1.5)$. This model is suitable for strain- or stress-controlled fatigue or fatigue-creep life prediction of ductile material.

6.10.5   Fatigue Toughness and Strain Energy

At high temperatures, the fatigue strength often depends on the total time the stress is applied rather than solely on the number of "loading" cycles. Under fluctuating stresses, the cyclic frequency affects both the fatigue life and the amount of creep. The principal method of studying creep-fatigue interactions has been to conduct strain energy-controlled fatigue tests with variable frequencies with and without a holding period (hold time) during some portion of the test [Zhu et al.]. According to [Ostergren] the fatigue toughness of a material, K_{ft}, is exploited in terms of strain energy done by inelastic deformation (plastic and creep deformations) as

$$K_{ft} \equiv \Delta\varepsilon_{inelastic} \, \sigma_{max} (2N_f)^{\alpha} \tag{6.10.2}$$

and $\quad \Delta\varepsilon_{inelastic} = \Delta\varepsilon_p + \Delta\varepsilon_{creep} \tag{6.10.3}$

where

K_{ft}: Fatigue toughness;

$\Delta\varepsilon_{inelastic}$: Inelastic strain range;

$\Delta\varepsilon_p$: Plastic strain range, including both mechanical and thermal strains;

$\Delta\varepsilon_{creep}$: Creep strain range;

σ_{max}: Maximum stress;

$2N_f$: Life cycles;

α: Exponent.

6.10.6　Inelastic Work Done Due to Cycling Loads-Constant Creep Strain Rate

The strain energy done in one cycle subjected to cyclic loads is

$$W_s = \int \sigma \, d\varepsilon = \int \sigma \frac{d\varepsilon}{dt} dt \tag{6.10.4}$$

$$W_s = \sigma \, \varepsilon \Big|_0^{\frac{2\pi}{\omega}} - \int_0^{\frac{2\pi}{\omega}} \left(\frac{d\sigma}{dt}\right) \varepsilon \, dt \tag{6.10.5}$$

$$\sigma = \left[E_\infty + \sum_{i=1}^{N} E_i \exp\left(-\frac{t}{\tau_i}\right) \right] \varepsilon_o \tag{6.10.6}$$

$$\frac{d\varepsilon_{creep}}{dt} = A \, \sigma^n \exp\left(\frac{-Q}{RT_k}\right) \tag{6.10.7}$$

If strain rate $d\varepsilon/dt$ is kept constant, the above equation can be rewritten as

$$W_s = \frac{d\varepsilon}{dt} \int \sigma \, dt \tag{6.10.8}$$

Term $d\varepsilon/dt$ in the above equation functions like the strain rate experienced in a dashpot, as shown in the standard linear solid model. Then, the integral becomes

$$\mu_d = \int \sigma \, dt \tag{6.10.9}$$

the viscosity (MPa-sec) that drives the fatigue process as argued by [Zhu et al.]. Assume that the stress waveform applied at a certain point of concern is known as a time series exhibited in Fig. 6.10.4. For simplicity, a sine wave is assigned to the stress

$$\sigma(t) = \sigma_m + \sigma_a \sin(\omega t) \tag{6.10.10}$$

though it can be of any shape such as a trapezoidal wave [Zhu et al.] as shown in Fig. 6.10.4. The total dynamic viscosity (MPa-sec) per cycle is then the area between the sine wave and the horizontal axis,

$$\mu_d = \int_0^{\frac{2\pi}{\omega}} [\sigma_m + \sigma_a \sin(\omega t)] dt, \quad \text{if } \sigma_m \geq \sigma_a \geq 0 \tag{6.10.11a}$$

$$\mu_d = \int_0^{\theta_+} [\sigma_m + \sigma_a \sin(\omega t)] dt + \int_0^{\frac{2\pi}{\omega}} [\sigma_m + \sigma_a \sin(\omega t)] dt, \quad \text{if } \sigma_a \geq \sigma_m \geq 0 \tag{6.10.11b}$$

$$\mu_d = \int_0^{\theta_+} [\sigma_m + \sigma_a \sin(\omega t)] dt, \quad \text{if } \sigma_m \leq 0 \ \& \ \sigma_a \geq |\sigma_m| \tag{6.10.11c}$$

or $\mu_d = 0$, $\quad$ if $\sigma_m \leq 0 \ \& \ \sigma_a \leq |\sigma_m|$ $\tag{6.10.11d}$

where

σ_m: Mean stress;

σ_a: Fluctuating stress amplitude;

ω: Rotating speed;

θ_+: Locating angle;

t: Time.

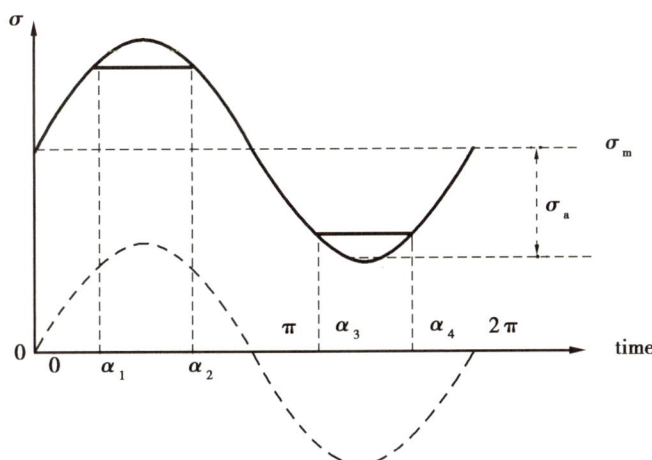

Fig. 6.10.4   Sine-Shaped Sine Wave without and with Holding Times

The above four equations for boundary conditions may have to be revised according to theory in accordance with the material creep behaviors as addressed in Section 6.10.1. Locating angle θ_+ is used for signalizing that only stresses in tension do a damage to the material, and calculated as

$$\theta_+ = \sin^{-1} \frac{-\sigma_m}{\sigma_a} \tag{6.10.12}$$

Note that the stress ratio, R, is

$$R = \frac{\sigma_{min}}{\sigma_{max}} = \frac{\sigma_m - \sigma_a}{\sigma_m + \sigma_a} \tag{6.10.13}$$

The inelastic work done due to dynamic viscosity (dynamic viscosity in an inelastic range) per cycle is then

$$W_{s,in} = \frac{d\varepsilon}{dt}\mu_d - 2\pi \frac{1}{2}\frac{\sigma_f^2}{E} = \frac{d\varepsilon}{dt}\mu_d - \frac{\pi\sigma_f^2}{E} \tag{6.10.14}$$

of which σ_f is the fatigue strength (limit) and the strain energy done ($\sigma_f^2/2E$) by a stress less than the fatigue strength is assumed to be in the elastic range and not to do any damage to the material. The total inelastic dynamic viscosity is then

$$\sum W_{s,in} = 2N_f\left(\frac{d\varepsilon}{dt}\mu_d - \frac{\pi\sigma_f^2}{E}\right) \tag{6.10.15}$$

Assume that the fatigue toughness follows the power law of inelastic dynamic viscosity [Zhu] as

$$K_{ft} \equiv \Delta\varepsilon_{inelastic}\,\sigma_{max}(2N_f)^a \tag{6.10.16}$$

$$K_{ft} \infty \left(\sum W_{s,in}\right)^a = \left\{(2N_f)\left[W_{s,in} - \frac{\pi\sigma_f^2}{E}\right]\right\}^a \tag{6.10.17}$$

Relating the above equation to Eq. (6.10.2) leads to

$$\Delta\varepsilon_{in}\,\sigma_{max}(2N_f)^a = k\left(W_{s,in} - \frac{\pi\sigma_f^2}{E}\right)^a \tag{6.10.18}$$

As enlightened by Eq. (6.10.2) in the LCF (low cycle fatigue) range and $\Delta\varepsilon_{in} = 2\varepsilon_{a,in}$, the above equation is rearranged to be

$$\varepsilon_{a,in} = \varepsilon_f'(2N_f)^c = \varepsilon_f'' \frac{\left(W_{s,in} - \dfrac{\pi\sigma_f^2}{E}\right)^a}{\sigma_{max}}(2N_f)^c \tag{6.10.19}$$

and $\quad \varepsilon'_f = \dfrac{\varepsilon''_f \left(W_{s,in} - \dfrac{\pi \sigma_f^2}{E} \right)^a}{\sigma_{max}}$ (6.10.20)

where

$\varepsilon_{a,in}$: Fluctuating stress amplitude in the inelastic range, $\varepsilon_{a,in} \approx \varepsilon_a$ in the LCF range;

ε'_f: Fatigue strain coefficient (Chapter 4);

ε''_f: Fatigue strain coefficient II;

a: Viscous exponent;

c: Fatigue strain exponent, and $c = a - \alpha$. (6.10.21)

Instead of staying constant as in Eq. (6.10.2), ε'_f (fatigue strain coefficient) is here rephrased with two new parameters, i.e. ε''_f and a. Substituting of Eq. (6.10.20) back into Eq. (6.10.2) leads to a predictive equation for crack initiation that accommodates the interaction between creep and fatigue,

$$\varepsilon_a = \frac{\sigma'_f - \sigma_M}{E}(2N_f)^b + \varepsilon''_f \left[\frac{\left(W_{s,in} - \dfrac{\pi \sigma_f^2}{E} \right)^a}{\sigma_{max}} \right] (2N_f)^c$$ (6.10.22)

Note that strain rate $d\varepsilon/dt$ is assumed to be constant in the above equation.

6.10.7   Inelastic Work Done Due to Cycling-Variable Creep Strain Rate

Assume that the variable strain rate follows the power law as described by Eq. (6.8.25). The strain energy done in one cycle can then be obtained by substituting Eq. (6.8.25) into Eq. (6.10.18),

$$\begin{aligned} W_s &= \int \sigma \frac{d\varepsilon}{dt}dt - \int \sigma \left[A\,\sigma^n\, t^m \, \exp\left(\frac{-Q}{RT_k}\right) \right] dt \\ &= \int_0^{2\pi} A \left[\sigma_m + \sigma_a \sin(\omega t) \right]^{n+1} t^m \, \exp\left(\frac{-Q}{RT_k}\right) \right] dt \end{aligned}$$ (6.10.23)

The integration in the above equation will be carried out for the four different cases with varying σ_m and σ_a, as demonstrated by Eq. (6.10.14). Again, the inelastic work done per cycle is then

$$W_{s,in} = W_s - 2\pi \left(\frac{\sigma_f^2}{2E} \right) = W_s - \frac{\pi \sigma_f^2}{E}$$ (6.10.24)

The hold time at either the high strain (stress) and/or the low strain (stress) level, depicted in Fig. 6.10.4, can be implemented by integrating Eq. (6.10.8) or Eq. (6.10.23) numerically with respective upper or lower limits specified accordingly.

6.11　Oxidation

Disintegration of a metal by its surrounding materials (fluids mainly) through a chemical reaction on the surface of the metal is called corrosion. Oxidation is a special case of corrosion and it is generally considered irreversible. Oxidation of metal during isothermal loading at the ambient temperature is hardly perceptible and is not an active failure mechanism. Excessive erosion or sedimentation of oxidized metal can either create or remove large vertical stresses upon the underlying substrate (metal).

Oxidation resistance is often the limiting factor that determines the life of high temperature structural metals and alloys. The substrate (metal) will expand or contract in the vertical direction as a direct result of the applied stress, and it will also deform in the horizontal direction as a result of Poisson's effect. Comparative oxidation resistance of some high-temperature materials in flowing air is given in Table 6.10.1. However, the accelerated attack caused by moisture or other fluids may expedite the oxidation process at elevated temperatures. Proper alloying elements may help reduce the oxidation attack. For example, Yttrium is the most commonly used reactive element to impart scale-spallation resistance to alumina forming alloys.

6.11.1　Strength of Oxides

Oxidation damage occurs and causes a change in the chemical composition of the material due to environmental factors when an oxide layer forms on the outer material surface. The oxidized material is more brittle than the original material. Mechanical properties of frequently observed oxides are listed in Table 6.11.1. Apparently the ultimate strength of material decreases nonlinearly with increasing thickness of the oxide, as shown in Fig. 6.11.1. Assume that the biaxial stress condition is met when the oxide is thin, and thus $\sigma_{33} = 0$ and $\sigma_{22} = \sigma_{11}$ in the plane stress state. Then the strains can be derived from Eqs. (2.6.10) and (2.6.8), respectively as

$$\varepsilon_{11} = \varepsilon_{22} = \frac{1 - \nu_{ox}}{E_{ox}} \sigma_{11} \tag{6.11.1}$$

and $\quad \varepsilon_{33} = \frac{-2\nu_{ox}}{1 - \nu_{ox}} \varepsilon_{11} = \frac{-2\nu_{ox}}{E_{ox}} \sigma_{11}$ $\tag{6.11.2}$

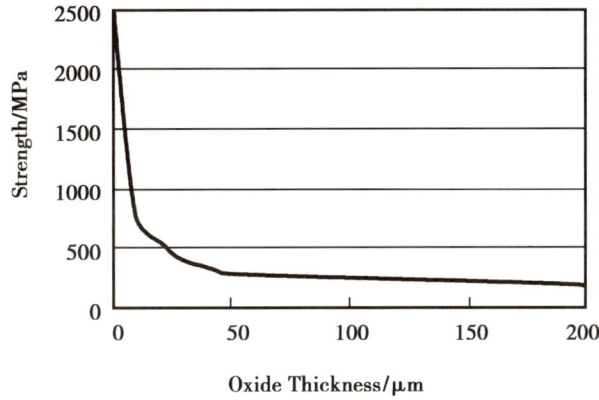

Fig. 6.11.1   **Schematic Drawing of Oxide Strength as a Function of Thickness [Robertson & Manning]**

Enlightened by Eq. (6.11.1), the failure stress and strain of an oxide are related to each other by the following biaxial stress state equation [Steiner & Konys],

$$\sigma_{ucs} = \frac{E_{ox}}{1 - \nu_{ox}} \varepsilon_{ucs} \quad (\text{in compression}) \tag{6.11.3}$$

$$\text{or} \quad \sigma_{uts} = \frac{E_{ox}}{1 - \nu_{ox}} \varepsilon_{uts} \quad (\text{in tension}) \tag{6.11.4}$$

Once an oxide gets exposed to a certain high working temperature, it may be disintegrated into small disilicide particles, covered by a loose, voluminous scale. This phenomenon is called pest oxidation. Pest oxidation could be eliminated by keeping the porosity of sintered material to very low levels [Schlichting] or by additional alloying elements [Zeitch].

6.11.2   Oxidation of Metals

An oxidation kinetic mechanism of metals comes with two different reaction periods: (a) initial transient period at a faster pace and (b) steady-state period afterwards. A general description of mass gain per unit area during an oxidation process can be described by the following equation:

$$(\Delta m - \Delta m_{in})^n = k_p (t - t_{in})^m = k_0 (t - t_{in})^m \exp\left(\frac{-Q_o}{RT_k}\right) \tag{6.11.5}$$

$$\text{and} \quad k_p = k_0 \exp\left(\frac{-Q_o}{RT_k}\right) \tag{6.11.6}$$

where

$\Delta m (\text{mg/cm}^2 \text{ or kg/m}^2)$: Steady-state mass change per unit area, $1 \text{ kg/m}^2 = 100 \text{ mg/cm}^2$;

Δm_{in}: Initial mass change in the initial transient reaction period, at a faster pace;

t (hour): Time;

t_{in} : Initial transient reaction period;

n : Exponent;

m : Exponent;

k_p ($kg^2/m^4/h$ or $mg^2/cm^4/h$) : Constant at a fixed temperature;

Q_o ($J/mole$) : Activation energy for oxide growth;

R ($= 8.314\ J/mole/ ℃$) : Universal gas constant;

T_k (K) : Exposure temperature;

k_0 : Constant of material oxidation.

Alloying elements chromium and silicon improve the resistance to heavy scaling by forming a light surface oxide (e.g. CrO) that is impervious to oxidizing atmospheres. However, both elements reduce the toughness and thermal shock resistance of the metal.

6.11.3   Oxidation of Cast Iron

Iron oxidizes to form three well known oxides, namely wustite (FeO), magnetite (Fe_3O_4) and hematite (Fe_2O_3) in proportions determined by reaction kinetics, where the predominant oxide being magnetite. Intermediate or mixed control oxidation may put exponent n in the range between 1 and 2. In general, the oxidation process at a given temperature can be expressed as [Encinas-Oropesa et al.]:

$$(\Delta m)^n = k_p\, t \quad (\text{Steady state only}) \tag{6.11.7}$$

which is a simplified version of Eq. (6.11.5), but time starts from the beginning of steady-state period only. This is quite the same for cast iron, pure iron, and low carbon steel, but an additional internal scale layer is formed upon cast iron, as being a mixture of Wustite and Fayalite due to the existence of silicon. Two distinct phenomena have been observed:

(a) $n = 1$: Linear oxidation normally takes place during the initial oxidation period. During this stage, oxidation is controlled by the diffusion rate of oxygen atoms from the bulky gas through the reaction surface.

(b) $n = 2$: After the oxide layer reaches a certain thickness (between 0.004 mm and 0.1 mm) or a certain amount of exposure time, the outward diffusion of metal ions and/or the inward diffusion of oxygen ions through the oxide layer become rate controlling. This diffusion controlled process is known as parabolic growth of oxidation ($n = 2$). In evaluating the parabolic rate constant at the moment when oxidation sets in a steady state, the data collected during the transient period (e.g. first 10 minutes) of oxidation initially, has to be omitted.

6.11.4   Oxidation of Stainless Steel

AISI 301S stainless steel is employed here to demonstrate the oxidation mechanism as a general concept for stainless steels. Contrary to oxidation at a lower temperature, exposure of AISI 301S at 800 ℃ shows a remarkable compliance with the parabolic growth rate. Though the final weight gain for these alloys was relatively higher compared to an exposure at lower temperatures, specimens exhibit only a parabolic behavior even after a 200 hours exposure [Raj]. It means that the initial oxidation is due to diffusion of the metal cation to the surface that forms oxide films. After then, a steady-state oxidation process consequently proceeds by diffusion of oxygen through the initial layers towards the metal as

$$(\Delta m)^2 = k_p\, t \tag{6.11.8}$$

From the experimental results [Raj], it is found that the main oxidation products are Fe_2O_3 and a mixture of Fe_2O_3 and spinel, and whereby Fe_3O_4 is detected in the outermost oxide layer. This is because the Fe_3O_4 kinetics is typically more active than Fe_2O_3. Inspection of the surface of the oxide scale covering the specimens (AISI 301S) after the isothermal exposure for 200 hours revealed that the part of the grown-up oxide spalled off. The finding tells that at all the test temperatures (700 ℃, 800 ℃ and 900 ℃), an oxide layer retards further oxidation. Stainless steel bent tubes or stamped shells are widely used for exhaust manifolds. Some stainless steels for high-temperature applications are addressed as follows:

(a) Austenitic AISI 304 and AISI 321 are rarely used because of their poor cyclic oxidation resistance due to oxide layer spalling and of their relatively high thermal expansion coefficients. For example, a two-layered structure scale, having inner $FeCr_2O_4/NiCr_2O_4$ and outer Fe_2O_3, appears on the surface of a duplex type 321 stainless steel in the hot air at 700 ℃ and the scale may spall off. Thus, only the austenitic refractory grade AISI 308Si (or 302B) can be used at a high temperature.

(b) Ferritic AISI 409 is the most common grade for exhaust line application but can be used only up to 850 ℃.

(c) Ferritic AISI 441 or Fe-14Cr-Nb grades are used for a temperature up to 950 ℃. Ferric AISI 441 affords the proper thermal fatigue resistance, even when compared with the refractory grade AISI 302B that is more sensitive to the detrimental effect of the holding time at a peak temperature.

Nevertheless, the formation of oxides on stainless steels may provide a protective layer preventing further atmospheric attack, allowing for the material to be used for sustained periods at both room and high temperatures. Such high-temperature corrosion as produced in the form of compacted oxide layer glazes can even reduce wear during high-temperature sliding contact.

6.11.5 Oxidation of Electrodeposited Coating

Similar to the pure metals, the oxidation kinetics of electrodeposited coating can be damaging. It is generally described using the growth time exponent "α" as put the in following equation:

$$\Delta m = k\, t^{\alpha} + C \tag{6.11.9}$$

where

k: Oxidation rate constant;

α: Oxidation time-growth exponent, $\alpha = 1/n$ as derived from simplified Eq. (6.11.5);

C: Constant value.

6.12 Thermomechanical Fatigue of Oxides

Oxidized material is more brittle and prone to crack nucleation. The material phase transforms with the elongation of exposure time. The thermal expansion capability of γ phase is much higher than that of α phase. The changes of phase content, especially the decrease of γ content, will produce a tensile effect upon the outer scale. In the heating or cooling process of a product (e.g. engine exhaust manifold or heat exchanger), the matrix will also produce tensile or compressive effects on the scale correspondingly, because of the different thermal expansion capability of scale relative to the matrix. Furthermore, oxidation weakens the surface of the substrate material and creating flaws for crack propagation in/between dissimilar materials (substrate and scale).

6.12.1 Thermomechanical Load Ratio

Induced interfacial stresses lead to scale cracks that expose the substrate (metal) to the environment (full of oxygen generally) and thus accelerate the oxidation process. The oxidation occurs spontaneously at higher temperatures, it happens to be either in-phase or out-of-phase thermomechanical fatigue (TMF). Simple TMF cycling as shown schematically in Fig. 6.11 may be applied in the laboratory to capture the TMF failure mechanism [Wu] [ASTM E 2368 (2010)] [ISO FDIS-12111 (2012)]:

    (a) In-phase (IP) cycles, having a 0° phase angle between thermal and mechanical loads;

    (b) Out-of-phase (OP) cycles, having a 180° phase angle;

    (c) Diamond phase (DP) cycle, as the diamond (dashed) shown in Fig. 6.12.1.

The OP and IP cycles represent two extreme conditions, where the maximum stress is reached at the "hot" end of IP and the "cold" end of OP-TMF (Out-of-phase Thermomechanical Fatigue) cycle. A thermomechanical load ratio, K_{TM}, is defined as the ratio of the mechanical strain amplitude and thermal strain amplitude as

$$K_{TM} = \frac{-\varepsilon_{mechanical}}{\varepsilon_{thermal}} \tag{6.12.1}$$

6.12.2　IP-TMF（In-Phase Thermomechanical Fatigue）

In-phase（IP）thermomechanical loading means that the temperature and mechanical load increase or decrease simultaneously, as identified in Fig. 6.12.1. Although oxidation may occur （at a high temperature）when the substrate is in tension at high temperatures, a combined effect of thermal expansion and mechanical stress is the ideal condition for creep in the IP-TMF （In-Phase Thermomechanical Fatigue）process. IP-TMF cycling leads to a creep relaxation in tension at the maximum temperature and plastic deformation in compression at the minimum temperature. In other words, the heated material tends to flow more in tension, but it cools and stiffens under compression. Creep of the substrate（metal）is usually dominantly significant under the IP-TMF loading.

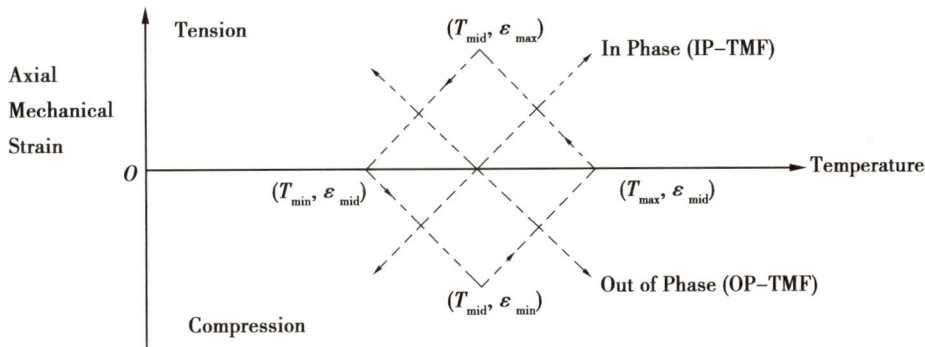

Fig. 6.12.1　Uniaxial Thermomechanical Fatigue Cycles Involved in Oxidation

6.12.3　OP-TMF（Out-of-Phase Thermomechanical Fatigue）

While the material is in compression subject to mechanical loadings, the oxide may form in the meantime during the hot durations of a loading cycle. This combination constitutes the OP-TMF （Out-of-Phase Thermomechanical Fatigue）loading. In the case of OP-TMF loading, creep is a minor damage mechanism but the fatigue complicated by oxidation turns out to be a new failure mechanism ［Zineb et al.］. Fatigue goes all the way while oxidation is more active at high temperatures. A layer of scale might build up as a result of oxidation that takes effect predominantly at high temperatures. This layer of scale is very brittle as it cools, causing early crack initiation and consequently resulting in accelerated crack propagation. Generally speaking, OP-TMF lives are shorter than IP-TMF lives ［Han et al.］.

When the mechanical stress difference between the substrate and oxide scale is much greater than the thermal stress difference, mechanical fatigue will be the sole driving cause of OP-TMF failure in this case, causing the material to fail before oxidation has much of an effect.

6.12.4　Buckling Delamination of Oxides

A buckling delamination may also occur at a lower temperature when the oxide is subject to shrinking substrate and thus cracks to expose new clean substrate (metal) surface to the environment [He et al.]. The buckling stress and strain can be obtained from elasticity theory [Cathcart] [Steiner & Konys], respectively as

$$\varepsilon_{buck} = 1.22 \frac{\delta_{ox}}{R_{cohesion}} \tag{6.12.2}$$

and

$$\sigma_{buck} = 1.22 \left(\frac{E_{ox}}{1 - \nu_{ox}} \right) \left(\frac{\delta_{ox}}{R_{cohesion}} \right) \tag{6.12.3}$$

where
E_{ox} : Young's modulus of oxide;
ν_{ox} : Poisson's ratio of oxide;
δ_{ox} : Thickness of oxide;
$R_{cohesion}$: Radius of the zone of decohesion.

6.12.5　Growth Stresses

As the oxide grows geometrically induced stresses may appear because of part curvatures. These are called growth stresses in oxidation. Note that there is no such a stress growth on a flat part surface.

6.12.6　Stresses in Oxide Scale

Consider a cylindrical test specimen (oxide/substrate) and assume that both the oxide and substrate are in a biaxial stress state (neglecting the interface stresses, i.e. $\sigma_{33} = 0$). Based on the fact that the radial displacement in the oxide is the same as that of the substrate for a perfect adhesion in the isothermal state, the mean hoop stress in the oxide is [Steiner & Konys]

$$\sigma_{hoop} = \left[\frac{\dfrac{E_{ox}}{1 - \nu_{ox}}}{1 + \dfrac{\delta_{ox}(1 - \nu_s)}{E_s \delta_s (1 - \nu_{ox})}} \right] \int_{T_{ox}}^{T} [\alpha_s(T) - \alpha_{ox}(T)] \, dT \tag{6.12.4}$$

where

E_{ox}: Young's modulus of oxide;

ν_{ox}: Poisson's ratio of oxide;

α_{ox}: Coefficient of linear thermal expansion of oxide, $\alpha_{ox} = \alpha_{ox}(T)$;

δ_{ox}: Thickness of oxide;

E_s: Young's modulus of the substrate;

δ_s: Thickness of the substrate;

ν_s: Poisson's ratio of substrate;

α_s: Coefficient of linear thermal expansion of the substrate, $\alpha_s = \alpha_s(T)$;

T_{ox}: Temperature, at which oxidation occurs;

T & $\hat{T}$: Temperature and its corresponding dummy variable.

It is known that TMF phenomenon is related to start-operate-stop cycling and not to the combustion cycles in a combustion engine. Integration temperature limits from T_{ox} to T in the above equation are thus defined in this manner. When $\delta_s \gg \delta_{ox}$ for a relatively thin oxide layer (i.e. relatively thick substrate), Eq. (6.12.4) reduces to

$$\sigma_{hoop} = \left(\frac{E_{ox}}{1 - \nu_{ox}} \right) \int_{T_{ox}}^{T} [\alpha_s(\hat{T}) - \alpha_{ox}(\hat{T})] \, d\hat{T} \tag{6.12.5}$$

Eq. (6.11.1) bears a part in the above equation, of which the principal stresses ε_{11} and ε_{22} are induced by the thermal variation. When the point of interest is located on the 2-axis, then ε_{11} (σ_{11}) is the hoop strain (stress) and $\varepsilon_{22}(\sigma_{22})$ is the radial strain (stress). The radial stress in a thin oxide is equal to the hoop stress according to the biaxial stress state, similar to that $\varepsilon_{11} = \varepsilon_{22}$ given in Eq. (6.11.1). Hence,

$$\sigma_{radial} = \sigma_{hoop} \tag{6.12.6}$$

Let $R_{cohesion}$ be the radius of cohesion. The radial stress at the interface between the substrate and a thin oxide layer can be calculated [Steiner & Konys]

$$\sigma_{radial, interface} = -\left(\frac{\delta_{ox}}{R_{cohesion}} \right) \sigma_{hoop} \tag{6.12.7}$$

Note that no plastic stress flow or creep phenomenon is expected in the substrate, as the stress level in the substrate is one order of magnitude lower than the stresses in the oxide as long as the oxide is thin. More research work on the growth stresses in oxidized tube subject to multiaxial oxidation strains is detailed in [Steiner, Konys, & Heck].

6.12.7   Spalling of Oxide Scales

Protective oxide scales are brittle once the working temperature goes below the brittle-to-ductile transition temperature. The energy release rate in terms of stress and elastic constants may be employed to detect the potential failure of the oxide as follows:

$$G = \left(\frac{\sigma_{ox}^2}{E_{ox}}\right)(1 - \nu_{ox})\, \delta_{ox} > \gamma_{surface} \tag{6.12.8}$$

Once the energy release rate (G) is larger than the surface fracture energy ($\gamma_{surface}$), spalling occurs. The surface fracture energy is a material parameter that varies with respect to the spalling spot that may be located at the interface between the substrate and oxide scale or between two subscales. The surface fracture energy required for spalling may be lowered by any defect such as porosities.

6.13   Thermal Barrier Systems

Ceramic-bonded-to-metal composites working as functionally graded material have attracted a great deal of attention for aerospace structures, gas turbines and aircraft engines. They function as an insulator for load-carrying hot components from the hot oxidative environment in combustor and turbine. Yttria that is partially stabilized zirconia (YPSZ) with a low thermal conductivity has been used as the top ceramic layer that protects the structural components from corrosion (including oxidation) and mechanical property degradation when it is subjected to high thermal load coupled with fatigue and/or creep phenomena. For example, a commercial EB-PVD 7YSZ thermal barrier coating, i.e. an Ni(Pt)Al chemically vapor deposited (CVD) platinum aluminide diffusion layer, has been applied to gas turbine blades [Smialek].

Nevertheless, a thermally grown oxide (TGO) that will form at the interface between bonding material and the top ceramic layer when getting exposed to high temperatures. The general failure pattern of TBC (Thermal Barrier Coating) is thermal spalling due to oxidation at or near the formed TGO interfaces with bonding cement layer. Mechanical creep parameters of some TBC components are listed in Table 6.13.1.

6.13.1   Thickness of Thermal Grown Oxide (TGO)

The total thickness of the thermal grown oxide layer (h_{tgo}) at time t can be computed from a phenomenological oxide growth kinetics in terms of temperature and accumulated time [Busso et al.] as

$$h_{tgo} = A_o\, t^q\, \exp\left[\frac{Q_o}{R}\left(\frac{1}{T_{k,ref}} - \frac{1}{T_{k,max}}\right)\right] \tag{6.13.1}$$

where

h_{tgo}: Thickness of the oxide;

t: Time;

A_o: Coefficient, $A_o = 10^{-6}$ m/s^q;

q: Exponent, e.g. $q = 0.332$;

Q_o(J/mole): Apparent activation energy, $Q_o = 767 \times 10^3$ J/mol;

$R(= 8.314$ J/mole/ ℃): Universal gas constant;

$T_{k,ref}$(K): Reference temperature, e.g. $T_{k,ref} = 2424$ K;

$T_{k,max}$(K): Maximum temperature of the thermal cycle.

The numeric data for oxidation parameters given above are for the TGO produced in the TBC system made of between MCrAlY (bond coat) and EBPVD YSZ (insulating ceramic layer); on a CMSX4 steel substrate.

The total oxide thickness (h_{tgo}) is divided into an internally grown portion of thickness $h_{tgo,in}$ and an externally grown portion of thickness $h_{tgo,out}$.

$$h_{tgo} = h_{tgo,in} + h_{tgo,out} \tag{6.13.2}$$

and

$$h_{tgo,in} = \frac{h_{tgo}}{R_{pb}} \tag{6.13.3}$$

where

$$R_{pb} \equiv \frac{h_{tgo}}{h_{tgo,in}} \tag{6.13.3a}$$

Parameter R_{pb} is called Pilling-Bedworth ratio or Bedworth ratio, defined as the ratio of the total thickness to the internal grown thickness, $R_{pb} = 1.28$, corresponding to the primary oxidation reaction between MCrAlY (bond coat) and EBPVD YSZ (insulating ceramic layer).

A TGO scale is usually orthotropic, or more specifically transversely isotropic. The normal strains adherent to the oxide scale [Busso et al.] in the plane are

$$\varepsilon_{11} = \varepsilon_{22} = \left(\frac{3r}{1 + 2r}\right) \ln \frac{R_{pb}}{3} \quad \text{(In-plane)} \tag{6.13.4}$$

Note that $r = 0.005/0.435 = 0.0115$ [Busso et al.] corresponds to the primary oxidation reaction between MCrAlY (bond coat) and EBPVD YSZ (insulating ceramic layer). It can be shown by the above equation that $\varepsilon_{33} > \varepsilon_{11}$ (or ε_{22}).

6.13.2   Nominal Stresses and Strains

Thermal spallation may occur due to the difference in thermal expansion coefficients among the substrate（metal usually）, bonding cement, and protecting oxide layer. As a general design guideline, the coefficient of linear thermal expansion of the bonding cement falls between the substrate and ceramic as

$$\alpha_c < \alpha_b < \alpha_s \tag{6.13.5}$$

As the temperature goes from T_0 to T_1, the thermal strains of individual "independent" layers （free of adhesion） due to thermal differentials are, respectively

$$\varepsilon_{th,c} = \alpha_c(T_1 - T_0) = \alpha_c \Delta T \quad \text{(Ceramic)} \tag{6.13.6}$$

$$\varepsilon_{th,b} = \alpha_b(T_1 - T_0) = \alpha_b \Delta T \quad \text{(Bonding Cement)} \tag{6.13.7}$$

and $\quad \varepsilon_{th,s} = \alpha_s(T_1 - T_0) = \alpha_s \Delta T \quad \text{(Substrate)} \tag{6.13.8}$

where
α_c: Coefficients of linear thermal expansion of ceramic;
α_b: Coefficients of linear thermal expansion of bonding cement;
α_s: Coefficients of linear thermal expansion of substrate;
$\varepsilon_{th,c}$, $\varepsilon_{th,b}$, $\varepsilon_{th,s}$: Thermal strains of in ceramic, bonding cement, and substrate, respectively;
T_0 & T_1: Initial temperature and instantaneous temperature, respectively;
ΔT: Temperature differential, $\Delta T = T_1 - T_0$.

Note that the thermal strains given above create no stress if the TBC specimen is not constrained. Next, consider the components（ceramic, bonding cement and substrate）of the TBC system are in adhesive constraints mutually. The force balance of these three distinct layers of materials in combination with their strain compatibilities under mutual constraining result in the corresponding stress and strain components in terms of their material properties as follows [Zhu and Miller]:

$$\sigma_c = \frac{[E_b E_c h_b(1-\nu_s)(\alpha_b-\alpha_c) + E_s E_c h_s(1-\nu_b)(\alpha_s-\alpha_c)]\Delta T}{E_c h_c(1-\nu_b)(1-\nu_s) + E_b h_b(1-\nu_s)(1-\nu_c) + E_s h_s(1-\nu_c)(1-\nu_b)} \tag{6.13.9}$$

$$\sigma_b = \frac{[E_b^2 h_b(1-\nu_s)(1-\nu_c)(\alpha_b-\alpha_c) + E_b E_s h_s(1-\nu_b)(1-\nu_c)(\alpha_s-\alpha_c)]\Delta T}{[E_c h_c(1-\nu_b)(1-\nu_s) + E_b h_b(1-\nu_s)(1-\nu_c) + E_s h_s(1-\nu_c)(1-\nu_b)](1-\nu_b)} -$$

$$\frac{E_b(\alpha_b-\alpha_c)\Delta T}{1-\nu_b} \tag{6.13.10}$$

$$\sigma_s = \frac{[E_b E_s h_b(1-\nu_s)(1-\nu_c)(\alpha_b-\alpha_c) + E_s^2 h_s(1-\nu_b)(1-\nu_c)(\alpha_s-\alpha_c)]\Delta T}{[E_c h_c(1-\nu_b)(1-\nu_s) + E_b h_b(1-\nu_s)(1-\nu_c) + E_s h_s(1-\nu_c)(1-\nu_b)](1-\nu_s)} -$$

$$\frac{E_s(\alpha_s-\alpha_c)\Delta T}{1-\nu_s} \tag{6.13.11}$$

$$\varepsilon_{c} = \frac{[E_{b} h_{b}(1 - \nu_{c})(1 - \nu_{s})(\alpha_{b} - \alpha_{c}) + E_{s} h_{s}(1 - \nu_{c})(1 - \nu_{b})(\alpha_{s} - \alpha_{c})]\Delta T}{E_{c} h_{c}(1 - \nu_{b})(1 - \nu_{s}) + E_{b} h_{b}(1 - \nu_{s})(1 - \nu_{c}) + E_{s} h_{s}(1 - \nu_{c})(1 - \nu_{b})}$$

$$(6.13.12)$$

$$\varepsilon_{b} = \frac{[E_{b} h_{b}(1 - \nu_{s})(1 - \nu_{c})(\alpha_{b} - \alpha_{c}) + E_{s} h_{s}(1 - \nu_{b})(1 - \nu_{c})(\alpha_{s} - \alpha_{c})]\Delta T}{E_{c} h_{c}(1 - \nu_{b})(1 - \nu_{s}) + E_{b} h_{b}(1 - \nu_{s})(1 - \nu_{c}) + E_{s} h_{s}(1 - \nu_{c})(1 - \nu_{b})} -$$
$$(\alpha_{b} - \alpha_{c})\Delta T \qquad (6.13.13)$$

$$\text{and} \quad \varepsilon_{s} = \frac{[E_{b} h_{b}(1 - \nu_{s})(1 - \nu_{c})(\alpha_{b} - \alpha_{c}) + E_{s} h_{s}(1 - \nu_{b})(1 - \nu_{c})(\alpha_{s} - \alpha_{c})]\Delta T}{E_{c} h_{c}(1 - \nu_{b})(1 - \nu_{s}) + E_{b} h_{b}(1 - \nu_{s})(1 - \nu_{c}) + E_{s} h_{s}(1 - \nu_{c})(1 - \nu_{b})} -$$
$$(\alpha_{s} - \alpha_{c})\Delta T \qquad (6.13.14)$$

The six stress and strain components given above are nominal stresses and strains without the influence of free edge effect.

6.13.3 Strain Isolation Coefficient and Normalized Adhesion Coefficient

The resultant nominal thermal expansion coefficient of the ceramic coating subject to the bonding cement and substrate can be written as the summation of the thermal strain in free state (ε_{c}) and the further strain extended by the bonding cement and substrate ($\varepsilon_{th,c}$) as

$$\alpha'_{c} = \frac{\varepsilon_{th,c} + \varepsilon_{c}}{\Delta T} \qquad (6.13.15)$$

Substituting Eqs. (6.13.6) and (6.13.12) into the above equation leads to resultant nominal thermal coefficient in terms of material constants,

$$\alpha'_{c} = \alpha_{c} + \frac{E_{b} h_{b}(1 - \nu_{c})(1 - \nu_{s})(\alpha_{b} - \alpha_{c}) + E_{s} h_{s}(1 - \nu_{c})(1 - \nu_{b})(\alpha_{s} - \alpha_{c})}{E_{c} h_{c}(1 - \nu_{b})(1 - \nu_{s}) + E_{b} h_{b}(1 - \nu_{s})(1 - \nu_{c}) + E_{s} h_{s}(1 - \nu_{c})(1 - \nu_{b})}$$

$$(6.13.16)$$

As thermal cycling continues, the following two engineering terms are in-situ defined to detect the TBC system health at the *i*th thermal cycle [Zhu and Miller]:

$$S_{i} = \frac{\alpha_{s} - \alpha'_{c,i}}{\alpha_{s} - \alpha'_{c,0}} \quad \text{(Strain isolation coefficient)} \qquad (6.13.17)$$

$$\text{and} \quad A_{i} = \frac{\alpha'_{c,i} - \alpha_{c}}{\alpha'_{c,0} - \alpha_{c}} \quad \text{(Normalized adhesion coefficient)} \qquad (6.13.18)$$

It is shown by Eq. (6.13.11), denoting the normalized adhesive coefficient, that the nominal strain isolation by a thin bonding cement will not be significant with a predominantly thick substrate as given in a general design practice, if the stress intensities between dissimilar materials are not taken into consideration. In fact the thickness of the bonding cement is a deciding parameter on the stress intensity factor. Thus, it is strongly recommended that finite element methods be employed to explore the edge effect due to dissimilar materials.

6.13.4 Maximum Shear Stress Criterion in Ceramic Layer

Spalling occurs when the shear stress between the ceramic and bonding cement exceeds the shear strength between them. The maximum shear stress has been derived by [Tien and Davidson] as

$$\tau_{max} = \frac{4 h_c}{L}\left(\frac{E_c}{1-\nu_c}\right) \varepsilon_c \qquad (6.13.19)$$

where
h_c: Thickness of ceramic;
L: length of adhesion between the ceramic and bonding cement;
E_c: Modulus of elasticity (Young's modulus) of ceramic;
ν_c: Poisson's ratio of ceramic;
τ_{max}: Maximum shear stress induced between the ceramic and bonding cement;
ε_c: Normal strain induced in the ceramic as constrained by the bonding/substrate, related to material constants by Eq. (6.13.12).

6.13.5 Pseudo-Crack Propagation Approach

A modified Paris equation based on the energy release rate (denoted by G) is given as follows [Brodin]:

$$\frac{dN}{da} = C(\lambda \Delta G)^n \qquad (6.13.20)$$

6.14 Thermomechanical Fatigue Life Prediction with Combined Creep and Oxidation

Thermomechanical fatigue (TMF) refers to the fatigue behavior of a material under both thermal and mechanical loads simultaneously. Crack initiation in the oxide scale may result from mechanical fatigue complicated by coupled creep and oxidation failure mechanisms. One attempt to predict the thermomechanical fatigue lifetime according to Fig. 6.14.1, based on ε-N principles, is made by [Jones et al.]. The resulting applicable fatigue parameters are listed in Table 6.14.1.

6.14.1 Additivity of Thermomechanical Fatigue Damage

The damage accumulation model is assumed to be a constitutive model of thermomechanical fatigue to combine together additively the damage resulting from the three failure mechanisms as

$$(2N_f)^{-1} = (2N_{f, \text{ mechanical}})^{-1} + (2N_{f, \text{ creep}})^{-1} + (2N_{f, \text{ oxidation}})^{-1} \tag{6.14.1}$$

where $2N_f$ is the fatigue life of the material, i.e. the number of loading cycles until failure. The contributions of $(2N_{f, \text{ mechanical}})^{-1}$ and $(2N_{f,\text{creep}})^{-1}$ may be accounted for according to Eq. (6.10.18) in a coupled manner, while $(2N_{f,\text{oxidation}})^{-1}$ can be calculated independently as most researchers did [Chai et al.] [Sehitoglu & Neu].

6.14.2 Impact of Oxidation on Fatigue Life

Fatigue parameters due to oxidation can be found by comparing fatigue tests done in the air full of oxygen and in an environment with no oxygen (argon, N_2, or vacuum). The effect of oxidation can reduce the fatigue life of a specimen by a whole order of magnitude as shown in Fig. 6.14.1, of which the applied temperature fluctuates between 100 ℃ and 650 ℃. Higher temperatures greatly increase the amount of damage from environmental factors. Based on the assumption that oxide cracks once the strain range exceeds a threshold ($\varepsilon_{a,\text{mech}} > \varepsilon_0$), the following oxidation damage equation [Neu & Sehitoglu] has been applied in a decoupled manner (i.e. no alias to creep or mechanical fatigue) as

$$(2N_{f,\text{oxidation}})^{-1} = \left(\frac{\phi_{\text{ox}} K_{\text{peff}}}{h_{\text{cr}}}\right)^{\frac{1}{\beta}} \left[\frac{2(\varepsilon_{a,\text{mech}})^{1+\frac{2}{\beta}}}{\left(\frac{d\varepsilon}{dt}\right)^{1-\frac{\Lambda}{\beta}}}\right] \tag{6.14.2}$$

$$\text{with}\quad \phi_{\text{ox}} = t_c^{-1} \int_0^{t_c} \exp\left\{-\frac{1}{2}\left[1 + \frac{\dfrac{d\varepsilon_{\text{th}}}{dt}}{\dfrac{d\varepsilon_{\text{mech}}}{dt}}\right]^2\right\} dt \tag{6.14.3}$$

$$\text{and}\quad K_{\text{peff}} = \int_0^{t_c} D_o \exp\left(\frac{-Q_{\text{ox}}}{RT}\right) dt \tag{6.14.4}$$

where

ε_0: Threshold strain for oxide cracking;

$(d\varepsilon_{\text{th}}/dt)/(d\varepsilon_{\text{mech}}/dt)$: Ratio of thermal strain rate to mechanical strain rate;

t_c: Cycle duration;

h_{cr}: A constant related to critical oxide thickness;

β: Mechanical strain range exponent;

λ: Thermal strain rate sensitivity exponent;

ξ_{ox}: Oxidation-phasing constant for thermal and mechanical strains;

Q_{ox}(J/mole): Activation energy for oxidation;

K_{peff}: Effective parabolic oxidation constant;

D_o: Scaling constant for oxidation.

As an example, oxidation parameters of SAE1070 (HR) steel are listed here as follows: $\beta = 1.5$; $\lambda = 0.75$; $\xi_{ox} = 2$; $E_{ox} = 156.5 \times 10^3$; $D_o = 6.95 \times 10^7$; $\varepsilon_o = 0$; $h_{cr} = 0.01536$. Based on Eq. (6.14.2), one can derive the following two extreme cases:

(a) When $(d\varepsilon_{th}/dt)/(d\varepsilon_{mech}/dt) = -1$, it is an OP-TMF oxidation process and $\phi_{ox} = 1$. The oxidation damage is most.

(b) When $(d\varepsilon_{th}/dt)/(d\varepsilon_{mech}/dt) = \infty$ or $-\infty$, it is an IP-TMF oxidation process and $\phi_{ox} = 0$. There is no oxidation damage.

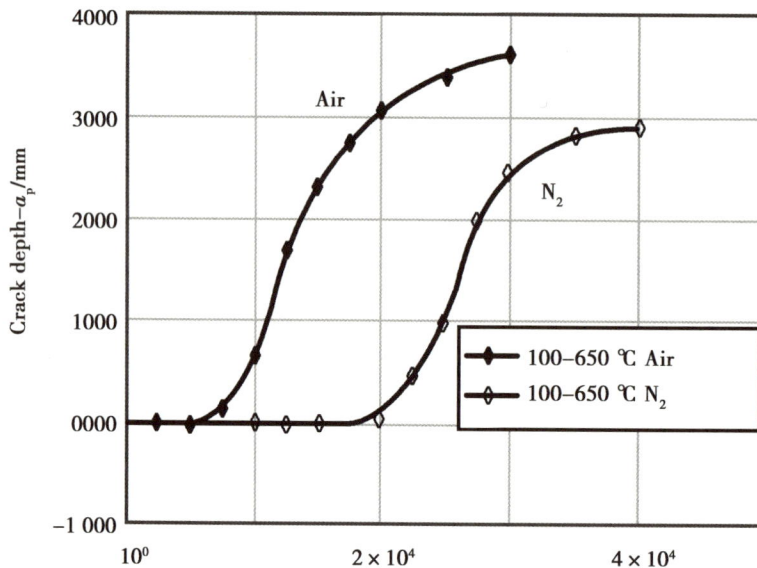

Fig. 6.14.1   Fatigue Life Reduction by Oxidation in the Air versus N_2 [Lamesle et al.]

6.14.3   Technical Challenge of Multiaxial Thermomechanical Fatigue

Numerous fatigue life prediction models have been developed for thermomechanical fatigue (TMF) life prediction. They are predominantly applicable to components under uniaxial mechanical loading conditions. Products have to endure multiaxial, non-isothermal loadings in the real world and their durability concern is complicated by coupled interactive effects from various damaging factors such as phase difference between shear and normal stresses, phase difference between thermal and mechanical loadings, edge effect, existing manufacturing defects, and non-isothermal working environments. Future product robustness will definitely resort to promising predictive models and test validation procedures involved in multiaxial thermomechanical fatigue.

References

ABULUWEFA H T, 2005. Kinetics of High Temperature Oxidation of High Carbon Steels in Multi-component Gases Approximating Industrial Steel Reheat Furnace Atmospheres[J]. University of Misurata, Libya.

ANTONIOUAND R, RADTKE, T. 1997. Mechanisms of Fretting Fatigue of Titanium Alloys[J]. Materials Science and Engineering, A,237, 229-240.

ARYA V K, 1999. Finite Element Elastic-Plastic-Creep and Cyclic Life Analysis of a Cowl Lip[J]. Fatigue and Fracture of Engineering Materials and Structures, 14(10): 967-977.

ASHBY M F, ABEL C A, 1995. Materials Selection to Resist Creep[J]. Philosophical Transactions of Royal Society of London, A, 351: 451-468.

BELLOWS R S, et al, 1999. Validation of the Step Test Method for Generating Haigh Diagrams for Ti-6Al-41 [J]. International Journal of Fatigue, 21(7): 687-697.

BRODIN H, et al, 2006. Thermal Barrier Coating Fatigue Assessment[J]. Siemens AG 2006.

BENDL K et al, 2004. Finite Element Analysis of Modules Made of Thermoplastic Materials and Elastomeric Gaskets for Powertrain Applications[J]. SAE 2004-01-0011.

BOYER H E, 1988. Atlas of Creep and Stress-Rupture Curves[J]. ASM International, Metals Park, OH, USA.

BROCK W, MARTIN R E, 2003. A Nonlinear Viscoelastic Characterization of Creep Rupture in Reinforced Plastic[J]. Advances in Polymer Technology, 3(3): 253-269.

BUSSO E P, QIAN Z Q, 2006. A Mechanistic Study of Microcracking in Transversely Isotropic Ceramic-Metal Systems[J]. Acta Materialia, 52: 325-338.

CATHCART J, 1975. Stress Effects and the Oxidation of Metals[M], TMS-AIME, New York.

CHAI C, et al, 1999. Recent Developments in the Thermomechanical Fatigue Life Prediction of Superalloys[J]. JOM, April 1999.

CRISTALLI C, AGOSTINI P, BERNARDI D, et al, 2017. Low Cycle Fatigue, Creep-Fatigue and Relaxation-Fatigue Tests on P91[J]. Journal of Physical Science and Application, 7(3): 18-26.

CHICOT D, et al, 2013. Mechanical Properties of Magnetite (Fe_3O_4), Hematite (α-Fe_2O_3) and Goethite (α-FeO · OH) by Instrumented Indentation and Molecular Dynamics Analysis[J]. Materials Chemistry and Physics, 129(3): 862-870.

CHRIST H, JUNG A, MAIER H, TETERUK R, 2003. Thermomechanical Fatigue-Damage Mechanisms and Mechanism-based Life Prediction Methods[J]. Sadhana, 28: 147-165.

CHRZANOWSKI M, 1988. A Strain Energy Governed Damage Law for High Temperature Low Cycle Fatigue [J]. RPI Report MML 88-5.

EVANS H E, TAYLOR M P, 2003. Delamination Processes in Thermal Barrier Coating Systems[J]. Journal of Corrosion Science and Engineering, 6: 011.

EVANS W J, SCREECH J E, WILLIAMS S W, 2008. Thermomechanical Fatigue and Fracture of INCO718 [J]. International Journal of Fatigue, 30: 257-267.

FAN Z, et al, 2006. A Life Prediction Model of Fatigue-Creep Interaction with Stress Controlled Fatigue[J]. Journal of Pressure Equipment and Systems, 4: 42-47.

FATEMI A, SOCIE D F, 1988. A Critical Plane Approach to Multiaxial Fatigue Damage Including Out-Of-Phase Loading[J]. Fatigue and Fracture of Engineering Materials and Structures, 11(3): 145-165.

FINDLEY W N, LAI J S, ONARAN K, 1976. Creep and Relaxation of Nonlinear Viscoelastic Materials[J]. Dover Publications, New York, NY, USA.

FINDLEY W N, 1960. Mechanism and Mechanics of Creep of Plastics[J]. SPEJ, 16: 57-65.

GENOVESE A, SHANKS R A, 2007. Time-temperature Creep Behavior of Poly (propylene) and Polar Ethylene Copolymer Blends[J]. Macromolecular Materials and Engineering, 292: 184-196.

GIANNAKOPOULOS A E, et al, 1999. Theory of Indentation of Piezoelectric Materials[J]. Acta Materialia. 47 (7): 2153-2164.

GOERTZEN W K, KESSLER M R, 2006. Creep Behavior of Carbon Fiber/Epoxy Matrix Composites[J]. Materials Science and Engineering, 421(1-2): 217-225.

GOSWAMI T, 2004. Development of Generic Creep-Fatigue Life Prediction Models[J]. Materials and Design, 25: 277-288.

GOYAL S, et al, 2014. Mechanistic Approach for Prediction of Creep Deformation, Damage and Rupture Life of Different Cr-Mo Ferritic Steels[J]. Materials at High Temperatures, 31(3):211-220.

GUEDES R M, 2011. A Viscoelastic Model for a Biomedical Ultra-high Molecular Weight Polyethylene Using the Time-Temperature Superposition Principle[J]. Polymer Testing, 30: 294-302.

GUEDES R M, 2008. Creep and Fatigue Lifetime Prediction of Polymer Matrix Composites Based on Simple Cumulative Damage Laws[J]. Composites Part A: Applied Science and Manufacturing, 39(11): 1716-1725.

HAHNER P, et al, 2007. Research and Development into a European Code-of Practice for Strain-controlled Thermomechanical Fatigue Testing[J]. International Journal of Fatigue, 30: 372-381.

HAN G, et al, 2011. Thermomechanical Fatigue Behavior of a Single Crystal Nickel-based Superalloy [J]. Materials Science and Engineering, A, 528(19-20): 6217-6224.

HE M Y, et al, 2003. Simulation of Stresses and Delamination in a Plasma-sprayed Thermal Barrier System upon Thermal Cycling[J]. Materials Science & Engineering, A, 345: 172-178.

HIDAKY Y, et al, 2000. High Temperature Tensile Behavior of FeO Scale[J]. Nippon Kinzoku Gakkaishi, 64 (5): 291-294。

HIEMENZ P C, 2007. Polymer Chemistry[M]. 2nd Edition. Florida: Taylor & Francis Group.

ISO 12111, 2011. Metallic Materials-Fatigue Testing-Strain-Controlled Thermomechanical Fatigue Testing Method[J]. BSI Standards Publication.

JEON H Y, KIM S H, YOO H K, 2002. Assessment of Long-term Performances of Polyester Geogrids by Accelerated Creep Test[J]. Polymer Testing, 21: 489-495.

JONES J, et al, 2014. Lifting the Thermomechanical Fatigue (TMF) Behavior of the Polycrystalline Nickel-Based Superalloy RR1000[J]. MATEC Web of Conferences 14, 19001.

JUNISBEKOV T M, 2003. Stress Relaxation in Viscoelastic Materials[M]. Science Pub Incorporated.

KALLURI S, 2013. Multiaxial and Thermomechanical Fatigue of Materials: A Historical Perspective and Some Future Challenges [J]. 13th International ASTM/ESIS Symposium on Fatigue and Fracture Mechanics, November 13-15, 2013, Jacksonville, Florida.

KANG H, LEE Y, CHEN J, et al, 2007. Thermomechanical Fatigue Damage Model for Variable Temperature and Loading Amplitude Conditions[J]. International Journal of Fatigue, 29: 1797-1802.

KASSNER M, 2008. Fundamentals of Creep in Metals and Alloys[M]. 2nd Edition. Elsevier.

KEATING M Y, MALONE L, SAUNDERS W, 2002. Annealing Effect on Semi-Crystalline Materials in Creep Behavior[J]. Journal of Thermal Analysis and Calorimetry, 69: 37-52.

LAMESLE P, SALEM M, LEROUX S, et al, 2000. Oxidation and Corrosion Effects on Thermal Behavior of Hot Work Tool Steel X38CrMoV5 (AISI H11)[J]. Ecole des Mines d'Albi -Campus Jarlard-Route de Teillet -81013 Albi cedex 09, France.

LANCASTER R J, WHITTAKER M T, WILLIAMS S J, 2013. A Review of Thermomechanical Fatigue Behavior in Polycrystalline Nickel Superalloys for Turbine Disc Applications [J]. Materials at High Temperatures, 30: 2-12.

LARSON F R, MILLER J, 1952. A Time-temperature Relationship for Rupture and Creep Stresses [J]. Transactions of the ASME, 74: 765-775.

LI R Z, 2000. Time-Temperature Superposition Method for Glass Transition Point of Plastic Materials[J]. Materials Science and Engineering, A, 278(1-2): 36-45.

LIU D, XU Q, LU Z, 2013. Research in the Development of Finite Element Software for Creep Damage Analysis[J]. Journal of Communication and Computer, 10: 1019-1030.

L'VOV G, LYSENKO S, GORASH E, 2008. Creep and Creep-Rupture Strength of Gas Turbine Components in View of Nonuniform Temperature Distribution[J]. Strength of Materials, 40(5): 525-530.

MARUYAMA K, et al, 2001. Strengthening Mechanisms of Creep Resistant Tempered Martensitic Steel[J]. ISIJ International, 41(6): 641-653.

MAZIASZ P J, et al, 2005. Overview of Creep Strength and Oxidation of Heat-Resistance Alloy Sheets and Foils for Compact Heat Exchangers[J]. Proceedings of GT2005, Reno-Tahoe, Nevada, USA.

MILLER, R A, 2009. History of Thermal Barrier Coatings for Gas Turbine Engine[J]. Thermal Barrier Coatings 11. Engineering Conference International. NASA 2009-215459.

MIYANO Y, NAKADA, M CAI H, 2008. Formulation of Long-term Creep and Fatigue Strengths of Polymer Composites Based on Accelerated Testing Methodology[J]. Journal of Composite Materials, 42(19-8): 1897-1919.

MIYANO Y, NAKADA M, SEKINE N, 2006. Accelerated Testing for Long-term Durability of FRP Laminates for Marine Use[J]. Journal of Composite Materials, 39(1): 5-20.

NAGESHA A, et al, 2010. A Comparative Study of Isothermal and Thermomechanical Fatigue on Type 316L (N) Austenitic Stainless Steel[J]. Materials Science and Engineering, A, 527(21-22): 5969-5975.

NAGL M, SAUNDERS S, GUTTMANN, V, 1994. Experimental Data on Oxide Fracture[J]. Materials at High Temperatures[J]. 12(2-3): 163-168.

NAGODE A, KOSEC L, ULE B, et al, 2011. Review of Creep Resistant Alloys for Power Plant Applications [J]. METALURGUA, 50(1): 45-48.

NEU R, SEHITOGLU H, 1989, Thermomechanical Fatigue, Oxidation and Creep: Part 1-Experiments[J]. Metallurgical Transactions, 20A: 1755-1767.

NEU R, SEHITOGLU H, 1989, Thermomechanical Fatigue, Oxidation and Creep: Part 2-Life Prediction[J]. Metallurgical Transactions, 20A: 1769-1783.

NILLES M, Van SCIVER S, 1988, Effects of Oxidation and Roughness on Cu Contact Resistance from 4 K to 290 K[J]. Advances in Cryogenic Engineering (Materials), 34: 443-450.

NUNN J, SAUNDERS S R J, BANKS J, 2005. Application of Thermography in the Evaluation of Early Signs of Failure of Thermal Barrier Coatings[J]. Proceedings of 6th International Conference on Microscopy of Oxidation, Birmingham University, April 2005: 219-226.

OGATA T, 2010. Creep-fatigue Damage and Life Prediction of Alloy Steels[J]. Materials at High Temperatures, 27(1): 11-19.

OSTERGREN W, 1967. A Damage Foundation Hold Time and Frequency Effects in Elevated Temperature Low Cycle Fatigue[J]. Journal of Testing and Evaluation, 4: 327-33.

PENNY R K, MARRIOTT D L, 1995. Design for Creep[M]. Springer Science and Business Media.

PERNOT J, NICHOLAS T, MALL S, 1994. Modeling Thermomechanical Fatigue Crack Growth Rates in Ti-24Al-11Nb[J]. International Journal of Fatigue, 16: 111-112.

PULIDO J, 2012. Reliability Analysis for Components under Thermal Mechanical Loadings[J]. 2012 Reliability and Maintainability Symposium, January 2012.

RAJ A K, 2013. On High-Temperature Materials: A Case on Creep and Oxidation of a Fully Austenitic Heat-Resistant Superalloy Stainless Steel Sheet[J]. Journal of Materials, Volume 2013, Article ID 124649, 6 pages.

REVIE R W UHLIG H H, 2008. Corrosion and Corrosion Control: An Introduction to Corrosion Science and Engineering, John Wiley and Sons, Hoboken, NJ, USA.

RIGNEY D V, 1997. PVD Thermal Barrier Coating Applications and Process Development for Aircraft Engines [J]. Journal of Thermal Spray Technology[J]. 6(2): 167-75.

ROBERTSON J, MANNING M, 1990. Journal of Materials Science & Technology, 6: 81-91.

SAKAI T, SOMIYA S, 2006. Estimating Creep Deformation of Glass-Fiber-Reinforced Polycarbonate [J]. Mechanics of Time Dependent Materials, 10(3): 185-199.

SAKANE M, ITOH T, 2005. Effect of Hydrostatic Stress on Low Cycle Fatigue Life[C]. ASME Pressure Vessels and Piping Conference, 41863: 279-285.

SCHLICHTINC J, 1978. High Temperature Oxidation of Disilicides in the System $MoSi_2$ [J]. Ceramurgia International, 4(4): 162-166.

SCHÜTZE M, 2010. 1.08 -Stress Effects in High Temperature Oxidation[J]. Shreir's Corrosion, 1: 153-179.

SEHITOGLU H, MAIER H, 2000. Thermomechanical Fatigue Behavior of Materials[J]. ASTM STP, 3: 1371.

SEIFERT T, et al, 2010. Thermomechanical Fatigue of 1.4849 Cast Steel-Experiments and Life Prediction Using a Fracture Mechanics Approach[J]. International Journal of Materials Research, 101(8): 942-950.

SEIFERT T, RIEDE H, 2009. Fatigue Life Prediction of High Temperature Components in Combustion Engines and Exhaust Systems [J]. EASC 2009, 4th European Automotive Simulation Conference, Munich, Germany, July 6-7.

SHCHERBINA O B, et al, 2014. Mechanical Properties of Nb_2O_5 and Ta_2O_5 Prepared by Different Procedures [J]. Inorganic Materials, 48(4): 433-438.

SHI L, NORTHWOOD D O, 1995. Recent Progress in the Modeling of High-Temperature Creep and Its Application to Alloy Development[J]. Journal of Materials Engineering and Performance, 1995, 4(2): 196-211.

SIHN S, TSAI S W, 2018. Automated Shift For Time-Temperature Superposition [J]. Department of Aeronautics and Astronautics, Stanford University Durand 381, Stanford, California, 94305, USA.

SMIALEK J L, 2011. Moisture-Induced TBC Spallation on Turbine Blade Samples[J]. Surface and Coatings Technology, 206: 1577-1585.

STEINER H, KONYS J, 2006. Stress in Oxidized Claddings and Mechanical Stability of Oxide Scales[M].

FZKA 7191, Forschungszen Karlsruhe.

STEINER H, KONYS J, HECK M, 2006. Growth Stresses in Oxidized Tube Subject to Multiaxial Oxidation Strains Oxidation of Metals, 66(1-2): 37-67.

STOOT F H, 1997. The Influence of Oxidation on the Wear of Metals and Alloys[J]. New Directions in Tribology, 391-401.

STRUIK L C E, 1978. Physical Aging in Amorphous Polymers and other Materials, Elsevier Scientific Publishing Company, 82(9): 1019.

TAKEDA M, et al, 2009. Physical Properties of Iron Oxide Scales on Si-Containing Steels at High Temperatures[J]. Materials Transactions, 50(9): 2242-2246.

TURNER S, 2001. Creep of Polymeric Materials[M]. Oxford: Elsevier Science Ltd.

VAN G M, PALMENM J, 1998. Time-Temperature Superposition for Polymer Blends[J]. Rheology Bulletin, 67(1): 5-8.

WILLIAMS M L, LANDEL R F, FERRY J D, 1955. The Temperature Dependence of Relaxation Mechanisms in Amorphous Polymers and Other Glass-Forming Liquids[J]. Journal of the American Chemical Society, 77 (14): 3701-3707.

WU X J, 2009. A Model of Nonlinear Fatigue-Creep/Dwell Interactions[J]. Journal of Engineering for Gas Turbines and Power, 131(3): 1-6.

YAGUCHI M, et al, 2010. Creep Strength of High Chromium Steels Welded Parts under Multiaxial Stress Conditions[J]. International Journal of Pressure Vessels and Piping, 87(6): 357-364.

ZACHARIAH K J, 2012. Creep Analysis of a Bolted Joint-A Sensitivity Study of Bolt Relaxation Due To Different Assembly Preloads, MS Thesis, Rensselaer Polytechnic Institute.

ZHANG J X, et al, 2009. Crack Appearance of Single-Crystal Nickel-Based Superalloys after Thermomechanical Fatigue Failure[J]. Scripta Materialia, 61: 1105-1108.

ZHU S, HUANG H, LI Y, et al, 2012. A Novel Viscosity-Based Model for Low Cycle Fatigue Creep Life Prediction of High-Temperature Structures[J]. International Journal of Damage Mechanics, 21: 1076-1099.

ZHU D M, MILLER R A, 1996. Evaluation of Oxidation Damage in Thermal Barrier Coating Systems[R]. Fall Meeting, the Electrochemical Society, San Antonio, Texas, Oct. 6-11.

ZINEB A, et al, 2010. Analysis of Thermomechanical Fatigue by Using Finite Element Post-Processing[J]. Australian Journal of Basic and Applied Sciences, 4(10): 4857-4869.

Problems

Problem 6.1　　Inconel 718 bolts in a steam-pipe flange are tightened so that the initial tensile stress is $\sigma_0 = 900$ MPa at the working temperature of 725 ℃. The length the bolts remains fixed in service. At 725 ℃, the steady-state creep strain rate of the steel follows the following equation: $d\varepsilon_{creep}/dt = 4.547\ 2 \times 10^{-34}\ \sigma^{9.71} t^{-0.468}$ (units are s^{-1}, MPa, and s, respectively) and the initial elastic modulus $E_0 = 175$ GPa. What is the stress in the bolts after 1500-hour operation under the same working temperature? What is the creep strain after 1500-hour operation? (Answer: $\sigma(1500) = 758$ MPa and $\varepsilon_{creep}(1\ 500) = 8.1 \times 10^{-4}$)

Table 6.10.1   Comparative Oxidation Resistance in Flowing Air

Material	$T/℃$	Fluid	Speed/($mm \cdot s^{-1}$)	Duration/h	Material Loss/μm
Haynes 188 (Ni-alloy)	982	Air	35.6	1008	15
	1093	Air	35.6	1008	33
	1149	Air	35.6	1008	203
	1204	Air	35.6	1008	>551
Haynes 230 (Ni-alloy)	982	Air	35.6	1008	18
	1093	Air	35.6	1008	33
	1149	Air	35.6	1008	86
	1204	Air	35.6	1008	201
Inconel 601 (Ni-alloy)	982	Air	35.6	1008	33
	1093	Air	35.6	1008	66
	1149	Air	35.6	1008	135
	1204	Air	35.6	1008	191
AISI 316 (Stainless Steel)	982	Air	35.6	1008	363
	1093	Air	35.6	1008	1737
	1149	Air	35.6	1008	2667
	1204	Air	35.6	1008	3566
AISI 446 (Stainless Steel)	982	Air	35.6	1008	58
	1093	Air	35.6	1008	368
	1149	Air	35.6	1008	551
	1204	Air	35.6	1008	592

Table 6.11.1　Mechanical Properties of Oxide Layers ［Busso & Qian］［Steiner & Konys］［Takada et al.］［Evans & Taylor］

Material	$T/℃$	E_T	ρ	ν	(σ,ε)	α	k	γ	$\gamma_{surface}$	R_{pb}	K_{IC}
FeCr₂O₄ (Inner Subscale)	23	233	—	0.31	—	10.5	—	—	5	2.07	1.5
	300	—	—	—	—	12.5	—	—	—	—	—
	500	—	—	—	—	18.5	—	—	—	—	—
	550	—	—	—	—	18.5	—	—	—	—	—
	600	—	—	—	—	17.5	—	—	—	—	—
FeO (Wustite)	23	—	—	0.3	—	12	10	—	—	—	—
	200	—	—	—	—	12.5	9.5	—	—	—	—
	400	—	—	—	—	13	8	—	—	—	—
	600	—	—	—	—	14	7	—	—	—	—
	700	—	—	—	—	17	—	—	—	—	—
	800	—	—	—	—	17	6	—	—	—	—
	1000	—	—	—	—	18	—	—	—	—	—
FeO · OH (α) (Goethite)	23	—	—	0.3	—	—	—	—	—	—	—
Fe₂O₃(α) (Hematite; Surface layer)	23	211	5.26	0.35	$\sigma_{uts}=350$	9	15	—	—	—	—
	200	—	—	—	—	10	7	—	—	—	—
	400	—	—	—	—	10.5	5	—	—	—	—
	600	—	—	—	—	11	3.5	—	—	—	—
	800	—	—	—	—	12.5	3	—	—	—	—
	1000	—	—	—	—	12	—	—	—	—	—
	1595 (T_m)	—	—	—	—	—	—	—	—	—	—
Fe₃O₄(25 μm Magnetite)	23	211	5.1	0.29	—	11	6	734	4.5	2.07	1.4
	200	—	—	—	—	—	4.5	—	—	—	—
	400	—	—	—	—	16	4	—	—	—	—
	500	—	—	—	—	24	—	—	—	—	—
	550	—	—	—	—	25	—	—	—	—	—
	600	—	—	—	—	17	3.5	—	—	—	—
	800	—	—	—	—	15	3.5	—	—	—	—

continued

Material	$T/℃$	E_T	ρ	ν	(σ,ε)	α	k	γ	$\gamma_{surface}$	R_{pb}	K_{IC}
Fe_2SiO_4	23	—	—	—	—	12	3.5	—	—	—	—
	200	—	—	—	—	9	3	—	—	—	—
	400	—	—	—	—	10	2.5	—	—	—	—
	600	—	—	—	—	10.5	2.3	—	—	—	—
	800	—	—	—	—	11.5	2	—	—	—	—
	1000	—	—	—	—	14.5	—	—	—	—	—
Cr_2O_3	550	—	—	—	—	7.3	—	—	—	—	—
NiO	500	—	—	—	—	17.1	—	—	—	—	—
$NiCr_2O_4$	23	233	—	0.31	—	10.5	—	—	—	—	1.5
EB-PVD YSZ	23	—	—	—	—	—	9.7	—	—	—	—
	1100	—	—	—	—	—	10.1	—	—	—	—
FeCrAlY(TBC Bond Coat)	23	200	—	0.3	$\sigma_{uts}=426$	—	13.6	—	—	—	—
	600	160	—	0.31	$\sigma_{uts}=362$	—	15.2	—	—	—	—
	800	145	—	0.32	$\sigma_{uts}=284$	—	16.1	—	—	—	—
	1000	120	—	0.33	$\sigma_{uts}=202$	—	17.2	—	—	—	—
	1100	110	—	0.33	$\sigma_{uts}=114$	—	17.6	—	—	—	—
TGO(Grown between YSZ & Platinum Aluminide)	23	400	—	0.23	—	7.9	—	—	—	—	—
	400	380	—	0.24	—	8.4	—	—	—	—	—
	800	355	—	0.25	—	9	—	—	—	—	—
	1100	320	—	0.25	—	9.6	—	—	—	—	—
Platinum Aluminide (Substrate)	23	200	—	0.3	—	13.6	—	—	—	—	—
	400	175	—	0.31	—	14.6	—	—	—	—	—
	800	145	—	0.32	—	16.1	—	—	—	—	—
	1100	110	—	0.33	—	17.6	—	—	—	—	—

Notes: $\gamma_{surface}$: Surface fracture energy.

R_{pb}: Pilling-Bedworth ratio that is the ratio of total thickness to internal grown thickness.

Table 6.13.1 Mechanical Creep Parameters of TBC (Thermal Barrier Coating) Components [Busso & Qian].

Material	$T/°C$	Stress/MPa	Strain Rate/s^{-1}	$A/(MPa^{-n}\ s^{m-1})$	$Q/$ $(J \cdot mol^{-1})$	n	m
TGO(Grown between YSZ & Pt−Al Based)	200−1100	$E=1$	—	6805	$424×10^3$	2.3	0
Pt−Al Based (TBC Substrate)	200−1100	$E=1$	—	13.3	$263×10^3$	4.1	0

Notes: Creep equation $\dfrac{d\varepsilon_{creep}}{dt} = A\left(\dfrac{\sigma - \sigma_{th}}{E}\right)^n t^m \exp^{\frac{-Q}{RT_k}}, \sigma > \sigma_{th}$.

σ_{th}: Stress threshold and $\sigma_{th} = 0$, if not specified.

E: Young's modulus; If given that $E = 1$, it means E is not specified.

Table 6.14.1 Fatigue ε-N Properties of Materials under Thermomechanical Fatigue [Jones et al.].

Material	T	$d\varepsilon/dt$	σ'_f	ε'_f	b	c	K'	n'	$\sigma_f@2N_f$	R
RR 1000(Ni Alloy)	300−700	—	989.5	—	−0.082	—	—	—	—	−1 (IP)

国家出版基金项目
NATIONAL PUBLICATION FOUNDATION

产品寿命预测力学与设计
Mechanics and Design for Product Life Prediction II

江永瑞 著

重庆大学出版社

图书在版编目(CIP)数据

产品寿命预测力学与设计 = Mechanics and Design
for Product Life Prediction：英文／江永瑞著. --
重庆：重庆大学出版社，2022.1
（自主品牌汽车实践创新丛书）
ISBN 978-7-5689-1917-3

Ⅰ.①产…　Ⅱ.①江…　Ⅲ.①汽车—零部件—产品寿
命—力学—研究—英文　Ⅳ.U463

中国版本图书馆 CIP 数据核字(2020)第 001261 号

产品寿命预测力学与设计

CHANPIN SHOUMING YUCE LIXUE YU SHEJI

（Ⅱ）

江永瑞　著
策划编辑：杨粮菊　鲁 黎

责任编辑：陈 力　张慧梓　　版式设计：杨粮菊
责任校对：邹 忌　　　　　　责任印制：张 策
*
重庆大学出版社出版发行
出版人：饶帮华
社址：重庆市沙坪坝区大学城西路 21 号
邮编：401331
电话：(023)88617190　88617185(中小学)
传真：(023)88617186　88617166
网址：http://www.cqup.com.cn
邮箱：fxk@ cqup.com.cn(营销中心)
全国新华书店经销
重庆升光电力印务有限公司印刷
*
开本：889mm×1194mm　1/16　总印张：60.5　总字数：1975 千
2022 年 1 月第 1 版　　2022 年 1 月第 1 次印刷
ISBN 978-7-5689-1917-3　总定价：368.00 元(全 3 卷)

Contents

Chapter 9　Structural Instability

Chapter 10　Composites-Micromechanics

Chapter 11   Thermal Loadings

Chapter 12   Moisture Diffusion

Chapter 7

Random Vibration Fatigue and Impact Engineering

7.1　Automotive Vibrations

Automotive vibration analysis utilizes displacement, velocity and acceleration, displayed as a time waveform, but also as a related energy spectrum such as power spectral density (PSD). The PSD is often derived from an FFT (Fast Fourier Transform), no matter whether a diagnostic vibration test or finite element analysis is conducted in the form of sinusoidal or random signals. Swept sine-wave (one-frequency-at-a-time) tests are performed to survey the structural response of a vehicle under test, while a random vibration test (all frequencies at once) is considered when replicating a real world environment, such as the road input to a moving vehicle. Switching between time and frequency is a common tool used for analysis. A full-scaled VPG (Virtual Proving Ground) model based on finite element methods [Chiang], simplified closed-form solution model of relevant structural components [Jazar], or quarter-car model [Türkay & Akçay] can be used for vibration analysis.

Automotive vibration testing help attune automotive products for structural soundness and paramount vehicle operation using methods such as resonant searches and dwells, fixture resonance evaluation, custom fixture design and fabrication, reproduction of sample road and/or event data, shock response spectrum testing, buzz/squeak/rattle testing, and ultimately product life prediction. Automotive testing of full vehicles has been proven to be an excellent means of improving product quality and customer satisfaction. The need to improve reliability and functionality of entire vehicles, as well as major sub-assemblies such as the instrument panel and seating system, has led to the creation of multiaxial test systems capable of accurately reproducing recorded road data, axial-torsional systems to determine fatigue characteristics of parts and assemblies that emulate operating vehicle performance in the test lab. One choice is the 4-poster system shown in Fig. 7.1.1, or instrumented alike, where independent actuators are used under each vehicle wheel to deliver the desired vertical-transverse-longitudinal excitations phased to replicate road conditions.

Vibrations at low frequencies, ranging from 0 to 80 Hz, directly affect ride performance and human body comfort. Physiological responses to automotive vibrations are complex and they can be classified roughly as follows:

    (1) Around 1 Hz: Car sick.
    (2) 4-10 Hz: Chest pain.
    (3) 8-12 Hz: Backaches.
    (4) 10-20 Hz: Headaches, eye strain, and irritations in the intestines and bladder.
    (5) 10-25 Hz: Eyes impaired due to compensatory head and eye movements.

Practicing engineers take advantage of the information about all kinds of resonant vibration modes to design products in order that the resonant frequencies (natural frequencies) stay far from the loading dominant frequencies. As described in ISO 2631, human comfort charts are generally made regarding the acceleration level in the frequency domain. One simple guideline is not to design something that has a natural frequency of 40 Hz or below because the propeller-driven craft will always have structure-born vibration that is typically 40 Hz or below. Ideally, resonant frequencies should not coincide with any of the principal harmonics of the vehicle. A vehicle component may fail qualification if low-damped resonances are encountered within avoid bands of a principal harmonic. Speed-sensitive vibrations are mainly caused by tires, which are out of round, out of balance or have bulges or flat spots. In addition, a car can also vibrate onerously at a certain speed only because of the damaged brakes, bent wheels, worn-out drivetrain components, and/or broken suspension or steering parts.

Fig. 7.1.1　Automotive Multiaxial Vibration Testing

7.2　Free Vibration

Free vibration occurs when a mechanical system is set in motion with an initial input and allowed to move freely. The free vibration of a viscous vibration system of one degree of freedom can be formulated as

$$M\left(\frac{\mathrm{d}^2 x}{\mathrm{d}t^2}\right) + C\left(\frac{\mathrm{d}x}{\mathrm{d}t}\right) + K x = 0 \tag{7.2.1}$$

where

M: Mass;

C: Damping coefficient;

K: Stiffness.

The above equation can be rewritten in another format as

$$\frac{d^2x}{dt^2} + 2\,\xi\,\omega_n\left(\frac{dx}{dt}\right) + \omega_n\,x = 0 \tag{7.2.2}$$

where

ξ: Damping ratio, also called damping factor;

ω_n: Undamped natural frequency.

The damping ratio is a system parameter, denoted by ξ, which can vary from undamped ($\xi=0$), underdamped ($\xi<1$) through critically damped ($\xi=1$) to overdamped ($\xi>1$). The mass tends to overshoot its starting position when it is even excited in a free vibration system, and then return, overshooting again. With such a cyclic motion, certain amount of energy in the system is dissipated, and the oscillations die towards zero in a free vibration system. This case is called underdamped. Otherwise, it is called overdamped. Damping ratio (damping factor) and undamped natural frequency can be defined by relating Eq. (7.2.2) to Eq. (7.2.1), respectively as

$$\xi = \frac{\frac{1}{2}\,C}{(M\,K)^{\frac{1}{2}}} \tag{7.2.3}$$

and $\quad \omega_n = \left(\frac{K}{M}\right)^{\frac{1}{2}} \tag{7.2.4}$

Note that only positive numbers can be taken for natural frequencies. Negative eigenvalues resulting from finite element analyses or other engineering calculations ought to be neglected. Applying a force to the mass and spring, which store energy (kinetic energy in mass and potential energy in spring), is similar to pushing a child on swing, a push is needed at the right moment when matching a specific natural frequency to make the motion (swing) get higher and higher. This phenomenon is called resonance and it occurs when $\xi=1$. Every structure can vibrate and has particular frequencies (resonance frequencies), at which it vibrates with the greatest amplitude. At resonance, $\xi=1$, and Eq. (7.2.3) can be rewritten as

$$C_{\text{critical}} = 2(M\,K)^{\frac{1}{2}} \tag{7.2.5}$$

Parameter C_{critical} is called critical damping coefficient. Damping effect, instead of storing energy, dissipates energy. Viscous damping has been used to describe the energy-dissipating characteristics of different types of vibration systems. The most used viscous damping model is linear, of which the viscous-damping coefficient relates the viscous-damping force to the vibration velocity as

$$F_d = -C\left(\frac{dx}{dt}\right) = -C\,v \tag{7.2.6}$$

where

$C(\text{NS/mm or NS/m})$: Damping coefficient or viscous-damping coefficient;

$F_d(\text{N})$: Viscous damping force;

$x(\text{mm or m})$: Vibration amplitude (displacement);

$v(\text{mm/s or m/s})$: Moving velocity;

$t(\text{s or h})$: Time.

When the above equation is met, the vibration mechanism is called a linear viscous damping system. Since the viscous damping force is proportional to the velocity, the more the motion, the more the damper dissipates the energy. Damping coefficient is a material property while damping ratio (factor) is a structural property. Traditionally damping coefficient C is obtained from experimental measurements of the free vibration of a viscous vibration system. The damping coefficient of material depends on the frequency of the forcing function. The unit for damping coefficient is NS/mm or NS/m.

The vibration of a continuous system such as a car engine can have infinitive numbers of natural frequencies. Vibration-induced damaging to a component affixed to a car engine is mostly done within the frequency range between 10 Hz and 1500 Hz. Two general guidelines for regulating subsystems attached to a car engine system such as sensors and actuators are:

(a) Any natural frequency falls between 10 Hz and 500 Hz are definitely not allowed.

(b) Any natural frequency falls between 500 Hz and 1500 Hz should be avoided.

The damping coefficient of metal is low, e.g. 1.515 NS/m for aluminum [Prandina et al.], but it is significantly higher for plastics. The damped natural frequency (ω_d) is lower than the undamped natural frequency (ω_n) and they are related to each other by the damping coefficient as

$$\omega_d = \omega_n(1 - \xi^2)^{\frac{1}{2}} = \omega_n\left(1 - \frac{C^2}{4\,M\,K}\right)^{\frac{1}{2}} \tag{7.2.7}$$

When natural frequencies are to be calculated for a plastics-based sensor affixed to a car engine, the damping coefficient of the sensor has to be considered. The temperature is another factor in addition to the damping coefficient. Plastic material may be softened and its damping coefficient may change to lower the associated natural frequencies.

An equivalent viscous damping factor ξ_e can be obtained by equating the energy dissipated per cycle for the following three nonviscous damping systems:

(A) Structural damping (i.e. hysteretic damping or $\tan \delta$): Internal friction of material.

(B) Coulomb damping: Dry friction damping.

(C) Fluid damping: Velocity-squared damping, in general.

7.3 Forced Vibration System: Self-Excitation Due to Unbalanced Mass

Forced vibration develops when a time-varying excitation such as a force, acceleration, velocity or displacement, is applied to a mechanical system. A vibration excitation may come from

(1) A moving part to a foundation, e.g. from an unbalanced Diesel engine cranktrain to the vehicle frame, as shown in Fig. 7.3.1 (a).

(2) On the other hand, the vibration of the mass may also come from the foundation motion, e.g. the road roughness shakes the vehicle frame that excite the engine vibration as illustrated in Fig. 7.3.1(b).

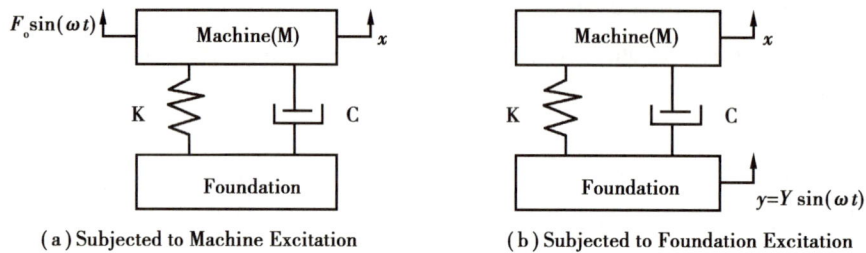

(a) Subjected to Machine Excitation   (b) Subjected to Foundation Excitation

Fig. 7.3.1   Vibration Isolation of Spring-and-Mass Systems with One Degree of Freedom

In light of Fig. 7.3.1 (a), of which unbalanced rotating machinery is installed onto a fixed foundation, one has the following forced viscously damped spring-and-mass system with one degree of freedom:

$$M\left(\frac{d^2x}{dt^2}\right) + C\left(\frac{dx}{dt}\right) + K x = F_o \sin(\omega t) \tag{7.3.1}$$

where

F_o: Input force (excitation force);

ω: Excitation frequency.

The above equation can be solved for the displacement, velocity, and acceleration of the steady-state forced vibration system as, respectively,

$$x = |X| \sin(\omega t - \phi) \tag{7.3.2}$$

$$\frac{dx}{dt} = \dot{x} = |X| \omega \cos(\omega t - \phi) \tag{7.3.3}$$

and $$\frac{d^2x}{dt^2} = \ddot{x} = -|X| \omega^2 \sin(\omega t - \phi) \tag{7.3.4}$$

The magnification factor of a viscously damped spring-and-mass system is defined as the ratio of the vibration amplitude to the "static deflection", i.e. F_o/K. Substituting Eqs. (7.3.2)-(7.3.4) into Eq. (7.3.1), one has

$$\frac{|X|}{F_o} = \frac{\dfrac{1}{K}}{\left\{\left[1 - \left(\dfrac{\omega}{\omega_n}\right)^2\right]^2 + \left(\dfrac{2\,\xi\,\omega}{\omega_n}\right)^2\right\}^{\frac{1}{2}}} \qquad (7.3.5a)$$

$$\text{or} \quad \frac{|X|}{\dfrac{F_o}{K}} = \frac{1}{\left\{\left[1 - \left(\dfrac{\omega}{\omega_n}\right)^2\right]^2 + \left(\dfrac{2\,\xi\,\omega}{\omega_n}\right)^2\right\}^{\frac{1}{2}}} \qquad (7.3.5b)$$

The magnification factor of a self-excitation system can reach 10 or more if the damping coefficient is as low as 0.05 or smaller. Note that the phase angle is

$$\phi = \tan^{-1}\left[\frac{2\,\xi\left(\dfrac{\omega}{\omega_n}\right)}{1 - \left(\dfrac{\omega}{\omega_n}\right)^2}\right] \qquad (7.3.6)$$

Plots of the vibration amplitude magnification and phase angle of a self-excited damped spring-and-mass system are given in Figs. 7.3.2 and 7.3.3, respectively. The phase angle is always 90° regardless of the magnitude of the damping coefficient, when the excitation frequency hits the natural frequency (frequency ratio = 1).

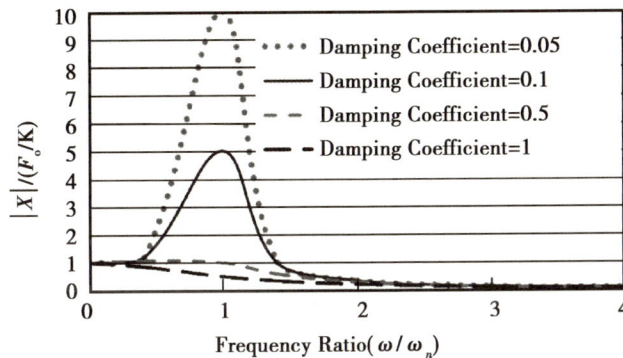

Fig. 7.3.2 Magnification of a Self-Excited Damped Spring-and-Mass System

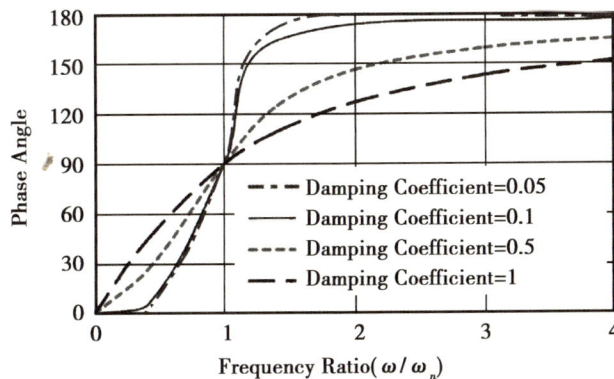

Fig. 7.3.3 Phase Angle of a Self-Excited Damped Spring-and-Mass System

7.4　Forced Vibration System: Transmissibility and Magnification

Vibration isolation is also used for reducing the magnitude of force transmission from a moving foundation to a part, e.g. from the suspension system to the seat and then to the passenger. Again, a damper may be used to reduce the magnification of the vibration. The concept of both transmissibility and magnification of a vibration source is introduced.

7.4.1　Transmissibility

Assume that the forced vibration of a viscous vibration system of one degree of freedom subjected to a sine forcing function from the foundation is

$$y = Y \sin(\omega t) \tag{7.4.1}$$

Both the foundation and the machine moves as depicted in Fig. 7.3.1(b). Taking the viscous force and spring force from both displacements into consideration, one has the following balanced dynamic equation

$$M \frac{d^2 x}{dt^2} + C\left(\frac{dx}{dt} - \frac{dy}{dt}\right) + K(x - y) = 0 \tag{7.4.2}$$

Vibration transmissibility is defined as the ratio of output vibration amplitude to the input amplitude of vibration. After Eq. (7.4.2) is solved for the x- and y-displacement, transmissibility can be written mathematically as

$$\mathrm{Tr} = \frac{|X|}{|Y|} = \frac{\left[1 + \left(\dfrac{2\xi\omega}{\omega_n}\right)^2\right]^{\frac{1}{2}}}{\left\{\left[1 - \left(\dfrac{\omega}{\omega_n}\right)^2\right]^2 + \left(\dfrac{2\xi\omega}{\omega_n}\right)^2\right\}^{\frac{1}{2}}} \tag{7.4.3}$$

where

Tr: Transmissibility;

X: Output vibration amplitude at the machine;

Y: Input vibration amplitude due to foundation excitation;

ω: Excitation frequency;

ω_n: Natural frequency, Eq. (7.2.4).

Note that the transmissibility is also a transfer function. The purpose of vibration isolation is to limit the force transmitted, i.e. reduction in vibration transmissibility. The transmissibility as described by Eq. (7.4.3) can be classified into three different zones:

(1) If $\omega/\omega_n < 2^{\frac{1}{2}} \approx 1.4142$, Tr>1 　　　　　　　　　　　　　　　(7.4.4)

(2) If $\omega/\omega_n = 2^{\frac{1}{2}} \approx 1.4142$, Tr=1 　　　　　　　　　　　　　　　(7.4.5)

(3) If $\omega/\omega_n > 2^{\frac{1}{2}} \approx 1.4142$, Tr<1 　　　　　　　　　　　　　　　(7.4.6)

When $\omega/\omega_n < 2^{\frac{1}{2}}$, an increase in damping results in vibration reduction. On the other hand, when $\omega/\omega_n > 2^{\frac{1}{2}}$, an increase in damping results in vibration promotion that is not desired.

Plots of the vibration amplitude magnification and phase angle of a vibration due to moving foundation are given in Figs. 7.4.1 and 7.4.2. As identified in Fig. 7.4.1, as well as by Eq. (7.4.7), the damping factor can be obtained in terms of the fundamental natural frequency (ω_1), the driving frequency, and their related phase angle. If there is no damping ($\xi = 0$), there is no phase angle between the input and output forcing functions ($\phi = 0$). At the resonance, $\omega/\omega_n = 1$,

$$\phi = \tan^{-1}\frac{\xi^{-1}}{2}　　　　　　　　　　　　　　　　(7.4.7)$$

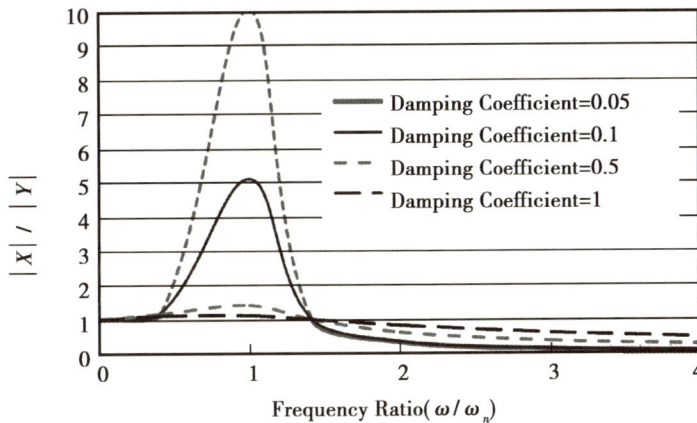

Fig. 7.4.1　Transmissibility from Moving Foundation to Damped Spring-and-Mass System

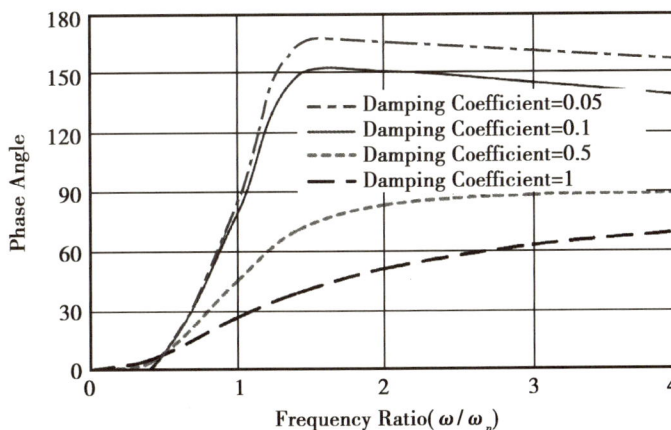

Fig. 7.4.2　Lag in Phase from Moving Foundation to Damped Spring-and-Mass System

The phase angle, ϕ, between the transmitted vibration and the input vibration $F_o \sin(\omega t)$ is a function of the damping ξ, as

$$\phi = \tan^{-1} \frac{2\xi\left(\dfrac{\omega}{\omega_n}\right)^3}{\left[1 - \left(\dfrac{\omega}{\omega_n}\right)^2\right] + \left[2\,\xi\left(\dfrac{\omega}{\omega_n}\right)\right]^2} \tag{7.4.8}$$

7.4.2 Transfer Function-SDOF

Taking the viscous force and spring force from both displacements into consideration, one has the following balanced dynamic equation subjected to the acceleration of the foundation,

$$M\left(\frac{d^2x}{dt^2} + \frac{d^2y}{dt^2}\right) + C\left(\frac{dx}{dt} - \frac{dy}{dt}\right) + K(x - y) = 0 \tag{7.4.9}$$

i.e. $$M\frac{d^2x}{dt^2} + C\left[\frac{d(x - dy)}{dt}\right] + K(x - y) = -M\frac{d^2y}{dt^2} \tag{7.4.10}$$

Let $z(t) = x(t) - y(t)$ $\tag{7.4.11}$

Then $$M\frac{d^2z}{dt^2} + C\frac{dz}{dt} + Kz = -M\frac{d^2y}{dt^2} \tag{7.4.12}$$

Let the ground motion input at the foundation of the system be specified in terms of ground acceleration. Assume that the excitation function $y(t)$ is sinusoidal,

$$\frac{d^2y}{dt^2} = A_{y,o} \exp(i\,\omega\,t) \tag{7.4.13}$$

By substituting the above equation into Eq. (7.4.12) and solving it for $z(t)$, one has

$$z(t) = \left(\frac{-M}{-M\omega^2 + i\,C\,\omega + K}\right) A_{y,o} \exp(i\,\omega\,t) \tag{7.4.14}$$

Next define the transfer function for such a SDOF (single degree of freedom) system for the relative motion between the mass displacement and the foundation acceleration as

$$H(\omega) \equiv \frac{z(t)}{\dfrac{d^2y}{dt^2}} \tag{7.4.15}$$

or $H(\omega) = \dfrac{-M}{-M\omega^2 + iC\omega + K}$ (7.4.16)

Dividing both the numerator and denominator on the right side of the above equation by M and applying Eqs. (7.2.3) and (7.2.4), the following transfer function can be obtained

$$H(\omega) = \frac{-\dfrac{1}{\omega_n^2}}{1 - \left(\dfrac{\omega}{\omega_n}\right)^2 + 2\xi\left(\dfrac{\omega}{\omega_n}\right)i}$$ (7.4.17)

Note that the transfer function is also called frequency response function (FRF), which relate the input loading (i.e. acceleration in this case) to the output response (i.e. displacement).

7.5   Damping Capacity and Quality Factor

Most commonly, vibration analysis is used to detect faults in rotating equipment such as fans, motors, pumps, and gearboxes etc., targeted at unbalance, misalignment, rolling element bearing faults and resonance conditions. Damping capacitor and quality factor are the two parameters that are often used to define the vibration behavior. Various damping parameters are also discussed here.

7.5.1   Damping Capacity

It is shown that among the various damping mechanisms that are generally encountered in a mechanical structure, only the "viscous component" actually accounts for energy loss. Damping is generally nonlinear for most materials even at a small strain. A measure of such damping is specific damping capacity, which is the ratio of the dissipated-energy to the stored-energy per cycle,

$$\psi = \frac{\Delta W}{W}$$ (7.5.1)

where
ψ: Damping capacity, also called specific damping capacity;
ΔW: Energy dissipated per cycle;
W: Energy stored per cycle.

The energy dissipated per cycle of a viscous system is integration of the viscous force against the differential displacement as

$$E_d = \int F_d \, dX = \int_0^{\frac{2\pi}{\omega}} C \, \dot{X}^2 \, dt \tag{7.5.2}$$

Substituting Eq. (7.3.3) into the above equation yields the energy dissipated per cycle

$$E_d = C \, \pi \, \omega \, | \, X \, |^2 \tag{7.5.3}$$

At resonance, $\omega = \omega_n = (K/M)^{\frac{1}{2}}$, the energy dissipated per cycle can be expressed in terms of the material parameters as

$$E_d = 2\pi \, K \, \xi \, | \, X \, |^2 \tag{7.5.4}$$

7.5.2 Quality Factor

The damping properties, which models the energy dissipation mechanisms present, can only be estimated from dynamic experiments. A vibration system of light damping is referred to having a high quality factor. The quality factor Q is defined as a measure of damping and mathematically it is

$$Q = \frac{1}{2\xi} \tag{7.5.5}$$

The quality factor is thus the ratio of the maximum dynamic response to the static response, also known as the dynamic amplification factor (DAF). As demonstrated by the vibration theory that the damping ratio (ζ) is related to the sharpness of the peak of the vibration magnitude. The damping ratio can be also determined by computing Q, calculated as the resonant frequency divided by the bandwidth that

$$Q = \frac{\omega_n}{\omega_2 - \omega_1} \tag{7.5.6}$$

where

ω_n: Natural frequency;

$\omega_2 - \omega_1$: Frequency bandwidth, frequency band between frequencies ω_1 and $\omega_2(\omega_2 > \omega_1)$.

When a vibration test is conducted, frequencies ω_1 and ω_2 are half power points on both sides of the peak (i.e. resonance point) measured -6 dB (Decibel) down from the peak. This is called half power bandwidth method. A dB value of data point x can be derived from

$$dB = 20 \, \lg \frac{x}{x_{ref}} \tag{7.5.7}$$

where

x: Data point;

x_{ref}: Reference point.

When comparing the motion of a mass to the motion of the base as illustrated in Fig. 7.3.1(b), base measurement is used as the reference point applied in the denominator and the mass response as the measurement applied in the numerator. The decibel scale allows us to see both large and small vibration amplitudes on the frequency scale. A level of -6 ($=-20\ \log(0.5)$) dB in the dB scale means the numerator is about half power of the reference value. When the response (numerator) and excitation (denominator) are equal, the level is 0 ($=-20\ \log(1)$) dB.

7.5.3   Structural Damping (Tan δ)

Materials may show significant amounts of hysteresis during cyclic loading. For example, elastomeric hysteresis is strain-rate dependent, and the strain-rate dependency is higher during loading than unloading. At a fixed strain the stress approaches the same equilibrium level with relaxation time for loading and unloading. Sinusoidal functions, for simplicity, are used to explain the dynamic behaviors of such materials. A sinusoidal strain amplitude as a function of time is given as

$$\varepsilon(t) = \varepsilon_0 \sin(\omega t) \tag{7.5.8}$$

One can have its corresponding stress amplitude as

$$\sigma(t) = \sigma_0 \sin(\omega t + \delta) \tag{7.5.9}$$

in which δ is the phase angle; $\delta = 0$ for elastic material and $\delta = 90°$ for fully viscous material.

Define the complex strain and stress as follows:

$$\varepsilon^*(t) = \varepsilon_0 \exp[i(\omega t + \delta)] \tag{7.5.10}$$

and $$\sigma^*(t) = \sigma_0 \exp[i(\omega t + \delta)] \tag{7.5.11}$$

The complex Young's modulus can be derived as

$$E^* = \frac{\sigma^*(t)}{\varepsilon^*(t)} = \frac{\sigma_0}{\varepsilon_0} \exp(i\delta) = \frac{\sigma_0}{\varepsilon_0} \cos\delta + i\frac{\sigma_0}{\varepsilon_0} \sin\delta = E' + iE'' \tag{7.5.12}$$

where

E': Storage modulus;

E'': Loss modulus.

The amplitude of complex Young's modulus is then

$$| E^* | = [(E')^2 + (E'')^2]^{\frac{1}{2}} \tag{7.5.13}$$

The stiffness of rubber consists of two parts due to its viscoelastic nature. Hysteresis loop showing its relations to storage and loss moduli and the phase angle is depicted in Fig. 7.5.1. The real component E' is called storage modulus and the imaginary component E'' is called loss modulus. Loss factor, also called loss tangent, is then defined as the ratio of the energy dissipated to the energy stored per cycle,

$$\tan \delta = \frac{E''}{E'} \tag{7.5.14}$$

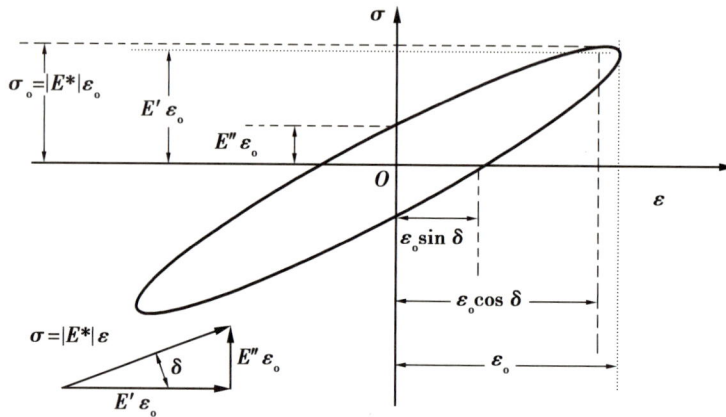

Fig. 7.5.1   Hysteresis Loop, Storage and Loss Moduli, and Phase Angle

Loss factor is a function of temperature and vibration frequency. A simplified relationship of loss factor to the viscous damping ratio in a linear viscous damping vibration system is

$$\tan \delta = 2 \xi \tag{7.5.15}$$

Thus, the quality factor of a solid is the inverse of its loss factor

$$Q = \frac{1}{2 \xi} = \frac{1}{\tan \delta} \tag{7.5.16}$$

The area of the perfect ellipse covered by one loop shown in Fig. 7.5.1 is

$$A_L = \pi E'' \varepsilon_o^2 \tag{7.5.17}$$

An expression similar to Eq. (7.5.13) can be defined for the complex shear modulus with a sinusoidal-varying shear stress as

$$G^* = G' + i G'' \tag{7.5.18}$$

The loss tangent is

$$\tan \delta = \frac{G''}{G'} \tag{7.5.19}$$

The complex Young's modulus is related to the complex shear modulus by the Poisson's ratio, ν, as

$$G^* = \frac{E^*}{2(1 + \nu)} \tag{7.5.20}$$

7.5.4   Fluid Damping

Fluid damping originates from viscous dissipation and fluid drag, i.e. the result of viscous shearing of the fluid at the surface of the contacting structure and flow separation. Fluid damping is motion dependent. The fluid damping is usually proportional to the velocity-squared as

$$F_{\mathrm{d}} = -\frac{1}{2} C_{\mathrm{d}} \rho A \dot{x}^2 \tag{7.5.21}$$

where

F_{d}: Damping force;

C_{d}: Effective drag coefficient;

ρ: Fluid density;

A: Frontal area; frontal projected area of the object in the moving direction.

Similar to Eq. (7.3.1), the equation of motion, accommodating the velocity-squared energy dissipation, is given as

$$M \frac{\mathrm{d}^2 x}{\mathrm{d}t^2} + \frac{1}{2} C_{\mathrm{d}} \rho A \frac{\mathrm{d}x^2}{\mathrm{d}t} + K x = F_{\mathrm{o}} \sin(\omega t) \tag{7.5.22}$$

Similar to Eq. (7.5.1), the energy dissipated per cycle is

$$E_{\mathrm{d}} = \int F_{\mathrm{d}} \, \mathrm{d}x = C_{\mathrm{d}} \rho A \int_0^{\frac{\pi}{\omega}} \dot{x}^3 \, \mathrm{d}t = \frac{4}{3} C_{\mathrm{d}} \rho A \mid X \mid^3 \omega^2 \tag{7.5.23}$$

At resonance, the equivalent viscous damping coefficient is [James et al.]

$$\xi_{\mathrm{e}} = \frac{2 C_{\mathrm{d}} \rho A \mid X \mid}{3\pi M} \tag{7.5.24}$$

7.5.5　Coulomb Friction

Consider a block sliding on the ground and subjected to a sinusoidal force, as shown in Fig. 7.5.2. Assume that the mass M is placed in a neutral force-free position initially. Following Coulomb's friction rule, the frictional damping force is

$$F_d = - \mu M g \qquad (7.5.25)$$

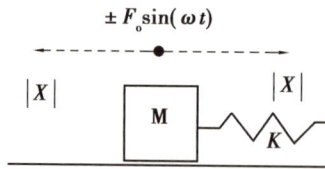

Fig. 7.5.2　Coulomb Damping as a Mass Subjected to a Sinusoidal Force

In other words, its energy dissipated per cycle (4 trips or 4 vibration amplitudes per cycle) is

$$E_d = 4 F_d | X | = 4 \mu M g | X | \qquad (7.5.26)$$

Relating the above equation into Eq. (7.5.3), one has the equivalent viscous damping coefficient as

$$C = \frac{4 F_d}{\pi \omega | X |} \qquad (7.5.27)$$

By equating the C given in the above equation to the second term on the left side of Eq. (7.2.3), one can obtain the equivalent damping factor as

$$\xi_e = \frac{2 \mu Mg}{\omega \omega_n \pi M | X |} \qquad (7.5.28)$$

7.5.6　Foam Damping Capacity

In low density closed cell foams, the pressure of air or other gas in the pores contributes to the overall stiffness. In open cell foams, air in the pores is free to escape as the material is stressed. Under quasi-static conditions or at low frequency, flow of air has little effect. The corresponding principle of the linear theory of viscoelasticity may then be applied to the foam as a composite with one mechanically active phase. So, given that [Gibson & Ashby]

$$\frac{E_{foam}}{E_{solid}} = \frac{\rho_{foam}^2}{\rho_{solid}^2} \qquad (7.5.29)$$

where

E_{foam}: Young's modulus of foam;

E_{solid}: Young's modulus of solid, which the foam is made from;

ρ_{foam}: Density of foam;

ρ_{solid}: Density of solid, which the foam is made from.

The same relationship held for corresponding viscoelastic foam of complex moduli

$$\frac{E_{\text{foam}}^*}{E_{\text{solid}}^*} = \frac{\rho_{\text{foam}}^{*2}}{\rho_{\text{solid}}^{*2}} \tag{7.5.30}$$

of which E_{foam}^* is the complex Young's modulus of foam and E_{solid}^* is the corresponding complex Young's modulus of solid. The related loss tangent is then

$$\tan \delta = \frac{\text{Im}\left[E_{\text{foam}}^*\right]}{\text{Re}\left[E_{\text{foam}}^*\right]} \tag{7.5.31}$$

7.6   Impact Factor and Surge

It is shown in Fig. 7.6.1 that an ideal piston is supported by a spring under a constant vertical load, e.g. its own weight-mass *gravity (mg). The balance between the potential energy and the dynamic energy leads to the following equation

$$m g\,(h\chi) = \frac{1}{2}k\chi^2 \tag{7.6.1}$$

The above equation can be solved for the spring deflection as

$$\chi = \frac{mg}{k}\left[1 + \left(1 + \frac{2h}{\frac{mg}{k}}\right)^{\frac{1}{2}}\right] = \chi_s\left[1 + \left(1 + \frac{2h}{\chi_s}\right)^{\frac{1}{2}}\right] \tag{7.6.2}$$

where $\chi_s = \dfrac{mg}{k}$ $\qquad\qquad\qquad\qquad\qquad\qquad\qquad\qquad$ (7.6.3)

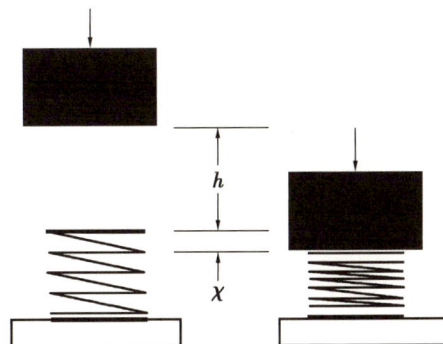

Fig. 7.6.1   Impact by a Mass Subject to a Constant Vertical Force Applied to a Spring

In fact, X_s is exactly the static deflection of the spring subject to a dead weight (mg) without the effect of impact. Thus, the force induced by the dropping weight is

$$F_X = k X = k X_s \left[1 + \left(1 + \frac{2h}{X_s} \right)^{\frac{1}{2}} \right] = m g \left[1 + \left(1 + \frac{2h}{X_s} \right)^{\frac{1}{2}} \right] \tag{7.6.4}$$

Term $1 + (1 + 2h/X_s)^{\frac{1}{2}}$ is the impact factor, which is herein the amplification factor of loading relative to a static application.

7.6.1 Impact Due to Suddenly Applied Load

Assume that the initial height is zero $(h = 0)$, i.e. a sudden load is applied, Eqs. (7.6.2) and (7.6.4) reduce to, respectively

$$X = 2X_s \tag{7.6.5}$$

and $F_X = 2 m g$ $\tag{7.6.6}$

It is shown in the above equation that the load is doubled as compared with a static load.

7.6.2 Impact on a Solid Foundation

If the spring is replaced by a solid ground, the spring-wise deflection is insignificant, i.e. $h \gg X_s$. In other words, $2h/X_s \gg 2 > 1$ and thus $1 + (1 + 2h/X_s)^{\frac{1}{2}} \approx (2h/X_s)^{\frac{1}{2}}$. Consequently, Eqs. (7.6.5) and (7.6.6) reduce to, respectively

$$X = X_s \left(\frac{2h}{X_s} \right)^{\frac{1}{2}} = (2 h X_s)^{\frac{1}{2}} \tag{7.6.7}$$

and $F_X = m g \left(\frac{2h}{X_s} \right)^{\frac{1}{2}}$ $\tag{7.6.8}$

7.6.3 Impact with Known Velocity

Again, with a known dead weight dropped from a height of h to an elastic foundation, its velocity at impact can be figured out using the equation balancing the potential energy and the dynamic energy as

$$m g h = \frac{1}{2} m v^2 \tag{7.6.9}$$

i.e. $h = \dfrac{\frac{1}{2}v^2}{g}$ 　　　　　　　　　　　　　　　　　　　　　(7.6.10)

Substituting the above equation into Eq. (7.6.8) leads to the impact force in terms of velocity at impact as

$$F_\chi = (k\ m\ v^2)^{\frac{1}{2}} \qquad\qquad (7.6.11)$$

with a deflection, derived from Eq. (7.6.7) and (7.6.8), as

$$\chi = \left(\dfrac{m\ v^2}{k}\right)^{\frac{1}{2}} \qquad\qquad (7.6.12)$$

Thus, the impact force and deflection are directly related to the dynamic energy $\left(\dfrac{1}{2}mv^2\right)$ of the dropping mass and the spring constant (mm/s) of the presumed elastic foundation.

7.6.4   Nominal Stress and Strain Induced by Impact

Take a case study on the impact of a rod with uniform cross-sectional area A and length L. The spring constant of the rod in the axial direction is then

$$k = \dfrac{AE}{L} \qquad\qquad (7.6.13)$$

The stress induced by the impact of a mass m on a rod is then derived by substituting the above equation into Eq. (7.6.4) as

$$\sigma = \dfrac{F_\chi}{A} = \dfrac{(k\ m\ v^2)^{\frac{1}{2}}}{A}\left(\dfrac{E}{A\ L}m\ v^2\right)^{\frac{1}{2}} = (\rho\ E)^{\frac{1}{2}}\ v \qquad\qquad (7.6.14)$$

The stress induced by the impact of a mass m on a rod is then derived by substituting Eq. (7.6.14) into Eq. (7.6.13) as

$$\varepsilon = \dfrac{\chi}{L} = \left(\dfrac{\rho}{E}\right)^{\frac{1}{2}}\ v \qquad\qquad (7.6.15)$$

The stress and strain induced by an impact of a dead weight on a rod in the axial direction are related to the material density and modulus of elasticity of the elastic foundation.

In general, the real impact-damaging stress and strain could be higher than what calculated using Eqs. (7.6.14) and (7.6.15), because of the local stress concentration due to non-uniform contact and inertia force of dropping mass. On the other hand, damping involved with the impact process may reduce the stress and strain levels. The strain energy ($1/2\sigma\varepsilon$, i.e. energy per unit volume) without any damping is exactly the dynamic energy, which can be derived from Eqs. (7.6.14) and (7.6.15)

$$\text{Strain energy} = \frac{1}{2}\sigma\,\varepsilon = \frac{1}{2}m\,v^2 \tag{7.6.16}$$

7.6.5 Spring Surge [Sorokin]

When one end of a helical spring is held to a fixed surface and the other end is subject to a cyclic load, a compression wave then propagates longitudinally between them. It is called surge. The wave propagation equation can be obtained similar to a longitudinal vibration of a rod. Assume that the motion of the free end is sinusoidal with amplitude u_0, i.e.

$$U\,(l,t) = u_0\sin(\omega\,t) \tag{7.6.17}$$

where z is the longitudinal coordinate of the spring cross-section of interest, measured from the fixed end. Let the displacement at the fixed end be

$$u\,(0,t) = 0 \tag{7.6.18}$$

Eqs. (7.6.17) and (7.6.18) are the boundary conditions at both ends to the following equation of longitudinal motion derived for a solid rod:

$$\left(\frac{E}{\rho}\right)\frac{\partial^2 u}{\partial z^2} = \frac{\partial^2 u}{\partial t^2} \tag{7.6.19}$$

Assume A_c is the cross-sectional area of the spring, then for the spring

$$E = \frac{k\,L}{A_c} \tag{7.6.20}$$

and

$$\frac{E}{\rho} = \frac{k\,L}{\rho\,A_c} \tag{7.6.21}$$

Substituting Eq. (7.6.21) into Eq. (7.6.19) and solving the new equation with Eqs. (7.6.17) and (7.6.18), one has

$$u(x,t) = \frac{\sin\left[\dfrac{\omega(x/L)}{(k/m_s)^{\frac{1}{2}}}\right]}{\sin\left[\dfrac{\omega}{(k/m_s)^{\frac{1}{2}}}\right]}[u_0\sin(\omega\,t)] \tag{7.6.22}$$

Note that $m_s = \rho A_c L$, which is the mass of the spring. The displacement goes infinitive, if the denominator of the above equation becomes zero. Making the denominator zero leads to its frequency in rad/s, i.e.

$$\omega_i = i \ \pi \left(\frac{k}{m_s}\right)^{\frac{1}{2}}, \ i = 1,2,3,\cdots \tag{7.6.23}$$

It means the resonance due to longitudinal wave propagation of a helical spring occurs, when the frequency of an external excitation has a frequency in Hz of

$$f_i = \frac{1}{2}i\left(\frac{k}{m_s}\right)^{\frac{1}{2}}, i = 1, 2, 3,\cdots \tag{7.6.24}$$

These are the natural frequencies of wave propagation in a helical spring, which is fixed at one end and driven at the other end. Its applications include reciprocating engine valves mounted on the camshaft and control valves for regulated pumping of engine oil. Eq. (7.6.24) is also valid for a helical spring fixed at both ends, as argued by [James et al.].

7.7 Random Vibration

A vibration may be random in nature for a variety of applications, such as vehicles traveling on rough roads or aircraft wings operating in the airfield where arbitrary loads may be encountered. In these cases, instantaneous vibration amplitudes are not highly predictable as the amplitude at any point in time is not related to that at another point in time. A random vibration test excites all the frequencies in a defined spectrum at any given time. When the integrity of a structure under a dynamic load is to be assessed, waveforms are usually measured in time domain but their corresponding vibration spectra are in the form of PSD (Power Spectral Density) computed from Fourier Transform (FT).

The sources of vibration in a vehicle are many, including the engine, driveline, tire contact patch and road surface, brakes, and wind. Vibrations are usually sensed at the steering wheel, the seat, armrests, pedals, and the floor, while some problems are sensed visually, such as the vibration of the rear-view mirror or header rail. Vibrations due to cooling fans, HVAC, alternator, and other engine accessories are sensed as acoustic noises.

In the real world of automotive engineering, it is more convenient to characterize mechanical vibrations in terms of acceleration, for its being easy to measure than velocity and displacement in the context, as detailed in USA MIL-STD-1540C. The acceleration waveform shown in Fig. 7.7.1

is for dashboard vibration of a vehicle traveling on Chicago Drive, Hudsonville, MI [Van Baren]. Note that $1G = 9.807 \text{ m/s}^2 = 9.807 \text{ N/kg}$. The waveform of acceleration can be used for durability analysis, even though vibrations are by no means repetitive or predictable. Random testing will cause all resonating frequencies to be excited at the same time, i.e. all frequency components will be examined against potential fatigue damage.

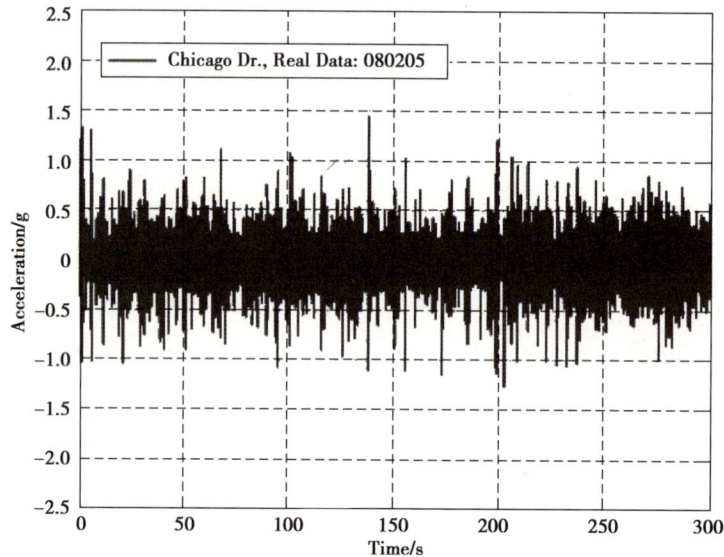

Fig. 7.7.1   Acceleration Time History Collected on Vehicle Dashboard While Driving on Chicago Drive, Hudsonville, MI [Van Baren]

7.7.1   Statistical in Nature

For a vibration ensemble to be random, the amplitude and starting phase of each sample would have to vary unpredictably. A random vibration process can be characterized using a probability distribution function with mean, standard deviation and other statistical parameters. Vibration amplitudes and means are averaged over a significant number of cycles and the cumulative effect is determined for this time period.

Automotive random vibration may consist of frequencies over a wide range of frequencies, e.g. going from 1 Hz to 2 kHz. The fatigue damage due to such a random loading function does not look at a specific frequency or amplitude at a specific moment in time but rather statistically investigates the structure's response. If the loading is a normal distribution function (ergodic stationary Gaussian function) the instantaneous acceleration in time share is given as follows:

(a) 68.3% falling between $\pm 1\sigma$ (7.7.1a)

(b) 95% falling between $\pm 2\sigma$ (7.7.1b)

(c) 99% falling between $\pm 2.575\sigma$ (7.7.1c)

(d) 99.73% falling between $\pm 3\sigma$ (7.7.1d)

(e) 99.99367% falling between $\pm 4\sigma$ (7.7.1e)

(f) 99.99994% falling between $\pm 5\sigma$ (7.7.1f)

When a signal is evaluated at $f(t)$ and $f(t+\Delta t)$ and their averaged values show no difference, the signal is stationary. Natural frequencies of a product should be extracted for checking against the excitation profile in order to warrant that it has no phenomenal resonance. As a design guideline, for example, the fundamental natural frequency of an engine part is expected to have a natural frequency 20% higher than the highest speed of the engine running at no load.

7.7.2 Power Spectral Density (PSD)

As a dynamic response measure, the power spectral density (PSD) of a function is used for quantifying the function's energy content distribution over a frequency range. It is capable of assessing the severity of damage due to random vibration. However, when a time series of data is transformed into PSD, the magnitude data are captured in the PSD signal while the phase information is lost.

There are three equivalent methods for formulating the PSD function of a random vibration process: (a) BP, (b) FT, and (c) FFT. The bandpass (BP) filter method is simple to use and can be easily understood, as demonstrated using Example 7.7.1. Since the bandpass filter method is inefficient, the Fourier transform (FT) method is applied in the automotive industry. Nevertheless the fast Fourier transform (FFT) is frequently used instead of FT.

A PSD shows how the functional power intensity is distributed over an applicable frequency range, in which a structure is subjected to a stochastic spectrum of harmonic loading functions. It can be plotted using the mean square acceleration per unit bandwidth versus frequency (unit: Acceleration^2/Hz). The unit is G^2/Hz as a general practice in the automotive engineering industry. The Hz value in G^2/Hz refers to a bandwidth rather than to the frequency in Hz along the horizontal axis. The amplitude is actually G_{rms}^2/Hz, of which the subscript (rms) means root-mean-square. Nevertheless, unit G_{rms}^2/Hz is frequently abbreviated as G^2/Hz.

7.7.3 Bandwidth Filter Method

To find the value of the power spectral density $S_{xx}(\omega)$ at frequency ω, one could insert between the transmission line and the resistor a bandpass filter, which passes only a narrow range of frequencies such as $\Delta\omega$ near the frequency of interest and then measure the total energy $E(\omega)$

dissipated across the resistor. The shape of a power spectral density function depends on the probability of loading for each frequency, and the variation in likely load magnitude as a function of its frequency. The value of the power spectral density at ω is then estimated to be power $\omega/\Delta\omega$. In an octative that has a band of $\Delta\omega$, the rms value of a design variable of interest such as strain (ε), then the strain PSD in the octative can be expressed as

$$S(f) = \frac{\varepsilon^2_{m,rms}}{\Delta f}$$

of which $\omega = 2\pi f$ is the frequency. The calculation procedure using bandpass filter method is demonstrated using Example 7.7.1.

Example 7.7.1   This example is based on the acceleration time series given in Fig. 7.7.1 [Irvine 2000] to illustrate how to generate PSD functions using the bandpass (BP) filter method.

Solution:

Three bandpass filters are employed to divide the power contents into three different sections: 10-20 Hz, 20-30 Hz, and 30-40 Hz. The G-loads measured via these three bandpass filters are given as follows:

Band filter	G-load	Bandwidth	Center	PSD	
10-20 Hz	0.68 G_{rms}	10 Hz	15 Hz	$(0.68)^2/10 = 0.046$	G^2/Hz
20-30 Hz	1.08 G_{rms}	10 Hz	25 Hz	$(1.08)^2/10 = 0.117$	G^2/Hz
30-40 Hz	0.73 G_{rms}	10 Hz	35 Hz	$(0.73)^2/10 = 0.053$	G^2/Hz
Unfiltered	—	—	1.49 G_{rms}	—	

The G-load between 10 Hz and 20 Hz is the root-mean-square value of the vibration amplitudes whose frequencies fall between 10 Hz and 20 Hz, so are the G-loads between 20 Hz and 30 Hz and the G-load between 30 Hz and 40 Hz. The overall G-load of the unfiltered signal is 1.49 G_{rms}, while $1.49\ G_{rms} \approx (0.68^2 + 1.08^2 + 0.73^2)^{\frac{1}{2}}\ G_{rms}$. These are depicted in Fig. 7.7.2. The more bandpass filters are used, the more accurately the PSD will embrace the power level.

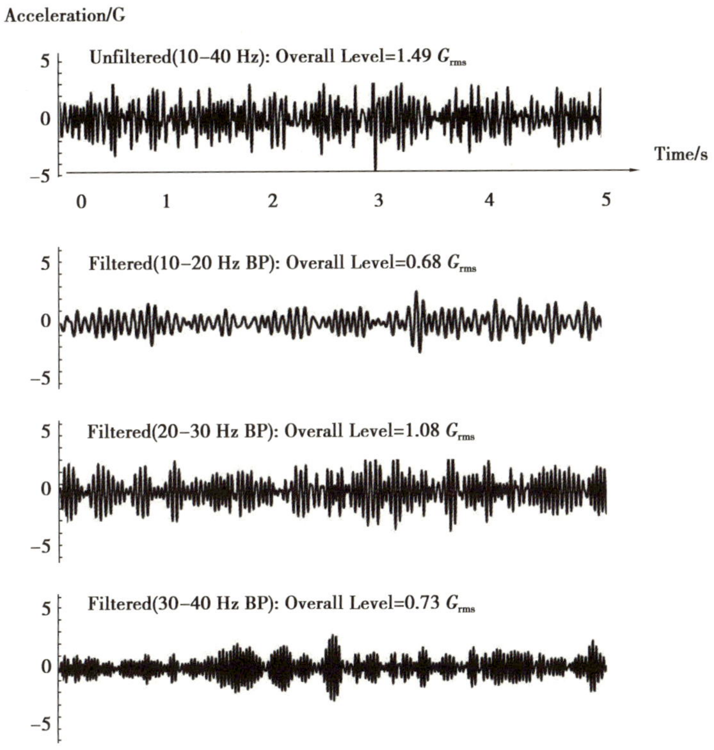

Fig. 7.7.2   Sample Acceleration Time Series Having Power Content between 10 Hz and 40 Hz as Unfiltered [Trvine]

7.7.4   Fourier Transform for Mechanical Vibrations

A Fourier Transform (FT) decomposes the time series of a signal into another signal in frequency domain. The term Fourier transform refers to both the frequency domain representation and the mathematical operation that associates the frequency domain representation with the function of time. The signal resulting from an FT operation is a real signal with power units (squared values) known as the power spectrum.

Let $u(t)$ be a loading or response function, e.g. displacement, velocity, acceleration, strain, or stress in the time domain of a mechanical vibration system. Assume that (1) $u(t)$ has period 2π, (2) $du(t)/dt$ exists, i.e. $u(t)$ is piecewise continuous, and (3) the integration of $u(t)$ over time is bounded by a finite number, M, i.e.

$$- M < \int_{-\infty}^{\infty} |u(t)| dt < M \tag{7.7.2}$$

Then, $u(t)$ has the complex Fourier series representation as

$$S(\omega) = \int_{-\infty}^{\infty} u(t) e^{-2\pi\omega t i} dt \tag{7.7.3}$$

At the points of continuity, $u(t)$ can be obtained using the following inverse Fourier transform

$$u(t) = \int_{-\infty}^{\infty} S(\omega) e^{2\pi\omega t i} d\omega \tag{7.7.4}$$

Differential equations formulated for structural vibrations are sometimes easier to analyze in the frequency domain, because a differentiation in the time domain corresponds to a multiplication by the corresponding frequency. Also, ordinary multiplication in the frequency domain means convolution in the time domain. Furthermore, the Fourier transform of a Gaussian function in the time domain is another Gaussian function in the frequency domain.

A Fast Fourier Transform (FFT) is often carried out instead of its corresponding Fourier Transform as a reasonable simplified approximation. An FFT algorithm computes the Discrete Fourier transformation (DFT) of a sequence of data. Let $x_0, \cdots, x_{N-1}$ represent a series of complex numbers in time series. The DFT is defined by the formula

$$X_k = \sum_{n=0}^{N-1} x_n e^{\frac{-2\pi k n i}{N}}, \quad k = 1, 2, \cdots, N-1 \tag{7.7.5}$$

and the corresponding inverse FFT is

$$x_n = \frac{1}{N} \sum_{n=0}^{N-1} X_k e^{\frac{2\pi k n i}{N}}, \quad k = 1, 2, \cdots, N-1 \tag{7.7.6}$$

When working in the linear elastoplastic range using the finite element method, a complex structure may be discretized as a linear system with multiple degrees of freedom that comprise a set of second-order differential equations as demonstrated in the finite element analysis [Cook]. Now let's consider the unbalanced rotating machinery given in Fig. 7.3.1(a) with an exponential loading function, $f(t) = F_o e^{i\omega t}$, the forced viscously damped spring-and-mass system with one degree of freedom is formulated as

$$M \frac{d^2 x}{dt^2} + C \frac{dx}{dt} + K_x = f(t) = F_o e^{i\omega t} \tag{7.7.7}$$

The displacement $x(t)$ can be solved in the time domain as

$$x(t) = \frac{F_o}{-M\omega^2 + iC\omega + K} e^{i\omega t} = X e^{i\omega t} \tag{7.7.8}$$

Next, solve Eq. (7.7.7) in the frequency domain. Since

$$FT \frac{dx}{dt} = i\omega [FT(x)] \tag{7.7.9}$$

and $FT \dfrac{d^2 x}{dt^2} = -\omega^2 [FT(x)]$　(7.7.10)

By taking the Fourier transform, Eq. (7.7.8) reduces to

$$(-M\omega^2 + Ci\omega + K) x(\omega) = F(\omega) \qquad (7.7.11)$$

then　$x(\omega) = (-M\omega^2 + Ci\omega + K)^{-1} F(\omega) = H(\omega) F(\omega) \qquad (7.7.12)$

or　$FT(x) = H(\omega) FT(f(t)) \qquad (7.7.13)$

where
$H(\omega)$: frequency response function (FRF), which is regarded as transfer function;
$x(\omega)$: Vector of displacement in the frequency domain, $x(\omega) = FT(x(t))$;
$F(\omega)$: Vector of forcing function in the frequency domain, $F(\omega) = FT(f(t))$.

There is a similarity between Eqs. (7.7.12) and (7.7.8). However, the frequency response function relates the output to the input directly as a transfer function in the frequency domain in Eq. (7.7.12). One special property of a stationary random vibration having a normal distribution function statistically is that the mean squared response can be calculated directly from the mean squared forcing function using the frequency response function (FRF)

$$(x_{rms})^2 = |H(\omega)|^2 (f_{rms})^2 \qquad (7.7.14)$$

where　$(x_{rms})^2 = E[x^2] = \lim\limits_{T \to 0} \dfrac{1}{T} \int_1^\infty x^2(t)\, dt \qquad (7.7.15)$

and　$(f_{rms})^2 = E[f^2] = \lim\limits_{T \to 0} \dfrac{1}{T} \int_0^\infty f^2(t)\, dt \qquad (7.7.16)$

where
x_{rms}: Mean squares response;
f_{rms}: Mean squared forcing function.

7.7.5　Example: G-Load and PSD for a Truck Turbocharger

An acceleration time history of the diesel engine- and road-induced vibrations collected on a commercial truck turbocharger is shown in Fig. 7.7.3. Data corresponding to peak G-loads are listed in Table 7.7.1. Generally the random vibration spectrum profile is displayed as a power spectral density (PSD) plot, which can be obtained from the G-load vibration profile through FFT (Fast Fourier Transform) as shown in Fig. 7.7.4.

The square root of the area under this PSD curve is equal to the acceleration's overall root-mean-square (RMS), namely G_{rms}, which quantifies the vibration energy intensity and it is a normalized probability density plot describing the mean square amplitude of each sinusoidal wave with respect to its corresponding "individual" natural frequency without any phase data. The spectrum of the RMS (Root Mean Square) acceleration response to a random PSD applied to a SDOF system of natural frequency ω_n and quality factor Q as [Miles]

$$G_{rms}(\omega) = \left[\frac{1}{2}\pi\omega_n QS_{aa}(\omega_n)\right]^{\frac{1}{2}} \tag{7.7.17}$$

Term $S_{aa}(\omega_n)$ is the PSD of acceleration in G^2/Hz at frequency ω_n, and Q is the dynamic amplification factor. The amplitude, i.e. the corresponding G-load, can be calculated in terms of the root mean square gravity via the property of normal probability density function, as

$$G\text{-load} = (2G_{rms}^2)^{\frac{1}{2}} \tag{7.7.18}$$

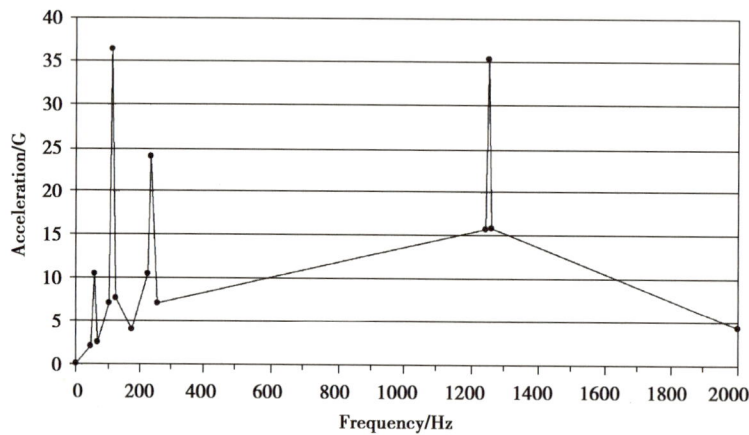

Fig. 7.7.3   G-Load of a Commercial Truck Turbocharger

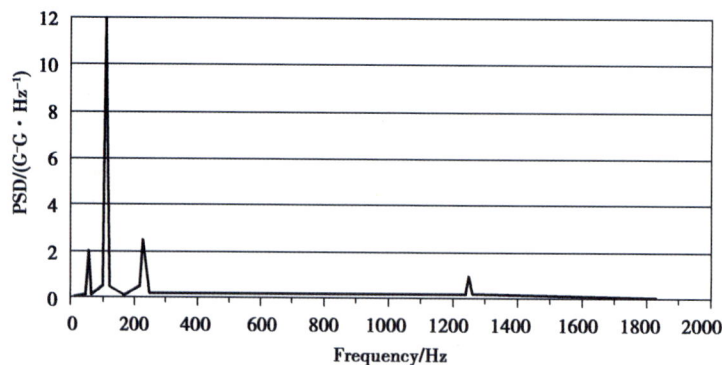

Fig. 7.7.4   Power Spectral Density Function of a Commercial Truck Turbocharger

How to regenerate a time signal from a PSD? One has to assume that the original process is "ergodic stationary Gaussian and random" such that the generated random phase angles can be added to the amplitude data given in the PSD. Thus, the Inverse Fourier Transform (IFT) is applied to configuring a statistically equivalent time history.

7.7.6   Gains in Acceleration and Displacement Responses

It is important to consider both the acceleration amplitude and the amount of strain energy during the vibration assessment, as fatigue fracture is also attributable to excessive strain energy that is proportional to displacement rather than acceleration. The damaging effect of acceleration is seen to reduce with the square of the frequency. When the high frequency reaches a certain level, high frequencies become less damaging than lower frequencies. Response spectra around natural frequencies are thus classified into two different operating requirements:

(a) VRS (Vibration Response Spectrum): The spectrum of peak oscillating absolute acceleration as the root mean square response, obtained by integrating the area under the PSD curve. Let Q be the quality factor, i.e. $Q = 2\xi$. Then, the VRS of the input acceleration for any SDOF system over natural frequency ω_n can be obtained from Eq. (7.3.5b) as

$$\mathrm{Gain}_{\mathrm{acceleration}}(\omega) = \frac{1}{\left\{\left[1 - \left(\dfrac{\omega}{\omega_n}\right)^2\right]^2 + \left[\left(\dfrac{\omega}{Q\,\omega_n}\right)^2\right]^2\right\}^{\frac{1}{2}}} \tag{7.7.19}$$

(b) SRS (Shock Response Spectrum) is used to determine the peak displacement amplitude of loading seen during an operating event, e.g. a vibration test. For fatigue problems, engineers are mostly interested in the displacement response. For example, a crack nucleation and its fatigue growth are dominantly controlled by the cyclic strain energy release rate and the displacement response provides a proportional relationship with the strain energy driving the failure. The SRS of displacement is thus employed to quantify the damaging effect of the input acceleration for any SDOF system over natural frequency ω_n, as derived from (7.4.15),

$$\mathrm{Gain}_{\mathrm{displacement}}(\omega) = \frac{\omega_n^{-2}}{\left\{\left[1 - \left(\dfrac{\omega}{\omega_n}\right)^2\right]^2 + \left[\left(\dfrac{\omega}{Q\,\omega_n}\right)^2\right]^2\right\}^{\frac{1}{2}}} \tag{7.7.20}$$

Extended from these VRS and SRS concepts, the fatigue damage spectrum (FDS) has been of great interest to researchers in the area of fracture mechanics and mechanical fatigue [Lalanne]. The FDS is calculated in the same way as the SRS but rather than simply finding the maximum displacement and strain energy response, the filtered displacement response is now the rainflow cycle counted and the fatigue damage obtained using a criterion given in the last chapter, e.g. ε-N curves, S-N curves, or the SWT equation.

7.8　Fatigue Analysis in Frequency Domain

A parallel approach to time-based fatigue analysis is to do fatigue analysis in the frequency domain, i.e. looking for fatigue damage spectrum (FDS). In the time domain, usually an engineer works with large load data, that requires significant computational power and labor, but one might feel more when being in control of the analysis process and routines. On the other hand, the rainflow cycle counting, typical of time domain fatigue analysis, can ruin the analysis accuracy if not sampled correctly. In the frequency domain, cycle counting can be assessed accurately by working with zero-cross frequencies, but stress risers may not be well captured during linearization. Note that the frequency spectrum for the random load can be transformed to time series data and then the deterministic signal is added directly to that time series as an "approximation", which is then cycle-counted using the rainflow algorithm.

Fatigue analysis in the frequency domain sometimes cannot be replaced by a time-domain analysis, when it is required to verify whether the structure will respond dynamically with the given environmental excitation load frequency history in the following categories:

（1）Aeroelastic structures, wings, blades, tall buildings, towers, bridges, pipelines, risers (that connecting the platform with the well at the sea bed in the offshore industry) and other structures subjected to VIV (Vortex-Induced Vibrations) and WIV (Wave-Induced Vibrations)

（2）Resonance-induced structural vibrations, typically with local machinery like vehicles, ships, steel frames, machinery foundation, and acoustic loads.

The techniques for estimating lifetime of a structure fall into two broad categories [Bishop & Sherratt] [Halfpenny & Bishop]: (a) those that estimate fatigue life directly based on a closed-form solution and (b) those that compute amplitude-mean (or range-mean) histograms as an intermediate stage as shown in Fig. 7.8.1.

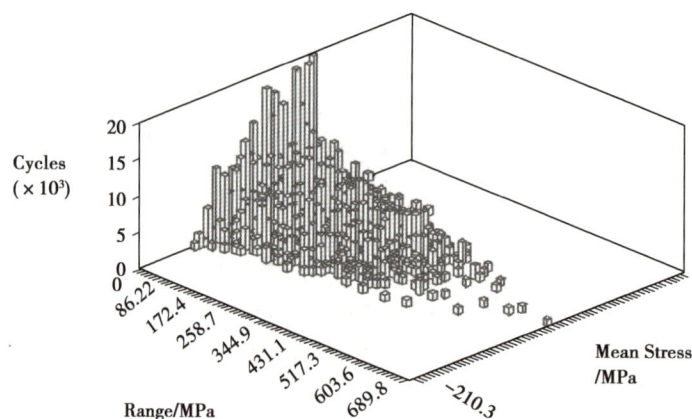

Fig. 7.8.1　Example Histogram as A function of Mean Value and Range [Halfpenny]

Random automotive loading of components under actual driving conditions causes dynamic stress/strain responses which can be better described and handled in the frequency domain. Power Spectrum Density (PSD) is usually the most concise and straightforward way of representing a random process. The fatigue analysis based on PSD using strain range mean (or strain amplitude) histograms as an intermediate stage is demonstrated here. The probability density function (PDF), obtained from PSD, is the cycle (reversal) counting mechanism in the frequency domain such as zero-cross frequencies, resembling the rainflow counting method in the time domain.

7.8.1　Dirlik Method

Dirlik method is based on a wide band time history that is to characterize it by smaller waves riding on a low frequency carrier. The fundamental assumption for applying the method is that the response time history is stationary with a normal distribution. The nth spectral moment m_n for a PSD is then formulated on the positive half-axis only as [Irvine]

$$m_n = \int_0^\infty \omega^n G(\omega) \, d\omega \tag{7.8.1}$$

where

ω: Frequency;

$G(\omega)$: One-sided PSD, for being positive side only.

Dirlik method uses a function of four moments of area of the PSD, which are m_0, m_1, m_2 and m_4 to characterize the rainflow counting algorithm statistically. This method has been found to be widely applicable in aircraft, wind turbine, railroad, and offshore oil industries and prominently outperforms other available methods applied in the frequency domain. Assume that $z(t)$ is the time series that represents the random process where it can be a series of acceleration, strain, stress, or temperature in the time domain. When $n=0$, the integration of the area beneath the PSD curve generates the variance of the random process as

$$\sigma_z^2 = m_0 = \int_0^\infty G(\omega) \, d\omega \tag{7.8.2}$$

Then the square root of m_0 is the standard deviation,

$$\sigma_z = m_0^{\frac{1}{2}} \tag{7.8.3}$$

Furthermore, the variance of the derivative of the variable in the time domain, i.e. $dz(t)/dt$, can be obtained as

$$(\sigma_{\frac{dz}{dt}})^2 = m_2 = \int_0^\infty \omega^2 G(\omega) \, d\omega \tag{7.8.4}$$

The great part of applying PSD to fatigue analysis is that the expected positive zero-crossing frequency (or rate), peak occurrence frequency, and the "mean" frequency can be identified statistically. Respectively, they are given as follows:

$$E[0] = \left(\frac{m_2}{m_0}\right)^{\frac{1}{2}} \tag{7.8.5}$$

$$E[p] = \left(\frac{m_4}{m_2}\right)^{\frac{1}{2}} \tag{7.8.6}$$

and $\quad E[z_{\text{mean}}] = \left(\frac{m_1}{m_0}\right)\left(\frac{m_2}{m_4}\right)^{\frac{1}{2}} \tag{7.8.7}$

where

m_0: The zero moment of area of the PSD;

m_1: The 1st moment of area of the PSD;

m_2: The 2nd moment of area of the PSD;

m_4: The 4th moment of area of the PSD;

$E[0]$: Positive zero-crossing frequency [Rice];

$E[p]$: Peak occurrence frequency [Rice];

$E[z_{\text{mean}}]$: Frequency of "mean" occurrence.

The equations listed above are given without derivations. They are important for determining the fatigue-life intensity. The detailed analytical derivation for these equations can be found in [Dirlik] and [Newland]. Note that p in the brackets given in the above equation means "peak frequency" or peak rate, i.e. number of strain (stress) amplitudes per unit time. $E[p]$ is the expected number of strain, stress, or G-load peaks depending on the case study. Spectral width is defined as the spread of the random process and it can be estimated using parameter α_i, which has the general form as

$$\alpha_i = \frac{m_i}{(m_0 \, m_2)^{\frac{1}{2}}} \tag{7.8.8}$$

e.g. $\quad \alpha_2 = \frac{m_2}{(m_0 \, m_2)^{\frac{1}{2}}} \tag{7.8.9}$

Spectral parameter α_2 is the negative of the correlation between the process and its second moment of area [Tovo]. It is used for spectral width estimation, ranging from 0 to 1. The higher the value of α_2, the narrower is the process in the frequency domain, and vice-versa. Another frequently used spectral parameter is called Vanmarcke's parameter, δ, which is defined as

$$\delta = (1 - \alpha_1^2)^{\frac{1}{2}} = \left[1 - \frac{m_1^2}{(m_0 \, m_2)} \right]^{\frac{1}{2}} \tag{7.8.10}$$

Based on the four moments of area of a PSD obtained from a random vibration, a cycle-counting (3-axis) histogram with mean strain (1-axis) and strain amplitude/range (2-axis) of the peaks can be determined from the Dirlik histogram formula $N_f(\varepsilon_a)$, which is comprised of exponential functions of normalized strain amplitude z. As formulated by [Dirlik], the number of fatigue cycles with strain amplitude ε_a occurring in the time duration Δt can be derived as follows:

$$2N_f(\varepsilon_a) = E[p] \Delta t p_d(z) \tag{7.8.11}$$

$$\text{with} \quad z = \left(\frac{\varepsilon_a^2}{m_0} \right)^{\frac{1}{2}} \tag{7.8.12}$$

$$p_d(z) = \frac{1}{2} \frac{G_1}{R_2} e^{-\frac{z}{R_2}} + \frac{G_2 z}{R_1^2} e^{-\frac{+z^2}{R_1^2}} + \frac{G_3 \, z \, e^{-\frac{1}{2}z^2}}{m_0^{\frac{1}{2}}} \tag{7.8.13}$$

$$G_1 = \frac{2\left(\dfrac{m_1}{m_0} \right) \left(\dfrac{m_2}{m_4} \right)^{\frac{1}{2}} - \dfrac{m_2^2}{m_0 \, m_4}}{1 + \dfrac{m_2^2}{m_0 \, m_4}} = \frac{2(E[z_{mean}] - \alpha_2^2)}{1 + \alpha_2^2} \tag{7.8.14}$$

$$R_1 = \frac{\dfrac{m_2}{(m_0 \, m_4)^{\frac{1}{2}}} - \dfrac{\dfrac{m_1}{m_0}}{\left(\dfrac{m_2}{m_4} \right)^{\frac{1}{2}}} - G_1^2}{1 - \dfrac{m_2}{(m_0 \, m_4)^{\frac{1}{2}}}} - G_1 + G_1^2 = \frac{\alpha_2 - E[z_{mean}] - G_1^2}{1 - \alpha_2 - G_1 + G_1^2} \tag{7.8.15}$$

$$G_2 = \frac{1 - \dfrac{m_2}{(m_0 \, m_4)^{\frac{1}{2}}} - G_1 + G_1^2}{1 - R_1} = \frac{1 - \alpha_2 - G_1 + G_1^2}{1 - R_1} \tag{7.8.16}$$

$$G_3 = 1 - G_1 - G_2 \tag{7.8.17}$$

$$R_2 = \frac{1.25(\alpha_2 - G_3 - G_2 \, R_1)}{G_1} \tag{7.8.18}$$

where

z: Normalized strain amplitude, defined as "Strain amplitude/Standard deviation";

$m_0^{\frac{1}{2}}$: Standard deviation;

$p(z)$: Probability density function that determines fatigue-life intensity;

Δt (s) : Time duration;

$\Delta\varepsilon$ or $\Delta\sigma$ (MPa) : Strain reversal range or stress reversal range (peak-to-peak);

ε_a : Strain amplitude, which is half the strain range as $\varepsilon_a = \dfrac{1}{2}\Delta\varepsilon$.

The equations given above for Dirlik method is based on the algorithm of ε-N fatigue cycles. If the stress range applies, $N(\sigma_a)$ and $z = \sigma_a/m_0^{\frac{1}{2}}$ are to be used in the above equations instead. The damage accumulated by a random load can be evaluated through the rule of linear damage accumulation [Palmgren-Miner] that the expected accumulated damage corresponding to each differential strain (stress) level. Let $M = 1$ (no repetition), then

$$E[D] = \sum_{i=1}^{N} \frac{n_i}{2N_{f,i}} = \int_0^{\infty} \frac{n(\varepsilon_a)}{2N_f(\varepsilon_a)} = d\varepsilon_a = \int_0^{\infty} \frac{p(z)\ n}{2N_f(\varepsilon_a)}\ d\varepsilon_a \qquad (7.8.19)$$

where

$E[D]$: Expected damage due to the random vibration;

n_i : Number of cycles at strain amplitude ε_a, accumulated in the ith load block;

$2N_{f,i}$: Number of cycles required to fail the material in the ith load block (i.e. at ε_a);

$2N_f(\varepsilon_a)$: Number of cycles that can fail the material at strain amplitude ε_a;

n : Number of total cycles.

As shown above, through the PDF one may determine the probability of a certain strain amplitude occurred in a certain differential interval $p(z)$, as $n(\varepsilon_a) = p(z)n$.

7.8.2   Direct Closed-Form Based on Von Mises Equivalent Strain (Stress)

Assume that someone would like to assess the lifetime estimation of a structure using a closed-form solution. One may herein consider the empirical Manson-Coffin equation based on the ε-N relationship, which has been in practice for fatigue analysis at high life cycles at a specified temperature with plastic strains only,

$$\varepsilon_a = \varepsilon_f'(2N_f)^c \qquad (7.8.20)$$

i.e. $2N_f(\varepsilon_a) = \left(\dfrac{\varepsilon_a}{\varepsilon_f'}\right)^{\frac{1}{c}} \qquad (7.8.21)$

Substituting the above equation into Eq. (7.8.19), one has

$$E[D] = \int_0^\infty \frac{p(z)\, n}{\left(\dfrac{\varepsilon_a}{\varepsilon_f'}\right)^{\frac{1}{c}}} d\varepsilon_a = \frac{n}{(\varepsilon_f')^{\frac{1}{c}}} \int_0^\infty (\varepsilon_a)^{\frac{1}{c}} p\left(\frac{\varepsilon_a}{m_0^{\frac{1}{2}}}\right) d\varepsilon_a$$

$$= \frac{\Delta T E[p]}{(\varepsilon_f')^{\frac{1}{c}}} \int_0^\infty (\varepsilon_a)^{\frac{1}{c}} p\left(\frac{\varepsilon_a}{m_0^{\frac{1}{2}}}\right) d\varepsilon_a \tag{7.8.22}$$

where

ΔT: Time duration for each load block in the random vibration;

$E[p]$: Expected peak rate, i.e. number of strain amplitudes per unit time.

The damage intensity, dD/dt, defined as the damage per unit time, can be written mathematically as

$$\frac{dD}{dt} = \frac{E[p]}{(\varepsilon_f')^{\frac{1}{c}}} \int_0^\infty \varepsilon_a^{\frac{1}{c}} p\left(\frac{\varepsilon_a}{m_0^{\frac{1}{2}}}\right) d\varepsilon_a \tag{7.8.23}$$

Then, Eq. (7.8.22) reduces to the damage done up to the point where the random vibration process reigns, as

$$E[D] \approx \Delta T \left(\frac{dD}{dt}\right) \approx \Delta T \left(\frac{\Delta D}{\Delta T}\right) \approx \Delta D \tag{7.8.24}$$

The Dirlik method [Dirlik, 1985] has long been considered to be one of the best approaches to material fatigue subjected to mechanical random vibration and has already been subject to other modifications, e.g., for the inclusion of the temperature effect [Zalaznik & Nagode]. The closed-form expression for the fatigue-life intensity can be derived in such a form [Slavic et al.] by substituting Eq. (7.8.13) into Eq. (7.8.23),

$$\frac{dD}{dt} = \frac{E[p]}{(\varepsilon_f')^{\frac{1}{c}}} \int_0^\infty (\varepsilon_a)^{\frac{1}{c}} p_d\left(\frac{\varepsilon_a}{m_0^{\frac{1}{2}}}\right) d\varepsilon_a$$

$$= \frac{E[p]\, m_0^{\frac{k}{2}}}{(\varepsilon_f')^{\frac{1}{c}}} \left[G_1\, R_2^k\, \Gamma(1+k) + 2^{\frac{k}{2}}\, \Gamma\left(1+\frac{k}{2}\right)(G_2|R_1|^k + G_3) \right] \tag{7.8.25}$$

of which $\Gamma(\ )$ is the Gamma function, which is defined as

$$\Gamma(z) = \int_0^\infty t^{z-1}\, e^{-t}\, dt \tag{7.8.26}$$

Thus $\quad \Gamma(1+k) = \int_0^\infty t^k\, e^{-t}\, dt \tag{7.8.27}$

and $\quad \Gamma\left(1 + \dfrac{k}{2}\right) = \int_0^\infty t^{\frac{k}{2}} e^{-t} \, dt$ $\qquad\qquad$ (7.8.28)

Exponent k in the above equations is the slope of ε-N curve or S-N curve. The error arises as the slope gets steeper, i.e. slope k of the S-N curve is significantly greater than 3 [Benasciutti & Tovo]. Estimate consistency is high for a relatively low value of k such as $k = 3$, when the S-N curve is applied.

Besides the closed-form solution given above, there are two ways of getting a response PSD to derive the spectral moments needed for the Dirlik method [Giovanani, M. et al.] [Teixeira et al.] [Cristofori et al.] [Nieslony & Bohm]:

(a) von Mises equivalent strain (stress) algorithm: Only the strain (stress) component having the maximum von Mises equivalent strain (stress) applies.

(b) Critical plane algorithm: Output PSD's of all strain (stress) components are to be projected onto the critical plane for further processing

7.8.3　Using von Mises Equivalent Strain (Stress)

The random vibration approach requires the evaluation of a frequency response function (FRF), also called transfer function usually going from acceleration (input) to strain (output) in the frequency domain, in terms of strains (or stresses) for a unit loading applied to every load channel that excites the structure. This can be accomplished by obtaining the FRFs through (a) modal superposition for harmonic analysis or (b) dynamic analysis in steady state. If modal superposition harmonic is the analysis of choice, modal results are combined to the modal participation factors to compose the FRFs. The detailed derivation will be addressed in Sections 7.10.2 and 7.10.3.

7.8.4　Using Equivalent PSD Projected onto the Critical Plane

The PSD output of every set of strain (or stress) components, $\{\varepsilon_{xx} \quad \varepsilon_{yy} \quad \varepsilon_{zz} \quad \varepsilon_{xy} \quad \varepsilon_{yz} \quad \varepsilon_{zx}\}$ or $\{\sigma_{xx} \quad \sigma_{yy} \quad \sigma_{zz} \quad \tau_{xy} \quad \tau_{yz} \quad \tau_{zx}\}$ of the loaded structure will be projected onto the critical plane in order to find out the most damaging location. Thus, the spectral fatigue damage method proposed herein involves a Monte Carlo enumeration step to find the critical plane orientation. Nevertheless, the variance method has been used to locate the critical plane position [Cristofori] [Nieslony]. By using the proposed technique, computationally expensive enumeration methods are avoided and greater accuracy in the fatigue damage estimate may result.

Grouping the frequency response functions of the strain (stress) components resulting from analysis, for all the input PSDs (e.g. FEA) or existing loading channels from experimental tests, leads to the following transfer function, also called transition coefficient matrix,

$$
[\boldsymbol{H}_{a\varepsilon}(\omega)]_{N\times 6} =
\begin{pmatrix}
\varepsilon_{xx,1}(\omega) & \varepsilon_{yy,1}(\omega) & \varepsilon_{zz,1}(\omega) & \varepsilon_{xy,1}(\omega) & \varepsilon_{yz,1}(\omega) & \varepsilon_{zx,1}(\omega) \\
\vdots & \vdots & \vdots & \vdots & \vdots & \vdots \\
[\varepsilon_{xx,n}(\omega) & \varepsilon_{yy,n}(\omega) & \varepsilon_{zz,n}(\omega) & \varepsilon_{xy,n}(\omega) & \varepsilon_{yz,n}(\omega) & \varepsilon_{zx,n}(\omega)] \\
\vdots & \vdots & \vdots & \vdots & \vdots & \vdots \\
\varepsilon_{xx,N}(\omega) & \varepsilon_{yy,N}(\omega) & \varepsilon_{zz,N}(\omega) & \varepsilon_{xy,N}(\omega) & \varepsilon_{yz,N}(\omega) & \varepsilon_{zx,N}(\omega)
\end{pmatrix}_{N\times 6}
$$

$$(7.8.29)$$

where

$[H_{a\varepsilon}(\omega)]_{N\times 6}$: Transition function matrix, made of N rows and 6 columns;

n: Index, $n = 1, 2, \cdots, N$;

N: Total number of PSD output spectra to be mapped onto the critical plane.

Note that the transfer function transforms the loading function to strains. Parameter N also stands for the number of degrees of freedom of the entire system, should the FEA is applied. The corresponding entire applied loads (i.e. force, displacement, acceleration, etc.) in the frequency domain is the input PSD, written as follows:

$$
[\boldsymbol{S}_{a\varepsilon}(\omega)]_{N\times N} =
\begin{pmatrix}
S_{1,1}(\omega) & S_{1,2}(\omega) & S_{1,3}(\omega) & \cdots & S_{1,N}(\omega) \\
S_{2,1}(\omega) & S_{2,2}(\omega) & S_{2,3}(\omega) & \cdots & S_{2,N}(\omega) \\
\vdots & \vdots & \vdots & & \vdots \\
S_{N-1,1}(\omega) & S_{N-1,2}(\omega) & S_{N-1,3}(\omega) & \cdots & S_{N-1,N}(\omega) \\
S_{N,1}(\omega) & S_{N,2}(\omega) & S_{N,3}(\omega) & \cdots & S_{N,N}(\omega)
\end{pmatrix}_{N\times N}
$$

$$(7.8.30)$$

Linear operations performed in one domain (time or frequency) have corresponding operations in the other domain. Pre- and post-multiplying the input matrix $[S_{a\varepsilon}(\omega)]_{N\times N}$ by $[H]_{N\times 6}$ results in the 6×6 strain (stress) PSD matrix at the point of interest of the structure in the global (x,y,z) coordinate system,

$$
[\boldsymbol{S}_{\varepsilon\varepsilon}(\omega)]_{6\times 6} = [\boldsymbol{H}_{a\varepsilon}(\omega)]_{6\times N}^{\mathrm{T}} \; [\boldsymbol{S}_{a\varepsilon}(\omega)]_{N\times N} \; [\boldsymbol{H}_{a\varepsilon}(\omega)]_{N\times 6} \tag{7.8.31}
$$

The strain (stress) components can be transformed from the global coordinate system to the local coordinate system attached to the critical plane, as demonstrated in Section 7.9. Then, different failure criteria such as SWT equation and Rivlin's function can be used for determining the potential life cycles and then subsequently substituted into Eq. (7.8.23) or Eq. (7.8.24) for calculating the total life cycles.

For simplicity, a scalar function for the failure criterion is looked for. Referring to Fig. 7.8.2, one can obtain the equivalent stress, which is a scalar, as

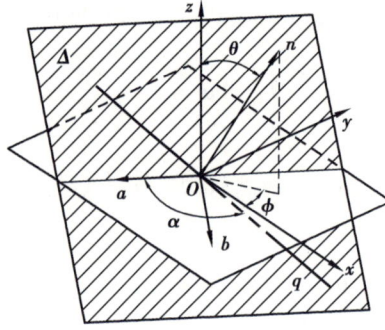

Fig. 7.8.2 **Transformations from the Global** (x,y,z) **Coordinate System to the Critical Plane** ［**Giovanni**］

$$\sigma'_{eq} = \sigma_{eq}(\omega)' = [\mathbf{T}_\sigma]^{\mathrm{T}}[\mathbf{S}_{\sigma\sigma}(\omega)]_{6\times6}[\mathbf{T}_\sigma] \tag{7.8.32}$$

and $\quad [\mathbf{T}_\sigma]^{\mathrm{T}} = \{l_c^2 \ m_c^2 \ n_c^2 \ 2l_c m_c \ 2m_c n_c \ 2n_c l_c\}$ (7.8.33)

where $\quad l_c = \sin\theta \cos\phi$ (7.8.34a)

$$m_c = \sin\theta \sin\phi \tag{7.8.34b}$$

and $\quad n_c = \cos\theta$ (7.8.34c)

Angles θ and ϕ are used for locating the norm of the critical plane relative to the global (x,y,z) coordinate system, starting from the z-axis. Note that the transformation matrix for strain transformation is different from that of stress transformation. It is

$$[\mathbf{T}_\varepsilon]^{\mathrm{T}} = \{l_c^2 \quad m_c^2 \quad n_c^2 \quad l_c m_c \quad m_c n_c \quad n_c l_c\} \tag{7.8.35}$$

and $\quad \varepsilon'_{eq} = \varepsilon_{eq}(\omega)' = [\mathbf{T}_\varepsilon]^{\mathrm{T}}[\mathbf{S}_{\varepsilon\varepsilon}(\omega)]_{6\times6}[\mathbf{T}_\varepsilon]$ (7.8.36)

7.8.5 Steinberg 3-Band Method for Quick Damage Checkup

Power spectral density (PSD) is a common way to represent the service load and can also be used to obtain a load spectrum. Based on the PSD, one can obtain the probability density function (PDF) of the strain (or stress) history. It is assumed that the loading and response (i.e. strain, stress, or any other damage parameter history) are statistically normally distributed in nature and it can be represented by a normal (Gaussian) distribution with "zero" mean, as demonstrated in Fig. 7.8.3. In other words, one can realize such a statistical distribution from the perspective of the likelihood that a certain level of load or response will fall within a certain standard deviation from the mean in a random vibration analysis.

The Steinberg 3-band method for damage calculation is frequently used due to its simplicity ［Mrsnik et al.］. Consider a structure subjected to a fluctuating load and let L_{1s}, L_{2s} and L_{3s} be its corresponding 3 fluctuating amplitudes of the input forcing function, which can be used as the input to the finite element analysis (FEA) of the structure at the loading points. Note that the load is arbitrarily assigned to the peak of the time series, as shown in Fig. 7.8.3, while the probability for the occurrence of each load is assumed to be appropriated according to the normal (Gaussian) distribution. The loading probability density function (or histogram) can then be classified as follows:

Loading	S. D.	Percentage (Occurrences)	Cumulative Probability
L_{1s}	$(0, \pm 1\sigma)$	68.27% (0.6827 n)	68.27%
L_{2s}	$(\pm 1\sigma, \pm 2\sigma)$	27.18% (0.2718 n)	95.45%
L_{3s}	$(\pm 2\sigma, \pm 3\sigma)$	4.33% (0.0433 n)	99.73%
Extremities		0.27%	100%

where

L_{1s}: Load within the ± 1 sigma of the standard probability density function;

L_{2s}: Load between the ± 1 sigma and ± 2 sigmas of the standard PDF;

L_{3s}: Load between the ± 2 sigmas and ± 3 sigmas of the standard PDF;

n: Number of cycles in each load block.

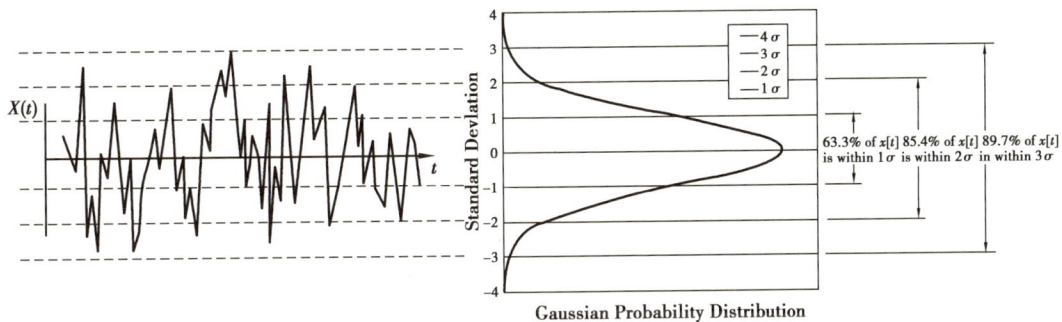

Gaussian Probability Distribution

Fig. 7.8.3   The 3-band Approximation to the Statistical Normal Distribution [Steinberg]

The estimated maximum strain (stress) levels at the three load levels, i.e. L_{1s}, L_{2s} and L_{3s}, can then be checked against its cumulative fatigue based on ε-N approach, S-N approach or others, in conjunction with damage accumulation models presented in Chapter 4 employed for the standard fatigue analysis procedure in the time domain. One algorithm to approach such a fatigue problem is to directly assume that the ± 3 sigma boundaries are right at the infinite life or fatigue limit. Since this algorithm sounds conservative in practice, further sophisticated methods are to be explored.

The percentage of occurrence for each load is the proportional share of cycles, as calculated using the corresponding Miner's fatigue damage cycle ratios that goes as follows:

$$100\% = M \sum_{i=1}^{3} \frac{n_i}{N_{fi}} = M\left(\frac{0.6827\ n}{N_{f1}} + \frac{0.2718\ n}{N_{f2}} + \frac{0.0433\ n}{N_{f3}}\right) \tag{7.8.37}$$

where

n_i: Number of cycles at the ith load level (block), and totally 3 levels in each load section;

n: Total number of cycles per load section;

M: Number of repeated load sections leading to failure;

N_{fi}: Number of fatigue cycles to failure resulting from physical tests (material property), corresponding to the $(\sigma_i, \varepsilon_i)$ load level, as calculated from FEA or measured data.

The fatigue life estimation is evaluated by comparing the calculated cumulative damage ratio to a specified cumulative damage index, e.g. 100% given in the above equation. M is therefore the total number of cycles to failure, i.e. life cycles. Assume that it takes H hours to complete a real-time test of each load block. Then, the life cycle in hours will be MH.

It can be assumed that for a zero-mean stationary random process that the induced strain (stress, fracture toughness, or strain energy) will be composed of both positive and negative peaks which correspond to a fully reversible stress cycle. The ε-N curve should then be adjusted accordingly for a load ratio of $R = -1$.

The next step is to figure out the number of applied cycles that the component is exposed to over time, n, in each load section. This can be calculated by applying the post-processing technique to the dynamic finite element analysis in frequency domain. Define the averaged frequency as the expected frequency in cycles per unit time at the structural location of concern. This can be accomplished by one of the following methods:

(a) Once the dynamic finite element analysis is carried out in the frequency domain, one can calculate the averaged frequency by dividing the velocity solution by the displacement solution for a given strain (or stress) level and convert the result to frequency in cycles per unit time, e.g. $f = \omega/2\pi$. This represents the number of positive zero crossings of the process per unit time. As for a narrow band stationary process, $E[p] = E[0]$, i.e. each positive zero crossing implies one cycle of vibration.

(b) Experimental Testing: The measured acceleration waveform is converted to a velocity waveform by an integration process. It was argued that stress (causing fatigue) is proportional to velocity, and thus the number of positive zero crossings of the process per unit time can be calculated accordingly. Technically speaking, the converted velocity waveform is run through a narrow-band fitter using a specific Q value, i.e. the quality factor shown in Eq. (7.5.13).

Next, one can compute the average number of cycles per load section by multiplying the averaged frequency by the time duration of the input random signal applied.

Example 7.8.1   Assume that the maximum root mean stress is 105 MPa of the applied random load, as obtained from finite element analysis. The *S-N* (root mean square stress versus cycles) curve of an aluminum alloy is given in Fig. 7.8.4. The fatigue lifetimes corresponding to three different load levels of the aluminum alloy are read as follows: $N_{f1} = 1.0 \times 10^{10}$ cycles at 35 MPa, $N_{f2} = 2.0 \times 10^8$ cycles at 70 MPa, and $N_{f3} = 1.8 \times 10^7$ cycles at 105 MPa, which are obtained from the shaker table test at three different fluctuating loads with $R = -1$. Each load section is set for 0.5 hour and the averaged frequency is 500 Hz. How soon do you expect to fail the specimen in such a random vibration test?

Solution:

The number of cycles per load case is $n = 500$ Hz×0.5 h = 500 Hz×1 800 s = 0.9×10^6 cycles. When applying Eq. (7.8.29), one has to determine which *S-N* curves (Fig. 7.8.4) should be used. The author's opinion is that 50% (reliability) is naive while 90% (reliability) is over-corrected, since the reliability is taken from a finite number of specimens without designated confidence interval for both curves. The good choice is to take the specimen from the production parts to test it to failure and it will fall between them.

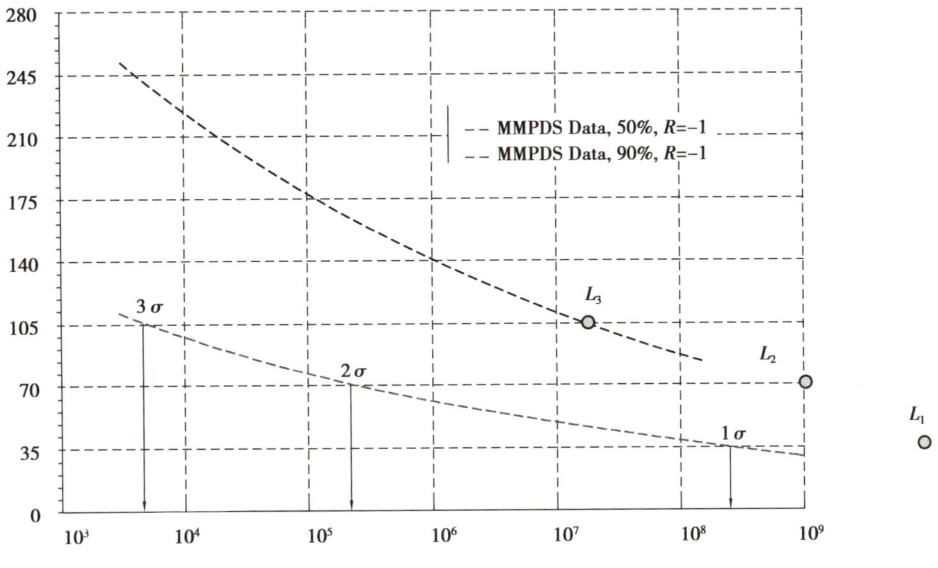

Fig. 7.8.4   *S-N* Curve for Aluminum Alloy 6061-T6 with Load Ratio $R = -1$

(a) Use the 90% *S-N* curve at points 1σ, 2σ, and $3\sigma_3$:

$$\text{Damage} = M\left(\frac{0.6827\ n}{N_{f1}} + \frac{0.2718\ n}{N_{f2}} + \frac{0.0433\ n}{N_{f3}}\right)$$

$$= M \frac{0.6827 \times 0.9 \times 10^6}{2.5 \times 10^8} + \frac{0.2718 \times 0.9 \times 10^6}{1.2 \times 10^5} + \frac{0.0433 \times 0.9 \times 10^6}{3.6 \times 10^3}$$

$$= M[0.00245772 + 2.0385 + 10.825]$$

$$= 12.866 \, M$$

Assume that the maximum damage can be allowed is 100%. Then

$$M = \frac{100\%}{12.866} = 0.0777 \quad \text{sections}$$

Hence, the specimen will survive at the shaker table for 0.0777 load section, i.e. 0.0389 h (= 0.5 h×0.0777).

(b) Use the 50% S-N curve at points L_1, L_2, and L_3:

$$\text{Damage} = M\left(\frac{0.6827 \, n}{N_{f1}} + \frac{0.2718 \, n}{N_{f2}} + \frac{0.0433 \, n}{N_{f3}}\right)$$

$$= M \frac{0.6827 \times 0.9 \times 10^6}{1.0 \times 10^{10}} + \frac{0.2718 \times 0.9 \times 10^6}{1.0 \times 10^9} + \frac{0.0433 \times 0.9 \times 10^6}{1.8 \times 10^7}$$

$$= M(0.000061443 + 0.00024462 + 0.002165)$$

$$= 0.002471063 \, M$$

Assume that the maximum damage can be allowed is 100%. Then

$$M = \frac{100\%}{0.002471063} = 404.7 \text{ sections}$$

Hence, the specimen will survive at the shaker table for 404.7 load section, i.e. 202.34 h (=0.5 h×404.7).

The 50% (reliability) S-N curve is too idealized to be true, while the 90% (reliability) curve is too conservative to be valid. An S-N curve should be obtained from test specimens obtained from production parts, and data are acquired on the axial fatigue test machine at the reliability of 90% with the confidence interval of 90% (i.e. $R = 90\%$ and $C = 90\%$), as required for automotive engineering practice.

Steinberg's 3-band method is here utilized for illustrating the basic concept of fatigue analysis for random processes, but it has three major drawbacks that hinder its accuracy. One is that the strain (stress) levels are lumped into 3 individual loads of 1-sigma, 2-sigma, and 3-sigma, while they are continuous distribution functions in reality. The 2nd is the assumption that each positive zero crossing implies a cycle of vibration, which works fine for a narrow band response such as Bendat, but is too conservative for a wide band response such as Dirlik method. Narrow band methods are to be addressed later. The 3rd issue is the assumption that the statistical probability density function is idealized to be normally distributed, while it may not be true. When the proper probability density function has been identified, the probability table given above should be revised accordingly.

7.8.6   Bendat Method

[Bendat] proposed in 1964 the first significant step towards a method of determining fatigue life from PSDs. Bendat method is based on a narrow band time history that is characterized by each peak having a corresponding valley of similar magnitude. It is shown by [Bendat] that the probability density function of peaks for a narrow band signal tended towards a Rayleigh distribution as the bandwidth reduced. The number of fatigue cycles at strain amplitude of ε_a occurring in the time duration Δt is given as follows [Bendat]:

$$2N(\varepsilon_a) = E[p]\Delta t p_b(z) \tag{7.8.38}$$

where $p_b(z) = \dfrac{1}{2}\left(\dfrac{z}{m_0^{\frac{1}{2}}}\right)e^{-\frac{1}{2}z^2} = \dfrac{1}{2}\left(\dfrac{\varepsilon_a}{m_0}\right)e^{-\frac{1}{2}\left(\frac{\varepsilon_a}{m_0^{\frac{1}{2}}}\right)^2}$ \hfill (7.8.39)

of which $p_b(z)$ has a Rayleigh distribution function. The range mean histogram provided by Bendat method contains no cycle mean data.

The Fatigue Damage Spectrum (FDS) is produced by plotting the individually calculated fatigue damage values for narrow frequency bands. Assume that the PSD data are available. The PSD data from a particular test run through a narrowband filter with a specific Q value, can be used for calculating the VRS (Vibration Response Spectrum), i.e. acceleration versus frequency. A specialized calculation tool such as Bendat method is then used to determine the fatigue damage for the data filtered for each frequency band. This is accomplished by using a rainflow counting algorithm to determine the fatigue cycles using strain (stress) peak-valley extremities. [Lalanne] was able to utilize this technology to create a closed form calculation to estimate the FDS directly from the acceleration PSD, given as follows:

$$\mathrm{FDS}(\omega_n) = \omega_n\,\Delta t\left[\frac{G^2\,Q\,S_{aa}(\omega_n)}{2\times(2\pi\omega_n)^3}\right]^{\frac{b}{2}}\Gamma\left(1+\frac{1}{2}\,b\right) \tag{7.8.40}$$

where
$\Delta t(\mathrm{s})$: Exposure duration in seconds;

G: Gravity, $1 \ G = 9.81 \ \text{N/s}^2$;

Q: Quality factor, i.e. Dynamic amplification factor;

$S_{aa}(\omega_n)$: PSD of applied acceleration in G^2/Hz;

$\Gamma(\ )$: Gamma function.

The above equation is derived using the following HCF (high cycle fatigue) equation [Basquin],

$$C = S^b N_f \tag{7.8.41}$$

where

C: Basquin coefficient, i.e. the intercept of the S-N curve with the y-axis;

S: Stress;

N_f: Fatigue cycle.

It has been proven that the Dirlik method is superior to the Bendat method for fatigue life prediction. However, both methods are subject to the fundamental assumption that the normality of selected vibration data has to be warranted. A lack of normality may lead to biased fatigue life estimation. For example, Dirlik method underestimates damage for some automotive components by up to 30%, as reported by [Quigley and Lee].

7.8.7 Zhao-Baker Method

[Zhao & Baker] proposed in 1993 the first significant step towards a method of determining fatigue life from PSDs based on both 2-parameter Weibull distribution and Rayleigh distribution. The number of fatigue cycles at strain amplitude of ε_a occurring in the time duration Δt is given as follows [Zhao & Baker]:

$$2N(\varepsilon_a) = E[p]\Delta t \ p_{zb}(z) \tag{7.8.42}$$

with $\quad p_{zb}(z) = \Psi \left[\eta \beta z^{\beta-1} \ e^{-\eta z^\beta} \right] + (1 - \Psi) \ \frac{1}{2} z e^{-\frac{1}{2} z^2} \tag{7.8.43}$

where

η: Coefficient in the 2-parameter Weibull function;

β: Exponent in the 2-parameter Weibull function;

Ψ: Weight for the 2-parameter Weibull function.

The probability density function $p(z)$ has a combination of weighted Weibull PDF and Rayleigh PDF, regulated by weighting parameter, Ψ. The relationships among the three parameters given above are listed here without analytic derivation as

$$\Psi = \frac{1 - \alpha_2}{1 - \left(\dfrac{2}{\pi}\right)^{\frac{1}{2}} \Gamma\left(1 + \beta^{-1}\right) \eta^{\frac{-1}{\beta}}} \tag{7.8.44}$$

$$\beta = 1.1 \qquad\qquad\qquad \text{if } \alpha_2 < 0.9 \qquad\qquad\qquad (7.8.45\text{a})$$

$$= 1.1 + 9\,(\alpha_2 - 0.9) \qquad\qquad \text{if } \alpha_2 \geqslant 0.9 \qquad\qquad\qquad (7.8.45\text{b})$$

and $\quad \alpha = d^{-\beta} \qquad\qquad\qquad\qquad\qquad\qquad\qquad\qquad\qquad\qquad (7.8.46)$

where

d is the root of the following equation.

$$\Gamma(1 + 3\,\beta^{-1})\,(1 - \alpha_2)\,d^3 + 3\,\Gamma(1 + \beta^{-1})\,(\rho\,\alpha_2 - 1)\,d + 3\left(\frac{1}{2}\,\pi\right)^{\frac{1}{2}} \alpha_2(1 - \rho) = 0$$

$$(7.8.47)$$

The correction factor in the above equation at $k = 3$, i.e. ρ, can be calculated as

$$\rho = 0.28 \qquad\qquad\qquad \text{If } \alpha_{0.75} < 0.5 \qquad\qquad\qquad (7.8.48\text{a})$$

$$= -0.4145 + 1.392\,\alpha_{0.75} \qquad \text{If } \alpha_{0.75} \geqslant 0.5 \qquad\qquad\qquad (7.8.48\text{b})$$

where $\quad \alpha_{0.75} = \dfrac{m_{0.75}}{(m_0\,m_{0.75})^{\frac{1}{2}}} \qquad\qquad\qquad\qquad\qquad\qquad (7.8.49)$

The value of $m_{0.75}$ can be obtained from Eq. (7.8.1). The closed-form expression for the fatigue-life intensity has been derived in the form [Slavic et al.] by substituting Eq. (7.8.43) into Eq. (7.8.23),

$$\frac{\mathrm{d}D}{\mathrm{d}t} = \frac{E[p]}{\varepsilon_{\mathrm{f}}'^{\frac{1}{c}}} \int_0^\infty \varepsilon_{\mathrm{a}}^{\frac{1}{c}}\,p_{\mathrm{bd}}\left(\frac{\varepsilon_{\mathrm{a}}}{m_0^{\frac{1}{2}}}\right)\mathrm{d}\varepsilon_{\mathrm{a}}$$

$$= \frac{E[p]\,m_0^{\frac{k}{2}}}{\varepsilon_{\mathrm{f}}'^{\frac{1}{c}}}\left[\Psi\,\alpha^{\frac{-k}{\beta}}\,\Gamma\!\left(1 + \frac{k}{\beta}\right) + (1 - \Psi)\,2^{\frac{k}{2}}\,\Gamma\!\left(1 + \frac{k}{2}\right)\right] \qquad (7.8.50)$$

7.9   Finite Element Methods in Frequency Domain

A transfer function is a mathematical representation for curve-fitting or to describe relationship of the output function to the input function. It describes the level of one signal relative to another signal, describing the behaviors of a known process or just a black box model. When a transfer function presented in the frequency domain, it is called frequency response function. Generally speaking, a transfer function is a complex-valued quantity, meaning the response of a vibrating system, e.g. the SDOF (Single Degrees of Freedom) system described by Eq. (7.3.5a), can be characterized by a magnitude and phase. The response to a dynamic system derived from finite element methods for continuous systems is frequently annotated in the frequency domain like a transfer function for MDOF (Multiple Degrees of Freedom). Transfer functions can be classified according to the response function as:

Response	Transfer Function	Damage
Displacement	Receptance	Fatigue
Velocity	Mobility	Impact
Acceleration	Inertance	Shock

PSD-based finite element analysis is such a type of frequency-domain analysis that a structure is subjected to a probabilistic spectrum of harmonic loading to obtain probabilistic distributions for dynamic response measures. A root-mean-square (RMS) formulation translates the PSD curve for each response quantity into a single, most likely value. Because PSD curves represent the continuous probability density function of each response measure, most of the integrated area will occur near the resonant frequencies of the structure. For accuracy, it is important to capture response at frequency steps near the natural modes of the structure. Via modal analysis or experiments, the transfer function from the acceleration function input at one point of the structure to the strain (or stress) levels at an output point can be deduced. A PSD output may be encouraged for each output point of interest to show strain and stress levels induced, including von Mises strain (stress) and principal strains (stresses), for the purpose of fatigue analysis.

7.9.1　Frequency Response Function: Force to Displacement

The dynamic analysis of mechanical vibrations can be determined both in the time and frequency domains. It is to characterize the vibration behaviors of a complex structure through the transfer function in the frequency domain for a control system design and/or structural health monitoring, while model parameters are identified from the response data obtained via finite element analysis. In the frequency domain the power spectrum density function is obtained via a "transfer function" technique. Essentially the frequency domain breaks down a signal into its constituent sinusoidal waves following Fourier's theory. The transfer function relates the amplitude of the input force (or moment) to the amplitude of the output strain (or stress) for each frequency of its corresponding sinusoidal wave.

When working in the linear elastoplastic range using the finite element method, a complex structure may be discretized as a linear system with multiple degrees of freedoms that comprise a set of second-order differential equations as demonstrated in the finite element analysis [Cook]:

$$[M]\left(\frac{\mathrm{d}^2 x}{\mathrm{d}t^2}\right) + [C]\left(\frac{\mathrm{d}x}{\mathrm{d}t}\right) + [K]\{x\} = \{f\} \tag{7.9.1}$$

where

$[M]$: Global mass matrix;

$[C]$: Global damping matrix;

$[K]$: Global stiffness matrix;

$\{x\}$: Vector of nodal displacements as the response function;

$\{f\}$: Vector of nodal forces as the excitation function.

For simplicity, If the input nodal load $\{f\}$ varies sinusoidally with respect to time t,

$$\{f\} = \{F\}\ \exp(i\ \omega\ t) \tag{7.9.2}$$

The displacement vector $\{x(t)\}$ in response for the forcing function can be solved in the time domain as

$$\{x(t)\} = \frac{\{F\}}{-[M]\ \omega^2 + [C]\ i\ \omega + [K]}\exp(i\ \omega\ t) = \{X\}\ \exp(i\ \omega\ t) \tag{7.9.3}$$

where

$\{F\}$: Vector of amplitudes of the input force;

$\{X\}$: Amplitude of the induced displacements;

ω (Hz or rad/s): Frequency.

It can be seen that solution $\{x(t)\}$ also varies sinusoidally with respect to time. Next, if Eq. (7.9.1) is solved in the frequency domain by taking the Fourier transform of both the forcing function and displacement response, one has

$$\{-[M]\ \omega^2 + [C]\ i\ \omega + [K]\}\ \{x(\omega)\} = \{F(\omega)\} \tag{7.9.4}$$

Let $[H(\omega)] = (-[M]\ \omega^2 + [C]\ i\ \omega + [K])^{-1}$ \hfill (7.9.5)

then $\{x(\omega)\} = [H(\omega)]\ \{F(\omega)\}$ \hfill (7.9.6)

and $\{x_{rms}\}^2 = [H(\omega)]^2\{F_{rms}\}^2$ \hfill (7.9.7)

where

$H(\omega)$: Frequency-response function, having both auto- and crossed-correlated spectra;

$x(\omega)$: Vector of displacement in the frequency domain, $x(\omega) = \text{FT}(x(t))$;

$F(\omega)$: Vector of forcing function in the frequency domain, $F(\omega) = \text{FT}(F(t))$;

$(x_{rms})^2$: Mean squared response;

$(F_{rms})^2$: Mean squared force.

Eqs. (7.9.3) and (7.9.6) are the corresponding counterparts in the time and frequency domains, respectively. Note that the phase information is truncated while using the PSD approach. There are two major empirical methods in practice for estimating load spectra: the narrow band method [Bendat] and the broad band method [Dirlik].

7.9.2 Damage Frequency Response: from Acceleration to Stress

The damage analysis can be done using von Mises stress. However, there are two different approaches, one is to derive the von Mises stress in the frequency domain and the other in the time domain.

The stressed point that is to be studied further for fatigue analysis has the stress response spectra as $S_{\sigma\sigma}(\omega)$ in the frequency domain, that can be related to a single acceleration excitation spectrum, $S_{aa}(\omega)$, in the frequency domain as [Newland]

$$[S_{\sigma\sigma}(\omega)] = H_{a\sigma}(\omega)[S_{aa}(\omega)]H_{a\sigma}(\omega)^{\mathrm{T}} \tag{7.9.8}$$

where

$S_{\sigma\sigma}(\omega)$: Stress response spectra;

$H_{a\sigma}(\omega)$: Transfer function, a frequency-response function from acceleration to stress.

Next consider the individual strained point, which comprises of six strain components in the 3-dimensional space, i.e. $S_{\sigma\sigma,xx}$, $S_{\sigma\sigma,yy}$, $S_{\sigma\sigma,zz}$, $S_{\sigma\sigma,xy}$, $S_{\sigma\sigma,xz}$, and $S_{\sigma\sigma,yz}$, as derived directly from finite element analysis in the frequency domain. The principal strains and corresponding von Mises strain in the frequency domain can be obtained, respectively as

$$\begin{Bmatrix} \sigma_1(\omega) \\ \sigma_2(\omega) \\ \sigma_3(\omega) \end{Bmatrix} = \text{Eigenvalues of} \begin{bmatrix} S_{\sigma\sigma,xx} & S_{\sigma\sigma,xy} & S_{\sigma\sigma,xz} \\ S_{\sigma\sigma,xy} & S_{\sigma\sigma,yy} & S_{\sigma\sigma,yz} \\ S_{\sigma\sigma,xz} & S_{\sigma\sigma,yz} & S_{\sigma\sigma,zz} \end{bmatrix} \tag{7.9.9}$$

and
$$\sigma(\omega)_{\text{von mises}} = \{[\sigma_1(\omega) - \sigma_2(\omega)]^2 + [\sigma_2(\omega) - \sigma_3(\omega)]^2 + [\sigma_3(\omega) - \sigma_1(\omega)]^2\}^{\frac{1}{2}} \tag{7.9.10}$$

Another method is to obtain the von Mises stresses in the time domain first [Preumont & Piefort] as

$$\sigma_{\text{eq}}^2 = \sigma_{xx}^2 + \sigma_{yy}^2 + \sigma_{zz}^2 - \sigma_{xx}\sigma_{yy} - \sigma_{yy}\sigma_{zz} - \sigma_{zz}\sigma_{xx} + 3(\tau_{xy}^2 + \tau_{yz}^2 + \tau_{zx}^2) \tag{7.9.11}$$

Then, the components of the stress response spectra, $S_{aa}(\omega)$, at a point subjected to a load at another point of the structure is a six independent stress tensor in the form of a 6×6 matrix:

$$[S_{aa}(\omega)]_{6\times6} = \begin{bmatrix} S_{xx,xx}(\omega) & S_{xx,yy}(\omega) & S_{xx,zz}(\omega) & S_{xx,xy}(\omega) & S_{xx,yz}(\omega) & S_{xx,zx}(\omega) \\ S_{yy,xx}(\omega) & S_{yy,yy}(\omega) & S_{yy,zz}(\omega) & S_{yy,xy}(\omega) & S_{yy,yz}(\omega) & S_{yy,zx}(\omega) \\ S_{zz,xx}(\omega) & S_{zz,yy}(\omega) & S_{zz,zz}(\omega) & S_{zz,xy}(\omega) & S_{zz,yz}(\omega) & S_{zz,zx}(\omega) \\ S_{xy,xx}(\omega) & S_{xy,yy}(\omega) & S_{xy,zz}(\omega) & S_{xy,xy}(\omega) & S_{xy,yz}(\omega) & S_{xy,zx}(\omega) \\ S_{yz,xx}(\omega) & S_{yz,yy}(\omega) & S_{yz,zz}(\omega) & S_{zx,xy}(\omega) & S_{zx,yz}(\omega) & S_{yz,zx}(\omega) \\ S_{zx,xx}(\omega) & S_{zx,yy}(\omega) & S_{zx,zz}(\omega) & S_{zx,xy}(\omega) & S_{zx,yz}(\omega) & S_{zx,zx}(\omega) \end{bmatrix}$$

$$(7.9.12)$$

Then, the expected value of σ_{eq}^2 can be rewritten as

$$E[\sigma_{eq}^2] = \sigma_{1\times6} Q_{6\times6} \sigma_{6\times1}^T = \text{Trace}\{[Q]_{6\times6} E[\{\sigma\}_{1\times6}\{\sigma\}_{6\times1}^T]\} \qquad (7.9.13)$$

where $\quad [Q]_{6\times6} = \begin{bmatrix} 1 & -\dfrac{1}{2} & -\dfrac{1}{2} & 0 & 0 & 0 \\ -\dfrac{1}{2} & 1 & -\dfrac{1}{2} & 0 & 0 & 0 \\ -\dfrac{1}{2} & -\dfrac{1}{2} & 1 & 0 & 0 & 0 \\ 0 & 0 & 0 & 3 & 0 & 0 \\ 0 & 0 & 0 & 0 & 3 & 0 \\ 0 & 0 & 0 & 0 & 0 & 3 \end{bmatrix} \qquad (7.9.14)$

$[Q]$ is called coefficient matrix. To conduct a fatigue analysis of the multiaxial stress in the frequency domain, it is imperative to obtain the PSD matrix of an equivalent von Mises stress of the whole structure as

$$E[\sigma_{eq}^2] = \int_0^\infty \text{Trace}\{[Q]S_{\sigma\sigma}(\omega)\} \, d\omega \qquad (7.9.15)$$

It has been assumed by some researchers that the above equation yields the expected value or the mean-square of the von Mises stress, which is equal for both time-domain and frequency-domain formulations [Mrsnik, 2016], as

$$\text{Trace}\{[Q] E[S_{\sigma\sigma}(\omega)]\} = \text{Trace}\{[Q]_{6\times6} E[\{\sigma\}_{1\times6}\{\sigma\}_{6\times1}^T]\} \qquad (7.9.16)$$

$$\text{Hence}, S_{\sigma\sigma,eq}(\omega) = \text{Trace}\{[Q] E[S_{\sigma\sigma}(\omega)]\} \qquad (7.9.17)$$

$$\text{Thus}, S_{\sigma\sigma,eq}(\omega) = \{\sigma\}_{1\times6}[Q]_{6\times6}\{\sigma\}_{6\times1}^T S_{aa}(\omega) \qquad (7.9.18)$$

The equivalent von Mises stress, as derived above, is a stationary zero-mean Gaussian process [Pitoiset & Preumont] for being in compliance with the input acceleration spectra; therefore, the existing frequency methods for fatigue-life calculations can be adopted.

As the fatigue damage intensity is calculated with frequency-domain counting methods, the characteristics of the equivalent stress-response spectrum are here identified for this purpose. The shape of the equivalent stress PSD can be characterized with a set of spectral moments as having been done for the forcing function using Eq. (7.9.2); for a stationary random vibration with a zero mean value, the nth spectral moment.

$$m_{\sigma,\text{equ},n} = \int_0^\infty \omega^n G_{\sigma,\text{equ}}(\omega) \, d\omega \quad (n = 0, 1, 2, \text{ or } 4) \tag{7.9.19}$$

where

$m_{\sigma,\text{equ},n}$: nth spectral moment of $G_{\sigma,\text{equ}}(\omega)$;

$G_{\sigma,\text{equ}}(\omega)$: One-sided equivalent stress PSD.

Again, the expected positive zero-crossing frequency of the spectral moment of $G_{\sigma,\text{equ}}(\omega)$, which can be used for counting the waveform, is given as follows:

$$E[0] = \frac{\left(\dfrac{m_{\sigma,\text{equ},2}}{m_{\sigma,\text{equ},0}}\right)^{\frac{1}{2}}}{2\pi} \tag{7.9.20}$$

The spectral width of spectral moment of $G_{\sigma,\text{equ}}(\omega)$, as defined for the spread of the random process, can be estimated using parameter α_2 as

$$\alpha_{\sigma,\text{equ},2} = \frac{m_{\sigma,\text{equ},2}}{\left(m_{\sigma,\text{equ},0} \, m_{\sigma,\text{equ},2}\right)^{\frac{1}{2}}} \tag{7.9.21}$$

7.9.3　Damage Frequency Response: From Acceleration to Strain

For strain response spectra at a specific output point of interest, $S_{\varepsilon\varepsilon}(\omega)$, in the frequency domain, can be related to a single acceleration excitation spectrum, $S_{aa}(\omega)$, in the frequency domain as [Newland]

$$[S_{\varepsilon\varepsilon}(\omega)] = [H_{a\varepsilon}(\omega)][S_{aa}(\omega)][H_{a\varepsilon}(\omega)]^{\mathrm{T}} \tag{7.9.22}$$

where

$S_{\varepsilon\varepsilon}(\omega)$: Strain response spectra;

$S_{aa}(\omega)$: Acceleration spectra;

$H_{a\varepsilon}(\omega)$: Transfer function, a frequency-response function from acceleration to strain.

Next consider the individual strained point, which comprises of six strain components in the 3-

dimensional space, i. e. $S_{\varepsilon\varepsilon,xx}$, $S_{\varepsilon\varepsilon,yy}$, $S_{\varepsilon\varepsilon,zz}$, $S_{\varepsilon\varepsilon,xy}$, $S_{\varepsilon\varepsilon,xz}$, and $S_{\varepsilon\varepsilon,yz}$, as derived from finite element analysis in the frequency domain. The principal strains and corresponding von Mises strain in the frequency domain can be obtained, respectively as

$$
\begin{Bmatrix} \varepsilon_1(\omega) \\ \varepsilon_2(\omega) \\ \varepsilon_3(\omega) \end{Bmatrix} = \text{Eigenvalues of} \begin{pmatrix} S_{\varepsilon\varepsilon,xx} & S_{\varepsilon\varepsilon,xy} & S_{\varepsilon\varepsilon,xz} \\ S_{\varepsilon\varepsilon,xy} & S_{\varepsilon\varepsilon,yy} & S_{\varepsilon\varepsilon,yz} \\ S_{\varepsilon\varepsilon,xz} & S_{\varepsilon\varepsilon,yz} & S_{\varepsilon\varepsilon,zz} \end{pmatrix} \tag{7.9.23}
$$

and $\quad \varepsilon(\omega)_{\text{von mises}} = \left\{ [\varepsilon_1(\omega) - \varepsilon_2(\omega)]^2 + [\varepsilon_2(\omega) - \varepsilon_3(\omega)]^2 + [\varepsilon_3(\omega) - \varepsilon_1(\omega)]^2 \right\}^{\frac{1}{2}}$

$$\tag{7.9.24}$$

7.9.4 Structural Health Diagnosis

Dynamic FEM can be used for detecting large flaws in a structure under random vibration as a tool for monitoring structural health. When the flaw size is small there is a need to use a high frequency wave with a small wavelength. Therefore, the FEM mesh has to be refined or it will lead to a coarse solution or increasing computational time.

A frequency-based damage-detection method (FBDD) was proposed [Kim et al., 2003] that there is proportionality between the damage d_j and vibration mode n as

$$
\sum_{j=1}^{J} F_{nj} d_j = \frac{(\Delta\omega_n)^2}{(\omega_{n,0})^2} \tag{7.9.25}
$$

and $\quad \Delta\omega_n \equiv \omega_{n,0} - \left[(\omega_{n,0})^2 - \delta(\omega_{n,0})^2 \right]^{\frac{1}{2}}$ $\tag{7.9.26}$

where
J: Number of finite elements;
d_j: Damage inflicted at location j;
F_{nj}: Sensitivity of vibration mode i at location j;
$\Delta\omega_n$: Fractional change in the natural frequency;
$\omega_{n,0}$: Natural frequency without damage;
δ: Fractional drop in the natural frequency.

By the spectral decomposition method, one can derive the structural response to a unit harmonic load using the transfer function with multi-degree of freedom as

$$
H_{ij}(\omega) = \sum_{n=1}^{N} = \frac{\phi_{ir} \phi_{jr}}{\omega_n^2 - \omega^2 + 2n\zeta_n\omega_n\omega} \tag{7.9.27}
$$

where

$H_{ij}(\omega)$: Displacement of the ith degree of freedom subjected to the unit load applied at the jth degree of freedom;

i: Measurement degree of freedom at the point of interest;

j: Excitation degree of freedom as the unit load is applied;

ω_n: Natural frequency;

ζ_n: Loss factor due to damping;

r: The rth modal shape corresponding to the rth eigenvalue;

ϕ_{ir} and ϕ_{jr}: Modal shapes at ith and jth degrees of freedom, respectively.

$H_{ij}(\omega)$ is a transfer function that the relationship between the steady-state ith displacement (output) in the finite element model and the jth force (input) in the forced vibration system. The transfer function is a complex-valued quantity that means the response of the dynamic relationship can be characterized by its magnitude and phase. The amplitude and phase angle inherent with the transfer function for the frequency response at point i excited by a simple unit harmonic load at point j can be expressed, respectively as

$$A_{ij}(\omega) = \left\{ \left[H_{ij,\text{real}}(\omega) \right]^2 + \left[H_{ij,\text{imaginary}}(\omega) \right]^2 \right\}^{\frac{1}{2}} \tag{7.9.28}$$

$$\vartheta_{ij}(\omega) = \tan^{-1}\left\{ \left[\frac{H_{ij,\text{imaginary}}(\omega)}{H_{ij,\text{real}}(\omega)} \right] \right\} \tag{7.9.29}$$

where

$H_{ij,\text{real}}(\omega)$: Real part of the transfer function;

$H_{ij,\text{imaginary}}(\omega)$: Imaginary part of the transfer function.

7.9.5　Spectral Finite Element Method

This method is essentially a frequency domain approach suitable for steady state harmonic or stationary random excitation problems. The method does not employ eigen-function expansions and, consequently, a major step of the traditional unit element analysis, namely, the determination of natural frequencies and mode shapes, is eliminated which automatically avoids the errors due to series truncation; this makes the method attractive for situations in which a large number of modes participate in vibration [Adhikari].

7.10　Diagnosis of Fatigue Damage Using Acoustic Emission

Wave in solid can be initiated from the abrupt strains generated by the variation of its internal structure. This phenomenon is known as an acoustic emission (AE). Acoustic emission applications vary from continuous in-service health-monitoring of processes, including diagnosis of fatigue damage, to new product examination that identifies and locates the presence of active defects.

7.10.1   Acoustic Emission

Acoustic emission is thus generally defined as transient mechanical waves generated by the rapid release of energy within an abrupt-strained material, when the material is subjected to an external stimulus, such as change in pressure, load, or temperature. The stress waves propagate acoustically to the surface and are recorded by sensors. Most frequencies of the released energy range from 100 kHz to 1 MHz for metals, and lower for softer materials such as plastics. A group of transducers can be used to record signals. The location of the origin can be identified by measuring the time for the sound to reach each individual transducer. A schematic drawing of acoustic emission test system is shown in Fig. 7.10.1. A typical acoustic emission apparatus consists of the following components: transducers converting strains to voltages (mainly piezoelectric crystals, e.g. PZT), preamplifiers (40 dB < amplification gain < 60 dB, generally), filter, amplifier, signal conditioner, cables, data acquisition and processing unit (e.g. computer), and analysis software (evaluating AE parameters).

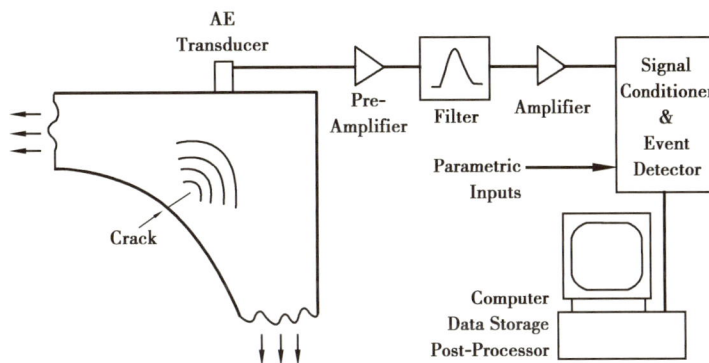

Fig. 7.10.1   Schematic Drawing of Acoustic Emission Test Setup

There are five basic acoustic emission signal parameters that can be used to characterize the onset of an unstable fatigue crack. They are the amplitude, rise-time, counts, duration, and relative energy (i.e. measured area under the rectified signal envelope, namely MARSE), as depicted in Fig. 7.10.2. Salient removal on part surface, elastic and plastic deformation, crack initiation, crack stable growth, and unstable growth yield different signals during different fatigue damage stages. "Cumulative counts" and "cumulative absolute energy" are two derivative parameters used for identifying the time history of fatigue crack growth.

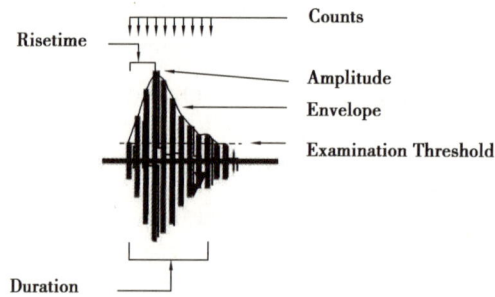

Fig. 7.10.2 Characteristics of a Burst Acoustic Emission

7.10.2 Fatigue Crack Initiation and Acoustic Emissions

Acoustic emission signals generated during a fatigue test can be triggered by various mechanisms, e.g. dislocation movement, cyclic softening, crack initiation, crack closure, and final separation. Cumulative acoustic emission hits is commonly used to characterize the degree of damage. High intensity of incoming signals means the existence of various crack courses, which are not related to a healthy structure. A 3-D plot of acoustic events versus cycles and stresses may be used for discriminating the signals due to different mechanisms: $z=f(x, y)$ with $x=$ cycles, $y=$ stresses, and $z=$ acoustic events. In general the signal can be divided into four stages along the cyclic loading axis:

(a) Stage Ⅰ: First several cycles before the cyclic loading (stress-strain curve) becomes stable. It occurs due to slip dislocation movement with cyclic hardening or softening.

(b) Stage Ⅱ (Incubation Stage): The material experiences steady micro-crack nucleation and dislocation movement with low strain amplitudes. The signal voltage (strain amplitude) is still smaller than the examination threshold.

(c) Stage Ⅲ (Stable Crack Propagation): Crack initiation is evidenced by the first appearance of the signal voltage (strain amplitude) apparently exceeding the examination threshold.

(d) Stage Ⅳ (Unstable Crack Propagation): The crack starts to grow with various physical phenomena such as crack-tip plastic deformation, fracture of hard inclusions, microcrack coalescence, transgranular cleavage, and fracture along the grain boundaries. The strain amplitude is high at this moment.

The first appearance of a high amplitude, high count, and low rise time means that acoustic emission signal virtually corresponds to the fatigue crack initiation. Mathematically, a weighting function may be taken to balance individual contributions from these three parameters to define the relative intensity of the acoustic emission signal as follows:

$$I_{AE} = w_1\, C(t)\ +\ w_2\, A(t)\ +\ w_3\, R(t)^{-1} \qquad\qquad (7.10.1)$$

where

$C(t)$: Normalized number of counts at time t;

$A(t)$: Normalized amplitude at time t;

$R(t)$: Normalized rise time at time t;

w_1, w_2, w_3: Weights put on the corresponding parameters, respectively.

The selection of w_1, w_2, and w_3 is subjective and need be defined scientifically. The following has been taken:

(a) $(w_1 = 1,\ w_2 = 0,\ w_3 = 0)$ was successfully applied to evaluating the fatigue life of Ti-6Al-4V by [Vlasic et al.].

(b) $(w_1 = 1/3,\ w_2 = 1/3,\ w_3 = -1/3)$ was suggested by [Keshtgar & Mohammad].

7.10.3   Kurtosis of AE Signals and Fatigue Crack Initiation

The relative energy of the AE (acoustic emission) signal, i.e. measured area under the rectified signal envelope (namely MARSE), and its derivatives can be used for fatigue life assessment. The histogram of a set of data is an effective graphical technique for showing both the associated skewness and kurtosis. The RMS of the AE signal is the vibration signal energy in time series and kurtosis is a measure of whether the data are heavy-tailed or light-tailed relative to a normal distribution. A time series with high kurtosis tends to have a heavy tail or more outliers, while a time series with low kurtosis tends to have a light tail, or lack of outliers.

(a) RMS Approach: For a sample of N data $(i = 1, 2, \cdots, N)$, the root mean square value (g_1) is estimated by

$$g_1 = \left[\frac{1}{N}\sum (x_i - x_{ave})^2\right]^{\frac{1}{2}} \qquad\qquad (7.10.2)$$

(b) Kurtosis Approach: For a sample of N data $(i = 1, 2, \cdots, N)$, the sample excess kurtosis (g_2) is calculated as

$$g_2 = \frac{m_4}{m_2} = \frac{\dfrac{\sum\limits_{i=1}^{N}(x_i - x_{ave})^4}{N}}{\dfrac{\sum\limits_{i=1}^{N}(x_i - x_{ave})^2}{N}} - 3 \qquad\qquad (7.10.3)$$

where

m_4: The fourth sample moment about the mean;

m_2: The second sample moment about the mean, i.e. the sample variance;

x_i: The ith value;

x_{ave}: Sample mean.

The kurtosis of a time series with standard normal distribution is exactly "3", i.e. the last term of the above equation. Vibration endurance tests are used to qualify vehicles and validate that they can withstand the expected service loads. In many practical situations such as the acceleration due to road irregularities, non-Gaussian tests are more realistic than Gaussian ones. It has been demonstrated by [Mohammad et al.] that the kurtosis of the AE signal is better correlated to the fatigue life (cycles) than the rms (root mean square) value. A test engineer can set a kurtosis value to create excitation signals that are more impulsive in their nature and content like the expected service loads.

7.10.4   Resonance Frequency and Fatigue Crack Initiation

Acoustic emission signals, as being related to the resonance at natural frequency, can be utilized to characterize the material fatigue behavior and predict the onset of crack. When a resonant frequency begins to decrease following decreasing structural stiffness, the onset of a reasonable-sized crack appears and tends to propagate. A study on Ti-6Al-4V alloy in high-cycle fatigue based on resonance was done by [Vlasic et al.].

7.10.5   Fatigue Crack Propagation and Acoustic Emission

Acoustic emissions have also been used for fatigue propagation tests. A recent study on the railway steel leads to an interesting conclusion that the acoustic emission rate correlates with the stable crack growth rate linearly [Mohammad et al.]. Thus, parameters $f(R)$ and m of Eq. (5.5.1) can be identified using the acoustic emission rate.

7.11   Diagnosis of Cracks Using Eddy Current

Material homogeneity and geometry discontinuities (such as cracks) disturb the trajectories of the eddy current and thus affect the magnitude and phase of the induced current. A probe is designed to make sense of the magnetic field induced by currents that produce a complex voltage in the coil, as shown in Fig. 7.11.1. The eddy current testing requires that the components of the potential difference across the coil or the changes in impedance be determined.

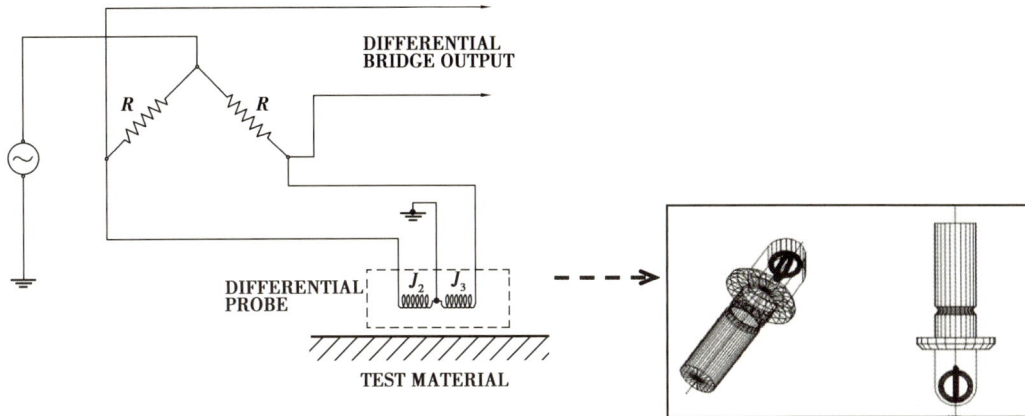

Fig. 7.11.1   Wheatstone Bridge Circuit for Eddy Current Probe with Orthogonal Coils for Crack Detection [**Lamtenzan et al.**]

7.11.1   Complex Impedance with Varying Inductive Reactance

Assume that a full Wheatstone bridge circuit typically contains four impedance arms: Z_1, Z_2, Z_3, and Z_4. Impedances Z_3 and Z_4 are the two impedances associated with the two orthogonal coils assembled in a differential "eddy current probe", as shown in Fig. 7.11.1 [Lamtenzan et al.]. Balance occurs when the potential difference across the differential bridge output circuit is zero, for which

$$\frac{Z_1}{Z_2} = \frac{Z_3}{Z_4} \tag{7.11.1}$$

or $$\frac{R_1 + j X_1}{R_2 + j X_2} = \frac{R_3 + j X_3}{R_4 + j X_4} \tag{7.11.2}$$

where

Z_1, Z_2, Z_3, Z_4: Electric impedances;

R_1, R_2, R_3, R_4: Electric resistances;

X_1, X_2, X_3, X_4: Inductive reactances.

Impedances Z_1 and Z_2 are purely resistivities with the same known value. Z_3 and Z_4 are the two frequency-dependent impedances of the probe coils and they are approximately equal to each other. The input electromotive force (EMF) to the bridge is an AC oscillator that varies in both frequency and amplitude. The difference in voltage between the two coils across the center of the bridge is amplified and passed through a demodulator that detects both in- and out-of-phase signals.

7.11.2 Detection of Cracks

The output signal is plotted as impedance diagram, or as a voltage plane trajectory diagram. The shape of the plane trajectory is a function of the nature of the discontinuity, and it is influenced by factors such as the test material conductivity, magnetic permeability, and geometry. Some of the factors that may affect the eddy current test are lift-off variations, probe canting angle, and noise measurement. The two-dimensional signal induced by each impedance that consists of real and imaginary components may be sampled and digitized with an analog-to-digital (A/D) converter. It is then computer-processed and then stored by a data acquisition system. Example output impedances in response to three different crack sizes obtained from an eddy current probe at 240 kHz are plotted in Fig. 7.11.2.

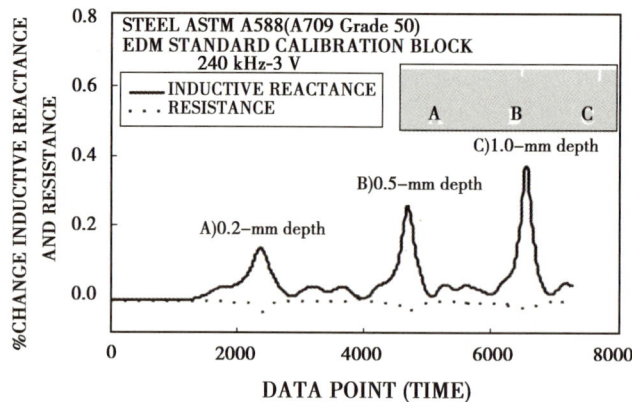

Fig. 7.11.2   Output Impedances from Standard Calibration Signals from Three Crack Sizes [**Lamtenzan et al.**]

The maximum probe response is observed when the crack is perpendicular to the direction of either winding coil. Minimal responses occur when the crack is at a 45° angle from the direction of the winding coil. Having approximately the same impedance, both coils are electrically connected to oppose each other. Assume that the two bridge arms have a resistance value of 50 Ω, the maximum sensitivity to changes in probe coil impedance occurs in coils with an impedance value of the same amount of electric resistance (i.e. 50 Ω). Consequently, the suitable probe frequency may range from 100-800 kHz.

7.11.3   Induction Penetration Strength

The depth of penetration of an induced eddy current field is not uniformly distributed throughout the test material but is most dense near the surface and decreases in magnitude with distance from the surface [Hagemaier]. The induction current density at a given depth x is given here [Libby], as

$$J = J_o e^{-x(\pi \sigma_o \mu f)^{\frac{1}{2}}} \tag{7.11.3}$$

The effective zone for flaw detection of the eddy current field, i.e. essentially the strength of the flaw response, is defined by the value of the standard depth of penetration. The standard depth of penetration (x_p) is hypothesized [Hagemaier] by letting the exponent in Eq. (7.11.3) equal to 1; as

$$x_p(\pi \sigma_o \mu f)^{\frac{1}{2}} = 1$$

i.e $x_p = (\pi \sigma_o \mu f)^{-\frac{1}{2}}$ (7.11.4)

where
σ_o: Conductivity of the test specimen material;
μ: Magnetic permeability of the test material;
f: Frequency of the pore source.

The standard depth of penetration is 0.9 mm in AISI type 304 stainless steel when it is used as the base material at the operating frequency of 250 kHz.

7.12   Diagnosis of Microcracks Using X-Rays

X-rays are a kind of super-powerful version of ordinary light. Due to their shorter wavelength, thousands of times shorter than that of ordinary light, X-rays tend to pass through materials made from lighter atoms with relatively few electrons (such as skin, built from carbon-based molecules), but they are stopped in their tracks by heavier atoms with lots of electrons (such as lead). Film radiography provides a permanent visible record of the internal condition of the subject via this characteristic, such as microcracks due to fatigue.

7.13   Diagnosis of Cracks Using Magnaflux

This is a nondestructive means to inspect material discontinuities such as cracks and near surface inclusions in ferromagnetic parts, such as iron engine blocks and steel transmission shafts. The detection of a crack is due to the visible accumulation of applied magnetics particles, which are drawn up in order between the south and north poles by the applied magnetics leakage flux across the opposite edges of the discontinuity. The magnetic field in the part is induced by the application of an electric current.

7.14 Constitutive Equations for Impact Engineering

When two vehicles collide, the damage is a function of the relative velocity between them. In general, the damage increases as the square of the velocity because it is the impact kinetic energy $[(1/2)mv^2]$ which is the variable of importance. The effect of high-speed impacts on products and standard test specimens are assessed using various tests, such as the Charpy test and Izod test. Both are standardized methods and used widely. Ductile materials like mild steel tend to be more brittle at a high loading rate or a low temperature.

7.14.1 Johnson-Cook Constitutive Equation

One promising equation to describe the constitutive stress-strain curve for impact is Johnson-Cook constitutive equation [1983], in which strain, strain rate, and temperature are effective factors. Johnson-Cook constitutive equation for the normal flow stress (σ) is portrayed using five material parameters, A, B, C, n, and m, as

$$\sigma = [A + B(\varepsilon_{eq}^{p})^{n}]\left\{1 + C\ln\left[\frac{\dfrac{d\varepsilon_{eq}^{p}}{dt}}{\left(\dfrac{d\varepsilon_{eq}^{p}}{dt}\right)_{0}}\right]\right\}\left[1 - \left(\frac{T - T_{room}}{T_{m} - T_{room}}\right)^{m}\right] \qquad (7.14.1)$$

where

T_{room}: Room temperature;

T_{m}: Melting point (temperature) of the material;

A: Yield strength at a strain rate of 1 s^{-1} and room temperature (T_{room});

B: Strain hardening coefficient at a strain rate of 1 s^{-1} and room temperature (T_{room});

n: Strain hardening exponent at T_{room};

C: Strain-rate hardening coefficient at T_{room};

m: Strain softening exponent with respect to temperature variation;

ε_{eq}^{p}: Equivalent plastic strain, e.g. von Mises equivalent plastic strain;

$d\varepsilon_{eq}^{p}/dt$: Equivalent plastic strain rate, e.g. von Mises equivalent plastic strain rate;

$(d\varepsilon_{eq}^{p}/dt)_{0}$: Reference equivalent plastic strain rate, usually at 1.0 s^{-1};

$(d\varepsilon_{eq}^{p}/dt)/(d\varepsilon_{eq}^{p}/dt)_{0}$: Normalized equivalent plastic strain rate.

Some available material parameters for Johnson-Cook Stress Model are listed in Table 7.14.1. The term "flow stress" means the onset of plastic flow of deformed material. It resembles the concept of von Mises stress, and physically it is an equivalent stress. Eq. (7.14.1) has been successfully applied in impact engineering areas such as metal cutting, car crashworthiness, metal forming, and explosive tests. The temperature rise, ΔT due to adiabatic heating can be calculated as,

$$\Delta T = \chi \left(\frac{\sigma_{eq}^p}{\rho C_p} \right) \tag{7.14.2}$$

where

χ: Coefficient, also called Taylor-Quinney parameter, to be obtained experimentally;

ρ: Density;

C_p: Specific heat.

The initial temperature is a given value. Local temperature rise is an extremely important phenomenon in the high strain impact events such as ballistic. Temperature cutoff at 1/2 of melting temperature (K) can be used in the numerical analysis with success. This reduces the computation time and numerical instability by deleting the elements such as "solid elements with lead", which are going in to semi-liquid state [Steinberg et al.]. Without the effects of strain rate and temperature, Eq. (7.14.1) reduces to an equation with strain-hardening only as

$$\sigma = A + B \, (\varepsilon_{eq}^p)^n \tag{7.14.3}$$

On the other hand the material dependency on the strain rate without considering the strain hardening (softening) and temperature effect reduces to

$$\sigma = A \left[1 + C \ln\left(\frac{d\varepsilon_{eq}^p}{dt} \right) \right] \tag{7.14.4}$$

Another relation between the dynamic stress σ and the strain rate $d\varepsilon/dt$ that has been in use is

$$\sigma = \sigma_o \left[1 + \left(\frac{d\varepsilon}{Ddt} \right)^{\frac{1}{q}} \right] \tag{7.14.5}$$

where

D: Constant (s^{-1});

q: Constant;

σ: Dynamic stress (MPa) at uniaxial strain rate, (s^{-1}).

7.14.2 Pressure Bar Test

An experimental setup based on pressure bars, called split Hopkinson test, is a well-established apparatus commonly utilized in the high-strain-rate testing of materials. Originally developed by [Kolsky], the concept has been modified as shown in Fig. 7.14.1 and has gained widespread applications in testing both ductile materials and composites at strain rates up to 10^4 s^{-1}.

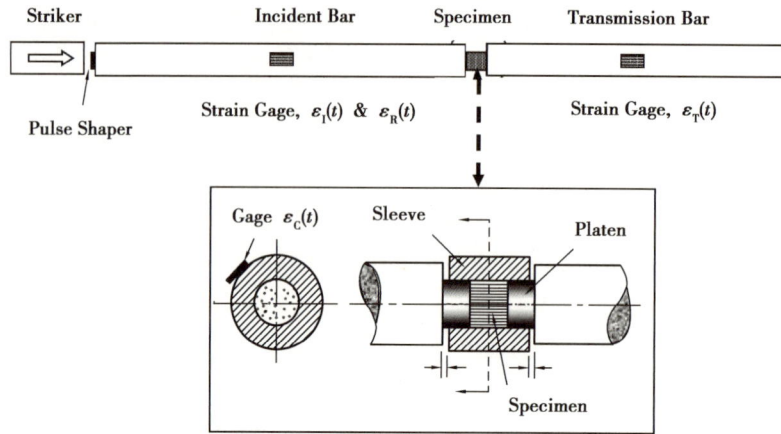

Fig. 7.14.1 Schematic Drawing of the Modified Pressure Bar Test Setup for Composites [Oguni & Ravichandran] under Multiaxial Impact Loading

The pulse duration equals the round-trip time of a longitudinal elastic bar wave in the striker bar. When the incident pulse gets to the specimen, part of the pulse goes through the specimen into the transmission bar, and the remaining is reflected back in the incident bar, depending on the degree of impedance mismatch at the bar-specimen interface. The strain gages provide time-resolved measures of the pulses in the incident and the transmission bars. For a specimen that is under mechanical equilibrium, [Kolsky] showed that the nominal strain rate $d\varepsilon(t)/dt$ and nominal stress in the specimen could be calculated using the following equations, respectively

$$\frac{d\varepsilon(t)}{dt} = -2\left(\frac{C_o}{L_s}\right)\varepsilon_R(t) \qquad (7.14.6)$$

and $\quad \sigma(t) = \left(\frac{A_T}{A_S}\right)E\varepsilon_T(t) \qquad (7.14.7)$

where

$\varepsilon(t)$: Strain induced in the specimen;

$\varepsilon_R(t)$: Reflected strain measured;

$\varepsilon_T(t)$: Transmitted strain measured;

L_s: Longitudinal length of the specimen;

C_o: Material constant, and $C_o = E/\rho$ (Young's modulus/density) for isotropic material;

A_T: Cross-sectional area of the transmission bar;

A_S: Cross-sectional area of the specimen.

It is assumed that the specimen is uniform and it undergoes a homogeneous deformation with no phase angle in delay. The circumferential stress due to lateral confinement, $\sigma_c(t)$ as measured, is designed to be in the elastic regime and it is related to axial stress $\sigma(t)$ in the composite by

$$\frac{\sigma(t)}{\sigma_c(t)} = \frac{(1-\nu)\,E_{22}\,R_i^2}{\nu_{12}(R_o^2 - R_i^2)}\left[1 + \frac{(1+\nu)\,R_o^2}{(1-\nu)\,R_i^2}\right] + \frac{1-\nu_{32}}{\nu_{12}} \tag{7.14.8}$$

where

$\sigma(t)$: Stress induced in the specimen;

$\sigma_c(t)$: Circumferential stress of the sleeve, as measured;

R_o and R_i: Outer and inner radii of the sleeve cylinder;

E & ν: Elastic modulus and Poisson's ratio of the sleeve;

E_{22}, ν_{12}, ν_{32}: Elastic modulus and Poisson's ratios of the composite lamina in the test.

7.15   Impact Damage

Impact is defined as the action of one object coming forcibly into contact with another. The magnitude of the energy absorbed during each impact is a function of the force magnitude, impact angle, and frictional effects. Impact damage plays an extremely important role in the energy release of any type of two-body or multi-body interactions. Large strains, high strain rates, and temperature rising are the expected key thermomechanical behaviors that need be investigated in order to assess an impact damage.

7.15.1   Johnson-Cook's Damage Model

An empirical constitutive relation developed by Johnson and Cook (J-C model) is widely used to capture strain rate sensitivity of the metals subjected to impact loads. For example, it has been used for describing the behavior of typical armor steel material under large strains and high strain rates with elevated temperatures. The failure model for predicting the material equivalent plastic strain in various stress-strain states at different strain rates and temperature levels, following Johnson-Cook's constitutive model, is denoted by the equivalent plastic strain as

$$\varepsilon_{eq,u} = \left[D_1 + D_2 \exp(D_3\,\sigma^*)\right]\left\{1 + D_4 \ln\left[\frac{\dfrac{d\varepsilon_{eq}^p}{dt}}{\left(\dfrac{d\varepsilon_{eq}^p}{dt}\right)_0}\right]\right\}\left[1 + D_5\left(\frac{T - T_{room}}{T_m - T_{room}}\right)\right] \tag{7.15.1}$$

where

$\varepsilon_{eq,u}$: Equivalent plastic strain;

D_1, D_2, D_3, D_4, & D_5: Failure parameters for John-Cook's Model (Tab. 7.15.1);

σ^*: Stress triaxiality factor, as $\sigma^* = \sigma_m/\sigma$ (Mean Stress/Flow Stress);

σ_m: Mean stress;

$(d\varepsilon_{eq}^p/dt)/(d\varepsilon_{eq}^p/dt)_0$: Normalized equivalent plastic strain rate.

The ratio of $(d\varepsilon_{eq}^p/dt)$ to $(d\varepsilon_{eq}^p/dt)_0$ in the above equation is called normalized damage-equivalent plastic strain rate. A scalar damage variable with scalar accumulation similar to the Miner's rule is defined as follows:

$$D = \int \frac{d\varepsilon_{eq}}{\varepsilon_{eq,u}} \approx \sum \frac{\Delta\varepsilon_{eq}}{\varepsilon_{eq,u}} \leqslant 100\ \% \tag{7.15.2}$$

Note that the differential equivalent strain $d\varepsilon_{eq}$ shown in the above equation consists mainly of plastic strain, which can be calculated using solid elements with reduced integration in the finite element analysis, as the plastic deformation prevails and the Poisson's ratio approaches 0.7. When $D>1$, the material is destroyed and the element is eroded. Another damage parameter of interest is called critical damage, namely D_c, at which the damage rate starts to grow dramatically as

$$\frac{dD}{dt} = \frac{D_c t}{\varepsilon_{eq,u} - \varepsilon_d} \qquad \text{when } \varepsilon \geqslant \varepsilon_d \tag{7.15.3a}$$

$$\frac{dD}{dt} = 0 \qquad \text{when } \varepsilon < \varepsilon_d \tag{7.15.3b}$$

where

D_c: Critical damage;

ε_d: Threshold equivalent strain where the critical damage starts.

On the other hand, when $\varepsilon < \varepsilon_d$, $dD/dt = 0$. It means that the damage varies linearly with respect to time in the early low-strained stage. As is demanded for regularizing the mesh for error reduction, remeshing based on the displacement at failure is required for the simulation prior to and post ductile necking of material. Three element eroding criteria are suggested for doing finite element simulations, when each individual element reaches:

    (1) The state, in which damage D is greater than its critical value as described by Eq.(7.15.3)

    (2) The temperature is higher than the critical temperature of the material

    (3) Johnson-Cook fracture criterion is met, i.e. Eq. (7.15.2)

The temperature rise in the high-speed impact-damaged areas can go beyond the melting temperature of the projectile and/or target material, such as lead in the bullet. Thus it could undergo phase transform from solid state to liquid state, due to that a pressure dependent material model better represents the actual behavior of lead rather than strain and strain rate dependent material model [Adams]. The ratio of the coefficient of expansion of a metal to its specific heat at constant pressure is constant at all temperatures [Dulieu-Smith & Stanley]. A thermodynamic state of a homogeneous material, which is not undergoing any chemical reaction or phase change, may be defined by two state variables in an equation of state [Anderson].

7.15.2   Failure Criteria Based on 3-Dimensional Solid Elements

There is a need to develop light-weight protective structures with a sufficient protection to prevent the damage occurring during extreme loading events such as blast and ballistic impacts. When a thin plate is hit by a low-speed bullet, tensile stresses induced by bending and necking may be significant. On the other hand, when a thick plate hit by a high-speed bullet, plugging occurs and thus shearing at the entrance side and spalling on the other side may show up. Largrangian methods combined with Johnson-Cook material model [LS-Dyna] can be used for such numerical simulations [Mohotti et al.]. However, Johnson-Cook failure model may not be able to handle the mixed failure modes where both tensile (petailing) and shear (plugging) stresses are significant contributors.

In the 3-dimensional state of stress based on solid elements, the principal stresses and mean stress (volumetric pressure) can be consolidated into the following two invariants (state variables) to describe the plastic large deformation,

$$\sigma^* = \frac{\sigma_m}{\sigma} = \frac{-(\sigma_1 + \sigma_2 + \sigma_3)}{3 \left| (\sigma_1^2 + \sigma_2^2 + \sigma_2^3 - \sigma_1 \sigma_2 - \sigma_2 \sigma_3 - \sigma_3 \sigma_1)^{\frac{1}{2}} \right|} \tag{7.15.4}$$

and

$$\frac{I_3}{\sigma^3} = \frac{\sigma_1 \sigma_2 \sigma_3}{\left| (\sigma_1^2 + \sigma_2^2 + \sigma_2^3 - \sigma_1 \sigma_2 - \sigma_2 \sigma_3 - \sigma_3 \sigma_1)^{\frac{3}{2}} \right|} \tag{7.15.5}$$

Another important consideration for the failure criterion is the lodge angle. The lodge angle that varies between -1 and 1 can be calculated using

$$-1 \leqslant \frac{27 J_3}{2 \sigma^3} \leqslant 1 \tag{7.15.6}$$

where

$$\frac{J_3}{\sigma^3} = \frac{I_3}{\sigma^3} + \frac{\sigma_m^3}{\sigma^3} - \frac{\sigma_m}{3 \sigma} \tag{7.15.7}$$

The significance of lodge angle and triaxiality inherent with failure test specimens is presented in Fig. 7.15.1. The material failure of solid elements in the 3-dimensional finite element analysis can be well predicted using Eqs. (7.15.4) and (7.15.5), combined with Eq. (7.15.6), according to

［DuBois et al.］. The failure criterion for predicting eroded solid elements is depicted in Fig. 7.15.2.

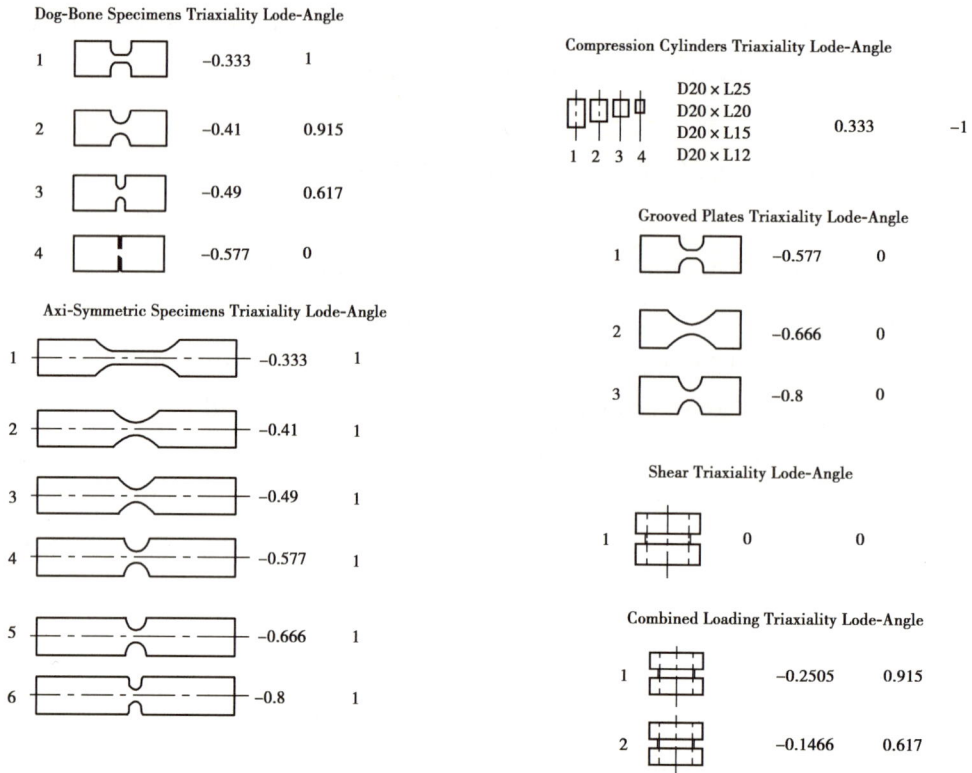

Fig. 7.15.1　Test Specimens-Triaxialities and Lode Angles

Fig. 7.15.2　Criteria for Eroded Solid Elements in High-Speed Impact Failure ［DuBois et al.］

7.15.3　Johnson-Holmquist Damage Model

In solid mechanics, the Johnson-Holmquist damage model is used to model the mechanical behavior of damaged brittle materials, such as ceramics, rocks, and concrete, over a range of strain rates. Such materials usually have high compressive strength but low tensile strength and tend to exhibit progressive damage under load due to the growth of microfractures [Johnson & Holmquist] resulting progressive damage.

7.16 Explicit Finite Element Analysis

When a dynamic problem is solved using explicit finite element methods, nodal accelerations are calculated directly from Newton's second law by using a mass matrix that is basically diagonal. This eliminates the need to generate and invert large matrices as the response of each node is now independent. Nodal velocities and displacements are then calculated directly from accelerations and the time increment that the solution has progressed through. The term "explicit" is used since the calculation only refers to values of force, displacement, velocity and acceleration at the start of each new time step. The disadvantage of this method is that time step size must be small for a stable solution. If too large, significant numerical errors will develop. This is why it is called conditionally stable. Explicit algorithms are used only when the time duration of the problem is short such as automotive crash problems.

Explicit solvers such as LS-DYNA and Abaqus Explicit are suitable for solving impact simulations such as car crash. In the explicit finite element code, Newton's equation of motion is formulated as follows:

$$M_{ij}\left(\frac{d^2 x_j}{dt^2}\right) + C_{ij}\frac{dx_j}{dt} + f_i(t) = p_i(t) \tag{7.16.1}$$

where

x_j: Displacement vector;

M_{ij}: Mass matrix;

C_{ij}: Damping matrix;

f_i: Internal nodal resistance vector, which is not dependent on x_j or the constitutive law;

p_i: External nodal force vector.

The above equation can be solved via the central difference method. For each time step,

$$\frac{dx_{j,n}}{dt} = \frac{x_{j,n+1} - x_{j,n-1}}{2\Delta t} \tag{7.16.2}$$

and $$\frac{d^2 x_{j,n}}{dt^2} = \frac{x_{j,n+1} - 2x_{j,n} - x_{j,n-1}}{(\Delta t)^2} \tag{7.16.3}$$

Plugging both equations given above into Eq. (7.16.1), one has

$$\mathbf{M}_{ij}(x_{j,n+1} - 2x_{j,n} - x_{j,n-1}) + \frac{1}{2}\Delta t\,\mathbf{C}_{i_j}(x_{j,n+1} - x_{j,n-1}) = (\Delta t)^2[p_{i,n} - f_{i,n}] \tag{7.16.4}$$

or $\left[\dfrac{M_{ij}}{(\Delta t)^2} + \dfrac{C_{ij}}{2\Delta t}\right]x_{j,n+1} = \left[\dfrac{2}{(\Delta t)^2}\right]M_{ij}\,x_{j,n} - \left[\dfrac{M_{ij}}{(\Delta t)^2} - \dfrac{C_{ij}}{2\Delta t}\right]x_{j,n-1} + p_{i,n} - f_{i,n}$ (7.16.5)

The above equation can be solved for the only unknown term $x_{j,n+1}$, i.e. the displacement vector at the next time step, given that the current and previous displacements are known. The efficiency and solution stability of an explicit solver will be increased by using only lumped mass matrices M_{ij} and modal damping $C_{ij} = \alpha\,M_{ij}$.

References

ADAMS, B, 2003. Simulation of Ballistic Impacts on Armored Civil Vehicles [D]. Eindhoven University of Technology.

ADHIKARI S, 2009. Doubly Spectral Finite Element Method for Stochastic Field Problems in Structural Dynamics [J]. 50th AIAA/ASME/ASCE/AHS/ASC Structures, Structural Dynamics & Materials Conference, 4-7 May 2009, Palm Springs, CA, USA.

ALBLAS J B, 1981. A Note on the Theory of Thermoelastic Damping [J]. Journal of Thermal Stresses, 4: 333-335.

ALLEN J J, SMITS A J, 2001, Energy Harvesting Eel [J]. Journal of Fluids and Structures, 15: 629-640.

ANDERSON O L, 2000. The Gruneisen Ratio for the Last 30 Years [J]. International Journal of Geophysics, 173: 279-294.

ARETZ M, VORLANDER M, 2014. Combined Wave and Ray Based Room Acoustic Simulations of Audio Systems in Car Passenger Compartments, Part Ⅰ: Boundary and Source Data [J]. Applied Acoustics, 76: 82-99.

ARETZ M, VORLANDER M, 2014. Combined Wave and Ray Based Room Acoustic Simulations of Audio Systems in Car Passenger Compartments, Part Ⅱ: Comparison of Simulations and Measurements [J]. Applied Acoustics, 76: 52-65.

ASTM E1049-85, 2005. Standard Practices for Cycle Counting in Fatigue Analysis [S]. ASTM International.

BAZ A, TEMPIA A et al, 2004. Active Piezoelectric Damping Composites [J]. Sensors and Actuators, A, Physics, 112(2-3): 340-350.

BENASCIUTTI D, 2012. Fatigue Analysis of Random Loadings: A Frequency-Domain Approach, LAP LAMBERT Academic Publishing.

BENASCIUTTI D, TOVO R, 2006. Comparison of Spectral Methods for Fatigue Analysis of Broadband Gaussian Random Processes[J]. Probabilistic Eng. Mechanics, 21: 287-299.

BENASCIUTTI D, TOVO R, 2005. Spectral Methods for Lifetime Prediction under Wide-Band Stationary Random Processes[J]. International Journal of Fatigue, 27(8): 867-877.

BENDAT J S,1964. Probability Functions for Random Responses[J]. NASA Report on Contract NAS-5-4590.

BIANCHI, S, et al, 2010. Detection of Stall Regions in a Low-Speed Axial Fan, Part 1: Azimuthal Acoustic Measurements[C]. in Proceedings of the 55th American Society of Mechanical Engineers Turbine and Aeroengine Congress, Glasgow, UK, GT2010-22753.

BIGONI D, NOSELLI G, 2011. Experimental Evidence of Flutter and Divergence Instabilities Induced by Dry Friction[J]. Journal of Mechanics and Physics of Solids, 59: 2208-2226.

BIROLINI A, 2007. Reliability Engineering[M]. Springer.

BISHOP N, SHERRAT F, 2000. Finite Element Based Fatigue Calculations[M]. NAFEMS.

BISHOP J E, KINRA V K, 1994. Elastothermodynamic Damping in Composite Materials[J]. Mechanics of Composites and Material Structures, 1: 75-93.

BISHOP N, HU Z, WANG R, et al, 1993. Methods for Rapid Evaluation of Fatigue Damage on the Howden HWP330 Wind Turbine[C]. British Wind Energy Conference, York.

BISHOP N, SHERRATT F, 1989. Fatigue Life Prediction from Power Spectral Density Data[J]. Environmental Engineering, 2.

BORELLO D, CORSINI A, DELIBRA G, et al, 2013. Numerical Investigation on the Aerodynamics of a Tunnel Ventilation Fan during Pressure Pulses[C]. Proceedings of the 10th European Turbomachinery Conference: 573-582, Lappeenranta, Finland.

BØRVIK T, DEYA S, CLAUSEN A H, 2009. Perforation Resistance of Five Different High-Strength Steel Plates Subjected to Small-Arms Projectiles[J]. International Journal of Impact Engineering, 36: 948-964.

BORVIK T, et al, 2005. Strength and Ductility of Weldox 460 E Steel at High Strain Rates, Elevated Temperatures, and Various Stress Triaxialities[J]. Engineering Fracture Mechanics, 72: 1071-1087.

BRACCESI C, CIANETTI F, LORI G, et al, 2015. Random Multiaxial Fatigue: A Comparative Analysis among Selected Frequency and Time Domain Fatigue Evaluation Methods[J]. International Journal of Fatigue, Vol. 74.

BRAR N S, et al, 2007. Constitutive Model Constants for Low Carbon Steels from Steels from Tension and Torsion Data[J]. CP955, Shock Compression of Condensed Matter-2007, American Institute of Physics.

BRODT M, LAKES R S, 1995. Composite Materials Which Exhibit High Stiffness and High Damping[J].

Journal of Composite Materials, 29: 1823-1833.

BUCKNALL C B, 1992. The Relevance of Impact Testing in the Material Science of Polymers[J]. Plastics Rubber and Composites Processing and Applications, 17(3): 7-12.

CARPINTERI A, et al, 2014. Reformulation in the Frequency Domain of a Critical Plane-Based Multiaxial Fatigue Criterion[J]. International Journal of Fatigue, 67: 55-61.

ČESNIK M, et al, 2016. Assessment of the Fatigue Parameters from Random Vibration Testing: Application to a Rivet Joint[J]. Journal of Mechanical Engineering, 62(7-8): 471-482.

CHIANG Y J, SHIH C D, LIN C C, et al, 2004. Multi-Variable Effects of Tire Structures and Suspension Alignments on Vehicle Pull[C]. Presented at the 23rd Annual Tire Society Conference, September: 20-21.

COOK R D, MALKUS D S, PLESHA M E, 2000. Concepts and Applications of Finite Element Analysis[M]. 3 rd Edition. John Wiley and Sons, NY, USA.

CRISTOFORI A, et al, 2011. A Stress Invariant Based Spectral Method to Estimate Fatigue Life under Multiaxial Random Loading[J]. International Journal of Fatigue, 33: 887-899.

CRONIN D S, BUI K, KAUFMANN C, 2003. Implementation and Validation of the Johnson-Holmquist Ceramic Material Model in LS-DYNA [C]. In Proc. 4th European LS-DYNA User Conference (DYNAmore), Ulm, Germany.

DIRLIK T, 1985. Application of Computers in Fatigue Analysis[D]. Thesis, University of Warwick.

DUBOIS P D, et al, 2010. Development, Implementation and Validation of 3-D Failure Model for Aluminum 2024 for High-Speed Impact Applications[C]. The 11th International LS-Dyna Users Conference, Dearborn, MI, USA.

DULIEU-SMITH J M, STANLEY P, 1998. On the Interpretation and Significance of the Grüneisen Parameter in Thermoelastic Stress Analysis[J]. Journal of Materials Processing Technology, 78: 75-83.

LEDOGAN Y, CIGEROGLU E, 2012. Vibration Fatigue Analysis of a Cantilever Beam Exposed to Random Loading[C]. The 15th International Conference on Machine Design and Production, Pamukkale, Denizili, Turkey.

ERTL M, KALTENBACHER M, 2011. Investigation of the Dynamics of Electromagnetic Valves by a Coupled Magnetomechanical Algorithm Including Contact Mechanics[J]. COMPEL, 30(2): 603-721.

FRIIS E A, LAKES R S, PARK J B, 1988. Negative Poisson's Ratio Polymeric and Metallic Foams[J]. Journal of Materials Science, 23: 4406-4414.

GAO Z, MOAN T, 2008. Frequency-Domain Fatigue Analysis of Wide-Band Stationary Gaussian Processes Using a Trimodal Spectral Formulation[J]. International Journal of Fatigue, 30(10-11): 1944-1955.

GIOVANANI M, et al, 2000. Random Vibration Fatigue: A Study Comparing Time Domain and Frequency Domain Approaches for Automotive Applications[J]. SAE 14M-0324.

GOLESTANI A, 2014. An Experimental Study of Buffet Detection on Supercritical Airfoils in Transonic Regime [J]. Proceedings of the Institution of Mechanical Engineers, Part G: Journal of Aerospace Engineering.

GRAFF K F, 1975. Wave Motion in Elastic Solids[M]. Oxford: Oxford University Press.

HA K, et al, 2004. Vibration Reduction of Switched Reluctance Motor by Experimental Transfer Function and Response Surface Methodology[J]. IEEE Transactions on Magnetics, 40(2): 577-580.

HAGEMAIER D J, 1990. Fundamentals of Eddy Current Testing[J]. American Society for Nondestructive Testing, Columbus, OH, USA.

HALFPENNY A, KIM, 2010. Rainflow Cycle Counting and Acoustic Fatigue Analysis Techniques for Random Loading[C]. RASD 2010 Conference, Southampton, UK.

HALFPENNY A, BISHOP N, 1997. Vibration Fatigue[M]. nCode International Ltd., 230 Woodbourn Road, Sheffield, S9 3LQ, UK.

HAN S H, AN D G, KWAK S J, et al, 2013. Vibration Fatigue Analysis for Multi-Point Spot-Welded Joints Based on Frequency Response Changes due to Fatigue Damage Accumulation[J]. International Journal of Fatigue, 48: 170-177.

HANSEN M H, 2004. Aeroelastic Stability Analysis of Wind Turbines Using an Eigenvalue Approach[J]. Wind Energy, 7: 133-143.

HIKI Y, TAMURA J, 1983. Internal Friction in Ice Crystals[J]. Journal of Physical Chemistry, 87: 4054-4059.

JAMES M L, et al, 1989. Vibration of Mechanical and Structural Systems[J]. Harper and Row, New York, NY, USA.

JAZAR R, 2009, Vehicle Dynamics: Theory and Applications[M]. Springer: Business Media Publishing Co.

JOHNSON G R, HOLMQUIST T J, 1994. An Improved Computational Constitutive Model for Brittle Materials [J]. High-Pressure Science and Technology, American Institute of Physics.

JOHNSON G R, HOLMQUIST T J, 1992. A Computational Constitutive Model for Brittle Materials Subjected to Large Strains[J]. Shock-Wave and High Strain-Rate Phenomena in Materials (Editors:M. Meyers, L. Murr, and K. Staudhammer), Marcel Dekker Inc., NY.

JOHNSON G R, COOK W H, 1985. Fracture Characteristic of Three Metals Subjected to Various Strain, Strain Rates, Temperatures, and Pressures[J].Engineering Fracture Mechanics, 21(1): 31-48.

JOHNSON G R, COOK W H, 1983. A Constitutive Model and Data for Metals Subjected to Large Strains, High

Strain Rates and High Temperatures[C]. Proceedings of the 7th International Symposium on Ballistics, The Hague, The Netherlands.

JUNG H, KIM I, JANG S, 2011. An Energy Harvesting System Using the Wind-Induced Vibration of a Stay Cable for Powering a Wireless Sensor Node[J]. Smart Materials and Structures, 20, 075001.

JUNG H, BAE S, 2005. Automotive Component Fatigue Life Estimation by Frequency Domain Approach[J]. Key Engineering Materials, Vols. 297-300: 1776-1783.

KIM J, et al, 2003. Damage Identification in Beam-Type Structures: Frequency-Based Method vs. Mode-Shape-Based Method[J]. Engineering Structures, 25: 57-67.

KIM S, LEE S, 2009. Prediction of Structure-Borne Noise Caused by the Powertrain on the Basis of the Hybrid Transfer Path[J]. Journal of Automobile Engineering, 223(4): 485-502.

KINRA V K, MILLIGAN V K, 1994. A Second Law Analysis of Thermoelastic Damping[J]. Journal of Applied Mechanics, 61: 71-76.

KIRK R G, 1988. Evaluation of Aerodynamic Instability Mechanisms for Centrifugal Compressors—Part Ⅰ: Current Theory[J]. Journal of Vibration and Acoustics, 110(2): 201-206.

KNANI K B, et al, 2007. Fatigue Damage Assessment of a Car Body-in-White Using a Frequency-Domain Approach[J]. International Journal of Materials and Product Technology, 30(1-3).

KOLSKY H, 1949. An Investigation of the Mechanical Properties of Materials at Very High Rates of Loading [J]. Proceedings of Royal Society, London, Vol. B62: 676-700.

KUMAR S M, 2000. Analyzing Random Vibration Fatigue[M]. ANSYS Advantage, Ⅱ(3).

LAKES R S, 1999. Viscoelastic Solids[M]. CRC Press LLC, Boca Raton, FL, USA.

LALWANI D, et al, 2009. Extension of Oxley's Predictive Machining Theory for Johnson and Cook Flow Stress Model[J]. Journal of Materials Processing Technology, 209: 5305-5312.

LALANNE C, 2002. Mechanical Vibration & Shock[M]. Vol. 5, Hermes Penton Ltd., London, UK.

LAMTENZAN D, et al, 2000. Detection and Sizing of Cracks in Structural Steel Using the Eddy Current Method [J]. FHWA-RD-00-018, November 2000, US Dept. of Transportation.

LAZAN B L, 1968. Damping of Materials and Members in Structural Mechanics[M]. Pergamon, New York, NY, USA.

LEE S, YOON D, PARK K, 2003. Aerodynamic Effect on Natural Frequency and Flutter Instability in Rotating Optical Disks[J]. Microsystem Technologies, 9(5): 369-374.

MANZATO S, et al, 2011. Model Updating Methodologies for Multibody Simulation Models: Application to a

Full-Scale Wind Turbine Model[J]. Linking Models and Experiments, 2: 349-358.

MATSUISHI M, ENDO T, 1968. Fatigue of Metals Subjected to Varying Stress [J]. Japan Soc. Mech. Engineering.

MATSUMOTO M, TREIN C, ITO Y, et al, 2006. Controlled Aerodynamic Instability Phenomena: An Alternative Approach for Wind Power Generation Systems[C]. The Nineteenth KKCNN Symposium on Civil Engineering, Japan.

MCKINNEY W, DELAURIER, J, 1981. The Windmill: An Oscillating-Wing Windmill[J]. Journal of Energy, 5(2): 109-115.

MEIROVITCH L, 1975. Elements of Vibration Analysis[M]. McGraw-Hill, New York, NY, USA.

MILES J W, 1954. On Structural Fatigue under Random Loading[J]. Journal of Aeronautical Sciences: 753.

MOHOTTI D, et al, 2010. Numerical Simulation of Impact and Penetration of Ogival Shaped Projectiles through Steel Plate Structures[D]. Department of Infrastructure Engineering, The University of Melbourne.

MOHAMMAD M, et al, 2012. Correlating Strain and Acoustic Emission Signals of Metallic Component Using Global Signal Statistical Approach[J]. Advanced Materials Research, 445: 1064.

MORMON K N, Nagtegaal J C, 1983. Finite Element Analysis of Sinusoidal Small-Amplitude Vibrations in Deformed Viscoelastic Solids[J]. International Journal of Numerical Methods in Engineering, 19(7): 1079-1103.

MRSNIK M, et al, 2016. Multiaxial Vibration Fatigue: A Theoretical and Experimental Comparison [J]. Mechanical Systems and Signal Processing, Vol. 76/77: 409-423.

MRSNIK M, SLAVIC J, BOLTEZAR M, 2013. Frequency-Domain Methods for a Vibration-Fatigue-Life Estimation: Application to Real Data[J]. International Journal of Fatigue, 47: 8-17.

MUTHU E, et al, 2012. Finite Element Simulation in Machining of Inconel 718 Nickel Based Super Alloy[J]. International Journal of Advanced Engineering Applications, 5(3): 22-27.

NASHIF A D, et al, 1985. Vibration Damping[M]. John Wiley and Sons, New York, NY, USA.

NEWLAND E, 1993. An Introduction to Random Vibrations and Spectral Analysis[J]. Longman Scientific & Technical, Essex.

NIESLONY A, BOHM M, 2012. Application of Spectral Method in Fatigue Life Assessment: Determination of Crack Initiation[J]. Journal of Theoretical and Applied Mechanics, 50(3): 819-829.

OHADI A R, MAGHSOODI G, 2007. Simulation of Engine Vibration on Nonlinear Hydraulic Engine Mounts [J]. Journal of Vibration and Acoustics, 129(4): 417-424.

OGUNI K, RAVICHANDRAN G, 1999. Dynamic Behavior of Fiber Reinforced Composites under Multiaxial Compression［C］. Proceedings of the 11th International Conference on Experimental Mechanics, Oxford, UK, Edited by I. M. Allison: 211-216.

PETRUCCI G, ZUCCARELLO B, 2004. Fatigue Life Prediction under Wide Band Random Loading［J］. Fatigue and Fracture of Engineering Materials and Structures, 27(12): 1183-1195.

PETRUCCI G, ZUCCARELLO B, 1999. On the Estimation of the Fatigue Cycle Distribution from Spectral Density Data［J］. Proceedings of the Institution of Mechanical Engineers, Part C, Journal of Engineering Science, 213(8): 819-831.

PITOISET X, PREUMONT A, 2000. Spectral Methods for Multiaxial Random Fatigue Analysis of Metallic Structures［J］. International Journal of Fatigue, 22(7): 541-550.

POTTER J M, WATANABE R T, 1989. Development of Fatigue Loading Spectra［M］. ASTM STP 1006, ASTM, West Conshohocken, PA: 150-171.

PRANDINA M, et al, 2009. Damping Identification in Multiple Degree-of-Freedom Systems Using an Energy Balance Approach［C］. The 7th International Conference on Modern Practice in Stress and Vibration Analysis, Journal of Physics: Conference Series 181, 012006.

REYNOLDS, DOUGLAS D, 2016. Engineering Principles of Mechanical Vibration［M］. 4th Edition, Bloomington, Indiana, USA.

RICE S O, 1954. Mathematical Analysis of Random Noise［M］. Selected Papers on Noise and Stochastic Processes, Dover, New York.

RITCHIE I G, PAN Z L, 1991. High Damping Metals and Alloys［M］. Metallurgical Transactions, 22, A: 607-616.

RITCHIE I G, et al, 1985. Internal Friction in Sonoston: A High Damping Mn-Cy-Based Alloy for Marine Propeller Applications［J］. Journal of Physics, 46: 409-415.

RYCHLIK I, 1996. Fatigue and Stochastic Loads［J］. Scand. J. Statistics, 23(4): 387-404.

SIMA M, OZEL T, 2010. Modified Material Constitutive Models for Serrated Chip Formation Simulations and Experimental Validation in Machining of Titanium Alloy Ti-6Al-4V［J］. International Journal of Machine Tool and Manufacture, 50 : 943-960.

SINGH R, 2000. Dynamic Design of Automotive Systems: Engine Mounts and Structural Joints［J］. Sadhana, 25(3): 319-330.

SLAVIC T, et al, 2011. Development of Next-Generation Vibration-Fatigue Software and Catia Integration for the Automotive Industry:117-125, Yugoslav SAE, Belgrade.

SMITH P, FURSE C, GUNTHER J, 2005. Analysis of Spread Spectrum Time Domain Reflectometry for Wire

Fault Location[J]. IEEE Sensors Journal, 5(6): 1469-1478.

ŠOLÍN K, DOLEŽEL I, 2003. Higher-Order Finite Element Methods[M]. Chapman & Hall/CRC Press.

SOROKIN S V, 2009. Linear Dynamics of Elastic Helical Springs: Asymptotic Analysis of Wave Propagation [J]. Proceedings of the Royal Society, A, Mathematical Physical and Engineering Science, 465(2105): 1513-1537.

STAAB G H, GILAT A, 1991. A Direct-Tension Split Hopkinson Bar for High Strain-Rate Testing[J]. Experimental Mechanics, 31: 232-235.

STEINBERG D S, 1988. Vibration Analysis for Electronic Equipment[M]. 2nd Edition, John Wiley & Sons.

STEINBERG D, COCHRAN S, GUINAN M, 1980. A Constitutive Model for Metals Applicable at High Strain Rate[J]. Journal of Applied Physics, 51(3): 1498-1504.

SUN C, SHI J, BAYERL D, et al, 2011. PVDF Microbelts for Harvesting Energy from Respiration[J]. Energy and Environmental Science, 4: 4508-4512.

TEIXEIRA G M, et al, 2013. Random Vibration Fatigue: Frequency Domain Critical Plane Approaches[C]. ASME, IMECE2013-62607.

TOVO R, 2002. Cycle Distribution and Fatigue Damage under Broad-Band Random Loading[J]. International Journal of Fatigue, 24(11): 1137-1147.

TUNA J M, 1986. Fatigue Life for Gaussian Random Loads at the Design Stage[J]. Fatigue and Fracture of Engineering Materials and Structures, 9(3): 169-184.

TÜRKAY S, AKÇAY H, 2004. A Study of Random Vibration Characteristics of a Quarter Car Model[J]. Journal of Sound and Vibration, 282: 111-124.

TVERDOKHLEHOV A, 1986. Resonant Cylinder for Internal Friction Measurement[J]. Journal of Acoustic Society, 80: 217-224.

UMBRELLO D, 2008. Finite Element Simulation of Conventional and High Speed Machining of Ti-6Al-4V Alloy [J]. Journal of Material Processing Technology, 196: 79-87.

UNGAR E E, KERWIN E M, 1962. Loss Factors of Viscoelastic Systems in Terms of Energy Concepts[J]. Journal of Acoustic Society, 34: 954-957.

VAN BAREN J, 2015. Fatigue Damage Spectrum: A New Tool to Accelerate Vibration Testing[J]. Sound & Vibration: 15-17.

VAN BAREN J, 2012. What is Random Vibration Testing? [J]. Sound and Vibration: 9-12.

VANMARCKE E H, 1972. Properties of Spectral Moments with Applications to Random Vibration[J]. Journal of Engineering Mechanics, ASCE, 98: 425-446.

VAROTO K G, MCCONNELL P S, 2008. Vibration Testing: Theory and Practice[M]. 2nd Edition, John Wiley & Sons, Hoboken, NJ, USA.

VLASIC F, et al, 2013. Study on High-Cycle Fatigue Behavior of Titanium Alloy Using Acoustic Method[J]. MeTal 2013, Brno, Czech Republic, EU; May 15-17.

VURAL M, et al, 2003. Large Strain Mechanical Behavior of 1018 Cold-Rolled Steel over a Wide Range of Strain Rates[J]. Metallurgical and Materials Transactions, A, 34: 2873.

WANG L, et al, 2010. Analytical Analysis Approach to Nonlinear Dynamic Characteristics of Hydraulically Damped Rubber Mount for Vehicle Engine[J]. Nonlinear Dynamics, 61(1-2): 251-264.

WILLIAMSON C, GODVARDHAN R, 2004. Vortex-Induced Vibrations [J]. Annual Review of Fluid Mechanics, Volume 36: 413-455.

WIRSCHING P H, LIGHT M C, 1980. Fatigue under Wide Band Random Loading[J]. Journal of Structural Division, ASCE: 1593-1607.

YıLDıRıM C, et al, 2013. Fatigue Assessment of High Frequency Mechanical Impact (HFMI): Improved Fillet Welds by Local Approaches[J]. International Journal of Fatigue, 52: 57-67.

YU Y, NAGANATHAN N G, DUKKIPATI R V, 2000. A Literature Review of Automotive Engine Mounting Systems[J]. Journal of Vehicle Design, 24: 32-57.

YUSOFF A R, et al, 2016. Power Spectrum Density (PSD) Analysis of Automotive Pedal-Pad[J]. Journal of Engineering Science and Technology, 11: 20-27.

ZALAZNIK A, NAGODE M, 2011. Frequency Based Fatigue Analysis and Temperature Effect[J]. Materials & Design, 32(10): 4794-4802.

ZHAO W, BAKER M J, 1992. On the Probability Density Function of Rainflow Stress Range for Stationary Gaussian Processes[J]. International Journal of Fatigue, 14(2): 121-135.

Table 7.14.1   Example Power Spectral Density (PSD) and Corresponding G-Load Peaks of an Engine Turbocharger (Truck).

Frequency/Hz	PSD/$(\mathrm{W} \cdot \mathrm{Hz}^{-1})$	G-Load $(1\ \mathrm{G} = 9.807\ \mathrm{m/s^2})$
1	0.01	0.1
45	0.1	2.1
55 (3300 RPM)	2	10.5
65	0.1	2.5
100	0.5	7.1
110 (6600 RPM)	12	36.3
120	0.5	7.7
170	0.1	4.1
220	0.5	10.5
230 (13800 RPM)	2.5	24
250	0.2	7.1
1240	0.2	15.7
1250 (75000 RPM)	1	35.4
1260	0.2	15.9
2000 (120000 RPM)	0.01	4.5

Table 7.14.2 Material Parameters for Johnson-Cook Stress Model〔Akbari-Mousavi et al.〕〔Johnson and Cook〕〔Jaspers et al.〕〔Muthu et al.〕〔Ocana et al.〕〔Rule〕〔SSAB〕.

Material	A/MPa	B/MPa	n	C	m	T_m/℃
Aliphatic Polyketone	27.8	177.3	0.378 6	0.029 5	0.655 220	
Al：1100（H14）	140	75.2	0.6474	0.0125	—	643
Al：2024（T3）	325	414	0.2	0.015	1.0	502
Al：2024（T6）	369	684	0.73	0.0083	1.7	502
Al：6061（T6）	293.4	121.3	0.23	0.002	1.34	582
Al：6063（T6）	261.2	126.8	0.301	0.0125	1.1	616
Al：6082（T6）	428.5	327.7	1.008	0.00747	1.31	582
Inconel 718	450	1700	0.65	0.017	1.3	1297
Inconel 718	1029	1478	0.33	0.06	1.44	1297
SAE 1006CD	350	275	0.36	0.02	1.0	—
SAE 1010CD	367	700	0.935	0.045	0.643	—
SAE 1018CD	560	300	0.32	—	0.55	—
SAE 1045	553.1	600.8	0.234	0.0134	1	1460
SAE 12L14	429.4	243	0.0868	0.021	0.874	1538
SAE 4150	1000	1785.4	0.14	0.0	0.85	1495
SAE 52100	2482.4	1498.5	0.19	0.027	0.66	—
SAE 4340	792	510	0.26	0.014	1.03	1520
AISI 304	350	275	1	0.022	1	1538
AISI 316L（Lowdε/dt）	248	1007	0.452	0.0727	0.259	1400
AISI 316L（dε/dt>10 s^{-1}）	245	580	0.587	0.117	0.733	1400
DP 590	430	824	0.51	0.17	—	—
RHA	900	545	0.26	0.014	1	—
Ti：CP Ti	—	—	—	—	—	1670
Ti：Ti-6Al-4V	884	599	0.36166	0.0335	1.041	1650
W	1510	177	0.12	0.016	1	3422
WC-Co（Tool）	0.003	8.0471	0.0003	0	0/179	1372

continued

Material	A/MPa	B/MPa	n	C	m	T_m/℃
AlN	850	310	0.29	0.013	0.21	2500
Al_2O_3	930	310	0.6	0	0.6	2054
B_4C	927	700	0.67	0.005	0.85	2450
SiC	960	350	0.65	0	1	2730
SiO_2(Silica)	930	88	0.7	0.003	0.35	1650
Weldox460E	499	382	0.458	0.0079	0.893	1527
Bullet-Cap and cover	206	505	0.42	0.01	1.67	916
Bullet-Hardened core steel	1200	50000	1.0	0	1.0	1527

Table 7.14.3   Failure Parameters of Johnson-Cook Stress Model at Room Temperature.

Material	D_1	D_2	D_3	D_4	D_5
Steel:SAE 12L14	0.2431	1.242	−2.525	0.003551	0.25
Steel-Hardened	0.051/0.85	0.018	−3.0	0.0002	0.55
Al:6063(T6)	0.2631	1.042	−2.312	0.04424	2.6
AlN	0.02	1.85	0	0	0
Al_2O_3	0.005	1	0	0	0
B_4C	0.001	0.5	−2.969	−0.014	1.014
SiC	0.48	0.48	0	0	0
SiO_2(Silica)	0.053	0.85	0	0	0
Weldox460 E	0.636	1.936	0	0	0

Chapter 8

Tribology

8.1 Dry Friction between Solids

Tribology is defined as the interdisciplinary study of contacting surfaces in relative motion and the resulting phenomena. It is intrinsically focused on friction, wear and lubrication, while tribology research in the automotive industry has been focused on reliability and energy consumption, ensuring the safe and continuous operation of mechanical components at high efficiency and minimum cost [Holmberg et al.]. As surface interactions involve [Holmberg et al.] [Jost] [Romig et al.], the multidisciplinary approaches to resolving tribology-related problems in the past can be classified as follows：

(a) Solid mechanics：Elastoplasticity, vibration, fatigue, creep, diffusion, and fracture.
(b) Thermal：Heat conduction and convection.
(c) Fluid mechanics：Elastohydrodynamic lubrication.
(d) Materials Science：Crystallization, amorphousness, corrosion, and phase transformation.
(e) Physics：Atomic-scale bond breaking, including electronic and photonic excitations.
(f) Chemistry：Chemical bond formation, adsorption, and dissociation.

Tribological interactions between two contacting solid surfaces may result in wear, denoted by the loss of material and types. Major wear types encountered in nature are subjected to abrasion, erosion, corrosion, cohesion, and frictional adhesion. Unpredictable friction should be regarded as an uncontrollable factor and eliminated as much as possible.

However, constructive friction such as automotive tire traction, brake traction, and force hysteresis of pedal systems should be put in control by design and constrained in a certain work range with a limited variance. The On/Off stiction of Gecko palms by nature is an adsorbing mechanism utilizing constructive friction.

8.1.1 Coefficient of Friction

The study of tribology is to look for solutions to the phenomena resulting from rubbing, including friction, wear, and lubrication. Rubbing friction is dictated by interaction of asperities, which are characterized by their mechanical and chemical properties. Friction is a measure of the resistance to relative motion between two surfaces in contact. A frictional force between two solids in contact with each other is related to the corresponding interactive normal force as follows [Coulomb's friction]：

$$F_f = \mu \, F_N \tag{8.1.1}$$

where

F_f: Frictional force, tangential to the surface;

F_N: Applied force, normal to the surface;

$\mu = \mu_S$: Static coefficient of friction, where there is no sliding;

$\mu = \mu_D$: Dynamic coefficient of friction, where there is sliding.

Friction is generally independent of the contact area unless the surfaces in contact are clean and have extremely low surface roughness. Coefficients of friction between different solid materials in dry contact are listed in Table 8.1.1. In general, μ_S (static coefficient of friction) is larger than μ_D (dynamic coefficient of friction).

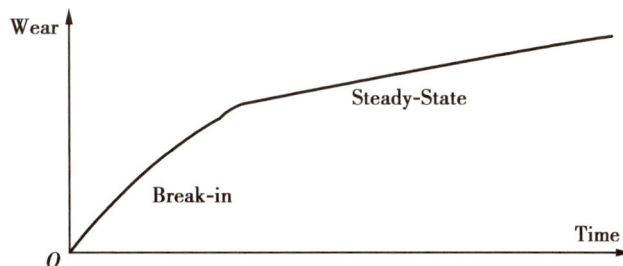

Fig. 8.1.1   Wear of Material

8.1.2   Dry Wear

A wear curve may be divided into two bi-linear segments: (a) break-in wear and (b) steady-state, as shown in Fig. 8.1.1. In the break-in period, also called running in period, the wear rate is dependent upon counter-face roughness. The wear rate depends on mechanical properties of the material, its ability to smooth the counter-face surface and transport a thin film of debris. After then, the steady-state wear kicks in. Coefficient of wear K is defined as a dimensionless parameter for the operation in steady state based on the following empirical wear equation [Lancaster]

$$K = \frac{V_w H}{F S} \tag{8.1.2}$$

where

K: Dimensionless wear coefficient, which is constant over a steady-state operation;

$V_w (\text{mm}^3)$: Volume of wear;

H (MPa): Hardness of surface, e.g. Vickers hardness (H_v);

F (N): Compressive force;

S (mm): Sliding distance.

Wear coefficient K can be used to predict component lifetimes, providing that the tribological system does not change the wear mode. Note that Brinell, Vickers, and Knoop hardness values are in kg/mm^2, which has been converted into MPa as 1 $\text{kg/mm}^2 = 9.807$ MPa while working with Eq. (8.1.2). The volume of wear is independent of the contact area for a given compressive force, but it is complicated by the temperature variation and lubrication condition. K/H is defined as the specific coefficient of wear, which shows the tendency of wear per applied pressure. According to [Yang, 2005] the specific coefficient of wear is inversely proportional to the travel distance. As derived from Eq. (8.1.2), it is written as follows:

$$\frac{K}{H} = \frac{V_w}{F\,S} \tag{8.1.3}$$

For an infinitesimal depth of wear (dh_w) on a contact surface of area A subjected to an incremental sliding distance (dS), the volume of wear $dV_w = A\ dh_w$. Eq. (8.1.3) can then be rewritten as

$$\frac{K}{H} = \frac{A\ dh_w}{F\ dS} = \frac{A\ dh_w}{F\ (V\ dt)} = \frac{dh_w}{dt}\left[\frac{1}{\left(\dfrac{F}{A}\right)V}\right] \tag{8.1.4}$$

where

h_w(mm): Depth of wear;

t (s): Time;

P (MPa): Contact pressure, $P = F / A$;

V (mm/s): Sliding speed;

dS (mm): Differential distance, and $dS = V\ dt$.

It is straightforward to derive the following two equations directly from Eq. (8.1.4),

$$\frac{dh_w}{dt} = \left(\frac{K}{H}\right) P\ V \tag{8.1.5}$$

and
$$\frac{dh_w}{dS} = \left(\frac{K}{H}\right) P \tag{8.1.6}$$

In light of Eq. (8.1.5), PV (MPa · mm/s) and K/H (MPa^{-1}) are the two factors that control the depth of wear. Nominal PV limits and specific wear coefficient K/H for some unlubricated bearing materials are given in Table 8.1.2. The wear pattern results from unidirectional sliding is very different from that due to reciprocating sliding and cyclic "start-stop" is usually more damaging than a continuous motion.

Besides the theory given above for "dry wear" the boundary (edge) effect [Strand] has to be also considered as shown in Fig. 8.1.2. The wear will be more severe on contact edges of a bearing pin subject to both normal-stress and shear-stress singularities attributed to both geometric and material factors.

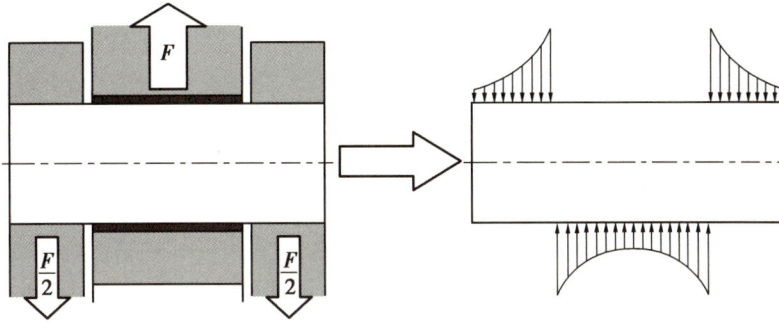

Fig. 8.1.2   Schematic Normal-Stress Profile on a Pin Bearing Joint Due to Boundary Effect

8.1.3   Wear Patterns

Mechanical wear is an interacting property between solids in a system, and it is not a material property. Wear patterns can be divided into the following five categories: abrasive/scuffing wear, adhesive/fretting wear, corrosive wear, erosive wear, and fatigue wear.

(a) Abrasive/scuffing wear: It functions like a machining process, in which a hard material cuts or plows a soft material. The direction of scars indicates scuffing (sliding) Direction. Energy loss contributes to friction loss.

(b) Adhesive/fretting wear: It is solid phase welding, by which material transferred from one part to another part via contact as its surface oxide films on the asperities break away. If the amplitude in oscillatory relative motion is small, it is called fretting wear. Galling is a phenomenon that the contact surfaces seize or freeze-up at high stresses like a press-fit literally after a certain amount of oscillatory relative motion.

(c) Erosive wear: It is abrasive wear assisted by "erosive" fluids such as acids.

(d) Corrosive wear: It is abrasive wear subjected to material degradation due to chemical or electrochemical reactions.

(e) Fatigue wear: It occurs when the dynamic shear stresses or strains in the sliding contact surface of an articulation exceed the shear fatigue limit under cyclic loads.

8.1.4   Good Wear

The hard material scratches the soft material. It has been recognized that a "dry" bearing must at least meet the following three requirements to be recognized to have good wear:

(1) $K/H \leqslant 10^{-9}$ MPa$^{-1} = 10^{-9}$ mm^3(N $\cdot$ mm) $= 10^{-6}$ mm^3/(N $\cdot$ m).

(2) $\mu_D \leqslant 0.2$.

(3) K (coefficient of wear) and μ (coefficient of friction) are literally not dependent upon the operating conditions, such as speed and temperature variations.

8.1.5　High- or Low-Speed Friction

Friction is not usually influenced by the sliding speed, except at an extremely low or high speed. At a relative high sliding speed the coefficient of friction generally decreases with increasing speed. Dry friction at an extremely low or high sliding speed can introduce dynamic instabilities such as brake squeal, glass harp, stick and slip of windshield wipers, and flutter between roller and cam. An effective description of such phenomena can be modeled using a coefficient of friction as a function of relative velocity.

8.1.6　Friction at Elevated Temperatures

Friction coefficients can be predicted as a function of yield strength, which decreases as the working temperature arises. Based on the observation that the yield strength of workpiece material dominates the ratio of the real contact area when it comes into contact with the metal-cutting tool, [Tao] provides the following equation as the first approximating equation for estimating the dry coefficient

$$\mu = \mu_a + \mu_b \exp\left[\frac{\left(\dfrac{\sigma_y(T)}{3}\right)^{\frac{1}{2}}}{100}\right] \tag{8.1.7}$$

where

σ_y: Yield strength and thus $\sigma_y/3^{\frac{1}{2}}$ is the stress flow strength of the workpiece.

T: Temperature.

Coefficients μ_a and μ_b can be obtained by curve fitting. The following data are provided for convenience by [Tao]:

Material	Coefficient μ_a	Coefficient μ_b
Al6061	1.22	−0.23
Al2024	1.21	−0.24
Ti	0.085	−0.094
Gray Iron	−1.34	0.37
Ductile Iron	0.80	−0.12

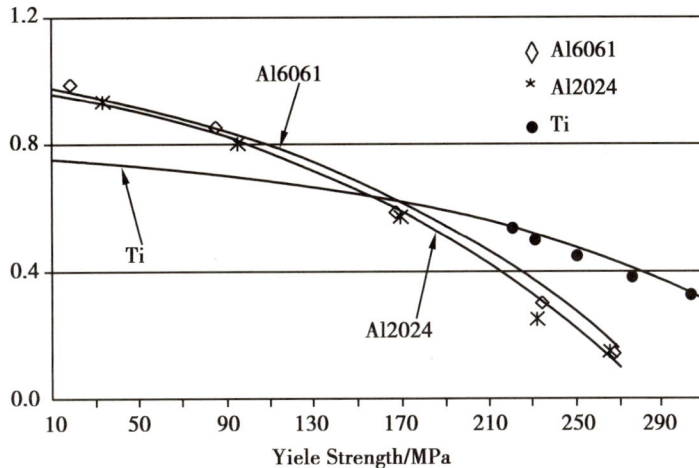

Fig. 8.1.3   Coefficient of Friction as a Function of Yield Strength [Tao]

8.1.7   Stick-Slip

Stick-slip is a phenomenon that spontaneous alternate stick and slip motions occur while two objects are sliding against each other. Noises generally accompany stick-slip through surface acoustic waves.

Typically, the static coefficient of friction between two surfaces is larger than the kinetic friction coefficient. A hypothesis to explain the stick-slip phenomenon is that once the applied energy is large enough to overcome the static friction, the reduction of the static friction to the dynamic friction can cause a sudden jump in the moving speed. The phenomenon accounts for some automotive noises such as the squeak of bearings and rattle of windshield wipers.

8.2   Surface Roughness

A surface profile may differ from the "form" as prescribed in the drawing in two ways. One is the macro-geometric deviation called waviness and the other is micro-geometric deviation called roughness. Stylus profilometer, optical interferometer, and atomic force microscope (AFM) are the three major tools frequently used for measuring material roughness. Randomly distributed asperities, having different size, are frequently used to represent the roughness in a statistical way. They interact with each other in a short time interval during sliding, as being constantly reformed by wear in the meanwhile.

The real contact area and its related contact stress distribution resulting from the applied compressive force between two surfaces in contact play an important role in the prediction of friction, wear, electrical contact resistance, and thermal contact resistance. The actual compressive stress due to contact is much larger than the nominal contact pressure, because the real contact area ranges from 1% to 30% while the diameter of a single contact "spot" ranges from 1 μm to 50 μm in most engineering applications [Stachowiak & Batcherlor], as schematically illustrated in Fig. 8.2.1.

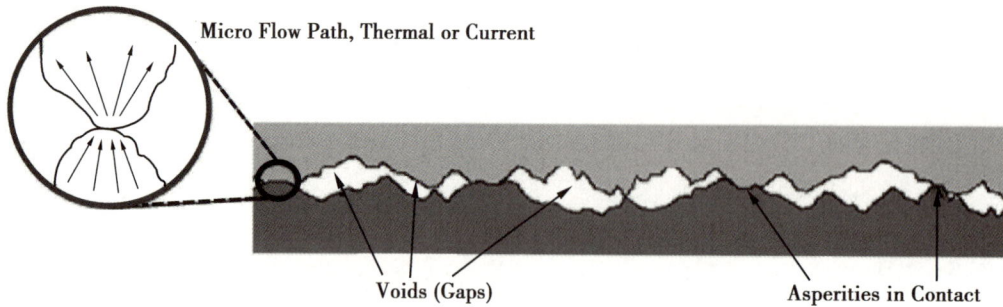

Fig. 8.2.1　Schematic 2-Dimensional Drawing of Two Surfaces in Contact [Wislon]

8.2.1　Spectral Moments of Surface Roughness

Spectral moments of a series of data are used to characterize the surface roughness, assume to be random, as for the random vibration [Irvine] [Greenwood & Williamson]. The average and nth spectral moment m_n, where $n = 0$, 2, or 4, are formulated on the positive x-axis using the measured discrete data [Irvine], respectively as

$$R_a = \frac{1}{N} \sum_{n=1}^{N} |z_n| \qquad (8.2.1)$$

$$m_0 = \frac{1}{N} \sum_{n=1}^{N} (z_n)^2 \qquad (8.2.2)$$

$$m_2 = \frac{1}{N} \sum_{n=1}^{N} \left(\frac{dz_n}{dx}\right)^2 \qquad (8.2.3)$$

and $\qquad m_4 = \frac{1}{N} \sum_{n=1}^{N} \left(\frac{d^2 z_n}{dx^2}\right)^2 \qquad (8.2.4)$

where

N: Number of data in total;

$z_n(\mu m)$: The nth amplitude, i.e., the nth height relative to the mean value;

x：Horizontal axis；

m_0，m_2，m_4：Spectral moments 0，2，and 4，respectively.

The derivatives in the above two equations can be calculated using the central finite difference method. Each "row along the x-axis" of data is used to obtain $m_{2,\text{row}}$ and $m_{4,\text{row}}$, and then the averaged values of all the rows are used to represent m_2 and m_4. As an example, the surface roughness in terms of root-mean-square height of a rotating shaft journal is expected to fall between 0.1 μm and 0.4 μm. The statistical characteristics, i.e., (a) height (root mean square), (b) apparent radius of curvature and (c) areal density of surface roughness, can then be calculated [McCool], respectively as

$$R_{\text{q}} = m_0^{\frac{1}{2}} \tag{8.2.5}$$

$$R_{\text{c}} = \frac{m_4}{6\pi \times 3^{\frac{1}{2}} m_2} \tag{8.2.6}$$

$$\eta_z = \frac{3 \, \pi^{\frac{1}{2}}}{8 \, m_4^{\frac{1}{2}}} \tag{8.2.7}$$

where

$R_{\text{q}}(\mu\text{m})$：Root-mean-square height；

$R_{\text{c}}(\mu\text{m})$：Apparent radius of curvature；

η_z：Areal density of asperities.

The following four equations can be used for calculating the four parameters in the 3-dimensional space,

$$R_{\text{a}} = \frac{1}{A} \int_0^{L_y} \int_0^{L_x} |z(x, y)| \, dx \, dy \tag{8.2.8}$$

$$m_0 = \frac{1}{A} \int_0^{L_y} \int_0^{L_x} [z(x, y)]^2 dx \, dy \tag{8.2.9}$$

$$m_2 = \frac{1}{A} \int_0^{L_y} \int_0^{L_x} \left\{ \left[\frac{\partial z(x, y)}{\partial x} \right]^2 + \left[\frac{\partial z(x, y)}{\partial y} \right]^2 \right\} dx \, dy \tag{8.2.10}$$

and $\quad m_4 = \frac{1}{A} \int_0^{L_y} \int_0^{L_x} \left\{ \left[\frac{\partial z^2(x, y)}{\partial x^2} \right]^2 + \left[\frac{\partial z^2(x, y)}{\partial y^2} \right]^2 \right\} dx \, dy \tag{8.2.11}$

8.2.2　Surface Roughness and Asperity Deformations

In order to determine the plastic deformation of asperities, of which each individual representative group is assumed to have a "peak radius." Following the derivations in ［Greenwood & Williamson］, one has the following two equations for elastic and fully plastic contact areas, respectively

$$A_{\text{elastic}} \propto \left(\frac{F}{E'}\right)\left(\frac{R_q}{R_c}\right)^{\frac{1}{2}} \tag{8.2.12}$$

and

$$A_{\text{plastic}} \propto \left(\frac{F}{H}\right) \tag{8.2.13}$$

where

E' (MPa): Apparent Young's modulus; the larger E' is, the smaller the contact area;

H (MPa): Indentation hardness of the softer material, i.e., a measure of plastic stress flow;

R_c (mm): Apparent radius of curvature; the smaller R_c is, the smaller the contact area;

R_q (mm): Root-mean-square height.

Plastic deformation will begin when the pressure at the asperity is greater than H ［Greenwood & Williamson］, and thus a plasticity index can be defined as the ratio A_{plastic} to A_{elastic}. According to Eq. (8.2.8) and Eq. (8.2.9), the plasticity index reduces to

$$\psi = \frac{E'}{H}\left(\frac{R_q}{R_c}\right)^{\frac{1}{2}} \tag{8.2.14}$$

where

(a) When $\psi > 1$, the asperities of the group are likely to deform plastically. Material is likely to flow and fills the valleys, resulting in more contact area and larger connecting (or adhesive) zone. It would take more tangential force for the two contacting solids to slide against each other, i.e., high coefficient of friction.

(b) When $\psi < 0.6$, the asperities of the group are likely to deform elastically, resulting in less friction.

A 3-dimensional thermomechanical asperity contact model developed by ［Liu & Wang］ was used to model the contact evolution of a steel ball sliding against a B_4C coated disc. Observations of wear initiation of AISI 52100 steel sliding against a thin boron carbide coating, as declared by ［Siniawski et al.］ are given as follows: "Prior to wear initiation, the contact pressure is a highly concentrated circular patch. As the wear begins and sliding increases, the contact pressure becomes distributed over a larger surface area, corresponding to the increasing size of the wear scar. Although the overall size of the contact area increases with sliding distance, the size of the contact area experiencing plastic deformation remains nearly constant once wear begins." A rough estimate of contact area in response to a compressive force F is

$$A_c = \left(\frac{3\ F\ R_c}{4\ E'}\right) \pi \tag{8.2.15}$$

8.3   Thermal Contact Conductance

Thermal contact conductance is the study of heat conduction between two solids in intimate contact with each other. The thermal contact conductance coefficient is defined to evaluate the performance and it is a tribological property indicating the thermal conductivity, i.e., the ability to conduct heat, between them. The thermal conductance coefficient can be also called an apparent convective heat transfer coefficient between the two solids, which is denoted as $h_c(W/m^2/℃)$.

8.3.1   As Part of Heat Conductance in Series

Thermal contact conductance is the study of heat conduction between solid bodies in contact. It is characterized using a thermal conductance coefficient $h_c(W/m^2/℃)$, which is similar to heat convection. For example, solids A and B are in contact with each other via a plane surface as shown in Fig. 8.3.1. The heat flow between the two bodies (a and b) in contact is found to be

$$q = \frac{T_1 - T_4}{\dfrac{X_a}{k_a\ A_a} + \dfrac{1}{h_c\ A_c} + \dfrac{X_b}{k_b\ A_b}} \tag{8.3.1}$$

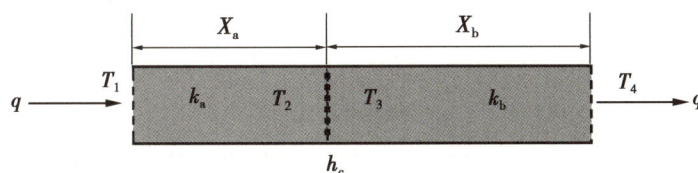

Fig. 8.3.1   Thermal Conductance in Series $(T_1 > T_2 > T_3 > T_4)$

The inverse of this interfacial conductance property is called thermal contact resistance. As demonstrated in the above equation, the combined overall heat flow resistance consists of three different resistances in series

$$R_a = \frac{X_a}{k_a A_a} \quad\quad\quad (8.3.2)$$

$$R_c = \frac{1}{h_c A_c} \quad\quad\quad (8.3.3)$$

$$R_b = \frac{X_b}{k_b A_b} \quad\quad\quad (8.3.4)$$

Measurement of the thermal contact conductance between two solid surfaces is complicated by the following hard-to-know factors [Madhusudana]:

(a) Contact pressure distribution.
(b) Interstitial structure and filling materials.
(c) Surface waviness and roughness.
(d) Degree of elastoplastic deformation.
(e) Surface cleanliness.

The interstitial contact exists in nature, resulting in relatively large separating gaps even if two bodies are put together with a high pressure. The gases/fluids filling these gaps will influence the heat flow across the interface. It is therefore difficult to figure out the real contact area. The applied contact pressure is the most influential factor, as it may close a good number of gaps.

8.3.2　What in h_c?

Even the smoothest surface reveals various asperities that limit the actual area of contact to as few as several discrete locations. Heat may pass through the interface via three paths:

(1) Conduction through the contact spots.
(2) Conduction through the gas trapped in the gap between surfaces.
(3) Radiation across the gap (not significant until the temperature is above 500 ℃).

An application to thermal contact resistances for a typical aluminum-ceramic interface with flycut and ground surfaces in microelectronics was studied by [Yovanovich], where the joint conductance is valid for a contact pressure falling between 0.007 MPa and 0.35 MPa. This pressure range accommodates well the practical microelectronic pressure range of 0.07 MPa and 0.17 MPa [Latham].

(a) Air in gaps: The least thermal contact conductance was found when air is present in interstitial gaps. In the contact pressure range of 0.007 MPa to 0.35 MPa, the thermal conductance varies from 3.75×10^3 W/m²/℃ to 5.26×10^3 W/m²/℃. Note that the data presented here are converted from thermal resistance data 2.67×10^{-4} W/m²/℃ to 1.9×10^{-4} W/m²/℃ given in [Yovanovich].

    (b) Grease in gaps: When silicon grease is placed in the gap, the thermal resistance is much smaller than the bare interface. The calculated thermal conductance varies from 3.0×10^4 W/m²/℃ to 4.7×10^4 W/m²/℃, which is an order of magnitude larger than those of a bare contact with air in the gaps.

    (c) Thermally conductive grease in gaps: If thermally conductive grease is used, the thermal conductance is raised to 1.54×10^5 W/m²/℃, which is much higher than "regular" grease in the gaps.

In light of the above observation, h_c consists of the following two mechanisms without considering the radiation effect

$$h_c = h_{c1} + h_{c2} \tag{8.3.5}$$

where

h_{c1}: Due to the conductivity from real contacts, e.g. asperity-typed contacts;

h_{c2}: Due to convection and conductivity with material (or vacuum) trapped in gaps.

8.3.3   Effect by Asperity-Typed Contacts

Surface waviness and roughness play an important role in deciding thermal conductance resistance. According to [Yovanovich] the thermal contact conductance due to asperity-typed contacts is

$$h_{c1} = 2.5 \left(\frac{k_a k_b}{k_a + k_b} \right) + \left(\frac{m_c}{R_{rms}} \right) \left(\frac{P_c}{H_c} \right)^{0.95} \tag{8.3.6}$$

where

k_a, k_b: Thermal conductivities of solid A and solid B, respectively;

m_c: Effective mean absolute asperity slope of the interface;

R_{rms}(μm): Root meansquare roughness;

P_c(MPa): Contact pressure;

H_c(MPa): Microhardness of solids, e.g. Vickers microhardness correlation coefficient.

The combined effective mean absolute asperity slope and root meansquare roughness are, respectively

$$m_c = (m_{1c}^2 + m_{2c}^2)^{\frac{1}{2}} \tag{8.3.7}$$

and $\quad R_{rms} = (R_{1rms}^2 + R_{2rms}^2)^{\frac{1}{2}} \tag{8.3.8}$

The heat-transfer effect resulting from contact pressure can be seen in Table 8.3.1. If the root meansquare roughness R_{rms} (μm) falls in the range between 0.216 μm and 9.6 μm, which is applicable to most surface roughness of metals, the mean absolute asperity slope (m_c) can be approximated by the following empirical equation according to [Antonetti]

$$m_c = 0.125 \ (R_{rms} \times 10^6)^{0.402} \qquad (\text{If } 0.216 \ \mu m < R_{rms} < 9.6 \ \mu m) \qquad (8.3.9)$$

8.3.4 Temperature Effect

The other influential factor is the working temperature. It is shown experimentally by [Berman] [Deutsch] [Niles et al.] [Salerno et al.] that the thermal contact conductance of metals increases according to a simple power law function of temperature as

$$h_c = h_{co} \ T^{\chi} \qquad (8.3.10)$$

where the exponent χ ranges from 0.25 to 0.75 for metals.

8.4 Electric Contact Conductance

When two surfaces are in intimate contact that carries electric current, they are called electric contact. Electric contact conductance is the study of electric conduction between two solids in intimate contact with each other. It is a tribological property indicating the electric conductivity, i.e., the ability to conduct electric current between them. The inverse of this property is called electric contact resistance. The three commonly used conductors are (a) copper, (b) aluminum, and (c) low-alloyed steel. Copper and aluminum have great electric conductivities, while steel (low-alloyed) is used primarily as a strengthening agent for conductors such as copper and aluminum.

8.4.1 Electric Impedance at Electric Contact

The contact is in fact made at only some asperities, of which the true contact area for conducting electricity is much less than the nominal contact area. Electric contacts are rated for the current carrying capacity while closed, or rated for the voltage breaking capacity while open or when opening (due to arcing). Constrictions that impede the electric current flow between them are termed electric contact resistance. Enlighted by Fig. 8.4.1, predictive models are developed to characterize the electric contact impedance at the interface [Holm] [Zhai].

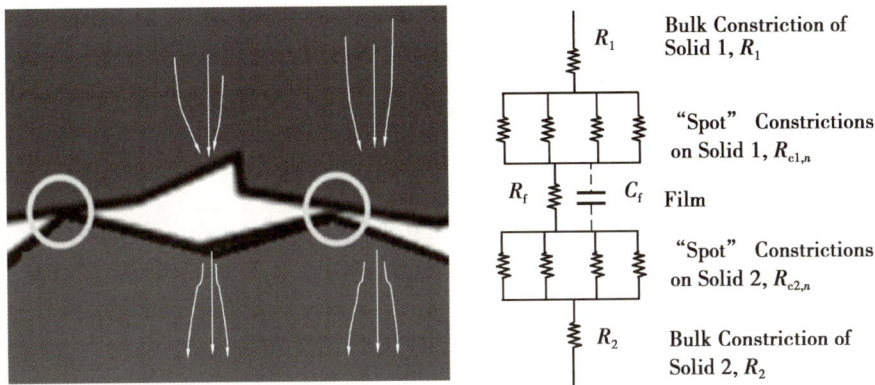

Fig. 8.4.1   Schematic Drawing of Electric Impedance at Electric Contact "Spot"

$$Z_c = R_1 + j\,\omega\,L_1 + \sum_{n=1}^{N} R_{1,n}^{-1} + (R_f^{-1} + j\,\omega\,C_f)^{-1} + R_2 + j\,\omega\,L_2 + \sum_{n=1}^{N} R_{2,n}^{-1} \qquad (8.4.1)$$

where

Z_c: Overall contact impedance;

R_1: Electric Resistance of bulk solid 1;

L_1: Inductance of bulk solid 1;

$R_{1,n}$: Electric resistance due to spotted-contact constriction on solid 1 at spot n;

R_f: Total electric resistance of film at contact spots;

$R_{2,n}$: Electric resistance of bulk solid 2;

L_2: Inductance of bulk solid 2;

R_2: Electric resistance due to spotted-contact constriction on solid 2 at spot n;

N, n: Total number of contact spots and numbering of spot, respectively.

Films covering surfaces need be electrically or mechanically removed before metal-to-metal contact can be formed. Consider a static case without the effect of time. The electric contact resistance can be derived from Eq. (8.4.1) as

$$R_c = R_1 + \frac{1}{\sum R_{c1,n} - 1} + R_f + R_2 + \frac{1}{\sum R_{c2,n} - 1} \qquad (8.4.2)$$

High electric contact resistance hinders electric connecting devices, such as electric breakers, contactors, relays, switches, connectors, and other special switching devices, from operating at a high efficiency. Increase in contact resistance can cause a high-voltage drop in the system or even result in failure.

8.4.2 Electric Contact Tarnish

Electric contact corrosion occurs and the contact can be tarnished. The corrosion reduces the contact area of contacting "spots", and it subsequently results in the contact resistance.

(a) Copper: Copper oxide forms immediately upon exposure to the atmosphere. Once stabilized, this oxide prevents the copper from further oxidation until it is heated above 88 ℃ (e.g., by bad connection). Once hearted, more oxides with high electric resistance are formed and these oxides continue to increase the heat until the conductor breaks. Oxides due to ammonium and SO_2 are damaging to the copper conductivity.

(b) Aluminum: Light-weighted aluminum may grow 20 Angstroms of Al_2O_3 in thickness after being exposed to the air in a few seconds and this oxide prevents further oxidation of the aluminum. It resists arcs pitting better than any other metal.

Once the corrosion layer cracks or delaminates, the compressive force may reduce dramatically. The dramatic increase in electric resistance due to compression relaxation, as shown in Fig. 8.4.2, may cause power loss, heat generation, loss of contactor capacity, interruption of current flow, or even sparkling fire. If vibration occurs such as the connectors installed in an electric vehicle, fretting corrosion at high temperatures could result in a catastrophic event. In other words, mechanical stability can provide electric stability in electric contact.

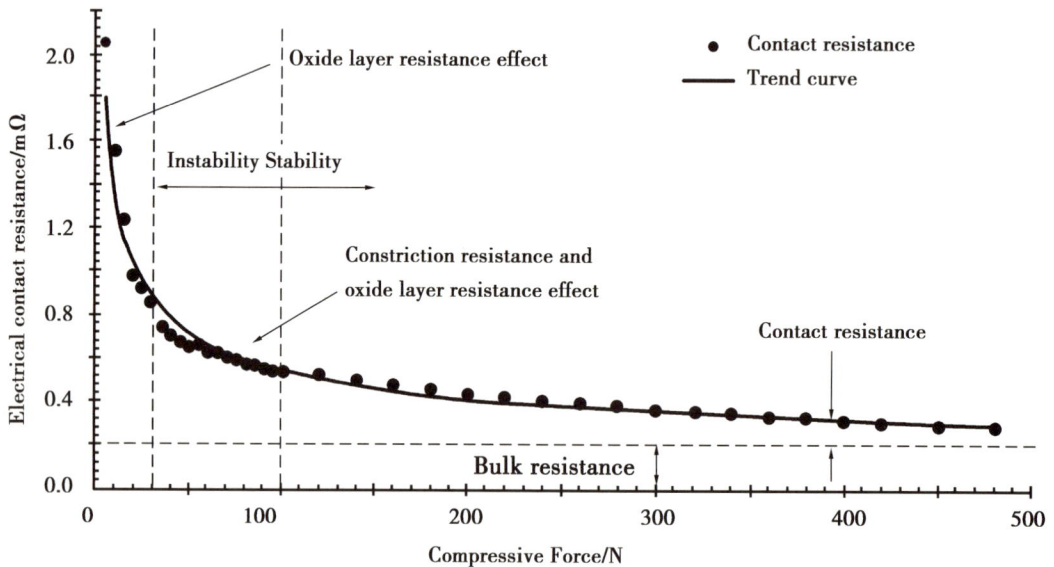

Fig. 8.4.2 Electrical Contact Resistance （10^{-3} Ω） of Copper Versus Compressive Force （N）［Zeroukhi et al.］

8.4.3   Attenuation of Contact Corrosion

An electric connector can survive in a harsh environment by the following multi-level attenuating mechanisms:

(a) Connector Housing: It restricts the access of the corrosive ambient the contact.

(b) Spacing between Asperities: The outer opposite surfaces, which are not mutually in contact might trap the corrosive media in the "pockets" peripherally, and prevent it from getting into the inner contact spots.

(c) Lubrication: Filling of the pockets by the dispersed lubricant provides another layer of attenuation.

8.4.4   Power Loss at Electric Contact

An investigation into the electric contact loss at the connecting joints to the electrodes of lithium battery assemblies for electric vehicles by [Taheri et al.] has shown a significant portion of the battery energy. The power loss ranges from 6% to 25%, depending on the surface geometry (waviness and toughness), contact conditions (e.g. pressure size, pressure distribution, and wetness), joint type, and applied material. The power loss due to the electric contact resistance, obtained from Eq. (8.4.2), can be described as follows:

$$P_{\text{loss}} = R_{\text{c}}(I_{\text{battery}})^2 \tag{8.4.3}$$

The power loss will be dissipated as heat. The following two dimensionless semi-empirical equations have been in use for calculating the power loss as a function of surface roughness and electromagnetic properties due to [Morgan] [Horn III et al.] [Lukie & Filipodia] and [Gross et al.], respectively

$$\frac{P_{\text{rough}}}{P_{\text{smooth}}} = 1 + 2\,\pi^{-1}\tan^{-1}\left[1.4\left(\frac{\delta}{R_{\text{rms}}}\right)^2\right] \tag{8.4.4}$$

and
$$\frac{P_{\text{rough}}}{P_{\text{smooth}}} = 1 + e^{1-\left(\frac{\frac{\delta}{2}}{R_{\text{rms}}}\right)^{1.6}} \qquad [\text{Groiss et al.}] \tag{8.4.5}$$

where

P_{rough}: Power loss of rough wire;

P_{smooth}: Power loss of smooth wire;

δ: Skin depth.

In a fast time-varying electromagnetic field, there is not enough time for each magnetic wave to penetrate into the conductor interior. The depth of penetration, called skin depth, is given as follows:

$$\delta = \left(\frac{2}{\omega \, \rho_{\mathrm{e}} \, \mu} \right)^{\frac{1}{2}} \tag{8.4.6}$$

where

δ: Skin depth;

ω: Frequency;

ρ_{e}: Electric conductivity of wire;

μ: Permeability.

8.4.5　Influence of Surface Roughness on RF Field

As the RF (Radio Frequency) electromagnetic field penetrates the surface and there the induced current will pass and cause RF loss. The loss induced by surface roughness is significant in many RF components, such as micro strip transmission line, wave guide, and RF resonator. When the surface current has more current paths in rough surface, incident waves experience more reflection, scattering, and absorption and thus result in unnecessary power consumption and aggravate the quality factor of transmission [Tsang] [Xu et al.].

8.4.6　Electric Contact in Wire Strands

Influences of intersecting angle and compressive force of wire strands on contact resistance in cable-in-conduit conductors have been extensively discussed by [Nakamura et al.].

8.5　Skin Friction

Friction between fluid flowing over solid surfaces is called skin friction. Colebrook's empirical equation has been used for calculating the friction factor, μ_{f}, for fluid flow in pipes, ducts, and conduits, as [Buzzelli]

$$\mu_{\mathrm{f}}^{-\frac{1}{2}} + 2 \log \left(\frac{0.27027027 \, R_{\mathrm{a}}}{D} + \frac{2.51 \, \mu_{\mathrm{f}}^{-\frac{1}{2}}}{R_{\mathrm{e}}} \right) = 0 \tag{8.5.1}$$

where

μ_{f}: Frictional factor;

R_a: Surface roughness;

D: Hydraulic diameter;

R_e: Reynolds number.

The above equation can be solved numerically for μ_f. Since the equation is asymptotic for both smooth and rough surfaces, a plot of $F(\mu_f) = \mu_f^{-1/2} + 2\,\log(0.27027027\,R_a/D + 2.51\mu_f^{-1/2}/R_e)$ using two columns of Excel spreadsheet, i.e., $[F(\mu_f)]$ versus $[\mu_f]$, will reveal the root (solution), at which $F(\mu_f) = 0$. The Reynolds number (R_e), ranging from 10^3 to 10^8 for most applications, is defined as

$$R_e = \frac{V D \rho}{\mu} \tag{8.5.2}$$

where

V: Flow speed of fluid;

ρ: Fluid density, e.g. 1000 kg/m^3 for water at 4 ℃;

μ: Dynamic viscosity, e.g. 2.82×10^{-4} N · S/m^2 for water at 100 ℃.

8.6   Solid Lubricants

Widely used solid lubricants include graphite (C), molybdenum disulfide (MoS_2), tungsten disulfide (WS_2), boron nitride (BN), Polytetrafluoroethylene (PTFE), and polychloro-fluoroethylene (PCTFE or PTFCE) that are lamellar in structure, resulting in good lubrication properties. DLC (diamond like coating), resin-bonded PTFE, and impregnating porous anodizing are effective bonded films to reduce the surface friction. After all, diamond has the lowest coefficient of friction among all natural materials.

8.7   Fluid Lubricants

Lubricants are used to protect moving parts in contact with each other. If the lubricant is too thin (low viscosity) the pump cannot provide enough pressure to support the workload. On the other hand, if too thick (high viscosity) the pump has a hard time to circulate the lubricant or the lubricant cannot penetrate into tiny gaps between contacting parts. This is why SAE ratings of lubricants, such as 5W30, are designed to protect parts in both cold winter and hot summer under various working conditions. Automotive fluid lubricants are classified into two major categories: mineral lubricants and synthetic lubricants. They are further classified into the following sub-categories:

(1) Mineral lubricants: Paraffinic oils having high flash and pour points while naphthenic

oils having low flash and pour points; and aromatic oils are not for lubricating automotive components.

(2) Synthetic lubricants: There are three popular groups of synthetic lubricants. (a) PAO (Polyalphaolefins) is the most popular synthetic lubricant. (b) PAG (Polyalkylene Glycols or Polyglycols in short) has a low coefficient of friction. (c) Silicones are characterized by their broad working temperature range (−73 ℃ to 300 ℃).

Although the viscosity of a lubricant is its major performance index, the lubrication system must also have the capacity to dissipate heat, to resist corrosion, to decrease oxidation rate, and to handle water or other foreign fluids. A general guide to bearing performance is based on the nominal bearing modulus, M, which is defined as:

$$M_{\text{bearing}} = \frac{\mu_d \omega}{P_b} \tag{8.7.1}$$

where

μ_d(MPa · s, Pa · s, or MPa · s): Dynamic or absolute viscosity; 1 MPa · s = 10^{-3} Pa · s;

ω (s^{-1}): Angular speed of the lubricant circulating around the axis of the journal bearing;

P_b(MPa): Bearing unit load, defined as the load divided by the projected bearing area.

The achievement of hydrodynamic lubrication requires three elements: (a) proper relative motion between sliding surfaces, (b) wedging action (resulting from eccentricity of journal bearing), and (c) lubricant properties. The onset of thick film lubrication occurs at a bearing modulus of 75 according to [Tafe]. Nominal bearing modulus M_{bearing}, which is a dimensionless parameter, has been employed to provide a general design guide for journal bearings. Application examples of bearing unit loads for plain journals are divided into two groups. One group works between 4 MPa and 20 MPa for reciprocating-loaded machines such as engine connecting rod bearings and crankshaft main bearings. The other group works between 0.5 MPa and 4 MPa for steady rotating loads such as electric motors, centrifugal pumps, and turbocharger turbines.

The demand of a certain viscosity grade is dependent upon rotating speed of the shaft, oil temperature, and workload. The reciprocal of viscosity is fluidity. Most traditional lubricant viscosity is defined as the kinematic viscosity, which is obtained by dividing the dynamic viscosity by mass density as

$$\mu_k = \frac{\mu_d}{\rho} \tag{8.7.2}$$

where

ρ: mass density;

μ_k: Kinematic viscosity;

8.7.1   Classification of Fluid Lubricants

Engine oils and gear oils are two major lubricants required for operating on-ground vehicles. Automotive lubricants are classified by SAE (Society of Automotive Engineers) according to their viscosities. The cold crank simulator tells the dynamic viscosity in Pa · s (Pascal Second), but a W grade must also meet the minimum requirement at 100 ℃ measured in mm^2/s. Typical lubricating characteristics of fluidic lubricants and other fluids of concern are listed in the following tables:

(1) Table 8.7.1: Engine Oils.
(2) Table 8.7.2: Gear and Compressor Oils.
(3) Table 8.7.3: Hydraulic and Transformer Oils.
(4) Table 8.7.4: Fuels.
(5) Table 8.7.5: Air and Water.
(6) Table 8.7.6: Other Fluids Related to Lubrication.

SAE 30 means that it meets the working requirement at 100 ℃, defined for operations at elevated temperatures. SAE 5W-30 means that the lubricant meets the 5W viscosity requirement at −17.8 ℃ (i.e., 0 °F) for operations at low temperatures in addition to the SAE 30 requirement at 100 ℃ for operations at elevated temperatures.

8.7.2   Mass Density of Lubricant

In reference to the mass density of petroleum oils at 15.6 ℃ (0.89 g/cm^3) the density at temperature T (℃) under the ambient pressure is approximated using

$$\rho_0 = 0.89 - 0.00063 (T - 15.6) \tag{8.7.3}$$

A commonly used formula that describes the density variation with respect to pressure is [Dowson and Higginson]

$$\rho = \rho_0 \frac{590 + 1.34 p}{590 + p} \tag{8.7.4}$$

where

ρ_0: Density under ambient pressure;

p (MPa or Pa): Pressure.

The formula applies to both mineral and synthetic lubricants, except for silicones of which the compressibility is much higher [Pirro & Wessol]. Thus the density of a lubricant can be predicted using Eqs. (8.7.3) and (8.7.4) successively.

Grease does not begin to flow while working as a lubricant until the applied viscous shear stress exceeds its corresponding yield point.

8.7.3　Viscosity of Lubricants

The viscosity of a lubricant varies exponentially with respect to working temperature and applied pressure. Theoretical formulae published for interactive effect of temperature and pressure on viscosity are given in Sections 8.7.3.1—8.7.3.4:

8.7.3.1　Based on Exponential Sum

One easy-to-use equation relating the viscosity to pressure and temperature is given as

$$\mu_d(P,T) = \mu_{d0} \exp[\alpha_\mu(P - P_o)]\exp[-\beta_\mu(T - T_o)]$$

$$= \mu_{d0} \exp[\alpha_\mu(P - P_o) - \beta_\mu(T - T_o)] \tag{8.7.5}$$

and
$$\mu_d(P,T) \approx \mu_{d0} \exp[\alpha_\mu P - \beta_\mu(T - T_o)] \text{ (Elastohydrodynamic Lubrication)} \tag{8.7.6}$$

where

μ_{d0} : Dynamic viscosity under the ambient pressure and at reference temperature;

α_μ : Pressure-viscosity coefficient, though it is an exponent;

β_μ : Temperature-viscosity coefficient, though it is an exponent;

T and T_o : Working and reference temperatures;

P and P_o : Working and reference pressure, as $P_o \ll P$ for elastohydrodynamic lubrication.

8.7.3.2　Based on Modulus Equations

Another widely used equation relating the viscosity to pressure is given by [Barus], which is a simplified version of Eq. (8.7.6),

$$\mu_d(p) = \mu_{d0} \exp(\alpha'_\mu P) \tag{8.7.7}$$

where $\mu_{d0} = 0.0088$ Pa · s at $T = 40$ ℃ and $\alpha'_\mu = 2 \times 10^{-8}$ Pa^{-1} = 2×10^{-2} MPa^{-1} for turbine oil T9, as an example given by [Liu].

Pressure-viscosity coefficient α'_μ of Eq. (8.7.7) is a function of the temperature and pressure [Barus], relating to temperature T and pressure P as

$$\alpha'_\mu(P,T) = \frac{\ln(\mu_d) - \ln(\mu_{d0})}{P - P_0} = \frac{1}{a_1 + a_2 T + (b_1 + b_2 T) P} \tag{8.7.8}$$

Note that the unit of $\alpha'_{\mu}(P, T)$ is the inverse of pressure, e.g. MPa^{-1} or mm^2/N. Plugging Eq. (8.7.8) into Eq. (8.7.7) yields

$$\mu_{d}(p) = \mu_{d0} \exp\left[\frac{P}{a_1 + a_2 T + (b_1 + b_2 T) P}\right] \tag{8.7.9}$$

where a_1, a_2, b_1, and b_2 are four constants. For paraffinic-based hydraulic oil, for instance, $a_1 = 33.7$ MPa, $a_2 = 0.329$ MPa/℃, $b_1 = 0.0263$, and $b_2 = 0.000315$ ℃$^{-1}$ [Knezevic & Savic]. So far, this is the most reliable approach. As an example, given that the pressure $P = 40$ MPa and $T = 50$ ℃, then dynamic viscosity ratio $\mu_d/\mu_{d0} = 1.97$. It means that under the pressure of 35 MPa and at the temperature of 40 ℃, the viscosity of paraffinic-based hydraulic oil is 1.97 times of that at atmospheric pressure and ambient temperature.

8.7.3.3 Vogel Equation for Influence of Temperature on Viscosity

The viscosity of a lubricant, synthetic or mineral, drops rapidly with an increasing temperature. A widely used equation relating the viscosity to temperature is called Vogel equation, given as

$$\mu_{d}(T) = \mu_{d0}\, e^{\frac{\beta}{T - T_o}} \tag{8.7.10}$$

where

μ_{d0} : Dynamic viscosity at T_o;

β (K): Exponent;

T (K) and T_o(K): Working and reference temperatures;

This equation is quite accurate. Some data of the three parameters of mineral oils, characterizing Vogel's equation, are listed as follows [Knezevic & Savic]:

Parameter	HM 32 Oil	HM 46 Oil	HM 68 Oil	HVL 46 Oil
$\mu_{d0}(Pa \cdot s)$	73.63×10^{-6}	63.33×10^{-6}	39.0×10^{-6}	116×10^{-6}
β (K)	797.7	879.8	1083.9	799.7
T_o(K)	177.4	177.8	166.2	176.7

8.7.3.4 Interactive Effect of Temperature and Pressure Based on Glass Transition Point

As both the temperature and pressure are quite influential factors, the following equation has been suggested as another general approach [Yasutomi et al.]

$$\mu_{d} = \mu_{dg}\, \exp\left\{\frac{-2.3\, C_1(T - T_g)[1 - B_1 \ln(1 + B_2\, p)]}{C_2 + (T - T_g)[1 - B_1 \ln(1 + B_2\, p)]}\right\} \tag{8.7.11}$$

of which μ_{dg} is the viscosity at the corresponding glass transition temperature. The above equation based on free volume theory estimates the viscosity at elevated temperatures as well [Bair]. The glass transition temperature T_g increases with respect to increasing pressure as

$$T_g = T_{go} \left[1 + A_1 \ln(1 + A_2 \, p) \right] \tag{8.7.12}$$

where T_{go} is the glass transition temperature under the ambient pressure. Eq. (8.7.12) is too tedious to be practical, because eight material parameters, i.e., T_{go}, A_1, A_2, μ_{dg}, B_1, B_2 C_1, and C_2, have to be obtained prior to calculating the dynamic viscosity. Specifically, the data for turbine oil T9 are [Bair] [Liu]: $\mu_{dg} = 10^7$ Pa · s, $T_{go} = -76\ ℃$, $A_1 = 228.3\ ℃$, $A_2 = 0.7645\ \text{GPa}^{-1}$, $B_1 = 0.188$, $B_2 = 25.84\ \text{GPa}^{-1}$, $C_1 = 11.45$, and $C_2 = 30.26\ ℃$.

8.7.4　Flash and Pour Points

The flash point of a volatile material is the lowest temperature, at which it evaporates to form an ignitable gaseous mixture in the air, if the ignition source is provided. The flash point of gasoline is generally around $-43\ ℃$ and the flash point of jet fuel is higher than $38\ ℃$. As the flash point of Diesel fuel is higher than $52\ ℃$, a glow plug that is an electrified heating device with a heating element at the tip with high electric resistance is required for heating up each combustion chamber to aid starting Diesel engines.

The pour point is the coldest temperature at which the lubricant will flow before solidification. In other words, it is the temperature at which a liquid becomes semi-solid and loses its flow characteristics.

8.8　Lubricated Friction

The Stribeck curve (Fig. 8.8.1) has been used to characterize lubricated friction between two surfaces in contact, defining respective regimes of friction during a lubricated sliding and rolling contacts. Four distinct regimes are identified as follows:

(Ⅰ) Boundary Lubrication (BL): The load is for 100% carried by the asperities in the contact area, protected by adsorbed molecules of the lubricant and/or a thin oxide layer.

(Ⅱ) Mixed Lubrication (ML): The load is carried by a combination of hydrodynamic pressure and contact pressure between the asperities of both surfaces.

(Ⅲ) Elastohydrodynamic Lubrication (EHL): The load is carried by hydrodynamic pressure as the asperities on both surfaces are completely separated by the lubricant. The surface may deform (expand) due to high pressure.

(Ⅳ) Hydrodynamic Lubrication (HL): The load is fully carried by fluid lubrication (FL) of which the film thickness may be optimized at a specific rotating speed. However, over-lubrication ($h_{\mathrm{film}} \gg h_{\mathrm{min}}$) may lead to churning, of which undesirable friction occurs in fluid.

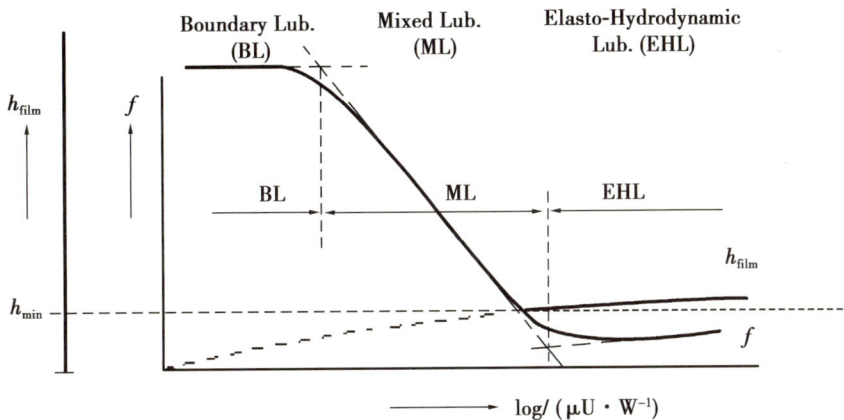

Fig. 8.8.1   Stribeck Curve of Lubricated Friction (f) and Fluid Film Buildup (h_{film})

Lubrication is governed by one of the two principles: hydrodynamic lubrication and boundary lubrication, as well as the mixed balance between them. The friction is mainly a function of viscosity (μ), sliding speed (U), operating load (W), surface roughness factor (λ), and working temperature. Its minimal value occurs in the EHL regime but close to ML, identified as the EHL→ML transition. This is the ideal design point for operating a journal bearing, but not practical. Temperatures are often limited by the lubricant used, as the journal bearing surface (either lead or tin Babbitt) is basically capable of working at temperatures approaching 150 ℃.

8.8.1   Hydrodynamic Lift Due to Viscosity

If two plates move relative to each other and fluid is trapped between them, the fluid will be dragged into the interface by viscosity which accounts for the adhesion between fluid and plates. A certain amount of fluid that enters a converging gap in this manner will see a pressure increase as the gap converges, $h_2 < h_1$, as depicted by the schematic drawing in Fig. 8.8.2(a). The fluid will create hydrodynamic lift forcing the surfaces apart like a wedge, also called hydroplaning. A similar hydroplaning effect for a journal bearing may occur as shown in Fig. 8.8.2(b). The rotating shaft is not centered in the bearing shell during a normal operation. This offset distance is referred to as the eccentricity of the bearing and creates a unique location corresponding to the minimum oil film thickness. Note that the viscosity shall generate heat that would raise the fluid temperature and lower the viscosity.

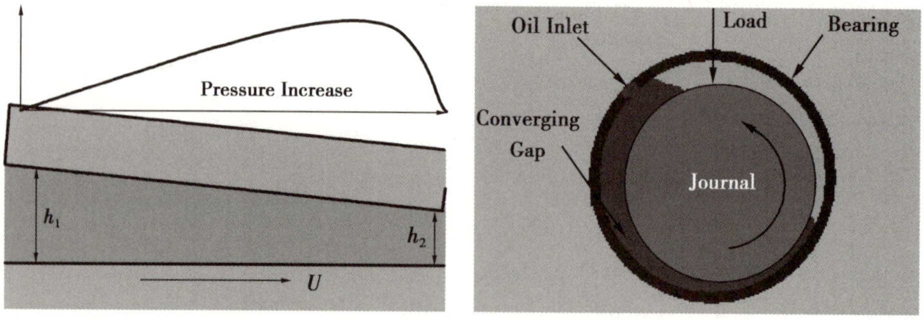

| (a) Hydroplaning (Wedging Effect) | (b) Hydrodynamic Journal Bearing |

Fig. 8.8.2   Hydrodynamic Lifts Created by Relative "Sliding" Motion〔after STLE〕

8.8.2   Hydrodynamic Lift Following Sliding Speed

If the speed is low there will be no pressure buildup in the lubricant. Hence the load is carried by the asperities in the contact area. When the speed goes up, a hydrodynamic pressure builds up in the lubricant and a mixed lubrication may be established such that the load is carried by a combination of the hydrodynamic pressure and the contact asperities. At a certain high sliding speed the hydrodynamic pressure is fully established such that the surface asperities are completely separated by a lubricant film.

8.8.3   Surface Roughness Factor

When two macroscopically smooth surfaces are put in contact with each other under pressure, the contact is made really at only some asperities, which experience extremely high stress. Relative sliding will cause the lubrication film to disperse among the asperities. The surface roughness factor, λ, is defined as the ratio of lubricant film thickness (h_{film}) to the combined surface roughness (Ra) of the two contact areas in sliding to each other, i.e.,

$$\lambda = \frac{h_{\text{film}}}{R_{\text{rms}}} \tag{8.8.1}$$

The combined surface roughness, Ra, is estimated from the two in-contact surface roughnesses, as

$$R_{\text{rms}} = \left[\frac{1}{2} \left(R_{\text{rms}1}^2 + R_{\text{rms}2}^2 \right) \right]^{\frac{1}{2}} \tag{8.8.2}$$

Note that Eq. (8.8.2) is established on the assumption that both surface roughnesses are normally-distributed individually. Consequently, a better polish is more beneficial to fatigue life in circumstances involving high-speed and slip in a bearing system. Aero-engine bearings are typically finished to have an rms surface roughness less than 0.05 μm [Braza], which is 10% of the lower limit of a functional film thickness, i.e., 0.5 μm. The following is to identify the four possible load-carrying mechanisms of a journal bearing:

(1) $0 < \lambda < 1.2$: Boundary lubrication, where solids are in contact with each other;

(2) $1.2 < \lambda < 3$: Partial lubrication, where solids are in contact with each other occasionally;

(3) $3 < \lambda < 10$: Elastohydrodynamic lubrication, where solids are separated;

(4) $5 < \lambda < 100$: Hydrodynamic lubrication.

The surface topography plays an important role in preventing adhesive wear due to the extreme high contact stress in asperities. This can be figured out by following the study done by [Nahm & Bamberger] that a rolling bearing element made of M-50 steel works at a maximum Herzian stress of 4800 MPa. When the rolling speed changes from 15.5 m/s to 25 m/s, the λ value increases from 1.48 to 2.48 and the fatigue life increases from 7.4×10^6 cycles to 26.9×10^6 cycles.

The effect of surface roughness was once examined by analyzing surface roughness of the bearing and rotating shaft before and after break-in for compressor journal bearings by [Hirayam et al.]. It shows that R_{rms} is 0.21 μm before break-in and 0.084 μm after the running-in operation.

8.8.4   Cavitation

There are two possible cavitation mechanisms: gaseous cavitation and vapor cavitation. They are addressed as follows:

(a) Gaseous Cavitation: Once the lubricant pressure falls below the atmospheric pressure, gases and air tend to come out of the lubricant. The cavities (gaseous cavitation voids) are carried by the circulating lubricant until they are dissolved in the lubricant again.

(b) Vapor Cavitation: If the applied load fluctuates at a high frequency following a high rotating speed, the lubricant pressure falling accordingly may cause formation of "near vacuum" vapor cavities by means of fast evaporation/boiling. When the lubricant pressure rises again, the vapor cavities contract at a high speed as squeezed and result in impact loads eroding the bearing material.

8.9   Hydrodynamic Lubrication

The rotation of the shaft in a journal bearing causes pumping of the lubricant, circulating around the bearing (Fig. 8.8.3), of which $z = 0$ is taken at the bearing middle in the axial direction. After the load is applied, the lubricant is squeezed through the wedge-shaped gap producing hydrodynamic pressure. Friction resistance in hydrodynamic bearings is a function of lubricant viscosity and shear rate. Shear rate increases with increasing rotating speed or decreasing film thickness. The coefficient of friction is usually less than 0.001.

8.9.1 Reynolds Equation for Lubricant Film

Under laminar and isothermal flow conditions, the narrow gap assumption for hydrodynamic lubrication can be utilized for simplifying Navies-Stokes equations to Reynolds equation as

$$\frac{\partial}{R_j^2 \partial \theta}\left[\frac{\rho\, h^3}{\mu_d}\left(\frac{\partial P}{\partial \theta}\right)\right] + \frac{\partial}{\partial z}\left[\frac{\rho\, h^3}{\mu_d}\left(\frac{\partial P}{\partial z}\right)\right] = \frac{6\,\hat{h}}{R_j}\left[\frac{\partial(\rho\, U)}{\partial \theta}\right] - \frac{6U}{R_j}\left[\frac{\partial(\rho\hat{h})}{\partial \theta}\right] + 12\frac{\partial(\rho\hat{h})}{\partial t} \quad (8.9.1)$$

where

$h(\theta, z)$: Nominal lubricant film thickness or mean lubricant film thickness;

$\hat{h}$: Local film thickness including the effect of surface roughness;

r, θ, z: Polar coordinates in radial, angular and axial directions, respectively;

R_j: Journal radius of rotating shaft;

μ_d: Lubricating film viscosity;

ρ: Density of lubricant;

U: Peripheral tangential velocity, $U = \omega R_j$; where ω is the rotating speed of the shaft;

P: Lubricating film pressure, $P = P(\theta, z)$;

t: Time.

The 2nd term of Eq. (8.9.1) means squeezing of the fluid in the axial direction. Angle φ (Fig. 8.9.1) is called attitude angle, which is the angle between x-axis (vertical axis) and line $O_s - O_b$ (shaft center-to-bearing center line). Nominal film thicknesses, $h(\theta)$ and $h_T(\theta)$, can be expressed as

$$h(\theta) = c + e \cos \theta = c\left[1 + e_c \cos \theta\right] \quad (8.9.2)$$

and $\quad h_T(\theta) = c + e \cos \theta + \delta_x \sin(\theta + \varphi) - \delta_y \cos(\theta + \varphi)$

$$= c\left[1 + e_c \cos \theta\right] + \delta_x \sin(\theta + \varphi) - \delta_y \cos(\theta + \varphi) \quad (8.9.3)$$

where

$h(\theta)$: Film thickness due to fluid pressure only;

$h_T(\theta)$: Film thickness due to fluid pressure and bearing deformation;

c: Radial clearance between the aligned shaft and bearing under no load, $c = R_b - R_j$;

R_b: Radius of bearing;

e: Eccentricity and $e = e(t)$, i.e., function of time;

e_c: eccentricity ratio;

δ_x: Elastic-deformation amount of bearing surface in x-direction;

δ_y: Elastic-deformation amount of bearing surface in y-direction;

θ: Angular position as film pressure develops.

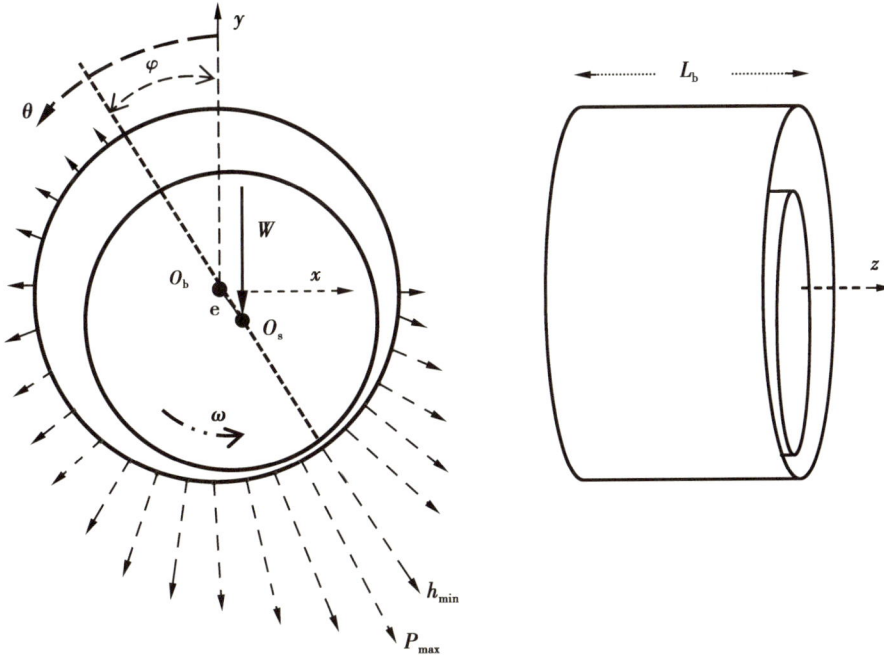

Fig. 8.9.1   Hydrodynamic Pressure of a Journal Bearing in Operation

Note that the dimensionless eccentric ratio is defined as

$$e_c \equiv \frac{e}{c} \tag{8.9.4}$$

The amounts of elastic deformations δ_x and δ_y are to be calculated using the finite element method, as the bearing is divided into numerous 3-dimensional solid elements. The total amount of compression (deformation) is

$$\delta = (\delta_x^2 + \delta_y^2)^{\frac{1}{2}} \tag{8.9.5}$$

where

δ: Radial elastic compression (deformation) along line O_b–O_s.

For oil lubricant, it is reasonable to assume that the nominal film thickness (i.e., no deformation of parts in contact), ρ and μ_d are independent of r, θ, z, and t. Thus, the Reynolds equation for an incompressible laminar flow without taking the surface roughness into consideration reduces to

$$\frac{\partial}{R_j^2 \, \partial \theta} \left[\frac{h^3}{\mu_d} \left(\frac{\partial P}{\partial \theta} \right) \right] + \frac{\partial}{\partial z} \left[\frac{h^3}{\mu_d} \left(\frac{\partial P}{\partial z} \right) \right] = 6h \left(\frac{\partial U}{\partial \theta} \right) - 6\omega \left(\frac{\partial h}{\partial \theta} \right) + 12 \left(\frac{\partial h}{\partial t} \right) \tag{8.9.6}$$

The three terms on the right-hand side of the above equation contributing to the hydrodynamic pressure have their physical attributes, respectively as

(1) $6h(\partial U/\partial\theta)$: Tangential velocity variation circumferentially.

(2) $6U(\partial h/\partial\theta)$: Wedge effect circumferentially.

(3) $12(\partial h/\partial t)$: Speed of squeezing lubricant film.

8.9.2　Tangential Speed U_x

The tangential and normal speeds of a point around on the journal can be formulated, respectively, as

$$U_x = \omega R_j + \left(\frac{de}{dt}\right) \sin\theta - e\left(\frac{d\varphi}{dt}\right)\cos\theta$$

$$= \omega R_j + C\sin\theta\left(\frac{de_c}{dt}\right) - C e_c \cos\theta\left(\frac{d\varphi}{dt}\right) \tag{8.9.7}$$

$$U_y = \omega\left(\frac{\partial h}{\partial\theta}\right) + \left(\frac{de}{dt}\right)\cos\theta + e\left(\frac{d\varphi}{dt}\right)\sin\theta$$

$$= \omega\left(\frac{\partial h}{\partial\theta}\right) + c\cos\theta\left(\frac{de_c}{dt}\right) + c e_c \sin\theta\left(\frac{d\varphi}{dt}\right) \tag{8.9.8}$$

Substituting Eqs. (8.9.4), (8.9.7), and (8.9.8) into Eq. (8.9.6), one has [Flores et al.]

$$\frac{\partial}{R_j^2 \partial\theta}\left[\frac{h^3}{\mu_d}\left(\frac{\partial P}{\partial\theta}\right)\right] + \frac{\partial}{\partial z}\left[\frac{h^3}{\mu_d}\left(\frac{\partial P}{\partial z}\right)\right] = 12c\left[\left(\frac{de_c}{dt}\right)\cos\theta + e_c\left(\frac{d\varphi}{dt} - \omega\right)\sin\theta\right] \tag{8.9.9}$$

8.9.3　Eccentricity Ratio and Attitude Angle

Time derivatives of both eccentricity ratio E and attitude angle φ can be obtained according to the mobility method provided by [Booker]. They are given here without a detailed derivation in Sections 8.9.3.1 and 8.9.3.2.

8.9.3.1　$W > 0$ (Downwards)

$$\frac{de_c}{dt} = \frac{2c^2 W}{\mu_d \pi^2 R_j L^3}[\pi\cos\varphi(1 - e_c\cos\varphi)^{\frac{5}{2}} + 4e_c\sin\varphi(1 - e_c\cos\varphi)^{\frac{3}{2}}] \tag{8.9.10}$$

and

$$\frac{d\varphi}{dt} - \omega = \frac{2c^2 W}{\mu_d \pi^2 R_j L^3}[-\pi\sin\varphi(1 - e_c\cos\varphi)^{\frac{5}{2}} + 4e_c\sin\varphi(1 - e_c\cos\varphi)^{\frac{3}{2}}]$$

$$\tag{8.9.11}$$

The above two simultaneous linear first-order differential equations can be solved numerically using such as Runge-Kutta method for the two unknowns E and φ.

8.9.3.2 $W < 0$ (Upwards)

$$\frac{\mathrm{d}e_c}{\mathrm{d}t} = \frac{2c^2 \, W}{\mu_d \, \pi^2 \, R_j \, L^3} [\,\pi \cos \varphi \,(1 + e_c \cos \varphi)^{\frac{5}{2}} + 4e_c \sin \varphi (1 + e_c \cos \varphi)^{\frac{3}{2}}] \qquad (8.9.12)$$

and $\quad \dfrac{\mathrm{d}\varphi}{\mathrm{d}t} - \omega = \dfrac{2c^2 \, W}{\mu_d \, \pi^2 \, R_j \, L^3} [\, -\pi \sin \varphi (1 + e_c \cos \varphi)^{\frac{5}{2}} + 4e_c \sin \varphi (1 + e_c \cos \varphi)^{\frac{3}{2}}]$

$$(8.9.13)$$

Again, the above two simultaneous linear first-order differential equations can be solved numerically using such as Runge-Kutta method for the two unknowns E and φ.

8.9.4   Force Components Resulting from Hydrodynamic Pressure

Load carried by the hydrodynamic pressure can be obtained by integrating the pressure distribution circumferentially first and then integrating the resultant axially. The two force components along and perpendicular to the attitude axis $(O_s - O_b)$ are respectively formulated as follows :

$$F_E = -\int_{-\frac{1}{2}L_b}^{\frac{1}{2}L_b} \left(\int_{\theta_i}^{\theta_o} P \, R_j \cos \theta_o \mathrm{d}\theta \right) \theta \, \mathrm{d}z \qquad \text{(Radially)} \qquad (8.9.14)$$

$$F_\varphi = -\int_{-\frac{1}{2}L_b}^{\frac{1}{2}L_b} \left(\int_{\theta_i}^{\theta_o} P \, R_j \sin \theta \, \mathrm{d}\theta \right) \theta \, \mathrm{d}z \qquad \text{(Circumferentially)} \qquad (8.9.15)$$

of which L_b is the bearing length. Through proper coordinate transformations, the forces in the (x, y, z) coordinates can be obtained as

$$F_x = F_E \cos \varphi - F_\varphi \sin \varphi \qquad\qquad\qquad (8.9.16)$$

$$F_y = F_E \cos \varphi + F_\varphi \sin \varphi \qquad\qquad\qquad (8.9.17)$$

8.9.5   Boundary Conditions

The above partial differential equation is not easy to solve. In case the journal bearing is of finite length, numerical analysis (e.g. finite element method) is recommended for calculating the hydrodynamic pressure. Boundary conditions along the z-axis are given as follows :

$$P = 0 \qquad \text{at } z = \pm \frac{1}{2} L_b \qquad\qquad\qquad (8.9.18)$$

and $\quad \dfrac{\partial P}{\partial z} = 0 \quad$ at $z = 0$ $\hfill (8.9.19)$

Assume that there is no slip at boundaries. The two boundary conditions of fluid flow velocities in response to the rotating speed of the shaft are given as follows:

$$U_x = U_b \text{ at the bearing bushing for } -\frac{1}{2}L_b \leqslant z \leqslant \frac{1}{2}L_b \hfill (8.9.20)$$

and $\quad U_x = U_j$ at the shaft journal for $\dfrac{1}{2}L_b \leqslant z \leqslant \dfrac{1}{2}L_b$ $\hfill (8.9.21)$

$U_b = 0$ at a stationary bearing bushing. The analytic solution to Eq. (8.9.6) for the region of positive pressure area, denoted by the pressure arrows directed outwards in Fig. 8.8.3, exists for two special cases: (a) infinitely long bearing and (b) significantly short bearing.

8.10　Infinitely Long Plain Bearings

Given an infinitely long bearing, lubricant flow in the axial direction is neglected. Sommerfeld solution applies and it is valid for a length-to-diameter ratio of 2 or more. Thus, the second term on the left-hand side of Eq. (8.9.9) is neglected, as a result, it reduces to

$$\frac{\partial}{R_j^2 \, \partial \theta} \left[\frac{h^3}{\mu_d} \left(\frac{\partial P}{\partial \theta} \right) \right] = 12c \left[\left(\frac{\mathrm{d}e_c}{\mathrm{d}t} \right) \cos \theta + e_c \left(\frac{\mathrm{d}\varphi}{\mathrm{d}t} - \omega \right) \sin \theta \right] \hfill (8.10.1)$$

8.10.1　Hydrodynamic Pressure on Infinitely Long Bearings

The pressure in the axial direction is constant, but its buildup varies in the circumferential direction [Flores et al.]. Eq. (8.10.1) can be solved using the boundary conditions prescribed by Eqs. (8.9.18) and (8.9.19) for

$$P(\theta) = \frac{6 \mu_d R_j^2}{c^2} \left\{ \frac{\dfrac{\mathrm{d}e_c}{\mathrm{d}t}}{e_c} \left[\frac{1}{(1 + e_c \cos \theta)^2} - \frac{1}{(1 + e_c)^2} \right] + \right.$$

$$\left. \frac{\left[\omega - \dfrac{\mathrm{d}\varphi}{\mathrm{d}t} \right] e_c \sin \theta \, (2 + e_c \cos \theta)}{(2 + e_c^2)(1 + e_c \cos \theta)^2} \right\} + P_o \hfill (8.10.2)$$

8.10.2 Integration Limits along the Circumferential Direction

The applicable pressure for calculating forces is assumably located between $0 \leqslant \theta \leqslant \pi$ for a journal bearing running in the steady state, as named Gumbel's boundary conditions:

$$\theta_i = 0 \tag{8.10.3}$$

and $\quad \theta_o = \theta_i + \pi = \pi \tag{8.10.4}$

8.10.3 Force Components for Infinitely Long Bearings

For the infinitely long bearing, Sommerfeld solution for a full film applies. The force components can be obtained by integration [Frene et al.] [Machado et al.] based on Eqs. (8.9.14) and (8.8.14), respectively as

$$F_E = \frac{12\pi \mu_d R_j^3 L_b}{c^2 (1 - e_c^2)^{\frac{3}{2}}} \left(\frac{de_c}{dt} \right) \tag{8.10.5}$$

and $\quad F_\varphi = \dfrac{12\pi \mu_d R_j^3 L_b e_c}{c^2 (2 + e_c^2)(1 - e_c^2)^{\frac{1}{2}}} \left(\omega - \dfrac{d\varphi}{dt} \right) \tag{8.10.6}$

8.11 Significantly Short Plain Bearings

For a significantly short bearing, Ocvirk solution may be applied. The axial flow (including the end leakage) is the major portion of the total flow change. There is no circumferential pressure gradient. After the first term is omitted and Eq. (8.9.9) reduces to

$$\frac{\partial}{\partial z} \left[\frac{h^3}{\mu_d} \left(\frac{\partial P}{\partial z} \right) \right] = 12c \left[\left(\frac{de_c}{dt} \right) \cos \theta + e_c \left(\frac{d\varphi}{dt} - \omega \right) \sin \theta \right] \tag{8.11.1}$$

8.11.1 Hydrodynamic Pressure on Signifcantly Short Plain Bearings

Eq. (8.10.7) can be solved for the pressure distribution by integration using the boundary conditions prescribed by Eqs. (8.9.18) and (8.9.19), as

$$P(\theta, z) = \frac{6 c \mu_d}{h^3} \left[\left(\frac{de_c}{dt} \right) \cos \theta + \left(\frac{d\varphi}{dt} - \omega \right) e_c \sin \theta \right] \left(z^2 - \frac{1}{4} L_b^2 \right) \tag{8.11.2}$$

The above equation is good for short bearings, of which $0.5 < L_b/R_j < 1.5$ is the application range.

8.11.2   Integration Limits along the Circumferential Direction

Since no negative pressure is accepted, the integration is taken around the half circle only. According to Eq. (8.9.9), $P(\theta, z)$ is always positive if the following condition is satisfied

$$\theta_i = \tan^{-1} \frac{\dfrac{\mathrm{d}e_c}{\mathrm{d}t}}{e_c\left(\omega - \dfrac{\mathrm{d}\varphi}{\mathrm{d}t}\right)} \tag{8.11.3}$$

and $\theta_o = \theta_i + \pi$ \hfill (8.11.4)

8.11.3   Force Components for Significantly Short Plain Bearings

For a significantly short bearing, Sommerfeld solution for a full film applied, the force components are [Frene et al.] [Machado et al.], respectively

$$F_E = \frac{\pi \, \mu_d \, R_j \, L_b^3 (1 + 2e_c^2)}{c^2 (1 - e_c^2)^{\frac{5}{2}}} \left(\frac{\mathrm{d}e_c}{\mathrm{d}t}\right) \tag{8.11.5}$$

$$F_\varphi = \frac{\pi \, \mu_d \, R_j \, L_b^3 \, e_c}{2c^2 (1 - e_c^2)^{\frac{3}{2}}} \left(\omega - 2\frac{\mathrm{d}\varphi}{\mathrm{d}t}\right) \tag{8.11.6}$$

8.12   Elastohydrodynamic Lubrication

Adhesion of oil to the two sliding elements creates a lubricant film and increases the pressure between them. As the area of contact is very small, the unit bearing load of a roller bearing may reach 35 MPa and the ball bearing pressure may reach 70 MPa. The lubricant viscosity rises considerably to prevent the lubricant from flowing away from the wearing surfaces. The pressure is sufficient to cause the lubricant to become a pseudo solid and thus the elastic deformation of the contact zones has to be taken into consideration in the design. The generated lubricant film completely separate the two wedged surfaces under the condition of fully elastohydrodynamic lubrication.

8.12.1　Effective Surface Roughness

The roughness between the wearing surfaces is a major consideration in Elastohydrodynamic Lubrication (EHL). Roughness of a surface is here defined for bearing surfaces as the arithmetic average difference between the high and low points of a surface, called centerline average (R_a) and it is calculated using Eq. (8.7.8) or Eq. (8.7.1). The film thickness-to-surface roughness ratio is used to estimate the bearing life. A full film thickness is perceived to exist when the ratio falls between 2 and 4, under which fatigue failure is due entirely to the subsurface stress. The combined surface roughness from bearing roughness and shaft surface roughness is

$$R_c^2 = R_{a,b}^2 + R_{a,s}^2 \tag{8.12.1}$$

where

R_c: Combined roughness from bearing roughness and shaft surface roughness;

$R_{a,b}$: Surface roughness of bearing;

$R_{a,s}$: Surface roughness of shaft.

Lubrication in gear teeth, roller bearings, ball bearings, cam-follower systems, engine piston/liner interaction, or engine piston skirt/liner interaction belongs to EHL, and sometimes it is in a mixed regime combining both EHL (Elastohydrodynamic Lubrication) and BL (Boundary Lubrication).

8.12.2　Mixed Lubrication Regime and Wear in Sliding Mode

As film thickness decreases relative to surface roughness, more asperities make contact. Film thickness-to-surface roughness ratio falls between 1 and 2, under which asperities undergo stress and contribute to failure. Contact between raised surface features such as asperities may occur and thus lead to a mixed lubrication regime, i.e., a mixture of boundary and fluid lubrications as shown in Fig. 8.12.1. The bearing load W can be divided between the oil film load and the solid contact load in the mixed lubrication regime. Therefore, the load W is equal to the value obtained by integrating the oil film pressure and the solid contact pressure as

$$W = \int p \, \mathrm{d}s + \int p_c \, \mathrm{d}s \tag{8.12.2}$$

where

W: Bearing load;

p: Lubricant film pressure;

p_c: Contact pressure between solids;

s: Bearing area.

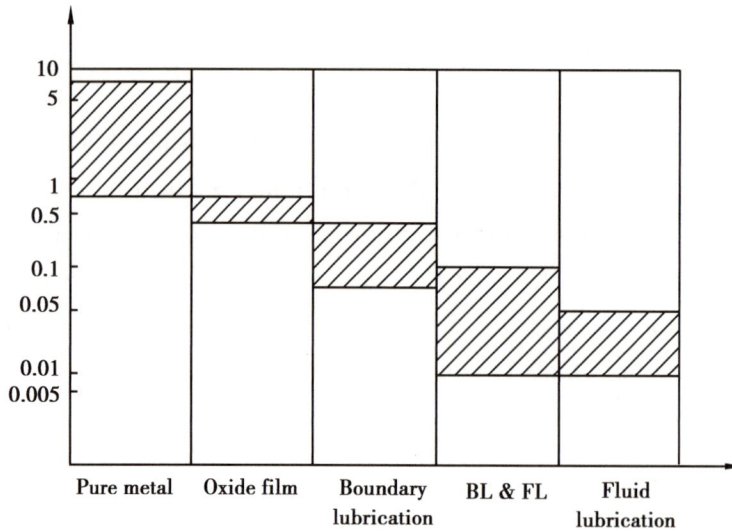

Fig. 8.12.1　Coefficient of Friction Subjected to Various Lubrication Conditions

8.12.3　Modified Reynolds Equation for Oil Film Pressure

Both dynamic viscosity μ_d and lubricant density ρ are functions of temperature and pressure. In the EHL regime, the contact pressure typically falls between 1 GPa and 3 GPa. When the Reynolds equation is incorporated with the micro-asperity effect in the mixed lubrication regime, it becomes ［Patir & Cheng］

$$\frac{\partial}{R_j^2 \, \partial\theta} \left[\phi_\theta \frac{\rho \, h^3}{\mu_d} \left(\frac{\partial P}{\partial\theta}\right) \right] + \frac{\partial}{\partial z}\left[\phi_z \frac{\rho \, h^3}{\mu_d} \left(\frac{\partial P}{\partial z}\right) \right]$$

$$= \frac{6U \, \phi_c}{R_j}\left[\frac{\partial(\rho \, \hat{h})}{\partial\theta}\right] + \frac{6UR_{rms}}{R_j}\left[\frac{\partial(\rho \, \phi_s)}{\partial\theta}\right] + 12 \, \phi_c \frac{\partial(\rho\hat{h})}{\partial t} \qquad (8.12.3)$$

where

ϕ_θ and ϕ_z: Correction factors of a pressurized flow along θ and z directions, respectively;

ϕ_s: Shear follow factor;

ϕ_c: Contact factor.

If the Reynolds equation is equipped with the oil filling and micro-asperity effect in the mixed lubrication regime, it becomes ［Patir & Cheng］

$$\frac{\partial}{R_j^2 \, \partial\theta}\left[\psi \, \phi_\theta \frac{\rho \, h^3}{\mu_d} \left(\frac{\partial P}{\partial\theta}\right) \right] + \frac{\partial}{\partial z}\left[\psi \, \phi_z \frac{\rho \, h^3}{\mu_d} \left(\frac{\partial P}{\partial z}\right) \right]$$

$$= \frac{6 \, U \, \phi_c}{R_j}\left[\frac{\partial(\psi \, \rho \, \hat{h})}{\partial\theta}\right] + 12 \, \phi_c \frac{\partial(\psi \, \rho \, \hat{h})}{\partial t} + \frac{6UR_c}{R_j}\left[\frac{\partial(\psi \, \rho \, \phi_s)}{\partial\theta}\right] \qquad (8.12.4)$$

where　ψ is the fill factor ［Krasser］ and it is defined as

$$\psi = \frac{V_{\text{lubricant}}}{V_{\text{total}}} \tag{8.12.5}$$

The film thickness due to the wedge effect of the fluid lubricant on the right-hand side of Eq. (8.12.5) will be

$$\hat{h} = \frac{1}{2}h\left[1 + \text{erf}\left(\frac{h}{2^{\frac{1}{2}} R_c} \right) + \frac{R_c}{(2\pi)^{\frac{1}{2}}} e^{-\frac{h^2}{R_c^2}} \right] \tag{8.12.6}$$

Parameters h (film thickness in hydrodynamic lubrication) and R_c (combined surface roughness) are to be derived from Eq. (8.9.2) and Eq. (8.12.2), respectively. The total film thickness in Eq. (8.9.3) is to be modified as follows:

$$h_{\text{T}}(\theta) = \hat{h} + \delta_x \sin(\theta + \varphi) - \delta_y \cos(\theta + \varphi) \tag{8.12.7}$$

If the lubricant pressure falls below its corresponding vapor pressure, "cavity bubbles" are induced. Once the bubbles collapse near/at the journal surface, localized stress (e.g. pressure) waves impinging on the solid surface will be strong enough to cause permanent plastic derogation. It is called cavitation damage. Letting P be the film pressure and $P_{\text{cavitation}}$ the cavitation pressure (i.e., vapor pressure in the cavitation region), one has the following two algorithms:

$$\text{If } P \leqslant P_{\text{cavitation}} \text{ or } \psi < 1, \text{ then } (r, z) \in \text{Cavitation Region} \tag{8.12.8}$$

$$\text{If } P > P_{\text{cavitation}} \text{ or } \psi = 1, \text{ then } (r, z) \in \text{Lubrication Region} \tag{8.12.9}$$

8.12.4 Solid Contact Regime

Solid contact pressure P_c may be calculated by applying an approximate expression based on Greenwood and Tripp's elastic contact theory for a surface roughness projection as

$$P_c = 4.4068 \times 10^{-5} k_c E_c \left(4 - \frac{\hat{h}}{R_a} \right)^{6.804} \tag{8.12.10}$$

and
$$\frac{1}{E_c} = \frac{1 - \nu_s^2}{E_s} + \frac{1 - \nu_b^2}{E_b} \tag{8.12.11}$$

where
P_c: Solid contact pressure;
k_c: Surface roughness constant according to the shape;
E_c: Composite Young's modulus combining E_s and E_b;
E_s: Modulus of elasticity of the shaft material;
E_b: Modulus of elasticity of the bearing material;

ν_s: Poisson's ratio of the shaft material;

ν_b: Poisson's ratio of the bearing material.

The friction force can be derived from the asperity contact force F_A and fluid friction f_H. As the contact condition changes, the coefficient of friction varies accordingly as shown in Fig. 8.12.1.

8.12.5　Approximate Elastohydrodynamic Lubrication Film Thickness

If the lubrication conditons are not well-known, the EHL (ElastoHydrodynamic Lubrication) film thickness between two sliding surfaces can be calculated using the following empirical equation [AGMA925] as the first approximation

$$h_c = 3.06 \left(\frac{G^{0.56} \; U^{0.69}}{W^{0.10}} \right) \tag{8.12.12}$$

where

h_c: Dimensionless central film thickness;

G: Material parameter;

U: Speed parameter;

W: Load parameter.

If the material, speed, and related load parameters are fixed, the film thickness depends on α_μ (pressure-viscosity coefficient) and μ_{d0} (dynamic viscosity under the ambient pressure and at a reference temperature) as [AGMA925]

$$h_c \propto \alpha_\mu^{0.56} \mu_{d0}^{0.69} \tag{8.12.13}$$

Example 8.12.1　The roller bearing for a gearset typically operates at 80 ℃. How much is the reliability improvement if PAO-320 (synthetic oil) or PAG-320 (synthetic oil) is used instead of the original lubricant ISO/VG-320 (mineral)?

Solution:

Rewrite Eq. (8.12.13) in a dimensionless form on the basis of the mineral oil (ISO/VG-320) as

$$\frac{h_c}{h_{c,VG}} \propto \left(\frac{\alpha_\mu}{\alpha_{\mu,VG}} \right)^{0.56} \left(\frac{\mu_{d0}}{\mu_{d0,VG}} \right)^{0.69}$$

The data of α_μ (pressure-viscosity coefficient) and μ_{d0} (dynamic viscosity) for these three lubricants are given as follows:

Parameters	$T/°C$	ISO/VG-320	PAO-320	PAG-320
$\alpha_\mu(MPa^{-1})$	50	0.021	0.013 4	0.011
	60	0.0194	0.0131	0.0105
	70	0.0182	0.0129	0.01
	80	0.0173	0.0126	0.0096
	90	0.0164	0.0124	0.0092
	100	0.0157	0.0122	0.0089
$\mu_{d0}(MPa \cdot s)$	50	159×10^{-9}	171×10^{-9}	229×10^{-9}
	60	95×10^{-9}	110.4×10^{-9}	164.6×10^{-9}
	70	60.4×10^{-9}	74.7×10^{-9}	121.8×10^{-9}
	80	40.5×10^{-9}	52.6×10^{-9}	92.4×10^{-9}
	90	28.4×10^{-9}	38.2×10^{-9}	71.7×10^{-9}
	100	20.6×10^{-9}	28.7×10^{-9}	56.7×10^{-9}

Plugging the above data into Eq. (a), one can obtain the following relative film thicknesses:

$T/°C$	ISO/VG-320	PAO-320	PAG-320
50	$h_{c,VG,50}$	$0.818h_{c,VG,50}$	$0.895h_{c,VG,50}$
60	$h_{c,VG,60}$	$0.844h_{c,VG,60}$	$0.912\ h_{c,VG,60}$
70	$h_{c,VG,70}$	$0.955h_{c,VG,70}$	$1.16h_{c,VG,70}$
80	$h_{c,VG,80}$	$1.003h_{c,VG,80}$	$1.27h_{c,VG,80}$
90	$h_{c,VG,90}$	$1.049h_{c,VG,90}$	$1.371h_{c,VG,90}$
100	$h_{c,VG,100}$	$1.092h_{c,VG,100}$	$1.463h_{c,VG,100}$

A plot of the relative film thickness of PAO-320 and PAG-320 with reference to ISO/VG-320 (mineral) as a function of temperature is given in Fig. 8.12.2.

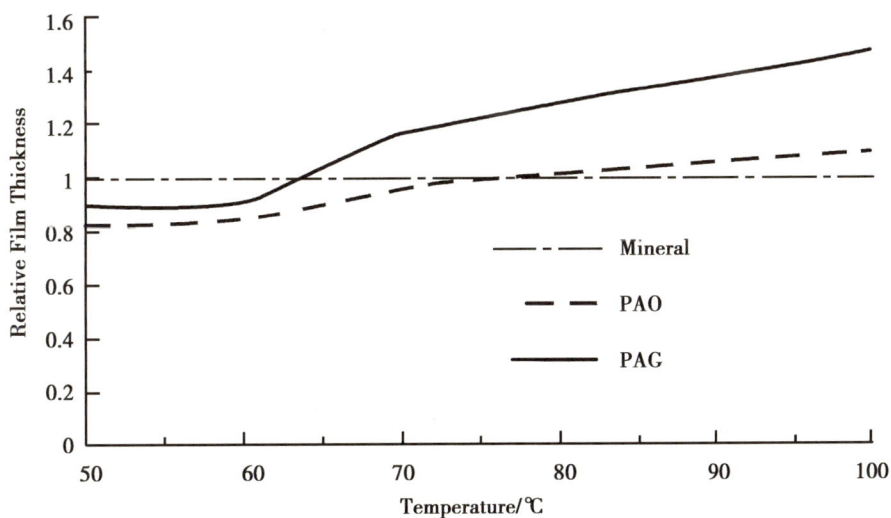

Fig. 8.12.2   Plot of Relative Film Thickness of PAO-320 and PAG-320 with Reference to ISO/VG-320 (Mineral) as a Function Temperature

According to DIN ISO 281, a 16% increase (i.e., PAG-320 versus VG-320 at 70 ℃) in the film thickness may result in a more than 400% improvement of bearing life, or specifically 129×10^3 hours with PAG-320 oil versus 31.5×10^3 hours with VG-320 oil.

A 27% increase (i.e., PAG-320 versus VG-320 at 80 ℃) in the film thickness will reduce the wear significantly. The probability of wear with PAG-320 oil is less than 5%, while 25% with a mineral oil, as addressed in AGMA 925-A03.

8.13 Thrust Bearings

Thrust bearings are designed to support predominantly axial thrust loads on rotating shafts, while journal bearings is for radial loads. A thrust bearing has two functional requirements:

(a) Preventing the shaft from drifting axially.
(b) Withstanding thrust loads.

Thrust bearings come in different varieties: ball bearings, roller bearings, fluid bearings, and magnetic bearings. The moving surface exerted against a thrust bearing is a shaft end, or a collar attached to it. Double helical and herringbone gears may help balance the thrust load.

8.13.1 Plain Thrust Bearing

A plain thrust bearing, also called thrust washer, operates like a "simple plate" operating in the mixed regime of elastohydrodynamic lubrication and boundary lubrication. Plain thrust bearings are adequate, if applied loads are light.

Separate contoured thrust washers or a flanged bearing of multi-piece assembly (usually 2 or 3 pieces) are used in heavy-duty Diesel engines to support higher thrust loads exerted by crankshafts. The bearing face of a thrust washer may have multiple tapered ramps and relatively small flat pads or curved surfaces having sine-waved contours circumferentially. Besides thrust bearings, there are two major concerns with regard to the mating crankshaft:

(a) Need of well-polished crankshaft thrust shaft ending faces.
(b) Need of crankshaft thrust shaft ending faces being well-aligned with journal axes.

8.13.2 Tilting-Pad Thrust Bearings

Tilting-pad thrust bearings are designed to take high axial loads from rotating shafts with minimum power loss. Lubricant supplied to the inside diameter of the rotating runner plate flows outwards by means of the centrifugal force. As the lubricant is dragged circumferentially in-between the runner plate and tilted pads on the stationary part, wedge effect builds up the hydrodynamic pressure because of pad tapering. Pads may be allowed to have their own ideal tilt angle custom-built for a specific need. A thrust bearing with 8 pads is shown in Fig. 8.13.1. Note that 6-, 8-, or 10-pad thrust bearings are also commercially available.

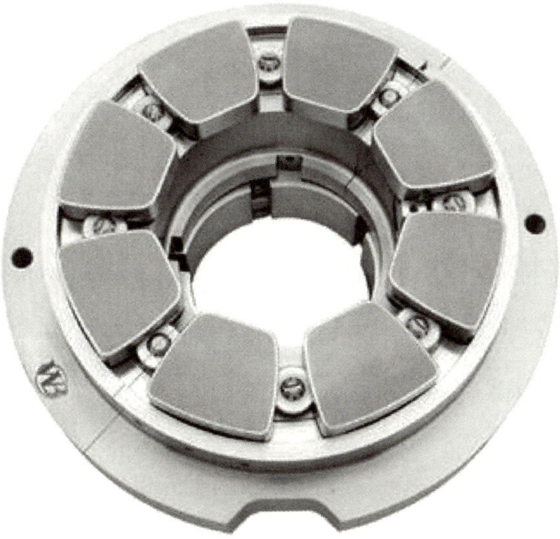

Fig. 8.13.1   Thrust Bearing Made of Eight Tilting Pads [after Waukesha Bearings]

8.13.3   Elastohydrodynamic Thrust Bearing

An elastohydrodynamic thrust bearing is a relative thin disk that has a number of repetitive segmental bearing elements, of which each has its own defining EHL (elastohydrodynamic lubrication work task. See the Kalsi thrust bearing shown in Fig. 8.13.2(a) [Kalsi Engineering]. Each bearing element is initially flat when just coming into contact with the mating plate with a minor axial thrust load. As the load increases, each bearing element deflected elastically and creates a gradual convergence between the EHL pockets. During rotation the lubricant is forced to get into the dynamic interface and generating a load-supporting wedged interfacial lubricant film, as seen in Fig. 8.13.2 (b), of which V is the circumferential velocity. Friction is typically in the range of 0.003 and 0.005 according to Kalsi Engineering. It also has high shock resistance.

The thrust bearing plate deforms and results in a wedged fluid distribution between the constrained stationary thrust plate and orbiting plate, as the axial load is applied. Additionally, the high lubricant pressure increases the deformation further and creates an elastohydrodynamic lubrication pocket at the thrust bearing [Ishii et al.].

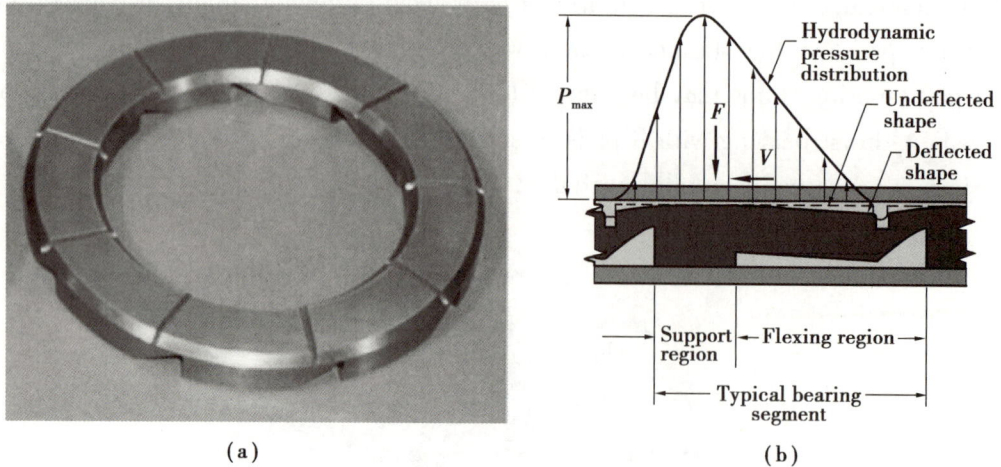

(a)   (b)

Fig. 8.13.2   Thrust Bearing Made of Nine Segments of Bearing Elements〔after Kalsi Engineering〕

8.13.4   Ball Thrust Bearing

Ball bearings are supported in a ring, generally used in applications with load axial loads.

8.13.5   Roller Thrust Bearing

Cylindrical or slight-tapered cylindrical roller bearings are arranged with their axis pointing to the axis of bearing. It has good load capacity but tends to wear out (relative to ball bearings) due to friction and non-uniformity of radial speed.

Spherical roller thrust bearings roll inside a house washer with a raceway of spherical shape often used in combination with spherical roller radial bearings. It has the highest load-capacity density among all bearings.

8.13.6   Magnetic Bearing

Magnetic force is employed to support the axial load. It is used for applications to systems of low drag at high speeds.

8.14   Thermohydrodynamic Lubrication

Friction generates heat in the lubricant. True thermohydrodynamic lubrication theory must meet both the Navier-Stokes/Reynolds equations and the heat equation. The thermal balance includes heat generation by the lubricant, the heat transfer from lubricant to the bearing walls, and heat carried away via lubricant circulation. In Cartesian coordinates system, thermal energy balance in the lubricating film leads to the following equation

$$\rho\, C_p\left[U_x\left(\frac{\partial T}{\partial x}\right) + U_y\left(\frac{\partial T}{\partial y}\right) + U_z\left(\frac{\partial T}{\partial z}\right)\right] = k\left(\frac{\partial^2 T}{\partial y^2}\right) + \mu_d\left[\left(\frac{\partial U_x}{\partial y}\right)^2 + \left(\frac{\partial U_z}{\partial y}\right)^2\right] \quad (8.14.1)$$

where

C_p: Specific heat of lubricant;

k: Thermal conductivity;

x: x-axis, along the circumference of bearing;

y: y-axis, along the oil film thickness;

z: Axial direction of the bearing;

U_x, U_y, U_z: Velocities in the axial, circumferential, and longitudinal directions.

According to experimental results that the temperature distribution over the fast revolving shaft is independent of the angular coordinate, the above equation reduces to

$$\rho\, C_p\left[U_x\left(\frac{\partial T}{\partial x}\right) + U_z\left(\frac{\partial T}{\partial z}\right)\right] = k\left(\frac{\partial^2 T}{\partial y^2}\right) + \mu_d\left[\left(\frac{\partial U_x}{\partial y}\right)^2 + \left(\frac{\partial U_z}{\partial y}\right)^2\right] \quad (8.14.2)$$

The term on the left hand side in the above equation represents the energy transfer due to convection, the first and second terms on right hand side represents the energy transfer due to conduction and energy transfer due to dissipation, respectively.

For simplicity, the temperature profile across the film thickness (y-axis) is represented by a second-order polynomial as:

$$T = a_0 + a_1 T + a_2 T^2 \quad (8.14.3)$$

The three constants, a_0, a_1 and a_2 can be obtained using the following three boundary conditions:

(a) $T = T_j$ when $y = 0$ (On the outer surface of the shaft)   (8.14.4)

(b) $T = T_b$ when $y = h$ (On the inner surface of the bearing)   (8.14.5)

(c) $T_m = \dfrac{\displaystyle\int_0^h T\mathrm{d}y}{h}$ (Averaged temperature, from 0 to h)   (8.14.6)

Substituting Eqs. (8.14.4)-(8.14.6) into Eq. (8.14.3) leads to

$$T = T_j - (4T_j + 2T_b - 6T_m)\left(\frac{y}{h}\right) + (3T_j + 3T_b - 6T_m)\left(\frac{y}{h}\right)^2 \quad (8.14.7)$$

Then substituting Eq. (8.14.7) into Eq. (8.14.3) yields

$$(6 \, T_{\mathrm{b}} + 6 \, T_{\mathrm{j}} - 12 \, T_{\mathrm{m}}) - \frac{\rho \, C_{\mathrm{p}} \, h^4}{120 \, k \, \mu_{\mathrm{d}}} \left[\frac{\partial p}{\partial x} \left(\frac{\partial T_{\mathrm{b}}}{\partial x} + \frac{\partial T_{\mathrm{j}}}{\partial x} - 12 \frac{\partial T_{\mathrm{m}}}{\partial x} \right) + \right.$$

$$\left. \frac{\partial p}{\partial z} \left(\frac{\partial T_{\mathrm{b}}}{\partial z} + \frac{\partial T_{\mathrm{j}}}{\partial z} - 12 \frac{\partial T_{\mathrm{m}}}{\partial z} \right) \right] + \frac{h^4}{12 \, k \, \mu_{\mathrm{d}}} \left[\left(\frac{\partial p}{\partial x} \right)^2 + \left(\frac{\partial p}{\partial z} \right)^2 \right] -$$

$$\frac{\rho \, C_{\mathrm{p}} \, h^2 (U_{\mathrm{b}} + U_{\mathrm{j}})}{2k} \left(\frac{\partial T_{\mathrm{m}}}{\partial x} \right) - \frac{\rho \, C_{\mathrm{p}} \, h^2 (U_{\mathrm{b}} - U_{\mathrm{j}})}{12k} \left(\frac{\partial T_{\mathrm{b}}}{\partial x} - \frac{\partial T_{\mathrm{j}}}{\partial x} \right) +$$

$$\frac{\mu_{\mathrm{d}} (U_{\mathrm{b}} - U_{\mathrm{j}})^2}{k} = 0 \tag{8.14.8}$$

The lubricant temperature at the inlet can be used for the initial values of T_{b} and T_{j}. The heat transfer within the bearing is governed by the following thermal conduction as

$$\rho \, C_{\mathrm{pb}} \left(\frac{\partial T}{\partial t} \right) = K \, \Delta T \tag{8.14.9}$$

As the temperature distribution over the fast revolving shaft is independent of the angular coordinate, Eq. (8.10.9) can be rewritten in the polar coordinate system without considering the variation around the circumference (θ-axis) as

$$\rho \, C_{\mathrm{pb}} \left(\frac{\partial T}{\partial t} \right) = k \left[\frac{\partial \left(\frac{\partial T}{\partial r} \right)}{r \, \partial r} + \frac{1}{r^2} \left(\frac{\partial^2 T}{\partial r^2} \right) + \left(\frac{\partial^2 T}{\partial z^2} \right) \right] \tag{8.14.10}$$

Considering the steady-state heat transfer only, i.e., $\partial T / \partial t = 0$, the above equation reduces to

$$\left(\frac{1}{r} \right) \frac{\partial \left(\frac{\partial T}{\partial r} \right)}{\partial r} + \frac{1}{r^2} \left(\frac{\partial^2 T}{\partial r^2} \right) + \left(\frac{\partial^2 T}{\partial z^2} \right) = 0 \tag{8.14.11}$$

Energy balance equation Eq. (8.14.8) and heat-conduction equation Eq. (8.14.11), in combination with Reynolds equation or pressure-distribution equations calculated using Reynolds equation, can be resolved numerically using finite element or finite different methods for the coupled solution.

8.15 Finite Element Methods for Lubrication

A method based on a combination of the Eulerian and Lagrangian formulation has been developed, called Arbitrary Lagrangian-Eulerian formulation (ALE) that offers freedom in moving the computational mesh and large distortions of the fluid continuum and can be handled with high resolution and accuracy. Nodes either follow the continuum as in the Lagrangian description, are fixed as in Eulerian description or move arbitrarily to get continuously rezoning capability. The result is a computational mesh that can avoid large mesh distortion with good resolution.

References

ACARY V, et al, 2011. A Formulation of the Linear Discrete Coulomb Friction Problem via Convex Optimization[J]. Journal of Applied Mathematics and Mechanics, 91(2): 155-175.

AGMA 925-A03, 2003. Effect of Lubrication on Gear Distress Surface, AGMA.

ARGYRIS J, LAXANDER A, SZIMMAT J, 1992. Petrov-Galerkin Finite Element Approach to Coupled Heat and Fluid-Flow[J]. Computer Methods in Applied Mechanics and Engineering, 94(2): 181-200.

ALLMATER H, et al, 2011. Predicting Friction Reliably and Accurately in Journal Bearings: A Systematic Validation of Simulation Results with Experimental Measurements[J]. Tribology International, 44(10): 1151-1160.

BA L, HE Z, GUO L, et al, 2015. Piston Ring-Cylinder Liner Tribology Investigation in Mixed Lubrication Regime: Part I - Correlation with Bench Experiment[J]. Industrial Lubrication and Tribology, 67(6): 520-530.

BAIR S, 2001. The Variation of Viscosity with Temperature and Pressure for Various Real Lubricants[J]. Journal of Tribology, 123(2): 433- 437.

BAJAJ M, et al, 2006. Multiscale Simulation of Viscoelastic Free Surface Flows[J]. Journal of Non-Newtonian Fluid Mechanics, 140(1-3): 87-107.

BRAUNOVIC M, KONCHITS V, MYSHKIN N, 2006. Fundamentals of Electrical Contacts[M]. Taylor & Francis Group, LLC, London, UK.

BARUS C, 1893. Isothermals, Isopiestics and Isometrics Relative to Viscosity[J]. American Journal of Science, 45: 87-96.

BIGONI D, NOSELLI G, 2011. Experimental Evidence of Flutter and Divergence Instability Induced by Dry Friction[J]. Journal of Mechanics and Physics of Solids, 59(10): 2208-2226.

BOLANDER N W, et al, 2005. Lubrication Regime Transitions at the Piston Ring-Cylinder Liner Interface[J]. Journal of Engineering Tribology, 219(1): 19-31.

BROSTOW W, CHONKAEW W, MENARD K. 2006. Connection between Dynamic Mechanical Properties and Sliding Wear Resistance of Polymers[J]. Materials Research Innovations, 10(4): 389-393.

BRUCE W R, 2012. Handbook of Lubrication and Tribology, Volume Ⅱ: Theory and Design[M]. 2nd Edition, CRC Press.

BUZZELLI, D, 2008. Calculating Friction in One Step[J]. Machine Design, June 19: 54-55.

CHANG W, ETSION I, BOGU D, 1988. Static Friction Coefficient Model for Metallic Rough Surface[J]. Journal of Tribology, 110: 57.

CHAUHAN A, SEHGAL R, SHARMA R K, 2011. Investigations on the Thermal Effects in Non-Circular Journal Bearings[J]. Tribology International, 44: 1765-1773.

CHUN S M, 2002. A Parametric Study on Bubbly Lubrication of High-Speed Journal Bearings[J]. Tribology International, 37: 1-13.

DAY S W, et al, 2003. Effect of Reynolds Number on Performance of a Small Centrifugal Pump[J]. Proceedings of FEDSM'03, Honolulu, Hawaii, USA, July 6-11.

DOWSON D, HIGGINSON G R, 1966. Elastohydrodynamic Lubrication: The Fundamentals of Roller and Gear Lubrication[M]. Pergamon, Oxford.

ELROD H G, 1981. A Cavitation Algorithm[J]. Journal of Lubrication Technology, 103(3): 350-354.

ERDEMIR A, DONNET C, 2006. Tribology of Diamond-Like Carbon Films: Recent Progress and Future Prospects[J]. Journal of Physics, D, Applied Physics, 39: R311-R327.

FELHOSI D, et al, 2008. Viscoelastic Characterization of an EPDM Rubber and Finite Element Simulation of Its Dry Rolling Friction[J]. Express Polymer Letters, 2(3): 157-164.

FEYZULLAH E, ŞAFFAK Z, 2008. The Tribological Behavior of Different Engineering Plastics under Dry Friction Conditions[J]. Materials and Design, 29: 205-211.

FLORES P, et al, 2006. Journal of Bearings Subjected to Dynamic Loads: The Analytic Mobility Method[J]. Mechanica Experimental, Vol. 13: 115-127.

FRENE J, et al, 1997. Hydrodynamic Lubrication: Bearings and Thrust Bearings[M]. Elsevier, Amsterdam, the Netherlands.

FULLER D D, 1984. Theory and Practice of Lubrication for Engineers[M]. Wiley-Interscience, NY.

GAWARKIEWICZ R, WASILCZUK M, 2007. Wear Measurements of Self-Lubricating Bearing Materials in Small Oscillatory Movement[J]. Wear, 263: 458-462.

GIVENS W, MICHAEL P, 2003. Fuels and Lubricants Handbook [C]. Edited by Totten, G., ASTM International.

GREENWOOD J A, WILLIAMSON J B P, 1966. Contact of Nominally Flat Surfaces[J]. Proceedings of the Royal Society of London, A, Vol. 295: 300-319.

GREENWOOD J A, TRIPP J H, 1970. The Contact of Nominally Flat Rough Surface[J]. Proc Inst Mech. Engr., Vol. 185: 625-633.

GROISS S, et al, 1996. Parameters of Lossy Cavity Resonators Calculated by the Finite Element Method[J]. IEEE Transactions on Magnetics, 32: 894.

GU X, TSANG L, BRAUNISCH H, 2007. Modeling Effects of Random Rough Interface on Power Absorption between Dielectric and Conductive Medium in 3-D Problem[J]. IEEE Transactions on Microwave Theory and Techniques, 55: 51.

HERZ H, 1881. On the Contact of Elastic Solids[J]. J. Reine Angnew Math., 92: 156-171.

HIRAYAM T, et al, 2006. Numerical Analysis for Mixed Lubrication in Journal Bearings of Rotary Compressors[C]. Internal Compressor Engineering Conference, July 17-20, Purdue University, IN, USA.

HOLM R, 1999. Electric Contacts: Theory and Applications[M]. 4th Edition, Springer, Berlin, Germany.

HOLMBERG K, ANDERSSON P, ERDEMIR A, 2012. Global Energy Consumption due to Friction in Passenger Cars[J]. Tribology International, 47: 221-234.

HORN Ⅲ A F, et al, 2010. Effect of Conductor Profile on the Insertion Loss, Phase Constant, and Dispersion in Thin High Frequency Transmission Lines[C]. DesignCon 2010, Santa Clara, CA.

HYMAN D, MEHREGANY M, 1999. Contact Physics of Gold Microcontacts for MEMS Switches[J]. IEEE Transactions on Components, Packaging, and Manufacturing Technology, 22: 357-364.

ISHII N, et al, 2012. Elasto-Hydrodynamic Lubrication Effect in Thrust-Slide Bearings of Scroll Compressors[C]. International Compressor Conference, Paper 2125, Purdue University, IN.

JACKSON R L, GREEN I, 2011. On the Modeling of Elastic Contact between Rough Surfaces[J]. Tribology Transactions, 54: 300-314.

JANG Y H, BARBER J R, 2003. Effect of Contact Statistics on Electrical Contact Resistance[J]. Journal of Applied Physics, 94: 7215.

JANNA W S, 1993. Introduction to Fluid Mechanics[M]. 3rd Edition, PWS-Kent, Boston, MA, USA.

JIA J H, et al, 2003. A Comparative Investigation of the Friction and Wear Behavior of Polyamide Composites under Dry Sliding and Water-Lubricated Condition[J]. Materials Science and Engineering, A356: 48-53.

JIA N, KAGAN V, 2001. Mechanical Performance of Polyamides with Influence of Moisture and Temperature-

Accurate Evaluation and Better Understanding[J]. Plastic Design Library (PDL)-Plastics Failure: Analysis and Prevention: 95-104, New York.

JOST H P, 2005. Tribology Micro Macro Economics: A Road to Economic Savings [J]. Tribology and Lubrication Technology, 61(10): 18-22.

KHEDKAR J, NEGULESCU I, MELETIS E, 2002. Sliding Wear Behavior of PTFE Composites[J]. Wear, 252: 361-369.

KIM B J, KIM K W, 2001. Thermo-Elastohydrodynamic Analysis of Connecting Rod Bearing in Internal Combustion Engine[J]. Journal of Tribology, 123: 444-454.

KNEZEVIC D, SAVIC V, 2006. Mathematical Modeling of Changing of Dynamic Viscosity, As a Function of Temperature and Pressure, of Mineral Oils for Hydraulic Systems [J]. Facta Universitatis, Mechanical Engineering, 4(1): 27-34.

KRASSER J, 1996. Thermo-Elasto-Hydrodynamic Analysis of Dynamically Loaded Journal Bearings [D]. Technology University of Graz.

LANCASTER J K, 1973. Dry Bearings: A Survey of Materials and Factors Affecting Their Performance[J]. Tribology: 219-251.

LANCASTER, J K. 1967. The Influence of Substrate Hardness on the Formation and Endurance of Molybdenum Disulphide Films[J]. Wear, 10: 103-117.

LIGTERINK D J, DEGEE A W, 1996. Measurement of Wear in Radial Journal Bearings[J]. Tribotest Journal, 3(1), September: 45-54.

LIU H, et al, 2010. Lubrication Analysis of Journal Bearing and Rotor System Using CFD and FSI Techniques[J]. Advanced Tribology: 40-41.

LUGT P M, MORALES-ESPEJEL G E, 2011. A Review of Elasto-Hydrodynamic Lubrication Theory [J]. Tribology Transactions, 54(3): 470-496.

LUKIE M V, FILIPOVIC D S, 2007. Modeling of 3-D Surface Roughness Effects with Application to μ-Coaxial Lines[J]. IEEE Transactions on Microwave Theory and Techniques: 518.

LUNDGREN J, GUDMUNDSON P, 1998. A Model for Moisture Absorption in Cross-Ply Composite Laminates with Cracks[J]. Journal of Composite Materials, 32(24).

LUO H, et al, 2001. Graphite Friction Coefficient for Various Conditions[J]. Science in China, Series A, Vol. 44: 248-252.

MACHADO M, et al, 2012. The Effect of the Lubricated Revolute Joint Parameters and Hydrodynamic Force

Models on the Dynamic Response of Planar Multibody Systems[J]. Nonlinear Dynamics, 69(1-2): 635-654.

MADHUSUDANA C V, 1999. Thermal Contact Conductance[M]. Springer-Verlag, New York.

MANGLIK R M, FANG P, 2001. Thermal Processing of Viscous Non-Newtonian Fluids in Annular Ducts: Effects of Power-Law Rheology, Duct Eccentricity, and Thermal Boundary Conditions[J]. International Journal of Heat and Mass Transfer, 45(4): 803-814.

MCCOOL J I, 1987. Relating Profile Instrument Measurements to the Functional Performance of Rough Surfaces [J]. Journal of Tribology, 109(2): 264-270.

MENS J, DEGEE A, 1991. Friction and Wear Behavior of 18 Polymers in Contact with Steel in Environments of Air and Water[J]. Wear, 149: 255-268.

MOLEWYK M, et al, 2014. In Situ Control of Lubricant Properties for Reduction of Power Cylinder Friction through Thermal Barrier Coating[J]. SAE 2014-01-1659.

MORGAN S P, 1949. Effect of Surface Roughness on Eddy Current Losses at Microwave Frequencies[J]. Journal of Applied Physics, 20: 352-362.

MULLER Q E, et al, 2008. Simulation of Dry and Lubricated Contacts in Multi-Body Systems[J]. Mécanique and Industries, 01/2008.

NAHM A H, BAMBERGER E N, 1980. Rolling Contact Fatigue Life of AISI M50 as a Function of Specific Film Thickness Ratio Using a High Speed Rolling Contact Rig[J]. Transactions of ASME International, 102: 534-538.

NAKAI A, IKEGAKI S, HAMADA H, et al, 2000. Degradation of Braided Composites in Hot Water[J]. Composites Science and Technology, 60: 325-331.

NAKAMURA K, et al, 2003. Influence of Intersecting Angles of Strands on Contact Resistance in Cable-in-Conduit Conductors[J]. IEEE Transactions on Applied Superconductivity, 13: 2392-2395.

NAKAMURA K, et al, 2007. Effects of Compressive Force between Strands on Contact Resistance in Cable-in-Conduit Conductors[J]. IEEE Transactions on Applied Superconductivity, 17: 2466-2469.

NEISSEL A, et al, 2013. Journal Bearings Lubrication Aspect Analysis Using Non-Newtonian Fluids[J]. Advances in Tribology, Article ID 212568, 9.

OGURI K, ARAI M, 1992. Two Different Low Friction Mechanisms of Diamond-like Carbon with Silicon Coating Formed by Plasma-Assisted Chemical Vapor Deposition[J]. Journal of Materials Research, 7(6): 1313-1316.

PADIR N, Cheng H S, 1979. Application of Average Flow Model to Lubrication between Rough Sliding Surfaces[J]. Journal of Lubrication Technology, ASME, 101: 220-230.

PAVAL V M K, RICHARD L, MIKHAIL S, 2006. Arbitrary Lagrangian-Eulerian （ALE） Methods in Compressible Fluid Dynamics[J]. Programs and Algorithms of Numerical Mathematics, 13: 178-183.

PIRRO D M, WESSOL A A, 2001. Lubrication Fundamentals[M]. 2nd Edition, Marcel Dekker, New York, NY.

PRIESTNER C, et al, 2012. Refined Simulation of Friction Power Loss in Crank Shaft Slider Bearings Considering Wear in the Mixed Lubrication Regime[J]. Tribology International, 46(1): 200-207.

PRITZKAU D, SIEMANN R, 2002. Experimental Study of RF Pulsed Heating on Oxygen Free Electronic Copper[J]. Phys. Rev. ST Accel. Beams, 5, 112002.

REYNOLDS O, 1886. On the Theory of Lubrication and Its Applications to Mr. Beauchamp Tower's Experiments, Including an Experimental Determination of Viscosity of Oliver Oil [J]. Philosophical Transactions of the Royal Society of London, 177: 157-234.

ROBERSON J, CROWE C, 1993. Engineering Fluid Mechanics[M]. 5th Edition, Houghton Mifflin, Boston, MA, USA.

ROBLES F, et al, 2011. Correlation between Laboratory Ball-on-Disk and Full-Scale Rail Performance Tests [J]. Wear, 270(7-8): 479-491.

ROH B H, et al, 2003. Noise Analysis of Oil-Lubricated Journal Bearings [J]. Journal of Mechanical Engineering Science, Proceedings of Institute of Mechanical Engineers, Part C, 217: 365-371.

ROMIG A D, JR, et al, 2003. Materials Issues in Microelectromechanical Devices: Science, Engineering, Manufacturability and Reliability[J]. Acta Materialia, 51(19): 5837-5866.

SAHOO P, CHOWDHURY S, 2000. A Fractal Analysis of Adhesive Friction between Rough Solids in Gentle Sliding[J]. Proceedings of Institute of Mechanical Engineers, J214: 583.

SANCHEZ-RUBIO M, et al, 2006. A New Focus on the Walther Equation for Lubricant Viscosity Determination [J]. Lubrication Science, 18(2): 95-107.

SCHMIDT A, 2000. Viscosity Pressure Behavior of Mineral and Synthetic Oils [C]. 12th International Colloquium Tribology 2000, Stuttgart, Germany.

SINIAWSKI S, et al, 2003. Wear Initiation of 52100 Steel Sliding against a Thin Boron Carbide Coating[J]. Tribology Letters, 15(1): 29-41.

SOMMERFELD A, 1904. Zur Hydrodynamischen Theorie der Schmiermittelreibung [J]. Z. Angew. Math. Phys., 50: 970155.

SONG Y, CHOI D, YANG H, et al, 2011. An Extremely Low Contact-Resistance MEMS Relay Using Meshed Drain Structure and Soft Insulating Layer[J]. Journal of Microelectromechanical Systems, 20: 204.

STACHOWIAK G, Batchelor A, 2005. Engineering Tribology[M]. Elsevier Butterworth-Heinemann, UK.

STANLEY H M, KATO T, 1997. FFT-Based Method for Rough Surface Contact[J]. Journal of Tribology, 119 (3): 481-485.

STEFANI F, REBORA A, 2009. Steadily Loaded Journal Bearings: Quasi-3D Mass-Energy-Conserving Analysis[J]. Tribology International, 42: 448-460.

Strand Henrik, 2005. Design, Testing, and Analysis of Journal Bearings for Construction Equipment[D]. Royal Institute of Technology, Stockholm, Sweden.

STRIBECK, R, 1902. Die wesentlichen Eigenschaften der Gleit- und Rollenlager (Characteristics of Plain and Roller Bearings)[J]. Zeit. Des, VDI 46.

SU F H, et al, 2007. Tribological and Mechanical Properties of Nomex Fabric Composites Filled with Polyfluo 159 Wax and Nano-SiO_2[J]. Composites Science and Technology, 67: 102-110.

TAHERI P, et al, 2011. Investigating Electric Contact Resistance Losses in Lithium Battery Assemblies for Hybrid and Electric Vehicles[J]. Journal of Power Sources, 196: 6525-6533.

TAO Z, 2002. Friction Analysis and Modeling in Metal Cutting Process at Elevated Temperatures[D]. Dept. of Mechanical Engineering Univ. of Pittsburgh, PA.

TIMSIT R, 2010. Constriction Resistance of Thin-film Contacts [J]. IEEE Transactions on Components, Packaging, and Manufacturing Technology, 33: 636.

TODOROVIC G, PARIKYAN T, 2002. Automated Generation of Crankshaft Dynamic Model to Reduce Engine Development Time[J]. SAE Paper Offer 03P-336.

TSANG L, 2004. Scattering of Electromagnetic Waves, Theories and Applications[J]. John Wiley & Sons, Seattle.

UNAL H, MIMAROĞLU A, 2005. Abrasive Wear Behavior of Polymeric Materials[J]. Materials and Design, 26: 750-710.

UNDERWOOD G, 2002. Wear Performance of Ultra-Performance Engineering Polymers at High PVs[J]. SAE 2002-01-0600.

ÜNLÜ S B, ATIK E YıLMAZ S S, 2009. Tribological Behavior of Polymer Based Journal Bearings Manufactured From Particle Reinforced Bakelite Composites[J]. Materials and Design, 30: 3896-3899.

ÜNLÜ S B, ATIK E, KOKSAL S, 2009. Tribological Properties of Polymer-Based Journal Bearings［J］. Materials and Design, 30: 2618-2622.

WANG J, CHUNG Y, 2013. Encyclopedia of Tribology［M］. Springer, New York.

WEI L, et al, 2013. EHD Mixed-Lubrication Analysis of Main Bearings for Marine Diesel Engine Based on Flexible Whole Block［J］. Advanced Shipping and Ocean Engineering, 2(3): 96-104.

WILSON W E, et al, 2010. Surface Treatment and Contact Resistance Considering Sinusoidal Elastic-Plastic Multi-Scale Rough Surface Contact［J］. Wear, 268: 190-201.

WOOD R, 2010. Tribological Design Constraints of Marine Renewable Energy Systems［J］. Philosophical Transactions of the Royal Society, A, 368(1929): 4807-4827.

WOYDT M, WÄSCHE R, 2010. The History of the Stribeck Curve and Ball Bearing Steels: The Role of Adolf Martens［J］. Wear, 268: 1542-1546.

XU C, et al, 2012. Analyzing Surface Roughness Dependence on Linear RF Losses［J］. Proceedings of LINAC 2012, Tel-Aviv, Israel.

YANG L J, 2005. A Test Methodology for the Determination of Wear Coefficient［J］. Wear, 259: 1453-1461.

YASUTOMI S, BAIR S, WINER W, 1984. An Application of a Free Volume Model to Lubricant Rheology［J］. Journal of Tribology, 106(2): 291-303.

YEN K, et al, 2004. Origin of Low-Friction Behavior in Graphite Investigated by Surface X-ray Diffraction［J］. Applied Physics Letters, 84(23): 4702-4704.

ZAIDI H, et al, 1991. Behavior of Graphite in Friction under Various Environments: Connections with Surface Reactivity［J］. Surface Science, 251/252: 778-781.

ZEROUKHI Y, et al, 2014. Dependence of the Contact Resistance on the Design of Stranded Conductors［J］. Sensors, 14: 13925-13942.

ZEROUKHI Y, et al, 2012. Mechanical-Electrical Identification of the Contact Resistance in the Stranded Electric Power Cable［J］. Journal of Achievements in Materials and Manufacturing Engineering, 55: 921-923.

ZHAI C, HANAOR D, PROUST G, et al, 2015. Stress-Dependent Electrical Contact Resistance at Fractal Rough Surfaces［J］. Journal of Engineering Mechanics, B4015001.

ZHANG P, LAU Y, TIMSIT R, 2012. On the Spreading Resistance of Thin-Film Contacts［J］. IEEE Transactions on Electron Devices, 59: 1936.

ZHANG P, LAU Y, GILGENBACH R, 2009. Analysis of Radio-Frequency Absorption and Electric and Magnetic Field Enhancements due to Surface Roughness［J］. Journal of Applied Physics, 105, 114908.

Table 8.1.1　Nominal Coefficients of Friction of Unlubricated Materials in Air ［Lancaster］［Materion Corporation］, Unless Otherwise Specified

Material	T/℃	μ_S on itself	μ_D on itself	μ_S on steel	μ_D on steel
Rubbers:					
Fluoroelastomer	23	—	—	0.67	0.33
TPC-ET（e.g. Hytrel）	23	—	—	0.27	0.22
Thermoplastics:					
ABS	23	0.37	—	0.5	—
FEP	23	—	—	—	0.08~0.3
LCP/30GF	23	—	—	0.09	0.12
PA6,6	23	0.41	0.15	0.52	0.25（s）
PA6,6/44PTFE	23	—	—	—	0.18
PA6,6/15PTFE/30GF	23	—	—	—	0.26
PC	23	0.52	—	0.5	0.31
PC/22PTFE	23	—	—	—	0.15
PC/15PTFE/30GF	23	—	—	—	0.20
PBI	23	—	—	0.28	0.24
PBT	23	0.4	—	0.4	—
PE-flexible	23	0.67	0.33	0.58	0.26
PE-rigid	23	0.45	0.11	0.22	0.10
PE-UHMW	23	0.2	0.15	0.16	0.14（s）
PEEK	23	—	—	—	0.36
PEEK/50PTFE	23	—	—	—	0.11
PEEK/8%ePTFE	23	—	—	—	0.13
PEEK/10%ePTFE	23	—	—	—	0.11
PEI	23	—	—	0.38	—
PES	23	—	—	0.35	0.62
PES-30GF	23	—	—	—	0.54
PET	23	0.17	0.22	0.125	0.19
PFA	23	—	—	—	0.21
PMMA	23	0.65	—	0.55	—

continued

Material	$T/℃$	μ_S on itself	μ_D on itself	μ_S on steel	μ_D on steel
POM（Acetal）	23	0.25	0.40	0.25	0.35
DuPont Delrin CL	23	—	—	0.10	0.20（n）
DuPont Delrin AF	23	—	0.17	0.08	0.14（n）
POM/22PTFE	23	—	—	—	0.15
POM/15PTFE/30GF	23	—	—	—	0.28
PP	23	0.4	—	0.3	—
PPS	23	0.23	0.4	0.23	0.40
	93	—	—	—	0.43
PS	23	0.52	—	0.45	—
PSU	23	0.67	—	0.45	0.35
PTFE	23	0.10~0.25	0.04~0.1	0.10~0.25	0.1（n）
PTFE/55Bronze/5MoS$_2$	23	—	—	—	0.13
PTFE/20CF/5Gr	23	—	—	—	0.12
PTFE/12.5GF/12.5MoS$_2$	23	—	—	—	0.09
PTFE/15GF	23	—	—	—	0.09
PTFE/15Gr	23	—	—	—	0.12
PU	23	—	—	—	—
PVC	23	0.58	0.40	0.58	0.40
PVDF	23	—	—	0.34	—
SAN	23	0.52	—	—	—
Thermoset Plastics：					
PI	23	—	—	—	0.50
PI/15Gr	23	—	0.3	0.04~0.24	0.20
PI/15MoS$_2$	23	—	—	—	0.20
Metals：					
Silver（Ag）	23	1.4	—	—	—
Aluminum（Al）	23	1.2	1.4	0.61	0.47
Gold（Au）	23	0.49	—	—	—

continued

Material	$T/℃$	μ_S on itself	μ_D on itself	μ_S on steel	μ_D on steel
Cadmium (Cd)	23	0.65	—	—	0.46
Chromium (Cr)	23	0.41	—	—	—
Copper (Cu)	23	1.0	0.68	0.53	0.36
Brass	23	—	—	0.43	0.44
Bronze (Dry)	23	—	—	—	0.35 (s)
Bronze (Mineral Oil)	23	—	—	—	0.16 (n)
C62300	23	—	—	—	0.25
C63000	23	—	—	—	0.30
C63020	23	—	—	—	0.28
C67300	23	—	—	—	0.11
C83600	23	—	—	—	—
C95510	23	—	—	—	0.31
C95900	23	—	—	—	0.15
Cu/Graphite	23	—	—	—	—
Cu-15Pb-8Sn	23	—	—	—	0.11
Steel (General)	23	0.76	0.5 (s)	0.76	0.50 (s)
Steel: AISI 4140 (dry)	23	0.42	0.42	—	—
Steel, Boron (dry)	23	—	—	0.38	—
Steel, Boron (wet)	23	—	—	0.33	—
Steel (Fe-Co-Cr-Mo)	23	—	—	—	0.20
Cast Iron (Fe-)	23	1.1	0.15	0.4	0.23
Lead (Pb)	23	—	—	0.95	0.95
Magnesium (Mg)	23	0.6	—	—	—
Nickel (Ni)	23	0.9	0.53	—	0.64
Ti-6Al-4V	23	—	—	—	0.25
Zinc (Zn; Pure)	23	0.6	—	—	—
Zinc (98% Zn; Rolled)	23	0.21	—	—	—
Zn-26.2Al-2.3Cu-..	23	—	—	—	0.10

continued

Material	$T/°C$	μ_S on itself	μ_D on itself	μ_S on steel	μ_D on steel
Zn-14.4Al-1.3Cu-..	23	—	—	—	0.12
Ceramics and Harder：					
CVD DLC	23	0.15	—	0.125	—
CVD DLC-Si	23	0.01	—	—	—
PCD (Polycrystalline diamond)	23	—	0.065	—	—
Glass	23	0.94	0.40	0.6	—
Graphite （in air）	23	0.1	—	—	—
	350	0.22	—	—	—
	500	0.4	—	—	—
Graphite （in a vacuum）	23	0.65	—	—	—
Plexiglas	23	—	—	0.45	—
SiC	23	—	—	0.19	—
WC	23	0.225	—	0.5	—

Notes：CVD：Chemical Vapor Deposition；

　　　（s）：Stick-slip may occur；

　　　（n）：No stick-slip problem.

Table 8.1.2　Nominal PV Limits and Wear Parameter K/H for Unlubricated Bearing Materials in Air, Unless Otherwise Specified ［Lancaster］［Mens & deGee］

Material	$T/°C$	PV	P/MPa	V	$K/H/(MPa^{-1})$	K	H_V
Thermosplastics：							
PA6,6 （Nylon）	23	105	3	1830	$a=0,\ b=18.8×10^{-9}$	—	—
PA6,6 （in H_2O）	23	—	—	—	$a=0,\ b=0.9×10^{-9}$	—	—
PA6,6/15PTFE	23	—	—	—	$a=0,\ b=0.55×10^{-9}$	—	—
PA6,6/15PTFE （in H_2O）	23	—	—	—	$a=0,\ b=0.7×10^{-9}$	—	—
PA6,6/15PTFE/20GF	23	—	—	—	$a=0,\ b=2×10^{-9}$	—	—
PC	23	—	7	—	—	—	—
PE	23	—	—	—	—	—	—
PE-UHMW	23	70	7	510	—	—	—
PEEK	23	120	59	2000	$a=0,\ b=14.8×10^{-9}$	—	—

continued

Material	$T/℃$	PV	P/MPa	V	$K/H/(\text{MPa}^{-1})$	K	H_V
PEEK/15PTFE	23	—	—	—	$a=0$, $b=0.6\times10^{-9}$	—	—
PEEK/15PTFE/20GF	23	—	—	—	$a=0$, $b=1.2\times10^{-9}$	—	—
PEI	23	—	—	—	$a=0$, $b=46.3\times10^{-9}$	—	—
PEI/15PTFE	23	—	—	—	$a=0$, $b=2.4\times10^{-9}$	—	—
PEI/15PTFE/20GF	23	—	—	—	$a=0$, $b=3\times10^{-9}$	—	—
PET	23	—	—	—	$a=0$, $b=21.8\times10^{-9}$	—	—
PET/15PTFE	23	—	—	—	$a=0$, $b=0.6\times10^{-9}$	—	—
PET/15PTFE/20GF	23	—	—	—	$a=0$, $b=1.8\times10^{-9}$	—	—
POM	23	90	7	5100	$a=0$, $b=2\times10^{-9}$	—	—
POM (in H_2O)	23	—	—	—	$a=0$, $b=0.8\times10^{-9}$	—	—
POM/15PTFE	23	—	—	—	$a=0$, $b=0.4\times10^{-9}$	—	—
POM/15PTFE (in H_2O)	23	—	—	—	$a=0$, $b=0.4\times10^{-9}$	—	—
POM-15PTFE-20GF	23	—	—	—	$a=0$, $b=4.1\times10^{-9}$	—	—
Delrin 100AF	23	438	—	—	—	2.0×10^{-7}	—
Delrin 500AF	23	438	—	—	—	—	—
Delrin 500CL	23	263	—	—	—	—	—
PPS	23	—	—	—	$a=0$, $b=37.5\times10^{-9}$	—	—
PPS/15PTFE	23	—	—	—	$a=0$, $b=2.9\times10^{-9}$	—	—
PPS/15PTFE/20GF	23	—	—	—	$a=0$, $b=3.4\times10^{-9}$	—	—
PTFE							
PTFE/40Bronze	23	—	—	—	$a=0$, $b=0.08\times10^{-9}$	—	—
PTFE/18CF/7Gr	23	—	—	—	—	8.5×10^{-5}	—
PTFE/20CF/5Gr	23	—	—	—	$a=0$, $b=0.12\times10^{-9}$	—	—
PTFE/25CF (High-E CF)	23	—	—	—	$a=0$, $b=0.2\times10^{-9}$	—	—
PTFE/25CF (High-σ_{uts} CF)	23	—	—	—	$a=0$, $b=8\times10^{-9}$	—	—
PTFE/25Coke	23	—	—	—	$a=0$, $b=1.7\times10^{-9}$	—	—

continued

Material	$T/^\circ C$	PV	P/MPa	V	$K/H/(MPa^{-1})$	K	H_v
PTFE/15GF	23	—	—	—	$a=0$, $b=0.14\times10^{-9}$	7.0×10^{-4}	—
PTFE/20GF/MoS$_2$	23	—	—	—	—	1.0×10^{-4}	—
PTFE/25GF	23	—	—	—	—	3.0×10^{-4}	—
PTFE/30GF	23	—	—	—	$a=0$, $b=62\times10^{-9}$	—	—
PTFE/15Gr	23	—	—	—	$a=0$, $b=0.68\times10^{-9}$	—	—
PTFE/33Gr	23	—	—	—	$a=0$, $b=0.05\times10^{-9}$	—	—
PTFE/30Mica	23	—	—	—	$a=0$, $b=3.1\times10^{-9}$	—	—
Wood	23	420	14	—	—	—	—
Thermoset Plastics：							
Frelon	23	350	10	710	—	—	—
Frelon（Al backing）	23	700	21	300	—	—	—
PF（Phenolics）	23	525	41.4	—	—	—	—
PI/20CF	23	—	—	—	$a=0$, $b=5\times10^{-9}$	—	—
Metals：							
Al	23	—	—	—	—	—	—
Al-4Si-1Cd	23	—	—	—	—	—	55
Al-20Si-1Cu	23	—	—	—	—	—	40
Al-6Sn-1Cu-1Ni	23	—	—	—	—	—	52
Al-11Sn-4Si-1.5Cu	23	—	—	—	—	—	60
Co	500	—	—	—	$a=0$, $b=10^{-9}\sim10^{-8}$	—	—
Cu	23	—	—	—	—	—	—
C90300	23	3152	34.5	1270	—	—	—
C90700	23	3503	34.5	1270	—	—	—
C93200	23	2627	27.6	3810	—	—	—
C93700	23	2977	27.6	5080	—	—	—
C95400	23	4378	41.4	1270	—	—	—
C95500	23	4729	48.3	1060	—	—	—
C95900	23	5254	55.2	508	—	—	—

continued

Material	$T/℃$	PV	P/MPa	V	$K/H/(MPa^{-1})$	K	H_v
Cu/Graphite	23	420	5	380	—	—	—
Bronze (Porous)	23	1750	31	—	—	—	—
Bronze/PTFE (Steel backing)	23	1790	249	2000	—	—	—
Cu-9Pb-5Sn	23	—	—	—	—	—	58
Cu-10Pb-10Sn	23	—	—	—	—	—	78
Cu-15Pb-8Sn	23	—	—	—	$a=0,\ b=19.3\times10^{-9}$	—	—
Cu-20Pb-5Sn	23	—	—	—	—	—	48
Cu-24Pb-4Sn	23	—	—	—	—	—	58
Cu-30Pb	23	—	—	—	—	—	40
Fe (Iron)	23	—	—	—	—	—	—
Iron (Porous)	23	1750	55	—	—	—	—
Tool steels	500	—	—	—	$a=0,\ b=10^{-8}\sim10^{-7}$	—	—
Ni	500	—	—	—	$a=0,\ b=10^{-8}\sim10^{-6}$	—	—
Pb	23	—	—	—	—	—	—
Pb-10Sb-6Sn-1Cu	23	—	—	—	—	—	26
Sn	23	—	—	—	—	—	—
Sn-7.5Sb-3.5Cu	23	—	—	—	—	—	24
Sn-8Sb-4Cu-1Cd	23	—	—	—	—	—	30
Zn	23	—	—	—	—	—	—
Zn-26.2Al-2.3Cu-..	23	—	—	—	$a=0,\ b=10.8\times10^{-9}$	—	—
Zn-14.4Al-1.3Cu-..	23	—	—	—	$a=0,\ b=40.2\times10^{-9}$	—	—
Ceramics and Harder:							
Ceramics	500	—	—	—	$a=0,\ b=10^{-8}\sim10^{-6}$	—	—
Cermets	500	—	—	—	$a=0,\ b=10^{-10}\sim10^{-8}$	—	—

Notes: PV (MPa · mm/s): Pressure · Velocity;

P (MPa): Pressure;

V (mm/s): Velocity;

K/H (MPa^{-1}): Wear coefficient / hardness, of which H_v is generally applied;

K: Wear coefficient, dimensionless;

H_v(MPa): Vickers hardness.

Table 8.3.1   Thermal Contact Conductance between Solids, h_c (W/m²/℃)

Materials A–B	$T_2 \to T_3$/℃	P_c/MPa	R_{rms}/μm	h_c/(W/m²/℃)
Aluminum/Aluminum	—	0.1~1	—	$2.2 \times 10^3 \sim 12 \times 10^3$
Aluminum/Aluminum	—	10	—	$25 \times 10^3 \sim 50 \times 10^3$
Aluminum/Iron	—	0.1~1	—	45×10^3
Copper/Copper	—	0.1~1	—	$10 \times 10^3 \sim 25 \times 10^3$
Copper/Copper	—	10	—	$20 \times 10^3 \sim 100 \times 10^3$
Magnesium/Magnesium	—	10	—	$25 \times 10^3 \sim 50 \times 10^3$
Steels: Stainless/Stainless	—	Evacuated Gaps	—	$2 \times 10^2 \sim 1.1 \times 10^3$
Steels: Stainless/Stainless	—	0.1~1	—	$2 \times 10^3 \sim 3.7 \times 10^3$
Steels: Stainless/Stainless	—	10	—	$2.5 \times 10^3 \sim 14.3 \times 10^3$
Ceramic/Ceramic	—	0.1~1	—	$5 \times 10^2 \sim 3 \times 10^3$

Notes: $T_2 \to T_3$ (℃): Temperature at thermal conduction between solids;

P_c (MPa): Contact pressure;

R_{rms} (μm): Surface roughness; rms-Root Mean Squared.

Table 8.7.1   Typical Thermomechanical Characteristics of Engine Oils （SAE J300）

Material	T/℃	ρ/(g·cm⁻³)	μ_d/(Pa·s)	α_μ	β_μ	α	k	γ
SAE 5W-20 (Mineral)	−40	(Pour Point)	—	—	—	—	—	—
	15.6	0.85	—	—	—	—	—	—
	40	—	0.038	—	—	—	—	—
	100	—	0.007	—	—	—	—	—
	214	(Flash Point)	—	—	—	—	—	—
SAE 5W-30 (Mineral)	−36	(Pour Point)	—	—	—	—	—	—
	−35	—	>60 (Pumping)	—	—	—	—	—
	−30	—	<6.6 (Cranking)	—	—	—	—	—
	15.6	0.86	—	—	—	—	—	—
	40	0.846	0.0534	0.016	0.042	734	0.126	2000
	100	—	0.0088	—	—	—	—	—
	150	—	>2.9(High shear)	—	—	—	—	—
	220	(Flash Point)	—	—	—	—	—	—

continued

Material	$T/°C$	$\rho /(\text{g} \cdot \text{cm}^{-3})$	$\mu_d/(\text{Pa} \cdot \text{s})$	α_μ	β_μ	α	k	γ
SAE 5W-30 (Synthetic)	−46	(Pour Point)	—	—	—	—	—	—
	−35	—	>60 (Pumping)	—	—	—	—	—
	−30	—	<6.6 (Cranking)	—	—	—	—	—
	15.6	0.865	—	—	—	—	—	—
	40	—	0.0487	—	—	—	—	—
	100	—	0.0088	—	—	—	—	—
	150	—	>2.9(High shear)	—	—	—	—	—
	218	(Flash Point)	—	—	—	—	—	—
SAE 5W-40	−35	—	>60 (Pumping)	—	—	—	—	—
	−30	—	<6.6 (Cranking)	—	—	—	—	—
	15.6	0.87	—	—	—	—	—	—
	150	—	>2.9(High shear)	—	—	—	—	—
SAE 5W-50 (Synthetic)	−46	(Pour Point)	—	—	—	—	—	—
	−35	—	>60 (Pumping)	—	—	—	—	—
	−30	—	<6.6 (Cranking)	—	—	—	—	—
	15.6	0.911	—	—	—	—	—	—
	40	—	0.1124	—	—	—	—	—
	100	—	0.0173	—	—	—	—	—
	238	(Flash Point)	—	—	—	—	—	—
SAE 10W-30 (Mineral)	−33	(Pour Point)	—	—	—	—	—	—
	−30	—	>60 (Pimping)	—	—	—	—	—
	−25	—	<7.0 (Cranking)	—	—	—	—	—
	15.6	0.875	—	—	—	—	—	—
	40	0.865	0.057	—	—	—	—	—
	100	—	0.0089	—	—	—	—	—
	210	(Flash Point)	—	—	—	—	—	—

continued

Material	$T/℃$	$\rho/(g \cdot cm^{-3})$	$\mu_d/(Pa \cdot s)$	α_μ	β_μ	α	k	γ
SAE 10W-40（Mineral）	−33	（Pour Point）	—	—	—	—	—	—
	−30	—	>60（Pumping）	—	—	—	—	—
	−25	—	<7.0（Cranking）	—	—	—	—	—
	15.6	0.872	—	—	—	—	—	—
	40	—	0.092	—	—	—	—	—
	100	—	0.0129	—	—	—	—	—
	150	—	>2.9(High shear)	—	—	—	—	—
	220	（Flash Point）	—	—	—	—	—	—
SAE 15W-40	−25	—	>60（Pumping）	—	—	—	—	—
	−20	—	<7.0（Cranking）	—	—	—	—	—
	−13	—	12.23	—	—	700	0.149	1760
	23	—	—	—	—	—	—	—
	67	—	0.0053	—	—	700	0.139	2080
	127	—	0.009	—	—	700	0.134	2340
	150	—	>3.7	—	—	—	—	—
SAE 20W-40	−20	—	>60（Pumping）	—	—	—	—	—
	−15	—	<9.5（Cranking）	—	—	—	—	—
	23	—	—	—	—	—	—	—
	150	—	>3.7(High shear)	—	—	—	—	—
SAE 20W-50	−20	—	>60（Pumping）	—	—	—	—	—
	−15	—	<9.5（Cranking）	—	—	—	—	—
	40	0.872	0.1448	—	—	—	—	—
	100	—	0.0163	—	—	—	—	—
SAE 25W-40	−15	—	>60（Pumping）	—	—	—	—	—
	−10	—	<13（Cranking）	—	—	—	—	—
	23	—	—	—	—	—	—	—
	150	—	>3.7(High shear)	—	—	—	—	—
SAE 0W	−40	—	>60（Pumping）	—	—	—	—	—
	−35	—	<6.2（Cranking）	—	—	—	—	—
	23	—	—	—	—	—	—	—

continued

Material	$T/°C$	$\rho /(g \cdot cm^{-3})$	$\mu_d/(Pa \cdot s)$	α_μ	β_μ	α	k	γ
SAE 5W	−35	—	>60 (Pumping)	—	—	—	—	—
	−30	—	<6.6 (Cranking)	—	—	—	—	—
	23	—	—	—	—	—	—	—
	40	—	0.015	—	—	—	—	—
SAE 10W	−30	—	>60 (Pumping)	—	—	—	—	—
	−25	—	<7.0 (Cranking)	—	—	—	—	—
	23	—	—	—	—	—	—	—
	40	—	0.015	—	—	—	—	—
SAE 15W	−25	—	>60 (Pumping)	—	—	—	—	—
	−20	—	<7.0 (Cranking)	—	—	—	—	—
	23	—	—	—	—	—	—	—
	40	—	0.03	—	—	—	—	—
SAE 20W	−20	—	>60 (Pumping)	—	—	—	—	—
	−15	—	<9.5 (Cranking)	—	—	—	—	—
	23	—	—	—	—	—	—	—
SAE 25W	−15	—	>60 (Pumping)	—	—	—	—	—
	−10	—	<13 (Cranking)	—	—	—	—	—
	23	—	—	—	—	—	—	—
SAE 10	23	0.87	0.112	—	—	—	—	—
SAE 20	20	0.88	0.125	—	—	—	—	—
	40	—	0.06	—	—	—	—	—
	150	—	>2.6	—	—	—	—	—
SAE 30	20	—	0.2	—	—	—	—	—
	40	0.88	0.092	—	—	—	—	—
	150	—	>2.9	—	—	—	—	—
SAE 40	20	0.88	0.319	—	—	—	—	—
	40	—	0.138	—	—	—	—	—
SAE 50	23	0.88	—	—	—	—	—	
	40	—	0.2	—	—	—	—	—
	150	—	>3.7	—	—	—	—	
SAE 60	23	—	—	—	—	—		
	40	—	0.3	—	—	—	—	—
	150	—	>3.7	—	—	—	—	—

Notes: γ (J/kg/°C) : Specific heat capacity at 0.1 MPa (100 kPa) constant pressure;

μ_d(Pa · s) : Dynamic viscosity as averaged at the ambient pressure;

α_μ(MPa^{-1}) : Pressure-dynamic viscosity coefficient, Eq. (8.7.6);

β_μ(°C^{-1}) : Temperature-dynamic viscosity coefficient, Eq. (8.7.6);

α (μm/m/°C) : Coefficient of linear thermal expansion.

Table 8.7.2　Typical Thermomechanical Characteristics of Gear, Screw, and Compressor Oils

Material	$T/^\circ\mathrm{C}$	$\rho/(\mathrm{g \cdot cm^{-3}})$	$\mu_\mathrm{d}/(\mathrm{Pa \cdot s})$	α_μ	β_μ	α	k	γ
ISO 3448 VG-22	−36	（Pour Point）	—	—	—	—	—	—
	15.6	0.864	—	—	—	—	—	—
	40	—	0.0183	—	—	—	—	—
	100	—	0.0035	—	—	—	—	—
	208	（Flash Point）	—	—	—	—	—	—
ISO 3448 VG-32 （AGMA 0）	−33	（Pour Point）	—	—	—	—	—	—
	15.6	0.868	—	—	—	—	—	—
	40	—	0.028	—	0.034	—	0.13	2000
	100	—	0.0047	—	—	—	—	—
	212	（Flash Point）	—	—	—	—	—	—
ISO 3448 VG-46 （AGMA 1）	−30	（Pour Point）	—	—	—	—	—	—
	15.6	0.871	—	—	—	—	—	—
	40	—	0.04	—	—	—	—	—
	100	—	0.006	—	—	—	—	—
	220	（Flash Point）	—	—	—	—	—	—
ISO 3448 VG-68 （AGMA 2）	−26	（Pour Point）	—	—	—	—	—	—
	15.6	0.878	—	—	—	—	—	—
	40	—	0.059	0.023	0.034	—	0.126	—
	100	—	0.0074	—	—	—	—	—
	242	（Flash Point）	—	—	—	—	—	
ISO 3448 VG-100 （AGMA 3）	−24	（Pour Point）	—	—	—	—	—	—
	15.6	0.88	—	—	—	—	—	—
	40	—	0.087	—	—	—	—	—
	100	—	0.0097	—	—	—	—	—
	250	（Flash Point）	—	—	—	—	—	—
ISO 3448 VG-150 （AGMA 4）	−24	（Pour Point）	—	—	—	—	—	—
	15.6	0.884	—	—	—	—	—	—
	40	—	0.13	—	—	—	—	—
	100	—	0.013	—	—	—	—	—
	256	（Flash Point）	—	—	—	—	—	—

continued

Material	$T/℃$	$\rho/(g \cdot cm^{-3})$	$\mu_d/(Pa \cdot s)$	α_μ	β_μ	α	k	γ
ISO 3448 VG-220 (AGMA 5)	-18	(Pour Point)	—	—	—	—	—	—
	15.6	0.9	—	—	—	—	—	—
	40	—	0.205	—	—	—	—	—
	100	—	0.017	—	—	—	—	—
	258	(Flash Point)	—	—	—	—	—	
ISO 3448 VG-320 (AGMA 6)	-15	(Pour Point)	—	—	—	—	—	—
	15.6	0.907	—	—	—	—	—	—
	40	—	0.29	—	—	—	—	—
	100	—	0.0215	—	—	—	—	—
	220	(Flash Point)	—	—	—	—	—	—
ISO 3448 VG-460 (AGMA 7C)	-15	(Pour Point)	—	—	—	—	—	—
	15.6	0.913	—	—	—	—	—	—
	40	—	0.414	—	—	—	—	—
	100	—	0.027	—	—	—	—	—
	215	(Flash Point)	—	—	—	—	—	—
ISO 3448 VG-680 (AGMA 8)	40	—	0.62	—	—	—	—	—
ISO 3448 VG-1000 (AGMA 8A)	40	—	0.92	—	—	—	—	—
	-42	(Pour Point)	—	—	—	—	—	—
SAE 75W-90 (PAO; Synthetic)	15.6	0.887	—	—	—	—	—	—
	40	—	0.097	—	—	—	—	—
	100	—	0.017	—	—	—	—	—
	195	(Flash Point)	—	—	—	—	—	
SAE 80W-90	-27	(Pour Point)						
	15.6	0.887	—	—	—	—	—	—
	40	—	0.12	—	—	—	—	—
	100	—	0.013	—	—	—	—	—
	218	(Flash Point)						
SAE 85W-140	-12	(Pour Point)	—	—	—	—	—	—
	15.6	0.901	—	—	—	—	—	—
	40	—	0.366	—	—	—	—	—
	100	—	0.027	—	—	—	—	—
	200	(Flash Point)	—	—	—	—	—	—

continued

Material	$T/\text{℃}$	$\rho/(\text{g} \cdot \text{cm}^{-3})$	$\mu_d/(\text{Pa} \cdot \text{s})$	α_μ	β_μ	α	k	γ
Synthetic PAG-46 (Compressor Oil)	−39	(Pour Point)	—	—	—	—	—	—
	15.6	1.035	—	—	—	—	—	—
	40	—	0.046	—	—	—	—	—
	100	—	0.008	—	—	—	—	—
	263	(Flash Point)	—	—	—	—	—	—
Synthetic PAG-100 (Compressor Oil)	−35	(Pour Point)	—	—	—	—	—	—
	15.6	1.048	—	—	—	—	—	—
	40	—	0.1	—	—	—	—	—
	100	—	0.0162	—	—	—	—	—
	275	(Flash Point)	—	—	—	—	—	—
Synthetic PAG-220 (Compressor Oil)	−33	(Pour Point)	—	—	—	—	—	—
	15.6	1.072	—	—	—	—	—	—
	40	—	0.22	—	—	—	—	—
	100	—	0.034	—	—	—	—	—
	280	(Flash Point)	—	—	—	—	—	—
Synthetic PAG-460 (Compressor Oil)	−30	(Pour Point)	—	—	—	—	—	—
	15.6	1.035	—	—	—	—	—	—
	40	—	0.46	—	—	—	—	—
	100	—	0.069	—	—	—	—	—
	280	(Flash Point)	—	—	—	—	—	—
Synthetic PAG-1000 (Compressor Oil)	−20	(Pour Point)	—	—	—	—	—	—
	15.6	1.07	—	—	—	—	—	—
	40	—	1.0	—	—	—	—	—
	100	—	0.146	—	—	—	—	—
	275	(Flash Point)	—	—	—	—	—	—
Turbine Oils	ISO 3448 VG 32, 46, 68, and 100 may be applied.							

Notes: γ (J/kg/℃): Specific heat capacity at 0.1 MPa (100 kPa) constant pressure;

μ_d(Pa · s): Dynamic viscosity as averaged at the ambient pressure;

α_μ(MPa^{-1}): Pressure-dynamic viscosity coefficient, Eq. (8.7.6);

β_μ(℃$^{-1}$): Temperature-dynamic viscosity coefficient, Eq. (8.7.6);

α (μm/m/℃): Coefficient of linear thermal expansion;

VG: Viscosity grade.

Table 8.7.3 Typical Thermomechanical Characteristics of Hydraulic and Transformer Oils

Material	$T/℃$	$\rho /(g \cdot cm^{-3})$	$\mu_d/(Pa \cdot s)$	α_μ	β_μ	α	k	γ
Mineral-HM32	15	0.879	—	—	—	—	—	—
	20.5	—	0.0702	—	—	—	—	—
	40	—	0.0262	—	—	—	—	—
	100	—	0.00433	—	—	—	—	—
Mineral-HM46	15	0.883	—	—	—	—	—	—
	20.5	—	0.1257	—	—	—	—	—
	40	—	0.0421	—	—	—	—	—
	100	—	0.00572	—	—	—	—	—
Mineral-HM68	15	0.887	—	—	—	—	—	—
	20.5	—	0.1928	—	—	—	—	—
	40	—	0.06334	—	—	—	—	—
	100	—	0.00734	—	—	—	—	—
Mineral-HVL68	15	0.879	—	—	—	—	—	—
	20.5	—	0.1085	—	—	—	—	—
	40	—	0.0408	—	—	—	—	—
	100	—	0.00681	—	—	—	—	—
Transformer Oil (Mineral)	−50	(Pour Point)	—	—	—	—	—	—
	15.6	0.88	—	—	—	750	0.126	1860
	40	—	0.019	—	—	—	—	—
	100	—	0.0022	—	—	—	—	—
	160	(Flash Point)	—	—	—	—	—	
	280	(Autoignition Point)	—	—	—	—	—	—
Synthetic PAO-320	−34	(Pour Point)	—	—	—	—	—	—
	15.6	0.876	—	—	—	—	—	—
	40	—	0.294	0.0134	—	—	—	—
	100	—	0.028	0.0122	—	—	—	—
	220	(Flash Point)	—	—	—	—	—	—

continued

Material	$T/^\circ\text{C}$	$\rho/(\text{g}\cdot\text{cm}^{-3})$	$\mu_{\text{d}}/(\text{Pa}\cdot\text{s})$	α_μ	β_μ	α	k	γ
Synthetic PAO-460	−27	(Pour Point)	—	—	—	—	—	—
	15.6	0.878	—	—	—	—	—	—
	40	—	0.423	—	—	—	—	—
	100	—	0.037	0.0122	—	—	—	—
	220	(Flash Point)	—	—	—	—	—	—
Synthetic PAO-680	−27	(Pour Point)	—	—	—	—	—	—
	15.6	0.88	—	—	—	—	—	—
	40	—	0.626	0.0134	—	—	—	—
	100	—	0.0515	0.0122	—	—	—	—
	220	(Flash Point)	—	—	—	—	—	—

Notes: γ (J/kg/℃): Specific heat capacity at 0.1 MPa (100 kPa) constant pressure;

μ_{d} (Pa·s): Dynamic viscosity as averaged at the ambient pressure;

α_μ (MPa^{-1}): Pressure-dynamic viscosity coefficient, Eq. (8.7.6);

β_μ (℃$^{-1}$): Temperature-dynamic viscosity coefficient, Eq. (8.7.6);

α (μm/m/℃): Coefficient of linear thermal expansion;

Hydraulic Oils: Lubricants used in hydraulic systems for transmitting power.

Table 8.7.4 Typical Thermomechanical Characteristics of Fuels

Material	$T/^\circ\text{C}$	$\rho/(\text{g}\cdot\text{cm}^{-3})$	$\mu_{\text{d}}/(\text{Pa}\cdot\text{s})$	α_μ	β_μ	α	k	γ
Diesel Fuel Oil (No. 2)	23	0.85	—	—	—	—	—	1750
	52	(Flash Point)	—	—	—	—	—	—
	256	(Autoignition Point)	—	—	—	—	—	—
Diesel Fuel Oil (No. 4)	23	0.85	0.0157	—	—	—	—	1750
Diesel Fuel Oil (No. 6)	23	0.85		—	—	—	—	1750
DME (Dimethyl Ether)	23	0.667	—	—	—	—	—	2990
	235	(Autoignition Point)	—	—	—	—	—	—
	248	(Boiling Point)	—	—	—	—	—	—

continued

Material	$T/℃$	$\rho/(g \cdot cm^{-3})$	$\mu_d/(Pa \cdot s)$	α_μ	β_μ	α	k	γ
Gasoline (a)	−43	(Flash Point)	—	—	—	—	—	—
	15.6	0.74	—	—	—	—	—	2220
	280	(Autoignition Point)						
Gasoline (b)	−43	(Flash Point)	—	—	—	—	—	—
	15.6	0.72	—	—	—	—	—	2220
	280	(Autoignition Point)	—	—	—	—	—	—
Gasoline (c)	−43	(Flash Point)	—	—	—	—	—	—
	15.6	0.68	—	—	—	—	—	2220
	280	(Autoignition Point)	—	—	—	—	—	—
Jet A Fuel	23	—	—	—	—	—	—	—
	> 38	(Flash Point)	—	—	—	—	—	—
	210	(Autoignition Point)	—			—	—	—
Jet A-1 Fuel	23	—	—	—	—	—	—	—
	> 38	(Flash Point)	—	—	—	—	—	—
	210	(Autoignition Point)	—	—	—	—	—	—
Jet B Fuel	> −23	(Flash Point)	—	—	—	—	—	—
	23	—	—	—	—	—	—	—
	210	(Autoignition Point)	—	—	—	—	—	—

Notes: γ (J/kg/℃): Specific heat capacity at 0.1 MPa (100 kPa) constant pressure;

μ_d(Pa · s): Dynamic viscosity as averaged at the ambient pressure;

α_μ(MPa^{-1}): Pressure-dynamic viscosity coefficient;

β_μ(℃$^{-1}$): Temperature-dynamic viscosity coefficient;

α (μm/m/℃): Coefficient of linear thermal expansion.

Table 8.7.5　Typical Thermomechanical Characteristics of Air and Water/Ice

Material	$T/^\circ\text{C}$	$\rho/(\text{g}\cdot\text{cm}^{-3})$	$\mu_\text{d}/(\text{Pa}\cdot\text{s})$	α_μ	β_μ	α	k	γ
Air (Dry)	−20	0.00137	1.51×10^{-5}	—	—	—	—	—
	0	0.00127	1.72×10^{-5}	—	—	—	—	—
	23	0.00117	1.82×10^{-5}	—	—	—	0.024	1005(C_p)
	60	0.00107	2.0×10^{-5}	—	—	—	0.029	—
	100	0.000954	2.17×10^{-5}	—	—	—	—	—
	140	0.000838	2.34×10^{-5}	—	—	—	—	—
	180	0.000765	2.50×10^{-5}	—	—	—	—	—
	200	0.000732	2.57×10^{-5}	—	—	—	—	—
H_2O (Ice)	−30	0.983854	—	—	—	—	—	—
	−20	0.993547	—	—	—	—	—	—
	−10	0.998117	—	—	—	—	—	—
	0(Ice)		—	—	—	—	2.18	2050
H_2O (Water)	0	0.998395	0.00179	—	—	—	—	4218
	4	0.999973	0.00155	—	—	—	—	—
	20	0.9982	0.001002	—	—	—	0.58	4182
	30	—	0.007978	—	—	—	—	—
	40	0.9922	0.000653	—	—	—	—	4178
	50	—	0.000547	—	—	—	—	—
	60	0.9832	0.000466	—	—	—	—	4184
	70	—	0.000404	—	—	—	—	—
	80	0.9718	0.000354	—	—	—	—	4196
	90	0.9668	0.000316	—	—	—	—	—
	100	0.9584	0.000282	—	—	—	—	4216
H_2O (Steam)	100	—	—	—	—	—	—	2080
	125	—	—	—	—	—	0.016	—
H_2O (Sea Water)	10	1.025	0.00135	—	—	—	—	—
	15	1.025	0.00121	—	—	—	—	—
	20	1.03	0.00107	—	—	—	—	3930
	104	(Boiling Point)						

Notes：γ (J/kg/℃)：Specific heat capacity at 0.1 MPa (100 kPa) constant pressure；

　　　μ_d(Pa·s)：Dynamic viscosity as averaged at the ambient pressure；

　　　α_μ(MPa^{-1})：Pressure-dynamic viscosity coefficient, Eq. (8.7.6)；

　　　β_μ(℃$^{-1}$)：Temperature-dynamic viscosity coefficient, Eq. (8.7.6)；

　　　α (μm/m/℃)：Coefficient of linear thermal expansion.

Table 8.7.6   Typical Thermomechanical Characteristics of Fluids.

Material	$T/\text{℃}$	$\rho/(\text{g}\cdot\text{cm}^{-3})$	$\mu_d/(\text{Pa}\cdot\text{s})$	α_μ	β_μ	α	k	γ
Gaseous:								
Ammonia	20	—	9.82×10^{-6}	—	—	—	—	—
	10	—	—	—	—	—	0.0157	—
Carbon Dioxide (CO_2)	20	0.00185	14.8×10^{-6}	—	—	—	—	$841(C_p)$
	50	—	—	—	—	—	0.0184	—
Carbon Monoxide (CO)	15	0.00185	117.2×10^{-6}	—	—	—	—	$841(C_p)$
Helium	−269	(Liquid)	0.00333	—	—	—	—	—
	0	—	18.5×10^{-6}	—	—	—	—	—
	23	0.00169	—	—	—	—	—	$5187(C_p)$
	27	—	20×10^{-6}	—	—	—	—	—
Hydrogen (H_2)	−196	(Liquid)	0.000158	—	—	—	—	—
	0	—	8.4×10^{-6}	—	—	—	—	—
	20	0.0008988	8.76×10^{-6}	—	—	—	0.1805	$14223(C_p)$
	27	—	9.0×10^{-6}	—	—	—	—	—
Methane (Natural Gas)	23	0.00678	—	—	—	—	—	$2208(C_p)$
Nitrogen (N_2)	0	—	16.7×10^{-6}					
	23	0.00118	—	—	—	—	—	$1041(C_p)$
	27	—	17.8×10^{-6}	—	—	—	—	—
Oxygen (O_2)	0	—	18.1×10^{-6}	—	—	—	—	—
	20	0.00135	20.2×10^{-6}	—	—	—	—	$916(C_p)$
Sulfur Dioxide (SO_2)	20	—	12.54×10^{-6}	—	—	—	—	—
Liquids:								
Alcohol, Ethyl	23	0.79	0.0012	—	—	1100	—	2440
	78	(Boiling Point)	—	—	—	—	—	—
Blood	37	—	0.0035	—	—	—	—	—
Brake Fluid	23	—	—	—	—	—	—	—
	149	(Flash Point)	—	—	—	—	—	—
	232	(Boiling Point)	—	—	—	—	—	—
	288	(Autoignition Point)	—	—	—	—	—	—
Power Steering Fluid	23	—	—	—	—	—	—	—
	177	(Flash Point)	—	—	—	—	—	—

continued

Material	$T/℃$	$\rho/(g \cdot cm^{-3})$	$\mu_d/(Pa \cdot s)$	α_μ	β_μ	α	k	γ
Ethylene Glycol (Engine Coolant)	23	—	—	—	—	—	—	—
	121	(Flash Point)	—	—	—	—	—	—
	190	(Boiling Point)	—	—	—	—	—	—
	399	(Autoignition Point)	—	—	—	—	—	—
Ethylene Glycol+ H_2O (60%/40%) (Engine Coolant)	23	—	—	—	—	—	—	—
	110	(Boiling Point)	—	—	—	—	—	—
	142	(Flash Point)	—	—	—	—	—	—
	145	(Flame Point)	—	—	—	—	—	—
Honey	23	—	2.2	—	—	—	—	—
Kerosene	23	0.82	0.0019	—	—	—	—	2090
	300	(Boiling Point)	—	—	—	—	—	—
Silicone Oil	55	0.91	0.0046	—	—	—	—	—
	301	(Flash Point)	—	—	—	—	—	—
Windshield Wiper Fluid	23	—	—	—	—	—	—	—
	32	(Flash Point)	—	—	—	—	—	—
	454	(Autoignition Point)	—	—	—	—	—	—
Glass	23	—	$10^{18} \sim 10^{21}$	—	—	—	—	—

Notes：γ (J/kg/℃)：Specific heat capacity at 0.1 MPa (100 kPa) constant pressure；

μ_d(Pa $\cdot$ s=NS/m^2)：Dynamic viscosity as averaged at the ambient pressure；

α_μ(MPa^{-1})：Pressure-dynamic viscosity coefficient, Eq. (8.7.6)；

β_μ(℃$^{-1}$)：Temperature-dynamic viscosity coefficient, Eq. (8.7.6)；

α (μm/m/℃)：Coefficient of linear thermal expansion.

Chapter 9

Structural Instability

9.1　Instability of Structural Behaviors

There are two major categories of continued behaviors that may lead to the sudden failure of a mechanical component: material fracture and structural instability. The two phenomena are due to different governing differential equations. As a structure works in the elastoplastic range and the loading function is conservative, there are two kinds of feasible structural instability-bifurcation and snapping. All of them are involved with geometric nonlinearity as shown in Fig. 9.1.1.

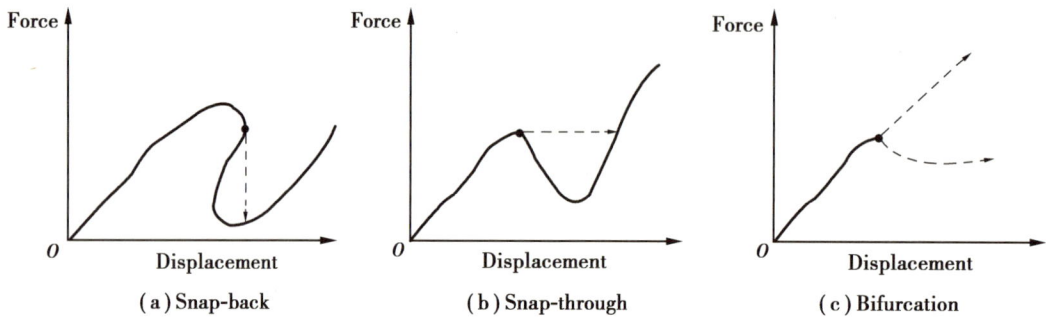

Fig. 9.1.1　Static Structural Instability-Bifurcation and Snapping

9.1.1　Bifurcation

When a structure is loaded, the transition from stability to instability can only occur at a critical point, at which two or more equilibrium branches intersect in mathematics. This phenomenon is called bifurcation. Buckling is a bifurcation where two or more equilibrium paths intersect in the solution to a set of equations of static equilibrium. Nevertheless, dynamic buckling is also feasible. What happens after the bifurcation point configures the post-buckling behavior.

Buckling is characterized by an excessive lateral deformation of a structural member right due to a high compressive load, by which the induced compressive stress at the point of failure is usually less than the compressive yield strength and ultimate compressive stress. It results in structural instability that may end up with a failure mode. One problem due to the thin section of a part is that the generated thin cross section may buckle locally. This phenomenon is called local buckling, which can be prevented using strengthening stiffeners.

9.1.2 Snapping

When a loaded structure reaches a limiting point, the load that can be carried by the related material reaches a maximum or minimum. When an equilibrium branch reaches a maximum or minimum, the inflexion due to influential factors may occur. What happens after snapping configures the post-snapping behavior? Snapping can be also divided into two different categories: snap-through and snap-back.

9.2 Buckling of Columns

When the compressive force is applied to a slender column the bending moment induced by its lateral deflection with or without any eccentricity may create a failure mode due to structural instability and it is called column buckling. As a long column exhibits unstable behaviors in the form of buckling, its critical buckling strength depends on the slenderness and boundary conditions and it is independent of material strength.

9.2.1 Buckling of Eccentric-Loaded Columns

When the applied force is not well aligned with the column centroid, the column is loaded eccentrically as identified in Fig. 9.2.1. If force F is the only applied force, the bending moment induced by the eccentricity of force and loading deflection is

$$M = - F(e + y) \tag{9.2.1}$$

where

e: Eccentricity, the distance from the centroidal axis (column) to load axis;

y: Lateral deflection due to the bending moment.

$$E I \frac{\mathrm{d}^2 y}{\mathrm{d}x^2} = - F(e + y) \tag{9.2.2}$$

i.e., $\quad \dfrac{\mathrm{d}^2 y}{\mathrm{d}x^2} + \lambda^2 (e + y) = 0 \tag{9.2.3}$

where $\quad \lambda \equiv \left(\dfrac{F}{EI}\right)^{\frac{1}{2}} \tag{9.2.4}$

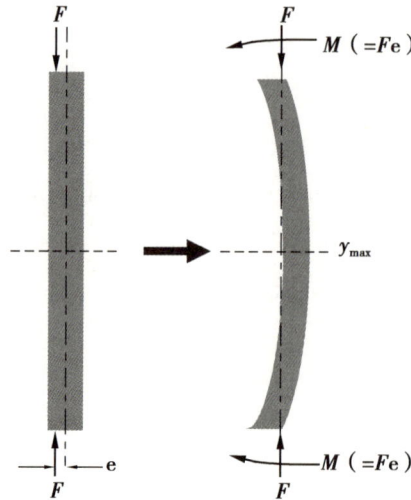

Fig. 9.2.1 Hinged Slender Column Loaded Eccentrically

The above Second order ordinary differential equation constitutes a boundary value problem and it can be solved for lateral deflection y as

$$y = c_1 \sin(\lambda\ x) + c_2 \cos(\lambda\ x) - e \qquad (9.2.5)$$

of which c_1 and c_2 are coefficients that can be obtained from the boundary conditions at both ends of the column.

9.2.1.1 Both Ends Hinged

Constants c_1 and c_2 in Eq. (9.2.5) can be resolved using the following two boundary conditions for the case of two hinged ends:

$$(a)\ y = 0 \text{ at } x = 0 \quad (\text{No deflection at } x = 0) \qquad (9.2.6)$$

$$(b)\ dy/dx = 0 \text{ at } x = \frac{1}{2}L\ (\text{Zero slope in the middle}) \qquad (9.2.7)$$

Substituting the above two equations into Eq. (9.2.5) leads to

$$y = \left[\tan\left(\frac{1}{2}\ \lambda\ L\right)\sin(\lambda\ x) + \cos(\lambda\ x) - 1\right]e \qquad (9.2.8)$$

The maximum deflection, bending moment, and stress occur at $dy/dx = 0$ that leads to $x = 1/2L$. Respectively, they are

$$y_{max} = y\left(\frac{1}{2}\ L\right) = \left(\sec\frac{\lambda L}{2} - 1\right)e \qquad (9.2.9)$$

$$M_{max} = F(e + Y_{max}) = F e \sec \frac{\lambda L}{2} \tag{9.2.10}$$

and $\quad \sigma_{max} = \dfrac{F}{A} + \dfrac{M_{max} C}{L} = \dfrac{F}{A} + \dfrac{F e C}{L} \sec \dfrac{\lambda L}{2}$

Substituting Eq. (9.2.4) into the above equation leads to the maximum allowable stress due to buckling in terms of the applied force, and Young's modulus, and geometric parameters,

$$\sigma_{max} = \frac{F}{A} \left\{ 1 + \frac{e C}{k^2} \sec \left[\frac{L}{2k} \left(\frac{F}{E A} \right)^{\frac{1}{2}} \right] \right\} \tag{9.2.11}$$

where

A: Cross-sectional area;

k: Radius of gyration, and $k \equiv (A/I)^{\frac{1}{2}}$. $\tag{9.2.12}$

C: Distance from the cross-sectional centroid to the outer surface;

$(eC)/k^2$: Eccentric ratio, defining the relative eccentricity scaled by the cross-section.

The maximum value for force F appear in the above equation is called critical buckling load and its corresponding stress is called critical buckling stress, respectively denoted by F_{cr} and $\sigma_{cr}(F_{cr}/A)$. Detailed derivations of critical buckling load F_{cr} and critical bucking stress σ_{cr} are to be discussed in Section 9.2.2.

Assume that the maximum stress never exceeds the yield strength. The secant formula in Eq. (9.2.11) for the maximum allowable stress due to buckling ($\sigma_{cr} = F_{cr}/A$) is to be further constrained by the following equation

$$\sigma_y \geqslant \frac{F_{cr}}{A} \left\{ 1 + \frac{e C}{k^2} \sec \left[\frac{L}{2 k E^{\frac{1}{2}}} \left(\frac{F_{cr}}{A} \right)^{\frac{1}{2}} \right] \right\} \tag{9.2.13}$$

9.2.1.2　Cantilevered Column

Constants c_1 and c_2 in Eq. (9.2.4) can be resolved using the following two boundary conditions for the case of cantilevered column (one clamped end and one free end):

(a) $y = 0$ at $x = 0$ (No deflection as fixed at $x = 0$) $\tag{9.2.14}$

(b) $\dfrac{dy}{dx} = 0$ at $x = 0$ (Zero slope as fixed at $x = 0$) $\tag{9.2.15}$

Substituting the above two equations into Eq. (9.2.4) leads to

$$y = [\lambda \sin(\lambda x) + \cos(\lambda x) - 1]e \tag{9.2.16}$$

The maximum moment occurs at $x = 0$ while the maximum deflection is at $x = L$. Substituting Eq. (9.2.16) into Eq. (9.2.1) yields

$$M_{max} = F(e + y_{max})$$

$$= Fe[\lambda \sin(\lambda L) + \cos(\lambda L)] \tag{9.2.17}$$

and

$$\sigma_{max} = \frac{F}{A} + \frac{M_{max}C}{I} = \frac{F}{A}\left\{1 + \left(\frac{F}{A}\right)^{-\frac{1}{2}}\left(\frac{e\ C\ E^{\frac{1}{2}}}{k}\right)\sin\left[\left(\frac{F}{A}\right)^{\frac{1}{2}}(kE^{\frac{1}{2}})^{-1}L\right]\right\}$$

$$= \frac{F}{A}\left\{1 + \left(\frac{F}{A}\right)^{-\frac{1}{2}}\left(\frac{e\ C\ E^{\frac{1}{2}}}{k}\right)\sin\left[\left(\frac{F}{A}\right)^{\frac{1}{2}}(kE^{\frac{1}{2}})^{-1}L\right]\frac{e\ C}{k^2}\cos\left[\left(\frac{F}{A}\right)^{\frac{1}{2}}(k\ E^{\frac{1}{2}})^{-1}L\right]\right\} \tag{9.2.18}$$

The corresponding critical buckling load and buckling stress (F_{cr} and σ_{cr}) given above are to be derived by the same token as the case with two hinged ends, but with different boundary conditions.

Assume that the maximum stress never exceeds the yield strength, the following equation will give another constraint to the allowable critical load F_{cr} and critical stress ($\sigma_{cr} = F_{cr}/A$) as

$$\sigma_y \geqslant \frac{F_{cr}}{A}\left\{1 + \left(\frac{F_{cr}}{A}\right)^{-\frac{1}{2}}\left(\frac{e\ C\ E^{\frac{1}{2}}}{k}\right)\sin\left[\left(\frac{F_{cr}}{A}\right)^{\frac{1}{2}}(k\ E^{\frac{1}{2}})^{-1}L\right]\frac{e\ C}{k^2}\cos\left[\left(\frac{F_{cr}}{A}\right)^{\frac{1}{2}}(k\ E^{\frac{1}{2}})^{-1}L\right]\right\} \tag{9.2.19}$$

9.2.2　Column Buckling without Eccentricity

The maximum force that can be carried by a slender column (or beam) without buckling depends on the values of constants c_1 and c_2 in Eq. (9.2.5) that can be resolved using the boundary conditions. When there is no eccentricity, the differential equation and its general solution can be reduced from Eqs. (9.2.3) and (9.2.5), respectively as

$$\frac{d^2y}{dx^2} + \lambda^2 y = 0 \tag{9.2.20}$$

and

$$y = c_1 \sin(\lambda x) + c_2 \cos(\lambda x) \tag{9.2.21}$$

9.2.2.1 Both Ends Hinged

The major interest is to find out the value of force F that would cause bucking due to bending. It means to find out a nontrivial $(x \neq 0)$ solution to this boundary-value problem. Consider the case with two hinged ends,

$$y(x = 0) = c_1 \sin(0) + c_2 \cos(0) = c_2 = 0 \tag{9.2.22}$$

and $$y(x = L) = c_1 \sin(\lambda L) + c_2 \cos(\lambda L) = 0 \tag{9.2.23}$$

Plugging Eq. (9.2.22) into Eq. (9.2.23), one has the following characteristic equation for column buckling without eccentricity

$$\sin(\lambda L) = 0 \tag{9.2.24}$$

The above eigenvalue equation is true if and only if

$$\lambda_n L = n \pi, \quad \text{where } n = 0, 1, 2, 3, \cdots \tag{9.2.25}$$

Substitution Eq. (9.2.4) into the above equation leads to

$$\left(\frac{F_n}{E I} \right)^{\frac{1}{2}} L = n \pi \tag{9.2.26}$$

i.e., $$F_n = \frac{n^2 \pi^2 E I}{L^2} \tag{9.2.27}$$

Define the critical buckling load for the case of two hinge ends as the lowest load given by the above equation with nontrivial solution, i.e., $n = 1$, and

i.e., $$F_{cr} = F_1 = \frac{\pi^2 E I}{L^2} \tag{9.2.28}$$

9.2.2.2 Cantilever Column

Again, it is intended to find out a nontrivial $(x \neq 0)$ solution to this boundary-value problem. Consider the case of cantilevered column,

$$y(x = 0) = c_1 \sin 0 + c_2 \cos 0 = c_2 = 0 \tag{9.2.29}$$

and $$\frac{dy}{dx}(x = L) = c_1 \lambda \cos(\lambda L) - c_2 \lambda \sin(\lambda L) = 0 \tag{9.2.30}$$

Plugging Eq. (9.2.29) into Eq. (9.2.30), one has the following characteristic equation for column buckling without eccentricity

$$\cos(\lambda L) = 0 \tag{9.2.31}$$

The above eigenvalue equation is true if and only if

$$\lambda_n L = n \pi, \quad \text{where } n = \frac{1}{2}, \frac{3}{2}, \frac{5}{2} \tag{9.2.32}$$

Substituting Eq. (9.2.4) into the above equation and letting $n = 1/2$ (the lowest) leads to

$$\left(\frac{F_{\frac{1}{2}}}{E\,I}\right)^{\frac{1}{2}} L = \frac{1}{2}\pi \tag{9.2.33}$$

i.e.,
$$F_{\frac{1}{2}} = \frac{\frac{1}{4}\pi^2 E\,I}{L^2} \tag{9.2.34}$$

9.2.2.3 Column Effective Length Factor

As generalized using the column effective length (K), the critical buckling load (F_{cr}), also called Euler's critical buckling load for columns [Euler] with various boundary conditions, is defined as

$$F_{cr} = \frac{\pi^2 E\,I}{(K\,L)^2} \tag{9.2.35}$$

Therefore, the critical buckling stress in response to various boundary conditions becomes

$$\sigma_{cr} = \frac{F_{cr}}{A} = \frac{\pi^2 E\,I}{A(K\,L)^2} \tag{9.2.36}$$

where

L: Rod length;

K: Column effective length factor;

σ_{cr}: Pseudo-critical stress due to buckling;

A: Cross-sectional area.

Note that Eq. (9.2.36) reduces to Eq. (9.2.28) by setting $K=1$ (i.e., having both ends hinged) and to Eq. (9.2.34) by setting $K=2$. The column effective length factor corresponding to different boundary conditions is given as follows [Kaewkulchai]:

	One End	The Other End
(1) $K=0.5$	Fixed	Fixed
(2) $K=0.6997$	Fixed	Hinged
(3) $K=1.0$	Fixed	Hinged and Guided
(4) $K=2.0$	Fixed	Free
(5) $K=1.0$	Hinged	Hinged
(6) $K=2.0$	Hinged	Guided

A hinged end is also called a simply-supported end. Note that either fixed or hinged end is allowed to move in the longitudinal direction when considering a buckling failure.

Stress σ_{cr} obtained from Eq. (9.2.36) is the maximum conceptual compressive stress, up to which the column could actually carry in the linear elastic range when limited by the buckling consideration only. It is a function of material elasticity and geometry, not related to the strength of material. Therefore, materials with a high strength will buckle just as quickly as a low-strength one. Should the eccentricity be involved, the critical load defined by Eq. (9.2.36) can be substituted into Eq. (9.2.11) for the case that both ends are fixed and into Eq. (9.2.18) for the case of cantilevered columns.

Example 9.2.1   A slender steel column of length 5000 mm is fixed at both ends and used to support a concentric axial load of 80 kN. Given that $E = 210$ GPa and $\sigma_y = 360$ MPa, determine the required minimum diameter (mm).

Solution:

By Eq. (9.2.29),

$$\sigma_{cr} = \frac{F_{cr}}{A} = \frac{\pi^2 E I}{A(K L)^2} = \frac{\pi^2 \times 210000 \times \dfrac{1}{2}\pi r^4}{\pi r^2 (0.5 \times 5000)^2} = 0.16581\, r^2$$

If safety factor $= 1.0$, then $\sigma_{cr} = \sigma_y$, i.e., $0.16581 r^2 = 360$. Thus, $r = 46.6$ mm ≈ 47 mm.

If safety factor $= 1.5$, then $\sigma_{cr} = 1.5\,\sigma_y$, i.e., $0.16581 r^2 = 1.5 \times 360$. Thus, $r = 57.1$ mm ≈ 58 mm.

If safety factor $= 2.0$, then $\sigma_{cr} = 2\,\sigma_y$, i.e., $0.16581 r^2 = 2 \times 360$. Thus, $r = 65.9$ mm ≈ 66 mm.

9.2.3 Inclusive Deflection in Buckling

However, deflection （δ） due to column flex also accounts for an effect like eccentricity. For a truly clamped ended column, as a special case, the post-buckling curve is stable and the relation between the deflection （δ） and the applied load level （F） exceeding the initial buckling load is ［Budiansky］

$$\frac{F}{F_{cr}} \approx 1 + \frac{\pi^2 \delta^2}{8 L^2} + \frac{3 \pi^4 \delta^4}{64 L^4} \tag{9.2.37}$$

Note that F_{cr} is calculated from Eq. （9.2.13） and δ can be obtained from finite element analysis or design handbooks. Note that $\sigma_{cr} = F_{cr}/A$.

9.2.4 Buckling Load versus Yielding of Material

Buckling is an eigenvalue problem as a function of the material and geometric stiffness. There are a number of buckling modes and corresponding modal shapes. The stress ratio corresponding to the lowest eigenvalue is the critical one. The ratio of the yield strength to the critical load is,

$$R_\sigma = \frac{\sigma_y}{\sigma_{cr}} \tag{9.2.38}$$

This is a design focus because of its unique interpretation, which is different from other failure criteria. It reflects the ratio of the maximum possible load a column could carry before it yields if no buckling is to take place. It is sometimes treated like a safety factor.

In bifurcation buckling, there are two equilibrium solutions at the bifurcation point, e.g. snap-through of a dome, the ordinary "static strength of materials" solution and the instability （buckling） solution may be resolved simultaneously.

Buckling is a critical state of stress and deformation, at which a slight disturbance causes a gross additional deformation, or perhaps a total structural failure of the part. Nevertheless, an interesting variation arises in the case of automotive applications. In the case of front end collision, the hood is expected to crumple in controlled buckling modes in order to absorb the energy of collision, as well as to save the passenger compartment. In such cases, we design for buckling, not against it.

9.2.5   Self-Buckling

A free stand-alone column will buckle under its own weight if its height exceeds a certain limiting length [Kato] [Cox et al.]

$$
H_{\mathrm{cr}} = 1.\ 986353 \left(\frac{E\ I}{\rho\ G\ A} \right)^{\frac{1}{3}}
\tag{9.2.39}
$$

where

I: Second moment of cross-sectional area;
ρ ($\mathrm{kg/m^3}$): Density;
G: Gravity, 1 G~9.807 $\mathrm{m/s^2}$;
A ($\mathrm{m^2}$): Cross-sectional area.

9.3   Buckling of Simply Supported Plates under Compression

A thin plate may exhibit a unstable behavior in the form of buckling and its critical buckling strength depends on the thickness and boundary conditions. Consider a plate, which is simply supported at the centroidal plane on all four sides. Eq. (9.2.4) for column buckling can be extended to the differential equation for plate buckling subjected to a uniform compression, i.e., the compressive force per unit length N_x as shown in Fig. 9.3.1. The governing equation and boundary conditions can be written as

$$
\frac{\partial^4 w}{\partial^4 x} + \frac{\partial^4 w}{\partial x^2\ \mathrm{d}y^2} + \frac{\partial\ w}{\partial y^4} + \frac{12\ (1-\nu^2)\ N_x}{E\ h^3} \left(\frac{\partial w^2}{\partial x^2} \right) = 0
\tag{9.3.1}
$$

and $w = 0$, If $x = 0$, $x = a$, $y = 0$, $x = b$ (9.3.2)

where
w (m): Out-of-plate deflection;
x, y (m): x-and y-coordinates in the midplane and having the origin at the plate centroid;
N_x(N/m): Force per unit length acting at the boundary perpendicular to the x-axis;
H (m): Thickness.

Note that N_x is here defined to have a positive value regardless of the compression status. Mathematically, the deflection can be represented by the interaction of two harmonic functions

$$
w = \sum_{i=1}^{I} \sum_{j=1}^{J} w_{ij}\ \sin\left(\frac{p\ \pi\ x}{a} \right)\ \cos\left(\frac{q\ \pi\ y}{b} \right)
\tag{9.3.3}
$$

where

w_{ij}: Coefficient of deflection corresponding to buckling mode (i, j);

a: Length of the plate, directed along the x-axis;

b: Width of the plate, directed along the y-axis;

i: Number of half sinewave-like curvatures along the x-axis (Fig. 9.3.1);

j: Number of half sinewave-like curvatures along the y-axis (Fig. 9.3.1).

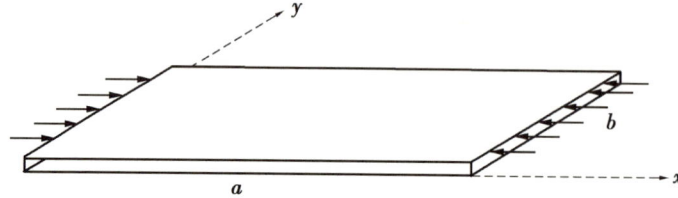

Fig. 9.3.1   Simply-Supported Plate Subjected to 1st Mode Buckling（Dashed Profile）

Plugging the above equation into Eq. (9.3.1) yields

$$\left(\frac{p^4 \pi^4}{a^4} + \frac{2 p^2 q^2 \pi^4}{a^2 b^2} + \frac{q^4 \pi^4}{b^4} \right) + \left[\frac{12(1 - \nu^2)}{E h^3} \right] \left[\frac{p^2 \pi^2}{a^2} \right] N_x = 0 \tag{9.3.4}$$

Thus, $\quad N_x = \left(\frac{p}{a} + \frac{q^2 a}{p b^2} \right)^2 \left[\frac{\pi^2 E h^3}{12(1 - \nu^2)} \right]$ $\tag{9.3.5}$

of which $p = 1, 2, \cdots, P$ and $q = 1, 2, \cdots Q$. The corresponding critical normal stress is

and $\quad \sigma_{xx,\text{cr}} = \frac{N_{x,\text{cr}}}{h} = \left(\frac{p b}{a} + \frac{q^2 a}{p b} \right)^2 \left[\frac{\pi^2 E}{12(1 - \nu^2)} \right] \left(\frac{h}{b} \right)^2$

$$= k_{\text{C}} \left[\frac{\pi^2 E}{12(1 - \nu^2)} \right] \left(\frac{h}{b} \right)^2 \tag{9.3.6}$$

where $\quad k_{\text{C}} = \left(\frac{p b}{a} + \frac{q^2 a}{p b} \right)^2 = \left[\frac{p}{\dfrac{a}{b}} + \frac{q^2}{p} \left(\frac{a}{b} \right) \right]^2$ $\tag{9.3.7}$

Eq. (9.3.6) gives the critical normal stress rendering the buckling of a simply-supported plate and it bears the same form as Eq. (9.2.2) for the critical load of column buckling. Critical normal stress $\sigma_{xx,\text{cr}}$ is proportional to parameter k_{C}, which is called buckling coefficient of a simply-supported plate, expressed as a function of aspect ratio a/b and half-wave numbers p and q.

The fundamental buckling mode, i.e., half wave along the y-direction ($\perp$ the loading direction), of such a thin plate is obtained by setting $q = 1$, since k_{C} increases with respect to q quadratically.

On the other hand, parameter p is the integer that exhibits how may half waves along "side a" of the plate. The buckling coefficient for the first 5 failure modes corresponding to $a/b = 1$, 2, and 3 at $q = 1$ are listed as follows:

a/b	p	q	k_C	
1	1	1	4.00	⟶Critical buckling load
1	2	1	6.25	
1	3	1	11.11	
1	4	1	18.06	
1	5	1	27.04	
2	1	1	6.25	
2	2	1	4.00	⟶Critical buckling load
2	3	1	4.69	
2	4	1	6.25	
2	5	1	8.41	
3	1	1	11.11	
3	2	1	4.69	
3	3	1	4.00	⟶Critical buckling load
3	4	1	4.34	
3	5	1	5.14	
4	1	1	18.06	
4	2	1	6.25	
4	3	1	4.34	
4	4	1	4.00	⟶Critical buckling load
4	5	1	4.20	

It is observed that the critical normal stress (least compressive stress) required to produce a buckling mode of a simply-supported plate does not necessarily correspond to mode $(p = 1, q = 1)$. Yet it depends very much on aspect ratio a/b, i.e., the "slenderness" of the plate. Given that $q = 1$, one can obtain the lowest k_C value at the moment when

$$\frac{dk_C}{dp} = 0 \tag{9.3.8}$$

i.e., $\quad p = \dfrac{a}{b} \tag{9.3.9}$

9.4 Buckling of Plates under Compression with Various Boundary Conditions

Steel plates are frequently used in automobiles, ships, and civil engineering infrastructures. Thin plates tend to buckle in the through-thickness direction when subjected to compressive loads. The critical buckling strength for rectangular plates subjected to normal compression at edges with various boundary conditions, including the simply supported, can be generally expressed in light of Eq. (9.3.6) as

$$\sigma_{xx,cr} = \frac{N_{x,cr}}{h} = k_C \left[\frac{\pi^2 E}{12(1-\nu^2)} \right] \left(\frac{h}{b} \right)^2 \qquad (9.4.1)$$

The lowest value of k_C corresponding to various boundary conditions are given as follows:

a-edge (‖x-axis)	b-edge (‖y-axis)	k_C
Free	Fixed	0.43
Free	Hinged	1.27
Hinged	Hinged	4.00
Fixed	Fixed	6.97

In order to assure that a plate will fail due to material yielding rather than buckling, the thickness-to-width ratio of the plate has to be constrained by the following equation

$$\sigma_{xx,cr} = k_C \left[\frac{\pi^2 E}{12 (1-\nu^2)} \right] \left(\frac{h}{b} \right)^2 > \sigma_y \qquad (9.4.2)$$

i.e.,
$$\frac{h}{b} > \left[\frac{k_C \pi^2 E}{12 (1-\nu^2) \sigma_y} \right]^{-\frac{1}{2}} \qquad (9.4.3)$$

of which σ_y is the yielding strength. A thin plate may exhibit an unstable behavior in the form of buckling, but it continues carrying loads right after the occurrence of buckling and usually has a post-buckling strength higher than the critical buckling strength. Thus, its design point may fall between the critical buckling strength and yield strength.

9.5 Buckling of Plates Subjected to In-Plane Shearing

The critical buckling strength for rectangular plates subjected to in-plane shearing with various boundary conditions can also be generally expressed in light of Eq. (9.3.6) as

$$\tau_{xy,cr} = k_C \left[\frac{\pi^2 E}{12(1-\nu^2)} \right] \left(\frac{h}{b} \right)^2 \qquad (9.5.1)$$

When in-plane shearing occurs, the pure shear stress may create two in-plane principal stresses and they are denoted as σ_1 (in tension) and σ_2 (in compression) for the large and small values, respectively. Buckling aligned with σ_2 loses the load-carrying capacity. On the other hand, the tension due to σ_1 continues to take more load and the plate works like a triangular truss with diagonal beams directed along σ_1. The phenomenon is called tension field action due to in-plane shear buckling.

9.6 Buckling of Plates Subjected to Mixed Loads

One failure criterion for buckling of rectangular plates subjected to mixed loads can be derived from the following formula

$$\left(\frac{\sigma_{xx}}{\sigma_{xx,\text{cr}}}\right) + \left(\frac{\tau_{xy}}{\tau_{xy,\text{cr}}}\right)^2 + \left(\frac{\sigma_{\text{b}}}{\sigma_{\text{b,cr}}}\right)^2 < 1 \qquad (9.6.1)$$

where

σ_{b} : Normal stress due to bending of the plate;

$\sigma_{\text{b,cr}}$: Critical normal stress in bending mode only.

9.7 Buckling Analysis by Finite Element Methods

From a finite-element analysis (FEA) point of view, a buckling analysis is used to find the lowest multiplication factor for the load that will make a structure buckle. The result of such an analysis is a number of buckling load factors (BLF), which resemble the stress ratio. The first BLF (the lowest factor) corresponds to the first buckling mode and is always the one of interest. If it is less than unity, then buckling will occur due to the load being applied to the structure.

The FEA is also used to find the shape of the buckled structure. A non-linear 3-D buckling analysis should be carried out, together with full displacement analyses, if the component is critical to the safe operation of a system. The approach to a non-linear buckling solution is achieved by applying the load slowly (dividing it into a number of small load increments). The model is assumed to behave linearly for each load increment, and the change in model shape is calculated at each increment. Stresses are updated from increment to increment, until the full applied load is reached.

9.7.1　Selection of Modeling Elements

It would be straightforward and error-proof to directly apply solid elements, isotropic or orthotropic, to structural buckling problems [Chiang & Tang] [Sadowski & Rotter] especially when dealing with various constraints (e.g. contacts), although finite elements based on shell and plate theories have been continuously tuned up for modeling structural buckling [Thai & Kim] [Rouzegar & Sharifpoor]. The formulation of each of these solid elements (i.e., 8-noded and 20-noded with various integration schemes) allows for nonlinear analysis with large strains and rotations, and employs the flow theory of plasticity. The reduced integration version of 20-noded solid element has the same number of through-thickness Gauss integration points as 8-noded (2×2×2)[Chiang & Tang], but yields more accurate results in stress analyses than the corresponding fully-integrated 20-noded brick element that boasts 3×3×3. Based on a thin tube, a comparison chart (radius/thickness=25) is presented in Fig. 9.7.1 by [Sadowski & Rotter], of which the vertical coordinate is the normalized bending moment and the horizontal axis the normalized curvature. It was found by [Sadowski & Rotter] that the 20-noded solid element with reduced integration provides very accurate buckling modeling for any radius/thickness ratio ranging from 10 to 50, while others don't always do.

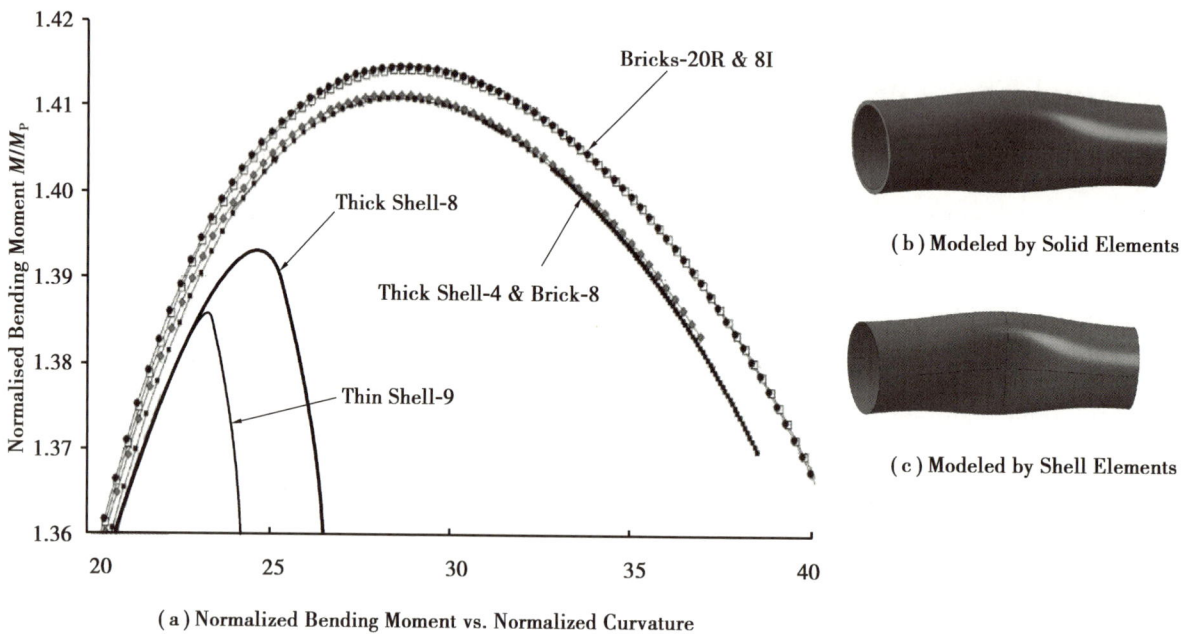

(a) Normalized Bending Moment vs. Normalized Curvature

Fig. 9.7.1　Accuracy Comparison of Buckling Analyses by Various Elements Using Abaqus [Sadowski & Rotter]

9.7.2　Linear Buckling by Finite Element Methods

Buckling failure is primarily characterized by a loss of structural stiffness (negative or null) and is not modeled by the usual linear finite element analysis, but by a finite element eigenvalue-eigenvector solution. Depending on the stress level of the element, a symmetric matrix appears to reflect the effect of geometric change on the element force vector from a known stress state. It is called geometric stiffness matrix, initial stress stiffness matrix, or stability coefficient matrix. It is necessary for a finite element formulation with large displacements to simulate structural instability, although it may be adequate to have only small strains. Thus, the general finite element formulation of buckling problems at least involves the construction of geometric stiffness matrix $[k_\sigma]$ in addition to the conventional elastic stiffness matrix $[k]$ as formulated in Chapter 3. A finite element formulation based on linear stress-strain terms is to get the elastic stiffness matrix, while other terms related to large displacements are to be considered for deriving the geometric stiffness matrix.

This stress stiffness matrix will lead to an eigenvalue equation due to the buckling load [Zhao et al.]. More specifically, the structure is first loaded with a reference load to find the reference stress stiffness matrix, $([k_\sigma])_{ref}$ and then an additional corresponding load vector is generated as

$$\{R\} = \lambda \ \{R\}_{ref} \tag{9.7.1}$$

which is to be applied to the structure, where λ represents an arbitrary multiplier to the original reference load vector and it is called buckling load factor (BLF). The conventional stiffness matrix and initial stress stiffness matrix (also called geometric stiffness matrix) are simultaneously combined to resist the buckling load as

$$([K] + \lambda_m [k_\sigma]_{ref})\{D\}_{ref} = \lambda_m \{R\}_{ref} \tag{9.7.2}$$

Where
$[K]$: Conventional stiffness matrix formulated as shown in Chapter 3;

$([k_\sigma])_{ref}$: Reference stress stiffness matrix, i.e., obtained from $\dfrac{1}{2}[B_N]$ in Eq. (3.14.7);

$\{D\}_{ref}$: Reference displacement vector;
$\{R\}_{ref}$: Reference load vector;
λ_m: Buckling load vector coefficient or buckling load factor (BLF) for the mth mode.

Next, introducing the associated buckling displacement shape for the mth mode, written as $\{\delta D\}$, into the above equation,

$$([K] + \lambda_m [K_\sigma]_{ref})(\{D\}_{ref} + \{\delta D\}) = \lambda_m\{R\}_{ref} \tag{9.7.3}$$

The comparison between Eq. (9.7.2) and Eq. (9.7.3) leads to

$$([K] + \lambda_m[K_\sigma]_{ref})(\{\delta D\}) = \{0\} \tag{9.7.4}$$

The combined stiffness is calculated as summation of elastic stiffness matrix and load factor multiplied by geometric stiffness matrix. When a structure is unstable, it means a small amount of load can render large displacement. In other words, the combined stiffness matrix is singular and this is purely an eigenvalue problem. Eq. (9.7.4) can be solved for eigenvalue λ_m, which can then be used for identifying the critical load that renders the onset of buckling [Earlis] for the mth mode, as implemented in Abaqus,

$$\{R\} = \lambda_m \{R\}_{ref} \tag{9.7.5}$$

The spatial distribution of the load is important while its relative magnitude is irrelevant. The buckling calculation gives a multiplier that scales the magnitude of the load up or down to the level that can cause buckling. The following steps are involved in linear elastic buckling analysis:

(a) Solve the assembled load-displacement (stress-strain) equations for linear elastic pre-buckling load state, i.e.,

$$[K]\{D\}_{ref} = \{R\}_{ref} \tag{9.7.6}$$

(b) The geometric stiffness matrix is then formulated at that pre-buckling stress-strain level in order to account for the right of stress-strain relationship.

(c) General eigenvalue calculation is performed for the combined elastic stiffness and geometric stiffness matrices, i.e., looking for λ_m using Eq. (9.7.4).

(d) The elastic buckling load factor is the lowest eigenvalue, i.e., λ_1. Nevertheless, the realistic buckling load may be even lower than $\lambda_1\{R\}_{ref}$, because the imperfection and other nonlinear behaviors in a structure may not have been considered yet.

Linear finite-element analysis does not provide enough information about buckling to make correct design decisions, especially when designing lightweight components [Pvorak]. It cannot predict the post-buckling behavior, but it provides the initial analysis preview that can be used as an input for the follow-up nonlinear buckling analysis.

9.7.3 Nonlinear Buckling Analysis

Two sources of nonlinearity (i.e., initial geometrical imperfection and material plasticity) and boundary restraints (e.g. realignment/misalignment, eccentricity of the load, and variation in contact boundaries such as contact areas and friction) have to be considered in nonlinear buckling analysis. However, buckling shape at the critical load obtained from the linear analysis without geometric imperfection, i.e., the result from Step (d) in Section 9.7.1, may be introduced into the nonlinear model with an imposed initial geometric imperfection. There is no eigenvalue calculation in nonlinear buckling analysis, because during the nonlinear run the overall structural stiffness matrix is to be updated between loading increments to incorporate deformations that affect the structural behavior and also to be checked if the load level at which a structure becomes unstable. As buckling begins, the structure undergoes a momentary loss of stiffness and the load control algorithm for nonlinear finite element analysis may invite numerical instabilities [Hilburger]. The use of traditional Newton-Raphson method based on load control for nonlinear finite element analysis to predict the structural behavior after buckling is not feasible in general. It is better dealt with using arc-length (displacement) control method, as illustrated in Fig. 9.7.2, by which points corresponding to consecutive load increments are evenly spaced along the load-displacement curve.

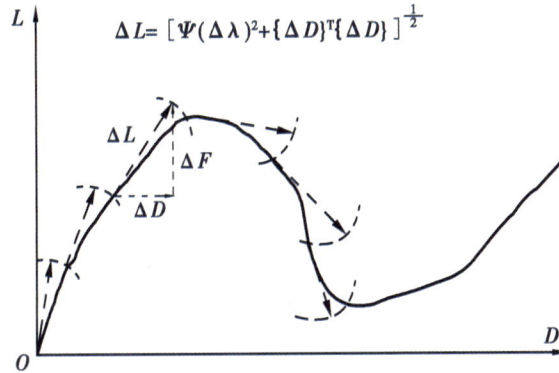

$$\Delta L = [\Psi(\Delta\lambda)^2 + \{\Delta D\}^T\{\Delta D\}]^{\frac{1}{2}}$$

Fig. 9.7.2   Iterations by Arc-Length Control for Nonlinear Buckling Analysis

Unlike the Newton-Raphson Method, the Arc Length method postulates a simultaneous variation in both the displacement vector $\{\Delta d\} = \{\Delta u, \Delta v, \Delta w\}$ and the buckling load factor $\Delta\lambda$. The main difference is that both Δu and $\Delta\lambda$ are unknowns in comparison with the Newton-Raphson method where the load, i.e., $\Delta\lambda\{R\}_{ref}$, is given and unknown displacement vector $\{\Delta d\}$ is to be solved iteratively. A scale factor, denoted by ψ, can be defined such that

$$(\Delta L)^2 = \psi(\Delta\lambda)^2 + \{\Delta D\}^T\{\Delta D\} \tag{9.7.7}$$

When $\psi = 1$, the method is also called the spherical arc-length method in the (λ, u, v, w) coordinate system and the radius of the spherical arc is ΔL. Otherwise, it is a hyper-ellipse arc control method. The analyst decides which value should be assigned to ψ and the next converged point is then obtained as the point of intersection between the equilibrium path and that hyper-elliptic arc. This iterative process to determine the next point of intersection is shown below in the pseudo-dimensional (D, λ) plane where the hyper-elliptic arc seemingly degenerates into an elliptic arc.

Due to buckling, the large deflection of cross sections causes the stress-strain relationship to get into nonlinear range, where modulus of elasticity as well as buckling load decreases considerably. Several cases have been chosen to illustrate those effects on the pre-buckling and post-buckling behaviors of aluminum sandwich foam plates [Nguyen et al.]. Metal foam core exhibits plastic deformation much sooner than the potential onset of buckling and results in a tremendously reduced critical buckling load. When the stress-strain relationship is nonlinear, tangent modulus of elasticity should be considered for calculating the buckling load. It is mainly due to geometric nonlinearity. In the post-buckling regime, as the global buckling proceeds, the shear deformation due to core's plastic deformation specially around loaded edges keep developing [Nguyen et al.] [Joubaneh et al.].

9.7.4 Thermal Buckling

Thermal buckling behavior of a structure can be understood using the application example done by [Audebert] on automotive transmission clutches and brake discs in light of finite element method [Yang]. The heat generated between friction surfaces in contact is not uniform. While rotating at the same angular velocity, the sliding speed is proportional to the radius of the contact point and thus non-uniform heat distribution is generated across the friction disc in combination with the physical constraints by design. As the temperature rises, the clutch and brake discs are then subjected to some potential failure modes, such as thermal distortion (including lateral runout, thickness variation, and thermal coning [Kao et al.]), thermoelastic instability [Zhao], and thermal buckling [Yang]. Thermal distortion mainly leads to the following problems: lateral runout, disc thickness variation (DTV) and thermal coning [Yang].

9.8 Aerodynamic Instability

When fluid flows, it interacts with the obstacles it reaches in its way by transferring a part of its energy to those interactions, which are converted into dynamic energy over the obstacles [Zhao et al.]. The energy may lead them to different levels of unstable vibration and/or motion, which are directly dependent on their aeroelastic and geometric characteristics such as buffeting, flutter, galloping, and Kármán vortex street [Bigoni]. On the other hand, the "obstacles" can also be driven into a controlled motion and used to extract energy from the flow as a positive contributing tool.

9.8.1 Risers

Risers are used for both seabed oil-drilling and environmental protection, as shown in Fig. 9.8.1. A riser is a slender structure that connects the off-shore floating platform with the well at the seabed and it may exceed 2 km in length. A riser can be excited by waves and underwater currents, and thus its vibration is subjected to vortex-induced vibrations (VIV) and wave-induced vibrations (WIV). VIV is a common phenomenon associated with long flexible structures, such as risers, chimneys, and bridge cables. The flow around such a slender structure is complex and fully 3-dimensional in nature for being fully coupled with the fluid motion.

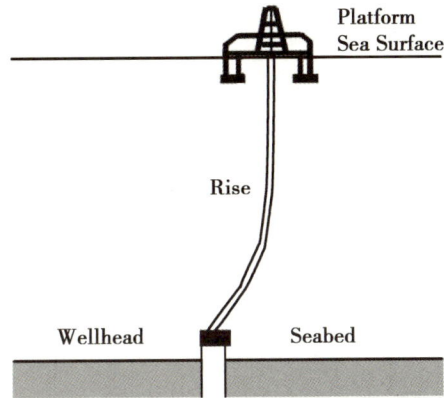

Fig. 9.8.1   Schematic Drawing of Offshore Riser from Drill Platform to Seabed

The eigen-frequencies associated with the fluid-structure interaction (FSI) in the coupled field are so low that low-order eigen-modes are, therefore, expected to be excited even in shallow current. Lock-in, also referred as synchronization, means that the riser moves together with the fluid excitation with a large damaging amplitude. The lock-in region is larger for a smaller mass ratio, which is defined as the ratio of the riser mass to corresponding fluid mass:

$$M_{\text{ratio}} = \frac{M_{\text{riser}}}{M_{\text{fluid}}} \tag{9.8.1}$$

It becomes critical as the mass ratio reaches unity [Williamson & Godvardhan]. In the neighborhood of lock-in, the vortex shedding frequency is dictated by the resonating eigen-frequency of the structure.

9.8.2   Rotating Disks

Flutter, buffeting, and vortex are top three typical phenomena of dynamic instability induced by aerodynamic flow of fluid. Interesting findings on flutter come from experiments on rotating disks [Lee et al.] and are given as follows:

(a) Pre-flutter: Aerodynamic effect by surrounding air reduces the natural frequencies and critical speeds of the vibration modes in pre-flutter regions.
(b) Onset of flutter: A natural frequency of the disk rotating at ambient atmospheric pressure is equal to that in vacuum at the flutter onset speed where the disk experiences aero-induced flutter.
(c) Post-flutter: Aerodynamic coupling between the disk and surrounding air increases the natural frequencies of the disk.

9.8.3 Aeroelastic Instability of Air Compressor

Industrial fan designers have asymptomatically assumed that a fan follows its steady-state characteristic curves even in the presence of a pressure pulse, as shown by the two black square dots in Fig. 9.8.2 [Borello et al.]. Nevertheless, aeroelastic instability analysis shows that a positive or negative pressure pulse shall cause the fan's operating point to depart from its steady state characteristic curves in a transient response [Kirk et al.], as denoted by the two red and blue circular dots in Fig. 9.8.2. This departure results in unsteady aerodynamic force variation by a factor of two compared with those associated with operation of the fan at its duty point, causing aeroelastic instability.

An axial flow fan fits with an anti-stall ring, as shown in Fig. 9.8.3. The anti-stall ring comprises an extension to the fan casing just over and upstream of the blades. The anti-stall casing incorporates static vanes, shown in yellow. As a fan approaches stall the flow though the fan is centrifuged upwards "along" the blades and the flow spills out of the fan inlet at stall. This process of redirecting the flow stabilizes the fan's performance, eliminating the drop in pressure.

9.8.4 Aeroelastic Instability of Aircraft Wing

An aeroelastic instability mechanism is a classical phenomenon of flutter involving the coupling of torsional and flapwise vibration modes due to geometric offsets of the center of mass relative to the center of elasticity in a wing cross-section (Fig. 9.8.4). For the torsional and flapwise modes to couple in a flutter mode, the modal frequencies must be sufficiently close. Structurally, it cannot occur until the "aspect ratio" exceeds the critical number as for a slender wing.

9.8.5 Aeroelastic Instability of Windmill Turbine

Wind turbine blades should be as light as possible to reduce the cost of energy, both because the cost of the blade itself is roughly proportional to the mass but also to minimize the gravity induced bending moments on the hub and to keep the total tower head mass down. A mass reduction at the tower top gives smaller bending moments in the tower and eases the stiffness requirements of the substructure to maintain the frequency of the first natural bending mode.

One aspect influencing the design criteria is the lower atmospheric turbulence and higher extreme wind speed offshore, which imply that ultimate loads will become relatively more important than fatigue loads for the flapwise strength of the blade.

- ● Unsteady computation, peak pressure across fan in extract mode with train departing
- ■ Fan duty point with +1000 Pa pressure pulse
- ▲ Fan duty point
- ◆ Fan duty point with −1000 Pa pressure pulse
- ▼ Unsteady computation, peak pressure across fan in extract mode with train approaching
- —— Experimental data
- —— +1000 Pa system curve
- —— System curve
- ······ −1000 Pa system curve

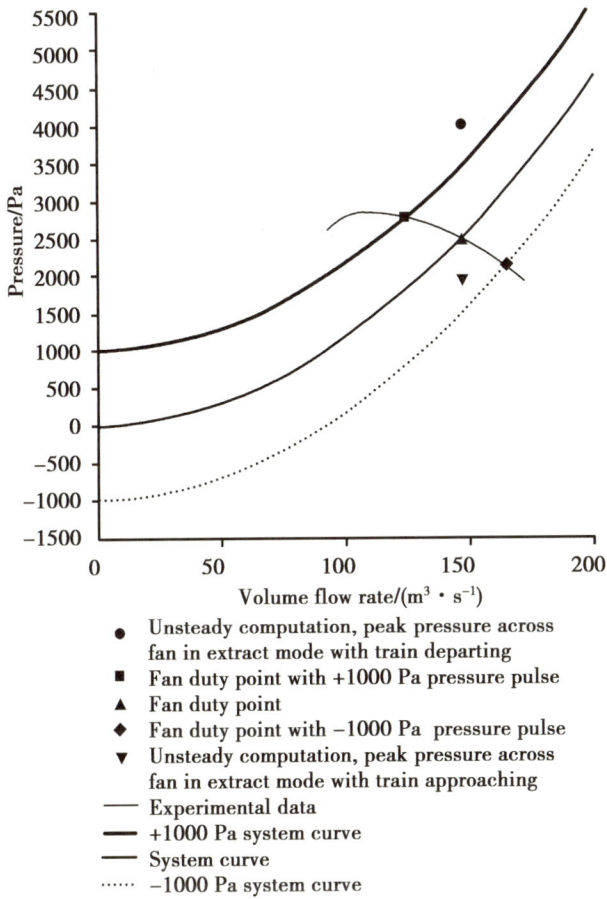

Fig. 9.8.2   Aeroelastic Instability of Air Compressor Induced by Unsteady Pressure Pulse [Kirk et al.]

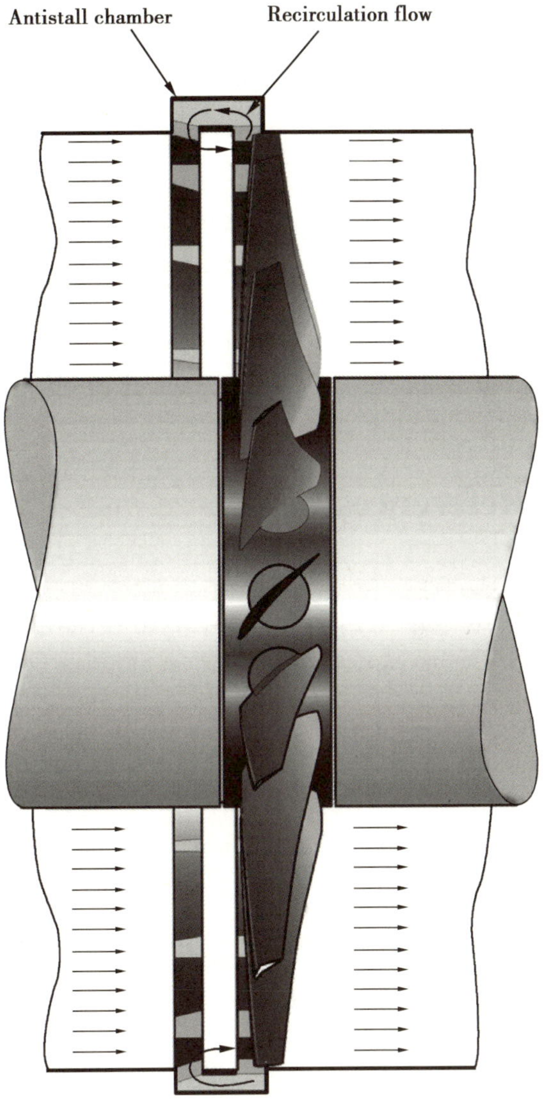

Fig. 9.8.3   Centrifugal Ring to Neutralize the Instability of an Axial Pump [Eurovent 1/11]

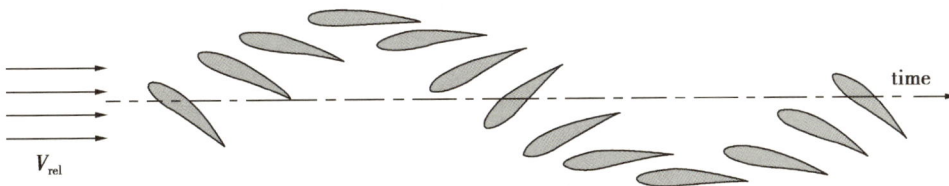

Fig. 9.8.4   Schematic Drawing of Classical Flutter Induced by Aeroelastic Instability [Hansen et al.]

9.8.6   Applications with Controlled Aerodynamic Instability

Structural instability caused by self-exciting aerodynamic flutter can be used as an effective input source for small-scaled energy harvesters, i.e., a controlled aerodynamic instability phenomenon is used intentionally and positively for generating electricity. Wind induced vibrations have been used to mechanically strain piezoelectric transducers to generate power [Allen & Smits] [Sun et al.], as well as to generate inductance power in electromagnetic transducers [Jung et al.].

In other fields, controlled aerodynamic instability can be utilized to make musical tones on ground-mounted devices, as well as on musical kites.

References

AUDEBERT N, BARBER J R, ZAGRODZKI P, 1998. Buckling of Automatic Transmission Clutch Plate due to Thermoelastic/Plastic Residual Stresses[J]. Journal of Thermal Stresses, 21(3): 309-326.

BIGONI D, 2012. Nonlinear Solid Mechanics: Bifurcation Theory and Material Instability[M]. Cambridge University Press.

BIGONI D, NOSELLI G, 1961. Experimental Evidence of Flutter and Divergence Instabilities Induced by Dry Friction[J]. Journal of the Mechanics and Physics of Solids, 59: 2208-2226.

BUDIANSKY B, 1974. Theory of Buckling and Post-Buckling Behavior of Elastic Structures[M]. Advances in Applied Mechanics, 14: 1-65.

CHIANG Y J, TANG C, 1995. Accuracy Assessment to Applying 20-Node Solid Elements to Pressurized Composite Shells[J]. Finite Elements in Analysis and Design, (20): 219-231.

COX S J, MCCARTHY C M, 1998. The Shape of the Tallest Column[J]. Society of Industrial and Applied Mathematics, 29: 547-554.

EARLS C J, 2007. Observations on Eigenvalue Buckling Analysis within a Finite Element Context[C]. Proceedings of Structural Stability Research Council, Annual Stability Conference, New Orleans, LA.

HILBURGER M W, 2012. Developing the Next Generation Shell Buckling Design Factors and Technologies[C]. Proceedings of the 53rd AIAA/ASME/ASCE/AHS/ASC Structures, Structural Dynamics, and Materials Conference, Honolulu, HI, AIAA Paper No. 2012-1686.

JONES R M, 2007. Buckling of Bars, Plates, and Shells[M]. CRC.

JOUBANEH E F, MOJAHEDIN A, KHORSHIDVAND A R, et al, 2015. Thermal Buckling Analysis of Porous Circular Plate with Piezoelectric Sensor-Actuator Layers under Uniform Thermal Load[J]. Journal of Sandwich Structures and Materials, 17(1): 3-25.

KATO K, 1915. Mathematical Investigation on the Mechanical Problems of Transmission Line[J]. Journal of Japan Society of Mechanical Engineers, 19: 41.

KAEWKULCHAI G, 1997. Design-Oriented Equations for Buckling of Slender Tapered Columns[D]. Master's Thesis, Department of Civil Engineering, Colorado State University.

KAO T K, RICHMOND J W, DOUARRE A, 2000. Brake Disc Hot Spotting and Thermal Judder: An Experimental and Finite Element Study[J]. International Journal of Vehicle Design, 23(3): 276-296.

KUO S Y, SHIAU L C, CHEN C Y, 2010. Thermal Buckling Behavior of Composite Laminated Plates[J]. Composite Structures, 92: 508-514.

NGUYEN T N, et al, 2007. Nonlinear Finite Element Method for Buckling and Post-Buckling of Aluminum Foam Sandwich Plates [C]. The 5th International Conference on Numerical Analysis in Engineering (NAE2007), Padang, Indonesia.

ROUZEGAR J, SHARIFPOOR R, 2017. Finite Element Formulations for Buckling Analysis of Isotropic and Orthotropic Plates Using Two-Variable Refined Plate Theory[J]. Iran Journal of Science and Technology Transactions of Mechanical Engineering, 41(3): 177-187.

SADOWSKI A, ROTTER J, 2013. Solid or Shell Finite Elements to Model Thick Cylindrical Tubes and Shells under Global Bending[J]. International Journal of Mechanical Sciences, 74: 143-153.

THAI H T, KIM S E, 2011. Levy-Type Solution for Buckling Analysis of Orthotropic Plates Based on Two Variable Refined Plate Theory[J]. Composite Structures, 93: 1738-1746.

YANG H Z, 2015. Finite Element Analysis of Thermal Buckling in Automotive Clutch and Brake Discs[D]. Electronic Theses and Dissertations. 1056, Mechanical Engineering Commons.

ZACCARIA D, et al, 2011. Structural Buckling under Tensile Dead Load[J]. Proceedings of the Royal Society, A, 467(2130): 1686-1700.

ZHAO J, MA B, LI H, et al, 2013. The Effect of Lubrication Film Thickness on Thermoelastic Instability under Fluid Lubricating Condition[J]. Wear, 303: 146-153.

Chapter 10

Composites-Micromechanics

10.1 Composite Materials

A composite is made of two or more different materials, of which the reinforcement does not chemically react with the matrix but are a distinct and integral part of the composite system. The reinforcement is strong and stiff forming a sort of backbone, while the matrix keeps the reinforcement in a set place. Composites provide design flexibility because many of them can be molded into complex shapes, while they are light and strong. These composite properties would not be possible without a superior strength of the fiber phase or the containing properties of the matrix phase, both are vital and essential.

10.1.1 Fiber-Reinforced Composites

Fibers are added to the matrix (e.g. resin of plastics) as a reinforcement to increase the tensile strength and stiffness of the finished part. Load transfer between an individual fiber and the matrix is schematically depicted in Fig. 10.1.1. The matrix may be rubber, plastics, metal, ceramics, or even cabin. The selection of reinforcement from a great number of fibers and particulates relies on the properties desired in the finished product. The top three basic types of fibrous reinforcements in use in the automotive industry are

(a) Glass fibers.
(b) Carbon-carbon fibers, graphite, carbon nanotubes.
(c) Natural fibers.

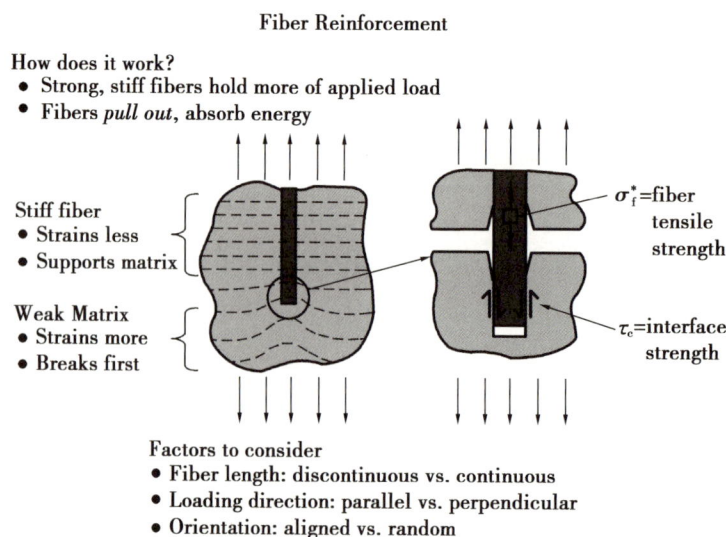

Fiber Reinforcement

How does it work?
• Strong, stiff fibers hold more of applied load
• Fibers *pull out*, absorb energy

Stiff fiber
• Strains less
• Supports matrix

Weak Matrix
• Strains more
• Breaks first

σ_f^*=fiber tensile strength

τ_c=interface strength

Factors to consider
• Fiber length: discontinuous vs. continuous
• Loading direction: parallel vs. perpendicular
• Orientation: aligned vs. random

Fig. 10.1.1　Schematic Drawing of Load Transfer Mechanism between Fibers and Matrix

Physical properties of fiber-reinforced composites are generally not isotropic in nature. Instead they are typically anisotropic, i.e., depending on the loading direction. For instance, the stiffness of a composite car-body panel often relies upon the orientation of fibers. The shape of fibers in a lamina can be one of the following:

(a) Continuous fibers: Unidirectional.
(b) Continuous fibers: Weave.
(c) Long fibers: Aligned.
(d) Long fibers: Radom.
(e) Short fibers: Random.
(f) Particulates.

Composite materials offer higher specific strength and stiffness than conventional homogeneous materials and they are in general very tolerant to environmental effects such as UV damage, moisture, chemical attack, and temperature extremes. They also provide outstanding durability potential and noise attenuation. The most popular fibrous reinforcement being used for automotive plastic parts is glass. E-glass fiber is widely accepted in the automotive industry since it is the least expensive among all glass fibers. In case glass fibers are not strong enough, carbon fibers are the next to be considered before going to metallic parts.

10.1.2   Natural Composites

Animal bones and tree trunks are typical strong natural composites. A bone is mainly made of hydroxyapatite matrix reinforced with collagen fibers. Wood is a composite made of long cellulose fibers (a polymer) held together by a much weaker matrix substance called lignin.

Natural fibers are also available from animals. For example, silky threads spun by a spider can be as strong as steel though they consist of a gel core encapsulated by a solid structure of aligned molecules.

10.1.3   Anisotropy, Orthotropy, and Isotropy

A lamina is a flat or curved arrangement of a composite material, such as power/particulates, short fibers, unidirectional fibers, or woven fibers, suspended in a matrix material. As shown in Fig. 10.1.2, each layer of the composite made of uniformly and unidirectional-arranged continuous fibers in the matrix is a lamina. The material characteristics, including mechanical, thermal, electric, magnetic, piezoelectric, piezomagnetic, electrostrictive, pyroelectric, pyromagnetic, and magnetostrictive properties of a lamina generally range from being isotropic to completely anisotropic, and its thickness depends on the material from which it is made. The mechanical properties of a lamina are known to have one of the following:

(a) Isotropy: A lamina with an infinite number of symmetry planes, i.e., every plane is a plane of symmetry, is isotropic, and requires only 2 elastic constants-generally E (Young's modulus) and ν (Poisson's ratio). It is basically homogenous material, e.g. pure copper.

(b) Transverse Isotropy: If the material properties along 1-axis and 2-axis are the same but not along 3-axis, then the composite is called transverse isotropic. Five constants are needed to describe this composite. Traditionally, 1-axis is aligned with the fiber direction and 2-axis is in the in-plane transverse direction.

(c) Orthotropy: An orthotropic material has at least 2 orthogonal planes of symmetry, where material properties are independent of direction within each plane, Fig. 10.1.2. Such materials require 9 independent variables (i.e., elastic constants) in their constitutive matrices, traditionally denoted by E_{11}, E_{22}, E_{33}, G_{12}, G_{23}, G_{31}, ν_{12}, ν_{23}, and ν_{31}. Most structural composite parts are made of orthotropic laminae.

(d) Anisotropy: A material without any planes of symmetry is fully anisotropic and requires 21 elastic constants to fully present its mechanical properties.

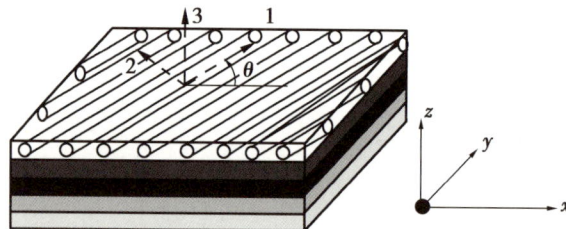

Fig. 10.1.2   Schematic Drawing of Unidirectional Continuous Fiber-Reinforced Lamina (Top Layer)

Orthotropic material properties can also be formed during manufacturing or application. One example of an orthotropic material is sheet metal formed during manufacturing by squeezing thick sections of metal between heavy rollers. This flattens and stretches its grain structure that causes the material to become anisotropic. The mechanical properties of sheet metal differ between the direction it is rolled in and those of the two transverse directions. Another example of an orthotropic material is rubber formed as applied by squeezing the rubber seal or stretching a rubber band. Again the molecular structure varies accordingly and it causes the material to become anisotropic. The mechanical properties of rubber differ between the direction it is squeezed or stretched in and those of the two transverse directions.

10.1.4   Fibrous Composites

Classification of fibrous composites according to the geometric shapes of its embedded hard materials can be divided into the following, as shown in Fig. 10.1.3:

(1) Matrix reinforced with long continuous unidirectional fibers.

(2) Matrix reinforced with weaves.

(3) Matrix reinforced with maps.

(4) Matrix reinforced with aligned short fibers.

(5) Matrix reinforced randomly with short fibers.

(6) Matrix reinforced with particulates.

(7) Matrix reinforced with powder.

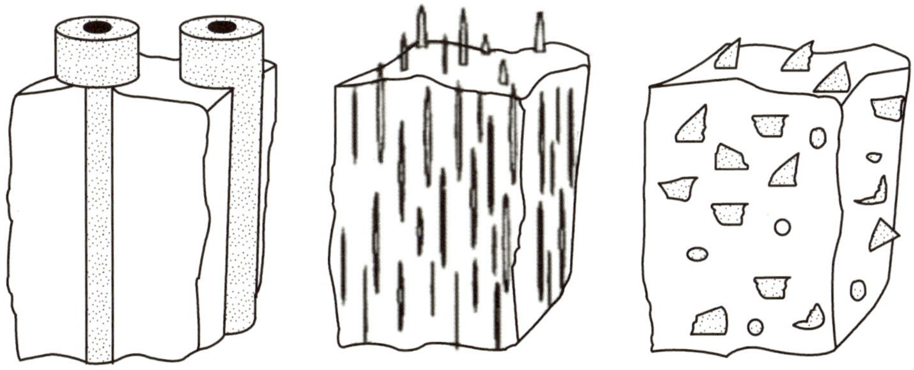

Continuous Fibers: Short Fibers   Particulates
UD, Mats, or Weaves   or Particulates   or Powder

Fig. 10.1.3   Schematic Drawings of Fibrous Composites

Elastoplastic and fatigue properties of the synthetic reinforcing fibers for automobiles are given in Tables 10.1.1-10.1.4.

10.1.5   Wettability

Wetting is the ability of the resin (liquid before being cures) to maintain contact with the surface of solid fibers and particulates. It mostly results from intermolecular interactions as active wetting or just mechanically bonded together as non-reactive wetting, when the two are brought together. The degree of wetting (wettability) is determined by a force balance between adhesive and cohesive forces. Wetting gets involved with three different material phases: solid, liquid, and unexpected gas. The surface force of the liquid resin is a predominant factor on wetting. It has drawn great attention in nano-engineering such as multi-wall carbon nanotubes.

Wettability is an index used for measuring the uniformity of embrace of fibers by the matrix. There are three primary methods applied for contact angle analysis: sessile drop method (Fig. 10.1.4), Wilhelmy plate or dynamic contact angle method (DCA), and wicking method for powders. Contact angle measurements are often the basis for estimating wetting properties of a material, as illustrated in Fig. 10.1.4.

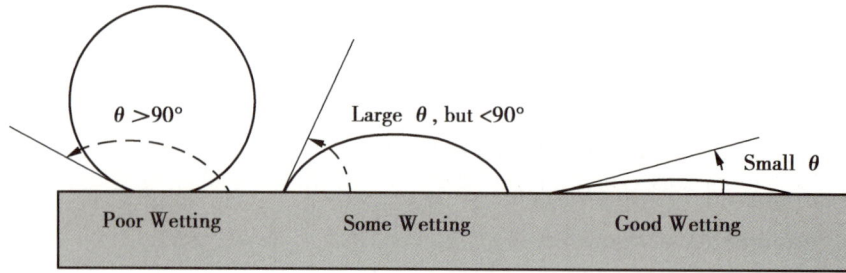

Fig. 10.1.4　Schematic Wetting of Different Fluids: A Liquid Droplet on a Solid Surface

10.1.6　Higher Mechanical and Thermal Properties with Higher Draw Ratios

The higher mechanical modulus of elasticity and thermal conductivity of a fiber along the fiber direction can be obtained, which is the attribute of the molecular orientation of polymer chains during ultra-drawing that improves the fiber quality toward an ideal single-crystal fiber. For example, UHMWPE (Ultra-high Molecular Weight Polyethylene) nanofibers with thermal conductivity values may go as high as $100 \ W/(m \cdot K)$, which is more than the conductivities of most cast irons and about half of pure metals. The longitudinal thermal conductivity along the fiber direction of such an orthotropic lamina is a function of the draw ratio of embedded fibers as demonstrated in Fig. 10.1.5.

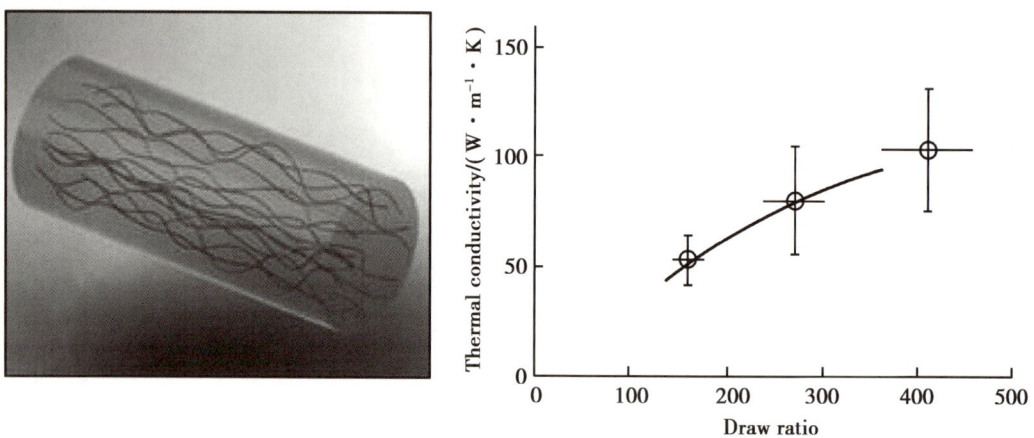

Fig. 10.1.5　Longitudinal Thermal Conductivity as a Function of Draw Ratio

10.1.7　Automotive Composites

Automotive composites accounts for about 50% of the thermoplastic and 24% of the thermoset polymers market worldwide. Glass-reinforced thermoplastic polymers (ABS, nylon, polyacetals, polypropylene, PVC, polycarbonates, polyacrylates, and polyurethanes） are a prominent material group for weight reduction because of the relatively low cost of the glass fiber, elightened by its fast cycle time and its ability to embrace parts integration. Carbon fiber reinforced polymers are more promising in weight reduction and strength enhancement, but they require breakthroughs in cost and manufacturing techniques to be cost effective for high volume production. Current applications include

(a) Composites with aligned fibers: composite springs, driveshafts, suspension arms, liquid fuel tanks, gas tanks, roofs, fenders, exterior doors, underbody, seat frames, wheel (rim), truck cargo boxes, and body panels, as shown in Fig. 10.1.6.

(b) Composites with random fibers: wheel shrouds, clutch plates, brake disks and pads, valve guides, engine rocker arm covers, engine oil pans, EV battery covers, door trims, brake pedal, gas accelerators, pump impellers, and most sensors.

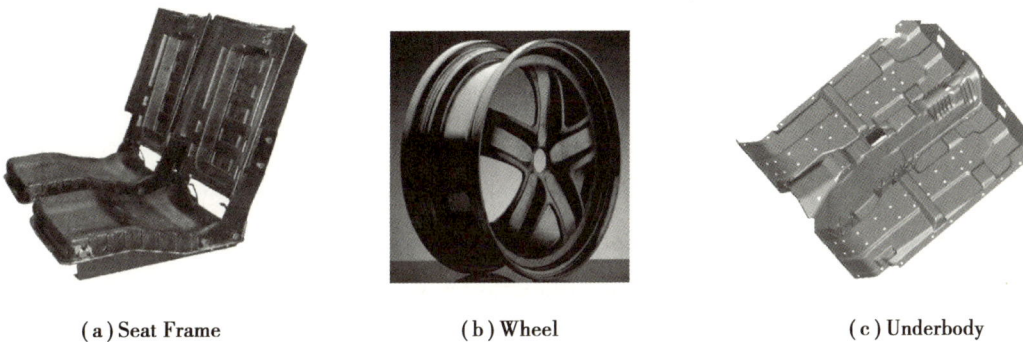

(a) Seat Frame   (b) Wheel   (c) Underbody

Fig. 10.1.6   Automotive Composites

Recently researchers have been interested in natural fiber-reinforced composites for automotive applications due to its acceptable formability, abundance, renewability, cost-effectiveness, and eco-friendliness [Ho].

Sustaining advances in plastics and polymer composites will expand and accelerate the benefits of the automotive composites. Some innovative ideas are given as follows: (1) electric car bodies made of specialty carbon fiber composites as light-weighted structural supercapacitors to power the car, (2) self-healing composites, and (3) smart fibrous composites such as intelligent lighting devices.

10.2   Weight and Volume Fractions

It is convenient to take the fiber content by weight for a wet-lay process to make thermoplastic composites, but it is customary for analysts to calculate mechanical properties based on the fiber content by volume. Data given in this chapter are fiber contents by weight, if not otherwise specified. Conversions between the content by weight (W_f) and the content by volume (V_f) are listed as follows:

$$W_f = \frac{V_f \, \rho_f}{V_f \, \rho_f + (1 - V_f) \, \rho_m} \tag{10.2.1}$$

and
$$V_f = \frac{W_f \, \rho_m}{W_f \, \rho_m + (1 - W_f) \, \rho_f} \tag{10.2.2}$$

where

ρ_f: Density of fibers;

ρ_m: Density of matrix;

V_f: Volume fraction of fibers;

V_m: Volume fraction of matrix;

W_f: Weight fraction of fibers;

W_m: Weight fraction of matrix.

All the alloy compositions and composite materials given in this book are in weight percentage unless stated otherwise. A variety of composites reinforced with fibers show a monotonic increase in stiffness with fiber content, i.e., approximately 38%-40% by weight; but a loss in tensile strength above a critical fiber content. The fiber volume fraction for a composite with inorganic fibers such as glass and carbon can be determined using the standard test method by ignition loss of cured resins according to ASTM D 2584, or calculated using Eq. (10.2.2).

10.3　Laminae Unidirectionally Reinforced with Continuous Fibers

When continuous fibers are processed into a composite lamina they are unidirectional-aligned in the longitudinal direction. All of the fibers run in the longitudinal direction of the composite lamina. This unidirectional fiber orientation creates a raw composite material that is highly anisotropic, as the properties (mechanical, thermal, electrical, and magnetic) are significantly different when evaluated in the direction of the fibers as opposed to the other two orthogonal directions: in-plane transverse or out-of-plane perpendicular to the fibers.

10.3.1　Young's Moduli of Composites Reinforced with Continuous Unidirectional Fibers

The Young' modulus of a continuous fiber-reinforced lamina along the fiber direction, i.e., 1-axis, can be estimated accurately using the rule of mixture as

$$E_{11} = E_f \, V_f + E_m \, V_m \tag{10.3.1}$$

where

E_m: Young's modulus of matrix;

E_f: Young's modulus of fibers.

On the other hand the rule of mixture may underestimate the Young's modulus along 2- and 3-axes. The semi-empirical Halpin-Tsai equation is herein recommended that

$$E_{22} = E_{33} = \cfrac{1 + \cfrac{\left(\dfrac{E_f}{E_m} - 1\right)}{\left(\dfrac{E_f}{E_m} + \zeta_2\right) V_f}}{1 - \cfrac{\left(\dfrac{E_f}{E_m} - 1\right)}{\left(\dfrac{E_f}{E_m} + \zeta_2\right) V_f}} E_m$$

$$= \frac{E_f(1 + V_f) + E_m(\zeta_2 - V_f)}{E_f(1 - V_f) + E_m(\zeta_2 + V_f)} E_m \qquad (10.3.2)$$

where parameter ζ_2 is a curve-fitting parameter that is an empirical factor to be used to make the equation conform to the experimental data. Parameter ζ_2 is related to packing pattern and fiber cross-section such as $\zeta_2 = 1$ for perfectly circular fibers packed rectangularly. In general,

$$\zeta_2 = 2 + 40 V_f^{10} \qquad (10.3.3)$$

10.3.2   Shear Moduli of Laminae Reinforced with Continuous Unidirectional Fibers

In-plane shear modulus G_{12} and out-of-plane shear modulus G_{23} can be obtained using Iosipestu shear test [Chiang]. The in-plane and shear moduli of a continuous fiber-reinforced lamina subjected to transverse and in-plane shear loadings in reference to fiber direction (1-axis) are calculated using the Halpin-Tsai equation [Hewitt & de Malherbe]

$$G_{12} = G_{21} = G_{13} = G_{31} = \frac{\left(\dfrac{G_f}{G_m} + \zeta_1\right) + \left(\dfrac{G_f}{G_m} - 1\right) V_f}{\left(\dfrac{G_f}{G_m} + \zeta_1\right) - \left(\dfrac{G_f}{G_m} - 1\right) V_f} G_m$$

$$= \frac{G_f \ (1 + V_f) + G_m \ (\zeta_1 - V_f)}{G_f \ (1 - V_f) + G_m \ (\zeta_1 + V_f)} \ G_m \qquad (10.3.4)$$

where $\zeta_1 = 1 + 40 \ V_f^{10}$ \qquad\qquad\qquad (10.3.5)

The out-of-plane shear modulus subject to out-of-plane loadings on the plane perpendicular to the fiber direction is

$$G_{23} = \frac{G_m \ B_m \ (G_f + G_m) + 2 \ G_f \ G_m - B_m \ (G_f - G_m) \ V_f}{B_m \ (G_f + G_m) + 2 \ G_f \ G_m - (B_m - 2 \ G_m) \ (G_f - G_m) \ V_f} \qquad (10.3.6)$$

where B_m is the bulk modulus of the matrix, given in terms of the Young's modulus and Poisson's ratio as

$$B_m = \frac{E_m}{3 \ (1 - 2 \ \nu_m)} \qquad (10.3.7)$$

10.3.3　Poisson's Ratios of Composites Reinforced with Continuous Unidirectional Fibers

In-plane and out-of-plane Poisson's ratios of a continuous fiber-reinforced lamina subjected to longitudinal loadings are calculated using the rule of mixture as

$$\nu_{12} = \nu_{13} = \nu_f \ V_f + \nu_m \ V_m \qquad (10.3.8)$$

While the out-of-plane Poisson's ratio subject to transverse loadings is

$$\nu_{23} = \frac{\zeta_2(3 - 4 \ \nu_{12}^2) - 1}{\zeta_2 + 1} \qquad (10.3.9)$$

where

ν_m: Young's modulus of matrix;

ν_f: Young's modulus of fibers;

ζ_2: Eq. (10.3.4).

10.4　Laminae Unidirectionally Reinforced with Short Fibers

Cost effective manufacturing often drives the use of discontinuous or "short" reinforcing elements in composites. These materials differ from continuous reinforced composites because the fibers do not extend throughout the entire material, as shown in Fig. 10.4.1. Therefore, load is not directly applied to each reinforcing element. If a chopped-fiber length is longer than the critical length, it is called a long fiber. The critical fiber length is defined as

$$L_c = \frac{\sigma_{uts,f}}{2\tau} d_f \qquad (10.4.1)$$

where τ is the smaller of the shear yield strength of matrix and the fiber-matrix bonding strength. i.e., $L_f > L_c$. For example, the critical fiber length of carbon-PAN fibers of a nominal cross-sectional diameter of 7.2 μm (0.0072 mm) is 1012 μm (1.012 mm). However, carbon-PAN fibers are usually chopped to a nominal length of 160 μm (0.16 mm) for easy molding.

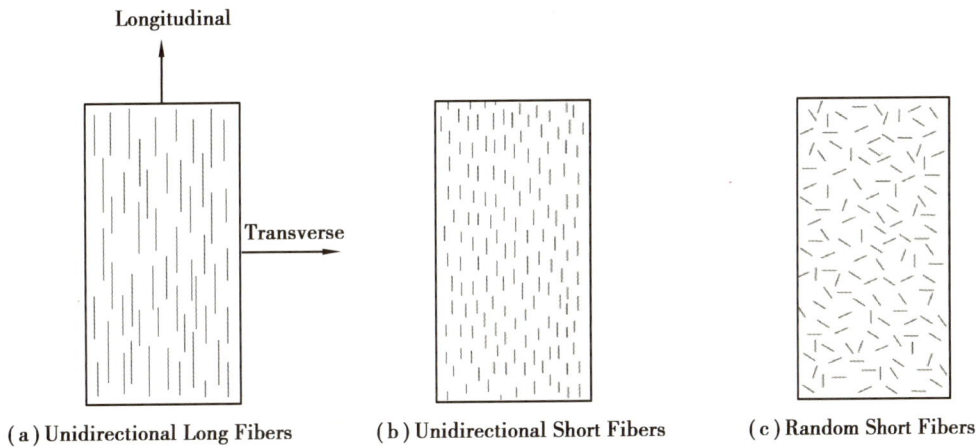

(a) Unidirectional Long Fibers   (b) Unidirectional Short Fibers   (c) Random Short Fibers

Fig. 10.4.1   Reinforcement of a Lamina

10.4.1   Young's Moduli of Laminae Reinforced with Unidirectional Short Fibers

In general the length has to be greater than 50 mm to be called E-glass fibers. Relatively long overlapping chopped fibers together with filaments or a binder and have the ability to move relative to each other, allowing the aligned reinforcement to more readily and easily stretch and move for greater, wrinkle-free conformability and faster layup than continuous fibers [Black]. The lamina is called an aligned discontinuous fiber-reinforced composite, Fig. 10.4.1(a). The lamina has such pseudo ductility akin to metal that a complex part can be formed while still meeting structural and strength requirements.

The elastic constants of a composite reinforced with unidirectional short fibers can be obtained from the Halpin-Tsai model as follows:

$$E_{11} = \frac{\left(\dfrac{E_f}{E_m} + \dfrac{2 L_f}{d_f}\right) + \dfrac{2L_f}{df}\left(\dfrac{E_f}{E_m} - 1\right) V_f}{\left(\dfrac{E_f}{E_m} + \dfrac{2 L_f}{d_f}\right) - \left(\dfrac{E_f}{E_m} - 1\right) V_f} E_m \qquad (10.4.2)$$

and
$$E_{22} = E_{33} = \frac{\left(\dfrac{E_f}{E_m} + 2\right) + 2\left(\dfrac{E_f}{E_m} - 1\right) V_f}{\left(\dfrac{E_f}{E_m} + 2\right) - \left(\dfrac{E_f}{E_m} - 1\right) V_f} E_m \qquad (10.4.3)$$

where

L_f: Fiber length;

d_f: Fiber diameter.

Another equation for E_{22} or E_{33} is the modified rule of mixture explored by ［Nielsen & Chen］ as

$$E_{22} = E_{33} = \frac{\dfrac{E_m}{\nu_m^2}}{(1 - V_f) + \dfrac{\dfrac{E_m}{\nu_m^2}}{E_f} V_f} \qquad (10.4.4)$$

The above equation has been proven to be quite accurate for aluminum composites reinforced with random short basalt fibers in predicting the Young's modulus ［Vannan & Vizhian］. The Poisson's ratio has been taken into consideration in Eq. （10.4.4）.

10.4.2　Shear Moduli of Composites Reinforced with Unidirectional Short Fibers

In-plane shear modulus G_{12} and out-of-plane shear modulus G_{23} can be obtained using Iosipescu test ［Chiang］. As the Halping-Tsai equation applies, they are respectively

$$G_{12} = G_{21} = \frac{\left(\dfrac{G_f}{G_m} + 1\right) + \left(\dfrac{G_f}{G_m} - 1\right) V_f}{\left(\dfrac{G_f}{G_m} + 1\right) - \left(\dfrac{G_f}{G_m} - 1\right) V_f} G_m$$

$$= \frac{G_f(1 + V_f) + G_m(1 - V_f)}{G_f(1 - V_f) + G_m(1 + V_f)} G_m \qquad (10.4.5)$$

and
$$G_{23} = G_{32} = \frac{\left(\dfrac{G_f}{G_m} + \zeta_3\right) + \left(\dfrac{G_f}{G_m} - 1\right) V_f}{\left(\dfrac{G_f}{G_m} + \zeta_3\right) - \left(\dfrac{G_f}{G_m} - 1\right) V_f} \, G_m$$

$$= \frac{G_f(1 + V_f) + G_m(\zeta_3 - V_f)}{G_f(1 - V_f) + G_m(\zeta_3 + V_f)} \, G_m \tag{10.4.6}$$

where
$$\zeta_3 = \frac{1 + \nu_m}{3 - \nu_m - 4\,\nu_m^2} \tag{10.4.7}$$

10.4.3   Poisson's Ratios of Composites Reinforced with Unidirectional Short Fibers

In-plane and out-of-plane Poisson's ratios of a continuous fiber-reinforced lamina subjected to longitudinal loadings are calculated using the rule of mixture as

$$\nu_{12} = \nu_{13} = \nu_f \, V_F + \nu_m \, V_m \tag{10.4.8}$$

The out-of-plane Poisson's ratio subject to transverse loadings is assumed to be the same as being reinforced by unidirectional fibers,

$$\nu_{23} = \frac{\zeta_3(3 - 4\,\nu_{12}^2) - 1}{\zeta_3 + 1} \tag{10.4.9}$$

10.5   Laminae Reinforced with Weaves

Resins reinforced with woven, braided, and knitted fabrics are becoming increasingly popular for various structural applications in the automotive, aerospace, and other industrial sectors. The majority of structures made from composites such as sailboards arc made from woven cloth rather than the simple uniaxial fibers. The reinforcement using weaves offer some advantages with respect to laminates made of unidirectional composites, including ease of lay-up, superior damage tolerance, and impact resistance of the resulting composite.

Woven fabrics are generally inhomogeneous and discontinuous objects. An orthogonal weave is considered an elastically orthotropic material with a very small deformation defined as an "orthotropic lamina" with two mutually perpendicular planes of symmetry. A planar weave exhibits no through-thickness feature other than the undulation resulting from weaving, as shown in Fig. 10.5.1. An orthogonal weave has tows woven at right angles in the plane of the fabric as follows:

(a) Weft direction (x-axis): Fill tows laid down in the direction at $\varphi=0°$.

(b) Warp direction (y-axis): Weft tows oriented at $\varphi=90°$ pass under and over the fill tows.

The total volume fraction rarely exceeds 40% in a given layer of woven fabric, and so the effective fiber fraction in either the warp or weft directions is unlikely to exceed 20%.

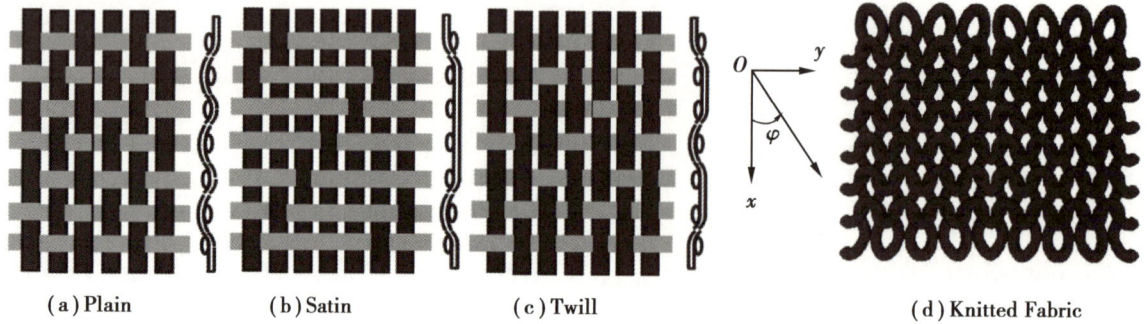

(a) Plain   (b) Satin   (c) Twill   (d) Knitted Fabric

Fig. 10.5.1   Three Simple Weave Patterns and One Knitted Fabric [Gay et al.]:
(a) Plain; (b) 5-Harness Satin (One Vertical+Four Horizontal-Filled Yarns);
(c) Twill (One Vertical+Two Horizontal-Filled Yarns); and (d) Knitted Fabric

10.5.1   Young's Moduli of Laminae Reinforced with Weaves

It's difficult to stretch a piece of plain-woven fiber glass cloth either in the warp direction (along y-axis shown in Fig. 10.5.1) or in the weft direction (along x-axis shown in Fig. 10.5.1), but to stretch easily it in the direction at 45° with respect to either direction. The stiffness and strength of fabric composites depend not only on the yarns and matrix properties, but also on material structural parameters as well, i.e., on fabric count and weave. The in-plane and out-of-plane Young's moduli of a lamina made of a plain weave can be approximated using the following equations:

$$E_{xx,w} = E_{11}\left(\frac{n_x}{n_x + n_y}\right) + E_{22}\left(\frac{n_y}{n_x + n_y}\right) \qquad \text{(In-plane)} \qquad (10.5.1)$$

$$E_{yy,w} = E_{11}\left(\frac{n_y}{n_x + n_y}\right) + E_{22}\left(\frac{n_x}{n_x + n_y}\right) \qquad \text{(In-plane)} \qquad (10.5.2)$$

and $\qquad E_{zz,w} = \dfrac{E_{11}}{5} \qquad\qquad\qquad\qquad\qquad\quad$ (Out-of-plane) $\qquad\qquad (10.5.3)$

where

n_x: Number of warped yarns aligned along x-axis per meter of width;

n_y: Number of filled yarns aligned along y-axis per meter of length;

E_{11}: Young's modulus of a lamina with continuous fibers, not woven, along the 1-axis;

E_{22}: Young's modulus of a lamina with continuous fibers, not woven, along the 2-axis.

Young's moduli E_{11} and E_{22} given in the above equations can be calculated using Eqs. (10.2.14) and (10.2.15) for the corresponding continuous unidirectional fibers. The stiffness obtained experimentally with a woven fabric is less than what described by the three equations given above. This is due to the curvature of yarns that makes the woven fabric more deformable and slippage between yarn and fill is not considered. Taking the interlaced lengths, fabric thickness and bending angle, [Morozov] derived the equation for the Young's modulus in the warp direction of a lamina with a plain reinforcing weave as follows:

$$E_{yy} = \frac{1}{2}E_{22} + \frac{E_{11}\left(t_1 + \dfrac{1}{4}t_2\right)}{2t_1 + t_2\left[\cos^4\alpha + \left(\dfrac{E_{11}}{E_{22}}\right)\sin^4\alpha + \left(\dfrac{E_{11}}{G_{12}} - 2\nu_{21}\right)\sin^2\alpha\,\cos^2\alpha\right]} \qquad (10.5.4)$$

Example 10.5.1   Consider the lamina reinforced with a plain weave as shown in both Fig. 10.5.1 (a) and Fig. 10.5.2, where $\alpha = 12°$ and $t_1 = 1/2t_2$. The in-plane mechanical properties of a unidirectional laminae of the same fiber volume ratio in the primary material coordinate system are given below: $E_{11} = 60$ GPa, $E_{22} = E_{33} = 13$ GPa, $G_{12} = G_{13} = 10.4$ GPa, and $\nu_{21} = 0.3$. Is the in-plane Young's modulus of this lamina (E_{xx}) higher than that of the [0°/90°] design which is 36.5 GPa.

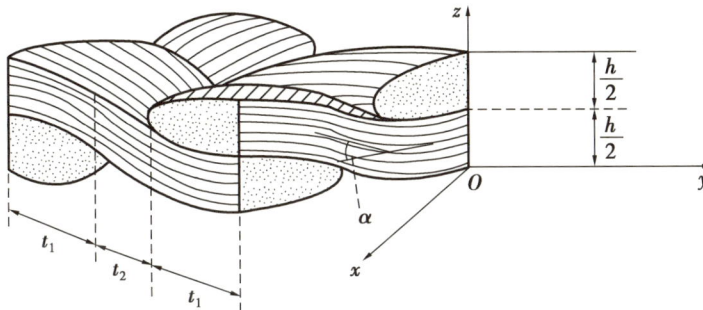

Fig. 10.5.2   Woven-Fabric Pattern for Formulating Elastic Moduli

Solution:

By Eq. (10.5.4), one has

$$E_{xx} = 23.5 \text{ GPa}$$

which is different from that of the [0°/90°] design, i.e., $E_{xx} = 36.5$ GPa

Thus, the in-plane Young's modulus of a woven lamina is less by 37%, i.e., (36.5 − 23.5) / 36.5, than that of a cross-ply lamina of the same material.

When yarns are scrolled in a higher curvature in a knitted fabric, their fibers are more stressed and damaged in the knitting process. The resulting knitted fabric has less strength and stiffness than their woven counterparts. If the weave is a knitted fabric, Young's moduli E_{11} and E_{22} of its corresponding continuous unidirectional fibers are obtained first using Eqs. (10.2.14) and (10.2.15). The effective modulus method based on the lamination theory may be then utilized to explore the in-plane effective moduli according to the knitting pattern [Kononova et al.].

10.5.2   Shear Moduli of Laminae Reinforced with Weaves

The shear moduli of a composite reinforced with weaves are highly nonlinear with prominent hysteresis. There are several ways of generating a state of in-plane shear in a composite to model the shear stress-strain relationship. Examples are the Iosipescu test [Iosipescu] [Chiang], 10° off-axis test [Pierron & Vautrin], [(45°, −45°)]$_{4s}$ tensile test [Baere], two- and three-railed shear test [Hussain & Adams], torsion of a rod [Ferry], and torsion of thin-walled tubes [Fujii & Lin]. The shear modulus of a lamina with plain weaves can also be calculated using Eq. (10.4.5) as the first approximation for the initial shear moduli,

$$G_{xy,w} \approx G_{12} = \frac{G_f(1 + V_f) + G_m(\zeta_1 - V_f)}{G_f(1 - V_f) + G_m(\zeta_1 + V_f)} G_m \tag{10.5.5}$$

and $$G_{xz,w} = G_{yz,w} \approx G_m \tag{10.5.6}$$

The in-plane shear modulus at an arbitrary angle, φ, measured from the x-axis, i.e., the weft direction (Fig. 10.5.1), can be calculated from the following equation [Penava et al.]

$$G_\varphi = 4 \sin^2\varphi \cos^2\varphi \ (E_{xx}^{-1} + E_{yy}^{-1} + 2\nu_{xy} E_{xx}^{-1}) + (\cos^2\varphi - \sin^2\varphi)^2 \ G_{xy}^{-1} \tag{10.5.7}$$

10.5.3   Poisson's Ratios of Composites Reinforced with Weaves

An attempt was made by [Sun et al.] to predict the Poisson's ratios of woven fabric. Nevertheless, it is more effective to calculate the Poisson's ratios directly from finite element analysis that can depict the construction of the weave of interest in details.

10.6   Laminae Reinforced with Mats

A mat is a lamina that consists of continuous (or very long) fibers placed onto the lamina plane, and thus the lamina is transversely isotropic, i.e., isotropic in its own plane as a randomly reinforced structure but anisotropic in an axis normal to the lamina. For loose-packed fabrics such as chopped strand mats, the total volume fraction of fibers is unlikely to exceed 10% and they are practically used to provide filler layers between the outer load bearing layers in a multiple-layered laminate.

10.6.1　Young's Moduli of Laminae Reinforced with Mats

If the continuous (or very long) fibers are randomly placed onto the lamina plane, the lamina is transversely isotropic, of which the in-plane and its out-of-plane Young's moduli are so much reduced as

$$E_{\mathrm{mat},11} = E_{\mathrm{mat},22} = \frac{3}{8} E_{11} + \frac{5}{8} E_{22} \qquad (\text{In-plane}) \qquad (10.6.1)$$

$$E_{33,\mathrm{R}} = \frac{E_{11}}{5} \qquad (\text{Out-of-plane}) \qquad (10.6.2)$$

Again, E_{11} and E_{22} are Young's moduli calculated using Eqs. (10.5.2) and (10.5.3) for continuous unidirectional fibers.

10.6.2　Shear Moduli of Laminae Reinforced with Mats

If the continuous (or very long) fibers are randomly placed onto the lamina plane, the shear modulus of such a transversely isotropic lamina reinforced can be calculated using Eq. (10.4.5) as

$$G_{12,\mathrm{mat}} = G_{12} = \frac{G_{\mathrm{f}} (1 + V_{\mathrm{F}}) + G_{\mathrm{m}} (\zeta_1 - V_{\mathrm{F}})}{G_{\mathrm{f}} (1 - V_{\mathrm{F}}) + G_{\mathrm{m}} (\zeta_1 + V_{\mathrm{F}})} G_{\mathrm{m}} \qquad (10.6.3)$$

and　　$G_{13,\mathrm{mat}} = G_{23,\mathrm{mat}} = G_{\mathrm{m}}$ 　　　　　　　　　　　　　　(10.6.4)

10.6.3　Poisson's Ratios Laminae Reinforced with Mats

A mat is used highly porous in nature, as it is flattened to shape the pre-form for a lamina. A finite element analysis is required to depict the construction of the specific mat of interest. For example, sintered stainless steel mats as shown in Fig. 10.6.1 are known to be able to exhibit negative through-thickness Poisson's ratios (ν_{13} or ν_{23}). PDMS, i. e., $CH_3 [Si (CH_3)_2 O]_n Si (CH_3)_3$, reinforced with a stainless steel mat at $V_{\mathrm{f}} = 60\%$ has a Poisson's ratio of -9.2, obtained experimentally [Jayanty]. The composite (PDMS/60% Steel Mat) has a thickness of 0.33 mm and a Young's modulus of 1.37 GPa. The thickness and Young's modulus of the mat (without PDMS) is 0.38 mm and 0.92 GPa. It means that the through-thickness compression is 0.05 mm after the composite is cured.

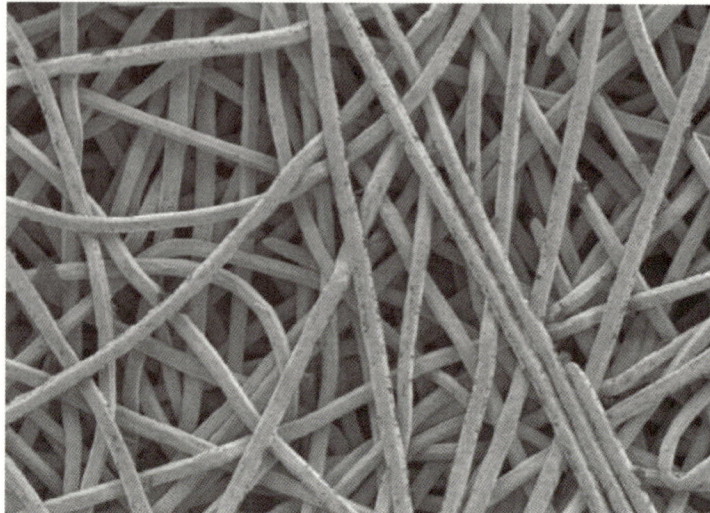

Fig. 10.6.1   Sintered Stainless Steel Mat with 60% Porosity〔Jayanty〕

Finite element analysis may be conducted to obtain the moisture diffusivities（in-plane or through-thickness）for the specific mat patterns of interest.

10.7   Composites Reinforced Randomly with Short Fibers

Plastics reinforced with short fibers are used for general structural applications. Recently plastics reinforced with short fibers are widely utilized in many structural parts in automobile, infrastructures, and electric devices due to their high specific strength, high specific stiffness, long fatigue life and high impact resistance as well as cost-effectiveness. For example, metal parts in the automobile such as intake manifolds, junction boxes, HVAC（Heating, Ventilating and Air Conditioning）cases, engine covers, sensors, actuators, and various structural parts have been replaced by equivalent stiffness short fiber-reinforced plastics（PA, PBT, PI, etc.）for weight reduction. In mobile phones, emphasizing slimness, traditional magnesium cases are replaced by short fiber-reinforced Polyphthalamide resin. They usually consist of discontinuous fibers randomly aligned in the 3-dimensional mode. However, fibers are directed as the mold flow pattern dictates. Fibers used for random reinforcement are short, ranging from 0.75 mm to 1.5 mm. Long fibers（ranging from 1.5 mm to 10 mm）are hard to mold, but they may render stronger composites than short fibers.

Non-uniform local material properties due to undesired fiber orientations may reduce the material stiffness, thermal expansion, heat conductivity, and failure profile. The importance of fiber orientation distribution has been addressed by〔Hine & Duckett〕based on glass fiber-reinforced ribbed PBT and PA6,6 plates. Each fiber length is approximately 0.2 mm. It was shown that the mold geometry is the primary factor which has influence on the fiber orientation and the matrix is secondary. The stiffness of the combined rib and web was found to depend on the average orientation of the two parts. The differential thermal expansion between the rib and web due to different fiber orientations may lead to significant warpage.

10.7.1   Young's Moduli of Composites Reinforced Randomly with Short Fibers

Unlike a unidirectional fiber-reinforced plastic whose tensile strength shows a monotonic increase with increasing fiber content, the tensile strength of a random fibers-reinforced plastic reaches its maximum value at a certain level of fiber content and then decreases. Similarly the tensile modulus of a random-fibers-reinforced plastic reaches its maximum value at another level of fiber content and then decreases. In general, the fiber content for maximum tensile modulus is not the same as that for maximum tensile strength. Higher volume of voids and poor bonding between fibers and matrix are due to the cause. The fiber volume fraction is generally less than 40%, as limited by mass-production manufacturing processes. A 3-dimensionally randomly oriented short-fiber lamina is presumably isotropic in the lamina plane, 1-2 plane or x-y plane. Its Young's modulus depends on the fiber's length (L_f) and it is generally

$$E = E_m \left[1 - V_f \left(1 - \frac{L_f}{2d_f} \right) \right] \qquad \text{(if } L_f < L_c \text{)} \qquad (10.7.1)$$

or $\qquad E = E_f V_f \left(1 - \frac{L_c}{2L_f} \right) + E_m (1 - V_f) \qquad \text{(if } L_f > L_c \text{)} \qquad (10.7.2)$

The other approach for a lamina made of short fibers is to take the elastic moduli being estimated by averaging the elastic moduli of the corresponding unidirectional lamina of the same constituents, around 360° to eliminate the dependence of aligning angle. Empirically, the elastic modulus is approximated by the Tsai-Pagano equation [Gibson] as

$$E_R = \frac{3}{8} E_{11} + \frac{5}{8} E_{22} \qquad (10.7.3)$$

The above equation is applicable to composites with a low volume fraction of fibers. The prediction is biased with a high volume fraction of fibers as an increase of the fiber content is accompanied by a non-proportional increase in concentration of defects within the composite.

The values of composite moduli, E_{11} and E_{22}, derived using the Nielsen-Chen model are given by Eqs. (10.4.2) and (10.4.3). It has been proven to be quite accurate by [Vannanl & Vizhian] for predicting the Young's modulus using aluminum composites reinforced with randomly-aligned basalt fibers.

10.7.2 Shear Moduli of Composites Reinforced Randomly with Short Fibers

For a 3-dimensionally randomly oriented short-fiber composite or lamina, its reduced pseudo-isotropic shear modulus is

$$G_R = \frac{E_{11}}{8} + \frac{E_{22}}{4} \qquad (10.7.4)$$

Again, E_{11} and E_{22} are Young's moduli calculated using Eqs. (10.5.2) and (10.5.3) for continuous unidirectional fibers.

10.7.3 Poisson's Ratios of Composites Reinforced Randomly with Short Fibers

For a composite reinforced with particulates, its pseudo-isotropic Poisson's ratio derived by [Pan] is

$$\nu = \frac{\nu_f V_f}{2\pi} + \nu_m \left(1 - \frac{V_f}{2\pi}\right) \qquad (10.7.5)$$

10.8 Composites Reinforced with Particulates and Powders

These are the least expensive and most widely used, such as automotive sensors and concretes. They fall in two categories depending on the size of the particles:

(1) Particulates are in the scale of minimeter and usually not regular-shaped. Large-particle composites act by restraining the movement of the matrix, if well bonded.

(2) Powders are in the form of micro-or even nano-scaled balls, either solid or hollow, having an averaged diameter between 10 and 150 μm such as MWCNT (Multi-Walled Carbon Nano Tubes). The matrix bears the major portion of the applied load and the small particles hinder dislocation motion, limiting plastic deformation.

Direct predictive equations for the pseudo-isotropic tensile modulus and Poisson's ratio of a composite reinforced with particulates have been of great interest to practitioners, as micro and nano reinforcements are gaining more applications in the real world.

10.8.1   Young's Moduli of Composites Reinforced with Particulates or Powders

With randomly oriented particulates or powders in 3-dimensional domain, the effective Young's modulus of the composites can be calculated according to [Hashin] as

$$E_C = \frac{9 \, G_C \, K_C}{G_C + 3 \, K_C} \tag{10.8.1}$$

where G_C is the shear modulus and K_C is the bulk modulus of the composites to be calculated [Gay et al.]. Let V_p be the volume fraction of particulates or powders in the composite, then

$$G_C = G_m + \frac{(G_p - G_m) \, V_p}{G_m + \psi_1(1 - V_p) \, (G_p - G_m)} \, G_m \tag{10.8.2}$$

and $\quad K_C = K_m + \dfrac{(K_p - K_m) \, V_p}{K_m + \psi_2(1 - V_p) \, (K_p - K_m)} \, K_m \tag{10.8.3}$

where $\quad \psi_1 = \dfrac{2(4 - 5 \, \nu_m)}{15 \, (1 - 2 \, \nu_m)} \tag{10.8.4}$

and $\quad \psi_2 = \dfrac{1 + \nu_m}{3 \, (1 - \nu_m)} \tag{10.8.5}$

K_C in Eq. (10.8.3) can be also expressed in terms of the Young's modulus and Poisson's ratio of the matrix as

$$K_C = \frac{E_m}{3 \, (1 - 2 \, \nu_m)} \left[1 + \left(\frac{1 - \nu_m}{1 + \nu_m} \right) \left(\frac{V_p}{V_m} \right) \right] \tag{10.8.6}$$

10.8.2   Shear Moduli of Composites Reinforced with Particulates or Powders

The corresponding shear modulus of a composite reinforced with particulates can be obtained using Eq. (10.8.3), which reduces to the following equations in terms of the Young's modulus, shear modulus and Poisson's ratio of the matrix [Mori & Tanka] [Hashin] [Gay et al.]:

$$G = \frac{E_m}{2 \, (1 + \nu_m)} \left[1 + \frac{15 \, (1 - \nu_m)}{2 \, (4 - 5 \, \nu_m)} \left(\frac{V_p}{V_m} \right) \right] \tag{10.8.7}$$

or
$$G = \frac{1 - 15\,(1 - \nu_m)\left(1 - \dfrac{G_p}{G_m}\right)V_p}{(1 - 5\,\nu_m) + 2\,(4 - 5\,\nu_m)\left(\dfrac{G_p}{G_m}\right)} \tag{10.8.8}$$

10.8.3 Poisson's Ratios of Composites Reinforced with Particulates or Powders

For a composite reinforced with particulates, its pseudo-isotropic Poisson's ratio derived by [Pan] is

$$\nu = \nu_f\left(\frac{V_p}{2\,\pi}\right) + \nu_m\left(1 - \frac{V_p}{2\,\pi}\right) \tag{10.8.9}$$

The above equation is quite accurate for a composite reinforced with particulates at a low level of reinforcement content.

10.9 Auxetic Composites: Negative Poisson's Ratios

A material having a negative Poisson's ratio (ν) is called auxetic. Auxetic materials in nature such as cow teat [Lee] and salamander skin [LaBarbera] are mostly due to naturally built-in microfibrous networks as composite structures.

10.9.1 Thickened as Stretched

An auxetic material is known to be anti-rubber [Delannay], as its cross-section is thickened when stretched. This can be understood by setting a negative ν value in the following equation for shear modulus

$$G = \frac{\dfrac{1}{2}E}{1 + \nu} \tag{10.9.1}$$

In the extreme case, $G = \infty$ if $\nu = -1$. On the other hand, rubber-like materials turn extremely thinner when stretched, as prescribed by the following equation for bulk modulus (K) with $\nu \to 0.5$:

$$K = \frac{E}{3(1 - 2\,\nu)} \tag{10.9.2}$$

10.9.2   Condensed as Compressed

The hardness of a material, denoted as H which is a presentation of its indentation resistance, is related to its Poisson's ratio as follows:

$$H \propto \left(\frac{E}{1-\nu^2}\right)^n \tag{10.9.3}$$

where

$n = 2/3$: Hertzian contact;

$n = 1$: Contact under a uniform pressure.

When Poisson's ratio falls in the range between -0.5 and -1, which is feasible for certain composite structures, the hardness is magnified significantly. In other words, the resistance to compression is tremendously enlarged with the resulting condensed material.

10.9.3   Composite Networks for Negative Poisson's Ratios

Certain composite networks may produce a through-thickness Poisson's ratio. Here is a simple one that the fiber network model resembles the random fiber network before compression where the sparse pointed-contact locations are considered to be much more rigid than non-contact points, as shown in Fig. 10.9.1(a). After it is compressed, it may result in a configuration as shown in Fig. 10.9.1(b) that the fiber network model is similar to reentrant honeycombs. Take a free body diagram of a "simply-supported beam" and assume that a uniform compressive pressure is applied to squeeze the mat. The "simply-supported beam" between two contact points will concave and pull in the two contact points and realign the contact zones. Obviously the compressed mat filled with random fibers render a geometrical structure like a honeycomb which will produce a negative Poisson's ratio, as claimed by [Tatlier & Berhan].

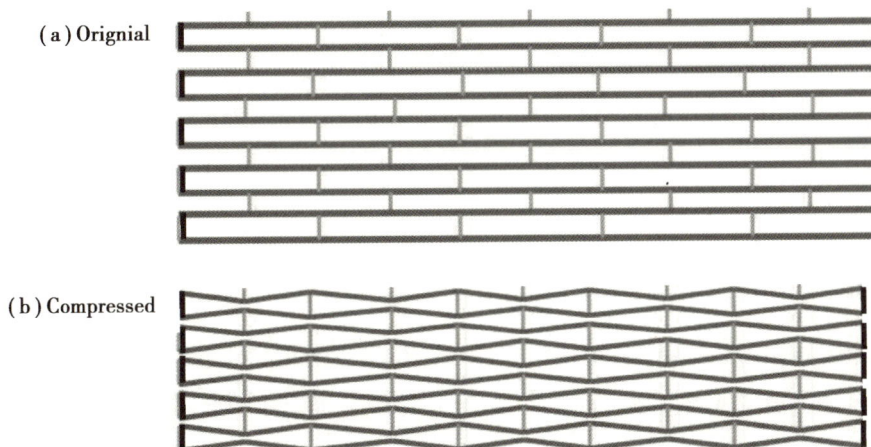

Fig. 10.9.1   Schematic Sample of Fiber-in-Contact Network of a Mat with Random Fibers

10.10   Lamination

A composite laminate is a stackup of laminae, i.e., layers of composite materials as shown in Fig. 10.10.1, which are joined to provide desired engineering properties, including stiffness, strength, fracture toughness, thermal conductivity, thermal expansion, dielectric constants, piezoelectric coefficients, pyroelectric coefficients, and sound insulation. The laminae in a laminate are permanently assembled using adhesives, heat, pressure, and/or even welding. For example, a vehicle windshield is usually made by laminating a plastic film of high fracture toughness between two layers of glass. Depending upon the stacking sequence of the individual layers, the laminate may exhibit desired or undesired coupling between in-plane and out-of-plane responses.

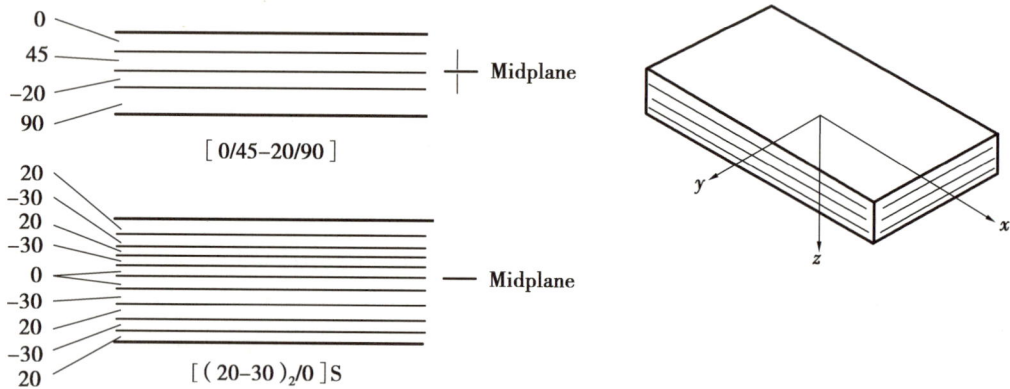

Fig. 10.10.1   Example Laminate Descriptions

10.10.1   Notation for Lamination

The stack is defined by the fiber direction of each ply, defined as the angle going from the 1-axis (primary material coordinate system) to the x-axis (global coordinate system), as shown in Fig. 10.10.1. Two example laminates are given. Subscript "s" behind bracket "]" stands for "symmetrical" implying that the listed sequences should be mirrored across the laminate's midline and subscript "2" behind parenthesis ")" means that sequence is to be repeated.

10.10.2   Classical Lamination Theory

When an arbitrary load is applied to a laminate, each through-thickness strain component may vary continuously across the boundary between two adjacent laminae, while each through-thickness stress component across the boundary will be discontinuous, more likely exhibiting a step function.

Assume that a laminate is a stack of N laminae, which have a set of ply orientations as $[\theta_1, \theta_2, \cdots, \theta_N]$. As simplified from Eq. (10.2.40), each ply of lamina in the local coordinate has the following in-plane stress-strain equation set

$$
\begin{Bmatrix} \sigma_{11} \\ \sigma_{22} \\ \tau_{12} \end{Bmatrix} = [c]_{3\times3} \{\varepsilon\} = \begin{bmatrix} c_{11} & c_{12} & 0 \\ c_{12} & c_{22} & 0 \\ 0 & 0 & c_{66} \end{bmatrix} \begin{Bmatrix} \varepsilon_{11} \\ \varepsilon_{22} \\ \varepsilon_{12} \end{Bmatrix}
\tag{10.10.1}
$$

A basic assumption in the classical laminate theory is that the strains resulting from curvature vary linearly in the thickness direction. Consequently, the total in-plane normal strains are a sum of those derived from membrane loads, hydrothermal loads, and bending loads

$$
\varepsilon_{ij} = \varepsilon_{ijo} + \varepsilon_{ij,h} + z\, \kappa_{ij}
\tag{10.10.2}
$$

i.e.,
$$
\varepsilon_{11} = \varepsilon_{11o} + \varepsilon_{11,h} + z\, \kappa_{11}
\tag{10.10.2a}
$$

$$
\varepsilon_{22} = \varepsilon_{22o} + \varepsilon_{22,h} + z\, \kappa_{22}
\tag{10.10.2b}
$$

and
$$
\varepsilon_{12} = \varepsilon_{12o} + z\, \kappa_{12}
\tag{10.10.2c}
$$

where

ε_{ijo} : Strain in the middle plane, $i = 1,\ 2$ and $j = 1,\ 2$;

$\varepsilon_{ij,h}$: Strain in the middle plane due to any thermal and/or moisture variations;

κ_{ij} : Curvature;

z : Through-thickness coordinate.

The stress-strain relationship of each lamina can be rotated to match the laminate axes (x, y, z) then as

$$
\begin{Bmatrix} \sigma_{xx} \\ \sigma_{yy} \\ \tau_{xy} \end{Bmatrix} = [Q]_{3\times3} \{\varepsilon\} = \begin{bmatrix} Q_{11} & Q_{12} & Q_{16} \\ Q_{12} & Q_{22} & Q_{26} \\ Q_{16} & Q_{26} & Q_{66} \end{bmatrix} \begin{Bmatrix} \varepsilon_{xx} \\ \varepsilon_{yy} \\ \varepsilon_{xy} \end{Bmatrix}
\tag{10.10.3}
$$

where

$$
Q_{11} = c_{11}\cos^4\theta + 2\,(c_{12} + 2c_{66})\sin^2\theta\cos^2\theta + c_{22}\sin^4\theta
\tag{10.10.4}
$$

$$
Q_{22} = c_{11}\sin^4\theta + 2\,(c_{12} + 2c_{66})\sin^2\theta\cos^2\theta + c_{22}\cos^4\theta
\tag{10.10.5}
$$

$$
Q_{12} = (c_{11} + c_{22} - 4c_{66})\sin^2\theta\cos^2\theta + c_{12}\,(\sin^4\theta + \cos^4\theta)
\tag{10.10.6}
$$

$$
Q_{66} = (c_{11} + c_{22} - 2c_{12} - 2c_{66})\sin^2\theta\cos^2\theta + c_{66}(\sin^4\theta + \cos^4\theta)
\tag{10.10.7}
$$

$$
Q_{16} = (c_{11} - c_{12} - 2c_{66})\sin\theta\cos^3\theta - (c_{22} - c_{12} - 2c_{66})\sin^3\theta\cos\theta
\tag{10.10.8}
$$

and $\quad Q_{26} = (c_{11} - c_{12} - 2c_{66}) \sin^3\theta \cos\theta - (c_{22} - c_{12} - 2c_{66}) \sin\theta \cos^3\theta$ (10.10.9)

After being reduced from 3-dimensional to in-plane 2-dimenssional in-plane properties, the elastic constants in Eqs. (10.2.29)-(10.2.38) become

$$c_{11} = \frac{E_{11}}{1 - \nu_{12}\nu_{21}}$$ (10.10.10)

$$c_{22} = \frac{E_{22}}{1 - \nu_{12}\nu_{21}}$$ (10.10.11)

$$c_{12} = c_{21} = \frac{\nu_{12}E_{22}}{1 - \nu_{12}\nu_{21}} = \frac{\nu_{21}E_{11}}{1 - \nu_{12}\nu_{21}}$$ (10.10.12)

and $\quad c_{66} = G_{12}$ (10.10.13)

Note that engineering shear strain doubles the size of the tensor shear strain,

$$\gamma_{xy} = 2\,\varepsilon_{xy}$$ (10.10.14)

Angle θ can be one of the following: θ_1, θ_2, $\cdots$ and θ_N, as the transformation is to be replicated for each ply. Plugging Eq. (10.10.2) into Eq. (10.10.3) leads to

i.e., $$\begin{Bmatrix} \sigma_{xx} \\ \sigma_{yy} \\ \tau_{xy} \end{Bmatrix} = \begin{bmatrix} (Q_{11})_n & (Q_{12})_n & (Q_{16})_n \\ (Q_{12})_n & (Q_{22})_n & (Q_{26})_n \\ (Q_{16})_n & (Q_{26})_n & (Q_{66})_n \end{bmatrix} \left(\begin{Bmatrix} \varepsilon_{11o} \\ \varepsilon_{22o} \\ \gamma_{12o} \end{Bmatrix} + \begin{Bmatrix} (\varepsilon_{11,h})_n \\ (\varepsilon_{22,h})_n \\ (\varepsilon_{12,h})_n \end{Bmatrix} \right) +$$
$$z \begin{bmatrix} (Q_{11})_n & (Q_{12})_n & (Q_{16})_n \\ (Q_{12})_n & (Q_{22})_n & (Q_{26})_n \\ (Q_{16})_n & (Q_{26})_n & (Q_{66})_n \end{bmatrix} \begin{Bmatrix} \kappa_{11} \\ \kappa_{22} \\ \kappa_{12} \end{Bmatrix}$$ (10.10.15)

Assume that the laminate is rectangular with a constant thickness. Given that the shear stresses in the middle plane and the curvatures of the composite are constant, the applied force resultants per unit length (along the width side) can be obtained by integrating stress components and "curvatures * z" in each lamina based on the above equation set along the out-of-plane direction, and then summing them up as follows:

$$\begin{Bmatrix} N_{xx} \\ N_{yy} \\ N_{xy} \end{Bmatrix} = \sum_{n=1}^{N} \begin{bmatrix} Q_{11} & Q_{12} & Q_{16} \\ Q_{12} & Q_{22} & Q_{26} \\ Q_{16} & Q_{26} & Q_{66} \end{bmatrix}_n \left(\int_{z_{k-1}}^{z_k} \begin{Bmatrix} \varepsilon_{11o} \\ \varepsilon_{22o} \\ \gamma_{12o} \end{Bmatrix} dz \right) + \sum_{n=1}^{N} \begin{bmatrix} Q_{11} & Q_{12} & Q_{16} \\ Q_{12} & Q_{22} & Q_{26} \\ Q_{16} & Q_{26} & Q_{66} \end{bmatrix} \left(\int_{z_{k-1}}^{z_k} \begin{Bmatrix} \kappa_{11} \\ \kappa_{22} \\ \kappa_{12} \end{Bmatrix} z dz \right) +$$
$$\sum_{n=1}^{N} \begin{bmatrix} Q_{11} & Q_{12} & Q_{16} \\ Q_{12} & Q_{22} & Q_{26} \\ Q_{16} & Q_{26} & Q_{66} \end{bmatrix} \left(\int_{z_{k-1}}^{z_k} \begin{Bmatrix} (\varepsilon_{11,h})_n \\ (\varepsilon_{22,h})_n \\ (\gamma_{12,h})_n \end{Bmatrix} dz \right)$$ (10.10.16)

$$\text{or} \quad \begin{Bmatrix} N_{xx} \\ N_{yy} \\ N_{xy} \end{Bmatrix} = \begin{bmatrix} A_{11} & A_{12} & A_{16} \\ A_{12} & A_{22} & A_{26} \\ A_{16} & A_{26} & A_{66} \end{bmatrix} \begin{Bmatrix} \varepsilon_{xxo} \\ \varepsilon_{yyo} \\ \gamma_{xyo} \end{Bmatrix} + \begin{bmatrix} B_{11} & B_{12} & B_{16} \\ B_{12} & B_{22} & B_{26} \\ B_{16} & B_{26} & B_{66} \end{bmatrix} \begin{Bmatrix} \kappa_{xx} \\ \kappa_{yy} \\ \kappa_{xy} \end{Bmatrix} +$$

$$\sum_{n=1}^{N} \begin{Bmatrix} (Q_{11})_n(\varepsilon_{11,h})_n(z_k - z_{k-1}) + (Q_{12})_n(\varepsilon_{22,h})_n(z_k - z_{k-1}) + (Q_{16})_n(\gamma_{12,h})_n(z_k - z_{k-1}) \\ (Q_{12})_n(\varepsilon_{11,h})_n(z_k - z_{k-1}) + (Q_{22})_n(\varepsilon_{22,h})_n(z_k - z_{k-1}) + (Q_{26})_n(\gamma_{12,h})_n(z_k - z_{k-1}) \\ (Q_{16})_n(\varepsilon_{11,h})_n(z_k - z_{k-1}) + (Q_{26})_n(\varepsilon_{22,h})_n(z_k - z_{k-1}) + (Q_{66})_n(\gamma_{12,h})_n(z_k - z_{k-1}) \end{Bmatrix}$$

$$(10.10.17)$$

with $\quad A_{ij} = \displaystyle\sum_{n=1}^{N} (Q_{ij})_n(z_n - z_{n-1}) \qquad$ (Extension Stiffness) $\qquad (10.10.18)$

and $\quad B_{ij} = \dfrac{1}{2}\displaystyle\sum_{n=1}^{N} (Q_{ij})_n(z_n^2 - z_{n-1}^2) \qquad$ (Coupling Stiffness) $\qquad (10.10.19)$

where

z_n: Distance from the midplane to the bottom of the nth lamina;

z_{n-1}: Distance from the midplane to the top of the nth lamina;

N: Total number of laminae;

N_{xx} & N_{yy}: Normal force per unit length, along the x-axis and y-axis, respectively;

N_{xy}: Shear force per unit length, acting on the cross-section normal to the x-axis and directed along the y-axis, and $N_{yx} = N_{xy}$.

Similarly, given that the shear stresses in the middle plane and the curvatures of the laminate are constant, the applied moment resultants per unit length (along the width side) can be obtained by integrating "stress components $*z$" and "curvatures $*z^2$" in each lamina based on Eq. (10.10.15) along the out-of-plane direction, and then summing them up as follows:

$$\begin{Bmatrix} M_{xx} \\ M_{yy} \\ M_{xy} \end{Bmatrix} = \sum_{n=1}^{N} \begin{bmatrix} Q_{11} & Q_{12} & Q_{16} \\ Q_{12} & Q_{22} & Q_{26} \\ Q_{16} & Q_{26} & Q_{66} \end{bmatrix} \int_{z_{k-1}}^{z_k} \begin{Bmatrix} \varepsilon_{xxo} \\ \varepsilon_{yyo} \\ \gamma_{xyo} \end{Bmatrix} z\, dz + \sum_{n=1}^{N} \begin{pmatrix} Q_{11} & Q_{12} & Q_{16} \\ Q_{12} & Q_{22} & Q_{26} \\ Q_{16} & Q_{26} & Q_{66} \end{pmatrix} \int_{z_{k-1}}^{z_k} \begin{Bmatrix} \kappa_{xx} \\ \kappa_{yy} \\ \kappa_{xy} \end{Bmatrix} z^2\, dz +$$

$$\sum_{n=1}^{N} \begin{bmatrix} Q_{11} & Q_{12} & Q_{16} \\ Q_{12} & Q_{22} & Q_{26} \\ Q_{16} & Q_{26} & Q_{66} \end{bmatrix} \int_{z_{k-1}}^{z_k} \begin{Bmatrix} (\varepsilon_{11,h})_n \\ (\varepsilon_{22,h})_n \\ (\gamma_{12,h})_n \end{Bmatrix} z\, dz \qquad\qquad (10.10.20)$$

$$\text{or} \quad \begin{Bmatrix} M_{xx} \\ M_{yy} \\ M_{xy} \end{Bmatrix} = \begin{bmatrix} B_{11} & B_{12} & B_{16} \\ B_{12} & B_{22} & B_{26} \\ B_{16} & B_{26} & B_{66} \end{bmatrix} \begin{Bmatrix} \varepsilon_{xxo} \\ \varepsilon_{yyo} \\ \gamma_{xyo} \end{Bmatrix} + \begin{bmatrix} D_{11} & D_{12} & D_{16} \\ D_{12} & D_{22} & D_{26} \\ D_{16} & D_{26} & D_{66} \end{bmatrix} \begin{Bmatrix} \kappa_{xx} \\ \kappa_{yy} \\ \kappa_{xy} \end{Bmatrix} +$$

$$\frac{1}{2}\sum_{n=1}^{N}\begin{cases}(Q_{11})_n(\varepsilon_{11,h})_n(z_k^2-z_{k-1}^2)+(Q_{12})_n(\varepsilon_{22,h})_n(z_k^2-z_{k-1}^2)+(Q_{16})_n(\gamma_{12,h})_n(z_k^2-z_{k-1}^2)\\(Q_{12})_n(\varepsilon_{11,h})_n(z_k^2-z_{k-1}^2)+(Q_{22})_n(\varepsilon_{22,h})_n(z_k^2-z_{k-1}^2)+(Q_{26})_n(\gamma_{12,h})_n(z_k^2-z_{k-1}^2)\\(Q_{16})_n(\varepsilon_{11,h})_n(z_k^2-z_{k-1}^2)+(Q_{26})_n(\varepsilon_{22,h})_n(z_k^2-z_{k-1}^2)+(Q_{66})_n(\gamma_{12,h})_n(z_k^2-z_{k-1}^2)\end{cases}$$

$$(10.10.21)$$

and $\quad D_{ij}=\frac{1}{3}\sum_{n=1}^{N}(Q_{ij})_n(z_n^3-z_{n-1}^3)$ （Bending Stiffness or Rigidity） $\quad(10.10.22)$

The existence of the coupling stiffness, i.e., [B] in Eqs. (10.10.17) and (10.10.21), means that an applied in-plane force may induce out-of-plane curved deformations while an applied out-of-plane moment may produce in-plane stretching or shortening.

10.10.3　Interlaminar Strain （Stress） Singularity

There is a weak strain (stress) singularity between two adjacent dissimilar laminae. This is called interlaminar strain (stress) singularity. The straightforward way to accurately predict interlaminar stresses using composites analysis is to create a mesh of 3-dimensional solid elements, with at least three elements across the thickness of each layer of the laminate. The interlaminar stresses can then be extracted directly from the full stress tensor, noting that σ_{zz}, τ_{xz}, and τ_{yz} are all continuous across the layer boundaries while the corresponding strains ε_{zz}, ε_{xz}, and ε_{yz} are not necessarily continuous across layer boundaries. Due to the fact that at a free edge the interlaminar strains (stresses) are singular, a comparative approach should be considered. Prognosis of interlaminar problems will be discussed in Chapter 15.

10.10.4　Through-the-Thickness Wave Propagation

It was shown by [Remillat et al.] using a combination of semi-analytical models and finite element time-stepping techniques that a cross-ply laminate may exhibit well-spaced bending, shear and symmetric fundamental modes, while featuring normal stresses for "[A] mode" are 3 times lower than composite laminates with the positive Poisson's ratio obtained from the classic lamination theory. It means that the through-thickness Poisson's ratio of a cross-ply laminate can be negative.

References

ADAMS D F, WALRATH D E, 1987. Further Development of the Iosipescu Shear Test Method [J]. Experimental Mechanics, 27(2): 113-119.

ADAMS D F, WALRATH D E, 1987. Current Status of the Iosipescu Shear Test Method [J]. Journal of Composite Materials, June: 494-507.

American Chemistry Council-Plastics Division, 2014. Technology Roadmap: Plastics and Polymer Composites for Automotive Markets[J]. American Chemistry Council.

ARCAN M, 1984. The Iosipescu Shear Test as Applied to Composite Materials: Discussion[J]. Experimental Mechanics, 24(1): 66-67.

ASTM STANDARD D5229/D5229M-92, 1992. Standard Test Methodology for Moisture Absorption Properties and Equilibrium Conditioning of Polymer Matrix Composite Materials[S]. American Society for Testing and Materials.

Automotive Composites Consortium, 1990. Test Procedures for Automotive Structural Composite Materials[M]. Troy, MI, USA.

BAERE I, et al, 2009. Modeling the Nonlinear Shear Stress-Strain Behavior of a Carbon Fabric Reinforced Polyphenylene Sulphide from Rail Shear and $[(45°, -45°)]_{4s}$ Tensile Test[J]. Polymer Composites, 30: 1016-1026.

BAKER D, RIALS T, 2013. Recent Advances in Low-Cost Carbon Fiber Manufacture from Lignin[J]. Journal of Applied Polymer Science, 130(2): 713-728.

BARNES J A, KUMOSA M, HULL D, 1987. Theoretical and Experimental Evaluation Iosipescu Shear Test [J]. Composites Science and Technology, 28: 251-268.

BARBERO E J, 2017. Introduction to Composite Materials Design, 3rd Edition, CRC Press.

BAUCHAU O A, 1972. Experimental Measurement of Elastic Shear Modulus of Graphite/Epoxy Tubes[J]. Journal of Composite Materials, 15: 151-156.

BERGER L, et al, 2012. Focal Project 4: Structural Automotive Components from Composite Materials[J]. Automotive Composites Consortium, Project ID #LM049.

BLACK S, 2012. Carbon Fiber Gathering Momentum[J]. Composites World.

BLACK S, 2008. Aligned Discontinuous Fibers Come of Age[J]. High Performance Composites.

BLUMENTRITT B F, VU B T, COOPER S L, 1975. Mechanical Properties of Discontinuous Fiber Reinforced Thermoplastics. Ⅱ. Random-in-Plane Fiber Orientation[J]. Polymer Engineering and Science, 15(6): 428-436.

BROUGHTON W R, KUMOSA M, HULL D, 1990. Analysis of the Iosipescu Shear Test as Applied to Unidirectional Carbon-Fiber Reinforced Composites[J]. Composites Science and Technology: 299-325.

BULGAKOV V E, KUHN G, 1995. High-Performance Multilevel Iterative Aggregation Solver for Large Finite-Element Structural Analysis Problems[J]. International Journal of Numerical Methods Eng., 38: 3529-3544.

BUNSELL A R, 2009. Handbook of Tensile Properties of Textile and Technical Fibers[M]. Woodhead Publishing Ltd.

CARUSO J, CHAMIS C, 1986. Assessment of Simplified Composite Micromechanics Using Three Dimensional Finite Element Analysis[J]. Journal of Composites Technology and Research, 18(3): 77-83.

CHAMIS C C, 1989. Mechanics of Composites Materials: Past, Present and Future[J]. Journal of Composites Technology and Research, 11: 3-14.

CHIANG Y J, 1996. Robust Design of the Iosipescu Shear Test Specimen for Composites[J]. Journal of Testing and Evaluation, 24(1): 1-11.

CHIANG Y J, 1996. Characterizing Simple-Stranded Wire Cables under Axial Loading[J]. Finite Elements in Analysis and Design, (24): 49-66.

CHRISTENSEN R M, WAALS F M, 1972. Effective Stiffness of Randomly Oriented Fiber Composites[J]. Journal of Composite Materials, (6): 518-532.

COLOMBAN P, et al, 2007. Micro-Raman and IR Study of the Compressive Behavior of Poly (Paraphenylene Benzobisoxazole) (PBO) Fibers in a Diamond-Anvil Cell[J]. J. Raman Spectroscopy, 38: 100.

COMPTON B G, LEWIS J A, 2014. 3D-Printing of Lightweight Cellular Composites[J]. Advanced Materials, 26(34): 5930-5935.

DANIEL I M, ISHAI O, 2007. Engineering Mechanics of Composite Materials[M]. 2nd Edition, Oxford University Press, New York, NY, USA.

DIZ J, HUMBERT M, 1992. Practical Aspects of Calculating the Elastic Properties of Polycrystals from the Texture According to Different Models[J]. Journal of Applied Crystallography, 25(6): 756-760.

DOE, 2013. Onboard Type Ⅳ Compressed Hydrogen Storage Systems, Current Performance and Cost[J]. Fuel Cells Technology Office Fact Record #13013U.S. Department of Energy.

FEHER L, FLACH A, NUSS V, et al, 2003. HEPHAISTOS: A novel 2.45 GHz Microwave System for Aerospace Composite Fabrication[C]. the 9th International Conference on Microwave and RF Heating, Loughborough University, Loughborough.

FERRY L, et al, 1999. Composites Science and Technology, 59(4): 575.

DELANNAY F, 2005. Elastic Model of an Entangled Network of Interconnected Fibers Accounting for Negative Poisson Ratio Behavior and Random Triangulation[J]. International Journal of Solids and Structures, 42: 2265-2285.

FUJII T, LIN F, 1995. Fatigue Behavior of a Plain-Woven Glass Fabric Laminate under Tension/Torsion Biaxial Loading[J]. Journal of Composite Materials, 29(5): 573-590.

GAY D, HOA S, TSAI S, 2003. Composite Materials Design and Applications[M]. CRC Press LLC.

GONZÁLEZ C, LORCA J, 2007. Virtual Fracture Testing of Composites: A Computational Micromechanics Approach[J]. Engineering Fracture Mechanics, 74: 1126-1138.

GIBSON A G, et al, 2006. Laminate Theory Analysis of Composites under Load in Fire[J]. Journal of Composite Materials, 40(7): 639-658.

GU B, CHEN Y, ZHOU J, 2011. Design, Manufacture and Performance Evaluation of Non-Asbestos Sealing Composites[M]. Advances in Composite Materials: Ecodesign and Analysis, Edited by Brahim Attaf.

HALPIN J C, TSAI S W, 1969. Effects of Environmental Factors on Composite Materials[J]. AFMLTR 67-423.

HALPIN J C, 1969. Stiffness and Expansion Estimates for Oriented Short Fiber Composites[J]. Journal of Composite Materials, 3:732-734.

HASHIN Z, 1964. Theory of Mechanical Behavior of Heterogeneous Media[J]. Applied Mechanics Review, 17(1): 1-9.

HERRERA RAMIREZ J M, et al, 2004. Micro-Raman Study of the Fatigue Fracture and Tensile Behavior of Polyamide (PA6,6) Fibers[J]. Journal of Raman Spectroscopy, 35: 1063-1072.

HEWITT R L, DE MALHERBE M C, 1970. An Approximation for the Longitudinal Shear Modulus of Continuous Fiber Composites[J]. Journal of Composite Materials, 4: 280-282.

HILL R, 1965. A Self-Consistent Mechanics of Composite Materials[J]. Journal of Mech. Phys. Sol., 13: 213-222.

HO H, TSAI M Y, MORTON J, et al, 1991. An Experimental Investigation of Iosipescu Specimen for Composite Materials[J]. Experimental Mechanics, 31(4): 328-336.

HO H, TSAI M Y, MORTON J, et al, 1993. Numerical Analysis of the Iosipescu Specimen for Composite Materials[J]. Composite Science and Technology, 46: 115-128.

HO H, MORTON J, FARLEY G L, 1994. Non-Linear Numerical Analysis of the Iosipescu Specimen for Composite Materials[J]. Composites Science and Technology, 50: 355-365.

HO H, TSAI M Y, MORTON J, et al. 1994. In-Plane Shear Testing of Graphite-Woven Fabric Composites[J]. Experimental Mechanics, 34(1): 45-52.

HO M P, et al, 2012. Critical Factors on Manufacturing Processes of Natural Fiber Composites [J]. Composites, Part B, 43: 3549-3562.

HOA S V, 2017. Factors Affecting the Properties of Composites Made by 4D Printing (Moldless Composites Manufacturing)[M]. Advanced Manufacturing: Polymer & Composites Science, 3(3): 101-109.

HOPCROFT M A, et al, 2010. What is the Young's Modulus of Silicon? [J]. Journal of Microelectromechanical Systems, 19(2): 229-238.

HUANG Z, 2001. Micromechanical Prediction of Ultimate Strength of Transversely Isotropic Fibrous Composites[J]. International Journal of Solids and Structures, 8: 4147-4172.

HUSSAIN A K, ADAMS D F, 1999. Development of a New Two-Rail Shear Test Fixture for Composite Materials[J]. Journal of Compo. Technol. Res., 21(4): 215.

IOSIPESCU N, 1967. New Accurate Procedure for Single Shear Testing of Metals[J]. Journal of Materials, 2(3): 537-566.

ISO, 2008. ISO 62: 2008(E), International Organization for Standardization.

JACOBSEN A, 2004. Characterization of Constitutive Behavior of Satin-Weave Fabric Composite[J]. Journal of Composite Materials, 38(7): 555-565.

JEONG J J, et al, 2014. Progressive Damage of Randomly Oriented Short Fiber Reinforced Composites[C]. 16th International Conference on Composite Materials, Dubai, UAE.

JEON Y, ALWAY-COOPER R, MORALES M, et al, 2013. Carbon Fibers[M]. Handbook of Advanced Ceramics, Editors: Somiya & Kaneno, 2nd Edition, Elsevier: 143-154.

JIA N, KAGAN V, 2001. Mechanical Performance of Polyamides with Influence of Moisture and Temperature: Accurate Evaluation and Better Understanding[J]. Plastics Failure: Analysis and Prevention, Plastic Design Library (PDL), New York, NY, USA: 95-104.

JONES, 1975. Mechanics of Composite Materials[M]. McGraw-Hill, New York, NY, USA.

JOVEN R, et al. 2010. Experimental Investigation of Tool/Part Interface during Curing of Composites[C]. Proceedings of the SAMPE 2010 Conference and Exhibition.

KIM H G, KWAC L K, 2009. Modeling on Constitutive Behavior for Short Fiber Reinforced Composites[J]. Journal of Mechanical Science and Technology, 23: 54.

KITAGAWA T, YABUKI K, YOUNG R J, 2001. An Investigation into the Relationship between Processing, Structure and Properties for High-Modulus PBO Fibers. Part 1. Raman Band Shifts and Broadening in Tension and Compression[J]. Polymer, 42(5): 2101-2112.

KITAGAWA T, MURASE H, YABUKI K, 1998. Morphological Study on Poly-p-phenylenebenzobisoxazole (PBO) Fiber[J]. Journal of Polymer Science, Part B, 36: 39-48.

KONONOVA O, et al, 2010. Mechanical Properties of Composites Reinforced by Cotton Knitted Fabric[C]. 7th International DAAAM Baltic Conference, 22-24 April, Tallinn, Estonia.

KRAUSE S J, 1988. Morphology and Properties of Rigid-Rod Poly(p-phenylene benzobisoxazole) (PBO) and Stiff-Chain Poly(2,5(6)-benzoxazole) (ABPBO) Fibers[J]. Polymer, 29(8): 1354-1364.

KUMOSA M, HULL D, 1987. Mixed-Mode Fracture of Composites Using Iosipescu Shear Test[J]. International Journal of Fracture, 35: 83-102.

CHOI J B, LAKES R S, 1996. Fracture Toughness of Re-entrant Foam Materials with a Negative Poisson's Ratio: Experiment and Analysis[J]. International Journal of Fracture, 80: 3269.

LAKES, RODERIC, 1987. Foam Structures with a Negative Poisson's Ratio[J]. Science, 235 (4792): 1038.

LEE S, MUNRO M, 1986. Evaluation of In-Plane Shear Test Methods for Advanced Composite Materials by the Decision Analysis Technique[J]. Composites, 17(1): 13-22.

LEE S, MUNRO M, 1990. Evaluation of Testing Techniques for the Iosipescu Shear Test for Advanced Composite Materials[J]. Journal of Composite Materials, 24: 419-440.

LEE S, MUNRO M, SCOTT R F, 1990. Evaluation of Three In-Plane Shear Test Methods for Advanced Composite Materials[J]. Composites, 21(6): 495-502.

LUO J J, DANIEL I M, 2004. Sublaminate-Based Lamination Theory and Symmetry Properties of Textile Composite Laminates[J]. Composites, B, 35(6-8): 483-496.

MEHTA P K, 1986. Concrete Structure, Properties and Materials[J]. Prentice-Hall, New Jersey.

MORI T, TANKA A, 1973. Averaged Stress in Matrix and Averaged Energy in Materials with Misfitting Inclusions[J]. Acta Metallurgica, 21: 571-574.

MORTON J, HO H, TSAI M Y, et al, 1992. An Evaluation of the Iosipescu Specimen for Composite Materials Shear Property Measurement[J]. Journal of Composite Materials, 26(5): 708-750.

National Research Council, 2012. Application of Light-Weighting Technology to Military Aircraft, Vessels and Vehicles[M]. The National Academies Press.

NORTHOLT M, BALTUSSEN J, 2001. The Tensile and Compressive Deformation of Polymer and Carbon Fibers [J]. Journal of Applied Polymer Science, 83: 508-538.

ODOM E, BLACKKETTER D, SURATNO B, 1994. Experimental and Analytical Investigation of the Modified Wyoming Shear-Test Fixture[J]. Experimental Mechanics, 34(1): 10-15.

OGALE A, ANDERSON D, LIN C, et al, 2002. Orientation and Dimensional Changes in Mesophase Pitch-Based Carbon Fibers[J]. Carbon, 40(8): 1309-1319.

ORNDOFF E, 1995. Development and Evaluation of Polybenzoxazole Fibrous Structures[R]. NASA Tech Memo 104814.

PAHR D H, BÖHM H J, 2008. Assessment of Mixed Uniform Boundary Conditions for Predicting the Mechanical Behavior of Elastic and Inelastic Discontinuously Reinforced Composites[J]. Computer Modeling in Engineering and Science, 34: 117-136.

PAN N, 1996. The Elastic Constants of Randomly Oriented Fiber Composite: A New Approach to Prediction[J]. Science and Engineering of Composite Materials, 5(2): 63-72.

PENAVA Ž, et al, 2014. Determination of the Elastic Constants of a Plain Woven Fabrics by Tensile Test in Various Directions[J]. Fibers and Textiles in Eastern Europe, 22(2): 57-63.

PIERRON F, VAUTRIN A, 1996. Measurement of the In-Plane Shear Strengths of Unidirectional Composites with the Iosipescu Test[J]. Composites Science and Technology, 56(4): 483-488.

PINDERA M J, IFJU P, POST D, 1990. Iosipescu Shear Characterization of Polymeric and Metal Matrix Composites[J]. Experimental Mechanics, 30(1): 101-108.

PAGANO N J, HALPIN J C, 1968. Influence of End Constraint in the Testing of Anisotropic Bodies [J]. Journal of Composite Materials, 2: 18-31.

PINDERA M J, et al, 1989. Mechanical Response of Aramid/Epoxy under Tensile, Compressive and Shearing Loading[J]. Journal of Reinforced Plastics and Composites, 8: 410-420.

PINDERA M J, CHOKSI G, HIDDE J S, et al, 1987. A Methodology for Accurate Shear Characterization for Unidirectional Composites[J]. Journal of Composite Materials, 21(12): 1164-1184.

PINDERA M J, HERAKOVICH C T, 1986. Shear Characterization of Unidirectional Composites with the Off-

Axis Tension Test[J]. Experimental Mechanics, 26(1): 103-112.

PINTADO P, CANAS J, MORTON J, 1986. Numerical Analysis of Notched Shear Specimens for Composites[J]. Journal of Reinforced Plastics and Composites, 10: 198-211.

PIGEON F, et al, 1992. Optical Fiber Young Modulus Measurement Using an Optical Method[J]. Electronics Letters, 28(11): 1034-1035.

PIGGOT M R, 1980. Load Bearing Composites[M]. Pergamon Press, Oxford, UK.

REMILLAT C, et al, 2008. Lamb Wave Propagation in Negative Poisson's Ratio Composites[J]. Proceedings of SPIE, The International Society for Optical Engineering.

RICHARDSON M, HAYLOCK B., 2012. Designer/Maker: The Rise of Additive Manufacturing, Domestic-Scale Production and the Possible Implications for the Automotive Industry[J]. Computer-Aided Design and Applications, 2: 33-48.

ROSEN B W, 1972. A Simple Procedure for Experimental Determination of the Longitudinal Shear Modulus of Unidirectional Composites[J]. Journal of Composite Materials, 6: 552-554.

SAID M A, et al, 2006. Investigation of Ultra Violet (UV) Resistance for High Strength Fibers[J]. Advances in Space Research, 37(11): 2052-2058.

SANDIA National Laboratories, 2013. Large Blade Manufacturing Cost Studies Using the Sandia Blade Manufacturing Cost Tool and Sandia 100-Meter Blades[J]. SAND2013-2734.

SIERAKOWSKI R L, 1997. Strain Rate Effects in Composites[J]. Applied Mechanics Reviews, 50(12): 741-761.

SORENSEN B F, JACOBSEN T K, 1998. Composites[J]. 29A: 1443-1451.

SRIVASTAVAL V K, SINGH S, 2012. A Micro-Mechanical Model for Elastic Modulus of Multi-Walled Carbon Nanotube/Epoxy Resin Composites[J]. International Journal of Composite Materials, 2(2): 1-6.

STONG A B, 2008. Fundamentals of Composite Manufacturing Materials, Methods, and Applications[M]. 2nd Edition, Society of Manufacturing Engineers, Dearborn, MI.

SULLIVAN J L, 1988. The Use of Iosipescu Specimens[J]. Experimental Mechanics, 28(3): 326-328.

SULLIVAN J, KAO B, VAN OENE H, 1984. Shear Properties and a Stress Analysis Obtained from Vinyl-ester Iosipescu Specimens[J]. Experimental Mechanics, 24(3): 223-232.

SWANSON S R, MERSICK M, TOOMBES G R. Comparison of Torsion Tube and Iosipescu In-Plane Shear Test Results for a Carbon Fiber-Reinforced Epoxy Composite[J]. Composites, 16(3): 185.

TATLIER M, BERHAN L, 2009. Modeling the Negative Poisson's Ratio of Compressed Fused Fiber Networks [J]. Physica Status Solidi, B, 246(9): 2018-2024.

TSAI S W, PAGANO J J, 1968. Composite Materials Workshop[J]. Technomic, Stamford, CT, USA.

TUTTLE M E, BRINSM H F, 1984. Resistance-Foil Strain-Gage Technology as Applied to Composite Materials [J]. Experimental Mechanics, March, 24(1): 54-65.

VANNAN E, VIZHIAN P, 2014. Prediction of the Elastic Properties of Short Basalt Fiber Reinforced Al Alloy Metal Matrix Composites[J]. Journal of Minerals and Materials Characterization and Engineering, 2(1): 61-69.

WALRATH D E, ADAMS D E, 1983. The Iosipescu Shear Test as Applied to Composite Materials[J]. Experimental Mechanics, 23(1): 105-110.

WALTER J D, PATEL H P, 1979. Approximate Expressions for the Elastic Constants of Cord-Rubber Laminates[J]. Rubber Chemistry and Technology, 52: 710-724.

WARREN C D, 2012. Lower Cost Carbon Fiber Precursors[J]. 2012 DOE Vehicle Technologies Office Annual Merit Review, Dept. of Energy, USA.

WARREN C D, EBERLE C, 2013. Barriers to Widespread Adoption of Carbon Fibers in High Volume Applications[J]. Presented to Southern Advanced Materials in Transportation Alliance (SAMTA), Oak Ridge, TN.

WEEKS C A, SUN C T, 1998. Modeling Non-Linear Rate Dependent Behavior in Fiber-Reinforced Composites [J]. Composites Science and Technology, 58(3-4): 603-611.

WHITNEY J M, MCCULLOUGH R L, 1990. Micromechanical Material Modeling[J]. Delaware Composite Design Encyclopedia, Vol. 2, Technomic Publishing Co., Lancaster, PA, USA.

WHITNEY J M, STANSBARGER D L, HOWELL H B, 1971. Analysis of the Rail Shear Test- Application and Limitations[J]. Journal of Composite Materials, 5: 24-34.

MILTON G W, 2002. The Theory of Composites[J]. Cambridge University Press, Cambridge, UK.

WU E M, 1971. Optimal Experimental Measurements of Anisotropic Materials[J]. Journal of Composite Materials, 5: 58.

WYCHERLEY G W, MESTAN S A, GRABOVAC I, 1990. A Method for Uniform Shear Stress-Strain Analysis of Adhesives[J]. Journal of Testing and Evaluation, 18(3): 203-209.

YOUNG R J, DAY R J, ZAKIKHANI M, 1990. The Structure and Deformation Behavior of Poly (p-phenylene benzobisoxazole) Fibers[J]. Journal of Materials Science, 25(1): 127-136.

ZENG D, XIA C, WEBB J, et al, 2014. Effect of Fiber Orientation on the Mechanical Properties of Long Glass Fiber Reinforced (LGFR)[J]. Composites, SAE 2014-01-1049.

ZOK F, LEVI C, 2001. Mechanical Properties of Porous-Matrix Ceramic Composites[J]. Advanced Engineering
Materials, 3(1-2): 15-23.

Problems

10.1   A sheet molding compound lamina, SMCR65 (65% of fibers in weight fraction or 44.6% in
volume fraction), contains Eglass fibers in a thermosetting epoxy matrix. Given that the material
properties for the constituents are $E_f = 72.4$ GPa, $\nu_f = 0.2$, and $E_m = 3.6$ GPa, $\nu_m = 0.35$.

Determine E_{11}, E_{22}, E_{33}, G_{23}, G_{31}, G_{12}, ν_{23}, ν_{31}, and ν_{12} of the lamina.

10.2   A cylindrical pressure vessel with closed ends has mean radius R and thin wall thickness t
and is subjected to internal pressure P. The vessel is made of helically wound high modulus fibers
in a low modulus matrix. The winding angle is $\pm\varphi$. Assume that the matrix modulus is so small that
the load (stresses) is taken by fibers, which are in pure tension. Determine the winding angle
independent of R, t and P.

10.3   A unidirectional boron/epoxy composite has the following material properties: $E_{11}^t = E_{11}^c =$
206 GPa, $E_{22}^t = E_{22}^c = 20.6$ GPa, and $G_{12} = 6.895$ GPa, $\nu_{12t} = \nu_{12c} = 0.3$. Here the superscripts t and c
represents tension and compression. At a point in the lamina, the strains are measured to be
$\varepsilon_{11} = 0.5\%$, $\varepsilon_{22} = -0.2\%$, and $\gamma_{12} = 0.3\%$. Determine the (a) principal directions of strains,
(b) principal directions of stresses, and (c) principal stresses.

10.4   The material properties for 3-M Scotchply (glass/epoxy) are $E_{11}^t = E_{11}^c = 38.6$ GPa, $E_{22}^t =$
$E_{22}^c = 20.6$ GPa, $G_{12} = 6.895$ GPa, $\nu_{12t} = \nu_{12c} = 0.30$. At a point in the lamina, the stresses are
measured to be $\sigma_{11} = 400$ MPa, $\sigma_{22} = 60$ MPa, and $\tau_{12} = 15$ MPa. Determine the (a) magnitude of
strains ε_{11}, ε_{22}, and γ_{12}, (b) magnitude of principal strains, (c) principal direction of strains,
(d) principal stresses, and (e) principal direction of stresses.

10.5   Determine the stiffness matrix in the x-y coordinate, when a unidirectional carbon/epoxy
lamina is subjected to $+45°$ and off-axis, but $-45°$ in-plane, loadings. The volume fraction for
fibers is 60%. The material properties for the constituents (fibers and matrix) are assumed to be
isotropic and given as $E_f = 220$ GPa, $\nu_f = 0.2$ and $E_m = 3.6$ GPa, $\nu_m = 0.35$.

10.6   Plot the longitudinal and transverse coefficients of thermal expansions for a unidirectional
glass-polyester lamina, as functions of fiber volume fraction, V_f. If $V_f = 60\%$, calculate the
longitudinal and transverse coefficients of thermal expansions. Given that $\alpha_f = 5 \times 10^{-6}$℃, $\alpha_m = 90 \times$
10^{-6}℃, $E_f = 72$ GPa, $E_m = 3.8$ GPa, $\nu_f = 0.20$, $\nu_m = 0.35$.

Table 10.1.1   Elastic Constants of Synthetic Fibers〔Valliappan〕〔Kinsella et al.〕〔Ogale et al.〕, where $G_{ij} = G_{ji}$ and $\nu_{ij}E_{jj} = \nu_{ji}E_{ii}$

Material-DAM	$T/℃$	ρ	E_{11}	E_{22}	E_{33}	G_{12}	G_{13}	G_{23}	ν_{12}	ν_{13}	ν_{23}
Al_2O_3(20 μm)	23	3.9	380	380	380	154	154	154	0.2	0.24	0.24
Basalt (25 mm × 18 μm)	23	2.7	88	88	88	—	—	—	0.2	0.2	0.2
Boron	23	2.45	420	420	420	170	170	170	0.2	0.2	0.2
Carbon（AS4）	23	—	210	—	—	—	—	—	0.2	0.2	0.2
Carbon（EC6）	23	1.79	294	—	—	—	—	—	0.2	0.2	0.2
Carbon: PAN (IM-7)	23	1.74	317	21	21	14	14	—	0.2	0.2	0.2
Carbon: PAN (T50)	23	1.64	410	12	12	—	—	—	0.2	0.2	0.2
Carbon: PAN (T300; 7 μm, AS-4)	23	1.76	230	15	15	9	9	4	0.2	0.2	0.2
Carbon: Pitch (P120)	23	1.75	827	—	—	—	—	—	0.2	0.2	0.2
Carbon: Pitch (d_f =9 μm; Heat-treated = 2600 ℃)	23	1.75	482	—	—	—	—	—	0.2	0.2	0.2
Carbon: Pitch (d_f =9 μm; Heat-treated = 2100 ℃)	23	1.75	412	—	—	—	—	—	0.2	0.2	0.25
Carbon: Pitch (d_f =9 μm; Heat-treated = 1500 ℃)	23	1.75	206	—	—	—	—	—	0.2	0.2	0.2

continued

Material-DAM	$T/°C$	ρ	E_{11}	E_{22}	E_{33}	G_{12}	G_{13}	G_{23}	ν_{12}	ν_{13}	ν_{23}
Carbon: Pitch ($d_f = 9$ μm; Heat-treated = 1200 ℃)	23	1.75	174	—	—	—	—	—	0.2	0.2	0.2
Carbon (Bulk)	23	1.64	124	124	124	—	—	—	0.2	0.2	0.2
	100	—	119	119	119	—	—	—	—	—	—
	200	—	107	107	107	—	—	—	—	—	—
	600	—	45	45	45	—	—	—	—	—	—
CNT: MWNT (Single)	23	1.4	1200	5	5	—	—	—	—	—	—
CNT: SWNT (Single)	23	1.4	1000	5	5	—	—	—	—	—	—
SWNT (Bulk; Measured)	23	1.4	1000	—	—	—	—	—	—	—	—
Glass-Advantex	23	2.62	—	—	—	—	—	—	0.2	0.2	0.23
Glass-AR	23	2.7	70	70	70	30	30	30	0.23	0.23	0.23
Glass-C Fiber	23	2.52	—	—	—	—	—	—	0.2	0.2	0.23
Glass-D Fiber	23	2.11	—	—	—	—	—	—	0.2	0.2	0.23
Glass-E Fiber	23	2.58	77	68	68	30	30	30	0.2	0.2	0.23
	538	—	81	—	—	—	—	—	—	—	—
Glass-E-CR Fiber	23	2.7	80.3	80.3	80.3	—	—	—	0.2	0.2	0.23
	538	—	81.3	81.3	81.3	—	—	—	—	—	—
Glass-NE Fiber	23	—	—	—	—	—	—	—	0.2	0.2	0.23
Glass-R Fiber	23	2.54	87	87	87	—	—	—	0.2	0.2	0.23
Glass-S1 Fiber	23	2.5	86	86	86	—	—	—	0.2	0.2	0.23
Glass-S2 Fiber	23	2.48	87	87	87	—	—	—	0.2	0.2	0.23
	538	—	89	89	89	—	—	—	—	—	—

continued

Material-DAM	$T/°C$	ρ	E_{11}	E_{22}	E_{33}	G_{12}	G_{13}	G_{23}	ν_{12}	ν_{13}	ν_{23}
Glass-S2 Yarn	23	2.48	74.2	24	24	7.6	7.6	—	0.22	0.22	0.3
Glass-T Fiber	23	—	84	84	84	—	—	—	0.2	0.2	0.23
Glass Fiber ($d_f=9.5$ μm)	23	2.6	41	41	41	—	—	—	0.2	0.2	0.23
	100	—	41	41	41	—	—	—	—	—	—
	150	—	39	39	39	—	—	—	—	—	—
	350	—	37	37	37	—	—	—	—	—	—
Graphite-AS4 ($d_f=0.3$ mm)	23	1.75	224	14	14	27	27	7	0.2	0.2	—
Graphite-HM	23	1.94	385	6.3	6.3	7.7	7.7	—	0.2	0.2	—
Kevlar-29 Fiber	23	1.44	61	4.2	4.2	2.9	2.9	2	0.32	0.32	0.4
	450（Decomposition temperature）										
Kevla-29 Yarn	23	1.44	53	2.4	2.4	1.6	1.6	—	0.36	0.36	0.36
Kevlar-49	23	1.44	154	7	7	5	5	—	0.32	0.32	0.4
	550（Decomposition temperature）										
Kevlar-149	23	1.47	186	10	10	5	5	—	0.32	0.32	0.4
Mica	23	2.7	231	—	—	—	—	—	0.23	0.23	0.23
Mo Fiber	23	—	—	—	—	—	—	—	—	—	—
M5	23	1.7	271	—	—	—	—	—	—	—	—
PA$_{(draw-ratio=1)}$	23	1.2	2.0	—	—	—	—	—	—	—	—
PA$_{(draw-ratio=3)}$	23	1.2	3.7	—	—	—	—	—	—	—	—
PA$_{(draw-ratio=4)}$	23	1.2	4.6	—	—	—	—	—	—	—	—
PA$_{(draw-ratio=5)}$	23	1.2	5.8	—	—	—	—	—	—	—	—
PBI	23	1.4	5.6	5.6	5.6	—	—	—	—	—	—
PBT	23	1.58	115	115	115	—	—	—	0.44	0.44	0.44
PE-Spectra 900 （UHMWPE）	23	0.97	60.4	4.7	4.7	1.65	1.65	—	0.3	0.3	0.4
	150（Decomposition temperature）										

continued

Material-DAM	$T/^{\circ}C$	ρ	E_{11}	E_{22}	E_{33}	G_{12}	G_{13}	G_{23}	ν_{12}	ν_{13}	ν_{23}
PE-Spectra 1000	23	0.97	120	6	6	2	2	2	0.3	0.3	0.4
PE-Spectra 2000	23	0.97	120	6	6	2	2	2	0.3	0.3	0.4
PE-dyneema	23	0.975	110	6	6	2	2	2	0.3	0.3	0.4
	150 (Decomposition temperature)										
Polyester	23	1.38	15	15	15	—	—	—	0.44	0.44	0.44
PP fiber	23	—	—	—	—	—	—	—	—	—	—
Saffil Fiber ($Al_2O_3/5\%SiO_2$)	23	3.3	300	300	300	126	126	126	0.19	0.19	0.19
SiC	23	3.2	410	410	410	169	169	169	0.21	0.21	0.21
Silica Fiber (Optical Fiber)	23	—	69	—	—	—	—	—	—	—	—
SiO_2(Fused)	23	2.3	74	74	74	31.3	31.4	31.4	0.18	0.18	0.18
Vectran-NT (LCP Fiber)	23	1.4	52	—	—	—	—	—	—	—	—
Vectran-HS	23	1.4	75	—	—	—	—	—	—	—	—
Vectran-HM	23	1.4	105	—	—	—	—	—	—	—	—
Zylon-HM (d_f = 11-13 μm)	23	1.56	280	—	—	—	—	—	—	—	—
	650 (Decomposition temperature)										
Zylon-AS (d_f = 11-13 μm)	23	1.54	180	—	—	—	—	—	—	—	—
	650 (Decomposition temperature)										

Notes: ρ (g/cm^3) : Density ;

d_f(mm) : Mean diameter of fibers ;

E_T & E_C (GPa) : Tensile and compressive moduli of elasticity ;

E_{11} , E_{22} , E_{33} (GPa) : Young's moduli in axial, transverse, and out-of-plane directions ;

G_{12} , G_{13} , G_{23} (GPa) : Shear moduli of a unidirectional lamina, and $G_{ij} = G_{ji}$;

σ_{uts} (MPa) & ε_{uts} : Ultimate tensile strength and strain ;

ν_{12} , ν_{13} , ν_{23} : Poisson's ratios of a unidirectional lamina and $\nu_{ij}E_{jj} = \nu_{ji}E_{ii}$;

AS : As spun ;

HM : High modulus ;

HS : High tensile strength ;

LCP : Liquid crystal polymer.

Table 10.1.2   Thermal Properties of Synthetic Fibers ［Wang et al.］

Material-DAM	$T/℃$	α_1	α_2	α_3	k_1	k_2	k_3	γ	β_1	β_2	β_3
$Al_2O_3(\rho=3.2)$	23	8.5	8.5	8.5	1	1	1	—	—	—	—
$Al_2O_3/5\%SiO_2$（Saffil）	23	5.2	5.2	5.2	—	—	—	—	—	—	—
Basalt	23	—	—	—	—	—	—	—	—	—	—
Boron （$\rho=2.4$）	23	5	5	5	—	—	—	—	—	—	—
Carbon：PAN （T300；$d_f=7$ μm；AS-4）	23	−0.3	9	9	15	0.533	0.533	710	—	—	—
Carbon （Pitch；Vapor-grown）	23	—	—	—	1200	—	—	837	—	—	—
Carbon：Pitch （P120）	23	−1.4	6.8	6.8	—	—	—	837	—	—	—
Carbon：Pitch （$d_f=9$ μm；Heat-treated=2600 ℃）	23	—	—	—	466	—	—	837	—	—	—
Carbon：Pitch （$d_f=9$ μm；Heat-treated=2100 ℃）	23	—	—	—	120	—	—	837	—	—	—
Carbon：Pitch （$d_f=9$ μm；Heat-treated=1500 ℃）	23	—	—	—	66	—	—	837	—	—	—
Carbon：Pitch （$d_f=9$ μm；Heat-treated=1200 ℃）	23	—	—	—	31	—	—	837	—	—	—
CNT （fiber of 8.84 mm×12.9 μm；Measured）	23	—	—	—	456	1.52	1.52	735	—	—	—

continued

Material-DAM	$T/℃$	α_1	α_2	α_3	k_1	k_2	k_3	γ	β_1	β_2	β_3
CNT：MWNT (Single unit；Measured)	−200	—	—	—	500	—	—	—	—	—	—
	−40	—	—	—	2800	—	—	—	—	—	—
	23	—	—	—	3000	1.52	1.52	735	—	—	—
	50	—	—	—	3200	—	—	750	—	—	—
	100	—	—	—	2500	—	—	775	—	—	—
	125	—	—	—	—	—	—	800	—	—	—
CNT：MWNT (Random；Thin Film)	23	—	—	—	—	—	—	710	—	—	—
	80	—	—	—	—	—	—	790	—	—	—
	100	—	—	—	—	—	—	875	—	—	—
	120	—	—	—	—	—	—	900	—	—	—
CNT：SWNT (Single unit；theoretical)	−228	—	—	—	31000	—	—	—	—	—	—
	−173	—	—	—	37000	—	—	—	—	—	—
	−73	—	—	—	19000	—	—	—	—	—	—
	23	—	—	—	3000	—	—	—	—	—	—
SWNT (Bulk；Random；Thin Film)	−173	—	—	—	60	—	—	—	—	—	—
	−40	—	—	—	190	—	—	—	—	—	—
	23	—	—	—	210	—	—	755	—	—	—
	80	—	—	—	—	—	—	810	—	—	—
	100	—	—	—	—	—	—	900	—	—	—
	125	—	—	—	—	—	—	1030	—	—	—
Glass-Advantex ($\rho=2.62$)	23	5.8	5.8	5.8	—	—	—	—	—	—	—
Glass-AR ($\rho=2.7$)	23	6.5	6.5	6.5	—	—	—	—	—	—	—
Glass-C ($\rho=2.52$)	23	6.3	6.3	6.3	—	—	—	787	—	—	—
Glass-D ($\rho=2.11$)	23	2.9	2.9	2.9	—	—	—	733	—	—	—

continued

Material-DAM	$T/^{\circ}C$	α_1	α_2	α_3	k_1	k_2	k_3	γ	β_1	β_2	β_3
Glass-E （$\rho=2.58$）	23	5.4	5.4	5.4	1.3	1.3	1.3	810	—	—	—
	538	—	—	—	—	—	—	—	—	—	—
Glass-E-CR （$\rho=2.7$）	23	5.9	5.9	5.9	—	—	—	—	—	—	—
Glass-NE	23	3.4	3.4	3.4	—	—	—	—	—	—	—
Glass-R （$\rho=2.54$）	23	3.8	3.8	3.8	—	—	—	732	—	—	—
Glass-S2 （$\rho=2.48$）	23	1.6	1.6	1.6	1.45	1.45	1.45	737	—	—	—
Graphite-AS4 （$\rho=1.75$）	23	−0.7	15	15	66	11.6	11.6	712	—	—	—
	80	—	—	—	85	—	—	785	—	—	—
	100	—	—	—	—	—	—	850	—	—	—
	125	—	—	—	120	—	—	900	—	—	—
Graphite-HM （$\rho=1.94$）	23	−1	10	10	8.6	8.6	8.6	710	—	—	—
Kevlar-29 （$\rho=1.44$）	23	−4	60	60	2.5	0.5	0.5	1230	—	—	—
Kevlar-49 （$\rho=1.44$）	23	−2	54	54	3.5	0.5	0.5	1230	—	—	—
Kevlar-149 （$\rho=1.47$）	23	—	—	—	4	0.5	0.5	1230	—	—	—
	550 （Decomposition temperature）										
PBT（$\rho=1.58$）	23	—	—	—	14	—	—	1500	—	—	—
PE-Spectra 900	−150	—	—	—	20	—	—	—	—	—	—
	−100	—	—	—	16	—	—	—	—	—	—
	23	—	—	—	12	0.3	0.3	—	—	—	—
PE-Spectra 2000	23	—	—	—	19	0.3	0.3	—	—	—	—
UHMWPE fiber （$E=151$ GPa）	−173	—	—	—	38	—	—	—	—	—	—
	−123	—	—	—	52	—	—	—	—	—	—
	23	—	—	—	—	—	—	—	—	—	—
UHMWPE fiber （$E=85$ GPa）	−173	—	—	—	30	—	—	—	—	—	—
	−123	—	—	—	36	—	—	—	—	—	—
	23	—	—	—	—	—	—	—	—	—	—

continued

Material-DAM	$T/℃$	α_1	α_2	α_3	k_1	k_2	k_3	γ	β_1	β_2	β_3
UHMWPE fiber ($E=51$ GPa)	−173	—	—	—	18	—	—	—	—	—	—
	−123	—	—	—	25	—	—	—	—	—	—
	23	—	—	—	—	—	—	—	—	—	—
UHMWPE fiber ($E=15$ GPa)	−173	—	—	—	7	—	—	—	—	—	—
	−123	—	—	—	13	—	—	—	—	—	—
	23	—	—	—	—	—	—	—	—	—	—
PE-dyneema ($\rho=0.975$)	−173	—	—	—	35	—	—	—	—	—	—
	−123	—	—	—	20	—	—	—	—	—	—
	23	−12	—	—	15	—	—	—	—	—	—
	200	—	—	—	4	—	—	—	—	—	—
PP fiber	23	6	6	6	—	—	—	—	—	—	—
SiC ($\rho=3.0$)	23	4	4	4	1	1	1	—	—	—	—
SiO$_2$(Fused)	23	0.55	0.55	0.55	1.6	1.6	1.6	740	—	—	—
Vectran-HS (LCP Fiber)	23	−5	75	75	1.5	0.18	0.18	1100	—	—	—
	100	—	—	—	2.0	—	—	1420	—	—	—
Zylon-HM (Polybenzoxazole)	23	−6	—	—	23	—	—	—	—	—	—
	650 (Decomposition temperature)										
Zylon-AS (Polybenzoxazole)	−100	—	—	—	16	—	—	—	—	—	—
	23	−6	—	—	19	—	—	—	—	—	—
	200	—	—	—	10	—	—	—	—	—	—
	650 (Decomposition temperature)										

Notes: α_1, α_2, α_3(μm/m/℃): Coefficients of linear thermal expansion of a unidirectional lamina;

k_1, k_2, k_3(W/m/℃): Thermal conductivities of a unidirectional lamina;

β_1, β_2, β_3(μm/m/%): Swelling coefficients of linear moisture expansion;

γ (J/kg/℃): Specific heat capacity.

Table 10.1.3 Orthotropic Mechanical Strengths of Synthetic Fibers

Material	$T/℃$	$(\sigma_{11u}, \varepsilon_{11u})$	$(\sigma_{22u}, \varepsilon_{22u})$	$(\sigma_{33u}, \varepsilon_{33u})$	$(\sigma_{12u}, \varepsilon_{12u})/(\sigma_{23u}, \varepsilon_{23u})/(\sigma_{13u}, \varepsilon_{13u})$
Al_2O_3	23	$\sigma_{11t}=2930$	—	—	—/—/—
$Al_2O_3/5\%SiO_2$ （Saffil; $V_f=5\%$）	23	$\sigma_{11t}=1500$	—	—	—/—/—
Basalt （25×0.018 mm）	23	(3800, 3.2%)	—	—	—/—/—
Carbon （AS4）	23	$\sigma_{11t}=2800$	—	—	—/—/—
Carbon （EC6）	23	$\sigma_{11t}=5000$	—	—	—/—/—
Carbon （M40A）	23	(2400, 0.6%)	—	—	—/—/—
Carbon: PAN （IM-7）	23	$\sigma_{11c}=-1100$; (4900, 1.7%)	—	—	—/—/—
Carbon: PAN （T300）	23	$\sigma_{11c}=-2800$; (3530, 1.5%)	—	—	—/—/—
Carbon: PAN （T50）	23	$\sigma_{11c}=-1600$	—	—	—/—/—
Carbon: Pitch （P120）	23	$\sigma_{11c}=-500$; (2250, 0.27%)	—	—	—/—/—
Carbon: Pitch （$d_f=9$ μm; HT at 2600 ℃）	23	(1900, 0.42%)	—	—	—/—/—
Carbon: Pitch （$d_f=9$ μm; HT at 2100 ℃）	23	(2700, 0.7%)	—	—	—/—/—
Carbon: Pitch （$d_f=9$ μm; HTat 1500 ℃）	23	(2300, 1.1%)	—	—	—/—/—

continued

Material	$T/℃$	$(\sigma_{11u}, \varepsilon_{11u})$	$(\sigma_{22u}, \varepsilon_{22u})$	$(\sigma_{33u}, \varepsilon_{33u})$	$(\sigma_{12u}, \varepsilon_{12u})/(\sigma_{23u}, \varepsilon_{23u})/$ $(\sigma_{13u}, \varepsilon_{13u})$
Carbon: Pitch ($d_f = 9$ μm; HT at 1200 ℃)	23	$(2000, 1.1\%)$	—	—	—/—/—
CNT: MWNT (Single cnt)	23	$\sigma_{11t} = 63000$	—	—	—/—/—
CNT: SWNT (Single cnt)	23	$(34000, 16\%)$	—	—	—/—/—
Glass-E	23	$\sigma_{11c} = -1080$; $(3200, 3.1\%)$	—	—	—/—/—
Glass-E-CR	23	$(3400, 4.8\%)$	—	—	—/—/—
Glass-R	23	$\sigma_{11t} = 3200$	—	—	—/—/—
Glass-S1	23	$\sigma_{11t} = 4000$	—	—	—/—/—
Glass-S2	23	$\sigma_{11c} = -1600$; $(4800, 4.8\%)$	—	—	—/—/—
Glass-T	23	$\sigma_{11t} = 4100$	—	—	—/—/—
Graphite-AS4	23	$\sigma_{11t} = 3700$	—	—	—/—/—
HMPE (Dyneema SK75)	23	$\sigma_{11t} = 3500$	—	—	—/—/—
Kevlar-29	23	$\sigma_{11t} = 2900$	—	—	—/—/—
Kevlar-49	23	$(-350, -0.63\%)$; $(3700, 2.8\%)$	—	—	—/—/—
Polyester	23	$\sigma_{11t} = 1300$	—	—	—/—/—
M5	23	$(3960, 1.4\%)$	—	—	—/—/—
Mo Fiber	23	$(826, 0.2\%)$; $(1000, 10\%)$	—	—	—/—/—

continued

Material	$T/℃$	$(\sigma_{11u},\ \varepsilon_{11u})$	$(\sigma_{22u},\ \varepsilon_{22u})$	$(\sigma_{33u},\ \varepsilon_{33u})$	$(\sigma_{12u},\ \varepsilon_{12u})/(\sigma_{23u},\ \varepsilon_{23u})/$ $(\sigma_{13u},\varepsilon_{13u})$
PE-Spectra 900	23	(2570, 5%)	—	—	350/—/—
PE-Spectra 1000	23	(3200, 4%)	—	—	—/—/—
PE-Spectra 2000	23	(3400, 3%)	—	—	—/—/—
PE-dyneema （HMPE；SK75）	23	$\sigma_{11t}=3400$	—	—	—/—/—
SiC	23	$\sigma_{11t}=3450$	—	—	—/—/—
Vectran-NT	23	(1100, 3.3%)	—	—	—/—/—
Vectran-HS	23	(3200, 3.8%)	—	—	—/—/—
Vectran-HM	23	(3000, 2.8%)	—	—	—/—/—
Zylon-HM （Polybenzoxazole； $d_f=12$ μm）	23	(−560, −0.23%)； (5800, 2.4%)	—	—	—/—/—
	650（Decomposition temperature）				
Zylon（AS） （Polybenzoxazole； $d_f=12$ μm）	23	(−470, −0.22%)； (5700, 3.8%)	—	—	—/—/—
	650（Decomposition temperature）				
Zylon（PBO） （Polybenzoxazole； $d_f=19$ μm）	23	$\sigma_{11t}=4200$	—	—	—/—/—
	650（Decomposition temperature）				

Table 10.1.4　Fatigue ε-N Properties of Engineering Fibers in the Longitudinal Direction〔Horikawa et al.〕〔Davies〕

Material	$T/℃$	$d\varepsilon/dt$	σ_f'	ε_f'	b	c	K'	n'	$\sigma_f@2N_f$	R
HMPE	23	—	—	—	—	—	—	—	2220@ 1.2×10^5	—
									2590@ 5.9×10^4	—
									2775@ 1.4×10^4	—

continued

Material	$T/℃$	$d\varepsilon/dt$	σ'_f	ε'_f	b	c	K'	n'	$\sigma_f@\,2N_f$	R
Kevlar-29	23	—	—	—	—	—	—	—	$1456@\,7.3\times10^5$	—
									$1820@\,2.6\times10^5$	—
Polyester	23	—	—	—	—	—	—	—	$882@\,2.1\times10^5$	—
									$945@\,1.5\times10^5$	—
									$1008@\,2\times10^4$	—
Zylon-AS	23	—	—	—	—	—	—	—	$1000@\,10^7$	0.1^+
									$1500@\,10^6$	0.1^+
									$1800@\,10^5$	0.1^+
									$2200@\,10^3$	0.1^+
Zylon-HM	23	—	—	—	—	—	—	—	$1750@\,10^7$	0.1^+
									$2000@\,10^6$	0.1^+
									$2300@\,10^5$	0.1^+
									$2800@\,10^3$	0.1^+

Chapter 11

Thermal Loadings

11.1　Thermal Effect

Material properties vary with temperature, which is a measure of energy content possessed by matter and it is representative of hotness or coldness. Automotive parts are expected to survive 10 years' service under the temperature variation between $-40\ ℃$ and $80\ ℃$. A common approach to precipitating latent defects is to let the vehicle system and components go through various environmental and operational stress tests before the manufacturing of products. Typical stresses induced in automotive components, including mechanical and electronic parts, consist of vibration loads due to on-road input and self-induced vibration with cycling temperatures. Automotive electronics are more subjected to fatigue-creep-oxidation threats at elevated temperatures. High-temperature fatigue is a major concern once the working temperature goes beyond 30%-40% of the absolute melting temperature（K）.

Heat related fatigue failure is called thermal fatigue, which usually involves mechanical stress, creep and oxidation, resulting from fluctuating temperatures. Thermal strains and stresses exist when subjected to external constraints such as rigid mountings, or due to internal constraints that are set up by a temperature gradient within the part. Thermomechanical fatigue involves simultaneous changes in both thermal strains/stresses, mechanical strains/stresses, and the related relative phase angle（out-of-phase fatigue case）.

Temperature gradients are likely to occur both along and through the material, causing high triaxial stresses, reducing material ductility in contrast to a ductility increase in a uniaxial-stressed case. There are a number of cleavaged facets on fracture surface in evidence, when material is subjected to high thermal gradients.

11.1.1　Flammability and Flash Point

The flash point of a material is a measure of how easy it is to ignite its vapor as the material evaporates into the atmosphere. A high flash point means lower flammability. Major codes related to flammability of automotive materials are standardized as follows:

（A）ISO 3795: Road vehicles, and tractors and machinery for agriculture and forestry.
（B）FMVSS302: Applied to cars, trucks, and buses.
（C）SAE J369: Flammability of polymeric interior materials horizontal test method.
（D）DIN 3795: Determination of burning behavior of interior materials in motor vehicles.
（E）GB8410（China）: Flammability test to interior material of motor vehicles.

The flammability ratings ranging from 0（inflammable）to 4（most flammable）according to HMIS （Hazardous Materials Identification System）, a standard for flammability ratings defined by US

Government, are listed as follows:

0: Materials will not burn, e.g. steel.

1: Materials that must be preheated before they will ignite, e.g. engine lubricating oil.

2: Materials that must be moderately heated or exposed to relatively high ambient temperatures before they will ignite, e.g. Diesel fuel.

3: Liquids and solids that can ignite under almost all temperature conditions, e.g. gasoline.

4: Materials which will rapidly vaporize at atmospheric pressure and normal temperatures, or are readily dispersed in the air and which burn readily, e.g. natural gas.

11.1.2   Glass Transition Point

A plot of specific volume versus temperature for elastomers and plastics has a temperature point (or region) where the curve undergoes a discontinuity. This point, called the glass transition temperature (T_g), depends on physical conditions, not on thermodynamics. Glass transition temperature T_g can be shifted to higher or lower values by blending with other compatible elastomers or plasticizers. The shifted T_g is approximated with reasonable accuracy by the following relationship [Neilsen]:

$$T_g = V_1 \, T_{g,1} + V_2 \, T_{g,2} \tag{11.1.1}$$

where $T_{g,1}$ and $T_{g,2}$ are the glass transition temperatures in K or ℃ (273.15 K = 0 ℃), and V_1 and V_2 are the volume fractions.

11.1.3   Curie Temperature

The Curie temperature, also called Curie point, is the temperature at which a material's permanent magnetism changes in accordance with induced magnetism.

11.1.4   0 K

The coldest theoretical temperature is absolute zero (0 K = −273.15 ℃), at which the thermal motion in matter would be zero.

11.2   Thermal Expansion

The coefficient of thermal expansion is used to determine the rate, at which a material expands as a function of temperature. A thermal expansion can be measured by linear variation, increasing volume, or area change. Coefficient of linear thermal expansion (CTE) of a orthotropic lamina is a widely used term for the purpose of engineering design and it is defined as the rate of change of the material length per unit length with respect to temperature variation.

$$\alpha_i = \frac{\dfrac{\mathrm{d}x_i}{\mathrm{d}T}}{x_i} \qquad (i = 1,\ 2,\ 3) \tag{11.2.1}$$

where

α_i (μmm/mm/℃ or μm/m/℃): Coefficient of linear thermal expansion along x_i-axis;

x_i: Length along x_i-axis, i.e., x_1-, x_2-, x_3-axes;

T: Temperature.

Contributions of thermal expansions to stress levels in the three primary material axes are described by Eqs. (11.2.1)-(11.2.6). In general, the ranges of coefficients of linear thermal expansion of different kinds of materials are given in Table 11.1.1. The coefficient of linear thermal expansion of water is 69 μm/m/℃. Some materials have low thermal expansion, such as ≈ 0 μm/m/℃ for YbGaHe, 0.59 μm/m/℃ for fused quartz, and 1 μm/m/℃ for diamond. Coefficients of linear thermal expansion of most thermoplastics without fibrous or particulate reinforcements are higher than 50 μm/m/℃ at room temperature and they increase significantly once the working temperature is elevated above glass transition points. Coefficients of linear thermal expansion of most metals for automotive applications range from 10 μm/m/℃ to 30 μm/m/℃.

11.2.1 Thermal Expansions of Fibrous Composites—Unidirectional Continuous Fibers

Assume that the fiber is transversely isotropic. In-plane and out-of-plane coefficients of linear thermal expansion of a continuous fiber-reinforced lamina, along and transverse to the fiber direction, are respectively [Ran et al.]

$$\alpha_1 = \frac{\alpha_f E_{f11} V_f + \alpha_m E_m V_m}{E_{f11} V_f + E_m V_m} = \frac{\alpha_f E_{f11} V_f + \alpha_m E_m V_m}{E_{11}} \tag{11.2.2}$$

and $$\alpha_2 = \alpha_3 = \alpha_m + \frac{a_1 + a_2}{a_3 + a_4 + a_5} \tag{11.2.3}$$

The five coefficients (a_1, a_2, a_3, a_4, a_5) appear in the above equation are calculated from the material properties of the fiber and matrix as

$$a_1 = V_f E_{f11} E_{f22} \nu_{f12} \left[(\nu_m^2 + V_m \nu_m)(\alpha_m - \alpha_{f1}) + 2V_f(\alpha_{f2} - \alpha_m) + V_f \nu_m^2(\alpha_m + \alpha_{f1} - 2\alpha_{f2}) \right] \tag{11.2.4}$$

$$a_2 = V_f E_{f11} E_m \left[2 V_m \nu_{f21}(1 - \nu_m \nu_{f12})(\alpha_m - \alpha_{f2}) + V_m \nu_{f12}(2 \nu_{f21} - \nu_m + \nu_m^2)(\alpha_m - \alpha_{f1}) \right]$$
$$(11.2.5)$$

$$a_3 = V_m E_{f11} E_m \left[\nu_{f21} + V_f(\nu_{f12} + \nu_{f21}) + V_m \nu_{f21} \nu_m - V_m(1 + 4 \nu_{f21}) \nu_{f12} \nu_m \right. \quad (11.2.6)$$

$$a_4 = V_m^2 E_m^2 \nu_{f12}(1 - \nu_m - 2 \nu_{f12} \nu_{f21}) \qquad (11.2.7)$$

and $\quad a_5 = V_f E_{f11} E_{f22} \nu_{f12} \left[1 + V_f(1 - 2 \nu_m^2) + V_m \nu_m \right] \qquad (11.2.8)$

where

E_{f11}, E_{f22}, E_{f33}: Young's moduli of the transversely isotropic fiber;

α_{f1}, α_{f2}, α_{f3}: Coefficients of linear thermal expansion of the fiber;

ν_{f12}, ν_{f21}: Poisson's ratios of the transversely isotropic fiber.

11.2.2   Thermal Expansions of Fibrous Composites—Unidirectional Short Fibers

In-plane and out-of-plane coefficients of linear thermal expansion of a lamina reinforced with unidirectional short fibers along and transverse to the fiber direction, respectively are

$$\alpha_1 = \frac{\alpha_f E_f V_f + \alpha_m E_m V_m}{E_{11}} \qquad (11.2.9)$$

$$\alpha_2 = (1 + \nu_f) \alpha_f V_f + (1 + \nu_m) \alpha_m V_m - \alpha_1 \nu_{12} \qquad (11.2.10)$$

and $\quad \alpha_3 = (1 + \nu_f) \alpha_f V_f + (1 + \nu_m) \alpha_m V_m - \alpha_1 \nu_{13} \qquad (11.2.11)$

Note that E_{11} given above is derived from Eq. (10.4.2).

11.2.3   Thermal Expansions of Fibrous Composites—Random Short Fibers

The coefficient of linear thermal expansion of a random short fiber-reinforced composite is approximated using the following equation

$$\alpha = \left\{ \left[V_f^{\frac{3}{2}} - V_f\left(1 - \frac{\alpha_f}{\alpha_m}\right) \right] \left[\frac{\dfrac{E_m}{E_f}}{1 - V_f^{\frac{1}{3}}} \left(1 - \frac{E_m}{E_f}\right) \right] + (1 - V_f^{\frac{2}{3}})\left(\frac{E_m}{E_f}\right) \right\} \alpha_m \qquad (11.2.12)$$

11.2.4   Thermal Expansions of Composites Reinforced with Weaves

Finite element analysis may be conducted to obtain the thermal expansions (in-plane or through-thickness) for the specific weave patterns of interest.

11.2.5 Thermal Expansions of Lamina Reinforced Randomly with Particulates/Powders

The coefficient of linear thermal expansion of a composite reinforced with particulates or powders is approximated using the following equation

$$\alpha = \left\{ \left[V_p^{\frac{2}{3}} - V_f\left(1 - \frac{\alpha_f}{\alpha_m}\right) \right] \frac{\frac{E_m}{E_f}}{1 - V_p^{\frac{1}{3}}\left(1 - \frac{E_m}{E_f}\right)} + (1 - V_p^{\frac{2}{3}})\left(\frac{E_m}{E_f}\right) \right\} \alpha_m \qquad (11.2.13)$$

11.2.6 Thermal Distortion Upon Cooling

A layered fibrous composite may get distorted due to the combined effect from the difference in coefficients of thermal contraction upon cooling from its curing temperature [Mallick], e.g. 177 ℃ for Ep/CF composite [Hoa]. The following example is an illustration.

Example 11.2.1　Referring to the material for a composite leaf spring for pickup trucks, the constituents of a lamina reinforced with rectangular-packed unidirectional E-glass fibers having the following mechanical properties:

$E_f = 80$ GPa, $E_m = 30$ GPa, $\nu_f = 0.2$, $\nu_m = 0.35$, $\alpha_f = 5.4\times10^{-6}℃$, $\alpha_m = 60\times10^{-6}℃$, $V_f = 60\%$.

Assume that the fiber cross-section is circular and the thickness of each lamina is h. When two plies of such laminae are stacked up to make a cross-ply laminate, i.e., [0°/90°], how will the laminate deform after it is cooled from the curing temperature to room temperature? Assume that the temperature distribution is uniform and cooled at the same rate.

Solution：

(1) Young's moduli for the Unidirectional lamina: Following Eqs. (10.3.2) and (10.3.3), one has

$$E_{11} = E_f V_f + E_m V_m = 80 \times 0.6 + 30 \times (1 - 0.6) = 60 \text{ GPa} = 60000 \text{ MPa} \qquad (a)$$

$$E_{22} = \frac{E_f(1 + V_f) + E_m(1 - V_f)}{E_f(1 - V_f) + E_m(1 + V_f)}E_m \quad (\text{since } \zeta_2 = 1 \text{ due to circular cross-section})$$

$$= \frac{80 \times (1 + 0.6) + 30 \times (1 - 0.6)}{80 \times (1 - 0.6) + 30 \times (1 + 0.6)} \times 30$$

$$= 52.5 \text{ GPa} = 52500 \text{ MPa} \tag{b}$$

(2) Poisson's Ratios: Following Eqs. (10.3.9) and (10.1.21), one has

$$\nu_{12} = \nu_f V_f + \nu_m V_m = 0.2 \times 0.6 + 0.35 \times (1 - 0.6) = 0.26 \tag{c}$$

and $\quad \nu_{12} E_{22} = \nu_{21} E_{11}$

$$0.26 \times 30000 = 80000 \times \nu_{21}$$

$$\nu_{21} = 0.0975 \tag{d}$$

(3) Assume that the material properties of fibers are isotropic. Shear moduli for the fibers and matrix are, respectively

$$G_f = \frac{E_f}{2 \times (1 + \nu_f)} = \frac{80}{2 \times (1 + 0.2)} = 33.333 \text{ GPa} = 33333 \text{ MPa} \tag{e}$$

$$G_m = \frac{E_m}{2 \times (1 + \nu_m)} = \frac{30}{2 \times (1 + 0.35)} = 11.111 \text{ GPa} = 11111 \text{ MPa} \tag{f}$$

Following Eq.(10.3.5), one has the in-plane shear modulus as follows:

$$G_{12} = \frac{G_f(1 + V_f) + G_m(\zeta_1 - V_f)}{G_f(1 - V_f) + G_m(\zeta_1 + V_f)} G_m \quad \text{where} \quad \zeta_1 = 1 + 40 \, V_f^{10} = 1.242$$

$$= \frac{33.333 \times (1 + 0.6) + 11.111 \times (1.242 - 0.6)}{33.333 \times (1 - 0.6) + 11.111 \times (1.242 + 0.6)}$$

$$= 1.79 \text{ GPa} = 1790 \text{ MPa} \tag{g}$$

(4) For $\theta = 0°$ ply: Following Eqs. (10.10.4)-(10.10.7) and Eqs. (10.10.10)-(10.10.13), one has

$$(Q_{11})_0 = c_{11} \cos^4\theta + 2 (c_{12} + 2c_{66}) \sin^2\theta \cos^2\theta + c_{22} \sin^4\theta$$

$$= c_{11} = \frac{E_{11}}{1 - \nu_{12} \nu_{21}} = \frac{60000}{1 - 0.26 \times 0.0975} = 61561 \text{ MPa} \tag{h}$$

$$(Q_{22})_0 = c_{11} \sin^4\theta + 2 (c_{12} + 2c_{66}) \sin^2\theta \cos^2\theta + c_{22} \cos^4\theta$$

$$= c_{22} = \frac{E_{22}}{1 - \nu_{12} \nu_{21}} = \frac{52500}{1 - 0.26 \times 0.0975} = 53865 \text{ MPa} \tag{i}$$

$$(Q_{12})_0 = (c_{11} + c_{22} - 4c_{66})\sin^2\theta\cos^2\theta + c_{12}(\sin^4\theta + \cos^4\theta)$$

$$= c_{12} = \frac{\nu_{12}E_{22}}{1 - \nu_{12}\nu_{21}} = 0.26 \times 53865 = 14005 \text{ MPa} \tag{j}$$

$$(Q_{66})_0 = (c_{11} + c_{22} - 2c_{12} - 2c_{66})\sin^2\theta\cos^2\theta + c_{66}(\sin^4\theta + \cos^4\theta)$$
$$= c_{66} = G_{12} = 1790 \text{ MPa} \tag{k}$$

Other $(Q_{ij})_0 = 0$

（5）For $\theta = 90°$ ply: Following Eqs. (10.10.4)-(10.10.7) and (10.10.10)-(10.10.13), one has

$$(Q_{11})_{90} = c_{11}\cos^4\theta + 2(c_{12} + 2c_{66})\sin^2\theta\cos^2\theta + c_{22}\sin^4\theta$$

$$= c_{22} = \frac{E_{22}}{1 - \nu_{12}\nu_{21}} = 53865 \text{ MPa} \tag{l}$$

$$(Q_{22})_{90} = c_{11}\sin^4\theta + 2(c_{12} + 2c_{66})\sin^2\theta\cos^2\theta + c_{22}\cos^4\theta$$

$$= c_{11} = \frac{E_{11}}{1 - \nu_{12}\nu_{21}} = 61561 \text{ MPa} \tag{m}$$

$$(Q_{12})_{90} = (c_{11} + c_{22} - 4c_{66})\sin^2\theta\cos^2\theta + c_{12}(\sin^4\theta + \cos^4\theta)$$

$$= c_{12} = \frac{\nu_{12}E_{22}}{1 - \nu_{12}\nu_{21}} = 14005 \text{ MPa} \tag{n}$$

$$(Q_{66})_{90} = (c_{11} + c_{22} - 2c_{12} - 2c_{66})\sin^2\theta\cos^2\theta + c_{66}(\sin^4\theta + \cos^4\theta)$$

$$= c_{66} = G_{12} = 1790 \text{ MPa} \tag{o}$$

Other $(Q_{ij})_{90} = 0$

（6）Laminate constants? Following Eqs. (10.10.18), (10.10.19), and (10.10.22), one has

$$A_{ij} = \sum_{n=1}^{2}(Q_{ij})_n(z_n - z_{n-1}) = (Q_{ij})_0(h - 0) + (Q_{ij})_{90}[0 - (-h)]$$

$$= h[(Q_{ij})_0 + (Q_{ij})_{90}] \tag{p}$$

$$B_{ij} = \frac{1}{2}\sum_{n=1}^{2}(Q_{ij})_n(z_n^2 - z_{n-1}^2) = \frac{1}{2}\{(Q_{ij})_0(h^2 - 0) + (Q_{ij})_{90}[0 - (-h)^2]\}$$

$$= \frac{1}{2} h^2 [(Q_{ij})_0 - (Q_{ij})_{90}] \tag{q}$$

and

$$D_{ij} = \sum_{n=1}^{2} \frac{(Q_{ij})_n (z_n^3 - z_{n-1}^3)}{3} = \frac{(Q_{ij})_0 (h^3 - 0) + (Q_{ij})_{90} [0 - (-h)^3]}{3}$$

$$= \frac{h^3 [(Q_{ij})_0 + (Q_{ij})_{90}]}{3} \tag{r}$$

Substituting the $(Q_{ij})_0$ and $(Q_{ij})_{90}$ data into the above two equations leads to

$$[A] = h \begin{bmatrix} 115426 & 29001 & 0 \\ 29001 & 115426 & 0 \\ 0 & 0 & 3580 \end{bmatrix} \quad (\text{N/mm}) \tag{s}$$

and

$$[B] = h^2 \begin{bmatrix} -3848 & 0 & 0 \\ 0 & 3848 & 0 \\ 0 & 0 & 0 \end{bmatrix} \quad (\text{N/mm}) \tag{t}$$

and

$$[D] = h^3 \begin{bmatrix} 38475 & 9667 & 0 \\ 9667 & 38475 & 0 \\ 0 & 0 & 1193 \end{bmatrix} \quad (\text{N/mm}) \tag{u}$$

(7) Thermal Strains? If constrained, the thermal strains due to temperature variation will be present

$$\begin{Bmatrix} (\varepsilon_{11,h})_0 \\ (\varepsilon_{22,h})_0 \\ (\gamma_{12,h})_0 \end{Bmatrix} = - \begin{Bmatrix} \alpha_1 \\ \alpha_2 \\ 0 \end{Bmatrix} \Delta T = - \begin{Bmatrix} 16.32 \times 10^{-6} \\ 32 \times 10^{-6} \\ 0 \end{Bmatrix} \Delta T \tag{v}$$

$$\begin{Bmatrix} (\varepsilon_{11,h})_{90} \\ (\varepsilon_{22,h})_{90} \\ (\gamma_{12,h})_{90} \end{Bmatrix} = - \begin{Bmatrix} \alpha_2 \\ \alpha_1 \\ 0 \end{Bmatrix} \Delta T = - \begin{Bmatrix} 32 \times 10^{-6} \\ 16.32 \times 10^{-6} \\ 0 \end{Bmatrix} \Delta T \tag{w}$$

Note that no in-plane shear strain is induced for each individual lamina. The equations for α_1 and α_2 can be obtained using Eqs. (11.2.8) and (11.2.9),

$$\alpha_1 = \frac{\alpha_f E_f V_f + \alpha_m E_m V_m}{E_{11}}$$

$$= \frac{5.4 \times 10^{-6} \times 80000 \times 0.6 + 60 \times 10^{-6} \times 30000 \times 0.4}{60000}$$

$$= 16.32 \times 10^{-6}$$

$$\alpha_2 = (1 + \nu_f)\, \alpha_f\, V_f + (1 + \nu_m)\, \alpha_m\, V_m - \alpha_1\, \nu_{12}$$

$$= (1 + 0.2) \times (5.4 \times 10^{-6}) \times 0.6 + (1 + 0.35) \times (60 \times 10^{-6}) \times 0.4 - (16.32 \times 10^{-6}) \times 0.26$$

$$= 32 \times 10^{-6}$$

（8）Substituting Eqs. （v）and （w）given above into Eq. （10.10.17）, the balanced equation set for forces per unit length induced by the thermal strains can be formulated as

$$
\begin{Bmatrix} 0 \\ 0 \\ 0 \end{Bmatrix} =
\begin{bmatrix} A_{11} & A_{12} & A_{16} \\ A_{12} & A_{22} & A_{26} \\ A_{16} & A_{26} & A_{66} \end{bmatrix}
\begin{Bmatrix} \varepsilon_{xxo} \\ \varepsilon_{yyo} \\ \gamma_{xyo} \end{Bmatrix} +
\begin{bmatrix} B_{11} & B_{12} & B_{16} \\ B_{12} & B_{22} & B_{26} \\ B_{16} & B_{26} & B_{66} \end{bmatrix}
\begin{Bmatrix} \kappa_{xx} \\ \kappa_{yy} \\ \kappa_{xy} \end{Bmatrix} +
$$

$$
\begin{Bmatrix} (Q_{11})_0(-\alpha_1 \Delta T)\,h + (Q_{12})_0(-\alpha_2 \Delta T)h \\ (Q_{12})_0(-\alpha_1 \Delta T)\,h + (Q_{22})_0(-\alpha_2 \Delta T)h \\ (Q_{16})_0(-\alpha_1 \Delta T)\,h + (Q_{26})_0(-\alpha_2 \Delta T)h \end{Bmatrix} +
$$

$$
\begin{Bmatrix} (Q_{11})_{90}(-\alpha_2 \Delta T)\,h + (Q_{12})_{90}(-\alpha_1 \Delta T)h \\ (Q_{12})_{90}(-\alpha_2 \Delta T)\,h + (Q_{22})_{90}(-\alpha_1 \Delta T)h \\ (Q_{16})_{90}(-\alpha_2 \Delta T)\,h + (Q_{26})_{90}(-\alpha_1 \Delta T)h \end{Bmatrix}
$$

i.e.,

$$
\begin{Bmatrix} 0 \\ 0 \\ 0 \end{Bmatrix} =
\begin{bmatrix} 115426 & 29001 & 0 \\ 29001 & 115426 & 0 \\ 0 & 0 & 3580 \end{bmatrix}
\begin{Bmatrix} \varepsilon_{xxo} \\ \varepsilon_{yyo} \\ \gamma_{xyo} \end{Bmatrix} +
\begin{bmatrix} -3848 & 0 & 0 \\ 0 & 3848 & 0 \\ 0 & 0 & 0 \end{bmatrix}
\begin{Bmatrix} \kappa_{xx} \\ \kappa_{yy} \\ \kappa_{xy} \end{Bmatrix} +
$$

$$
h\, \Delta T
\begin{Bmatrix} 61561 \times (-16.32 \times 10^{-6}) + 14005 \times (-32 \times 10^{-6}) \\ 14005 \times (-16.32 \times 10^{-6}) + 53865 \times (-32 \times 10^{-6}) \\ 0 \end{Bmatrix} +
$$

$$
h\, \Delta T
\begin{Bmatrix} 53865 \times (-32 \times 10^{-6}) + 14005 \times (-16.32 \times 10^{-6}) \\ 14005 \times (-32 \times 10^{-6}) + 61561 \times (-16.32 \times 10^{-6}) \\ 0 \end{Bmatrix} \tag{x}
$$

（9）Similarly, the balanced equation set for moments per unit length induced by the thermal strains can be derived from Eq. （10.10.21）as

$$
\begin{Bmatrix} 0 \\ 0 \\ 0 \end{Bmatrix} = \begin{bmatrix} B_{11} & B_{12} & B_{16} \\ B_{12} & B_{22} & B_{26} \\ B_{16} & B_{26} & B_{66} \end{bmatrix} \begin{Bmatrix} \varepsilon_{xxo} \\ \varepsilon_{yyo} \\ \gamma_{xyo} \end{Bmatrix} + \begin{bmatrix} D_{11} & D_{12} & D_{16} \\ D_{12} & D_{22} & D_{26} \\ D_{16} & D_{26} & D_{66} \end{bmatrix} \begin{Bmatrix} \kappa_{xx} \\ \kappa_{yy} \\ \kappa_{xy} \end{Bmatrix} +
$$

$$
\frac{1}{2} \begin{Bmatrix} (Q_{11})_0(-\alpha_1\Delta T)\ h^2 + (Q_{12})_0(-\alpha_2\Delta T)\ h^2 \\ (Q_{12})_0(-\alpha_1\Delta T)\ h^2 + (Q_{22})_0(-\alpha_2\Delta T)\ h^2 \\ (Q_{16})_0(-\alpha_1\Delta T)\ h^2 + (Q_{26})_0(-\alpha_2\Delta T)\ h^2 \end{Bmatrix} -
$$

$$
\frac{1}{2} \begin{Bmatrix} (Q_{11})_{90}(-\alpha_2\Delta T)\ h^2 + (Q_{12})_{90}(-\alpha_1\Delta T)\ h^2 \\ (Q_{12})_{90}(-\alpha_2\Delta T)\ h^2 + (Q_{22})_{90}(-\alpha_1\Delta T)\ h^2 \\ (Q_{16})_{90}(-\alpha_2\Delta T)\ h^2 + (Q_{26})_{90}(-\alpha_1\Delta T)\ h^2 \end{Bmatrix}
$$

i.e.,

$$
\begin{Bmatrix} 0 \\ 0 \\ 0 \end{Bmatrix} = \begin{bmatrix} -3848 & 0 & 0 \\ 0 & 3848 & 0 \\ 0 & 0 & 0 \end{bmatrix} \begin{Bmatrix} \varepsilon_{xxo} \\ \varepsilon_{yyo} \\ \gamma_{xyo} \end{Bmatrix} + \begin{bmatrix} 38475 & 9667 & 0 \\ 9667 & 38475 & 0 \\ 0 & 0 & 1193 \end{bmatrix} \begin{Bmatrix} \kappa_{xx} \\ \kappa_{yy} \\ \kappa_{xy} \end{Bmatrix} +
$$

$$
\frac{1}{2} h^2 \Delta T \begin{bmatrix} 61561 \times (-16.32 \times 10^{-6}) + 14005 \times (-32 \times 10^{-6}) \\ 14005 \times (-16.32 \times 10^{-6}) + 53865 \times (-32 \times 10^{-6}) \\ 0 \end{bmatrix} +
$$

$$
\frac{1}{2} h^2 \Delta T \begin{bmatrix} 53865 \times (-32 \times 10^{-6}) + 14005 \times (-16.32 \times 10^{-6}) \\ 14005 \times (-32 \times 10^{-6}) + 61561 \times (-16.32 \times 10^{-6}) \\ 0 \end{bmatrix} \qquad (y)
$$

(10) There are six independent equations in equation set (x) and equation set (y), that can be solved for six unknowns. The results for curvatures are

$$k_{xx} = -k_{yy} \neq 0$$

$$k_{xy} = 0.0$$

Thus, the laminate looks like a horse saddle once it is cooled down from cure temperature to room temperature, as shown below:

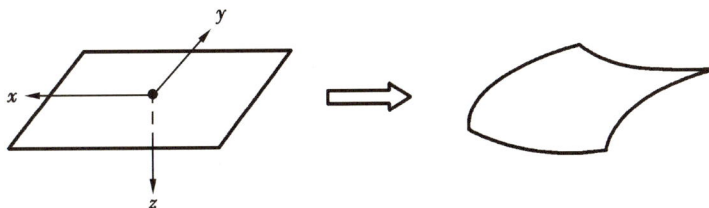

11.2.7 Coefficient of Volumetric Thermal Expansion

"Coefficient of thermal expansion" sometimes means coefficient of volumetric thermal expansion, which is the rate of change of the material volume per unit volume with respect to temperature variation

$$\alpha_V = \frac{1}{V}\left(\frac{dV}{dT}\right) \tag{11.2.14}$$

where

α_V : Coefficient of volumetric thermal expansion;

V : Volume.

The coefficient of linear thermal expansion of a homogeneous material is one third the coefficient of volumetric thermal expansion for exactly isotropic materials under small expansions, i.e., $\alpha_V = 3\alpha$.

11.3 Specific Heat Capacity

The energy required to increase the temperature of a unit mass of material by a unit temperature is called specific heat capacity, also called heat capacity in short. The heat capacities of water and air at room temperature are 4181.3 J/kg/℃ and 1012 J/kg/℃ (i.e., 4181.3×10^6 N · mm/T/℃ and 1012×10^6 N · mm/T/℃, where metric ton T is related to kg by T = 1000 kg), respectively. The heat energy is related to the heat capacity as

$$Q = \gamma \, M \, \Delta T \tag{11.3.1}$$

where

Q (J) : Heat energy;

γ (N · mm/T/℃ or J/kg/℃) : Heat capacity or specific heat capacity;

M (T or kg) : Mass;

ΔT (℃) : Temperature variation.

The specific heat capacity of a crystalline polymer usually increases linearly with the temperature up to their melting points, whereas the degree of transformation into an amorphous polymer rises up to about 100% at the glass transition temperature range.

The specific heat of a fibrous composite regardless of its reinforcement pattern (aligned or random) can be obtained from the rule of mixture as

$$\gamma_c = \frac{\gamma_f V_f \rho_f + \gamma_m (1 - V_f) \rho_m}{\rho_c} \qquad (11.3.2)$$

where

ρ_c : Density of the composite;

γ_p : Specific heat capacity of particulates or powders.

The specific heat of EP/CF composites, regardless of the reinforcement structures such as weaves and unidirectional laminae, increases linearly with the increasing temperature in the range between 0 ℃ and 200 ℃ [Joven et al.].

11.4   Thermal Conductivity

Where there is a temperature gradient between two domains of the same solid or between two solids in contact, there is an energy transfer from the domain of a high temperature to the domain of a low temperature. It occurs due to vibrating atoms and molecules interacting with neighboring atoms and molecules and transferring energy by means of heat mostly to the neighboring particles. The phenomenon is called thermal conduction. Consider an orthotropic lamina, whose primary material axes are denoted by (x_1, x_2, x_3). The thermal conductivities, k_i, where $i = 1, 2,$ or 3, is defined as the coefficient that relates the heat-transfer rate per unit area to the normal temperature gradient along the ith primary material axis in an orthotropic lamina,

$$q_i = - k_i A_i \frac{\partial T}{\partial x_i} \qquad (i = 1, 2 \text{ and } 3) \qquad (11.4.1)$$

where

k_{ii} (N/s/℃ or W/m/℃) : Thermal conductivities;

A_i : Surface area perpendicular to x_i-axis;

q_i : Heat transfer rate along x_i-axis and $\perp A_i$;

T : Temperature;

$\partial T / \partial x_i$: Temperature gradient along x_i-axis and $\perp A_i$.

Light-weighted aluminum alloys have excellent thermal conductivities and have been in use for structural components with their heat-sinking capability such as housing for power electronics boards and engine blocks. For example, the thermal conductivity of A380 alloy is 96 W/m/℃ or 96 N/s/℃. Thermal contact conductance, as addressed in Chapter 8, is the study of heat conduction between solid bodies in contact.

11.4.1 Thermal Conductivities of Laminae Reinforced Unidirectionally with Continuous Fibers

The thermal conductivity of a continuous fiber-reinforced lamina in the 1-axis can be obtained from the rule of mixture as follows:

$$k_1 = k_f V_f + k_m V_m \tag{11.4.2}$$

Thermal conductivities in the transverse (in-plane) and out-of-plane directions can be obtained from Halpin-Tsai equation:

$$k_2 = k_3 = \frac{\left(\dfrac{k_f}{k_m} + \zeta_2\right) + \left(\dfrac{k_f}{k_m} - 1\right) V_f}{\left(\dfrac{k_f}{k_m} + \zeta_2\right) - \left(\dfrac{k_f}{k_m} - 1\right) V_f} k_m \tag{11.4.3}$$

where parameter ζ_2 is related to packing pattern and fiber cross-section, as shown by Eq. (10.5.4).

Thermal conductivies in both in-plane transverse and out-of-plane directions are significantly smaller than the along-the-fiber thermal conductivity in a unidirectional lamina. This is very profound for highly anisotropic laminae such as pitch carbon laminae. This phenomenon places limits on most composites for applications with a limited heat dissipation capacity.

11.4.2 Thermal Conductivities of Laminae Reinforced Unidirectionally with Short Fibers

Again the Halping-Tsai equation is applied, and k_1 and k_2 resemble E_{11} and E_{22} respectively,

$$k_1 = \frac{\left(\dfrac{k_f}{k_m} + \dfrac{2 L_f}{d_f}\right) + 2\left(\dfrac{L_f}{d_f}\right)\left(\dfrac{k_f}{k_m} - 1\right) V_f}{\left(\dfrac{k_f}{k_m} + \dfrac{2 L_f}{d_f}\right) - \left(\dfrac{k_f}{k_m} - 1\right) V_f} k_m \tag{11.4.4}$$

and $$k_2 = \frac{\left(\dfrac{k_f}{k_m} + \zeta_2\right) + 2\left(\dfrac{k_f}{k_m} - 1\right) V_f}{\left(\dfrac{k_f}{k_m} + \zeta_2\right) - \left(\dfrac{k_f}{k_m} - 1\right) V_f} k_m$$

$$= \frac{k_f(1 + 2V_f) + k_m(\zeta_2 - 2 V_f)}{k_f(1 - V_f) + k_m(\zeta_2 + V_f)} k_m \tag{11.4.5}$$

11.4.3   Thermal Conductivities of Laminae Reinforced Randomly with Short Fibers

The thermal conductivity of a random fiber-filled composite (k) can be approximated using the following equation

$$k = \left[1 - a^{-1} + \frac{1}{2}\pi b^{-1} - ab^{-1}(b^2 - a^2)^{-\frac{1}{2}} \ln \left| \frac{b + (b^2 - a^2)^{\frac{1}{2}}}{a} \right| \right] k_m \qquad (11.4.6)$$

where $a = \dfrac{1}{2}\left(\dfrac{\pi \rho}{V_f} \right)^{\frac{1}{2}}$ $\qquad\qquad\qquad\qquad\qquad\qquad\qquad (11.4.7)$

and $b = \rho \left(\dfrac{k_m}{k_f} - 1 \right)^{\frac{1}{2}}$ $\qquad\qquad\qquad\qquad\qquad\qquad\qquad (11.4.8)$

11.4.4   Thermal Conductivities of Composites Reinforced with Weaves

A special case study is on expoy/carbon fibre (EP/CF) composites, of which carbon fibers have much higher thermal conductivity than the polymeric matrix, i. e., 24.0 W/m/K for graphite carbon fibers versus 0.17-0.79 W/ W/m/K for most epoxy matrices. Thus, fiber orientation, configuration, and volume fraction are factors that may affect the heat propagation in composite parts. The thermal conductivities of EP/CF composites, regardless of the reinforcement structures such as weaves and unidirectional laminae, increase linearly with the increasing temperature in the range between 0 ℃ and 200 ℃ [Joven et al.].

Finite element analysis may be conducted to obtain the thermal conductivities (in-plane or through-thickness) for the specific weave patterns of interest.

11. 4. 5   Thermal Conductivities of Composites Reinforced with Particulates or Powders

The thermal conductivity of a composite reinforced with particulates is approximated using the following equation

$$k = \frac{k_m V_p^{\frac{2}{3}}}{1 - V_p^{\frac{1}{3}}\left(1 - \dfrac{k_m}{k_f} \right)} + k_m(1 - V_p^{\frac{2}{3}}) \qquad (11.4.9)$$

11.5　Thermal Shock and Cold Shock

Thermal shock occurs when a thermal gradient causes different portions of a part to expand nonuniformly. Thermal shock resistance is a measure of robustness of a material's resistance to differential expansions. Consider the case that a thin plate of finite thickness is suddenly exposed to a convective medium of different temperature and thus the heat flows along the x_3-axis, i.e., in the through-thickness direction. The governing equation for heat transfer along the through-thickness direction can be written as

$$\frac{\partial T(x_3,\ t)}{\partial t} = \left(\frac{k_{33}}{\rho\ C_{\mathrm{p}}}\right)\left[\frac{\partial^2 T(x_3,\ t)}{\partial x_3^2}\right] \tag{11.5.1}$$

or

$$\frac{\partial T(x_3,\ t)}{\partial t} = D_{33}\left[\frac{\partial^2 T(x_3,\ t)}{\partial x_3^2}\right] \tag{11.5.2}$$

where

$$D_{33} = \frac{k_{33}}{\rho\ C_{\mathrm{p}}} \tag{11.5.3}$$

Parameter $D_{33}(\mathrm{m^2/s}$ or $\mathrm{mm^2/s})$ is called thermal diffusivity along the thickness direction. It is the ratio of the time derivative of temperature to the temperature-distribution curvature along the x_3-axis, as indicated by Eq. (11.5.1) or Eq. (11.5.2) for thermal diffusion resembles Eq. (12.2.12) for moisture diffusion. Assume that the temperature of the convective medium temperature is T_∞ and the initial temperature of the plate is T_0. Then, the above equation can be solved for the temperature in terms of x_3 and T [Carslaw & Jaeger] [Lu & Fleck],

$$T(x_3,\ t) - T_0 \doteq (T_\infty - T_0)\left(1 - 2\sum_{n=1}^{\infty}\frac{\sin(\beta_n)\cos\dfrac{\beta_n\ z}{H}}{\beta_n + \sin\beta_n\ \cos\beta_n}\ \mathrm{e}^{-\frac{\beta_n^2\ D_{33}\ t}{H^2}}\right) \tag{11.5.4}$$

of which β_n is to be solved from the following equation

$$\beta_n\ \tan\beta_n = \frac{h_3 H}{D_{33}} \tag{11.5.5}$$

where $(h\ H/D_{33})$ is called Biot number, which is non-dimensional heat transfer coefficient for orthotropic material. For example,

　　(a) If the lamina is insulated without any heat transfer, $h = 0$ and $h\ H/D_{33} = 0$. Then Eq. (11.5.5) yields $\beta_n = n\ \pi$ and Eq. (11.5.4) leads to $T(z,\ T) = T_0$.
　　(b) If the heat is perfectly conducted, $h = \infty$ and $h\ H/D_{33} = \infty$. Then Eq. (11.5.5) yields

$\beta_n = (n+1/2)\pi$ and Eq. (11.5.4) leads to

$$T(x_3, t) - T_0 = (T_\infty - T_0)\left[1 - \frac{4}{\pi}\sum_{n=0}^{\infty}\frac{(-1)^n}{2n+1}\ e^{\frac{-D_{33}(2n+1)^2\pi^2 t}{4H^2}}\cos\frac{(2n+1)\pi z}{2H}\right]$$

$$(11.5.6)$$

The small stress induced by the temperature variation as shown above due to thermal diffusion can be attributed two contributors: (a) the uniform strain variation due to the temperature difference between the lamina and the ambient temperature and (b) the strain variation due to temperature variation across the lamina thickness H, as

$$\sigma_{11}(z, t) = \sigma_{22}(z, t) = -(E_{11}^{-1} - \nu_{12}E_{11}^{-1})(\alpha_1 + \nu_{12}\alpha_2)(T - T_0) +$$

$$\frac{(E_{11}^{-1} - \nu_{12}E_{11}^{-1})(\alpha_1 + \nu_{12}\alpha_2)}{2H}\int_{-\frac{1}{2}H}^{\frac{1}{2}H}(T - T_0)\,dx_3 \qquad (11.5.7)$$

Substituting Eq. (11.5.4) into the above equation leads to a general expression of stress distribution across the lamina thickness,

$$\sigma_{11}(z, t) = \sigma_{22}(z, t) = -2(E_{11}^{-1} - \nu_{12}E_{11}^{-1})(\alpha_1 + \nu_{12}\alpha_2)(T_\infty - T_0)$$

$$\sum_{n=1}^{\infty}\left[\left(\frac{\sin\beta_n}{\beta_n + \sin\beta_n\cos\beta_n}\right)\cos\left(\frac{\beta_n z}{H}\right) - \frac{\sin\beta_n}{\beta_n}\ e^{\frac{-\beta_n^2 D_{33} t}{H^2}}\right] \qquad (11.5.8)$$

Two extreme cases related to the stress are given below:

  (a) If the lamina is insulated without any heat transfer, $h = 0$ and $hH/D_{33} = 0$. Then Eq. (11.5.3) yields $\beta_n = n\pi$ and Eq. (11.5.4) leads to $T(z, T) = T_0$. Thus, $\sigma_{11}(z, t) = \sigma_{22}(z, t) = 0$ according to Eq. (11.5.8).

  (b) If the heat is perfectly conducted, $h = \infty$ and $h/D_{33} = \infty$. Then Eq. (11.5.5) yields $\beta_n = (n+1/2)\pi$ and Eq. (11.5.8) leads to

$$\sigma_{11}(z, t) = \sigma_{22}(z, t) = -(E_{11}^{-1} - \nu_{12}E_{11}^{-1})(\alpha_1 + \nu_{12}\alpha_2)(T_\infty - T_0)$$

$$\frac{4}{\pi}\sum_{n=0}^{\infty}\left\{\left[\frac{(-1)^n}{2n+1}\cos\frac{(2n+1)\pi z}{2H} - \frac{2}{(2n+1)^2\pi}\right]e^{\frac{-D_{33}(2n+1)^2\pi^2 t}{4H^2}}\right\}$$

$$(11.5.9)$$

A dimensionless stress can be obtained by dividing both sides in Eq. (11.5.9) by $[(E_{11}^{-1}-\nu_{12}E_{11}^{-1})(\alpha_1+\nu_{12}\alpha_2)(T_\infty-T_0)]$,

$$\sigma(z, t) = \frac{\sigma_{11}(z, t)}{(E_{11}^{-1} - \nu_{12}E_{11}^{-1})(\alpha_1 + \nu_{12}\alpha_2)(T_\infty - T_0)}$$

$$= \frac{\sigma_{22}(z,\,t)}{(E_{11}^{-1} - \nu_{12}\,E_{11}^{-1})\,(\alpha_1 + \nu_{12}\,\alpha_2)\,(T_\infty - T_0)}$$

$$= \frac{-4}{\pi} \sum_{n=0}^{\infty} \left\{ \left[\frac{(-1)^n}{2n+1} \cos\frac{(2n+1)\pi z}{2H} - \frac{2}{(2n+1)^2\,\pi} \right] e^{\frac{-D_{33}\,(2n+1)^2\,\pi^2\,t}{4\,H^2}} \right\}$$

$$(11.5.10)$$

If $T_\infty > T_0$, it is a hot shock and the two surface layers experience compressive stresses in transience, while a tensile zone is created in the neighborhood of the central plane of the plate; and vice versa for a cold shock. The transient tensile stresses at the outer surface induced under a cold shock test are evidenced by the crack nucleation at the outer surface and the nonstationary propagation into the inner compressive zone.

11.6　Heat Convection

Thermal transfer between an object and its environment due to fluid-exchange motion is called heat convection, also called convective heat transfer. It is essentially the transfer of heat via mass transfer. Consider a solid that is exposed to fluid. The heat convection from the high-temperature solid object of to the low-temperature fluid is proportional to the exposed surface and the temperature difference between them,

$$q = h\,A\,(T_W - T_\infty) \tag{11.6.1}$$

where

q (W): Heat transfer rate;

h (N/s/mm/℃ or W/mm^2/℃): Convective heat transfer coefficient;

A (m^2): Surface area perpendicular to the flow direction of the fluid;

T_W(℃): Temperature of solid-object wall in contact with the fluid;

T_∞(℃): Temperature of fluid in contact with the solid-object wall.

The above equation is applicable to the case with a heat-transfer direction in perpendicular to the flat plane. Convective heat transfer coefficient h (W/m^2/℃) is also simply called heat transfer coefficient. The general defining equation is applicable to a differential element of heat transfer surface area dA for which the heat transfer rate is dq, i.e.,

$$\mathrm{d}q = (T_W - T_\infty)\,h\,\mathrm{d}A \tag{11.6.2}$$

If the heat convection occurs in nature, it is called natural convection, though it may be affected by buoyancy forces due to gravitational fields, when thermal energy expands the fluid and thus influences its own heat transfer. Another form of convection is the forced convection, in which the fluid is forced to flow by use of a pump, fan, or other external means. Nevertheless, a convective process also moves heat by diffusion in parallel to macro convection.

11.6.1   Fluid Film Temperature

A fluid film temperature is an approximation to the temperature of a fluid inside a convection boundary layer on a solid. As a general practice, it is defined as the average of surface temperature T_s of the solid and surrounding bulk temperature of free-stream fluid T_b,

$$T_f = \frac{1}{2}(T_s + T_b)$$
(11.6.3)

The fluid film temperature is often used as the temperature, at which fluid properties are calculated when using Prandtl number, Nusselt number, Reynolds number or Grashof number to calculate a heat transfer coefficient by convection. The flow rate of the "convective heat transfer fluid" or media is used for determining the highest temperature occurring in the heating system. This temperature occurs in the heater. It is important to maintain a high flow rate by convection inside the heating tube. This will reduce the difference between the wall/tube film temperature and the bulk temperature of the fluid.

11.6.2   Natural Convection

When the fluid is in contact with a hot surface its molecules separate and scatter further, causing the fluid to be less dense. The less dense fluid is displaced consequently when the cooler fluid gets denser and sinks. This heat transfer phenomenon in the absence of an "external" source is called natural convection.

As a natural convection is due to thermal energy that expands the fluid, it is affected by buoyancy forces subject to gravitational fields, thus also influencing its own transfer. A different conceptual measure of natural convection is to assess connective heat transfer coefficient in Eq. (11.6.1) for natural convection through the Nusselt number (Nu), which is the ratio between the convective and the conductive heat transfer as

$$Nu \equiv \frac{\text{Convective heat transfer}}{\text{Conductive heat transfer}} = \frac{h\,D}{k}$$
(11.6.4)

where
Nu: Nusselt number;
h (W/m^2/℃): Convective heat transfer coefficient;
k (W/m/℃): Thermal conductivity of fluid, $k = 0.026$ W/m/℃ at 27 ℃ for dry air;

D (m): Characteristic dimensional length, e.g. ball diameter and length of cylinder.

The Nusselt number depends on the geometrical shape of the heat sink and the air flow in a natural air convention. For natural convection on a flat surface of an isothermal plate the formulae of Nu are related to the Rayleigh number (Ra) as

$$\text{Vertical Fins:} \quad Nu = 0.59\ Ra^{\frac{1}{4}} \quad \text{(Laminar flow)} \tag{11.6.5}$$

$$Nu = 0.14\ Ra^{\frac{1}{3}} \quad \text{(Turbulent flow)} \tag{11.6.6}$$

$$\text{and} \quad \text{Horizontal Fins:} \quad Nu = 0.54\ Ra^{\frac{1}{3}} \quad \text{(Laminar flow upwards)} \tag{11.6.7}$$

$$Nu = 0.27 Ra^{\frac{1}{4}} \quad \text{(Laminar flow downwards)} \tag{11.6.8}$$

$$Nu = 0.14 Ra^{\frac{1}{3}} \quad \text{(Turbulent flow)} \tag{11.6.9}$$

where V, ρ, and μ_d are the flow speed, density and dynamic viscosity of fluid, respectively. If $Ra < 10^6$ the heat flow is laminar and otherwise the flow is turbulent. Rayleigh number (Ra) can be obtained from the following equation

$$Ra = Pr\ Gr \tag{11.6.10}$$

where Prandtl number (Pr) and Grashof number (Gr) are calculated as

$$Pr = \frac{\mu_d\ C_p}{k} = \frac{\text{Heat Dissipation}}{\text{Heat Conduction}} \tag{11.6.11}$$

$$\text{and} \quad Gr = \frac{D^3\ \rho^2\ g\ \beta\ (T_W - T_\infty)}{\mu_d^2} = \frac{D^3\ g\ \alpha_v(T_W - T_\infty)}{\mu_k^2} \tag{11.6.12}$$

where

μ_d: Dynamic viscosity of fluid, $\mu_d = 1.81 \times 10^{-5}$ Pa $\cdot$ s (20 ℃) and 1.86×10^{-5} Pa $\cdot$ s (30 ℃);

μ_k: Kinematic viscosity of fluid, $\mu_k = \mu_d / \rho$;

ρ (kg/m³): Density of fluid, $\rho = 0.00117$ g/cm³ $= 1.17$ kg/m³;

g: Gravity, 1 g $= 9.807$ N/s²;

C_p(J/kg/℃): Specific heat of fluid, $C_p = 1005$ J/kg/℃ for dry air;

$$\alpha_v(\text{K}^{-1}): \text{Coefficient of volume expansion of fluid as } \alpha_v = 1/T_a; \tag{11.6.13}$$

T_a(℃): Air temperature.

The Archimedes number (Ar), named after the ancient Greek scientist Archimedes, is used to determine the motion of fluids due to density differences. It is a dimensionless number defined as the ratio of external buoyancy forces to internal viscous/inertia forces [Incropera]. When analyzing potentially mixed convection of fluid, the Archimedes number parameterizes the relative strength of free and forced convection by representing the ratio of Grashof number (Gr) to the square of Reynolds number (Re)

$$Ar = \frac{Gr}{Re^2} \tag{11.6.14}$$

where $Re = \dfrac{V D \rho}{\mu_d}$ \hfill (11.6.15)

where V is the fluid flow velocity. Reynolds number shows the contrast between flow inertia and viscosity for checking if friction due to kinetic viscosity is important. Parameter Ar indicates the contribution of natural convection as follows:

(a) When $Ar \gg 1$, natural convection dominates.
(b) When $Ar \ll 1$, forced convection dominates.

Various models for different conditions of heat convection can be found in [Welty et al.].

11.6.3   Iterative Solution

Convective heat transfer problems are usually solved iteratively in a numerical analysis. The procedure may be divided into the following steps:

(a) Taking an initial guess for temperature T_w.
(b) Solving Eq. (11.6.6) for Gr.
(c) Solving Eq. (11.6.5) for Pr.
(d) Ra is then obtained using Eq. (11.6.4), i.e., $Ra = Gr\,Pr$.
(e) The Nu value of each individual vertical or horizontal fin exposed to the air is calculated using Eqs. (11.6.3)-(11.6.7).
(f) Convective heat transfer coefficient h is obtained using Eq. (11.6.2).
(g) The obtained h value is utilized in combination with the given (expected) heat transfer rate (q) to estimate the new T_w as

$$T'_w = T_\infty + \frac{q}{h\,A} \tag{11.6.16}$$

(h) Check if $T'_w \cong T_w$. If yes, T'_w is the answer. If no, repeat steps (a)-(h) until $T'_w \cong T_w$.

Example 11.6.1   A 3-Watt LED is assembled onto a 40 mm× 40 mm × 6 mm aluminum heat sink with 4 fins, of which 30 mm long and 4 mm wide each. Assume that the room temperature is 23 ℃. What is the heat sink temperature in the steady state?

Solution:

(a) Taking an initial guess for temperature, $T_w = 93$ ℃.

(b) Solving Eq. (11.6.6), $Gr = \dfrac{D^3 \, g \, \beta \, (T_w - T_\infty)}{\mu_k^2}$

$$= \frac{0.04^3 \times 9.81 \times (273 + 23)^{-1} \times (93 - 23)}{(1.5 \times 10^{-5})^2}$$

$$= 6.6 \times 10^5.$$

(c) Solving Eq. (11.6.5) for Pr, $Pr = \dfrac{\mu_d \, C_p}{k} = \dfrac{1.825 \times 10^{-5} \times 1005}{0.026} = 0.705.$

(d) Ra is then obtained using Eq. (11.6.10), i. e., $Ra = Gr \ Pr = 6.6 \times 10^5 \times 0.705 = 4.6 \times 10^5$, which is less than 10^9. Thus, the theory of laminar flow applies.

(e) The Nu value of each individual vertical and horizontal fin exposed to the air is calculated using Eq. (11.6.4) c: $Nu = 0.54 \ Ra^{\frac{1}{4}} = 0.54 \times (4.6 \times 10^5)^{\frac{1}{4}} = 14.06.$

(f) The convection heat transfer coefficient (h) is obtained using Eq. (11.6.2) that

$$h = \frac{Nu \ k}{D} = \frac{14.06 \times 0.026}{0.04} = 9.17 \ \text{W/m}^2/\text{℃}.$$

(g) The obtained h-value is employed together with the expected heat transfer rate to estimate the new T_w as

$$T'_w = T_\infty + \frac{q}{h \ A} = 23 + \frac{3}{9.17 \times 0.0112} = 52.2 \ \text{℃}.$$

(h) Since $T'_w(52.2 \ ℃) \neq T_w(93 \ ℃)$. Repeat steps (a)-(h) until $T'_w \cong T_w$.

After several iterations, $T_w = 54$ ℃.

11.6.4 Forced Convection

Forced convection [Welty et al.] is a heat transfer mechanism by fluid, in which fluid motion is generated by unnatural external sources such as pumps and fans. It is also called heat advection.

Numerical analysis based on forced convection theories typically yields fairly accurate results, but not for natural connection.

11.6.4.1 Forced Laminar Flow in a Tube

The film heat transfer coefficient (convective heat transfer coefficient) for the laminar flow in a tube of diameter D with smooth surface conditions is related to the Nusselt number as [Sieder & Tate]

$$Nu = 1.86(Re\ Pr)^{\frac{1}{3}}\left(\frac{D}{L}\right)^{\frac{1}{3}}\left(\frac{\mu_{db}}{\mu_{ds}}\right)^{0.14} \tag{11.6.17}$$

where

Re: Reynolds number;

D: Inner diameter of the tube;

L: Length;

μ_{db}: Dynamic viscosity of bulk fluid temperature;

μ_{ds}: Dynamic viscosity of film at the wall surface temperature.

Note that h can be derived using Eq. (11.6.2) as

$$h = \frac{Nu\ k}{D} \tag{11.6.18}$$

11.6.4.2 Forced Turbulent Flow in a Tube

The principal difference between laminar and turbulent flow, as far as heat transfer is concerned, is that an additional mechanism of heat transfer in the radial and azimuthal directions becomes available in turbulent flow, also called eddy transport. Turbulent flow results in a much faster heat transfer rate, which in turn would result in a higher heat transfer coefficient. The convective heat transfer coefficient (h) for the turbulent flow in a tube with smooth surface conditions is calculated using the following equation:

$$q = h\ A\ (T_w - T_b) = h\ A\ T_{sub} \tag{11.6.19}$$

where

T_w: Tube wall (outer) temperature;

T_b: Fluid bulk temperature;

T_{sub}: Subcooling temperature, $T_{sub} = T_w - T_b$. \qquad\qquad (11.6.20)

Convective heat transfer coefficient h may be derived from each individual heat exchanger. The heat transferred from the inner fluid to the outer surface of the tube, e.g. automotive coolant is hotter than radiator tubes, is [Sieder and Tate]

$$Nu = 0.023 \ Re^{0.8} \ Pr^{\frac{1}{3}} \ \left(\frac{\mu_{db}}{\mu_{ds}}\right)^{0.14} \tag{11.6.21}$$

or $\qquad h = \dfrac{0.023 \ k^{0.67} \ \rho^{0.8} \ C_p^{0.33}}{\mu_{db}^{0.47} \ D^{0.2}} \tag{11.6.22}$

where μ_{db} is the dynamic viscosity of bulk fluid temperature and μ_{ds} is the dynamic viscosity of film (fluid) at the pipe wall surface temperature. Eq. (11.6.21) is valid for a heat exchange under the following conditions: $0.6 \leqslant Pr \leqslant 160$, $Re \geqslant 10000$, and $L/D \geqslant 10$, where L is the tube length and D is the inner radius of the tube.

On the other hand, if the heat is transferred from the outer surface of the tube wall to the inner fluid as a cooler, i.e., outer air cooler than automotive radiator tubes,

$$Nu = 0.023 \ Re^{0.8} \ Pr^{0.4} \ \left(\frac{\mu_{db}}{\mu_{ds}}\right)^{0.14} \tag{11.6.23}$$

or $\qquad h = \dfrac{0.023 \ k^{0.6} \ \rho^{0.8} \ C_p^{0.4}}{\mu_{db}^{0.4} \ D^{0.2}} \tag{11.6.24}$

11.6.5　Heat Transfer Coefficient in Nucleate Boiling

Nucleate boiling is characterized by the incidence and growth of bubbles on a heated surface (e.g. cooking pan). Bubbles rise from discrete points on a surface, whose temperature is only slightly above the liquid's saturation temperature and the number of nucleation sites is increased by an increasing surface temperature. The bubbles grow until they reach some critical size, at which point they separate from the wall and are carried into the main fluid stream. There the bubbles collapse because the temperature of bulk fluid is not as high as that at the heat transfer surface, where the bubbles were created. The period is called nucleate boiling stage, of which the heat transfer rate rises, as shown in Fig. 11.6.1. Boiling is a very efficient mode of heat transfer before it reaches the critical heat flux point. As more nucleation sites become active, increasing bubble formation causes bubble interference and coalescence. The heat transfer coefficient starts to reduce at a certain point (called critical heat flux point) as the surface temperature rises further, although the product of the heat transfer coefficient and the temperature difference (the heat flux) is still increasing (Fig. 11.6.1). Note that water's saturation temperature is 100 ℃ at 1 bar and 120.4 ℃ at 2 bar, while the saturation temperature of a 50-50 percent mixture of water and the antifreeze liquid [BASF Glythermin (ethylene-glycol with some additives)] as engine coolant is 130.7 ℃.

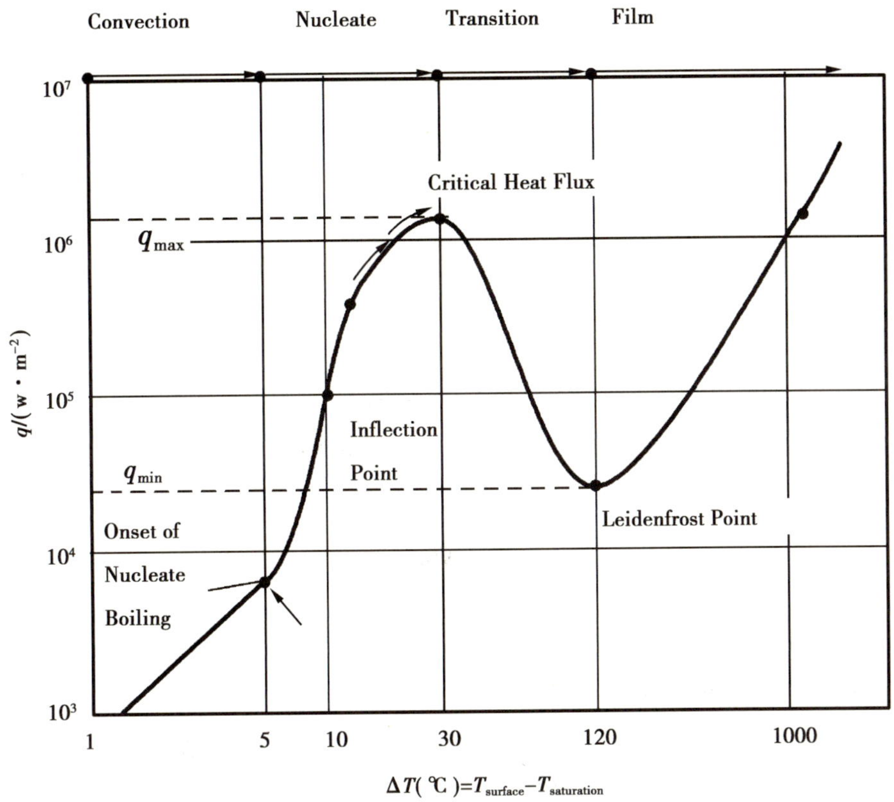

Fig. 11.6.1   Four Heat Transfer Stages of Boiling Water at 1 atm

Consider the flow of nucleate boiling water, sub cooled or saturated at pressures up to about 20 Map, under conditions when the nucleate boiling contribution predominates over forced convection. The following empirical equation exhibits a simple correlation between the temperature variation and heat transfer [Rohsenow et al.]

$$\Delta T = 22.5 \left(\frac{\mathrm{d}q}{\mathrm{d}A}\right)^{\frac{1}{2}} e^{\frac{-P}{8.7}} \tag{11.6.25}$$

i.e., $\dfrac{\mathrm{d}q}{\mathrm{d}A} = 0.001975(\Delta T)^2 e^{\frac{P}{4.35}}$ (11.6.26)

where

ΔT (℃): Temperature difference;

$\mathrm{d}q/\mathrm{d}A$ (W/mm^2): Heat flux;

P (MPa): Pressure of water.

The correlation uses an additive approach to describe the components of the heat flux consisting of one part from forced convection (q_{fc}) and one part from the contribution of nucleate boiling (q_{nb}) as expressed by the following equation [Chen]

$$q = q_{\text{fc}} + q_{nb} = h_{\text{fc}}(T_{\text{w}} - T_{\text{b}}) + h_{nb}(T_{\text{w}} - T_{\text{sat}}) \tag{11.6.27}$$

where

h_{fc}: Convective heat transfer coefficient before nucleate boiling;

h_{nb}: Nucleate boiling heat transfer coefficient;

T_{w}: Wall temperature;

T_{b}: Bulk fluid temperature;

T_{sat}: Saturation temperature of liquid.

The nucleate boiling heat transfer coefficient h_{nb} is derived from a dimensionless Nusselt number relationship presented by [Forster and Zuber] and the anal equation is given as [Chen]

$$h_{nb} = 0.00122 \frac{k^{0.79} C_{\text{pb}}^{0.45} \rho_{\text{b}}^{0.49}}{\sigma^{0.5} \mu_{\text{b}}^{0.29} i_{\text{lv}}^{0.24} \rho_{\text{v}}^{0.24}} \Delta T_{\text{sat}}^{0.24} \Delta p_{\text{sat}}^{0.75} S \tag{11.6.28}$$

where

$\Delta T_{\text{sat}}(\text{℃})$: Wall superheat and $\Delta T_{\text{sat}} = T_{\text{w}} - T_{\text{sat}}$;

$\Delta p_{\text{sat}}(\text{Pa})$: Elevated pressure at wall beyond the pressure at T_{sat} and $\Delta p_{\text{sat}} = p_{\text{w}} - p_{\text{sat}}(T_{\text{sat}})$;

$C_{\text{pb}}(\text{J/kg/℃})$: Heat capacity of bulk liquid;

σ (N/m): Surface tension;

$\mu_{\text{b}}(\text{Pa·s})$: Dynamic viscosity of bulk liquid;

$i_{\text{lv}}(\text{J/kg})$: Latent heat of vaporization (Enthalpy);

$\rho_{\text{b}}(\text{kg/m}^3)$: Density of bulk liquid;

$\rho_{\text{v}}(\text{kg/m}^3)$: Density of vapor (bubble);

S: Suppression factor, accounting for suppressing nucleate boiling by the flow field.

Suppression factor S is employed here to quantify the suppression of nucleate boiling by the flow field and defined as [Chen]

$$S = \left(\frac{T_{\text{v}} - T_{\text{sat}}}{T_{\text{w}} - T_{\text{sat}}}\right)^{0.99} \tag{11.6.29}$$

where $(T_{\text{v}} - T_{\text{sat}})$ is called effective superheat effect. The temperature of a bubbled vapor (T_{v}) is lower than the wall temperature T_{w}, but higher than T_{sat} during the nucleate boiling stage. Thus, $S < 1$. Since the exponent is 0.99 (≈ 1) in the above equation, approximately

$$T_{\text{v}} \approx T_{\text{sat}} + S(T_{\text{w}} - T_{\text{sat}}) \tag{11.6.30}$$

11.6.6   Onset of Nucleate Boiling

The amount of superheat that is needed to activate the bubble vapors depend on many different factors such as vapor size, vapor shape, temperature profile of thermal boundary layer at wall, and surface tension of fluid, and contact angle of vapor bubbles against the wall [Crowe]. The following equation for predicting onset of nucleate boiling has been in use for years and has been proven to be reasonably accurate [Hsu]:

$$\Delta T_{sat,ONB} \equiv T_{w,ONB} - T_{sat}$$

$$= \frac{4 \sigma T_{sat} h_b}{K_b i_{lv} \rho_{lv}} \left[1 + \left(1 + \frac{K_b i_{lv} \rho_{lv} \Delta T_{sub}}{2 \sigma T_{sat} h_b} \right) \right]^{\frac{1}{2}} \qquad (11.6.31)$$

where inlet subcooling is the temperature difference between the wall temperature and bulk fluid temperature, $\Delta T_{sub} = T_w - T_b$. Hence ΔT_{sub} is not only part of the convective heat transfer correlation but also the onset of nucleate boiling (ONB) condition as shown in the above equation. A table of predicted ONB temperatures of 50-50 percent mixture of water and antifreeze liquid [BASF Glythermin (ethylene-glycol with some additives)] and suppression factors at different speeds, are listed as follows [Ohrby]:

Speed/$(m \cdot s^{-1})$	$T_{ONB}/℃$	S
0.25	134	0.8340
1.00	136	0.6338
3.00	139	0.4266
5.00	141	0.3331

The saturation temperature of the coolant mixture is 130.7 ℃ at 2-bar pressure. The boiling point for the pure antifreeze liquid is around 225.4 ℃, while 120.4 ℃ for pure water at 2-bar pressure. Therefore, at the boiling point of the mixture the generated bubbles mainly consist of water vapor. Values for water vapor should be assumed for the properties of bubbles in the analysis.

11.6.7 Critical Heat Flux

The initiation and actual mechanisms leading to the maximum heat transfer phenomenon at the critical heat flux (CHF) point (Fig. 11.6.1) and then getting into departure of nucleate boiling (DNB) stage (also called transition stage) is not yet completely understood by researchers [Ohrby].

11.6.8 Convective Heat Transfer Coefficients of Object in the Air

Data for convective heat transfer coefficients of objects exposed to the air are given in Table 11.6.1. When no more information about the air and process of interest is available, the following equation may be used for a rough estimate of the convective heat transfer coefficient against the airflow speed V relative to the object

$$h = 10.5 + 10\ V^{\frac{1}{2}} - V \tag{11.6.32}$$

11.7 Combined Heat Conduction and Convection

The overall heat transfer coefficient is to be estimated and then employed in calculating the rate of heat transfer q from the fluid at an average bulk temperature T_i through a solid wall to a second fluid at an average bulk temperature T_o, where $T_i > T_o$. Plate and tubular heat exchangers are the most widely applied.

11.7.1 Flat Panel Exchanger (In Series)

Consider a flat panel that is cooled by fluid on each side, as shown in Fig. 11.7.1(a). The heat transfer between the solid walls and fluid on both sides can be obtained using Eq. (11.6.1), respectively

$$q_a = h_a A\ (T_{wa} - T_a) \tag{11.7.1}$$

and $\quad q_b = h_b A (T_{wb} - T_b) \tag{11.7.2}$

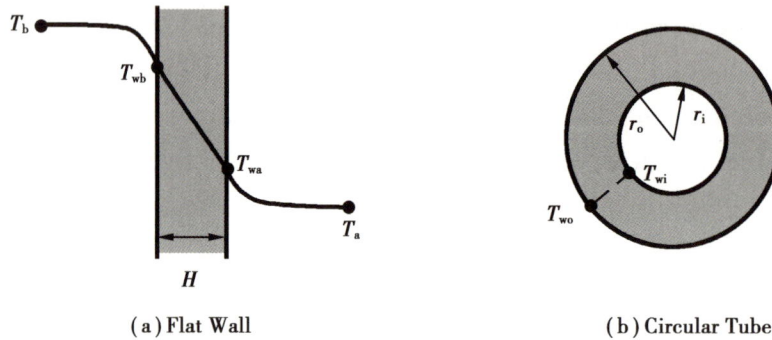

(a) Flat Wall   (b) Circular Tube

Fig. 11.7.1   Conductors with Convective Heat Transfer: (a) Flat Wall and (b) Circular Tube

The heat conduction within the wall from one side to the other along the z-axis can be derived from Eq. (11.4.1)

$$q_z = - k\ A\ \left(\frac{\Delta T}{\Delta z}\right) = - k\ A\ \frac{T_{wb} - T_{wa}}{H} \tag{11.7.3}$$

The overall temperature variation from fluid a and fluid b can be calculated from Eqs. (11.7.1) - (11.7.3),

$$T_b - T_a = (T_b - T_{wb}) + (T_{wb} - T_{wa}) + (T_{wa} - T_a)$$

$$= \frac{q_b}{h_b A_b} + q_z \left(\frac{H}{k A_w}\right) + \frac{q_a}{h_a A_a}$$

$$= \frac{q_b}{h_b A_b} + q_z \left(\frac{H}{k A_w}\right) + \frac{q_a}{h_a A_b}$$

$$= \left(\frac{1}{h_b A_b} + \frac{H}{k A_w} + \frac{1}{h_a A_b}\right) q \tag{11.7.4}$$

of which $q_b = q_z = q_a = q$ is presumed for an isolated conservative system. Note that q_b, q_z, and q_a are scalar flow rates of energy along the through-thickness direction, having the unit of watt. Eq. (11.7.4) then reduces to

$$q = \left(\frac{1}{h_b A_b} + \frac{H}{k A_w} + \frac{1}{h_a A_b}\right)^{-1} (T_b - T_a) = h A (T_b - T_a) \tag{11.7.5}$$

where $$\frac{1}{h A} = \frac{1}{h_b A_b} + \frac{H}{k A_w} + \frac{1}{h_a A_b} \tag{11.7.6}$$

where area A is the apparent area for heat transfer between these two fluid cooling effects.

11.7.2   Thermal Resistance

The thermal resistance can be defined as the retardation of heat transfer rate between two temperature levels, i.e., T_2 and T_1,

$$q = \frac{T_2 - T_1}{R} \tag{11.7.7}$$

For two or more heat transfer processes including conduction and convection connected in series, the thermal resistance in terms of heat transfer coefficients added up inversely can be written as

$$R = (h A)^{-1}$$
$$= (h_1 A_1)^{-1} + (h_2 A_2)^{-1} + \cdots + (h_m A_m)^{-1} + H_a(h_a A_a)^{-1} +$$
$$H_a(h_a A_a)^{-1} + \cdots + H_n(h_n A_n)^{-1} \tag{11.7.8}$$

11.7.3　Heat Exchange in Parallel

For multiple heat transfer processes in parallel, the overall hear transfer coefficient (h) and the thermal resistance (R) are related to each other as

$$R = (h\,A)^{-1}$$
$$= (h_1\,A_1)^{-1} + (h_2\,A_2)^{-1} + \cdots + (h_m\,A_m)^{-1} +$$
$$\left(\frac{k_a\,A_a}{H_a}\right)^{-1} + \left(\frac{k_b\,A_b}{H_b}\right)^{-1} + \cdots + \left(\frac{k_n A_n}{H_n}\right)^{-1} \tag{11.7.9}$$

11.7.4　Tubular Heat Exchanger with Clean Wall

A precise heat transfer coefficient representing the heat conduction through the tube wall, as shown in Fig. 11.6.1(b), can be estimated considering the curved wall thickness of the tube. The thermal flow can be divided into three heat exchange processes:

(a) Heat convection from fluid to the inner wall of the tube,
(b) Heat conduction transfer through the tube wall, and
(c) Heat convection from the outer tube wall to the outside fluid.

First consider process (b). Assume that the temperature variation from the inner wall to the outer wall is linear and thus $dT \approx \delta T = T_{wo} - T_{wi}$. When Eq. (11.4.1) is formed in the polar coordinate system, the heat transfer rate per unit axial length becomes

$$q = -k\,(2\pi r)\,\frac{dT}{dr} \tag{11.7.10}$$

The integration of the above equation from the inner radius to the outer radius leads to

$$q = \frac{-2\pi\,k\,\delta\,T}{\ln\dfrac{r_o}{r_i}} = \left(\frac{2\pi\,k}{\ln\dfrac{r_o}{r_i}}\right)(-\delta T)$$

$$= \left(\frac{2\pi\,k}{\ln\dfrac{r_o}{r_i}}\right)(T_{wi} - T_{wo}) \tag{11.7.11}$$

where

r_i: Inner radius of the tube;

r_o: Outer diameter of the tube;

k: Thermal conductivity;

T_{wi}: Temperature at the inner wall;

T_{wo}: Temperature at the outer wall;

δT: Temperature variation between the two walls.

The heat exchange is quite related to the surface area of transfer. It is often desired to define an overall heat transfer coefficient (per unit length) at the output temperature, i.e., T_{wo} in this case,

$$q = \frac{k}{r_o \ln \dfrac{r_o}{r_i}} A_o (T_{wi} - T_{wo}) \qquad (11.7.12)$$

Define $\quad q = h_{wo} A_o (T_{wi} - T_{wo}) \qquad (11.7.13)$

Then, $\quad h_{wo} = \dfrac{k}{r_o \ln \dfrac{r_o}{r_i}} \qquad (11.7.14)$

The heat transfer rates at outer and inner surfaces are equal

Then $\quad q = h_{wo} A_o (T_{wi} - T_{wo}) = h_{wi} A_i (T_{wi} - T_{wo}) \qquad (11.7.15)$

and $\quad h_{wi} = h_{wo} \left(\dfrac{A_o}{A_i} \right) \qquad (11.7.16)$

When the inner-wall convection, the wall conduction, and the outer-wall convection are put in series, the overall thermal resistance at the output can be calculated as

$$q = \left(\frac{1}{h_o A_o} + \frac{H}{k A_o} + \frac{1}{h_i A_i} \right)^{-1} (T_i - T_o) = h A_o (T_i - T_o) \qquad (11.7.17)$$

Hence $\quad R = \dfrac{1}{h A_o} = \dfrac{1}{h_o A_o} + \dfrac{1}{h_{wo} A_o} + \dfrac{1}{h_i A_i}$

$$= \frac{1}{h_o A_o} + \frac{r_o \ln \dfrac{r_o}{r_i}}{k A_o} + \frac{1}{h_i A_i}$$

$$= \frac{1}{A_o} + \frac{r_o \ln \dfrac{r_o}{r_i}}{k} + \frac{h_o}{h_i \, r_i} \tag{11.7.18}$$

and

$$h = \frac{1}{h_o} + \frac{r_o \ln \dfrac{r_o}{r_i}}{k} + \frac{\dfrac{r_o}{r_i}}{h_i} \tag{11.7.19}$$

The overall differential heat transfer rate based on the outer differential surface area dA_o for an irregular shape can then be defined using Eq. (11.7.17) as

$$dq = h \, (T_i - T_o) \, dA_o = \frac{T_i - T_o}{\dfrac{1}{h_o} + \dfrac{r_o \ln \dfrac{r_o}{r_i}}{k} + \dfrac{r_o}{h_i \, r_i}} \, dA_o \tag{11.7.20}$$

11.7.5   Overall Heat Transfer Coefficient with Fouling Layers

If there are fouling deposits on the wall, they have two more thermal resistances to deal with, R_i and R_o, in units of $(\mathrm{m}^2{}^{\circ}\mathrm{C} / \mathrm{W})$, and these resistances can be taken into consideration as being in series with tube wall and films,

$$dq = h_{\mathrm{all}}(T_i - T_o) \, dA_o = \frac{T_i - T_o}{\dfrac{1}{h_o} + \dfrac{r_o \ln \dfrac{r_o}{r_i}}{k} + \dfrac{r_o}{h_i \, r_i} + R_i \left(\dfrac{r_o}{r_i}\right) + R_o A_o} \, dA_o \tag{11.7.21}$$

Finally, the area required for maintaining the required temperature difference $(T_i - T_o)$ is dependent on the required heat transfer rate (q_{need}) as

$$A_o = \int dA_o = \int_0^{q_{\mathrm{need}}} \frac{1}{h_{\mathrm{all}}(T_i - T_o)} \, dq \tag{11.7.22}$$

11.8   Heat Exchange by Design

Consider a simplified heat exchanger consisting of two different fluid channels, denoted as a and b, of the same length L, as shown in Fig. 11.8.1. The exchanged heat is carried away by fluid flow. In light of Eq. (11.7.3), the heat transfer rates per unit length of both fluid channels can be

written as

$$q_a = \gamma \left[T_b(z) - T_a(z) \right] \tag{11.8.1}$$

and $\quad q_b = \gamma \left[T_a(z) - T_b(z) \right] \tag{11.8.2}$

$$q_z = - k \, A \, \frac{\Delta T}{\Delta z} = - k \, A \, \frac{T_{wb} - T_{wa}}{H} \tag{11.8.3}$$

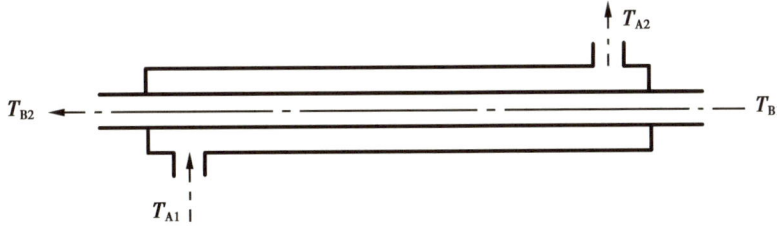

Fig. 11.8.1   Fluid Temperature Distribution along the Tube with Uniform Wall Temperature

Next consider the mass flow of fluids in a counterblow heat exchange. Both channels are aligned in the axial direction z. The heat taken away by the flow masses are

$$Q_a = v_a \, C_{pa} \left(\frac{dT_a}{dz} \right) \tag{11.8.4}$$

and $\quad q_b = v_b \, C_{pb} \left(\frac{dT_b}{dz} \right) \tag{11.8.5}$

Equating Eq. (11.8.4) to Eq. (11.8.2) and Eq. (11.8.5) to Eq. (11.8.3) leads to two coupled simultaneous differential equations in terms of axis z only, as

$$v_a \, C_{pa} \left(\frac{dT_a}{dz} \right) = \gamma \left[T_b(z) - T_a(z) \right] \tag{11.8.6}$$

and $\quad v_b \, C_{pb} \left(\frac{dT_b}{dz} \right) = \gamma \left[T_a(z) - T_b(z) \right] \tag{11.8.7}$

The above two equations can be solved simultaneously as

$$T_a(z) = C_1 + \frac{C_2(v_a \, C_{pa})}{v_a \, C_{pa} + v_b \, C_{pb}} \, e^{\frac{-z \gamma (v_a \, C_{pa} + v_b \, C_{pb})}{v_a \, C_{pa} \, v_b \, C_{pb}}} \tag{11.8.8}$$

$$T_b(z) = C_3 + \frac{C_4(v_b \, C_{pb})}{v_a \, C_{pa} + v_b \, C_{pb}} \, e^{\frac{-z \gamma (v_a \, C_{pa} + v_b \, C_{pb})}{V_a \, C_{pa} \, v_b \, C_{pb}}} \tag{11.8.9}$$

where C_1, C_2, C_3 and C_4 are coefficients resulting from integrations. These constants can be resolved using the temperatures measured at the inlets and outlets as given by the following boundary conditions:

$$T_a(0) = T_{a0} \quad (\text{at } z = 0) \tag{11.8.10}$$

$$T_a(L) = T_{aL} \quad (\text{at } z = L) \tag{11.8.11}$$

$$T_b(0) = T_{b0} \quad (\text{at } z = 0) \tag{11.8.12}$$

and $\quad T_b(L) = T_{bL} \quad (\text{at } z = L) \tag{11.8.13}$

Note that $C_3 = C_1$ and $C_4 = C_2$. The total heat transfer rate between the two fluid channels can be obtained by integrating the expressions for the time rate of change of internal energy per unit length as

$$Q_a = \int_0^L q_a \, dz = v_a \, C_{pa} \, (T_{aL} - T_{a0}) \tag{11.8.14}$$

and $\quad Q_b = \int_0^L q_b \, dz = v_b \, C_{pb} \, (T_{bL} - T_{b0}) \tag{11.8.15}$

Define the average temperature of both fluid channels as

$$\overline{T}_a(z) = \int_0^L T_a(z) \, dz = C_1 - \frac{C_2(v_b \, C_{pb})}{\gamma \, (v_a \, C_{pa} + v_b \, C_{pb})^2} \left[1 - e^{\frac{-z \gamma \, (v_a \, C_{pa} + v_b \, C_{pb})}{v_a \, C_{pa} v_b \, C_{pb}}} \right] \tag{11.8.16}$$

and $\quad \overline{T}_b(z) = \int_0^L T_b(z) \, dz = C_1 - \dfrac{C_2(v_a \, C_{pa})}{\gamma \, (v_a \, C_{pa} + v_b \, C_{pb})^2} \left[1 - e^{\frac{-z \gamma \, (v_a \, C_{pa} + v_b \, C_{pb})}{v_a \, C_{pa} v_b \, C_{pb}}} \right] \tag{11.8.17}$

Eqs. (11.8.17) and (11.8.18) can be rewritten as

$$Q_a = \int_0^L q_a \, dz = v_a \, C_{pa} \, L \, (\overline{T}_b - \overline{T}_a) \tag{11.8.18}$$

and $\quad Q_b = \int_0^L q_b \, dz = v_b \, C_{pb} \, L \, (\overline{T}_a - \overline{T}_b) \tag{11.8.19}$

The quantity $(\overline{T}_a - \overline{T}_b)$ is known as the log mean temperature difference due to the exponential forms of Eqs. (11.8.16) and (11.8.17) and it is a measure of the effectiveness of the heat exchanger in heat transfer.

11.9   Heat Radiation

When the heat transfer is due to the thermal motion of charged particles within atoms that has been converted to electromagnetic radiation and travels at the speed of light, it is called heat radiation or thermal radiation. Thermal radiation emitted by a body as an emitter (i.e., heat source) at any temperature consists of a wide range of frequencies, but the major amount of heat transfer takes place in form of electromagnetic waves mainly in the infrared region. The dominant frequency range of the emitted radiation shifts to higher frequencies as the temperature of the emitter increases. In other words, the total amount of radiation of all frequencies increases as the temperature rises. Radiative power output from an wall can be calculated using the following formula

$$q_r = \epsilon \, S_B \, A \, (T_w^4 - T_a^4) \tag{11.9.1}$$

where

ϵ : Emissivity of radiating surface that is dimensionless;

$S_B(W/m^2/°C^4)$: Stepfan-Boltzmann constant ($S_B = 5.670\ 373 \times 10^{-8}\ W/m^2/°C^4$);

A (m^2) : Radiating surface area;

$q_r(W$ or $J/s)$: Heat transfer per unit time;

T_w and $T_a(K)$: Temperatures of emitting wall plane and air, respectively.

The total amount of energy leaving the wall surface as radiant heat depends on the absolute temperature and on the nature of the surface as described by the above equation. Radiation does play a significant role once the temperature goes above 500 °C [Olsen et al.]. The emissivity of the surface of a material, varying from 0 to 1, is its effectiveness in emitting energy as heat radiation. Data of radiative emissivity of some example materials are given in Table 11.9.1. Eq. (11.6.1) can also be written in the generalized form for heat transfer rate as demonstrated in Section 11.6,

$$q_r = h_r \, A \, (T_w - T_a) \tag{11.9.2}$$

where $h_r = \dfrac{\epsilon \, S_B(T_w^4 - T_a^4)}{T_w - T_a} = \epsilon \, S_B(T_w + T_a) \, (T_w^2 + T_a^2) \tag{11.9.3}$

The overall heat transfer coefficient, including radiation, is the summation of the heat transfer coefficient of combined heat conduction and convection (h) and the heat transfer coefficient due to radiation (h_r),

$$h_{\text{all}} = h + h_{\text{r}} \tag{11.9.4}$$

11.9.1 Black Body

The black body is defined as an extreme object that absorbs all radiation that falls on its surface and thus $\epsilon = 1$. However, there is no such a thing like the black body in nature. The radiation energy per unit time from a black wall is proportional to the fourth power of the absolute temperature as

$$q_{\text{r}} = S_{\text{B}} A T_{\text{w}}^4 \tag{11.9.5}$$

11.9.2 Thermal Radiation for a Grey Body with Only Two Surfaces

In general, the heat transfer rate, i.e., $q_{\text{r}} = dQ/dt$, via thermal radiation for a grey body with only two flat surfaces can be written as

$$q_{\text{r}} = \frac{S_{\text{B}} (T_1^4 - T_2^4)}{\dfrac{1 - \epsilon_1}{A_1 \epsilon_1} + \dfrac{1}{A_1 F_{1 \to 2}} + \dfrac{1 - \epsilon_2}{A_2 \epsilon_2}} \tag{11.9.6}$$

where

T_1 and T_2: Temperatures of surface 1 and surface 2, respectively;

ϵ_1 and ϵ_2: Emissivities of surface 1 and surface 2, respectively, material properties;

A_1 and A_2: Surface areas of surface 1 and surface 2, respectively;

$F_{1 \to 2}$: View factor from surface 1 to surface 2.

11.9.3 External Heating

The thermal reaction of a mechanical or structural element against external heating is practically a transient heat transfer process, through which the heat of fire transmits to the outer surface of the brace by convection and radiation followed by conduction into the internal, e.g. structural steel tube and concrete casing shown in Fig. 11.9.1. Convective and radiative heat fluxes can be calculated [Lu et al.] as

$$q_{\text{convection}} = h_{\text{f}} A (T_{\text{f}} - T_{\text{s}}) \tag{11.9.7}$$

$$q_{\text{radiation}} = \epsilon_{\text{f}} \epsilon_{\text{m}} A S_{\text{B}} [(T_{\text{f}} + T_\infty)^4 - (T_{\text{s}} + T_\infty)^4] \tag{11.9.8}$$

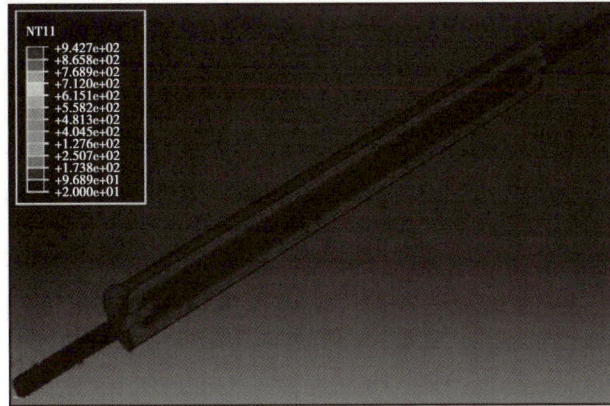

Fig. 11.9.1   Heat Distribution from the Exterior Surface to the Inner Surfaces

As an example for a composite subjected to a standard fire exposure, the following values are proposed by [EC4] for finite element analysis: $h_f = 25$ W/(m^2 · °C), $\epsilon_f = 0.8$ for fibers, and $\epsilon_m = 0.7$ for the matrix, such as the one given in Fig. 11.9.2:

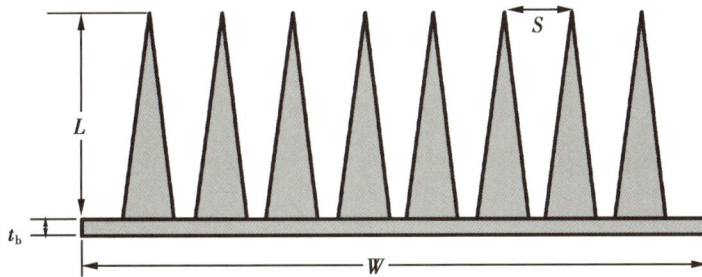

(a) Dimensions

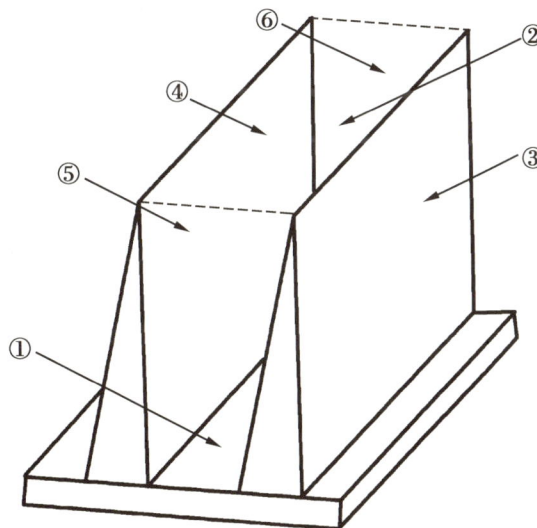

(b) Facets

Fig. 11.9.2   An Ideal Heat Sink with Triangular Fins

11.9.4　Example Radiation Boundary Conditions of Heat Transfer in V-Channel Domain

The radiation heat transfer coefficient （h_r） of heat exchanger fins can be formulated in form of the convection heat transfer coefficient. Based on Stefan Boltzman equation, the heat transfer coefficient, q, is defined as follows:

$$q_r = \frac{A_i \, F_{i \to \infty} \, S_B \, (T'^4 - T'^4_\infty)}{T_s - T_\infty}(T_s - T_\infty) \tag{11.9.9}$$

or

$$q_r = A_i \, F_{i \to \infty} \, h_r \, (T_s - T_\infty) \tag{11.9.10}$$

where

$$h_r = \frac{S_B \, (T'^4_s - T'^4_\infty)}{T_s - T_\infty} \tag{11.9.11}$$

where

$F_{i \to \infty}$: Gray body shape factor, from surface i to the ambient ∞ ;

A_i : Area of surface i ;

$T_s(\text{℃})$: Surface temperature;

$T'_s(\text{℃})$: $T'_s = T_s + 273$;

$T_\infty(\text{℃})$: Ambient temperature;

$T'_\infty(\text{℃})$: $T'_\infty = T_\infty + 273$.

Assuming that all external surfaces of the heat sink is black body, and both fin and base temperature distributions are uniform. Body shape factor $F_{all \to \infty}$ of the heat sink shown in Fig. 11.9.1 ［Donglyoul］ is given as follows:

$$F_{all \to \infty} = \frac{2C_{net}}{t_h(S + 2L)} \tag{11.9.12}$$

where C_{net} is a combined effective resistance coefficient to the heat radiation, formulated as

$$C_{net} = \frac{(R_a + R_b + R_c)(R_c + R_d + R_e) - R_e^2}{[(R_a + R_b + R_c)(R_c + R_d + R_e) - R_e^2] - R_b[R_b(R_b + R_d + R_e) + R_e R_d] - R_b[R_b(R_b + R_d + R_e) + R_e R_d]} \tag{11.9.13}$$

and

$$R_a = \frac{1 - \epsilon}{\epsilon A_3} \tag{11.9.14}$$

$$R_b = \frac{2(1 - \epsilon)}{\epsilon A_1} \tag{11.9.15}$$

$$R_c = \frac{1}{A_1 \, F_{13} + 2 \, A_3 \, F_{35}} \tag{11.9.16}$$

$$R_{\mathrm{d}} = \frac{2}{A_1 \, F_{12} + 2 \, A_1 \, F_{15}} \tag{11.9.17}$$

$$R_{\mathrm{e}} = \frac{1}{A_1 \, F_{13}} \tag{11.9.18}$$

where

R_{a}, R_{b}, R_{c}, R_{d}, R_{e}: Surface resistances to radiation;

A_1, A_3: Areas of surfaces 1 and 3, respectively;

F_{ij}: Shape factor from surface i to surface j.

11.10　Finite Element Formulation for Heat Transfer

The thermal response of a product can seriously impact its structural performance. For example, the shuttle orbiter has a Thermal Protection System (TPS) designed to protect it during reentry. The TPS on the orbiter consists of ceramics-based composite tiles, carbon fiber-reinforced carbon composites, and insulation blankets that protect the aluminum structure of the orbiter from extreme heat. The application of finite element methods will provide promising solutions.

The advent of electric vehicles renders finite element methods for solving coupled magneto-electro-thermo-mechanical problems, because the magnetic driving forces due to magnets and electric motors, the power-electronics parts, and the mechanical performance of the structural system, all rely on the heat transfer within the EV system. In order to accurately figure out the thermal fatigue life of each components, the temperature distribution over the material has to be calculated. Due to thermodynamic state variables, e. g. metallurgical phase change, generally vary with the temperature. These state variables must be also considered when doing finite element analysis in the field of heat transfer.

11.10.1　Governing Equation for Heat Transfer

Let us consider a domain full of temperature-dependent heat transfer. The balance of the heat transfer in the x-, y-, and z-directions and the inner heat generation (or consumption) render a temperature variation according to the following equation

$$\frac{\partial q_x}{\partial x} + \frac{\partial q_y}{\partial y} + \frac{\partial q_z}{\partial z} + Q = \rho \, \gamma \left(\frac{\partial T}{\partial t} \right) \tag{11.10.1}$$

where

q_x: Heat flow through the unit area in the x-direction;

q_y: Heat flow through the unit area in the y-direction;

q_z: Heat flow through the unit area in the z-direction;

$Q(x, y, z, t)$: Inner heat-generation rate per unit volume, a function of x, y, z and t;

P: Material density;

γ: Heat capacity.

Similar to Eq. (11.6.1), the heat flow components can be expressed according to Fourier's law as follows:

$$q_x = - k_x \left(\frac{\partial T}{\partial x} \right) \tag{11.10.2}$$

$$q_y = - k_y \left(\frac{\partial T}{\partial y} \right) \tag{11.10.3}$$

$$q_z = - k_z \left(\frac{\partial T}{\partial z} \right) \tag{11.10.4}$$

where

k_x: Thermal conductivity coefficient of the media in the x-direction;

k_y: Thermal conductivity coefficient of the media in the y-direction;

k_z: Thermal conductivity coefficient of the media in the z-direction.

Substitution of Eqs. (11.10.3)-(11.10.5) into Eq. (11.10.1) yields the following basic heat transfer equation:

$$\frac{\partial}{\partial t}\left(k_x \frac{\partial T}{\partial x} \right) + \frac{\partial}{\partial t}\left(k_y \frac{\partial T}{\partial y} \right) + \frac{\partial}{\partial t}\left(k_z \frac{\partial T}{\partial z} \right) + Q = \rho \, \gamma \left(\frac{\partial T}{\partial t} \right) \tag{11.10.5}$$

11.10.2　Boundary Conditions

Boundary conditions can be one of the following types:

(1) Prescribed temperature (Surface A): $\quad T_s = T_A(x, y, z, t)$ $\hfill$ (11.10.6)

(2) Prescribed heat flow (Surface B): $\quad q_x n_x + q_y n_y + q_z n_z = - q_B$ $\hfill$ (11.10.7)

(3) Heat convection (Surface C): $\quad q_x n_x + q_y n_y + q_z n_z = h \, (T_C - T_e)$ $\hfill$ (11.10.8)

(4) Radiation (Surface D): $\quad q_x n_x + q_y n_y + q_z n_z = \sigma \, \varepsilon \, T_D^4 - \alpha \, q_r$

$\hfill$ (11.10.9)

where

h: Convective heat transfer coefficient;

T_s: Specified surface temperature;

T_e: Specified convective heat exchange temperature;

σ: Stefan-Boltzmann constant;

ε: Surface emission coefficient;

α: Surface absorption coefficient;

q_r: Incident radiant heat flow per unit surface area;

n_x, n_y, n_z: Unit directions normal to the body surface aligned with x-, y-, and z-directions.

11.10.3   Initial Conditions

As heat transfer is a dynamic phenomenon, it is necessary to specify an initial temperature field for the geometric domain at the very beginning moment ($t=0$):

$$T(x, y, z, 0) = T_0(x, y, z) \qquad (11.10.10)$$

11.10.4   Finite Element Discretization

Based on the finite element discretization, the continuum is meshed into a set of discrete elements connected at nodes. Global equations for the domain are assembled from discrete "finite element" equations based on connectivity information. For the convenience but without losing the general realization, the finite element derivation for the 20-node solid element is demonstrated here. Note that 20-node solid elements are the most widely used finite elements for 3-dimensional heat transfer. The temperature of a finite element is obtained through the interpolation of the temperatures of the element's nodes ranging from T_1, T_2, T_3, $\cdots$, to T_{20} using shape functions N_i ($i=1, 2, 3, \cdots, 20$) as

$$T = [N]\{T\} \qquad (11.10.11)$$

where $[N] = [N_1, N_2, N_3, \cdots, N_{20}]$ $\qquad (11.10.12)$

$\{T\}^{\mathrm{T}} = \{T_1, T_2, T_3, \cdots, T_{20}\}$ $\qquad (11.10.13)$

In other words,

$$T = \sum_{i=1}^{20} N_i T_i \qquad (11.10.14)$$

By differentiating the above equation with respect to the three body coordinates (ξ, η, ζ) associated with the element of interest, and stacking them into a vector column, one has

$$
\begin{Bmatrix} \dfrac{\partial T}{\partial \xi} \\[2mm] \dfrac{\partial T}{\partial \eta} \\[2mm] \dfrac{\partial T}{\partial \zeta} \end{Bmatrix}_{3\times1} = \sum_{i=1}^{20} \begin{Bmatrix} \dfrac{\partial N_i}{\partial \xi} \\[2mm] \dfrac{\partial N_i}{\partial \eta} \\[2mm] \dfrac{\partial N_i}{\partial \zeta} \end{Bmatrix}_{3\times1} T_i
\tag{11.10.15}
$$

Following Eq. (3.2.14), one has

$$
\begin{Bmatrix} \dfrac{\partial T}{\partial x} \\[2mm] \dfrac{\partial T}{\partial y} \\[2mm] \dfrac{\partial T}{\partial z} \end{Bmatrix} = [L] \begin{Bmatrix} \dfrac{\partial T}{\partial \xi} \\[2mm] \dfrac{\partial T}{\partial \eta} \\[2mm] \dfrac{\partial T}{\partial \zeta} \end{Bmatrix}
\tag{11.10.16}
$$

Substituting Eq. (11.10.15) into Eq. (11.10.16) leads to

$$
\begin{Bmatrix} \dfrac{\partial T}{\partial x} \\[2mm] \dfrac{\partial T}{\partial y} \\[2mm] \dfrac{\partial T}{\partial z} \end{Bmatrix} = [L] \sum_{i=1}^{20} \begin{Bmatrix} \dfrac{\partial N_i}{\partial \xi} \\[2mm] \dfrac{\partial N_i}{\partial \eta} \\[2mm] \dfrac{\partial N_i}{\partial \zeta} \end{Bmatrix}_{3\times1} T_i = \sum_{i=1}^{20} [L] \begin{Bmatrix} \dfrac{\partial N_i}{\partial \xi} \\[2mm] \dfrac{\partial N_i}{\partial \eta} \\[2mm] \dfrac{\partial N_i}{\partial \zeta} \end{Bmatrix}_{3\times1} T_i
\tag{11.10.17}
$$

or
$$
\begin{Bmatrix} \dfrac{\partial T}{\partial x} \\[2mm] \dfrac{\partial T}{\partial y} \\[2mm] \dfrac{\partial T}{\partial z} \end{Bmatrix} = [B_{\mathrm{T}}] \{T\}
\tag{11.10.18}
$$

Here, $\{T\}$ is a vector of temperatures at nodes and $[B_{\mathrm{T}}]$ is a matrix for temperature-gradient interpolation. Applying the Galerkin method to (11.10.6), one has

$$
\iiint_V \left[\frac{\partial q_x}{\partial x} + \frac{\partial q_y}{\partial y} + \frac{\partial q_z}{\partial z} + Q - \rho\,\gamma \left(\frac{\partial T}{\partial t} \right) \right] N_i \, \mathrm{d}V = 0
\tag{11.10.19}
$$

Applying the divergence theorem to the first three terms, one has

$$\iiint_V \rho \, \gamma \left(\frac{\partial T}{\partial t} \right) N_i \, dV - \iiint_V \left[\frac{\partial N_i}{\partial x} \quad \frac{\partial N_i}{\partial y} \quad \frac{\partial N_i}{\partial z} \right] \{q\} - \iiint_V Q \, N_i dV + \iint_S \{q\}^{\text{T}} \{n\} \, N_i \, dS = 0$$

$$(11.10.20)$$

where $\{q\}^{\text{T}} = \{q_x \quad q_y \quad q_z\} = - k [B_{\text{T}}] \{T\}$ (11.10.21)

After the boundary conditions, i.e., Eqs. (11.10.7)-(11.10.10), are plugged into the above equation, the discretized equations become

$$\iiint_V \rho \, \gamma \left(\frac{\partial T}{\partial t} \right) N_i \, dV - \iiint_V \left[\frac{\partial N_i}{\partial x} \quad \frac{\partial N_i}{\partial y} \quad \frac{\partial N_i}{\partial z} \right] \{q\}$$

$$= \iiint_V Q \, N_i \, dV - \iint_A \{q\}^{\text{T}} \{n\} \, N_i \, dS + \iint_B q_s \, N_i \, dS -$$

$$\iint_C h \, (T - T_e) \, N_i \, dS - \iint_D (S_B \, \epsilon \, T_D^4 - \alpha \, q_r) \, N_i \, dS$$ (11.10.22)

The discretized finite element equations for the 3-dimensional heat transfer can be written in matrix form as

$$[C] \left\{ \frac{dT}{dt} \right\} + ([K_c] + [K_h] + [K_r]) \{T\} = \{R_{\text{T}}\} + \{R_Q\} + \{R_q\} + \{R_h\} + \{R_r\}$$

$$(11.10.23)$$

Let $$[C] \left\{ \frac{dT}{dt} \right\} + [K] \{T\} = \{R\}$$ (11.10.24)

$$[C] = \iiint_V \rho \, \gamma \, [N]^{\text{T}} \, [N] \, dV$$ (11.10.25)

$$[K] = ([K_c] + [K_h] + [K_r])$$ (11.10.26)

and $$\{R\} = \{R_{\text{T}}\} + \{R_Q\} + \{R_q\} + \{R_h\} + \{R_r\}$$ (11.10.27)

where $$[K_c] = \iiint_V k \, [B_{\text{T}}]^{\text{T}} [B_{\text{T}}] \, dV$$ (11.10.28)

$$[K_h] = \iint_C h \, [N]^{\text{T}} \, [N] \, dS$$ (11.10.29)

$$[K_r] = \iint_D S_B \epsilon \, T^4 \, [N]^{\text{T}} \, dS$$ (11.10.30)

$$[R_{\text{T}}] = - \iint_A \{q\}^{\text{T}} [N][N]^{\text{T}} \, dS$$ (11.10.31)

$$[R_Q] = \iiint_V Q \; [n]^T \; dV \tag{11.10.32}$$

$$[R_q] = \iint_B q_s \; [N]^T \; dS \tag{11.10.33}$$

$$[R_h] = \iint_C h \; T_e \; [N]^T \; dS \tag{11.10.34}$$

$$[R_r] = \iint_D \alpha \; q_r \; [N]^T \; dS \tag{11.10.35}$$

Matrix $[C]$ is called heat capacity matrix, $\{R\}$ is the vector of thermal nodal loads, and matrix $[K]$ including the three heat-transfer mechanisms: heat conduction, convection and radiation. The predominant numerical method for analysis of heat transfer problems, even using the finite element method, remains the finite difference method. Time integration schemes based on finite difference methods, as well as the related converging stability and solution accuracy, are detailed in [Bathe et al.] and [Bergheau & Fortunier].

11.10.5　Different Analysis Types

Equations for different types of problems can be deducted from the above general equation as follows:

(a) Stationary Linear Problem

$$([K_c] + [K_h])\{T\} = \{R_Q\} + \{R_q\} + \{R_h\} \tag{11.10.36}$$

(b) Stationary Nonlinear Problem

$$([K_c] + [K_h] + [K_r])\{T\} = \{R_Q(T)\} + \{R_q(T)\} + \{R_h(T)\} + \{R_r(T)\} \tag{11.10.37}$$

(c) Transient Linear Problem

$$[C] \left\{ \frac{dT(t)}{dt} \right\} + ([K_c] + [K_h(t)])\{T(t)\} = \{R_Q(t)\} + \{R_q(t)\} + \{R_h(t)\} \tag{11.10.38}$$

(d) Transient Nonlinear Problem

$$[C] \left\{ \frac{dT(t)}{dt} \right\} + ([K_c(T)] + [K_h(T, t)] + [K_r(T)] \{T\}$$

$$= \{R_Q(T, t)\} + \{R_q(T, t)\} + \{R_h(T, t)\} + \{R_r(T,t)\} \tag{11.10.39}$$

11.11   Thermomechanical Analysis of Bolts for Disc Brake

As the speed of bullet trains increases, the durability of bolts that secure the integrity of the braking mechanism subject to various thermomechanical loadings is of great concern. A schematic drawing of basic disk-brake components is demonstrated in Fig. 11.11.1(a).

11.11.1   Transient Heat Transfer Analysis

The initial situation rises to the challenge of predicting the temperature distribution over the parts including the disk and brake pads. The axisymmetric or periodic model was not applicable for this case because the disk and brake pads cannot be analyzed simultaneously. Some researchers looked into the feasibility of utilizing "rigid bodies with temperature degrees of freedom" for a fully-coupled thermomechanical analysis in three-dimensional modes under a high-speed rotation, as implemented using Abaqus/Explicit codes by [Fujii & Saito].

It is assumed that in-situ contact conditions do not change in the braking event, i.e., no wear problem between the brake lining and disk, because all parts are made rigid members. Hence, each elemental node has only one degree of freedom in the temperature domain and the stable time increment increased by the order to two and the associated simultaneous equations can be solved with reasonable size of time increment as a practical approach. A resulting thermal temperature distribution obtained by [Fujii & Saito] is plotted in Fig. 11.11.1(b).

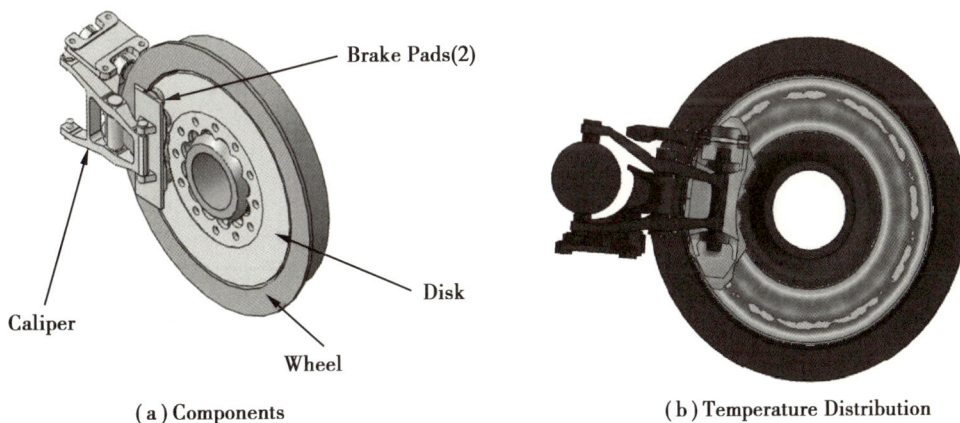

(a) Components

(b) Temperature Distribution

Fig. 11.11.1   Design Configurtation of Train Disk Brake Mechanism [Fujii & Saito]

11.11.2   Thermomechanical Analysis

The initial prescribed angular velocity is calculated from the deceleration-versus-time relationship as applied to the wheel axis. The required braking force was derived from the linear deceleration of the vehicle. The spontaneous heat generated by friction due to the braking force is obtained from the force and the respective velocity, and then applied onto the contact surfaces between the disk and brake pads.

After the calculated temperature profile is validated by full-scaled physical tests, the temperature profile is transferred to the "elastoplastic" disk using Abaqus Standard to predict the fluctuating loss of fastening force of the bolts due to material creep and varying elastoplastic modulus. The conductive heat transfer between the parts was considered using thermal contact properties as described in Section 8.3.

11.11.3 Loading Cyles

Follow the procedure described in Chapter 4.

11.11.4 Damage Accumulation

Follow the procedure described in Chapter 4.

11.12 Example Boundary Conditions of Heat Transfer in Diesel Engine

The cycle lifetime of an internal combustion engine and its related exhaust system are relatively short, so that creep damage plays only a minor role. However, high strain amplitudes arise due to the constrained thermal strains, so that cracks nucleate in an early stage. The lifetime limiting damage mechanism is therefore the growth of these cracks under cyclic loading. The crack growth rates depend on cycle times, strain amplitudes, mean stress, temperature and the environment [Seifert & Riede].

The change of temperature of node i of a differential mass (dm_i) based on finite element method for heat transfer may occur through thermal conductance, convective heat transfer, and thermal radiations in a time span Δt, as generally described by the following equation:

$$C_v \, dm_i \, \frac{T_{i,t+\Delta t} - T_{i,t}}{\Delta t} = \sum_s \left[K_{is}(T_{s,t+\Delta t} - T_{s,t}) \right] + \sum_f \left[h_{if}(T_f - T_{i,t+\Delta t}) \, dA_{if} \right] +$$

$$\sum_r \left[h_{ir}(T_r - T_{i,\,t+\Delta t}) \, dA_{ir} \right] + \sum_k q_{ik} \qquad (11.12.1)$$

where

dm_i: Differential mass of node i;

C_v: Heat capacity;

K_{is}: Thermal conductivity from solid contact s;

h_{if}: Convective heat transfer coefficient from fluid f;

dA_{if}: Differential area in contact with fluid f;

h_{ir}: Heat transfer coefficient due to thermal radiation source r;

dA_{ir}: Differential area exposed to thermal radiation source r;

q_{ik}: Heat conduction between node i and its adjacent node k of the same part.

A set of example data of temperature boundary conditions and heat transfer coefficients for the calculated temperature distribution around a Diesel engine valve [Sharmal et al.] is given in Table 11.12.1.

11.12.1   Cylinder Head

The desire for increasing engine power, reducing emission, and cutting down fuel consumption for diesel engines has created stringent demands on the cylinder head design. It is often observed that the limiting design factor is given by the thermal mechanical fatigue strength of the cylinder head. The material model formulation in finite element analysis is based on a continuum-damage-mechanics approach in order to account for the tension/compression anomaly of cast iron [Zieher et al.].

A cylinder head receives the heat not only from in-cylinder burning gases during the combustion period, but also in the exhaust process-from burned gases flowing through exhaust valve and along exhaust ports. Thus, a cylinder head gets exposed to the burnt gas as subjected to three different heat-transfer mechanisms: (a) convective heat transfer (b) thermal radiation, and (c) heat conduction, while various channels of coolant flow are used to dissipate the heat.

11.12.1.1   Convective Heat Transfer between Cylinder Head and Burnt Gas

Assume that the cylinder head temperature is independent of the engine crank angle (θ). The averaged convective heat flux $dq_{ave,h}/dA$ (heat transfer per unit area) between the burnt gas and a certain point of the cylinder head wall is estimated using the following equation:

$$\frac{dq_{ave}}{dA} = (4\pi)^{-1} \int_0^{4\pi} \frac{dq(\theta)}{dA} \, d\alpha$$

$$= (4\pi)^{-1} \int_0^{4\pi} h(\theta) \, [T_g(\theta) - T_h] \, d\alpha$$

$$= (4\pi)^{-1} \int_0^{4\pi} h(\theta) \ T_g(\theta) \ d\theta - (2\pi)^{-1} T_h \int_0^{4\pi} h(\theta) \ d\theta$$

$$\approx h_{ave} \ T_{g,ave} - h_{ave} \ T_h$$

$$= h_c (T_{g,app} - T_h) \tag{11.12.2}$$

of which

$$h_{cov} = h_{ave} = (4\pi)^{-1} \int_0^{4\pi} h(\theta) \ d\theta \tag{11.12.3}$$

$$T_{g,app} = \frac{1}{4 \pi \ h_{ave}} \int_0^{4\pi} h(\theta) \ T_g(\theta) \ d\theta \tag{11.12.4}$$

where

θ: Engine crank angle;

$T_g(\text{℃})$: Burnt gas temperature;

$T_{g,app}(\text{℃})$: Apparent gas temperature averaged over an engine crank cycle, i.e., 4π;

$T_h(\text{℃})$: Cylinder head temperature;

$h(\text{℃})$: Convective heat transfer coefficient;

$h_{cov} = h_{ave}(\text{℃})$: Convective heat transfer coefficient averaged over an engine crank cycle.

11.12.1.2　Thermal Radiation Impinging upon Cylinder Head by Burnt Gas

Next, consider the thermal radiation impinging upon a differential area （dA）of the cylinder head, by means of Eqs. （11.9.1）and （11.9.2）one has the following:

$$q_r = h_r \ dA(T_w - T_a) \tag{11.12.5}$$

and $\quad h_r = \epsilon \ S_B(T_w + T_a) \ (T_w^2 + T_a^2) \tag{11.12.6}$

The overall heat transfer coefficient between the burnt gas and cylinder head, including convective heat transfer and thermal radiation, is then［Kassab et al.］

$$h_{all} = h_c + h_r = h_c + \epsilon \ S_B(T_w + T_a) \ (T_w^2 + T_a^2) \tag{11.12.7}$$

11.12.1.3　Heat Dissipation of Cylinder Head into Coolant

Forced convection is the dominant heat-transfer mechanism between coolant and its contacting solid part surfaces such as the liner, flow channels in the cylinder block, and flow channels in the cylinder head. One of the widely used equations to describe the turbulent flow in the cylinder head ［Dittus-Boelter］ is

$$Nu = 0.023 \ Re^{0.8} \ Pr^{0.4} \tag{11.12.8}$$

The related convective heat transfer coefficient is then calculated using Eq. (11.6.18) as

$$h = \frac{k\,Nu}{D}$$

(11.12.9)

where the characteristic dimension D can be the diameter of the channel. When nucleate boiling occurs, the heat flux (dq/dA) is related to the temperature change by Eq. (11.12.2).

It has been noted that water vaporizes overwhelmingly to bubbled vapors on a hot surface reducing the ability of heat to transfer from hot metal, while pure ethylene glycol as a coolant alone has a specific heat capacity about one half that of water. A practical coolant is a 50/50 mixture of water and ethylene glycol by mass and has a specific heat capacity of about 3140 J/(kg · ℃), which is three quarters that of pure water.

On the other hand, ethylene glycol disrupts hydrogen bonding when dissolved in water. Pure ethylene glycol freezes at about −12 ℃, but when mixed with water, the mixture does not readily crystallize, and therefore the freezing point of the mixture is depressed. Specifically, a mixture of 50% ethylene glycol and 50% water by volume freezes at −38 ℃, and its boiling points are 107 ℃ at 1 atm and 120 ℃ at 2 atm, respectively.

11.12.1.4 Heat Transfer between Cylinder Head and Liner

Heat conduction between the cylinder head and liner is carried out through in-between gaskets. Usually both contact conductance between the cylinder head and gasket is not as significant as other heat-transfer mechanisms in an engine, and so is the contact conductance between the cylinder liner and gasket.

11.12.1.5 Heat Dissipation of Cylinder Head into Ambient Air

Heat convection follows Eq. (11.9.10) with film heat transfer coefficient h between the cylinder head and moving air.

11.12.2 Heat Transfer in Engine Piston

The piston heat that comes from burnt gas is dissipated in two ways. Though part of the heat is transferred through the liner to the coolant, an engine oil jet shall remove most heat from a piston. For a high-speed direct injection diesel engine, there is an extensive impingement of fuel sprays on to the piston bowl. The fuel spray deposition on the piston bowl surface is in the form of a thin film that did not experience bulk boiling [Ladommato et al.]. An increase in the operating temperature leads to a significant reduction in unburned hydrocarbon emission, a significant increase in smoke emission, and no significant change in the emission of oxides of nitrogen.

11.12.2.1 Piston Crown Exposed to Burnt Gas

Similar to the cylinder head exposed to burnt gas, the heat transfer from the burnt gas to the piston crown can be obtained through convective heat transfer and thermal radiation by the same token as detailed in Section 11.11.1, and

$$\frac{\mathrm{d}q_{\mathrm{ave}}}{\mathrm{d}A} = h_{\mathrm{c}} [T_{\mathrm{g,app}} - T_{\mathrm{h}}] \tag{11.12.10}$$

11.12.2.2 Heat Dissipation of Piston by Engine Oil Jet

The majority of piston heat is carried away by engine oil jet. The rate and type of nozzle spray are influential factors besides the piston gallery geometry. The Nusselt and Reynolds number can be calculated, respectively as follows:

$$Nu = C_{\mathrm{nu}} Re^{\mathrm{m}} \tag{11.12.11}$$

and

$$Re = \frac{D V_{\mathrm{p}}}{\mu_{\mathrm{d}}} \tag{11.12.12}$$

where

C_{Nu} and m: Coefficient and exponent to be obtained from spray test by regression;

D: Piston gallery (under) diameter;

V_{p}: Mean piston speed.

11.12.2.3 Heat Transfer While Piston in Contact with Liner

The conductance between the piston skirt and the liner through part-time contact is given by the following formula:

$$k = \left(\frac{T_{\mathrm{con}}}{T_{\mathrm{cycle}}} \right) k_{\mathrm{P-L}} \left(\frac{1}{2} D \right) \psi \tag{11.12.13}$$

where

$T_{\mathrm{con}} / T_{\mathrm{cycle}}$: Ratio of the contact time to the cycle duration during a combustion cycle;

$k_{\mathrm{P-L}}$: Contact conductance between the piston and liner;

D: Liner bore diameter;

ψ: Contact angle circumferentially between the piston and liner.

11.12.3   Heat Transfer via Cylinder Liner

The objective of studying the heat transfer via cylinder liner is two folds: (1) achievement of uniformity in jacket cooling and (2) reduction of liner distortion.

11.12.3.1   Heat Dissipation of Cylinder Liner by Coolant

The equation employed to simulate the turbulent flow of coolant in the liner jacket [Dittus-Boelter] is the same as the one used for cylinder head and it is

$$Nu = 0.023\ Re^{0.8}\ Pr^{0.4} \tag{11.12.14}$$

Heat flux going to cylinder liner, flow velocity of coolant, and coolant mixture fraction (i.e., water and glycol) are also key influential parameters.

11.12.3.2   Heat Dissipation of Cylinder Liner Bore by Engine Oil

On the wall of a liner bore is splashed continuously with engine oil of a lower temperature and the engine oil is scraped off at a downward stroke.

11.12.4   Heat Transfer from Burnt Gas to Engine Block

A thermostat is located between the engine block and the thermal radiator. Its temperature-sensitive spring valve stays closed during engine warm-up. When the thermostat is closed, it prevents coolant from leaving the engine until the correct running temperature is reached. Hoses are used to connect the engine block and the water pump to the radiator.

Nowadays, the engine block is manufactured in one piece with the water jackets cast into the block and cylinder head. The water jacket is a collection of passages within the block (and head). These passages let the coolant circulate around the "hot spots" (valve seats and guides, cylinder walls, combustion chamber, etc.) in order to cool them off. The equation employed to simulate the turbulent flow in the engine block [Dittus-Boelter] is the same as the one used for cylinder head and it is

$$Nu = 0.023\ Re^{0.8}\ Pr^{0.4} \tag{11.12.15}$$

11.12.5   Heat Transfer from Burnt Gas to the Exhaust Manifold and Other Runners

The high run-away velocity of the burnt gas in the exhaust system creates pulsating turbulence following the valve operation. A mixing equation with dissipation coefficients has been proposed to calculate the instantaneous apparent velocity [Descombes et al.] as

$$V(t) = \frac{\displaystyle\sum_{i=0}^{\infty} p_i \, V(t - i \, \Delta t)}{\displaystyle\sum_{i=0}^{\infty} p_i} \qquad (11.12.16)$$

where

$V(t)$ and $V(t-i \, \Delta t)$: Speed at time t and time $(t-i\Delta t)$, respectively;

p_i: Dissipation coefficient.

A simplified model derived from the above equation for only one dissipation coefficient, i.e., p, is

$$V(t) = p \, V(t - \Delta t) + (1 - p) \, V(t) \qquad (11.12.17)$$

By which the Reynolds number and Nusselt number can be calculated, respectively as

$$Re = \frac{\rho \, V \, D}{\mu_d} \qquad (11.12.18)$$

and $\quad Nu = 1.6 \, Re^{0.4} \qquad (11.12.19)$

The Nusselt number calculated above using the instantaneous speed is to be summed up for calculating the averaged Nusselt number over a combustion cycle (Nu_{cycle}). The related convective heat transfer coefficient is then calculated using Eq. (11.12.9) as

$$h = \frac{k \, Nu_{cycle}}{D} \qquad (11.12.20)$$

References

ANTONETTI V, WHITTLE T, SIMONS R, 1991. An Approximate Thermal Contact Conductance Correlation [J]. HTD-Vol. 170, Experimental/Numerical Heat Transfer in Combustion and Phase Change, 15(1): 131-134.

ASTM E1354. Standard Test Method for Heat and Visible Smoke Release Rates for Materials and Products[J]. Using an Oxygen Consumption Calorimeter.

BATHE K, et al, 1979. Finite Element Formulation and Solution of Nonlinear Heat Transfer[J]. Nuclear Engineering and Design, 51: 389-401.

BERGHEAU J, FORTUNIER R, 2013. Finite Element Simulation of Heat Transfer[M]. Wiley, NY.

BERMAN R, 1956. Some Experiments on Thermal Contact at Low Temperatures [J]. Journal of Applied Physics, 27(4): 318-323.

BORMAN G, NISHIWAKI K, 1987. A Review of Internal Combustion Engine Heat Transfer[J]. Prog. Energy Combust. Sci., 13(1): 1-46.

BOSCO, N, KURTZ, S. 2010. Quantifying the Thermal Fatigue of CPV Modules [J]. AIP Conference Proceedings, 1277 : 225-228.

CAMPBELL N, et al, 2002. Predictions for Nucleate Boiling-Results from a Thermal Bench Marking Exercise under Low Flow Conditions[J]. SAE 2002-01-1028.

CAMPBELL W E, THOMAS U B, 1947. The Oxidation of Metals[J]. Journal of Electrochemical Society, 91 (1): 623-640.

CARSLAW H S, JAEGER J C, 1959. Conduction of Heat in Solids[M]. Oxford University Press, Oxford, UK.

CENGEL Y A, GHAJAR A J, 2010. Heat and Mass Transfer: Fundamentals and Applications [M]. 4th Edition, McGraw-Hill, NY.

CHEN J C, 1966. Correlation for Boiling Heat Transfer to Saturated Fluids in Convective Flow[J]. Industrial and Engineering Chemistry, Process Design and Development, 5(3): 322-329.

CHRIST H, JUNG A, MAIER, H, et al, 2003. Thermomechanical Fatigue-Damage Mechanisms and Mechanism-Based Life Prediction Methods[J]. Sadhana, 28(1-2): 147-165.

CROWE C T, 2006. Multiphase Flow Handbook[M]. CRC Taylor and Francis, Boca Raton, FL.

DARYABEIGI K, et al, 2010. Combined Heat Transfer in High-Porosity High-Temperature Fibrous Insulations: Theory and Experimental Validation[J]. AIAA Paper 2010-4660.

DEUTSCH M, 1979. Thermal Conductance in Screw-Fastened Joints at Helium Temperatures[J]. Cryogenics, 19(5): 273-274.

DESCOMBES G, et al, 2003. Study of the Interaction between Mechanical Energy and Heat Exchanges Applied to IC Engines[J]. Applied Thermal Engineering, 23(16): 2061-2078.

DITTUS F W, BOELTER L M K, 1930. Heat Transfer in Automobile Radiators of the Tubular Type[D]. University of California, Berkeley, Publ. Eng., 2: 443.

DOGAN E, 2005. Thermoeconomic Optimization of Baffle Spacing for Shell and Tube Heat Exchangers[J]. Energy Conservation and Management, 47(11-12): 1478-1489.

DONGLYOUL S, 1999. Thermal Design and Evaluation Methods for Heat Sink[J]. E-CIM Team, Corporate Technical Operations.

EC4, 2005. Eurocode 4: Design of Composite Steel and Concrete Structures, Part 1-2: General Rules-Structural Fire Design[J]. BS EN 1994-1-2, British Standards Institution, London, UK.

ENCINAS-OROPESA A., et al, 2008. Effects of Oxidation and Hot Corrosion in a Nickel Disc Alloy[J]. Superalloys 2008, The Minerals, Metals and Materials Society.

FAGHRI A., et al, 2010. Advanced Heat and Mass Transfer[M]. Global Digital Press, Columbia, MO, USA.

FARROKHZAD M A, KHAN T I, 2013. High Temperature Oxidation Behavior of Nanostructured Cermet Coatings in a Mixed CO_2-O_2 Environment[J]. International Symposium on Advanced Materials, ISAM.

FLETCHER L S, 1988. Recent Developments in Contact Conductance Heat Transfer[J]. Journal of Heat Transfer, 110(4b): 1059-1070.

GANESH V K, NAIK N K, 1994. Thermal Expansion Coefficients of Plane-Wave Fabric Laminates[J]. Composites Science and Technology, 51: 387-408.

GEMBAROVIC J, TAYLOR R E, 2007. A Method for Thermal Diffusivity Determination of Thermal Insulators [J]. International Journal of Thermophysics, 28(6): 2164-2175.

HENRY A, CHEN G, 2008. High Thermal Conductivity of Single Polyethylene Chains Using Molecular Dynamics Simulations[J]. Physics Review Letters, 101(23), PRL 101, 235502.

HAJMOHAMMADI M, et al, 2013. A New Configuration of Bend Tubes for Compound Optimization of Heat and Fluid Flow[J]. Energy, 62(dec.1): 418-424.

HOA S V, 2017. Advanced Manufacturing: Polymer and Composites Science, Factors Affecting the Properties of Composites Made by 4D Printing (Moldless Composites Manufacturing)[J]. Advanced Manufacturing: Polymer & Composites Science, 3(3): 101-109.

HOLMAN J P, 1997. Heat Transfer[M]. 8th Edition, McGraw-Hill Book Company, NY.

HSU H C, et al, 2008. Thermo-Hygro-Mechanical Design and Reliability Analysis for CMOS Image Sensor[J]. Journal of Thermal Stresses, 31(10): 917-934.

HSU Y Y, 1962. On the Size Range of Active Nucleation Cavities on a Heating Surface[J]. Journal of Heat Transfer, 83(30): 207-213.

INCROPERA F P, DEWITT D P, BERGMAN T L, et al, Fundamentals of Heat and Mass Transfer[M]. 6th Edition, John Wiley & Sons, Hoboken, NJ, USA.

KAJIWARA H., et al, 2002. An Analytical Approach for Prediction of Piston Temperature Distribution in Diesel Engines[J]. JSAE Review, 23(4): 429-434.

KAKAC S, LIU H, 2002. Heat Exchangers: Selection, Rating and Thermal Design[M]. 2nd Edition, CRC Press.

KHARE G, CHANDRA N, SILVAIN J, 2008. Application of Eshelby's Tensor and Rotation Matrix for the Evaluation of Thermal Transport Properties Composites [J]. Mechanics of Advanced Materials and Structures, 15(2): 117-129.

KASSAB R K, et al, 2012. Experimental and Finite Element Analysis of a T-Joint Welding[J]. Journal of Mechanical Engineering and Automation, 2: 411-421.

KITTEL P, 1995. Modeling Thermal Contact Resistance[M]. Cryocoolers: Plenum Press.

KWOK T, et al, 2015. Four-Dimensional Printing for Freeform Surfaces: Design Optimization of Origami and Kirigami Structures[J]. Journal of Mechanical Design, 137(11): 1-10.

LADOMMATOS N, XIAO Z, ZHAO H, 2005. The Effect of Piston Bowl Temperature on Diesel Exhaust Emissions[J]. PI MECH ENG D-JAVT, Journal of Automobile Engineering, 219(3): 371-388.

LAMBERT M A, FLETCHER L S, 1997. Thermal Contact Conductance of Spherical Rough Metals[J]. Journal of Heat Transfer.

LATHAM C A, 1996. Thermal Resistance of Interface Materials as a Function of Pressure [J]. Electronics Cooling, 2(2): 35.

LEE K S, ASSANIS D N, 1990. Measurements and Predictions of Steady-State and Transient Stress Distributions in a Diesel Engine Cylinder Head[J]. SAE 1999-01-0973.

LIM T C, 2002. Unified Practical Bounds for the Thermal Conductivity of Composite Materials[J]. Materials Letters, 54(2002): 152-157.

LU H, et al, 2011. FE Modeling and Fire Resistance Design of Concrete Filled Double Skin Tubular Columns [J]. Journal of Constructional Steel Research, 67(11): 1733-1748.

MADHUSUDANA C V, LING F F, 1995. Thermal Contact Conductance[M]. Springer, NJ.

MALLICK P K, 1988. Fiber-Reinforced Composites[M]. Mercel Dekker, New York, USA.

NEILSEN L E, 1962. Mechanical Properties of Polymers[M]. Rheinhold, New York.

OHRBY F, 2014. Numerical Modeling of Subcooled Nucleate Flow Boiling in Engine Cooling Systems, Master Thesis[M]. Chalmers University of Technology, Goteborg, Sweden.

OLSEN E L, et al, 2002. Modeling of Constriction Resistance in Coated Joints[J]. Journal of Thermophysics and Heat Transfer, 16: 207-216, AIAA.

PRADHAN N, et al, 2009. The Specific Heat and Effective Thermal Conductivity of Composites Containing Single-Wall and Multi-Wall Carbon Nanotubes[J]. Nanotechnology, 20(24): 245705.

PRADERE C, et al, 2013. Thermal Properties of Carbon Fibers at Very High Temperature[J]. Carbon, 47(3): 737-743.

RAN Z, et al, 2014. Determination of Thermal Expansion Coefficients for Unidirectional Fiber-Reinforced Matrix[J]. Chinese Journal of Aeronautics, 27(5): 1180-1187.

ROHSENOW W, et al, 1998. Handbook of Heat Transfer[M]. 3rd Edition, McGraw-Hill, NY.

ROSEN B W, HASHIN Z, 1970. Effective Thermal Expansion Coefficients and Specific Heat of Composite Materials[J]. International Journal of Engineering, 8(2): 157-173.

SALERNO L J, et al, 1994. Thermal Conductance of Pressed Metallic Contacts Augmented with Indium Foil or Apiezon Grease at Liquid Helium Temperatures[J]. Cryogenics, 34(8): 649-654.

SCHAPERY R A, 1968. Thermal Expansion Coefficient of Composite Materials Based on Energy Principles[J]. Journal of Composite Materials, 2(3): 380-404.

SEIFERT T, RIEDE H, 2009. Fatigue Life Prediction of High Temperature Components in Combustion Engines and Exhaust Systems [M]. EASC 2009, 4th European Automotive Simulation Conference, Munich, Germany, July 6-7.

SHARMAL S, SAINI P K, SAMRIA N, 2013. Modeling and Analysis of Radial Thermal Stresses and Temperature Field in Diesel Engine Valves with and without Air Cavity [J]. International Journal of Engineering, Science and Technology, 5(3): 93-105.

SHARP K, BOGDANOVICH A, SCHUSTER J, et al, 2007. Through-Thickness Thermal Conductivity in Composites Based on 3-D Fiber Architectures[J]. SAE 2007-01-3931.

SHEN S, HENRY A, TONG J, et al, 2010. Polyethylene Nanofibres with Very High Thermal Conductivities [J]. Nature Nanotechnology, 5(4): 251-255.

SHINGARE A P, TOTLA N B, 2016. Simulation of Jacket Cooling of a Liner of Four Cylinder Diesel Engine for Genset Application[J]. International Engineering Research Journal: 1276-1283.

SKELTON R P, 1993. Cyclic Hardening, Softening and Crack Growth during High Temperature Fatigue[J]. Materials Science and Technology, 9: 1001-1008.

STEINER H, KOBOR A, GEBHARD L, 2005. A Wall Heat Transfer Model for Subcooled Boiling Flow[J]. International Journal of Heat and Mass Transfer, vol 48: 4161-4173.

SUN H, LI R, CEHNIER E, et al, 2012. On the Modeling of Aiding Mixed Convection in Vertical Channels

[J]. International Journal of Heat and Mass Transfer, 48(7): 1125-1134.

TAYLOR R A, 2012. Socioeconomic Impacts of Heat Transfer Research[J]. International Communications in Heat and Mass Transfer, 39(10): 1467-1473.

TAYLOR R A, 2011. Applicability of Nanofluids in High Flux Solar Collectors[J]. Journal of Renewable and Sustainable Energy, 3(2): 1-8.

TORREGROSA A, OLMEDA P, BROATCH A, et al, 2006. A Concise Wall Temperature Model for DI Diesel Engines[J]. Applied Thermal Engineering, 26(11-12): 1320-1327.

WAGONER G, BACON R, 1989. Elastic Constants and Thermal Expansion Coefficients of Various Carbon Fibers[J]. Extended Abstracts of 19th Biennial Carbon Conference: 296-297.

WANG X J, et al, 2013. Thermal Conductivity of High-Modulus Polymer Fibers[J]. Macromolecules, 46 (12): 4937-4943.

WANG Y C, et al, 2012. An Experimental Study of Mechanical Properties of Fiber-Reinforced Polymers and Steel-Reinforcing Bars at Elevated Temperatures[J]. Composites and Structures, 80(1): 131-140.

WELTY J R, et al, 2007. Fundamental of Momentum, Heat and Mass Transfer[M]. 5th Edition, John Wiley and Sons, New York, NY, USA.

WILLIAMSON M, MAJUMDAR A, 1992. Effect of Surface Deformations on Contact Conductance[J]. Journal of Heat Transfer, 114(4): 802-810.

YALVAC S, TATISTCHEFF E M, 1989. An Analytical Model for Estimating the Coefficient of Thermal Expansion of Random Fiber Reinforced Composites[J]. Journal of Reinforced Plastics and Composites, 8 (5): 472-483.

YOKOTA H, et al, 1999. Computer Simulation for Estimating the Effective Thermal Conductivity of Composite Materials[J]. Japan J. of Thermophysical Properties, 13: 240-245.

YOVANOVICH M M, 1981. New Contact and Gap Correlations for Conforming Rough Surfaces[J]. AIAA-81-1164, AIAA 16th Thermophysics Conference, Palo Alto, CA., June.

ZIEHER F, LANGMAYR F, JELATANCEV A, et al, 2005. Thermal Mechanical Fatigue Simulation of Cast Iron Cylinder Heads[J]. SAE 2005-01-0796.

ZIMMER M., et al, 2012. Through-Thickness Thermal Conductivity Prediction Study on Nanocomposites and Multiscale Composites[J]. Materials Sciences and Applications, 3(3): 131-138.

Table 11.1.1　Coefficients of Linear Thermal Expansion, α (μm/m/℃), of Generic Automotive Materials at Room Temperature

Plastics	Metals	Ceramics	Diamond	Quartz	YbGaHe
$\alpha > 50$	$10 < \alpha < 30$	$3 < \alpha < 10$	$\alpha < 1$	$\alpha \approx 0.5$	$\alpha \approx 0$

Table 11.1.2　Thermal Conductivities and Convective Heat Transfer Coefficients of Fluids

Material	T(State)/℃	Convection	$h/(\mathrm{W \cdot m^{-2} \cdot ℃^{-1}})$	$k/(\mathrm{W \cdot m^{-1} \cdot ℃^{-1}})$
Air	23	Free	$5 \sim 25$	0.026
	23	Forced	$10 \sim 200$	—
Water	23	Free	$20 \sim 100$	—
	23	Forced	$50 \sim 10^4$	—
	100 (Boiling)		$3 \times 10^3 \sim 10^5$	—
	Condensed water vapor		$5 \times 10^3 \sim 10^5$	—
Water (Deionzied)	23	—	—	—
	55	$V = 0.157$ m/s	3046	—
		$V = 0.314$ m/s	4929	—
		$V = 0.471$ m/s	6865	—
		$V = 0.628$ m/s	9037	—
		$V = 0.785$ m/s	12872	—
		$V = 0.942$ m/s	16714	—
Silicone Oil	23	—	—	—
	55	$V = 0.157$ m/s	709	—
		$V = 0.314$ m/s	1222	—
		$V = 0.471$ m/s	1714	—
		$V = 0.628$ m/s	2058	—
		$V = 0.785$ m/s	2708	—
		$V = 0.942$ m/s	2984	—
Water (Deionzied) Silicone Coil (75%/25%)	23	—	—	—
	55	$V = 0.157$ m/s	4023	—
		$V = 0.314$ m/s	7186	—
		$V = 0.471$ m/s	9553	—
		$V = 0.628$ m/s	13238	—
		$V = 0.785$ m/s	18490	—
		$V = 0.942$ m/s	20313	—

Table 11.1.3 Data of Radiative Emissivities of Commonly Used Materials

Material	$T(\text{K}/℃)$	Polished	Oxidized	Weathered	Anodized	General
Metals:						
Ag	310(27 ℃)	0.02	0.04	—	—	—
Al	310(27 ℃)	0.04	0.11	0.40 (24-ST)	0.94 (at 538 ℃)	—
	530(347 ℃)	0.05	0.12	0.32 (24-ST)	0.42 (at 538 ℃)	—
	800(517 ℃)	0.08	0.18	0.27 (24-ST)	0.60 (at 538 ℃)	—
Al Foil	310(27 ℃)	—	—	—	—	0.03
Cu	310(27 ℃)	0.04	0.87	—	—	—
Non-Metals:						
Asphalt	310 (27 ℃)	—	—	—	—	0.88
Brick	310 (27 ℃)	—	—	—	—	0.90
Glass	310 (27 ℃)	—	—	—	—	0.95
H_2O-Ice	310 (27 ℃)	—	—	—	—	0.97
H_2O-Snow	310 (27 ℃)	—	—	—	—	0.85
H_2O-Water	310 (27 ℃)	—	—	—	—	0.96

Table 11.1.4 Example Data of Temperature Boundary Conditions and Heat Transfer Coefficients for Calculating Temperature Distribution of a Diesel Engine Valve[Sharmal et al.]

(a) Temperature B. C.	Full Load	3/4 Load	Half Load	No Load
T_g(Gas side)	1000	800	600	400
T_s(Valve seat side)	300	120	120	120
T_a(Air side)	25	25	25	25
T_b(Bush side)	80	80	80	80
T_{ex}(Exhaust gas side)	290	270	250	230
(b) Heat Transfer Coefficient	Full Load	3/4 Load	Half Load	No Load
h_g(Gas side)	290	232.5	203.48	174.4
h_w(Water side)	1859.2	1859.2	1859.2	1859.2
h_a(Air side)	23	23	23	23
h_b(Bush side)	1745	1745	1745	1745
h_{ex}(Exhaust gas side)	175	175	175	175

Notes: Units for the temperature and heat transfer coefficient are ℃ and $\text{W}/(\text{m}^2 \cdot ℃)$, respectively.

Chapter 12

Moisture Diffusion

12.1　Moisture Concentration

Plastics, rubber and wood expand when they are exposed to moisture and the content of moisture at equilibrium increases with an increasing temperature. When moisture absorption takes place in a constrained part, mechanical strains and the corresponding stresses will build up due to moisture expansion. These are called hygroscopic stresses. Similarly, hygroscopic stresses also build up in a composite made of different constituents due to the mismatches in their swelling coefficients of linear moisture expansion.

12.1.1　Driving Force for Moisture Diffusion

The driving force for moisture diffusion results from the gradient in the moisture concentration. $C_m = C_m(x_1, x_2, x_3, t)$, the mixture weight fraction content in percentile (%), is defined as

$$C_m = \frac{100(W - W_{dry})}{W_{dry}} \quad (\% \text{ by weight}) \tag{12.1.1}$$

where
C_m: Moisture concentration at time t, i.e., $C_m = C_m(t)$;
W: Weight of the sample at time t, i.e., $W = W(t)$;
W_{dry}: Dry weight.

Saturated moisture concentration $C_{m,sat}$, also called equilibrium moisture content, has the same physical meaning as solubility. Its value is typically a constant as a material property, when water immersion conditioning is applied. The saturated moisture concentration is a function of temperature and moist condition. It is in an exponential relationship with relative humidity (H_R) if the humid air conditioning is applied. Mathematically,

$$C_{m,sat} = \text{Constant} \quad (\text{Liquid Immersion}) \tag{12.1.2}$$

and

$$C_{m,sat} = a \ (H_R)^b \quad (\text{Humid Air}) \tag{12.1.3}$$

where H_R is the relative humidity. Coefficient a and exponent b are material constants to be determined experimentally. For example, $a = 3.3225$ and $b = 1.3402$ for epoxy adhesive FM-300 [Huo et al.], i.e.,

$$C_{m,sat} = 3.3225 \ H_R^{1.3402} \quad (\text{Humid Air}) \tag{12.1.4}$$

Note that FM-300 is widely used as the adhesive layer for "gluing" two composite laminae together.

12.1.2   Influence of Moisture Content on Mechanical Properties

Plastics and natural materials are subject to water sorption and their mechanical performances deteriorate with the increasing moisture content. Studies of moisture ageing of polymeric composites have shown that hydrothermal exposures have great impact on the strengths of fibers, matrix, and their interface. When water molecules diffuse into thermoplastic polymers it acts as a plasticizer where they pose in a free state. Plasticization softens the matrix and lowers its glass transition temperature, modulus of elasticity, and mechanical strength. On the other hand, long-term ageing of some thermoset plastics such as epoxy [Zhou & Lucas], water molecules can bond strongly with the polymer chains and render additional cross-linking that increases the glass transition temperature and hardens the modulus of elasticity.

Since the mechanics properties of plastics are greatly influenced by the level of moisture, it is important to analyze properties at various moisture levels and working temperature. As shown in Fig. 12.1.1, both the tensile modulus and yield strength in tension of Nylon-6 reduce nonlinearly with respect to the water content [Jia & Kagan]. Thus, the effect of moisture can be a major factor in products that were exposed to different environmental conditions, in contrast to which molded specimens are usually sealed in special bags to preserve their dry-as-molded state while the moisture content remains approximately at 0.2%.

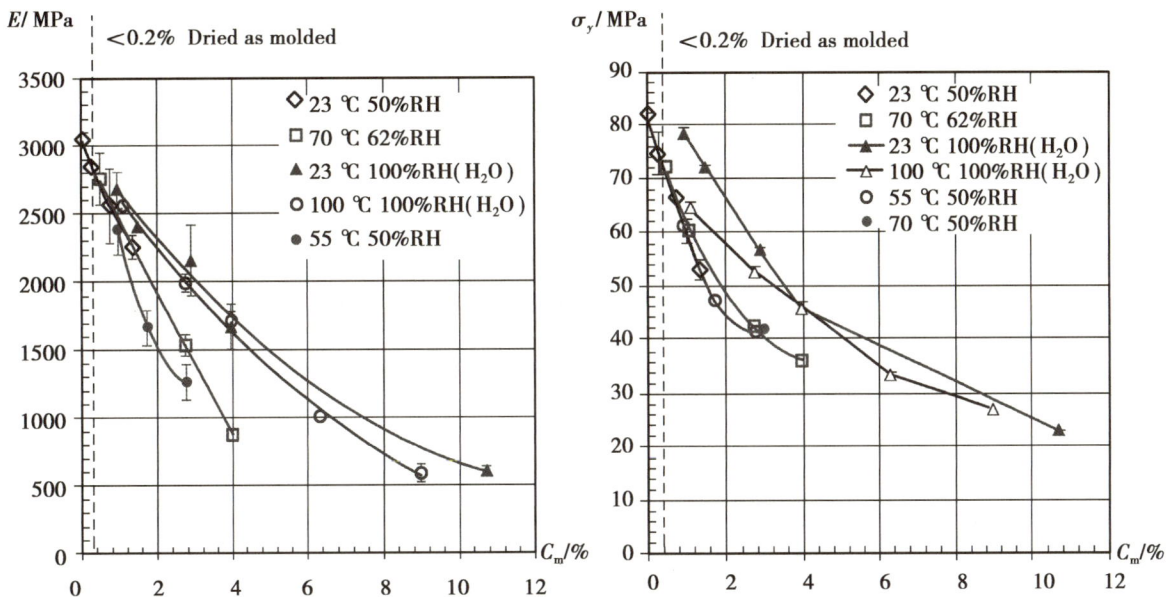

Fig. 12.1.1   Tensile Modulus of Elasticity and Yield Strength of PA-6 as a Function of Moisture Content [BASF]

Carbon fibers are reportedly inert to humid environments [Liao et al.], while glass fibers are sensitive to moisture exposure. The strength decrease of glass fiber typically results from surface corrosion through an ion exchange mechanism [Schmitz]. Water has been found to accelerate the rate of crack growth in glass fibers because water not only reduces the surface fracture energy of the glass fiber but also reduces the energy required to break the Si-O bond [Michalske & Bunker].

Polymers and their interfaces with other materials exhibit a wide range of responses to hygrothermal exposure that reflects the diversity of chemical and structural effects.

12.2 Moisture Diffusivities of Absorption

For homogeneous materials and orthotropic composites, the moisture diffusion follows Fick's second law of diffusion,

$$\frac{\partial C_m}{\partial t} = \frac{\partial \left[D_{ij} \left(\frac{\partial C_m}{\partial x_j} \right) \right]}{\partial x_i} \tag{12.2.1}$$

where

x_i or x_j (mm or m): Cartesian coordinates in 3-dimensional space;

D_{ij} (mm^2/s or m^2/s): Diffusivity or diffusion coefficient;

i: Index, ranging from 1 to 3;

j: Index, ranging from 1 to 3;

t(s): Time.

The analytical solution to Eq. (12.2.1) can be obtained using the method of separation of variables and the moisture content varies as a function of time. At the initial stages of the diffusion process, it obeys Fick's law. Fick's law that governs moisture diffusion is similar to Fourier's law that governs heat transfer. The difference between heat transfer and mass diffusion is the continuity of primary variables, or saying temperature versus moisture concentration, at the interface for layered multi-material system.

The temperature distribution is always continuous at the interface between different materials for heat transfer, while the moisture concentration is discontinuous at the interface of different materials for moisture diffusion due to different saturated moisture concentrations for different materials.

12.2.1 Moisture Diffusivities of 3-Dimensional Orthotropic Composites

For an orthotropic composite the moisture diffusivities are aligned with primary fiber orientations, i.e., 1- longitudinal, 2- transverse, and 3- out-of-plane, and Eq. (12.2.1) is explicitly expressed as

$$\frac{\partial C_m}{\partial t} = \frac{\partial \left[D_{11}\left(\frac{\partial C_m}{\partial x_1} \right) \right]}{\partial x_1} + \frac{\partial \left[D_{22}\left(\frac{\partial C_m}{\partial x_2} \right) \right]}{\partial x_2} + \frac{\partial \left[D_{33}\left(\frac{\partial C_m}{\partial x_3} \right) \right]}{\partial x_3} \tag{12.2.2}$$

or

$$\frac{\partial C_m}{\partial t} = D_{11}\left(\frac{\partial^2 C_m}{\partial x_1^2} \right) + D_{22}\left(\frac{\partial^2 C_m}{\partial x_2^2} \right) + D_{33}\left(\frac{\partial^2 C_m}{\partial x_3^2} \right) \tag{12.2.3}$$

where

$D_{11}(\text{mm}^2/\text{s}, \text{m}^2/\text{s})$: Diffusivity along the primary material axis;

$D_{22}(\text{mm}^2/\text{s}, \text{m}^2/\text{s})$: Diffusivity along the in-plane transverse axis;

$D_{33}(\text{mm}^2/\text{s}, \text{m}^2/\text{s})$: Diffusivity in through-thickness (out-of-plane) direction.

Moisture diffusivities D_{11}, D_{22}, and D_{33} are material properties and they are not direction-dependent anymore in Eq. (12.2.3) for isotropic materials, while they are in Eq. (12.2.2). They may be expressed in terms of the fiber and matrix diffusion coefficients by the rule of mixture for a unidirectional lamina as

$$D_{11} = D_f V_f + D_m V_m \tag{12.2.4}$$

and

$$D_{22} = D_{33} = D_m \, f(D_f, D_m, V_f, V_m) \tag{12.2.5}$$

where

$D_f(\text{mm}^2/\text{s}, \text{m}^2/\text{s})$: Diffusivity of fiber, e.g. glass fiber;

$D_m(\text{mm}^2/\text{s}, \text{m}^2/\text{s})$: Diffusivity of matrix, e.g. epoxy;

V_f: Volume fraction of fiber;

V_m: Volume fraction of matrix.

For glass and carbon fiber reinforcements for most automotive composites, D_f is negligible compared with D_m. Thus the above two equations reduce to [Roe et al.]

$$D_{11} = D_m V_m \tag{12.2.6}$$

and

$$D_{22} = D_{33} = D_m \left[1 - 2\left(\frac{V_f}{\pi} \right)^{\frac{1}{2}} \right] \tag{12.2.7}$$

12.2.2　Retardation of Moisture Diffusion in Fiber-Reinforced Composites

The diffusion coefficients in a unidirectional fiber reinforced lamina are orthotropic and they are fiber orientation-dependent. These coefficients may be expressed in terms of the fiber and matrix diffusion coefficients by the rule of mixture, using an analogy with thermal conductivity, as shown by Eqs. (12.2.4)-(12.2.7). The contrasts of moisture diffusion of composite resins to their respective corresponding fiber-reinforced composites are demonstrated in Figs. 12.2.1 and 12.2.2.

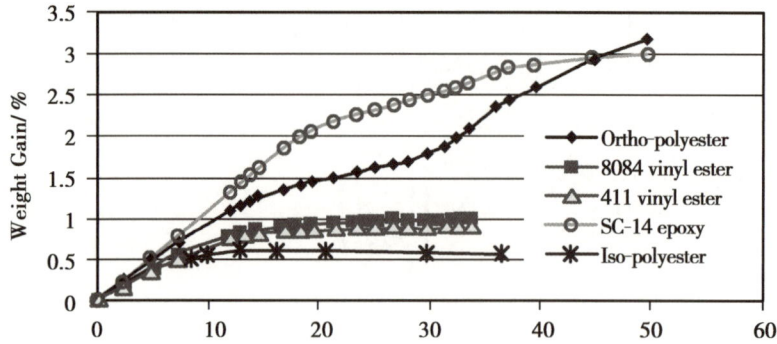

Fig. 12.2.1   Moisture Diffusion into Different Composite Resins

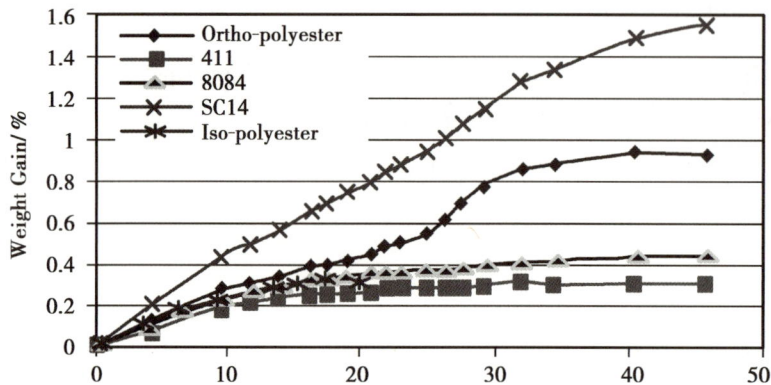

Fig. 12.2.2   Moisture Diffusion into Composites Reinforced with Fibers

Composites reinforced with natural fibers exhibit higher diffusivities than the counterparts reinforced with synthetic fibers. Addition of natural fibers to composite leads to a higher rate of swelling and higher degree of water absorption due to an increase in the cellulose content. For hybrid composites the layer sequence has an effect on moisture gain, and subsequently on tensile and impact properties.

12.2.3   Thin Laminae

If a classical closed form solution is required for a lamina immersed in a solution (e.g. water), then its averaged out-of-plane (through-thickness) diffusion coefficient may be calculated without sophisticated finite element analysis [Huo et al.], instead applying the following approximating equation [Roe et al.]

$$D_{33,\text{ave}} = D_{33}\left[1 + \left(\frac{h_3}{h_1}\right)\left(\frac{D_{11}}{D_{33}}\right)^{\frac{1}{2}} + \left(\frac{h_3}{h_2}\right)\left(\frac{D_{22}}{D_{33}}\right)^{\frac{1}{2}}\right]^2 \tag{12.2.8}$$

where h_1, h_2, and h_3 are length, width, and thickness of the lamina, respectively. D_{22} and D_{33} are supposedly the same if it is a uniform lamina (i.e., transversely isotropic). Note that the moisture diffusion contribution from edges, called the edge correction factor, has been taken into consideration in the above equation.

Assume that there is no voids (i.e., $V_f = 1 - V_m$), then D_{11} and D_{22} as a function of V_f can be tabulated using Eqs. (12.2.6) and (12.2.7) such as

$V_f(=1-V_m)$	D_{11}	D_{22}
10%	$0.9D_m$	$0.643D_m$
20%	$0.8D_m$	$0.495D_m$
30%	$0.7D_m$	$0.382D_m$
40%	$0.6D_m$	$0.286D_m$
50%	$0.5D_m$	$0.202D_m$

Eq. (12.2.8) is valid for thin plates. When the finite element method is employed for predicting the moisture concentration of a plate having a significant thickness, the boundary conditions of moisture diffusivities have to be modified accordingly [Huo et al.] such as

$$D_{33,ave} = D_{33} h(h_1, h_2, h_3) P(C_m) \tag{12.2.9}$$

where

P: Pattern function of diffusivity as a function of nodal moisture concentration;

$h(mm)$: Thickness factor, e.g. edge correction factor.

Parameter $h(h_1, h_2, h_3)$ is to be determined experimentally in order to properly denote the dependence of diffusivity on the specimen thickness (h_3) and the other two dimensions (h_1 & h_2). Pattern parameter $P(C_m)$ describes the diffusion activity at two different stages. When nodal moisture concentration increases in the low moisture stage, the diffusivity decreases significantly. It gradually reaches a constant value, as the moisture concentration gets to the material solubility value.

On the composite high-voltage insulators for replacing ceramics, vinyl ester performs better than epoxy with regard to water absorption while both perform far better than polyester. The diffusivities of these three plastics reinforced with E-glass fibers [Kumosa et al.] with edge correction factors are given in Table 12.2.1.

12.2.4   Moisture Diffusivities of Homogeneous Material

The diffusivity of homogeneous material is generally regarded to be dependent only upon temperature, as expressed in the Arrhenius-type equation [Loh et al.]:

$$D_m = D_{mo} \exp\left[\frac{-Q_d}{R T_k}\right] \tag{12.2.10}$$

where

$D_{mo}(\text{mm}^2/\text{s})$: Diffusivity coefficient, a constant;

$Q_d(\text{J/mol})$: Activation energy for diffusion;

$R(= 8.314 \text{ J}/(\text{mole} \cdot \text{°C}))$: Universal gas constant;

$T_k(\text{K})$: Temperature in Kelvin.

When the moisture absorption of a material follows the above Arrhenius equation, it is called Fickian moisture diffusion. It signifies that for reactants to diffuse into base products, they must first acquire a minimum amount of energy, called the activation energy Q_d. For example, $D_{mo} = 9.2166 \text{ m}^2/\text{s}$ and $Q_d/R = 5523.3$ for water to pervade epoxy adhesive FM-300 [Huo et al.], i.e.,

$$D_m = 9.2166 \exp\left(\frac{-5523.3}{T_k}\right) \tag{12.2.11}$$

Eqs. (12.2.3)-(12.2.11) can be used for calculating moisture diffusions of a unidirectional lamina in the material axis system. Some example moisture-diffusion curves are illustrated in Fig. 12.2.3. In both unsaturated and saturated conditions, the moisture concentration at the interface of a layered bi-material system is not necessarily continuous.

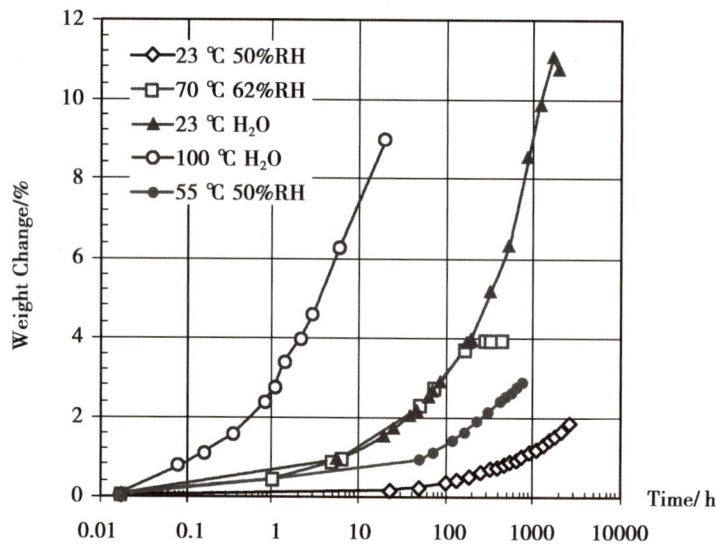

Fig. 12.2.3 Water Diffusion into Injection-Molded PA6/33GF Composite (33% GF by Weight) [Jia et al.] [BASF]

In natural materials, the change of moisture content often leads to storage of water between the fibers, causing a significant swelling of wood transverse to the fiber direction. An approximating equation for the saturated (equilibrium) concentration of moisture of wood given by [Eckelman] is

$$C_{m,sat} = \left[\frac{-\ln(1 - H_R)}{8.1 \times 10^{-5}(T + 273.3)}\right]^{0.638} \quad (\% \text{ by weight}) \tag{12.2.12}$$

where

$C_{m,sat}$: Saturated concentration of moisture, of which the unit is % by weight;

H_R : Relative humidity, $H_R = 0.5$, which means 50% relative humidity;

$T(\,^\circ\!C\,)$: Temperature.

Example 12.2.1   Given that $H_R = 50\%$, how much is the moisture concentration after a 24-hour test (ASTM D 570 or ISO-62), for this red wood at room temperature (23 ℃)?

Solution:

$$
C_{m,sat} = \left\{ \left[\frac{-\ln(1 - H_R)}{8.1 \times 10^{-5}(T + 273.15)} \right]^{0.638} \right\}\% = \left\{ \left[\frac{-\ln(1 - 50\%)}{8.1 \times 10^{-5}(23 + 273.15)} \right]^{0.638} \right\}\%
$$

$$
= 8.55\%
$$

12.2.5   Thin-Film Diffusion

Plastics used in enclosures of electronic devices consist of flexible polymer chains, which have spaces between the chains as free voids within a plastic. Moisture diffusion in epoxy molding compounds (EMCs) is one of the major reliability concerns in plastic-encapsulated microcircuits (PEMs). The difference between the external and internal relative humidity (RH) environments of the device provides the diffusion mechanism for water vapor ingress. Once ambient air containing moisture is trapped in the device during assembly, a temperature drop during shipping or storage can yield water vapor condensation within the device, which may pervade the plastic housing either through structural defects or via direct permeation through the polymer material.

Long term moisture exposure has been shown to affect the mechanical performance of polymeric composite structures. Moisture diffusion is so slow in plastic composites reinforced with carbon or glass fibers that thin parts may reach moisture equilibrium while thick parts will never become fully soaked. Consider a thin plate (e.g. PCB) having a uniform through-thickness moisture diffusion, as depicted in Fig. 12.2.4. For a one-dimensional case involving a single diffusion parameter, Eq. (12.2.3) reduces to

$$
\frac{\partial C_m(z,\ t)}{\partial t} = D_{zz} \left[\frac{\partial^2 C_m(z,t)}{\partial z^2} \right] \tag{12.2.13}
$$

where a material of thickness h is exposed to moisture at the boundaries $z = 1/2H$ and $z = -1/2H$. Corresponding to the governing equation, Eq. (12.2.13), there are three boundary conditions, one initial condition, and one finial condition, which are described as follows:

(a) Boundary conditions:

$$
\frac{\partial C_m(0,t)}{\partial z} = 0 \tag{12.2.14}
$$

$$C_m\left(\frac{1}{2}h,t\right) = C_{m,sat} \tag{12.2.15}$$

$$C_m\left(-\frac{1}{2}h,t\right) = C_{m,sat} \tag{12.2.16}$$

(b) Initial condition: $\quad C_m(z,0) = C_0 \tag{12.2.17}$

(c) Final condition: $\quad C_m(z, t_{sat}) = C_{m,sat} \tag{12.2.18}$

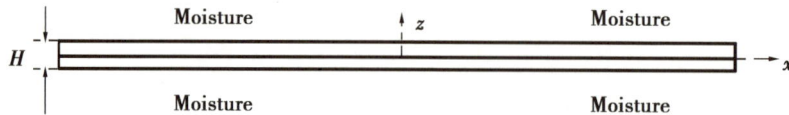

Fig. 12.2.4   One-Dimensional Moisture Diffusion in a Uniform Through-Thickness Thin Plate

Saturated moisture content $C_{m,sat}$ is the equilibrium moisture concentration resulting from the final asymptotic value on the diffusion curve. Applying the separation-of-variables method and the boundary and initial/final conditions, one can obtain the solution to Eq. (12.2.13) as

$$C_m(z,t) - C_0 = (C_{m,sat} - C_0)\left\{1 - \frac{4}{\pi}\sum_{n=0}^{\infty}\frac{(-1)^n}{2n+1}e^{\frac{-D_m(2n+1)^2\pi^2 t}{4H^2}}\cos\left[\frac{(2n+1)\pi z}{2H}\right]\right\} \tag{12.2.19}$$

The moisture concentration, $C_m(z,t)$, at any particular depth can be determined at each time step based on the above one-dimensional moisture diffusion model. A plot of $C_m(z,t)$ versus $t^{\frac{1}{2}}$, based on the relationship described by Eq. (12.2.19), yields an asymptotic curve as shown in Fig. 12.2.5. Assume that the initial moisture content is zero, i.e., $C_m(z, 0)$. Eq. (12.2.19) can then be integrated along the thickness ($z=-1/2H$ to $z=1/2H$) of the thin film in bulky mode to obtain the mass change,

$$m_m(t) = m_{m,sat}\left\{1 - \frac{8}{\pi^2}\sum_{n=0}^{\infty}(2n+1)^{-2}\exp\left[\frac{-D_m(2n+1)^2\pi^2 t}{4H^2}\right]\right\} \tag{12.2.20}$$

where

m_m: Mass of moisture absorbed in the thin film at time t;

$m_{m,sat}$: Mass of the thin film with saturated concentration of moisture.

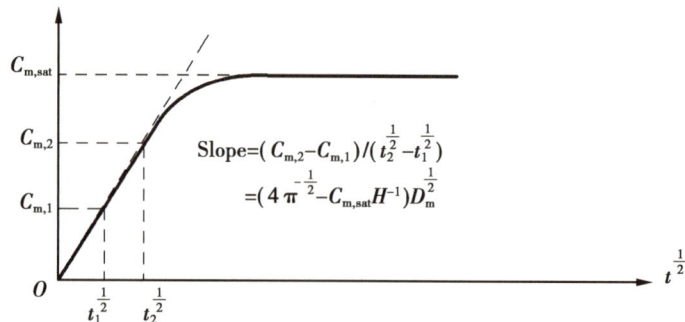

Fig. 12.2.5   Asymptotic Moisture Diffusion via Material Voids: Fickian Behavior

The use of 20 summands as given in the above equation is considered sufficient [ISO], i.e., $\infty \approx$ 20 here. The absolute weight gain of the sample may be calculated as a function of time after the moisture concentration is obtained. In general, the moisture mass absorbed in the early stage is much less than the saturated mass, i.e., $m_{\mathrm{m}}(t) < 1/2 m_{\mathrm{m,sat}}$. Then, Eq. (12.2.20) reduces to [Shirangi et al.]

$$m_{\mathrm{m}}(t) = 4\left(\frac{D_{\mathrm{m}} t}{\pi H^2}\right)^{\frac{1}{2}} m_{\mathrm{m,sat}} \tag{12.2.21}$$

12.2.6   Determination of Diffusivities

The diffusion coefficient D_{m} can be determined experimentally from the initial linear region of the Fickian diffusion curve starting from $t = 0^+$ at a fixed temperature as shown in Fig. 12.2.5. Enlightened by Eq. (12.2.21), which shows a measure of $m_{\mathrm{m}}(t)/m_{\mathrm{m,sat}}$ with respect to $t^{\frac{1}{2}}$, one can have the slope at the very starting point as

$$\text{Slope} = 4\left(\frac{D_{\mathrm{m}} t}{\pi H^2}\right)^{\frac{1}{2}} \tag{12.2.22}$$

In the mean while one can derive the "2-point" slope as $(C_{\mathrm{m,2}} - C_{\mathrm{m,1}})/\left(t_2^{\frac{1}{2}} - t_1^{\frac{1}{2}}\right)$, by arbitrarily taking two points as shown in Fig. 12.2.5. Equating the "2-point" slope to the initial slope leads to

$$D_{\mathrm{m}} = \left[\frac{\pi^{\frac{1}{2}} h(C_{\mathrm{m,2}} - C_{\mathrm{m,1}})}{4\left(t_2^{\frac{1}{2}} - t_1^{\frac{1}{2}}\right) C_{\mathrm{m,sat}}}\right]^2 = \frac{\pi H^2}{16 C_{\mathrm{m,sat}}^2}\left[\frac{C_{\mathrm{m,2}} - C_{\mathrm{m,1}}}{t_2^{\frac{1}{2}} - t_1^{\frac{1}{2}}}\right]^2 \tag{12.2.23}$$

where
$C_{\mathrm{m,1}}$: Moisture uptake at time t_1;
$C_{\mathrm{m,2}}$: Moisture uptake at time t_2;
H: Thickness of the thin plate (e.g. PCB);
$C_{\mathrm{m,sat}}$: Saturated moisture content.

Diffusivity D_{m} of Eq. (12.2.20) applies to an infinite sheet of fixed thickness only, while it is also a function of temperature as shown in Eq. (12.2.11). Since the sample's length and width are not significantly large when compared to the thickness for some applications, a correction is required for including the effect of the increased uptake due to the open sides. The ratios of the width (W) and the length (L), to the thickness (h) of specimens used in moisture absorption tests are preferably larger than 100 according to the ASTM standard [ASTM]. The corrected diffusivity is to be approximated using the "apparent diffusivity", $\check{D}_m$, that can be obtained from the "thick-plate" diffusion test of a plate of length L, width W, and thickness h [Springer] as

$$D_m = \frac{\check{D}_m}{\left(1 + \dfrac{H}{W} + \dfrac{H}{L}\right)^2} \tag{12.2.24}$$

or

$$D_m = \frac{\dfrac{\pi H^2}{16 C_{m,sat}^2}\left[\dfrac{C_{m,2} - C_{m,1}}{t_2^{\frac{1}{2}} - t_1^{\frac{1}{2}}}\right]^2}{\left(1 + \dfrac{H}{W} + \dfrac{H}{L}\right)^2} \tag{12.2.25}$$

Note that Eq. (12.2.11) has to be utilized instead of the above equation if the diffusivities along the primary material axes (i.e., D_{11}, D_{22} and D_{33}) are known.

12.2.7 Coating Diffusion of Circular Fibers

Assume that the optical fiber consists of two layers. Namely, a solid circular glass fiber of radius a surrounded by plastic coating of radius b. Because the fiber is cylindrically symmetric, the moisture content in the plastics coating can be represented by $C_m(r,t)$, where r is the radius and t is time. For calculating how the moisture pervades the plastic coating, the boundary conditions for such a geometric configuration can be configured as follows:

(1) External moisture concentration kept constant:

$$C_m(b,t) = C_{m,b} \tag{12.2.26}$$

(2) Impermeable glass/plastics interface:

$$\frac{\partial C_m(a, t)}{\partial r} = 0 \tag{12.2.27}$$

where

a: Radius of the solid glass fiber or inner radius of the plastic coating;

b: External radius of the plastic coating;

$C_{m,b}$: Moisture content at the external boundary of plastic coating.

The solution to the governing equation, Eq. (12.2.13), for the diffusion problem with the above two corresponding boundary conditions in cylindrical symmetry is [Crank]

$$1 - \frac{C_m(r,t)}{C_{m,b}} = \pi \sum_{n=1}^{\infty} \left\{\frac{Y_0(r\,\alpha_n)J_1(a\,\alpha_n) - J_0(r\,\alpha_n)Y_1(a\,\alpha_n)}{J_0(b\,\alpha_n)^2 - J_1(a\,\alpha_n)^2}\right\} \tag{12.2.28}$$

where J_i and Y_i are Bessel functions of order i, $i = 0$, 1, $\cdots$, ∞, α_n is the nth positive root of the following equation.

$$Y_0(b\,\alpha)J_1(a\,\alpha) - J_0(b\,\alpha)Y_1(a\,\alpha) = 0 \tag{12.2.29}$$

Note that the boundary condition given by Eq. (12.2.26) may not hold for the reality, since a wetted plastic coating can be in adjacent contact to dry glass. $C_m(a, t)$ has to be known as a boundary condition as a function of time. The effective concentration of water vapor can be obtained from strength tests at the interface, because the ultimate strength (σ_{us}) of the fiber coating at the interface depends on the level of the moisture content in situation, as proposed by [Mrotek et al.]

$$\sigma_{us} = A + B\,e^{-CC_m} \tag{12.2.30}$$

where

A: Constant;

B: Coefficient;

C: Exponent coefficient.

Moisture diffusion into a composite via its matrix resin leads to material degradation including lowering the glass transition temperature (T_g), reducing the tensile strength, and softening the stiffness. Furthermore, it can aggravate the interfacial bonding between fibers and the matrix [Schultheisz et al.]. A plot of the tensile strength of three different kinds of coating materials, i.e., silicone, acrylate and polyimide, is presented in Fig. 12.2.6.

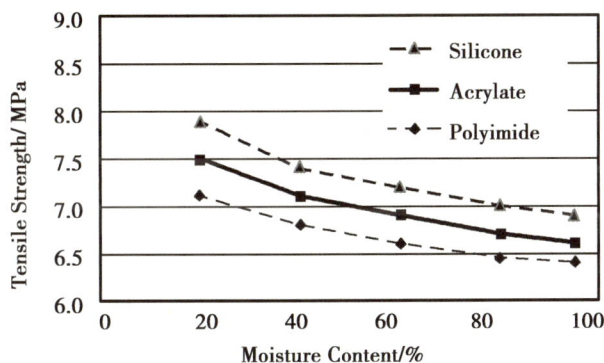

Fig. 12.2.6   Tensile Strength of Plastic Coatings of Optical Fiber as a Function of Moisture Content [**Mrotek et al.**]

12.3   Non-Fickian Moisture Absorption

Thermoset polymers frequently display non-fickian moisture sorption behaviors. A non-fickian sorption process involves two stages: (1) an initial linear increase with respect to the square root of time following Fick's model and then (2) a deviation from Fick's model without stabilization of the mass uptake [Yagoubi et al.]. For example, a schematic plot of moisture absorption curve of a thin EMC (Epoxy Molding Compound) disk resulting from the exposure to 85 ℃/85% RH environments is presented as the solid line in Fig. 12.3.1. The absorption process can be divided into two distinct stages [Carter & Kibler]:

(1) Voids-filling stage: The moisture diffusion in the EMC follows the Fickian law up to a point at which the water fills up the micro voids. This is called virtual saturation and the affective mechanosorptive strain is recoverable.

(2) Hydrogen-bonding stage: After the point of virtual saturation, water pervades the EMC linearly with respect to $t^{\frac{1}{2}}$ (t: time) due to the hydrogen bonding between the water and the EMC. Irrecoverable mechanosorptive strains are observed.

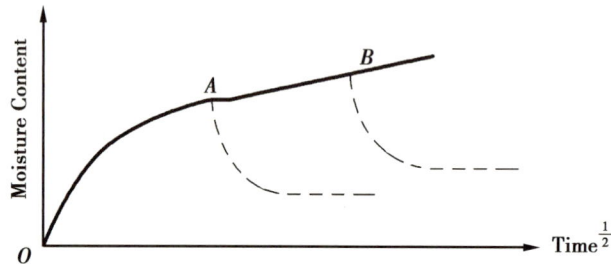

Fig. 12.3.1 **Schematic Drawing of Moisture Content of EMC (Epoxy Molding Compound) as Water Absorbing (Solid Line) and Desorbing (Dashed Line)**

A relaxation process is assumed to fit the hydrogen-bonding stage, which is the first order in terms of the moisture content difference. The differential equation for the relaxation process [Shao & Kouadio] is assumed to be

$$\frac{dC_{m,R}}{dt} = k_R(C_{m,\infty} - C_{m,R}) \tag{12.3.1}$$

where

$C_{m,R}$: Moisture content on the relaxation;

k_R: Constant as the rate of relaxation;

$C_{m,\infty}$: Moisture content at time $t = \infty$.

Note that $C_{m,\infty}$ is the moisture content at the very final moment, while $C_{m,sat}$ is the moisture content at virtual saturation. Solving Eq. (12.3.1) leads to

$$C_{m,R} = C_{m,\infty}[1 - \exp(k_R t)] \tag{12.3.2}$$

Let's consider a thin plate again. Assume that the moisture content resulting from both processes

(void filling and hydrogen bonding) are additive, then the total moisture content is to be obtained from Eqs. (12.2.18) and (12.3.2) by superposition,

$$C_{\mathrm{m}}(z,t) - C_0 = (C_{\mathrm{m,sat}} - C_0)\left\{1 - \frac{4}{\pi}\sum_{n=0}^{\infty}\frac{(-1)^n}{2n+1}\mathrm{e}^{\frac{-D_{\mathrm{m}}(2n+1)^2\pi^2 t}{4h^2}}\cos\frac{(2n+1)\pi z}{2h}\right\} + C_{\mathrm{m},\infty}[1 - \exp(k_{\mathrm{R}}t)]$$

$$(12.3.3)$$

12.4   Moisture Diffusivities of Desorption

Materials lose their moisture content when the environmental temperature rises or the environmental humidity is lowered. This process is called desorption. "Sorption" means absorption and/or desorption existing in the process.

Samples of EMC (epoxy molding compound) with a higher starting moisture content ends with a higher final residual content after desorption [Shirangi et al.], as depicted in Fig. 12.3.1 using the dashed lines. One desorption curve starts before the virtual saturation and the other starts after the virtual saturation. A significant permanent deformation of the sample dimensions may occur due to such irreversible residual moisture content.

An experiment conducted on moisture absorption for EMCs at 85℃/85% RH showed that moisture absorption experiences a two-stage diffusion process. Moisture absorption exhibits both distinct sorption mechanisms: mobile fluid and bound fluid in the material. The latter is called the non-Fickian diffusion process, which is nonreversible even by the immediate followed desorption at the same temperature, at least for a period of 2 weeks according to some experiments done by [Fan et al.]. However, desorption at a higher temperature, falling between 100-260 ℃, causes more bound water removed; modeling of experimental data from [Placette et al.] shows that it follows Fickian diffusion in reflow process.

12.5   Moisture Diffusivities of Fibrous Composites

Reductions in mechanical performance and fatigue life of a fibrous composite due to moisture exposure must be accounted for in the product design stage.

12.5.1   Moisture Diffusivities of Laminae with Continuous Unidirectional Fibers

The mechanical properties of a composite materials may suffer when it is exposed to moisture for a prolonged period of time. In the case the thickness of the specimen is within an applicable limits, namely ranging from 0.5-8 mm. The predictive equations given by [Shen & Springer] are listed as follows:

$$D_{11} = D_m(1 - v_f) \tag{12.5.1}$$

and

$$D_{22} = D_{33} = D_m\left[1 - 2\left(\frac{v_f}{\pi}\right)^{\frac{1}{2}}\right] \tag{12.5.2}$$

where D_m is the diffusivity of the matrix. Experimentally D_m can be determined using the following equation [Shen & Springer] [Carter & Kibler]

$$D_A = D_x\left\{\left[\left(\frac{h_2}{h_1}\right)\left(\frac{D_y}{D_x}\right)^{\frac{1}{2}} + \left(\frac{h_3}{h_1}\right)\left(\frac{D_z}{D_x}\right)^{\frac{1}{2}}\right]\right\}^2 \tag{12.5.3}$$

$$D_x = D_{11}\cos^2\alpha + D_{22}\sin^2\alpha \tag{12.5.4}$$

$$D_y = D_{11}\cos^2\beta + D_{22}\sin^2\beta \tag{12.5.5}$$

and

$$D_z = D_{11}\cos^2\beta + D_{22}\sin^2\gamma \tag{12.5.6}$$

where

D_m: Moisture diffusivity of the matrix;

D_A: Apparent moisture diffusivity of the lamina under test;

D_x, D_y, D_z: Moisture diffusivities of the lamina along the x-, y-, and z-axis;

h_1, h_2, h_3: Length, width, and thickness of the lamina;

α, β, γ: Angles between the Cartesian plane of a lamina and the fiber direction.

Substituting Eqs. (12.5.1) and (12.5.2) into Eqs. (12.5.4)-(12.5.5), then subsequently into Eq. (12.5.3), and taking an inverse, one has

$$D_m = D_A\left\{(1 - V_f)\cos^2\alpha + \left[1 - 2\left(\frac{V_f}{\pi}\right)^{\frac{1}{2}}\right]\sin^2\alpha\right\}^{-1}$$

$$\left\{1 + \left(\frac{h_2}{h_1}\right)\left[\frac{(1 - V_f)\cos^2\beta + \left[1 - 2\left(\frac{V_f}{\pi}\right)^{\frac{1}{2}}\right]\sin^2\beta}{(1 - V_f)\cos^2\alpha + \left[1 - 2\left(\frac{V_f}{\pi}\right)^{\frac{1}{2}}\right]\sin^2\alpha}\right]^{\frac{1}{2}} + \right.$$

$$\left. \left(\frac{h_3}{h_2}\right)\left[\frac{(1 - V_f)\cos^2\gamma + \left[1 - 2\left(\frac{V_f}{\pi}\right)^{\frac{1}{2}}\right]\sin^2\gamma}{(1 - V_f)\cos^2\alpha + \left[1 - 2\left(\frac{V_f}{\pi}\right)^{\frac{1}{2}}\right]\sin^2\alpha}\right]^{-2}\right\} \tag{12.5.7}$$

On the other hand, if D_m is known for the lamina, the apparent moisture diffusivity of a lamina can be calculated using the equation given above. According to the ASTM standard, if the ratio between the width and the thickness of a continuous unidirectional composite used in moisture absorption tests is larger than 100, the edge effect will be minimized. One typical example is PCB. In other words, the moisture diffusion process will occur essentially only in the through-thickness for a very thin fibrous lamina [ASTM] [Kumosa et al.].

12.5.2　Moisture Diffusivities of Laminae with Unidirectional Short Fibers

Assume that the moisture diffusivities of composites reinforced with aligned short fibers are the same as those for unidirectional continuous fibers. Based on the fact that the moisture diffusivity of fibers (e.g. glass or carbon) is relatively much smaller than the matrix. Thus,

$$D_{11} = D_m(1 - v_f) \qquad (12.5.8)$$

and
$$D_{22} = D_{33} = D_m\left[1 - 2\left(\frac{v_f}{\pi}\right)^{\frac{1}{2}}\right] \qquad (12.5.9)$$

12.5.3　Moisture Diffusivities of Composites Reinforced with Weaves

Finite element analysis may be conducted to obtain the moisture diffusivities (in-plane or through-thickness) for the specific weave patterns of interest.

12.5.4　Moisture Diffusivities of Laminae Reinforced with Mats

Finite element analysis may be conducted to obtain the moisture diffusivities (in-plane or through-thickness) for the specific mat patterns of interest.

12.5.5　Moisture Diffusivities of Composites Reinforced Randomly with Short Fibers

Based on the fact that the moisture diffusivity of fibers (e.g. glass or carbon) is relatively much smaller than the matrix. Then,

$$D = D_m(1 - v_f) \qquad (12.5.10)$$

where
D_m is the moisture diffusivity of the matrix.

12.5.6　Moisture Diffusivities of Composites Reinforced with Particulates or Powders

Based on the fact that the moisture diffusivitiy of particulates or powders (e.g. glass or carbon) is relatively much smaller than the matrix. Then,

$$D = D_m(1 - v_f)$$ (12.5.11)

where

D_m is the moisture diffusivity of the matrix.

12.6　Swelling Coefficients of Fibrous Composites

Moisture expansion occurs in response to increased moisture content in the material and the coefficient of linear moisture expansion is also called swelling coefficients. It is expected that the moisture causes the matrix to swell and become more compliant while the fibers passively resist the swelling stresses exerted by the matrix. Reduction in strength is generally attributed to the weakening of the interfacial bonding between the matrix and reinforcing fibers.

12.6.1　Swelling Coefficients of Laminae with Continuous Unidirectional Fibers

Swelling coefficients of a continuous fiber-reinforced lamina along and perpendicular to the fiber direction are, respectively

$$\beta_1 = \frac{\beta_f E_f V_f + \beta_m E_m V_m}{E_{11}}$$ (12.6.1)

$$\beta_2 = (1 + v_f)\beta_f V_f + (1 + v_m)\beta_m V_m - \beta_1 v_{12}$$ (12.6.2)

and　$$\beta_3 = (1 + v_f)\beta_f V_f + (1 + v_m)\beta_m V_m - \beta_1 v_{13}$$ (12.6.3)

where
β_1: Coefficient of linear moisture expansion in the 1-diretcuion;
β_2: Coefficient of linear moisture expansion in the 2-diretcuion;
β_3: Coefficient of linear moisture expansion in the 3-diretcuion;
β_f: Coefficient of linear moisture expansion of fiber;
β_m: Coefficient of linear moisture expansion of matrix.

If the moisture diffusion of fibers are much less than that of the matrix, then the above three equations reduce to

$$\beta_1 = \beta_m V_m \left(\frac{E_m}{E_{11}} \right) \tag{12.6.4}$$

$$\beta_2 = (1 + v_m) \beta_m V_m \tag{12.6.5}$$

and $\quad \beta_3 = (1 + v_m) \beta_m V_m \tag{12.6.6}$

12.6.2 Swelling Coefficients of Composites Reinforced with Unidirectional Short Fibers

In-plane and out-of-plane swelling coefficients of a lamina reinforced with unidirectional short fibers along and transverse to the fiber direction, respectively are

$$\beta_1 = \frac{\beta_f E_f V_f + \beta_m E_m V_m}{E_{11}} \tag{12.6.7}$$

$$\beta_2 = (1 + v_f) \beta_f V_f + (1 + v_m) \beta_m V_m - \beta_1 v_{12} \tag{12.6.8}$$

and $\quad \beta_3 = (1 + v_f) \beta_f V_f + (1 + v_m) \beta_m V_m - \beta_1 v_{13} \tag{12.6.9}$

Again, E_{11} given above is derived from Eq. (10.4.2).

12.6.3 Swelling Coefficients of Composites Reinforced with Weaves

Finite element analysis may be conducted to obtain the selling coefficinets (in-plane or through-thickness) for the specifice weave patterns of interest.

12.6.4 Swelling Coefficients of Laminae Reinforced with Mats

Finite element analysis may be conducted to obtain the swelling coefficients (in-plane or through-thickness) for the specifice mat patterns of interest.

12.6.5 Swelling Coefficients of Composites Reinforced Randomly with Short Fibers

The swelling coefficient of moisture expansion of a random fiber-reinforced composite is approximated using the following equation

$$\beta = \left\{ \left[V_f^{\frac{2}{3}} - V_f \left(1 - \frac{\beta_f}{\beta_m} \right) \right] \left[\frac{\frac{E_m}{E_f}}{1 - V_f^{\frac{1}{3}} \left(1 - \frac{E_m}{E_f} \right)} \right] + (1 - V_f^{\frac{2}{3}}) \left(\frac{E_m}{E_f} \right) \right\} \beta_m \tag{12.6.10}$$

12.6.6　Swelling Coefficients of Composites Reinforced with Particulates and Powders

The swelling coefficient of moisture expansion of a composite reinforced with particulates or powders is approximated using the following equation

$$\beta = \left\{ \left[V_f^{\frac{2}{3}} - V_f \left(1 - \frac{\beta_f}{\beta_m} \right) \right] \left[\frac{\frac{E_m}{E_f}}{1 - V_f^{\frac{1}{3}} \left(1 - \frac{E_m}{E_f} \right)} \right] + \left(1 - V_f^{\frac{2}{3}} \right) \left(\frac{E_m}{E_f} \right) \right\} \beta_m \qquad (12.6.11)$$

12.7　Moisture at Interface

Another concern is the moisture at interface between two dissimilar materials. The moisture absorption of water pervading the EMC at the interface between EMC and a thin copper layer (Cu/EMC) reduces the fracture toughness at the interface [Shirangi et al.]. Proper annealing after desorption may partially recover the interfacial facture toughness before the absorption reaches the saturation point. After it gets into hydrogen bonding stage beyond the virtual saturation point, the loss of interfacial fracture toughness is permanent. The following is the interfacial fracture toughness (in shear mode- Mode Ⅱ) based on 3-point bending tests at different sorption stages [Shrangi et al.]:

(1) 58.7 J/m^2: Dry.
(2) 26.3 J/m^2: Virtual saturation point.
(3) 44.9 J/m^2: Dried after virtual saturation.
(4) 28.8 J/m^2: Dried after hydrogen-bonding develops at the interface.

As demonstrated above, the recoverability depends very much on the materials. For example, the loss of interfacial fracture toughness between organo-silicate glass film stacks is recoverable [Lin et al. 2007], while the interfacial fracture toughness for epoxy-based underfill adhesive is not recoverable [Ferguson and Qu].

12.8　Finite Element Methods for Moisture Diffusion and Related Strain Analysis

As described above, the approach based on classical closed-form solutions for analyzing the time required to condition test specimens is limited, allowing only simple geometry and an assumption that the variation of diffusivity is independent of the flow path or direction. Therefore, the finite element method is desired. Finite element analysis can be conducted for complex geometric shapes, moisture diffusion pathways, and varying moisture boundary conditions at different temperature levels.

12.8.1   Moisture Contents and Temperature as Nodal Potentials

Since the temperature is a prominent factor that has influence on the moisture diffusion, the finite element formulation moisture diffusion had better include the finite element formulation for temperature as being coupled. The selection of moisture content and temperature as potentials has the advantage that the same mathematical formulation represents both diffusion transfer and capillary transfer with a single required diffusivity [Calbureanu et al.].

Let vector $\{C_m\}$ and $\{T\}$ represent the nodal moisture content and temperature in the primary material axes. Then, vectors $\{\dot{C}_m\}$ and $\{\dot{T}\}$ contains the rates of change of nodal moisture content and temperature. The finite element formulation for moisture concentration is similar to what is given in Section 11.10 for temperature. The derivation will be simplified. Assume that the 20-noded linear solid element is applied. The moisture content and temperature defined in the x, y, and z directions of the global Cartesian coordinates can be interpolated by

$$C_m = \sum_{i=1}^{20} N_i \, C_{m,i} \tag{12.8.1}$$

$$T = \sum_{i=1}^{20} N_i \, T_i \tag{12.8.2}$$

Note that C_i and T_i are discrete variables at individual nodes. Parameter N_i is the interpolation function, called shape function, that relates the discrete nodal value at node i to the continuous variable. The elemental moisture content (variable) can be obtained from nodal moisture content using the shape function, $\{N\}$, in the form of matrix as

$$\{C_m\} = \{N\} \{C_{m1} \quad C_{m2} \quad C_{m3} \quad \cdots \quad C_{m20}\}^T \tag{12.8.3}$$

and $\quad \{N\} = \{N_1 \quad N_2 \quad N_3 \quad \cdots \quad N_{20}\}$ $\hspace{2cm}$ (12.8.4)

Similarly, the elemental temperature in terms of discrete nodal temperature can be expressed as

and $\quad \{T\} = [N] \{T_1 \quad T_2 \quad T_3 \quad T_4 \quad T_5 \quad T_6 \quad T_7 \quad T_8\}^T$ $\hspace{1cm}$ (12.8.5)

Differentiating the moisture content term on the left side of Eq. (12.8.3) and the temperature term on the left side of Eq. (12.8.5) with respect to time, one has the moisture content and temperature gradients, respectively as follows

$$
\begin{Bmatrix} \dfrac{\partial C_m}{\partial x} \\[2mm] \dfrac{\partial C_m}{\partial y} \\[2mm] \dfrac{\partial C_m}{\partial z} \end{Bmatrix} = [B_T]\{C_m\} \tag{12.8.6}
$$

and

$$
\begin{Bmatrix} \dfrac{\partial T}{\partial x} \\[2mm] \dfrac{\partial T}{\partial y} \\[2mm] \dfrac{\partial T}{\partial z} \end{Bmatrix} = [B_T]\{T\} \tag{12.8.7}
$$

Matrix $[B_T]$ contains the derivatives of shape functions, as shown in Eq. (11.10.18) for 20 noded elements,

$$
\begin{Bmatrix} \dfrac{\partial T}{\partial x} \\[2mm] \dfrac{\partial T}{\partial y} \\[2mm] \dfrac{\partial T}{\partial z} \end{Bmatrix} = [L] \sum_{i=1}^{20} \begin{Bmatrix} \dfrac{\partial N_i}{\partial \zeta} \\[2mm] \dfrac{\partial N_i}{\partial \eta} \\[2mm] \dfrac{\partial N_i}{\partial \zeta} \end{Bmatrix}_{3\times1} T_i = \sum_{i=1}^{20} [L] \begin{Bmatrix} \dfrac{\partial N_i}{\partial \zeta} \\[2mm] \dfrac{\partial N_i}{\partial \eta} \\[2mm] \dfrac{\partial N_i}{\partial \zeta} \end{Bmatrix}_{3\times1} T_i = [B_T]\{T\} \tag{12.8.8}
$$

Assume that D_{11}, D_{22}, and D_{33} are not coordinate-dependent and subscripts 1, 2, and 3 are used to denote the primary material coordinate system. The moisture transfer is governed by dimensional conservation of mass equation, namely Eq. (12.8.8), given as follows:

$$
\frac{\partial C_m}{\partial t} = D_{11}\left(\frac{\partial^2 C_m}{\partial x_1^2}\right) + D_{22}\left(\frac{\partial^2 C_m}{\partial^2 x_2}\right) + D_{33}\left(\frac{\partial^2 C_m}{\partial x_3^2}\right) \tag{12.8.8a}
$$

where

$$
D_{11} = D_{11}(C_m, T) \tag{12.8.9}
$$

$$
D_{22} = D_{22}(C_m, T) \tag{12.8.10}
$$

and $\qquad D_{33} = D_{33}(C_m, T)$ （12.8.11）

Similarly, the thermal conduction (heat diffusivity) is governed by

$$
[\rho \gamma + \rho \, C_m \, \gamma_m]\left(\frac{\partial T}{\partial t}\right) = k_{11}\left(\frac{\partial^2 T}{\partial x_1^2}\right) + k_{22}\left(\frac{\partial^2 T}{\partial x_2^2}\right) + k_{33}\left(\frac{\partial^2 T}{\partial x_3^2}\right) \tag{12.8.12}
$$

When the moisture content of a material is in liquid state, moisture diffusivities D_{ii} and thermal conductivities $k_{ii}(i=1, 2$ and $3)$ in the liquid state are used directly. The thermal conductivities are functions of both content of moisture and temperature,

$$k_{11} = k_{11}(C_m, T) \tag{12.8.13}$$

$$k_{22} = k_{22}(C_m, T) \tag{12.8.14}$$

and $\quad k_{33} = k_{33}(C_m, T) \tag{12.8.15}$

where

$\rho(\text{kg/m}^3, \text{T/mm}^3)$: Density of the base material;

$\gamma(\text{J/kg/℃})$: Specific heat of base material;

$\gamma_m(\text{J/kg/℃})$: Specific heat of moisture, e.g. water;

$k_{11}, k_{22}, k_{33}(\text{W/m/℃}$ or $\text{W/mm/℃})$: Thermal conductivities in the $(1, 2, 3)$ coordinate system.

12.8.2   Finite Element Formulation

Assume that $D_{ii}(i=1, 2$ and $3)$ is independent of temperature but follows the Fickian behavior in the moisture absorption process. Then,

$$\frac{\partial C_m}{\partial t} = D_{xx}\left(\frac{\partial^2 C_m}{\partial x^2}\right) + D_{yy}\left(\frac{\partial^2 C_m}{\partial y^2}\right) + D_{zz}\left(\frac{\partial^2 C_m}{\partial z^2}\right) \tag{12.8.16}$$

The finite element formulation based on solid elements resulting from the Galerkin's weighted residual method, as applied to the above equation, is given as follows:

$$[K]\{C_m\} + [M]\{\dot{C}_m\} = \{F\} \tag{12.8.17}$$

where

$$[K] = \iiint_V [B_T]^T[D][B_T]dV \tag{12.8.18}$$

$$[M] = \iiint_V [B_T]^T[B_T]dV \tag{12.8.19}$$

and $\quad \{F\} = \iint_S [N]^T\{S\}dS \tag{12.8.20}$

Matrix $[K]$ is the moisture diffusivity matrix, $[M]$ is the moisture flow velocity matrix, and $[F]$ is the applied nodal moisture contents (working as forcing functions) on the boundary surfaces. Diffusivity matrix $[D]$ is made of the three diffusivities aligned with the primary material coordinate system,

$$[D] = \begin{pmatrix} D_{11} & 0 & 0 \\ 0 & D_{22} & 0 \\ 0 & 0 & D_{33} \end{pmatrix}$$

(12.8.21)

Eq. (12.8.16) can be solved for the transient responses using the backward finite difference scheme, which is unconditional stable with small steps, in the time domain [Cook et al.] described as follows:

$$(\Delta t [K] + [M]) \{C_{\mathrm{m}}\}_{t+\Delta t} = [M] \{C_{\mathrm{m}}\}_t + \{F\}_{t+\Delta t}$$

(12.8.22)

12.8.3　Strains due to Moisture with the Dual Stage Model

The finite element method can be used for modeling the dual stage model of moisture absorption that Fickian and non-Fickian diffusion occur simultaneously throughout the process [Placette et al.]. The total strain can be considered as being composed of distinct strains due to different physical phenomena, which are assumed to be related to different mechanisms acting in series [Santaoja et al.]:

$$d\varepsilon = d\varepsilon_{\mathrm{elastic}} + d\varepsilon_{\mathrm{h}} + d\varepsilon_{\mathrm{creep}} + d\varepsilon_{\mathrm{fick}} + d\varepsilon_{\mathrm{non\text{-}fick}}$$

(12.8.23)

where

$d\varepsilon_{\mathrm{elastic}}$: Elastic strain;

$d\varepsilon_{\mathrm{h}}$: Strain due to hygroexpansion (variation in moisture content);

$d\varepsilon_{\mathrm{creep}}$: Creep strain for viscoelastic deformation;

$d\varepsilon_{\mathrm{fick}}$: Mechanosorptive strain-Frickian moisture sorption (recoverable);

$d\varepsilon_{\mathrm{non\text{-}fick}}$: Mechanosorptive strain-Nonfickian moisture sorption (irrecoverable).

As being implemented for problem-solving using finite element methods, the above equation can be rewritten in terms of incremental time steps

$$\Delta\varepsilon_{\mathrm{elastic}} + \Delta\varepsilon_{\mathrm{creep}} + \Delta\varepsilon_{\mathrm{fick}} = \Delta\varepsilon - \Delta\varepsilon_h - \Delta\varepsilon_{\mathrm{non\text{-}fick}}$$

(12.8.24)

Note that the stiffness matrix for strain and stress calculations will be updated after each time step as material moduli and Poisson's ratios, i.e., E_{ii}, G_{ij}, and ν_{ij}, are functions of the moisture content and temperature.

12.8.4　Water-Vapor Pressure as Potential for Moisture Diffusion

Another feasible way to formulate finite element analysis for moisture diffusion is to utilize water-vapor pressure as the moisture transfer potential in the diffusion regime and suction pressure in the capillary flow regime.

12.9 Moisture Diffusivities and Thermal Conductivities under Vapor Pressure

Complex couplings exist between thermal conductivities (namely heat diffusivities) and moisture diffusivities in the two preceding governing equations. Both moisture diffusivities due to moisture gradients and thermal conductivities due to temperature gradients are functions of moisture content and temperature, as illustrated in Section 12.8. There are two possibilities while dealing with D_{ii} ($i = 1$, 2 and 3):

- (a) When the moisture content of a material is saturated, liquid diffusivities D_{ii} are to be used directly.
- (b) When the moisture content of a material is below the vapor saturation level, the moisture diffusivities and the thermal conductivities are determined with the following equations:

$$D_{ii} = \frac{\mu_{ii}(H_R)\ P_{vapor}(T)}{\rho \left[\dfrac{\partial f_{ii}(H_R)}{\partial H_R} \right]} \quad \text{for } i = 1, 2 \text{ and } 3 \tag{12.9.1}$$

where

H_R: Relative humidity;

$\mu_{ii}(H_R)$: Water vapor permeability, $i = 1$, 2 and 3;

$P_{vapor}(T)$: Vapor saturation pressure;

$f_{ii}(H_R)$: Sorption isotherm function, $i = 1$, 2 and 3.

The sorption isotherm function $f_{ii}(H_R)$ may be obtained applying the chain rule of Fick's steady-state diffusion equation with the gradient of the water-vapor pressure as the driving-force potential [Calbureanu et al.] along the primary material axes.

The thermal conductivities can be obtained as a function of relative humidity, permeability and vapor pressure from the following equation:

$$k_{ii} = \frac{H_R\ \mu_{ii}(H_R) \left[\dfrac{\partial P_{vapor}(T)}{\partial H_R} \right]}{\rho} \quad \text{for } i = 1, 2 \text{ and } 3 \tag{12.9.2}$$

Since other components due to enthalpy transport by moisture diffusion are generally small, they are therefore neglected. In the term $[\rho\ \gamma + \rho\ C_m\ \gamma_m]$ on the left side of Eq. (12.8.12), the heat capacity of dry material is given by $\rho\ \gamma$ and the heat capacity of the accumulated moisture is given by $\rho\ C_m \gamma_m$. Latent transport of heat is included at the boundaries of the layers.

12.10　Corrosion

Obtaining the stress distribution in the vicinity of corrosion defects is a decisive phase in understanding the structural integrity of corroded components under high internal pressure. Localized corrosion includes crevice corrosion, pitting, stress corrosion cracking, and intergranular corrosion. Identifying the shape of the defect and its corresponding corrosion mode is considered as a critical factor to predict the remaining life of a corroded part in the structural assessment.

12.10.1　Electrochemical Corrosion

The material (usually metal) with the lower positive electrochemical potential loses ions to balance the electron flow and thus acts as an anode. The mating material with higher positive electrochemical potential acts as a cathode receiving ions. This is called galvanic corrosion. The severity of galvanic corrosion depends upon the difference in electric potentials.

There are two major distinct localized galvanic corrosions. One is crevice corrosion, which occurs at a narrow gap or crevice between two material (metal and non-metal) surfaces. The other one is pitting corrosion, which appears because of defect, impurity and/or scratch. An existing pit may cause a common stress corrosion form that is called stress corrosion cracking, which occurs under a prolonged tensile stress.

12.10.2　Chemical Corrosion

Chemical corrosion is generated by chemical reactions, which has nothing to do with galvanic effect (i.e., electric current). For example, steel pipes can be corroded by acids (e.g. chlorite), Carbon Dioxide (CO_2), and hydrogen sulphide (H_2S). A chemical corrosion can be complicated by mechanical loading. For example,

(a) Prolonged tensile stress occurring in H_2S environment may result in sulphide stress as hydrogen diffuses into the steel.

(b) A combination of tension and chlorite (HCl) may result in chlorite stress cracking.

12.10.3　Corrosion Fatigue

Mechanical stresses may increase corrosion especially on the joints and connecting collars. This results in damage to the protective corrosion films allowing localized corrosion to take place. This is called corrosion fatigue, which behaves like the fatigue of oxides described in Chapter 6.

12.10.4 Generalized Governing Equation for Electrochemical Corrosion

The corrosion is generally attributed to four different mechanisms [Liu & Kelly]: diffusion, migration, convection, and reaction. The reactive rate of material corrosion is fundamental as a material property, while diffusion flow is the main activating venue, which is assisted by the migration due to the electromagnetic field and the convection subject to the fluid flow. Fluid velocity also plays a crucial role in corrosion. The higher the velocity is, the higher the corrosion rate up to the limit of diffusion at the specific temperature.

As an extension of Fick's law of diffusion for the case where the diffusing particles move with respect to the fluid by electro-magneto-static forces, the Nernst-Planck differential equation based on mass conservation that is used to describe the motion of a charged chemical species in a fluid solution can be adopted as the generalized governing equation for corrosion [Nernst] [Planck] [Jones]

$$
\frac{\partial C_m}{\partial t} = D\left[\left(\frac{\partial^2 C_m}{\partial x^2}\right) + \left(\frac{\partial^2 C_m}{\partial y^2}\right) + \left(\frac{\partial^2 C_m}{\partial z^2}\right)\right] \quad \text{(Diffusion)} +
$$

$$
\frac{z\,e}{k_B\,T_k} D\,C_m\left[\left(\frac{\partial^2 \phi}{\partial x^2}\right) + \left(\frac{\partial^2 \phi}{\partial y^2}\right) + \left(\frac{\partial^2 \phi}{\partial z^2}\right) + \left(\frac{\partial^2 A}{\partial x\,\partial t} + \frac{\partial^2 A}{\partial y\,\partial t} + \frac{\partial^2 A}{\partial z\,\partial t}\right)\right] \quad \text{(Migration)} -
$$

$$
C_m\left[\left(\frac{\partial v}{\partial x}\right) + \left(\frac{\partial v}{\partial y}\right) + \left(\frac{\partial v}{\partial z}\right)\right] \quad \text{(Convection or Advection)} + R_m \quad \text{(Reaction)}
$$

$$(12.10.1)$$

where

t: Time;

c_m: Species concentration of mass transfer, i.e., moisture concentration or temperature;

D_m: Diffusivity of species m;

z_m: Valence of ionic species m;

A: Magnetic vector potential;

E: Elementary charge;

k_B: Boltzmann constant;

ϕ: Electric potential;

v: Velocity of fluid;

R_m: Reactive rate of homogeneous production of material m, i.e., source or sink.

The above equation can be applied to nanofiltration, which is a pressure-driven membrane process that is able to separate ions as described by the equation given above, by presenting pores on a nanometric scale with fixed charges. R_m describes the creation or destruction of the quantity. When $R_m > 0$, it means that a chemical reaction is creating more of the species. On the other hand, a chemical reaction is destroying the species for $R_m < 0$. For heat transport, $R_m > 0$ might occur if thermal energy is being generated such as by chemical reaction like rubber curing or by friction.

References

ADAMSON M J, 1980. Thermal Expansion and Swelling of Cured Epoxy Resin Used in Graphite/Epoxy Composite Materials[J]. Journal of Materials Science, 15: 1736-1745.

Astm standard D5229/D5229M-92, 1992. Standard Test Methodology for Moisture Absorption Properties and Equilibrium Conditioning of Polymer Matrix Composite Materials[J]. Physical Review B, 2010, 791(5): 897-899.

BANFIELD S J, CASEY N F, NATARAJA R, 2005. Durability of Polyester Deepwater Mooring Rope[J]. OTC 17510, 2005 Offshore Technology Conference Proceedings.

BARBERO E J, LONETTI P, 2001. An Inelastic Damage Model for Fiber Reinforced Laminates[J]. Journal of Composite Materials, 36: 941-962.

BARJASTEH E, NUTT S, 2012. Moisture Absorption in Unidirectional Hybrid Composites[J]. Composites, A, 43(1): 158-164.

BASF, 2004. Effects of Moisture Conditioning Methods on Mechanical Properties of Injection Molded Nylon 6[J]. Journal of Reinforal Plastic & Composites, 23(7): 729-737.

CALBUREANU M, et al, 2000. The Finite Element Analysis of Water Vapor Diffusion in a Brick with Vertical Holes[J]. Mathematical Models for Engineering Science (ISBN: 58 978-960-474-252-3): 57-62.

CERVENKA A J, et al, 2005. Micromechanical Phenomena during Hygrothermal Ageing of Model Composites Investigated by Raman Spectroscopy. Part Ⅱ: Comparison of the Behavior of PBO and M5 Fibers Compared with Twaron[J]. Composites, Part A, 36(7): 1020-1026.

CHEN X, ZHAO S, 2005. Moisture Absorption and Diffusion Characterization of Molding Compound[J]. Journal of Electronic Packaging, 127: 460-465.

CARTER H, KIBLER K, 1978. Langmuir Type Model for Anomalous Moisture Diffusion in Composite Resin[J]. Journal of Composite Materials, 12(2): 118-131.

COOK R D, MALKUS D S, PLESHA M E, 1993. Concepts and Applications in Finite Element Analysis[M]. 4th Edition, McGraw-Hill, New York, NY, USA.

CRANK J, 1975. The Mathematics of Diffusion[M]. Oxford University Press, Oxford, U.K.

DARVISHI H, et al, 2013. Mathematical Modeling, Moisture Diffusion, Energy Consumption and Efficiency of Thin Layer Drying of Potato Slices[J]. Journal of Food Process Technol., 4(3).

ECKELMAN C A, 2004. The Shrinking and Swelling of Wood and Its Effect on Furniture[J]. FNR 163, Dept. of Forestry and Natural Resources, Purdue Univ., West Lafayette, IN 479071.

FAN X J, SUHIR E, 2010. Editors. Moisture Sensitivity of Plastic Packages of IC Devices[J]. Springer US.

FAN X, LEE S, HAN Q, 2009. Experimental Investigations and Model Study of Moisture Behaviors in Polymeric Materials[J]. Microelectronics Reliability, 49: 861-871.

FAN X J, ZHANG G Q, VAN DRIEL W D, et al, 2008. Interfacial Delamination Mechanisms during Reflow with Moisture Preconditioning[J]. IEEE Transactions on Components and Packaging Technologies, 31(2): 252-259.

FAN X J, ZHOU J, ZHANG G Q, 2004. Multi-Physics Modeling in Virtual Prototyping of Electronic Packages-Combined Thermal, Thermomechanical and Vapor Pressure Modeling[J]. Microelectronics Reliability, 44: 1967-1976.

FERGUSON T, QU J, 2006. Predictive Model for Adhesion Loss of Molding Compounds from Exposure to Humid Environment[C]// Electwnic Componenty and Technology Conference, Proceedings. 56th IEEE. Proceedings of ECT: 1408-1414.

FRANKE B, et al, 2016. Moisture Diffusion in Wood-Experimental and Numerical Investigations[C]. WTCE// world conference on Timber Engineering.

GUERIBZA D, et al, 2013. A Moisture Diffusion Coupled Model for Composite Materials[J]. European Journal of Mechanics, A/Solids, 42: 81-89.

HE Y, ALAM Z, 2013. Moisture Absorption and Diffusion in an Underfill Encapsulant at $T>T_g$ and $T<T_g$[J]. Journal of Thermal Analysis and Calorimetry, 113: 461.

HUO Z, et al, 2015. Modeling of Concentration-Dependent Moisture Diffusion in Hybrid Fiber-Reinforced Polymer Composites[J]. Journal of Composite Materials 49(3): 321-333.

JIA N, KAGAN V, 2001. Mechanical Performance of Polyamides with Influence of Moisture and Temperature—Accurate Evaluation and Better Understanding[J]. Plastics Failure: Analysis and Prevention: 95-104, Plastic Design Library (PDL), New York, NY.

JONES D A, 1996. Principles and Prevention of Corrosion[M]. 2nd Edition, Prentice-Hall, Inc., Upper Saddle River, NJ.

KANG S, DELWICHE S, 2001. Moisture Diffusion Coefficients of Single Wheat Kernels with Assumed Simplified Geometry[J]. Transactions of the ASAE, 43(6): 1653-1659.

KARBHARI V M, ZHANG S, 2003. E-Glass/Vinylester Composites in Aqueous Environments-I, Experimental Results[J]. Applied Composite Materials, 10: 19-48.

KOLLEGAL M G, SRIDHARAN S, 1998. Strength Prediction of Plain Woven Fabrics[J]. Journal of Composite Materials, Vol. 34.

KOLLEGAL M G, SRIDHARAN S, 1998. A Simplified Model for Plain Woven Fabrics[J]. Journal of Composite Materials, Vol. 34.

KUMOSA L, et al, 2005. An Investigation of Moisture and Leakage Currents in GRP Composite Hollow Cylinders[J]. IEEE Transactions on Dielectrics and Electrical Insulation, 12(5): 1043-1059.

KUMOSA L, et al, 2004. Moisture Absorption Properties of Unidirectional Glass/Polymer Composites Used in Composite (Non-Ceramic) Insulators[J]. Composites Part A: Applied Science and Manufacturing 35(9): 1049-1063.

LEGER R, ROY A, GRANDIDIER J, 2010. Non-Classical Water Diffusion in an Industrial Adhesive[J]. International Journal of Adhesion and Adhesives, 30(8): 744-753.

LEKATOU A, et al, 1997. Effect of Water and Its Activity on Transport Properties of Glass/Epoxy Particulate Composites[J]. Journal of Composites, Part A, 28(3): 223-236.

LI M, 2000. Temperature and Moisture Effects on Composite Materials for Wind Turbine Blades[D]. Master Thesis, Montana State University, Bozeman, Montana.

LI S, LEE J, CASTRO J, 2002. Effective Mass Diffusivity in Composites[J]. Journal of Composite Materials, 36(14): 1709-1724.

LIAO K, et al, 1999. Long-Term Environmental Fatigue of Pultruded Glass-Fiber Reinforced Composites under Flexural Loading[J]. International Journal of Fatigue, 25: 485-495.

LIN Y C, 2006. Investigation of the Moisture-Desorption Characteristics of Epoxy Resin[J]. Journal of Polymer Research, 13(5): 369-374.

LIN Y C, et al, 2007. Water Diffusion and Fracture Toughness between Organosilicate Glass Film Stacks[J]. Acta Materialia, 55: 2455-2464.

LIU C, KELLY R G, 2014. The Use of Finite Element Methods (FEM) in the Modeling of Localized Corrosion [J]. The Electrochemical Society Interface, 23(4): 47.

LOH W K, et al, 2005. Modeling Anomalous Moisture Uptake, Swelling and Thermal Characteristics of a Rubber Toughened Epoxy Adhesive[J]. International Journal of Adhesion & Adhesives, 25(1): 1-12.

LU X, HOFSTRA P, BAJKAR R, 1998. Moisture Absorption, Dielectric Relaxation, and Thermal Conductivity Studies of Polymer Composites[J]. Journal of Polymer Science, Part B: Polymer Physics, 36: 2259-2265.

MICHALSKE T A, BUNKER B C, 1987. The Fracturing of Glass[J]. Scientific American, 257(6): 78-85.

MROTEK J L, et al, 2001. Diffusion of Moisture Through Optical Fiber Coatings[J]. Journal of Lightwave Technology, 19(7): 988-993.

NAKAI A, IKEGAKI S, HAMADA H, et al, 2000. Degradation of Braided Composites in Hot Water[J]. Composites Science and Technology, 60(3): 325-331.

NERNST W, 1888. Zur Kinetik der in Lösung befindlichen Körper[J]. Zeitschr f Phys Chem, 2(1): 613-637.

OGAWA T, et al, 1993. Determination of Diffusion Coefficient of Water in Polymer Films by TGA[J]. Journal of Applied Polymer Science, 50(6): 981-987.

PIERRON F, POIREET Y, VAUTRIN A, 2002. A Novel Procedure for Identification of 3D Moisture Diffusion Parameters on Thick Composites: Theory, Validation and Experimental Results[J]. Journal of Composite

Materials, 36(19): 2219-2243.

PLACETTE M D, FAN X J, ZHAO J H, et al, 2012. Dual Stage Modeling of Moisture Diffusion and Desorption in Epoxy Mold Compounds[J]. Microelectronics Reliability, 52(7): 1401-1408.

PLANCK M, 1890. Uber die Erregung von Elektricität und Wärme in Elektrolyten[J]. Wied Ann Phys, 275 (2): 161-186.

ROE N, et al, 2013. Advanced Moisture Modeling of Polymer Composites[J]. Journal of Reinforced Plastics and Composites, 32(7): 437-449.

SANTAOJA K, et al, 1991. Mechanosorptive Structural Analysis of Wood by the ABAQUS Finite Element Program[M]. Espoo: Technical Research Centre of Finland, Research Notes 1276, 49.

SCHULTHEISZ R C, et al, 1997. Effect of Moisture on E-Glass/Epoxy Interfacial and Fiber Strengths[J]. Composite Materials: Testing and Design, Vol. 13, ASTM STP 1242: 257-286.

SCHMITZ G K, METCALFE A G, 1966. Stress Corrosion of E-Glass Fibers[J]. Industrial and Engineering Chemistry Product Research, 5: 1-8.

SHAO Y, KOUADIO S, 2002. Durability of Fiberglass Composite Sheet Piles in Water[J]. Journal of Composites for Construction, 6(4): 280.

SHEN C H, SPRINGER G S, 1976. Moisture Absorption and Desorption of Composite Materials[J]. Journal of Composite Materials, 10: 2-20.

SHI X, ZHANG Y, ZHOU W, et al, 2008. Effect of Hygrothermal Aging on Interfacial Reliability of Silicon/Underfill/FR-4 Assembly[J]. IEEE Transactions on Components and Packaging Technologies, 31: 94-103.

SHIRANGI M H, et al, 2008. Mechanism of Moisture Diffusion, Hydroscopic Swelling and Adhesive Degradation in Epoxy Molding Compounds[M]. IMAPS 2008, 41st Symposium on Microelectronics.

SONG Y S, YOUNG J R, GUTOWSKI T G, 2009. Life Cycle Energy Analysis of Fiber-Reinforced Composites [J]. Composites, Part A, 40: 1257-1265.

SPRINGER, G S. 1981. Environmental Effects on Composite Materials[M]. Chapter 13, Technomic Publishing Company, Inc..

STELLRECHT E, HAN B, PECHT M G, 2004. Characterization of Hygroscopic Swelling of Mold Compounds and Plastic Packages[J]. IEEE Transactions on Components and Packaging Technologies, 27(3): 499-506.

TAKAHASHI M K, 1990. AC Impedance Measurements of Moisture in Interfaces between Epoxy and Oxidized Silicon[J]. Journal of Applied Physics, 67(7): 3419-3429.

TSAI Y I, et al, 2009. Influence of Hygrothermal Environment on Thermal and Mechanical Properties of Carbon Fiber/Fiberglass Hybrid Composites[J]. Composites Science and Technology, 69(3-4): 432-437.

VAUTHIER E, et al, 1998. Interactions between Hygrothermal Ageing and Fatigue Damage in Unidirectional Glass/Epoxy Composites[J]. Composites Science & Technology, 58(5): 687-692.

WANG W, et al, 2006. Study of Moisture Observation in Natural Fiber Plastic Composites[J]. Composites Science and Technology, 66(3-4): 379-386.

WATERS P, VOLINSKY A, 2007. Stress and Moisture Effects on Thin Film Buckling Delamination[J]. Experimental Mechanics, 47(1): 163-170.

WEITSMAN Y J, 2006. Anomalous Fluid Absorption in Polymeric Composites and Its Relation to Fluid Induced Damage[J]. Composites Part A: applied science and Manufacturing, 37(4): 617-623.

WEIDE-ZAAGE K, et al, 2005. Moisture Diffusion in Printed Circuit Boards: Measurements and Finite Element Simulations[J]. Microelectronics Reliability, 45: 1662-1667.

WEI Y, et al, 2011. Hygroscopic Dimensional Changes of Self-Adhering and New Resin-Matrix Composites during Water Sorption/Desorption Cycles[J]. Dental Materials, 27(3): 259-266.

WU W L, ORTS W J, MAJKZAK C J, 1995. Water Absorption at a Polyimide/Silicon Wafer Interface[J]. Polymer Engineering & Science, 12: 1000-1004.

XIE B, FAN X J, SHI X Q, et al, 2009. Direct Concentration Approach of Moisture Diffusion and Whole Field Vapor Pressure Modeling for Reflow Process: Part Ⅱ—Application to 3-D Ultrathin Stacked-die Chip Scale Packages[J]. Journal of Electronic Packaging, 31(3).

YAGOUBI J E., et al, 2012. A Fully Coupled Diffusion-Reaction Scheme for Moisture Sorption-Desorption in an Anhydride-Cured Epoxy Resin[J]. Polymer, 53: 5582-5595.

YANG Y, et al, 2012. Recycling of Composite Materials[J]. Chemical Engineering and Processing: Process Intensification, 51(1): 53-68.

ZHOU J, LUCAS J P, 1999. Hygrothermal Effects of Epoxy Resin[J]. Polymer, 40(20): 5505-5522.

ZHOU Q, et al, 2000. Moisture Diffusion in Larch Wood[J]. BioResources, 6(2): 1196-1203.

Table 12.1.1　Diffusivities of Materials（Wetting）

Material	Conditioning/($^\circ$C · %)	$C_{m,max}$	$D_{11}/(mm^2 \cdot s^{-1})$	$D_{22}/(mm^2 \cdot s^{-1})$	$D_{33}/(mm^2 \cdot s^{-1})$
Potato Chip [Sravishi et al.]	22 $^\circ$C/RH=65%	—	$1.0 \sim 3.8 \times 10^{-2}$	$1.0 \sim 3.8 \times 10^{-2}$	$1.0 \sim 3.8 \times 10^{-2}$
Wheat-Pearled[Kang & Delwiche]	—				
Grandin	22 $^\circ$C/RH= 65%	—	62×10^{-6}	62×10^{-6}	62×10^{-6}
Amidon	22 $^\circ$C/RH=65%	—	41×10^{-6}	41×10^{-6}	41×10^{-6}
Renville	22 $^\circ$C/RH=65%	—	55×10^{-6}	55×10^{-6}	55×10^{-6}
Jagger	22 $^\circ$C/RH=65%	—	55×10^{-6}	55×10^{-6}	55×10^{-6}
TAM107	22 $^\circ$C/RH=65%	—	70×10^{-6}	70×10^{-6}	70×10^{-6}

continued

Material	Conditioning/($^\circ$C $\cdot$ %)	$C_{m,max}$	D_{11}/(mm^2 $\cdot$s^{-1})	D_{22}/(mm^2 $\cdot$s^{-1})	D_{33}/(mm^2 $\cdot$s^{-1})
Madsen	22 $^\circ$C/RH=65%	—	43×10^{-6}	43×10^{-6}	43×10^{-6}
Rely	22 $^\circ$C/RH=65%	—	47×10^{-6}	47×10^{-6}	47×10^{-6}
Penawawa	22 $^\circ$C/RH=65%	—	44×10^{-6}	44×10^{-6}	44×10^{-6}
Vanna	22 $^\circ$C/RH=65%	—	44×10^{-6}	44×10^{-6}	44×10^{-6}
Wood-Glulam [Franke et al.]	20 $^\circ$C/RH=65%	—	1042×10^{-6}	289×10^{-6}	161×10^{-6}
Acrylate[Mrotek et al.]	25 $^\circ$C/RH=95%	—	0.52×10^{-6}	0.52×10^{-6}	0.52×10^{-6}
PA6[Abachal et al.]	40 $^\circ$C/Immersed	—	2.26×10^{-6}	2.26×10^{-6}	—
	50 $^\circ$C/Immersed	—	3.81×10^{-6}	3.81×10^{-6}	3.81×10^{-6}
	60 $^\circ$C/Immersed	—	7.92×10^{-6}	7.92×10^{-6}	7.92×10^{-6}
Polyimide[Ogawa et al.]	25 $^\circ$C/RH=95%	—	0.2×10^{-6}	0.2×10^{-6}	0.2×10^{-6}
Epoxy SC14	50 $^\circ$C/Immersed	3%	2.47×10^{-6}	2.47×10^{-6}	2.47×10^{-6}
Polyester (Iso)	50 $^\circ$C/Immersed	0.6%	5.72×10^{-6}	5.72×10^{-6}	5.72×10^{-6}
Polyester (Ortho)	50 $^\circ$C/Immersed	1.8%	3.72×10^{-6}	3.72×10^{-6}	3.72×10^{-6}
Vinylesteer 411	50 $^\circ$C/Immersed	0.88%	4.22×10^{-6}	4.22×10^{-6}	4.22×10^{-6}
Vinylesteer 8084	50 $^\circ$C/Immersed	0.98%	3.67×10^{-6}	3.67×10^{-6}	3.67×10^{-6}
Polyester/E-Glass (V_f=55.8%) [Kumosa]	20 $^\circ$C/RH=65%	—	2.423×10^{-6}	0.879×10^{-6}	0.879×10^{-6}
Epoxy/E-Glass (V_f=53.1%) [Kumosa]	20 $^\circ$C/RH=65%	—	1.95×10^{-6}	0.71×10^{-6}	0.71×10^{-6}
Vinylester/E-Glass (V_f=56.9%) [Kumosa]	20 $^\circ$C/RH=65%	—	2.15×10^{-6}	0.78×10^{-6}	0.78×10^{-6}
Vinylester/E-Glass (V_f=52.5%)	23 $^\circ$C/Immersed	0.405%	—	—	—
	40 $^\circ$C/Immersed	0.438%	—	—	—
[Karbahari & Zhang]	60 $^\circ$C/Immersed	0.533%	—	—	—

Note: The solution for "RH (relative humidity)" is H_2O and "immersed", if not mentioned otherwise.

国家出版基金项目

NATIONAL PUBLICATION FOUNDATION

产品寿命预测力学与设计
Mechanics and Design for Product Life Prediction　Ⅲ

江永瑞　著

重庆大学出版社

图书在版编目(CIP)数据

产品寿命预测力学与设计 = Mechanics and Design
for Product Life Prediction：英文／江永瑞著. --
重庆：重庆大学出版社，2022.1
（自主品牌汽车实践创新丛书）
ISBN 978-7-5689-1917-3

Ⅰ.①产…　Ⅱ.①江…　Ⅲ.①汽车—零部件—产品寿
命—力学—研究—英文　Ⅳ.U463

中国版本图书馆 CIP 数据核字(2020)第 001261 号

产品寿命预测力学与设计
CHANPIN SHOUMING YUCE LIXUE YU SHEJI
（Ⅲ）
江永瑞　著
策划编辑:杨粮菊　鲁　黎
责任编辑:陈　力　张慧梓　版式设计:杨粮菊
责任校对:邹　忌　　　　责任印制:张　策
*
重庆大学出版社出版发行
出版人:饶帮华
社址:重庆市沙坪坝区大学城西路 21 号
邮编:401331
电话:(023)88617190　88617185(中小学)
传真:(023)88617186　88617166
网址:http://www.cqup.com.cn
邮箱:fxk@ cqup.com.cn（营销中心）
全国新华书店经销
重庆升光电力印务有限公司印刷
*
开本:889mm×1194mm　1/16　总印张:60.5　总字数:1975 千
2022 年 1 月第 1 版　2022 年 1 月第 1 次印刷
ISBN 978-7-5689-1917-3　总定价:368.00 元(全 3 卷)

Chapter 15　Failure of Composites

Chapter 16　Indentation Engineering and Fretting Fatigue

Index

Chapter 13

Elastomeric Composites

13.1   Introduction to Rubber Failure

The mechanical response of elastomeric materials is known to depend greatly on their ability to crystallize under stress, on the difference between the glass transition and the usage temperature, on the density of permanent and transient crosslinks, and on the filler. Rubber and resilient foam are widely used for a variety of applications, such as seals and gaskets, shock mounts, vibration isolators and tires. The mechanical and chemical properties of these materials allow them to act as excellent seals against moisture, pressure and heat. They also have excellent energy absorption and dissipation capabilities.

13.1.1   Designing with Rubber

The strengths of rubbers are considerably lower than those of metals, plastics or even wood, but their elasticity is much greater. The major property of rubbers, which distinguishes them from other solid materials, is their incompressibility. Most rubber products are used mainly as dampers and seals.

Rubber dampers may work as vibration isolators that act as a spring with good damping properties. A vibration isolator is usually stiff in the loading direction but soft in the other two orthogonal directions. These transversely isotropic characteristics allow the isolator to move laterally with relatively low stiffness yet to carry significant axial load due to their high vertical stiffness. The high vertical stiffness is achieved by having thin layers of rubber reinforced by metal (mainly steel) shims. A typical vibration damper for road bridges is shown in Fig. 13.1.1.

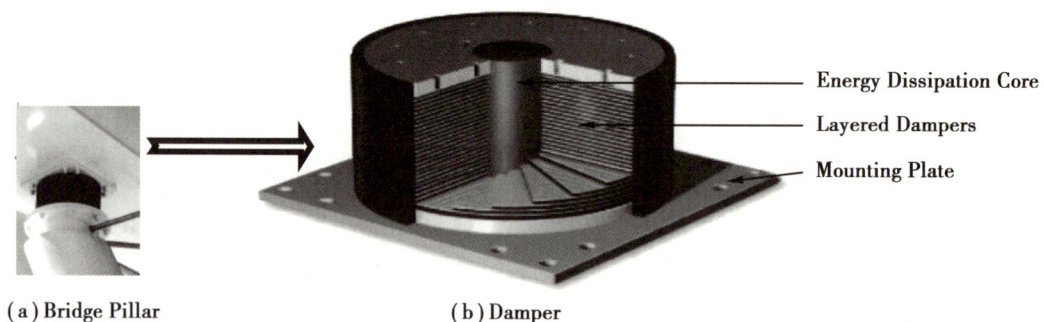

(a) Bridge Pillar   (b) Damper

Fig. 13.1.1   A Vibration Isolator for Road Bridges [**Dynamic Isolation Systems, Inc., Reno, Nevada, USA.**]

Mechanical seals are used in industrial pumps, compressors, engines, and other applications to provide a leakproof seal between parts. Squeeze type seals operate by distorting under compressive load, and the hardness specified for such an application must be sufficient to ensure adequate retention of the sealing pressure. Dimensional variations due to contact with fluids can be adjusted to achieve a small positive swell, which can maintain seal efficiency, by compensating for wear and compression set. The choice of compound will depend on the effects of the fluids with which the seal is in contact, the operating temperature, and mechanical conditions such as pressure, relative velocity, and abrasion. In seals, resilience is important because it allows a dynamic seal to adapt to variations without creep in the sealing surface.

13.1.2   Failure Modes of Rubber Products

Common causes of failure include chemical attacks, thermal degradation, ozone, fatigue, wear, abrasive flaking or peeling of seal face, tear/nibbling/extrusion, compression set, extensional set, explosive decompression by entrapped gas, and buckling. For example, extensive tests of three different sealing materials (HNBF, FKM, FEMP) for heavy-duty engine coolants by [Hertz] has concluded that HNBR is not a suitable elastomer for high temperature service (up to 150 ℃) in the three coolants examined. Absent data to the contrary, data based on 40 cycles (1000 hours) of testing indicates FEPM (FFKM) and FKM are suitable materials for the coolant studied. However, the increasing trend in fluoride ion, and associated reduction in pH, indicates longer term testing and validation of FKM in hot coolant are warranted [Hertz].

13.2   Constitutive Equations of Elastomers

Rubber, an elastomer, is said to be hyperelastic because it possesses the property of a strain energy density function (strain energy per unit mass), which is a scalar function of strain tensor formed with respect to the homogeneous stress-free natural state, such that the rate of change of the strain energy density function is equal to the rate of work done by stresses. In other words, the derivative of the strain energy density function with respect to a strain component determines the corresponding stress component.

The stress-stretch behavior of rubber depends on the state of stretch. Numerous constitutive models have been proposed to characterize the observed behavior. The static material behavior of elastomers is generally modeled using the following three material models: Rivlin strain energy density function, Ogden model, and Davis-De-Thomas model.

When the three axes of the coordinate system are coincident with the principal directions of material deformation, the three invariants can be expressed explicitly in terms of Cauchy-Green strain tensor as [Fung]

$$I_1 = \lambda_1^2 + \lambda_2^2 + \lambda_3^2 \tag{13.2.1}$$

$$I_2 = \lambda_1^2 \lambda_2^2 + \lambda_2^2 \lambda_3^2 + \lambda_3^2 \lambda_1^2 \tag{13.2.2}$$

and $\quad I_3 = \lambda_1^2 \lambda_2^2 \lambda_3^2 \tag{13.2.3}$

where the principal stretch ratios, λ_i, are defined by the principal strains, $\varepsilon_{ii}(i=1, 2, 3)$ as

$$\lambda_i = 1 + \varepsilon_{ii}, \quad i = 1, 2, 3 \tag{13.2.4}$$

In terms of Lagrange-Green strains in a general Cartesian coordinate system, these three invariants can be expressed using engineering strains, ε_{ij},

$$I_1 = 3 + 2 (\varepsilon_{11} + \varepsilon_{22} + \varepsilon_{33}) \tag{13.2.5}$$

$$I_2 = 3 + 4 (\varepsilon_{11} + \varepsilon_{22} + \varepsilon_{33}) - 4 (\varepsilon_{11}^2 + \varepsilon_{22}^2 + \varepsilon_{33}^2) + 4 (\varepsilon_{11} \varepsilon_{22} + \varepsilon_{22} \varepsilon_{33} + \varepsilon_{33} \varepsilon_{11}) \tag{13.2.6}$$

and $\quad I_3 = 1 + 2 (\varepsilon_{11} + \varepsilon_{22} + \varepsilon_{33}) - 4 (\varepsilon_{12}^2 + \varepsilon_{23}^2 + \varepsilon_{31}^2) + 4 (\varepsilon_{11} \varepsilon_{22} + \varepsilon_{22} \varepsilon_{33} + \varepsilon_{33} \varepsilon_{11}) +$

$$8 \varepsilon_{11} \varepsilon_{22} \varepsilon_{33} - 8 (\varepsilon_{11} \varepsilon_{23}^2 + \varepsilon_{22} \varepsilon_{31}^2 + \varepsilon_{33} \varepsilon_{12}^2) + 16 \varepsilon_{12} \varepsilon_{23} \varepsilon_{31} \tag{13.2.7}$$

In incompressible elastomers, $I_3 = 1$ while the first invariant (I_1) is by far the stronger contributor to strain energy density than the second invariant (I_2). Define the volume change ratio, J, in Cartesian coordinate system as

$$J = (1 + \varepsilon_{11}) (1 + \varepsilon_{22}) (1 + \varepsilon_{33}) \tag{13.2.8}$$

Plugging Eq. (13.2.4) into the above equation yields

$$J = \lambda_1 \lambda_2 \lambda_3 \tag{13.2.9}$$

13.2.1 Rivlin Model

Rivlin model states that elastic strain energy of stressed elastomers (isotropic and incompressible), can be represented by a strain energy density function, W, in terms of the invariants of Cauchy-Green strain tensor,

$$W (I_1, I_2) = \sum_{i=0}^{p} \sum_{j=0}^{q} A_{ij}(I_1 - 3)^i (I_2 - 3)^j \tag{13.2.10}$$

where I_1 and I_2 are the first and second strain invariants of motion, which can be expressed in terms of nonlinear strain components as described by Eqs. (13.2.5) and (13.2.6). In order to satisfy the condition of incompressibility the third invariant, I_3, has to be exactly one,

$$I_3 = \lambda_1^2 \, \lambda_2^2 \, \lambda_3^2 = J^2 = 1 \quad (\text{Volume change ratio} = 1) \tag{13.2.11}$$

Based on the invariants defined by Eqs. (13.2.1)-(13.2.5), a true stress component, called the second Piola-Kirchhoff stress or Cauchy-Green stress, can be determined [Chen et al.] [Swanson] [Fung] differentiating the strain energy term with respect to the corresponding strain component,

$$\sigma_{ij} = \frac{\partial W}{\partial \varepsilon_{ij}} = \frac{\partial W}{\partial I_1} \frac{\partial I_1}{\partial \varepsilon_{ij}} + \frac{\partial W}{\partial I_2} \frac{\partial I_2}{\partial \varepsilon_{ij}} + \frac{\partial W}{\partial I_3} \frac{\partial I_3}{\partial \varepsilon_{ij}} \tag{13.2.12}$$

Each stress component given in the above equation can be derived substituting Eqs. (13.2.5)-(13.2.7) into Eq. (13.2.10), then successively into Eq. (13.2.12). The bulk modulus of material is defined as the stiffness in resistance to the change of volume under hydrostatic pressure,

$$\frac{\Delta V}{V} = \frac{-P}{B} \tag{13.2.13}$$

because $\quad J = \lambda_1 \, \lambda_2 \, \lambda_3 = (1 + \varepsilon_{11})(1 + \varepsilon_{22})(1 + \varepsilon_{33})$, and

$$\frac{-P}{B} = \frac{\Delta V}{V} = (1 + \varepsilon_{11})(1 + \varepsilon_{22})(1 + \varepsilon_{33}) - 1 = \lambda_1 \, \lambda_2 \, \lambda_3 - 1$$

The bulk modulus based on Rivlin's equation can be derived substituting the above equation into Eq. (13.2.12), setting $\sigma_{11} = \sigma_{22} = \sigma_{33} = -P$, as

$$B = \frac{2(A_{10} + A_{01})}{1 - 2\nu} \tag{13.2.14}$$

The bulk modulus become infinitive as the Poisson's ratio approaches 1/2. Commonly performed experiments to identify the material properties are: (a) uniaxial tension, (b) uniaxial compression, (c) planar shear, and (d) biaxial tension. It is suggested that tests be conducted at room temperature at a strain rate of 5.08 mm/min (or 0.2 inch per minute). Softening of the elastomers after cyclic loading occurs as a result of changes in the rubber phase, not due to rubber/carbon black interface. This phenomenon is called Mullin's effect [Mullins and Tobin]. When obtaining the material coefficients A_{ij}, one has to cycle the specimen up to the maximum stretch a few times before recording the test data. ASTM Designation E412-87 describes test methods for rubber property in tension (Annual Book of ASTM Standards) and it is generally valid for tensile strains up to 300% (also called 300% modulus); while ASTM designation D575-88 (Annual Book of ASTM Standards) presents test methods for rubber property in compression. Calculations for hyperelastic material constants will be illustrated here using the uniaxial tensile test for simple models such as Neo-Hookean law and Mooney-Rivlin's equation.

13.2.2 Neo-Hookean Law

When $p=1$ and $q=0$, Rivlin equation is called Neo-Hookean law and the equation reduces to

$$W(I_1, I_2) = A_{10}(I_1 - 3) + D(I_3 - 1)^2 \tag{13.2.15}$$

The unit for A_{10} is the same as stress. For example, $A_{10} = 214$ kPa (i.e., 31 Psi) at 104 ℃ (220 ℉) is used for modeling bladder compound as Neo-Hookean material in a tire-forming process.

Based on the uniaxial tensile test using dumbbell specimens with circular cross-sections, the relationship of principal extension ratios can be obtained using the incompressibility equation, Eq. (13.2.5), as

$$\lambda_2 = \lambda_3 = \lambda_1^{-\frac{1}{2}} \tag{13.2.16}$$

where λ_1 is principal extension ratio in loading direction, and λ_2 and λ_3 are principal extension ratios in the other two directions. Hence

$$I_1 = \lambda_1^2 + 2\lambda_1^{-1} \tag{13.2.17}$$

and $\quad I_2 = 2\lambda_1 + \lambda_1^{-2} \tag{13.2.18}$

The true stress, force per current area, in the loading direction can be derived substituting Eq. (13.2.15) into Eq. (13.2.6),

$$\sigma_{\text{true}} = 2A_{10}(\lambda_1 - \lambda_1^{-2}) \tag{13.2.19}$$

Assume the original radius of the circular cross-section of the specimen is r. Then the new radius after deformation is λ_2. Now that the cross-sectional area ratio is $[\pi(r\lambda_2)^2]/(\pi r)^2 = \lambda_2^2 = \lambda_1^{-1}$, the engineering stress (force per original unit area) is

$$\sigma_{11} = \frac{\sigma_{\text{true}}}{1 + \varepsilon_{11}} = \sigma_{\text{true}} \lambda_1^{-1} = 2A_{10}(1 - \lambda_1^{-3}) \tag{13.2.20}$$

When loaded at a small strain,

$$\lambda_1^{-3} = (1 + \varepsilon_{11})^{-3}$$

$$= 1 - 3\,\varepsilon_{11} + \text{higher order terms of } \varepsilon_{11}$$

$$\approx 1 - 3\,\varepsilon_{11} \tag{13.2.21}$$

As ε_{11} is small in the early stage of stretching, substituting the above equation into Eq. (13.2.20) yields the initial Young's modulus ($E = \sigma_{11}/\varepsilon_{11}$ for uniaxial loading) and shear modulus ($G = E/3$ for incompressible material),

$$E \approx 6\,A_{10} \tag{13.2.22}$$

and $\quad G \approx 2\,A_{10} \tag{13.2.23}$

13.2.3   Mooney-Rivlin's Equation

When $p = q = 1$ and only the first two terms are considered, Rivlin equation is called Mooney-Rivlin's equation and could be rewritten as

$$W(I_1, I_2) = A_{10}(I_1 - 3) + A_{01}(I_2 - 3) + C\,(I_3^{-2} - 1) + D\,(I_3 - 1)^2 \tag{13.2.24}$$

Again A_{10} and A_{01} are material properties and have the same unit as stress. The two hydrostatic parameters can be obtained, respectively as

$$C = \frac{1}{2}\,A_{10} + A_{01} \tag{13.2.25}$$

and $\quad D = (5\,\nu - 2)\,A_{10} + \dfrac{(11\,\nu - 4)\,A_{01}}{2 - 4\,\nu} \tag{13.2.26}$

Poisson's ratio ν approaches 0.5, e.g. 0.49, 0.499, 0.4999, etc., for near-incompressible material, while $\nu = 0.5$ for totally incompressible material. Parameter C and D are provided for a numerical treatment without "deadly" constraints in the finite element analysis. Typical data for tire rubber components based on Rivlin-Mooney equation are listed in Table 13.2.1. The true stress, i.e., Piola-Kirchhoff stress, corresponding to Eq. (13.2.24) for near-incompressible model based on Mooney-Rivlin equation becomes

$$\sigma_{\text{true}} = 2\,A_{10}(\lambda_1 - \lambda_1^{-2}) - 2\,A_{01}\,C - 4\,[\,D\,J^2(J^2 - 1) - C\,J^{-4}\,]\,C^{-1} \tag{13.2.27}$$

Simultaneously, the true stress corresponding to Eq. (13.2.24) for totally incompressible model based on Mooney-Rivlin equation reduces to

$$\sigma_{\text{true}} = 2 A_{10}(\lambda_1 - \lambda_1^{-2}) \tag{13.2.28}$$

How to obtain the hyperelastic material properties from tensile tests? The relationship of principal extension ratios for the uniaxial tensile test can be obtained using the incompressibility equation. Similarly based on the equations for invariants such as Eqs. (13.2.17)-(13.2.18), one has the true stress and engineering stress, respectively, as

$$\sigma_{\text{true}} = 2 \left(A_{10} + \frac{A_{01}}{\lambda_1} \right) \left(\lambda_1^2 - \frac{1}{\lambda_1} \right) \tag{13.2.29}$$

Assume the original radius of the circular cross-section of the specimen is r. Then the new radius after deformation is $r\lambda_2$. Now that the cross-sectional area ratio is $\left[\pi (r\lambda_2)^2 \right] / (\pi r)^2 = \lambda_2^2 = \lambda_1^{-1}$, the engineering stress (force per original unit area) is

$$\sigma_{11} = \frac{\sigma_{\text{true}}}{1 + \varepsilon_{11}} = \frac{\sigma_{\text{true}}}{\lambda_1^{-1}} = 2 \left(A_{10} + \frac{A_{01}}{\lambda_1} \right) \left(\lambda_1 - \frac{1}{\lambda_1^2} \right) \tag{13.2.30}$$

Again, when loaded at a small strain,

$$\lambda_1^{-2} = (1 + \varepsilon_{11})^{-2}$$

$$= 1 - 2 \varepsilon_{11} + \text{higher order} (\varepsilon_{11})$$

$$\approx 1 - 2 \varepsilon_{11} \tag{13.2.31}$$

As ε_{11} is small in the early stage of stretching, substituting the above equation into Eq. (13.2.30) yields the initial Young's modulus and shear modulus,

$$E \approx 6(A_{10} + A_{01}) \tag{13.2.32}$$

and $\quad G = \dfrac{E}{3} \approx 2(A_{10} + A_{01}) \tag{13.2.33}$

13.2.4　Yeoh's Equation

Because the influence of I_2 on the material behavior is significantly smaller than I_1, another equation was proposed by Yeoh to model the rubber behavior using the first three terms of Rivlin's equation based on I_1 only,

$$W (I_1) = A_{10}(I_1 - 3) + A_{20}(I_1 - 3)^2 + A_{30}(I_1 - 3)^3 \tag{13.2.34}$$

The true stress, force per current area, in the loading direction can be derived substituting Eq. (13.2.15) into Eq. (13.2.6),

$$\sigma_{\text{true}} = 2\,A_{10}(\lambda_1 - \lambda_1^{-2}) + \text{higher order terms } of\ \lambda_1 \tag{13.2.35}$$

As ε_{11} is small in the early stage of stretching, substituting the above equation into Eq. (13.2.20) yields the initial Young's modulus and shear modulus,

$$E \approx 6\,A_{10} \tag{13.2.36}$$

and

$$G \approx 2\,A_{10} \tag{13.2.37}$$

13.2.5　Ogden's Equation

Another model being used for analysts in the rubber industry is Ogden's equation. It is represented by the strain energy density function, W, in terms of the principal extension ratios, i.e., λ_1, λ_2, and λ_3, directly as

$$W = \sum_{i=1}^{n} \frac{2B_i}{A_i^2}\,(\lambda_1^{Ai} + \lambda_2^{Ai} + \lambda_3^{Ai} - 3) + K[\,(J-1) - \ln J\,] \tag{13.2.38}$$

where
A_i: Material constant, non-integer;
B_i: Material constant;
K: Bulk modulus.

Note that $2B_i/A_i^2$ must be positive in order to secure a positive strain energy function in the pure shear test. Parameters A_i and B_i can be obtained by regression modeling of test data.

13.2.6　Fractional-Exponent Model

Finally a promising model for large but not-so-large deformations in rubber filled with carbon black is Fractional-Exponent model [Davies, De, and Thomas]. An energy model with non-integer exponents was proposed as

$$W = \frac{A}{2\left(1 - \dfrac{1}{2}n\right)}\,(I_1 - 3 + C^2)^{\left(1 - \frac{n}{2}\right)} + K\,(I_1 - 3)^2 \tag{13.2.39}$$

where parameters A and K are material constants related to the content of black carbon and the degree of cross-linking. Parameter C is of the initial strain value at which the breakdown of the carbon black structure begins; a small value is usually assumed, e.g. 0.001 or 0.01. Exponent n

indicates the rate at which the carbon black breaks down. The upsweep of the stress-strain curve is governed by K, which shows the finite extensibility of the rubber cross-linking network. In general this model is valid for a not-so-large strain, falling in the range of 0.1% and 100%. Most engineering applications such as engine mounting devices, suspension bushings, and tires, fit right into this range.

For simple tensile and compressive tests, the first derivative of the energy with respect to I_1 is given as

$$\frac{\partial W}{\partial I_1} = \frac{\sigma}{2(\lambda + \lambda^2)} \qquad (13.2.40)$$

or $\qquad \sigma = \frac{\partial W}{\partial I_1} \left[2(\lambda + \lambda^2) \right] \qquad (13.2.41)$

in which σ is the engineering stress. Substituting the energy term, W, in Eq. (13.2.39) into Eq. (13.2.40) yields

$$\frac{W}{\partial I_1} = \frac{1}{2}A (I_1 - 3 + C^2)^{-\frac{n}{2}} + 2K(I_1 - 3) = \frac{\sigma}{2(\lambda + \lambda^2)} \qquad (13.2.42)$$

Parameter K has little impact on the stress response when the strain is not large, saying $\leqslant 40\%$. The above equation can be transformed into the log scale, with $2K(I_1-3)$ being discarded for small strains, as

$$\ln\left(\frac{1}{2}A\right) - \frac{1}{2}n \ln(I_1 - 3 + C^2) = \ln\left(\frac{\sigma}{2(\lambda + \lambda^2)}\right) \qquad (13.2.43)$$

The above equation can be used to numerically calculate $\ln\frac{1}{2}A$ and $\frac{1}{2} \cdot n$, and thus solved for A and n using linear regression for a given group of stress-strain data. $\ln(I_1 - 3 + C^2)$ and $\ln[\sigma/(2\lambda+2\lambda^2)]$ are independent and dependent variables in the linear regression. The residues after being filtered by $\frac{1}{2}A (I_1-3+C^2)^{-n/2}$ will be used as the dependent variable to do the linear regression for K with $2(I_1-3)$ as the independent variable. The shear modulus of the material can be related to the shear strain γ by

$$G = A(\gamma^2 + C^2)^{-\frac{n}{2}} + 4K\gamma^2 \qquad (13.2.44)$$

Of course the Young's modulus is related to the shear modulus as $E = 3G$.

13.2.7   Selection of Hyperelastic Models

Mooney-Rivlin model is good for modeling elastomeric materials for an application at a strain level up to 100%, which is true for most vibration isolators for on-ground vehicles. Fractional-Exponent equation is quite accurate up to a moderate size of strain, which is higher than 100%, that is, it is valid for most elastomers for on-ground vehicles. Yeoh's equation and Ogden equation are generally good for modeling elastomeric materials applied at an extreme high strain level.

13.3   Penalty Function Method for Finite Element Analysis of Elastomers

Implementation of the Rivlin's equation, Eq. (13.2.1), infinite element analysis is generally conducted using a model with terms up to order three. In order to accommodate the incompressibility of rubber, with Poisson's ratio being 0.5, a penalty parameter may be used to formulate the energy equations, as shown in the following equation:

$$W_G = W + \frac{1}{2} \alpha G I_3^2$$

$$= \left[\sum_{i=1}^{3} \sum_{j=0}^{3} A_{ij} (I_1-3)^i (I_2-3)^j \right] + \frac{1}{2} \alpha G I_3^2$$

$$= A_{10} (I_1 - 3) + A_{01} (I_2 - 3) + A_{20} (I_1 - 3)^2 + A_{11} (I_1 - 3)(I_2 - 3) +$$

$$A_{02} (I_2 - 3)^2 + A_{30} (I_1 - 3)^3 + A_{21} (I_1 - 3)^2(I_2 - 3) +$$

$$A_{12} (I_1 - 3)(I_2 - 3)^2 + A_{03} (I_2 - 3)^3 + \frac{1}{2} \alpha G I_3^2 \qquad (13.3.1)$$

where $G(I_3)$, called the penalty function [Malkus], is spurious with null value in theory. The relationship between the penalty number, α, and the bulk modulus is a clue to estimate the penalty number. Thus, in theoretical formulation, $W_G = W+0 = W$. For example [Swanson],

$$G(I_3) = I_3 - 1 \qquad (13.3.2)$$

The above equation is used here to illustrate the calculation of the penalty number (α) in terms of the bulk modulus. Similar to the format in defining the Young's modulus, $E = d\sigma/d\varepsilon$, the bulk modulus given by Eq. (13.2.13) can be rewritten in a differential form as

$$B = \frac{dP_G}{d(J - 1)} \qquad (13.3.3)$$

where $J = I_3^{\frac{1}{2}}$ as shown in Eq. (13.2.11), such that $(J-1)$ is the volumetric strain. The hydrostatic pressure associated with the new strain energy form in Eq. (13.3.3), P_G, resembling a normal stress, can be derived as,

$$P_G = \frac{\partial W_G}{\partial(J-1)} \tag{13.3.4}$$

Substituting Eq. (13.3.4) into Eq. (13.3.3), and then into the above equation, one has

$$P_G = \frac{\partial\left[W + \dfrac{1}{2}\alpha(I_3-1)^2\right]}{\partial(J-1)}$$

$$= \frac{\partial\left[W + \dfrac{1}{2}\alpha(J^2-1)^2\right]}{\partial(J-1)}$$

$$= 2\alpha(J^3 - J) \tag{13.3.5}$$

Note that $P = \partial W/\partial(J-1) = 0$ per Eq. (13.2.10), because there is no volume change associated with the strain energy term, W. Substituting the above equation into Eq. (13.2.3) yields

$$B = 2\alpha(3J^2 - 1) = 4\alpha \tag{13.3.6}$$

The penalty function shown in Eq. (13.3.2) is one of the many available. Another penalty function has been applied is $G(I_3) = \dfrac{1}{2}\ln I_3$, which can be added to the strain energy density function, W, for finite element formulations. Be aware that $J^2 = I_3 = 1$, due to incompressibility. The value taken for α has been empirical. A number between 5×10^3 and 10^5 could be a good choice. The penalty number, α, is limited by the computational precision of computer, e.g. should be less than 10^6 for computations using double precision. Only nearly incompressible is numerically possible.

13.4 Rubber Degradation due to Cycling

Softening due to stretch-cycling occurs in both unfilled and filled elastomers is called Mullins effect. However, the effect is far more pronounced in filled elastomers and therefore is frequently identified as a filled-rubber phenomenon. Stress softening is maximal in the first cycle but it reduces in subsequent cycles until the stretch reaches a constant value after several cycles, and hereinafter referred to as hysteresis like plastics, as shown in Fig. 13.4.1.

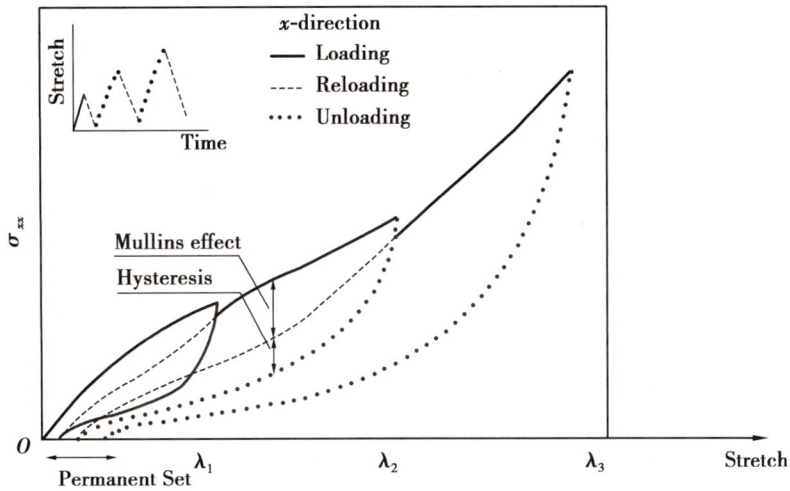

Fig. 13.4.1   Schematic Stress-Strain Curves Showing the Mullins Effect and Hysteresis Observed in Cyclic Uniaxial Tensile Tests〔Dargazany & Itskov〕

Thus, the mechanical properties of rubber have to be measured after it passed a few large-deformation cycles (i.e., the stretch-softening stage) that is to rearrange molecular networks prior to its reaching equilibrium, as given in Fig. 13.4.2. In other words, the material properties of elastomers for finite element analysis and other methods should be taken after an initial transition period in order to capture the influence of Mullins effect. Listed as follows are two set of material parameters based on Odgen model, i.e., Eq. (13.2.38) for $n = 1$, 2 and 3, before and after Mullins effect〔Chung & Kim〕:

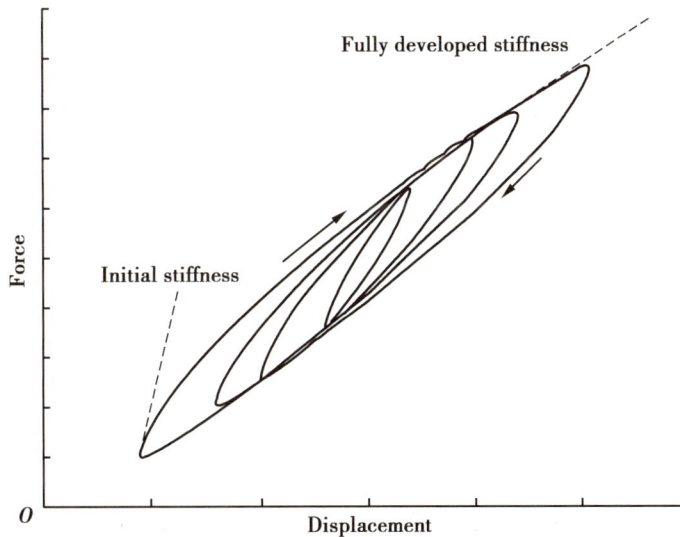

Fig. 13.4.2   Rubber Stiffness (Dashed Slope Lines) Measured at Force-Displacement Loops after Removing Mullins Effect

Mullins Effect	$2B_1$	A_1	$2B_2$	A_2	$2B_3$	A_3
Before	0.556	2.5786	5.643	0.1068	6.284	0.1120
After	0.410	2.5786	4.161	0.1068	4.635	0.1120

Rubber is isotropic in the virgin state but it becomes anisotropic after being loaded in one direction for a long time while being stress-free in other directions. This phenomenon is generally referred to as induced anisotropy.

13.5 Elastomeric Dynamics

The stress-stretch (or stress-strain) behavior of rubber (an elastomer) exhibits different kinds of dependency on time. Three major distinct material properties have been observed and they are strain hardening, stress relaxation, and hysteresis. Strain hardening demonstrates that the stress level is found to increase with increasing strain rate. Stress relaxation shows that the stress will approach an equilibrium state when the material is held at a constant strain for a certain amount of time. Hysteresis means the unloading recovery path does not follow the loading path on the stress-stretch curve. The loss due to hysteresis is present even at quasi-static conditions for filled rubber exposed to a harmonic excitation.

Because all the rubber properties are time-dependent, viscoelastic models are chosen to describe their behaviors. When stress is applied to viscoelastic material, the viscous effect causes a lag of strain behind stress. The stress induced in linear viscoelastic material is described as

$$\sigma(t) = \int_0^t E(t-\tau) \frac{d\varepsilon(\tau)}{d\tau} \, d\tau \qquad (13.5.1)$$

where

$\sigma(t)$: Accumulated stress level at time t;

$E(t-\tau)$: Modulus of elasticity with time delay $t-\tau$;

$d\varepsilon(\tau)$: Differential strain at time τ, where $0 \leqslant \tau \leqslant t$.

Mechanical hysteresis losses in rubber compounds and fibers of a tire manifest itself in internal heat generation, causing the temperature of a running tire to go above the ambient temperature. Hysteresis loss Φ per cycle per unit volume under a sinusoidal-varying displacement is illustrated here using a sinusoidal function as follows

$$\Phi = \pi \, \sigma_o \, \varepsilon_o \sin \delta = \pi \, E'' \, \varepsilon_o^2 = \frac{\pi \, E'' \, \sigma_o^2}{|E^*|^2} \qquad (13.5.2)$$

where σ_o and ε_o are stress and strain amplitudes, respectively. Note that tandδ is the loss tangent. The amount of the hysteresis loss given in Eq. (13.5.2) is the area of eaqch ellipse shown in Fig. 13.4.2. The coefficient of rolling resistance can be viewed as the drag force to pull the free rolling tire divided by the normal load, is referred to power loss by the equation

$$f_r = \frac{f\left(\sum H\right)}{V_v\, W_w} \tag{13.5.3}$$

in which $\sum H$ means the summation of all the energy loss per cycle of tire rotation for the entire tire and f is the number of cycles per second. V_v is the linear vehicle speed (in m/s) and W_w is the normal load (in Newton) at the wheel/tire.

13.5.1   Maxwell Model

As shown in Fig. 13.5.1, a spring and a dashpot are arranged in a series, in which E is the spring rate, η is dashpot viscosity, $\sigma(t)$ is the applied stress, and $\varepsilon(t)$ is the induced strain. In light of the stress balance and strain compatibility, in analogy to the force balance and displacement compatibility, one can have the following two equations

$$\sigma = \sigma_{dashpot} = \sigma_{spring} \tag{13.5.4}$$

and

$$\varepsilon = \varepsilon_{dashpot} + \varepsilon_{spring} \tag{13.5.5}$$

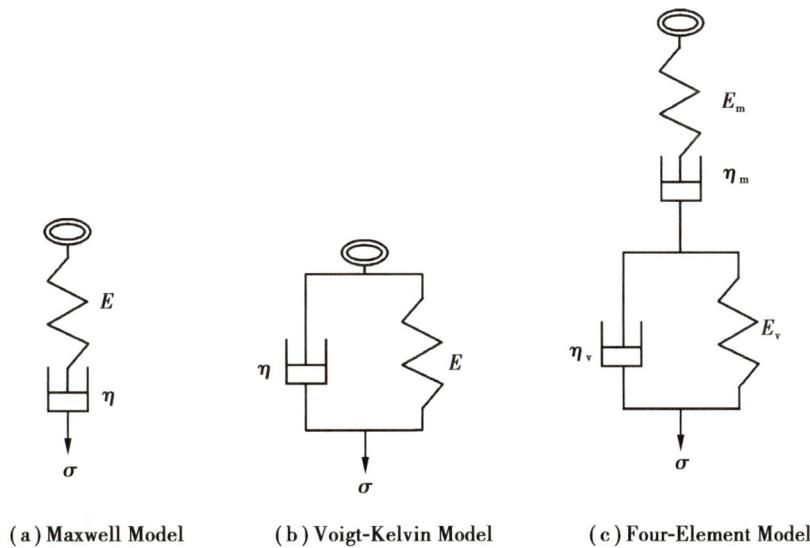

(a) Maxwell Model   (b) Voigt-Kelvin Model   (c) Four-Element Model

Fig. 13.5.1   Viscoelastic Models

The constitutive functions for spring and dashpot are

$$\sigma_{\text{spring}} = E\varepsilon_{\text{spring}} \tag{13.5.6}$$

and $\quad \sigma_{\text{dashpot}} = \eta \dfrac{\text{d}\varepsilon_{\text{dashpot}}}{\text{d}t} \tag{13.5.7}$

Differentiating Eq. (13.5.4) with respect to time and substituting Eqs. (13.5.5)-(13.5.7) into the derivative equation, one has

$$\frac{\text{d}\sigma(t)}{\text{d}t} + \frac{E}{\eta}\,\sigma(t) = E\,\frac{\text{d}\varepsilon(t)}{\text{d}t} \tag{13.5.8}$$

13.5.2 Voigt-Kelvin Model

The spring and dashpot are arranged in parallel. In light of the force balance and displacement compatibility, one can have the following two equations,

$$\sigma = \sigma_{\text{dashpot}} + \sigma_{\text{spring}} \tag{13.5.9}$$

and $\quad \varepsilon = \varepsilon_{\text{dashpot}} = \varepsilon_{\text{spring}} \tag{13.5.10}$

with the same constitutive functions as shown in Eq. (13.5.6) and Eq. (13.5.7). Differentiating Eq. (13.5.10) with respect to time and substituting Eqs. (13.5.7)-(13.5.9) into the derivative equation give

$$\frac{\text{d}\varepsilon(t)}{\text{d}t} + \frac{E}{\eta_{\cdot}}\,\varepsilon(t) = \frac{\sigma(t)}{\eta} \tag{13.5.11}$$

13.5.3 Four-Parameter Model

The viscoelastic characteristics of linear amorphous rubber or plastics can be represented using a four-parameter model [Hewitt] [Progelhof & Throne], which is a combination of Maxwell model and Voigt-Kelvin model in series,

$$\frac{\text{d}^2\sigma(t)}{\text{d}t^2} + \left(\frac{E_{\text{m}}}{\eta_{\text{m}}} + \frac{E_{\text{m}}}{\eta_{\text{v}}} + \frac{E_{\text{v}}}{\eta_{\text{v}}}\right)\frac{\text{d}\sigma(t)}{\text{d}t} + \frac{E_{\text{m}}E_{\text{v}}}{\eta_{\text{m}}\eta_{\text{v}}}\,\sigma(t) = E_{\text{m}}\frac{\text{d}^2\varepsilon(t)}{\text{d}t^2} + \left(\frac{E_{\text{m}}E_{\text{v}}}{\eta_{\text{v}}}\right)\frac{\text{d}\varepsilon(t)}{\text{d}t} \tag{13.5.12}$$

This is a crude qualitative description of the viscoelastic response of linear amorphous rubber or plastics. At a fixed uniform tensile load with zero initial velocity and zero initial acceleration, $\sigma(t) = \sigma_{\text{o}}$, $\text{d}\sigma(t)/\text{d}t = 0$, $\text{d}^2\sigma(t)/\text{d}t^2 = 0$, the four-element equation reduces to a differential equation for strain only

$$\frac{\mathrm{d}^2 \varepsilon(t)}{\mathrm{d}t^2} + \left(\frac{E_\mathrm{v}}{\eta_\mathrm{v}}\right) \frac{\mathrm{d}\varepsilon(t)}{\mathrm{d}t} = \frac{E_\mathrm{m} E_\mathrm{v}}{\eta_\mathrm{m} \eta_\mathrm{v}} \sigma_\mathrm{o} \tag{13.5.13}$$

Consider the initial conditions for the strain and strain rate. Since there is no immediate response of strain in Voigt-Kelvin model, the initial strain is

$$\varepsilon(t) = \frac{\sigma_\mathrm{o}}{E_\mathrm{m}} \tag{13.5.14}$$

Simultaneously, since η_m and η_v are in series the initial strain rate may be

$$\frac{\mathrm{d}\varepsilon(t)}{\mathrm{d}t} = \frac{\sigma_\mathrm{o}}{\eta_\mathrm{m}} + \frac{\sigma_\mathrm{o}}{\eta_\mathrm{v}} \tag{13.5.15}$$

The four-element equation, Eq. (13.5.13), can be solved for the strain history as

$$\varepsilon(t) = \frac{\sigma_\mathrm{o}}{E_\mathrm{m}} + \frac{\sigma_\mathrm{o}}{E_\mathrm{v}} \left(1 - e^{\frac{-E_\mathrm{v} t}{\eta_\mathrm{v}}}\right) + \frac{\sigma_\mathrm{o} t}{\eta_\mathrm{v}} \tag{13.5.16}$$

or
$$\varepsilon(t) = \left[\frac{1}{E_\mathrm{m}} + \frac{1}{E_\mathrm{v}} \left(1 - e^{\frac{-E_\mathrm{v} t}{\eta_\mathrm{v}}}\right) + \frac{t}{\eta_\mathrm{v}}\right] \sigma_\mathrm{o} = \frac{\sigma_\mathrm{o}}{E_\mathrm{app}(t)} \tag{13.5.17}$$

where $E_\mathrm{app}(t)$ is called an apparent modulus as a function of time, referring to Eq. (13.5.1),

$$\frac{1}{E_\mathrm{app}(t)} = \frac{1}{E_\mathrm{m}} + \frac{1}{E_\mathrm{v}} \left(1 - e^{\frac{-E_\mathrm{v} t}{\eta_\mathrm{v}}}\right) + \frac{t}{\eta_\mathrm{v}} \tag{13.5.18}$$

The first three curve segments shown in Fig. 13.5.2 follows the three terms of Eq. (13.5.16). The above equation exhibits an additive superposition of different contributing strain components in form of material compliances, when rewritten as follows

$$S_\mathrm{app}(t) = S_\mathrm{m} + S_\mathrm{retard}(t) + S_\mathrm{creep} \tag{13.5.19}$$

where the apparent compliance, Maxwell spring compliance, and Voigt-Kelvin spring compliance are, respectively,

$$S_\mathrm{app}(t) = \frac{1}{E_\mathrm{app}(t)} \tag{13.5.20}$$

$$S_\mathrm{m} = \frac{1}{E_\mathrm{m}} \tag{13.5.21}$$

$$S_\mathrm{retard}(t) = \frac{1 - e^{\frac{-E_\mathrm{v} t}{\eta_\mathrm{v}}}}{E_\mathrm{v}} \tag{13.5.22}$$

and $\qquad S_{\text{creep}}(t) = \dfrac{t}{\eta_v}$ $\qquad\qquad$ (13.5.23)

After the fixed load is removed at time $t = t_1$, the strain becomes

$$\varepsilon(t_1) = \frac{\sigma_o}{E_m} + \frac{\sigma_o t_1}{\eta_v} + \frac{\sigma_o}{E_v}\left(1 - e^{\frac{-E_v t_1}{\eta_v}}\right) \qquad\qquad (13.5.24)$$

and $\qquad \dfrac{d\varepsilon(t_1)}{dt} = \dfrac{\sigma_o}{\eta_v} - \dfrac{\sigma_o}{E_v} e^{\frac{-E_v t_1}{\eta_v}}$ $\qquad\qquad$ (13.5.25)

After solving Eq. (13.5.13) with the conditions at time t_1 listed above, one has the strain recovery process, as shown in Fig. 13.5.2,

$$\varepsilon(t_1) = \frac{\sigma_o}{E_v}\left[\left(1 - e^{\frac{-E_v t_1}{\eta_v}}\right)e^{\frac{-E_v(t-t_1)}{\eta_v}} + t_1\right] \qquad\qquad (13.5.26)$$

As depicted in Fig. 13.5.2, the response of the four-element model, under a fixed load with zero initial conditions and after the load getting removed later, consists of six different stages in the mechanics evolution:

(a) Hookean elastic strain;
(b) Retarded elastic strain;
(c) Newtonian viscous fluid;
(d) Hookean spring back;
(e) Retarded recovery;
(f) Permanent set.

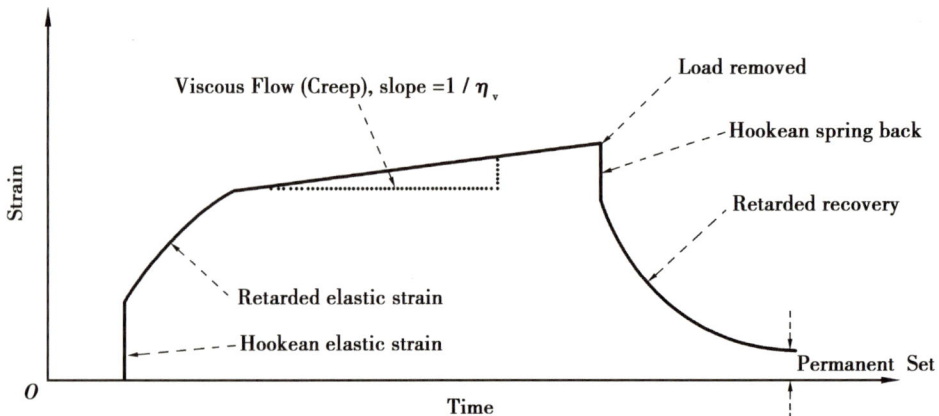

Fig. 13.5.2 **Response of Rubber Based on Four-Element Model under a Constant Load**

13.5.4　Temperature-Dependent Rubber Viscoelasticity

The material behavior of elastomers including rubber is split into three regions according to temperature variation: a glassy, a transition and a rubber region, as shown in Fig. 13.5.3 [Sjöberg]. The dynamic modulus of elasticity and loss factor vary as:

(1) Crystalline (glassy) rubber ($T < T_g$): Rubber is crystalline rendering a high dynamic shear modulus and low loss factor when it works at a temperature below T_g.

(2) Glass transition point ($T = T_g$): The glass transition point is the temperature, where the change of shear modulus magnitude is the greatest and results in a maximum value of loss factor.

(3) Rubbery region ($T > T_g$): As the temperature goes beyond the glass transition point, the material enters the transition region where it becomes rubbery and its dynamic shear modulus magnitude decreases. Dynamic shear modulus magnitude and loss factor both exhibit moderate changes with temperature once the rubbery region is reached. A plot of monotonic stress-strain curves at -5 ℃, 23 ℃, and 50 ℃ with the loading rate at 0.001 s^{-1} are shown in Fig. 13.5.4(a). Another plot at 23 ℃ with two different loading rates in Fig. 13.5.4(b) shows the material gets stiffer when the loading rate is higher.

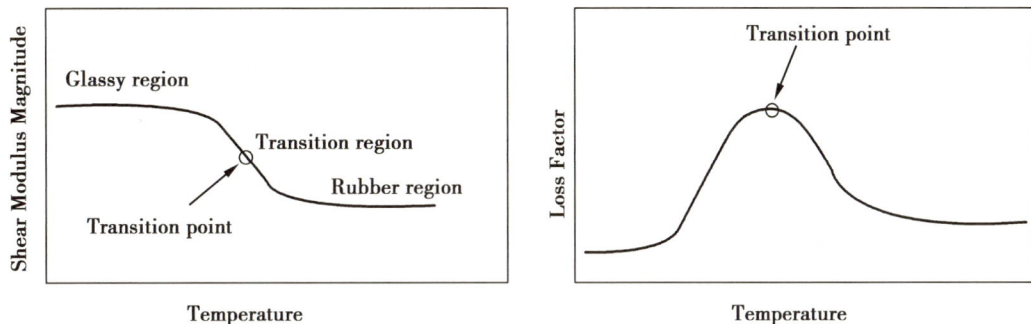

Fig. 13.5.3　Schematic Drawing of Temperature-Dependent Properties of Elastomers

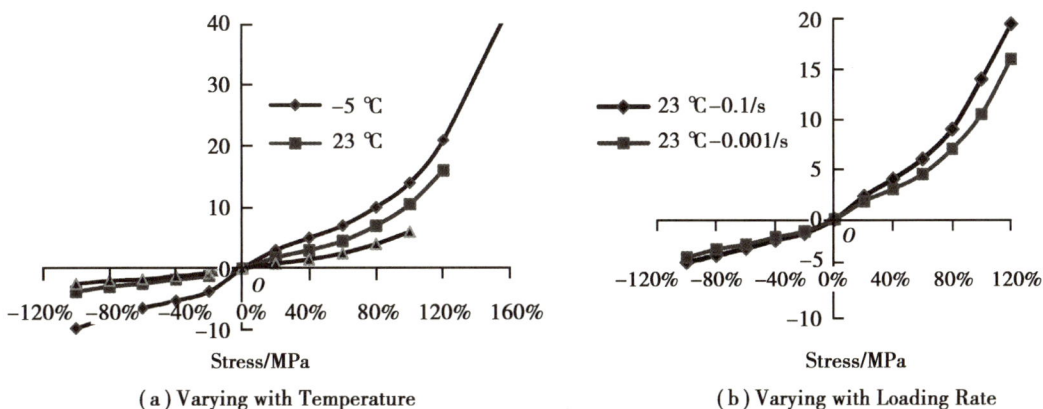

(a) Varying with Temperature　　(b) Varying with Loading Rate

Fig. 13.5.4　Monotonic Stress (MPa)-Strain Curves of SBR [Brown et al.]

Another aspect of rubber is its viscoelasticity, which is its temperature-dependent tendency, especially the creep (viscous flow) behavior in the rubbery region. It has been shown by [Debruyne & Vanhoutte] that the creep compliance increases with rising temperature in the following temperature range: $T_g < T < (T_g + 100 \ °C)$. The shift factor follows Williams-Landel-Ferry empirical equation,

$$\log_{10}(S_{\text{creep}}) = \frac{-C_1(T - T_{\text{ref}})}{C_2 + (T - T_{\text{ref}})}$$

$$= \frac{-17.4\ (T - T_g)}{51.6 + (T - T_g)} \quad \text{for } T_g < T < T_g + 100\ °C \qquad (13.5.27)$$

where

$T\ (°C)$: Temperature;

$T_g(°C)$: Glass transition temperature of material, and $T_g \approx -70\ °C$ for most tire rubber;

$T_{\text{ref}}(°C)$: Reference temperature;

$C_1(°C)$: Constant, and $C_1 = 17.44$ for rubber, if $T_{\text{ref}} = T_g$;

$C_2(°C)$: Constant, and $C_2 = 51.6\ °C$ for rubber, if $T_{\text{ref}} = T_g$.

The major application of the shift factor is to replace a high-speed vibration test of rubber product (e.g. tires) by a low-speed vibration test at a lower temperature [Gehman]. For example, the shift factor given by Eq. (13.5.27) shows that $\log_{10}(S_{\text{creep}}) = -11.3$ at 25 °C and $\log_{10}(S_{\text{creep}}) = -10.0$ at 0 °C. Thus, the vibration speed is allowed to go from 10 m/min at 25 °C down to 0.5 m/min, i.e., $10 / \log_{10}^{-1}(11.3 / 10)$ m/s, at 0 °C to validate the product function if a high-speed test machine is not available.

13.5.5   Amplitude-Dependent Rubber Vibration

Typical hysteresis loops of a filled rubber for cyclic excitation with different amplitudes is shown in Fig. 13.4.1. It is demonstrated that the rubber stiffness decreases with increasing vibration amplitude, as exhibited in Fig. 13.5.5.

13.5.6   Frequency-Dependent Rubber Vibration

It is demonstrated in Fig. 13.5.6 that the rubber stiffness decreases with increasing vibration amplitude.

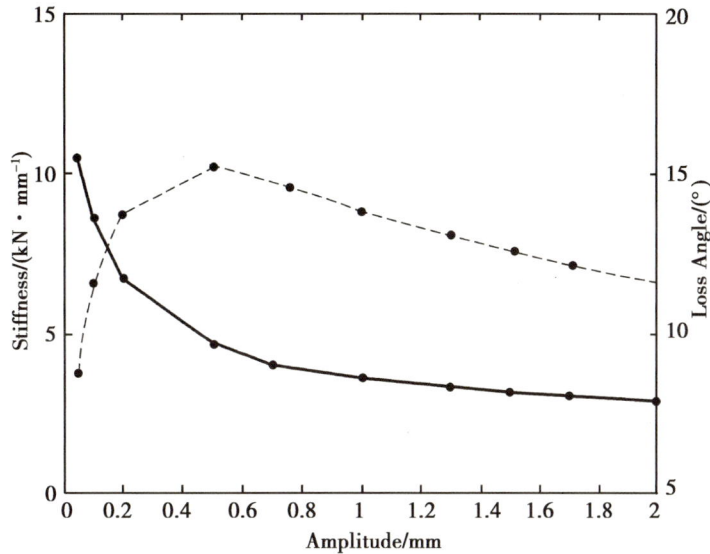

Fig. 13.5.5 Vibration Amplitude-Dependent Mechanical Properties of Elastomers [Sjöberg 2002]

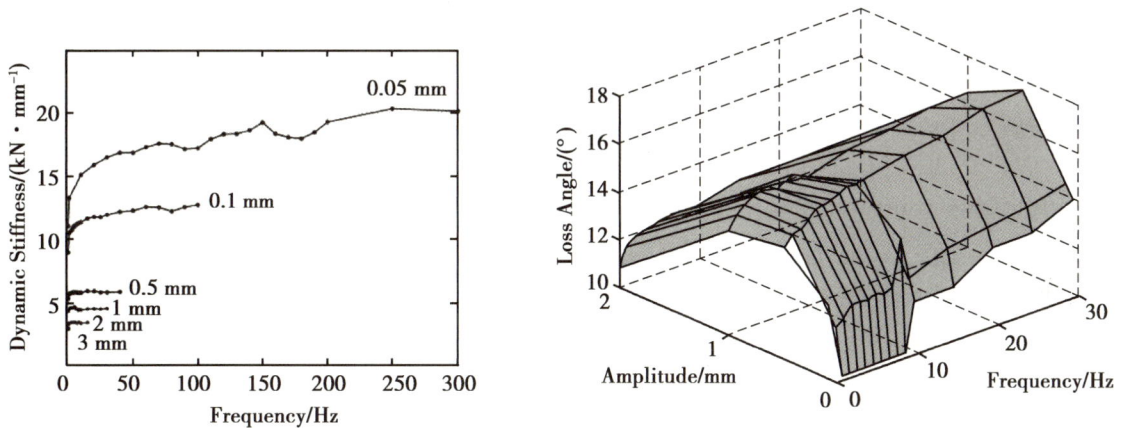

Fig. 13.5.6 Frequency-Dependent Mechanical Properties of Elastomers [Sjöberg 2000]

13.6 Fatigue of Rubber

Structural rubber components such as engine mounts are expected to meet two functional requirements: (a) Absorption of loads caused by operation of the engine and by excitation from the road surface and (b) Vibration isolation and damping. Since each rubber component is subject to complex loading conditions and harsh working environments, its fatigue strength is suggested to be considered in an early design phase before building the first round of prototypes.

13.6.1 Strain-Based Crack Nucleation Criteria for Rubber Fatigue under Uniaxial Loading

The following equation based on strain-life curves can be used to estimate the life of a rubber compound or product (e.g. mounting pads for shock absorbers) resulting from a HCF (High Cycle Fatigue) tests

$$2N_f = \left[(1-R)^{q-1} \left(\frac{\varepsilon_a}{\varepsilon_o} \right) \right]^k e^{\left(\frac{E_a}{R_a} \right)} (T^{-1} - T_o^{-1}) \tag{13.6.1}$$

where

T (K) : Temperature;

R : Load ratio;

ε_a : Working strain amplitude;

ε_o : Reference strain amplitude, which can be the strain at fracture [Woo et al.] ;

E_a : Energy term;

q : Exponent;

k : Exponent.

In general, either the equivalent strain (i.e., von Mises strain) or principal strain instead of normal strain would work better for modeling the ε_a-N curve [Harbor]. Since the model is applicable to HCF only, it is not suitable to fit the curve with LCF (Low Cycle Fatigue) data or mixed LCF-HCF data. When $R=0.5$, $T=T_o$, Eq. (13.6.1) deforms to

$$\varepsilon_a = \varepsilon_o 0.5^{1-q} (2N_f)^{\frac{1}{k}} \tag{13.6.2}$$

Lifetime estimation by the above equation is an empirical approach. Reference strain amplitude ε_o can be used for the need such as ultimate strength for fatigue or creep fracture limit for creep failure. The following is derived for natural rubber at fatigue limit [Woo et al.]

$$2N_f = 4466 \left(\frac{\varepsilon_a}{\varepsilon_{uts}} \right)^{-3.85} \tag{13.6.3}$$

Since each rubber product has its own specific rubber compound and working environment, it must be tested for its own market need. For reference, the following is a list of fatigue lives of different example rubber compounds based on the strain-life criterion:

$$\varepsilon_a = 0.000036 (2N_f)^{-6.277} \qquad \text{for CR (Chloroprene) [Suryatal et al.])}$$

$$\varepsilon_a = 0.8091 (2N_f)^{-0.099} \qquad \text{for SBR (Styrene-Butadiene Rubber) [Brown et al.]}$$

$$\varepsilon_a = 0.00001292(2N_f)^{-0.4545} \quad \text{for NR (Natural Rubber)} \; [\text{Harbor et al.}]$$

The strain-cycle curve of SBR for tracked vehicle pads at 23 ℃, described by Eq. ($13.6.2_a$) is depicted in Fig. 13.6.1 [Brown et al.]. The strain amplitude versus fatigue cycle of vulcanized chloroprene rubber, rated at Shore A hardness 66, subjected to uniaxial loading are listed as follows [Suryatal et al.]:

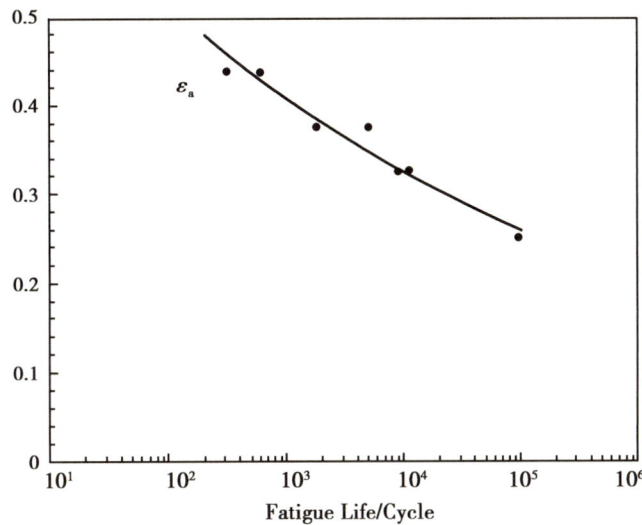

Fig. 13.6.1   Strain-Cycle Curve of SBR for Tracked Vehicle Pads at 23 ℃ [Brown et al.]

Strain	Life Cycles
25%	7.20×10^5
50%	3.36×10^5
65%	1.68×10^5
75%	8.80×10^4
85%	4.00×10^4
100%	3.21×10^4
125%	1.60×10^4

Eq. (13.6.2) is valid once the strain energy release rate goes beyond the threshold (Fig. 13.6.2). Other factors that have a significant influence on the fatigue life of rubber are listed as follows:

(1) Mean Strain: A higher tensile mean strain does more damage as a function of R (load ratio) demonstrated in Fig. 13.6.2 and Eq. (13.6.1).

(2) Strain Amplitude: Larger strain amplitude does more damage.

(3) Annealing Strain: It is shown by [Roland] that annealing under a static strain on fatigue life and tensile strength can improve the fatigue strength of unfilled polyisoprene. The improvement depends on the strain amplitude and statically strained rest period-the

ratio of maximum to minimum fatigue life is about 250%.

(4) Load Sequence: A decreasing-load sequence reduces the residual ultimate strength to a greater degree than an increasing-load sequence [Sun et al.].

(5) Loading frequency: Loading frequency has a great influence on the fatigue life of amorphous rubbers, but little effect on the fatigue life of rubber that exhibits strain crystallization under isothermal conditions over a frequency range of 10^{-3} to 50 Hz [Ellul].

(6) Ozone: The fatigue life of rubber can be shortened significantly as exposed to ozone for a long time during a fatigue test. Ozone reacts chemically with carbon-carbon double bonds in the rubber, causing scission of the chain.

(7) Oxygen: The mechanical fatigue crack growth threshold (Fig. 13.6.2) is lowered as referenced to testing in vacuum and oxidative aging occurs, when exposed to oxygen.

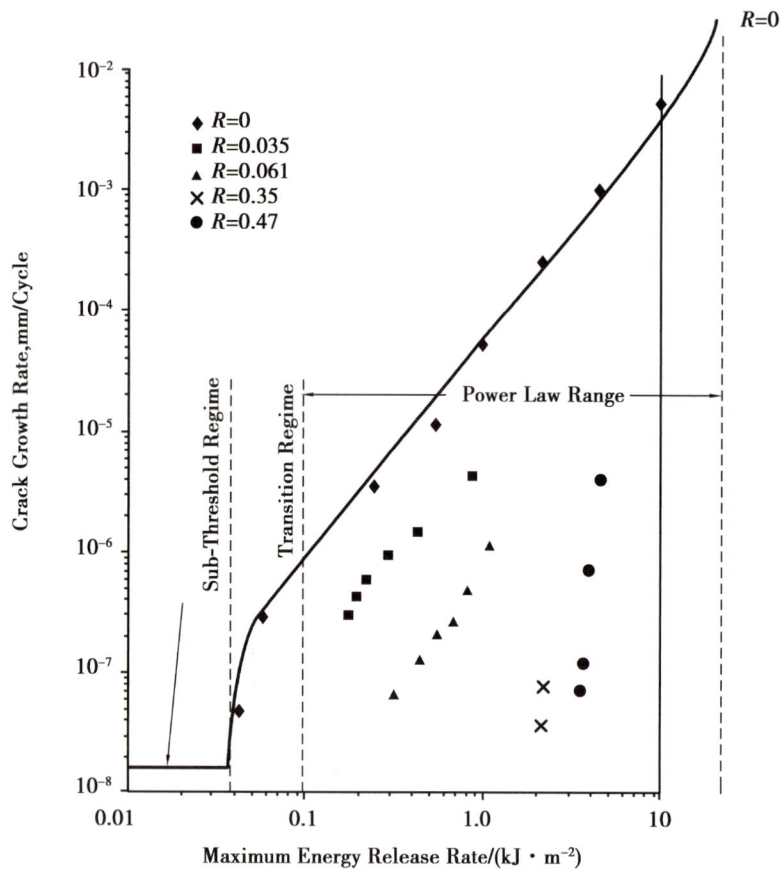

Fig. 13.6.2 Fatigue Crack Growth Rate of Unfilled Natural Rubber [Lindley]

13.6.2 Rubber Fatigue under Multiaxial Loadings: Crack Nucleation Criterion

The influence of multiaxial loadings on the rubber fatigue is still not well understood. The fatigue cycling under different combinations of biaxial loadings due to [Cadwell et al.] are listed as follows:

Shear Strain	Normal Strain	Lifetime (Cycles)
$-25\% < \gamma < 25\%$	$\varepsilon = 0$	7×10^6
$-25\% < \gamma < 25\%$	$\varepsilon = -12.5\%$	20×10^6
$-25\% < \gamma < 25\%$	$\varepsilon = 25\%$	12×10^6
$0 < \gamma < 50\%$	$\varepsilon = 0\%$	1×10^6
$0 < \gamma < 50\%$	$\varepsilon = -12.5\%$	2×10^6
$0 < \gamma < 50\%$	$\varepsilon = 25\%$	2×10^6
$75\% < \gamma < 125\%$	$\varepsilon = 0$	15×10^6
$75\% < \gamma < 125\%$	$\varepsilon = -12.5\%$	2×10^6
$75\% < \gamma < 125\%$	$\varepsilon = 25\%$	40×10^6

It has been argued by veteran researchers [Ro 1989], [Abraham et al. 2005] [Harbor et al. 2008] that the strain energy density is a better criterion than the strain-or stress-based criterion for predicting crack nucleation (crack initiation). A criterion inspired by the strain energy method is given as follows [Chen et al.]:

$$\Delta\sigma_c \Delta\varepsilon_{c,\max} + \Delta\tau_c \Delta\gamma_c = K(2N_f)^d \qquad (13.6.4)$$

where

K: Coefficient;

d: Exponent;

$\Delta\sigma_c$: Normal stress range on the critical plane;

$\Delta\varepsilon_{c,\max}$: Maximum principal strain on the critical plane;

$\Delta\tau_c$: Shear stress range on the critical plane;

$\Delta\gamma_c$: Shear strain range on the critical plane.

13.6.3   Crack Propagation Based on Strain Energy Release Rate in Rubber

The strain energy density can be considered as a measure of the energy release rate of preexisting flaws in relation with the phenomena observed during the propagation of microscopic defects. This also suggests that the energy release rate is the proper criterion for estimating the fatigue crack propagation in rubber compounds subjected to multiaxial loadings.

It was reported [Stevenson et al.] that fatigue crack growth under a combination of compression and shear loadings can be predicted, though the method is considered slightly conservative. It is based on analytical estimates of individual energy release rates of small cracks in axial compression G_c, and in shear G_s, which are combined to obtain a total energy release rate G according to the following rule [Stevenson]

$$G = (G_c^2 + G_s^2)^{\frac{1}{2}} \qquad (13.6.5)$$

It is thus feasible to predict the crack growth rate with mixed modes (mode-I and mode-II) using the finite element methods as proven by [Busfield et al.] for the case study on $R=0$. The variation of the crack growth rate versus the maximum energy release rate at various load ratios is depicted in Fig. 13.6.2.

Nevertheless, a simple model for crack propagation with different rubbers as a function of temperature at $R=0$ is given by [Young] & [Mars & Fatemi] as follows:

$$\frac{\mathrm{d}a}{\mathrm{d}t} = B\ G^F \tag{13.6.6}$$

such as

$$\frac{\mathrm{d}a}{\mathrm{d}t} = 12.0 \times 10^{-18} G^{1.35} \qquad (\mathrm{BR}) \tag{13.6.6a}$$

$$\frac{\mathrm{d}a}{\mathrm{d}t} = 0.12 \times 10^{-18} G^{3.42} \qquad (\mathrm{BIIR}) \tag{13.6.6b}$$

$$\frac{\mathrm{d}a}{\mathrm{d}t} = 3.39 \times 10^{-14} G^{1.91} \qquad (45\mathrm{BIIR}/45\mathrm{NR}/10\mathrm{EPDM}) \tag{13.6.6c}$$

$$\frac{\mathrm{d}a}{\mathrm{d}t} = 0.95 \times 10^{-14} G^{1.96} \qquad (60\mathrm{BIIR}/35\mathrm{NR}/5\mathrm{EPDM}) \tag{13.6.6d}$$

$$\frac{\mathrm{d}a}{\mathrm{d}t} = 0.85 \times 10^{-18} G^{3.31} \qquad (\mathrm{CIIR}) \tag{13.6.6e}$$

$$\frac{\mathrm{d}a}{\mathrm{d}t} = 4.46 \times 10^{-12} G^{1.35} \qquad (\mathrm{NR}) \tag{13.6.6f}$$

$$\frac{\mathrm{d}a}{\mathrm{d}t} = 1.38 \times 10^{-14} G^{2.12} \qquad (50\mathrm{NR}/50\mathrm{BR}) \tag{13.6.6g}$$

where
a (m): Crack length;
G (J/m^2): Energy release rate;
B: Fatigue coefficient;
F: Fatigue exponent.

13.6.4　Energy-Based Criterion for Rubber Fatigue Limit

A protocol using thermal measurements to predict the fatigue lifetime throughout an energy-based criterion constitutes a very efficient prediction of the deterministic fatigue limit curve (Wöhler curve) with only one sample and within one day [Marcos et al.].

13.6.5   Critical Plane Method for Fatigue of Rubber

The critical plane is obtained by finding the direction that maximizes the normal stress variance. It is found that the direction of maximal normal stress is shown to coincide with one of the principal directions in the case of proportional stress components. This may not be true in the case of non-proportional loading. Nevertheless, the critical plane method allows the cases involving multiple out-of-phase load inputs, or crack closure to be treated with high accuracy [Barbash & Mars].

The shear stress and normal stress are not correlated in the critical plane. In other words, the three energy release rates G_I (mode-I), G_{II} (mode II), and G_{III} (mode III) associated with the critical plane can work validly on the crack extension, independently of one another or with mixed modes. A flow chart for predicting the fatigue crack growth (FCG) of rubber utilizing the critical plane method is depicted in Fig. 13.6.3.

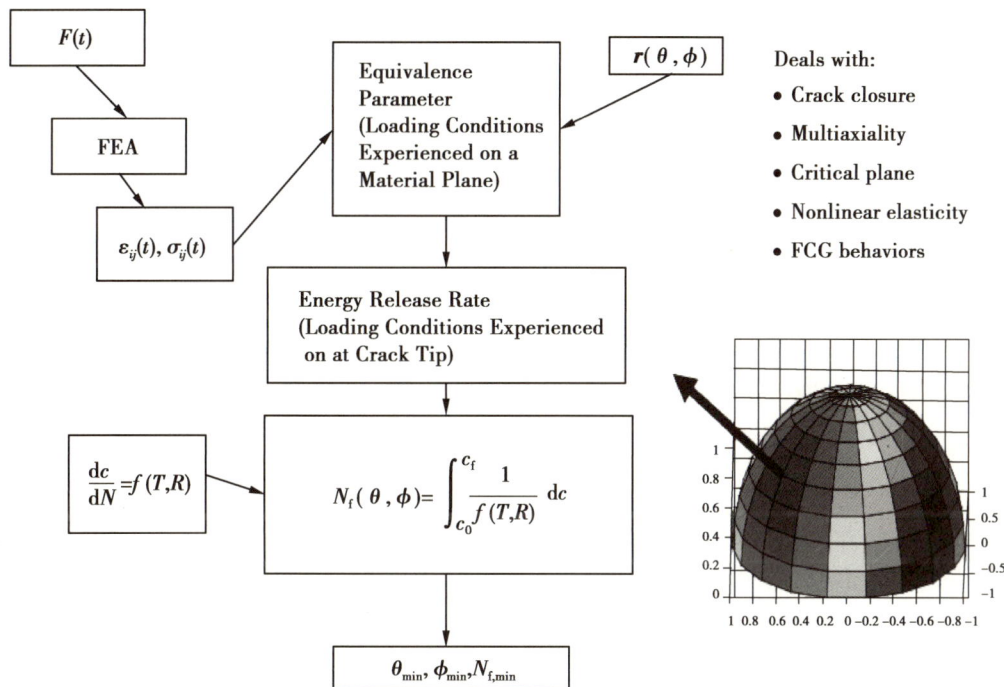

Fig. 13.6.3   Flow Chart for Predicting the Fatigue Crack Growth of Rubber Using the Energy Release Rate at the Critical Plane

13.7   Rubber Composites

Automotive tires, seals, hoses, engine mounts, shock absorbers, and vibration isolators, are rubber based composites, which turn into high-tech systems as soon as their material properties are tuned by embedded inclusions. For instance, carbon black or mica particles are filled into the rubber matrix to compound materials with specific properties on the microscopic scale and a sophisticated weave of embedded steel fibers controls the footprint of the tire on the belt edge, preventing separation.

13.7.1 Rubber Reinforced with Carbon Black

Anti-vibration automotive parts are often mad of rubber reinforced with carbon black. Use of carbon black reinforced natural rubber is very common in automotive applications especially suspension top cups, cab mounts, suspension bushes, engine mounts, etc. The reinforcement that leads to an increase of stiffness, hardness, compressive strength, tensile strength, shear strength, creep resistance, and hysteresis comes from the filler-rubber and filler-filler interactions. Carbon black particulates are strongly bonded to other elementary particles to form aggregates of the size of 100 nanometers. Part of rubber is trapped inside the aggregates and shielded from macroscopic deformation. Carbon black types are classified according to the specific surface, i.e., the outer surface per unit mass. Fatigue damage initially occurs generally on carbon black agglomerates or oxides (e. g. ZnO), but both types of inclusions have their own distinct crack nucleation mechanisms. The nucleation by carbon black agglomerates more likely initiates crack propagation that yields failure [Huneau et al.].

13.7.2 Rubber Reinforced with MWNTs

The volume electric resistivity of the NR/MWNTs composite decreases with the increasing content of MWNTs (Multi-walled Nanotubes) and the electrical percolation threshold is reached at less than 1phr of MWNTs (phr=parts of filler by weight per hundred parts of rubber). The stiffness is improved considerably upon incorporation of MWNTs in the natural rubber matrix as shown in Fig. 13.7.1, but the main factor for reinforcement of natural rubber MWNTs appears to be their high aspect ratio rather than strong interfacial interaction with rubber [Bokobza].

13.7.3 Rubber-Cord Laminae

As pointed out by [Lee et al.], the damage initiation, as well as the eventual structural failure of angle-plied, cord-rubber composite laminae, can be fulfilled on the basis of a " strain-controlled" process. The failure mode appears to be controlled by the interfacial separation between the cord and matrix and the fatigue life is linearly proportional to the inverse of the dynamic creep rate, i.e., the time required to increase cyclic strain by a unit amount. The gross failure subjected to a low-frequency loading function occurs when the total strain accumulation, i.e., cumulative creep strain, reached the static failure strain, regardless of the associated stress amplitude. An increased load level results in a decrease of fatigue life by simply shortening the time to reach the critical level of strain for gross failure.

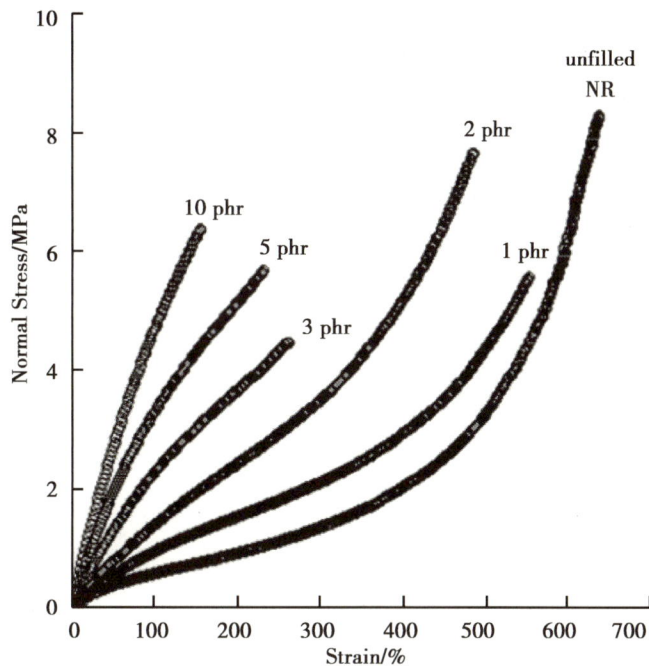

Fig. 13.7.1 Stress-strain Curves of Rubber Reinforced with MWNTs [Bokobza]

13.7.4 Laminated Rubber Composites

Laminated rubber, or elastomeric, bearing fatigues are subjected to repeated cycles of loading. Fatigue in these elements is characterized by the formation of cracks typically originating at the interface of the steel-rubber laminae at the outermost edge of the laminate then propagating at an inclination toward the center of the bearing under subsequent cycling. The presence of fatigue cracks alters the bulging surface of the rubber layers, thereby degrades the stiffness properties of the bearings. Past experimental studies have shown the stiffness degradation of laminated rubber bearings can be significant, i.e., reductions on the order of 20%-30%. To date, much of the analytical and experimental research has been focused on the determination of the initiation of fatigue cracking to establish replacement schedules for elastomeric bearing components in aerospace and rail applications.

13.8　Curing Mechanics of Rubber

The tire-curing process, or other rubber products, has been more art than science to manufacturing engineers due to its complexity. Many factors have impact on the state of cure, such as rubber compound, compounding variables, cross-linking during vulcanization, die temperature, press-on time, post-cure requirements, geometric shapes and cooling environment [Chiang].

13.8.1　Kinetics of Rubber Cure with No Reversion

Empirical models are regression models that fit the data assuming a particular functional form, where the parameters are estimated from the experimental data using non-linear parameter estimation procedures. A number of empirical models that have been used for modeling sulfur vulcanization in rubber. The kinetics of rubber cure can be divided into two periods, when no reversion is involved at the ending. One is the induction period and the other is vulcanization period. A generalized empirical kinetic model to describe such a polymerization process was proposed by [Kamal & Ryan] as

$$\frac{\mathrm{d}\psi}{\mathrm{d}t} = [k_1 + k_2 \psi(t)]^m [1 - \psi(t)]^n \qquad (13.8.1)$$

where

$\psi(t)$: Degree of cure as a function of time, and $0 \leqslant \psi(t) \leqslant 1$;

k_1, k_2: Coefficients;

m, n: Exponents, of which $m < 1$ and $n \geqslant 1$.

The above equation can be solved for the time required for a certain cure level,

$$t = \int_0^\psi \frac{\mathrm{d}\psi}{[k_1 + k_2 \psi(t)]^m [1 - \psi(t)]^n}$$

In view of the complexity of introducing Eq. (13.8.1) into the finite element formulation, [Toth et al.] suggested two simplified equations to represent the two distinct time periods as

$$\psi \approx 0 \qquad \text{when } 0 \leqslant t \leqslant t_A \qquad (13.8.2)$$

and $\qquad \dfrac{\mathrm{d}\psi}{\mathrm{d}t} = k_2 \psi(t)^m [1 - \psi(t)]^n \qquad \text{when } t_A \geqslant t \qquad (13.8.3)$

The above equation is called Piloyan equation. Exponent m is to be derived from experimental data. However, most rubber-based compounds exhibit a common feature that $m = 1/2$, which exhibits asymptotical curing curves without reversion, as observed by [Toth et al.]. Solution to Eq. (13.8.3) with $n = 1$ becomes

$$t = \int_0^\psi \frac{d\psi}{\psi^m(1-\psi)} \tag{13.8.4}$$

13.8.2   Kinetics of Rubber Cure with No Reversion

Without considering the induction period explicitly, [Rimondi] proposed an exponential formula for conversion of sulphur into the cross-linked compounds,

$$\psi(t) = 1 - \frac{e^{(-kt)^m}}{n} \tag{13.8.5}$$

where

$\psi(t)$: Degree of cure as a function of time, and $0 \leqslant \psi(t) \leqslant 1$;

k: Coefficient as a function of temperature;

n: Constant and $n \geqslant 1$.

The above equation is capable of modeling reversion and it is applicable to the formation of strong cross-linked compound, weak cross-linked compound, and disruptive weak cross-linked compound.

13.8.3   Section Modulus during Curing

As rubber cure proceeds, the shear modulus increases in the curing stage as depicted in Fig. 13.8.1. A typical rheometer cure curve, which is calibrated with a torque curve that represent the shearing modulus, obtained from an Oscillating Disk Rheometer (ODR) for accelerated sulfur vulcanization may finish up with distinct endings:

Curve A: Cure to maximum torque with reversion;

Curve B: Cure to equilibrium torque;

Curve C: Cure with no equilibrium or maximum torque.

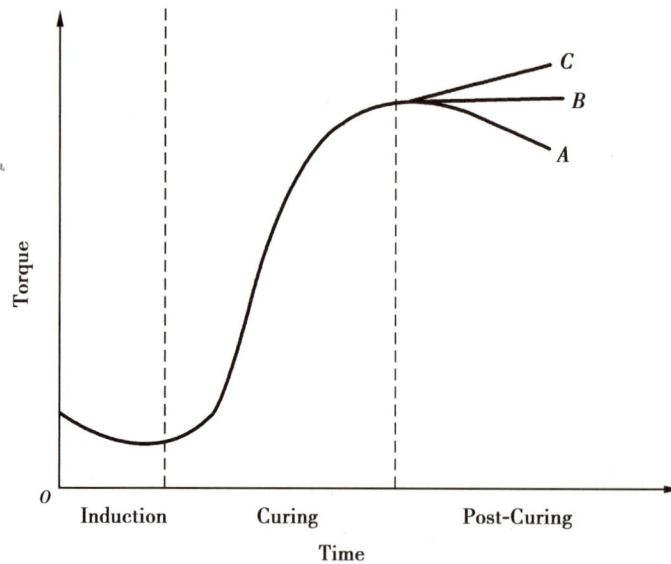

Fig. 13.8.1   Schematic Drawing of Torque Curve (Shear Modulus) from Oscillating Disk Rheometer

13.8.4   Examination of Rubber Cure Using Weibull Distribution Functions

A statistical examination of rubber cure based on Weibull distribution functions was first conducted by [Chiang et al.]. It has been proven using Weibull distribution functions that there exist mixed modes in rubber resilience for a cure curve without reversion: viscous effect and cross-linking. It appears that a single 2-parameter Weibull distribution function is adequate to embrace the mixed modes associated with a non-reverted cure curve. The scale factor decreases, as the cure temperature is elevated higher. The probability density function of the degree of cure is also explored. The higher the environmental temperature, the more coherent is the central tendency of cure rate. A quality vs. productivity chart is proposed as a practical approach to decision-making on rubber cure.

References

ABRAHAM F. et al, 2005. The Effect of Minimum Stress and Stress Amplitude on the Fatigue Life of Non Strain Crystallizing Elastomers[J]. Materials & Design, 26(3): 239-245.

ANDREINI G, et al, 2010. Comparison of Sine Versus Pulse Waveform Effects on Fatigue Crack Growth Behavior of NR, SBR AND BR COMPOUNDS[J]. Rubber Chemistry and Technology, 83(4): 391-403.

ASSAAD M C. 1991. Mechanics of the Dynamic Flex Test[J]. Tire Science and Technology, 19(4): 237-247.

AYOUB G, ZAÏRI F, NAÏT-ABDELAZIZ M, et al, 2014. A Visco-Hyperelastic Damage Model for Cyclic Stress-Softening, Hysteresis and Permanent Set in Rubber Using the Network Alteration Theory [J].

International Journal of Plasticity, 54: 19-33.

BALWIN J M, et al, 2004. Passenger Tires Inflated with Nitrogen Age Slower: Part 2 of 2[J]. Rubber and Plastics News, September 20, 2004.

BARBASH K P, MARS W V, 2016. Critical Plane Analysis of Rubber Bushing Durability under Road Loads[J]. Sae World Congress & Exhibition.

BAUMAN J T, 2008. Fatigue, Stress, and Strain of Rubber Components[J]. A Guide for Design Engineers, Hanser Publishers, Munich.

BECKER A, DORSCH V, KALISKE M, et al, 1998. A Material Model for Simulating the Hysteretic Behavior of Filled Rubber for Rolling Tires[J]. Tire Science and Technology, 26(3): 132-148.

BERGSTROM J S, 2005. Modeling of the Dynamic Mechanical Response of Elastomers[J]. Tire Science and Technology, 33(2): 120-134.

BLOW C M, 1982. Rubber Technology and Manufacture[M]. 2nd Edition, Butterworth Scientific, London, UK.

BOKOBZA L, 2012. Multiwall Carbon Nanotube-Filled Natural Rubber: Electrical and Mechanical Properties[J]. Express Polymer Letters, 6(3): 213-223.

BOYCE M C, ARRUDA E M, 2000. Constitutive Models of Rubber Elasticity: A Review [J]. Rubber Chemistry and Technology, 73(3): 504-523.

BRINK U, STEIN E, 1996. On Some Mixed Finite Element Methods for Incompressible and Nearly Incompressible Finite Elasticity[J]. Computational Mechanics, 19(1): 105-119.

CHARLTON D J, YANG J, 1994. A Review of Methods to Characterize Rubber Elastic Behavior for Use in Finite Element Analysis[J]. Rubber Chemistry and Technology, 67(3): 481-503.

CEMBROLA R J, DUDEK T J, 1985. Cord/Rubber Material Properties [J]. Rubber Chemistry and Technology, 58: 830-856.

CHEN X, XU S, HUANG D, 1999. A critical plane-strain energy density criterion of multiaxial low-cycle fatigue life under non-proportional loading[J]. Fatigue & Fracture of Engineering Materials & Structures, 22 (8): 679-686.

CHIANG Y J, SHIH C D, LIN C C, et al, 2004. Multi-variable Effects of Tire Structures and Suspension Alignments on Vehicle Pull[J]. Presented at the 23rd Annual Tire Society Conference (Sept. 20-21, 2004).

CHIANG Y J, et al, 2004. Examination of Tire Cure by Weibull Distribution Functions [J]. International Journal of Materials and Product Technology, 20 (1-3): 210-219.

CHIANG Y J, SHIH C D, LIN C C, et al, 2000. Multi-Variable Effects on Sealing Pressure between Tires and Rims[J]. International Journal of Vehicle Design, 23(1-2): 78-93(16).

CHIANG Y J, TANG C. 1995. Accuracy Assessment to Applying 20-Node Solid Elements to Pressurized Composite Shells[J]. Finite Elements in Analysis and Design, 20(4): 219-231.

CHUNG J, KIM N. 2016. Numerical Methods of Multiaxial Fatigue Life Prediction for Elastomers under Variable Amplitude Loadings[J]. Fatigue & Fracture of Engineering Materials & Structures, 39(7): 866-887.

CLAMROTH R, 1981. Determination of Viscoelastic Properties by Dynamic Testing[J]. Polymer Testing, 2(4): 263-286.

DENG P, WARN G P, 2015. Modeling the Compression Stiffness Degradation in Circular Elastomeric Bearings due to Fatigue[J]. Journal of Engineering Mechanics, 142(1): 04015057.

MARK J E, ERMAN B, ROLAND M, 2013. The Science and Technology of Rubber[M]. 4th Edition, NIPPON GOMU KYOKAISHI.

GENT A N, 2001. Engineering with Rubber: How to Design Rubber Components[M]. 3rd Edition, Hanser Publications, Cincinnati, OH.

GREEN A E, ZERNA W, 1954. Theoretical Elasticity[M]. Oxford University Press, Oxford, UK.

HAGGBLAD B, SUNDBERG J A, 1983. Large Strain Solutions of Rubber Components[J]. Computers and Structures, 17(5-6): 835-843.

HAN I, CHUNG C, KIM J, et al, 1996. Dynamic Simulation of the Tire Curing Process[J]. Tire Science and Technology, 24(1): 50-76.

HARBOR R, et al, 2008. Fatigue Life Analysis and Predictions for NR and SBR under Variable Amplitude and Multiaxial Loading Conditions[J]. International Journal of Fatigue, 30(7): 1231-1247.

HERTZ D L, 2010. Effects of Thermal Cycling on Elastomers in High Temperature Coolant[J]. ICEF2010-35074, September 12-15, 2010, San Antonio, Texas, USA.

HEWITT N L. 1984. The Use of Viscoelastic Series for Compound Design[J]. Rubber World.

HUNEAU B, et al, 2016. Fatigue Crack Initiation in a Carbon Black-Filled Natural Rubber[J]. Rubber Chemistry and Technology Macromolecule, 37(13): 5011-5017.

KAMAL M R, 1974. Thermoset Characterization for Moldability Analysis[J]. Polymer Engineering and Science, 14(3): 231.

KENNEDY R H, MCMINN M S, 2000. Tire Temperature Prediction during Post-Cure Inflation[J]. Tire Science and Technology, 28(4): 248-263.

KIM W D, LEE H J, KIM J Y, et al, 2004. Fatigue Life Estimation of an Engine Rubber Mount[J]. International Journal of Fatigue, 26(5): 553-560.

KIM Y, SALEEB A, CHANG T, 1994. Implementation of Material Stiffness Coefficients in Finite Element Applications to Rubber[J]. Tire Science and Technology, 22(4): 223-241.

KRAMER O, PERRY J D, 1994. Dynamic Mechanical Properties[M]. Science and Technology of Rubber, 2nd Edition. Academic Press.

LAKE G J, 2001. Application of Fracture Mechanics to Crack Growth in Rubber-Cord Laminates[J]. Rubber Chemistry and Technology, 74(3): 509-524.

LEBEL M C, 1999. New Development in Carbon Black Surface Chemistry Technology Improves Tire Performance and Vehicle Fuel Economy[J]. SAE 1999-01-0788.

LEE B L, et al, 1998. Fatigue of Cord-Rubber Composites: Ⅱ. Strain-Based Failure Criteria[J]. Rubber Chemistry and Technology, 71(5): 866-888.

LETALLCE P, RAHIER C. Numerical Models of Steady Rolling for Non-Linear Viscoelastic Structures in Finite Deformations[J]. International Journal for Numerical Methods in Engineering, 37(7): 1159-1186.

LI Q, et al, 2009. Fatigue Life Prediction of a Rubber Mount Based on Test of Material Properties and Finite Element Analysis[J]. Engineering Failure Analysis, 16(7): 2304-2310.

LINDLEY P B, 1973. International Journal of Fracture, 9: 449.

LIU Y, WAN Z, TIAN Z, et al, 1999. Fatigue of Unidirectional Cord-Rubber Composites[J]. Tire Science and Technology, 27(1):48-47.

LUO R K, WU W X, 2006. Fatigue Failure Analysis of Anti-Vibration Rubber Spring[J]. Engineering Failure Analysis, 13(1): 110-116.

LUX F, STUMPF H, 1996. Light Weight Tire Concept[J]. Tire Science and Technology, 24(2): 119-131.

MALKUS D S, 1980. Finite Elements with Penalties in Nonlinear Elasticity [J]. International Journal of Numerical Methods in Engineering, 16(1): 121-136.

MARCO Y, et al, 2017. Fast Prediction of the Wohler Curve from Thermal Measurements for a Wide Range of NR and SBR Compounds[J]. Rubber Chemistry and Technology, 90(3): 487-507.

MARS W, FATEMI A, 2004. Factors That Affect the Fatigue Life of Rubber: A Literature Survey[J]. Rubber Chemistry and Technology, 77(3): 391-412.

MESCHKE G, HELNWEIN P, 1994. Large-Strain 3D Analysis of Fiber-Reinforced Composites Using Rebar Elements: Hyperelastic Formulation for Cords[J]. Computational Mechanics, 13(4): 241-254.

MOONEY M, 1940. A Theory of Large Elastic Deformations[J]. Journal of Applied Physics, 11(9): 582-592.

MULLINS L, 1948. Effect of Stretching on the Properties of Rubber[J]. Rubber Chemistry and Technology, 21: 281-300.

ALEXEFF V, 1968. Tire Manufacturing Methods[J]. US, US3375150 A[P].

OCHI M, HATO S, ABE T, 1992. Numerical Analysis of Deformation of Rubber Composite Material (Tensile Deformation under Plane Strain)[J]. JSME International Journal, Series I, 35(4): 404-412.

OGDEN R W, 1972. Large Deformation Isotropic Elasticity: On the Correlation of Theory and Experiment for Incompressible Rubberlike Solids[J]. Proceedings of the Royal Society, 326(1567): 565-584.

PEEKEN H, DOPPER R, ORSCHALL B, 1987. A 3-D Rubber Material Model Verified in a User-Supplied Subroutine[J]. Computers and Structures, 26(1-2): 181-189.

PROGELHOF R C, THRONE J L, 1988. Engineering Properties of Polymers[J]. Hanser Publishers, Sherwood Technologies Inc.

RIDHA R A, SATYAMURTHY K, HIRSCHFELT L R, et al, 1985. Contact Loading of a Rubber Disk[J]. Tire Science and Technology, 13(1): 3-15.

RIMONDI G, TOTH W J, KOUNAVIS J, 1996. Predictive Model for Reversion-Type Cures[J]. Tire Science and Technology, 24(1): 77-91.

RIVLIN R S, SAWYERS K N, 1976. Strain-Energy Function for Elastomers[J]. Transactions of Society of Rheology, 20(4): 545-557.

RIVLIN R S, THOMAS A G, 1953. Rupture of Rubber: I. Characteristic Energy for Tearing[J]. Journal of Polymer Science, 10(3): 291-318.

RIVLIN R S, 1948. Large Elastic Deformations of Isotropic Materials: IV. Further Development of the General Theory[J]. Philosophical Transactions of the Royal Society of London, 241(835): 379-397.

SEGALMAN D J, 1981. Modeling Tire Energy Dissipation for Power Loss Calculations[J]. SAE Transactions, 810162.

SIMO J C, 1987. On a Fully Three-Dimensional Finite Strain Viscoelastic Damage Model: Formulation and Computational Aspects[J]. Computer Methods in Applied Mechanics and Engineering, 60(2): 153-173.

SJÖBERG M, 2002. On Dynamic Properties of Rubber Isolators[J]. Dept. of Vehicle Engineering, Royal Institute of Technology, Stockholm, TRITA-FKT 2002:39, ISSN 1103-470X.

SJÖOBERG M, 2000. Dynamic Behavior of a Rubber Component in the Low Frequency Range-Measurements and Modeling[J]. Proceedings of the 7th International Conference of Sound and Vibration, Garmisch-Partenkirchen, 5: 2955-2962.

STEVENSON A, 1986. Rubber Chemistry and Technology[J]. 59: 208.

SUN C, GENT A, MARTENY P, 2000. Effect of Fatigue Step Loading Sequence on Residual Strength[J]. Tire Science and Technology, 28(4): 196-208.

SURYATAL B, et al, 2015. Fatigue Life Estimation of an Elastomeric Pad by ε-N Curve and FEA[J]. Journal of Surface Engineered Materials and Advanced Technology, 5(2): 85-92.

SWANSON S R, 1985. A Constitutive Model for High Elongation Elastic Materials[J]. Journal of Engineering Materials and Technology, 107(2): 110-114.

THOMAS A G. 1975. Factors Influencing the Strength of Rubbers[J]. Rubber Chemistry and Technology, 48 (5): 902-912.

TOTH W J, CHANG J P, ZANCHELLI C, 1991. Finite Element Evaluation of the State of Cure in a Tire[J]. Tire Science and Technology, 19(4): 178-212.

TRELOAR L R G, 1976. The Mechanics of Rubber Elasticity [Iand Discussion][J]. Proceedings of the Royal Society of London, A, 351(1666): 301-330.

TRELOAR L R G, 1944. Stress-Strain Data for Vulcanized Rubber under Various Types of Deformation[J]. Rubber Chemistry and Technology, 17(4): 813-825.

VALLEE G E, SHUKLA A, 1996. A Study of the Dynamic Behavior of Elastomeric Materials Using Finite Elements[J]. Journal of Engineering Materials and Technology, 118(4).

WANG Y, et al, 2008. Fatigue Life Prediction of Vulcanized Natural Rubber under Proportional and Non-Proportional Loading[J]. Fatigue and Fracture of Engineering Materials and Structures, 31(1): 38-48.

WOO C S, et al, 2013. The Effect of Maximum Strain on Fatigue Life Prediction for Natural Rubber Material[J]. International Journal of Mechanical and Mechatronics Engineering, 7(4): 621-626.

WOO C S, KIM W D, 2006. Heat-Aging Effects on the Material Properties and Fatigue Life Prediction of Vulcanized Natural Rubber[J]. Journal of Soft Materials, 2(2006): 7-12.

YAN J, STRENSKOWSKI J S, 2006. A Finite Element Analysis of Orthogonal Rubber Cutting[J]. Journal Materials Processing Technology, 174(1-3): 102-108.

YEOH O H, 2012. Some Forms of the Strain Energy Function for Rubber [J]. Rubber Chemistry and Technology, 66(5): 754-771.

YEOH O H, 2012. Characterization of Elastic Properties of Carbon Black-Filled Rubber Vulcanizate [J]. Rubber Chemistry and Technology, 63(5): 792-805.

ZINE A, et al, 2006. Prediction of Rubber Fatigue Life under Multiaxial Loading[J]. Fatigue and Fracture of Engineering Materials and Structures, 29(3): 267-278.

Table 13.1.1 Rivlin-Mooney Constants for a Typical Passenger-Car Tire [Cho et al.]

Component	A_{10}/MPa	A_{01}/MPa
Tread	0.579	0.145
Cappy	0.699	0.175
Belt	1.085	0.271
Carcass	0.616	0.154
Shoulder	0.726	0.182
Sidewall	0.524	0.131
Chafer (Rim)	1.112	0.278
Chafer (Gum)	0.974	0.244
Apex	1.581	0.395
Bead	11478	2669

Chapter 14

Dielectric Materials

14.1　Introduction

Electronic Control Units (ECUs) and related sensors/actuators built upon electromagnetic materials are core components in modern cars. Without these devices, the electric motor or engine motor could not run properly, the instrument cluster displaying vehicle speed, engine RPM, fuel level, oil level, and related warning lights would not function, and for the most there would be no information system. A standard car may have as many as 100 ECUs installed throughout the vehicle. Each ECU has its own power electronics module and it may range from something that controls the complexity of the electric motor/engine speed to a relatively simple component that controls the electric windows. Even certain fundamental components are based on sensors such as key fobs whose data need be processed through an ECU.

Mechanics of electromagnetic materials is here defined as a branch of engineering mechanics, with emphasis on the fundamental physics of these electromagnetic materials including theoretical models and test validation, for characterizing the material properties and potential failure mechanisms in the presence of electro-magneto-thermo-mechanical coupling and dissipative effects.

14.1.1　Classification of Electromagnetic Materials

There are 32 kinds of crystals as classified according to the crystal structure in terms of the number of available rotating axes and reflection planes that can be applied without altering the crystal identity. Twenty-one crystal structures out of the thirty-two are nonsymmetrical and they are ferroelectric. Ferroelectricity is a property of certain nonconducting or semi-conducting materials (e.g. dielectric crystals) that exhibit spontaneous electric polarization, i.e., separation of the center of positive and negative electric charge making one side of the crystal positive and the opposite side negative. The polarization can be reversed in direction by the application of an appropriate electric field. Ferroelectricity is named after ferromagnetism that is often observed in ferrous materials [*Encyclopedia Britannica*, 7-20-1998]. Ferroelectricity occurs not only in the crystalline region of semi-crystalline materials, but it also appears in certain amorphous polymers.

Besides crystal 432(cubic), the other twenty nonsymmetrical crystal structures (i.e., 1, 2, m, 222, mm2, 4, −4, 422, 4 mm, −42 m, 3, 32, 3 m, 6, −6, 622, 6 mm, −62 m, 23, −43 m) show the piezoelectric effect: a mechanical strain generates an electric potential and/or an electric potential produces a mechanical strain.

Ten, including 1, 2, m, mm2, 3, 3 m, 4, 4 mm, 6, and 6 mm crystal structures, out of these twenty piezoelectric crystals exhibit spontaneous polarization because of having a dipole in each unit cell. They are called "polar" or pyroelectric. As a subset of piezoelectric materials, pyroelectric materials made of these ten crystal structures have such significant phenomena, by which either a temperature difference generates an electric potential (Seebeck effect) or an electric potential produces a temperature difference (Peltier effect).

14.1.2 From Dielectrics to Ferroelectrics

Important electromagnetic materials and selected applications are re-cast in Fig. 14.1.1 from [Currie 2004] and [Aggarwal et al.].

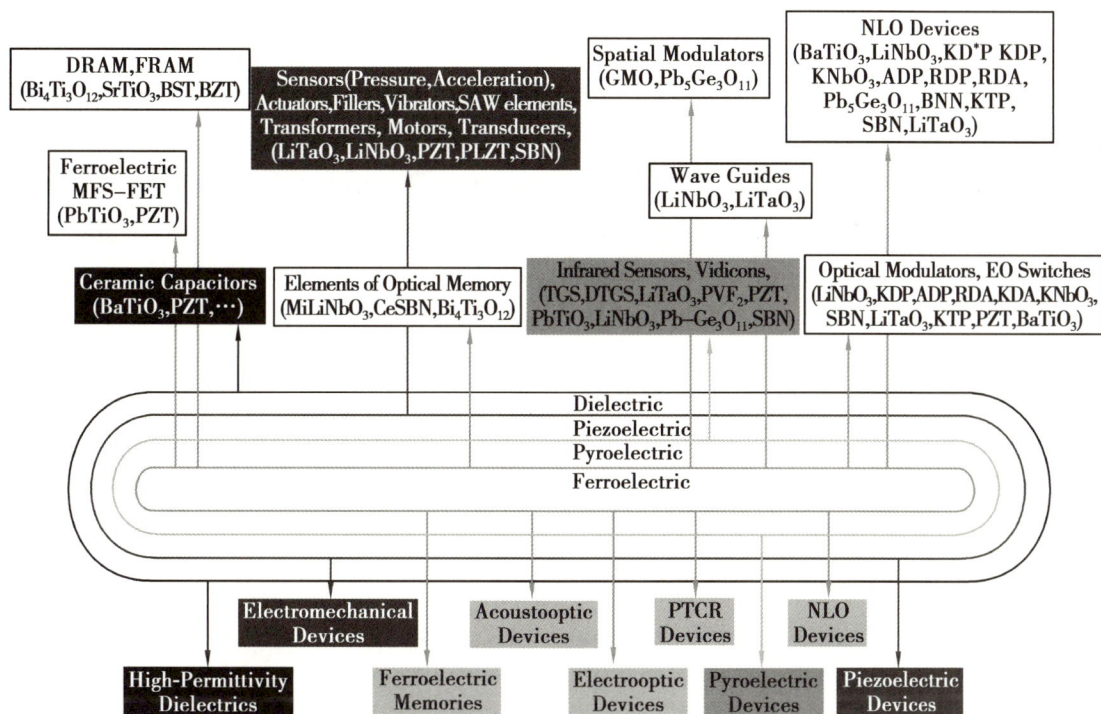

Fig. 14.1.1 Application of Electromagnetic Materials [Curie 2004]

Ferroelectrics, the inner core of dielectric materials with permanent dielectric polarization is exhibited in Fig. 14.1.1. It means that ferroelectrics have a spontaneous electric polarization that can be changed or reversed by the application of an external electric or magnetic field. Polarization ceases when the applied electric or magnetic field disappears. Ferroelectric materials are generally nonferrous crystals/polycrystals and crystalline ceramics, while ferromagnetic materials usually contain iron and exhibit a permanent magnetic moment. Although ferroelectricity and ferromagnetism are analogous, they are two distinct phenomena.

14.1.3　Application

Important parameters and properties of magnetic field sensors and actuators include bandwidth, full scale range, linearity, hysteresis, temperature coefficient of sensitivity, bias stability, offset features, long term stability, noise, resistance to the environment factors, power consumption, size, cost, etc. By combining those magnetostrictive amorphous ferromagnetic ribbons with piezoelectric materials, for example, one can fabricate an electromagnetic laminated composite that shows an extremely high sensitivity for electromagnetic field detection[García-Arribas et al.].

One crucial application of ferroelectric materials is modern wireless communication tools. Each wireless communication tool has its own corresponding frequency band, e.g. GSM (0.9~1.8 GHz) for the wireless phone service and Wi-Fi (2.4~2.48 GHz) for internet service. If each service has its own RF circuits, it comes with some major commercial disadvantages—high cost, high weight, and more power consumption. A solution to overcome the integration obstacles consists in tunable microwave devices based on a stackup of piezoelectric and piezomagnetic materials as a composite, which exhibits multiferroic properties. When an electric field is applied to the piezoelectric lamina of such a composite, it induces a magnetic field in the piezomagnetic (magnetostrictive) lamina thanks to the mechanical coupling between adjacent laminae[Salemi et al.].

Practical smart material systems include piezoelectric materials, magnetostrictive materials, electrostrictive materials, shape memory alloys, electrorheological fluids, and optical fibers. Magnetostrictives, electrostrictives, shape-memory alloys and electrorheological fluids are used as actuators while optical fibers are used primarily as sensors[Harris and Ounaies].

14.1.4　Electro-Magneto-Thermo-Mechanical Coupling

Although electromagnetic devices are characterized by electric and magnetic fields in practice, they are seriously influenced by other types of physical and chemical phenomena such as the change of a material's electrical and/or magnetic properties due to thermal effects, creep, corrosive environments, mechanical vibrations, material degradation, and others. An approach to the stress-strain analysis of a product component involving coupled electro-magneto-thermo-mechanical complication is depicted in Fig. 14.1.2[ANSYS]. In addition to what presented in this figure, an entire process for lifetime estimation of an EV electro-magneto-thermo-mechanical component may involve.

(1) Loading: Driving cycles, environmental condition, loads, and true road profile.
(2) Parasitics: Copper/iron losses, magnetic saturation, EMI (electromagnetic interference), and others, which have to be integrated simultaneously into the coupling calculation, including power electronics and electromagnetic components (e.g. magnets, electric motors

and transformers).

(3)Material degradation: Moisture, creep, and oxidation are the top affecting factors.

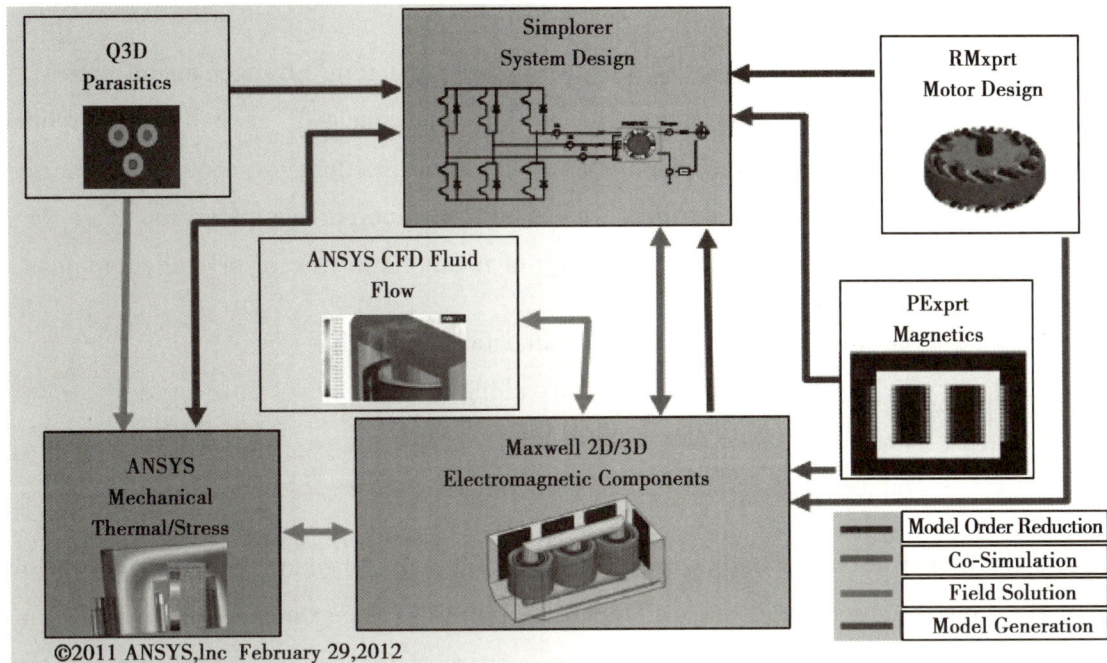

Fig. 14.1.2　Suggested Stress-Strain Analysis of an Electro-Magneto-Thermo-Mechanical Component [Ansys, Inc.]

14.1.5　Thermocouple

When two different metallic wires are joined at both ends, they become a thermocouple. The joining contact is called junction. Three interesting effects are observed in a thermocouple:

(a)Seeback Effect: If the two junctions of a thermo-couple are placed at different temperatures, an emf will be produced and its size is proportional to the temperature difference. In other words, voltage will be developed across two dissimilar metallic junctions due to a temperature difference.

(b)Peltier Effect: It is a reverse of Seeback effect. If an electric current goes through a thermo-couple, one end will turn hot while the other will turn cold. The absorption and evolution of heat depend on the direction of current flow. It means that an electric potential leads to a temperature difference.

(c)Thomson Effect: When an electric current passing through a single electric wire, there is a difference of temperature along the wire. It is basically the Peltier effect, when applied to one wire.

Note that the three physical phenomena of thermocouples is completely different from electro-magneto-thermo-mechanical coupling effect.

14.2 Crystallographic Elasticity

A crystal is a fundamental substance that has a regularly repeating arrangement of atoms, ions, and molecules in a 3-dimensional solid. It can be homogeneous, crystalline (directionally dependent), or semicrystalline. Crystallographic planes and directions are commonly described by Miller indices based on three-integer triples "*h k l*" for the morphology of crystals, as shown in Fig. 14.2.1. Symbolically, the following is a group of notations in use for crystallographics:

(a) [*h k l*]: The direction of crystal designated by the 3 indices *h*, *k* and *l*.
(b) <*h k l*>: The group of directional vectors along [*h k l*].
(c) (*h k l*): The crystal plane perpendicular to [*h k l*].
(d) {*h k l*}: The group of crystal planes perpendicular to [*h k l*].

Many physical properties of crystalline materials are anisotropic because the arrangement of the atoms in the crystal lattice varies in different directions. As an example, the orientation of a crystal has significant effects on the fabrication properties of the silicon wafer, and so, locating crystal orientation with respect to the material coordinate system (1, 2, 3) is an important part of the specified crystal. An arbitrary-oriented crystal is generally anisotropic with 21 independent elastic constants.

For cubic, tetragonal and orthorhombic crystals the obvious choice is to use the orthogonal lattice basis vectors a[1 0 0], b[0 1 0] and c[0 0 1] crystal axes, as shown in Fig. 14.2.1. When [1 0 0] is aligned with the x-axis, [0 1 0] is aligned with the y-axis, and [0 0 1] is aligned with the z-axis in a cubic crystal such as silicon, the constitutive (i.e., stress-strain) equations become orthotropic by default. The (x, y, z) coordinate system is thereby replaced by the (1, 2, 3) coordinate system in terms of the primary material axes, when applied to an orthotropic composite. For a crystal such as silicon that has cubic symmetry conditions, a general anisotropic crystal (composite) having 21 independent elastic constants reduces to an orthotropic material having 9 independent elastic constants in the primary material coordinate system. Thus, Eqs. (10.2.10) and (10.2.40) apply to such crystals. Then the apparent stress-strain relationship can be obtained from the corresponding elastic constants using the following nine equations: Eqs. (10.2.29)-(10.2.37) for orthotropic materials.

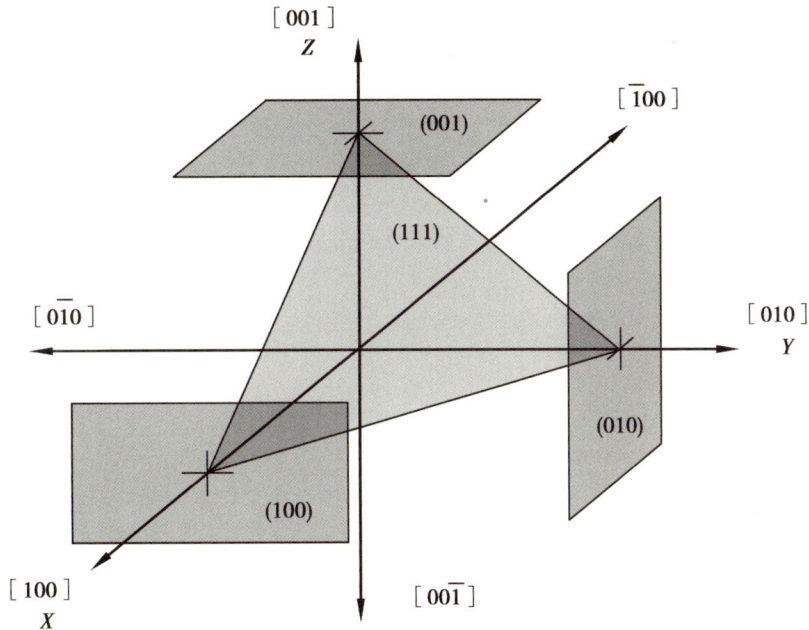

Fig. 14.2.1   Crystallographics by Miller Indices and the (x, y, z) Coordinate System[Hopcroft]

Traditionally the six stress and strain components are expressed as $(\sigma_1, \sigma_2, \sigma_3, \sigma_4, \sigma_5, \sigma_6)$ and $(\varepsilon_1, \varepsilon_2, \varepsilon_3, \varepsilon_4, \varepsilon_5, \varepsilon_6)$, respectively; and so, the 9 independent elastic constants of a crystal orthotropy denoted by $c_{11}, c_{22}, c_{33}, c_{12} = c_{21}, c_{23} = c_{32}, c_{31} = c_{13}, c_{44}, c_{55}, c_{66}$, and other $c_{ij} = 0$ are derived accordingly. Note that the traditional notations for presenting crystallographic stress and strain components are related to their orthotropic counterparts as

$$(\sigma_1, \sigma_2, \sigma_3, \sigma_4, \sigma_5, \sigma_6) = (\sigma_{11}, \sigma_{22}, \sigma_{33}, \sigma_{23}, \sigma_{31}, \sigma_{12}) \tag{14.2.1}$$

and $\quad (\varepsilon_1, \varepsilon_2, \varepsilon_3, \varepsilon_4, \varepsilon_5, \varepsilon_6) = (\varepsilon_{11}, \varepsilon_{22}, \varepsilon_{33}, \varepsilon_{23}, \varepsilon_{31}, \varepsilon_{12}) \tag{14.2.2}$

The above two equations are different from certain existing commercial finite element analysis codes in the sequential order of shear stresses and strains, respectively. In order to clear the confusion and build a "big picture" for product design, some traditional composites notations are given as follows:

Abaqus: $\quad (\sigma_1, \sigma_2, \sigma_3, \sigma_4, \sigma_5, \sigma_6) = (\sigma_{11}, \sigma_{22}, \sigma_{33}, \sigma_{12}, \sigma_{13}, \sigma_{23}) \tag{14.2.3}$

Ansys: $\quad (\sigma_1, \sigma_2, \sigma_3, \sigma_4, \sigma_5, \sigma_6) = (\sigma_{11}, \sigma_{22}, \sigma_{33}, \sigma_{12}, \sigma_{23}, \sigma_{13}) \tag{14.2.4}$

14.2.1   Elastic Constants of a Crystal

How to obtain the elastic constants of a crystal? Experimental values may diverge from the crystal properties at the nanoscale (≈ 0.1 μm), where lattice defects andsurface effects dominate the mechanical response of the sample[Sharpe]. Assume that its crystal indices[1 0 0],[0 1 0],and [0 0 1] are well-aligned with material (1, 2, 3) axes. When the crystal is subjected to a uniaxial tensile (or compression) test along the [h k l] direction, the corresponding Young's modulus (E_{hkl}) in response to the applied load can be calculated as [Nye]

$$E_{hkl}^{-1} = s_{11} - [2(s_{11} - s_{12}) - s_{55}](m^2 n^2 + n^2 p^2 + m^2 p^2) \qquad (14.2.5)$$

where

$$m = \frac{h}{h^2 + k^2 + l^2} \qquad (14.2.6)$$

$$n = \frac{k}{h^2 + k^2 + l^2} \qquad (14.2.7)$$

$$p = \frac{l}{h^2 + k^2 + l^2} \qquad (14.2.8)$$

and $\quad s_{55} = \dfrac{1}{2G_{31}}$

Note that the directional cosines m, n, and p are the cosines of the angles between the direction of E_{hkl}, [h k l], and the corresponding orthotropic material coordinate system (1, 2, 3), respectively. Compliance "s_{55}" is used according to the traditional composites' notation, instead of the crystal annotation. The following three equations can be derived directly from Eq. (14.2.3):

$$E_{100}^{-1} = s_{11} \qquad (14.2.9)$$

$$E_{110}^{-1} = s_{11} - \frac{s_{11} - s_{12}}{2} + \frac{1}{4}s_{55} \qquad (14.2.10)$$

$$E_{111}^{-1} = s_{11} - \frac{2(s_{11} - s_{12}) + s_{55}}{3} \qquad (14.2.11)$$

Once the three "Young's moduli" are obtained from the uniaxial test, they can be solved for E_{11}, v_{12} and G_{23} using Eqs. (10.2.12), (10.2.15) and (10.2.18) based on the material coordinate system, denoted by (1, 2, 3). By the same token, the other elastic constants can be obtained using six more uniaxial tests. Most electromagnetic solids (e.g. silicon wafers) are not pure material (silicon); a certain amount of chemical impurities is usually added to control the solid (wafer's) electromagnetic properties. This procedure is called "doping." The changes are typically a 1%-3% decrease for heavy doping levels and are usually ignored for engineering calculations of elastic constants [Hopcroft et al.]. There are more ways to obtain the elastic constants from other test methods [Nye].

As an example, the elastic constants of silicon crystal re-examined by [Hopcroft et al.] using the following two different "crystal alignments" with respect to the material coordinate system reveal that

Elastic Constant	$[1\ 0\ 0],[0\ 1\ 0]\ \&[0\ 0\ 1]$ aligned with $(1, 2, 3)$ axes	$[1\ 1\ 0],[-1\ 1\ 0]\ \&[0\ 0\ 1]$ aligned with $(1, 2, 3)$ axes
E_{11}	130 GPa	169 GPa
E_{22}	130 GPa	169 GPa
E_{33}	130 GPa	130 GPa
v_{23}	0.28	0.36
v_{31}	0.28	0.28
v_{12}	0.28	0.064
G_{12}	79.6 GPa	50.9 GPa
G_{23}	79.6 GPa	79.6 GPa
G_{31}	79.6 GPa	79.6 GPa

A polysilicon film is a layer of silicon that has been deposited by CVD (chemical vapor deposition) or other low-temperature processes. The film is composed of distinct grains of silicon with certain prevalent defects and thus its elastic modulus will be further affected by the presence of grain boundaries, impurities, and dislocations[Maluf]. The pseudo-isotropic elastic constants of a polysilicon film are $E_{polysilicon} = 160$ GPa and $v_{polysilicon} = 0.22$[Sharpe].

14.2.2   Equivalent Stiffness for Crystalline Structures

The Voigt average modulus E_V based on the isostrain assumption and Reuss average modulus E_R based on the isostress assumption are supposed to yield the upper and lower theoretical bounds on the true value of a pseudo-isotropic polysilicon film[Diz & Humbert], respectively as

$$E_V = \frac{(c_{11} - c_{12} + 3c_{44})(c_{11} + 2c_{12})}{2c_{11} + 3c_{12} + c_{55}} \tag{14.2.12}$$

and $\quad E_R = \dfrac{5}{3s_{11} + 2s_{12} + s_{44}} \tag{14.2.13}$

where

$$c_{44} = 2\ G_{23};$$

$$c_{55} = 2\ G_{31}.$$

These coefficients are defined following the notations used for Eq. (10.2.40). For a polysilicon film, $E_V = 166$ GPa and $E_R = 159$ GPa. The E_R value is sometimes presented as the aggregate elastic modulus for a polysilicon film as a conservative approach [Diz & Humbert] for stress analysis or eve for fatigue life prediction. Another aggregate Young's modulus and shear modulus provided by [Watt] based on the Voigt-Reuss averaging scheme is given as follows:

$$E_{\mathrm{w}} = \frac{2c_{11} + c_{33} + 2c_{12} + 4c_{13}}{9} \tag{14.2.14}$$

and

$$G_{\mathrm{w}} = \frac{7c_{11} + 2c_{33} + 12c_{44} - 5c_{12} - 4c_{13}}{30} \tag{14.2.15}$$

of which $c_{44} = 2G_{23}$, following the crystalline notations.

14.3 Electromagnetism

Research after mechanics of electromagnetic materials in the automotive industry has been at a quick pace as the product life prediction and failure prevention of electronic components are of great concern with the advent of electric vehicles and autonomous vehicles. The constitutive laws for electricity and magnetism can be described by the following two relationships [Ikeda]

$$\boldsymbol{D} = \epsilon\, \boldsymbol{E} = \epsilon_{\mathrm{o}}\, \boldsymbol{E} + \boldsymbol{P} \tag{14.3.1}$$

and $\boldsymbol{B} = \mu\, \boldsymbol{H} = \mu_{\mathrm{o}}\, \boldsymbol{H} + \mu_{\mathrm{o}}\, \boldsymbol{M}$ (14.3.2)

where

$\boldsymbol{D}$ (C/m^2 or Coulombs/meter^2): Electric displacement, a vector;

$\boldsymbol{P}$ (C/m^2): Polarization density of the material, i.e., a vector;

$\boldsymbol{E}$ (V/m or N · m/C): Electric field intensity, a vector;

ϵ (C/N/m^2, A · s/N/m^2 or FV/N/m^2): Absolute permittivity;

ϵ_{o}(C/N/m^2): Permittivity of vacuum volume, a constant;

$\epsilon_{\mathrm{o}}\boldsymbol{E}$(C/m^2): Polarization density of the vacuum volume;

$\boldsymbol{B}$ (T or W/m^2): Magnetic flux density (or magnetic displacement), a vector;

$\boldsymbol{H}$ (A/m): Magnetic field intensity, a vector;

$\boldsymbol{M}$ (A/m): Magnetization of the material, a vector;

μ (H/m or N/A^2): Absolute magnetic permeability, a tensor;

μ_{o}(H/m or N/A^2): Permeability of vacuum volume, a constant;

$\mu_{\mathrm{o}}\boldsymbol{H}$ (A/m): Magnetization of the vacuum volume, i.e., a vector.

Notes: A—Ampere, C—Coulomb, F—Farad, H—Henry, m—meter, N—Newton, s—second, T—Tesla, V—Volt, W—Weber.

Variables D (C/m^2) and B (Wb/m^2) are the electric displacement and magnetic flux density (magnetic displacement) respectively, named in the related concept of displacement current and electromagnetism in dielectrics. Variable D is equivalent to electric flux density for being the specific capacity of electric induction and variable B is the measure of how much the magnetic flux penetrates a fixed known area. Variable P is the macroscopic polarization density of both the permanent and induced electric dipole moments in the material and variable M stands for the macroscopic magnetization of both the permanent and induced magnetic dipole moments in the material. Permittivity is the measure of the ability of a material to support the formation of an electric field within itself, while permeability for magnetic field. The opposite of magnetic permeability is magnetic reluctance.

14.3.1 Maxwell Equations

Electromagnetic fields are governed by the Maxwell's equations[James Clerk Maxwell, 1873] in a time-varying field, by which bilateral couplings between electric and magnetic field quantities are given as follows[Ulaby]:

$$\nabla \cdot D = \rho_f \qquad \text{(Gauss Law)} \qquad (14.3.3)$$

$$\nabla \times E = \frac{-\partial B}{\partial t} \qquad \text{(Farady's law)} \qquad (14.3.4)$$

$$\nabla \cdot B = 0 \qquad \text{(Gauss Law for Magnetism)} \qquad (14.3.5)$$

and $\quad \nabla \times H = J + \dfrac{\partial D}{\partial t} \qquad \text{(Ampere's Law)} \qquad (14.3.6)$

where

ρ_f(C/m^3 or Coulombs/meter^3): Electric charge density in free space;

J (A/m^2): Current density, i.e., amount of current flow per unit area.

Parameters such as ∇ ,D,E,B, and H denoted by bold italic characters are vectors in the space. Note that ∇ is the operator of gradient, defined in the Cartesian coordinate system (x, y, z) as

$$\nabla = \left(\frac{\partial}{\partial x}\right) i + \left(\frac{\partial}{\partial y}\right) j + \left(\frac{\partial}{\partial z}\right) k \qquad (14.3.7)$$

Note that (i, j, k) are directional unit vectors correspond to the (x, y, z) coordinates. Electric fields and magnetic fields are coupled when they because they vary respect to time, as demonstrated in Eqs. (14.3.3) and (14.3.6). In the linear range, the Maxwell equations can be rewritten as follows:

$$\nabla \cdot \boldsymbol{E} = \frac{\rho_{\mathrm{v}}}{\epsilon} \tag{14.3.8}$$

$$\nabla \times \boldsymbol{E} = -\frac{\partial \boldsymbol{B}}{\partial t} \tag{14.3.9}$$

$$\nabla \cdot \boldsymbol{B} = 0 \tag{14.3.10}$$

and $\quad \nabla \times \boldsymbol{B} = \mu \boldsymbol{J} + \mu \epsilon \left(\dfrac{\partial \boldsymbol{E}}{\partial t} \right) \tag{14.3.11}$

Permeability can be interpreted as the ratio of the electric charge density to the mass density. For a good conductor working in the linear range, the Maxwell equations can be further rewritten as follows:

$$\nabla \cdot \boldsymbol{E} = 0 \tag{14.3.12}$$

$$\nabla \times \boldsymbol{E} = -\frac{\partial \boldsymbol{B}}{\partial t} \tag{14.3.13}$$

$$\nabla \cdot \boldsymbol{B} = 0 \tag{14.3.14}$$

and $\quad \nabla \times \boldsymbol{B} = \mu \boldsymbol{J} + \mu \epsilon \left(\dfrac{\partial \boldsymbol{E}}{\partial t} \right) \tag{14.3.15}$

Under the assumption that material response is linear with field strength, the following generalized relationship in the frequency domain can be derived from the Maxwell's equations:

$$\nabla x (\mu_{\mathrm{r}}^{-1} \nabla \times \boldsymbol{E}) - \frac{\omega^2}{C_{\mathrm{o}}^2} [\epsilon_{\mathrm{r}} - i (\omega \rho_{\mathrm{e}} \epsilon_{\mathrm{o}})^{-1}] \boldsymbol{E} = 0 \tag{14.3.16}$$

where

ω: Operating angular speed ($= 2\pi f$, of which f is frequency);

ρ_{e}($\Omega \cdot$ m or ohm.meter): Electric resitivity;

μ_{r}(H/m or N/A^2): Relative magnetic permeability of the material;

ϵ_0(8.854×10^{-12}F/m, C/V/m, or C^2/N/m^2): Electric permittivity of vacuum;

ϵ_{r}: Relative permittivity of the material, also called dielectric constant if $\epsilon_{\mathrm{r}} > 1$;

C_{o}(m/s): Light speed in the vacuum;

∇: $\left(\dfrac{\partial}{\partial x} \right) \boldsymbol{i} + \left(\dfrac{\partial}{\partial y} \right) \boldsymbol{j} + \left(\dfrac{\partial}{\partial z} \right) \boldsymbol{k}$ in the Cartesian coordinate system (x, y, z).

The above equation can be solved for electric field strength vector $\boldsymbol{E}$ (not electromotive force $\boldsymbol{E}$) at a specific operating frequency, since each of the material properties, i.e., ρ_{e}, μ_{r}, and ϵ_{r}, may vary as a function of frequency. Nevertheless, it is not always necessary to consider the variation when the device works in a relatively narrow frequency range. Note that electric field strength vector $\boldsymbol{E}(V/m)$ is not electromotive force E (V), which is also called electric potential.

14.3.2   Continuity Equation

Another important equation in addition to the four Maxwell equations is the continuity equation, which relates the electric charge to the current density ($\boldsymbol{J}$), as

$$\nabla \cdot \boldsymbol{J} + \frac{\partial \rho_e}{\partial t} = 0 \tag{14.3.17}$$

14.3.3   Electric Conductivity

Electricity is the flow of electrons in a circuit. The conductivity equation that describes the relationship between the current density ($\boldsymbol{J}$) and electric field strength ($\boldsymbol{E}$) is generally depicted as

$$\boldsymbol{J} = \sigma_e \boldsymbol{E} \tag{14.3.18}$$

of which σ_e(S/m or Siemens/meter) is the electric conductivity as a material property. The above equation can be reversed to obtain the Ohm's law

$$\boldsymbol{E} = \rho_e \boldsymbol{J} \tag{14.3.19}$$

and $\sigma_e = \rho_e^{-1}$. $\tag{14.3.20}$

14.3.4   Electromagnetic Force Vector

Note that there are only four independent equations among the five governing equations of electromagnetics, i.e., Eqs. (14.3.2), (14.3.3), (14.3.4), (14.3.5), and (14.3.17). Vectors $\boldsymbol{B}$ and $\boldsymbol{E}$ are the fundamental electromagnetic field vectors, which define the electromagnetic force vector $\boldsymbol{F}$ acting on the electric charge q moving with a velocity $\boldsymbol{V}$ in an electromagnetic field according to Lorenz force equation, given as

$$\boldsymbol{F} = q(\boldsymbol{E} + \boldsymbol{V} \times \boldsymbol{B}) \tag{14.3.21}$$

14.3.5   Energy in the Electric Field

The total energy per unit volume at a certain moment stored by a nonstationary electromagnetic field, in which the electric field and the magnetic field are coupled and both vary with time, can be calculated as

$$
U_{em} = \frac{\frac{1}{2}\varepsilon |E|^2 + \frac{1}{2}|B|^2}{\mu}
\tag{14.3.22}
$$

14.3.6 Skin Depth

In a fast-varying field, the magnetic field does not penetrate through to the interior of the material, as "beauty is just skin deep" prescribes. When an electromagnetic wave with a sinusoidally time-varying field of angular speed of ω impinges perpendicularly upon a conductor surface from the air (or vacuum), the wave strength attenuates to e^{-1} of the original magnitude after it travels a certain distance[Griffiths]

$$
\begin{aligned}
d_S &= \{Re[j\,\omega\,\mu_o\,\mu_r(\rho_e^{-1} + j\,\omega\,\varepsilon_o\,\epsilon_r)]^{\frac{1}{2}}\}^{-1} \\
&= \omega^{-1}\left\{\frac{1}{2}\mu_o\,\mu_r[-1 + (\omega\,\rho_e\,\varepsilon_o\,\epsilon_r)^2]\right\}^{-\frac{1}{2}}
\end{aligned}
\tag{14.3.23}
$$

The characteristic length, d_S, given above is called skin depth, which depends not only on the electric conductivity and magnetic permittivity, but also on the frequency of the incident wave in radiation. Skin depths for good conductors such as silver and copper are very small for a wide range of frequencies.

14.3.7 Numerical Analysis in Electromagnetic Field

Typical applications of numerical analysis in the electromagnetic field include integrated circuits, capacitors, inductors, insulators, coils, electric motors, sensors, and actuators, with dedicated tools for extracting performance parameters such as resistance, capacitance, inductance, impedance, force, and torque. For example, the AC/DC module of[COMSOL Multiphysics] can be used for simulating electric, magnetic, and electromagnetic fields in static and low-frequency applications, as demonstrated in Fig. 14.3.1.

Fig. 14.3.1   Magnetic Flux Density and Norm on the Ferromagnetic Core, around Which a 50 Hz AC Coil Wound[COMSOL Multiphysics]

Material properties and constitutive relations are defined in terms of permittivity, permeability, conductivity, and remnant fields. Material properties are allowed to be spatially varying, time-dependent, anisotropic, and having core losses. Both electric and magnetic media can include nonlinearities such as **B-H** (magnetic flux density versus magnetic field intensity) curves, or even be described by implicitly given equations. The "fresh" relationship between the magnetizing force and the magnetic flux produced in a material is typically plotted as *B-H* curves, as shown in Fig. 14.3.2.

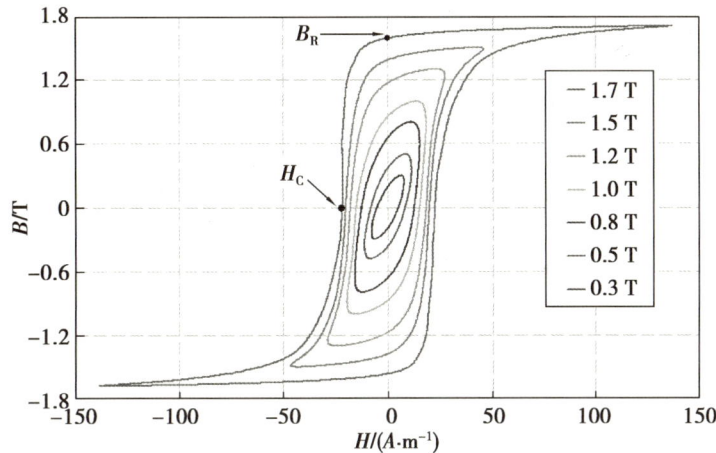

Fig. 14.3.2   Fresh *B-H* Curves at Different Magnetic Induction Levels

The skin depth is used to assure the quality of meshing (for finite element methods and boundary element methods) in the numerical analysis of electromagnetic wave travelling in a solid. The following meshing scheme is suggested[COMSOL Multiphysics]:

(a) If the skin depth is smaller than the object, it is advised to use boundary layer meshing to resolve the strong variations in the fields in the direction normal to the boundary, with a minimum of one element per skin depth and a minimum of three boundary layer elements.

(b) If the skin depth is larger than the effective wavelength in the medium, it is sufficient to resolve the wavelength in the medium itself with five elements per wavelength.

When an infinite element layer is added to the outside of a finite-sized modeling domain, the field equations are automatically scaled to represent a "possibly" infinite domain with a finite-sized model and avoids artificial truncation effects from the model boundaries.

14.4   Polarization

An applied electric field will polarize the material by orienting the dipole moments of polar molecules in opposite direction when working at a temperature below Curie point (T_c): the process leading to a macroscopic net polarization is called poling, i.e., aligning dipole moments. The Curie point is the temperature, above which the material is paraelectric (nonpolar). As an example, at a temperature between 5 ℃ and 120 ℃ (T_c), the natural piezoelectric crystal or polycrystal of $BaTiO_3$ exhibits a tetragonal symmetry that leads to a dipole moment in a ferroelectric phase, but it will be reshaped into a cubic perovskite structure at a temperature higher than T_c. Nevertheless, these dielectric materials possess polarization in nature, but they have no electric dipoles in the absence of an applied electrical field.

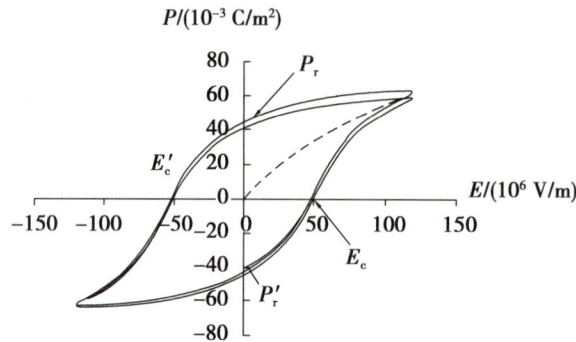

Fig. 14.4.1   Typical Piezoelectric Hysteresis Loop for PVDF[Harrison & Ounaies]

14.4.1   Dielectric Permittivity

A material develops a dielectric polarization when an electric field is applied, but a substance that has such a natural charge separation even in the absence of a field is called a polar material. After being exposed to an electricfield of 10^6 V/m (MV/m) or higher, the temperature of a ferroelectric material may rise above the Curie point and the spontaneous polarizations appear. A typical piezoelectric hysteresis loop for polarizing PVDF[Harrison & Ounaies] is shown in Fig. 14.4.1. Parameters E_c and E_c' are coercive electric field intensities required to reduce the polarization to zero, while P_r and P_r' are remnant polarizations when the electric field is zeroed. E_c and E_c are usually not equal, so are P_r and P_r'.

Permittivity is the key physical parameter of a dielectric that presents the amount of reduction of effective electric field as shown in Eq. (14.3.1). The relative permittivity (ϵ_r) of material is also called dielectric constant or dielectrics, if it is greater than one. The permittivity of an isotropic homogeneous material is related to its relative permittivity as

$$\epsilon = \epsilon_r \epsilon_o = (1 + \chi_e) \epsilon_o = \epsilon_o + \chi_e \epsilon_o \qquad (14.4.1)$$

and $\epsilon_r = 1 + \chi_e$ \qquad (14.4.2)

where

$\epsilon(C/N/m^2)$: Permittivity, i.e., free-body dielectric constant;

$\epsilon_\mathrm{o}(\mathrm{C/N/m^2})$: Permittivity of the vacuum, $\epsilon_\mathrm{o}=8.854\times10^{-12}$ C/N/m^2;

ϵ_r: Relative permittivity of the material, also called relative dielectric constant;

χ_e: Electric susceptibility.

The unit of a dipole moment is C · m (Coulomb · meter), named after force moment N · m (Newton · meter). The susceptibility of a homogeneous electric conductor is defined as the degree of polarization (P) of a material when it is exposed to an electric field. Following Eqs. (14.4.1) and (14.4.2), one has

$$P = \epsilon E - \epsilon_0 E = (\epsilon - \epsilon_0)E = \chi_\mathrm{e} \epsilon_0 E = (\epsilon_\mathrm{r} - 1)\epsilon_0 E \tag{14.4.3}$$

of which P (C/m^2 or μC/m^2) is the polarization. Polarization is the dipole moment per unit volume (C · m/m^3), utilized to quantify the degree of material polarization. No polarization is produced in a perfect conductor ($\chi_\mathrm{e}=0$). It is reasonable to assume that $\chi_\mathrm{e} \approx 0$ for good electric conductors such as silver and copper. The ferroelectric polarization has been well documented for ceramic crystals. Mechanical orientation, thermal annealing and high voltage treatment have all been shown to be effective in inducing crystalline phase transformations. A typical *P-E* curve describing the nonlinear hysteresis relationship between polarization and electric field of polymer PVDF is depicted in Fig. 14.4.1.

The dashed line in Fig. 14.4.1 gives the initial "nearly-proportional" property between polarization and the applied electric field intensity. After then, a ferroelectric performance curve, namely *P-E*, shows the hysteresis effect in the cyclic test, which can be used as a memory function. Ferroelectric materials are indeed used for ferroelectric RAM (FeRAM) memory chips for computers.

14.4.2 Loss Tangent (tan δ) of Permittivity

When a dielectric material is placed between two charged electrode plates having an electric field intensity E, the polarization of the dielectric produces an electric field intensity E_p that is opposite to E, the resulting electrical field is

$$E_\mathrm{e} = E - E_\mathrm{p} \tag{14.4.4}$$

Polarization is a charge motion in an alternating field (either electric or magnetic), resembling an electric current that is out of phase with the voltage by 90 degrees if there is no power loss. A useful tool for dealing with the power loss due to electric polarization is to use the complex permeability

$$\epsilon = \epsilon' + i \epsilon'' \tag{14.4.5}$$

where

$$|\epsilon| = [(\epsilon')^2 + (\epsilon'')^2]^{\frac{1}{2}} \tag{14.4.6}$$

$$\epsilon' = \epsilon (1 - \tan^2 \delta)^{\frac{1}{2}} \tag{14.4.7}$$

and $\quad \epsilon'' = \epsilon \tan \delta \tag{14.4.8}$

While at low frequencies in a linear dielectric the main electric field (due to ϵ') and the auxiliary electric field (due to ϵ'') are simply proportional to each other through lumped scalar permittivity ϵ. At high frequencies these quantities will react to each other with a certain amount of phase, namely δ. Parameter $\tan \delta$ is thus the variable that provides a measure of how much power is lost in a material versus how much is stored when exposed in an electric field. The loss factor (f_L) is defined as the loss tangent times the dielectric constant in the polariztaion process as a measure of energy dissipation in an alternation field,

$$f_L = \epsilon_r \tan \delta \tag{14.4.9}$$

When a dielectric is placed in an alternating electric field of intensity E and frequency f, an energy dissipation occurs and the electric field is attenuated accordingly. The power dissipated per unit volume of the dielectric material is

$$w_L = (\epsilon_r \tan \delta) \epsilon_o f E^2 \tag{14.4.10}$$

The power dissipated as heat. One application is the radio-frequency welding of polymers. Note that the power factor is defined as $\sin \delta$, which has the same value as loss tangent $\tan \delta$ when loss angle δ is small.

14.4.3　Ageing

Ageing is the tendency of a ceramic to change back to its original state prior to polarization. Ageing of piezoelectric or pyroelectric ceramics is a logarithmic function with time. For example, stretching the polymer essentially enables the amorphous strands to be well-aligned in the film plane and facilitates uniform rotation of the crystallites by applying an electric field. Semicrystalline fluoropolymers such as PVDF (polyvinylidene fluoride), copolymers of PVDF and TrFE (trifluoroethylene), and TFE (tetraflouoroethylene) are the first discovered piezoelectric polymers [Kawai]. Amorphous polyimides containing polar functional groups have been synthesized and investigated for potential use as piezoelectric sensors at elevated temperatures. Fresh and cyclic-fatigued polarization curves obtained by [Young & Hinkley] are depicted in Fig. 14.4.2. It shows that the capacity of polarization reduces significantly after the cyclic fatigue test while doped films show stronger resistance to cycling than the undoped.

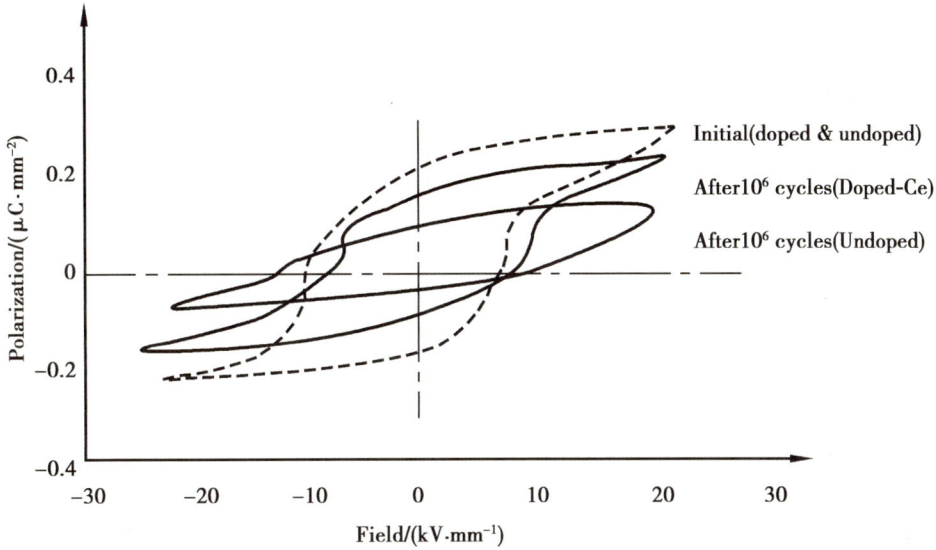

Fig. 14.4.2   Initial and Cyclic-Fatigued *P-E* Curves of Piezoelectric Polyimide Films[Young & Hinkley]

14.4.4   Dissipation Factor and Mechanical Q_m

Electrical potential energy is dissipated in any dielectric material. In a capacitor made of a dielectric placed between two conductors, the typical lumped elemental model consists of an ideal capacitor in series with a resistor called equivalent series resistance (R_{ES}). The dissipation factor (DF) is defiend as a measure of the dielectric loss-rate of energy due to oscillation in the material. Assume that there is no dipole relaxation. The loss is dissipated in the form of heat via R_{ES}. Typically, DF ranges from 0.1% to 0.2% for low-k (low dielectric constant) dielectrics (dielectric constants) and from 1% to 2% for high-k dielectrics. The dissipation factor has the same value as loss tangent when loss angle δ is small, i.e.

$$DF \approx \tan \delta \approx \delta \text{ (for small } \delta) \tag{14.4.11}$$

Quality factor Q is the reciprocal of dissipation factor, as it represents the quality of oscillation. Mechanical Q_m, as one of the quality factors, is defined as the ratio of reactance to resistance in the equivalent series circuit representing the mechanical vibrating resonant systems.

14.5   Electro-Magneto-Thermo-Mechanical Coupling

In light of the orthotropic elasticity of materials given in Chapters 1 and 10 and the electromagnetic theories in Section 14.2, one can write the total electro-magnetic-thermo-mechanical energy per unit volume of an orthotropic electromagnetic material based on thermodynamics as

$$U = \sigma_{ij} \, \varepsilon_{ij} + D_m \, E_m + B_m \, H_m + (\delta\theta) \; T + \text{Interactive terms} \tag{14.5.1}$$

where

$U(\mathrm{J})$: Total energy per unit volume;

$\sigma_{ij}(\mathrm{MPa\ or\ Pa})$: Stress components;

ε_{ij}: Strain components;

$E_{m}(\mathrm{V/m\ or\ N\cdot m/C})$: Electric field intensity; vector $\boldsymbol{E}=(E_1, E_2, E_3)^{\mathrm{T}}$;

$D_{m}(\mathrm{C/m}^2)$: Electric displacement; vector $\boldsymbol{D}=(D_1, D_2, D_3)^{\mathrm{T}}$;

$H_{m}(\mathrm{A/m,\ or\ Weber/m/Henry})$: Magnetic field intensity; vector $\boldsymbol{H}=(H_1, H_2, H_3)^{\mathrm{T}}$;

$B_{m}(\mathrm{Tesla\ or\ Weber/m}^2)$: Magnetic flux density (displacement); vector $\boldsymbol{B}=(B_1, B_2, B_3)^{\mathrm{T}}$;

$T(\mathrm{^\circ C\ or\ K})$: Temperature;

$\delta(\mathrm{J/m}^3/\mathrm{^\circ C\ or\ J/kg/^\circ C})$: Entropy change of a pure substance as an intensive property.

Subscript "i" "j", or "m" ranges from 1 to 3 as an index. The incremental reversible transfer of heat into the substance, regarded as a thermodynamic system, is then calculated as

$$\delta(\mathrm{Heat}) = T\,\delta\,\theta \tag{14.5.2}$$

The unit for entropy change $\delta\theta$ is $\mathrm{J/m}^3/\mathrm{^\circ C}$, i.e., $\mathrm{N\cdot m/m}^3/\mathrm{^\circ C}$, when applied to Eq. (14.5.1), though it may be $\mathrm{J/kg/^\circ C}$ or even $\mathrm{J/^\circ C}$ for other applications. Entropy is conserved for a reversible process, which means that the process does not deviate from thermodynamic equilibrium, when producing the maximum work.

14.5.1　Functional Variables

Next one can arbitrarily choose a set of independent "functional factors" that builds up Eq. (14.5.1). Here are ε_{kl}, E_{m}, and T. Since $\sigma_{ij}=\sigma_{ij}(\varepsilon_{kl}, E_{m}, T)$, $D_{m}=D_{m}(\varepsilon_{kl}, E_{m}, T)$, $B_{m}=B_{m}(\varepsilon_{kl}, E_{m}, T)$, and $\delta\theta=\delta\theta(\varepsilon_{kl}, E_{m}, T)$, their differential forms with respect to these three functional variables are, respectively

$$\mathrm{d}\sigma_{ij} = \left(\frac{\partial\sigma_{ij}}{\partial\varepsilon_{kl}}\right)\mathrm{d}\varepsilon_{kl} + \left(\frac{\partial\sigma_{ij}}{\partial E_{n}}\right)\mathrm{d}E_{n} + \left(\frac{\partial\sigma_{ij}}{\partial H_{n}}\right)\mathrm{d}H_{n} + \left(\frac{\partial\sigma_{ij}}{\partial\mathrm{T}}\right)\mathrm{d}T \tag{14.5.3}$$

$$\mathrm{d}D_{m} = \left(\frac{\partial D_{m}}{\partial\varepsilon_{kl}}\right)\mathrm{d}\varepsilon_{kl} + \left(\frac{\partial D_{m}}{\partial E_{n}}\right)\mathrm{d}E_{n} + \left(\frac{\partial D_{m}}{\partial H_{n}}\right)\mathrm{d}H_{n} + \left(\frac{\partial D_{m}}{\partial\mathrm{T}}\right)\mathrm{d}T \tag{14.5.4}$$

$$\mathrm{d}B_{m} = \left(\frac{\partial B_{m}}{\partial\varepsilon_{kl}}\right)\mathrm{d}\varepsilon_{kl} + \left(\frac{\partial B_{m}}{\partial E_{n}}\right)\mathrm{d}E_{n} + \left(\frac{\partial B_{m}}{\partial H_{n}}\right)\mathrm{d}H_{n} + \left(\frac{\partial B_{m}}{\partial\mathrm{T}}\right)\mathrm{d}T \tag{14.5.5}$$

and $$\mathrm{d}(\delta\theta) = \left[\frac{\partial(\delta\theta)}{\partial\varepsilon_{kl}}\right]\mathrm{d}\varepsilon_{kl} + \left[\frac{\partial(\delta\theta)}{\partial E_{n}}\right]\mathrm{d}E_{n} + \left[\frac{\partial(\delta\theta)}{\partial H_{n}}\right]\mathrm{d}H_{n} + \left[\frac{\partial(\delta\theta)}{\partial\mathrm{T}}\right]\mathrm{d}T \tag{14.5.6}$$

The above four equations can be rewritten in the matrix format to explore the two-factor interaction that

$$
\begin{Bmatrix} \mathrm{d}\sigma_{ij} \\ \mathrm{d}D_m \\ \mathrm{d}B_m \\ \mathrm{d}(\delta\theta) \end{Bmatrix} =
\begin{bmatrix}
\dfrac{\partial\sigma_{ij}}{\partial\varepsilon_{kl}} & \dfrac{\partial\sigma_{ij}}{\partial E_n} & \dfrac{\partial\sigma_{ij}}{\partial H_n} & \dfrac{\partial\sigma_{ij}}{\partial T} \\[2ex]
\dfrac{\partial D_m}{\partial\varepsilon_{kl}} & \dfrac{\partial D_m}{\partial E_n} & \dfrac{\partial D_m}{\partial H_n} & \dfrac{\partial D_m}{\partial T} \\[2ex]
\dfrac{\partial B_m}{\partial\varepsilon_{kl}} & \dfrac{\partial B_m}{\partial E_n} & \dfrac{\partial B_m}{\partial H_n} & \dfrac{\partial B_m}{\partial T} \\[2ex]
\dfrac{\partial(\delta\theta)}{\partial\varepsilon_{kl}} & \dfrac{\partial(\delta\theta)}{\partial E_n} & \dfrac{\partial(\delta\theta)}{\partial H_n} & \dfrac{\partial(\delta\theta)}{\partial T}
\end{bmatrix}
\begin{Bmatrix} \mathrm{d}\varepsilon_{kl} \\ \mathrm{d}E_n \\ \mathrm{d}H_n \\ \mathrm{d}T \end{Bmatrix}
\tag{14.5.7}
$$

The four partial differentiation terms on the diagonal of the tensor matrix given above, i.e., $\partial\sigma_{ij}/\partial\varepsilon_{kl}$, $\partial D_m/\partial E_n$, $\partial B_m/\partial H_n$, and $\partial(\delta\theta)/\partial t$, have no cross-functional coupling. The physical meanings of them are given as follows:

$$
\frac{\partial\sigma_{ij}}{\partial\varepsilon_{kl}} \equiv c_{ijkl} \qquad (\text{Mechanical stiffness}) \tag{14.5.8}
$$

$$
\frac{\partial D_m}{\partial E_n} \equiv \epsilon_{mn} \qquad (\text{Electric permittivity}) \tag{14.5.9}
$$

$$
\frac{\partial B_m}{\partial H_n} \equiv \mu_{mn} \qquad (\text{Magnetic permeability}) \tag{14.5.10}
$$

$$
\frac{\partial(\delta\theta)}{\partial t} \equiv C_v \qquad (\text{Specific heat capacity}) \tag{14.5.11}
$$

where

$c_{ijkl}(\text{GPa or MPa})$: Mechanical stiffness, 4th order tensor;

$\epsilon_{mn}(\text{C/N/m}^2)$: Electric permittivity, 2nd order tensor;

$\mu_{mn}(\text{C/N/m}^2)$: Magnetic permeability, 2nd order tensor;

$C_v(\text{J/m}^3/\text{℃})$: Specific heat capacity per volume, scalar.

The above four equations display the structural, electric, magnetic, and thermal material properties, respectively. All of these four coefficients are highly temperature-dependent, as shown in Tables 14.5.1 and 14.5.2. Specific heat capacity per unit volume C_v is a scalar. The others are tensors that can be rewritten in the short forms according to the primary material axes (1, 2, 3) in the orthotropic domain, respectively as

$$
[c] = [c_{ij}] =
\begin{bmatrix}
c_{11} & c_{12} & c_{13} & 0 & 0 & 0 \\
c_{12} & c_{22} & c_{23} & 0 & 0 & 0 \\
c_{13} & c_{23} & c_{33} & 0 & 0 & 0 \\
0 & 0 & 0 & c_{44} & 0 & 0 \\
0 & 0 & 0 & 0 & c_{55} & 0 \\
0 & 0 & 0 & 0 & 0 & c_{66}
\end{bmatrix}
\tag{14.5.12}
$$

$$[\boldsymbol{\epsilon}] = [\boldsymbol{\epsilon}_{mn}] = \begin{bmatrix} \epsilon_1 & 0 & 0 \\ 0 & \epsilon_2 & 0 \\ 0 & 0 & \epsilon_3 \end{bmatrix} \qquad (14.5.13)$$

$$\text{and} \quad [\boldsymbol{\mu}] = [\boldsymbol{\mu}_{mn}] = \begin{bmatrix} \mu_1 & 0 & 0 \\ 0 & \mu_2 & 0 \\ 0 & 0 & \mu_3 \end{bmatrix} \qquad (14.5.14)$$

where

$[c]_{6\times6}$: Stiffness, c_{ij} (GPa, MPa or Pa) ;

$[\boldsymbol{\epsilon}]_{3\times3}$: Electric permittvities (dielectric constants) ϵ_{ij} ($\epsilon_o = 8.854$ pC/N/m^2) ;

$[\boldsymbol{\mu}]_{3\times3}$: Magnetic permeabilities μ_{ij} (μN $\cdot$ s/C^2, i.e., 10^{-6} N $\cdot$ s/C^2).

Notes: A—Ampere, C—Coulomb, F—Farad, H—Henry, m—meter, N—Newton, s—second, T—Tesla, V—Volt, W—Weber.

14.5.2　Interactive Effects between Variables

All the other differentiation terms off the diagonal of the matrix in Eq. (14.5.7) embrace interactive effects. Thanks to the assumption that the process is reversible, there are only six independent coefficients for the twelve terms off the diagonal. They are defined using their reciprocal differentiation relationships as follows:

$$\frac{\partial \sigma_{ij}}{\partial E_m} \equiv - e_{ijn} \text{ and } \frac{\partial D_m}{\partial \varepsilon_{kl}} = e_{ijn} \qquad \text{(Piezoelectric effect)} \qquad (14.5.15)$$

$$\frac{\partial \sigma_{ij}}{\partial H_m} \equiv - q_{ijm} \text{ and } \frac{\partial B_m}{\partial \varepsilon_{ij}} \equiv q_{ijm} \qquad \text{(Piezomagnetic effect)} \qquad (14.5.16)$$

$$\frac{\partial \sigma_{ij}}{\partial T} \equiv - \eta_{ij} \text{ and } \frac{\partial(\delta\theta)}{\partial \varepsilon_{ij}} \equiv \eta_{ij} \qquad \text{(Thermomechanical effect)} \qquad (14.5.17)$$

$$\frac{\partial D_m}{\partial H_n} = \frac{B_m}{\partial E_n} \equiv m_{mn} \qquad \text{(Magnetoelectric effect)} \qquad (14.5.18)$$

$$\frac{\partial D_m}{\partial T} = \frac{\partial(\delta\theta)}{\partial E_m} \equiv p_m \qquad \text{(Pyroelectric effect)} \qquad (14.5.19)$$

$$\frac{\partial B_m}{\partial T} = \frac{\partial(\delta\theta)}{\partial H_m} \equiv \kappa_m \qquad \text{(Pyromagnetic effect)} \qquad (14.5.20)$$

where

e_{ijm}(C/m or N/V/m): Piezoelectric coefficient in stress form, a 3rd order tensor;

q_{ijm}(N/A/m): Piezomagnetic coefficient, a 3rd order tensor;

η_{ij}(MPa/℃): Thermal-stress gradient, a 2nd order tensor;

m_{mn}(pNs/V/C, i.e., 10^{-12} N · s/V/C): Magnetoelectric coefficient, a 2nd order tensor;

p_{m}(μC/m²/℃): Pyroelectric coefficient, a vector;

κ_{m}(10^{-3}N/A/m/℃): Pyromagnetic coefficient, a vector.

The relationships exhibited in the above equations are called Maxwell-Callen equations. The parameters given above are namely electro-magneto-thermo-mechanical coupling coefficients. For example, "$\partial \sigma_{ij}/\partial E_m$" means that an applied electric field produces stresses (via strains) and "$\partial D_m/\partial \varepsilon_{kl}$" means that an applied strain generates electric displacement that is supposedly generated by electric field only for a nonpiezoelectric material. Assume that the converse piezoelectric effect and piezoelectric effect are reversible, they shall share the same piezoelectric coefficient in magnitude. A negative sign "−" is assigned to "$\partial \sigma_{ij}/\partial E_m$" due to the traditional sign convention of naming strain and stress tensors. A negative sign "−" is also assigned to "$\partial \sigma_{ij}/\partial H_m$" and "$\partial \sigma_{ij}/\partial T$", respectively for the same reason.

Reference data for frequently used piezo- and pyro-crystals and ceramics are listed in Table 14.5.1, while the data for synthesized laminae/composites are listed in Table 14.5.2. All the data are highly temperature-dependent. Coefficients e_{ijm}, q_{ijm}, η_{ij}, m_{mn}, p_m, and κ_m are the six parameters herein employed to present the distinct phenomena of linear cross-functional interactions. They can be rewritten in the short forms according to the primary material axes (1, 2, 3) in the orthotropic domain, respectively as

$$[\boldsymbol{e}] = [\boldsymbol{e}_{ij}]_{3\times6} = \begin{bmatrix} e_{11} & e_{12} & e_{13} & e_{14} & e_{15} & e_{16} \\ e_{21} & e_{22} & e_{23} & e_{24} & e_{25} & e_{26} \\ e_{31} & e_{32} & e_{33} & e_{34} & e_{35} & e_{36} \end{bmatrix} \tag{14.5.21}$$

$$[\boldsymbol{q}] = [\boldsymbol{q}_{ij}]_{3\times6} = \begin{bmatrix} q_{11} & q_{12} & q_{13} & q_{14} & q_{15} & q_{16} \\ q_{21} & q_{22} & q_{23} & q_{24} & q_{25} & q_{26} \\ q_{31} & q_{32} & q_{33} & q_{34} & q_{35} & q_{36} \end{bmatrix} \tag{14.5.22}$$

$$\{\boldsymbol{\eta}\} = \{\boldsymbol{\eta}_n\}_{6\times1} = \begin{Bmatrix} \eta_{11} \\ \eta_{21} \\ \eta_{31} \\ \eta_{41} \\ \eta_{51} \\ \eta_{61} \end{Bmatrix} = [\boldsymbol{c}]\{\boldsymbol{\alpha}\}, \text{ of which} \{\boldsymbol{\alpha}_m\}_{6\times1} = \begin{Bmatrix} \alpha_1 \\ \alpha_2 \\ \alpha_3 \\ 0 \\ 0 \\ 0 \end{Bmatrix} \tag{14.5.23a \& b}$$

$$[m] = [m_{ij}]_{3\times3} = \begin{bmatrix} m_{11} & m_{12} & m_{13} \\ m_{21} & m_{22} & m_{23} \\ m_{31} & m_{32} & m_{33} \end{bmatrix} \qquad (14.5.24)$$

$$\{p\} = \{p_n\}_{3\times1} = \begin{Bmatrix} p_1 \\ p_2 \\ p_3 \end{Bmatrix} \qquad (14.5.25)$$

$$\text{and} \quad \{\kappa\} = \{\kappa_n\}_{3\times1} = \begin{Bmatrix} \kappa_1 \\ \kappa_2 \\ \kappa_3 \end{Bmatrix} \qquad (14.5.26)$$

where

$[e]_{3\times6}$: Piezoelectric coefficients in stress form e_{ij} (C/m or N/V/m) ;

$[d]_{3\times6}$: Piezoelectric coefficients in strain form d_{ij} (C/N or m/V) ;

$[q]_{3\times6}$: Piezomagnetic coefficients q_{ij} (N/A/m) ;

$[m]_{3\times3}$: Magnetoelectric coefficient m_{ij} (pNs/V/C, i.e., 10^{-12} N · s/V/C) ;

$\{\eta\}_{6\times1}$: Thermal-stress coefficient η_{ij} (MPa/℃ or Pa/℃) ;

$\{\alpha\}_{6\times1}$: Coefficient of linear thermal expansions α_m (℃$^{-1}$) ;

$\{p\}_{6\times1}$: Pyroelectric coefficients p_m (μC/m^2/℃) ;

$\{\kappa\}_{6\times1}$: Pyromagnetic coefficients κ_m (10^{-3}N/A/m/℃).

Notes: A—Ampere, C—Coulomb, F—Farad, H—Henry, m—meter, N—Newton, s—second, T—Tesla, V—Volt, W—Weber.

14.5.3 Gibbs Free Energy Function

The interactive effects given in Eqs. (14.5.15)-(14.5.20), which are given without a derivation, are to be further characterized using the Gibbs free energy function, denoted as G_e. It is termed as magneto-electric enthalpy that has three dependent responses, i.e., stress σ_{ij}, electric displacement D_m. and magnetic flux density B_m. G_e can be obtained by subtracting the electric energy and thermal energy due to temperature variation per unit volume from the total strain energy per unit volume as given below [Gibbs] [Ikeda] :

$$G_e(\varepsilon_{ij}, E_m, H_m, T) = U_o - D_m E_m - B_m H_m - (\delta\theta)T - \text{Interactive terms} \qquad (14.5.27)$$

In other words, G_e is a function of the following three independent variables: ε_{ij}, E_m and H_m, in addition to the temperature variation as a thermodynamic potential. Presenting Eq. (14.5.27) in its differential form, one has

$$dG_e(\varepsilon_{ij},\ E_m,\ T) = dU_o - D_m\ dE_m - B_m\ dH_m - (\delta\theta)\,dT$$

$$= \left(\frac{\partial U_o}{\partial\varepsilon_{ij}}\right) d\varepsilon_{ij} - D_m\ dE_m - B_m\ dH_m - \delta\theta\ dT$$

$$= \sigma_{ij}\ d\varepsilon_{ij} - D_m\ dE_m - B_m\ dH_m - \delta\theta\ dT \tag{14.5.28}$$

On the other hand, by taking a partial differentiation of $G_e(\varepsilon_{ij},\ E_k,\ T)$, given by Eq. (14.5.27), with respect to the other three independent variables without considering its explicit content such as the U_o and others, one has the following equation[Gibbs]

$$dG_e(\varepsilon_{ij},\ E_k,\ H_m,\ T) = \left(\frac{\partial G_e}{\partial\varepsilon_{ij}}\right) d\varepsilon_{ij} + \left(\frac{\partial G_e}{\partial E_m}\right) dE_m + \left(\frac{\partial G_e}{\partial H_m}\right) dH_m + \left(\frac{\partial G_e}{\partial T}\right) dT \tag{14.5.29}$$

Comparing the above equation with Eq. (14.5.28) leads to the following four equations

$$\frac{\partial G_e}{\partial\varepsilon_{ij}} = \sigma_{ij} \tag{14.5.30}$$

$$\frac{\partial G_e}{\partial E_m} = - D_m \tag{14.5.31}$$

$$\frac{\partial G_e}{\partial H_m} = - B_m \tag{14.5.32}$$

and $\quad \dfrac{\partial G_e}{\partial T} = - \delta\theta \tag{14.5.33}$

Next taking further differentiations of the terms on both sides of Eq. (14.5.30) with respect to E_m and another differentiation of both sides of Eq. (14.5.31) with respect to ε_{ij}, one has the following two equations

$$\frac{\partial^2 G_e}{\partial\varepsilon_{ij}\partial E_m} = \frac{\partial\sigma_{ij}}{\partial E_m} \tag{14.5.34}$$

and $\quad \dfrac{\partial^2 G_e}{\partial\varepsilon_{ij}\partial E_m} = - \dfrac{\partial D_m}{\partial\varepsilon_{ij}} \tag{14.5.35}$

Thus, $\quad \dfrac{\partial\sigma_{ij}}{\partial E_m} = - \dfrac{\partial D_m}{\partial\varepsilon_{ij}} = - e_{ijm} \tag{14.5.36}$

By the same token, the following relationships can be obtained from all other combinations of Eqs. (14.5.30)-(14.5.33)

$$\frac{\partial \sigma_{ij}}{\partial H_m} = -\frac{\partial B_m}{\partial \varepsilon_{ij}} = -q_{ijm} \tag{14.5.37}$$

$$\frac{\partial \sigma_{ij}}{\partial T} = -\frac{\partial(\delta\theta)}{\partial \varepsilon_{ij}} = -\eta_{ij} \tag{14.5.38}$$

$$\frac{\partial D_m}{\partial H_n} = \frac{\partial B_m}{\partial E_n} = m_{mn} \tag{14.5.39}$$

$$\frac{\partial D_m}{\partial T} = \frac{\partial(\delta\theta)}{\partial E_m} = p_m \tag{14.5.40}$$

$$\frac{\partial B_m}{\partial T} = \frac{\partial(\delta\theta)}{\partial H_m} = \kappa_m \tag{14.5.41}$$

Exactly the above six equations are Eq. (14.5.15)-(14.5.20). It warrants that each two-factor interaction due to electro-magneto-thermo-mechanical coupling is a two-way conversion of energy as long as the system is conservative and reversible.

14.5.4   Constitutive Equations

The thermodynamic potential for an electromagnetic material working in the linear orthotropic domain, including strains, electric charges, magnetic inductions, and thermal entropy with various electro-magneto-thermo-mechanical coupling effects can be obtained by subtracting the electric energy, magnetic energy, thermal energy, and the energy terms due to their interactive effects per unit volume from the total strain energy per unit volume [Gibbs] [Ikeda] [Sunar et al.]. Once the explored linear interactive effects are included in the Gibbs free energy function, it can be rewritten in matrix form as follows:

$$G_e(\varepsilon_{ij}, E_m, H_m, T) = \frac{1}{2}\{\varepsilon\}^T[c]\{\varepsilon\} - \frac{1}{2}\{E\}^T[\epsilon]\{E\} - \frac{1}{2}\{H\}^T[\mu]\{H\} - T\delta\theta -$$
$$\{\varepsilon\}^T[e]^T\{E\} - \{\varepsilon\}^T[q]^T\{H\} - \{\varepsilon\}^T\{\eta\}T -$$
$$\{E\}^T\{p\}\,T - \{H\}^T[m]\{E\} - \{H\}^T\{\kappa\}T \tag{14.5.42}$$

As long as it is a conservative reversible system, introducing Eqs. (14.5.30)-(14.5.33) that $\partial G_e/\partial \varepsilon_{ij} = \sigma_{ij}$, $\partial G_e/\partial E_m = -D_m$, $\partial G_e/\partial H_m = -B_m$, and $\partial G_e/\partial T = -\delta\theta$ to the above equation leads to the following four constitutive equations:

$$\{\sigma\}_{6\times1} = [c]_{6\times6}\{\varepsilon\}_{6\times1} - [e]^T_{6\times3}\{E\}_{3\times1} - [q]^T_{6\times3}\{H\}_{3\times1} - \{\eta\}_{6\times1}T \tag{14.5.43}$$

$$\{D\}_{3\times1} = \{e\}_{3\times6}\{\varepsilon\}_{6\times1} + [\epsilon]_{3\times3}\{E\}_{3\times1} + [m]_{3\times3}\{H\}_{3\times1} + \{p\}_{3\times1}T \tag{14.5.44}$$

$$\{B\}_{3\times1} = [q]_{3\times6}\{\varepsilon\}_{6\times1} + [m]_{3\times3}\{E\}_{3\times1} + [\mu]_{3\times3}\{H\}_{3\times1} + \{\kappa\}_{3\times1}T \qquad (14.5.45)$$

$$\text{and}\quad 0 = \{\varepsilon\}^{\mathrm{T}}_{1\times6}[\eta]_{6\times1} + \{E\}^{\mathrm{T}}_{1\times3}\{p\}_{3\times1} + \{H\}^{\mathrm{T}}_{1\times3}\{\kappa\}_{3\times1} \qquad (14.5.46)$$

When the primary material axes as an orthogonal system are well-aligned with the principal direction of polarization in the above four equations, they can be condensed into one equation as follows:

$$\text{or}\quad
\begin{Bmatrix}
\sigma_{11} \\ \sigma_{22} \\ \sigma_{33} \\ \tau_{12} \\ \tau_{23} \\ \tau_{31} \\ D_1 \\ D_2 \\ D_3 \\ B_1 \\ B_2 \\ B_3 \\ \delta\theta
\end{Bmatrix}
=
\begin{bmatrix}
c_{11} & c_{12} & c_{13} & 0 & 0 & 0 & -e_{11} & -e_{21} & -e_{31} & -q_{11} & -q_{21} & -q_{31} & -\eta_1 \\
c_{12} & c_{22} & c_{23} & 0 & 0 & 0 & -e_{12} & -e_{22} & -e_{32} & -q_{12} & -q_{22} & -q_{33} & -\eta_2 \\
c_{13} & c_{23} & c_{33} & 0 & 0 & 0 & -e_{13} & -e_{23} & -e_{33} & -q_{13} & -q_{23} & -q_{33} & -\eta_3 \\
0 & 0 & 0 & c_{44} & 0 & 0 & -e_{14} & -e_{24} & -e_{34} & -q_{14} & -q_{24} & -q_{34} & 0 \\
0 & 0 & 0 & 0 & c_{55} & 0 & -e_{15} & -e_{25} & -e_{35} & -q_{15} & -q_{25} & -q_{35} & 0 \\
0 & 0 & 0 & 0 & 0 & c_{66} & -e_{16} & -e_{26} & -e_{36} & -q_{16} & -q_{26} & -q_{36} & 0 \\
e_{11} & e_{12} & e_{13} & e_{14} & e_{15} & e_{16} & \epsilon_{11} & 0 & 0 & m_{11} & 0 & 0 & p_1 \\
e_{21} & e_{22} & e_{23} & e_{24} & e_{25} & e_{26} & 0 & \epsilon_{22} & 0 & 0 & m_{22} & 0 & p_2 \\
e_{31} & e_{32} & e_{33} & e_{34} & e_{35} & e_{36} & 0 & 0 & \epsilon_{33} & 0 & 0 & m_{33} & p_3 \\
q_{11} & q_{12} & q_{13} & q_{14} & q_{15} & q_{16} & m_{11} & 0 & 0 & \mu_{11} & 0 & 0 & \kappa_1 \\
q_{21} & q_{22} & q_{23} & q_{24} & q_{25} & q_{26} & 0 & m_{22} & 0 & 0 & \mu_{22} & 0 & \kappa_2 \\
q_{31} & q_{32} & q_{33} & q_{34} & q_{35} & q_{36} & 0 & 0 & m_{33} & 0 & 0 & \mu_{22} & \kappa_3 \\
\eta_1 & \eta_2 & \eta_3 & 0 & 0 & 0 & p_1 & p_2 & p_3 & \kappa_1 & \kappa_2 & \kappa_3 & 0
\end{bmatrix}
\begin{Bmatrix}
\varepsilon_{11} \\ \varepsilon_{22} \\ \varepsilon_{33} \\ \varepsilon_{12} \\ \varepsilon_{23} \\ \varepsilon_{31} \\ E_1 \\ E_2 \\ E_3 \\ H_1 \\ H_2 \\ H_3 \\ T
\end{Bmatrix}$$

$$(14.5.47)$$

The equation presented above is to characterize electromagnetic materials that exhibit reversible behavior in the near domain only, when subjected to mechanical stresses and temperature variations. It does not apply to irreversible processes such as

(a) Transport processes, e.g. heat conduction, electrical conduction;

(b) Dissipative processes, e.g. mechanical friction, viscoelastic/viscoplastic deformations, electric hysteresis, magnetic hysteresis.

14.6   Piezoelectricity

Piezoelectricity is due to asymmetries in the crystallographic structure or due to polarization when stressed. Polarization may be produced in the force direction or perpendicular to it, depending on the stressed material. Piezoelectric materials are as a subset of ferroelectric materials. Although polarization of piezoelectric polymers is not so significant as piezoelectric ceramics and single crystal materials, polymers are uniquely qualified to fit niche areas where single crystals and ceramics are incapable of performing as effectively.

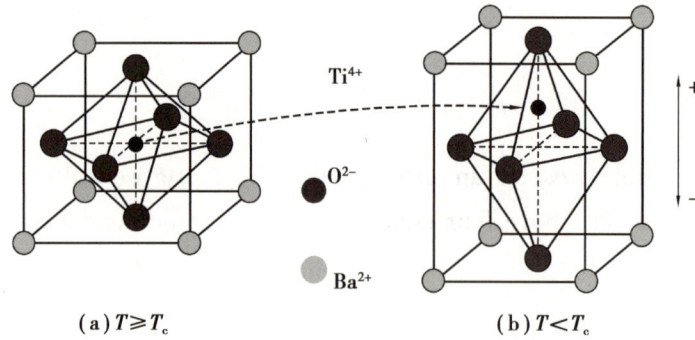

(a) $T \geqslant T_c$ (b) $T < T_c$

Fig. 14.6.1 How the Piezoelectric Effect of Barium Titanate (BaTiO$_3$) Rendered by Nature

Polarization is a measure of the degree of piezoelectricity in a given material. For example, the Curie point of barium titanate (BaTiO$_3$) is about 130 ℃. Once above 130 ℃, a non-piezoelectric cubic phase stays stable with balanced electric charges, as the center of positive charge (Ba^{2+} and Ti^{4+}) coincides with the center of the negative charge (O^{2-}). When it is cooled below the Curie point, a tetragonal structure forms as shown in Fig. 14.6.1, where the center of positive charge is displaced relative to the O^{2-} ions and thus renders the apparent electric dipoles. Perovskite is the name for a group of piezoelectric materials with a general formula similar to BaTiO$_3$ (barium titanate), such as CaTiO$_3$ (calcium titanate), PbTiO$_3$ (lead titanate), PbZr$_x$Ti$_{1-x}$O$_3$ (PZT: lead zirconate titanate), Pb$_{1-x}$La$_x$(Zr$_y$T$_{1-y}$)$_{1-x/4}$O$_3$ (PLZT: lead lanthanum zirconate titanate), and PbMg$_{1/3}$Nb$_{2/3}$O$_3$ (PMN: lead magnesium niobate). The direct and converse piezoelectric effects with piezo electric material loading in tension and compression are illustrated in Fig. 14.6.2.

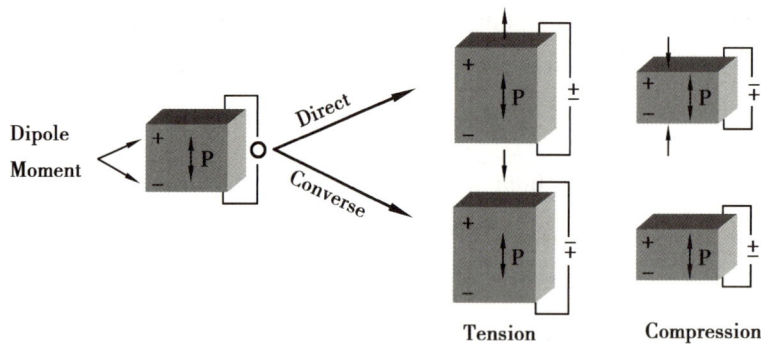

Fig. 14.6.2 Signed Direct and Converse Piezoelectric Effects Based on the Original Dipole Moment

14.6.1 Constitutive Equations-Generating Electric Displacement

In a piezoelectric material that is free of electric field at a constant temperature, a change in polarization results from applied stresses $\{\sigma\}$ or strains $\{\varepsilon\}$. Assume that the linear relationship between the polarization and $\{\sigma\}$ or strains $\{\varepsilon\}$ prevails. Given that both the electric field and strain applied remain constant, the polarization of the generalized orthotropic material in a vector format with three orthogonal components in the primary material coordinate system, $(1, 2, 3)$ in the "stress-charge" form can be obtained from Eqs. (14.5.30) and (14.5.31) as the following two coupled equations,

$$\{D\} = [e]_{3\times6}\{\varepsilon\}_{6\times1} + [\epsilon]_{3\times3}\{E\}_{3\times1} \qquad \text{(Direct piezoelectric effect)} \qquad (14.6.1)$$

and $\quad \{\sigma\} = [c]_{6\times6}\{\varepsilon\}_{6\times1} - [e]_{6\times3}\{E\}_{3\times1} \qquad \text{(Converse piezoelectric effect)} \qquad (14.6.2)$

Simultaneously, they can be rewritten into the following two coupled equations

$$\{D\} = [d]_{3\times6}\{\sigma\}_{6\times1} + [\epsilon]_{3\times3}\{E\}_{3\times1} \qquad \text{(Direct piezoelectric effect)} \qquad (14.6.3)$$

and $\quad \{\varepsilon\} = [s]_{6\times6}\{\sigma\}_{6\times1} + [d]^{T}_{6\times3}\{E\}_{3\times1} \qquad \text{(Converse piezoelectric effect)} \qquad (14.6.4)$

of which $\quad [d] = [d_{ij}]_{3\times6} = \begin{bmatrix} d_{11} & d_{12} & d_{13} & d_{14} & d_{15} & d_{16} \\ d_{21} & d_{22} & d_{23} & d_{24} & d_{25} & d_{26} \\ d_{31} & d_{32} & d_{33} & d_{34} & d_{35} & d_{36} \end{bmatrix} \qquad (14.6.5)$

where

$d_{3\times6}$: Matrix for the direct piezoelectric effect in strain form, where $[d] = [d_{ij}]$;

$d_{ij}(\text{C/N or m/V})$: Piezoelectric strain charge coefficient that can be positive.

As an example, a poled piezoelectric ceramic such as $BaTiO_3$ and tetragonal PZT can be written in an expanded format similar to Eq. (3.2.11) in the "strain charge" form as [ANSI IEEE 176]

$$\begin{Bmatrix} \varepsilon_{11} \\ \varepsilon_{22} \\ \varepsilon_{33} \\ \varepsilon_{23} \\ \varepsilon_{31} \\ \varepsilon_{12} \end{Bmatrix} = \begin{bmatrix} s_{11} & s_{12} & s_{13} & 0 & 0 & 0 \\ s_{12} & s_{22} & s_{23} & 0 & 0 & 0 \\ s_{13} & s_{23} & s_{33} & 0 & 0 & 0 \\ 0 & 0 & 0 & s_{44} & 0 & 0 \\ 0 & 0 & 0 & 0 & s_{55} & 0 \\ 0 & 0 & 0 & 0 & 0 & s_{66} \end{bmatrix} \begin{Bmatrix} \sigma_{11} \\ \sigma_{22} \\ \sigma_{33} \\ \sigma_{23} \\ \sigma_{31} \\ \sigma_{12} \end{Bmatrix} + \begin{bmatrix} 0 & 0 & d_{31} \\ 0 & 0 & d_{32} \\ 0 & 0 & d_{33} \\ 0 & d_{24} & 0 \\ d_{15} & 0 & 0 \\ 0 & 0 & 0 \end{bmatrix} \begin{Bmatrix} E_1 \\ E_2 \\ E_3 \end{Bmatrix} \qquad (14.6.6)$$

and $\quad \begin{Bmatrix} D_1 \\ D_2 \\ D_3 \end{Bmatrix} = \begin{bmatrix} 0 & 0 & 0 & 0 & d_{15} & 0 \\ 0 & 0 & 0 & d_{24} & 0 & 0 \\ d_{31} & d_{32} & d_{33} & 0 & 0 & 0 \end{bmatrix} \begin{Bmatrix} \sigma_{11} \\ \sigma_{22} \\ \sigma_{33} \\ \sigma_{23} \\ \sigma_{31} \\ \sigma_{12} \end{Bmatrix} + \begin{bmatrix} \epsilon_{11} & 0 & 0 \\ 0 & \epsilon_{22} & 0 \\ 0 & 0 & \epsilon_{33} \end{bmatrix} \begin{Bmatrix} E_1 \\ E_2 \\ E_3 \end{Bmatrix} \qquad (14.6.7)$

The above equation can be rewritten in crystallographic coordinate system as

$$\{D_1 \quad D_2 \quad D_3\}^{T} = [d]\{\sigma_{11} \quad \sigma_{22} \quad \sigma_{33} \quad \sigma_{23} \quad \sigma_{31} \quad \sigma_{12}\}^{T} + [\varepsilon]\{E_1 \quad E_2 \quad E_3\}^{T}$$

$$(14.6.8)$$

While measuring the piezoelectric coefficients of a crystal, one usually aligns the applied field with a-axis or c-axis. It is called the longitudinal coefficient, which may not be well aligned with the primary material axes (1, 2, 3). When measured in the direction perpendicular to the field, it is known as the transverse coefficient. In the particular case of tetragonal symmetry (axis "3" is the polar axis). Matrix $[d]$ and matrix $[e]$ are 3rd rank tensors, while matrix $[s]$ and matrix $[c]$ are 4th rank tensors. Coefficient d_{ij} can be either positive or negative. The first subscript of d_{ij} is the direction of the electric field or charge displacement while the second subscript gives the direction of the mechanical deformation. The primary material axes as an orthogonal system must be aligned with the principal direction of polarization in Eqs. (14.6.3) and (14.6.4), which can be condensed into one equation as follows:

$$
\text{or} \quad
\begin{Bmatrix}
\sigma_{11} \\
\sigma_{22} \\
\sigma_{33} \\
\tau_{12} \\
\tau_{23} \\
\tau_{31} \\
D_1 \\
D_2 \\
D_3
\end{Bmatrix}
=
\begin{bmatrix}
c_{11} & c_{12} & c_{13} & 0 & 0 & 0 & -e_{11} & -e_{21} & -e_{31} \\
c_{12} & c_{22} & c_{23} & 0 & 0 & 0 & -e_{12} & -e_{22} & -e_{32} \\
c_{13} & c_{23} & c_{33} & 0 & 0 & 0 & -e_{13} & -e_{23} & -e_{33} \\
0 & 0 & 0 & c_{44} & 0 & 0 & -e_{14} & -e_{24} & -e_{34} \\
0 & 0 & 0 & 0 & c_{55} & 0 & -e_{15} & -e_{25} & -e_{35} \\
0 & 0 & 0 & 0 & 0 & c_{66} & -e_{16} & -e_{26} & -e_{36} \\
e_{11} & e_{12} & e_{13} & e_{14} & e_{15} & e_{16} & \epsilon_{11} & 0 & 0 \\
e_{21} & e_{22} & e_{23} & e_{24} & e_{25} & e_{26} & 0 & \epsilon_{22} & 0 \\
e_{31} & e_{32} & e_{33} & e_{34} & e_{35} & e_{36} & 0 & 0 & \epsilon_{33}
\end{bmatrix}
\begin{Bmatrix}
\varepsilon_{11} \\
\varepsilon_{22} \\
\varepsilon_{33} \\
\varepsilon_{12} \\
\varepsilon_{23} \\
\varepsilon_{31} \\
E_1 \\
E_2 \\
E_3
\end{Bmatrix}
\quad (14.6.9)
$$

Example 14.6.1 The d_{ij} data of quartz-α crystal (right handed quartz) are given in Table 14.5.1. Formulate the piezoelectric effects when the quartz is loaded in the a-axis, m-axis, and c-axis, respectively, without any external electric field.

Solution:

Without $\{E\}$, the piezoelectric effect described by Eq. (14.6.2) can be rewritten as

$$D_1 = d_{11}\sigma_{11} + d_{12}\sigma_{22} + d_{13}\sigma_{33} + d_{14}\sigma_{12} + d_{15}\sigma_{23} + d_{16}\sigma_{31}$$

$$D_2 = d_{21}\sigma_{11} + d_{22}\sigma_{22} + d_{23}\sigma_{33} + d_{24}\sigma_{12} + d_{25}\sigma_{23} + d_{26}\sigma_{31}$$

$$D_3 = d_{31}\sigma_{11} + d_{32}\sigma_{22} + d_{33}\sigma_{33} + d_{34}\sigma_{12} + d_{35}\sigma_{23} + d_{36}\sigma_{31}$$

The piezoelectric tensor for quartz-α is tabulated as follows:

$$
[d] = [d_{ij}]_{3\times 6} =
\begin{bmatrix}
d_{11} & d_{12}=d_{11} & 0 & d_{14} & 0 & 0 \\
0 & 0 & 0 & 0 & d_{25}=-d_{14} & d_{26}=-2d_{11} \\
0 & 0 & 0 & 0 & 0 & 0
\end{bmatrix}_{3\times 6}
\begin{array}{l}
a\text{-axis}(i=1) \\
m\text{-axis}(i=2) \\
c\text{-axis}(i=3)
\end{array}
$$

Thus $D_1 = d_{11}\sigma_{11} + d_{11}\sigma_{22} + d_{14}\sigma_{12}$ (Crystallographic coordinate system)

$\qquad = d_{11}\sigma_{11} + d_{11}\sigma_{22} + d_{14}\sigma_{31}$ (Primary material coordinate system-composites)

$\quad D_2 = - d_{14}\sigma_{23} - 2d_{11}\sigma_{31}$ (Crystallographic coordinate system)

$\qquad = - d_{14}\sigma_{12} - 2d_{11}\sigma_{23}$ (Primary material coordinate system-composites)

and $D_3 = 0$

since $(\sigma_1, \sigma_2, \sigma_3, \sigma_4, \sigma_5, \sigma_6) = (\sigma_{11}, \sigma_{22}, \sigma_{33}, \sigma_{23}, \sigma_{31}, \sigma_{12})$ for crystallographic coordinates
and $(\sigma_1, \sigma_2, \sigma_3, \sigma_4, \sigma_5, \sigma_6) = (\sigma_{11}, \sigma_{22}, \sigma_{33}, \sigma_{12}, \sigma_{23}, \sigma_{32})$ for primary material coordinates.

Note that $d_{11} = -2.3$ and $d_{14} = -0.7$ can be obtained from Table 14.5.1.

Piezoelectric strain (stress) charge coefficients decrease significantly at cryogenic temperatures as shown in Tables 14.5.1 and 14.5.2, but do not vanish. However, they may be de-poled at an elevated temperature, depending on the material.

14.6.2   Constitutive Equations-Generating Electric Displacement

Given that both the electric displacement and strain (stress) level applied remain constant, the polarization of the generalized orthotropic material in a vector format with three orthogonal components in the primary material coordinate system, (1, 2, 3) in strain-charge form can be written into another two coupled equations,

$$\{E\} = - [g]\{\sigma\} + [\epsilon]^{-1}\{D\} \qquad \text{(Direct piezoelectric effect)} \qquad (14.6.10)$$

and $\{\varepsilon\} = [s]\{\sigma\} + [g]^{\mathrm{T}}\{D\}$ (Converse piezoelectric effect)   (14.6.11)

In the stress-charge form, they are

$$\{E\} = - [h]\{\varepsilon\} + [\epsilon]^{-1}\{D\} \qquad \text{(Direct piezoelectric effect)} \qquad (14.6.12)$$

and $\{\sigma\} = [c]\{\varepsilon\} - [h]^{\mathrm{T}}\{D\}$ (Converse piezoelectric effect)   (14.6.13)

where

  $[g]$: Matrix for the direct piezoelectric effect in strain form, $[g] = [g_{ij}]$;
  $g_{ij}(\mathrm{N/V}$ or $\mathrm{m^2/C})$: Piezoelectric strain voltage coefficient;
  $[h]$: Matrix for the direct piezoelectric effect in stress from, $[h] = [h_{ij}]$;
  $h_{ij}(\mathrm{N/C}$ or $\mathrm{V/m})$: Piezoelectric stress voltage coefficient.

These are the four different expressions for piezoelectric coefficients: d_{ij}, e_{ij}, g_{ij}, and h_{ij}, which are used by researchers at their convenience.

In summary, piezoelectricity is a physical phenomenon that the positive ions of a dielectric material are displaced in the direction of the field and negative ions are displaced in the other direction when exposed to an external electric field. It is a measure of the degree of electro-mechanical polarization in a given dielectric. In a piezoelectric material, a change in polarization results from an applied strain ε_{ij} or stress σ_{ij} under the conditions of constant temperature and zero electric field. If the stress and strain tensors can be annotated in another way [Department of Defense Test Standard] as

$$(\sigma_{11}, \sigma_{22}, \sigma_{33}, \sigma_{23}, \sigma_{31}, \sigma_{12}) \rightarrow (\sigma_1, \sigma_2, \sigma_3, \sigma_4, \sigma_5, \sigma_6) \qquad (14.6.14)$$

and $\quad (\varepsilon_{11}, \varepsilon_{22}, \varepsilon_{33}, \varepsilon_{23}, \varepsilon_{31}, \varepsilon_{12}) \rightarrow (\varepsilon_1, \varepsilon_2, \varepsilon_3, \varepsilon_4, \varepsilon_5, \varepsilon_6) \qquad (14.6.15)$

then, the following four equations for $[d], [e], [g],$ and $[h]$ can be established as

$$d_{ij} = \frac{\partial D_i}{\partial \sigma_j} = \frac{\partial \varepsilon_i}{\partial E_j} \qquad \text{(C/N or m/V)} \qquad (14.6.16)$$

$$e_{ij} = \frac{\partial D_i}{\partial \varepsilon_j} = -\frac{\partial \sigma_i}{\partial E_j} \qquad \text{(C/m or N/V/m)} \qquad (14.6.17)$$

$$g_{ij} = -\frac{\partial E_i}{\partial \sigma_j} = \frac{\partial \varepsilon_i}{\partial D_j} \qquad \text{(m/C or V} \cdot \text{m/N)} \qquad (14.6.18)$$

and $\quad h_{ij} = -\frac{\partial E_i}{\partial \varepsilon_j} = -\frac{\partial \sigma_i}{\partial D_j} \qquad \text{(N/C or V/m)} \qquad (14.6.19)$

A high g_{ij} favors a large voltage output, and is looked after for sensors. The output voltage is obtained by multiplying the calculated electric field intensity, according to Eq. (14.6.17), by the thickness of ceramic between electrodes. The relationship between charge constants d_{ij} and voltage constant g_{ij} are given as follows:

$$d_{33} = \epsilon_{33}\, \epsilon_0\, g_{33} \qquad (14.6.20)$$

$$d_{31} = \epsilon_{33}\, \epsilon_0\, g_{31} \qquad (14.6.21)$$

and $\quad d_{15} = \epsilon_{11}\, \epsilon_0\, g_{15} \qquad (14.6.22)$

Thus, d_{ij} is the short circuit charge density per applied mechanical stress, while g_{ij} is the open circuit electric filed per applied mechanical stress.

14.6.3 Electroelasticity

Piezoelectricity is a physical phenomenon that the electricity results from mechanical strains in materials lacking a center of symmetry on the atomic or molecular scale and conversely mechanical strains are induced due to an applied electrical field and polarization of the material in a piezoelectric material. Consider a piezoelectric material that has neither piezomagnetic effect nor pyromagnetic effect. Assume that it works in a linear range, then the induced strains are given as follows:

$$\{\varepsilon\}_{6\times1} = [s]_{6\times6}\{\sigma\}_{6\times1} + [d]_{6\times3}[E]_{3\times1} + \{\alpha\}\Delta T + \{\beta\}\Delta C_m \qquad (14.6.23)$$

where

$[s]$: Compliance matrix of s_{ij};

$s_{ij}(MPa^{-1})$: Compliance coefficient (4th rank tensor) in the (1, 2, 3) coordinate system;

$\{\alpha\}$: Vector of linear thermal expansions;

$\alpha_k(m/m/℃)$: Coefficients of linear thermal expansion;

$\{\beta\}$: Vector of linear moisture expansion;

$\{\beta_k\}$: Coefficients of linear moisture expansion;

ΔT (℃): Temperature variation;

ΔC_m: Moisture-content variation.

The above equation can be rewritten in an explicit format expanded with condensed tensor notations as the following three equations:

$$\varepsilon_{11} = \frac{1}{E_{11}}\sigma_{11} + \frac{-v_{21}}{E_{22}}\sigma_{22} + \frac{-v_{31}}{E_{33}}\sigma_{33} + d_{11} E_1 + d_{12} E_2 + d_{13} E_3 + \alpha_1 \Delta T + \beta_1 \Delta C_m$$

$$(14.6.24)$$

$$\varepsilon_{22} = \frac{-v_{12}}{E_{11}}\sigma_{11} + \frac{1}{E_{22}}\sigma_{22} + \frac{-v_{32}}{E_{33}}\sigma_{33} + d_{21} E_1 + d_{22} E_2 + d_{23} E_3 + \alpha_2 \Delta T + \beta_2 \Delta C_m$$

$$(14.6.25)$$

$$\varepsilon_{33} = \frac{-v_{13}}{E_{11}}\sigma_{11} + \frac{-v_{23}}{E_{22}}\sigma_{22} + \frac{1}{E_{33}}\sigma_{33} + d_{31} E_1 + d_{32} E_2 + d_{33} E_3 + \alpha_3 \Delta T + \beta_3 \Delta C_m$$

$$(14.6.26)$$

$$\varepsilon_{23} = \frac{\tau_{23}}{2 G_{23}} + d_{41} E_1 + d_{42} E_2 + d_{43} E_3 \qquad (14.6.27)$$

$$\varepsilon_{31} = \frac{\tau_{31}}{2 G_{23}} + d_{51} E_1 + d_{52} E_2 + d_{53} E_3 \qquad (14.6.28)$$

$$\varepsilon_{12} = \frac{\tau_{12}}{2 G_{12}} + d_{61} E_1 + d_{62} E_2 + d_{63} E_3 \qquad (14.6.29)$$

Each subscript i, j, or k used above takes 1, 2, or 3 according to the applied primary material coordinate system (1, 2, 3). The first subscript of d_{ij} means the direction of the electric field or charge displacement, while the second subscript stands for the direction of the mechanical deformation. Subscript "33" means that the electric field and the mechanical stress are both along the polarization axis. Subscript "31" says that the compressive stress (mechanical pressure) is applied at a right angle to the polarization axis, but the voltage goes along the polarization axis. Subscript "15" implies that the applied stress is in shearing mode and that the resulting electric field is oriented perpendicular to the polarization axis, as shown in Eq. (14.6.28).

Plane (1, 2) can be attached to the surface of the lamina of concern and the 3-axis is normal to the surface in the application for a laminated product. Based on such a coordinate system, some specific characteristics of piezoelectric materials observed are given as follows:

(a) Poled polymer films are transversely isotropic as they are usually designed to be. In other words, there are only five independent d_{ij} components and they are d_{31}, d_{32}, d_{33}, d_{15} and d_{24}. If the film is poled and biaxially oriented like a layer of graphite, $d_{31} = d_{32}$ (no in-plane shear variation) and $d_{15} = d_{24}$ (no out-of-plane shear variation). Thus, there are only three independent piezoelectric strain constants: d_{13}, d_{33}, d_{15}.

(b) Most natural biopolymers possess symmetry in matrix $[d]$, which leads to a matrix having only two shear piezoelectricity components, i.e., $d_{13} = d_{31}$ (in-plane shear) and $d_{15} = d_{51}$ (out-of-plane shear).

14.6.4 Data Acquisition for Piezoelectric Coefficients

Original piezoelectric ceramics exhibit a random orientation of dipoles rendering a null polarization. In order to obtain a preferential axis (polar axis) a polling process is first identified. Heating the material close to the temperature slightly above the Curie point, applying a strong electric field ($\geqslant 10^6$ V/m) aligned with the polar axis, and then cooling the material while being exposed to the electric field. The constitutive equation for electric charge density D, on the analogy of the B-field in ferromagnetism as shown in Fig. 14.6.3, can be related to the applied stress and electric field intensity.

Electrical poling is accomplished by applying an electric field across the thickness of the polymer as depicted in Fig. 14.6.3. An electric field strength, $\{E\}$, on the order of 50×10^6 V/m (50 MV/m) is typically sufficient to affect crystalline orientation. Polymer poling can be accomplished using a direct contact method or a corona discharge. Eq. (14.6.7) can be expanded to the following three equations for practical application in material data acquisitions:

$$D_1 = \epsilon_{11} E_1 + \epsilon_{12} E_2 + \epsilon_{13} E_3 + d_{11} \sigma_{11} + d_{12} \sigma_{22} + d_{13} \sigma_{33} + d_{14} \tau_{23} + d_{15} \tau_{31} + d_{16} \tau_{12}$$

$$(14.6.30)$$

$$D_2 = \epsilon_{21} E_1 + \epsilon_{22} E_2 + \epsilon_{23} E_3 + d_{21} \sigma_{11} + d_{22} \sigma_{22} + d_{23} \sigma_{33} + d_{24} \tau_{23} + d_{25} \tau_{31} + d_{26} \tau_{12}$$

$$(14.6.31)$$

$$D_3 = \epsilon_{31} E_1 + \epsilon_{32} E_2 + \epsilon_{33} E_3 + d_{31} \sigma_{11} + d_{32} \sigma_{22} + d_{33} \sigma_{33} + d_{34} \tau_{23} + d_{35} \tau_{31} + d_{36} \tau_{12}$$

$$(14.6.32)$$

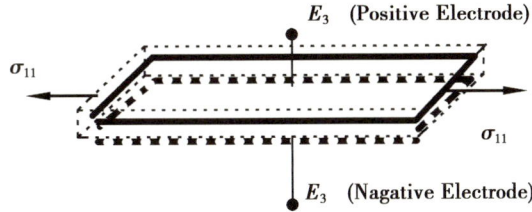

Fig. 14.6.3　Parameter d_{31} Obtained Using a Piezoelectric Lamina. (Positive: Upper Surface; Negative: Lower Surface)

Special skills are required for identifying parameter d_{33} [Jordan et al.]. Piezoelectric strain coefficient d_{31} can be obtained by applying a longitudinal force to polymer electrodes (lamina) while charge Q is generated on the surface of the electrodes. For a simple electrode shown in Fig. 14.6.3, one has

$$d_{31} = \frac{\dfrac{Q}{w L}}{\dfrac{F}{w h}} \qquad (14.6.33)$$

where

　d_{31}(C/N; pC/N): Piezoelectric strain charge constant;

　Q(C): Coulomb;

　w (m): Width;

　L (m): Length;

　h (m): Thickness.

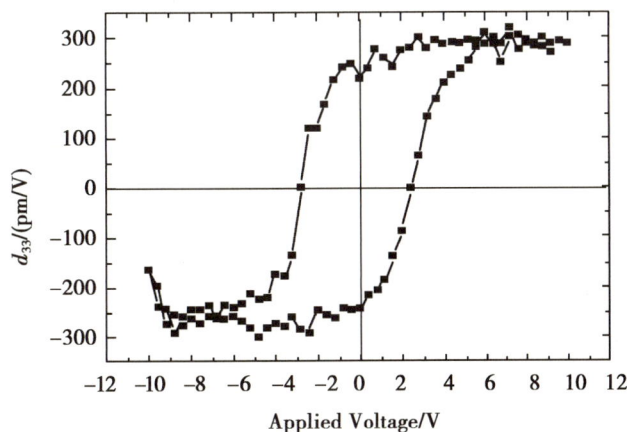

Fig. 14.6.4　Piezoelectric Pseudo-Hysteresis Loop of d_{33} in 1 μm PZT Film [Yang et al.]

When a quasi-static mechanical pressure is applied to the sample, the electric charge analyzed for d_{33} measurement the mechanical stress is perpendicular to electrode while for d_{31} measurement mechanical stress is parallel to electrodes. In general, the piezoelectric coefficients are much smaller than those of bulk ceramics due to the clamping to the substrate [Kholkin et al.]. The pseudo piezoelectric hysteresis loop of d_{33} in 1 μm PZT film is given in Fig. 14.6.4, as coupled with a substrate.

14.6.5　Transduction Efficiency

The conversion of mechanical energy into electrical energy and vice versa is regarded as the electromechanical coupling coefficient, which is a measure of transduction efficiency defined as

$$\text{either}\quad k^2 = \frac{\text{Mechanical energy converted into electric energy}}{\text{Input mechanical energy}} \qquad (14.6.34a)$$

$$\text{or}\quad k^2 = \frac{\text{Electrical energy converted into mechanical energy}}{\text{Input electric energy}} \qquad (14.6.34b)$$

Electromechanical coupling coefficient k (mainly k_{33}, k_{31}, k_p, and k_{15}) is a numerical measure of the conversion efficiency from electrical form to mechanical form in piezoelectric materials or vice versa:

(a) k_{33} is appropriate for a long thin bar, electroded at both ends, and polarized along the length, and vibrating in a simple length expansion and contraction.

(b) k_{31} relates to a long thin bar, electroded on a pair of long faces, polarized in thickness, and vibrating in simple length expansion and contraction.

(c) k_{15} describes the energy conversion in a thickness shear vibration.

(d) k_p signifies the coupling of electrical and mechanical energy in a thin round disc, polarized in thickness and vibrating in radial expansion and contraction.

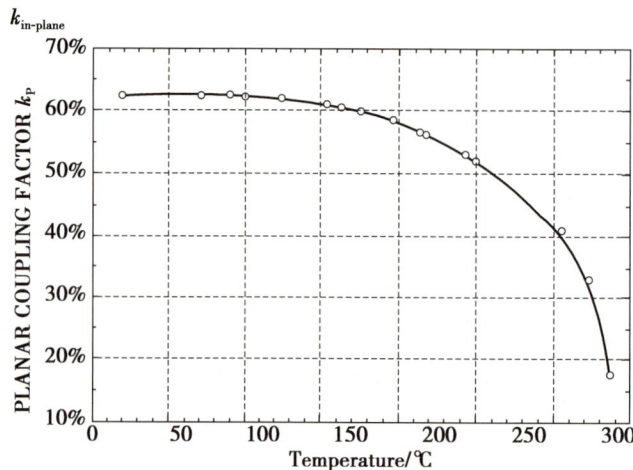

Fig. 14.6.5　In-Plane Electromechanical Coupling Factor Decreases with Increasing Temperature of a Soft PZT Disk ($R = 10$ mm & $h = 1$ mm) [Miclea et al.]

For example, electromechanical coupling coefficient k_{31}, which appears to be the major coupling effect for most piezoelectric materials, can be calculated directly from the following equation

$$k_{31} = \frac{d_{31}}{(\sigma_{11} \epsilon_3)^{\frac{1}{2}}} \qquad (14.6.35)$$

Transduction efficiency varies, such as k_{31} = 34%, 33%, 12%, 5.4%, and 4.9% for PZT, 75PVDF/25TrFE copolymer (mol%), PVDF, Nylon-7, and Nylon-11, respectively[Harrison & Quannies]. It is shown in Fig. 14.6.5 by[Miclea et al.] that the transduction efficiency of a soft PZT ($PbNb_{0.02} Li_{0.007} (Zr_{0.51} Ti_{0.463}) O_3$) disk, having a radius of 10 mm and height of 1 mm, decreases with an increasing temperature, ranging from room temperature up to the Curie point (≈ 350 ℃).

However, when a force (vector) is applied in one direction, there will be three strain components involved. Let's consider the electric displacement along the 3-axis, i.e., D_3, subjected to a force F_3 applied in this direction. Following Eqs. (3.5.24)-(3.5.29) and assuming the force is uniformly distributed over the entire area A, one has

$$\varepsilon_{11} = - v_{31} \frac{\sigma_{33}}{E_{33}} \qquad (14.6.36)$$

$$\varepsilon_{22} = - v_{32} \frac{\sigma_{33}}{E_{33}} \qquad (14.6.37)$$

and $$\varepsilon_{33} = \frac{\sigma_{33}}{E_{33}} \qquad (14.6.38)$$

where $$\sigma_{33} = \frac{F_3}{A} \qquad (14.6.39)$$

Thus, $D_3 = e_{33} \varepsilon_{33} + e_{31} \varepsilon_{11} + e_{32} \varepsilon_{22}$

$$= e_{33} \frac{\sigma_{33}}{E_{33}} - e_{31} v_{31} \frac{\sigma_{33}}{E_{33}} - e_{32} v_{32} \frac{\sigma_{33}}{E_{33}} \qquad (14.6.40)$$

Since e_{33} is positive and e_{31} and e_{32} are negative for most piezoelectric crystals, spontaneous and piezoelectric polarization caused by straining aid each other for tensile strain and oppose for compressive strain. Therefore, the transduction efficiency subjected to uniaxial loading can be a mixed index.

14.6.6 Piezoelectric Sensors and Transducers

Piezoelectric materials are used as vibrating elements for time keeping, as emitters of sound (speakers) or ultrasound, and as microphones (amplifiers), or other sensors and actuators such as force transducer, strain gages, pressure transducers, accelerometers, and acoustic emission sensors[Gautschi]. When a PZT composite is made from mixing two different constituents at a certain ratio and its piezoelectric constants of the composite reach the maximum (e.g. 53.5 PbTiO/46.5PbZrO), it is called morphotropic phase boundary (MPB). Some PZT-based piezoelectric composites at or close to the morphotropic phase boundary have been used exclusively in electromechanical devices and transducers. As implemented in piezoelectric microphones and piezoelectric pickups for electrically amplified guitars, the detection of pressure variations in the form of sound is a common sensor application of piezoelectric cells. Piezoelectric sensors are excellent ultrasonic transducers for medical imaging, as well as industrial nondestructive testing that demands acute response at high frequencies.

Langasite (LGS), $LiNbO_3$(LN), AlN, and YCOB[yttrium calcium oxyborate; $YCa_4O(BO_3)_3$] are the most widely used piezoelectric materials for high-temperature applications (>600 ℃) due to their stable performance at elevated temperatures [Zu et al.]. YCOB-based devices in particular, including accelerometers, ultrasound transducers, and acoustic emission sensors give rise to a highly steady and reliable operation even at temperatures over 1000 ℃.

PVDF is the most used among all piezoelectric materials. Properties of PVDF Piezoelectric films are listed as follows:

-Flexibility (possibility of application on curved surfaces);
-High mechanical strength;
-Dimensional stability;
-High and stable piezoelectric coefficients over time up to approximately 90 ℃;
-Characteristic chemical inertness of PVDF;
-Continuous polarization for great lengths spooled onto drums;
-Thickness between 9 microns and 1 mm.

Examples of applications of PVDF[Piezotech Arkema, 9 Rue de Colmar F-68220, Hesingue, France] include

(a) Pressure pick-ups: distribution of pressure on surface, localization of impacts, accelerometers, and keyboards;
(b) Robotics: artificial sensitive skin, pressure sensors;
(c) Acoustic components: microphones, ultrasonic detectors, hydrophones, and sonars.

There are two ways to make connection to metalized PVDF: (1) adhesive joints (e.g. silver-loaded epoxy) and (2) mechanical connections with crimps or folds.

Zinc oxide is a semiconducting piezoelectric material that has been used in MEMS (microelectromechanical systems) as sensors and actuators and in communications as SAW (surface acoustic wave), and thin-film FBAR (bulk acoustic wave resonator) devices[Molarius et al.].

The schematic drawing of a simplified piezoelectric transducer is given in Fig. 14.6.6. When the piezoelectric plate of a force transducer is under pressure, i.e., subject to force F_z shown in figure, it absorbs mechanical energy, enduring compressive strain change, and experiencing polarization changes, consequently resulting in a surface charge on the two capacitor plates. At all times, while the polarization proceeds due to the variation in mechanical strain, the following phenomena develop:

$$\sigma_{zz} = \frac{F_z}{A} \qquad \text{(Mechanical Strain, nominal)} \qquad (14.6.41)$$

$$p_{pi} = \frac{\partial \boldsymbol{P}}{\partial \sigma_{zz}} \qquad \text{(Piezoelectric polarization)} \qquad (14.6.42)$$

$$\delta Q = A\ \delta \boldsymbol{P} = A\ p_{pi}\ \delta \sigma_{zz} \qquad \text{(Piezoelectric charge)} \qquad (14.6.43)$$

$$I = \frac{dQ}{dt} = -p_{pi}\ A\left(\frac{\partial \sigma_{zz}}{\partial t}\right) \qquad \text{(Piezoelectric current)} \qquad (14.6.44)$$

$$\delta \boldsymbol{E} = \frac{-\delta \boldsymbol{P}}{\epsilon} = \frac{-\delta \boldsymbol{P}}{\epsilon_o \chi_e} \qquad \text{(Piezoelectric electric field strength)} \qquad (14.6.45)$$

and $\quad \delta V = h\ \delta \boldsymbol{E} = h\left(\frac{\delta \boldsymbol{P}}{\epsilon}\right) = \left(\frac{h\ p_{pi}}{\epsilon}\right) \delta \sigma_{zz} \quad$ (Piezoelectric electric voltage) $\qquad (14.6.46)$

where

   I (A): Electric current;
   $\boldsymbol{p}$ (C/m^2): Polarization;
   p_{pi}(C/m^2/℃): Piezoelectric polarization coefficient;
   A (m^2): Electrode area;
   F_z(N): Force, applied;
   $\delta \sigma_{zz}$(MPa): Stress variation due to force F_z;
   $\delta \boldsymbol{E}$: Change of electric field strength;
   δV: Change of electric voltage (voltage gradient);
   h: height, i.e., distance between the two capacitor plates.

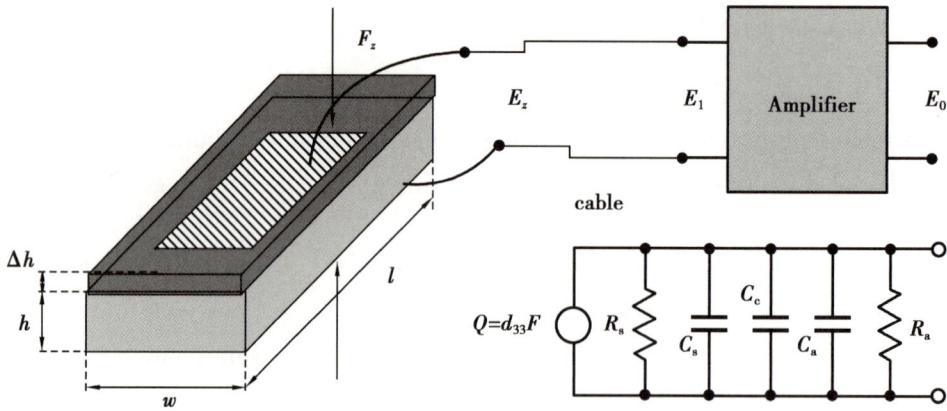

Fig. 14.6.6 A Schematic Drawing of a Force Transducer and Its Equivalent Circuit

Example 14.6.2   The cubic piezoelectric material (PbTiO$_3$) of 10 mm each side, which is sandwiched between two electrode plates (Fig. 14.6.6), has the following electro-magneto-mechanical properties: Piezoelectric voltage coefficient $g = -8 \times 10^{-3}$ (V/m)/(N/m^2), and Dielectric constant $\epsilon_3 = 600\ \epsilon_o$, where $\epsilon_o = 8.85 \times 10^{-12}$ C/N/m^2.

What is piezoelectric charge constant d_{33}, if the measured electric voltage in an open circuitry is 850 V, when $F_z = -1\ 000$ N (in compression)?

Solution:

Following Eq. (14.6.45), one has

$$\delta E_3 = \frac{-\delta P_3}{\epsilon_3} = -d_{33}\frac{\delta \sigma_{33}}{\epsilon_3} = \frac{-d_{33}\left(\dfrac{-1\ 000}{0.01^2}\right)}{600 \times 8.85 \times 10^{-12}}$$

$$= 82.9 \times 10^3 \text{ V/m} = 1\ 883.24 \times 10^{12} d_{33}\text{V/m}$$

By Eq. (14.6.46),

$$\delta V = h\delta E_3$$

i.e. $850\ V = 0.01 \times (1\ 883.24 \times 10^{12} d_{33})$

Thus, $d_{33} = 45.1 \times 10^{-12}$ C/N = 45.1 pC/N

14.6.7   Piezoelectric Actuators and Motors

Piezoelectric materials are widely utilized in smart actuators or motors because of their high generative forces, quick electromechanical response, wide working bandwidth, and relatively low power requirements. Some single crystals and ceramics are electromagnetic dielectrics in nature. After a piezoelectric cell receives an electrical pulse, it applies a force to an opposing part (e.g. a ceramic plate) and activates the part to move in the prescribed direction-linear or rotary. A piezoelectric motor provides inherent braking and the ability to eliminate servo dither when it comes to a steady-state position in transition from a transient dynamic state. The effort delivered by a piezoelectric actuator (motor) in the industrial applications may range from 0.4 kg · f (single piezoelectric cell) to 3.2 kg · f (eight-cell actuator), while the speed ranges from several μm/s to 250 mm/s[Nanomotion].

The synthetic materials extensively used in practice are not crystalline but ceramics, while the natural piezoelectric materials frequently used are quartz and tourmaline.

14.7   Electrostriction

Electrostriction is a property of dielectric materials, of which positive ions will be displaced in the direction of the field and negative ions will be displaced in the opposite direction when they are exposed to an external electric field. Electrostriction applies to all crystal symmetries, while the piezoelectric effect only applies to the 20 piezoelectric families.

14.7.1   Electrostrictive Elasticity

Electrostriction is a prominent elastic deformation of a dielectric material under the force exerted by an electrostatic field. The mechanical strain caused by the relative displacement of ions in the crystal is proportional to the quadratics of polarization. This nonlinear "non-piezoelectric" effect is traditionally theorized using the electrostrictive coefficient as follows:

$$\varepsilon_{ij} = Q_{ijkl} P_k P_l \qquad (14.7.1)$$

where

ε_{ij}: Strain induced by the electric field;

Q_{ijkl}: Electrostrictive coefficient, a polarization-related 4th order tensor;

P_k: Polarization vector k;

P_l: Polarization vector l.

Electrostriction is a one-sided relationship between electric field and deformation, while piezoelectricity is two-sided. Each Q_{ijkl} is a polarization-related electrostrictive coefficient, a component of the 4th rank electrostrictive tensor. Both ε-P and ε-E curves are accepted as a method to determine the electrostrictive coefficients for materials with a high dielectric response, where the strains can be accurately measured. In the particular case of the tetragonal symmetry that 3-axis is the polar direction as appearing in barium titanate, Eq. (14.7.1) reduces to [Devonshire]

$$\varepsilon_{33} = Q_{33} P_3^2 = \left(\frac{0.111 \text{ m}^4}{C^2}\right) P_3^2 \qquad \text{(Barium titanate crystal)} \qquad (14.7.1a)$$

$$\text{and} \quad \varepsilon_{11} = Q_{31} P_3^2 = \left(\frac{0.044 \text{ m}^4}{C^2}\right) P_3^2 \qquad \text{(Barium titanate crystal)} \qquad (14.7.1b)$$

Coefficients $Q_{33} = 0.111 \text{ m}^4/C^2$ and $Q_{31} = 0.044 \text{ m}^4/C^2$ 2 were obtained by aligning the three primary material axes (1, 2, 3) with [100], [010] and [001], respectively in the test [Berlincourt & Jaffe] while the crystal was poled along the 3-axis. The quadratic electrostriction effect can be observed for any amount of applied electric field intensity, having a prominent contrast to the piezoelectric effect. Electrostrictive deformation is associated with the following engineering parameters: Young's modulus, Poisson's ratio, the relative dielectric constant in the absence of deformation, (ϵ_r), and other derivative dielectric coefficients that describe the change in the dielectric tensor with deformation[Shkel & Klingenberg].

14.7.2　Piezorestrictive Materials

A class of ferroelectrics is piezorestrictive and they are called relaxor ferroelectrics such as PMN (lead magnesium niobate or $Pb(Mg_{\frac{1}{3}}Nb_{\frac{2}{3}})O_3$), PZN (lead zinc niobate or $Pb(Zn_{\frac{1}{3}}Nb_{\frac{2}{3}})O_3$), PMN-PT (lead magnesium niobate-lead titanate), PLZT (lead lanthanum zirconate titanate), and electron-irradiated $P(VDF\text{-}TrFE)$—poly(vinylidene fluoride-trifluoroethylene) copolymer, for exhibiting high electrostrictive coefficients. Relaxors show high strain responses and are actively investigated for transducer and dielectric applications. The spontaneous strain activation plays an important role in the process of the formation of stable ferroelectric domains and also in their switching.

Herein the ε-E (strain-electric field intensity) relationship is employed to determine the electrostrictive coefficients for materials with a high dielectric response. When a relaxor is exposed to an electric field, the induced strain may be attributed to both piezoelectric and electrostrictive effects. It can be formulated in the "strain charge" form as follows:

$$\{\varepsilon\} = [s]\{\sigma\} + [d]_{6\times3}^T[E] + [d']_{6\times3}^T\{E\}^T\{E\} \qquad \text{(Strain charge form)} \qquad (14.7.2)$$

$$\text{or} \quad \varepsilon_{ij} = s_{ijkl}\,\sigma_{kl} + d_{jim}E_m + d'_{iklm}E_k E_l \qquad (14.7.3)$$

of which d'_{ijkl} is the electrostriction strain coefficient. It can also be formulated in the "stress charge" form as follows:

$$\{\sigma\} = [c]\{\varepsilon\} - [e]_{6\times3}^{T}\{D\} + [e']_{6\times3}^{T}\{E\}^{T}\{E\} \quad \text{(Stress charge form)} \quad (14.7.4)$$

$$\text{or} \quad \sigma_{ij} = c_{ijkl}\,\varepsilon_{kl} - e_{jim}\,D_m + e'_{iklm}\,E_k\,E_l \quad (14.7.5)$$

of which e'_{ijkl} is the electrostriction stress coefficient. If only the electrorestictive effect is to accounted for, $[d]$ and $[h]$ can be omitted in the above equations. Both 4th rank tensors, d'_{iklm} and e'_{iklm}, can be expressed as [Shkel]:

$$d'_{iklm} = \frac{1}{2}\,\epsilon_o\left(\frac{\partial\epsilon_{ij}}{\partial\varepsilon_{kl}}\right)\bigg|_{E,\,T=\text{constant}} \quad (14.7.6)$$

$$e'_{iklm} = \frac{1}{2}\,\epsilon_o\frac{\partial\epsilon_{ij}}{\partial\sigma_{kl}}\bigg|_{E,\,T=\text{constant}} \quad (14.7.7)$$

where

ϵ_o: Permittivity of free space;

ϵ_{ij}: Dielectric constant, i.e., relative permittivity in tensor $[\epsilon]$;

T: Temperature, kept constant;

E: Electric field intensity, kept constant.

The induced electrostrictive strain and stress can also be written in terms of polarization as

$$\varepsilon_{ij} = s_{ijkl}\,\sigma_{kl} + g_{ijk}\,E_{ij}\,P_k + Q_{ijkl}\,P_k\,P_l \quad (14.7.8)$$

and $\quad \sigma_{ij} = c_{ijm}\,\varepsilon_{ij} - (h_{ijm})^{T}\,D_m + q_{ijkl}\,E_k\,E_l \quad (14.7.9)$

14.7.3   Hydrostatic Pressure Effect

It is shown that the application of external fields enhances piezoelectric-electrostritive coefficients of PZT or $BaTiO_3$ along the nonpolar directions, which is related to the phase transitions that are accompanied by huge shear piezoelectric coefficients, resulting an enhancement of longitudinal piezoelectric coefficient "d_{33}" [Liang et al.]. While in the orthorhombic phase, the highest piezoelectric-electrostritive response of d_{33} in crystallographic coordinate systems went over 500 pC/N as observed in $BaTiO_3$ when an electric field was applied along [001], which is a no-polar direction. Thus, the hydrostatic pressure effect on the dielectric, piezoelectric, and piezorestrictive properties is similar to temperature, suggesting a common underlying mechanism for the piezoelectric anisotropy and its enhancement. The piezoelectric-electrostritive effect under hydrostatic pressure is termed as d_h. Data of certain materials for hydrostatic pressure coefficient are given in Table 14.5.1. Direct piezoelectric-electrostritive effect is measured in the chamber under isotropic hydrostatic pressure. Considering only the electric displacement along the 3-axis, i.e., D_3, one has the polarization due to a hydrostatic pressure as

$$D_3 = (d_{31} + d_{32} + d_{33}) \, p \equiv d_{\mathrm{h}} \, p \qquad (14.7.10)$$

where p is the pressure, bearing a negative-stress value for being in compression.

14.8 Pyroelectricity

When polarization is induced by temperature variation instead of mechanical strain and works as a function of temperature, the material is called "pyroelectric". Pyroelectric materials are also piezoelectric. Thus, pyroelectricity involves power conversion in three different energy states: mechanical (kinematic), thermal, and electric. Being regarded as the physical inverse of pyroelectric effect, the electrocaloric effect is a phenomenon, in which a material shows a reversible temperature change under an applied electric field.

Pyroelectric materials can be born natural or synthesized. Bone and tendon are typical natureborn pyroelectric materials. One important man-made example is the gallium nitride semiconductor. Triglycine sulfate (TGS), lithium niobate (LN), lithium tantalate (LT), lead titanate (PT), lead zirconate titanate (PZT), polyvinylidene fluoride (PVDF), PVDF/MWCT, and polyvinylidene fluoride-trifluoroethylene copolymer (P(VDF-TrFE)) are well-known pyroelectric materials.

14.8.1 Pyroelectric Effect

Pyroelectrics can be repeatedly heated and cooled, analogously to a heat engine, to generate usable electrical power [Kouchachvili & Ikura]. The pyroelectric effect is analogous to the piezoelectric effect, but it refers to change in temperature causing change in spontaneous polarization and resulting change in electric charge or voltage. The pyroelectric coefficient of a homogeneous isotropic material working in the linear range may be described as the change in the spontaneous polarization with respect to temperature variation with respect to time ($℃/s$). Consider the simplified capacitor of an IR detector having nanowires in a 1-3 composite as shown in Fig. 14.8.1. When an IR detector absorbs radiation both temperature and polarization change, and hence it results in a surface charge on the capacitor plates. At all times, as the polarization proceeds due to the temperature change, the following phenomena develop:

$$P = \frac{\partial \boldsymbol{P}}{\partial T} \qquad (14.8.1)$$

$$\delta Q = A \, \delta \boldsymbol{P} = A \, p \, \delta T \qquad \text{(Pyroelectric charge)} \qquad (14.8.2)$$

$$I = \frac{dQ}{dt} = -pA\left(\frac{\partial T}{\partial t}\right) \qquad \text{(Pyroelectric current)} \qquad (14.8.3)$$

$$\delta E = \frac{\delta P}{\epsilon_o} = \frac{\delta P}{\epsilon_o \chi_e} \qquad \text{(Pyroelectric electric field strength)} \qquad (14.8.4)$$

and $\delta V = L \, \delta E = L\left(\frac{\delta p}{\epsilon}\right) = \left(\frac{Lp}{\epsilon}\right)\delta T \qquad$ (Pyroelectric electric voltage) $\qquad (14.8.5)$

where

I (A) : Electric current, i.e., time rate of change of charge passing through a specific area;
p_{py} (C/m^2) : Polarization;
p ($C/m^2/°C$) : Pyroelectric polarization coefficient-gradient with respect to temperature;
A (m^2) : Electrode area, Fig. 14.8.1;
δT (°C) : Temperature variation;
δE (V/m) : Change of electric field strength;
δV (V) : Change of electric voltage (voltage gradient);
L (m or μm) : Length (height) between the two electrode plates.

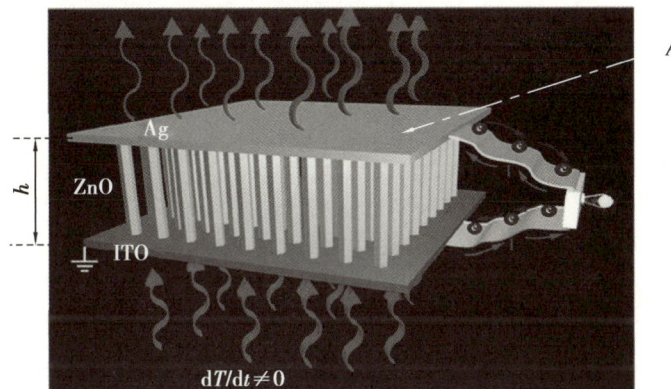

Fig. 14.8.1   Pyroelectric Effect of a 1-3 Composite with ZnO Nanowires[Yang et al.]

Pyroelectric polarization coefficients of several materials are given in Table 14.5.1. The higher the positive voltage gradient, the profounder the pyroelectric effect is. In light of the above equations the "voltage gradient" can be improved by increasing polarization (high polarization coefficient) and decreasing susceptibility (low dielectric constant). The other important properties to look for in pyromagnetic materials or devices (e.g. sensors and actuators) are low dielectric loss and low specific heat. Conversely, the temperature variation of a pyroelectric material can be derived from the applied current as

$$\delta T = T_f - T_i = -\int_{T_i}^{T_f} I_p \, dt \qquad (14.8.6)$$

Note that the frequency of the temperature fluctuation is also an influential factor. Electric charge density D of an orthotropic pyroelectric material that works in the linear range can then be related to the applied strain (stress), electric field strength, and temperature variation as simplified from Eqs. (14.5.43)-(14.5.44),

$$\{D\}_{3\times1} = [e]_{3\times6}\{\varepsilon\}_{6\times1} + [\epsilon]_{3\times3}\{E\}_{3\times1} + [p]_{3\times1}T \qquad (14.8.7)$$

$$\text{or} \quad \{D\}_{3\times1} = [d]_{3\times6}\{\sigma\}_{6\times1} + [\epsilon]_{3\times3}\{E\}_{3\times1} + \{p\}_{3\times1}T \qquad (14.8.8)$$

where

$\{p\}$: Pyroelectric coefficient column containing of p_i;
$p_i(\text{C/m}^2/\text{℃})$: Pyroelectric coefficients;
T: Temperature variation.

14.8.2 Penetration Depth of Temperature Wave

With the cyclic-leaded system by heat radiation, the temperature change rate and the power generation rate are smaller than a one-time quasi-static power generation. It is observed that higher power densities are generated at low-frequency heating[Mane et al.].

The penetration depth of temperature wave, also called thermal diffusion length, is influenced by the frequency as follows[Hammes & Regtien][Chang et al.]:

$$d_{\mathrm{p}} = \left(\frac{2D_{\mathrm{w}}}{f}\right)^{\frac{1}{2}} = \left[\frac{2\left(\dfrac{C_{\mathrm{v}}}{k}\right)}{f}\right]^{\frac{1}{2}} \qquad (14.8.9)$$

where

d_{p}: Penetration depth of temperature wave, also called thermal diffusion length;
D_{w}: Diffusivity of the media, where the temperature wave propagates;
C_{v}: Specific heat capacity;
k: Thermal conductivity;
f: Modulation frequency of the thermal flux.

Optimization of the pyroelectric film thickness should be checked against the penetration depth of the temperature wave [Bravina et al.] at all the applicable frequencies [Mane et al.] and temperature levels. Size effects are considered in the conceptual design stage as the dependence of pyroelectric response on the layers' thicknesses.

14.8.3 Pyroelectric Power Generation

A strong pyroelectric or pyromagnetic effect has the potential to be used in small power generation systems for energy harvesting at a working temperature lower than that of internal combustion engines.

The pyroelectric coefficient strongly increases with the wire radius decrease and diverges at critical radius corresponding to the size-driven transition into paraelectric phase. Pyroelectric ZnO nanowire arrays have been experimentally proven to be effective with converting thermal energy into electricity, as schematically depicted in Fig. 14.8.1. The pyroelectric coefficient for ZnO nanowire falls between 0.05 Vm^2/W and 0.08 Vm^2/W [Yang et al.]. Pyroelectric materials, such as bismuth telluride (Bi_2Te_3), have also been used for small-scaled refrigeration based on the heat-electricity exchange mechanism.

One study by [Xie et al.] concludes that the power density is keenly dependent upon the surface area and the pyroelectric coefficient of the material, underlining the importance of maximizing these parameters. It predicted that a thin film, made of PVDF, PZT-5A, or PMN-PT, with a large area and a significantly enhanced pyroelectric coefficient can generate nearly three orders of magnitude improved peak power density under similar boundary conditions.

Example 14.8.1   A pyroelectric lamina, suggested for an application in an energy harvester [Zakharov et al.], has the following material properties: dielectric constant ϵ_r = 1800 ϵ_o, pyroelectric strain charge coefficient p_{py} = 238×10^{-6} $m^{-2}/°C$, and thickness h = 127 μm. How much is the theoretical generation rate of voltage (V/°C)?

Solution:

By Eq. (14.8.5),

$$\delta V = \left(\frac{h\,p_{py}}{\epsilon}\right)\delta T = \left(\frac{127 \times 10^{-6} \times 238 \times 10^{-6}}{1800 \times 8.854 \times 10^{-12}}\right) \times 1 \ °C = 1.9 \ V/°C$$

Another kind of electric harvesters generates thermoelectric energy mainly relying on the Seebeck effect, which utilizes the temperature difference between the two ends of a device for driving the diffusion of electric charge carriers. However, in an environment that the temperature is spatially uniform, the pyroelectric effect is the choice, which is based on the spontaneous polarization in certain orthotropic solids due to a time-dependent temperature variation.

14.8.4   Hysteresis of Pyroelectric Polarization

A new model presented by [Morozovska et al.] for pyroelectric response has shown that the pyroelectric hysteresis loops of ferroelectrics-semiconductor films with charged defects can be successfully modeled using six coupled equations, as shown in Fig. 14.8.2. In addition to the validation of pyroelectric effect, the modeling effectiveness for the hysteresis of piezoelectric effect and permittivity are also demonstrated. Please see [Morozovska et al.] for details of derivation. Parameter E_c is the coercive field.

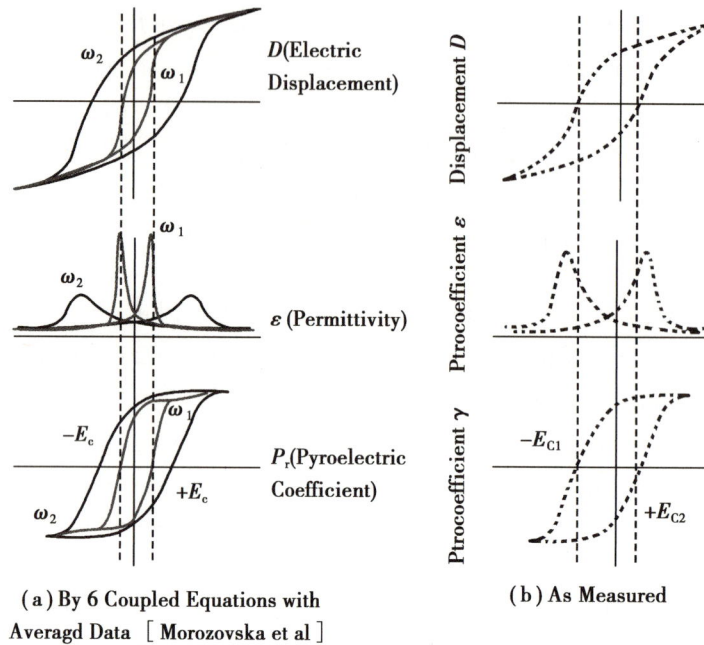

(a) By 6 Coupled Equations with Averagd Data [Morozovska et al]

(b) As Measured

Fig. 14.8.2   Hysteresis Loops of Polarization as Functions of Applied Field and Loading Frequency [Lang] [Morozovska]

14.8.5   Pyroelectric Sensors

Pyroelectric materials can be used for enhancing the performance of traditional sensors, such as pyroelectric infrared (PIR) sensors for motion detection. Objects, including human beings, animals, trees, and roads, generate heat in the form of infrared radiation (IR). The pyroelectric sensor is made of crystalline material that generates a surface electric charge when exposed to heat. The output voltage is a function of the amount of infrared radiation sensed. Filter window is added to the device to limit incoming radiation to the 8-14 μm range that is most sensitive to human body radiation, because the peak in emission of the black-body curve for objects at 27 ℃ (300 K) occurs around 10 μm. Consequently, IR detectors with high sensitivity in this wavelength region can easily detect human beings and other warm-blooded animals. A large pyroelectric coefficient and small values of dielectric permittivity are in demand for such a IR detector.

Noncontact temperature meters in furnaces, melted glass or metal, films, and heat loss assessment in buildings are application examples for pyroelectric materials. The pyroelectric materials have been also extensively applied for the purpose of measuring the cement pavement temperature using "smart cement composites", such as plain cement, cement/PVA (polyvinyl alcohol), cement /PVA/steel fibers, and cement/silica fumes/pitch-based carbon fibers [Wen and Chung]. The pyroelectric coefficient decreases with increasing frequencies in the range between 10 kHz and

1 MHz, as expected. Development of pyroelectric temperature sensors using Lithium Niobate ($LiNbO_3$) has also been of interest to researchers for high-resolution thermometry.

14.8.6 Figures of Merit for Pyroelectric Materials

The figure of merit (FOM) put forward and explored beyond the material properties is of great interest to those who select materials for the design of sensors, actuators, acoustic effect, heat detector, infrared detector, and thermal harvesting devices. As a design objective function, it may vary with the goal to achieve. The top three FOMs used for selection of materials for heat and infrared detection are

$$F_{om,i} = \frac{p}{\rho \, C_p} \qquad \text{(Maximizing current generated)} \qquad (14.8.10)$$

$$F_{om,v} = \frac{p}{C_p \, \epsilon'}$$

$$= \frac{p}{C_p [\epsilon \, \epsilon_o (1 - \tan^2 \delta)^{\frac{1}{2}}]} \qquad \text{(Maximizing voltage generated)} \qquad (14.8.11)$$

$$\text{and} \quad F_{om,d} = \frac{p}{\dfrac{C_p}{\epsilon''^{\frac{1}{2}}}}$$

$$= \frac{p}{\dfrac{C_p}{(\epsilon \, \epsilon_o \tan^2 \delta)^{\frac{1}{2}}}} \qquad \text{(Maximizing detectivity)} \qquad (14.8.12)$$

where

$F_{om,i}$: Figure of merit for high current detectivity;

$F_{om,v}$: Figure of merit for high voltage responsivity;

$F_{om,d}$: Figure of merit for high detectivity.

Thus, the general guidelines to look for important properties of a pyroelectric sensor is to have a low dielectric constant, low power loss, low specific heat, and high pyroelectric coefficient.

A typical application of energy harvesting devices is for battery-free wireless networking, which is a maintenance-free mechanism. Pyroelectric materials are of great interest for energy harvesting devices because they have the potential to operate at a high thermodynamic efficiency without a bulky heat sink, when compared with thermoelectric ones. If the pyroelectric element is placed onto a substrate that works as a heat sink, which has a relatively infinite thermal conductivity referring to that of semiconductors, the equations for figures of merit, i.e., Eqs. (14.8.11)-(14.8.13), are then to be revised by replacing heat capacity C_p by thermal conductivity k[Lee et al.].

14.9 Piezomagnetism

Piezomagnetism is a physical phenomenon that the positive ions of a dielectric material are displaced in the direction of the field and negative ions are displaced in the other direction, causing a mechanical displacement when exposed to an external magnetic field. A magnetic material undergoes only a small volume change on magnetization, usually on a micro scale (10^{-6}). The magnetic induction of an isotropic homogeneous material is related to the magnetic field intensity as

$$\boldsymbol{B} = \mu \, \boldsymbol{H} = \mu_o(1 + \chi_m)\boldsymbol{H} = \mu_o \boldsymbol{H} + \mu_o \chi_m \boldsymbol{H}$$

$$= \mu_o \boldsymbol{H} + \mu_o \boldsymbol{M}$$

$$= \mu_o \boldsymbol{H} + \boldsymbol{J} \tag{14.9.1}$$

or $\quad \boldsymbol{B} = \mu_o \mu_r \boldsymbol{H} \tag{14.9.2}$

with $\quad \mu = \mu_o(1 + \chi_m) = \mu_o \mu_r \tag{14.9.3}$

$$\boldsymbol{M} = \chi_m \boldsymbol{H} \tag{14.9.4}$$

and $\quad \mu_r = 1 + \chi_m \tag{14.9.5}$

where

μ (H/m or N/A^2): Permeability of the material and vacuum volume;
μ_o(H/m or N/A^2): Permeability of the vacuum volume, $\mu_o = 4\pi \times 10^{-7}$ H/m;
μ_r: Relative permeability of the material, dimensionless;
χ_m: Magnetic susceptibility, which is the dimensionless volumetric susceptibility;
$\boldsymbol{M}$ (A/m): Magnetization of the material;
$\boldsymbol{J}$ (T): Magnetization intensity or degree of magnetic polarization.

14.9.1 Magnetic Susceptibility

Magnetic susceptibility is a dimensionless proportionality factor that indicates magnetization intensity of a material in response to an applied magnetic field, as demonstrated by Eq. (14.9.1). The magnetic susceptibility of a crystal or poled lamina is usually not a scalar quantity. It is more likely to be transversely isotropic, or orthotropic sometimes. Magnetic response $\boldsymbol{M}$ is thus dependent upon the orientation of the sample and can occur in directions other than that of the applied magnetic field $\boldsymbol{H}$. In these cases, volume susceptibility is defined as a 2nd rank tensor,

$$\{M\}_{3\times1} = [\chi_m]_{3\times3}\{H\}_{3\times1} \tag{14.9.6}$$

or $\quad M_i = \chi_{m,ij} H_j \quad (i, j = 1, 2, 3)$ $\hfill (14.9.7)$

Dimension 3×3 means that the component of magnetization in the ith direction will result from the external field applied in the jth direction. However, the relationship between M and H is quite nonlinear in ferromagnetic crystals and synthetic laminae. To accommodate this, a more general definition of differential susceptibility applies as follows

$$\chi_{m,ij} = \frac{\partial M_i}{\partial H_j} \tag{14.9.8}$$

This may induce a magnetic anisotropy incidentally. It means that $\chi_{m,ij}$ is direction-dependent upon the material's magnetic properties. The dipole moment of a magnetically anisotropic material tends to align with the easy-going direction, which consequently turns out to be the energetically favorable polarization axis under spontaneous magnetization. The strongest piezomagnet known is uranium dioxide[Jaime et al.].

14.9.2   Electro-Magneto-Elasticity

For a piezomagnetic material working in the linear orthotropic domain, the strains induced by the coupled mechanical energy, electric energy, and magnetic energy can be obtained from Eqs. (14.5.43)-(14.5.45) by neglecting the thermal term as[Buchanan 2003]

$$\{\sigma\}_{6\times1} = [c]_{6\times6}\{\varepsilon\}_{6\times1} - [e]_{6\times3}^{\mathrm{T}}\{E\}_{3\times1} - [q]_{6\times3}^{\mathrm{T}}\{H\}_{3\times1} \tag{14.9.9}$$

$$\{D\}_{3\times1} = [e]_{3\times6}\{\varepsilon\}_{6\times1} + [\boldsymbol{\epsilon}]_{3\times3}\{E\}_{3\times1} + \{m\}_{3\times3}\{H\}_{3\times1} \tag{14.9.10}$$

and $\quad \{B\}_{3\times1} = [q]_{3\times6}\{\varepsilon\}_{6\times1} + [m]_{3\times3}\{E\}_{3\times1} + [\mu]_{3\times3}\{H\}_{3\times1}$ $\hfill (14.9.11)$

where

$\{q\}$: Piezomagnetic coefficient column containing q_{ij};
$q_{ij}(\mathrm{N/A/m})$: Piezomagnetic coefficient in the (1, 2, 3) coordinate system;
$\{m\}$: Magneto-electric coefficient column containing m_{ij};
$m_{ij}(\mathrm{N \cdot s/V/C})$: Magneto-electric coefficient in the (1, 2, 3) coordinate system;
$\{\mu\}$: Magnetic permeability coefficient column containing μ_{ij};
$\mu_{ij}(\mathrm{N \cdot s/C^2})$: Magnetic permeability coefficient in the (1, 2, 3) coordinate system.

A piezoelectric material and a piezomagnetic material are usually fabricated into composite laminae in order to make a piezoelectric-piezomagnetic material. However, such a composite made only of piezoelectric and piezomagnetic phases would be susceptible to brittle fracture because the constituents are usually brittle ceramics. A three-phase magneto-electro-elastic composite lamina consisting of piezoelectric and piezomagnetic phases separated by polymer matrix would have greater ductility and formability. Electro-magnetic performances of $Ep/BaTiO_3/(CoFe_2O_4)$ laminae, i. e., epoxy (matrix) reinforced with $BaTiO_3$ (piezoelectric fibers) and $CoFe_2O_4$ (piezomagnetic matrix), have been studied [Jaesang et al.]. The material properties of the constituents and the effect of reinforcement on piezoelectric and electromagnetic material properties are given in Tables 14.5.1 and 14.5.2.

14.9.3　Loss Tangent (tan δ) of Permeability

A useful tool for dealing with the polarization due to magnetic effects is to use the complex permeability

$$\mu = \mu' + i\,\mu'' \tag{14.9.12}$$

where

$$|\mu| = [(\mu')^2 + (\mu'')^2]^{\frac{1}{2}} \tag{14.9.13}$$

$$\mu' = \mu\,(1 - \tan^2\delta)^{\frac{1}{2}} \tag{14.9.14}$$

and　$\mu'' = \mu\,\tan\delta$ (14.9.15)

While at low frequencies in a linear material the main magnetic field (due to μ') and the auxiliary magnetic field (due to μ'') are simply proportional to each other through lumped scalar permeability μ. At high frequencies these quantities will react to each other with a certain amount of phase, namely δ. Parameter $\tan\delta$ is thus the variable that provides a measure of how much power is lost in a material versus how much is stored when exposed in the magnetic field.

14.10　Magnetostriction

Magnetostriction means that the shape of a solid made of ferromagnetic material changes due to the magnetostrictive strain nonlinearly when exposed to a magnetic field. Ferromagnetic materials placed in a magnetic field produce microscopic distortion in the molecular structure, which causes a change of their dimensions [Temposonics]. This physical phenomenon is due to the existence of high numbers of tiny little elementary magnets forming the ferromagnetic material. These particles show a tendency towards parallel arrangement within a limited field, even without being influenced by an external magnetic field. However, such an induced magnetostrictive strain may result in

(a) Energy loss due to frictional heating in susceptible ferromagnetic cores;

(b) Discernible humming noise (e.g. transformers and high-powered electric devices) when the magnetic field is subjected to an oscillating AC;

(c) Shape or dimensional change during the process of magnetization. For an applied magnetic field of 60 Hz in an AC electrical device, the maximum elongation change occurs at 120 Hz that produces the humming noise at 120 Hz.

The property can be quantified by the magnetostrictive coefficient (Λ), which is defined as the fractional change in length as the magnetization of the material increases from zero to the saturation value. Several magnetostrictive materials are given in Table 14.10.1[Grössingerl et al.]. As presented in the table, a magnetostrictive coefficient can be positive (extension) or negative (contraction), depending on the crystallographic alignment with the magnetic field. Note that a crystal is orthotropic in nature. The reciprocal effect of the magnetorestriction is called Villari effect, which is defined as the change of the susceptibility of a ferromagnetic material in response to an applied magnetic field.

Magnetostrictive materials can convert magnetic energy into mechanical strain energy and vice versus. Magnetostrictive materials can convert magnetic energy into mechanical energy and vice versa, and are used to build actuators and sensors. Magnetostriction is a phenomenon mainly found in ferromagnetic materials such as iron, nickel, cobalt and their alloys.

Temposisonics[MTS] is a contactless position sensor with absolute linear displacement, working on the magnetostrictive principle.

Another application example is the magnetostrictive actuator in use for generating ultrasonic vibrations in an ultrasonic cleaning device.

14.11   Pyromagnetism

For a pyromagnetic material working in the linear orthotropic domain, the strains induced by the coupled mechanical energy, electric energy, and magnetic energy can be obtained from Eqs. (14.5.43)-(14.5.45) as

$$\{\sigma\}_{6\times1} = [c]_{6\times6}\{\varepsilon\}_{6\times1} - [e]^{\mathrm{T}}_{6\times3}\{E\}_{3\times1} - [q]^{\mathrm{T}}_{6\times3}\{H\}_{3\times1} - [\eta]_{6\times1}T \qquad (14.11.1)$$

$$\{D\}_{3\times1} = [e]_{3\times6}\{\varepsilon\}_{6\times1} + [\epsilon]_{3\times3}\{E\}_{3\times1} + [m]_{3\times3}\{H\}_{3\times1} + [p]_{3\times1}T \qquad (14.11.2)$$

and $\{B\}_{3\times1} = [q]_{3\times6}\{\varepsilon\}_{6\times1} + [m]_{3\times3}\{E\}_{3\times1} + [\mu]_{3\times3}\{H\}_{3\times1} + [\kappa]_{3\times1}T \qquad (14.11.3)$

Recently both classical closed-form solution [Kim et al.] and numerical methods have been a focused study on electro-magneto-thermo-elastic equations for deriving pyroelectric and pyromagnetic coefficients of functionally graded multilayered multiferroic composites[Nan et al.].

Being regarded as the physical inverse of pyromagnetic, the magnetocaloric effect is a phenomenon, in which a material shows a reversible temperature change under an applied magnetic field.

14.12 Domain Engineering in Ferroelectrics

Ferroelectrics may be polarized to create a multi-domain structure[Hirohashi et al.]. Three different directions of polarization in orthorhombic $BaTiO_3$ as revealed by the etching technique at 0 ℃ by[Cameron] is shown in Fig. 14.12.1. Corresponding to the three polarization directions, it shows three distinct appearances: (a) smooth region, (b) rough region, and (c) intermediate.

Smooth region: Negative dipoles at the surface

Rough region: Positive dipoles at the surface

Intermediate: Dipoles parallel to the surface

Fig. 14.12.1 Multi-Domain BaTiO₃ Crystal[Cameron]

14.12.1 Domain Switching

Ferroelectric ceramics (e. g. barium titanate, lead zirconate titanate, and lead magnesium niobate) are widely used as sensors, computer memories, switches, actuators, and ultrasonic transducers for their electro-mechanical and dielectric properties. Domain switching is the phenomenon wherein the ferroelectric material changes from one state of polarization to another under electrical or mechanical loads[Donahue & Porter][Li et al.], but it is highly temperature-dependent.

14.12.2 Domain Wall Motion

A domain wall is an interface separating two magnetic domains in magnetism. It is a transition space of a finite thickness between two different magnetic moments (vectors) with an angular displacement of 180° (or 90°) apart. The width of the domain wall varies owing to the two opposing energies associated with the two magnetic moments that create it.

Spin Hall effect can be used to create pure spin currents at a heavy-metal/ferromagnetic interface that can drive magnetization switching and domain wall motion in an adjacent ferromagnetic film [Emori et al.]. In these same materials, broken inversion symmetry can lift the chiral degeneracy and generate new topological spin textures such as spin-spirals and skyrmions. This chiral ferromagnetism can persist at room temperature and can be engineered simply by appropriately designing interfaces between magnetic and nonmagnetic materials.

14.12.3   Electromagnetic Interference

EMI (electromagnetic interference) is the disruption of operation of an electronic device when it is in the vicinity of an electromagnetic field (EM field) in the radio frequency (RF) spectrum that is caused by another electronic device. EMI (Electromagnetic interference), whether intentional or not, may cause a wide spectrum of difficulties ranging from momentary inconveniences to system failures in automotive electronic devices.

The well-known equations for electromagnetic shielding effectiveness (EMSE) are based on the assumption that the shielding material is a good conductor. Integrated circuits are often a source of EMI, but they usually couple their energy to larger objects such as heat sinks, circuit board planes and cables to radiate significantly. Before bring any shielding stuff (e. g. conductive gaskets) into action, the following options may offer an engineer a comprehensive choice [Wikipedia-"Electromagnetic Interference, obtained 9-26-2017]:

(a) Use of bypass or decoupling capacitors on each active device (connected across the power supply, as close to the device as possible);

(b) Rise time control of high-speed signals using series resistors, and;

(c) IC power supply pin filtering.

14.12.4   Domain-Average Engineering

Domain-average engineering may make a substantial increase of piezoelectric coefficients in multi-domain ferroelectric system such as what observed in piezoelectric single crystals PZN-PT and PMN-PT[Park & Shrout][Wada et al.] as those schematically depicted in Fig. 14.12.2.

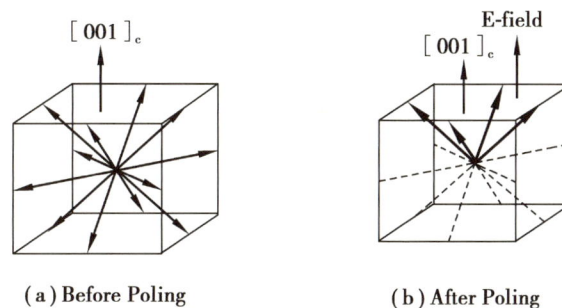

(a) Before Poling   (b) After Poling

Fig. 14.12.2   Domain Average Polarization of KNbO₃ to Comb Polarization Directions[Wada et al.]

14.12.5　Domain Patterning

An space arrangement of domain distributions may create a "composite polarization" that is well tailored for a special serve purpose such as achieving optical superlattices or suppressing mode resonators by varying the inherent impedance. This approach is called domain patterning technology. There are ten important connectivity patterns in diphasic solids, ranging from a 0-0 unconnected checkerboard pattern to a 3-3 pattern in which both phases are three dimensionally self-connected[Newhham et al.]. Composites are a combination of an active material such as piezoelectric ceramics and a passive material such as a polymer or epoxy. One basic relationship between the active and passive material is commonly referred to as connectivity. Connectivity is a convenient notation for illustrating the number of dimensions through which a material is continuous. Connectivity of a piezoelectric composite is shown as a combination of two numbers such as 1-3, 2-2 or 0-3 where the first digit represents the active material and the second digit represents the passive material. When a composite is 1-3 connected within, it means that the piezoelectric material is continuous in one direction. The connectivity relationship is the origin of some of the benefits of these composites.

An example of domain patterning engineering is shown in Fig. 14.12.3, of which individual zinc oxide nanobelt is a promising specialty piezoelectric material for nanosensors and nanoactuators, since each nanobelt has a perfect single crystalline structure and it is free of dislocation. Surface facets of ZnO nanobelts[Kong & Wang][Zhao] are given as follows:

(a) Growing along c-axis[0001]: Top surface ($2\bar{1}\bar{1}0$) and side surface ($01\bar{1}0$) exhibit no piezoelectric property across thickness;

(b) Growing along b-axis[$01\bar{1}0$]: Top surface ($2\bar{1}\bar{1}0$) and side surface (0001) exhibit no piezoelectric property across thickness;

(c) Growing along a-axis[$2\bar{1}10$]: Top surface (0001) and side surface ($0\bar{1}10$) exhibit piezoelectric effect across thickness.

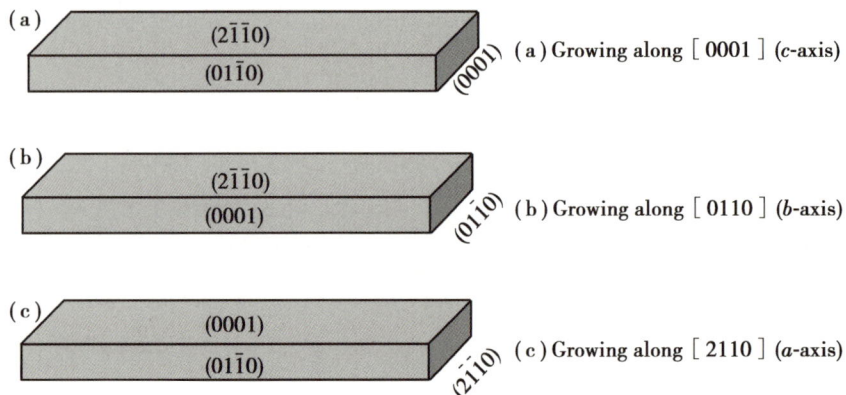

(a) ($2\bar{1}\bar{1}0$)　($01\bar{1}0$)　($000\bar{1}$)　(a) Growing along [0001] (c-axis)

(b) ($2\bar{1}\bar{1}0$)　(0001)　($01\bar{1}0$)　(b) Growing along [0110] (b-axis)

(c) (0001)　($01\bar{1}0$)　($2\bar{1}10$)　(c) Growing along [2110] (a-axis)

Fig. 14.12.3　Individually Domain-Patterned ZnO Nanobelts[Zhao et al.]

14.13   Fibrous Electromagnetic Laminae

There are important connectivity patterns in diphasic solids in a composite, ranging from a 0-0 (unconnected checkerboard pattern) to a 3-3 pattern (three dimensionally self-connected) [Newnham et al.]. One basic relationship between the active and passive material is commonly referred to as connectivity. Connectivity is used for annotating the number of dimensions through which a material is continuous. The family of interconnectivity of piezoelectric composites are depicted in [Newnham]'s original schematic drawings shown in Fig. 14.13.1. Connectivity of a piezo-electric composite is shown as a combination of two numbers such as 1-3, 2-2 or 0-3, where the first digit represents the active material and the second digit represents the passive material. For example, a composite has 1-3 connectivity, which means that the piezo-electric materials are continuous-connected in one direction.

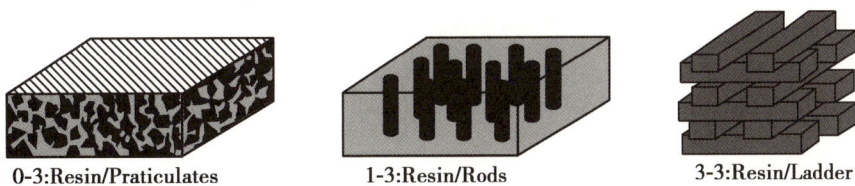

0-3:Resin/Praticulates   1-3:Resin/Rods   3-3:Resin/Ladder

Fig. 14.13.1   Interconnectivity of Piezoelectric Composites: 0-3, 1-3, and 3-3 [Newnham]

Nowadays, the concept of connectivity relationship for piezo-electric materials can then be extended to all electromagnetic materials, rendering the rule that "1+1>2" reign in the piezo- and/or pyro-performance in regard of electro-magneto-thermo-mechanical coupling functionalism in addition to the structural enhancement based on micromechanics.

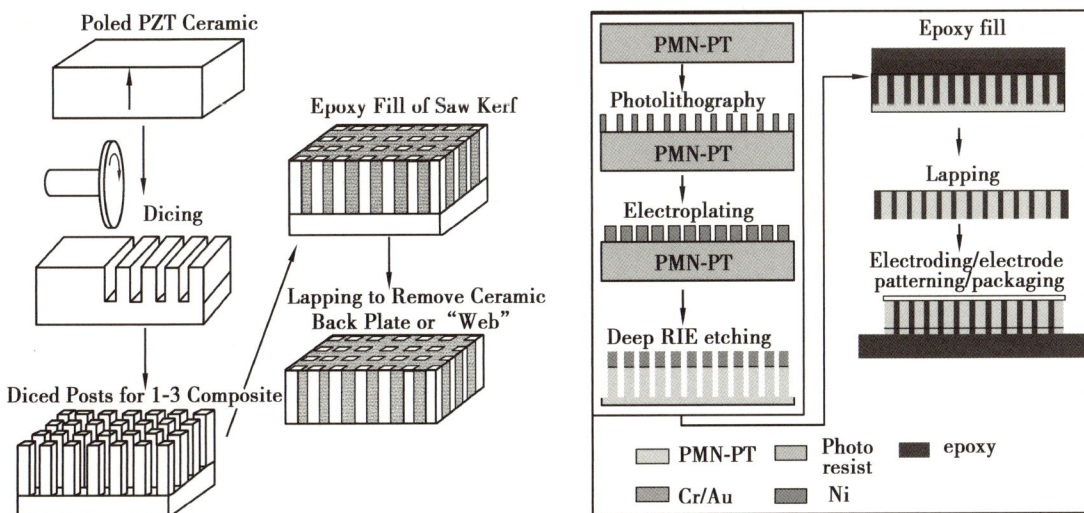

Fig. 14.13.2   Fabrication of Unidirectional Fibrous Electromagnetic Laminae [Jiang et al.]

14.13.1　Fabrication of Fibrous Electromagnetic Laminae

The 1-3 is a lamina reinforced with unidirectional fibers. Two ways of fabricating such unidirectional fibrous electromagnetic laminae are demonstrated in Fig. 14.13.2[Jiang et al.]. A schematic drawing of the transducer assembly based on the Ep/PMN-PT lamina is shown in Fig. 14.13.3[Jiang et al.].

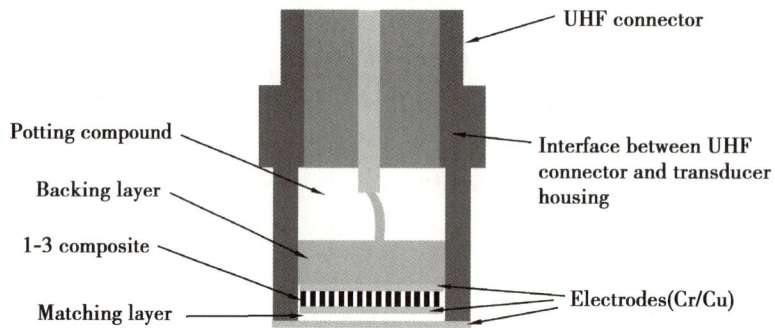

Fig. 14.13.3　10 MHz PMN-PT Fibrous-Composite Transducer Assembly[Jiang et al.]

14.13.2　Micromechanics for Fibrous Laminae

There are two types of fibrous laminae, or saying MFCs (Macro-fiber Composites). One is MFC-d_{31} that has the polarization in the thickness direction and the other is MFC-d_{33} that has the polarization parallel to the piezo fiber direction. In the polarization of a unidirectional lamina,

　　(a)d_{33}: called longitudinal piezoelectric coefficient;
　　(b)d_{3q}: called transverse piezoelectric coefficient.

The fiber direction is designated 1-axis in the primary material coordinate system attached to an individual lamina, as shown in Fig. 14.13.4.

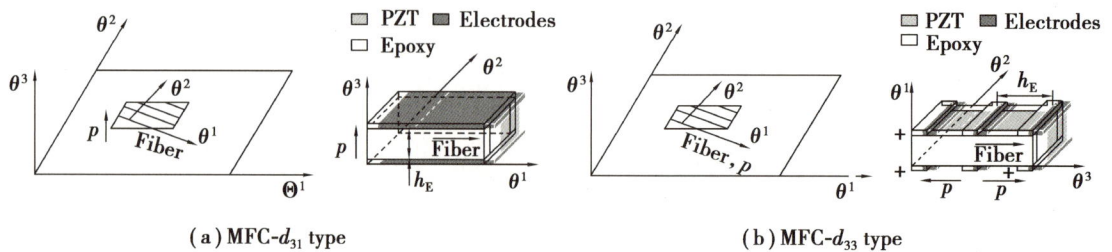

(a) MFC-d_{31} type　　　　　　　　　　(b) MFC-d_{33} type

Fig. 14.13.4　Lamination of Piezoelectric Fibrous Laminae

14.14   Electromagnetic Laminae Reinforced with Particulates

The demand for flexible electronic devices that can be bent and even folded, leads engineers to get focused on laminated films made of electromagnetic materials. Since engineering plastics have such merits except for their inherent low dielectric constants, conventional polymer-based dielectric materials are made into thin composite laminae that embrace high dielectric ceramic powder such as $LiTaO_3$ or PZT. On the other hand, magnetoelectroelastic materials are inherently brittle and prone to cracking, laminae are one form to reduce such a risk.

Researchers have been also focused on the individual and interrelated dielectric and pyroelectric properties of 0-3 nm (nanometer) composite films. For example, both the pyroelectric coefficient and dielectric constant generated by PVDF/MWCNT films increase with an increasing temperature much faster than pure PVDF films as demonstrated in Table 14.5.1[Edwards et al.], so does the power loss accompanying the increase in dielectric constant (i.e., increasing $\tan \delta$). This keen increase in PDVF films reinforced with MWCNT, having outside diameter (7-15 nm) × length (0.5-10 μm), is attributed to the formation of a continuous network that allows efficient current to flow through the material[Guggilla & Edwards].

14.14.1   Dielectric Constant

The model raised by [Yamada et al.] for PVDF reinforced with PZT as a 0-3 composite is generally applicable to generic particulates-reinforced resin, as

$$\epsilon_{\text{eff}} = \epsilon_{\text{m}} \left[1 + \frac{\eta \, v_{\text{f}}(\epsilon_{\text{f}} - \epsilon_{\text{m}})}{\eta \, \epsilon_{\text{m}} + v_{\text{m}}(\epsilon_{\text{f}} - \epsilon_{\text{m}})} \right] \qquad (14.14.1)$$

where

v_{f}: Volume fraction of reinforcing material, i.e., particulates, particles or powders;

v_{m}: Volume fraction of matrix, i.e., resin; $v_{\text{m}} = 1 - v_{\text{f}} - v_{\text{void}}$;

ϵ_{eff}: Effective dielectric constant;

ϵ_{f}: Dielectric constant of reinforcing material;

ϵ_{m}: Dielectric constant of matrix;

η: Parameter, depending on the particulate shape and orientation in the composite film.

Another frequently used formula for the effective dielectric constant of particulates-reinforced plastics with limited volume of particulates ($v_{\text{f}} < 50\%$) regardless of their shapes is

$$\epsilon_{\text{eff}} = \frac{\epsilon_m v_m + \epsilon_f v_f \left(\dfrac{3\epsilon_m}{\epsilon_f + 2\epsilon_m}\right) \left[1 + 3v_f \left(\dfrac{\epsilon_f - \epsilon_m}{\epsilon_f + 2\epsilon_m}\right)\right]}{v_m + v_f \left(\dfrac{3\epsilon_m}{\epsilon_f + 2\epsilon_m}\right) \left[1 + 3v_f \left(\dfrac{\epsilon_f - \epsilon_m}{\epsilon_f + 2\epsilon_m}\right)\right]} \qquad (14.14.2)$$

14.14.2 Piezoelectric Coefficient

[Yamada et al.] proposed a model to characterize the electric permittivities, piezoelectric constants, and elastic moduli of a composite, where the ellipsoidal particles of piezoelectric materials are dispersed uniformly a plastic medium. The model shows good agreement with experimental data for PVDF/PZT composites. The effective piezoelectric coefficient in the through-thickness direction is

$$d_{33,\text{eff}} = \frac{p_{\text{ratio}} v_f d_{33,p}}{1 + \dfrac{\epsilon_f}{\dfrac{\epsilon_m - 1}{\eta}}} \qquad (14.14.3)$$

where

p_{ratio}: Poling ratio;

v_f: Volume fraction of particulates in the lamina;

$d_{33,p}$: Piezoelectric constant of reinforcing particulates;

η: Parameter attributed to the shape particulates, e.g. $\eta = 4\pi/r$ for spheres.

14.14.3 Pyroelectric Coefficient

Research of the 0-3 composite of thermoplastic elastomer polyurethane (PU) reinforced with PZT particulates by[Lam et al.] reveals a formula for the effective pyroelectric coefficient that includes the influence of the conductivities of reinforcements and matrix, as

$$p_{\text{py},c} = v_f p_{\text{py},f} \left\{1 - \left[\frac{v_m}{3v_f \epsilon_m + v_m(\epsilon_f + 2\epsilon_m)}\right] \left[\frac{\omega^2 \lambda^2 (\epsilon_f - \epsilon_m) + \lambda (k_2 - k_1)}{1 + \omega^2 \lambda^2}\right]\right\} \qquad (14.14.4)$$

and $\quad \lambda = \dfrac{3v_f \epsilon_m + v_m(\epsilon_f + 2\epsilon_m)}{3v_f k_m + v_m(k_f + 2k_m)} \qquad (14.14.5)$

where

$p_{\text{py},c}$: Effective pyroelectric coefficient of the composite;

$p_{py,f}$: Pyroelectric coefficient of particulates;

k_f: Thermal conductivity of particulates, e.g. PZT;

k_m: Thermal conductivity of the matrix.

The above equation shows that high conductivities enhance the pyroelectricity of a 0-3 composite as evidenced by the pyroelectric coefficient of PU/PZT lamina that exhibits more than tenfold of that of PVDF/PZT lamina.

14.15   Laminated Piezo-and Pyro-Composites

Piezoelectric laminates are used in a variety of applications that require relatively high force and larger displacement than single element piezoelectric transducers can produce. These include micro-positioning systems, solid-state pumps/switches, noise isolation mounts, ultrasonic drills and stacked ultrasonic transducers[Martin][Sherrit et al.].

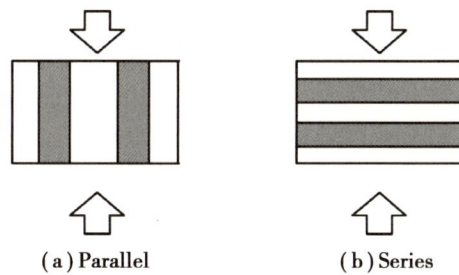

(a) Parallel   (b) Series

Fig. 14.15.1   Parallel and Series Connections in a 2−2 Composite

14.15.1   Dielectrics in Laminates

The combined effective dielectric constants for both in-parallel and in-series connections in a 2−2 composite (Fig. 14.15.1) are, respectively

$$\epsilon_{eff} = v_f \, \epsilon_f + v_m \, \epsilon_m \qquad \text{(In Parallel)} \qquad (14.15.1)$$

$$\frac{1}{\epsilon_{eff}} = \frac{v_f}{\epsilon_f} + \frac{v_m}{\epsilon_m} \qquad \text{(In Series)} \qquad (14.15.2)$$

14.15.2   Piezoelectricity in 2-Layered Laminates

Considering only piezoelectric-electrostritive coefficient d_{33}, for the 2-layered composite and following the rule of mixture for composites (Chapter 10), one has the effective d_{33eff} for the two different application cases, in parallel and in series, as shown in Fig. 14.15.1, respectively

$$d_{31eff} = v_f \, d_{31f} + v_m \, d_{31m} \qquad \text{(In Parallel)} \qquad (14.15.3)$$

$$d_{33\text{eff}} = \frac{v_\text{f}\, d_{33\text{f}}\, s_{33\text{m}} + v_\text{m}\, d_{33\text{m}}\, s_{33\text{f}}}{v_\text{f}\, s_{33\text{m}} + v_\text{m}\, s_{33\text{f}}} \qquad (\text{In Parallel}) \qquad (14.15.4)$$

$$\text{and} \quad d_{33\text{eff}} = \frac{v_\text{f}\, d_{33\text{f}}\, \epsilon_{33\text{m}} + v_\text{m}\, d_{33\text{m}}\, \epsilon_{33\text{f}}}{v_\text{f}\, \epsilon_{33\text{m}} + v_\text{m}\, \epsilon_{33\text{f}}} \qquad (\text{In Series}) \qquad (14.15.5)$$

where

$d_{31\text{eff}}$: Effective d_{31} for the composite;

$d_{33\text{eff}}$: Effective d_{33} for the composite;

v_f : Volume fraction of material f, conventionally used for the piezoelectric material;

v_m : Volume fraction of material m;

$d_{31\text{f}}$ and $d_{32\text{f}}$: d_{31} and d_{32} for material f;

$d_{31\text{m}}$ and $d_{32\text{m}}$: d_{31} and d_{32} for material m;

$\epsilon_{31\text{f}}$ and $\epsilon_{32\text{f}}$: ϵ_{31} and ϵ_{32} for material f;

$\epsilon_{31\text{m}}$ and $\epsilon_{32\text{m}}$: ϵ_{31} and ϵ_{32} for material m.

The combined coefficient $d_{\text{h,eff}}$ for 2-2 composite—Fig. 14.15.1(a), i.e., arranged in parallel, under hydrostatic pressure is

$$d_{\text{h,eff}} = d_{33\text{eff}} + 2\, d_{31\text{eff}} = \frac{v_\text{f}\, d_{33\text{f}}\, s_{33\text{m}} + v_\text{m}\, d_{33\text{m}}\, s_{33\text{f}}}{v_\text{f}\, s_{33\text{m}} + v_\text{m}\, s_{33\text{f}}} + 2(v_\text{f}\, d_{31\text{f}} + v_\text{m}\, d_{31\text{m}}) \qquad (14.15.6)$$

14.15.3   Piezo-and Pyro-Electric Stackups

Recently, a hybrid laminated composite was proposed and studied for harvesting quasi-static temperature variations[Zakharov et al.]. It consists of (a) a pyroelectric lamina and (b) a PZT-A1 fiber-reinforced Ti-Ni-Cu (a shape memory material) lamina, as schematically depicted in Fig. 14.15.2. When the temperature varies, large thermally induced strain generated by the SMA layer is transmitted to the piezoelectric layer that in turn generates an electric voltage. In this way thermally induced strain is converted into useful voltage with neither complex electronics nor cold source management system. Note that the SMA generates much larger strains than piezoelectric material. This is useful when the harvester is expected to even work with a narrow temperature variation.

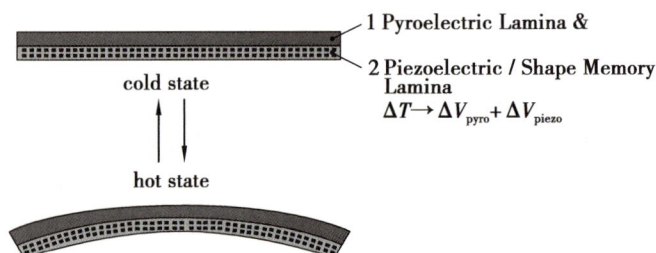

Fig. 14.15.2   A Laminate Combining Pyroelectric-Piezoelectric-Shape Memory Effects

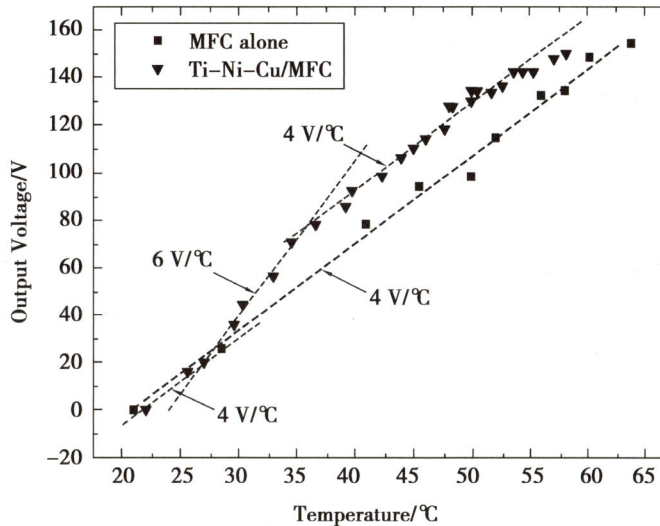

Fig. 14.15.3　Output Voltages Versus Temperature Increase〔Zakharov et al.〕

Physical tests were conducted by〔Zakharov et al.〕to see if the pyroelectric lamina makes a difference. The results are replotted in Fig. 14.15.3. The curve marked with dotted boxes is for the PZT-A1 fiber-reinforced Ti-Ni-Cu (a shape memory material) lamina only, named "MFC" by the authors. The other curve marked with dotted triangles is done using a test involving both laminae, called "composite" here. It is observed that the composite does outperform the MFC by 2 ℃ in voltage generation, which is coincident with the theoretical result calculated in Example 14.5.1. The harvesters are put in 21 ℃ water with a constant increase in temperature. As "heat transfer" is slower than "electric conduction", the composite does not deviate from the MFC curve until 30 ℃ and shows a continued increase due to "pyro-electric voltage" subjected to thermoelastic straining of the MFC, and then resumes the "pyro" slope from 40 ℃ on.

14.16　Finite Element Methods for Piezoelectricity

A practical application of piezoelectric effect to designing large bandwidth power piezoelectric transducers involves the 3-dimensional structure and sophisticated couplings of material behaviors. It is quite difficult, if not impossible, to analyze such a transducer using closed-form solutions based on equivalent circuits or the related numerical methods. The finite element method is by-far the most promising tool for modeling such a sophisticated mechanism inherent with both geometric and material nonlinearities in the time-varying domain.

14.16.1　Electric Field Intensity-Electric Displacement Relationship

Based on the finite element discretization, the piezoelectric continuum is meshed into a set of discrete elements and nodes. Variable electric potential ϕ_ϵ (a scalar) at any location of the element can be related to nodal electric potential $\phi_{\epsilon i}$ ($i = 1, 2, \cdots, 20$) of the element using the global Cartesian coordinates as follows:

$$\phi_\epsilon = \sum_{i=1}^{20} N_i \phi_{\epsilon i} \qquad (14.16.1)$$

The above equation is formulated using the shape functions applied to the 20-node solid element, i.e., Eqs. (3.2.7a)-(3.2.7c). By differentiating the above equation with respect to the three body coordinates (ξ, η, ζ) associated with the element of interest, and stacking them into a vector column, one has

$$\begin{Bmatrix} \dfrac{\partial \phi_\epsilon}{\partial x} \\[2mm] \dfrac{\partial \phi_\epsilon}{\partial y} \\[2mm] \dfrac{\partial \phi_\epsilon}{\partial z} \end{Bmatrix}_{3\times1} = \sum_{i=1}^{20} \begin{bmatrix} L_{11} & L_{12} & L_{13} \\ L_{21} & L_{22} & L_{23} \\ L_{31} & L_{32} & L_{33} \end{bmatrix} \begin{Bmatrix} \dfrac{\partial \phi_\epsilon}{\partial \xi} \\[2mm] \dfrac{\partial \phi_\epsilon}{\partial \eta} \\[2mm] \dfrac{\partial \phi_\epsilon}{\partial \zeta} \end{Bmatrix} = \sum_{i=1}^{20} [L] \begin{Bmatrix} \dfrac{\partial N_i}{\partial \xi} \\[2mm] \dfrac{\partial N_i}{\partial \eta} \\[2mm] \dfrac{\partial N_i}{\partial \zeta} \end{Bmatrix}_{3\times1} \phi_{\epsilon i}$$

i.e. $$\begin{Bmatrix} \dfrac{\partial \phi_\epsilon}{\partial x} \\[2mm] \dfrac{\partial \phi_\epsilon}{\partial y} \\[2mm] \dfrac{\partial \phi_\epsilon}{\partial z} \end{Bmatrix}_{3\times1} = \sum_{i=1}^{20} [B_{\epsilon i}]_{3\times1} \phi_{\epsilon i} = [B_\epsilon]_{3\times20} \{\phi_{\epsilon i}\}_{20\times1} \qquad (14.16.2)$$

where

$$[B_\epsilon]_{3\times20} = [[B_\epsilon]_{3\times1} [B_{\epsilon2}]_{3\times1} [B_{\epsilon2}]_{3\times1} \cdots [B_{\epsilon20}]_{3\times1}] \qquad (14.16.3)$$

Note that the summation in Eq. (14.16.2) means a stackup of all the 20-node nodes. The electric field intensity E is a vector in the space that is related to its corresponding electrical potential ϕ_ϵ (scalar) by

$$E = -\,\mathrm{grad}(\phi_\epsilon) = \nabla \phi_\epsilon = \left(\frac{-\partial \phi_\epsilon}{\partial x}\right) i + \left(\frac{-\partial \phi_\epsilon}{\partial y}\right) j + \left(\frac{-\partial \phi_\epsilon}{\partial z}\right) k \qquad (14.16.4)$$

Substituting Eq. (14.16.2) into the above equation, one may compute the gradient of the potential as

$$\begin{Bmatrix} E_x \\ E_y \\ E_z \end{Bmatrix} \begin{Bmatrix} \dfrac{\partial \phi_\epsilon}{\partial x} \\[2mm] \dfrac{\partial \phi_\epsilon}{\partial y} \\[2mm] \dfrac{\partial \phi_\epsilon}{\partial z} \end{Bmatrix} = \sum_{i=1}^{20} [L] \begin{Bmatrix} \dfrac{\partial N_i}{\partial \xi} \\[2mm] \dfrac{\partial N_i}{\partial \eta} \\[2mm] \dfrac{\partial N_i}{\partial \zeta} \end{Bmatrix} \phi_{\epsilon i} \qquad (14.16.5)$$

or $\quad \{E\} = \begin{Bmatrix} E_x \\ E_y \\ E_z \end{Bmatrix} = \begin{Bmatrix} \dfrac{\partial \phi}{\partial x} \\[4pt] \dfrac{\partial \phi}{\partial y} \\[4pt] \dfrac{\partial \phi}{\partial z} \end{Bmatrix} = \displaystyle\sum_{i=1}^{20} \{B_{\epsilon i}\}_{3\times1} \phi_{\epsilon i} = [B_\epsilon]_{3\times20} \{\phi_\epsilon\}_{20\times1}$ $\hspace{2em}(14.16.6)$

where $\quad \{\phi_\epsilon\}_{20\times1} = \{\phi_{\epsilon 1}, \phi_{\epsilon 2}, \cdots, \phi_{\epsilon 20}\}^{\mathrm{T}}_{20\times1}$ $\hspace{4em}(14.16.7)$

Note that the $\phi_{\epsilon i}$ value at every node is stacked up to form column vector $\{\phi_\epsilon\}$, i.e., nodal electric displacements of the entire element, so is $\{B_{\epsilon i}\}_{3\times1}$ stacked up to make $[B_\epsilon]_{3\times20}$. Next, consider the electric displacement that can be calculated from the electric field intensity using Eq. (14.6.6). It is

$$\{D\}_{3\times1} = [\epsilon]_{3\times3} \{E\}_{3\times1} + [d]_{3\times6} \{\sigma\}_{6\times1} \hspace{3em}(14.16.8)$$

14.16.2　Piezoelectric Element Formulation

The differential electric-field energy density of the electric field in the linear range, without initial stress or initial strain, is

$$\mathrm{d}U_{\mathrm{E}} = \{E\}^{\mathrm{T}}\{\mathrm{d}D\}$$

$$= \{E\}^{\mathrm{T}}_{3\times1}([d]_{3\times6}\{\mathrm{d}\sigma\}_{6\times1} + [\epsilon]_{3\times3}\{\mathrm{d}E\}^{\mathrm{T}}_{3\times1})$$

$$= \{E\}^{\mathrm{T}}_{3\times1}[d]_{3\times6}\{\mathrm{d}\sigma\}_{6\times1} + \{E\}^{\mathrm{T}}_{3\times1}[\epsilon]_{3\times3}\{\mathrm{d}E\}_{3\times1}$$

$$= \{E\}^{\mathrm{T}}_{1\times3}[d]_{3\times6}[c]_{6\times6}\{\mathrm{d}\varepsilon\}_{6\times1} + \{E\}^{\mathrm{T}}_{1\times3}[\epsilon]_{3\times3}\{\mathrm{d}E\}_{3\times1} \hspace{2em}(14.16.9)$$

Plugging Eq. (14.16.6) and Eq. (14.16.8) into the above equation and completing the integrations and adding the initial electric field intensity $\{E_{\mathrm{o}}\}$ and initial electric displacement vector $\{D_{\mathrm{o}}\}$, one has the following electric-field energy density ($\mathrm{J/m^3}$ or $\mathrm{N \cdot mm/mm^3}$) as

$$U_{\mathrm{E}} = \iiint_V \mathrm{d}U_{\mathrm{E}}$$

$$= \iiint_V \{E\}^{\mathrm{T}}\{\mathrm{d}D\}$$

$$= \frac{1}{2}\{E\}^{\mathrm{T}}\{\epsilon\}\,\{E\} + \{E\}^{\mathrm{T}}[d]\,\{\sigma\} + \{E\}^{\mathrm{T}}\{D_{\mathrm{o}}\} - \{E\}^{\mathrm{T}}[\epsilon]\,\{E_{\mathrm{o}}\}$$

$$= \frac{1}{2}\{\phi_\epsilon\}^{\mathrm{T}}[B_\epsilon]^{\mathrm{T}}\{\epsilon\}[B_\epsilon]\,\{\phi_\epsilon\} + \{\phi_\epsilon\}^{\mathrm{T}}[B_\epsilon]^{\mathrm{T}}[d][c][B]\,\{\phi\} +$$

$$\{\phi_\epsilon\}^T[B_\epsilon]^T\{D_o\} - \{\phi_\epsilon\}^T[B_\epsilon]^T[\epsilon]\{E_o\} \tag{14.16.10}$$

Simultaneously, the strain energy density (J/m^3 or $N \cdot mm/mm^3$) without any other external forcing functions (e.g. body force) is given by Eq. (11.13.13)

$$U_o = \iiint_V dU_o = \iiint_V \{\sigma\}^T\{d\varepsilon\}$$

$$= \frac{1}{2}\{\varepsilon\}^T[c]\{\varepsilon\} - \{\varepsilon\}^T[c]\{\varepsilon_o\} + \{\varepsilon\}^T\{\sigma_o\}$$

$$= \frac{1}{2}\{\phi\}^T[B]^T[c][B]\{\phi\} - \{\phi\}^T[B]^T[c]\{\varepsilon_o\} + \{\phi\}^T[B]^T\{\rho_o\} \tag{14.16.11}$$

Furthermore, the total potential of a continuum with volume domain V and surface domain S consists of four parts, i. e. strain energy, and works done by body forces $\{b\}$, surface tractions $\{S\}$ and concentrated forces $\{Q\}$,

$$\Pi = \iiint_V U_o \, dV - \iiint_V \{g\}^T\{b\} \, dV - \iint_S \{g\}^T\{S\} \, dS - \{\Phi\}^T\{F_c\} + \iiint_V U_E \, dV \tag{14.16.12}$$

Since the concentrated forces in $\{F_c\}$ are usually expressed in the global Cartesian coordinate system and independent of integration, the total displacement vector for the entire structure $\{\Phi\}$ is used as its corresponding displacement. Substituting Eq. (14.16.10) and Eq. (14.16.11) into the above equation yields

$$\Pi = \iiint_V \left(\frac{1}{2}\{\phi\}^T[B]^T[c][B]\{\phi\} - \{\phi\}^T[B]^T[c]\{\varepsilon_o\} + \{\phi\}^T[B]^T\{\sigma_o\}\right) dV -$$

$$\iiint_V \{\phi\}^T[N]^T\{b\} \, dV - \iint_S \{\phi\}^T[N]^T\{S\} \, dS - \{\Phi\}^T\{F_c\} +$$

$$\iiint_V \left(\frac{1}{2}\{\phi_\epsilon\}^T[B_\epsilon]^T\{\epsilon\}[B_\epsilon]\{\phi_\epsilon\} - \{\phi_\epsilon\}^T[B_\epsilon]^T[\epsilon]\{E_o\} + \{\phi_\epsilon\}^T[B_\epsilon]^T\{D_o\}\right) dV +$$

$$\iiint_V \{\phi_\epsilon\}^T[B_\epsilon]^T[d][c][B]\{\phi\} \, dV \tag{14.16.13}$$

The integration (summation) means that the contribution from all elements are assembled. Thus the total potential of the entire structure can be obtained by approximating the integration using the summation as

$$\Pi = \frac{1}{2}\sum\{\phi\}^T[k]\{\phi\} - \sum\{\phi\}^T\{f\} - \sum\{\Phi\}^T\{F_c\} +$$

$$\frac{1}{2} \sum \{\phi_\epsilon\}^{\mathrm{T}} [k_\epsilon] \{\phi\} + \sum \{\phi_\epsilon\}^{\mathrm{T}} [k_e] \{\phi\} - \sum \{\phi_\epsilon\}^{\mathrm{T}} \{q\} \qquad (14.16.14)$$

where $\quad [k] = \iiint_V [B]^T_{60\times6} [c]_{6\times6} [B]_{6\times60} \, \mathrm{d}V \qquad (14.16.15)$

$$\{f\} = \iiint_V [B]^{\mathrm{T}} [c] \{\varepsilon_o\} \, \mathrm{d}V - \iiint_V [B] \{\sigma_o\} \, \mathrm{d}V + \iiint_V [N]^{\mathrm{T}} \{b\} \, \mathrm{d}V + \iint_S [N]^{\mathrm{T}} \{S\}$$

$$(14.16.16)$$

$$[k_\epsilon] = \iiint_V [B_\epsilon]^{\mathrm{T}}_{20\times3} \{\epsilon\}_{3\times3} [B_\epsilon]_{3\times20} \mathrm{d}V \qquad (\text{Dielectric constants}) \qquad (14.16.17)$$

$$[k_e] = \iiint_V [B_\epsilon]^{\mathrm{T}}_{20\times3} [d]_{3\times6} [c]_{6\times6} [B]_{6\times60} \mathrm{d}V \qquad (\text{Piezoelectric effect}) \qquad (14.16.18)$$

$$\{q\} = \iiint_V ([B_\epsilon]^{\mathrm{T}} [\epsilon] \{E_o\} - [B_\epsilon]^{\mathrm{T}} \{D_o\}) \mathrm{d}V \qquad (14.16.19)$$

and $\quad \{F_c\}$: Collection of applied concentrated forces.

Subscript "ϵ" means that the matrix comes from dielectric constants as shown in Eq. (14.16.17), while subscript "p" means that the matrix originates from piezoelectric effect where the electromechanical coupling effect is denoted by $[d]_{3\times6} [c]_{6\times6}$ in Eq. (14.16.19).

14.16.3   Global Coupled Equations for Static Analysis

The next step is to do the stacking of the elemental displacements $\{\phi\}$ into a vector column to form the total displacement vector $\{\Phi\}$ and the elemental electric potentials $\{\phi_\epsilon\}$ into a vector column to form the total electric potential $\{\Phi_\epsilon\}$ according to the sequence of element numbers. Eq. (14.16.14) can be rewritten as

$$\Pi = \frac{1}{2} \{\Phi\}^{\mathrm{T}} [K] \{\Phi\} - \{\Phi\}^{\mathrm{T}} \{F\} +$$

$$\frac{1}{2} \{\Phi_\epsilon\}^{\mathrm{T}} [K_\epsilon] \{\Phi_\epsilon\} + \{K_e\}^{\mathrm{T}} \{\Phi_\epsilon\} - \{\Phi_\epsilon\}^{\mathrm{T}} \{Q_\epsilon\} \qquad (14.16.20)$$

The elements in stiffness $[K]$, $[K_\epsilon]$, or $[K_e]$ will be arranged according to the solution scheme. Taking the first derivatives with respect to the total displacement vector $\{\Phi\}$ and total electric potential vector $\{\Phi_\epsilon\}$, respectively leads to the following coupled equations.

$$\begin{bmatrix} [K] & [K_e]^{\mathrm{T}} \\ [K_e] & [K_\epsilon] \end{bmatrix} \begin{Bmatrix} \{\Phi\} \\ \{\Phi_\epsilon\} \end{Bmatrix} = \begin{Bmatrix} \{F\} \\ \{Q\} \end{Bmatrix} \qquad (14.16.21)$$

where

$[K]$: Assembled $[k]$, i.e., Total structural stiffness matrix;

$[K_\epsilon]$: Assembled $[k_\epsilon]$, total dielectric constant matrix;

$[K_e]$: Assembled $[k_e]$, total piezoelectric coefficient matrix;

$\{D\}$: Total electric displacement vector;

$\{\Phi_\epsilon\}$ Total electric potential vector;

$\{F\}$: Directed $\{F_c\}$ +Assembled $\{f\}$ (Generalized nodal forces);

$\{Q_\epsilon\}$: Directed $\{Q_{\epsilon,c}\}$ +Assembled $\{q\}$ (Generalized nodal charges).

The generalized matrices and vectors of consistent piezoelectric properties given in the above set of equations are obtained as follows:

$$[k] = \iiint_V [B]^T[c][B]\ \mathrm{d}V \qquad (\text{Structural stiffness})$$

$$[k_\epsilon] = \iiint_V [B_e]^T[\epsilon][B_e]\ \mathrm{d}V \qquad (\text{Dielectric constants})$$

$$[k_e] = \iiint_V [B_e]^T_{20\times3}[d]_{3\times6}[c]_{6\times6}[B]_{6\times60}\ \mathrm{d}V$$

$$= \iiint_V [B_e]^T_{20\times3}[e]_{3\times6}[B]_{6\times60}\ \mathrm{d}V \qquad (\text{Piezoelectricity})$$

Assume that surface charge density, i.e., the component of the electric displacement D_n normal to the residing surface, is given, one can derive the "charge force" q by integrating the D_n over the corresponding surface area. As an example for analyzing a capacitor that has a flat surface, q can be obtained by multiplying D_n by the area A. The sum of the charges on the boundaries of the elements will yield the total electrode charge.

14.16.4   Global Coupled Equation for Dynamic Analysis

The coupled dynamic equations for the piezoelectric and mechanical effects, either discretized using 20-node or 8-node solid elements in the global Cartesian (x, y, z) coordinate system, can be written in terms of the nodal displacements and electric potentials (i.e., electric field strength) in matrix form as

$$\begin{bmatrix} [M] & [0] \\ [0] & [0] \end{bmatrix} \begin{Bmatrix} \left\{\dfrac{\mathrm{d}^2\Phi}{\mathrm{d}t^2}\right\} \\ \left\{\dfrac{\mathrm{d}^2\Phi_\epsilon}{\mathrm{d}t^2}\right\} \end{Bmatrix} + \begin{bmatrix} [C] & [0] \\ [0] & [0] \end{bmatrix} \begin{Bmatrix} \left\{\dfrac{\mathrm{d}\Phi}{\mathrm{d}t}\right\} \\ \left\{\dfrac{\mathrm{d}\Phi_\epsilon}{\mathrm{d}t}\right\} \end{Bmatrix} + \begin{bmatrix} [K] & [K_e] \\ [K_e] & -[K_\epsilon] \end{bmatrix}^T \begin{Bmatrix} \{\Phi\} \\ \{\Phi_e\} \end{Bmatrix} = \begin{Bmatrix} \{F\} \\ \{Q_\epsilon\} \end{Bmatrix}$$

$$(14.16.22)$$

where

[M]: Consistent mass matrix;
[C]: Structural damping coefficients matrix.

The mass and damping matrices given in the above set of equations are to be obtained using the following equations:

$$[M] = \text{Assembled}[m], \text{ where}[m] = \iiint_V \rho[N]^T[N]\mathrm{d}V \qquad (14.16.23)$$

$$[C] = \text{Assembled}[c_f], \text{ where } [c_f] = \iiint_V c_f[B]^T[B]\mathrm{d}V \qquad (14.16.24)$$

where

[M]: Elemental mass matrix;
ρ: Density;
[c_f]: Elemental damping matrix of the structure;
c_f: Elemental damping coefficient of the structure-structural damping.

Matrix [c_f] in the above equation is the structural damping matrix, while the damping induced by the electric charges (e.g. dielectric loss) is neglected here. Most material properties applied to the above equation are temperature-dependent. A detailed derivation of finite element formulation is given in[Bendigeril et al.].

Coupled dynamical equations given by Eq. (14.16.22) for linear piezoelectric effect can be solved either in frequency domain using harmonic function expansion or in time domain to integrate step-by-step. One need identify the objective of the analysis before making a choice. Generally speaking, a frequency domain formulation is appropriate for investigating static deformations, modal shapes, resonance frequencies and steady state vibrations, while a time domain formulation is ideal for examining transient responses and local disturbances of a short time duration.

14.17   Finite Element Methods for Coupled Piezoelectricity and Piezomagnetics

Electro-magneto-mechanical behaviors of a material that exhibits piezoelectric and piezomagnetic effects can be utilized for enhancing the performance of pyro-sensors under a prescribed thermal condition. Due to the structural complexity, a finite element method for coupled electric, magnetic, and thermal effects becomes a mandate. By finite element methods, the composite continuum is meshed into a set of discrete elements and nodes. The discretized coupled dynamic equations for the piezoelectric and piezomagnetic effects, discretized using either 20-noded or 8-noded solid elements, can be written in terms of the nodal displacement, electric potential and magnetic potential in the matrix form as

$$
\begin{bmatrix} [M] & [0] & [0] \\ [0] & [0] & [0] \\ [0] & [0] & [0] \end{bmatrix} \begin{Bmatrix} \left\{ \dfrac{d^2 \Phi}{dt^2} \right\} \\ \left\{ \dfrac{d^2 \Phi_\epsilon}{dt^2} \right\} \\ \left\{ \dfrac{d^2 \Phi_\mu}{dt^2} \right\} \end{Bmatrix} + \begin{bmatrix} [C] & [0] & [0] \\ [0] & [0] & [0] \\ [0] & [0] & [0] \end{bmatrix} \begin{Bmatrix} \left\{ \dfrac{d\Phi}{dt} \right\} \\ \left\{ \dfrac{d\Phi_\epsilon}{dt} \right\} \\ \left\{ \dfrac{d\Phi_\mu}{dt} \right\} \end{Bmatrix} +
$$

$$
\begin{bmatrix} [K] & [K_e]^T & [K_q]^T \\ [K_e] & -[K_\epsilon] & -[K_m]^T \\ [K_q] & -[K_m] & -[K_\mu] \end{bmatrix} \begin{Bmatrix} \{\Phi\} \\ \{\Phi_\epsilon\} \\ \{Q_\mu\} \end{Bmatrix} = \begin{Bmatrix} \{F\} \\ \{Q_\epsilon\} \\ \{Q_\mu\} \end{Bmatrix}
$$

$$(14.17.1)$$

where

$[K_\mu]$: Pyromagnetic constants matrix, where subscript μ stands for pyromagnetism;

$[K_q]$: Pyromagnetic and structural coupling matrix;

$[K_m]$: Magnetoelectric effects—Pyroelectric/pyromagnetic coupling matrix;

$[\phi_\mu]$: Nodal magnetic vector potentials ($V \cdot s/m$);

$\{\Phi_\mu\}$: Total nodal magnetic vector potentials—the assembled;

$\{Q_\mu\}$: Total nodal magnetic fluxes—both the assembled and directly applied $\{Q_{\mu,c}\}$.

The matrices and vectors given in the above set of equations are obtained as follows:

$$
[K_\mu]: \text{Assembled}[k_\mu], \text{ where } [k_\mu] = \iiint_V [B_\mu]_{20\times3}^T [\mu]_{3\times3} [B_\mu]_{3\times20} dV \qquad (14.17.2)
$$

$$
[k_q] = \iiint_V [B]_{60\times6}^T [q]_{6\times3} [B_\mu]_{3\times20} dV \qquad (14.17.3)
$$

and

$$
[k_m] = \iiint_V [B_e]_{20\times3}^T [m]_{3\times3} [B_\mu]_{3\times20} dV \qquad (14.17.4)
$$

Most material properties applied to the above equation are temperature-dependent. The detailed derivation of such a finite element formulation is given in [Kondaiah et al.]. Note that without the disturbance of electric field, i.e., $\partial E/\partial t = 0$, the magnetic vector potential is related to magnetic field by

$$
\{B\} = \nabla x \{\phi_\mu\} \qquad (14.17.5)
$$

Again, coupled dynamical equation set given by Eq. (14.17.1) for linear pyromagnetic effect can be solved either in frequency domain using harmonic function expansion or in time domain to integrate step-by-step. One need identify the objective of the analysis before making a choice. Generally speaking, a frequency domain formulation is appropriate for investigating static deformations, modal shapes, resonance frequencies and steady state vibrations, while a time domain formulation is ideal for examining transient responses and local disturbances of a short time duration.

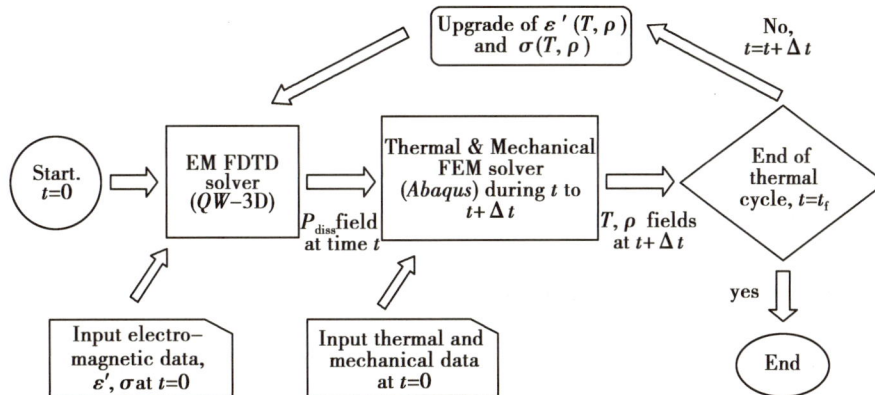

Fig. 14.17.1   Procedure for Finite Element Simulation of Microwave Sintering[Bogachev et al.]

Finite element simulation of microwave sintering at a macroscopic scale with changing geometry of processed powder compacts based on the electro-magneto-thermo-mechanical coupling is depicted in Fig. 14.17.1.

References

ABOUDI J, 2001. Micromechanical Analysis of Fully Coupled Electro-Magneto-Thermo-Elastic Multiphase Composites[J]. Smart Materials and Structures, 10(10): 867-877.

AGGARWAL M D, et al, 2010. Pyroelectric Materials for Uncooled Infrared Detectors: Processing, Properties, Applications, NASA/TM-2010-216373, Marshall Space Flight Center.

ARJUN A, et al, 2011. A Novel Approach to Recycle Energy Using Piezoelectric Crystals[J]. International Journal of Environmental Science and Development, 2(6): 488-492.

BENDIGERIL C, et al, 2011. Detailed Formulation and Programming Method for Piezoelectric Finite Element [J]. International Journal of Pure and Applied Sciences and Technology, 7(1): 1-21.

BERLINCOURT D, JAFFE H, 1958. Elastic and Piezoelectric Coefficients of Single-Crystal Barium Titanate [J].Physics Reviews, 111(1): 143-148.

BIENKOWSKI A, SZEWCZYK R, 2004. The Possibility of Utilizing the High Permeability Magnetic Materials in Construction of Magnetoelastic Stress and Force Sensors[J]. Sensors and Actuators, 113(3): 270-276.

BOESING M, et al, 2010. Vibration Synthesis for Electrical Machines Based on Force Response Superposition [J]. IEEE Transactions on Magnetics, 46(8): 2986-2989.

BOGACHEV, et al, 2011. An Iterative Routine for Macroscopic Modeling of Electromagnetic, Thermal, Mechanical Phenomena in Microwave Sintering[M]. AMPERE.

BOZORTH R M, 1993.Ferromagnetism[M]. Wiley-IEEE Press.

BRAVO-IMAZ I, et al, 2013. Magnetoelastic Viscosity Sensor for On-Line Status Assessment of Lubricant Oils, IEEE Transactions on Magnetics, 49(1): 113-116.

BRAVINA S, et al, 2006. Predicted and Realized Improved Performances of PZT-Films-Silicon Based Structures for Integrated Pyrosensorics[J]. Integrated Ferroelectrics, 80(1): 3-9.

BROWN K, 2004. Metal Oxide Varistor Degradation Fleviton[M]. IAEI Magazine.

BUCHANAN R C, 2004.Ceramic Materials for Electronics[M]. 3rd Edition, Marcel Dekker, Inc, Cincinnati, Ohio.

BYER R L, ROUNDY C B, 1972. Pyroelectric Coefficient Direct Measurement Technique and Application to a NSEC Response Time Detector[J]. IEEE Ferroelectrics, 19(2): 333-338.

CAFISO S, et al, 2013. Experimental Analysis for Piezoelectric Transducers Applications into Roads Pavements [J].Advanced Materials Research, 684: 253-257.

CALISKAN V, et al, 2003. Analysis of Three-Phase Rectifiers with Constant-Voltage Loads [J]. IEEE Transactions on Circuits and Systems I: Fundamental Theory and Applications, 50(9): 1220-1226.

CHANG D, KANG S, YOON Y, 1998. Response of Thin Film Pyroelectric Sensors[J]. IEEE Transactions on Ultrasonics, Ferroelectrics, Frequency Control, 45(5): 213-216.

CHEN J, et al, 2011. Validation and Verification of Life Prediction Technology for Electromechanical Products [J]. Applied Mechanics and Materials, 58-60: 1690-1695.

CHEN, X, MAI, Y, 2012. Fracture Mechanics of Electromagnetic Materials-Nonlinear Field Theory and Applications[M]. Imperial College Press (World Scientific).

CHU Y, LEE R, PSYK V, et al, 2012. Determination of the Flow Curve at High Strain Rates Using Electromagnetic Punch Stretching[J]. Journal of Materials Processing Technology, 212(6): 1314-1323.

CORREA M A, et al, 2010. Tailoring the Magneto-Impedance Effect of NiFe/Ag Multilayer[J]. Journal of Physics, D Applied Physics, 43(29): 295004.

DAVIM J P, 2011.Mechatronics[M]. John Wiley & Sons, NYC.

DAVIS G T, 1993. Piezoelectric and Pyroelectric Polymers[M]. in Polymers for Electronic and Photonic Applications, Edited by C. P. Wong, Academic Press, Boston, MA: 435.

DEAN C, et al, 1999. System Dynamics: Modeling and Simulation of Mechatronic Systems [M]. Wiley-Interscience, NYC.

DEVONSHIRE A F, 1949. XCVI. Theory of Barium Titanate-Part Ⅰ [J]. Journal of The London, Edinburgh, Dublin Philosophical Magazine and Journal of Science, Series 7: 40(309).

DEPARTMENT of DEFENSE TEST STANDARD, 2010. Destructive Physical Analysis for Electronic, Electromagnetic, Electromechanical Parts, MIL-STD-l580B w/change 2, DOD, USA.

DONAHUE M J, PORTER D G, 2002. Analysis of Switching in Uniformly Magnetized Bodies [J]. IEEE Transactions on Magnetics, 38 (5): 2468-2470.

DONG S, et al, 2009. Tunable Features of Magnetoelectric Transformers [J]. IEEE Transactions on Ultrasonics, Ferroelectrics, Frequency Control, 56(6): 1124-1127.

EDWARDS M E, et al, 2012. Pyroelectric Properties of PVDF: MWCNT Nanocomposite Film for Uncooled Infrared Detectors[J]. Materials Sciences and Applications, 3(12): 851-855.

ERHART J, 2013. Experiments to Demonstrate Piezoelectric and Pyroelectric Effects[J]. *Physics Education*, 48(4): 438.

FERNANDEZ E, et al, 2010. Differences in the Magneto-Impedance of FeNi/Cu/FeNi Multilayers with Open and Closed Magnetic Path[J].IEEE Transactions on Magnetics, 46(2): 658-661.

FERRARA A, et al, 2015. Physics-Based Stability Analysis of MOS Transistors[J]. Solid-State Electronics, 113: 28-34.

FERNÁNDEZ E, et al, 2012. High Performance Magneto-impedance in FeNi/Ti Nanostructured Multilayers with Opened Magnetic Flux[J]. Journal of Nanoscience and Nanotechnology, 12(9): 7496-7500.

FIEBIG M, 2005. Revival of the Magnetoelectric Effect[J]. Journal of Physics, D, 38: R123.

FONTEYN K, et al, 2010. FEM for Directly Coupled Magneto-Mechanical Phenomena in Electrical Machines [J]. IEEE Transactions on Magnetics, 46(8): 2923-2926.

FURLANI E P, 2001.Permanent Magnet and Electromechanical Devices: Materials, Analysis and Applications [M]. Academic Press, San Diego, CA.

FURUKAWA T, 1989. Ferroelectric Properties of Vinylidene Fluoride Copolymers[J]. Phase Transitions, 18: 143-211.

GARCIA-ARRIBAS A, et al, 2013. Tailoring the Magnetic Anisotropy of Thin Film Permalloy Microstrips by Combined Shape and Induced Anisotropies[J]. European Physics Journal B, 86(4): 1-7.

GARCIA-ARRIBAS A, et al, 1992. Anisotropy Field Distribution in Amorphous Ferromagnetic Alloys from

Second Harmonic Response[J]. Journal of Applied Physics, 71(6): 3047-3049.

GARDNER D S, et al, 2009. Review of On-Chip Inductor Structures with Magnetic Films [J]. IEEE Transactions on Magnetics, 45: 4760-4766.

GAUTSCHI G H, 2002. Piezoelectric Sensorics Force, Strain, Pressure, Acceleration and Acoustic Emission Sensors Materials and Amplifiers[M]. Emerald Group Pubilshing Limited, Springer.

GERHARD R, 2016. Piezoelectricity and Electrostriction [M]. Part of the series: Polymers and Polymeric Composites, 489-507.

GRANT I S, PHILLIPS W R, 2008. Electromagnetism[M]. 2nd Edition, John Wiley & Sons, NY.

GRIFFITHS D J, 2007. Introduction to Electrodynamics [M]. 3rd Edition, Pearson Education, Dorling Kindersley.

GRÖSSINGERL R, et al, 2013. Materials with High Magnetostriction [J]. International Symposium on Advanced Materials (ISAM 2013).

GUGGILLA P, EDWARDS M, 2016. Dielectric, Conductance and Pyroelectric Characterization of MWCNT: PVDF Nanocomposite: Thin Films for Multiple Device Applications[J]. International Journal of Composite Materials,6(5): 145-151.

GUTIÉRREZ J, et al, 2013. Improving the Magnetoelectric Response of Laminates Containing High Temperature Piezopolymers[J]. IEEE Transactions on Magnetics, 49(1): 42-45.

HAMMES P, REGTIEN P, 1995. Thermal and Electrical Behavior of PVDF Infrared Matrix Sensor-Pyroelectric Sensor[J]. Ferroelectrics, 163: 15-28.

HANA P, BURIANOVA L B, PANOS S, 2004. The Dynamic Method of Determination of the Piezoelectric Hydrostatic Coefficients[J]. Sensors and Actuators A, 110(1-3): 318-322.

HASSISON J, OUNAILES Z, 1999. Piezoelectric Polymers[J]. CASE Report No, 2001-43, NASA/CR-2001-211422 I, USA.

HATTORI T, TAKAHASHI Y, IIJIMA M, et al, 1996. Piezoelectric and Ferroelectric Properties of Polyurea-5 Thin Films Prepared by Vapor Deposition Polymerization[J]. Journal of Applied Physics, 79(3): 1713-1721.

HAYES P R, et al, 2008. Electromagnetic Interference Risk Analysis[J]. IEEE Engineering in Medicine and Biology Magazine, 27(6): 39-41.

IKEDA T, 1996. Fundamentals of Piezoelectricity[M]. Oxford University Press, Oxford, UK.

JAESANG L, JAMES G, BOYD I V, et al, 2005. Effective Properties of Three-Phase Electro-Magnetoelastic

Composites[J]. International Journal of Engineering Science, 43(10): 790-825.

JAIME M, et al, 2017. Piezomagnetism and Magnetoelastic Memory in Uranium Dioxide [J]. Nature Communications, 8(1): 99.

JAIN M K, GRIMES C A, 2001. A Wireless Magnetoelastic Micro-Sensor Array for Simultaneous Measurements of Temperature and Pressure[J]. Magnetics IEEE Transactions on, 37(4): 2022-2024.

JAMES R D, WUTTIG M, 1998. Magnetostriction of Martensite[J]. Philosophical Magazine, A, 77(5): 1273-1299.

JIANG X, PAN E, 2014. Exact Solution of the 2D Polynomial Inclusion Problem in Anisotropic Magnetoelectroelastic Full-, Half-, Bilateral-Planes[J]. International Journal of Solids and Structures, 41 (16-17): 4361-4382.

JIANG X, SNOOK K, HACKENBERGER W S, 2007. Single Crystal Piezoelectric Composites for Advanced NDE Ultrasound[J]. Proc Spie 6531.

JIN J, et al, 2011. Multiferroic Polymer Composites with Greatly Enhanced Magnetoelectric Effect under a Low Magnetic Bias[J]. Advanced Materials, 23(33): 3853-3858.

JIN J M, 2014.The Finite Element Method in Electromagnetics[M]. 3rd Edition, Wiley, NY.

JORDAN T L, QUNAIES Z, TURNER T L, 1997. Complex Piezoelectric Coefficients of PZT Ceramics: Method for Direct Measurement of d_{33}, Materials Research Society Symposia Proceedings, 459(1): 231.

KARNOPP D C, MARGOLIS D L, ROSENBERG R C, 2006.System Dynamics: Modeling and Simulation of Mechatronic Systems[M]. 4th Edition, John Wiley & Sons, NYC.

KAWAI H, 1969. Piezoelectricity of Poly(vinylidene fluoride)[J]. Japanese Journal of Applied Physics, 8: 975-976.

KING-SMITH R D, VANDERBILT D, 1993. Theory of Polarization of Crystalline Solids[J]. Physic Review B Condensed Matter, 47(3): 1651.

KIM J Y, LI Z, BALTAZAR A, 2012. Pyroelectric and Pyromagnetic Coefficients of Functionally Graded Multilayered Multiferroic Composites[J]. Acta Mechanica, 223(4): 849-860.

KITTEL C, 2005.Introduction to Solid State Physics[M]. 8th Edition, Wiley.

KONDAIAH P, et al, 2013. Pyroelectric and Pyromagnetic Effects on Behavior of Magneto-Electro-Elastic Plate,Coupled Systems Mechanics, 2(1): 1-22.

KONOWROCKI R, et al, 2016. An Influence of the Stepping Motor Control and Friction Models on Precise Positioning of the Complex Mechanical System[J]. Mechanical Systems and Signal Processing, 70(MAR): 397-413.

KOUCHACHVILI L, IKURA M, 2007. Pyroelectric Conversion-Effects of P(VDF-TrFE) Preconditioning on Power Conversion[J]. Journal of Electrostatics, 65(3): 182.

LABARBERA M, 1994. Poisson's Ratio of a Crossed Fiber S: the Skin of Aquatic Salamanders[J]. Journal of Zoology, 232: 231-252.

LANG S B, 2005. Pyroelectricity: From Ancient Curiosity to Modern Imaging Tool[J]. Physics Today, 58(8): 31-36.

LANG S B, DAS-GUPTA D K, 2000. Pyroelectricity: Fundamentals and Applications[J]. Ferroelectrics Review, 2(4): 217-354.

LEE F Y, NAVID A, PILON L, 2012. Pyroelectric Waste Heat Energy Harvesting Using Heat Conduction, Applied Thermal Engineering, 37(5): 30-37.

LEE H J, SARAVANOS D A, 1997. The Effect of Temperature Dependent Material Nonlinearities on the Response of Piezoelectric Composite Plates, NASA/TM-97-206216.

LI J Y, et al, 2005. Domain Switching in Polycrystalline Ferroelectric Ceramics[J]. Nature Materials, 4(10): 776-781.

LEE S C, 1991. Poisson's Ratio in Skin[J]. Bio-Medical Materials and Engineering, 1(1): 19.

LIANG L, et al, 2012. Pressure and Electric Field Effects on Piezoelectric Responses of $KNbO_3$[J]. Journal of Applied Physics, 112(6): 193.

LIN R, et al, 2010. End-Winding Vibrations Caused by Steady-State Magnetic Forces in an Induction Machine [J]. IEEE Transactions on Magnetics, 46(7): 2665-2674.

LUO F, YE H, 2004. Advanced DC/DC Converters[J]. CRC Press.

LYNCH C S, 1993. Polyvinylidene Fluoride (PVDF) Elastic, Piezoelectric, Pyroelectric, Dielectric Coefficients and Their Non-linearities[J]. Journal of Ferroelectrics, 150(1): 331-342.

MAEDA H, FUKADA E, 2010. Effect of Water on Piezoelectric Dielectric and Elastic Properties of Bone[J]. Biopolymers, 21(10): 2055-2068.

MAJID W H A, 1994. Pyroelectric Activity in Cyclic and Linear Polysiloxane Langmuir-Blodgett Films[J]. University of Sheffield, UK.

MALUF N, 2000. An Introduction to Microelectromechanical Systems Engineering[J]. Artech House, Boston, MA.

MANE P, et al, 2011. Cyclic Energy Harvesting from Pyroelectric Materials[J]. IEEE Transactions on Ultrasonics, Ferroelectrics, Frequency Control, 58(1): 10-17.

MARTIN G E, 1964. Vibrations of Coaxially Segmented Longitudinally Polarized Ferroelectric Tubes[J]. JASA, 36(8): 1496-1506.

MARTINEZ J, et al, 2016. A 2D Magnetic and 3D Mechanical Coupled Finite Element Model for the Study of the Dynamic Vibrations in the Stator of Induction Motors[J]. Mechanical Systems and Signal Processing, 66/67: 640-656.

MAUGIN G A, et al, 1992. Theory of Elastic Inhomogeneities in Electromagnetic Materials[J]. International Journal of Engineering Science, 30(10): 1441-1449.

MCKEOWN S A, 1999. Mechanical Analysis of Electronic Packaging Systems[M]. Marcel Dekker, NYC, NY.

MICLEA C, et al, 2007. Effect of Temperature on The Main Piezoelectric Parameters of a Soft PZT Ceramic [J]. Romanian Journal of Information Science and Technology, 10(3): 243-250.

MILLITHALER P, et al, 2015. Structural Dynamics of Electric Machine Stators: Modeling Guidelines and Identification of Three-Dimensional Equivalent Material Properties for Multi-Layered Orthotropic Laminates [J]. Journal of Sound and Vibration, 348: 185-205.

MISCHENKO A S, ZHANG Q, SCOTT J F, et al, 2006. Giant Electrocaloric Effect in Thin-Film $PbZr_{0.95}Ti_{0.05}O_3$[J]. Science, 311(5765): 1270-1271.

MOGENIER G, et al, 2010. Identification of Lamination Stack Properties: Application to High-Speed Induction Motors[J]. IEEE Transactions on Industrial Electronics, 57(1): 281-287.

MOROZOVSKA A N, et al, 2004. Semiconductor Physics[J]. Quantum Electronics & Optoelectronics, 7: 251.

MOUBARAK P, et al, 2012. A Self-Calibrating Mathematical Model for the Direct Piezoelectric Effect of a New MEMS Tilt Sensor[J]. IEEE Sensors Journal, 12(5): 1033-1042.

MURALT P, 2001. Micromachined Infrared Detectors Based on Pyroelectric Thin Films[J]. Report on Progress in Physics, 64(10): 1339-1388.

NAN C, et al, 2008. Multiferroic Magnetoelectric Composites: Historical Perspective, Status, and Future Directions[J]. Journal of Applied Physics, 103: 031101.

NARANJO B, GIMZEWSKI J K, PUTTERMAN S, 2005. Observation of Nuclear Fusion Driven by a Pyroelectric Crystal[J]. Nature, 434 (7037): 1115-1117.

NEWNHAM R E, et al, 1978. Connectivity and Piezoelectric-pyroelectric Composites[J]. Materials Research Bulletin, 13(5):525-536.

NICHOLLS D, 2007. An Introduction to the RIAC 217Plus Component Failure Rate Models[J]. The Journal of The Reliability Information Analysis Center, 1st Quarter, 2007.

NUTARO J J, 2010. Building Software for Simulation: Theory and Algorithms, with Applications in C^{++}[M].

John Wiley & Sons, NYC.

NYE J F, 1985. Physical Properties of Crystals: Their Representation by Tensors and Matrices[M]. Oxford University Press, Oxford, U K.

ODEGARD G M, 2004. Constitutive Modeling of Piezoelectric Polymer Composites[J]. Acta Materialia, 52 (18): 5315-5330.

OMOTE K, OHIGASHI H, KOGA K, 1997. Temperature Dependence of Elastic, Dielectric and Piezoelectric Properties of "Single Crystalline" Films of Vinylidene Fluoride Trifluoroethylene Copolymer[J]. Journal of Applied Physics, 81(6): 2760.

OOTAO Y, ISHIHARA M, 2011. Exact Solution of Transient Thermal Stress Problem of the Multilayered Magneto-Electro-Thermoelastic Hallow Cylinder[J]. Journal of Solid Mechanics and Materials Engineering, 5(2): 90-103.

OR Y T, et al, 2003. Modeling of Poling, Piezoelectric and Pyroelectric Properties of Ferroelectric 0-3 Composites[J]. Journal of Applied Physics, 94(5): 3319-3325.

PRIYA S, 2010. Criterion for Material Selection in Design of Bulk Piezoelectric Energy Harvesters [J]. Ultrasonics Ferroelectrics and Frequency Control IEEE Transactions on, 57(12): 2610-2612.

SAITO Y, et al, 2004. Lead-Free Piezoceramics[J]. Nature, Nature Publishing Group, 432(7013): 81-87.

SAITO A, et al, 2016. Equivalent Orthotropic Elastic Moduli Identification Method for Laminated Electrical Steel Sheets[J]. Mechanical Systems and Signal Processing, 72-73(May): 607-628.

SAKKA M, et al, 2011. DC/DC Converters for Electric Vehicles, Electric Vehicles-Modeling and Simulations, Editor: Seref Soylu, INTECH.

SALAHUN E, et al, 2002. Correlation between Magnetic Properties of Layered Ferromagnetic/Dielectric Material and Tunable Microwave Device Applications[J]. Journal of Applied Physics, 91(8): 5449-5455.

SAY M G, 1984. Alternating Currents[M]. 5th Edition, Halsted Press.

SCHMIDT R M, et al, 2014. The Design of High Performance Mechatronics[M]. 2nd Edition, IOS Press.

SEBALD G, GUYOMAR D, AGBOSSOU A, 2011. On Thermoelectric and Pyroelectric Energy Harvesting, Smart Materials and Structures, 18(12): 125006(1-7).

SHABANA Y M, RISTINMAA M, 2011. Micromechanical Modeling of Smart Composites Considering Debonding of Reinforcements[J]. International Journal of Solids and Structures, 48(22-23): 3209-3216.

SHERRIT S, et al, 2000. Analysis of the Impedance Resonance of Piezoelectric Stacks[C]. IEEE Ultrasonics Symposium (Cat. No. OOCH 37121), San Juan, Puerto Rico.

SHKEL Y M, 2007. Electrostriction: Material Parameters and Stress/Strain Constitutive Relations [J]. Philosophical Magazine, 87(11): 1743-1767.

SHKEL Y M, KLINGENBERG D J, 1996. Material Parameters for Electrostriction[J]. Journal of Applied Physics, 80(8): 4566-4572.

SHINDO Y, 2003.Mechanics of Electromagnetic Material Systems and Structures[M]. WIT Press Computational Mechanics. Incorporated.

SUNAR M, AL-GARNI A Z, ALI M H, et al, 2002. Finite Element Modeling of Thermopiezomagnetic Smart Structures[J]. AIAA Journal, 40: 1846-1851.

SZEWCZYK R, 2006. Modeling of the Magnetic and Magnetostrictive Properties of High Permeability Mn-Zn Ferrites[J]. Journal of Physics-PRAMANA, 67(6): 1165.

SZOLC T, et al, 2013. An Investigation of the Dynamic Electromechanical Coupling Effects in Machine Drive Systems Driven by Asynchronous Motors[J]. Mechanical Systems and Signal Processing, 49: 118-134.

TAKASE Y, LEE J W, SCHEINBEIM J I, et al, 1991. High-Temperature Characteristics of Nylon-11 and Nylon-7 Piezoelectrics[J]. Macromolecules, 24: 6644-6652.

TASAKA S, TOYAMA T, INAGAKI N, 1994. Ferro-and Pyroelectricity in Amorphous Polyphenylethernitrile [J]. Japanese Journal of Applied Physics, 33(11A): 5838-5844.

VAN D G M, et al, 2012. Material Parameters for the Structural Dynamic Simulation of Electrical Machines [C]. XXth International Conference on Electrical Machines (ICEM): 2994-3000.

VILLACORTA B, HUBING T, 2014. Analysis of the Electromagnetic Shielding Mechanisms of Plane Waves in Generally Lossy Materials[J]. Technical Report: CVEL-13-044, Clemson University.

WANG H, et al, 2013. Toward Reliable Power Electronics-Challenges, Design Tools and Opportunities[J]. IEEE Industrial Electronics Magazine, 7(2):17-26.

WATT J P, 1987. Polyxstal: a FORTRAN Program to Calculate Average Elastic Properties of Minerals from Single-Crystal Elasticity Data[J]. Computers & Geosciences, 13(5): 441-462.

WATTIAUX D, et al, 2006. Prediction of the Dynamic Behavior of Electromagnetic Relays Submitted to Mechanical Shocks[C]. ASME 8th Biennial Conference on Engineering Systems Design and Analysis, Torino, Italy.

WEN S, CHUNG D, 2003. Pyroelectric Behavior of Cement-Based Materials [J]. Cement and Concrete Research, 33(10): 1675-1679.

WU R, et al, 2013. Overview of Catastrophic Failures of Freewheeling Diodes in Power Electronic Circuits[J]. Microelectronic Reliability, 53(9-11): 1788-1792.

KU Y. 1991.Ferroelectric Materials and Their Applications[J]. Japanese Journal of Applied Physics, 56(10s): QT001-QT001.

YAMADA T, et al, 1982. Primary and Secondary Pyroelectric Effects in Ferroelectric 0-3 Composites[J]. Journal of Applied Physics, 53 (4): 4328-4332.

YANG J S, et al, 2003. Piezoelectric and Pyroelectric Properties of Roti, TiO_3 Films for Micro-Sensors and Actuators[J]. Integrated Ferroelectrics, 54(1): 515-525.

YANG J S, MAUGIN G A, 2003.Mechanics of Electromagnetic Solids[M], 2003 Edition, Springer (Kluwer Academic Publishers).

YANG J S, MAUGIN G A, 2000.Mechanics of Electromagnetic Materials and Structures[M]. Proceedings of the Symposium on the Mechanics of Electromagnetic Materials and Structures of the ASME Mechanics and Materials Conference.

YANG S, et al, 2011. An Industry-Based Survey of Reliability in Power Electronic Converters[J]. IEEE Transaction on Industry Applications, 47(3): 1441-1451.

YANG Y, et al, 2012. Pyroelectric Nanogenerators for Harvesting Thermoelectric Energy[J]. NANO Letters, 12(6): 2833-2838.

YOUNG J A, HINKLEY J A, 1999. Molecular Modeling of the Poling of Piezoelectric Polyimides[J]. Polymer, 40(10): 2787-2795.

ZAKHAROV D, et al, 2013. Combined Pyroelectric, Piezoelectric and Shape Memory Effects for Thermal Energy Harvesting[J]. Journal of Physics: Conference Series. 476(1): 012021.

ZHANG Q M, et al, 2011. Solar Micro-Energy Harvesting with Pyroelectric Effect and Wind Flow[J]. Sensors and Actuators A, 168(3): 335-342.

ZHANG Q M, et al, 1998. Giant Electrostriction and Relaxor Ferroelectric Behavior in Electron-Irradiated Poly (vinylidene fluoride-trifluoroethylene) Copolymer[J]. Science, 280(5372): 2101-2104.

ZHAO G, CHEN Y, LI D, et al, 2014. Failure Mechanism Analysis of Electromagnetic Relay under Mechanical Impact[J]. Applied Mechanics and Materials, 473: 39-45.

ZHAO M, et al, 2004. Piezoelectric Characterization of Individual Zinc Oxide Nanobelt Probed by Piezoresponse Force Microscope[J]. Nano Letters, 4(4): 587-590.

ZIRKL M, et al, 2011. An All-Printed Ferroelectric Active Matrix Sensor Network Based on Only Five Functional Materials Forming a Touchless Control Interface[J]. Advanced Materials, 23(18): 2069-2074.

ZU H F, et al, 2014. Properties of Single Crystal Piezoelectric $Ca_3TaGa_3Si_2O_{14}$ and $YCa_4O(BO_3)_3$ Resonators at High-Temperature and Vacuum Conditions[J]. Sensors and Actuators A, 216(3): 167-175.

Table 14.5.1   Electro-Magneto-Thermo-Mechanical Coupling Properties of Crystals [Aggarwal et al.] [Byer & Roundy] [efunda] [Edwards et al.] [Hooker] [Jaesang et al.] [Lang] [Lee & Saravanos] [Majid] [Muralt] [Newnham] [Park & Shrout] [Piezo Systems, Inc] [Wada et al.] [Xu] [Yang et al.].

Material	$T/°C$	$E_{ij}/c_{ij}/s_{ij}$	ϵ_r	d_{ij}	e_{ij}	g_{ij}	h_{ij}	p_i/κ_i	μ_{ij}	q_{ij}	m_{ij}
AlN	25	$c_{11}=390$	$\epsilon_{33}=10$	$d_{31}=-1.5$	$e_{15}=-0.4$	—	—	—	—	—	—
		$c_{22}=390$	—	—	$e_{31}=-0.6$	—	—	—	—	—	—
		$c_{33}=410$	—	—	$e_{33}=1.7$	—	—	—	—	—	—
		$c_{44}=122$	—	—	—	—	—	—	—	—	—
		$c_{55}=122$	—	—	—	—	—	—	—	—	—
		$c_{66}=126$	—	—	—	—	—	—	—	—	—
		$c_{12}=149$	—	—	—	—	—	—	—	—	—
		$c_{13}=999$	—	—	—	—	—	—	—	—	—
		$c_{23}=99$	—	—	—	—	—	—	—	—	—
		others $=0$	—	—	—	—	—	—	—	—	—
	2000	T_c	—	—	—	—	—	—	—	—	—
	25	$c_{33}=373$	$\epsilon_{33}=10.5$	$d_{31}=-1.5$	$e_{31}=-0.6$	—	—	—	—	—	—
		$c_{13}=108$	—	—	$e_{33}=1.46$	—	—	—	—	—	—
AlPO$_4$−α (α-Berlinite)	25	—	—	—	—	—	—	—	—	—	—

continued

Material	$T/^\circ C$	$E_{ij}/c_{ij}/s_{ij}$	ϵ_r	d_{ij}	e_{ij}	g_{ij}	h_{ij}	p_i/κ_i	μ_{ij}	q_{ij}	m_{ij}
Ba$_2$NaNb$_5$O$_{15}$ (Orthorhombic 2 mm) [efunda]	25	$s_{11}=5.3$	$\epsilon_{11}=240$	$d_{15}=42$	—	—	—	$p_3=-100$	—	—	—
		$s_{22}=5.1$	$\epsilon_{22}=250$	$d_{24}=52$	—	—	—	—	—	—	—
		$s_{33}=8.1$	$\epsilon_{33}=50$	$d_{31}=-7$	—	—	—	—	—	—	—
		$s_{44}=15.4$	others $=0$	$d_{32}=-6$	—	—	—	—	—	—	—
		$s_{55}=15$	—	$d_{33}=37$	—	—	—	—	—	—	—
		$s_{66}=13$	—	others $=0$	—	—	—	—	—	—	—
		$s_{12}=-2$	—	—	—	—	—	—	—	—	—
		$s_{13}=-1.2$	—	—	—	—	—	—	—	—	—
		$s_{23}=-1.3$	—	—	—	—	—	—	—	—	—
		others $=0$	—	others $=0$	—	—	—	—	—	—	—
BaTiO$_3$ (Tetragonal 4 mm) [efunda]	25	$s_{11}=8$	$\epsilon_{11}=2600$	$d_{15}=392$	—	—	—	$p_3=-200$	$\mu_{11}=5$	—	—
		$s_{22}=8$	$\epsilon_{22}=2600$	$d_{24}=392$	—	—	—	—	$\mu_{33}=10$	—	—
		$s_{33}=14$	$\epsilon_{33}=110$	$d_{31}=-34$	—	—	—	—	others $=0$	—	—
		$s_{44}=16.4$	others $=0$	$d_{32}=-34$	—	—	—	—	—	—	—
		$s_{55}=16.4$	—	$d_{33}=90$	—	—	—	—	—	—	—
		$s_{66}=8$	—	others $=0$	—	—	—	—	—	—	—
		others $=0$	—	—	—	—	—	—	—	—	—
	130	T_c	—	—		—	—	—	—	—	—

BaTiO₃ (Poled uniaxially) [efunda]	25	$s_{11}=9.1$	$\epsilon_{11}=1450$	$d_{15}=260$	—	—	—	—	—	$\mu_{11}=5$	—	—
		$s_{22}=9.1$	$\epsilon_{22}=1450$	$d_{24}=260$	—	—	—	—	—	$\mu_{33}=10$	—	—
		$s_{33}=9.5$	$\epsilon_{33}=1700$	$d_{31}=-78$	—	—	—	—	—	others = 0	—	—
		$s_{44}=23$	others = 0	$d_{32}=-78$	—	—	—	—	—	—	—	—
		$s_{55}=23$	—	$d_{33}=190$	—	—	—	—	—	—	—	—
		$s_{66}=24$	—	$k_{15}=0.5$	—	—	—	—	—	—	—	—
		others = 0	—	$k_{31}=0.21$	—	—	—	—	—	—	—	—
		—	—	others = 0	—	—	—	—	—	—	—	—
	130	T_{c}	—	—	—	—	all = 0	all = 0	all = 0	—	—	—
BaTiO₃ (Piezoelectric lamina)	25	$c_{11}=166$	$\epsilon_{11}=1265$	—	$e_{15}=11.6$	—	—	—	$\mu_{11}=5$	—	—	—
		$c_{22}=166$	$\epsilon_{22}=1265$	—	$e_{31}=-4.4$	—	—	—	$\mu_{22}=5$	—	—	—
		$c_{33}=162$	$\epsilon_{33}=1423$	—	$e_{33}=18.6$	—	—	—	$\mu_{33}=10$	—	—	—
		$c_{44}=43$	others = 0	—	others = 0	—	—	—	others = 0	—	—	—
		$c_{55}=43$	—	—	—	—	—	—	—	—	—	—
		$c_{66}=45$	—	—	—	—	—	—	—	—	—	—
		$c_{12}=77$	—	—	—	—	—	—	—	—	—	—
		$c_{13}=78$	—	—	—	—	—	—	—	—	—	—
		$c_{13}=78$	—	—	—	—	—	—	—	—	—	—
		others = 0	—	—	—	—	—	—	—	—	—	—
	130	T_{c}	—	—	—	—	—	—	—	—	—	—

continued

Material	$T/°C$	$E_{ij}/c_{ij}/s_{ij}$	ϵ_r	d_{ij}	e_{ij}	g_{ij}	h_{ij}	p_i/κ_i	μ_{ij}	q_{ij}	m_{ij}
$BiFeO_3$	25	—	—	—	—	—	—	—	—	—	—
$Bi_4Ti_3O_{12}$	25	—	—	—	—	—	—	—	—	—	—
$Bi_2VO_{5.5}$ (Bulky Ceramic)	25	—	—	—	—	—	—	$p_3 = -900$	—	—	—
C_dS (Cubic 43 m)	25	$s_{11} = 20.7$ $s_{22} = 20.7$ $s_{33} = 17$ $s_{44} = 66.5$ $s_{55} = 66.5$ $s_{66} = 61.4$ $s_{12} = -10$ $s_{13} = -5.8$ symmetric others $= 0$	$\epsilon_{11} = 9.4$ $\epsilon_{22} = 9.4$ $\epsilon_{33} = 10.3$ others $= 0$	$d_{15} = -14$ $d_{24} = -14$ $d_{31} = -5$ $d_{32} = -5$ $d_{33} = 10.3$ others $= 0$	—	—	—	$p_3 = -4.0$	—	—	—
$CdSe$	25	—	—	—	—	—	—	$p_3 = -3.5$	—	—	—
$(CH_2CF_2)_n$	25	—	—	—	—	—	—	$p_3 = -27$	—	—	—

Material	Temp	Elastic (c or s)	ϵ	d				μ	q	
CoFe$_2$O$_4$ (Piezomagnetic lamina [Aboudi 2001])	25	$c_{11}=286$	$\epsilon_{11}=9$	all $=0$	—	—	—	$\mu_{11}=-590$	$q_{15}=560$	all $=0$
		$c_{22}=286$	$\epsilon_{22}=9$	—	—	—	—	$\mu_{22}=157$	$q_{24}=560$	—
		$c_{33}=270$	$\epsilon_{33}=10.5$	—	—	—	—	$\mu_{33}=157$	$q_{31}=580$	—
		$c_{44}=45$	others $=0$	—	—	—	—	others $=0$	$q_{32}=580$	—
		$c_{55}=45$	—	—	—	—	—	—	$q_{33}=700$	—
		$c_{66}=57$	—	—	—	—	—	—	others $=0$	—
		$c_{12}=173$	—	—	—	—	—	—	—	—
		$c_{13}=170$	—	—	—	—	—	—	—	—
		$c_{23}=170$	—	—	—	—	—	—	—	—
		Symmetric	—	—	—	—	—	—	—	—
		others $=0$	—	—	—	—	—	—	—	—
Cymbal Composite	25	—	—	$d_{33}=15000$	—	—	—	—	—	—
		—	—	$d_{14}=2.6$	—	—	—	—	—	—
		—	—	$d_{25}=2.6$	—	—	—	—	—	—
		—	—	$d_{36}=2.6$	—	—	—	—	—	—
		—	—	others $=0$	—	—	—	—	—	—
Gallium Arsenide (Cubic 43 m)	25	$s_{11}=12.6$	$\epsilon_{11}=4.5$	—	—	—	—	—	—	—
		$s_{22}=12.6$	$\epsilon_{22}=4.5$	—	—	—	—	—	—	—
		$s_{33}=12.6$	$\epsilon_{33}=4.7$	—	—	—	—	—	—	—
		$s_{44}=18.6$	others $=0$	—	—	—	—	—	—	—
		$s_{55}=18.6$	—	—	—	—	—	—	—	—
		$s_{66}=18.6$	—	—	—	—	—	—	—	—
		$s_{12}=-4.2$	—	—	—	—	—	—	—	—
		$s_{13}=-4.2$	—	—	—	—	—	—	—	—
		symmetric	—	—	—	—	—	—	—	—
		others $=0$	—	—	—	—	—	—	—	—
	550	T_c	—	—	—	—	—	—	—	—

continued

Material	$T/^\circ\mathrm{C}$	$E_{ij}/c_{ij}/s_{ij}$	ϵ_r	d_{ij}	e_{ij}	g_{ij}	h_{ij}	p_i/κ_i	μ_{ij}	q_{ij}	m_{ij}
GaN	25	$c_{11}=390$	$\epsilon_{33}=9.2$	—	$e_{15}=-0.3$	—	—	$p_3=-70$	—	—	—
		$c_{22}=390$	—	—	$e_{14}=0.4$	—	—	—	—	—	—
		$c_{33}=400$	—	—	$e_{31}=-0.5$	—	—	—	—	—	—
		$c_{44}=105$	—	—	$e_{33}=0.73$	—	—	—	—	—	—
		$c_{55}=105$	—	—	others$=0$	—	—	—	—	—	—
		$c_{66}=105$	—	—	—	—	—	—	—	—	—
		$c_{12}=145$	—	—	—	—	—	—	—	—	—
		$c_{13}=145$	—	—	—	—	—	—	—	—	—
		$c_{23}=106$	—	—	—	—	—	—	—	—	—
		others$=0$	—	—	—	—	—	—	—	—	—
	2000	T_c	—	—	—	—	—	—	—	—	—
GaPO$_4$ (Gallium Orthophosphate)	25	—	—	—	—	—	—	—	—	—	—
InN	25	$c_{11}=190$	$\epsilon_{33}=15.1$	—	$e_{31}=-0.5$	—	—	—	—	—	—
		$c_{22}=190$	—	—	$e_{33}=0.95$	—	—	—	—	—	—
		$c_{33}=180$	—	—	—	—	—	—	—	—	—
		$c_{44}=10$	—	—	—	—	—	—	—	—	—
		$c_{55}=10$	—	—	—	—	—	—	—	—	—

Material	T (°C)	Elastic / Compliance	ϵ	d	g	p
InN	-150	$c_{66} = 10$ $c_{12} = 104$ $c_{13} = 104$ $c_{23} = 100$ others $= 0$	—	—	—	—
KH_2PO_4 (Tetragonal 42 m)	25	$s_{11} = 18$ $s_{22} = 18$ $s_{33} = 20$ $s_{44} = 78$ $s_{55} = 78$ $s_{66} = 160$ others $= 0$	$\epsilon_{11} = 42$ $\epsilon_{22} = 42$ $\epsilon_{33} = 21$ others $= 0$	$d_{14} = 1.3$ $d_{25} = 1.3$ $d_{36} = 21$ others $= 0$	—	—
$KNaC_4H_4O_6 \cdot 4H_2O$ (Orthorhombic 222; R_o chelle Salt Potassium sodium tartrate; 1st discovered piezoelectric material)	25	$s_{11} = 52$ $s_{22} = 37$ $s_{33} = 36$ $s_{44} = 150$ $s_{55} = 350$ $s_{66} = 104$ $s_{12} = -16$	$\epsilon_{11} = 205$ $\epsilon_{22} = 10$ $\epsilon_{22} = 10$ others $= 0$	$d_{14} = 345$ $d_{25} = 54$ $d_{36} = 12$ others $= 0$	$g_{31} = -13.7$ $g_{33} = 16.6$	$p_3 = -238$

continued

Material	$T/°C$	$E_{ij}/c_{ij}/s_{ij}$	ϵ_r	d_{ij}	e_{ij}	g_{ij}	h_{ij}	p_i/κ_i	μ_{ij}	q_{ij}	m_{ij}
KNaC$_4$H$_4$O$_6$ · 4H$_2$O (Orthorhombic 222; R$_o$ chelle Salt Potassium sodium tartrate; 1st discovered piezoelectric material)		$s_{13}=-12$ others $=0$	—	—	—	—	—	—	—	—	—
	25	—	—	$d_{31}=52$	—	—	—	—	—	—	—
KNbO$_3$		—	—	$d_{33}=31$	—	—	—	—	—	—	—
		—	—	$k_{31}=31\%$	—	—	—	—	—	—	—
		—	—		—	—	—	—	—	—	—
La$_3$Ga$_{5.5}$Nb$_{0.5}$O$_{14}$ (Langanite)	25	—	—	—	—	—	—	—	—	—	—
La$_3$Ga$_5$SiO$_{14}$ (Langasite)	25	—	—	—	—	—	—	—	—	—	—
La$_3$Ga$_{5.5}$Ta$_{0.5}$O$_{14}$ (Langatite)	25	—	—	—	—	—	—	—	—	—	—
Li$_2$B$_4$O$_7$ (Lithium Tetraborate)	25	—	—	—	—	—	—	—	—	—	—
	25	$c_{11}=203$	$\epsilon_{11}=85$	$d_{15}=69$	$e_{15}=3.72$	—	—	—	$p_3=-83$	—	—
LiNbO$_3$ (Trigonal 3 m) [Peng & Cohe]		$c_{22}=203$	$\epsilon_{22}=85$	$d_{22}=21$	$e_{22}=2.4$	—	—	—	—	—	—
		$c_{33}=242$	$\epsilon_{33}=28.7$	$d_{31}=-1$	$e_{31}=-0.22$	—	—	—	—	—	—
		$c_{44}=60$	others $=0$	$d_{33}=6$	$e_{33}=1.33$	—	—	—	—	—	—

Material		Elastic / other constants			
LiNbO₃ (Trigonal 3 m) [Peng & Cohe]	$c_{55}=60$	$c_{66}=75$	$c_{12}=57.3$	$c_{13}=75.2$	$c_{14}=9$
	symmetric				
	T_c = 1142.3				
Li₂SO₄ · 2H₂O	25	$\epsilon_{33}=8$	$p_3=86.3$	others = 0	others = 0
	25	$c_{11}=233$	$\epsilon_{11}=54$	$d_{33}=8$	$p_3=-176$
		$c_{22}=103$	$\epsilon_{33}=43$		
LiTaO₃ (Lithium Tantalate)		$c_{33}=276$	$t_8<0.01$	others = 0	
	T_c = 603				
	T_m = 1 650				
Mg₃B₇O₁₃Cl	25				
	T_c = 265				
NaBi(TiO₃)₂	25				

continued

Material	$T/^\circ C$	$E_{ij}/c_{ij}/s_{ij}$	ϵ_r	d_{ij}	e_{ij}	g_{ij}	h_{ij}	p_i/κ_i	μ_{ij}	q_{ij}	m_{ij}
$NaNO_2$	25	—	$\epsilon_{11}=8$	—	—	—	—	$p_3=-120$	—	—	—
$(NH_2CH_2COOH)_3 \cdot$	25	—	—	—	—	—	—	—	—	—	—
H_2SO_4	49	T_c	—	—	—	—	—	—	—	—	—
	−125	T_c	—	—	—	—	—	—	—	—	—
$NH_4H_2PO_4$	25	$s_{11}=18$	$\epsilon_{11}=56$	$d_{14}=12$	—	—	—	—	—	—	—
		$s_{22}=18$	$\epsilon_{22}=56$	$d_{25}=12$	—	—	—	—	—	—	—
(Tetragonal 42 m)		$s_{33}=44$	$\epsilon_{33}=15.4$	$d_{36}=52$	—	—	—	—	—	—	—
		$s_{44}=116$	others $=0$	others $=0$	—	—	—	—	—	—	—
		$s_{55}=116$			—	—	—	—	—	—	—
		$s_{66}=166$			—	—	—	—	—	—	—
		others $=0$			—	—	—	—	—	—	—
	190	T_m	—	—	—	—	—	—	—	—	—
$Pb_5Ge_3O_{11}$	25	—	40	—	—	—	—	$p_3=-100$	—	—	—
		—	$t_\delta=0.0005$	—	—	—	—	—	—	—	—
$PbNb_2O_6$	25	—	$\varepsilon_h=225$	$d_h=67$	$d_h=34$	—	—	—	—	—	—
$PbTiO_3$	25	—	190	$d_{33}=84$	—	—	—	$p_3=-180$	—	—	—
	650	T_c	—	$t_\delta=0.01$	—	—	—	—	—	—	—
$Pb\left(Zn_{\frac{1}{3}}Nb_{\frac{2}{3}}\right)$	25	—	—	$d_{33}=250$	—	—	—	—	—	—	—
$O_3\text{-}PbTiO_3$		—	—	$k_{33}=0.9$	—	—	—	—	—	—	—

Material	Temperature	ε	d	g	p_3	Transition
$PbZr_{0.95}Ti_{0.05}O_3$	25	—	—	—	$p_3=-268$	—
PEO	25	8	all $=0$	—	all $=0$	—
PLZT (9/65/35)	25	—	$d_{31}=-265$	$g_{31}=-13.7$	—	—
PMN/25%PT (Ceramics)	25	—	$d_{33}=2100$	—	$p_3=-746$	—
PMN/25%PT[0 0 1]	25	—	$d_{33}=961$	—	$p_3=-1790$	—
PMN/25%PT[0 1 1]	25	—	$d_{33}=2500$	—	$p_3=-1187$	—
PMN/30%PT	25	—	$d_{33}=2800$	—	$p_3=-416$	T_c 150
PMN/33%PT[0 0 1]	25	—	$d_{33}=5820$	—	$p_3=-568$	—
PMN/33%PT[0 1 1]	25	—	$d_{33}=2940$	—	$p_3=-883$	—
PMN/33%PT[011]	-35	—	—	—	—	T_g

continued

Material	$T/°C$	$E_{ij}/c_{ij}/s_{ij}$	ϵ_r	d_{ij}	e_{ij}	g_{ij}	h_{ij}	p_i/κ_i	μ_{ij}	q_{ij}	m_{ij}
PVDF-β film（PVF$_2$） ［Bar-Cohen et al.］ ［Edwards et al.］ ［Elling et al.］ ［Furukawa］［Odegard］	25	$c_{11}=3.8$	$\epsilon_{11}=7.4$	$d_{15}=-23$	—	$g_{31}=216$	—	$p_3=-27$	—	—	—
		$c_{22}=3.2$	$\epsilon_{22}=9.3$	$d_{24}=-27$	—	$g_{33}=-330$	—	—	—	—	—
		$c_{33}=1.2$	$\epsilon_{33}=7.6$	$d_{31}=21$	—	—	—	—	—	—	—
		$c_{44}=0.7$	$\epsilon_h=13$	$d_{32}=2.3$	—	—	—	—	—	—	—
		$c_{55}=0.9$	others$=0$	$d_{33}=-30$	—	—	—	—	—	—	—
		$c_{66}=0.9$		$d_h=-6$	—	—	—	—	—	—	—
		$c_{12}=1.9$	—	$k_{31}=0.12$	—	—	—	—	—	—	—
		$c_{13}=1.0$	—	others$=0$	—	—	—	—	—	—	—
		$c_{23}=0.9$	—	—	—	—	—	—	—	—	—
		others$=0$	—	—	—	—	—	—	—	—	—
	165	—	—	$d_{31}=35$	—	—	—	$p_3=-45$	—	—	—
	175	T_m	—	—	—	—	—	—	—	—	—
PVDF film（9～50 μm） ［Edwards et al.］	35	—	$\epsilon_{33}=12.9$	—	—	—	—	$p_3=-1.2$	—	—	—
		—	$t_δ=0.036$	—	—	—	—	—	—	—	—
	45	—	$\epsilon_{33}=13.6$	—	—	—	—	$p_3=-4.4$	—	—	—
		—	$t_δ=0.057$	—	—	—	—	—	—	—	—

Material	Temp				$\epsilon_{33}=14.4$ $t_\delta=0.077$ ...			p_3		
PVDF film (9~50 μm) [Edwards et al.]	55	—	—	—	$\epsilon_{33}=14.4$ / $t_\delta=0.077$	—	—	$p_3=-21$	—	—
	65	—	—	—	$\epsilon_{33}=15.2$ / $t_\delta=0.105$	—	—	$p_3=-74$	—	—
	75	—	—	—	$\epsilon_{33}=16.2$ / $t_\delta=0.135$	—	—	$p_3=-283$	—	—
	35	—	—	—	$\epsilon_{33}=28.9$ / $t_\delta=0.47$	—	—	$p_3=-640$	—	—
	45	—	—	—	$\epsilon_{33}=35.6$ / $t_\delta=0.55$	—	—	$p_3=-991$	—	—
PVDF/MWCNT Film [Edwards et al.]	55	—	—	—	$\epsilon_{33}=44.3$ / $t_\delta=0.68$	—	—	$p_3=-1\,891$	—	—
	65	—	—	—	$\epsilon_{33}=57$ / $t_\delta=0.87$	—	—	$p_3=-3\,946$	—	—
	75	—	—	—	$\epsilon_{33}=74.7$ / $t_\delta=1.12$	—	—	$p_3=-9\,684$	—	—
60PVDF/40TrFE	25	—	—	$d_{33}=-20$	$\epsilon_{33}=10$	—	—	—	$p_3=-50$	—
LB film (10 nm) [Majid]		—	—	—	$t_\delta=0.015$	—	—	—	—	—

continued

Material	$T/^\circ C$	$E_{ij}/c_{ij}/s_{ij}$	ϵ_r	d_{ij}	e_{ij}	g_{ij}	h_{ij}	p_i/κ_i	μ_{ij}	q_{ij}	m_{ij}
80PVDF/20TrFE [Petty et al.]	25	—	$\epsilon_{33}=7$	$d_{33}=-20$	—	—	—	$p_3=-31$	—	—	—
		—	$t_\delta=0.015$	—	—	—	—	—	—	—	—
PVDF/TrFE Spun coating [Furukawa & Seo]	25	—	11	$d_{31}=7.5$	—	—	—	$p_3=-41$	—	—	—
		—	$t_\delta=0.018$	$d_{32}=7.5$	—	—	—	—	—	—	—
[Kohler et al.]		—	—	$d_{33}=-40$	—	—	—	—	—	—	—
	110	T_c	—	—	—	—	—	—	—	—	—
PT[Xu]	25	—	200	$d_{31}=-4.2$	—	—	—	$p_3=-268$	—	—	—
		—	—	$d_{33}=50$	—	—	—	—	—	—	—
PZN（0 0 1）	25	—	—	$d_{33}=83$	—	—	—	—	—	—	—
		—	—	$k_{33}=0.38$	—	—	—	—	—	—	—
PZN（1 1 1）	25	—	—	$d_{33}=1100$	—	—	—	—	—	—	—
		—	—	$k_{33}=0.85$	—	—	—	—	—	—	—
PZN/4.5%PT （Crystal）	25	$s_{11}=82$	$\epsilon_{11}=3100$	$d_{15}=140$	—	—	—	—	—	—	—
		$s_{22}=82$	$\epsilon_{22}=3100$	$d_{31}=-970$	—	—	—	—	—	—	—
		$s_{33}=108$	$\epsilon_{33}=5200$	$d_{33}=2000$	—	—	—	—	—	—	—
		$s_{44}=15.6$	others$=0$	—	—	—	—	—	—	—	—

PZN/4.5%PT (Crystal)	$s_{55}=15.6$	$s_{66}=15.9$	$s_{12}=-1.44$	$s_{13}=-0.88$	$s_{23}=-0.88$	others $=0$
PZN/8%PT(0 0 1)	25	$\epsilon_{33}=7000$	$d_{31}=-1400$			
			$d_{33}=2500$			
			$k_{33}=0.94$			
	160					T_c
PZN/8%PT (1 1 1)	25	$\epsilon_{33}=1000$	$d_{31}=-29$			
			$d_{33}=84$			
			$k_{33}=0.39$			
	160					T_c
PZT (PbTiO$_3$) (Pb(Zr$_{0.3}$Ti$_{0.7}$)O$_3$) [Yang et al.]	25	600				
	490					T_c
		$t_\delta=0.008$				
PZT-1 μm film (Pb(Zr$_{0.52}$Ti$_{0.48}$)O$_3$) [Yang et al.]	25	1400		$p_3=-120$		
		$t_\delta=0.02$				
PZT (PbZrO$_3$)	25					
	230					T_c

continued

Material	$T/^\circ\mathrm{C}$	$E_{ij}/c_{ij}/s_{ij}$	ϵ_r	d_{ij}	e_{ij}	g_{ij}	h_{ij}	p_i/κ_i	μ_{ij}	q_{ij}	m_{ij}
PZT (1 μm film; Pb($Zr_{0.7}Ti_{0.3}$)O_3) [Yang et al.]	25	—	800	—	—	—	—	$p_3 = -180$	—	—	—
		—	$t_8 = 0.02$	—	—	—	—	—	—	—	—
	25	$s_{11} = 12$	$\epsilon_{11} = 930$	$d_{15} = 440$	—	—	—	—	—	—	—
		$s_{22} = 12$	$\epsilon_{22} = 930$	$d_{24} = 440$	—	—	—	—	—	—	—
		$s_{33} = 15$	$\epsilon_{33} = 425$	$d_{31} = -60$	—	—	—	—	—	—	—
		$s_{44} = 45$	others $= 0$	$d_{32} = -60$	—	—	—	—	—	—	—
		$s_{55} = 45$	—	$d_{33} = 150$	—	—	—	—	—	—	—
		$s_{66} = 30$	—	others $= 0$	—	—	—	—	—	—	—
		$s_{12} = -3.3$	—	—	—	—	—	—	—	—	—
		$s_{13} = -5$	—	—	—	—	—	—	—	—	—
PZT-2[efunda]	-150	$s_{23} = -5$	—	—	—	$g_{31} = 10$	—	—	—	—	—
		others $= 0$	—	$d_{11} = -70$	—	—	—	—	—	—	—
		—	—	$d_{33} = 180$	—	—	—	—	—	—	—

25	$s_{11}=12$	$\epsilon_{11}=1450$	$d_{15}=500$		
	$s_{22}=12$	$\epsilon_{22}=1450$	$d_{24}=500$		
	$s_{33}=16$	$\epsilon_{33}=1200$	$d_{31}=-85$		
	$s_{44}=39$	$t_{\delta}=0.004$	$d_{32}=-85$		
	$s_{55}=39$	others $=0$	$d_{33}=225$		
	$s_{66}=33$	—	$k_{15}=0.71$		
	$s_{12}=-4$	—	$k_{33}=0.334$		
	$s_{13}=-5.3$	—	$k_{33}=0.70$		
	others $=0$	—	others $=0$		
150	—	—	$d_{31}=-100$		
	—	—	$d_{33}=300$		
	—	—	—		
250	—	—	$d_{31}=-125$		
	—	—	$d_{33}=360$		
328	T_{c}	—	—		
-150	—	—	$d_{31}=-100$		
	—	—	$d_{33}=240$		
	—	—	—		

PZT-4
[Lee & Saravanos]

continued

Material	$T/^\circ\mathrm{C}$	$E_{ij}/c_{ij}/s_{ij}$	ϵ_r	d_{ij}	e_{ij}	g_{ij}	h_{ij}	p_i/κ_i	μ_{ij}	q_{ij}	m_{ij}
	25	$c_{11}=99$	$\epsilon_{11}=1530$	$d_{15}=584$	$e_{15}=12.3$	$g_{31}=-13.7$	—	$p_3=-238$	all$=0$	all$=0$	all$=0$
		$c_{22}=99$	$\epsilon_{22}=1530$	$d_{24}=584$	$e_{31}=-7.2$	$g_{33}=24$	—	—	—	—	—
		$c_{33}=87$	$\epsilon_{33}=1500$	$d_{31}=-190$	$e_{31}=-7.2$	—	—	—	—	—	—
		$c_{44}=21$	others$=0$	$d_{32}=-154$	$e_{33}=16$	—	—	—	—	—	—
		$c_{55}=21$		$d_{33}=350$	—	—	—	—	—	—	—
		$c_{66}=23$		$k_{31}=0.35$	—	—	—	—	—	—	—
		$c_{12}=54$		$k_{33}=0.72$	—	—	—	—	—	—	—
		$c_{13}=51$		others$=0$	—	—	—	—	—	—	—
		$c_{23}=51$		—	—	—	—	—	—	—	—
		others$=0$	—	—	—	—	—	—	—	—	—
PZT-5A [Lee & Saravanos] [Aboudi]	150	—	—	$d_{31}=-290$	—	—	—	—	—	—	—
		—	—	$d_{33}=390$	—	—	—	—	—	—	—
	250	—	—	$d_{31}=-275$	—	—	—	—	—	—	—
		—	—	$d_{33}=440$	—	—	—	—	—	—	—
	365	T_c	—	—	—	—	—	—	—	—	—
	-150	—	—	$d_{31}=-130$	—	—	—	—	—	—	—
		—	—	$d_{33}=290$	—	—	—	—	—	—	—
		—	—	—	—	—	—	—	—	—	—

25	$s_{11}=17$	$\epsilon_{11}=3130$	$d_{15}=-740$	$e_{31}=22$	$g_{31}=-13.7$	—
	$s_{22}=17$	$\epsilon_{22}=3130$	$d_{24}=-740$	$e_{33}=30$	$g_{33}=19$	—
	$s_{33}=21$	$\epsilon_{33}=3800$	$d_{31}=-274$	—	—	—
	$s_{44}=44$	$t_{\delta}=0.012$	$d_{32}=-274$	—	—	—
	$s_{55}=44$	others $=0$	$d_{33}=593$	—	—	—
	$s_{66}=43$	—	$k_{15}=-0.68$	—	—	—
	$s_{12}=-4.8$	—	$k_{31}=0.44$	—	—	—
	$s_{13}=-8.5$	—	$k_{33}=0.75$	—	—	—
	$s_{23}=-8.5$	—	others $=0$	—	—	—
	others $=0$	—	—	—	—	—
120	—	—	$d_{31}=-500$	—	—	—
	—	—	$d_{33}=925$	—	—	—
150	—	—	$d_{31}=0$	—	—	—
	—	—	$d_{33}=0$	—	—	—
170	—	—	de-poled	—	—	—
193	T_c	—	—	—	—	—

PZT-5H

continued

Material	$T/°C$	$E_{ij}/c_{ij}/s_{ij}$	ϵ_r	d_{ij}	e_{ij}	g_{ij}	h_{ij}	p_i/κ_i	μ_{ij}	q_{ij}	m_{ij}
PZT-5J [efunda]	25	$s_{11}=16$	$\epsilon_{11}=2720$	$d_{15}=670$	—	—	—	—	—	—	—
		$s_{22}=16$	$\epsilon_{22}=2720$	$d_{24}=670$	—	—	—	—	—	—	—
		$s_{33}=23$	$\epsilon_{33}=2600$	$d_{31}=-220$	—	—	—	—	—	—	—
		$s_{44}=47$	others $=0$	$d_{32}=-220$	—	—	—	—	—	—	—
		$s_{55}=47$		$d_{33}=500$	—	—	—	—	—	—	—
		$s_{66}=42$		others $=0$	—	—	—	—	—	—	—
		$s_{12}=-4.5$			—	—	—	—	—	—	—
		$s_{13}=-5.9$			—	—	—	—	—	—	—
		$s_{23}=-5.9$			—	—	—	—	—	—	—
		others $=0$			—	—	—	—	—	—	—
PZT-7A [Odegard]	25	$c_{11}=148$	$\epsilon_{11}=460$	$d_{15}=360$	$e_{15}=9.2$	—	—	—	—	—	—
		$c_{22}=148$	$\epsilon_{22}=460$	$d_{24}=360$	$e_{24}=9.2$	—	—	—	—	—	—
		$c_{33}=131$	$\epsilon_{33}=235$	$d_{31}=-60$	$e_{31}=-2.1$	—	—	—	—	—	—
		$c_{44}=25.4$	others $=0$	$d_{32}=-60$	$e_{32}=-2.1$	—	—	—	—	—	—
		$c_{55}=25.4$		$d_{33}=150$	$e_{33}=9.5$	—	—	—	—	—	—
		$c_{66}=35.9$		$k_{31}=0.4$	others $=0$	—	—	—	—	—	—
		$c_{12}=76.2$		$k_{33}=0.53$	—	—	—	—	—	—	—
		$c_{13}=74.3$		others $=0$	—	—	—	—	—	—	—
		$c_{23}=-4.6$		—	—	—	—	—	—	—	—
		others $=0$		—	—	—	—	—	—	—	—

—	—	—	—	—	—	—	—	—	—	—	—	—
—	—	—	—	—	—	—	—	—	—	—	—	—
—	—	—	—	—	—	—	—	—	—	—	—	—
—	—	—	—	—	—	—	—	—	—	—	—	—
—	—	—	—	—	—	—	—	—	—	—	—	—
—	—	—	—	—	—	—	—	—	—	—	—	—

Material	Temp	s	ε	d
PZT-8 (Uniaxial) [efunda]	25	$s_{11}=12$	$\epsilon_{11}=1290$	$d_{15}=330$
		$s_{22}=12$	$\epsilon_{22}=1290$	$d_{24}=330$
		$s_{33}=14$	$\epsilon_{33}=1000$	$d_{31}=-97$
		$s_{44}=32$	others $=0$	$d_{32}=-97$
		$s_{55}=32$		$d_{33}=227$
		$s_{66}=30$		others $=0$
		$s_{12}=-5$		
		$s_{13}=-5$		
		$s_{23}=-5$		
		others $=0$		
SiO$_2$-α (α-Quartz; Trigonal 32)	25	$s_{11}=12.8$	$\epsilon_{11}=4.5$	$d_{11}=-2.3$
		$s_{22}=12.8$	$\epsilon_{22}=4.5$	$d_{12}=2.3$
		$s_{33}=9.6$	$\epsilon_{33}=4.7$	$d_{14}=-0.7$
		$s_{44}=20$	others $=0$	$d_{25}=0.7$
		$s_{55}=20$		$d_{26}=4.6$
		$s_{66}=29$		others $=0$
		$s_{12}=-1.8$		

continued

Material	$T/^{\circ}\mathrm{C}$	$E_{ij}/c_{ij}/s_{ij}$	ϵ_r	d_{ij}	e_{ij}	g_{ij}	h_{ij}	p_i/κ_i	μ_{ij}	q_{ij}	m_{ij}
SiO₂-α (α-Quartz; Trigonal 32)		$s_{13}=-1.2$	—	—	—	—	—	—	—	—	—
		$s_{14}=-4.5$	—	—	—	—	—	—	—	—	—
		$s_{24}=4.5$	—	—	—	—	—	—	—	—	—
		$s_{56}=-9$	—	—	—	—	—	—	—	—	—
		symmetric	—	—	—	—	—	—	—	—	—
		others = 0	—	—	—	—	—	—	—	—	—
	550	T_c	—	—	—	—	—	—	—	—	—
Sr₀.₃Ba₀.₇Nb₂O₆	25	—	400	—	—	—	—	$p_3=-600$	—	—	—
Sr₀.₄₆Ba₀.₆₄Nb₂O₆	25	—	$\epsilon_{33}=43$	—	—	—	—	$p_3=-430$	—	—	—
Sr₀.₅Ba₀.₅Nb₂O₆	25	—	$\epsilon_{33}=55$	—	—	—	—	$p_3=-550$	—	—	—
		—	$t_b=0.003$	—	—	—	—	—	—	—	—
Sr₀.₇₃Ba₀.₂₇Nb₂O₆	25	—	$\epsilon_{33}=112$	—	—	—	—	$p_3=-2800$	—	—	—
Tellurium Oxide (Tetragonal 422) [Efunda]	25	$s_{11}=115$	$\epsilon_{11}=23$	$d_{14}=8.13$	—	—	—	—	—	—	—
		$s_{22}=115$	$\epsilon_{22}=23$	$d_{25}=-8.1$	—	—	—	—	—	—	—
		$s_{33}=10.3$	$\epsilon_{33}=25$	others = 0	—	—	—	—	—	—	—
		$s_{44}=38$	others = 0	—	—	—	—	—	—	—	—
		$s_{55}=38$	—	—	—	—	—	—	—	—	—
		$s_{66}=15$	—	—	—	—	—	—	—	—	—

Material	T (°C)	Elastic constants	ϵ, $\tan\delta$	d	e	p
Tellurium Oxide (Tetragonal 422) [Efunda]	25	$s_{12}=-105$; $s_{23}=-2.1$; $s_{31}=-2.1$; symmetric; others $=0$				
Terfenol-D ($Tb_x Dy_{1-x} Fe_2$)	25					
$Tb_2(MoO_4)_3$	163; 25	T_c	$\epsilon_{33}=35$			
TGS (Triglycine Sulfate)	50	T_c	$t_\delta=0.025$			$p_3=-350$
Tourmaline	25					$p_3=-4.0$
ZnO (Hexagonal 6 mm) [King-Smith & Vanderbilt] [Zhao et al.]	25	$c_{11}=216$; $c_{22}=219$; $c_{33}=209$; $c_{44}=44$; $c_{55}=44$	$\epsilon_{11}=9.2$; $\epsilon_{22}=9.2$; $\epsilon_{33}=12.6$; others $=0$	$d_{15}=-11$; $d_{24}=-11$; $d_{31}=-5.4$; $d_{32}=-5.4$; $d_{33}=20$	$e_{15}=-0.37$; $e_{24}=-0.37$; $e_{31}=-0.62$; $e_{32}=-0.62$; $e_{33}=0.96$	$p_3=-9.4$

continued

Material	$T/^\circ\text{C}$	$E_{ij}/c_{ij}/s_{ij}$	ϵ_r	d_{ij}	e_{ij}	g_{ij}	h_{ij}	p_i/κ_i	μ_{ij}	q_{ij}	m_{ij}
ZnO （Hexagonal 6 mm） [King-Smith & Vanderbilt] [Zhao et al.]		$c_{66}=45$	—	others $=0$	others $=0$	—	—	—	—	—	—
		$c_{12}=-120$	—	—	—	—	—	—	—	—	—
		$c_{13}=-104$	—	—	—	—	—	—	—	—	—
		$c_{31}=-104$	—	—	—	—	—	—	—	—	—
		symmetric	—	—	—	—	—	—	—	—	—
		others $=0$	—	—	—	—	—	—	—	—	—
	1975	T_m	—	—	—	—	—	—	—	—	—
ZnS （Hexagonal 6 mm） [Efunda]	25	$s_{11}=11.1$	$\epsilon_{11}=8.7$	$d_{15}=-2.8$	—	—	—	$p_3=-9.4$	—	—	—
		$s_{12}=-4.56$	$\epsilon_{22}=8.7$	$d_{24}=-2.8$	—	—	—	—	—	—	—
		$s_{13}=-1.4$	$\epsilon_{33}=8.7$	$d_{31}=-1.13$	—	—	—	—	—	—	—
		$s_{22}=11.1$	others $=0$	$d_{32}=-1.13$	—	—	—	—	—	—	—
		$s_{33}=8.47$		$d_{33}=3.23$	—	—	—	—	—	—	—
		$s_{44}=34.4$	—	others $=0$	—	—	—	—	—	—	—
		$s_{55}=34.4$	—	—	—	—	—	—	—	—	—

											—
											—
											—
$s_{66}=31.4$	—	—	—	—	—	—	—	—	—	—	—
symmetric	—	—	—	—	—	—	—	—	—	—	—
others $=0$	—	—	—	—	—	—	—	—	—	—	—

ZnS (Hexagonal 6 mm) [Efunda]

Units: Stiffness/Compliance: c_{ij} (GPa), s_{ij} (10^{-3} GPa^{-1})

Dielectric: ϵ_{ij} (ϵ_o) and $\epsilon_o = 8.85$ pC/M/m^2; $t_\delta = \tan\delta$ (at 1 kHz)

Piezoelectric: d_{ij} (pC/N or pm/V), e_{ij} (C/m or N/V/m), g_{ij} (10^{-3} Vm/N or m/C),
h_{ij} (N/C or V/m)

Piezomagnetic: μ_{ij} (μNs/C^2); q_{ij} (N/A/m); m_{ij} (pNs/V/C)

Pyroelectric: p_i (μC/m^2/ °C)

Pyromagnetic: κ_i (10^{-3} N/A/m/°C)

Notes: $p=10^{-12}$, $\mu=10^{-6}$

Table 14.5.2   Electro-Magneto-Thermo-Mechanical Coupling Properties of Composite Laminae-Matrix, Inclusions, and Related Additives [Aggarwal et al.] [Hooker]

Material	$T/^\circ C$	c_{ij}/s_{ij}	ϵ_r	d_{ij}	e_{ij}	g_{ij}	h_{ij}	p_{py}	μ_{ij}	q_{ij}	m_{ij}
Cement Paste	25	—	—	$d=0.066$	—	$g=0.22$	—	$p_3=-0.002$	—	—	—
100%Expoxy Lamina [Hooker]	25	$c_{11}=5.53$	$\epsilon_{11}=11.3$	all=0	all=0	—	—	—	$\mu_{11}=0.01$	all=0	all=0
		$c_{22}=5.53$	$\epsilon_{22}=11.3$	—	—	—	—	—	$\mu_{33}=0.01$	—	—
		$c_{33}=5.53$	$\epsilon_{33}=11.3$	—	—	—	—	—	others=0	—	—
		$c_{44}=1.28$	others=0	—	—	—	—	—	—	—	—
		$c_{55}=1.28$	—	—	—	—	—	—	—	—	—
		$c_{66}=1.28$	—	—	—	—	—	—	—	—	—
		$c_{13}=2.97$	—	—	—	—	—	—	—	—	—
		$c_{23}=2.97$	—	—	—	—	—	—	—	—	—
		others=0	—	—	—	—	—	—	—	—	—
Ep/40%BaTiO$_3$ /20%CoFe$_2$O$_4$	25	$c_{11}=16$	$\epsilon_{11}=33.2$	—	$e_{15}=1.9$	—	—	—	$\mu_{11}=315$	$q_{15}=0.72$	$m_{11}=0.00$
		$c_{22}=16$	$\epsilon_{33}=591$	—	$e_{31}=1.65$	—	—	—	$\mu_{33}=35.6$	$q_{31}=7.93$	$m_{33}=103$
		$c_{33}=80$	others=0	—	$e_{33}=9.1$	—	—	—	others=0	$q_{33}=59.3$	others=0
		$c_{44}=6$	—	—	others=0	—	—	—	—	others=0	—
		$c_{55}=6$	—	—	—	—	—	—	—	—	—
Ep/40% BaTiO$_3$/20% CoFe$_2$O$_4$ 20%CoFe$_2$O$_4$(V_f) [Hooker]		$c_{12}=9$	—	—	—	—	—	—	—	—	—
		$c_{13}=9$	—	—	—	—	—	—	—	—	—
		others=0	—	—	—	—	—	—	—	—	—

Material	T (°C)				
Ep/40%BaTiO₃/40% CoFe₂O₄ V_f [Hooker]	25	$c_{11}=17$, $c_{12}=9.4$, $c_{13}=9.4$, $c_{33}=87.2$, $c_{44}=6$, $c_{55}=6.3$, others$=0$	$\epsilon_{11}=26.5$, $\epsilon_{33}=0.27$, others$=0$	$e_{15}=1.9$, $e_{31}=1.71$, $e_{33}=5.45$, others$=0$	$\mu_{11}=314$, $\mu_{33}=65$, others$=0$; $q_{15}=0.72$, $q_{31}=15.1$, $q_{33}=118$, others$=0$; $m_{11}=0.00$, $m_{33}=103$, others$=0$
Ep/80%PMN (Fibrous, V_f; 1-3 composite)	25	$e_{11}=8.3$, $e_{22}=15.4$, $e_{23}=15.4$, $g_{12}=3.2$, $g_{23}=3.2$, $v_{12}=0.31$, others$=0$		$d_{11}=2000$, $d_{12}=-195$	
Ep/80%PZT-5A (Fibrous, V_f; 1-3 composite)	25	$e_{11}=53$, $e_{22}=61$, $e_{23}=61$, $g_{12}=21$, $g_{23}=21$, $v_{12}=0.38$, others$=0$		$d_{11}=399$, $d_{12}=-190$	

continued

Material	$T/^\circ\mathrm{C}$	c_{ij}/s_{ij}	ϵ_r	d_{ij}	e_{ij}	g_{ij}	h_{ij}	p_{py}	μ_{ij}	q_{ij}	m_{ij}
Graphite Fiber [Odegard]	25	$c_{11}=244$	$\epsilon_{11}=12$	—	all$=0$	—	—	—	—	—	—
		$c_{22}=24$	$\epsilon_{22}=12$	—	—	—	—	—	—	—	—
		$c_{33}=24$	$\epsilon_{33}=12$	—	—	—	—	—	—	—	—
		$c_{44}=11$	others$=0$	—	—	—	—	—	—	—	—
		$c_{55}=27$	—	—	—	—	—	—	—	—	—
		$c_{66}=27$	—	—	—	—	—	—	—	—	—
		$c_{12}=6.7$	—	—	—	—	—	—	—	—	—
		$c_{13}=6.7$	—	—	—	—	—	—	—	—	—
		$c_{23}=9.7$	—	—	—	—	—	—	—	—	—
		others$=0$	—	—	—	—	—	—	—	—	—
PZT-5A/ 60% BatiO$_3$ Film [Aboudi]	25	$c_{11}=200$	$\epsilon_{11}=900$	—	$e_{15}=0$	—	—	$p_3=-124$	$\mu_{11}=150$	$q_{15}=180$	$m_{11}=6$
		$c_{22}=200$	$\epsilon_{22}=900$	—	$e_{31}=-3.5$	—	—	$\kappa_3=-5.92$	$\mu_{22}=150$	$q_{31}=200$	$m_{22}=6$
		$c_{33}=190$	$\epsilon_{33}=7500$	—	$e_{31}=-3.5$	—	—		$\mu_{33}=75$	$q_{32}=200$	$m_{33}=2500$
		$c_{44}=45$	others$=0$	—	$e_{33}=11$	—	—	—	—	$q_{33}=260$	—
		$c_{55}=45$	—	—	—	—	—	—	—	—	—
		$c_{66}=45$	—	—	—	—	—	—	—	—	—
		$c_{12}=110$	—	—	—	—	—	—	—	—	—
		$c_{13}=110$	—	—	—	—	—	—	—	—	—
		$c_{23}=110$	—	—	—	—	—	—	—	—	—
		others$=0$	—	—	—	—	—	—	—	—	—

Material	T	Elastic constants	Dielectric		Piezoelectric	
Si (LaRC) [Odegard]	25	$c_{11}=484$, $c_{22}=484$, $c_{33}=484$, $c_{44}=192$, $c_{55}=192$, $c_{66}=192$, $c_{12}=99.1$, $c_{13}=99.1$, $c_{23}=99.1$, others$=0$	$\epsilon_{11}=2.8$, $\epsilon_{22}=2.8$, $\epsilon_{33}=2.8$, others$=0$		all$=0$	
SiC [Odegard]	25	$c_{11}=484$, $c_{22}=484$, $c_{33}=484$, $c_{44}=192$, $c_{55}=192$, $c_{66}=192$, $c_{12}=99.1$, $c_{13}=99.1$, $c_{23}=99.1$, others$=0$	$\epsilon_{11}=10$, $\epsilon_{22}=10$, $\epsilon_{33}=10$, others$=0$		all$=0$	
UPE/49%PZT/1%C (V_f) (UPE: Unsaturated Polyester)	25					$d_{33}=25$

Table 14.10.1　Magnetostrictirve Coefficients

Crystal/Ceramics	Magnetostrictive Coefficient $(\Lambda_{ij})/(\mu m \cdot m^{-1})$		
	(1, 1, 1)	(1, 0, 0)	No alignment identified
Co	—	—	60
Fe	−21	20	—
Ni	−24	−46	—
Terfenol D $(Tb_x Dy_{1-x} Fe_2)$	1640	90	—
Metglass $(Fe_{81} Si_{3.5} B_{13.5} C_2)$	—	—	20

Chapter 15

Failure of Composites

15.1 Fracture Modes of Composites

As fibrous composites are not only used in form of bulky plastics reinforced with random fibers, flat and curved laminae, or variations thereof, but also involve woven or braided constructions. Fibrous composites are rarely used in a unidirectional form. Most commonly, laminae (or tows) are taken as the building blocks in laminates (or woven forms) that are composed of layers at various fibrous orientations as shown in Fig. 15.1.1.

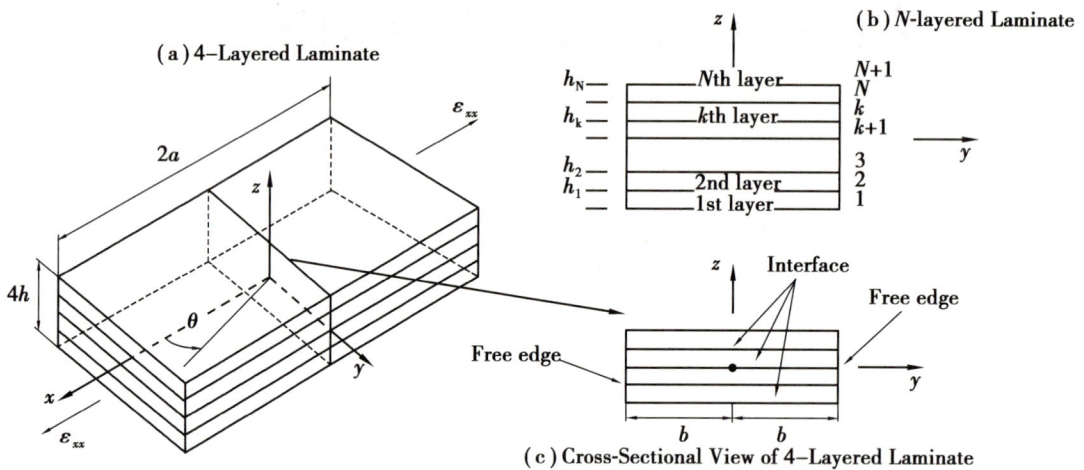

Fig. 15.1.1 Laminate as a Stackup of Laminae

Possible defects include broken fibers, fiber slacks, fiber misalignments, debonding, resin rich pockets, cracks, and porosity. The failure of a composite may be initiated by such local defects, although its global effective moduli do not related much to such defects. Damage occurs at all scales ranging from the molecular structure on a microscale up to various buckling behaviors as a whole. Each failure mode of a fibrous composite has a scale of action. The first well-educated theorization is to figure out the scale for such a particular mode of failure and then to characterize it on that scale in the global loading system.

15.1.1 Mode-I Stress Intensity Factor in Orthotropic Materials

Similar to Eqs. (5.3.1)-(5.3.3), stress expressions in terms of stress intensity factor Mode-I in the polar coordinate system with the origin at the crack tip and having an existing crack size of "a" in a orthotropic lamina are

$$\sigma_{xx} = \frac{K_{\text{I}}}{(2\pi r)^{\frac{1}{2}}} \text{Re}\left\{ \frac{s_1 s_2}{s_1 - s_2}\left[\frac{s_2}{(\cos\theta + s_2\sin\theta)^{\frac{1}{2}}} - \frac{s_1}{(\cos\theta + s_1\sin\theta)^{\frac{1}{2}}} \right] \right\} + O\left(r^{\frac{1}{2}}\right)$$

$$(15.1.1)$$

$$\sigma_{yy} = \frac{K_{\text{I}}}{(2\pi r)^{\frac{1}{2}}} \text{Re}\left\{ \frac{1}{s_1 - s_2}\left[\frac{s_1}{(\cos\theta + s_2\sin\theta)^{\frac{1}{2}}} - \frac{s_2}{(\cos\theta + s_1\sin\theta)^{\frac{1}{2}}} \right] \right\} + O\left(r^{\frac{1}{2}}\right)$$

$$(15.1.2)$$

$$\tau_{xy} = \frac{K_{\text{I}}}{(2\pi r)^{\frac{1}{2}}} \text{Re}\left\{ \frac{s_1 s_2}{s_1 - s_2}\left[\frac{1}{(\cos\theta + s_2\sin\theta)^{\frac{1}{2}}} - \frac{1}{(\cos\theta + s_1\sin\theta)^{\frac{1}{2}}} \right] \right\} + O\left(r^{\frac{1}{2}}\right)$$

$$(15.1.3)$$

where

$$K_{\text{I}} = \sigma_{yyo}(\pi a)^{\frac{1}{2}}$$

$$(15.1.4)$$

$$x = a + r\cos\theta$$

$$(15.1.5)$$

$$y = r\sin\theta$$

$$(15.1.6)$$

and $\quad s_1 = -s_2 = \left[\frac{E_{11}}{2E_{22}} - \left(\frac{E_{11}}{4G_{12}} - \frac{v_{12}}{2} \right) \right]^{\frac{1}{2}} + i\left[\frac{E_{11}}{2E_{22}} + \left(\frac{E_{11}}{4G_{12}} - \frac{v_{12}}{2} \right) \right]^{\frac{1}{2}}$ $\quad(15.1.7)$

Stress σ_{yyo} is the in-plane normal stress at the crack tip and $O(r^{\frac{1}{2}})$ represents the higher order terms. It must be emphasized that the stress intensity factor of Mode-I defined above by Eq. (15.1.4) has stress singularity of $-1/2$ and takes the same expression as that of isotropic case. Based on the in-plane stress transformation, the angle at any angle θ is

$$\sigma_\theta = \sigma_{xx}\sin^2\theta + \sigma_{yy}\cos^2\theta - 2\tau_{xy}\sin\theta\cos\theta$$

$$= \frac{K_{\text{I}}}{(2\pi r)^{\frac{1}{2}}}\text{Re}\left\{ \frac{s_1 s_2}{2(s_1 - s_2)}\left[\frac{1 + s_2^2 + (1 - s_2^2)\cos(2\theta) + 2 s_2\sin(2\theta)}{s_2(\cos\theta + s_2\sin\theta)^{\frac{1}{2}}} - \right. \right.$$

$$\left. \left. \frac{1 + s_1^2 + (1 - s_1^2)\cos(2\theta) + 2 s_1\sin 2\theta}{s_1(\cos\theta + s_1\sin\theta)^{\frac{1}{2}}} \right] \right\} + O\left(r^{\frac{1}{2}}\right)$$

$$(15.1.8)$$

Note that $d\dfrac{\sigma_\theta}{d\theta} = 0$ will lead to the maximum (or minimum) value of stress at θ_{max}, which can be expressed as

$$\theta_{\text{max}} = \text{function}(s_1, s_2) = \text{function}(E_{11}, E_{22}, G_{12}, v_{12})$$

$$(15.1.9)$$

Thus, it can be concluded that the maximum (minimum) stress due to Mode-I fracture in orthotropic materials does not necessarily happen at $\theta = 0$, which is true for isotropic materials.

15.1.2   Mode-II Stress Intensity Factor in Orthotropic Materials

Stress expressions in terms of stress intensity factor of Mode-II in the polar coordinate system with the origin at the crack tip and having an existing crack size of "a" in an orthotropic lamina are

$$\sigma_{xx} = \frac{K_{II}}{(2\pi r)^{\frac{1}{2}}} \mathrm{Re} \left\{ \frac{1}{s_1 - s_2} \left[\frac{s_2^2}{(\cos\theta + s_2\sin\theta)^{\frac{1}{2}}} - \frac{s_1^2}{(\cos\theta + s_1\sin\theta)^{\frac{1}{2}}} \right] \right\} + O\left(r^{\frac{1}{2}}\right)$$

$$(15.1.10)$$

$$\sigma_{yy} = \frac{K_{II}}{(2\pi r)^{\frac{1}{2}}} \mathrm{Re} \left\{ \frac{1}{s_1 - s_2} \left[\frac{1}{(\cos\theta + s_2\sin\theta)^{\frac{1}{2}}} - \frac{1}{(\cos\theta + s_1\sin\theta)^{\frac{1}{2}}} \right] \right\} + O\left(r^{\frac{1}{2}}\right)$$

$$(15.1.11)$$

$$\tau_{xy} = \frac{K_{II}}{(2\pi r)^{\frac{1}{2}}} \mathrm{Re} \left\{ \frac{1}{s_1 - s_2} \left[\frac{s_1}{(\cos\theta + s_1\sin\theta)^{\frac{1}{2}}} - \frac{s_2}{(\cos\theta + s_2\sin\theta)^{\frac{1}{2}}} \right] \right\} + O\left(r^{\frac{1}{2}}\right)$$

$$(15.1.12)$$

where $K_{II} = \tau_{yxo}(\pi a)^{\frac{1}{2}}$ $(15.1.13)$

Stress τ_{yxo} is the in-plane shear stress at the crack tip and $O\left(r^{\frac{1}{2}}\right)$ represents the higher order terms. It must be emphasized that the stress intensity factor of Mode-II defined above by Eq. (15.1.13) has stress singularity of $-1/2$ and takes the same expression as that of isotropic case. Similar to the Mode-I fracture, it can be derived that the maximum (minimum) stress due to Mode-II in orthotropic materials does not necessarily happen at $\theta = 0$, which is true for isotropic materials.

15.1.3   Mode-III Stress Intensity Factor of in Orthotropic Materials

Stress expressions in terms of stress intensity factor of Mode-III in the polar coordinate system with the origin at the crack tip and having an existing crack size of "a" in an orthotropic lamina are

$$\tau_{zx} = \frac{-K_{III}}{(2\pi r)^{\frac{1}{2}}} \mathrm{Re} \left[\frac{s_3}{(\cos\theta + s_3\sin\theta)^{\frac{1}{2}}} \right] + O\left(r^{\frac{1}{2}}\right) \qquad (15.1.14)$$

and $$\tau_{yz} = \frac{K_{III}}{(2\pi r)^{\frac{1}{2}}} \mathrm{Re} \left[\frac{1}{(\cos\theta + s_3\sin\theta)^{\frac{1}{2}}} \right] + O\left(r^{\frac{1}{2}}\right) \qquad (15.1.15)$$

where $K_{\mathrm{III}} = \tau_{yzo}(\pi a)^{\frac{1}{2}}$ (15.1.16)

and $s_3 = i\left(\dfrac{G_{31}}{G_{33}}\right)^{\frac{1}{2}}$ (15.1.17)

Stress τ_{yzo} is the out-of-plane shear stress at the crack tip and $O\left(r^{\frac{1}{2}}\right)$ represents the higher order terms. It must be emphasized that the stress intensity factor of Mode-III defined above by Eq. (15.1.16) has stress singularity of $-1/2$ and takes the same expression as that of isotropic case.

15.2   Fracture Toughness of Composites

The critical value of the fracture mechanics J_{IC} defines the point, at which large-scale plastic yielding during propagation takes place under mode-one loading as described in Chapter 5. The energy release rate is related to the stress intensity factors and J-integral only for the straight ahead growth for a composite lamina

$$J_{\mathrm{IC}} = G_{\mathrm{IC}} = \frac{K_{\mathrm{IC}}^2}{(2\,E_{11}\,E_{22})^{-\frac{1}{2}}}\left[\left(\frac{E_{11}}{E_{22}}\right)^{\frac{1}{2}} + \frac{E_{11}}{2G_{12}} - v_{12}\right]^{\frac{1}{2}}$$ (15.2.1)

where

$J_{\mathrm{IC}}(\mathrm{J/m}^2,\ \mathrm{J/cm}^2,\ \text{or } \mathrm{J/mm}^2)$: Critical J-integral around a crack tip of the lamina;
G_{IC} : Strain energy release rate;
K_{IC} : Stress Intensity Factor.

As described above, fracture toughness is measured in terms of the energy absorbed per unit crack extension and thus the fibers that are capable of absorbing energy around the crack tip can give rise to an increase in the fracture toughness of fiber-reinforced matrix.

15.2.1   Fiber Pull-Out Mode

Consider crack creation through a matrix containing short fibers of length l_{f}, such that the fibers are pulled out of the matrix fibers subjected to a uniform tensile stress as shown in Fig. 15.2.1. The work is done against friction or by shearing the matrix along the fibers. Following the shear-lag model one can calculate the work done pulling out a single fiber by integrating the product of applied force $f(x)$ and differential travel distance $\mathrm{d}x$ as

$$W_{\mathrm{f}} = \int_0^{\frac{1}{2}l_{\mathrm{f}}} f(x)\,\mathrm{d}x = \int_0^{\frac{1}{2}l_{\mathrm{f}}} \pi\,d_{\mathrm{f}}\left(\frac{1}{2}\,\tau_{y,\mathrm{matrix}}\right)x\,\mathrm{d}x = \frac{\pi\,d_{\mathrm{f}}\,l_{\mathrm{f}}^2\,\tau_{y,\mathrm{matrix}}}{16}$$ (15.2.2)

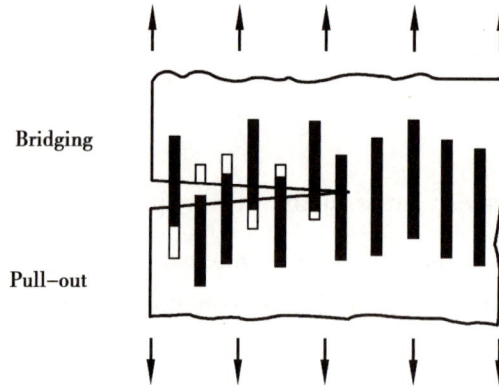

Fig. 15.2.1　Shear-Lag Model of Fiber Pull-Out around the Crack Tip

where

$f(x)$: Force function along the x-axis, i.e., pulling direction;

l_f: Fiber length;

$1/2 l_f$: Average distance of fiber travel before pullout;

$1/2\, \tau_{y,\mathrm{matrix}}$: Average shear stress experienced by a fiber at the first debonding via pullout;

d_f: Fiber diameter;

$\tau_{y,\mathrm{matrix}}$: Shear yield strength of the matrix.

Assume that the number of fibers per unit area (N) along the crack extension is proportional to the volume fraction of fibers,

$$N = \frac{V_f}{\frac{1}{4}\pi\, d_f^2} \tag{15.2.3}$$

of which V_f is the volume fraction of fibers. Thus, the strain energy release rate, i.e., work done per unit area, along the crack extension is

$$G = W_f\, N = \left(\frac{\pi\, d_f\, l_f^2\, \tau_{y,\mathrm{matrix}}}{16}\right)\left(\frac{V_f}{\frac{1}{4}\pi\, d_f^2}\right)$$

$$= \frac{1}{4}\, V_f\, l_f^2 \left(\frac{\tau_{y,\mathrm{matrix}}}{d_f}\right) \tag{15.2.4}$$

A long fiber is harder to get pulled out of the matrix than a short one. When the fiber length reaches a certain critical value, a long fiber may break before it gets pulled out. Therefore, the maximum work per unit area required to extend the crack by pull-out is limited by the critical fiber length as

$$G_{\max} = \frac{1}{4} V_f\, d_f \left(\frac{\sigma_{\mathrm{uts,fiber}}^2}{\tau_{y,\mathrm{matrix}}}\right) \tag{15.2.5}$$

of which $\sigma_{\text{uts,fiber}}$ is the ultimate tensile strength of fibers. Given that the critical fiber length for pulling out a fiber before it fractures is determined using the shear-lag approach as

$$l_{\text{f,critical}} = \left(\frac{\sigma_{\text{uts,fiber}}}{\tau_{y,\text{matrix}}} \right) d_{\text{f}} \qquad (15.2.6)$$

of which $l_{\text{f,c}}$ is the critical fiber length. Thus,

$$G_{\text{max}} = \frac{1}{4} V_{\text{f}} l^2_{\text{f,critical}} \left(\frac{\tau_{y,\text{matrix}}}{d_{\text{f}}} \right) = \frac{1}{4} \left(\frac{\sigma^2_{\text{uts,fiber}}}{\tau_{y,\text{matrix}}} \right) V_{\text{f}} d_{\text{f}} \qquad (15.2.7)$$

15.2.2   Fibers-with-Defects Mode

On the other hand, if the fibers are so weakened by defects that the averaged effective critical fiber length of the fibers reduces from $l_{\text{f,critical}}$ to l^*_{c}, which accounts for the lowered effective fiber strength, as

$$l^*_{\text{c}} = l_{\text{f,critical}} \left(1 - \frac{\sigma^*_{\text{uts,fiber}}}{\sigma_{\text{uts,fiber}}} \right) \qquad (15.2.8)$$

where

l^*_{c} : Adjusted critical fiber length on account of effectiveness of defects;

$\sigma^*_{\text{uts,fiber}}$: Ultimate tensile strength of fibers on account of effectiveness of defects.

Parameter l^*_{c} is also interpreted as the fiber length between defects. The following two possible extreme outcomes can be obtained from the above equation:

(a) $\sigma^*_{\text{uts,fiber}} = 0$ for extremely weak fibers or defect-weakened fibers, as $l^*_{\text{c}} = l_{\text{f,critical}}$;

(b) $\sigma^*_{\text{uts,fiber}} = \sigma_{\text{uts,fiber}}$: $l^*_{\text{c}} = 0$, i.e., no pull-out.

If $0 < \sigma^*_{\text{uts,fiber}} < \sigma_{\text{uts,fiber}}$, the fraction of fiber pull-out will be $l^*_{\text{c}} / l_{\text{f,critical}}$, which may be asserted in the equation for the maximum work done per unit area as

$$
\begin{aligned}
G_{\text{max}} &= \left(\frac{l^*_{\text{c}}}{l_{\text{f}}} \right) \left[\frac{1}{4} V_{\text{f}} (l^*_{\text{c}})^2 \left(\frac{\sigma_{y,\text{matrix}}}{d_{\text{f}}} \right) \right] \\
&= \frac{\frac{1}{4} V_{\text{f}} (l^*_{\text{c}})^3 \sigma_{y,\text{matrix}}}{l_{\text{f}} d_{\text{f}}} \\
&= \frac{\frac{1}{4} V_{\text{f}} (l_{\text{f,critical}})^3 \left(\dfrac{1 - \sigma^*_{\text{uts,fiber}}}{\sigma_{\text{uts,fiber}}} \right)^3 \sigma_{y,\text{matrix}}}{l_{\text{f}} d_{\text{f}}}
\end{aligned}
\qquad (15.2.9)
$$

15.2.3 Interfacial Strain Energy Release Rate of Two Dissimilar Materials

The critical strain energy release rate criterion for predicting an interfacial failure is more realistic than the average shear stress failure criterion, as demonstrated by[Scheer & Nairn]. It is assumed that the interfacial debonding occurs when $G=G_{12C}$, where G_{12C} is the critical energy release rate at the interface, i.e., interfacial toughness, as the load is applied in the longitudinal direction of the fiber. By applying the pseudo-static interfacial load up to debonding between the glass fiber and epoxy in a composite, they discovered a limiting solution to the energy release rate of a frictionless interface between two dissimilar materials regardless of wetted lengths as shown in Fig. 15.2.2. [Liu & Nairn] added a quadratic term with respect to temperature variation to Scheer-Nairn equation. The Scheer-Nairn-Liu equation is

$$G = \frac{1}{2} R_f \left\{ \frac{1}{2} \left[E_{11}^{-1} + \left(\frac{V_f}{V_m} \right) E_m^{-1} \right] \sigma_{11f}^2 + (\alpha_{1f} - \alpha_m) \sigma_{11f} \Delta T + \left[\frac{D_o^2}{C_o} + \frac{V_m(\alpha_{1f} - \alpha_{2f})^2}{V_f A_o} \right] \Delta T^2 \right\}$$ (15.2.10)

where

R_f: Radius of the fiber, assumed to have a circular cross-section;
V_f: Volume fraction of the fiber;
V_m: Volume fraction of matrix;
σ_{11f}: Nominal normal stress along the fiber;
α_{1f}: Coefficient of linear thermal expansion along the fiber;
α_{2f}: Coefficient of linear thermal expansion transverse to the fiber;
α_m: Coefficient of linear thermal expansion of matrix;
v_m: Poisson's ratio of matrix;
v_{12f}: Poisson's ratio of the fiber;
v_{23f}: Poisson's ratio in the fibrous cross-section;
ΔT: Temperature variation.

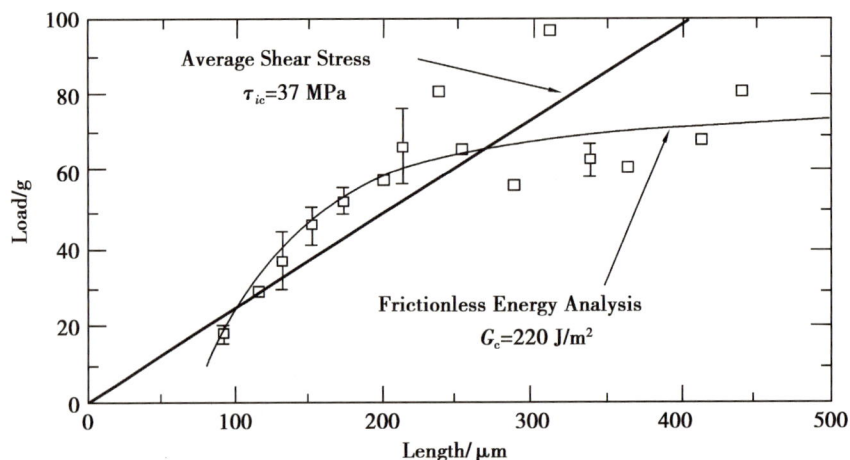

Fig. 15.2.2 Interfacial Energy Release Rate between Glass Fiber and Epoxy[Liu & Nairn]

This analytical expression for energy release rate is useful for debond growth that is independent of debond length. It is applicable to isotropic matrix reinforced with transversely isotropic fibers such as carbon fibers and the related material coefficients A_o, C_o, and D_o are given as follows:

$$A_o = \frac{\left(\dfrac{V_m}{V_f}\right)(1 - v_{23})}{E_{22}} + \frac{1 - v_m}{E_m} + \frac{1 + v_m}{V_f E_m} \tag{15.2.11}$$

$$C_o = \frac{1}{2}\left[E_{11}^{-1} + \left(\frac{V_f}{V_m}\right)E_m^{-1}\right] - \left(\frac{V_m}{V_f}\right)\frac{\left(\dfrac{v_{12}}{E_{11}} + \dfrac{V_f v_m}{V_m E_m}\right)^2}{A_o} \tag{15.2.12}$$

$$\text{and}\quad D_o = \frac{1}{2}(\alpha_{1f} - \alpha_m) + \left[\frac{\left(\dfrac{V_m}{V_f}\right)\left(\dfrac{v_{12}}{E_{11}} + \dfrac{V_f v_m}{V_m E_m}\right)}{A_o}\right](\alpha_{2f} - \alpha_m) \tag{15.2.13}$$

15.3   Failure Analysis of Composite Laminae

One major limiting factor in the design of composite laminae is their compressive strength. The compressive strength of a unidirectional-reinforced composite or lamina is roughly 50% of its tensile strength. Its compressive strength has also been consistently and considerably lower than its theoretical value. Localized softening like the failure surfaces of a free unconfined lamina compressed at both ends reveal local axial splitting due to a transverse tension that eventually cause the specimen to split macroscopically. Microscopic splitting weakens the not-so-well-reinforced surrounding matrix and leads to fiber breaking, fiber buckling and fiber kinking (Fig. 15.3.1), and subsequent fiber failure [Oguni & Ravichandran]. The axial splitting is manifested as a catastrophic drop in the stress as seen from the stress-strain response of the unconfined composite. A typical failure profile of unidirectional lamina is shown in Fig. 15.3.2, of which data points obtained from a wound tube having a diameter of 60 mm and thickness of 2 mm by [Hutter et al., 1974] and curved-fitted by [Pinho et al., 2006].

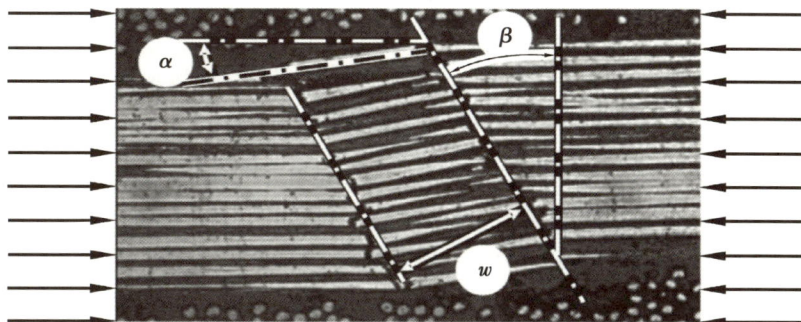

Fig. 15.3.1   Crack Initiated at an Angle (β) due to Kink Band Formation Subjected to Initial Misalignment [Pinho et al.] under Longitudinal Compression

15.3.1　Generalized Failure Criterion

A 3-dimensional failure model including both tensile and compressive loadings is required in light of Fig. 15.3.2. In case each individual fiber is transversely isotropic, the quadratic failure criterion for fibers extended from Tsai-Wu failure criterion can be applied to such a failure mode,

$$
\left(\frac{1}{\sigma_{11,\mathrm{uts}}} - \frac{1}{\sigma_{11,\mathrm{ucs}}}\right)\sigma_{11} + \left(\frac{1}{\sigma_{22,\mathrm{uts}}} - \frac{1}{\sigma_{22,\mathrm{ucs}}}\right)(\sigma_{22} + \sigma_{33}) + \frac{\sigma_{11}^2}{\sigma_{11,\mathrm{uts}}\,\sigma_{11,\mathrm{ucs}}} -
$$

$$
\frac{2\sigma_{11}(\sigma_{22} + \sigma_{33})}{3(\sigma_{11,\mathrm{uts}}\,\sigma_{11,\mathrm{ucs}}\,\sigma_{22,\mathrm{uts}}\,\sigma_{22,\mathrm{ucs}})^{\frac{1}{2}}} +
$$

$$
\frac{(\sigma_{22} + \sigma_{33})^2}{\sigma_{22,\mathrm{uts}}\,\sigma_{22,\mathrm{ucs}}} + \frac{\tau_{23}^2 - \sigma_{22}\,\sigma_{33}}{\tau_{23,\mathrm{uss}}^2} + \frac{\tau_{12}^2 + \tau_{31}^2}{\tau_{12,\mathrm{uss}}^2} \leqslant 1 \tag{15.3.1}
$$

where

$\sigma_{11,\mathrm{uts}}(\sigma_{11,\mathrm{ucs}})$: Ultimate tensile (compressive) strength along the fiber;

$\sigma_{22,\mathrm{uts}}(\sigma_{22,\mathrm{ucs}})$: Ultimate tensile (compressive) strength along the 2-axis;

$\sigma_{33,\mathrm{uts}}(\sigma_{33,\mathrm{ucs}})$: Ultimate tensile (compressive) Strength along the 3-axis;

$\tau_{12,\mathrm{uss}}, \tau_{23,\mathrm{uss}}$: Ultimate in-plane & out-of-plane shear strengths, respectively.

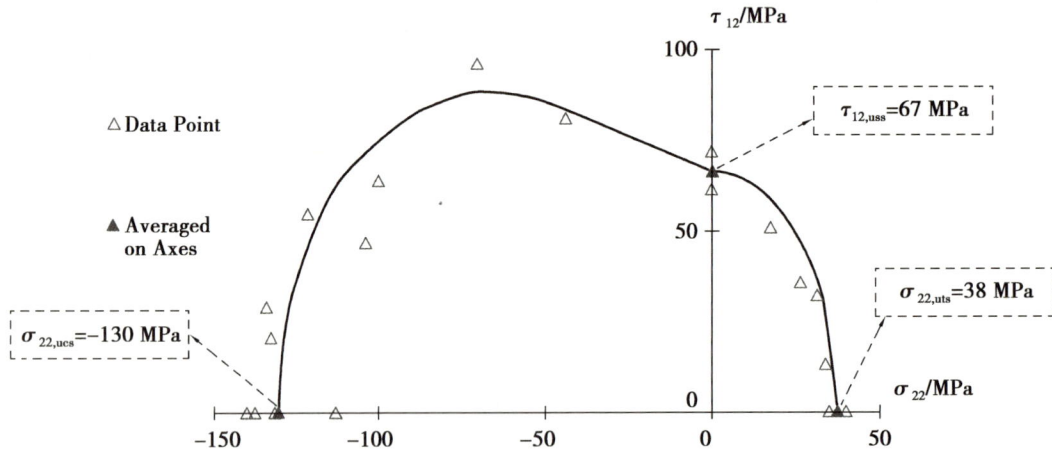

Fig. 15.3.2　Failure Profile Resulting from Compression/Tension-Torsion Tests[Hutter et al., 1975] and Follow-Up Curve Fitting[Pinho et al., 2006]

The Tsai-Wu failure criterion is applicable to most composite structures under multiaxial loadings such as pressure vessels and submersibles, though it is valid only for moderately anisotropic composites. In order to include the interaction between the stress component along the fiber direction and the other two directions, the polynomial failure profile based on Eq. (15.3.1) can also be written as[Christensen][Tsai & Hahn]

$$\left(\frac{1}{\sigma_{11,\text{uts}}} - \frac{1}{\sigma_{11,\text{ucs}}}\right)\sigma_{11} + \left(\frac{1}{\sigma_{22,\text{uts}}} - \frac{1}{\sigma_{22,\text{ucs}}}\right)(\sigma_{22} + \sigma_{33}) + \frac{\sigma_{11}^2}{\sigma_{11,\text{uts}}\sigma_{11,\text{ucs}}} +$$

$$\frac{\sigma_{22}^2}{\sigma_{22,\text{uts}}\sigma_{22,\text{ucs}}} + F_{12}\sigma_{11}(\sigma_{22} + \sigma_{33}) + \frac{\tau_{12}^2}{\tau_{12,\text{uss}}^2} \leqslant 1 \tag{15.3.2}$$

Interactive coefficient F_{12} can be determined from a biaxial-loaded test on a unidirectional lamina, with that $\sigma_{11} = \sigma_{22} = \sigma_{o}$ and other stress components being zero,

$$F_{12} = (2\sigma_o^2)^{-1}\{1 - (\sigma_{11,\text{uts}}^{-1} - \sigma_{11,\text{ucs}}^{-1} + \sigma_{22,\text{uts}}^{-1} - \sigma_{22,\text{ucs}}^{-1})\sigma_o -$$

$$[(\sigma_{11,\text{uts}}\,\sigma_{11,\text{ucs}})^{-1} + (\sigma_{22,\text{uts}}\,\sigma_{22,\text{ucs}})^{-1}]\sigma_o^2\} \tag{15.3.3}$$

Due to the complexity of a biaxial-loaded test in practice, F_{12} can also be determined in a tensile (or compressive) test at $45°$ degree to the 1-axis (in the primary material coordinate system) of the lamina up to failure. The biaxial stress applied in Eq. (15.3.3) is to be replaced by $\sigma_{45}/2$. Thus,

$$F_{12} = \left(\frac{2}{\sigma_{45}^{-2}}\right)\left\{1 - \frac{(\sigma_{11,\text{uts}}^{-1} - \sigma_{11,\text{ucs}}^{-1} + \sigma_{22,\text{uts}}^{-1} - \sigma_{22,\text{ucs}}^{-1})\sigma_{45}}{2} - \right.$$

$$\left.\frac{[(\sigma_{11,\text{uts}}\,\sigma_{11,\text{ucs}})^{-1} + (\sigma_{22,\text{uts}}\,\sigma_{22,\text{ucs}})^{-1} + (\tau_{12,\text{uss}}\,\tau_{12,\text{uss}})^{-1}]\sigma_{45}^2}{4}\right\} \tag{15.3.4}$$

15.3.2   Matrix-Controlled Failure Criteria

The Tsai-Wu failure criterion does not decompose into separate matrix-and fiber-controlled modes, whereas others do. For composites with high anisotropy, there are two independent failure criteria at the lamina level proposed. They are the matrix-controlled failure and the fiber-controlled failure. A matrix-controlled failure criterion for unidirectional laminae based on the failure parameters derived from strength denominators of the laminae is given as follows:

$$\left(\frac{1}{\sigma_{22,\text{uts}}} - \frac{1}{\sigma_{22,\text{ucs}}}\right)(\sigma_{22} + \sigma_{33}) + \frac{(\sigma_{22} + \sigma_{33})^2}{\sigma_{22,\text{uts}}\,\sigma_{22,\text{ucs}}} + \frac{\tau_{23}^2 - \sigma_{22}\,\sigma_{33}}{\tau_{23,\text{uss}}^2} + \frac{\tau_{12}^2 + \tau_{31}^2}{\tau_{12,\text{uss}}^2} \leqslant 1 \quad (15.3.5)$$

Finite element-based techniques using solid elements[Chiang] are attractive for simulation of the matrix-dominated failure modes in composites. Such models account for the micro-mechanical damage in the matrix through nonlinear interlaminar stress-strain relations. Fracture mechanics-based and stress-based failure criteria can be used to predict the matrix-dominated failures [Makeev et al.].

15.3.3 Fiber-Initiated Failure Criteria

A fiber-controlled failure criterion for unidirectional laminae based on the failure parameters derived from strength denominators of the laminae is given as follows:

$$\frac{\sigma_{11}^2}{\sigma_{11,\text{uts}}\,\sigma_{11,\text{ucs}}} + \left(\frac{1}{\sigma_{11,\text{uts}}} - \frac{1}{\sigma_{11,\text{ucs}}}\right)\sigma_{11} \leqslant 1 \tag{15.3.6}$$

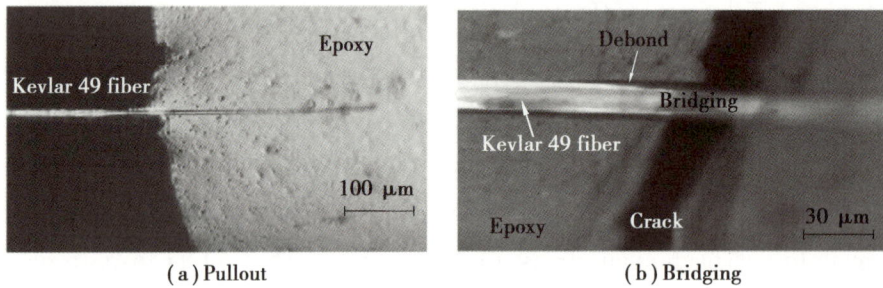

(a) Pullout   (b) Bridging

Fig. 15.3.3   Debonding between Matrix and Fibers: (a) Pullout and (b) Bridging[Lei et al.]

15.3.4 Failure Criterion Fiber-Matrix Interface

Two distinct failure modes at the interface between fibers and the matrix are demonstrated in Fig. 15.3.3: (a) pullout and (b) bridging. The typical axial stress distribution along a single fiber subject to a pull-out test is depicted in Fig. 15.3.4. The fiber-matrix interface mainly exhibits shear separation behavior but is complicated by opening mode. The failure criterion proposed by [Camanho & Dávila] is employed here:

$$\left(\frac{\sigma_{22}}{\sigma_{22,\text{uts}}}\right)^2 + \left(\frac{\tau_{12}}{\tau_{12,\text{uss}}}\right)^2 \leqslant 1 \tag{15.3.7}$$

where

σ_{22}: Normal stress in the opening mode, i.e., mode-I fracture;

τ_{12}: Shear stress in the sliding mode, i.e., mode-II fracture;

$\sigma_{22,\text{uts}}$: Ultimate tensile stress in the opening mode, perpendicular to the fiber;

$\tau_{12,\text{uss}}$: Ultimate shear stress in the sliding mode, along the fiber axis.

As a damage tolerance in a lamina, cracks in the matrix must either arrest at the fiber/matrix interface or deflect onto it to create a bridging mode. Fibers bridging across the two crack faces are one of the causes of an increasing R-curve. Conditions for the deflection to the interface are determined using the two energy release rates associated with two distinct hypotheses based on mode-I fracture energy: (1) penetration across the interphase boundary (G_{Id}) and (2) deflection into the boundary (G_{Ip}), respectively. This mechanism has been discussed by [Sorensen and Jacobsen] and denoted that the effect of fiber bridging on G_{Ip} values can depend on the specimen arm stiffness. Mathematically[Berry],

$$G_{IC} = \frac{n F \delta}{2 b a} \tag{15.3.8}$$

and $C = K a^n$ \hfill (15.3.9)

where

    n: Empirical constant;

    F: Force applied;

    δ: Crack opening;

    a: Crack length;

    b: Crack width and $2b$ for a two-sided surface crack;

    K: Empirical constant;

    C: Compliance, and $C \equiv \delta / F$.

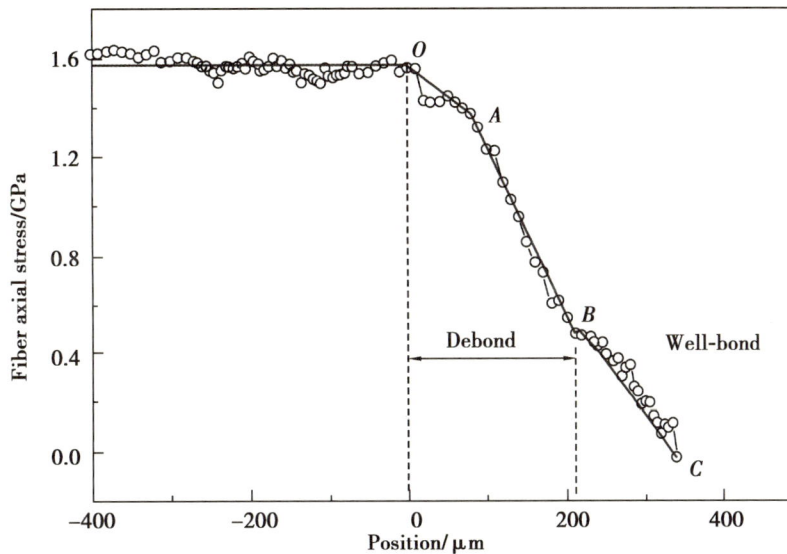

Fig. 15.3.4   Stress Distribution Obtained from a Pullout Test[Lei et al.]

The key material property emerged in the ratio of G_{Id} to G_{Ip}, i.e., G_{Id}/G_{Ip} is the elastic mismatch, to which elastic constants are applied[Zok & Levi] as

$$R_{mismatch} = \frac{E_f - E_m}{E_f + E_m} \tag{15.3.10}$$

Bridging tends to occur with a higher elastic mismatch (R_{mismatch}). This is attributed to the effect of a larger crack tip opening displacement on breaking fibers in the bridging zone in more flexible specimens. The stiffer samples show a smaller bridged zone and lower toughness. The low failure strain of the high modulus fibers in the bridging zone may be responsible for this.

On the other hand, once fibers begin to fail, the subsequent behavior is dictated by the nature and extent of inelastic deformation within the surrounding matrix and the effect of the stress concentration in neighboring fibers.

When a crack in the matrix propagates vertically across an unbroken fiber as embedded, the bridging fiber will show partial debonding across both sides of the matrix crack. The formation of bridging fiber can be regarded as two fiber-pullout processes, as described by [Piggot] model. The interfacial strength depends on mechanical interlock, chemical bond, van der Waal force, and electrostatic attraction. Interface parameters such as fiber diameter, contact angle, embedded fiber length, and wettability are also of concern for the given fibers and matrix. Without considering the stress singularity between dissimilar materials and friction between the fiber and matrix, [Piggot] gave the interfacial shear stress along the embedded fiber under a pull-out load as

$$\tau_{12} = \left\{ \frac{n \cos h\left[\dfrac{n(L-x)}{r}\right]}{2 \sin h\left(\dfrac{nL}{r}\right)} \right\} \sigma_{11,x=0} \qquad (15.3.11)$$

where

    L: Fiber length;

    r: Fiber radius;

    $\sigma_{11,x=0}$: Pull-out stress at the $x=0$ (Fig. 3.8) with the loading point at the free surface;

    n: Aspect ratio, a constant as a function of fiber geometry/material and matrix material.

15.3.5   Interfacial Shear Strength

The tensile strength of the matrix reinforced with well-aligned unidirectional fibers can be obtained from the modified Kelly-Tyson-Bowyer-Bader equation, in which the interfacial shear strength between the matrix and fiber is taken into consideration as

$$\sigma_{11,\text{uts}} = \chi \left\{ \sum_{i=1} \frac{\tau_{12,\text{us}} L_{\text{f},i} V_{\text{f},i}}{d_{\text{f}}} + \sum_{j=1} \left[\sigma_{\text{f,uts}} V_{\text{f},j} \left(1 - \frac{\sigma_{\text{f,uts}} d_{\text{f}}}{4 \tau_{12} L_{\text{f},j}} \right) \right] \right\} + (1 - V_{\text{f},j}) \sigma_{\text{m,uts}}$$

$$(15.3.12)$$

where

$\sigma_{f,uts}$: Ultimate tensile strength of fibers;

$\sigma_{m,uts}$: Ultimate tensile strength of matrix;

$\chi \leqslant 1$: Fiber-alignment factor; $\chi = 1$ for a perfect alignment;

$\tau_{12,us}$: Interfacial shear strength between the matrix and fiber;

$L_{f,j}$: Fiber length;

$V_{f,j}$: Volume fraction;

i, j : Indices for fiber groups.

15.3.6   Micromechanics of Failure

Based on micromechanics of failure (MMF), a constituent-based methodology for predicting failure and life of composites was studied by [Ha]. The six starting strengths for evaluating an evolving failure profile are:

(a) Tensile and compressive strengths of fibers;

(b) Tensile and compressive strengths of the matrix;

(c) Normal and shear strengths for the fiber/matrix interface.

Matrix and fiber constituent failures, as well as interfacial cohesion damage, are taken into account to determine the failure envelope of a unidirectional ply. Micro-stresses in the matrix, fibers and interface are calculated from macro-scaled stresses using a micromechanics approach. The methodology is illustrated in Fig. 15.3.5[Ha et al.].

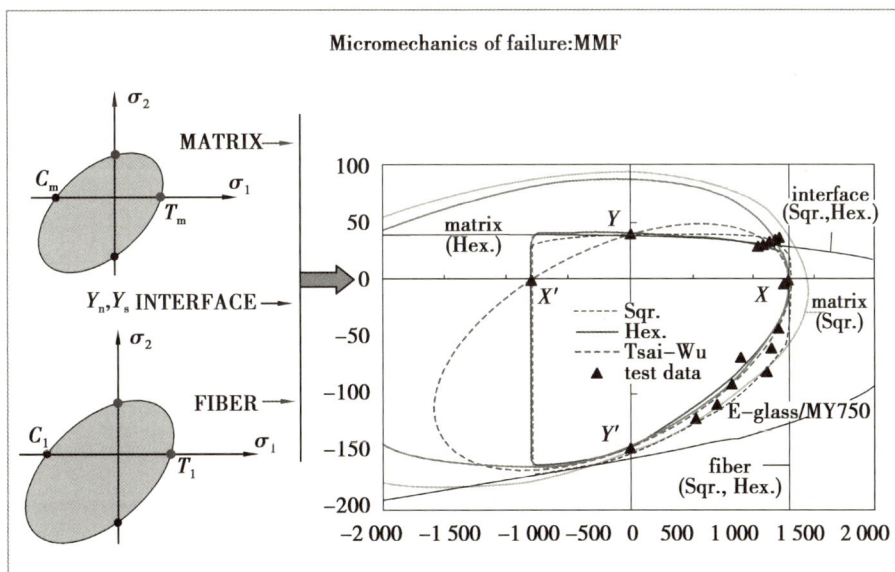

Fig. 15.3.5   Failure Profile Defined Using Micromechanics Model[Ha et al.]

15.4　Interlaminar Strength

The main advantage of composite materials is that a designer can choose the material according to the directional stiffness and strength in a specific direction. At a certain loading condition, so much accumulated damage at the micro and lamina levels in the form of localized failure modes that the laminate cannot sustain anymore may comprise the ultimate load. The failure in such a broad and total sense is called progressive damage criterion for laminates. This process may include the in-plane and the out-of-plane failure modes for the laminate although both types of failure modes are traditionally taken to be uncoupled on the excuse of an isotropy of effects between them. Interlaminar stress components of the $[0/90]_S$ laminate (Fig. 15.1.1) subjected to a uniform strain (ε_{xx}) are plotted in Fig. 15.4.1, where there are only three significant components while the other three don't respond.

Interlaminar stresses, i.e., σ_{zz}, τ_{xz}, and τ_{yz} due to the load transfer between two adjacent layers, are created by the mutual constraint between them as they are "glued" together with strain continuities. Consider shear stress τ_{yz} (i.e., shear stress acting on the cross-section perpendicular to y-axis with force directed along out-of-plane z-axis) along the y-axis. Since there is no $\tau_{yz,b}$ at the free edge ($y=b$), a high shear stress gradient near the free edge is expected to balance the "unbalanced shear effect" accumulated from the lamina center ($y=0$), as depicted in Fig. 15.1.1.

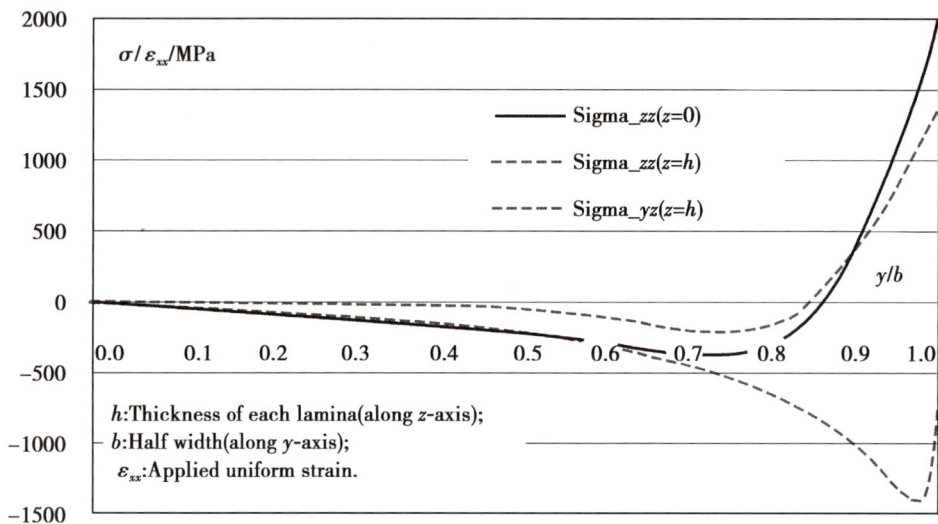

Fig. 15.4.1　Interlaminar Stresses of the $[0/90]_S$ Laminate Subjected to a Uniform Strain ε_{xx} : $\sigma_{zz}(z=0)$, $\sigma_{zz}(z=h)$ & $\sigma_{yz}(z=h)$ are plotted as $\sigma_{xz}(z=0) = \sigma_{yz}(z=0) = \sigma_{xz}(z=h) = 0$

15.4.1　Interlaminar Stresses at Free Edges

When two composite laminae are bonded together, interlaminar stress singularities arise between them, even at free-boundary edges or corners without any crack. Each asymptotic stress components σ_{ij} at the interface between two laminae due to an edge effect can be described [Mohammed & Liechti] by

$$\sigma_{ij} = \sum_{n=0}^{N} K_n \, r^{-\lambda_n} f_{ij,n}(\theta) \qquad\qquad (15.4.1)$$

where

K_n: Stress intensity factors;

λ_n: Stress singularity, a complex number, but no singularity if the real part of $\lambda_n \leqslant 0$;

r: Radius of the point of interest originating from the singular tip (free-boundary edge);

$f_{ij,n}(\theta)$: Function of angle θ, referring to the x-axis.

Note that exponent λ_n is the order of stress singularity, which is determined by a combined effect of laminar materials, fiber angles, and edge geometry. Coefficient K_n given in Eq. (15.4.1) dominates only the local region near an interfacial edge or corner, and it is called intensity of singularity or free edge intensity factor.

Delamination is one of the major failure modes in laminated composite materials and their associated interlaminar stresses are highly nonlinear as shown by Eq. (15.4.1). It's common to assume that out-of-plane modulus E_{33} is equal to in-plane transverse modulus E_{22}, making its measurement of lesser importance. This is not the case, however, for the interlaminar tensile strength. Differences in manufacturing methods can also affect the bond strength between the plies of a composite laminate and produce significant differences between the interlaminar tensile strength and the in-plane tensile strength transverse to the fiber direction.

15.4.2 Ramberg-Osgood Equation

The following Ramberg-Osgood equations are proposed for the assessment of highly nonlinear shear stress-strain relations in the x-z and y-z material planes, respectively

$$\gamma_{xz} = \frac{\tau_{xz}}{G_{xz}} + \left(\frac{\tau_{xz}}{K_{xz}}\right)^{\frac{1}{n}} \qquad\qquad (15.4.2)$$

and $\quad \gamma_{yz} = \dfrac{\tau_{yz}}{G_{yz}} + \left(\dfrac{\tau_{yz}}{K_{yz}}\right)^{\frac{1}{n}} \qquad\qquad (15.4.3)$

where

G_{xz} and G_{yz}: Shear moduli;

K_{xz} and K_{yz}: Constants, which are material parameters;

n: Exponent, which is a material parameter.

15.4.3 Control of Interlaminar Singularities

An interlayer can be inserted between laminae to defuse the residual stress due to the difference in the coefficients of thermal expansion and Poisson's ratios. One major application is the three-layered journal bearings for engine crankshafts.

There exhibits strong stress singularities between the two belts of a passenger tire and at the interface between the upper tire belt and tire tread. Belt edge strips, also called belt wedges, are employed to lower the free edge effect between the two belts. A nylon overlay is placed on top of both tire belts such that the dynamic effect of the nylon cap ply may restrain expansion of the belt bundle during highway speed operation.

15.5 Failure Criteria for Composites with Random Fibers

Assume that the matrix is homogeneous and isotropic and the matrix strength under uniaxial compression is larger than the strength under uniaxial tension, as most polymers do.

15.5.1 Modified von Mises Failure Criterion

A modified version of von Mises failure criterion suggested by [Christensen] is granted here for predicting the matrix failure in a composite reinforced with random fibers:

$$\frac{\sigma_{eq}^2}{\sigma_{uts}\,\sigma_{ucs}} + \left(\frac{1}{\sigma_{uts}} - \frac{1}{\sigma_{ucs}}\right) I_1 \leqslant 1 \qquad (15.5.1)$$

and $\quad I_1 = \sigma_1 + \sigma_2 + \sigma_3 \qquad (15.5.2)$

where

σ_{eq} : Equivalent stress subjected to loadings, e.g. von Mises stress;

σ_{uts} : Ultimate tensile stress from uniaxial test;

σ_{ucs} : Ultimate compressive stress from uniaxial test;

I_1 : The first stress invariant of loaded stresses;

σ_1, σ_2, σ_3 : The 3 principal stresses.

When the porosity of a composite is significant for composites reinforced with particulates or powders, the ultimate tensile strength used in the above equation has to be modified as a function of porosity [Metha],

$$\sigma_{uts} = \sigma_{uts,0}\,\exp(-a\,V_{voids}) \qquad (15.5.3)$$

where σ_{uts}: Tensile strength of material at a porosity P;

$\quad\quad\sigma_{uts,0}$: Tensile strength of material at zero porosity;

$\quad\quad a$: Material constant.

15.5.2   Loss Factor

The tensile stress-strain relationship as generalized for a composite reinforced with short fibers is given as follows[Gu et al.]:

$$\sigma_{comp} = C_\theta \, C_f \, C_i \, V_f \, \sigma_f(\varepsilon_c) + V_m \, E_m \, \varepsilon_m \tag{15.5.4}$$

and $$\sigma_f(\varepsilon_c) = \left\{ 1 + \left[\left(\frac{E_m}{E_f} \right)^{\frac{1}{2}} - 1 \right] \frac{\tan h\left[\beta_s \left(\frac{L_f}{d_f} \right) \right]}{\beta_s \left(\frac{L_f}{d_f} \right)} \right\} (E_f \varepsilon_c - \sigma_{thermal}) \tag{15.5.5}$$

of which[Kim & Kwac][Cox][Nairna & Mendels],

$$\beta_s = \left[\frac{8G_m}{\left(E_f \ln \frac{2S_f}{d_f} \right)} \right]^{\frac{1}{2}} \frac{1}{d_f} = \left(\frac{4E_m}{E_f(1+v_m)\ln \frac{2S_f}{d_f}} \right)^{\frac{1}{2}} \frac{1}{d_f} \tag{15.5.6}$$

$$\sigma_{thermal} = \frac{2(\alpha_m - \alpha_f) \, E_m \, \Delta T}{(1+v_m) + (1+v_f) \dfrac{E_m}{E_f}} \tag{15.5.7}$$

and $$C_f = 1 - V_f^2 \tag{15.5.8}$$

where

$\quad C_\theta$: Correction factor for fiber orientation, as $C_\theta = 1$ and 0.5 for reinforcements with well-and random-aligned fibers, respectively;

$\quad C_f$: Loss factor due to fiber occupation;

$\quad C_i$: Correction factor for the fiber-matrix interface;

$\quad \beta_s$: Shear lag parameter;

$\quad S_f$: Mean center-to-center separation of fibers normal to their common axial direction;

$\quad \Delta T$: Temperature variation, from the melting point of the matrix to working temperature;

$\quad \sigma_{thermal}$: Thermal stress between the fiber and matrix material due to ΔT.

When aspect ratio L_f/d_f is smaller than the critical value, the debonding between fibers and the matrix will occur. Otherwise, the fiber breaks. A simplifed equation can be applied as the first approximation to finding out the critical shear stress to buckle or break the long fiber,

$$\tau_{\text{critical}} = \left[\frac{\ln\left(\dfrac{2L_f}{d_f}\right) - 1.75}{2\left(\dfrac{L_f}{d_f}\right)^4} \right] E_f \qquad (15.5.9)$$

15.5.3 Failure Subjected to Impact

When plastics reinforced randomly with short fibers are exposed to low-velocity impact, a significant damage may develop inside the composite part. The impact damage may cause a reduction of the mechanical performance of such composites, and thus a progressive damage model with modified stiffness has been of great interest to researchers[Jeong et al.].

15.6 Fatigue of Composites under Multiaxial Loadings

It was found that the transverse strain-induced failure due to voids/defects in a unidirectional composite of glass-fiber/epoxy is more likely to occur than that for the pure matrix under uniaxial loading[Asp et al.] regardless of the fiber volume fraction. The location of the maximum dilatation energy density in the matrix lies close to the fiber/matrix interface. In the case of an off-axis unidirectional laminate subjected to mechanical fatigue, microscopic defects may cause an unstable crack propagation and sudden failure, whereas in multidirectional laminates the damage evolution process is more progressive as being involved with several damage mechanisms, including the growth of micro-scale defects, off-axis crack nucleation and propagation, and interlaminar delamination between plies, as schematically illustrated in Fig. 15.6.1.

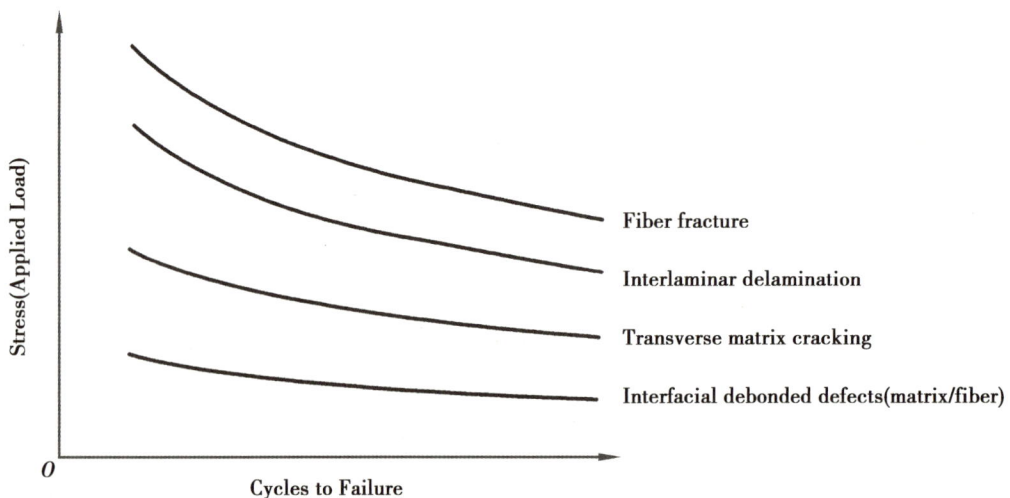

Fig. 15.6.1   Relative Cycling Fatigue Failure Modes of Fibrous Laminates

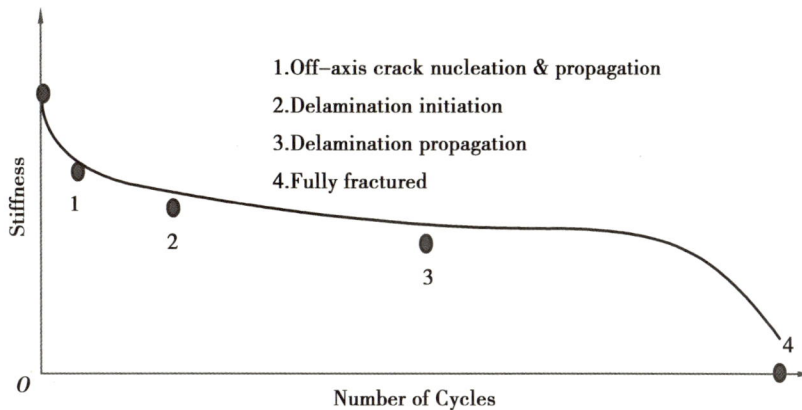

Fig. 15.6.2   Reduction in Stiffness of Multidirectional Laminates under Mechanical Fatigue[Quaresimin et al.]

15.6.1   Stiffness and Fatigue Damage

When a multidirectional composite laminate is subjected to mechanical fatigue, microscopic defects embedded in a composite can induce a quick drop of structural stiffness in the very early stage, as shown in Fig. 15.6.2. The first event of damage on the micro scale prior to the initiation of a visible off-axis crack is the initiation of micro-cracks in the matrix, inclined of a certain angle with respect to the fiber's direction. In case of a $[0/90]_s$ cross-ply composite is loaded axially along the 0° fibers, the initial off-axis crack path nucleates in the 90° ply and its potential crack path is perpendicular to the 0° ply as shown in Fig. 15.6.3(a). The off-axis crack nucleates and propagates as shown in Fig. 15.6.3(b) and more off-axis cracks may develop sub-sequentially. In the meanwhile the longitudinal crack along the fiber axis of 0° ply is activated and it is then followed by multiple delaminations between the two plies as shown in Fig. 15.6.3 (c) and Fig. 15.6.3.(d). As delaminations grow longer and/or wider, the entire structural stiffness goes down further and eventually leads to a catastrophic failure. Therefore, the design against stiffness of a composite can be divided into three stages:

(a) Designing against multiple intralaminar debonding (Point 1 in Fig. 15.6.2);
(b) Designing against multiple interlaminar delamination (Point 2 in Fig. 15.6.2);
(c) Designing against total fracture (Point 3 in Fig. 15.6.2).

Due to the demand of energy savings and high structural rigidity, the automotive industry has been actively engaged with introducing laminated and woven composites as primary load-carrying components. The failure criteria of these materials under fatigue loading, however, is not yet fully explored. Designing against stiffness degradation and strength degradation under mechanical fatigue has yet to be defined for different automotive components, which consist of multidirectional plies.

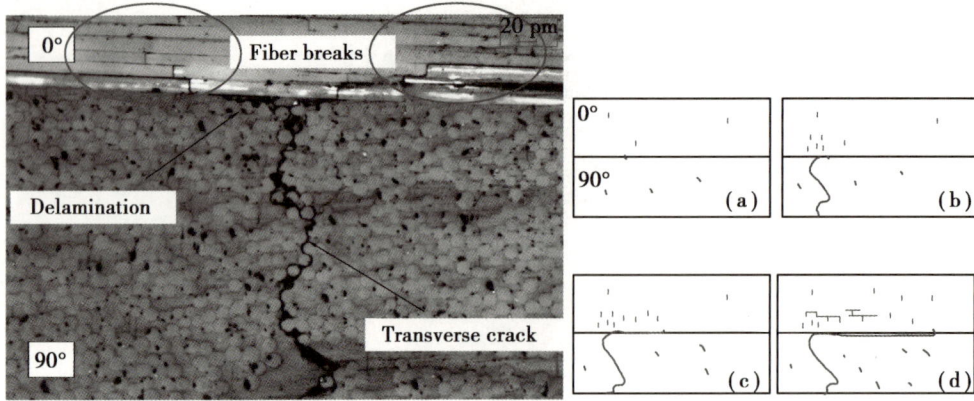

Fig. 15.6.3 **Sequential Crack Patterns of [0/90]ₛ Cross-Ply Composite under Mechanical Fatigue** [Quaresimin et al.]: (a) → (b) → (b) → (c) → (d).

15.6.2 Intralaminar Damage Nucleation under Fatigue Loading

Based on the algorithm of damage accumulation, [Zhang et al.] applied a cycle-by-cycle damage evolution law in terms of elastic energy, stress ratio, and evolutionary damage of each load block to assess the fatigue life of angle-plied laminates. Under the plane-stress assumption with small perturbations in the linear elastic range, the strain energy done per cycle expressed in the primary material coordinates (1, 2, 3) can be written as follows:

$$
W_{se} = \frac{\frac{1}{2}\sigma_{11}^2}{E_{11}(1 - D_{11})} + \frac{\frac{1}{2}\sigma_{22}^2}{E_{22}(1 - D_{22})} - \frac{v_{12}\sigma_{11}^2\sigma_{22}^2}{E_{11}} + \frac{\frac{1}{2}\tau_{12}^2}{G_{12}(1 - D_{12})} \tag{15.6.1}
$$

where

W_{se} (J/m³ or J/mm³): Strain energy;

E_{11}, E_{22}, G_{12} (Pa or MPa): In-plane Young's moduli and shear modulus;

σ_{11}, σ_{22}, τ_{12} (Pa or MPa): In-plane stress components in the primary material coordinates;

D_{11}: Dimensionless damage along the 1-axis, i.e., induced by fiber breakage;

D_{22}: Dimensionless damage along the 2-axis, i.e., induced by matrix breakage in tension;

D_{12}: Dimensionless damage in shear (1-2 plane), i.e., breakage at fiber/matrix interface.

D_{11}, D_{22} and D_{12} are damage metrics that begin with zeros for a robust material and they will accumulate iteratively with respect to the progressively applied load. The variation of the strain energy per cycle with respect to each individual dimensionless damage parameter can be written as

$$
\frac{\partial W_{se}}{\partial D_{11}} = \frac{\frac{1}{2}\sigma_{11}^2}{E_{11}(1 - D_{11})^2} \tag{15.6.2}
$$

$$\frac{\partial W_{se}}{\partial D_{22}} = \frac{\frac{1}{2}\sigma_{22}^2}{E_{22}(1-D_{22})^2} \tag{15.6.3}$$

$$\text{and} \quad \frac{\partial W_{se}}{\partial D_{12}} = \frac{\frac{1}{2}\tau_{12}^2}{G_{12}(1-D_{12})^2} \tag{15.6.4}$$

By Eq. (15.6.2), the updated stiffness, i.e., $E_{11}(1-D_{11})^2$, reduces with respect to decreasing damage parameter D_{11} due to fatigue cycling. In other words, dD_{11}/dN is the growth of damage due to cycling, so are dD_{22}/dN and dD_{12}/dN. It is herein assumed that

$$\frac{dD_{11}}{dN} = f(D_{11}, N, R, \sigma_{11}) \tag{15.6.5}$$

$$\frac{dD_{22}}{dN} = f(D_{22}, N, R, \sigma_{22}) \tag{15.6.6}$$

$$\text{and} \quad \frac{dD_{12}}{dN} = f(D_{12}, N, R, \tau_{12}) \tag{15.6.7}$$

where

N: Cycles to failure;

R: Stress ratio.

When the conceptual general failure criterion, i.e., Eq. (15.3.1), is applied to the intralaminar failure, the resulting stress flow reduces to

$$\sigma_{eq} = \left[\frac{\sigma_{11}^2}{\sigma_{11,uts}\,\sigma_{11,ucs}} + (\sigma_{11,uts}^{-1} - \sigma_{11,ucs}^{-1})\,\sigma_{11} + (\sigma_{22,uts}^{-1} - \sigma_{22,ucs}^{-1})\,\sigma_{22} + \right.$$

$$\left. \frac{-\sigma_{22}^2}{\sigma_{22,uts}\,\sigma_{22,ucs}} + F_{12}\,\sigma_{11}\,\sigma_{22} + \frac{\tau_{12}^2}{\tau_{12,uss}^2} \right]^{\frac{1}{2}} \tag{15.6.8}$$

The physical meaning of the stress flow for orthotropic materials given above resembles the von Mises stress for 2-dimensional isotropic homogeneous materials. Eqs. (4.5.10)-(4.5.12) can be applied to individual stress components, i.e., σ_{11}, σ_{22} and τ_{12}, for fatigue life estimation. For example, along the fiber direction,

$$\varepsilon_{11a} = \frac{\sigma_{11f}' - \sigma_{11m}}{E_{11}(1-D_{11})}(2N_f)^{b_{11}} + \varepsilon_{11f}'(2N_f)^{c_{11}} \tag{15.6.9}$$

$$\varepsilon_{22a} = \frac{\sigma'_{22f} - \sigma_{22m}}{E_{22}(1 - D_{22})}(2N_f)^{b_{22}} + \varepsilon'_{22f}(2N_f)^{c_{22}} \tag{15.6.10}$$

$$\text{and} \quad \gamma_{12a} = \frac{\tau'_{12f} - \tau_{12m}}{G_{12}(1 - D_{12})}(2N_f)^{b_{12}} + \gamma'_{12f}(2N_f)^{c_{12}} \tag{15.6.11}$$

Parameter D_{ij} accounts for the damage corresponding to each failure mode, i.e., D_{11} for mode-I along the fiber direction, D_{22} for mode-I transverse to the fiber direction, and D_{12} for mode-II. It is process dependent and $D_{ij0} = 0$ initially at time $= 0$. $D_{ij} < 1$ before the structure loses the entire stiffness. Initially $D_{ij0} = 0$ initially at time $= 0$. Then,

$$D_{ij} = \sum \Delta D_{ij} \tag{15.6.12}$$

where $\quad \Delta D_{ij} = f(2N_f, \Delta t_{ij}, \sigma_{ija}, R_{ij}) \tag{15.6.13}$

The above equation tells that diffusion damage interval ΔD_{ij} is a function of cycle $2N_f$, hold-time duration Δt_{ij} (e.g. creep phenomenon), stress amplitude σ_{ija}, and stress ratio R_{ij}. It can be understood that $\Delta t_{11} \neq \Delta t_{22} \neq \Delta t_{12}$, $\sigma_{11a} \neq \sigma_{22a} \neq \tau_{12a}$ and $R_{11} \neq R_{22} \neq R_{12}$ in a general case, especially if the loading is nonproportional. As proposed by [Zhang et al.], the damage growth rate equation is prescribed following the form of the Kachanov-Rabotnov equation [Rabotnov],

$$\frac{dD_{ij}}{dN} = \frac{A_{ij}\left(\dfrac{\sigma_a^*}{1 - \sigma_m^*}\right)^{n_{ij}}}{(1 - D_{ij})^{B_{ij}}} \tag{15.6.14}$$

$$\sigma_a^* = \frac{\sigma_a}{\sigma_{eq}} \tag{15.6.15}$$

$$\text{and} \quad \sigma_m^* = \frac{\sigma_m}{\sigma_{eq}} \tag{15.6.16}$$

where

A_{ij}: Coefficient, to be obtained from regression of test data;

B_{ij}: Exponent, to be obtained from regression of test data;

n_{ij}: Exponent, to be obtained from regression of test data;

σ_a^* : Dimensionless stress amplitude;

σ_m^* : Dimensionless mean stress;

σ_{eq}: Equivalent stress, which can be obtained from Eq. (15.6.8).

Note that A_{ij}, B_{ij}, and n_{ij} are material-dependent. After Eq. (4.5.15) is derived, dD/dN can be approximated using $\Delta D/\Delta N$.

15.6.3 Intralaminar Debonding of Laminates under Fatigue Loading

If there is a perfect bonding between the matrix and fibers, the principal stresses developed in the matrix at the boundary can be used for predicting the direction of first crack propagation in the matrix. However, the wetting between the matrix and fibers has never been so perfect. The debonding defects increase with respect to increasing fatigue cycling as shown in Fig. 15.6.4. Both the stiffness and strength decrease with increasing defects. Assume that the design against stiffness degradation is defined the moment when interlaminar debonding cannot be contained. Using microscopic assessment of the fracture surfaces under various types of loading, [Hahn & Johannesson] proposed a fracture toughness-based fully-debonding failure criterion as follows:

$$g\left(\frac{G_{\mathrm{I}}}{G_{\mathrm{IC}}}\right) + (1 - g)\left(\frac{G_{\mathrm{I}}}{G_{\mathrm{IC}}}\right)^{\frac{1}{2}} + \frac{G_{\mathrm{II}}}{G_{\mathrm{IIC}}} = 1 \qquad \text{(Fully deboned)} \qquad (15.6.17)$$

and $g = \dfrac{G_{\mathrm{IC}}}{G_{\mathrm{IIC}}}$ (15.6.18)

where

$\sigma_{1,\mathrm{uts}}$: Tensile strength in the principal direction in the opening mode;

$\sigma_{1,\mathrm{uts}}$: Tensile strength in the principal direction in the opening mode;

G_{IC} : Fracture toughness in opening mode;

G_{IIC} : Fracture toughness in shear mode.

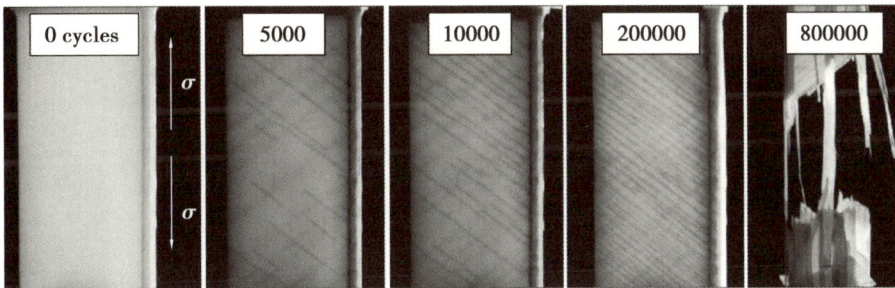

Fig. 15.6.4   Increase in Debonding Defects in a $[0/60_2/0/-60_2]_s$ Epoxy/GF Laminate as Fatigue Cycling Proceeds[Quaresimin et al.]

Assuming quadratic interactions between tractions acting in the critical plane (i.e., plane of failure) as proposed by[Davila et al.] and modified by[Camanho et al.], a conservative failure criterion for crack-initiation in laminated composites under biaxial static and in-phase fatigue loading conditions, is given as follows:

$$(1 - g)\left(\frac{\sigma_{22}}{\sigma_{22,\mathrm{uts}}}\right) + g\left(\frac{\sigma_{22}}{\sigma_{22,\mathrm{uts}}}\right)^2 + \left(\frac{\tau_{12}}{\tau_{12,\mathrm{uss}}}\right)^2 = 1 \quad (\sigma_{22} > 0) \qquad (15.6.19)$$

and $\quad \left(\dfrac{\tau_{12}}{\tau_{12,\mathrm{uss}}}\right)^2 = 1 \quad (\sigma_{22} \leqslant 0)$ (15.6.20)

The two equations given above are formulated on the basis of a linear relationship between the shear stress and shear strain that results in term $(\tau_{12}/\tau_{12,\mathrm{uss}})^2$. However, the shearing modulus is quite nonlinear for most fibrous composites, instead of term $(\tau_{12}/\tau_{12,\mathrm{uss}})^2$ the following energy expression has been proposed: $Q(\tau_{12})/Q(\tau_{12,\mathrm{uss}})$, of which

$$Q(\tau_{12}) = 2\int_0^{\tau_{12}} \tau_{12}\, \mathrm{d}\gamma_{12} \tag{15.6.21}$$

and $\quad \gamma_{12} = \gamma_{12}(\tau_{12})$ (15.6.22)

Therefore, when the shear stress-strain relationship is nonlinear, instead of Eqs. (15.6.19) and (15.6.20) the following two equations apply

$$(1-g)\left(\dfrac{\sigma_{22}}{\sigma_{22,\mathrm{uts}}}\right) + g\left(\dfrac{\sigma_{22}}{\sigma_{22,\mathrm{uts}}}\right)^2 + \dfrac{Q(\tau_{12})}{Q(\tau_{12,\mathrm{uss}})} = 1 \quad (\sigma_{22} > 0) \tag{15.6.23}$$

and $\quad \dfrac{Q(\tau_{12})}{Q(\tau_{12,\mathrm{uss}})} = 1 \quad (\sigma_{22} \leqslant 0)$ (15.6.24)

When the stress-strain relationship is linear, the operating shear energy, i.e., Eq. (15.6.16), its corresponding shear energy at failure, and their shear energy ratio become, respectively

$$Q(\tau_{12}) = 2\int_0^{\tau_{12}} \tau_{12}\, \mathrm{d}\gamma_{12} = 2\int_0^{\tau_{12}} \tau_{12}\, \mathrm{d}\dfrac{\tau_{12}}{G_{12}} = \dfrac{\tau_{12}^2}{G_{12}} \tag{15.6.25}$$

Crack Initiation Locus

$$Q(\tau_{12,\mathrm{uss}}) = 2\int_0^{\tau_{12,\mathrm{uss}}} \tau_{12}\, \mathrm{d}\gamma_{12} = 2\int_0^{\tau_{12,\mathrm{uss}}} \tau_{12}\, \mathrm{d}\left(\dfrac{\tau_{12}}{G_{12}}\right) = \dfrac{\tau_{12,\mathrm{uss}}^2}{G_{12}} \tag{15.6.26}$$

and $\quad \dfrac{Q(\tau_{12})}{Q(\tau_{12,\mathrm{uss}})} = \left(\dfrac{\tau_{12}}{\tau_{12,\mathrm{uss}}}\right)^2$ (15.6.27)

The above equation tells us the derivations of Eq. (15.6.21) and the last term of Eq. (15.6.19) are based on linear elasticity. The following Ramberg-Osgood equations are proposed for assessing the highly nonlinear shear stress-strain relation in the 1-2 material plane,

$$\gamma_{12} = \dfrac{\tau_{12}}{G_{12}} + \left(\dfrac{\tau_{12}}{K_{12}}\right)^{\frac{n_a+1}{n_a}} \tag{15.6.28}$$

Substituting the above equation into Eq. (15.6.15) yields

$$Q(\tau_{12}) = \frac{\tau_{12}^2}{G_{12}} + \left(\frac{2 K_{12}}{n_{12} + 1}\right) \left[\left(\frac{\tau_{12}}{K_{12}}\right)^{\frac{n_u+1}{n_u}}\right]$$

(15.6.29)

This work conducted by [Makeev et al.] shows that simulating the matrix-dominated failure modes in thin laminated composites based on the algorithm of matrix-ply crack initiation using elastoplastic 3-dimensional finite element analysis is practical as verified with test results. The data of the example EP/CF (8552/IM7) composite constituents used in the study by [Makeev et al.] are given below:

E_{11} = 171 GPa, $\qquad E_{22}$ = 8.96 GPa, $\qquad E_{33} = E_{22}$;

v_{12} = 0.32, $\qquad\qquad v_{12} = v_{12}$, $\qquad\qquad v_{23}$ = 0.5;

G_{12} = 5.31 GPa, $\quad G_{13} = G_{12}$, $\qquad\qquad G_{23} = \dfrac{E_{22}}{2(1 + v_{23})}$;

K_{12} = 260 MPa, $\quad K_{13}$ = 260 MPa, $\quad K_{23} = \left(\dfrac{G_{23}}{G_{12}}\right) K_{12}$;

n_{12} = 0.203;

$\sigma_{22,\text{uts}}$ = 98.6 MPa, $\tau_{12,\text{uss}}$ = 113 MPa;

G_{IC} = 277.4 J/m^2, G_{IIC} = 788.9 J/m^2.

15.6.4   Intralaminar Debonding of Woven Laminates under Fatigue Loading

In light of the concept of damage accumulation, [Movaghghar & Lvov] applied a cycle-by-cycle damage evolution law on the basis of elastic energy, stress ratio, and evolutionary damage of each load block to assessing the fatigue life of woven composites. The damage done each cycle is calculated as

$$N_f^{-1} = m \ (n + 1) \left\{ \frac{1}{2} \left[\sigma_{xx,w} \left(\frac{\sigma_{xx,w}}{E_{xx,w}} - \frac{v_{xy,w} \ \sigma_{yy,w}}{E_{yy,w}} \right) + \right. \right.$$

$$\left. \left. \sigma_{yy,w} \left(\frac{\sigma_{yy,w}}{E_{yy,w}} - \frac{v_{xy,w} \ \sigma_{xx,w}}{E_{xx,w}} \right) + \frac{\tau_{xy,w}^2}{G_{xy,w}} \right] \right\}^n$$

(15.6.30)

where

N_f: Final fatigue life cycles;

$\sigma_{xx,w}$, $\sigma_{yy,w}$, $\tau_{xy,w}$: Stresses applied to the woven lamina;

$E_{xx,w}$, $E_{yy,w}$, $G_{xy,w}$: Elastic moduli of a woven lamina, as obtained by Eqs. (10.5.1)-(10.5.3);

m: curve-fitting coefficient;

n: Damage exponent.

Subscript w is used for "weave" while subscripts x and y are used to denote the weaving directions, of which y is aligned with the warped direction and x is perpendicular to y, as shown in Fig. 10.5.1. Elastic moduli of a woven lamina, $E_{xx,w}$, $E_{yy,w}$, and G_{xy}, can be obtained from Eqs. (10.5.1)-(10.5.3) or other similar equations. Eq. (15.6.25) has been calibrated with experimental data from reversed cyclic bending experiments on woven glass/epoxy laminates by [Movaghghar & Lvov].

15.6.5 Designing against Interlaminar Debonding under Fatigue Loading

Enlightened by mode-I double cantilever beam experiments for the total life prediction that describes the crack growth in all three growth regions of interlaminar delamination, including the slow stage, stable stage and unstable stage, [Chen et al.] formulated the following equation for designing against interlaminar debonding under fatigue

$$\frac{\mathrm{d}a}{\mathrm{d}N} = A\left(\frac{G_{Imax}}{G_{IR}}\right)^{n}\left\{\frac{\left[1-\left(\frac{G_{Ith}}{G_{Imax}}\right)^{n_1}\right]}{\left[1-\left(\frac{G_{Imax}}{G_{IR}}\right)^{n_2}\right]}\right\} \qquad (15.6.31)$$

where

  a: Crack length;

  N: Number of cycles;

  G_{Ith}: Mode-I strain energy release rate at the Ith load block in the loading history;

  G_{Imax}: Maximum mode-I strain energy release rate;

  G_{IR}: Interlaminar fracture resistance, which is a material property;

  A: Damage coefficient;

  n: Damage exponent;

  n_1: Damage exponent;

  n_2: Residual damage exponent.

Exponent D_1 is used to accounts for the Ith load block as measured by the "maximum" damaging load block in terms of interlaminar fracture resistance. The above damage accumulation is based on interlaminar strain energy release rates done by individual load blocks, while the concept is quite similar to the Paris equation.

15.6.6 Procedure for Fatigue Analysis of Composites

A fatigue calculation process for composites subjected to proportional loadings is illustrated in detail in Fig. 15.6.5 as described in [Ncode]. At each calculation point (element, layer, section point) the stress tensor history is constructed based on an appropriate FE solution and the applied loads. The normalized stress tensor, which has been calibrated previously using experimental ε-N or S-N curves in combination with the orientation tensor for that calculation point, is passed to the fatigue model, e.g. Eqs. (15.6.12)-(15.6.15). The fatigue model is used to generate a unique ε-N, S-N curve, or energy release rate, for that location, as a function of the microstructure and stress-strain state. The final step is then a conventional stress-life fatigue calculation based on rainflow cycle counting and linear damage accumulation as described in Chapter 4.

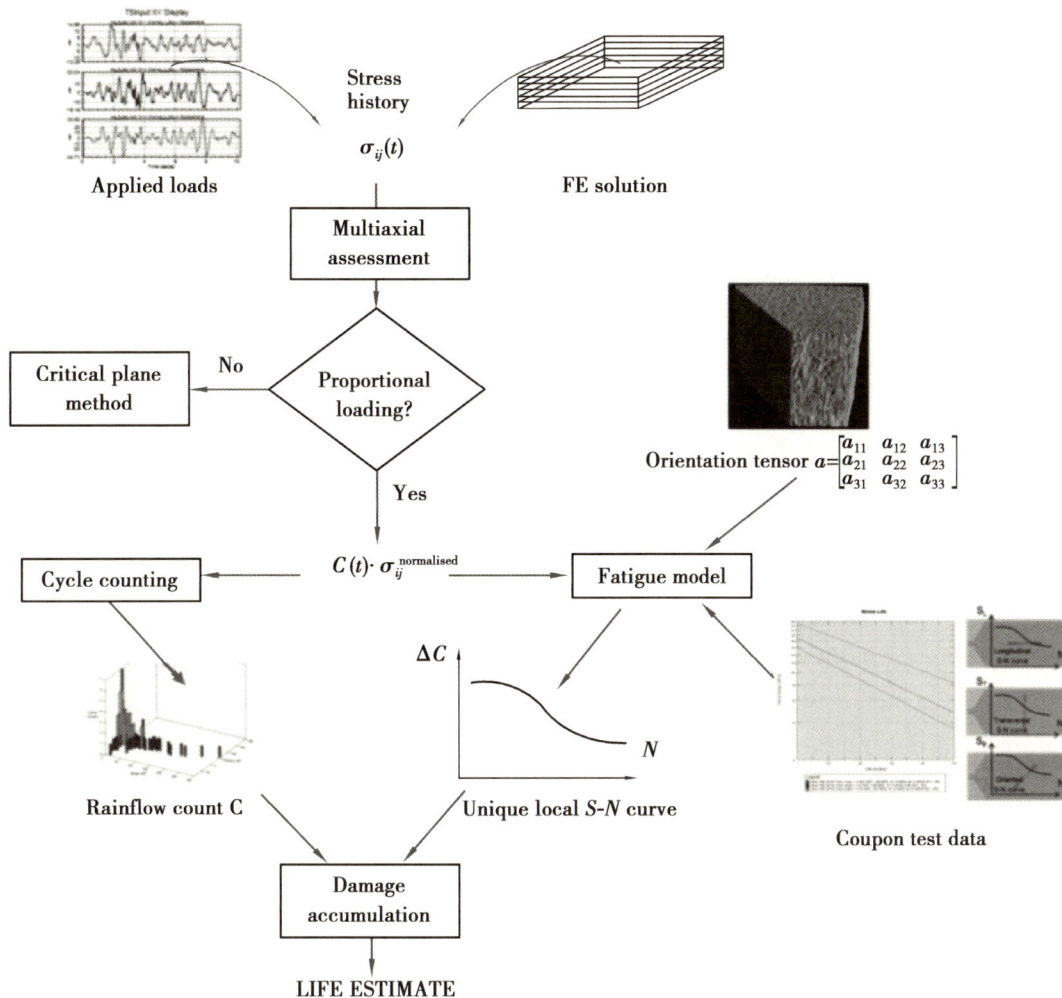

Fig. 15.6.5　Fatigue Analysis of Composites under Multiaxial Loadings[Ncode]

15.7　Creep-Fatigue of Composites under Multiaxial Loadings

Polymeric resins are widely used as matrices and adhesives in fiber-reinforced composites with applications in a variety of areas, such as automotive, aerospace, marine, wind turbine (power generation), and civil engineering industries. For instance, most standards for buried structures (e.g. pipes) made of glass fiber-reinforced polymeric composites demand a reliable lifetime more than 10000-hours creep tests in order to extrapolate life data for two decades with a high level of confidence. Creep fatigue in the long run is of great concern, especially for the parts used in load-carrying structures that work at elevated temperatures. At room temperature, each polymer tends to exhibit its own distinct creep behavior, which can be accurately predicted within the linear range of its stress-strain curve based on the theory of linear viscoelasticity. However, the synergistic interactive effect between creep and fatigue mechanisms on the damage evolution in the material is far from being well understood.

It has been observed that there are two major competing factors that have great influences on the creep-fatigue life of polymeric composites, i.e., damage evolution and internal heating, especially in a localized "hot spot." Numerous studies concerning the creep fatigue life prediction in polymers provide an account of various damage-localization mechanisms, including crazing, shear-band formation, and even voids. The onset of these mechanisms depends on a number of factors, such as temperature, strain rate, hydrostatic pressure, and strain-induced crystallization [Vinogradov & Schumacher]. Recently, [Miyano et al. 2006] utilized the time-temperature superposition principle to formulate the long-term creep and fatigue strengths of polymer composites and developed the related accelerated testing methodology while [Guedes 2008] constituted the creep and fatigue life prediction of polymer-based composites using simple cumulative damage law like Miner's rule for fatigue analysis.

15.7.1　Creep Fatigue of Amorphous Resin-Based Composites

The viscoelastic behavior of an amorphous resin-based composite, such as Ep/CF, may occur at a temperature both above and under the glass transition point (T_g) and it can be expressed in terms of strain, strain rate, and temperature. The time-temperature superposition principle based on creep rupture strength described in Section 6.7 can be used to predict the creep-fatigue life of such a composite, as its creep-fatigue behavior is dominated by the matrix (polymer).

15.7.2　Creep Fatigue of Crystalline Resin-Based Composites

The crystallinity of matrix can be found in some resins for composites, such as PEEK and PVDF. At room temperature, PVDF or PEEK is a semicrystalline polymer having a directional alignment of its long molecular chains, by which the material shows orthotropic behaviors with respect to two in-plane material directions, i.e., along (1-axis) and perpendicular to (2-axis) the orientation of the molecular chains[Vinogradov & Holloway]. Furthermore, Polyvinylidene fluoride (PVDF) is a piezoelectric material that can convert mechanical energy to the electrical energy and vice versa. When an electric field of up to 100 kV/mm is applied at an elevated temperature, typically 103 ℃, PVDF tends to form a permanent polarization. It can be integrated into an electromechanical design as an smart element capable of sensing and responding intelligently to external stimuli. The approach by the time-temperature superposition principle based on isotropic materials given by [Guedes] and [Miyano et al.] and other researchers is not applicable for such cases. The time-temperature superposition principle based on orthotropic behaviors either with or without the piezoelectric effect is yet to be discovered.

15.8   Modeling Composite Failures Using Finite Element Methods

Fracture of a laminated composite, including matrix crack, fiber-matrix debonding, fiber wrinkling, and interlaminar singularities, is a complex of both interior and exterior conditions, of which detailed discrete nature of damage that progressively interacts with applied loads are crucial to finite element analysis. Applying interface elements in the cohesive zone is effective for representing discrete fractures and good predictions can be made as long as the correct failure mechanism is captured. The progressive failure analysis on a multiscale algorithm, which aligns the macroscopic with microscopic damage and failure mechanisms, is expected to be implemented in the extended finite element method. A finite element technique to prompt its practical application to the progressive failure analysis of composite laminates has to predict the stiffness reduction and the number of cycles to failure before the final failure.

15.8.1   Interface Elements for Composites Fatigue

Interface elements available in various commercial FEA codes can be used to model both delamination failure modes and discrete transverse cracks. For example, Abaqus provides stress components to the USDFLD subroutine in order to compute the degradation factors (damage variables) and failure flags based on the modes of failure. The calculated principal stress components in the primary material coordinate system and the related strain energy release rates are used for predicting the onset of crack initiation and fully debonded damage, respectively shown in Fig. 15.6.3.

Strength-based failure criteria, such as Eqs. (15.8.7) and (15.8.8), are employed to establish initiation of a crack "smeared" over an individual finite element. If a failure criterion is met, the element is assumed broken and removed for the rest of the analysis. In other words, the element loses its tensile stiffness (E_{22}) in the transverse material direction as well as the shear stiffnesses (G_{12} and G_{23}) in plane 1-2 and plane 2-3. Therefore the stress-strain relationships for formulating the elemental stiffness at the next loading step reduce to

$$\begin{pmatrix} \varepsilon_{11} \\ \varepsilon_{22} \\ \varepsilon_{33} \\ \varepsilon_{23} \\ \varepsilon_{31} \\ \varepsilon_{12} \end{pmatrix} = \begin{pmatrix} s_{11} & s_{12} & s_{13} & 0 & 0 & 0 \\ s_{12} & s_{22} & s_{23} & 0 & 0 & 0 \\ s_{13} & s_{23} & s_{33} & 0 & 0 & 0 \\ 0 & 0 & 0 & s_{44} & 0 & 0 \\ 0 & 0 & 0 & 0 & s_{55} & 0 \\ 0 & 0 & 0 & 0 & 0 & s_{66} \end{pmatrix} = \begin{pmatrix} \sigma_{11} \\ \sigma_{22} \\ \sigma_{33} \\ \sigma_{23} \\ \sigma_{31} \\ \sigma_{12} \end{pmatrix} \tag{15.8.1}$$

where

$$s_{11} = \frac{1}{E_{11}} \tag{15.8.2}$$

$$s_{22} = \frac{1}{(1-d)E_{22}} \tag{15.8.3}$$

$$s_{33} = \frac{1}{E_{33}} \tag{15.8.4}$$

$$s_{12} = \frac{-v_{21}}{E_{22}} = s_{21} = \frac{-v_{12}}{E_{11}} \tag{15.8.5}$$

$$s_{13} = \frac{-v_{31}}{E_{33}} = s_{31} = \frac{-v_{13}}{E_{11}} \tag{15.8.6}$$

$$s_{23} = \frac{-v_{32}}{E_{33}} = s_{32} = \frac{-v_{23}}{E_{22}} \tag{15.8.7}$$

$$s_{44} = \frac{\frac{1}{2}\tau_{23}}{(1-d)G_{23}} + \frac{1}{2}\left[\frac{\tau_{23}}{(1-d)K_{23}}\right]^{\frac{1}{n_o}} \tag{15.8.8}$$

$$s_{55} = \frac{\frac{1}{2}\tau_{31}}{G_{31}} + \frac{1}{2}\left(\frac{\tau_{31}}{K_{31}}\right)^{\frac{1}{n_o}} \tag{15.8.9}$$

and $\quad s_{66} = \frac{\frac{1}{2}\tau_{12}}{(1-d)G_{12}} + \frac{1}{2}\left[\frac{\tau_{12}}{(1-d)K_{12}}\right]^{\frac{1}{n_o}} \tag{15.8.10}$

Modeling using Abaqus 3-dimensional 8-noded solid elements with reduced integration (C3D8R) for assessing the fatigue of composites is demonstrated to be effective by [Makeev et al.]. Each element has a single integration point so that the damage is representative of the entire element.

15.8.2   Iterative Steps in Nonlinear Analysis with Partial Collapsed Elements

It is assumed that damage ratio d due to tension goes from 0% to 100% as fast as practically possible to allow for convergence of the numerical procedure. Damage ratio d is expressed in terms of the time steps used in the commercial FEA codes such as Abaqus that

$$d = 0 \qquad\qquad \text{when } t < t_f \qquad\qquad (15.8.11a)$$

$$d = \left(\frac{t - t_f}{\Delta t_r}\right)(1 - k_f) \qquad \text{when } t_f < t < (t_f + \Delta t_r) \qquad (15.8.11b)$$

and $\quad d = (1 - k_f) \qquad \text{when}(t_f + \Delta t_r) < t \qquad\qquad (15.8.11c)$

where

> d: Damage ratio, starting from 0% to 100%;
>
> t: Current time step;
>
> t_f: Time step at which the crack-initiation starts;
>
> k_f: Remaining stiffness ratio, which is small enough to present the fully debonded state;
>
> Δt_r: Incremental time step accounting for damage relaxation, as determined from convergence requirements.

Note that K_f cannot be zero, but it is small. If $K_f = 0$, some compliances presented in Eq. (15.8.1) will be numerically singular. In the meanwhile, damaged elements must withstand compression to prevent overlapping. However, It is generally neglected in order to accelerate convergence as the effect of compressive stresses in the damaged elements are very minor [Makeev et al.].

15.9   Pressurized Isotropic Cylinders

One major application of pressurized cylinders is the gas tank for natural gas engines and the other is the H_2 tank for electric vehicles.

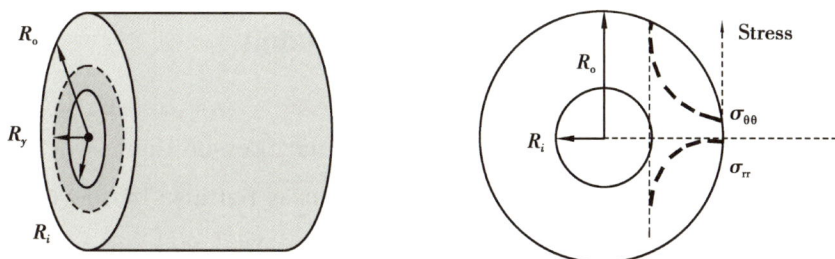

Fig. 15.9.1   A Cylinder under Internal Pressure Only

15.9.1　Pressurized Cylinder with Elastic Deformation

Consider a cylinder under both internal and external pressures, as shown in Fig. 15.9.1. Upon the linear elasticity, the radial, hoop (circumferential) and radial stresses at radius r in the wall $(R_i \leqslant r \leqslant R_o)$ are, respectively,

$$\sigma_{rr} = \frac{R_i^2 P_i - R_o^2 P_o - \dfrac{(P_i - P_o)R_i^2 R_o^2}{r^2}}{R_o^2 - R_i^2} \qquad \text{(Radial)} \tag{15.9.1}$$

$$\sigma_{\theta\theta} = \frac{R_i^2 P_i - R_o^2 P_o + \dfrac{(P_i - P_o)R_i^2 R_o^2}{r^2}}{R_o^2 - R_i^2} \qquad \text{(Hoop)} \tag{15.9.2}$$

and $\quad \sigma_{zz} = \dfrac{R_i^2 P_i}{R_o^2 - R_i^2} \quad$ (Longitudinal, closed-ended cylinders only) $\tag{15.9.3}$

Let $\quad k = \dfrac{R_o}{R_i}$ $\tag{15.9.4}$

Then $\quad \sigma_{rr} = \dfrac{P_i - k^2 P_o - \dfrac{(P_i - P_o)R_o^2}{r^2}}{k^2 - 1} \qquad \text{(Radial)} \tag{15.9.5}$

$$\sigma_{\theta\theta} = \frac{P_i - k^2 P_o + \dfrac{(P_i - P_o)R_o^2}{r^2}}{k^2 - 1} \qquad \text{(Hoop)} \tag{15.9.6}$$

and $\quad \sigma_{zz} = \dfrac{P_i}{k^2 - 1} \qquad \text{(Longitudinal)} \tag{15.9.7}$

15.9.2　Yielding Limit of a Single-Cylindered Conduit

Consider a conduit made of a single cylinder under internal pressure only. The allowable internal pressure for the cylinder is limited not only by wall thickness but also by the yield strength of the cylinder material. As no outer pressure is applied, the material yielding will commence at the inner surface first (Fig. 15.9.1). The flow stress induced by the internal pressure is a combination of the three principal stresses,

$$\sigma = (\sigma_{rr}^2 + \sigma_{\theta\theta}^2 + \sigma_{zz}^2)^{\frac{1}{2}} \tag{15.9.8}$$

Plugging Eqs. (15.9.5)-(15.9.7) into the above equation yields

$$\sigma = \frac{(3^{\frac{1}{2}} + k_y^{-4})P_i}{1 - k^{-2}} \tag{15.9.9}$$

Assume that the fluid pressure in the conduit is constant, the yielding strength can be used as the upper control limit and the internal pressure can be carried by the conduit is

$$P_i \leqslant \frac{\sigma_y(1 - k^{-2})}{3^{\frac{1}{2}} + k_y^{-4}} \qquad (\text{Closed-ended}) \tag{15.9.10}$$

$$\text{or} \quad P_i \leqslant \frac{\sigma_y(1 - k^{-2})}{3^{\frac{1}{2}}} \qquad (\text{Open-ended}) \tag{15.9.11}$$

If $k = 1.5$ ($R_o = 1.5R_i$), $P_i \leqslant 0.321\sigma_y$, i.e., the maximum pressure can be carried by an open-ended conduit is $0.321\sigma_y$. On the other hand if an internal pressure of 150 MPa is expected, the yield strength has to be higher than 468 MPa. This would demand an expensive material because a conduit cannot be formed without a great ductility, residual stress, and rough surface (stress riser). This calls for the need of compound cylinders. Note that a cylinder wall is considered thick if it is 10% of the cylinder radius or more.

15.9.3 Pressurized Cylinder with Elastoplastic Deformation

When a material is experiencing an elastoplastic deformation, its flow stress in terms of von Mises equivalent stress is related to its strain flow as

$$\sigma = \sigma_y + E_p \, \varepsilon_p + E_{creep} \, \varepsilon_{creep} \tag{15.9.12}$$

where

σ_y: Yield strength;

E_p: Elastoplastic modulus;

E_{creep}: Creep modulus.

The flow stress induced by the internal pressure is a combination of the three principal stresses,

$$\sigma = (\sigma_{rr}^2 + \sigma_{\theta\theta}^2 + \sigma_{zz}^2)^{\frac{1}{2}} \tag{15.9.13}$$

Consider a cylinder under internal pressure only. Assume that some material in the cylinder yields, starting from R_i to R_y ($R_i \leqslant r \leqslant R_y$) as shown in Fig. 15.9.1, undergoes an elastoplastic deformation with strain hardening but no creep. By Eqs. (15.9.9)-(15.9.11) with $P_o = 0$, the maximum internal pressure, a plastic deformation stops at R_p, is

$$|P_{i,y}| = \frac{\sigma_y(1 - k_y^{-2})}{3^{\frac{1}{2}}} \quad \text{(Open-ended cylinder)} \quad (15.9.14)$$

$$\text{or} \quad |P_{i,y}| = \frac{\sigma_y(1 - k_y^{-2})}{(3 + k_y^{-4})^{\frac{1}{2}}} \quad \text{(Closed-ended cylinder)} \quad (15.9.15)$$

where

$|P_{i,y}|$: Absolute value of pressure as radius R_y reaches yielding point, i.e., $r \to R_y$;

k_y: Ratio to measure the extension of yield starting from the internal, $k_y \equiv R_y/R_i$.

The radial and hoop stresses at a point between R_i and R_p are, respectively,

$$\sigma_{rr} = -\frac{1}{2}\sigma_y \left[\frac{\left(1 - \frac{R_p^2}{R_o^2}\right) + \ln\left(\frac{R_p^2}{r^2}\right) + (1 - v^2)\left(\frac{E_p}{E}\right)\left(\frac{R_p^2}{r^2} - \frac{R_p^2}{R_o^2}\right)}{(1 - v^2)\left(\frac{E_p}{E}\right) + 1} \right] \quad (15.9.16)$$

$$\text{and} \quad \sigma_{\theta\theta} = \frac{1}{2}\sigma_y \left[\frac{\left(1 + \frac{R_p^2}{R_o^2}\right) - \ln\left(\frac{R_p^2}{r^2}\right) + (1 - v^2)\left(\frac{E_p}{E}\right)\left(\frac{R_p^2}{r^2} - \frac{R_p^2}{R_o^2}\right)}{(1 - v^2)\left(\frac{E_p}{E}\right) + 1} \right] \quad (15.9.17)$$

Note that the elastic radial and hoop stresses in the region between R_p and R_o can still be calculated using Eqs. (15.9.5) and (15.9.6). With regard to the stress concern, the critical stress location is usually the inner surface of the cylinder, where maximum tensile hoop stress occurs.

15.10 Press-Fit

Press-fitted joints are widely used in mechanical engineering to transmit a torque through the joint of two parts such as the engine crankshaft and the mating torque-transmitting gear because of their high efficiency and easy implementation.

15.10.1 Press-Fit with Elastic Deformation

In a press-fit with a radial interference (δ_r), the outer surface of the inner cylinder (called shaft if its inner radius is zero) is compressed and the inner surface of the outer cylinder (or called hub) is expanded, as shown in Fig. 15.10.1. The critical-stressed location is usually the inner surface of the hub, where the maximum flow stress occurs due to the maximum tensile hoop stress if the materials are the same for both.

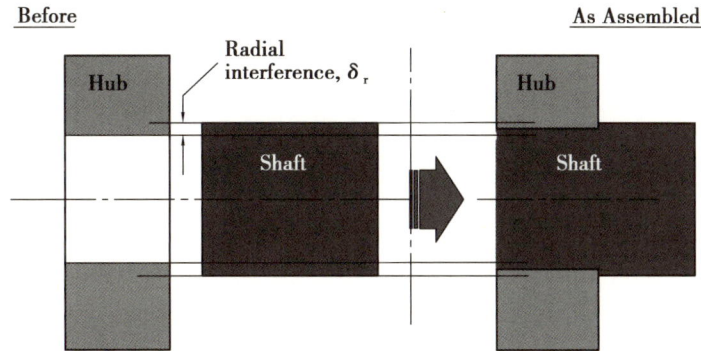

Fig. 15.10.1   Schematic Drawing of Press-Fit with a Radial Interference (δ_r)

When two cylinders are put together with an interference fit (i.e., press-fit) without any plastic deformation and creep, the radial strains in the radial direction in the elastic range is then

$$\varepsilon_{rr,1} = \frac{\sigma_{rr,1} - \nu_1 \sigma_{\theta\theta,1}}{E_1} \tag{15.10.1}$$

and $$\varepsilon_{rr,2} = \frac{\sigma_{rr,2} - \nu_1 \sigma_{\theta\theta,2}}{E_2} \tag{15.10.2}$$

where

  E_1 & ν_1: Young's modulus and Poisson's ratio of cylinder 1(inner)
  E_2 & ν_2: Young's modulus and Poisson's ratio of cylinder 2(outer).

Subscripts 1 and 2 are used to denote the inner and outer cylinders, respectively. Let P_c denote the contact pressure between the two cylinders. P_c is the outer pressure on cylinder 1 (inner cylinder), as well as the inner pressure on cylinder 2(outer cylinder). Assume that the sum of the radial compression of the inner cylinder and radial expansion of the outer cylinder at the interface radius (R_c) is equivalent to the initial interference (δ_c). Thus

$$\varepsilon_{rr,1} R_c + \varepsilon_{rr,2} R_c = \delta_c \tag{15.10.3}$$

Subscript c denotes "in-contact". Substituting Eqs. (15.9.5) and (15.9.6) into Eqs. (15.10.1) and (15.10.2), and then subsequently into Eq. (15.10.3) yields the interfacial pressure acting on the contact surface as installed,

$$P_c = \frac{\dfrac{\delta_r}{R_c}}{\dfrac{\dfrac{1 + k_1^{-2}}{1 - k_1^{-2}} - v_1}{E_1} + \dfrac{\dfrac{1 + k_2^{-2}}{1 - k_2^{-2}} + v_2}{E_2}} \tag{15.10.4}$$

where

$$k_1 \equiv \frac{R_{o,1}}{R_{i,1}};$$

$$k_2 \equiv \frac{R_{o,2}}{R_{i,2}};$$

$R_{o,1}$ & $R_{i,1}$: Outer and inner radii of the conduit (cylinder 1);

$R_{o,2}$ & $R_{i,2}$: Outer and inner radii of the jacket (cylinder 2).

If both the conduit and jacket are made of the same material, then the contact pressure as installed becomes

$$P_c = \frac{\left(\dfrac{\delta_r}{R_c}\right) E}{\dfrac{1 + k_1^{-2}}{1 - k_1^{-2}} + \dfrac{1 + k_2^{-2}}{1 - k_2^{-2}}} \tag{15.10.5}$$

If heating or cooling a part to achieve a shrink fit is needed, the temperature difference between cylinders 1 and 2 is then

$$\Delta T = \frac{\delta_r}{R_c \alpha} \tag{15.10.6}$$

of which α is the coefficient of linear thermal expansion of the heated (or cooled) part. The radial and tangential stresses as installed will be formulated inserting Eq. (15.10.4) into Eqs (15.9.5) and (15.9.6), respectively for inner cylinder (cylinder 1) and outer cylinder (cylinder 2) as

$$\sigma_{rr,1} = \frac{P_c\left(-k_1^2 + \dfrac{R_o^2}{r^2}\right)}{k_1^2 - 1} \quad (R_{i,1} \leqslant r \leqslant R_{o,1}) \tag{15.10.7}$$

$$\sigma_{\theta\theta,1} = \frac{-P_c\left(k_1^2 + \dfrac{R_o^2}{r^2}\right)}{k_1^2 - 1} \quad (R_{i,1} \leqslant r \leqslant R_{o,1}) \tag{15.10.8}$$

$$\sigma_{rr,2} = \frac{P_c\left(\dfrac{1 - R_o^2}{r^2}\right)}{k_2^2 - 1} \quad (R_{i,2} \leqslant r \leqslant R_{o,2})$$

(15.10.9)

$$\text{and} \quad \sigma_{\theta\theta,2} = \frac{P_c\left(1 + \dfrac{R_o^2}{r^2}\right)}{k_2^2 - 1} \quad (R_{i,2} \leqslant r \leqslant R_{o,2})$$

(15.10.10)

15.10.2 Grip and Torque Capacity of Press-Fit Joints

The grip force and torque capacities available will be, respectively,

$$F_{max} = 2\pi R_c L P_c \mu$$

(15.10.11)

$$\text{and} \quad T = F R_c = 2\pi R_c^2 L P_c \mu$$

(15.10.12)

where

μ: Coefficient of friction;

L: Contact length.

This is the pressure generated as installed without considering the fitness selection, dimensional variations, surface roughness[Yang] or free-boundary effect[Sen & Aksakal].

Example 15.10.1   An AISI 4140 steel shaft of 200 mm in diameter is to have a press fit in a GJL280 cast iron disk of 500 mm in diameter and 250 mm in thickness. Assume that the allowable tangential stress in the disk is 35 MPa and the coefficient of friction between the steel and cast iron is 0.15. Find:

(a) the required diametric interference of metal;
(b) the force required to press the parts together;
(c) the torque capacity.

Solution:

According to the literature available the mechanical properties of AISI 4410 and GJL 280 cast iron at room temperature are

AISI 4410: $E_1 = 206000$ MPa and $v_1 = 0.29$
GJL 280 Cast Iron: $E_2 = 124000$ MPa and $v_2 = 0.22$

The hoop stress exerted on the iron disk (cylinder 2 here) is due to the press-fit pressure $P_{i,2}$ with no external pressure ($P_{o,2} = 0$). By Eq. (15.10.3) and setting $r = R_{1,2}$, as the maximum radial stress is on the internal surface of the outside cylinder, one has

$$\sigma_{\theta\theta,2} = \frac{P_c\left(1 + \dfrac{R_o^2}{r^2}\right)}{k_2^2 - 1}$$

i.e. $$35 = \frac{P_c\left(1 + \dfrac{250^2}{100^2}\right)}{\left(\dfrac{250}{100}\right)^2 - 1}$$

Thus $P_c = 25.345$ MPa

Note that P_c is the contact pressure between the steel shaft and iron disk. By Eq. (15.10.14), the contact pressure as installed is related to the amount of radial interference as follows:

$$P_c = \frac{\dfrac{\delta_r}{R_c}}{\dfrac{\left(\dfrac{1 + k_1^{-2}}{1 - k_1^{-2}} - v_1\right)}{E_1} + \dfrac{\left(\dfrac{1 + k_2^{-2}}{1 - k_2^{-2}} + v_2\right)}{E_2}}$$

given that $k_1 = \dfrac{R_{o,1}}{R_{i,1}} = \infty$, $k_1^{-2} = 0$. As $k_2 = \dfrac{R_{o,2}}{R_{i,2}} = \dfrac{250}{100}$, $k_2^{-2} = 0.16$;

$$25.345 = \frac{\dfrac{\delta_r}{100}}{\dfrac{1 - 0.29}{206000} + \dfrac{\left(\dfrac{1 + 0.16}{1 - 0.16} + 0.22\right)}{124000}}$$

$\delta_r = 0.0415$ mm (Radial interference)

and $\delta_d = 2\delta_r = 0.083$ mm (Diametric interference).

The inserting force and torque capacity available will be, respectively,

$$F = 2\pi R_c L P_c \mu = 2\pi \times 100 \times 250 \times 25.345 \times 0.12 \text{ N} = 477\ 741 \text{ N} = 477.741 \text{ kN}$$

and $$T = 2\pi R_c^2 L P_c \mu = 2\pi \times 100^2 \times 250 \times 25.345 \times 0.12 \text{ N} \cdot \text{mm} = 47\ 774\ 159 \text{ N} \cdot \text{mm}$$

$$= 47.774 \text{ kN} \cdot \text{m}$$

15.10.3   Influence of Tolerance and Surface Roughness on Press-Fit Friction

Dimensional tolerances of the shaft and hub have to be considered and calculated according to statistical tolerance analysis.

15.10.4   Influence of Surface Roughness and Lubrication on Press-Fit Friction

Tolerances (min. and max. dimensions) of shaft and hub have to be considered. Surface roughness depending on the machining condition has also influence on the interfacial friction, and hence on the maximum torque transmission.

The interference should be corrected for the effect of surface roughness, whose generic probability density function is plotted in Fig. 15.10.2. The flattening of roughness peaks under high mounting pressure is generally estimated to be 10% of the R_z-value where $R_z \approx 6R_a$ according to [ISO 6336-2]. Assume that the surface roughness is of a normal distribution statistically. The average reductions for the purpose of correction in both radial and diametric interferences are, respectively, given below:

$$\Delta\delta_r = 10\% \text{ of}\{R_{z1}, R_{z2}\} = 0.1(R_{z1} + R_{z2}) = 0.1(6R_{a1} + 6R_{a2}) = 0.6(R_{a1} + R_{a2})$$

$$\approx 0.6(R_{rms1}^2 + R_{rms2}^2)^{\frac{1}{2}} \tag{15.10.13}$$

and $\Delta\delta_d = 2\Delta\delta_r$ $\hspace{4cm}$ (15.10.14)

where

$\Delta\delta_d$: Additional diametric interference due to surface conditions;
$\Delta\delta_r$: Additional radial interference due to surface conditions;
R_{z1} & R_{z2} : Heights from the crest to the valley;
R_{a1} & R_{a2} : Arithmetic averages;
R_{rms1} & R_{rms2} : Root means squared values.

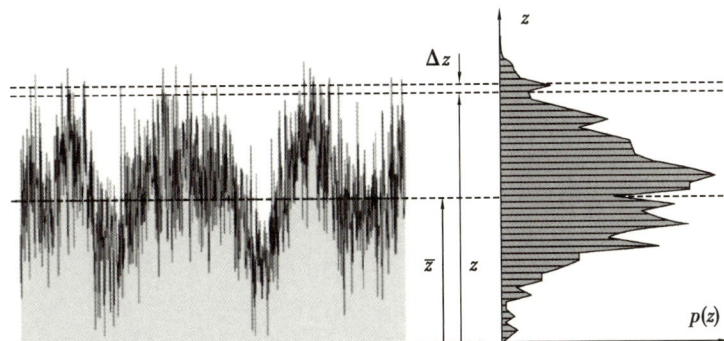

Fig. 15.10.2   **Measured Surface Roughness of a Bearing Pin with Exaggerated z-Scale and Its Probability Density Function $p(z)$**

Then the following data should be used for δ_r in the equations derived above:

$$\delta_{r,\text{effective}} = \delta_{r,\text{original}} - \Delta\delta_r \qquad (15.10.15)$$

For example, if the surface roughness of shaft $R_{a1} = 0.32$ μm and that of the bore $R_{a2} = 0.8$ μm, then $\Delta\delta_r = 0.6(0.32+0.8) = 0.672$ μm and $\Delta\delta_d = 1.344$ μm.

Approximate values for coefficients of friction of commonly used materials are listed in Table 8.1.1. With different lubricants and various surface roughness for a press-fit joint of steel on steel, the static coefficient of friction may vary from 0.047 to 0.26[Stamenković et al.]. It is suggested that the nominal coefficient of friction of a lubricated press-fit joint with good surface roughness falls in the range between 0.05 and 0.1.

15.10.5 Stress Concentration around a Press-Fit Joint

A stress concentration appears on the edges in the contact zone due to free-edge stress intensity, also called free-boundary effect, at a press-fit joint should be taken into consideration as a design parameter[Parsons & Wilson], see Fig. 15.10.3. It is mostly pronounced in the hub (external cylinder) and the stress intensity increase in $\sigma_{rr,2}$ is more severe than $\sigma_{\theta\theta,2}\sigma_{rr,1}$ and $\sigma_{\theta\theta,1}$ according to[Pérez et al.]. The variation of stress intensity can be more complex if the hub and shaft are made of two dissimilar materials. The finite element method is more effective due to the hardship with setting up the boundary conditions for a complex joint based on closed-form solutions.

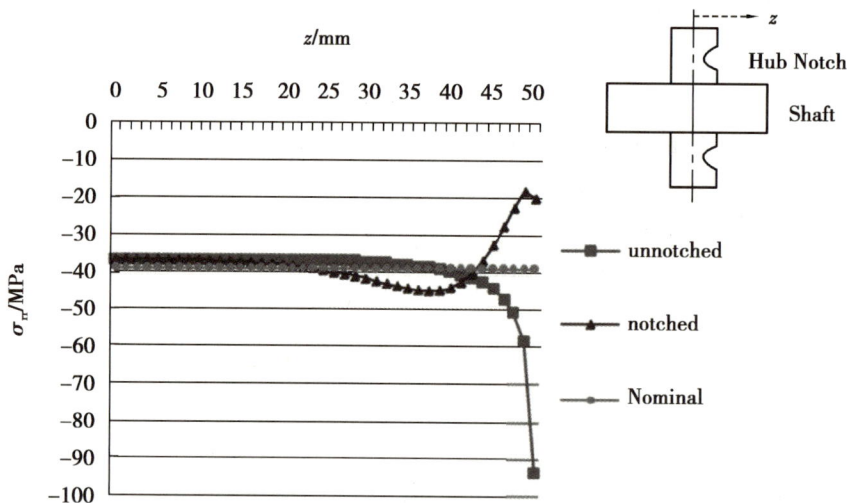

Fig. 15.10.3 Stress Concentration at a 100 mm Press-Fitted Joint[Parsons & Wilson 1970]

15.11   Compound Isotropic Cylinders

A typical example of compound cylinders is the fuel conduit in the high-pressurized common rail system of a Diesel engine. Because the inner radius of the outer cylinder (i.e., outside jacket) is slightly smaller than the outer radius of the inner cylinder (i.e., conduit), the outside jacket is heated and fitted onto the conduit. When the assembly cools down to the room temperature, a compound cylinder is formed. This gives the same effect as that obtained by shrinking a hoop over an inner cylinder. This is known as self-hooping or autofrettage. It allows the cylinder to operate at higher fluid pressure. For a given "autofrettage fluid pressure" a given amount of inelastic deformation is produced and therefore in service the same fluid pressure may be used without causing any additional inelastic deformation.

15.11.1   Compound Cylinders-Elastic Contact Mechanics

The conduit (inner cylinder) is subjected to a "solid" external pressure that leads to a compressive hoop stress at the interface as installed. The compressive hoop stress is intentionally used to relieve the hoop stress level (in tension) due to internal fuel pressure (P_{fluid}). When the fluid pressure is applied to the inner surface of the conduit (namely cylinder 1 as denoted in the following equation), it will exert an additional contact pressure on the inner surface of the jacket (namely cylinder 2), after[Ragab & Bayomi], as

$$P_{c,\text{fluid}} = \frac{\dfrac{2P_{\text{fluid}}}{(k_1^2 - 1)E_1}}{\dfrac{\dfrac{1 + k_1^{-2}}{1 - k_1^{-2}} - v_1}{E_1} + \dfrac{\dfrac{1 + k_2^{-2}}{1 - k_2^{-2}} + v_2}{E_2}} \tag{15.11.1}$$

where

P_{fluid}: Fluid pressure;

$P_{c,\text{fluid}}$: Contact pressure between the conduit and jacket due to fluid pressure.

When free body diagrams are drawn for both cylinders (conduit and jacket), the loading functions will be obtained by superposition as

Conduit (Cylinder 1) : $P_{i,1} = P_{\text{fluid}}$ $\tag{15.11.2}$

$P_{o,1} = P_c + P_{c,\text{fluid}}$ $\tag{15.11.3}$

Jacket (Cylinder 2): $P_{i,2} = P_c + P_{c,\text{fluid}}$ (15.11.4)

$$P_{o,2} = 0 \tag{15.11.5}$$

where

     $P_{i,1}$ & $P_{o,1}$: Inner and outer pressures exerted on cylinder 1 (conduit);

     $P_{i,2}$ & $P_{o,2}$: Inner and outer pressures exerted on cylinder 2 (jacket).

Substituting Eqs. (15.10.4) and (15.10.9) into the above four equations and then into Eqs. (15.9.5) and (15.9.6), one can obtain the radial and hoop stresses for both the conduit (cylinder 1) and jacket (cylinder 2) as follows:

Then $\sigma_{rr,1} = \dfrac{P_{\text{fluid}} - k_1^2(P_c + P_{c,\text{fluid}}) - \dfrac{[P_{\text{fluid}} - (P_c + P_{c,\text{fluid}})]R_{o,1}^2}{r^2}}{k_1^2 - 1}$ (15.11.6)

$$\sigma_{\theta\theta,1} = \frac{P_{\text{fluid}} - k_1^2(P_c + P_{c,\text{fluid}}) - \dfrac{[P_{\text{fluid}} - (P_c + P_{c,\text{fluid}})]R_{o,1}^2}{r^2}}{k_1^2 - 1} \tag{15.11.7}$$

$$\sigma_{rr,2} = \frac{P_c + P_{c,\text{fluid}} - \dfrac{(P_c + P_{c,\text{fluid}})R_{o,2}^2}{r^2}}{k_2^2 - 1} \tag{15.11.8}$$

and $\sigma_{\theta\theta,2} = \dfrac{P_c + P_{c,\text{fluid}} - \dfrac{(P_c + P_{c,\text{fluid}})R_{o,2}^2}{r^2}}{k_2^2 - 1}$ (15.11.9)

of which $(P_c + P_{c,\text{fluid}})$ is the contact pressure after being installed and pressurized and it can be obtained from Eqs. (15.10.4) and (15.10.9),

$$P_c + P_{c,\text{fluid}} = \frac{\dfrac{\delta_r}{R_c} + \dfrac{2P_{\text{fluid}}}{(k_1^2 - 1)E_1}}{\dfrac{\left(\dfrac{1 + k_1^{-2}}{1 - k_1^{-2}} - v_1\right)}{E_1} + \dfrac{\left(\dfrac{1 + k_2^{-2}}{1 - k_2^{-2}} + v_2\right)}{E_2}} \tag{15.11.10}$$

Example 15.11.1   A shrink-fitted compound cylinder is subjected to an internal pressure of 60 MPa. Both inner conduit and outer jacket are made of AISI 4140 steel. Before the fluid is admitted, the internal and external diameters of the assembly are 120 mm and 200 mm, respectively, and the diameter at the autofrettage junction is 160 mm. After shrinking, the contact pressure at the junction was 8 MPa, plot the resultant stress distribution in each cylinder after the fluid has been admitted.

Solution:

With the same material ($E = 206000$ and $v = 0.29$ for AISI 4140 steel) for the conduit and jacket, the additional contact pressure produced by the internal fluid pressure can be derived from Eq. (15.11.3) as

$$
P_{c,\text{fluid}} = \frac{\dfrac{2P_{\text{fluid}}}{k_1^2 - 1}}{\dfrac{1 + k_1^{-2}}{1 - k_1^{-2}} + \dfrac{1 + k_2^{-2}}{1 - k_2^{-2}}}
$$

$$
= \frac{\dfrac{2 \times 60}{\dfrac{16}{9} - 1}}{\dfrac{25}{7} + \dfrac{44}{9}} = 18.24 \text{ MPa}
$$

where $k_1 = \dfrac{80}{60} = \dfrac{4}{3}$ and $k_2 = \dfrac{100}{80} = \dfrac{5}{4}$.

Thus $P_c + P_{c,\text{fluid}} = 8 \text{ MPa} + 18.24 \text{ MPa} = 26.24 \text{ MPa}$

Plugging $P_{\text{fluid}} = 60$ MPa, $P_c = 8$ MPa, $P_c + P_{c,\text{fluid}} = 26.24$ MPa, $k_1 = 4/3$ and $k_2 = 5/4$ into Eqs. (15.11.8)-(15.11.11), one has the following radial and tangential stress distributions for the conduit ($60 \leqslant r \leqslant 80$)

$$
\sigma_{rr,1} = \frac{P_{\text{fluid}} - k_1^2(P_c + P_{c,\text{fluid}}) - [P_{\text{fluid}} - (P_c + P_{c,\text{fluid}})]\left(\dfrac{R_{o,1}^2}{r^2}\right)}{k_1^2 - 1}
$$

$$
= \frac{60 - \dfrac{16}{9} \times (26.24 - 0) - (60 - 26.24) \times \left(\dfrac{80}{r}\right)^2}{\dfrac{16}{9} - 1} = 17 - 43.41 \times \left(\dfrac{80}{r}\right)^2
$$

$$
\sigma_{\theta\theta,1} = \frac{P_{\text{fluid}} - k_1^2(P_c + P_{c,\text{fluid}}) + [P_{\text{fluid}} - (P_c + P_{c,\text{fluid}})]\left(\dfrac{R_{o,1}^2}{r^2}\right)}{k_1^2 - 1}
$$

$$= \frac{60 - \dfrac{16}{9} \times 26.24 + (60 - 26.24) \times \left(\dfrac{80}{r}\right)^2}{\dfrac{16}{9} - 1} = 17 + 43.41 \times \left(\dfrac{80}{r}\right)^2$$

and the following radial and tangential stress distributions for the jacket ($80 \leqslant r \leqslant 100$)

$$\sigma_{rr,2} = \frac{(P_c + P_{c,\text{fluid}}) - (P_c + P_{c,\text{fluid}})\left(\dfrac{R_{o,2}^2}{r^2}\right)}{k_2^2 - 1}$$

$$= \frac{26.24 - 26.24 \times \left(\dfrac{100}{r}\right)^2}{\dfrac{25}{16} - 1} = 46.65 \times \left[1 - \left(\dfrac{100}{r}\right)^2\right]$$

and $\quad \sigma_{\theta\theta,2} = \dfrac{(P_c + P_{c,\text{fluid}}) - (P_c + P_{c,\text{fluid}})\left(\dfrac{R_{o,2}^2}{r^2}\right)}{k_1^2 - 1}$

$$= \frac{26.24 - 26.24 \times \left(\dfrac{100}{r}\right)^2}{\dfrac{25}{16} - 1} = 46.65 \times \left[1 - \left(\dfrac{100}{r}\right)^2\right]$$

Now, one can plot the stress distributions against the thickness accordingly for both the conduit and jacket.

15.11.2 Design of Compound Cylinders of the Same Materials by Equal Shear Stress

When both conduit and jacket are made of the same material and the fluid pressure does not fluctuate, it makes sense to have the same maximum shear stress for both the conduit and jacket. Note that the maximum shear stress happens to be at the inner surface of each component (conduit or jacket).

$$\tau_{\max,1} = \left.\frac{\sigma_{rr,1} - \sigma_{\theta\theta,1}}{2}\right|_{r = R_{i,1}} \tag{15.11.11}$$

and $\quad \tau_{\max,2} = \left.\dfrac{\sigma_{rr,2} - \sigma_{\theta\theta,2}}{2}\right|_{r = R_{i,2}}$ \hfill (15.11.12)

Let $E_1 = E_2$ and $v_1 = v_2$. Substitute Eq. (15.11.1) into Eqs. (15.11.6)-(15.11.10) and subsequently into Eqs. (15.11.11) and (15.11.12). Letting $\tau_{max,1} = \tau_{max,2}$ will lead to the relationship between P_c and P_{fliud} as

$$P_c + P_{c,fluid} = \frac{P_{fluid}(1 - k_1^{-2})^2}{(1 - k_1^{-2}) + (1 - k_2^{-2})} \tag{15.11.13}$$

Plugging the above equation back into Eqs. (15.11.6)-(15.11.9) and subsequently into Eqs. (15.11.11) and (15.11.12), one has

$$\tau_{max} = \tau_{max,1} = \tau_{max,2} = \frac{P_{fluid}}{(1 - k_1^{-2}) + (1 - k_2^{-2})} \tag{15.11.14}$$

i.e. $\quad \tau_{max} = \dfrac{P_{fluid}}{\left[1 - \left(\dfrac{R\,R_{o,1}}{R_{i,1}}\right)^{-2}\right] + \left[1 - \left(\dfrac{R_{o,2}}{R_{i,2}}\right)^{-2}\right]}$

$$= \frac{P_{fluid}}{\left[1 - \left(\dfrac{R_c}{R_{i,1}}\right)^{-2}\right] + \left[1 - \left(\dfrac{R_{o,2}}{R_c}\right)^{-2}\right]} \tag{15.11.15}$$

of which R_c is the nominal value for both $R_{o,1}$ and $R_{i,2}$ at the interface. By setting $d\tau_{max}/dR_c = 0$ for the purpose of optimization, one has the following design parameter R_c,

$$R_c = (R_{i,1}\,R_{o,2})^{\frac{1}{2}} \tag{15.11.16}$$

Putting the derived R_c in the above equation back into Eq. (15.11.15), one has

$$\tau_{max} = \frac{1}{2}\,P_{fluid}\left(\frac{R_{o,2}}{R_{o,2} - R_{i,1}}\right) \tag{15.11.17}$$

The maximum shear stress produced by the fluid pressure (P_{fluid}) in the conduit is proportional to the outer diameter of the jacket but inversely proportional to the total thickness (conduit and jacket). Nevertheless, a thicker compound cylinder with a fixed outside radius means less fluid flow.

15.12 Pressurized Orthotropic Vessels

Composite pressure vessels are widely used in automotive, commercial, and aerospace industries, such as hydrogen/fuel tanks, portable oxygen storage boxes/bottles, and rocket motor cases. They are frequently made of a filament overwrap of fiberglass, carbon fiber, or Kevlar in customized resin systems. Typical pressure vessels are designed to have a cylindrical section in the middle, with two spherical caps at both ends or with optional polar openings.

15.12.1　Filament Winding

Techniques for filament-wound composite pressure vessel can be classified into two main types: (a) geodesic winding[Kim et al.] and (b) in-plane winding[Teng et al.]. A forming process consists of the following steps:

(1) Fibers are impregnated with a resin by drawing them through an in-line resin.
(2) Impregnated fibers are then positioned onto a mandrel by a winding machine to form the desired shape. Depending on the desired properties of the product, winding patterns such as hoop and helical windings can be aligned.
(3) Each ply is pressed to remove any entrapped air and wrinkles before the layup is sealed at the edges to form a vacuum seal.
(4) Finally, the "wetted pressure vessel" is removed from the winding machine and placed in an oven, where the resin is cured under well-conditioned environment including temperature control, appropriate moisture level, and timing.

The shape of end caps plays a vital role in the design, because they will endure high stress levels, including both the fracture[Mayes & Hansen] and buckling[Librescu & Maalawi] failure modes. Moreover, slippage tendency of the fibrous band at the ending edges must be taken into consideration, especially when utilizing the in-plane winding technique[DiVita et al.].

15.12.2　Buckling Criterion

The objective of buckling analysis is to estimate the maximum pressure that a thin-walled structure can withstand before it becomes elastically unstable. Buckling failure may come before the fatigue limit is reached for a thin structure. The Windenburg-Trilling equation has been used for conventional isotropic thin cylinder to determine the critical buckling pressure,

$$P_{critical} = \frac{2.42E\left(\dfrac{h}{D}\right)^{\frac{5}{2}}}{(1-\mu^2)^{\frac{3}{4}}\left[\dfrac{L}{D} - 0.45 \times \left(\dfrac{h}{D}\right)^{\frac{1}{2}}\right]} \tag{15.12.1}$$

where

$P_{critical}$: Critical pressure;

D: Outside diameter of the cylinder;

h: Thickness of the cylinder;

L: Length of the cylinder;

μ: Poisson's ratio of the material.

The above equation can be also used for predicting the bucking pressure of a thin-walled filament-wound structure using equivalent material properties that $E \approx E_{xx}$ and $\mu \approx \mu_{12}$. Specifically for a single-layered composite (i.e., lamina),

$$E \approx E_{xx} = \frac{E_{11}}{\cos^4\theta + \left(\dfrac{E_{11}}{E_{22}}\right)\sin^4\theta + \dfrac{1}{4}\left[\left(\dfrac{E_{11}}{E_{22}} - 2\mu\right)\sin^2 2\theta\right]} \qquad (15.12.2)$$

$$E_{yy} = \frac{E_{11}}{\sin^4\theta + \left(\dfrac{E_{11}}{E_{22}}\right)\cos^4\theta + \dfrac{1}{4}\left[\left(\dfrac{E_{11}}{E_{22}} - 2\mu\right)\sin^2 2\theta\right]} \qquad (15.12.3)$$

and $\mu \approx \mu_{12}$

of which the x-axis is aligned with the longitudinal direction of the cylinder while θ is the fiber angle ranging from x-axis to 1-axis.

Example 15.12.1   Let's consider a single-layered filament-wound pressure vessel, which is 10 mm thick, 343 mm long, and 670 mm in diameter. The carbon fiber-reinforced epoxy has the following mechanical properties: $E_{11} = 130$ GPa, $E_{22} = 11$ GPa, and $\mu_{12} = 0.27$. How much is the critical pressure when it is under an external pressure?

Solution:

Applying Eq. (15.12.2),

$$E \approx E_{xx} = \frac{E_{11}}{\cos^4\theta + \left(\dfrac{E_{11}}{E_{22}}\right)\sin^4\theta + \dfrac{1}{4}\left[\left(\dfrac{E_{11}}{E_{22}} - 2\mu\right)\sin^2 2\theta\right]}$$

$$= \frac{130 \times 10^3}{\cos^4 45° + 11.82\sin^4 45° + \dfrac{1}{4}(11.82 - 2 \times 0.27) \times \sin^2(2 \times 45°)}\text{MPa}$$

$$= 28174 \text{ MPa}$$

Plugging the equivalent material properties into Eq. (15.12.1) leads to the critical pressure,

$$P_{\text{crtical}} = \cfrac{2.42 \times 18174 \times \left(\cfrac{10}{670}\right)^{\frac{5}{2}}}{(1 - 0.27^2)^{\frac{3}{4}} \times \left(\cfrac{343}{670} - 0.45 \times \cfrac{10}{67}\right)^{\frac{1}{2}}} \text{MPa} = 3.87 \text{ MPa}$$

15.12.3 Fatigue and Fracture Analysis of Pressurized Cylinders

Failure analysis of a pressurized cylinder due to fatigue fracture subjected to either in-plane strains (stresses), out-of-plane strains (stresses), or interlaminar strains (stresses) can be conducted using the 3-dimenisional finite element method theorized in Chapter 3 to obtain the strains (stresses). Then apply the failure theories given in this Chapter.

References

ASP L E, BERGLUND L A, GUDMUNDSON P, 1995. Prediction of Matrix-Initiated Transverse Failure in Polymer Composites[J]. Composites Science and Technology, 56(9): 1089-1097.

ASTM D 5528-13 2013. Mode Ⅰ Interlaminar Fracture Toughness of Unidirectional Fiber-Reinforced Polymer Matrix Composites, ASTM International, PA, USA.

ASTM D 6671-13 2013. Mixed Mode Ⅰ-Mode Ⅱ Interlaminar Fracture Toughness of Unidirectional Fiber Reinforced Polymer Matrix Composites, ASTM International, PA, USA.

ASTM D 7905-14 2014. Determination of the Mode Ⅱ Interlaminar Fracture Toughness of Unidirectional Fiber-Reinforced Polymer Matrix Composites, ASTM International, PA, USA.

ATTAPORN W, KOGUCHI H, 2009. Intensity of Stress Singularity at a Vertex and along the Free Edges of the Interface in 3D-Dissimilar Material Joints Using 3D-Enriched FEM, CMES, 39(3): 237-262.

CAMANHO P P, DAVILA C G, PINHO S T, et al, 2006. Prediction of In Situ Strengths and Matrix Cracking in Composites under Transverse Tension and In-Plane Shear[J]. Composites, Part A, 37(2): 165-176.

CHAPELLE D, PERREUX D, 2006. Optimal Design of a Type 3 Hydrogen Vessel: Part Ⅱ Analytic Modeling of the Cylindrical Section[J]. International Journal of Hydrogen Energy, 31(5): 627-638.

CHEN H, SHIVAKUMAR K, ABALI F, 2006. A Comparison of Total Fatigue Life Models for Composite Laminates[J]. Fatigue and Fracture of Engineering Materials and Structures, 29(1): 31-39.

CHIANG Y J, ROWLANDS R E, 1991. Finite Element Analysis for Mixed-Mode Fracture of Bolted Composite

Joints[J]. Journal of Composites Technology and Research, 13(4): 227-235.

CHIANG Y J, 1991. Crack-Speed Calculations for Unidirectional Laminae [J]. Journal of Composites Technology and Research, 13(3): 183-186.

CHIN J, et al, 2007. Temperature and Humidity Ageing of Poly(phenylene-2-6-benzobisoxazole Fibers: Chemical and Physical Characterization[J]. Polymer Degradation and Stability, 92(7): 1234-1246.

CHRISTENSEN R M, 2007. A Comprehensive Theory of Yielding and Failure for Isotropic Materials[J]. Journal of Engineering Materials and Technology, 129(2): 173-181.

CHRISTENSEN R M, 1997. Stress Based Yield/Failure Criteria for Fiber Composites[J]. International Journal of Solids Structures, 34(5): 529-543.

CORMIER L, JONCAS S, NIJSSEN R P, 2015. Effects of Low Temperature on the Mechanical Properties of Glass Fibre-Epoxy Composites: Static Tension, Compression, $R=0.1$ and $R=-1$ Fatigue of $\pm45°$ Laminates, Wind Energy, 19(6): 1023-1041.

CUI W, WISNOM M R, JONES M, 1994. Effect of Step Spacing on Delamination of Tapered Laminates[J]. Composites Science and Technology, 52(1): 39-46.

DANIEL I M, 2014. Failure of Composite Materials under Multiaxial Static and Dynamic Loading[J]. Procedia Engineering, 88(2014): 10-17.

DAVID E, 2005. An Overview of Advanced Materials for Hydrogen Storage[J]. Journal of Materials Processing Technology, 162-163: 169-177.

DAVIES P, et al, 2010. Tensile Fatigue Behavior of PBO Fibers, Journal of Materials Science, 45(23): 6395-6400.

DIVITA G, MARCHETTI M, MORONI P, et al, 1992. Designing Complex-Shape Filament-Wound Structures [J]. Composites Manufacturing, 3(1): 53-58.

FOUND M S, 1985. A Review of the Multiaxial Fatigue Testing of Fiber Reinforced Plastics[J]. Multiaxial Fatigue, ASTM STP 853, Edited by K. Miller and M. Brown, ASTM International, West Conshohocken, PA, 318-395.

GUEDES R M, 2011. Creep and Fatigue in Polymer Matrix Composites[M]. Woodhead Publishing.

GUEDES R M, 2008. Creep and Fatigue Lifetime Prediction of Polymer Matrix Composites Based on Simple Cumulative Damage Laws[J]. Composites, A, 39(11): 1716-1725.

GUERRERO M A, BETEGON C, BELZUNCE J, 2008. Fracture Analysis of a Pressure Vessel Made of High Strength Steel (HSS)[J]. Engineering Failure Analysis, 15: 208-219.

HA S K, JIN K K, HUANG Y, 2008. Micromechanics of Failure (MMF) for Continuous Fiber Reinforced Composites[J]. Journal of Composite Materials, 42(18): 1873-1895.

HALN H T, 1975. On Approximations for Strength of Random Fiber Composites[J]. Journal of Composite Materials, 9(4): 316-326.

HASHIN Z, 1981. Failure Criteria for Unidirectional Fiber Composites[J]. Journal of Applied Mechanics, 48(4): 329-334.

HEARLE J, LOMAS B, COOKE W, 1998.Atlas of Fiber Fracture and Damage to Textiles[M]. 2nd Edition, Woodhead Publishing, 1998.

HINTON M J, KADDOUR A S, SODEN P D, 2002. A Comparison of the Predictive Capabilities of Current Failure Theories for Composite Laminates, Judged against Experimental Evidence[J]. Composites Science and Technology, 62(12-13): 1725-1797.

HORIKAWA, et al, 2005. Fatigue Strength of Poly(p-phenylene benzobisoxazole) (PBO) Fibers[J]. Japan Journal of Materials Science, 54(8): 875-880.

IARVE E V, et al, 2011. Mesh-Independent Matrix Cracking and Delamination Modeling in Laminated Composites[J]. International Journal For Numerical Methods in Engineering, 88(8): 749-773.

ISLAM M S, KOGUCHI H, 2010. Characteristics of Singular Stress Distribution at a Vertex in Transversely Isotropic Piezoelectric Dissimilar Material Joints[J]. Journal of Solid Mechanics and Material Engineering, 4(7): 1011-1026.

JEONG J J, et al, 2014. Progressive Damage of Randomly Oriented Short Fiber Reinforced Composites[C]. 16th International Conference on Composite Materials, Dubai, UAE.

JU J H, et al, 2008. An Initial and Progressive Failure Analysis for Cryogenic Composite Fuel Tank Design[J]. Journal of Composite Materials, 42(6): 569-592.

KIM J S, et al, 2012. Durability Evaluation of a Composite Bogie Frame with Bow-Shaped Side Beams[J]. Journal of Mechanical Science and Technology, 26(2): 531-536.

KIM U, et al, 2005. Optimal Design of Filament Wound Structures under Internal Pressure Based on the Semi-Geodesic Path Algorithm[J]. Composite Structures, 67(4): 443-452.

KUMOSA L, et al, 2001. An Evaluation of the Critical Conditions for the Initiation of Stress Corrosion Cracking in Unidirectional E-Glass/Polymer Composites[J]. Composites Science and Technology, 61(4): 615-623.

LAFITTE M H, BUNSELL A R, 1982. The Fatigue Behavior of Kevlar-29 Fibers[J]. Journal of Materials Science, 17(8): 1300-1308.

LECHAT C, 2006. Mechanical Behavior of Polyethylene Terephthalate and Polyethylene Naphthalate Fibers under Cyclic Loading[J]. Journal of Materials Science, 41(6): 1745-1756.

LECLERC C, et al, 2006. Role of Skin/Core Structure and Inclusions in the Fatigue Crack Initiation and Propagation in Organic Fibers[J]. Journal of Materials Science, 41(20): 6830-6842.

LEE L H, 1969. Strength-Composition Relationships of Random Short Glass Fiber-Thermoplastics Composites [J]. Polymer Engineering and Science, 9(3): 213-224.

LEI Z K, et al, 2013. Micromechanics of Fiber-Crack Interaction Studied by Micro-Raman Spectroscopy: Bridging Fiber[J]. Optics and Lasers in Engineering, 51(4): 358-363.

LEI Z K, WANG Q, QIU W, 2013. Stress Transfer of Kevlar 49 Fiber Pullout Test Studied by Micro Raman Spectroscopy[J]. Applied Spectroscopy, 67(6): 600-605.

LIBRESCU L, MAALAWI K, 2007. Material Grading for Improved Aeroelastic Stability in Composite Wings [J]. Journal of Mechanics of Materials and Structures, 2(7): 1381-1394.

LU T J, HUTCHINSON J W, 1995. Effect of Matrix Cracking and Interface Sliding on the Thermal Expansion of Fiber-Reinforced Composites[J]. Composites, 26(6): 403-414.

MAIMI P, CAMAHNO P P, MAYUGO J A, et al, A Continuum Damage Model for Composite Laminates: Part I-Constitutive Model[J]. Mechanics of Materials, 39(10): 897-908.

MAKEEV A, SEON G, LEE E, 2010. Failure Predictions for Carbon/Epoxy Tape Laminates with Wavy Plies [J]. Journal of Composite Materials, 44(1): 95-112.

MAKSIMOV R, URZHUMTSEV Y, 1970. Vibrocreep of Polymeric Materials[J]. Mechanics of Composite Materials, 6(4): 561-564.

MAYES S J, HANSEN A C, 2004. Composite Laminate Failure Analysis Using Multicontinuum Theory[J]. Composites Science and Technology, 64(3-4): 379-394.

MENEGHETTI G, QUARESIMIN M, RICOTTA M, 2010. Influence of the Interface Ply Orientation on the Fatigue Behavior of Bonded Joints in Composite Materials[J]. International Journal of Fatigue, 32: 82-93.

MIYANO Y, NAKADA M, SEKINE N, 2006. Accelerated Testing for Long-Term Durability of FRP Laminates for Marine Use[J]. Journal of Composite Materials, 39(1): 5-20.

MIWA M, et al, 1979. Temperature Dependence of the Tensile Strength of Glass Fiber-Epoxy and Glass Fiber-Unsaturated Polyester Composites[J]. Journal of Applied Polymer Science, 23(10): 2957-2966.

MORTAZAVIAN S, FATEMI A, 2015. Fatigue Behavior and Modeling of Short Fiber Reinforced Polymer

Composites Including Anisotropy and Temperature Effects[J]. International Journal of Fatigue, 77(aug): 12-27.

MOVAGHGHAR A, LVOV G I, 2012. A Method of Estimating Wind Turbine Blade Fatigue Life and Damage Using Continuum Damage Mechanics[J]. International Journal of Damage Mechanics, 21(6): 810-821.

MOVAGHGHAR A, LVOV G I, 2011. An Energy Model for Fatigue Life Prediction of Composite Materials Using Continuum Damage Mechanics[J]. Applied Mechanics and Materials, 110-116: 1353-1360.

NAIRNA J A, MENDELS D A, 2001. On the Use of Planar Shear-Lag Methods for Stress-Transfer Analysis of Multilayered Composites[J]. Mechanics of Materials, 33(6): 335-362.

PERING G A, FARREL P V, SPRINGER G S, 1989. Degradation of Tensile and Shear Properties of Composites Exposed to Fire or High Temperatures[J]. Journal of Composite Materials, 14(1): 54-68.

PHILLIPPIDIS T, THEOCARIS P, 1999. Fatigue Prediction under Multiaxial Stress[J]. Journal of Composites Materials, 33(17): 1578-1599.

PINHO S, IANNUCCI L, ROBINSON P, 2006. Physically-Based Failure Models and Criteria for Laminated Fiber-Reinforced Composites with Emphasis on Fiber Kinking: Part Ⅰ: Development[J]. Composites, A, 37(1): 63-73.

PINHO S, IANNUCCI L, ROBINSON P, 2006. Physically-Based Failure Models and Criteria for Laminated Fiber-Reinforced Composites with Emphasis on Fiber Kinking: Ⅱ: FE Implementation[J]. Composites, A, 37(5): 766-777.

PUCK A, SCHÜRMANN H, 1998. Failure Analysis of FRP Laminates by Means of Physically Based Phenomenological Models[J]. Composites Science and Technology, 62(12-13): 1633-1662.

QUARESIMIN M, 2016. A Damage-Based Approach for the Fatigue Design of Composite Structures[J]. 37th Risø International Symposium on Materials Science, 139: 012006.

QUARESIMIN M, et al, 2010. Fatigue Behavior and Life Assessment of Composite Laminates under Multiaxial Loadings[J]. International Journal of Fatigue, 32(1): 2-16.

REN W, 2002. Creep Behavior of a Continuous Strand, Ewirl Mat Reinforced Polymeric Composite in Simulated Automotive Environments for Durability Investigation; Part Ⅰ: Experimental Development and Creep-Rupture[J]. Materials Science and Engineering A, 334(1-2): 312-319.

ROBBINS D H, REDDY J N, 2008. Adaptive Hierarchical Kinematics in Modeling Progressive Damage and Global Failure in Fiber-Reinforced Composite Laminates[J]. Journal of Composite Materials, 42(2): 143-172.

STARINK M J, SYNGELLAKIS S, 1999. Shear Lag Model for Discontinuous Composite: Fiber End Stressed and Weak Interface Layers[J]. Materials Science and Engineering A, 270(2): 270-277.

TALREJA R, SINGH C V, 2012.Damage and Failure of Composite Materials[M]. Cambridge University Press, New York.

TANAKA K, et al, 2004. Influences of Stress Waveform and Wet Environment on Fatigue Fracture Behavior of Aramid Single Fiber[J]. Composites Science and Technology, 64(10/11): 1531-1537.

TSAI S, HAHN H, 1980.Introduction to Composite Materials[M]. Technomic Publishing Company.

TAY T E, 2005. Damage Progression by the Element Failure Method (EFM) and Strain Invariant Failure Theory (SIFT)[J]. Composites Science and Technology, 65(6): 935-944.

TENG T L, YU C M, WU Y Y, 2005. Optimization Design of Filament-Wound Composite Pressure Vessels[J]. Mechanics of Composite Materials, 41(4): 333-340.

THEOCARIS P, PHILLIPPIDIS T, 1991. On the Validity of the Tensor Polynomial Theory with Stress Interaction Terms Omitted, Acritical Assessment[J]. Composites Science and Technology, 40: 181-191.

TSAI S W, WU E M, 1971. A General Theory of Strength for Anisotropic Materials[J]. Journal of Composite Materials, 5(1): 58-80.

VINOGRADOV A, SCHUMACHER S, 2001. Cyclic Creep of Polymers and Polymer-Matrix Composites[J]. Mechanics of Composite Materials, 37(1): 29-34.

VINOGRADOV A, HOLLOWAY F, 1999. Electro-Mechanical Properties of the Piezoelectric Polymer PVDF [J]. Ferroelectrics, 226(1): 169-181.

XU L R, et al, 2005. Free-Edge Stress Singularities and Edge Modifications for Fiber Pushout Experiments[J]. Journal of Composite Materials, 39(12): 1103-1125.

YERRAMALLI C S, WAAS A M, 2002. Compressive Splitting Failure of Composites Using Modified Shear Lag Theory[J]. International Journal of Fracture, 115(1): 27-40.

ZAGO A, SPRINGER G, QUARESIMIN M, 2001. Cumulative Damage of Short Fiber Reinforced Thermoplastics[J]. Journal of Fiber-Reinforced Plastic Composites, 20(7): 596-605.

ZHANG J, WANG F, 2010. Modeling of Damage Evolution and Failure in Fiber-Reinforced Ductile Composites under Thermomechanical Fatigue Loading[J]. International Journal of Damage Mechanics, 19(7): 851-875.

ZHENG J Y, LIU P F, 2008. Elastoplastic Stress Analysis and Burst Strength Evaluation of Al-Carbon Fiber/

Epoxy Composite Cylindrical Laminates[J]. Computational Materials Science, 42(3): 453-461.

Problems

P15.12.1: Consider a single-layered filament-wound pressure vessel, which is 12 mm thick, 400 mm long, and 720 mm in diameter. The E-glass fiber-reinforced epoxy has the following mechanical properties: $E_{11} = 60$ GPa, $E_{22} = 12$ GPa, and $\mu_{12} = 0.3$. How much is the critical pressure when it is under an external pressure?

Chapter 16

Indentation Engineering and Fretting Fatigue

16.1 Hardness by Indentation

Indentation hardness measures the resistance of a sample to material deformation due to a constant compression load from a sharp object. It takes a resistance to deformation with various kinds of permanent shape change. Though it is not a "mechanics of materials" property employed for a deepened derivative analysis (e.g. finite element methods), hardness is related to such key mechanical properties as yield strength, tensile strength, and Young's moduli. Hardness may be employed to explore material ductility, elastic stiffness, yield strength, tensile strength, plasticity, toughness, viscoelasticity, and viscosity. The top three types of hardness measurements in use are scratch hardness, indentation hardness, and rebound hardness.

16.1.1 Hardness by Indentation

Indentation tests have been used for measuring hardness[Tabor]. Indentation tests, depending on the indentation scale, can be classified into three categories: macro-indentation, micro-indentation, and nano-indentation. There are several different measures on hardness depending on the indentation tools and calculation methods:

(A) Brinell Hardness (H_B): Spherical Indenter;

(B) Knoop Hardness (H_K): Pyramidal Indenter;

(C) Rockwell Hardness (H_R): Spheroconical Indenter;

(D) Vickers Hardness (H_V): Rectangular Pyramidal Indenter;

(E) Martens Hardness (H_M): Indenters listed above can be used, though often Vickers;

(F) Shore Hardness (Shore A or D): Diamond-Tipped Hammer (Rebound hardness).

Material hardness offers a comparative measure of material resistance to deformation and would-be wear, but it is not a fundamental material property. Recently, indentation tests have been explored further for mechanical properties other than hardness such as elastoplastic properties, viscoelastic and viscoplastic properties, fracture roughness, and creep of materials[Poon et al.][Kang et al.]. Although kgf/mm^2 has been the unit for Knoop hardness and Vickers hardness, MPa is also recommended as it is compatible with other material properties such as stress and strength. Hardness of different kinds of materials are given in Tables 16.1.1-16.1.4, respectively for non-ferrous metals, the ferrous, ceramics and harder, and biomaterials.

Fig. 16.1.1   Various Types of Indenters: Vickers, Berkovich, Cube Corner, Spherical, and Flat End [Zwick]

16.1.2   Microindentation Hardness

A diamond indenter of specific geometry is impressed into the surface of the test specimen using a known applied force, nominally set between 0.01 N and 10 N ($\approx$ 0.001 to 1 kgf) following ASTM E384 specification. Various types of indenters are displayed in Fig. 16.1.1. Knoop micro-hardness (H_K, using pyramidal indenter) and Vickers micro-hardness (H_V, using pyramidal indenter) are two most commonly used microindentation hardness test methods. In a general microindentation hardness testing of steel, the typical test load is around 2 N ($\approx$ 0.2 kgf) producing an indentation depth of about 0.05 mm (50 μm).

16.1.3   Hardness at Elevated Temperatures

With the increasing demand for materials to withstand high temperatures, a need arises for a rapid, inexpensive method for measuring mechanical properties at elevated temperatures. Hot hardness gives a good indication of the potential usefulness of an alloy for high-temperature strength applications. In an extensive review of hardness data at different temperatures, [Westbrook] has shown that the temperature dependence of hardness may be expressed by

$$H = A \, e^{-\alpha T} \tag{16.1.1}$$

where

$H(\text{kgf/mm}^2)$: Hardness;

$T(\text{K})$: Temperature;

A and α: Coefficient and exponents (constants).

The concept of temperature-dependent hardness has been employed for measuring the in-situ operating temperature of a moving part, e.g. an engine piston.

16.1.4　Thermal Drift

Thermal drift is defined as the change in the displacement signal when the normal force applied to the indenter is maintained constant, while the material does not exhibit time dependent mechanical properties.

16.2　Elastoplastic Properties by Indentation

Indentation itself is perhaps the most commonly applied means of testing the elastoplastic properties of materials. Regression functions are generated to map the indentation load-depth curve to the elastoplastic stress-strain curve. Knowledge of the relationship between the indentation load and the true (projected) contact area is essential for extracting the mechanical properties from instrumented indentation.

16.2.1　Flow Stress

The term "flow stress" means the onset of plastic flow of deformed materials. It resembles the concept of von Mises stress, and physically it is an equivalent stress. Johnson-Cook equation has been successfully applied to impact engineering such as metal cutting, car crashworthiness, metal forming, and explosive tests. Without the effects of strain rate and temperature, Eq. (4.117) can be rewritten as a special case of Holomann equation, also called Ludwig equation,

$$\sigma - A = B(\varepsilon_{\mathrm{p}})^{n} \tag{16.2.1}$$

The applied load increases as the indentation proceeds. The typical plot of a monotonic stress-strain curve (or σ-ε curve) of steel in compression is depicted schematically in Fig. 16.2.1(a), while its related schematic drawing of the contact stress distribution is presented in Fig. 16.2.1 (b). Point ($\sigma_{29\%}$, 29%) is identified arbitrarily for the indentation study [Giannakopoulos & Suresh].

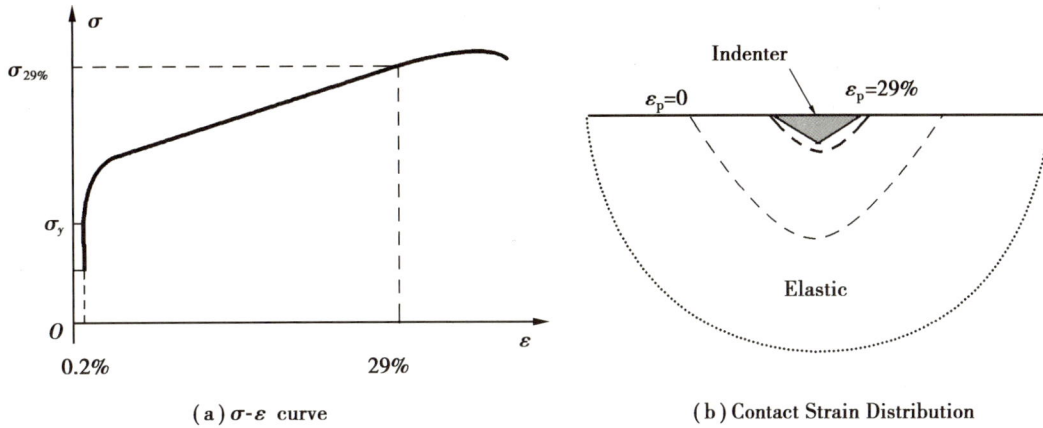

(a) σ-ε curve

(b) Contact Strain Distribution

Fig. 16.2.1   Schematic Drawings of Elastoplastic Stress-Strain Curve and Contact Strain Distribution of Steel in Compression

16.2.2   Force-Depth Relationship: Semi-Empirical Approach

The typical plot of an indentation load-versus-depth curve (or F_z-h curve) is depicted schematically in Fig. 16.2.2. The load is applied by electromagnetic force, which is controlled by varying the electric current. As the exerting force keeps growing, a curve concaved upwards is obtained. After the load is released at the set value, the specimen may exhibit a permanent displacement. An electric capacitive sensor and/or LVDT (Linear Variable Differential Transformer) may be used to measure the displacement. The Young's modulus, yield strength, and ultimate strength can be estimated from several loading-unloading curves, with the digitized information of the last 50%-90% portion of each loading-unloading curve.

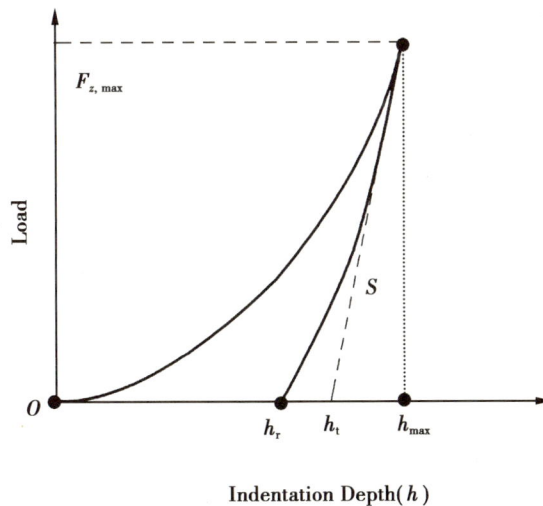

Indentation Depth(h)

Fig. 16.2.2   A Typical Load-Depth Curve with an Indentation

A force-depth (F_z-h) regression equation can be utilized for formulating elastoplastic material properties. Detailed three-dimensional, large-strain, plasticity simulations by [Giannakopoulos &

Suresh] reveal that the tip radius of the sharp indenter, R, has a negligible effect on indentation and the *P-h* curve provided the depth of penetration of the indenter into the material, $h > R/40$. In addition, adhesion and friction between the indenter and the substrate were found to have only a slight effect on the hardness and the F_z-h curve. As observed in the experimental tests and as shown in Fig. 16.2.2, the applied force is described as a function of the penetration depth as

$$F_z = C\,h^2 \tag{16.2.2}$$

Using a fixed value to characterize the stress-strain curve, e.g. at strain $= 29\%$ [Giannakopoulos & Suresh], a regression model for constant C can be derived as an empirical model. When $0.5 \leqslant p_{ave}/\sigma_y \leqslant 3$,

$$C = \frac{F_z}{h^2} = M_1\,\sigma_{29\%}\left(1 + \frac{\sigma_y}{\sigma_{29\%}}\right)\left[M_2 + \ln\left(\frac{E_{eq}}{\sigma_y}\right)\right] \tag{16.2.3}$$

and $\quad p_{ave} = \dfrac{F_{z,\max}}{A_{\max}} \tag{16.2.4}$

where

F_z: Indentation load (force) applied;

$F_{z,\max}$: Maximum indentation load (force);

p_{ave}: Pressure at final, averaged;

$A_{\max}$: Maximum true contact area;

σ_y: Yield strength;

$\sigma_{29\%}$: Characteristic plastic strength (ε_p) at 29%;

E_{eq}: Effective Young's modulus;

M_1 and M_2: Coefficients, varying with respect to the indenter.

Parameter p_{ave} is also called "hardness" by Berkovich indentation, when it is expressed in "GPa". The above equation is valid when $0.5 \leqslant p_{ave}/\sigma_y \leqslant 3$. If $(p_{ave}/\sigma_y) < 0.5$, it experiences an elastic deformation. If $(p_{ave}/\sigma_y) > 3$, it is elasto-perfectly plastic deformation. M_1 and M_2 are regression coefficients that vary with the indenter as shown in Table 16.2.1.

16.2.3   Equivalent Young's Modulus

Unknown constants in Table 16.2.1 for circular conical indenters vary with another feature-apex angle. The effective Young's modulus can be derived from the contact between indenter and the test material as

$$E_{eq} = \left(\frac{1 - v_{indenter}^2}{E_{indenter}} + \frac{1 - v^2}{E}\right)^{-1} \tag{16.2.5}$$

where

E_{eq}: Equivalent Young's modulus;

$v_{indenter}$: Poisson's ratio of indenter;

$E_{indenter}$: Young's modulus of indigene;

v: Poisson's ratio of test specimen;

E: Young's modulus of test specimen.

Note that $E_{indenter} = 900$ GPa and $v_{indenter} = 0.02$ for the Berkovich diamond pyramid indenter [Jayaraman et al.]. Equivalent Young's modulus E_{eq} was found to be related to the variation of the force required to create a differential depth as

$$E_{eq} = \frac{C^* \left(\dfrac{dF_z}{dh}\right)}{A_{max}^{\frac{1}{2}}} \qquad (16.2.6)$$

of which C^* is a constant and its value varies with the indenter, as shown in Table 16.2.1. After the equivalent Young's modulus is calculated from the measured data using (16.2.6), the Young's modulus of the test specimen can be obtained from Eq. (16.2.5). Finite element method can be used as a tool for deriving Eq. (16.2.6) iteratively [Fu et al.].

16.2.4   Plastic Strain and Residual Depth of Penetration

The residual depth of penetration, h_r, upon complete unloading (see Fig. 16.2.2) from the maximum penetration depth, can be approximated by

$$\frac{h_r}{h_{max}} = 1 - D^* S \qquad (16.2.7)$$

and $S \equiv \dfrac{P_{ave}}{E_{eq}} \qquad (16.2.8)$

where

h_r: Residual depth of penetration (Fig. 16.2.2);

D^*: Proportionality coefficient (Table 16.2.1);

S: Slope, tangent to the loading curve (NOT unloading curve) as denoted in Fig. 16.2.1.

Simultaneously, one can calculate S from Fig. 16.2.2 as

$$S = \frac{P_{max}}{h_{max} - h_t} \qquad (16.2.9)$$

The residual depth of penetration is indicative of plastic deformation with strain hardening. Define

$$E_{apparent} = \frac{\sigma_{29\%} - \sigma_y}{29\%} \tag{16.2.10}$$

of which the final loading point $\sigma_{29\%}$ is determined arbitrarily at strain = 29%. The apparent Young's modulus is the slope of an elastoplastic stress-strain curve after yielding point. The interpolation equation for the plastic deformation is formulated in the dimensionless form in terms of h_r/h_{max} as [Giannakopoulos & Suresh]

$$\frac{E_{apparent}}{E_{eq}} = \frac{\sigma_{29\%} - \sigma_y}{29\% \, E_{eq}} = 1 - 0.142 \left(\frac{h_r}{h_{max}}\right) - 0.957 \left(\frac{h_r}{h_{max}}\right)^2 \tag{16.2.11}$$

The above equation holds for Vickers, Berkovich, and circular conical indenters according to [Giannakopoulos & Suresh]. Two extreme cases are given as follows:

(a) When $h_r/h_{max} = 0$, $\sigma_{29\%} - \sigma_y = 29\% \, E_{eq}$ ➔ $E_{apparent} = E_{eq}$ (Linear elastic deformation)
(b) When $h_r/h_{max} = 1$, $\sigma_{29\%} = \sigma_y$ ➔ $E_{apparent} = 0$ (Perfect plastic deformation)

16.2.5 Energy for Penetration

The integrated area under the F_z-h curve (Fig. 16.2.2) is a measure of the total work done by the applied penetration force on the specimen material,

$$W_{total} = \int_0^{h_{max}} F_z(h) \, dh = \int_0^{} C \, h^2 dh = \frac{Ch_{max}^3}{3}$$

$$= \frac{F_{z,max} \, h_{max}}{3} = \frac{F_{z,max}^{\frac{3}{2}}}{3C^{\frac{1}{2}}} \tag{16.2.12}$$

It was revealed by [Stillwell & Tabor] that the ratio of work done in the plastic range to the total work is equivalent to the dimensionless residual depth,

$$\frac{W_{plastic}}{W_{total}} = \frac{h_r}{h_{max}} \tag{16.2.13}$$

Given that $W_{plastic} = W_{total} - W_{elastic}$, the work done in the elastic range can be obtained as

$$\frac{W_{elastic}}{W_{total}} = 1 - \frac{W_{plastic}}{W_{total}} = 1 - \frac{h_r}{h_{max}} \tag{16.2.14}$$

By plugging Eq. (16.2.7) into the above equation, one has

$$\frac{W_{elastic}}{W_{total}} = 1 - \frac{h_r}{h_{max}} = 1 - (1 - D^* S) = D^* S$$

$$= \frac{D^* P_{max}}{h_{max} - h_t} \tag{16.2.15}$$

16.2.6 Pile-Up or Sink-In

The work-hardening exponent has been found to be a main factor affecting the pileup/sink-in phenomena of various steels [Ahn & Kwon]. As for the effect of strain hardening on the true contact area resulting from pile-up or sink-in, the following general empirical guidelines are given by [Giannakopoulos & Suresh] in light of Eq. (16.2.12) as:

(1) When $7/8 < h_r/h_{max} \leqslant 1$, pile-up occurs, resulting that $A > A_{app}$;

(2) When $7/8 < h_r/h_{max} \leqslant 1$, sink-in occurs, resulting that $A \leqslant A_{app}$;

(3) When $h_r/h_{max} = 7/8$, and $A = A_{app}$; for Vickers indenter.

$$A = A_{app} \approx 24.5h^2 \tag{16.2.16}$$

where

A: True contact area;

A_{app}: Apparent contact area.

Through three-dimensional finite element analysis, the following relationship for the dimensionless maximum contact area is derived for elastoplastic materials [Giannakopoulos & Suresh],

$$\frac{A_{max}}{h_{max}^2} = 9.96 - 12.64\ (1-S) + 105.42\ (1-S)^2 - 229.57\ (1-S)^3 + 157.67\ (1-S)^4$$

$$\tag{16.2.17}$$

Example 16.2.1 Ultrahigh strength SAE 1070 steel is tested using the Berkovich indentation to validate its material properties ($E = 210$ GPa, $\sigma_y = 2610$ MPa $= 2.61$ GPa, and hardness $= 9.5$ GPa) that are obtained from the uniaxial test. Assume that the Poisson's ratio of the steel is $v = 0.3$. The following data are acquired from the indentation test: $F_{z, max} = 0.1$ N, $h_{max} = 0.733 \times 10^{-3}$ mm ($= 0.733$ μm), $h_r = 0.567 \times 10^{-3}$ mm ($= 0.567$ μm), $dF_z/dh = 752$ N/mm (at the beginning of unloading).

Solution

Converting all the units into (N, s, mm, MPa) system, then follow the steps given below:

(1) The slope of loading curve: By Eq. (16.2.7)

$$\frac{h_r}{h_{max}} = 1 - D^* S$$

$$\frac{0.567 \times 10^{-3}}{0.733 \times 10^{-3}} = 1 - 4.678 S$$

$$S = 0.04841$$

(2) Work done in the elastic range: By Eq. (16.2.13),

$$\frac{W_{\text{elastic}}}{W_{\text{total}}} = 1 - \frac{h_{\text{r}}}{h_{\text{max}}} = 1 - \frac{0.567 \times 10^{-3}}{0.733 \times 10^{-3}} = 22.65\%$$

(3) Maximum contact area: By Eq. (16.2.16),

$$\frac{A_{\text{max}}}{h_{\text{max}}^2} = 9.96 - 12.64(1 - S) + 105.42 (1 - S)^2 - 229.57(1 - S)^3 + 157.67(1 - S)^4$$

$$\frac{A_{\text{max}}}{(0.733 \times 10^{-3})^2} = 9.96 - 12.64 \times (1 - 0.04841) + 105.42 \times (1 - 0.04841)^2 -$$

$$229.57 \times (1 - 0.04841)^3 + 157.67 \times (1 - 0.04841)^4$$

$$A_{\text{max}} = 13.36 \times 10^{-6} \text{ mm}^2 = 13.36 \ \mu\text{m}^2$$

(4) Equivalent Young's modulus: By Eq. (16.2.6),

$$E_{\text{eq}} = \frac{C^* \left(\dfrac{\mathrm{d}F_z}{\mathrm{d}h} \right)}{A_{\text{max}}^{\frac{1}{2}}}$$

$$= \frac{0.8569 \times 752}{(13.36 \times 10^{-6})^{\frac{1}{2}}} = 176276 \text{ MPa} \approx 176.3 \text{ GPa}$$

(5) Young's modulus of test specimen: By Eq. (16.2.5),

$$E_{\text{eq}} = \left(\frac{1 - v_{\text{indenter}}^2}{E_{\text{indenter}}} + \frac{1 - v^2}{E} \right)^{-1}$$

$$176276 = \left(\frac{1 - 0.02^2}{900000} + \frac{1 - 0.3^2}{E} \right)^{-1}$$

$$E = 199463 \text{ MPa} \approx 199.5 \text{ GPa}$$

(6) Hardness (pressure, averaged): By Eq. (16.2.8),

$$S = \frac{p_{\text{ave}}}{E_{\text{eq}}}$$

$$0.04841 = \frac{p_{ave}}{176276}$$

$$p_{ave} = 0.04841 \times 176276 = 8533.5 \text{ MPa} = 8.5335 \text{ GPa}$$

(7) Yield strength: By Eq. (16.2.10),

$$\frac{\sigma_{29\%} - \sigma_y}{0.29 E_{eq}} = 1 - 0.142\left(\frac{h_r}{h_{max}}\right) - 0.957\left(\frac{h_r}{h_{max}}\right)^2$$

$$= 1 - 0.142 \times \frac{0.567 \times 10^{-3}}{0.733 \times 10^{-3}} - 0.957 \times \left(\frac{0.567 \times 10^{-3}}{0.733 \times 10^{-3}}\right)^2$$

$$= 0.317534$$

Thus, $(\sigma_{29\%} - \sigma_y) = 0.317534 \times 0.29 E_{eq} = 0.317534 \times 0.29 \times 199463 = 18367$ MPa

16.2.7 Meyer's Law

The mean pressure between the surface of the indenter and the indentation is equal to the load divided by the projected area of the indentation. Meyer proposed that this mean pressure should be taken as the measure of hardness instead of contact surface area. Meyer proposed an empirical equation relating the load to the size of the indentation, which is called Meyer's law

$$F_z = kd^m \tag{16.2.18}$$

where

F_z (kgf or N): Indenting force;

k: Constant;

d (mm): Characteristic diameter based on the projected area under the mean pressure;

m: Exponent, $m = 2$ for strain-hardened metals and $m = 2.5$ for fully annealed metals.

A hardness number is traditionally expressed in kgf/mm^2 (kilogram-force per square millimeter), of which the area of the denominator can be projected pressure area (e.g. Brinell test) as postulated using Meyer's law or real-contact surface area (e.g. Vickers test). To convert a traditional hardness number to SI units, it has to be multiplied by the standard gravity (9.80665) to get the hardness in MPa (N/mm^2) and furthermore divided by 1000 to get the hardness in GPa.

16.3 Brinell Hardness

The ball indentation technique has the potential to be a substitute for a standard uniaxial compression-tension test, specially in the case of mini- and micro-scaled specimens such as films or property-gradient materials such as coatings and welds. Spherical tungsten-carbide indenters of 10 mm in diameter are used in Brinell tests. It is commonly used for measuring hardness of metallic material with a known applied load of 500, 1500, or 3000 kgf. Note that 1 kgf = 9.807 N. The recommended impression size is in the range of 2.5 mm to 4.75 mm. When a spherical ball is pushed against a flat surface as illustrated in Fig. 16.3.1, the instantaneous radius of the intersecting circular cross-section, called chordal radius, is ideally

$$Z = R - (R^2 - X^2)^{\frac{1}{2}} \qquad (16.3.1)$$

where

Z: Depth of indentation, ideally;
X: Chordal radius of indentation;
R: Radius of ball.

The force is maintained for a specific dwell time, normally 10-15 s. After the dwell time is complete, the indenter is removed leaving a round indent in the sample. The Brinell hardness number is a function of the test force divided by the curved surface area of the indent. Accordingly, Brinell formula for hardness for a spherical ball can be obtained as

$$H_B = \frac{F_z}{2\pi RZ} = \frac{F_z}{2\pi R[R - (R^2 - X^2)^{\frac{1}{2}}]} \ (\text{kgf/mm}^2) \qquad (16.3.2)$$

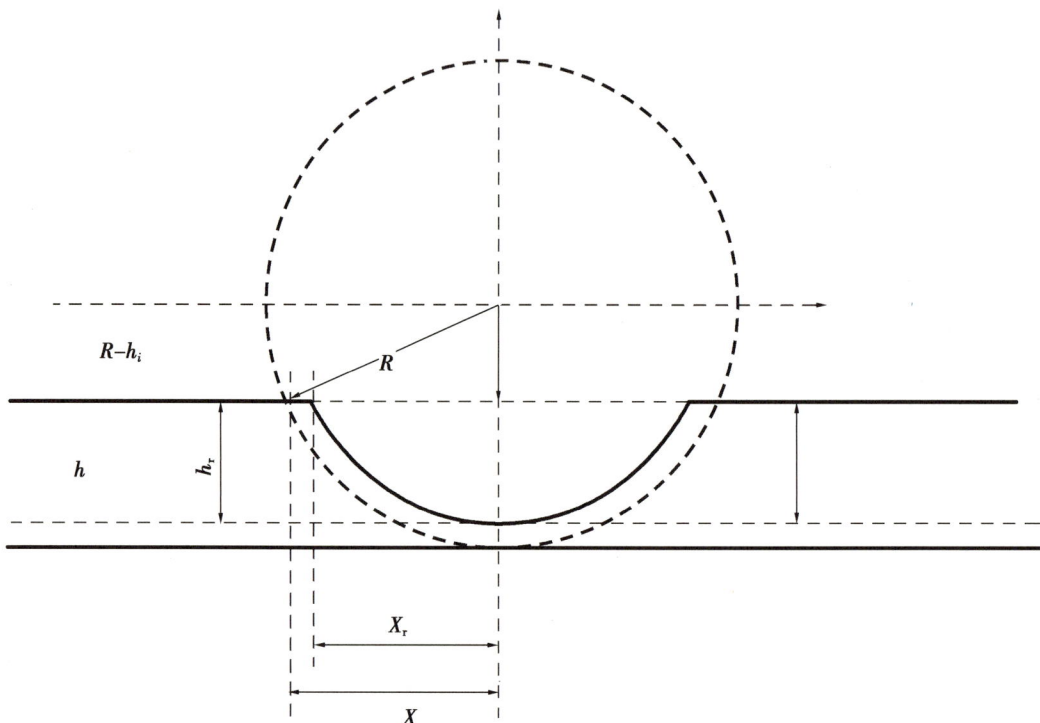

Fig. 16.3.1 Ball Indentation onto a Flat Surface

16.3.1   Normal Stress

As depicted in Fig. 16.3.1, the average pressure exerted onto the specimen is equal to the total force divided by the chordal area (πX^2) as

$$\sigma_{zz,\text{ave}} = \frac{F_z}{\pi X^2} \tag{16.3.3}$$

of which F_z is the force of indentation. The true tensile stress of interest induced on the indented edge is [Jeon et al.]

$$(\sigma_{xx})_{\max} = (\sigma_{yy})_{\max} = \sigma_{\text{rr}} = \frac{\sigma_{zz,\text{ave}}}{3} = \frac{F_z}{3\pi X^2} \tag{16.3.4}$$

Note that σ_{rr} is the true tensile stress in the polar coordinate system.

16.3.2   Shear Stress

Next consider the true strain associated with an indentation depth of h. The displacement, W (variation of length form the reference surface to the bottom of the dent), along the loading axis under the indenter is the difference between the depth of indentation (h) and the theoretical indenter penetration in the vertical direction

$$W \approx h - \left[R - (R^2 - X^2)^{\frac{1}{2}} \right] \tag{16.3.5}$$

By taking a differentiation of the vertical displacement (W) with respect to the horizontal axis (X), one has the true shear strain [Ahn & Kwon] as a function of ratio X/R,

$$\gamma = \text{function}\left\{ \frac{\dfrac{X}{R}}{\left[1 - \left(\dfrac{X}{R}\right)^2 \right]^{\frac{1}{2}}} \right\} = \text{function}\left\{ \tan \frac{X}{R} \right\} = f\{\tan \theta\} \tag{16.3.6}$$

of which θ is the contact angle between the indenter and the specimen, $\theta \approx X/R$. According to [Jeon et al.], the true tensile strains induced is in the same form of the shear strain and they are proportional to $\tan \theta$ as

$$(\varepsilon_{xx})_{\max} = (\varepsilon_{yy})_{\max} = \varepsilon_{\text{rr}} = \beta \tan \theta \tag{16.3.7}$$

where β is the proportionality. $\beta = 0.10$ leads to a robust modeling of structural steels [Ahn & Kwon] while $\beta = 0.14$ has been identified for a great variety of materials [Jeon].

16.3.3　Young's Modulus of a Homogeneous Material

As indentation is proceeding, shown in Fig. 16.2.2, the equation of elastic deformation (indentation force versus indentation depth) without considering friction in the early stage can be described by Herzian contact theory

$$F_z = \frac{4}{3}\left(\frac{E_s}{1-v_s^2} + \frac{E_i}{1-v_i^2}\right) R^{\frac{1}{2}} h^{\frac{3}{2}} \qquad (16.3.8)$$

where

E_s & E_i: Young's moduli of test specimen and indenter, respectively;

v_s & v_i: Poisson's ratios of test specimen and indenter, respectively.

$E_i = 1140$ GPa and $v_i = 0.07$ for diamond indenter. The slope of the curve of the indentation force versus the indentation depth at the maximum load in the elastic range, S, is obtained by taking a differentiation of force F_z against depth h as

$$S = \left(\frac{dF_z}{dh}\right)\Bigg|_{h_{max}} = 2\left(\frac{E_s}{1-v_s^2} + \frac{E_i}{1-v_i^2}\right) R^{\frac{1}{2}} h^{\frac{1}{2}} \qquad (16.3.9)$$

Eqs. (16.3.8) and (16.3.9) can be solved for the Young's modulus and Poisson's ratio of the specimen, which are the only two unknowns. The applied compressive force and indentation depth are to be measured as an indentation test goes on. Several different forces and depths may be taken in order to find the best-fit solution for the Young's modulus and Poisson's ratio of the specimen by regression.

16.3.4　Relationship of Yield and Tensile Strengths to Brinell Hardness of Steel

When a load of 3000 kgf (1 kgf = 9.807 N) is applied, the tensile strength of specimen material can be approximated using the Brinell hardness data by the following regression models:

$$\sigma_{uts} = \begin{cases} 0.362H_B, & \text{if } H_B \leqslant 176 \text{ kgf/mm}^2(\text{i.e. } 1717 \text{ MPa}) & (16.3.10) \\ 0.345H_B, & \text{if } H_B > 176 \text{ kgf/mm}^2(\text{i.e. } 1717 \text{ MPa}) & (16.3.11) \end{cases}$$

For example, given that one kind of steel has a Brinell hardness of 200 kgf/mm² (i.e., 1961.4 MPa), then its ultimate tensile strength $\sigma_{uts} \approx 0.345 \times 1961.4$ MPa = 677 MPa, based on Eq. (16.3.11).

16.4　Knoop Hardness

Pyramidal diamond indenters are used in Knoop hardness tests, as shown in Fig. 16.4.1. It can be applied to thin plastic sheets, thin metal sheets, electrodeposits, and ceramics. The indenter is an extended pyramid with the length-to-width ratio of 7:1. Its respective face angles are 172.5° for the long edge and 130° for the short edge. The Knoop hardness of a material is defined as the ratio of the load (N) to the impression area (mm^2) created by the indenter as per [ISO 9385] [ASTM 384]

$$H_{K} = \sigma_{zz,\text{ave}} = C\frac{F_z}{L^2} \quad (\text{kgf/mm}^2 \text{ or MPa}) \tag{16.4.1}$$

where

　　C: Dimensionless correction factor and typically $C = 14.229$ for $H_K(\text{kgf/mm}^2)$;

　　L (mm): Indentation length along its long edge;

　　F_z (N or kgf): Force.

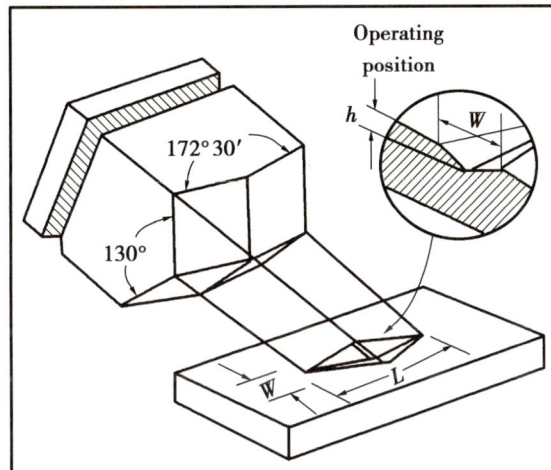

Fig. 16.4.1　Indenter and Impression Mark Resulting from a Knoop Hardness Test

The applied force is maintained for a specific dwell time, normally 10-15 s. After the dwell time is complete, the indenter is removed, leaving an elongated diamond shaped indent in the sample. Knoop hardness testing is used for measurement over small areas. The indentation depth is approximately 1/30 of the long dimension, thus called microhardness. The Knoop hardness can be calculated from the diagonal size L of the indentation using the following approximate equation (ISO 9385):

$$H_K(\text{kgf/mm}^2) = \frac{14.229F_z}{L^2} \quad (F_z: \text{kgf and } L: \text{mm}) \tag{16.4.2}$$

or $\quad H_{\mathrm{K}}(\mathrm{MPa}) = \dfrac{1.451 F_z}{L^2} (F_z: \mathrm{N} \text{ and } L: \mathrm{mm})$ $\qquad$ (16.4.3)

where

$\quad L\ (\mathrm{mm})$: Diagonal size of Knoop indenter.

The Knoop hardness number is a function of the test force divided by the projected area of the indent, as calculated using the above two equations. Size L of the indent is determined optically by measuring the longest diagonal of the diamond shaped indent. A typical Knoop hardness is specified, for example, as follows: 520 H_{K} 0.5, where 520 is the calculated hardness and 0.5 is the test force in kgf. Again, to convert a Knoop hardness number to SI units, it has to be multiplied by the standard gravity (9.80665) to get the hardness in MPa ($\mathrm{N/mm^2}$) and furthermore divided by 1000 to get the hardness in GPa.

16.5　Rockwell Hardness

Spheroconical indenters are used in Rockwell tests (Fig. 16.5.1). The major load is first applied for a specified time period (dwell time) and then it is released leaving the load maintained at minor level. The Rockwell hardness scale is determined by measuring the depth of penetration of the indenter under the major load compared to the penetration made by a much smaller preload. The resulting Rockwell number represents the difference in depth from the zero reference position as a result of the application of the major load.

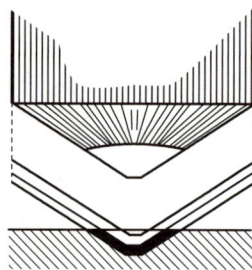

Fig. 16.5.1　Depth Difference Measured by Spheroconical Indenter for Rockwell Hardness

There are different scales for Rockwell hardness, designated by single letters. Each of these scales use different loads or indenters. Rockwell R (H_{RR}), Rockwell C (H_{RC}), and Rockwell A (H_{RA}) are the top three common practices based on Rockwell hardness testing[ASTM D2240][ISO 868] as they are applied according to the ascending "softness-to-hardness" of test specimens:

$\quad H_{\mathrm{RR}}$: To measure soft bearing metals, plastics and other similar soft materials.
$\quad H_{\mathrm{RC}}$: To measure steel, hard cast iron, and other materials having $H_{\mathrm{RR}} > 100$.
$\quad H_{\mathrm{RA}}$: To measure thin steel, shallow case hardened steel, and cemented carbide.

16.6   Shore Hardness

A diamond-tipped hammer in a graduated glass tube is allowed to fall from a known height on the specimen to be tested, and the hardness number depends on the height to which the hammer rebounds. As a hardness measure, the harder the material is the higher the rebound. If the indenter completely penetrates the sample, a reading of "0" is obtained. If no penetration occurs at all, a reading of "100" results. The reading is dimensionless. It is a measure of material elasticity. There are two measures of Shore hardness according to the "hardness" of materials:

Shore A durometer (H_A): Elastic materials such as rubber and soft plastics;

Shore D durometer (H_D): "Hard" rubber and plastics.

16.7   Vickers Hardness

Square-bottomed pyramidal diamond indenters that have a 136° face angle are commonly used in Vickers tests[Smith & Sandland, Vickers Ltd.], as shown in Fig. 16.7.1. It is utilized to observe the questioned material's ability to resist plastic deformation and used as a standard measure. The Vickers test can be used for all metals and has one of the widest scales among hardness tests.

16.7.1   Vickers Hardness Calculation-Direct

The "macro" diamond pyramid hardness is generally obtained using a nominal applied load of 50 kgf for a 30 s duration in practice, though the applied force may vary from 5 kgf to 120 kgf. In contrast, the load on the Vickers microhardness indenter usually ranges from a few grams to several kilograms. The Vickers hardness is defined as the ratio of the indentation force F_z to indentation area A_s, created at height h

$$H_V = \frac{F_z}{A_s(h)} \tag{16.7.1}$$

Rectangular pyramidal indenters are used in Vickers tests. The hardness number is determined by the load over the surface area of the indentation and not the area normal to the force. The surface area of the resulting indentation can be obtained using the included angle of the Vickers indenter 22° to the horizontal plane,

$$A_s(h) = \frac{d_d^2}{2 \cos 22°} \approx \frac{d_d^2}{1.8544} \tag{16.7.2}$$

where

F_z: Force of indentation;

d_d: Averaged diagonal length of the "rectangular" indentation on the horizontal plane; $d_d = d_1 = d_2$ for square indenters or $d_d = (d_1 + d_2)/2$, as shown in Fig. 16.7.1.

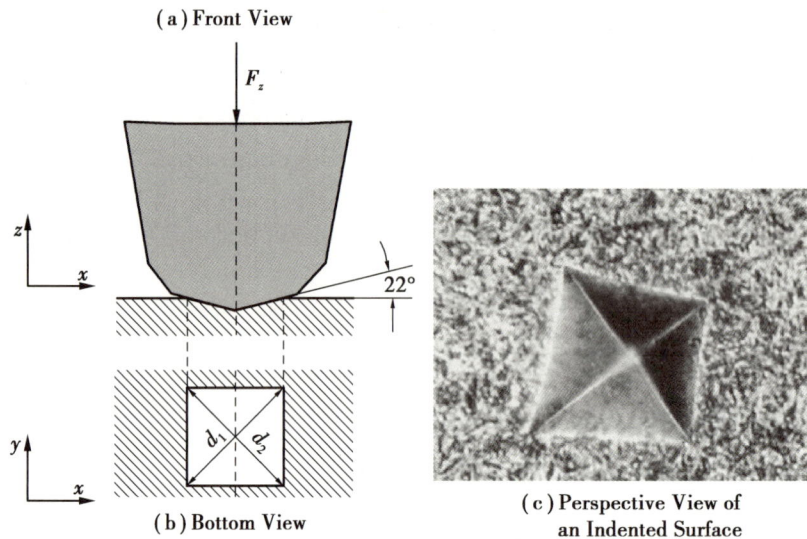

(a) Front View

(b) Bottom View

(c) Perspective View of an Indented Surface

Fig. 16.7.1 Indenter and Impression Mark Resulting from a Vickers Hardness Test

Thus, the Vickers hardness can be calculated using the following equation [ASTM E384]

$$H_V(\text{kgf/mm}^2) = \frac{1.8544F_z}{d_d^2} \qquad (16.7.3)$$

or $$H_V(\text{MPa}) = \frac{0.1891F_z}{d_d^2} \qquad (16.7.4)$$

The context of a given Vickers hardness is illustrated using a term like "$525H_V 10/20$", which means that $H_V = 525$ kgf/mm^2, $F_z = 10$ kgf, and loading duration $= 20$ s.

16.7.2 Relationship between Vickers Hardness and Yield/Tensile Strengths

The tensile strength of steel is related to Vickers hardness nearly linearly, as shown in Fig. 16.7.2. The yield strength (MPa) of carbon steel can be "roughly" approximated using Vickers hardness [Lin] as follows:

$$\sigma_Y(\text{MPa}) = 3.33\ H_V - 212.9, \quad \text{If } H_V \text{ is in kgf/mm}^2 \qquad (16.7.5)$$

or $$\sigma_Y(\text{MPa}) = 0.335\ H_V - 212.9, \quad \text{If } H_V \text{ is in MPa} \qquad (16.7.6)$$

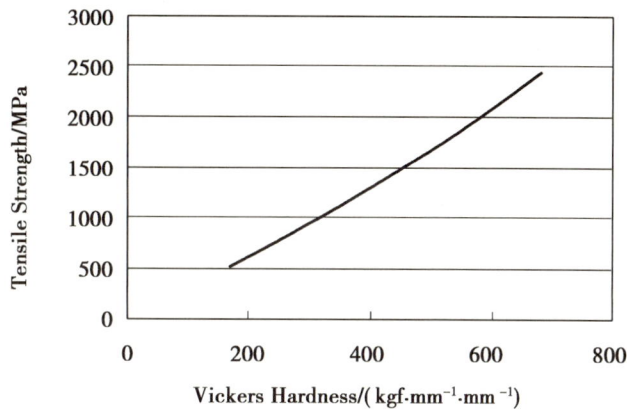

Fig. 16.7.2   Tensile Strength of Materials versus Vickers Hardness（10 kgf; Diamond Pyramid Hardness）

16.8   Martens Hardness

Indentation tests for Martens hardness, H_M, may be carried out with Vickers indenter and others. It is defined as the ratio of the test force F_z to the surface area $A_s(h)$ of the indenter penetrating beyond the zero-point of the contact, as given in Eq. (16.4.3). One way to calculate the hardness and other related material properties is to use the slope of loading-unloading curve. A data-acquisition process for Martens hardness and its related material properties is given in Fig. 16.8.1 [Zwick].

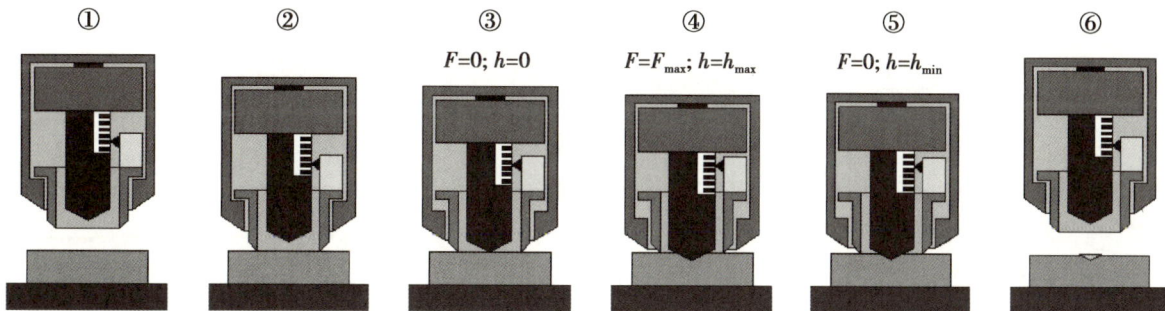

Fig. 16.8.1   Schematic Operating Sequence of an Indentation Test for Martens Hardness [Zwick Materials Testing]

16.8.1   Hardness Calculation Using Loading Slope

It is not easy to estimate the diameter of indentation automatically. Martens hardness is determined from the force-indentation depth curve following the increasing applied force, preferably after reaching and holding the specified maximum [ISO/DIS 14577]. Based on the Vickers indenter geometry, the contact area is related to the indentation depth as

$$A_s(h) = \frac{4 \sin\left(\frac{1}{2}\alpha\right)}{\cos^2\left(\frac{1}{2}\alpha\right)} h^2 \tag{16.8.1}$$

of which α is the angle between opposite faces of the pyramidal vertex of Vickers indenter. Given that $\alpha = 136°$, Eq. (16.8.1) reduces to

$$A_s(h) = 26.43h^2 \tag{16.8.2}$$

The following equation can be derived from the regression of a "nearly" parabolic F_z-h curve obtained by indentation [Wang et al.]

$$h = S_m F_z^{\frac{1}{2}} \tag{16.8.3}$$

or $\quad F_z = \dfrac{h^2}{S_m^2}$ (16.8.4)

S_m is the slope of $F_z^{\frac{1}{2}}$ evaluated against the indentation depth, which turns out to be fairly a constant in the applicable range taken for analysis. The data taken meticulously between 50% and 90% of the total load are quite congruent for calculating S [Wang et al.]. Note that Martens hardness is defined as $F_z/A_s(h)$. Thus,

$$H_M \equiv \frac{F_z}{A_s(h)} = \frac{h^2}{S_m^2 A_s(h)} \tag{16.8.5}$$

Substituting Eq. (16.8.2) into the above equation leads to

$$H_M = \frac{0.037838}{S_m^2} (\text{MPa}) \tag{16.8.6}$$

The unit of parameter S_m is usually $\mu\text{m}/\text{N}^{\frac{1}{2}}$ ($= 10^{-3} \text{mm}/\text{N}^{\frac{1}{2}}$) as derived from a micro-scaled indentation depth. Two sample F_z-h (Newton-μm) curves, respectively for Al-20Sn-Cu and Al-6Sn-Cu, are portrayed in Fig. 16.8.2.

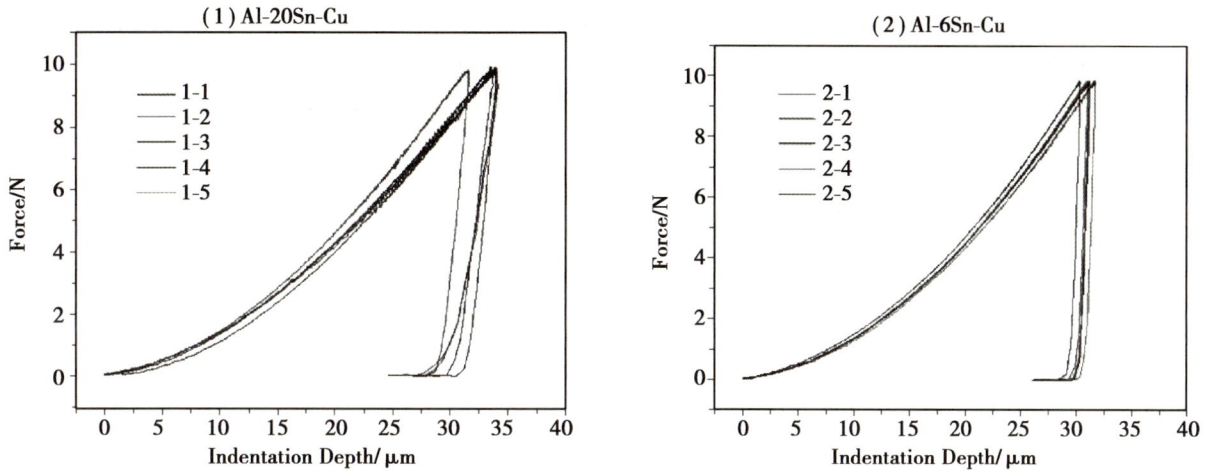

Fig. 16.8.2   Load-Deflection Curves for Two Bearing Materials, 5 Measurements Each

16.8.2   Estimating Young's Modulus Based on Unloading Curve

Indentation depth h has to be revised according to the load range, apparatus frame compliance, mounting and testing conditions of the sample[Oliver and Pharr]. As observed in Fig. 16.8.3, the elastic deformation will be recovered after the indentation is released. Assume that an elastic displacement for a simple punch geometry appearing in the unloading recovery related to the load following the power law as

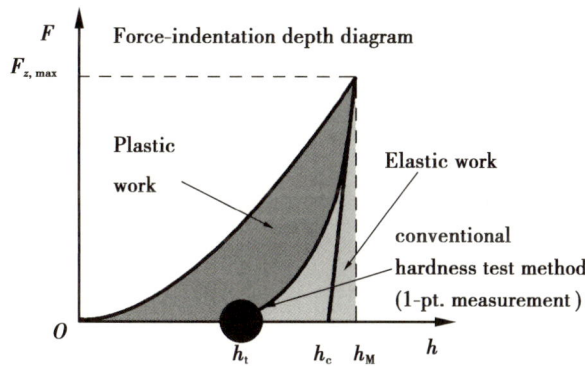

Fig. 16.8.3   Work Done as Loading-Unloading Proceeds[Zwick]

$$F_z = F_{z,M}\left(\frac{h - h_o}{h_M - h_o}\right)^m \tag{16.8.7}$$

where

α: Constant;

m: Exponent, varying with the indenter geometry as

$\qquad m = 1$ for flat indenter

$\qquad m = 1.5$ for paraboloidal indenter, and

$m = 2$ for conical indenter;

h_o: Starting point, usually $h_o = 0$ when calibrated properly.

Note that point M is the last loading point denoted in Fig. 16.2.1. Given that S is the slope measured at h_M,

$$S = \left(\frac{dF_z}{dh}\right)\Bigg|_{h_{MS}} = m\,(h_M - h_o)^{-1}\,F_{z,M} \tag{16.8.8}$$

As the unloading process begins at point M on the F_z-h curve, the tangent depth h_t can be estimated from the slope S, Fig. 16.2.1,

$$h_t = h_M - \frac{F_{z,M}}{S} \tag{16.8.9}$$

Consequently, the contact depth h_c at load step M is

$$h_c = h_M - \Lambda(h_M - h_t) \tag{16.8.10}$$

where

Λ: constant, depending on the indenter as;

$\Lambda = 1$ for flat indenter ($m = 1$ for Eq. (16.8.6)), i.e., point h_c is point h_t;

$\Lambda = 0.75$ for paraboloidal indenter ($m = 1.5$ for Eq. (16.8.7));

$\Lambda = 0.72$ for conical indenter ($m = 2$ for Eq. (16.8.7)).

Point h_r in Fig. 16.8.3 is approximated by h_c in Eq. (16.8.10) with regard to the estimation of A_p. Reduced elastic modulus E_r, indicative of the combined "composite" stiffness including the specimen and indenter, is[Chicot et al.]

$$E_r = \frac{\pi^{\frac{1}{2}}}{2\,\beta\,\gamma A_p^{\frac{1}{2}}}\left(\frac{dF_z}{dh}\right)\Bigg|_{h = h_M} \tag{16.8.11}$$

where

β: Constant related to indenter geometry as $\beta \approx 1.05$ for Vickers indenter[Antunes et al.];

γ: Correction factor for Poisson's ratio as $\gamma = 1.07$ for Vickers indenter on steels;

A_p: Projected area at the intersecting plane of undeformed sample plane and indenter.

Correction factor due to Poisson's ratio of the tested material in response to the indenter geometry is given as[Hay]

$$\gamma = \frac{\dfrac{1}{4} + 0.0387\left[\dfrac{1 - 2v}{(1 - v)\pi}\right]\cot\psi}{\left\{\dfrac{1}{2} - 0.2078\left[\dfrac{1 - 2v}{(1 - v)\pi}\right]\cot\psi\right\}^2} \tag{16.8.12}$$

As $\psi = 70.3°$ and $v = 0.29$ for mild carbon steels, $\gamma = 1.07$ for running Vickers indenter on steel samples. Parameter A_p is the projected area of contact on the undeformed sample plane. For $h > 6~\mu m$, the projected area of contact subject to Vickers indenter is valid for the following relationship:

$$A_p = 24.56~h_c^2 \qquad (16.8.13)$$

Note that h_c is the contact depth, which is shorter than the measured indentation depth h. The indentation hardness of material, also called Meyer hardness, is defined as the ratio of the applied force to the projected area of contact, and namely

$$H_{IT} = \frac{F_z}{A_p} \qquad (16.8.14)$$

Reduced elastic modulus E_r is a composite stiffness combining both the sample stiffness and indenter stiffness. They are related to one another by the following equation

$$\frac{1}{E_r} = \frac{1 - v_s^2}{E_s} + \frac{1 - v_i^2}{E_i} \qquad (16.8.15)$$

16.8.3   Estimating Young's Moduli of Composite Laminae

Many models were proposed to separate the elastoplastic properties of the layered composites according to the measured nanoindentation data. One of the empirical equations developed by [Doerner & Nix] is

$$\frac{1}{E_c} = \frac{1}{E_f} + \left(\frac{1}{E_{sb}} - \frac{1}{E_f} \right) e^{-\chi(\frac{t}{h})} \qquad (16.8.16)$$

where

E_c, E_f, E_{sb}: Young's moduli of a layered composite, film, and substrate, respectively;
χ: Constant;
t: Film thickness;
h: Depth of penetration.

16.8.4   Is Martens Hardness Tester a Universal Tool?

As demonstrated in Fig. 16.8.4, Martens hardness testers could be a starting point leading to a universal tool for evaluating elastoplastic properties of various materials, except rubbers.

H_{M}/MPa

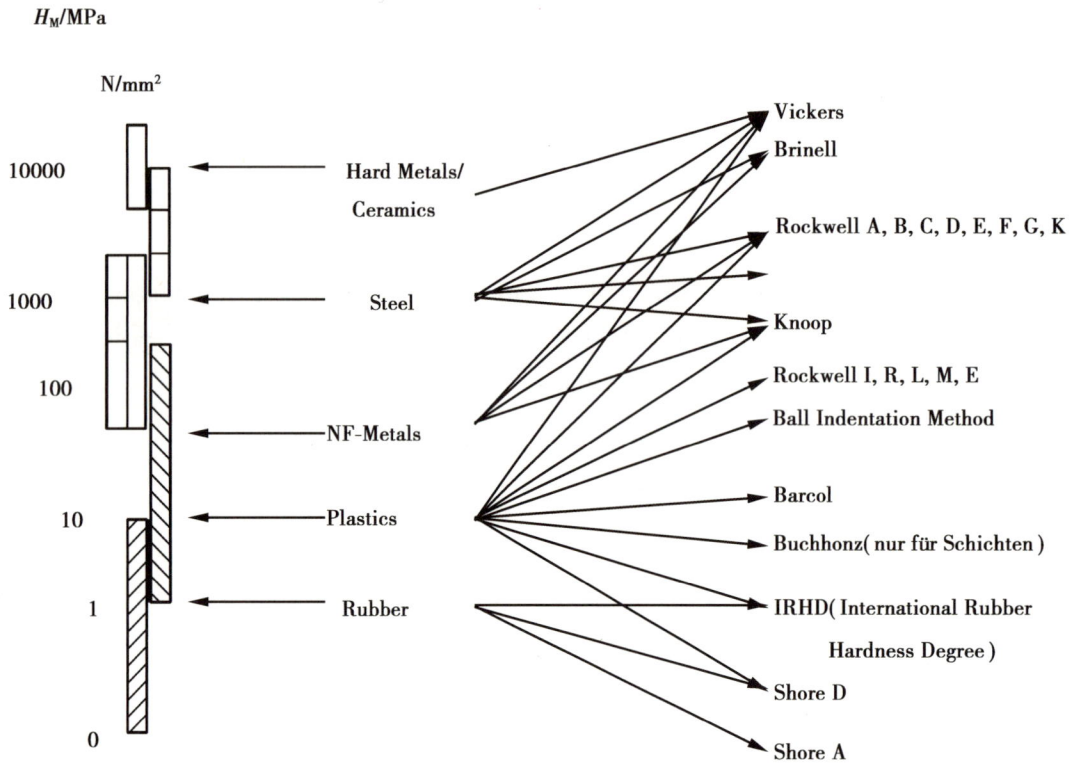

Fig. 16.8.4　Mapping of Materns Hardness (H_{M}) to Others〔Zwick Materials Testing〕

16.9　Estimating Yield and Tensile Strengths by Indentation

There is no universal representative strain in Vickers indentation. The mean pressure-based representative strain is in the range between 0.08 and 0.25, while Martens hardness-based representative strain lies between 0.025 and 0.095〔Hemot et al.〕. In light of the concept of flow stress, a regression model similar to Eq. (16.2.2) can be derived following the F_z-h curve from indentation

$$\sigma = \sigma_{\mathrm{Y}} + K \left(\varepsilon_{\mathrm{eq}}^{p} \right)^{n} \tag{16.9.1}$$

For the case of elastic strain-hardening material with strain gradient effect,〔Gao〕proposed the following equation based on a mean-pressure approach, relating the applied force to the indentation depth, as

$$F_z = F_{zo} + \sigma_{\mathrm{Y}} \, h^2 \left\{ \frac{49}{3} + 12.25 \left(\frac{E \cot \psi}{\sigma_{\mathrm{Y}}} \right)^{n} + \frac{49}{3n} \left[\left(\frac{E \cot \psi}{\sigma_{\mathrm{Y}}} \right)^{n} - 1 \right] \right\} \tag{16.9.2}$$

Yield strength σ_{Y} and strain exponent n can be obtained by the regression model by the above equation using test data based on $\psi = 70.3°$ for Vickers indenter.

16.10   Estimating Residual Stress by Indentation

Residue stresses can be found and calculated using the continuous indentation method. Define a linear contact ratio as

$$c \equiv \left(\frac{A}{A_{\text{nom}}} \right)^{\frac{1}{2}} \tag{16.10.1}$$

where

> A: Area in contact as measured;
>
> A_{nom}: Area in contact when no residue stress is present;
>
> c: Linear contact ratio.

If $c < 1$, sinking-in occurs during indentation; whereas if $c > 1$, pile-up shows up. Nevertheless, residual stresses have no effect on the hardness of a material according to experiments by [Carlsson et al.], but they do have an effect on the linear contact ratio c. A tensile residual stress yields a smaller value of the area ratio, as compared to indentation of a residue stress-free material; whereas, a compressive residual stress tends to increase the c value. A mathematical regression model derived by [Carlsson et al.] is

$$c^2 = c_1 + c_2 \ln \left[\frac{E \tan \beta}{(1 - v^2)(\sigma_{\text{Y}} + \sigma_{\text{Res}})} \right] \tag{16.10.2}$$

where

> E: Young's modulus;
>
> v: Poisson's ratio;
>
> σ_{Y}: Yield strength;
>
> σ_{Res}: Residual strength;
>
> β: Included angle;
>
> c_1: Constant;
>
> c_2: Constant; $c_2 = 0.32$, if $5 < (E \tan \beta)/[(1-v^2)(\sigma_{\text{Y}} + \sigma_{\text{Res}})] < 400$.   (16.10.3)

If there is no residue stress ($\sigma_{\text{Res}} = 0$), $c \rightarrow c_{\text{o}}$, i.e.,

$$c_{\text{o}}^2 = c_1 + c_2 \ln \left[\frac{E \tan \beta}{(1 - v^2)\, \sigma_{\text{Y}}} \right] \tag{16.10.4}$$

Thus, $c^2 = c_{\text{o}}^2 - c_2 \ln \left(1 + \dfrac{\sigma_{\text{Res}}}{\sigma_{\text{Y}}} \right)$ (16.10.5)

One concern of applying the above equation is that the determination of the contact ratio relies on the dimensional measurement accuracy for successive indentations, though optical methods may be used.

16.11   Estimating Fracture Toughness by Indentation

The fracture toughness of a thin film or brittle material is frequently assessed using Vickers testers. In general, K_{IC} can be calculated as[Antis et al.],

$$K_{IC} = \alpha \left(\frac{E}{H_V} \right)^{\frac{1}{2}} a^{\frac{3}{2}} F_z \qquad (16.11.1)$$

where

F_z: Load;
E: Young modulus;
H_V: Vickers hardness;
a: Crack length measured from the indent center;
α: Constant of calibration; $\alpha \approx 0.016$.

Among a good number of regression models for estimating the fracture toughness by indentation of cemented carbides[Sergejev & Antonov], the above equation is a good approach.

16.12   Estimating Creep Properties by Indentation

Assume the material is under a uniaxial steady-state viscoelastic deformation and the threshold stress is zero. Then, the strain rate on the right side of Eq. (7.4.1), can be estimated herein using the following equation

$$\dot{\varepsilon} = A \, \sigma^n \exp\left(\frac{-Q}{R\,T_k} \right) \qquad (16.12.1)$$

Taking a natural log of each term in the above equation and replacing the flow stress by a hardness, e.g. Knoop hardness (MPa) that is related to the flow stress by a constant in light of Eq. (16.4.1), one has

$$\ln(H_K) = \frac{Q}{n\,R}(T_k^{-1}) + \frac{\ln \dot{\varepsilon} - \ln A}{n} \qquad (16.12.2)$$

Keep the strain rate at a fixed value, $\dot{\varepsilon} = $ constant, the last term of the above equation, $(\ln \dot{\varepsilon} - \ln A)/n$, is then a constant. Thus, the activation energy Q can be obtained by the regression of T_k^{-1} against $\ln(H_K)$.

Use of indentation instruments is significantly limited for long term measurements such as creep because of thermal drift. In general, two main approaches have been employed to minimize the effect of thermal drift. One is to introduce a stabilization period before the measurement (though such thermal stabilization can take several hours); the other method is to perform the indentation quickly, within a few seconds.

16.13   Estimating Viscoelastic and Viscoplastic Properties by Indentation

Consider the three-element viscoelastic model as shown in Fig. 16. 13. 1. A spherical-tip indentation tester can be utilized to identify the parameters of the viscoelastic model [Cheng et al.]. Assume that the indenter is much more rigid than the test specimen. If the test specimen is fully elastic, the load-deflection (F_z-h) curve can be calculated as

$$F_z = \frac{4ER^{\frac{1}{2}}}{3(1 - v^2)} h^{\frac{3}{2}} \tag{16.13.1}$$

where

R: Radius of indenter tip;
E: Young's modulus of the test specimen;
v: Poisson's ratio of the test specimen.

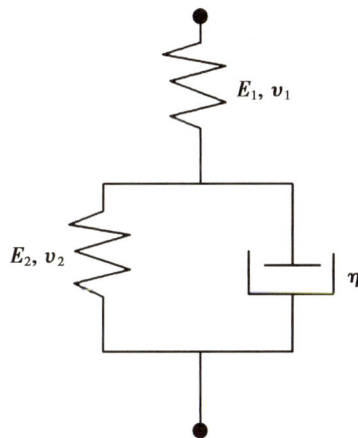

Fig. 16.13.1   A Schematic Drawing of a Three-Element Viscoelastic Model

When the spherical indenter tip is subjected to a sudden push against a half space of viscoelastic material (i.e., the specimen flat surface), the F_z-h relaxation model can be described by

$$F_z = \frac{4 E_1 R^{\frac{1}{2}}}{3(1 - v_1^2)} h^{\frac{3}{2}} (A e^{-\alpha t} + B e^{-\beta t} + C) \tag{16.13.2}$$

where

$$\alpha = \frac{E_1(1+v_2)+E_2(1+v_1)}{2\eta(1+v_2)(1+v_1)} \tag{16.13.3}$$

$$\beta = \alpha\left[\frac{1+v_1}{3(1-v_1)} + \frac{2(1-2v_1)(1+v_1)E_2}{12(1-v_1)(1+v_2)+3(1-v_1^2)\left(\dfrac{E_1}{E_2}\right)}\right] \tag{16.13.4}$$

$$A = \frac{1}{2(1-v_1)\left[1+\dfrac{1+v_2}{(1+v_1)\left(\dfrac{E_1}{E_2}\right)}\right]} \tag{16.13.5}$$

$$C = \frac{\dfrac{\left[9+6(1+v_2)\left(\dfrac{E_1}{E_2}\right)\right]}{4}}{\left[3(1-v_1)+(1+v_2)\left(\dfrac{E_1}{E_2}\right)\right]\left[(1+v_1)+(1+v_2)\left(\dfrac{E_1}{E_2}\right)\right]} \tag{16.13.6}$$

$$B = 1 - A - C \tag{16.13.7}$$

The two viscoelastic exponents and three viscoelastic coefficients are given above. Detailed derivations are presented in [Cheng et al.]. Note that $A+B+C=1$, i.e., Eq. (16.13.7) is established because Eq. (16.13.2) reduces to Eq. (16.13.1) at $t=0$. It means the viscoelastic behavior has no time effect at the very initial moment when the load is applied. For incompressible materials, such as rubbers, polymers work above their glass transition points, and high speed fracture mechanisms; due to $v_1=v_2=0.5$, Eq. (16.13.1) becomes

$$F_z(t,h) = \frac{4E_1 R^{\frac{1}{2}}}{3(1-v_1^2)}h^{\frac{3}{2}}\left[\frac{E_1}{E_1+E_2}e^{-\frac{(E_1+E_2)t}{3\eta}} + \frac{E_2}{E_1+E_2}\right] \tag{16.13.8}$$

Note that $B=0$ in Eq. (16.13.7), i.e., $A+C=1$, for incompressible materials. For a given penetration depth h_o, regression methods may be used for estimating the five material properties E_1, v_1, E_2, v_2 and η. It is an advantage to use the following two initial conditions:

$$F_z(0,h_o) = \frac{4E_1 R^{\frac{1}{2}}}{3(1-v_1^2)}h^{\frac{3}{2}} \tag{16.13.9}$$

and

$$F_z(\infty,h_o) = \frac{4E_1 R^{\frac{1}{2}}}{3(1-v_1^2)}h^{\frac{3}{2}}C \tag{16.13.10}$$

Note that C is derived from Eq. (16.13.6). After the five parameters are obtained, Boltsmann's superposition rule may be used to calculate the resulting load from an incremental displacement. Take an incremental differential in accordance with Eq. (16.13.1),

$$\mathrm{d}F_z = \frac{2E_1 R^{\frac{1}{2}}}{1 - v_1^2} h^{\frac{1}{2}} (Ae^{-\alpha t} + Be^{-\beta t} + C)\,\mathrm{d}h \tag{16.13.11}$$

Integration of the above equation with dummy variable τ (to the scale of t) ends in

$$F_z(t) = \int_0^t R^{\frac{1}{2}} h(\tau)^{\frac{1}{2}} \left[\frac{2E_1}{1 - v_1^2} (Ae^{-\alpha(t-\tau)} + Be^{-\beta(t-\tau)} + C) \right] \mathrm{d}h(\tau) \tag{16.13.12}$$

Rewritten as

$$F_z(t) = \int_0^t R^{\frac{1}{2}} h(\tau)^{\frac{1}{2}} G(t - \tau)\,\mathrm{d}h(\tau) \tag{16.13.13}$$

where

$G(t-\tau)$ is the relaxation modulus of elasticity, given as

$$G(t - \tau) = \frac{2E_1}{1 - v_1^2} [Ae^{-\alpha(t-\tau)} + Be^{-\beta(t-\tau)} + C] \tag{16.13.14}$$

16.14   Fretting Fatigue

Fretting fatigue, also called contact fatigue, is defined as damage resulting from parts clamped together under a normal load with a small relative motion of the contact surfaces, generally ranging from 0.5 μm to 50 μm[Venkatesh et al.]. Of common design concern are occurrences of contact fatigue in bolted joints, tapered joints, shaft couplings, flanges and dovetail slots. Significance of contact friction on the fretting fatigue is demonstrated in Fig. 16.14.1. The problem of fretting fatigue is very complex, involving

(a) High stress gradients: The fretting shear stress distribution is quite shallow, typically extending less than 0.125 mm into the surface with maximum shear stress magnitude in the vicinity of a contact edge[Conner]. The "edge of contact" is the initial location of fretting fatigue. Stress intensities are magnified in the vicinity of edge due to its boundary effect. There is also a clear variation in fatigue life with contact size[Bellows et al.], as shown in Fig. 16.14.1 that presents test data for an Al-4Cu alloy for sliding bearings [Antoniouand & Radtke].

(b) Non-proportional multiaxial loading: Loading is likely to be non-proportional in the neighborhood of the contact, even if the external loads are applied in a proportional fashion. This feature is caused by the non-linear nature of the friction at the contact interface[Nowell et al.].

(c) Initiated cracks will experience a variable load ratio as they grow away from the contact patch.

(d) Material degradation and transformation: The material properties may become orthotropic as the normal contact stress hardens the material in the normal direction. It may end up with $E_{33} > E_{22} = E_{33}$, in the working stress-strain curve.

(e) Corrosion: The fatigue damage resulting from fretting is not caused by visible corrosion, but by small shear stress initiated by fatigue cracks at the edges of the contact zones. Formation of oxide debris by corrosion will reduce the fatigue strength.

(f) Surface finish effects: The contact adhesion hysteresis is due to mechanical effect such as microplasticity of asperities or chemical reactions[Chowdhury et al.].

If the strain energy release rate needed to debond the two contact surfaces exceeds the threshold, it is called a strong adhesion. An adhesive contact produces a singular stress field at the contact perimeter. Contact fatigue failure may also result from the cracks propagating under the applied normal stresses (Mode-I) and shear stresses (Mode-II) through both components[Barquins & Maugis] in a strong adhesion.

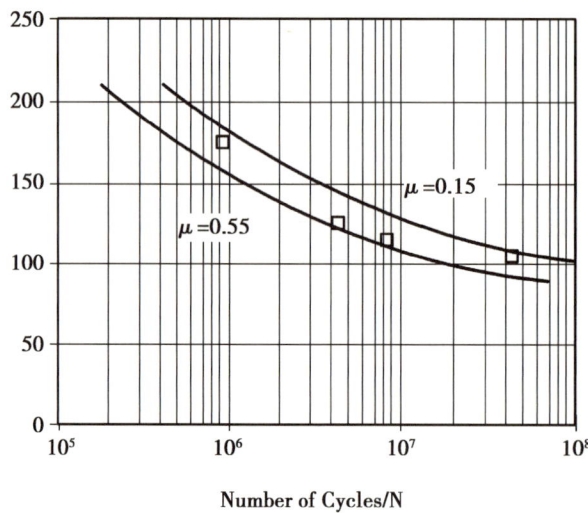

Fig. 16.14.1 Influence of Contact Friction on the Fatigue Life Based on Inconel 600 Material.[Helmi & Attia]

16.14.1 Configurable Mechanics Approach to Fretting Fatigue Life Prediction

It has been validated by[Neu et al.] that the Fatemi-Socie (FS) parameter is an effective tool for predicting the crack nucleation and initial growth direction of fatigue cracks. It is based on shear initiation along critical planes and defined as[Nowell et al.]

$$\Gamma = \frac{1}{2}\Delta\gamma\left(1 + \frac{\beta\,\sigma_{max}}{\sigma_y}\right) \tag{16.14.1}$$

where

$\Delta \gamma$: Shear strain range on the critical plane;

σ_{max}: Maximum value of direct stress across the critical plane;

σ_y: Yield stress;

β: Coefficient, measuring the strain hardening.

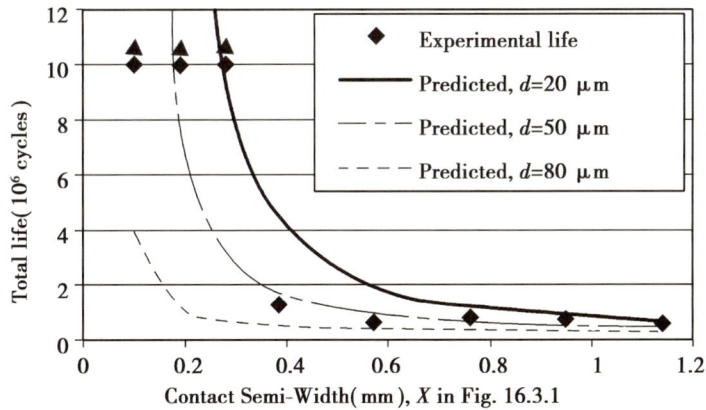

Fig. 16.14.2　Fatigue Life of Al-4Cu Alloy with Respect to Contact Size[Antoniouand & Radtke] and Spherical Size of the Indenter[Antoniouand & Radtke][Nowell et al.]

16.14.2　Crack Propagation by Normal Fretting Fatigue-Mode I

Assume that a ball is pushed against a flat surface as shown in Fig. 16.3.1. The Mode-I stress intensity factor at the contact edge corresponding to the oscillatory normal contact due to contact adhesion hysteresis is[Giannakoulos et al.]

$$\Delta K_{\mathrm{I}} = K_{\mathrm{I},max} - K_{\mathrm{I},min} = \frac{F_{z,max} - F_{z,min}}{2 X_{max}(\pi X_{max})^{\frac{1}{2}}} = \frac{3\pi\, G_{\mathrm{I},th}\, D}{8 X_{max}(\pi\, X_{max})^{\frac{1}{2}}} \qquad (16.14.2)$$

where

D: Diameter of the sphere, shown in Fig. 16.3.1;

X_{max}: Maximum chordal radius of indentation, Fig. 16.3.1;

$F_{z,max}$: Maximum push force during the oscillatory normal contact;

$F_{z,min}$: Minimum push force during the oscillatory normal contact;

$G_{\mathrm{I},th}$: Threshold strain energy release rate (Mode-I).

16.14.3　Crack Propagation by Tangential Fretting Fatigue-Mode II

The Mode-II stress intensity factor at the contact edge in response to the oscillatory normal contact due to contact adhesion hysteresis in the tangential direction is[Giannakoulos et al.]

$$\Delta K_{\text{II}} = \frac{\mu \, F_{z,\max} \left[1 - \left(\dfrac{X_{\text{r}}}{X_{\max}} \right)^3 \right]}{X_{\max} (\pi \, X_{\max})^{\frac{1}{2}}} \qquad (16.14.3)$$

where

μ: Coefficient of friction;

$\mu F_{z,\max}$ is then the sheer force;

X_{r}: Inner chordal radius of indentation, given in Fig. 16.3.1.

Friction is also an influential factor, as shown by Eq. (16.14.3). Nevertheless, deep compression produced may hold the micro-cracked tips in high compression preventing propagation.

16.14.4 Crack Propagation by Torsional Fretting Fatigue-Mode Ⅲ

The Mode-Ⅲ stress intensity factor at the contact edge in response to the normal contact force $(F_{z,\max})$ and subjected to a twisting torque (M_z) due to contact adhesion hysteresis in the circumferential direction is [Giannakoulos et al.]

$$\Delta K_{\text{Ⅲ}} = \frac{3 \, M_z}{4 \, X_{\max}^2 (\pi \, X_{\max})^{\frac{1}{2}}} \qquad (16.14.4)$$

or $\quad \Delta K_{\text{Ⅲ}} \approx 2 \min \left[\frac{3 \, M_z^m}{4 \, X_{\text{r}}^2 (\pi \, X_{\text{r}})^{\frac{1}{2}}}, \left(\frac{G_{\text{Ith}} E}{1 + v} \right)^{\frac{1}{2}} \right] \qquad (16.14.5)$

All the parameters in the above equation are defined before except that

$$M_z^m = M_z - \left(\frac{3 \, \mu \, F_{z,\max} \, X_{\max}}{8} \right) \left[\frac{1}{2} \pi - a \sin \left(\frac{X_{\text{r}}}{X_{\max}} \right) - \left(\frac{X_{\text{r}}}{X_{\max}} \right) \left(\frac{2 \, X_{\text{r}}^2}{X_{\max}^2} - 1 \right) \left(1 - \frac{X_{\text{r}}^2}{X_{\max}^2} \right)^{\frac{1}{2}} \right]$$

$$(16.14.6)$$

16.14.5 Fretting Fatigue Using Finite Element Methods

In fretting fatigue, nucleation processes are relatively fast, due to the strong tractions exerted upon the contacting surfaces [Sinclair et al.]. Under these circumstances, most of the component life is due at the ending of the propagation stage. The X-FEM has been proven to be able to accurately estimate the stress intensity factor on relatively coarse meshes [Giner et al.]. Furthermore, no remeshing is required for crack growth simulations even applied to complete or incomplete contact fretting problems.

References

AHN J H, KWON D, 2001. Derivation of Plastic Stress-Strain Relationship from Ball Indentations: Examination of Strain Definition and Pileup Effect[J]. Journal of Materials Research, 16(11): 3170-3178.

SINCLAIR G, CORMIER N, GRIFFIN J, et al, 2002. Contact Stresses in Dovetail Attachments: Finite Element Modeling[J]. Journal of Engineering for Gas Turbines and Power, 124(1): 182-189.

ANTIS G R, et al, 1981. A Critical Evaluation of Indentation Techniques for Measuring Fracture Toughness[J]. Journal of the American Ceramics Society, 64(9): 533-538.

ANTUNES J M, et al, 2006. Three-Dimensional Numerical Simulation of Vickers Indentation Tests [J]. International Journal of Solid and Structure, 43(3-4): 784-806.

ASIF S, et al, 2001. Quantitative Imaging of Nanoscale Mechanical Properties Using Hybrid Nanoindentation and Force Modulation[J]. Journal of Applied Physics, 90(3): 1192.

BHATTACHARYA A, NIX W, 1988. Analysis of Elastic and Plastic Deformation Associated with Indentation Testing of Thin Films on Substrates[J]. International Journal of Solids and Structures, 24(12): 881-891.

BOLSHAKOV A, PHARR G, 1998. Influences of Pileup on the Measurement of Mechanical Properties by Load and Depth-Sensing Indentation Techniques[J]. Journal of Materials Research, 13(4): 1049.

BOUZAKIS K D, MICHAILIDIS N, 2008. Indenter Tip Geometries and Calibration Procedures: Deviations in Determining Coatings and Other Material's Mechanical Properties [J]. ICMEN, October 1-3, 2008, Chalkidiki, Greece.

BOUZAKIS K D, MICHAILIDIS N, 2005. Hardness Determination, by Means of an FEM Supported Simulation of Nanoindentation and Applications in Thin Hard Coatings[J]. Surface & Coatings Technology, 200(1-4): 867-871.

BOUZAKIS K D, et al, 2003. The Effect of Surface Roughness and Indenter Tip Geometry on the Determination Accuracy of Thin Hard Coatings Stress-Strain Laws by Nanoindentation [J]. Journal of Materials Characterization, 49: 149-156.

BOUZAKIS K D, et al, 2001. Thin Hard Coatings Stress-Strain Curves D Termination through an FEM Supported Evaluation of Nanoindentation Test Results[J]. Surface and Coating Technology, 142: 102-109.

BULL S J, 2005. Nano-Indentation Coatings[J]. Journal of Physics, D: Applied Physics, 38(24): R393.

CHEN L, XIA X, SERIVEN L E, et al, 2005. Spherical-Tip Indentation of Viscoelastic Materials [J]. Mechanics of Materials, 37(1): 213-226.

CHEN X, YAN J, KARLSSON M, 2005. On the Determination of Residual Stress and Mechanical Properties by Indentation[J]. Materials Science and Engineering, 416(1-2): 139-149.

CHEN X, VLASSAK J J, 2001. Numerical Study on the Measurement of Thin Film Mechanical Properties by Means of Nanoindentation[J]. Journal of Materials Research, 16(10): 2974.

CHENG L, XIA X, SCRIVEN L E, et al, 2005. Spherical-Tip Indentation of Viscoelastic Material[J]. Mechanics of Materials, 37: 213-226.

CHENG L, et al, 2000. Flat Punch Indentation of Viscoelastic Material[J]. Journal of Polymer Science Part B: Polymer Physics, 38(1): 10-12.

CHENG Y T, CHENG C M, 2004. Scaling, Dimensional Analysis, Indentation Measurements[J]. Materials Science and Engineering, 44(4-5): 91.

CHENG Y T, CHENG C M, 1998. Scaling Approach to Conical Indentation in Elastoplastic Solids with Work Hardening[J]. Journal of Applied Physics, 84(3): 1284.

CHICOT D, et al, 2013. Mechanical Properties of Porosity-Free Beta Tricalcium Phosphate (-TCP) Ceramic by Sharp and Spherical Indentations[J]. New Journal of Glass and Ceramics, 3(1): 16-28.

CHOLLACOOP N, DAO M, SURESH S, 2003. Depth-Sensing Instrumented Indentation with Dual Sharp Indentation[J]. Acta Materialia, 51(13): 3713-3729.

CHROMIK R R, et al, 2003. Measuring the Mechanical Properties of Pb-Free Solder and Sn-Based Intermetallics by Indentation[J]. JOM, 55(6): 66-69.

CHUDOBA T, et al, 2000. Determination of Elastic Properties of Thin Films by Indentation Measurements with a Spherical Indenter[J]. Surface and Coatings Technology, 127(1): 9-17.

CRISTALLI C, et al, 2017. Low Cycle Fatigue, Creep Fatigue and Relaxation Fatigue Tests on P91[J]. Journal of Physical Science and Application, 7(20): 18-26.

DAO M, et al, 2001. Computational Modeling of the Forward and Reverse Problems in Instrumented Sharp Indentation[J]. Acta Materialia, 49(19): 3899-3918.

DATSKO J, et al, 2001. On the Tensile Strength and Hardness Relation for Metals[J]. Journal of Materials Engineering and Performance, 10(6): 718-722.

DEAN J, et al, 2011. Use of Nanoindentation to Measure Residual Stresses in Surface Layers[J]. Acta Materialia, 59(7): 2749-2761.

DEBOER M P, GERBERICH W W, 1996. Microwedge Indentation of the Thin Film Fine Line- I : Mechanics [J]. Acta Materialia, 44: 3169-3175.

DEBOER M P, GERBERICH W W, 1996. Microwedge Indentation of the Thin Film Fine Line-Ⅱ: Experiment [J]. Acta Materialia, 44(8): 3177-3187.

DOERNER M F, NIX W D, 1986. Interpreting the Data from Depth-Sensing Indentation Instruments[J]. Journal of Materials Research, 1(4): 601-609.

DOWNING S, SOCIE D, 1982. Simple Rainflow Algorithm[J]. International Journal of Fatigue, 4(1): 31-40.

DURST K, et al, 2006. Indentation Size Effect in Metallic Materials: Modeling Strength from Pop-In to Macroscopic Hardness Using Geometrically Necessary Dislocations[J]. Acta Materialia, 54(9): 2547-2555.

ELMUSTAFA A, KOSE S, STONE D, 2011. The Strain-Rate Sensitivity of the Hardness in Indentation Creep [J]. Journal of Materials Research, 14(2): 926-936.

FANG L, et al, 2008. Continuous Electrical In-Situ Contact Area Measurement during Instrumented Indentation [J]. Journal of Materials Research, 23(9): 2480-2485.

FENG G, NGAN A, 2002. Effect of Creep and Thermal Drift on Modulus Measurement Using Depth-Sensing Indentation[J]. Journal of Materials Research, 17(3): 660-668.

FIELD S S, SWAIN M V, 1995. Determining the Mechanical Properties of Small Volumes of Material from Submicrometer Spherical Indentation[J]. Journal of Material Research, 10(1): 101-102.

FISCHER-CRIPPS A C, 2006. Critical Review of Analysis and Interpretation of Nanoindentation Test Data[J]. Surface and Coatings Technology, 200(14-15): 4153-4165.

FOLLANSBEE P, SINCLAIR G, 1984. Quasi-Static Normal Indentation of an Elastic-Plastic Half-Space by a Rigid Sphere, Part Ⅰ: Analysis[J]. International Journal of Solids and Structures, 20(1): 81-91.

FRANCIS H A, 1976. Phenomenological Analysis of Plastic Spherical Indentations[J]. Transactions of ASME: 272-281.

FU K, et al, 2015. On the Determination of Representative Stress-Strain Curve of Metallic Materials Using Instrumented Indentation[J]. Mechanics and Design, 65: 989-994.

GAO X L, 2006. An Expanding Cavity Model Incorporating Strain-Hardening and Indentation Size Effects[J]. International Journal of Solids and Structures, 43(21): 6615-6629.

GAO Y F, et al, 2008. Effective Elastic Modulus of Film-on-Substrate System under Normal and Tangential Contact[J]. Journal of Mechanical Physics in Solids, 56: 402-416.

GAO H, CHIU C, LEE J, 1992. Elastic Contact versus Indentation Modeling of Multilayered Materials[J]. International Journal of Solids and Structures, 29(20): 2471-2492.

GERBERICH W W, et al, 1998. Elastic Loading and Elastoplastic Unloading from Nanometer Level Indentations for Modulus Determinations[J]. Journal of Materials Research, 13(2): 421-439.

GIANNAKOPOULOS A E, 2003. The Influence of Initial Elastic Surface Stresses on the Instrumented Sharp Indentation[J]. Journal of Applied Mechanics, 70(5): 638-643.

GIANNAKOPOULOS A E, SURESH S, 1999. Determination of Elastic Properties by Instrumented Sharp Indentation[J]. Scripta Materialia, 40(10): 1191-1198.

GINERA E, et al, 2008. Extended Finite Element Method for Fretting Fatigue Crack Propagation [J]. International Journal of Solids and Structures, 45(22-23): 5675-5687.

GIANNAKOPOULOS A E, SURESH S, 1999. Theory of Indentation of Piezoelectric Materials [J]. Acta Materialia, 47(7): 2153-2164.

GLINKA G, KAM J, 1987. Rainflow Counting Algorithm for Very Long Stress Histories [J]. International Journal of Fatigue, 9(4): 223-228.

HAGGAG F M, et al, 1996. Using Portable/In-Situ Stress-Strain Microprobe System to Measure Mechanical Properties of Steel Bridges during Service[C]. Nondestructive Evaluation of Bridges and Highway, 65-75.

HAGGAG F M, 1993. In-Situ Measurements of Mechanical Properties Using Novel Automated Ball Indentation System[J]. ASTM Special Technical Publication.

HAGGAG F M, 1989. Field Indentation Microprobe for Structural Integrity Evaluation: US19890323967[P]. 1989-08-01.

HAN S M, SAHA R, NIX W D, 2006. Determining Hardness of Thin Films in Elastically Mismatched Film-on-Substrate System Using Nanoindentation[J]. Acta Materialia, 54(6): 1571.

HAY J C, et al, 1999. A Critical Examination of the Fundamental Relations Used in the Analysis of Indentation Data[J]. Journal of Materials Research, 14(6): 2296-2305.

HERBERT E G, et al, 2001. On the Measurement of Stress-Strain Curves by Spherical Indentation[J]. Thin Solid Films, 398-399: 331-335.

HERMANN K, 2010. CIRP Sponsored International Comparison on Nanoindentation[J]. Metrologia, 47: S50-S58 (CIRP STC-S Meeting, January 26, 2007, Paris, France).

HERMANN K, et al, 2000. Progress in Determination of the Area Function of Indenters Used for Nanoindentation[J]. Thin Solid Films, 377-378: 394-400.

HEMOT X, et al, 2014. Study of the Concept of Representative Strain and Constraint Factor Introduced by Vickers Indentation[J]. Mechanics of Materials, 68(1): 1-14.

HILL R. 1898. Similarity Analysis of Creep Indentation Tests[J]. Proceedings of Royal Society of London, A, 1992(436): 617.

HUBER N, et al, 2001. Determination of Poisson's Ratio by Spherical Indentation Using Neural Networks, Part I: Theory[J]. Journal of Applied Mechanics, 68(2): 218.

HUBER N, TSAGRAKIS I, TSAKMAKIS C, 2000. Determination of Constitutive Properties of Thin Metallic Films on Substrates by Spherical Indentation Using Neural Networks[J]. International Journal of Solids and Structures, 37(44): 5499-6516.

HUNTER S C, 1960. The Hertz Problem for a Rigid Spherical Indenter and a Viscoelastic Half-Space[J]. Journal of Mechanical Physics in Solids, 8(4): 219-234.

HUTANU R, et al, 2005. Intergranular Strain and Texture in Steel Luders Bands[J]. Acta Materialia, 53 (12): 3517-3524.

JANG J, 2009. Estimation of Residual Stress by Instrumented Indentation: A Review[J]. Journal of Ceramic Processing Research, 10(3): 391-400.

JAKES J E, et al, 2008. Nanoindentation Near the Edge[J]. Journal of Material Research, 24(3): 1016-1031.

JAYARAMAN S, et al, 1998. Determination of Monotonic Stress-Strain Curve of Hard Materials from Ultra-Low-Load Indentation Tests[J]. International Journal of Solids and Structures, 35(5): 365-381.

JEON E, et al, 2005. Determining Representative Stress and Representative Strain in Deriving Indentation Flow Curves Based on Finite Element Analysis[J]. Key Engineering Materials, 297-300(Pt3): 2152-2157.

JEON E, et al, 2005. Optimum Definition of True Strain beneath a Spherical Indenter for Deriving Indentation Flow Curves[J]. Materials Science and Engineering, A419: 196-201.

JIN H, LEWIS J L, 2004. Determination of Poisson's Ratio of Cartilage in Indentation Test Using Different-Sized Indenters[J]. Journal of Biomechanical Engineering, 126(2): 138-145.

JOHNSON K L, 1970. Correlation of Indentation Experiments[J]. Journal of Mechanical Physics in Solids, 18 (2): 115-126.

KANG J, BECKER A, SUN W, 2015. Determination of Elastic and Viscoplastic Material Properties Obtained from Indentation Tests Using a Combined Finite Element Analysis and Optimization Approach[J]. Journal of Materials: Design and Applications, 229(3): 175-188.

KERMOUCHE G, et al, 2007. Cone Indentation of Time-Dependent Materials: The Effect of the Indentation Strain Rate[J]. Mechanical Materials, 39(1): 24-38.

KERMOUCHE G, et al, 2006. A New Index to Estimate the Strain Rate Sensitivity of the Glassy Polymers Using Conical/Pyramidal Indentation[J]. Philosophical Magazine, 86(33-35): 5667-5677.

KIM J Y, et al, 2008. Evaluating Plastic Flow Properties by Characterizing Indentation Size Effect Using a Sharp Indenter[J]. Acta Materialia, 56(14): 3338-3343.

KIM J H, et al, 2007. Characterization of Mechanical Properties of Brittle Coating Systems by Various Indentation Techniques[J]. Key Engineering Materials, 352: 53-58.

KIM J Y, et al, 2006. Determination of Tensile Properties by Instrumented Indentation Technique: Representative Stress and Strain Approach[J]. Surface Coating Technology, 201: 4278-4283.

KING R B, 1987. Elastic Analysis of Some Punch Problems for a Layered Medium[J]. International Journal of Solids and Structures, 23(12): 1657-1654.

KLAPPERICH C, et al, 2001. Nanomechanical Properties of Polymers Determined from Nanoindentation Experiments[J]. Journal of Tribology, 123(3): 624-631.

KNAPP J A, et al, 1999. Finite Element Analysis Modeling of Nanoindentation[J]. Journal of Applied Physics, 85(3): 1460-1474.

KNOOP F, PETERS C G, EMERSON W B, 1939. A Sensitive Pyramid-Diamond Tool for Indentation Measurements[J]. Journal of Research of the National Bureau of Standards, 23(1): 39-61.

KOGUT L, KOMVOPOULOS K, 2004. Analysis of the Spherical Indentation Cycle for Elastic-Perfectly Plastic Solids[J]. Journal of Materials Research, 19(2): 3641-3653.

KOMVOPOULUOS K, YE N. Three-Dimensional Contact Analysis of Elastic-Plastic Layered Media with Fractal Surface Topographies[J]. Journal of Tribology, 123(3): 632-640.

KRAL E, et al, 1993. Elastic-Plastic Finite Element Analysis of Repeated Indentation of a Half-Space by a Rigid Sphere[J]. Journal of Applied Mechanics, 60(4): 829-841.

KRIESE M D, et al, 1998. Nanomechanical Fracture-Testing of Thin Films[J]. Engineering Fracture Mechanics, 61(1): 1-20.

KUCHARSKI S, MROZ Z, 2007. Indentation of Yield Stress and Plastic Hardening Parameters from a Spherical Indentation Test[J]. International Journal of Mechanical Sciences, 49(11): 1238-1250.

LEE Y H, et al, 2005. Prediction of Stress Directionality from Pile-Up Morphology around Remnant Indentation [J]. Scripta Materialia, 51(9): 887-891.

LEE Y H, KWON D, 2001. Estimation of Biaxial Surface Stress by Instrumented Indentation with Sharp Indenters[J]. Acta Materialia, 52(6): 1555-1563.

LEROY G, EMBURY J, EDWARDS G, et al, 1981. A Model of Ductile Fracture Based on the Nucleation and Growth of Voids[J]. Acta Metallurgica, 29(8): 1509-1522.

LI B, et al, 2009. Characterization of Nonlinear Material Parameters of Foams Based on Indentation Tests[J]. Materials and Design, 30(7): 2708-2714.

LI H, RANDALL N X, VLASSAK J J, 2010. New Methods of Analyzing Indentation Experiments on Very Thin Films[J]. Journal of Materials Research, 25(4): 728-734.

LI H, VLASSAK J J, 2009. Determining the Elastic Modulus and Hardness of an Ultra-Thin Film on a Substrate Using Nanoindentation[J]. Journal of Materials Research, 24(3): 1114.

LI X D, BHUSHAN B, 1999. Evaluation of Fracture Toughness of Ultra-Thin Amorphous Carbon Coatings Deposited by Different Deposition Techniques[J]. Thin Solid Films, 355-356: 330-336.

LI X D, BHUSHAN B, 1999. Measurement of Fracture Toughness of Ultra-Thin Amorphous Carbon Films[J]. Thin Solid Films, 315(1-2): 214-221.

LIU Y, NGAN A H W, 2001. Depth Dependence of Hardness in Copper Single Crystals Measured by Nanoindentation[J]. Scripta Materialia, 44(2): 237-241.

LOUBET J L, et al, 2000. Measurement of the Loss Tangent of Low-Density Polyethylene with a Nanoindentation Technique[J]. Journal of Materials Research, 15(5): 1195-1198.

LOUBET J L, GEORGES J M, MARCHESINI O, et al, 1984. Vickers Indentation Curves of Magnesium Oxide (MgO)[J]. Journal of Tribology, 106(1): 43-48.

LU H, et al, 2003. Measurement of Creep Compliance of Solid Polymers by Nanoindentation[J]. Mechanics of Time-Dependent Materials, 7(3): 189-207.

LU J, SURESH S, RAVICHANDRAN G, 2003. Dynamic Indentation for Determining the Strain Rate Sensitivity of Metals[J]. Journal of Mechanical Physics in Solids, 51(11/12): 1923-1938.

LU Y, et al, 2008. Finite Element Analysis of Cylindrical Indentation for Determining Plastic Properties of Materials in Small Volumes[J]. Journal of Physics D: Applied Physics, 41(11): 115415.

MA D, XU K, HE J, 1997. Numerical Simulation for Measuring Yield Strength in Thin Metal Films by Nanoindentation Method[J]. Transactions of Nonferrous Metals Society of China, 7(3): 66-69.

MA D, et al, 1997. A New Method on Evaluating the Yield Strength of Metal Films Using Depth-Sensing Indentation Instrument[J]. Acta Metallurgical Sinica, 34(6): 661-666.

MA L, et al, 2002. Self-Similarity Simplification Approaches for the Modeling and Analysis of Rockwell Hardness Indentation[J]. Journal of Research of National Institute of Standard and Technology, 107(5):

401-412.

MALZBENDER J, 2003. Comment on Hardness Definitions[J]. Journal of the European Ceramics Society, 23 (9): 1355-1359.

MASSON R, GATT J, BARON D, 2007. Micro-Indentation Test on Nuclear Fuel: Numerical Investigations [J]. Transactions, SMiRT 19, Toronto, ON, Canada.

MCELHANEY K W, et al, 1998. Determination of Indenter Tip Geometry and Indentation Contact Area for Depth-Sensing Indentation Experiments[J]. Journal of Materials Research, 13(5): 1300-1306.

MENCIK J, et al, 1997. Determination of Elastic Modulus of Thin Layers Using Nanoindentation[J]. Journal of Materials Research, 16(10): 2475-2484.

NAKAMURA T, et al, 2000. Determination of Properties of Graded Materials by Inverse Analysis and Instrumented Indentation[J]. Acta Materialia, 48(17): 4293-4306.

NEU R W, et al, 2000. Fretting Fatigue: Current Technology and Practices[J]. Edited by D. Hoeppner, V. Chandrasekaran, C. Elliott: 369-388. ASTM STP 1367, West Conshohocken, PA.

NIX W D, GAO H, 1998. Indentation Size Effects in Crystalline Materials: A Law for Strain Gradient Plasticity [J]. Journal of Mechanical Physics in Solids, 46(3): 411-425.

NOHAVA J, et al, 2009. Ultra Nanoindentation Method with Extremely Low Thermal Drift: Principle and Experimental Results[J]. Journal of Materials Research, 24(3): 873-882.

NOWELL D, et al, 2006. Recent Developments in the Understanding of Fretting Fatigue[J]. Engineering Fracture Mechanics, 73(2): 207-222.

O'CONNOR K M, CLEVELAND P A, 1993. Indentation Creep Studies of Cross-Linked Glassy Polymer Films [J]. MRS Spring Meeting, 308: 308-495.

ODEGARD G M, et al, 2005. Characterization of Viscoelastic Properties of Polymeric Materials through Nanoindentation[J]. Experimental Mechanics, 45(2): 130-136.

OLIVER W C, PHARR G M, 2004. Measurement of Hardness and Elastic Modulus by Instrumented Indentation: Advances in Understanding and Refinement to Methodology[J]. Journal of Materials Research, 19(1): 3-20.

OLIVER W C, PHARR G M, 1992. An Improved Technique for Determining Hardness and Elastic Modulus Using Load and Displacement Sensing Indentation Experiments[J]. Journal of Materials Research, 7: 1564-1583.

PAGLIARO P, et al, 2009. Known Residual Stress Specimens Using Opposed Indentation [J]. Journal of

Engineering Materials and Technology, 131(3): 10.

PANICH N, et al, 2006. Finite Element Analysis of the Critical Ratio of Coating Thickness to Indentation Depth of Soft Coating on a Harder Substrate by Nanoindentation[J]. Science Asia, 32(4): 216-226.

PARK K, et al, 2004. Quasi-Static and Dynamic Nanoindentation Studies on Highly Cross Linked Ultra-High-Molecular-Weight Polyethylene[J]. Biomaterials, 25(12): 2427-2436.

PARK Y J, PHARR G M, 2004. Nanoindentation with Spherical Indenters: Finite Element Studies of Deformation in Elastic-Plastic Transition Regime[J]. Thin Solid Films, 447(none): 246-250.

PAVLINA E J, VAN T C J, 2008. Correlation of Yield Strength and Tensile Strength with Hardness for Steels [J]. Journal of Materials Engineering and Performance, 17(6): 888-893.

PHARR G M, BOLSHAKOV A, 2002. Understanding Nanoindentation Unloading Curves [J]. Journal of Materials Research, 17(10): 2660.

PHARR G M, et al, 1992. On the Generality of the Relationship among Contact Stiffness, Contact Area, Elastic Modulus during Indentation[J]. Journal of Materials Research, 7(3): 613-617.

POON B, RITTEL D, RAVICHANDRAN G, 2008. An Analysis of Nanoindentation in Linearly Elastic Solids [J]. International Journal of Solids and Structures, 45(24): 6018-6033.

PRIME M B, et al, 2004. Laser Surface-Contouring and Spline Data-Smoothing for Residual Stress Measurement[J]. Experimental Mechanics, 44(2): 176-184.

PRIME M B, 2001. Cross-Sectional Mapping of Residual Stresses by Measuring the Surface Contour after a Cut [J]. Journal of Engineering Materials and Technology, 123(2): 162-168.

PUTHOFF J B, et al, 2009. Investigation of Thermally Activated Deformation in Amorphous PMMA and Zr-Cu-Al Bulk Metallic Glasses with Broadband Nanoindentation[J]. Journal of Materials Research, 24(3): 1279-1290.

QINN G D, BRADT R C, 2007. On the Vickers Indentation Fracture Toughness Test[J]. Journal of American Ceramic Society, 90(3): 673-680.

QU S, HUANG Y, PHARR G M, et al, 2006. The Indentation Size Effect in the Spherical Indentation of Iridium: A Study via the Conventional Theory of Mechanism-Based Strain Gradient Plasticity [J]. International Journal of Plasticity, 22(7): 1265-1286.

QU S, et al, 2004. The Indenter Tip Radius Effect on the Nix-Gao Relation in Micro-and Nanoindentation in Hardness Experiments[J]. Journal of Materials Research, 19(11): 3423-3434.

RANDALL N X, 2002. Direct Measurement of Residual Contact Area and Volume during the Nanoindentation of

Coated Materials as an Alternative Method of Calculating Hardness[J]. Philosophical Magazine A, 82(10): 1883-1892.

RANDALL N X, et al, 1998. Combining Scanning Force Microscopy with Nanoindentation for More Complete Characterization of Bulk and Coated Materials[J]. Surface and Coating Technology, 108(1-3): 489-495.

SAHA R, NIX W D, 2002. Effects of the Substrate on the Determination of Thin Film Mechanical Properties by Nanoindentation[J]. Acta Materialia, 50(1): 23-38.

SAKAI M, 2009. Substrate-Affected Indentation Contact Parameters of Elastoplastic Coating/Substrate Composites[J]. Journal of Materials Research, 24(3): 831-843.

SAKAI M, HAKIRI N, MIYAJIMA T, 2006. Instrumented Indentation Microscope: A Powerful Tool for the Mechanical Characterization in Microscales[J]. Journal of Materials Research, 21(9): 2298-2303.

SAKAI M, et al, 2003. Linear Strain Hardening in Elastoplastic Indentation Contact[J]. Journal of Materials Research, 18(9): 2087-2096.

SAKAI M, NAKANO Y, 2002. Elastoplastic Load-Depth Hysteresis in Pyramidal Indentation[J]. Journal of Materials Research, 17(8): 2161-2173.

SANCHEZ E Z, et al, 1999. Cross-Sectional Nanoindentation: A New Technique for Thin Film Interfacial Adhesion Characterization[J]. Acta Materialia, 47(17): 4405-4413.

SCHUH C A, NIEH T G, 2004. A Survey of Instrumented Indentation Studies on Metallic Glasses[J]. Journal of Materials Research, 19(1): 46-57.

SERGEJEV F, ANTONOV M, 2006. Comparative Study on Indentation Fracture Toughness Measurements of Cemented Carbides[J]. Proc. Estonian Acad. Sci. Eng, 12(4): 388-398.

SHUMAN D J, et al, 2007. Calculating the Elastic Modulus from Nanoindentation and Microindentation Reload Curves[J]. Material Characterization, 58(4): 380-389.

SMITH R L, SANDLAND G, 1922. An Accurate Method of Determining the Hardness of Metals, with Particular Reference to Those of a High Degree of Hardness[J]. Proceedings of the Institution of Mechanical Engineers, I: 623-641.

SPINO J, ROUSSEAU F, 2003. Room-Temperature Microindentation Behavior of LWR-Fuels, Part I: Fuel Microhardness[J]. Journal of Nuclear Materials, 322(2-3): 204-216.

STAUSS S, et al, 2003. Determining the Stress-Strain Behavior of Small Devices by Nanoindentation in Combination with Inverse Methods[J]. Microelectronic Engineering, 67-68(1): 818-825.

STILLWELL N A, TABOR D, 1961. Proc. Phys. Soc, 78: 169.

STONE D S, et al, 2010. Analysis of Indentation Creep[J]. Journal of Materials Research, 25(4): 611-621.

STROJNY A, et al, 1998. Techniques and Considerations for Nanoindentation Measurements of Polymer Thin Film Constitutive Properties[J]. Journal of Adhesion Science and Technology, 12(12): 1299-1321.

SURESH S, GIANNAKOPOULOS A E, 1998. A New Method for Estimating Residual Stresses by Instrumented Sharp Indentation[J]. Acta Materialia, 46(16): 5755.

SWADENER J G, GEORGE E P, PHARR G M, 2002. The Correlation of the Indentation Size Effect Measured with Indenters of Various Shapes[J]. Journal of Mechanical Physics in Solids, 50(4): 681-694.

SYED A, et al, 2001. Quantitative Imaging of Nanoscale Mechanical Properties Using Hybrid Nanoindentation and Force Modulation[J]. Journal of Applied Physics, 90(11): 5838-5838.

SYED A, et al, 1999. Nanoindentation and Contact Stiffness Measurements Using Force Modulation with a Capacitive Load-Displacement Transducer[J]. Review of Scientific Instruments, 70(5): 2408-2413.

STRADER J H, et al, 2006. An Experimental Evaluation of the Constant Relating the Contact Stiffness to the Contact Area in Nanoindentation[J]. Philosophical Magazine, 86(33-35): 5285-5298.

TABOR D, 2000. The Hardness of Metals[M]. Oxford University Press, UK.

TALJAT B, ZACHARIA T, KOSEL F, 1998. New Analytical Procedure to Determine Stress-Strain Curve from Spherical Indentation Data[J]. International Journal of Solids and Structures, 35(33): 4411-4426.

TARDIEU A, CONSTANTINESCU A, 2000. On the Determination of Elastic Coefficients from Indentation Experiments[J]. Inverse Problems, 16(3): 577-588.

THOULES M D, 1998. An Analysis of Spalling in Microscratch Test[J]. Engineering Fracture Mechanics, 61(1): 75-81.

THURN J, MORRIS D, COOK R, 2002. Depth-Sensing Indentation at Macroscopic Dimensions[J]. Journal of Materials Research, 17(10): 2679-2690.

TING T C T, 1966. The Contact Stresses between a Rigid Indenter and a Viscoelastic Half-Space[J]. Journal of Applied Mechanics, 33(4): 845-854.

TOOTORELLI P F, 1993. Mechanical Properties of Chromic Scales[J]. Journal of Physique Ⅳ, C9-Ⅲ, 3(c9): 943-949.

TSUI T Y, PHAR G M, 1999. Substrate Effects on Nanoindentation Mechanical Property Measurement of Soft Films on Hard Substrates[J]. Journal of Materials Research, 14(1): 292-301.

TSUI T Y, et al, 1999. Indentation Plastic Displacement Field: Part Ⅰ. The Case of Soft Films on Hard

Substrates[J]. Journal of Materials Research, 14: 2196-2203.

TSUI T Y, et al, 1999. Indentation Plastic Displacement Field: Part Ⅱ. The Case of Hard Films on Soft Substrates[J]. Journal of Materials Research, 14: 2196-2209.

TUNVISUT K, et al, 2002. Determination of the Mechanical Properties of Metallic Thin Films and Substrates from Indentation Tests[J]. International Philosophical Magazine A, 82(10): 2013-2029.

TYULYUKONSLIY E, HUBER N, 2006. Identification of Viscoelastic Material Parameters from Spherical Indentation Data: Part Ⅰ. Neural Networks[J]. Journal of Materials Research, 21(3): 664-676.

UNDERWOOR J H, 1973. Residual Stress Measurement Using Surface Displacements around an Indentation [J]. Experimental Mechanics, 13(9): 373-380.

VAIDYANATHAN R, et al, 2001. Study of Mechanical Deformation in Bulk Metallic Glass through Instrumented Indentation[J]. Acta Materilaia, 49(18): 3781-3789.

VAN DOMMELEN J A W, et al, 2010. Mechanical Properties of Brain Tissue by Indentation: Interregional Variation[J]. Journal of the Mechanical Behavior of Biomedical Materials, 3(2): 158-166.

VAN V K J, GOULDSTONE A, 2001. Mechanical Properties of Thin Films Quantified via Instrumented Indentation[J]. Surface Engineering, 107(2): 140-145.

VENKATESH T A, et al, 2001. An Experimental Investigation of Fretting Fatigue in Ti-6Al-4V: The Role of Contact Conditions and Microstructure[J]. Metallurgical and Materials Transactions, 32A(5): 1131-1146.

VLACHOS D E, et al, 2001. 3-D Modeling of Nanoindentation Experiment on a Coating Substrate System[J]. Computational Mechanics, 27(12): 138-144.

VLASSAK J J, et al, 2003. The Indentation Modulus of Elastically Anisotropic Materials for Indenters of Arbitrary Shape[J]. Journal of Mechanical Physics in Solids, 51(9): 1701-1721.

VLASSAK J J, NIX W D, 1992. A New Bulge Test Technique for the Determination of Young's Modulus and Poisson's Ratio[J]. Journal of Materials Research, 7(12): 3242-3249.

VU-QUOC L, ZHANG X, LESBURG L, 2000. A Normal Force-Displacement Model for Contacting Spheres Accounting for Plastic Deformation: Force-Driven Formulation[J]. Journal of Applied Mechanics, 67(2): 363-371.

WARREN P D, et al, 1995. Determining the Fracture Toughness of Brittle Materials by Hertzian Indentation [J]. Journal of the European Ceramic Society, 15(3): 201-207.

WILDE H R, WEHRSTEDT A, 2000. Introduction of Martens Hardness H_M[J]. Materialprüfung, 42(11-12): 468-470.

WITHERS P J, 2007. Residual Stress and Its Role in Failure[J]. Reports on Progress in Physics, 70(12):

2211-2264.

WREDENBERG F, LARSSON P L, 2009. Scratch Testing of Metals and Polymers: Experiments and Numerics [J]. Wear, 266 (1-2): 76-83.

YAN W, et al, 2008. Determination of Plastic Yield Stress from Spherical Indentation Slope Curve [J]. Materials Letters, 62(15): 2260-2262.

YAN W, et al, 2006. Analysis of Spherical Indentation of Superelastic Shape Memory Alloys[J]. International Journal of Solids and Structures, 44(1): 1-17.

YANG S, ZHANG Y, ZENG K, 2004. Analysis of Nanoindentation Creep for Polymeric Materials[J]. Journal of Applied Physics, 95(7): 3655-3666.

YE N, KOMVOPOULOS K, 2003. Indentation Analysis of Elastic-Plastic Homogeneous and Layered Media: Criteria for Determining the Real Material Hardness[J]. Journal of Tribology, 125(4): 685-691.

ZENG K, 1996. Controlled Indentation: A General Approach to Determine Mechanical Properties of Brittle Materials[J]. Acta Materialia, 44(3): 1127-1141.

Table 16.1.1   Nominal Material Hardness and Melting Points of Elements[Harris et al.][Samsonov].

Element	H_B/MPa	H_K/MPa	H_V/MPa	T_m/℃
Ag (Annealed)	206	—	250	962
Ag (Electro-deposited)	—	—	980	962
Al (Pure)	184	—	—	660
Al 1050 (O; Annealed)	184	—	—	660
Al 6061 (T6)	950	—	1070	660
Al 356.0 (F)	—	—	500	660
Al 356.0 (T6)	—	—	750	660
Au (Cast)	189	—	—	1063
Au (Foil)	—	680	—	1063
B	—	4900	—	2076
Be	—	1670	—	1287
Bi	70	—	—	271.4
C	—	>7000	—	3527

continued

Element	H_B/MPa	H_K/MPa	H_V/MPa	T_m/℃
Ca	416	—	—	842
Cd	196	—	—	321
Cu（Rolled）	520	—	—	1084.6
Cu	—	356	—	1084.6
Cr（Annealed）	688	1060	—	3380
Co	—	1043	—	1495
Co（Annelaed）	1291	—	—	1495
Fe	—	608	—	1538
Ga	63	—	—	29.7646
Ge	—	—	—	938.25
In	9.8	—	—	156.6
Ir	1670	—	—	2446
Li	5	—	—	180.54
Mg（Cast）	44	—	—	650
Mn	196	—	—	1246
Mo（Annealed）	1340	—	—	2623
Nb（Annealed）	735	—	—	2477
Ni	—	638	—	1453
Ni（Annealed）	1050	—	—	1453
Pd（Cast）	310	—	—	1555
Pt（Annealed）	300	—	—	1768
Ti（Annealed）	1028	—	—	1670
V（Annealed）	742	—	—	1900
Zn（Cast）	500	—	—	420
Zr	333	—	—	1855

Note：1 kgf/mm^2 = 9.807 MPa.

Table 16.1.2   Nominal Material Hardness of Ferrous Materials (Meting Points Falling between 1425–1540 ℃)

Material	H_B/(kgf · mm^{-2})	H_K/(kgf · mm^{-2})	H_V/(kgf · mm^{-2})	H_R/(kgf · mm^{-2})
	(10 mm WC; 3000 kg)	—	—	(120°cone 150 kg)
Steel, *Plain*:				
SAE 1006 (HR)	86	—	—	80-90H_{RB}
SAE 1006 (CD)	95	—	—	—
SAE 1008 (HR)	86	—	—	—
SAE 1008 (CD)	95	—	—	—
SAE 1010 (HR)	95	—	—	—
SAE 1010 (CD)	105	—	—	—
SAE 1018 (HR)	116	—	—	—
SAE 1018 (CD)	126	—	—	—
SAE 1020 (HR)	118	126.5	—	—
SAE 1022 (HR)	121	—	—	—
SAE 1022 (CD)	137	—	—	—
SAE 1038 (HR)	149	—	—	—
SAE 1038 (CD)	163	—	—	—
SAE 1045 (HR)	163	—	—	—
SAE 1045 (CD)	179	—	—	—
SAE 1045 (ACD)	170	—	—	—
SAE 1117 (HR)	121	—	—	—
SAE 1117 (CD)	137	—	—	—
SAE 11415 (HR)	178	—	—	—
SAE 1141 (HR)	187	—	—	—
SAE 1141 (CD)	212	—	—	—
SAE 1144 (HR)	197	—	—	—
SAE 1144 (CD)	217	—	—	—
SAE 1212 (HR)	121	—	—	—
SAE 1212 (CD)	167	—	—	—
SAE 12L14 (HR)	121	—	—	—

continued

Material	$H_B/(\text{kgf} \cdot \text{mm}^{-2})$	$H_K/(\text{kgf} \cdot \text{mm}^{-2})$	$H_V/(\text{kgf} \cdot \text{mm}^{-2})$	$H_R/(\text{kgf} \cdot \text{mm}^{-2})$
SAE 12L14（CD）	163	—	—	—
SAE 1215（HR）	121	—	—	—
SAE 1215（CD）	163	—	—	—
SAE 4037（Annealed/CD）	174-217	—	—	—
SAE 4130（Annealed/CD）	187-229	—	—	—
SAE 4140（Annealed/CD）	187-229	—	—	—
SAE 8620（HR/CD）	179-235	—	—	—
SAE 8630（Annealed/CD）	174-229	—	—	—
White Cast Iron	415	—	—	$43H_{RC}$
Nitrided Surface	750	—	—	—
Steel, Stainless:				
AISI 302 HQ（Annealed）	150-180	—	—	$80\text{-}90H_{RB}$
AISI 303（Annealed）	160-180	—	—	$83\text{-}95H_{RB}$
AISI 304 HQ（Annealed）	150-180	—	—	$80\text{-}90H_{RB}$
AISI 316（Annealed）	150-180	—	—	$80\text{-}90H_{RB}$
AISI 316L（Annealed）	140	—	—	$80\text{-}90H_{RB}$
AISI 410（Annealed）	150-200	—	—	$80\text{-}90H_{RB}$
AISI 347L（Annealed）	180	—	—	—
AISI 416（Annealed）	190-220	—	—	$90\text{-}95H_{RB}$
AISI 630（Bars Cond. A）	320	—	—	$33H_{RC}$
AISI 630（Cond. H 1025）	352	—	—	$37H_{RC}$
AISI 630（Cond. H 900）	415	—	—	$43H_{RC}$

Table 16.1.3   Nominal Material Hardness and Melting Points of Ceramics and Harder Materials

Ceramics and Harder	Mohs Value	$H_K/(\text{kgf} \cdot \text{mm}^{-2})$	$T_m/\text{°C}$
Talc ($3MgO\text{-}4SiO_2\text{-}H_2O$)	1	—	1500
Gypsum ($CaSO_4\text{-}2H_2O$)	2	32	130
Calcite ($CaCO_3$)	3	135	839
Fluorite (CaF_2)	4	163	1360
Barrium titanate ($BaTiO_3$)	—	200	1625
Magnesia (MgO)	—	370	2852
Borosilicate glass (B-glass)	—	420	1649
Apatite ($CaF_2\text{-}3Ca_3(PO_4)_2$)	5	430	1660
Soda lime glass (Na-glass)	—	530	568
Feldspar ($K_2O\text{-}Al_2O_3\text{-}6SiO_2$)	6	560	842
Quartz-silica fused (SiO_2)	7	880	1650
Iron carbide (Fe_3C)	—	1030	1227
Spinel ($MgAl_2O_4$)	—	1140	2135
Zirconia (ZrO_2)	—	1160	2715
Aluminum nitride (AlN)	—	1200	2500
Beryllium oxide (BeO)	—	1250	2530
Topaz ($(AlF)_2 SiO_4$)	8	1350	1650
Yttrium aluminum garnet (YAG)	—	1370	1965
Titanium nitride/Co (TiN/Co)	—	1410-1810(depending on Co content)	
Zirconium diboride (ZrB_2)	—	1550	3246
Chromium carbide (Cr_3C_2)	—	1740	1895
Molybdenum carbide (MoC)	—	1800	2692
Titanium nitride (TiN)	9	1800	2930
Tungsten carbide (WC)	—	1880	2870
Tantalum carbide (TaC)	—	2010	3880
Alumina (Al_2O_3)	—	2100	2054

continued

Ceramics and Harder	Mohs Value	$H_K/(\text{kgf} \cdot \text{mm}^{-2})$	$T_m/{}^\circ\text{C}$
Zirconium carbide (ZrC)	—	2100	3532
Beryllium carbide (Be$_2$C)	—	2410	2100
Silicon carbide (SiC)	—	2480	2300
Aluminum diboride (AlB$_2$)	—	2510	1655
Vanadium carbide (VC)	—	2700	2810
Boron carbide (B$_4$C)	—	2500	2440
Titanium carbide (TiC)	—	3000	3160
Silicon nitride (Si$_3$N$_4$)	—	3400	1900
Wurtzite boron nitride (wBN)	—	3400	2700
Cubic boron nitride (cBN)	—	4500	2700
Gallium arsenide (GaAs)	—	7500	1238
Diamond film	—	6500	—
Diamond (C)	10	7000-10000	3650

Table 16.1.4 Nominal Material Hardness and Melting Points of Bio-Materials

Bio-Material	H_B/MPa	$H_K/(\text{kgf} \cdot \text{mm}^{-2})$	H_V/MPa	$T_m/{}^\circ\text{C}$
Dentin	—	6.8	—	—
Enamel, Tooth	—	34.3	—	—

Note: A bone does not exactly melt, while it is likely to fall apart as it consists of very solid but porous matrix of mineral crystals: hydroxyapatite or $Ca_{10}(PO_4)_6(OH)_2(s)$ partly bound with some organic material (mostly collagen).

Table 16.2.1 Regression Constants for Different Indenters

Indenter	Included Tip Angle	M_1	M_2	C^*	D^*
Vickers pyramid	136°	7.143	−1	0.8757	5
Berkovich	130.6°	6.618	−0.875	0.8569	4.678
Circular conical	—	—	—	0.8865	—

Index